The Indian Conveyancer

Kolkata
Eastern Law House Private Ltd.
54 Ganesh Chunder Avenue
Kolkata 700 013

New Delhi
Eastern Law House Private Ltd.
36 Netaji Subhash Marg, Daryaganj
New Delhi 110 002

The Indian Conveyancer

by

P.C. Mogha BA, LLB

Former Chief Justice Vindhya Pradesh, Rewa, Law and Revenue Minister, Jammu and Kashmir State, formerly Legal Remembrancer and Secretary to Government, U.P. Judicial and Legislative Departments, Government Conveyancer, Member of the U.P. Legislative Council, and Member of the faculty of Law of the Agra University and Author of the Law of Pleadings in India.

FIFTEENTH EDITION

by

S.N. Dhingra
Former Judge, High Court at Delhi

Narendra Kumar
Member (Judicial), Delhi VAT Appellate Tribunal

Ritika Mogha Nahata LLM

Kolkata New Delhi
EASTERN LAW HOUSE

EASTERN LAW HOUSE PRIVATE LTD.
54 Ganesh Chunder Avenue
Kolkata 700 013
Tel: (033) 4063-2301
Email: mail@elh.co.in
www.elh.co.in

First Edition	1938
Second Edition	1941
Third Edition	1949
Fourth Edition	1953
Fifth Edition	1959
Sixth Edition	1964
Seventh Edition	1968
Eighth Edition	1978
Ninth Edition	1984
Tenth Edition	1987
Reprint with Supplement	1992
Eleventh Edition	1997
Twelfth Edition	2000
Thirteenth Edition	2004
Fourteenth Edition	2009
Fifteenth Edition	2022
FIRST REPRINT	2023
SECOND REPRINT	2025

ISBN 978-81-7177-372-5

Published by Ritika Mogha Nahata
and printed at Mudrak, Noida, U.P.

LATE SRI P. C. MOGHA

PREFACE TO THE FIFTEENTH EDITION

In 1976, when I entered the legal profession, Mogha's Indian Conveyancer became very helpful to me in drafting deeds, agreements, partnerships, settlements, wills, power of attorneys, etc. The first edition of this book came in January 1938, today, we are in the year 2021. In this journey of time, this book has seen 14 editions, the 15th edition is in your hands. As we know in this universe, the only constant thing is 'change'. Since independence, laws in India have been given new interpretations and several new laws have been enacted. Ways of commerce have changed, emergence of new areas in the field of law and commerce has taken place. Globalisation of commerce and business had impacted drafting of instruments and deeds in a great way. Sincere efforts have been made to update the book in its 15th edition and to make it useful for today's professionals. New chapters on insolvency, bankruptcy and intellectual property rights have been added. In this effort, Shri Narendra Kumar, Member (Judicial), Delhi VAT Appellate Tribunal and Ritika Mogha Nahata, LL.M, have taken great pains to ensure the latest law is incorporated in the same. Efforts have been made to make it practicable and useful for the readers and users. All suggestions of users for the improvement of the book are welcome.

Ms. Kriti Madan, Advocate and Aaditya Gambhir, Advocate worked hard to ensure that this edition meets the expectations of users.

Justice (Retd.) S.N. Dhingra

PREFACE TO THE FIRST EDITION

A long preface or introduction or apology is not needed for the publication of a book of this kind, as its want has been long felt by the legal profession in the Country. The work of Conveyancing in the mofussil is in the hands of untrained deed writers having no knowledge of law and pleaders are rarely consulted. When they are consulted in complicated cases, they find it difficult to give proper advice about the forms and language of the draft as neither have they had any training in the art of Conveyancing, nor is there any book which gives precedents suited to Indian conditions. There are excellent books of English precedents, and, in the absence of an Indian book, pleaders depend on them; but as the precedents are generally overlanden with technical expressions of English law which are neither required nor understood even by lawyers in this Country, the pleaders find it somewhat difficult to adapt them properly to their needs. The result is that either they produce drafts full of expressions which are not fully understood and most of which are not necessary, or in their attempt to simplify and curtail the draft they omit something which is essential and produce a draft wanting in an essential ingredient.

In this book, forms for deeds of everyday use in India have been set out in simple language, devoid of highly technical expressions, as far as possible but no attempt has been made to revolutionise the entire system. English forms have been adopted but have been modified so as to omit all that is not required according to the Indian law by reason of any covenants or conditions being implied by statutory provisions, and to add some others which being implied by English Law are omitted there but are necessary as there is no corresponding implied covenant in Indian law. In the Introductory portion of the book general principles of Conveyancing have been stated, and in the preliminary notes appended to the subject, so far as it is necessary for conveyancing purposes, has been briefly stated, and the points to be borne in mind in drawing a conveyancing on the subject have been shown. It is also indicated what modifications in the English precedents are necessary and why. Provisions of Stamp and Registration laws have also been referred to. These notes will be found very useful and it is recommended that, before drawing up any conveyance and referring to the relevant precedents in the book, the draftsman should study these notes.

The precedents are arranged in groups according to subjects on the model of English books of Precedents, and are alphabetically arranged.

As this is the first book of its kind in India, the author is not fully confident that it contains all that is required and that there is no room for improvement. He will feel grateful to any lawyer who will point out any errors, shortcomings or defects which he may come across, or will kindly make suggestions as to any class of precedents which may usefully be added.

LUCKNOW
January 1, 1938 **P.C. MOGHA**

TABLE OF CONTENTS

MORTGAGE, CHARGE, HYPOTHECATION AND PLEDGE

SALE

SERVICE CONTRACTS

TRUSTS INCLUDING SETTLEMENTS, ENDOWMENTS AND WAQFS

INTRODUCTION

Part I—Preliminary

Conveyancing in India

Conveyancing has never been practised as an art in India. This work had upto 1980s generally been in the hands of scribes (deed writers) who have had no legal education or training, but were only conversant with certain set forms of various kinds of deeds, in common use in the country, and acquired by experience the knack of adapting them to their requirements.

In Presidency towns, conveyancing used to be done by solicitors trained in the English system of conveyancing.

Need of Legislation

This work can properly be performed by a person, who has adequate knowledge of law and legal training. The person assigned this work must have knowledge of intricacies of law of concerned branches of law, like Transfer of Property Act, Indian Stamp Act, Indian Succession Act, Hindu Succession Act, Indian Registration Act in addition to various personal laws applicable to the concerned parties. Bar Council of India needs to look into this aspect so that the work of conveyancing is performed only by a competent person. In this way, the standard of conveyancing shall improve, which in turn would certainly reduce the litigation and avoid harassment that follows due to faulty conveyancing by incompetent persons.

Furthermore, an Act of legislature, on the lines of English Acts,[1] laying down what a conveyance should, and what it need not contain, and providing a set of authoritative forms, seems to be an urgent necessity in this country. Until such legislation is passed, it should be the endeavour of

---

1 Namely, the Conveyancing Act 1881 (Sec. 2, interpretation of various terms) and the Law of Property Act 1925. The latter Act contains among other things (many of which are covered by our Transfer of Property Act, Trusts Act, Contract Act, Registration Act etc.) standard forms in the same manner as our Civil Procedure Code contains standard forms of pleadings, etc. Its Sec. 46 empowers the Lord Chancellor to prescribe other forms of agreements as well. Its Secs. 61, 62 and 63 also contain rules of interpretation applicable to deeds generally, subject to special provisions to the contrary as may be specified in a deed. Some other provisions which may be usefully adapted is one in Sec.15 ("The persons expressed to be parties to any conveyance shall, until the contrary be proved, be presumed to be of full age at the date thereof").

every lawyer who has anything to do with conveyancing to make an intelligent study of the subject and in adapting the English forms to his needs, he should try to strip them of all unnecessary verbiage and expressions which are unknown in this country and draft his conveyances with due regard to the requirement of Indian law and in language which is intelligible, not only to a lawyer, but also to a layman. Legislation for shortening the language of deeds and on their interpretation on the lines of what has been provided for statutes in the General Clauses Acts can also be considered.

What is Conveyancing

Conveyancing, a branch of law, deals with mode and form to embody and express intention of the parties for transfer of a property.

Sec. 2(10) of Indian Stamps Act, 1899, defines conveyance as under:

"Conveyance" includes a conveyance or sale and every instrument by which property, whether movable or immovable or any estate or interest in any property, is transferred inter vivos and which is not otherwise specifically provided for by Schedule I or Schedule I-A.

Form of Conveyance

The form in which a conveyance is drafted is immaterial but as English forms have, by long usage, obtained a sort of sanctity, the same may be retained with necessary alterations.

It may be noted that in England deeds are drafted either as deeds poll or as indentures.

What are Deeds Poll

A deeds poll is a legal document binding only one person or several persons acting jointly to express an active intention. It is, strictly speaking, not a contract because it binds only one party and expresses an intention instead of a promise. They are chiefly used for the purpose of granting powers of attorney, Will and for exercising power of appointment or setting out an arbitrator's award. They are drawn in first person.

Indentures Bilateral

Indentures are those deeds in which there are two or more parties. Indentures were so called as at one time they were indented or cut with an uneven edge at the top. This practice of indenting deeds has ceased long ago and even in England the practice of calling them indentures has largely fallen into disuse.

Indian Usage

In India, the Stamp Act, 1899 uses the word "instrument" for every document by which any right or liability is, or purports to be, created, transferred, limited, extended, extinguished or recorded, vide Sec. 2(14). In the Registration Act, 1908 the word "document" has been used instead.

In this book, for the sake of uniformity, the word "deed" has been used generally.

Simple Words

In English conveyances several words in Old English form are used, e.g. "witnesseth". "doth covenant", etc. We can however as well use their modern equivalents, e.g., "witnesses", "covenants", etc.

Paragraphs, Punctuation and Capitals

In England, deeds were formerly all written in one paragraph without punctuation, but the practice of dividing the deed into paragraphs is now growing. As the division of a deed into paragraphs makes it more easily intelligible, this practice is recommended. The commencement of every important part of a deed is marked by putting the first word or phrase in capital letters and this was very necessary when the deed was not divided into paragraphs as a reader who wanted to refer only to a particular part could easily find what he wanted without having to read the whole. With the division of deed into paragraph the use of capital letters is not absolutely necessary but is continued in practice.

Although a free use of punctuation marks is not desirable, as a mistake in punctuation sometimes alters the sense, yet a full stop or semicolon, as may be proper, at the end of each paragraph would be suitable. The language of the deed should be such that the intention of the parties should be clearly understood without the aid of punctuations.

As already noticed above, a deed poll is generally drawn in the first person and an indenture always in the third person.

Deeds poll generally commence with:

"Know all men by these presents", or

"To all whom these presents shall come Greeting"

If there are recitals, the date is written at the end of the deed in the testimonium clause, thus:

"IN WITNESS WHEREOF I the said ——— have hitherto set my hand this ——— day of ———."

The form in which deeds poll and other deeds (hitherto known as indentures) are drafted will be given later under appropriate headings and the exact requirements of such forms will be dealt with in the preliminary notes. The most common and important transactions for which deeds are required are those of various kinds of transfer of immovable property. The general requirements of all deeds of transfer are dealt with in the next part.

Use of Figures and Words

In order to avoid mistake, date, sums and numbers should be preferably stated in words or in words as well as in figures.

Part II—General Requirements of Deeds of Transfer

In this part, it is proposed to deal with the general requirements of all deeds of transfer and to notice the various clauses, of which a deed of transfer is generally composed, and to show in what way each clause should be framed.

The particular and special requirements of particular kinds of transfer deeds and any modifications necessary in the case of a particular kind of transfer will be noticed in the "preliminary note" to the precedents relating thereto.

Division of Deed

An ordinary deed of transfer may conveniently be divided into the following parts:

(a) Description of the deed;
(b) Date;
(c) Parties;
(d) Recitals;
(e) Testatum;
(f) Consideration;
(g) Receipt;
(h) Operative words;
(i) Parcels;
(j) Exceptions and Reservations (if any);
(k) Habendum;
(l) Covenants (if any);
(m) Testimonium;
(n) Signatures of executants;
(o) Signatures of witnesses and attesting witnesses, (wherever attestation is required).

The part of the deed which precedes the habendum is termed "the premises".[1]

Each of these parts will now be separately considered.

a) Description of the Deed

All deeds should be described by the name of the transaction which they evidence, such as "THIS DEED OF MORTGAGE", "THIS DEED OF SALE", "THIS LEASE", "THIS DEED OF GIFT", etc.

When the deed is of a complex character and evidences different transactions known by different legal names or the conveyancer is not sure as to what name should properly be given to the deed, it would be best to describe it simply as "THIS DEED". The description is usually written in capitals. The heading of the deed, though relevant, does not determine its character.

b) Date

After the description of the deed is stated, the date on which it is executed, is required to be stated.

The date of execution may be stated like this:

"THIS LEASE made on the first day of February one thousand nine hundred and ninety nine or "1st February, 1999"

The date is strictly speaking not an essential part of the deed and a deed is perfectly valid if it is undated or the date given is an impossible one, e.g. the 30th day of February. In case no date has been given, oral evidence can be led and such evidence would always be admissible to prove the date of execution if it becomes necessary to determine it.

It is, however, always a matter of great importance to know the date from which a particular deed operates. In India, the period for registration of a deed being 4 months from the date of execution (*see* Sec. 23, Registration Act, 1908) the date of execution is always the first matter for inquiry by the Registering Officer. Similarly, in the case of a deed of transfer of land in respect of which mutation of names is necessary, the date of execution is ascertained for mutation purposes. The date is further important for the purposes of the application of law of limitation.

---

1 Black's Law Dictionary (1992 Edn) defines "premises" (in conveyancing) as "that part of a deed which precedes the *habendum*, in which are set forth the names of the parties with their titles and additions, and in which are recited such deeds, agreements, or matters of fact as are necessary to explain the reasons upon which the present transaction is founded; and it is here, also, the consideration on which it is made is set down and the certainty of the thing granted".

In view of the extreme importance of the date of execution, and of the great risk in leaving the same to be determined by oral evidence, a deed should always be dated, and this should be regarded as an essential requirement.

The date of a deed is the date on which it is signed by the party or parties executing it. When there is only one party to a deed, as in the case of deed poll, or when all the parties sign it on one and the same date, or when, though there are several parties to a deed, all do not sign and those who sign do so on one date, there is no difficulty. But if several parties to a deed sign it on different dates, the question is which date should be entered as the date of deed. The practice is to regard the last of such dates as the date of the deed. This does not, however, seem to be universally correct as there might be a person or persons who execute a deed only for the sake of the formality and the deed operates even without their signature.

For example, in the case of a sale deed, the transfer operates on its execution by the vendor and even without the purchaser's signature on the deed, or when a person is impleaded as a party to a deed simply in order to give him notice of the transaction to obtain his consent though such consent is not legally necessary to validate the transaction. In all such cases the dates on which such person or persons sign the deed may be discarded from consideration, because the date of deed is really the date on which the deed operates.

In order to avoid mistake and risk of forgery, the date should, be written in words and not in figures. Figures may be added within parenthesis, if desired, thus—

"The First day of March Two Thousand Twenty One (the 1st March, 2021)".

In every case, in which a deed is executed by more than one person, the date on which each signs the deed must be shown in the deed, preferably against his signature.

c) Parties to the Deed

i) Transferee

After the date, the names and description of the parties to the deed are mentioned. As to who are the necessary and proper parties to a deed, depends on the circumstances of each case.

In England, the custom is to make both the transferor and the transferee parties to all deeds of transfer. This was necessary in former times as no person could take an interest under an indenture who was not named as a party therein. But ever since the passing of the Real Property Act, 1845 (later replaced by the Law of Property Act 1925) an estate or interest in any property and the benefit of a condition or covenant respecting the same may be taken, although the transferee is not named as a party [*see* Sec. 5 of the 1845 Act, now Sec. 56 of the 1925 Act]. The practice of naming the transferee as a party, however, still continues.

In India, except in the case of leases which, under section 107 of the Transfer of Property Act, 1882, are required to be executed both by the lessor and the lessee, the transferee is not a necessary party to any deed of transfer, and in the forms used in Indian languages, transferees are not normally named as parties and they do not execute the deeds.

But in all cases, where any covenant has to be made by the transferee also, the transferee becomes a necessary party.

Even though a transferee is not a necessary party and a deed will not be invalid or ineffective if he is not mentioned as such (except in the case of a lease), he is certainly a proper party and it is always advisable to make him a party.

Generally, the person or persons conveying interest or right or title in the property is or are to be described first i.e. as First Party. Thereafter, the person or persons in whose favour right or interest or title is conveyed is or are to be described as Second Party.

ii) Third Person

Sometimes it is necessary or expedient, in order to validate a transfer or to give a complete title to the transferee, or to avoid possible disputes or doubts in that regard, to obtain the consent or concurrence of a third person. In such cases, such third person may also be joined as a party. For instance, prior to the enactment of the Hindu Succession Act 1956, [Sec. 14(1)], a reversioner used to be joined in the case of a transfer by a Hindu widow of absolute title in her husband's property. Again, in the case of sale of lessee's right the lessor may be joined if the lessee has no power to transfer his rights without the lessor's permission. (Such permission is generally required under rent control laws; its absence may result in the lessee forfeiting his protection under such laws).

Sometimes other persons also make some covenants in the deed and are joined for this purpose. In all such cases the transferor is placed first, any person whose concurrence is necessary or who enters into any covenant comes next, and the transferee last.

If different portions of the estate transferred are owned by different persons as the mortgagor and mortgagee, lessor and lessee, reversioner and life owner and full estate is transferred by all such persons, the person who has the legal estate should be placed first, and those who have the equitable estate should be placed next.

iii) Description

Full description of the parties should follow the names so as to prevent difficulty in proper identification.

In India, father's name or husband's name, occupation and address of residence including municipal or house number, street, city and pincode and in the case of resident of a rural area the village, sub-division, tehsil and/or development block, district or Post Office etc., are generally regarded as sufficient to identify a man. However, nowadays Aadhar No. and PAN No. should be given to identify the person.

It should not be considered necessary to specify the caste or religion as it is desirable to discourage emphasis on communal or caste distinctions in our republic. But where the transferor is a member of a scheduled caste or scheduled tribe for whose protection the statute places restrictions on his right to transfer, it may be necessary to mention such caste or tribe while reciting the fact of permission for the transfer having been obtained from the competent authority.

iv) Juridical Person

A party to a transfer need not be a living individual but may be a company or association or body of individuals (Sec. 5, Transfer of Property Act, 1882), or an idol[1] or a corporation sole or aggregate[2] or in fact, any juridical person capable of holding property and entering into contracts. "Guru Granth Sahib" is a "juristic person".[3]

---

1 *Bhopatrao* v. *Shri Ram Chandra*, 96 IC 1004; see *Angurbala* v. *Debabrata*, AIR 1951 SC293 (In a Hindu religious endowment the entire ownership of the dedicated property is transferred to the deity or the institution itself as a juristic person, and the *shebait* or *mahant*—unlike a trustee under the English Law in whom the property vests for the benefit of *cestui que trust*—is a mere manager).

2 *Board of Trustees, Ayurvedic and Unani Tibia College* v. *State of Delhi*, AIR 1962 SC 458 (para 9). A company is a Corporation aggregate (Sec. 34, Companies Act, 1956); it has a legal personality distinct from its shareholders (*Charanjit Lal* v. *Union of India*, AIR 1951 SC 41, para 43). For illustrations of corporation sole see the Administrators—General Act 1963 (Sec. 5) and the Charitable Endowments Act 1890 (Sec. 3). Universities, State Electricity Boards, Life Insurance Corporation of India and nationalised banks are instances of corporations aggregate.

3 *Shiromani Gurdwara Prabandhak Committee* v. *Som Nath Dass*, (2000) 4 SCC 146.

A court is not a juridical person capable of holding property or entering into contracts, and security bonds which are given to courts must, therefore, be made in favour of the presiding judge of the court and his successor in office but not in favour of the court.[1]

The very words "juristic person" connote recognition of an entity to be in law a person which otherwise it is not. In other words, it is not an individual natural person but an artificially created person which is to be recognised to be in law as such.

Care should be taken that companies, associations and corporations are described by their correct names. It is better also to refer to the Act under which they are registered or incorporated thus:

"The Bengal Sugar Mills Limited, a company within the meaning of the Companies Act, 1956/2013, and having its registered office at Howrah";

"The Arya Pratinidhi Sabha, a society registered under the Societies Registration Act, 1860";

"The University of Lucknow a body incorporated under the U.P. State Universities Act 1973".

v) Idol

As an *idol* has to act through some natural person,[2] the name of the latter should be disclosed, thus:

"The idol of Sri Kishori Ramanji Maharaj installed in the temple at Brindaban, district Mathura, acting through its Sarbarkar, Ram Lal, son of Shiam Lal ...."

vi) Persons under Legal Disability

Persons under legal disability (namely minors, persons of unsound mind and persons disqualified from contracting by any law to which they are subject) cannot enter into a contract and therefore cannot transfer property (See Sec. 7 Transfer of Property Act read with Secs. 11 and 12 Contract Act and Sec. 3 Majority Act).[3] They cannot by themselves even take a transfer, if the same involves entering into any covenant, as all contracts made by them are void. But if no promise is made by the person under disability as a consideration of the transfer or where there remains

---

1 *Raghuber Singh* v. *Jai Indra Bopander Singh*, AIR 1919 PC 55, ILR 42 All 158, (See precedent, No. 10, page 233, under BOND).

2 *Angurbala* v.*Debabrata*, AIR 1951 SC 293.

3 See discussion of case law in *Manik Chandra* v. *Ram Chandra*, AIR 1981 SC 519, (1980) 4 SCC 22.

nothing for the minor to do there is nothing to make the contract unenforceable at his instance.[1]

However, some statutory obligations are attached to a transferee even in the absence of a specific covenant on their part, e.g., in Transfer of Property Act, Sec. 55(5) in a case of sale and Sec. 109 in a case of lease. Thus, a lease in favour of a minor is not enforceable even at his instance if he himself, and not his guardian, is the executant.[2] Sec. 68 of Contract Act lays down an exception to the effect that a person who supplies necessaries to a person under disability is entitled to reimbursement from the latter's property.

vii) Minors

Minors are persons—male or female—who are below the age of 18 years. A transfer of his or her immovable property can (except short-term lease for which no permission is required, as hereinafter stated) be made only by his natural guardian or guardian appointed by will or other instrument or appointed or declared by the court under the Guardians and Wards Act with the permission of the court. Even for transfer of movables or for lease for a short-term, it is necessary that the transfer should be for the benefit of the minor or for the realisation, protection or benefit of his estate and that there should be no personal covenant binding the minor. The powers of a testamentary guardian may be further restricted by the terms of the Will or other instrument by which he has been appointed as guardian (Sec. 28, Guardians and Wards Act).

The usual form is ....

"AB, a minor, acting through CD his guardian."

The authority of the guardian should be *either* recited in the recital, thus:

"The Vendor is a minor and the said CD is the certificated guardian of his property appointed by order of the District Judge of Agra dated ....".

Or it may be shortly stated in the heading itself thus:

---

1 *Raghava Chariar* v. *Srinivasa*, (1917) 40 Mad 308 (FB) (if minor has fulfilled his part of the contract the other party cannot resist its enforcement on the ground of voidness); *Zafar Ahsan* v. *Zubaida Khatun*, (1929) 27 All LJ 1114; *Bhaggabhor Mandal* v. *Mohini Mohan*, AIR 1918 Cal 1027; *Daniel* v. *Mariamma*, AIR 1951 Mad 466; *Bholanathv. Balbhadra*, AIR 1964 All 527; *The Great American Insurance Co.* v. *Mandanlal*, (1935) 59 Bom 656 (per Beaumont C.J.)

2 *Jaykant* v. *Durgashankar*, AIR 1970 Guj 106

"AB, a minor, acting through CD his guardian appointed by the District Judge, Agra, by order dated ....".

Or "AB, a minor, acting through his father and natural guardian CD."

In case of transfer of a minor's property, the circumstances which give the guardian or *Karta* power to make the transfer should be mentioned in the recitals, e.g. in case of natural guardian or manager of a Hindu family, the legal necessity of the transfer.

The powers of a natural guardian of a Hindu minor are now defined in Sec. 8 of the Hindu Minority and Guardianship Act, 1956. In fact, it gives statutory recognition to certain powers enjoyed by natural guardian under the old Hindu law. Under that provision, the natural guardian shall not mortgage or charge or transfer by sale, gift, exchange or otherwise any part of the immovable property of the minor; or lease any part of such property for a term exceeding five years or for a term exceeding more than one year beyond the date on which the minor will attain majority, except with the previous permission of the court. Such permission should be referred to in the recitals thus:

"The District Judge of Agra has by order dated .... in Miscellaneous Case No. .... of .... permitted the said AB to make the said sale".

If the guardian in his personal capacity also joins in making a conveyance, the two may be described thus:

"AB acting for himself and as guardian of CD, a minor", *or*

"AB, etc., and CD, etc., a minor acting by his guardian the said AB".

A transfer of immovable property by a guardian in contravention of sub-sec. (1) or sub-sec. (2) of Sec. 8 of the Hindu Minority and Guardianship Act or Sec. 28 or Sec. 29 of the Guardians and Wards Act is voidable, at the instance of the minor or any person claiming under him.

The other party as well as a minor, however, can enforce a contract for sale of property entered into by a natural guardian if the contract is for the benefit of the minor.[1] The restriction imposed under Sec. 8 is against alienation of minor's property by a natural guardian but the latter can purchase any property without Court's permission if the purchase is for the minor's benefit.[2] In *Nangali Amma Bhavani Amma* v. *Gopalkrishnan Nair*,[3] it was held that the alienation made in violation of Section 8(2) is voidable,

1 *Manik Chand* v. *Ram Chander*, AIR 1981 SC 519.

2 *Than Singh* v. *Barelal*, AIR 1974 MP 24.

3 (2004) 8 SCC 785.

and that holding it to be void would not only be contrary to the plain words of the statute but would also deprive the minor of the right to affirm or ratify the transaction upon attaining majority.

The position under Mohammadan Law was clarified in *Meethiyan Sidhiqu* v. *Mohd. Kunju Pareeth Kutty*,[1] wherein the Apex Court held that unless mother is appointed by the father as guardian of his minor children's estate or is so appointed by the Judge, she has no power to intermeddle with their immovable property. She must apply to the court for sanction in order to deal with the property, otherwise all his dealings with property are ipso facto void (para 9).

When a sale is to be made on behalf of the minor, the necessary ingredients are that the sale must be for the benefit of the estate of minor and, therefore, the competent person entitled to alienate the minor's property would be, subject to the above condition, either the natural guardian or the property guardian appointed by the court.

viii) Mentally Ill Persons

A mentally ill person means a person who is in need of treatment by reason of any mental disorder other than mental retardation. A manager appointed by the court can alone transfer such person's property with the permission of the court.

Since no specific provision is available in any Statutes to deal with the procedure for such appointment of Guardian to a victim lying in 'comatose state', High Court of Kerela in *Shobha Gopalakrishnan* v. *State of Kerala*,[2] has laid down certain 'Guidelines' which may be kept in mind while dealing with transfer of property of such person.

ix) Insolvent

Earlier, the property of an insolvent vested in the official assignee in the Presidency towns and in the official receiver elsewhere, and the official assignee or the official receiver alone could transfer it (Sec. 68, Presidency Towns Insolvency Act, 1909, and Sec. 59 of the Provincial Insolvency Act, 1920).

As the property vested in the official receiver (Sec. 56) or the official assignee (Sec. 51), the transfer could be made by him in his own name, and the fact of the insolvency of the owner and the vesting of the property in the transferor could be mentioned in the recitals.

---

1 (1996) 7 SCC 436.
2 (2019) 2 KLJ 549.

However, with the enactment of The Insolvency and Bankruptcy Code, 2018, The Presidency Towns Insolvency Act, 1909 and the Provincial Insolvency Act, 1920 stands repealed.

Now, fresh procedure has been laid for insolvency resolution in respect of corporate, partnership firms and individuals.

Where the Adjudicating Authority rejects the resolution plan for non-compliance with requirements specified therein, it has to pass an order requiring the corporate debtor to be liquidated in the manner as laid down in Chapter III of the Code.

Order regarding liquidation can also be passed under sub-section (2) and (4) of section 33 of the Code.

When a liquidation order has been passed, no suit or other legal proceeding can be instituted by or against the corporate debtor. However, Liquidator is empowered to institute suit or other legal proceedings, on behalf of the corporate debtor, though with the prior approval of the Adjudicating Authority. (See sub-sec.(5) of Sec.33 of the Code).

On the passing of the bankruptcy order, the estate of the bankrupt vests in the bankruptcy trustee; the estate shall be divided among his creditors; the creditor of the bankrupt indebted in respect of any debt claimed as bankruptcy debt cannot initiate any action against the property of the bankrupt in respect of such debt; any such creditor cannot commence any suit or other legal proceedings, except with the leave of the Adjudicating Authority and on such terms as may be imposed. (See sec.128).

Chapter V provides as to how the estate of the bankrupt is to be administered and distributed.

x) Trustees

If a property vests in trustees, the transfer should be by the trustees themselves in their own name, as

"AB, CD and EF trustees of the estate of XY",

The facts showing how the estate came to be vested in the trustees should be mentioned in the recitals.

The powers of trustees in regard to transfer of trust property depend on the terms of the trust deed. See precedents of "Miscellaneous Clauses and Conditions of Trust" under TRUSTS, *post*.

xi) Hindu Coparcenary

The manager or *Karta* may execute the deed in his name alone or all members of the coparcenary may join it. In either case, the fact of the property being joint family property should be mentioned in the recitals.

In *Madhavrao Ramchandra More* v. *Rajendra Sahakari Griha Nirman Sanstha Maryadeet*,[1] Court ruled that as per the legal position, the transactions entered into by the *karta* of the Hindu Joint Family are binding on the undivided share of the minors as well as other members of the family, not only when they are executed for the legal necessity but also for the benefit of joint family.

See "(*d*) Recitals", page 18 *post*.

xii) Attorney

An attorney may be made party either in his own name (Sec. 2, Power of Attorney Act, 1882), thus:

"AB attorney of CD",

Or the name of the principal may be shown as a party, thus:

"CD acting by his attorney AB."

The latter form is preferable.

xiii) Firm

Every partner has, under Sec. 19 of the Partnership Act, 1932, an implied authority to bind the firm by acts done to carry on the business of the firm in the usual way. In case of emergency a partner may do any reasonable act (Sec. 21). The acts mentioned in Sec. 19(2), including transfers of immovable property must be done by all the partners; other acts done and instruments executed by one partner must be done and executed by him *in the firm's name or in any other manner expressing or implying an intention to bind the firm (Sec. 22), thus:*

"AB, etc., a partner of and acting for and on behalf of the firm carrying on business under the name and style of —— (*firm's name*)"

"Firm —— acting through AB, etc., its managing partner".

It may, however, be added that strictly speaking, a firm, unlike a corporation, is not a juridical person[2] and only its partners are juridical persons. Hence, if it is desired to execute a deed of transfer in the firm name, it should be ensured that the deed is signed either by all its partners or by a partner holding a power of attorney on behalf of all partners.

---

1 2018 (5) ABR 626, 2018 (6) Bom CRI 28.

2 See *Dullichand* v. *C.I.T.*, AIR 1956 SC 354.

Section 18 of the Partnership Act postulates that "subject to the provisions of the Act, a partner is the agent of the firm for the purposes of the business of the firm." Section 19(1) postulates that "subject to the provisions of Section 22, the act of a partner which is done to carry on in the usual way, the business of the kind carried on by the firm, binds the firm.

The operation of Sections 18 and 19(1) is subject to the exceptions engrafted in sub-section (2) of Section 19, which provides that in the absence of any usage or custom of trade to the contrary, the implied authority of a partner does not empower him to submit a dispute relating to the business of the firm to arbitration, or open a banking account on behalf of the firm in his own name, or compromise or relinquish any claim or portion of a claim by the firm, or withdraw a suit or proceeding filed on behalf of the firm, or admit any liability in a suit or proceeding against the firm, or buy or sell property for or on behalf of the firm or enter into partnership on behalf of the firm.

xiv) Government

Contracts made in exercise of the power of the Union and all assurances of property vested in the Union are to be expressed in the name of the President, while those relating to a State are to be made in the name of the Governor[1] of that State, as laid down by Article 299(1) of the Constitution.

Notifications under Article 299(1) authorising Secretaries of the various Ministries of the Government of India and the Secretaries to Government of the various departments in the States as well as some heads of department and various other officers for entering into contracts or executing assurances of property on behalf of the President or the Governor, as the case may be, have been issued from time to time.

If the contract or transfer is not made in accordance with Article 299

---

1 While the agreement or the deed of lease, sale etc. may at the outset mention the President or the Governor so that it may be expressed in his name it is customary to add within brackets the words "(hereinafter called the Government of India/the State Government/the said Government)", as the case may be, so that the office of the President or the Governor may not have to be referred to repeatedly in subsequent clauses. It is sufficient to give it only in the beginning for fulfilling the constitutional requirement. See, e.g., the agreement quoted in *Laxmanrao* v. *Telecom Distt. Manager*, AIR 1998 Kant 67 (para 5).

of the Constitution, it is void.[1] Such a contract is not capable of being ratified, nor does estoppel become applicable, nor can there be implied contract between the Government and another person.[2] A formal contract in accordance with Article 299 is, however, necessary only when Government acts in its executive capacity and not when a particular statutory authority, as distinguished from the Union or the States, enters into contract in exercise of a statutory power, such as a contract whereby a licence is granted for vend of liquor after acceptance of bid at an auction under the relevant State excise law,[3] unless the statutory provision itself contemplates or requires that a formal deed between the contractor and the Government be executed.[4] Moreover, contract with Government or a public corporation will not stand in the way of a citizen pleading promissory estoppel against the Government or such corporation on the basis that on the assurance or promise made by the latter, he has acted to his prejudice.[5] Estoppel is, however, inoperative to defeat a statutory obligation of an unconditional character. Invalidity based on public policy is a good defence to the objection of consent.[6]

It is well settled that Article 299 does not by itself prohibit a contract with Government coming into existence without a formal deed as it can, notwithstanding the use of the word "executed" in that Article, result from correspondence between an authorised officer of Government, acting expressly on behalf of Government, and a private party, e.g., when a tender for purchase of goods in pursuance of an invitation issued by or on behalf of Government is accepted in writing by the authorised officer on behalf of Government.[7]

1 *Bihar Fishermen Society* v. *Sipahi Singh*, (1977) 4 SCC 145; *Bhikraj Jaipuria* v. *Union of India*, AIR 1962 SC 113, (1962) 2 SCJ 479, (1962) 2 SCR 880; *State of W. Bengal* v. *B.K. Mandal,* AIR 1962 SC 779; *State of U.P.* v. *Murari Lal & Bros.*, AIR 1971 SC 2210, (1971) 2 SCC 449; *Union of India* v. *N.K. Private Ltd.*, AIR 1972 SC 915, (1973) 1 SCJ 107; *K.P. Chowdhry* v. *State of M.P.,* AIR 1967 SC 203; *K.N. Vidhyadharan* v. *State of Kerala*, AIR 1980 Ker 212.

2 *Mulamchand* v. *State of M.P.*, (1968) 3 SCR 214, AIR 1968 SC 1218; *State of Haryana* v. *Lal Chand, (*1984) 3 SCC 634 (para 10).

3 State of Haryana, supra (para 10).

4 *K.P. Chowdhry,* supra; *Mulamchand,* supra; (distinguished on this ground in *State of Haryana*, supra, para 11).

5 *Motilal Padampat Sugar Mills* v. *State of U.P.*, AIR 1979 SC 621, (1979) 2 SCC 409; *Gujarat S.F.C.* v. *Lotus Hotel*, AIR 1983 SC 848, (1983) 3 SCC 379; *Union of India* v. *Godfrey Philips,* AIR 1986 SC 806; *State of Bihar* v. *Usha Martin Industries Ltd.*, 1987 (Supp) SCC 710.

6 *Union Carbide Corporation* v. *Union of India*, (1991) 4 SCC 584 (para 107).

7 *Union of India* v. *A.L. Rallia Ram*, AIR 1963 SC 1685.

However, as clause (1) of Article 299 adds that all such contracts and all assurances of property shall be executed on behalf of the President or the Governor by such persons and in such manner as he may direct or authorize. It is open to the Government concerned to direct that contracts of a specified class shall be made only through formal deed.

Even in the absence of a valid contract, where a party has done something for or supplied something to the Government under an informal agreement and the Government has taken advantage thereof, the Government can be required to compensate the other party (the former) under section 65 and 70 Contract Act.[1]

In *Food Corpn. of India* v. *Babulal Agrawal*,[2] Clause 8 of the agreement provided that upon completion of the plinths etc., the premises would be handed over to the defendant under a lease agreement to be executed between the parties in the prescribed proforma. So, it is obvious that the agreement itself was not a lease deed requiring registration. It only creates a right of getting another document executed creating rights and liabilities in respect of immovable property.

It is in the interest of the public that the question whether a binding contract has been made between the State and a private individual, should not be left to dispute and litigation.

xv) Reference Labels of Parties

In order to avoid the repetition of the full name and description at every place, the parties are generally referred to in the body of the deed by some easy and convenient names which generally have reference to the character in which they join in the deed, such as "the vendor", "the purchaser", "the lessor", "the lessee".

If no such name is adopted, the parties can be referred to as "the party of the first part" (or "the first party"), "the party of the second part" (or "the second party"), "the said AB", "the said CD", but it is always preferable to give each party some short name for reference. Whatever short name is adopted the party should be referred to throughout *by the same name.*

The form, in which the parties will be described in the beginning of the deed. would thus be as follows:

"This SALE DEED is made on the ——— day of ——— BETWEEN AB, etc. (hereinafter called 'the vendor') of the one part and CD, etc., (hereinafter called 'the purchaser'), of the other part."

---

1 *State of W. Bengal* v. *B.K. Mondal*, AIR 1962 SC 779, (1962) 2 SCJ 479, (1962) 2 SCR 880; *New Marine Coal Co.* v. *Union of India*, AIR 1964 SC 152.

2 (2004) 2 SCC 712.

If the transferor alone is made a party, this clause will run as follows:

"This SALE DEED is made on the ——— day of ——— by AB etc., (hereinafter called 'the vendor')."

If there are more than two parties, instead of the words "of the one part" and "of the other part" the words "of the first part", "of the second part", "of the third part", etc., should be used.

d) Recitals

Recitals are of two kinds:

(1) *Narrative* recitals, which relate the past history of the property transferred and set out facts and instruments necessary to show the title and the relation of the parties to the subject matter of the deed; and

(2) *Introductory* recitals, which explain the motive for the preparation and execution of the deed.

i) Narrative Recitals

If the transferor is an absolute owner of the property transferred, his title and the mode in which he acquired it need not generally be recited, but when he is not an absolute owner, recitals showing the extent of his interest and the title, under which he holds it, will be necessary.

So also when the transferor transfers under some power given to him by another instrument or by any special law, such instrument or law must be recited; e.g., in the case of a transfer by a guardian of a minor, the fact of his appointment as such guardian by a deed or order of court and, in the latter case, the fact of his having obtained the permission of the court to make the transfer, must be recited. Similarly, in a transfer of leasehold or mortgagee rights, the lease or mortgage, under which the transferor holds, should be recited.

When the transferor is authorized to transfer only in certain circumstances, it would be advisable to narrate those circumstances in the recital to avoid future disputes, although their omission in the recital cannot estop the transferee from proving them if the transfer is impugned.

For instance, in case of a *Karta* of a Hindu coparcenary, he should better recite the legal necessity for which the transfer is being made.

ii) Introductory Recitals

Among the introductory recitals, which come after the narrative recitals, the chief one is of the agreement which the deed is intended to give effect to. If the agreement is in writing, it is not necessary to give particulars of the date and place of such agreement but it may be expressed in brief and general terms. Any other recital which may be necessary to connect the narrative recitals with the rest of the deed by showing why and how the state of things previously existing is about to be altered by the deed, should also be entered.

The tendency of the modern conveyancers is to do away with recitals, and in simple cases of sale, lease or gift no recitals are generally needed. But recitals are necessary whenever the deed itself does not clearly imply for what purpose any person joining in it is made a party or whenever the covenants, into which he enters, show that he has only a qualified interest in the property transferred. It is unnecessary to recite conclusions of law or negative events.

Order of Recitals

If it is necessary to have numerous and lengthy recitals, they should be inserted in chronological order. In the case of narrative recitals, the different instruments and acts which ultimately result in vesting the property in the transferor, should be recited in strict, chronological order. When the property comes to the transferor partly under one and partly under another title, each title should be traced separately and in chronological order.

Facts and events contained in the introductory recitals also should be inserted in the sequence in which they have happened or occurred.

Form of Recitals

Recitals generally begin with the word "Whereas", but, when there are several recitals, one can either repeat the word before every one of them, by beginning the second and subsequent ones with the words "And Whereas", or divide the recitals into numbered paragraphs with the word "Whereas" at the top thus:

"Whereas—

1.

2.

etc."

Caution while Inserting Recitals

Recitals should be inserted with great caution because they may control the operative part of the deed if the same is ambiguous, and may operate as estoppel by estopping the parties and their representatives from showing the existence of a different state of things from that stated in the recitals. In any case, they may be good evidence of the facts recited, either as admissions under Sec. 21 or as substantive evidence under Sec. 32 or corroborative previous statements under Sec. 157 of the Evidence Act, though as admissions they are not ordinarily admissible in evidence against persons not parties to the document.[1]

If, however, the operative part of the deed is clear and unambiguous, nothing contained in the recital will control it. Conveyancers should, therefore, take the greatest care to avoid unnecessary recitals and to ensure that all recitals are both correct and judicious.

e) Testatum

The next division of a deed consists of the operative part. It commences with a witnessing clause termed the "testatum", which refers to the introductory recitals of the agreement (if any) and also states the consideration (if any) and recites acknowledgement of its receipt. The witnessing clause usually begins with the words "Now this deed witnesses". These words of testatum are of no importance as affecting the operation of the deed and their sole use is to direct attention to the object which the deed is intended to effect. If the deed is intended to serve several objects, use the words "as follows" after the testatum, thus:

"Now this deed witnesses as follows:

1.

2.

etc."

f) Consideration

As lawful consideration is essential element of contract (section 10 Contract Act), it is advisable to express consideration in an agreement. An agreement made without lawful consideration is void, section 25.

Section 2(d) of Indian Contract Act defines consideration as under:

"When, at the desire of the promisor, the promisee or any other person has done or abstained from doing, or does or abstains from doing, or promises to do or to abstain from doing something, such act or abstinence or promise is called a consideration for the promise".

For example, A promises to pay Rs.1 lac as a personal contribution for the purpose of constructing a temple, but he fails to pay. Steps having been

---

1 *Abdur Rahim Khan* v. *Fakir Md. Shah*, AIR 1946 Nag 401, ILR 1946 N 518.

taken by the other party for construction of the temple, A shall be liable to pay this amount and the sum of Rs.1 lac shall fall within the definition of consideration.

Mentioning of consideration is necessary in many cases of transfer for ascertaining the stamp duty payable on the deed as Sec. 27 of the Indian Stamp Act requires that the consideration should be fully and truly set forth in the deed. The penalty for omission to comply with this requirement is a fine which may extend to Rs.5,000 (*vide* Sec. 64).

g) Receipt

Acknowledgment of receipt of consideration may be embodied in the deed itself instead of passing a separate receipt. Thus:

"Now this deed witnesses that in pursuance of the aforesaid agreement and in consideration of Rs. —— paid by the purchaser to the vendor before the execution hereof, the receipt of which the vendor hereby acknowledges".

h) Operative Words

Then follow the real operative words, which vary according to the nature of the estate and of the transaction. What words are necessary in a particular kind of transaction will be dealt with in the preliminary note to the precedents relating to that kind of transaction.

i) Parcels

This is a technical expression meaning description of the property transferred and it follows the operative words. Care must be taken, on the one hand, to include in the particular description or in general words, all the lands, etc., which are intended to pass so that no doubt may arise as to the extent and operation of the deed; and, on the other hand not insert words which will pass more than what is intended.

Great care should be taken in describing the property, as a slight mistake or omission may cause immense loss to a party and if the property is described both in the body and the schedule, a conflict between the two should be carefully avoided.

In English conveyancing, different technical words such as Messuage, Tenement, Hereditament are used to denote different kinds of property. In India, however, there is no need to use such technical words. Instead, words of ordinary use such as, land, house, trees, etc., should be used, and so long as the description is sufficient to show with certainty what the subject-matter of a conveyance is. Care should always be taken that the whole interest conveyed is clearly and fully described.

If the description is a short one, it may be given in the body of the deed in full but if it is a long one it is better to give it in details in a schedule at the foot of the deed, describing it shortly in the body of the deed and referring to the schedule, thus:

"The house known as Glenco and situated at Naini Tal and fully described in the Schedule hereto".

The practice of entering the full description in a schedule is a convenient one and should generally be followed as it makes the reading of the deed easier and clearer.

Map: Sometimes it is necessary to have a map or a plan of the property in order to avoid mistake about its identity and to indicate the actual property conveyed, with greater definiteness and precision. In such cases, such plan or map should be appended to the deed and referred to in the parcels, stating how the property transferred has been shown on it, e.g., by being coloured, or by coloured boundaries or by letters, etc., thus:

"Which land is for greater clarity (*or*, by way of further identification), delineated on the plan annexed hereto and thereon shown as coloured red (*or*, with its boundaries coloured blue) (*or*, thereon marked with letters ABCDE)".

It is always desirable to make it clear whether the description in the deed controls the plan or vice versa. The words "for greater clarity" or "by way of further identification" are added to indicate that the description controls the plan. If plan is intended to control description, we may say thus:

"All that portion of the compound of house known as No. ——— Clyde Road, Lucknow, which is indicated by letters ABCD on the plan annexed hereto and which contains an area of 1500 sq. m. approximately".

A map referred to in a transfer deed is treated as incorporated in the deed, and if it is drawn to scale and demarcates the boundaries clearly, it is not permissible to attempt to correct them with reference to revenue records.[1]

General Words: After a specific description of the property conveyed, there formerly came what were known as the "general words" giving minute details of the easements and legal incidents intended to be conveyed, but this is unnecessary in India in view of the provision of Sec. 8 of the Transfer of Property Act, which lays down that unless a different intention

1 *K.S. Nanji & Co.* v. *Jatashankar*, AIR 1961 SC 1474.

is expressed or necessarily implied, a transfer of property passes forthwith to the transferee all the interest which the transferor is then capable of passing in the property and the legal incidents thereof. Hence, if it is intended to exclude any easement or legal incident, it should be expressly mentioned. Likewise, if it is intended to include in the transfer any right, the inclusion of which is not implied by these provisions, the same should be specifically mentioned, e.g., if a garden attached to a house is transferred with the house, the same should be specifically mentioned. No fixed rule can be laid down as to how a particular kind of property should be described in the parcels, but care should be taken that the description used is full, sufficient, precise, definite and unambiguous.

As laid down in Sec. 3, Transfer of Property Act, standing timber, growing crops or grass are not included in immovable property, hence, if they are also to be transferred specific mention should be made in that behalf.

The following are the particulars usually necessary for the description of different kinds of property in India—

Agricultural land: The numbers and areas of the plots, and the names of the village, pargana, tehsil and district should be given. The tenure on which the land is held, with the amount of revenue, if any, fixed on the land, should be given.

If the land is a part of a plot, the area transferred and its position with reference to a map (to be annexed to the deed) should be clearly stated and, if possible, boundaries may also be given.

Non-agricultural land: The exact situation, area and boundaries of the land should be given. If any number is assigned to it in municipal or village register, the same should also be given.

House: It should be described by its name, if any. The number of the house, if there is one, and the name of the street in which it is situate, should also be given as well as its boundaries. If there are any separate out-houses, stables, garages or gardens or open land attached to it, the same should be mentioned, unless the description of the house as given in the deed is wide enough to include them. Sometimes, the area of the land is also given. If house alone is transferred (and not the land covered by it, e.g., when the land belongs to another person), the fact should be made clear in the deed, by adding the words "but without the land occupied by the said house" after the description of the house. Sometimes, the length and breadth of the house or of the whole compound are also entered. It is not necessary to mention specifically the fixtures and fittings of the house, e.g., doors, windows, etc., and other things provided for permanent use therewith, nor any easement annexed to it (Sec. 8 of the Transfer of Property Act), but if there are any machineries fixed in the house and they are included, they should be specifically mentioned.

Trees: These pass with the land on which they stand, but if they are separately transferred, they should be described correctly by their position and their species.

Grove: The name, if any, with the correct position of the grove and the number, if any, in village or municipal registers should be given. The area and the boundaries should also be mentioned.

Area: Wherever area is given, care should be taken that it is correct. To be on the safe side, it is advisable that after the area the word "approximately" or the words "more or less" may be added so that there may not be any trouble if the area is found to be incorrect.

The normal rule is that in case of conflict, a description by fixed boundaries should be preferred to a description by area which would be rejected as *falsa demonstratio.*[1] Where, however, in a deed the boundaries of the land conveyed and the area marked in the plan disagreed, but the parties had always treated the area marked in the plan as the true area conveyed, this conduct of the parties was held to be relevant for upholding the plan in preference to the boundaries recited.[2] The boundaries stated in the description of the property at the foot of the deed should be read along with the document as a whole including any plan annexed thereto.

Description of the property to be conveyed should, as far as practicable, be the same as in former title deeds. If the description in former title deeds is found to be wrong or has been changed owing to change of circumstances, the correct present description should be given and a reference may, if necessary, be made connecting the parcels with the former description, thus:

"The house now known as Hari Bhawan situate at Naini Tal which was formerly known as Endcliffe."

For forms of parcels *see* under General Forms *post.*

j) Exceptions and Reservations

All exceptions and reservations out of the property transferred should follow the parcels.

---

1 *Plestin K.A.B. Co-op. Society* v. *Govt. of Palestine*, AIR 1948 PC 207.

2 *Watchman* v. *Attorney General of East Africa Protectorate*, (1919) AC 533 PC; referred to with approval in *Godhra Electricity Co.* v. *State of Gujarat*, (1975) 1 SCC 199.

An *exception* is something in existence at the date of transfer which, if not expressly excepted, would pass with the property as described in the parcels, such as trees.

A *reservation* is something not in existence at the date of the transfer but is newly created by the grant, e.g. when the vendor reserves a right of way over the property. But since both "excepting and reserving" are used in practice it is immaterial whether what follows is an exception or a reservation.

Strictly speaking, as a reservation operates as a new grant by the transferee to the transferor, deed should be executed by the transferee also, otherwise on reservation of an easement no legal easement is created but only an equitable right.

k) Habendum

This is the familiar "to have and to hold" (in Latin, *habendum et tenendum*) clause of the English precedents. In India such phrases as "to have and hold" or such an expression as "to the use of the purchaser" are not strictly necessary but there is no harm in continuing the established practice.

See Preliminary Notes to SALE, page 784 *post* on "Habendum, when Several Purchasers".

l) Covenants and Undertakings

If the parties to a transfer enter into covenants, such covenants should be entered after the Habendum. While drafting covenants, regard should be had to the statutorily implied covenants which operate subject to any contract to the contrary. For instance, provisions of Sec. 55 (sale), Secs. 65 and 67 (mortgage), Sec. 108 (lease) of the Transfer of Property Act should be kept in mind which deal with implied rights and liabilities of the parties.

Where several covenants follow each other, they may run on as one sentence, each being introduced with the words "and also" or by the words "Firstly", "secondly", etc. or they may be set out in paragraph form with the heading:

"The vendor hereby covenants with the purchaser as follows—"

It is better to put in the transferor's and the transferee's covenants separately, and any covenants mutually entered into by the parties with each other may be inserted separately. If the transferor's and transferee's covenants are separately mentioned in the deed, care should be taken that no covenant, which should really be the covenant of one party, is entered in the covenants of the other. For example, if a lessee is given the right to cut trees of a certain kind and not to cut trees of a different kind, the latter covenant is a covenant by the lessee and the former is a covenant by the lessor and both should not be inserted in one covenant by either. When it is found inconvenient or awkward to split up, what really is one covenant into two parts, it is better to insert such a covenant as a mutual covenant by the parties.

Sometimes the terms and conditions of a transfer cannot be conveniently separated into transferor's covenants and transferee's covenants. In such cases, it would be better to include all the covenants under one head as parties' covenants thus: "The parties aforesaid hereto hereby mutually agree with each other as follows:"

m) Testimonium

The last part of a deed is the testimonium which sets forth the fact of the parties having signed the deed. This is not an essential part of the deed, but as it marks the close of the deed there is no harm in continuing the established practice. The usual English form of testimonium is as follows:

"In witness whereof the parties hereto have hereunto set their respective hands and seals the day and year first above written."

The use of seals is not common in India except in cases of companies and corporations, and the proper form in simple language would be somewhat as follows:

"In witness whereof the parties hereto have signed this deed on the date first above written."

n) Signatures and Attestation

After testimonium should follow the signatures of the executants and those of attesting witnesses. If the executant is not competent to contract or is a juristic person, the deed must be signed by the person competent to contract on his or its behalf. Thus if the deed is executed:

i) on behalf of a minor or a mentally ill person, it must be signed by his natural guardian or where a guardian has been appointed by a competent court, then by such guardian, as guardian of ————;

ii) by a firm, then by any partner or partners of the firm, authorised (impliedly under Sec. 19 Partnership Act or expressly by power of attorney), on behalf of the firm;

iii) by a corporation, such as a university or a local authority or other statutory corporation, then by a person or the persons authorized in this behalf by or under the statute incorporating such body. Whether it is also to be sealed, depends on the provisions of the relevant statute;

iv) by a company or co-operative society or a society registered under the Societies Registration Act, 1860, then by a person authorized in this behalf by or under the articles of association or rules or regulations or bye-laws, as the case may be.

Sec. 21 of Companies Act, 2013 provides that save as otherwise provided in this Act, a document or proceeding requiring authentication by a company; or contracts made by or on behalf of a company may be signed by any key managerial personnel or an officer or employee of the company, duly authorized by the Board in this behalf.

Sub-sec. (1) of sec. 22 provides that a bill of exchange, hundi or promissory note shall be deemed to have been made, accepted, drawn or endorsed on behalf of a company if made, accepted, drawn, or endorsed in the name of, or on behalf of or on account of, the company by any person acting under its authority, express or implied.

Sub-sec.(2) provides that a company may, by writing under its common seal, if any, authorize any person, either generally or in respect of any specified matters, as its attorney, to execute other deeds on its behalf in any place either in or outside India.

Provided that in case a company does not have a common seal, the authorization under this sub-section shall be made by 2 directors or by a director and the Company Secretary, wherever the company has appointed a Company Secretary.

A deed signed by such an attorney on behalf of the company and under his seal shall bind the company.

v) by a trustee or mutwalli, then by such person describing himself as such;

vi) by an attorney, then by such person describing himself as such and mentioning the date of the deed of the power of attorney;

vii) by the Government, then by the person authorized in this behalf under Article 299 of the Constitution of India, by and on behalf of the President or the Governor, as the case may be, specifying the official designation and preferably notification or government order under which the authority is conferred. (The other party may well insist on seeing such notification or authorization).

Sign

The word “sign” means “to write one’s name on, as in acknowledging authorship”. Sec. 3 (56), General Clauses Act, 1897, extends its meaning, with reference to a person who is unable to write his name, to include “mark”. The document must be signed by a person in such a way as to acknowledge that he is the party contracting, and it is not very material in what part of the document the signature appears.

The execution of a deed is necessary under the Transfer of Property Act in cases of mortgage, lease, gift[1] of immovable property and transfer of actionable claims, and the omission of the signature of the executant, will therefore, make the deed invalid. However, in case of lease, execution of a deed is not necessary if the tenancy in from month to month or for a term upto one year which may be created orally, accompanied by delivery of possession, Section 107, Transfer of Property Act. But in case of sale, there is no such necessity if the property is movable or if the immovable property is sold for less than one hundred rupees.

A deed of transfer need not be signed by the transferee, even though he is mentioned as a party. All conditions and covenants are binding upon him without his executing the conveyance if he consents to it by entering upon the land granted under the conveyance. But if the deed contains any special covenant by the transferee or any reservation (which legally amounts to a re-grant by the transferee), it is always proper to have it signed by the transferee also.

Attestation

Attestation is necessary in case of some deeds, e.g., mortgage, gift, bond, Will and revocation of Will. In other cases, though it is not necessary, it is except in the case of negotiable instruments, always safe to have the signature of the executants attested. Attestation in India, whenever required by law, should be by at least two witnesses, who should have seen the executant sign the deed or should have received from the executant a personal acknowledgment of his signature but it is not necessary that both the witnesses should have been present at the same time.

A deed is normally signed at the end on the right side of its last page and the attesting witnesses may sign on the left side. If both the parties sign, transferor may sign on the right and the transferee on the left and witnesses to each signature may sign below the signature.

However, as noted earlier, the place at which the signatures occur has no legal effect. It is also expedient to ensure that preceding pages are also initialled or signed by the parties.

---

1 The Transfer of Property Act is, however, not exhaustive, nor is it universally applicable. Muslim gifts are thus governed by Muslim law, vide Sec. 129, Transfer of Property Act. A deed is not necessary for a gift by a Muslim, but if deed is executed it requires registration.

Section 68 of the Indian Evidence Act, 1872 provides as to how execution of a document, required by law to be attested, is to be proved.

It provides that if a document is required by law to be attested, it shall not be used as evidence until one attesting witness at least has been called for the purpose of proving its execution, if there be an attesting witness alive, and subject to the process of the court and capable of giving evidence;

Provided that it shall not be necessary to call an attesting witness in proof of the execution of any document, not being a Will, which has been registered in accordance with the provisions of the Indian Registration Act, 1908 (16 of 1908), unless its execution by the person by whom it purports to have been executed is specifically denied.

Section 63 of the Succession Act, 1925 requires a Will to be attested by two or more witnesses.

Forms of Attestation

There is no particular form of attestation but it should appear clearly that a witness intended to sign as an attesting witness. The practice in Indian forms is to write the word "Witness" above the signature. In English forms, between the signatures of the executants and witnesses the words "in the presence of" are added. It has been held that the signature of the scribe or of an identifying witness or of a third party approving the transaction or of the registering officer at the bottom of a deed does not by itself, amount to attestation.[1] If the scribe intends to sign as an attesting witness, this should clearly appear from the deed by the addition of the word "Witness", or otherwise. The intention to attest is necessary for any such person to be treated as an attesting witness.[2]

In the case of a will it is further noteworthy that while the testator may sign or affix his mark himself or direct some other person to sign on his behalf, the attestor is not allowed to so delegate his authority to any other person to sign or make a mark on his behalf.[3]

Illiterate Persons

Illiterate persons, who are not able to sign, may either put their pen mark or thumb mark. Only the latter is in vogue in modern deeds. As a

---

1 *Sarkar Barnard* v. *Alak Manjary*, AIR 1925 PC 89, 26 BLR 737, 83 IC 170; *Girja Dutt* v. *Gangotri*, AIR 1955 SC 346; *M.L. Abdul Jaffar* v. *Venkatashastri*, AIR 1969 SC 1147.

2 *Badri Prasad* v. *Abdul Karim*, (1913) ILR 35 All 254; *Dhyan Chand* v. *Savitri Devi*, AIR 1998 HP 37; *Shamu Patter* v. *Abdul Kadir*, (1908) ILR 31 Mad 215, (1908) 18 MLJ 219.

3 *Nagulapati Lakshamma* v. *Mupparaju*, (1998) 5 SCC 285 (case law on 'sign').

thumb mark is more satisfactory for identification purposes, the executant or witness should put his thumb mark (as per usage, left thumb mark in the case of males and right thumb mark in the case of females, and if that hand or thumb is defective or injured then of the other thumb), and the scribe or another person should make an endorsement above or under the mark to show whose mark and of which hand's thumb it is.

Deeds by Pardanashin Ladies

Where the executant cannot herself read a deed, it should be explained to her by the scribe or any other person before her signature or mark is obtained. This is necessary in the case of *pardanashin* ladies, as courts afford special protection to them and in all cases in which a deed executed by such a lady is used against her, insist on clear proof that it had been executed by her after fully understanding the terms and the effect thereof and that she had independent advice in the matter. The person reading and explaining the deed to the executant should certify the fact at the foot, thus:

"This deed was read over and explained by me to the executant before he/she executed it."

It appears that the Scheduled Banks, while dealing with ladies, have introduced a system by which they get an endorsement from the lady stating "she does not observe *purdah*". This might be availed as admission on her part, if an occasion arises.

These precautions apart, the terms of such deeds should also not appear to be loaded against such executants so as to give suspicion of fraud.[1] Although mere absence of an endorsement on the deed that the executant was a blind person is not fatal to the validity of the deed,[2] yet it is safer and expedient to mention any such fact.

Errors and Omissions

Any errors or omissions detected after engrossing a deed on stamped paper but before its completion by signature may be corrected, and the corrections initialled by the parties signing the deed. It is better and safer to have these noted in a memorandum before the testimonium or to execute a separate supplementary deed.

Endorsement and Supplemental Deeds

When a deed or agreement becomes necessary in pursuance of, or in relation to, a prior deed, this is effected either by endorsement on the prior

1 *Mahiruddin* v. *Mt. Rythun Nessa*, AIR 1998 Gau 22.

2 *Nooruddin* v. *Umairathu Beevi*, AIR 1998 Ker 171.

deed when a short writing would be sufficient, or by a separate deed described as "supplemental" or "intended to be read as annexed to the prior deed" in which case, detailed recitals of the prior deed are unnecessary. For example, if a lessee transfers his rights under the lease to another person such transfer, or if it is intended to alter any covenants in the lease or to surrender the lease, such agreement, may be endorsed on the lease itself (*see* precedents under "Lease"); if a mortgage is redeemed on receipt of mortgage money, the reconveyance may be endorsed on the mortgage deed (*see* precedents under "Mortgage"); and appointment of new trustees and revocation of trusts are usually made by endorsements on the deed of trust (*see* precedents under "Trust"). The same thing can also be done by a separate deed if a short writing is not considered sufficient and the deed, either by reason of large recitals or on account of lengthy covenants, promises to be a lengthy and detailed one. The matter is purely one of convenience, but mostly in contracts with the Government, a supplemental deed becomes necessary either because a new term of agreement is sought to be added or because modification of the existing terms has been subsequently agreed upon.

Endorsements which are of general use and for which no supplemental deed is necessary relate to part payment or acknowledgment of a debt by a debtor. What is necessary for such an endorsement is that the intention should be expressed by use of specific words. Endorsements are also common for negotiating a negotiable instrument or transfer of a bill of exchange or a policy of insurance or Government securities. Again, no particular form of endorsement is necessary in such cases. What is necessary is that the words should clearly show the transfer of interest in favour of a particular person.

Form of Endorsement

The endorsement may begin either by saying "This deed made on this ——— day of ——— between the within named ——— and the within named ————," or directly thus: "The parties to the within written deed hereby agree as follows". The operative part of the deed then follows, usually without any recitals unless any recital is also absolutely necessary in order to make the deed intelligible. The original deed on which the endorsement is made is referred to in the endorsement as the "within written deed" and the parties, recital, covenant, etc., in the original deed are referred to as "within named lessor" or "within named parties" or "within mentioned covenants" or "within recited ————" or "within described house" or "the garden described in the schedule to the within written deed", etc. If after one endorsement another is made, the reference in the latter to the former endorsed deed shall be made by the use of the word "above" instead of "within". After the operative part of the endorsement, the usual testimonium clause shall be added, ending with signatures of executants and of attesting witnesses, if necessary.

Form of Supplemental Deed

The form shall be the usual form of deed or agreement in which after the names of parties should be inserted the words "supplemental (*or*, intended to be read as annexed) to a deed of ——— dated ——— and made between the parties hereto (*or*, between ——— and ———) hereinafter called the "Principal deed". If the particulars of the principal deed are somewhat lengthy, it is more convenient to refer to the principal deed in the first recital and to say that this deed is supplemental to that deed, thus "Whereas this deed is supplemental to a deed of sale made, etc..... hereinafter called the "Principal deed". If the supplemental deed is supplemental to several deeds, each should be mentioned specifically. Then should follow such recitals as are considered absolutely necessary in order to make the deed intelligible for facts leading to the execution of the supplemental deed, but recitals about the contents of the principal deed are not necessary. After that, should follow the usual operative part and covenants, etc. When referring to matters or persons mentioned in the principal deed, we should say "——— mentioned (*or*, recited) in the principal deed".

Precedents of endorsement and supplemental deeds are given under the heads of the principal deeds, e.g. Lease, Sale, Trust, etc., and all deeds given under the head "rectification and modification" are supplemental deeds.

Stamp Duty

Under Section 35 of the Stamp Act, Instrument not duly stamped is inadmissible in evidence. However, the objection related to deficiency of stamp duty of a document has to be decided before proceeding further. In that eventuality, the document requires to be impounded, appropriately valued and adequately stamped before the trial in the matter could proceed. It is also a settled position of law that whenever any objection has been raised regarding admissibility of any material in evidence, the Court ought to first rule upon such objections before proceeding with trial of the suit. In *National Small Industries Corp. Ltd.* v. *Super Packers*,[1] the trial court kept

1 (2019) 264 DLT 473.

the question of insufficiency of stamp duty on the hire purchase agreements open. Hon'ble Judge of High Court observed that the court was only required to impound the documents and should have either called upon the appellant to pay the stamp duty to the extent the documents are insufficiently stamped and if the party did not agree with the direction, the Court could have impounded the documents and sent it to the collector for adjudication, but at the same time adjourned the proceedings, which was not done. Hence the rejection of the hire purchase agreements being insufficiently stamped and inadmissible in evidence was clearly erroneous.

Stamp Duty - by whom payable

Section 29 of the Stamp Act provides which party, in the absence of an agreement to the contrary, will bear the stamp duty payable on an instrument.

This may be kept in view while drafting a deed. Only when the party other than the one mentioned in Sec. 29 is to bear the stamp duty, specific provision be made in the deed.

Section 29 is not exhaustive of all the instruments on which the stamp duty is leviable under the Stamp Act. In cases of instruments not provided for in Sec. 29, the stamp duty will be borne by the person who has agreed to pay it.

Stamp Duty on endorsements and supplemental deeds

All endorsements or supplemental deeds should be stamped according to the nature of the transaction which they evidence, e.g., if it is for receipt of money, it should be stamped as a receipt; if it is an agreement, it should be stamped as an agreement. Some documents, if endorsed on prior deeds are exempt from stamp duty, e.g., receipt of mortgage money endorsed on mortgage deed, or transfer of a bill of exchange or policy of insurance or securities of Government of India endorsed on those papers.

Registration

Whether a deed is required to be compulsorily registered (Sec. 17, Registration Act) will be shown in the Preliminary Note to each deed. Even some documents not compulsorily registerable may be, voluntarily got registered (Sec. 18).

Proviso to Sec. 49 provides that an unregistered document requiring compulsory registration may be used in evidence for a contract, in a suit for specific performance or as evidence of any collateral transaction not required to be effected by registered instrument, but not as evidence of the transaction itself.

Sec. 60(2) provides that the Sub Registrar's endorsement made while registering a document is admissible for proving the facts mentioned therein.[1]

Part III—Precautions

Beside knowing the general requirements of deeds of transfer and the various components which compose a deed, it is also necessary to know some other essential requirements of drafting especially in light of rules of constructions of documents. In this part, it is proposed to point out the precautions which are to be taken in drafting a document, and in the next part, to note the various rules of interpretation of documents which may help a conveyancer to a scientific drafting of deeds.

The object of writing a deed is that the parties should remain bound to their contractual obligations. The deed has, therefore, to be drawn up in a manner as to give no chance to any party to the deed, to resile from the rights and obligations created under the deed. In the words of Sir James Fitzjames Stephen, "in drafting it is not enough to gain a degree of precision which a person reading in good faith can understand, but it is necessary to attain if possible a degree of precision which a person reading in bad faith cannot misunderstand."[2] To achieve this objective the following precautions should be observed:

(1) The deed should contain all the material facts leading to the agreement along with the terms and conditions settled between the parties.

(2) The intention of the parties should be made clear by plain and simple reading of the document as a whole and there should be no ambiguity or inconsistency between paragraphs or clauses of the deed.

(3) The words and expressions should be used in their primary natural and grammatical meanings and the same words and expressions should have same meaning throughout.

(4) The recitals should be kept at the minimum and drafted in consonance with the operative part, otherwise some recital may be interpreted to control the operative part.

---

1 *Gopal Das* v. *Sri Thakurji*, AIR 1943 PC, folld. in *S. Rathnammal* v. *Mottadu*, 1998 AIHC 3094 (Mad).

2 *Sant Ram* v. *Rajinder Lal* AIR 1978 SC 1601, (1979) 2 SCC 274 (para 8), (1979) 1 SCWR 175.

Part IV—Rules of Construction of Deeds

Relevancy of precedents for interpreting other documents

Unless the language of two documents is identical, an interpretation placed by courts on one document is no authority for the proposition that a document differently drafted, though using partially similar language, should be similarly interpreted.[1] Judicial interpretation of similar documents in the past can[2] and ought[3] to be relied on, but as the effect of the words used must inevitably depend on the context and would be conditioned by the tenor of each document, such decisions are not very useful unless the words used are identical.[4]

Description of deed not conclusive

As will be seen under the various Preliminary Notes, such as under LICENCE and under MORTGAGE, *post*, the description given to a transaction by the parties in the deed is not conclusive. It is the substance and not the form that has to be seen. A document described as licence may be construed as a lease, a deed described as a sale with a condition of re-purchase may be construed as a mortgage, a deed described as family settlement may be construed to be a partition, and so on. Numerous cases under the Stamp Act also show that sometimes parties deliberately mis-describe a deed, in order to avoid the need for registration or to evade stamp duty. "The document is weighed by its content, not the title".[5]

Construction of Deed a question of law or a mixed question of law and fact

The interpretation of written document is, as stated in Halsbury,[6] "generally speaking, a matter of law". But the ascertainment of the meaning of technical or commercial terms used in a written contract, and also, in order to enable the construction of the document, the surrounding circumstances of the particular case, are questions of fact; where there is a latent ambiguity in a written instrument, the question of which meaning was intended is also a question of fact.[7] Sections 91 and 92 Evidence Act also point to the same.

---

1 *Abdulla Ahmad* v. *Animendra K. Mitter*, AIR 1950 SC 15.

2 *Ram Gopal* v. *Nandlal,* AIR 1951 SC 139 (para 23).

3 *State of Orissa* v. *Titaghur Paper Mills*, AIR 1985 SC 1293, (1985) Supp. SCC 280.

4 *Shapoor F. Mazda* v. *Durga Prosad*, AIR 1961 SC 1236.

5 *Shyam Sunder* v. *Delta International Ltd.*, AIR 1998 Cal 233 (DB), Follg. *Inderjeet Singh* v. *Karam Chand Thapar*, (1995) 6 SCC 166 (para 13), AIR 1996 SC 247.

6 4th Edn. Vol. 12, para 1461.

7 The references to judge and jury in Halsbury (*ibid*) are irrelevant in the Indian context, hence replaced here by questions of law and of fact respectively.

Thus, the construction of a document of title or of a document which is the foundation of the rights of the parties, necessarily raises a question of law.[1]

Sections 91, 92 Evidence Act

A deed constitutes the primary evidence of the terms of a contract, or of a grant, or of any other disposition of property (Sec. 91, Evidence Act). The law forbids any contradictions of, or any addition, subtraction or variation in a written document by any extrinsic evidence,[2] though such evidence will be admissible to explain any ambiguity, etc. (Sec. 92, Evidence Act). The document should therefore contain all the terms and conditions, preceded by a recital of all relevant and material facts.

In cases of uncertainty, the rules embodied in provisos 2 and 6 to section 92 Evidence Act can be invoked for construing a deed.[3] Proviso 6 enables the court to examine the facts and surrounding circumstances to which the language of the document may be related, while proviso 2 permits evidence of any separate oral agreement, on which the document is silent and which is not inconsistent with its terms.

Literal Construction

The rules laid down in respect of construction of deeds are founded in law, reason and commonsense; they shall operate according to intention of parties, if by law, they may and will, effectuate the intention.

But, it is not always possible to be guided by the meaning of the words as found in the dictionary while construing an agreement; the intention of the parties has to be given necessary weightage and it is not possible to give a wider and liberal meaning merely because one of the parties is a public

---

1 *Sir Chuni Lal Mehta* v. *Century Spinning and Manufacturing Co. Ltd.,* AIR 1962 SC 1314; *I.C.I. India Pvt. Ltd.* v. *C.I.T.,* AIR 1972 SC 1524; ("The construction of a contractual document is a matter of law, not a question of fact); *Kameshwaramma* v. *S. Subba Rao,* AIR 1963 SC 884 (Construction of documents of title is a matter of law. But revenue records are not documents of title, whatever be their evidentiary value); *J.G. Chakravarty* v. *Bhowmik,* AIR 1978 SC 139 (Basic documents such as deeds of trust go to the root of the matter: Their construction is a question of law); *Tenkasi Senkunda* v. *N. Kuttralinga Mudaliar,* 1998 AIHC 2226 (Mad), (following AIR 1963 SC 884 and AIR 1978 SC 139 ibid) (Interpretation of documents involving title is a question of law).

2 *T.N. Electricity Board* v. *N. Raju Reddiei*, AIR 1996 SC 2025, 2027 (para 7) (re: contract); *General Assurance Society Ltd.* v. *Chand Mull Jain*, AIR 1966 SC 1644, 1649 (re: contract of insurance); *State Bank of India* v. *Agents and Manufacturers*, AIR 1998 Delhi 184 (re: description of risk in contract of insurance).

3 *Timblo Irmaos Ltd.* v. *Jorge A.M. Sequeira*, AIR 1977 SC 734.

authority.[1] While interpreting the terms of an insurance policy the view favouring the policyholder is preferred.[2]

If the intention of the parties can be gathered from the words and expressions used in a deed, such an intention does not require to be determined in any other manner except giving the words their normal or natural and primary meaning.[3] It is the dominant intention of the document as disclosed from its whole tenor, that must guide the construction of its contents.[4]

In a case[5] relating to power of attorney, the Supreme Court enumerated the following well known rules of interpretation of deeds, some of which are of general application:

"*firstly*, that a word used in a document has to be interpreted as a part of and in the context of the whole;

secondly, that the purpose of the powers conferred by the power of attorney has to be ascertained having regard to the need which gave rise to the execution of the document, the practice of the parties, and the manner in which the parties themselves understood the purpose of the document; and

thirdly, that powers which are absolutely necessary and incidental to the execution of the ascertained objects of the general powers given must be necessarily implied."

The question of interpretation of a deed arises only when there is some sort of patent or latent ambiguity. The cardinal rule again is that clear and unambiguous words prevail over any hypothetical considerations of supposed intention.[6]

Thus where the words "*malikmustakil*" being strong, clear and unambiguous were used in a compromise deed in respect of properties given to a widow, and those words were not qualified by any other words or circumstances appearing in the document it was held that the estate given to

---

1 *L.I.C.* v. *Raj Kumar*, (1999) 3 SCC 465 (para 15), AIR 1999 SC 2346.

2 *L.I.C.* v. *Raj Kumar*, *ibid* (para 16) Follg. *Shashi Gupta* v. *L.I.C.*, AIR 1995 SC 1367, 1995 Supp (1) SCC 754.

3 *Krishna Beharilal* v. *Gulabchand*, AIR 1971 SC 1041 (1043); *V.S. Talwar* v. *Prem Chandra Sharma*, (1984) 2 SCC 420; *D.D.A.* v. *D.C. Kaushik*, AIR 1973 SC 2609, (1973) 2 SCC 825; see also *Suresh Kumar Prasad* v. *Syed Imam Ali*, AIR 1986 Patna 353.

4 *Nai Babu* v. *L. Ramnarayan*, AIR 1978 SC 22, (1978) 1 SCC 58; *Puzhakkal Kuttappu*v. *C. Bhargavi*, (1977) 1 SCC 17 (whether mortgage or lease).

5 *Timblo Irmaos Ltd.* v. *Jorge A.M. Sequeira*, AIR 1977 SC 734, (1977) 3 SCC 474 (para 13).

6 *Union of India* v. *Kishorilal*, AIR 1959 SC 1362.

her was an absolute one.[1] In construing documents, one must have regards, not to the presumed intention of the parties, but to the meaning of the words they have used.

If two interpretations of the document are possible, the one which would give effect and meaning to all its parts should be adopted, and for the purpose, the words creating uncertainty[2] or illegality[3] in a document can be ignored.

Commercial contracts liberally construed

In respect of contracts which are commercial documents, including arbitration agreements, it has further been held that while interpreting them it would not be right to apply strict rules of construction which are ordinarily applicable to a conveyance and other formal documents. The meaning of such a contract must be gathered by adopting a commonsense approach and it must not be thwarted by a narrow, pedantic and legalistic interpretation.[4]

Ambiguous or redundant words in an agreement ought to be ignored. The rule of statutory interpretation that no words used by the legislature are useless and that meaning should be spelt out from the context is not applicable to a contract.[5]

In *Central Bank of India, Ltd, Amritsar* v. *Hartford Fire Insurance Co., Ltd.*,[6] Hon'ble Apex Court, held as under:

"7. ....it is the court's duty to give effect to the bargain of the parties according to their intention and when that bargain is in writing the intention is to be looked for in the words used unless they are such that one may suspect that they do not convey the intention correctly. If those words are clear, there is very little that the court has to do. The court must give effect to the plain meaning of the words however it may dislike the result."

---

1 *Krishna Beharilal* v. *Gulabchand*, AIR 1971 SC 1041, (1971) 1 SCC 837, (1971) 1 SCWR 614.

2 *Delhi Development Authority* v. *Durga Chand Kaushish*, AIR 1973 SC 2609, (1973) 2 SCC 825 (proviso to covenant No. 9 suffered from vice of uncertainty, hence ignored, and the earlier operative part of the demise, which was clear, given effect to); *Abdul Ghaffar* v. *Raghubir Singh*, 1979 ALJ 1140.

3 *Kissenlal Verma* v. *Khaleda*, AIR 1977 (NOC) 159 (Cal.).

4 *Union of India* v. *D.N. Revri and Co.*, (1976) 4 SCC 147.

5 *Ghaziabad Development Authority* v. *Unique Construction*, AIR 1997 All 341 (DB) (para 5).

6 AIR 1965 SC 1288.

Document to be read as a whole

A document must be read as a whole for finding out its true meaning, and it is not permissible to pick a clause or a sentence and to construe the document on its basis.[1] Even the description or title given to the document by the parties is not decisive if the document read as a whole leads to a different conclusion.[2] Where the words used are not clear and unambiguous the intention will have to be ascertained. The most essential thing is to collect the intention of the parties from the expressions they have used in the deed itself.[3]

What if the intention so collected will not square with the words used? The answer is that the intention prevails.[4]

The maxim "False grammar does not vitiate a deed" (*Grammatica falsa non vitiat chartam*) has been approved in *Whirlpool Corpn.* v. *Registrar of Trade Marks*,[5] where in it was extended even to statutory interpretation. Similarly, "*Falsa grammatica non vitiat concessionem*", *i.e.*, false or bad grammar does not vitiate a grant. Again *falsa orthographia non vitiat chartam concessionem, i.e.*, false spelling does not vitiate a deed or grant.[6] In other words, mistakes of language will not make a deed void when the intent of the parties is plainly apparent. Thus, in *Whirlpool, supra*, the Supreme Court ascertained the true meaning of the incorrect sentence from a reading of the statute as a whole (para 68 of the S.C.C. report).

Other verbal mistakes are also not necessarily fatal if the true intention can be reasonably ascertained. Thus, '*falsa demonstratione legatum non perimitur*', and '*falsa demonstratio non nocet, cum de corpore (persona) constat*', *i.e.*, when the part of document is true and the true part describes the subject with sufficient certainty, the part which is false does not vitiate the document (Mere false description does not make an instrument inoperative).

These maxims should not, however, lead to complacency or want of care on the part of the draftsman.

---

1 *State of Orissa* v. *Titaghur Paper Mills*, AIR 1985 SC 1293, (1985) Supp SCC 280; *Sita Ram* v. *Board of Revenue*, AIR 1979 All 301; *Kaluram Jain* v. *Mahabir Prasad*, 1978 ALJ 399.

2 *Padmaraja* v. *Dhanvathi*, (1972) 2 SCC 100.

3 *Ram Gopal* v. *Nand Lal*, AIR 1951 SC 139 (Hindu widow relinquishing all rights in certain properties and receiving under a Tamaliknama only two items of property as malik. Her full ownership could not be whittled down to life estate merely because of the circumstances that the motive was to provide for her maintenance).

4 Odger's Construction of Deeds and Statutes 5th Ed., p.31; *Goodlittle d. Edwards* v. *Balley*, (1772) 2 Cow. 597.

5 (1998) 8 SCC 1 (para 12), AIR 1999 SC 22.

6 Black's Law Dictionary, 6th edn., p. 600.

As observed by the Privy Council[1] "the form of expression, the literal sense is not to be so much regarded as the real intention of the parties which the transaction discloses".

Surrounding Circumstances

In construing a document whether in English or in an Indian language, the fundamental rule is to ascertain the intention from the words used. The surrounding circumstances are to be considered only for the purpose of finding out the intended meaning of the words which have actually been employed.[2] Plain language cannot be changed by surrounding circumstances.[3]

In case, the terms are not unambiguous, it is legitimate to take into account the surrounding circumstances for ascertaining the intention of the parties.[4] The social milieu, the actual life situations and the prevailing conditions of the country are also relevant circumstances.[5] How the parties or their representatives-in-interest treated the transaction may be relevant.[6] As observed by the Supreme Court,[7] "the test of the pudding is in the eating and the true scope of the instrument can readily be ascertained from what actually happened instead of merely depending upon expressions which the parties might have under some mistaken notion loosely used" and that not merely the words used but the substance has to be seen. The court is to look through or behind the documents, and to get at the reality.[8]

As observed by the Court of Appeal[9] "the first task of the Court was always to construe the particular words of the particular contract against the factual background known to the parties at or before the time when the contract was entered into". A subsequent declaration of intention by the author of an instrument is, however, inadmissible for the purpose of

---

1 *Hunooman Prasad* v. *Mst. Babooee*, (1856) 6 MIA 393 (PC).

2 *M.N. Aryamurthi* v. *M.L. Subbaraya Setty*, AIR 1972 SC 1279, (1972) 4 SCC 1.

3 *Central Bank of India* v. *The Hartford Fire Insurance Co. Ltd.*, AIR 1965 SC 1288.

4 *Syed Abdul Khader* v. *Rami Reddy*, AIR 1979 SC 553; *Abdulla Ahmad* v. *Animendra K. Mitter*, AIR 1950 SC 15; *C.N. Arunachala Mudaliar* v. *C.A. Muruganath*, 1954 SCR 243, AIR 1953 SC 495 (paras 16, 18); *M.P. Peria Karuppan Chettier* v. *C.I.T.*, (1975) 3 SCC 439; *C.I.T.* v. *Maharaja Bahadur Singh*, AIR 1987 SC 518, (1986) 4 SCC 512 (517); *State of Orissa* v. *Orient Paper Mills*, AIR 1977 SC 687, (1977) 2 SCC 77.

5 *Sant Ram* v. *Rajinder Lal*, (1979) 2 SCC 274.

6 *Puzhakkal Kuttappu* v. *C. Bhargavi*, (1977) 1 SCC 17; *Godhra Electricity Co.* v. *State of Gujarat*, (1975) 1 SCC 199.

7 *Sharad Vasant Kotak* v. *Ramnik Lal*, (1998) 2 SCC 171 (para 20 at p. 187) (words "for diverse other causes and considerations" construed).

8 *Tata Engg. & Loco Co.* v. *Bharat Mining Corpn.*, AIR 1980 Bom 168.

9 *Charter Reinsurance Co.* v. *Fagan*, (1996) 1 All ER 406.

construing it,[1] but if both parties have subsequently agreed to a particular interpretation, it would be admissible.[2] Evidence is admissible to show that the writing did not represent the real nature of the transaction but was only an illusory, fictitious and colourable device which cloaked something else, and that the apparent state of affairs was not the real state of affairs. Such evidence is not barred by Sec. 92 Evidence Act,[3]vide provisos to that section (See Sec. 91 to 100 of that Act on exclusion of oral by documentary evidence).

Headings and sub headings

In a case of ambiguity or doubt, the heading or sub-heading may be referred to as an aid to construe the provision "but even in such a case it could not be used for cutting down the wide application of the clear words used in the provision". They cannot be referred to for the purpose of construing the provision when the words used in the provision are clear and unabmiguous.[4]

Legal terms in legal sense

If a legal term such as "heirs" has been used in a Will, it must be construed in the legal sense (unless a contrary intention is clearly expressed) as including all legal heirs and cannot normally be limited to "issues" only.[5]

The Ejusdem Generis rule

General words following words conferring specifically enumerated powers cannot be construed so as to enlarge the restricted powers mentioned therein.[6]

The converse rule

Specific intances do not derogate from the width of the general power initially conferred.[7]

---

1 *Bati Maharani* v. *Collector*, 17 All 198.

2 *Godhra Electricity Co.* v. *State of Gujarat*, (1975) 1 SCC 199.

3 *Krishna Bai* v. *Appasaheb*, AIR 1979 SC 1880, (1979) 4 SCC 60.

4 *Frick India Ltd.* v. *Union of India*, (1990) 1 SCC 400; *Union of India* v. *Raman Iron Foundry*, (1974) 2 SCC 231 (para 9 at p. 240).

5 *N. Krishnammal* v. *R.E. Rambaram*, AIR 1979 SC 1298 (para 16), (1979) 3 SCC 273 (para 15).

6 *Adaikappa Chettiar* v. *Thomas Cook & Sons*, AIR 1933 PC 78, 64 MLJ 184 (case of power of attorney).

7 *Timblo Irmaos Ltd.* v. *Jorge A.M. Sequeira,* AIR 1977 SC 734 (para 18), (1977) 3 SCC 474 (case of power of attorney).

Intention to prevail

A cardinal rule of construction of documents is that the intention of the contracting parties should be determined from the document as a whole,[1] and not from any particular part or clause or clauses[2] read out of context,[3] or from the description of the document or the form in which it is dressed.[4] The court must have regard to the declared object of the document which is often contained in the preamble, (*i.e.*, the recitals, *ante*) but the title given to a document is not conclusive. The preamble may be looked into for ascertaining the object of the document in case of ambiguity, but if the operative words are clear they cannot be controlled by the recitals in the preamble.[5] As stated in Halsbury[6] the best construction of deeds is to make one part of the deed expound the other so as to make all the parts agree. Therefore, while drafting a document, care has to be taken that the various parts of the deed bring out the same intention of the parties.

Executed and Executory Contracts

Sometimes, a contract is completed in two parts. At first an executory contract is executed and later on an executed contract. In such cases too, the

---

1 Halsbury's laws of England, 4th Edn. Vol. XII p. 606 para 1469; *Syed Abdul Khader* v. *Rami Reddy*, AIR 1979 SC 553, (1979) 2 SCC 601; *C.I.T.* v. *Jagannath Jew*, AIR 1977 SC 1523, (1977) 2 SCC 519; *State of Orissa* v. *Titaghur Paper Mills*, AIR 1985 SC 1293, (1985) supp. SCC 280 (para 117).

2 *Abdul Kader Laskar* v. *State of West Bengal*, AIR 1967 Cal 99; *Shambhu Prasad Singh* v. *Mst. Phool Kumari*, AIR 1971 SC 1337; *State of Bihar* v. *Charusila Dasi*, AIR 1959 SC 1002

3 *Jayadayal Poddar* v. *Bibi Hazra*, (1974) 1 SCC 3; *Ramkishan Lal* v. *Kamalnarayan*, AIR 1963 SC 890 (despite the words "*Kul huq haquq samet milkiyat*" it was held that the intention was not to make the co-sharer absolute owner of the benefits of the deity).

4 *Shri Tarkeshwar Sio Thakur Jiu* v. *Dar Dass Dey & Co.*, AIR 1979 SC 1669, (1979) 3 SCC 106 (deed described as licence held to be lease); *Sarjug Barhi* v. *Devendra*, AIR 1979 SC 1967, (1980) 1 SCC 14 (deed described as sale held to be lease); *State of Orissa* v. *Titaghur Paper Mills*, AIR 1985 SC 1293 (the end result of document not by itself conclusive); *Bhopal Sugar Industries Ltd.* v. *S.T.O.*, (1977) 3 SCC 147 (contract title to be one of agency, held to be one of sale); *Undayilli Nagarathnam* v. *Reddy*, (1976) 4 SCC 20 (deed titled settlement deed, held to be one of lease); *C.I.T.* v. *Alagappa Textile Ltd.*, (1980) 1 SCC 214 (deed by a company purporting to appoint another company as "manager", held to be a loan agreement with conferment of superior powers of management on the creditor and not one of appointment of the other company as "manager" who would be subordinate to the board of directors of the former); *C.I.T.* v. *Panipat Woolen Mills*, (1976) 2 SCC 5 (deed titled a sole selling agency agreement, held to be a joint venture, as an agent could not be given a share in profits of the principal).

5 *Padmaraja* v. *Dhanavathi*, (1972) 2 SCC 100 (para 6); *Beli Ram* v. *Ch. Mohd. Afzal*, AIR 1948 PC 168.

6 *Atikulla K. Nawabjada* v. *Mohd. Mobarak Hossein*, AIR 1949 Cal 174, 52 CWN 304.

same language should be used, so that a different intention may not be made out by difference in language. It should be remembered that a deed is primarily construed from the words and expressions used in it and not on the basis of antecedent contract. In case of any difference between the preliminary contract and final contract the terms of the latter must prevail.[1] In some cases, the ground for such a view has been stated to be merger of the earlier contract into the latter,[2] or that the first contract was merely a provisional one.[3] (See also the next sub-heading "*Reference to earlier deeds*", in this context).

Conflict between different parts

A document has to be read harmoniously as a whole with attending circumstances giving effect to all the clauses contained in it which manifest the intention of the person who executed it.[4]

Where, however, in the same document there seems to be some difference in different clauses with regard to the purport or intention, attempt should first be made to reconcile all the clauses so that none of them is rendered nugatory, meaningless or futile,[5] the principle *ut res magis valeat quam pereat* (that the thing may have effect than be destroyed) being applicable. As laid down in Halsbury, "it is a rule of construction applicable to all written instruments that the instrument must be construed as a whole in order to ascertain the true meaning of its several clauses, and the words of each clause must be so interpreted as to bring them into harmony with the other provisions of the instrument if that interpretation does no violence to the meaning of which they are naturally susceptible. The best construction of deeds is to make one part of the deed expound the other, so to make all the parts agree. Effect must, as far as possible, be given to every word and every clause". If, however, there is a clear conflict and such reconciliation is not possible then the earlier clause must override the later

---

1 *Kandal Rao Naidu* v. *Dhanakoti Ammal,* AIR 1938 Mad 81, 1937 MWN 1027, 176 IC 173; see however, *Agarwal Engg. Co.* v. *Technoimpex*, (1977) 4 SCC 367 (para 17).

2 *The Knight Sugar Co. Ltd.* v. *The Alberata Railway & Irrigation Co.*, 173 UC 88 (PC).

3 *Laxam Waman* v. *Balmukund Jainarain*, AIR 1954 Nag 142; *State of Punjab* v. *Okara Grain Buyers Syndicate Ltd.*, AIR 1964 SC 669.

4 *Naramadaben* v. *Pranjivandas Thakker*, (1997) 2 SCC 255, JT 1996 (9) SC 273; *Keshav Kumar* v. *Flowmote Ltd.*, (1994) 2 SCC 10; *Tamboli Ramanlal* v. *Ghanchi Chimanlal*, 1993 SCC Supp (1) 295 (See also case law under "Intention to Prevail" above)

5 *Ramanna D. Shetty* v. *International Airport Authority*, AIR 1979 SC 1628, (1979) 3 SCC 489.

clause and not vice versa.[1] Lord Wrenbury stated the rule in the following terms:

"If in a deed an earlier clause is followed by a later clause which destroys altogether the obligation created by the earlier clause, the later clause is to be rejected as repugnant and the earlier clause prevails".[2] However, if the terms of a conveyance are self-contradictory and one part must be rejected it is legitimate to lean towards the rejection of that part which is inconsistent with the contract for carrying out which the conveyance was being executed.[3]

Where in a contract of sale of goods it was expressly provided that the price was exclusive of sales tax and at another place it was mentioned that the sales tax payable should be shown as an extra item, it was held that the former was a fundamental term while the latter was merely matter of procedure. Hence an omission in regard to the latter cannot absolve the purchaser from his liability under the former.[4]

Reference to earlier deeds

Mere reference to some earlier transaction in a document does not amount to an incorporation, in that document, of the terms and conditions relating thereto. Before the terms and conditions of an agreement can be said to have been incorporated into another document, the same must clearly show that the parties thereto intended to incorporate them.[5]

Previous and subsequent conduct of parties

In England, just as negotiations between the parties previous to the formation of a contract are inadmissible to prove the intention of the parties,[6] likewise subsequent conduct of the parties has been held to be inadmissible to construe the contract.[7] The American and other foreign courts have, however, received subsequent actings as admissible guides to

---

1 *Sahebzada Md. Kamgash Shah* v. *Jagdish Chandra,* AIR 1960 SC 953 (para 13); *Radha Sunder* v. *M.J. Rahim,* AIR 1959 SC 24; *Jaggavarapu Krishna Reddy* v. *Jaggavarapu Chittemma*, 1998 AIHC 3834 (AP).

2 *Forbes* v. *Git*, (1922) 1 AC 256, AIR 1921 PC 209, followed in *Radha Sunder, supra* and distinguished in *Central Bank of India* v. *H.F. Insurance Company*, AIR 1965 SC 1288.

3 *N.S. Krishnaswami Ayyangar* v. *Perumal*, AIR 1950 PC 105.

4 *Hind Tobacco Co.* v. *C.C.R.A.*, AIR 1972 SC 899, (1972) 1 SCC 726, (1972) 1 SC 899.

5 *Himalaya House Co.* v. *C.C.R.A.*, AIR 1972 SC 899, (1972) 1 SCC 726, (1972) 1 SC 899.

6 *Prenn* v. *Simmonds*, (1971) 3 All ER 237, HL.

7 *James Miller & Partners Ltd.* v. *Whitworth Street Estate Ltd.*, (1970) 1 All ER 39, (1973) 2 WLR 683 HC.

interpretation.[1] Corbin on Contracts[2] points out that it is true that one party cannot build up his case by making an interpretation in his own favour but the concurrence therein by the other party can be used by the former against the latter. This concurrence may be evidenced by the other party's express assent thereto, by his acting in accordance with it, by his receipt without objection of performances that indicated it, or by saying nothing when he knows that the first party is acting on reliance upon the interpretation. Such evidence has been held to be admissible.[3]

Evidence of acts done under a deed can, in case of doubt as to its true meaning, be a guide to the intention of the parties particularly when acts are done shortly after the date of the instrument.[4]

Ancient Documents

The initial intention to be gathered from an ancient document when the provisions are reasonably clear cannot, however, be readily altered to suit changing conditions over the years. In interpreting ancient documents the Courts have to be cautious to guard against warping of the issue by reference to subsequent conduct of the parties or their representatives, which may vary for imponderable reasons, bona fide or otherwise.[5] Contemporaneous usage may legitimately be resorted to for ascertaining the meaning of an ancient document which is ambiguous,[6] but if there is a deed which says, according to its true construction, one thing, you cannot say that the deed means something else, merely because the parties have gone on for a long time so understanding it.[7]

Proviso

A proviso is normally an excepting or a qualifying clause and the effect of it is to except out of the preceding clause upon which it is

1 *Godhra Electricity Co.* v. *State of Gujarat*, (1975) 1 SCC 199 (para 11 and 12)
2 Cited in *Godhra Electricity Co*. Supra (para 11).
3 *Godhra Electricity Co.*, supra (para 18), relying inter alia, on *Abdulla Ahmed* v. *A.K. Mitter*, AIR 1950 SC 15.
4 Halsbury's *Laws of England* (III Edn.) para 343, p. 274 relied on by Mahajan J. In Abdulla Ahmed, supra.
5 *Saffani Md. Mohideen* v. *Sethusubramania Pillai*, (1974) 1 SCC 615.
6 *Attorney General* v. *Drummerd*, (1842) 1 Dr. & War 353 (per Sugden L.C.); *Hulada Pd.* v. *Kalidas*, AIR 1914 Cal 813, 42 C 536.
7 *Saddler* v. *Biggs*, (1853) 4 HLC 453, 10 ER 531 (per Lord Cranwarth L.C.); *N.E. Rly Co.* v. *Lord Hastings*, 1900 AC 260; *Attorney General* v. *Rochester Corporation*, (1854) 5 De, G.M. & G 797, 43 ER 1079; *Drummond* v. *Attorney General*, (1849) 2 HLC 837, 9 ER 1312.

engrafted, something which but for the proviso would be within it.[1] If the main clause is clear and the contingency mentioned in the proviso does not arise the proviso is not attracted at all and its language should not be referred to for construing the main clause in a manner contradictory to its import.[2]

Clause modifying statutory rights and liabilities

Some statutory provisions define rights and liabilities of parties subject to the contrary. This gives the parties the option to contract themselves out of their statutory rights. Such clauses are strictly construed against the person claiming exemption from the statutory liability[3] and should therefore be drafted in categorical terms so that there may be no scope for doubt about the intention of the parties.

Deed partly void

The fact that a clause in the deed is not binding on the ground that it is unauthorised cannot *ipso facto* render the whole deed void unless it forms such an integral part of the transaction as to render it impossible to sever the good from the bad.[4]

Recitals when to be looked into

As a general rule of construction of documents, the recitals are not looked into, if the terms of the deed are otherwise clear.[5] If in a deed the operative part is clear, or the intention of the parties is clearly made out, whether consistent with the recitals or not, the recitals have to be disregarded. It is only when the terms of a deed are not clear or are ambiguous or the operative part creates a doubt about the intention of the parties that the recitals may be looked into to ascertain their real intention.[6] If there are several recitals in a deed, and there is at the same time some ambiguity in the operative part of the deed, it may be resolved by giving preference to such a recital as may appear to be the most important to convey the intention of the parties. An ambiguity in the recitals, when the terms of the contract or the intention of the parties is clear from the operative part, has no importance. If the recitals refer to an earlier

---

1 *Angurbala* v. *Debabrata*, AIR 1951 SC 293; *Dibyasingh Malana* v. *State of Orissa*, AIR 1989 SC 1737; *C.I.T.* v. *Indo Mercantile Bank Ltd.*, AIR 1959 SC 713.

2 *Angurbala*, supra.

3 *Karanpura Development Co.* v. *Kamakshya Narain Singh,* AIR 1956 SC 446.

4 *Karanpura Development Co.*, supra.

5 *Beli Ram & Bros.* v. *Ch. Mohd. Afzal*, AIR 1948 PC 168.

6 *Union of India* v. *Amarendra Nath Sarkar*, AIR 1967 Cal 119.

transaction evidenced by a deed, such reference does not amount to an incorporation of the terms and conditions of the earlier deed unless the parties so intended.[1]

Unanticipated Contingency

Sometimes the terms of the agreement provide elaborately for many things, but do not include an express provision to meet a contingency which the parties presumably never anticipated but which has since occurred. The rule of construction applicable in such case has been stated to be that the court is not to make a new agreement for the parties or to speculate how they would have dealt with the new contingency had they anticipated it; but that (except in cases when the intervening event produces frustration) the court should take the words of the agreement as they stand and apply them, as best as it can, to the new situation which has caused the difficulty.[2]

Contracts in Standard Form

These days, it is common for big corporations to obtain contracts in standard form, from the consumers of their goods and services. In such cases the consumer has hardly any option but to sign such standard agreements. These agreements are often one-sided and contain onerous terms or impose obligations on the party to whom they are handed over for signature or exclude or restrict the liability of the corporation supplying the document for signature. Hence, the courts interpret them strictly against the supplier of the form and may sometimes relieve the other party from its unduly onerous obligations.[3] Where, however, the parties' bargaining capacity is evenly balanced, there is little scope for claiming such relief.[4] The Competition Commission[5] can also grant relief against unfair terms of a contract in such cases.

In these standard printed forms, words not applicable are deleted according to the requirements of each individual transaction. A question often arises, whether reference may be made to the deleted words for interpreting the terms of the contract. The true rule is that the court must

---

1 *Himalaya House Co.* v. *Chief Controlling Revenue Authority*, (1972) 1 SCC 726, AIR 1972 SC 899.

2 *L.C. Ltd.* v. *G.B. Ollivant Ltd.*, 13 ITR (Supp.) 23, per Lord Simon, followed in *Shamlal Pragnarain* v. *C.I.T.*, 1955 ALJ 122 (FB).

3 *L.I.C.* v. *C.E.R. Centre,* (1995) 5 SCC 482, AIR 1995 SC 1811; *Pawan Alloys* v. *U.P.S.E.B.*, (1997) 7 SCC 251 (para 45 to 49, giving extracts from text books on law of Contract such as Chitty, Cheshire, Anson).

4 *Pawan Alloys*, supra; *Bihar SEB* v. *Green Rubber Ind.*, (1990) 1 SCC 731.

5 Monopolies and Restrictive Trade Practice Act has been repealed by Competition Act.

first look at the clause in its actual form without looking at the deleted words, and only if that clause is ambiguous then for solving the ambiguity assistance may be derived by looking at the deleted words.[1] But if the words of the clause in its actual form are clear, a different intention cannot be ascribed to the contracting parties by inferring it from the deletion of certain other words.[2] If something is added in handwriting or by typewriter to a printed form such addition should prevail over the language in print.[3]

Where an arbitration clause was deleted in the notice inviting tenders and the agreement entered into by parties but it was not deleted from the standard contract form which was made applicable, it was held that the deletion held good.[4]

Draftsman to be careful in the choice of words and expressions

The language of a deed, in order to convey the intention of the parties, should be simple, so that no other meaning except the primary and natural meaning may be imputed. The sentences should be grammatically correct. The court while construing a document would give to the words used their natural and grammatical meanings.[5] In construing contracts, the courts cannot give the words of the contract an entirely different meaning even to avoid superfluity. The parties' intention must be found out from the language in which the parties to the agreement chose to express themselves. This can easily be achieved if in drafting a document the same words and expressions are used to convey the same meaning in different clauses of the deed. Use of different words and language or substituted words, even though the meaning may be same, should be avoided. A draftsman, unlike a literary writer or orator, cannot indulge in the luxury of 'elegant variation'.[6]

As pointed out in *L.I.C.* v. *Dharam Vir*,[7] "when the same clause of a

1 *H.M. Kamaluddin Ansari & Co.* v. *Union of India*, (1983) 4 SCC 417 (substitution of certain words held significant).

2 *Louis Dreyfus et Cie* v. *Parnaso Cia*, (1959) 1 All ER 502, (1959) 2 WLR 405 (per Diplock J.)

3 *China Cotton Exporters* v. *B.R. Cotton Mills*, AIR 1961 SC 1295; *Moolchand Kesarimall* v. *Associated. Agencies*, AIR 1942 Mad 139; *Ganpatrai* v. *Modi Bros.*, 85 CLJ 136.

4 *State of Kerala* v. *N.E. Thomas*, AIR 1997 Ker 126 (DB), following *State of Kerala* v. *Abrahem*, AIR 1989 Ker 61 (FB); also see *M. Dayanand Reddy* v. *A.P. Industrial Infrastructure*, AIR 1993 SC 2268; *K. Sasidharan Co.* v. *K.S. Film Development Corporation*, AIR 1994 SC 2534.

5 *Sohanlal Pachisia & Co.* v. *Bilasrav Khemani*, AIR 1954 Cal 179 (para 17)

6 Fowler's Modern English Usage, (Oxford) does not recommend elegant variation for users of the language. Dictionaries of synonyms such as Roget's Thesarus are available for that purpose.

7 (1998) 7 SCC 348.

contract uses two different expressions, ordinarily those different expressions convey different meanings and both the expressions cannot be held to be conveying one and the same meaning". Because, if any inconsistency arises in the literal construction of the words used, the courts in their attempt to reconcile the inconsistency may interpret the clauses in a manner which may not be according to the actual intention of the contracting parties. If the inconsistency cannot be resolved by attributing natural and grammatical meanings, the courts may give the words any other reasonably possible construction that may resolve the inconsistency.[1]

Whether plant and machinery embedded in the earth is movable property or immovable property depends upon the facts and circumstances of each case, and the Court has to take into consideration whether the intention of the party, when it decided to embed the machinery, was to make such embedding temporary or permanent. In the instant case, the machineries which have been embedded in the earth to constitute a fertilizer plant are definitely embedded permanently with a view to utilise the same as a fertiliser plant. The plant and machinery of the fertiliser plant are immovable property and cannot be treated as movables.[2]

Blank spaces in Deed

Care should be taken, particularly while executing a contract in standard form, not to leave any blank space unfilled. Illustration (b) of Section 93 of the Evidence Act provides that evidence cannot be given of facts which would show how the blanks were meant to be filled. A deed containing blanks thus stands the risk of being declared void on the ground of uncertainty,[3] vide Sec. 29 of the Contract Act.

Material alteration in deed after execution

A motivated interpolation in a solemn document completely vitiates the document.[4]

If an alteration is made by erasure, interlineations or otherwise in a material part of a deed after its execution by or with the consent of any party thereto or person entitled thereunder, but without the consent of the party or parties liable thereunder, the deed is thereby made void,[5] with effect from the date of such alteration.

1 *Raneegunge Coal Association Ltd.* v. *Tata Iron and Steel Co. Ltd.*, AIR 1940 PC 151 (153).

2 *Duncans Industries Ltd.* v. *State of U.P.*, (2000) 1 SCC 633.

3 *I.T.C. Classis Finance Ltd.* v. *Grapco Mining and Co. Ltd.*, AIR 1997 Cal 397.

4 *Valiammal Rangarao Ramachar* v. *Muthukumaraswamy*, (1982) 3 SCC 508.

5 *Arumugam* v. *M.S. Narasaich*, AIR 1998 Mad 67 (Promissory note became void, hit by Sec. 87, Negotiable Instruments Act).

A material alteration is one which varies the rights, liabilities or legal position of the parties or otherwise varies the legal effect which was originally unascertained and as such void, or may otherwise prejudice the party bound by the deed as originally executed.[1] However, an alteration which is not material i.e., which does not vary the legal effect of the deed in its original state, but which merely expresses that which was implied by law in the deed as originally written, or which carries out the intention of the parties already apparent on the fact of the deed and does not otherwise prejudice the party liable thereunder, will not make the deed void.[2] An agreement modified on a date subsequent to its signing and execution was however, held to be valid if the modification was consented to by both parties.[3]

1 *Nathulal* v. *Gomti Kaur*, AIR 1940 PC 160 (but alterations held immaterial); *Ramlagan* v. *Akleshwar*, AIR 1958 Pat 211; *Seth Loonkaran* v. *Ivan John*, AIR 1977 SC 336, (1977) 1 SCC 319; *Valiammal R. Ramacharn*v. *Muthu Kumaraswamy Gounder*, (1982) 3 SCC 508.

2 *Kalianna Grounder* v. *Palani Grounder*, (1970) 1 SCC 56, AIR 1970 SC 1942.

3 *State of Gujarat* v. *Inderjit Parakh*, 1987 (Supp) SCC 280.

GENERAL FORMS

Forms of Formal Parts of Deeds

1. COMMENCEMENT

1. Commencement of Deed between Two Parties, without Recitals

THIS "DEED OF SALE", "MORTGAGE", "LEASE", "GIFT", *as the case may be*, or "THIS TRUST DEED", "THIS SETTLEMENT" made on the —— day of —— BETWEEN AB, etc. (hereinafter called the ———) of the one part AND CD, etc. (hereinafter called the ———) of the other part WITNESSES as follows:

(1) ....

(2) ....

etc.

2. Commencement of Deed between Several Parties with Recitals

THIS ——— (*as in above form No.*1) is made[1] BETWEEN AB, etc., (hereinafter called the ———) of the first part AND CD, etc., (hereinafter called the ———) of the second part AND EF, etc., (hereinafter called the ———) of the third part, etc. WHEREAS, etc.

NOW THIS DEED WITNESSES that, etc., (*or*, as follows:)

3. Form in First Person

I, AB, etc., in consideration of ——— hereby transfer to CD, etc. All that——— and covenant as follows:

4. Agreement between Two Parties with Recitals

THIS (*or*, AN) AGREEMENT made on the —— day of ——— BETWEEN AB, etc., of the one part AND CD, etc., of the other part. WHEREBY it is agreed as follows:

5. Agreement between Three Parties with Recitals

THIS AGREEMENT is made on the ——— day of ——— BETWEEN AB, etc., of the first part AND CD, etc., of the second part AND EF, etc., of the third part. WHEREAS, etc.

---

1 "made" or "is made", both forms are prevalent; either may be used.

NOW IT IS hereby agreed as follows:

(*or,* NOW THESE PRESENTS WITNESS and parties hereto hereby agree as follows:)

6. Deed Poll without Recitals

i) BY THIS DEED of (Adoption or Power of Attorney, etc.) I, AB, etc.———

ii) THIS DEED of (Adoption or Power of Attorney, etc.,) made by me, AB, etc., WITNESSES that in pursuance of ——— I ——— (using the first person).

7. Deed Poll with Recitals

THIS DEED, etc., is made on the ——— day of ——— by me, AB, etc.,

WHEREAS, etc.,

NOW THIS DEED WITNESSES that (*or*, as follows:)

8. Old form of Deed Poll

KNOW ALL MEN by these presents that I, etc.

9. Old form with Recitals

TO ALL TO WHOM THESE PRESENTS SHALL COME GREETING, WHEREAS, etc. Now, I ————, etc.

10. Commencement of a Supplemental Deed

THIS DEED made, etc., BETWEEN, etc., supplemental (*or*, intended to be read as annexed) to the deed of ———— dated the ——— and made between, etc., hereinafter called the principal deed (and another deed of ——— dated the ——— between, etc., hereinafter called the ———, etc.).

Or

THIS DEED made BETWEEN, etc., supplemental (*or*, intended to be read as annexed) to the several deeds the particulars and natures of which together with the names and descriptions by which the same are hereinafter referred to, are specified in the schedule hereto.

Parties in special cases

1. Minor

AB, etc., a minor acting through his father and natural guardian CD, etc., (*or*, through CD, guardian of his property appointed by the court of the

District Judge of Agra by order dated ————————).

2. Mentally ill person[1]

AB, etc., a mentally ill person acting through CD, guardian of his property appointed by the court of District Judge of Agra by order dated —————.

3. Receiver

AB, etc., receiver of the property of CD, etc., an insolvent, appointed as such by order of the court of District Judge, Agra dated —————.

4. Official Receiver

AB, etc., official receiver of the District of Agra acting on behalf of CD, etc., an insolvent under an order of Civil Judge of Agra dated ——— vesting the property of the said insolvent in him.

5. Trustees

AB, etc., CD, etc., trustees of the estate of XY, etc., (*or* trustees of the Agra College) under deed of trust dated ————.

6. Mutwalli

AB, etc., CD, etc., EF, etc., mutwallis of the waqf known as ——— and appointed as such by the deed of waqf dated ——— executed by ——.

7. Attorney

AB, etc., acting through his attorney CD, etc., appointed as such by a general power of attorney dated —— and registered at —— on ——.

8. Firm (by all Partners)

AB, etc., CD, etc., and EF, etc., carrying on business in partnership together as ——— at ——— under the name and style of ———.

See also Part II of the Introduction *ante*, precedents given under "*(c) Parties to the Deed - (iv) Juridical Person*", etc.

Testimonium

1. Parties signing on one date

In witness whereof the parties hereto have signed this deed on the day and the year first above written.

---

1 The Lunacy Act, 1912 has been replaced by the Mental Health Act, 1987 which uses the expression "mentally ill person" instead of "lunatic" used in the former.

2. Parties signing on different dates

i) In witness whereof the parties have signed this deed hereunder on the dates respectively mentioned against their signatures.

ii) In witness whereof the said AB (*or*, the vendor, mortgagor, etc.) has signed this deed on the ———, and the said CD (*or*, the purchaser, mortgagee, etc.) on the ———.

3. Deed executed by a Company

In witness whereof AB acting on behalf and under authority of the said ——– (Company or Corporation) in this behalf and the said parties hereto have, etc., (*as in preceding forms*)

4. Deed executed by other Corporation

In witness whereof X, the duly appointed officer for this purpose of the said ——— Corporation has signed this deed on behalf of the said Corporation on the ——— and the said AB has signed this deed on the ———.

5. Deed Executed by Attorney

i) In witness whereof the said AB by XY his attorney has signed this deed on the ———.

ii) In witness whereof XY as attorney for the above named AB by virtue of a power of attorney executed by the said AB and dated the —— and registered at the office of ——— on the ——— has signed this deed on the ———.

6. Deed executed by Government

In witness whereof AB Collector of Agra for and on behalf of the Governor of Uttar Pradesh and the said AB have, etc.

7. Deed executed by Guardian

In witness whereof the said AB as guardian of the vendor and in the name and on behalf of the vendor has signed, etc.

8. Deed executed by Municipal Board or other Statutory Authority

In witness whereof the said AB, etc., (*designation*) for and on behalf of the said Municipal Board (*or other specified authority*) has signed this deed and the said Board (*or authority*) has affixed its common seal on this deed on the ——.

9. Deed Poll

In witness whereof I, the said AB, have signed this deed on the —— (*or*, on the day and year first above written).

10. Deed by an Illiterate Person

In witness whereof the said AB being an illiterate person has affixed his thumb mark on the ———, etc.

Consideration and Receipt

1. Consideration Paid before Execution

In consideration of the sum of Rs. ——— paid by the ——— to the ——— before the execution of this deed (the receipt of which the —— hereby acknowledges).

2. Consideration to be Paid at the time of Registration[1]

In consideration of the sum of Rs. ———— to be paid by the —— to the ——— at the time of registration of this deed.

3. Consideration when Transferor is a Minor

In consideration of the sum of Rs. ——— paid by the ——— to AB, the guardian of the ———— (the receipt of which the said AB hereby acknowledges).

4. Consideration Set Off against Debt due to the Transferee

In consideration of the sum of Rs. ———— due to the ——— from the ——— under a mortgage deed dated ———— from the payment whereof and from all claims and demands in respect whereof the ——— hereby releases the ———.

5. Consideration left for Payment to Creditors

In consideration of the sum of Rs. ——— left by the vendor with the purchaser for payment to XY on account of a debt due to him from the vendor under a mortgage deed dated ——— (*or*, for payment to the various persons mentioned in the first Schedule hereto).

---

1 When consideration is paid before the Sub-Registrar, the acknowledgment of receipt is furnished by the Sub-Registrar's endorsement also and though no separate receipt of acknowledgment in the body of the deed is strictly necessary, yet it is customary and expedient for the sake of completeness to mention it in the deed too.

6. Consideration Partly Paid in cash, Partly left for Mortgagee, and Partly Set Off

In consideration of the sum of Rs. ——— out of which the sum of Rs. ——— has been credited by the purchaser to himself on account of a debt due to him under the bond dated ———, from the payment and from all claims and demands in respect whereof the purchaser hereby releases the vendor, and the sum of Rs. ——— has been retained by the purchaser for payment to one XY due under a mortgage deed dated ———, and the remaining sum of Rs. ——— has been agreed to be paid by the purchaser to the vendor in cash at the time of the registration of this deed.

7. Details in Schedule[1]

In consideration of the sum of Rs. ——— which has been agreed to be paid in the manner detailed in the schedule (or the first schedule) to this deed.

8. Agreed to be Paid Subsequently

In consideration of the sum of Rs. ——— agreed to be paid by the purchaser to the vendor in the manner provided in this deed.

9. Appearing from the Recitals

In consideration of the premises (*or*, of the covenant by ——— hereinafter contained) (*or*, of the payments hereinbefore recited).

10. Premium and Rent in Lease

In consideration of the payment by the lessee of Rs. ——— as premium (the receipt of which the lessor hereby acknowledges) and the rent reserved and of the covenants contained in this deed.

11. Paid by several Purchasers separately

In consideration of the sum of Rs. ——— paid by the purchasers in equal shares (*or*, in the following proportions, *i.e.* by X Rs.———, by Y Rs.—— and by Z Rs. ———).

12. Natural Love and Affection

In consideration of the natural love and affection of the donor for the donee.

---

1 This form is convenient and is generally adopted in sale deeds where the details are long.

Parcels[1]

1. Agricultural Land

All those plots of land specified with reference to their *khasra* numbers and areas in the schedule and situate in village —— pargana —— tehsil ——— district———.

2. Non-Agricultural Land

i) The plot of land containing an approximate area of ——— hectares/ acres/bighas/square metres situate in village —— pargana —— tahsil—— district ——— and bounded on the east by ———, on the west by ———, on the north by ———, and on the south by ———.

ii) The plot of land measuring approximately ——— metres north-south and ——— metres east - west (*or*, ——— metres on the north side, ——— metres on the south side, ——— metres on the east side and —— metres on the west side) and containing an area of ——— square metres approximately and situate in —— street, in the town of ——— and bounded as follows:

On the east by ———

On the west by ———

On the north by ———and

On the south by ———.

3. Land, by Reference to Plan (which is controlled by Description)

The plot of land, etc. (*as in forms given above*), and for greater clearness delineated on the plan annexed hereto and thereon shown with its boundaries coloured red (*or*, thereon coloured red) (*or*, thereon marked with letters ABCDE).

4. Land (when Plan Controls the Description)

All that piece of land situate at ——— on the ——— side of the road leading from ——— to ——— and which as to its position, dimensions and boundaries is shown on the plan annexed hereto and thereon coloured red.

5. Groves

i) ALL that grove of mango and other fruit and timber trees situate in village ———, pargana, ——— tehsil ———, district ——— and bearing khasra No. ——— and containing an approximate area of —— acres and

1 *See* Part II of the Introduction, *ante* sub-head (i) Parcels.

bounded as follows:

ii) ALL that grove of fruit trees and garden of flower and other plants situate at ———, containing an area of ——— approximately (together with the *pucca* well and *kothi* standing in the said grove) and bounded as follows:

iii) ALL that one-fourth share in Bhumidhari Khata number ——— in village ——— pargana ——— tahsil ——— and district ——— consisting of plot numbers ———— area ———— hectares/acres/ bighas, as assessed to the sum of Rs. ——— as land revenue.

6. House

i) ALL that *pucca* built house known as No. ——— street and situate in the city of ——— (*or*, situate in *mohalla* ——— of ——) and bounded on the east by ———, on the west by ———, on the north by ——— and on the south by———.

ii) ALL that *pucca* built house (*or*, house built partly *kucha* and partly *pucca*) situate in village ——— pargana ———, tahsil/thana ——, district ——— and standing on plot No. ——— in the *khasra* abadi.

iii) ALL that bungalow known as No. ——, on —— road, and situate in the city of ———— together with out-houses, garage, stables, garden, well and tennis court and other appurtenances thereof, the whole of which premises are shown on the plan annexed hereto with their boundaries marked with letters ———.

7. Shop

ALL that shop situate in Bazar ———— in the city of ———— and bearing No. ——— in the municipal register and bounded, etc. (*as in form of House above*).

8. Right of Way

Together with the right in common with the other persons having the like right to the use of the passage on the east of the said premises for going to and coming from the public road on the east of the said passage.

9. Right to Use Common Staircase

Together with the free right in common with the occupier of the house to the west of the demised premises to use the staircase between the demised premises and the said house on the west.

10. Right to Common Compound

Together with the free right of using in common with the lessor and occupiers of adjoining houses the common compound shown on the said plan as coloured blue.

11. Right to Drainage

Together with the free right to passage and running of water and sullage from the demised premises through the drain running from ——— to ——— and shown on the said plan by letters ABCD.

12. Fixtures and Fittings

Together with the fixtures and fittings therein and specified in the schedule hereto.

13. Mill and Machinery

ALL that mill, engine house, lands and buildings known as the —— Mill situate at ———— AND also ALL the engines, mill gear and fixed and movable machinery, implements and utensils placed upon or used in or about the said premises or any part thereof (all of which machinery, implements and utensils are respectively specified in the ——— Schedule hereto).

14. Rice Mill

ALL that rice mill and the building in which it is installed, known as ——— Mill, situate in —————, together with the godown, land and outbuildings appurtenant thereto, together also with the machinery belonging to the said mill and the right of taking and using the water of the adjoining stream called the ——— usually enjoyed therewith.

15. Cement Factory

ALL that piece of land situate at ——— with the kilns, warehouses and other buildings and erections standing thereon and used as a cement factory known as ——— together with the machinery and furniture now in or about the said premises specified in the ——— Schedule hereto.

16. Minerals

[Note: Leases and licences relating to mines and minerals are now governed by the Mines and Minerals (Development and Regulation) Act 1957 and the rules made thereunder. See Note under LEASE, *post* (General Forms)]

17. Business with Goodwill

ALL that business of a chemist carried on by the said —— at ——— under the name of David and Co., and the goodwill thereof and the exclusive right to use the name of David and Co. for the purpose of carrying on the said business, together with the benefit of all contracts and engagements entered into with the said ——— in respect of the said business and all book debts now owing to the said ——— in respect of the said business and all trade fixtures and fittings and utensils now in or upon the premises.

18. Stock in Trade

ALL their stock in trade, goods and effects in or upon their business premises and used and employed by them in or in connection with the said business.

19. Policy of Life Insurance

ALL that policy of insurance dated the ——— day of ——— and numbered ——— granted by the Life Insurance Corporation of India, insuring the life of ——— in the sum of Rs. ——— at or under the annual premium of Rs. ——— and all the bonuses and additional sums of money to become payable or to be received under or by virtue of the said policy and all benefits and advantages thereof.

20. Share in Partnership

ALL the share or interest of the said ——— in the goodwill of the said partnership and the gains and profits which have arisen or which will henceforth arise therefrom and in the goods, stock in trade, furniture, capital, account books and all other property and effects of the said partnership.

21. Share in Company[1]

ALL those ——— ordinary equity/preference shares of Rs. ——— each, of registered folio No.——— and bearing distinctive numbers ——— to ——— of the ——— Company Limited (held in my name *or*, jointly with ——— and ———.

22. Furniture

ALL the household furniture and things specified in the schedule hereto and being in the said house (*or*, house known as ———).

---

1 For transfer of shares, only prescribed forms are used now. Under the depository system, transfer of shares has been further simplified.

23. Growing Crops

ALL the crop of wheat/paddy/maize and grass now growing in and upon the said land (*or*, the plots of land mentioned below) with full liberty for the ——— his servants, workmen and agents either with or without tractor, trolleys, carts, donkeys or other means of transport at all reasonable times hereafter so long as the said crop shall be growing, standing or lying on the said land to enter upon the same to see the state of such crops or for the purpose of cutting, reaping and carrying away the same and for all other necessary purposes.

24. Timber[1]

ALL the trees of ——— (*kind of trees*) (*or*, ALL the trees of all kinds) standing and growing on ——— (*describe the plot of land or grove*) with full liberty to the ———, his servants, agents and workmen from the ——— day of ——— to the ——— day of ——— at all reasonable times to fell, cut down, grub up, saw and work up the said trees and wood and also to have free ingress and egress with or without horses, carts, lorries and other means of transport to enter into and upon the said premises for the purpose of taking and carrying away the said trees and wood.

25. Annuity

ALL that annuity of yearly sum of Rs. ——— payable during the life of ——— by half-yearly payments on the ——— and on the ——— in every year (*or, as the case may be*) and the arrears and future payments thereof and all remedies and powers whatsoever for the recovery thereof.

26. Bond

ALL that bond dated ——— executed by ——— in favour of ——— for Rs. ——— and all moneys now or hereafter to become due and payable thereupon or by virtue thereof and all the right, title and interest of the said ——— in the same.

27. Debts

ALL those debts due and owing to the said ——— which are specified in the first column of the schedule hereto with the names of the persons from whom they are due mentioned in the second column of the said schedule opposite such debts respectively (with the benefit of all security therefor).

---

1 Cutting of trees is now subject to various statutory restrictions designed in the interests of afforestation and environmental conservation.

28. Decretal Debt

ALL that decree for the sum of Rs. ——— dated the ——— day of —— and passed by the court of ——— at —— in suit No. ———— of ——— between AB plaintiff and CD defendant and all benefits and advantages whatsoever obtainable in respect of the same.

29. Final Decree for Sale

ALL the benefit and advantage of the final decree for sale, full particulars of which are given in the schedule hereto, together with the decretal debt due under the said decree and further interest that may be due under the same and also with the security thereof and all the right and interest of the said AB as decree-holder under the said decree.

30. Rent

ALL that amount due to the said AB on account of rent from the tenants named in the first column of the schedule hereto which amounts are more particularly mentioned in the second column of the said schedule opposite the names of the tenants respectively (with the benefit of all security for the same).[1]

31. Benefit of Restrictive Covenants

Together with the benefit so far as the said AB can assign the same of all the covenants and conditions contained in the deed of —— dated —— and made between ———— and ———— in respect of the user of the premises thereby transferred.

32. Interpretation Clause

The references to the parties herein shall, whenever such an interpretation would be requisite to give the fullest possible scope and effect to any covenant herein contained, include their respective successors and assigns.

---

1 Portion within brackets is not necessary and may be dispensed with in territories in which Transfer of Property Act is in force (vide Sec.8)

ACKNOWLEDGMENT

Preliminary Note

Acknowledgment serves to renew the liability, vide Sec. 18 Limitation Act. It does not create a new right. In order that this may be binding, the liability in question must be subsisting.[1] There must be indication of existence of a jural relationship between the parties from the words used in acknowledgment to make it effective in law. Even if not expressly denoted, this should be capable of being inferred by implication.

In order that acknowledgment may be availed under Sec. 18, it must be in writing and signed by the party who or on whose behalf it is made.[2] It can provide a fresh cause of action and may be made the basis of a suit, if it implies a promise to pay.[3]

Acknowledgment also operates as a fresh contract to repay the amount as held by the Hon'ble Supreme Court in the judgment in the case of *Syndicate Bank* v. *R. Veeranna*,[4]

Part payment of a debt also has the effect to extend the limitation under Sec. 19, provided it is acknowledged in writing and signed by the person making it. It is necessary for this purpose that the acknowledgment be made within the period prescribed for the enforcement of the right. Acknowledgment of liability under Section 18 of the Limitation Act must be made prior to the expiry of the period of limitation of suit.[5]

To amount to acknowledgment the admission need not be unconditional.[6] It may be sufficient despite omission to specify the exact nature of the property or right or accompanied by refusal to pay, deliver, perform or permit to enjoy.

It is open to maintain a suit on the footing of 'Account stated', such as an endorsement on the creditor's *bahikhata* by the debtor or a person authorised on his behalf. In every case, however, the acknowledgment must appear to be a conscious act of the person liable. Acknowledgement in the balance sheet by the defendant extends the period of limitation.[7]

For stamp duty, see Article 1 of Schedule 1 to the Stamp Act.

---

1 *Lakshmiratan Cotton Mills Co. Ltd.* v. *Aluminium Corporation of India Ltd.*, AIR 1971 SC 1482.

2 *Inam Ali Khan* v. *Hazi Mohd. Idris*, 1986 All C J 212.

3 *Hiralal* v. *Badku Lal*, AIR 1953 SC 225

4 (2003) 2 SCC 15.

5 *J.C. Budh Raja* v. *Chairman Orissa Mining Corporation Ltd.*, (2008) 2 SCC 444.

6 *P.C. Bhandari v. New Victoria Mills,* AIR 1979 All 1.

7 *Shahi Exports Pvt. Ltd.* v. *CMD Buildtech Pvt. Ltd.*, 2013, (202) DLT 735.

PRECEDENTS[1]

1—Acknowledgment Requiring Stamp Duty

This is to acknowledge that a sum of Rs. ——— has been found due from me on the basis of an account settled between AB and myself.

Dated——— (Signed) ——— Address————

2—Acknowledgment to Save Limitation

I have received your letter dated———demanding Rs. ——— due from me on account of a bond dated———executed by me in favour of ———.

I shall be obliged if you will kindly wait for three months more, within which time I hope to be able to pay the said amount due from me.

3—Acknowledgment of Part Payment

I hereby acknowledge that I have this ——— day of ——— paid Rs.2000 (Rupees Two thousand only) in part payment of the debt of Rs.10,000 (Rupees Ten thousand only) I borrowed from AB on a pronote executed by me in his favour on ———

4—Acknowledgment by Endorsement

This day I have paid Rupees two hundred in part payment of the within mentioned pronote debt.

---

1 There are numerous other forms in which an acknowledgment may be made. It may be a mere receipt or an agreement. Where there is any question relating to any right in immovable property, suitable form may be adapted from other precedents given in this book.

ADOPTION

Preliminary Note

The Hindu Adoption and Maintenance Act, 1956 has changed the concept of adoption under the old law. The object of adoption as earlier understood was principally religious and not material.[1] The Act makes no mention of the object of adoption; it is immaterial for determining the validity of adoption under the Act. The Act prescribes the conditions for a valid adoption.

Deed of Adoption, not necessary

In order to make a valid adoption by a Hindu, only certain formal ceremonies are necessary and a deed of adoption is not essential.[2] In view of section 16 of the Hindu Adoption and Maintenance Act, a registered deed purporting to record an adoption made, if signed both by the person giving and the person taking the child in adoption, affords a rebuttable presumption of the factum of adoption.[3] If there is any inherent defect in adoption it cannot, however, be cured by such deed.

Other salient features of the Act

The Act applies to "Hindus", which expression, for the purposes of the statute, includes Sikhs, Jains and Buddhists by religion and also all other Indians excepting Muslims, Christians, Parsis and Jews (Sec.2). It further has an overriding effect over all the prevailing concepts of adoption laid down by courts in cases of different caste Hindus or the widows of different communities on the basis of customs or usages, or texts or rules (Sec. 4).

All adoptions made after the commencement of the said Act are to be governed by the provisions of the Act. Any adoption which contravenes its provisions will be invalid in law (Sec. 5).

Any male 'Hindu' who is major and is of sound mind may adopt, but if he has a wife living, he can adopt only with her consent, unless she has renounced the world or has ceased to be a Hindu or is of unsound mind. If he has more than one wife, consent of all is necessary (Sec. 17).

An adoption without the concurrence of wife is void.[4] An adoption by a

---

1 *V.T.S. Chandrashekhar* v. *Kulandaivalu*, AIR 1963 SC 185.

2 The statement of law herein is subject to any State amendments of the Hindu Adoption and Maintenance Act. For instance, in U.P., a registered deed recording an adoption is compulsory, and that both the person giving and the person taking the child in adoption should make and sign it [Sec. 16(2)].

3 *Jai Singh* v. *Shakuntala*, AIR 2002 SC 1428.

4 *Krushna Chandra Sahu* v. *Pradipa Das*, AIR 1982 Ori 114.

widow is adoption to her deceased husband as well.[1]

A female 'Hindu', if major and of sound mind, whether unmarried or widow, may as well adopt. Earlier a married woman had no right to adopt a child, unless she was divorced, or the marriage had been dissolved, or the husband had renounced the world or had ceased to be a Hindu or had been adjudicated to be a mentally ill person.

As per Personal Laws (Amendment) Act, 2010, section 8 stand amended. It provides that any female Hindu, who is of sound mind and is not a minor, has capacity to take a son or daughter in adoption.

It provides that, if she has a husband living, she shall not adopt a son or a daughter except with the consent of her husband unless the husband has completely and finally renounced the world or has ceased to be a Hindu or has been declared by a court of competent jurisdiction to be of unsound mind.

Sub-sec. (2) of Sec.9 has also been substituted by new sub-section and same reads as under:

"(2) Subject to the provisions of sub-section (4), the father or mother, if alive, shall have equal right to give a son or daughter in adoption.

Provided that such right shall not be exercised by either of them save with the consent of the other unless one of them has completely and finally renounced the world or has ceased to be a Hindu or has been declared by a court of competent jurisdiction to be of unsound mind.

In *Ghisalal* v. *Dhapubai*,[2] it has been held that consent should either be in writing or reflected by affirmative positive act voluntarily and willingly done by the wife. Consent of wife cannot be presumed, simply because she was present at the time of adoption.

The law now permits adoption of a boy or a girl and even an orphan, provided he or she is a 'Hindu', and has not already been adopted, and subject to a custom or usage to the contrary, is unmarried and has not completed the age of 15 years (Sec. 10).

Some other conditions as given in Sec. 11 are:

1. If a boy is adopted, there should be no living son or son's son or son's son's son to the adoptive father or mother.
2. If a girl is adopted, there should be no living daughter or son's daughter.
3. The adoptive father or mother must be at least 21 years older to the female or male child respectively.
4. There should be actual giving and taking ceremony but *Datta Homam* is not necessary. So long as the intention to adopt is manifest, no particular form is necessary.[3]

---

1 *Sawan Ram* v. *Kala Wanti*, (1967) 3 SCR 687.

2 (2011) 2 SCC 298, AIR 2011 SC 644.

3 *Lakshman Singh Kothari* v. *Rup Kanwar*, AIR 1961 SC 1378, (1962) 1 SCR 4.

In *Nilima Mukherjee* v. *Kanta Bhusan Ghosh*,[1] the Apex Court observed that mere having a joint bank account would not prove adoption in the absence of any other cogent evidence.

Sec.12 lays down the effect of adoption on the families of the adoptive father and natural father and forbids divesting of property already vested.[2]

The adoption is to the person adopting, though the wife of the adopter also becomes the adoptive mother (Sec. 14). However, if the adoption is by a widower or by a widow or by an unmarried person their subsequent marriages will only result in their spouse acquiring the relationship of a step-mother or step-father as the case may be.

There is no divesting of property vested in the adopted child or the adoptive father or mother. The child becomes a member of the adoptive family and severs his connections with the family of his birth (Sec.12).

Does a child adopted by a widow become the child of the deceased husband for all purposes including succession?

The view taken by the Allahabad High Court in *Subash Misir* v. *Thagai Masir*,[3] is that in the absence of any provision to the contrary it is not unreasonable to infer from Secs. 12 and 13 that the child adopted would be the son of the widow as well as her deceased husband. On the opening of succession a second time when the widow dies the heir of the husband would preferentially be the adopted son and not the reversioner.[4]

Under the Hindu Succession Act 1956 the widow becomes the absolute owner of the husband's property vested in her. Merely by adopting a child she would not be deprived of any of her rights in the property. The adoption would come into play and the adopted child would get the rights to which he is entitled after her death as is clear from the scheme of Sec. 12 proviso (c), Hindu Adoption and Maintenance Act, 1956. Where the persons giving the child in adoption intend to limit the power of the adoptive parents to dispose of their property *inter vivos* or by will, it is open to the parties to agree to the contrary, vide Sec. 13.

However, the agreement would require to be registered under Sec. 17 (1) (b) of the Registration Act.[5]

In *Saroja* v. *Santhilkumar*,[6] all rituals were followed, adoption deed was registered, photographs and negatives were on record, it was held that adoption could not be disbelieved.

In absence of registered deed, adoption must be proved by some cogent

1 (2001) 6 SCC 660, AIR 2001 SC 2725.
2 *Namdev* v. *Chandrakant*, AIR 2003 SC 1735.
3 A 1967 All 148.
4 *Sawan Ram* v. *Kalawanti*, AIR 1967 SC 1761.
5 *Dinaji* v. *Daddi*, (1990) 1 SCC 1.
6 AIR 2011 SC 642.

evidence (Sec. 193).[1] Evidence of relevant witnesses is enough. It is not necessary that everyone who is present at the time of adoption should be examined (Sec. 194).[2]

Form of Deed

In the deed of adoption the child to be adopted should be fully described, his/her age and the consent of his/her mother if alive should be stated, as also the consent of the wife of the adoptive father.

The ceremony of giving, as to who gave the child in adoption and that of, taking the child in adoption should be described, as under the present law this is the only required ceremony. The deed should better be in the form of a Deed Poll and should be executed by the person making the adoption. No deed is usually executed by the person giving the child in adoption but there could be no objection to such a deed. However, a declaration from such a person would be in the fitness of things.

Agreements before Adoption

Under the Act the adopted child continues to have the property which vested in him or her before the adoption subject to the obligations, if any, attaching to the property including the obligation to maintain relatives in the family of his or her birth [Sec. 12, proviso (b)]. The adopted child also does not divest any person of any estate which vested in him or her before the adoption [proviso (c)]. The adoption does not deprive the adoptive father or mother of the power to dispose of his or her property by transfer *inter vivos* or by will (Sec. 13). Sec. 17 prohibits any person from receiving or agreeing to receive any payment or other reward in consideration of the adoption of any person. A pre-adoption agreement, if any, must therefore be drafted keeping these points in view. There is nothing to prevent the person to be adopted giving up the whole or part of the property which vested in him before adoption. But that should not be the consideration for the adoption being made.

There is no provision for adoption in the personal law of Muslims, Christians, Parsis and Jews in India. Nor does there exist any general law of adoption applicable to all communities. Persons belonging to these communities, as also foreigners,[3] can, however, "Adopt" a child from orphanages or children's homes through the procedures provided under the Guardians and Wards Act and the Juvenile Justice (Care and Protection of Children) Act, 2000. Section 41(2) of the 2000 Act (as amended by Amendment Act 33 of 2006) provides that adoption shall be resorted to for the rehabilitation of children as are orphaned, abandoned, neglected and abused. These laws, however, merely authorize the custody of the child to a proper person and make him responsible for the child's appropriate

---

1 *Rahasa* v. *Gukulnanda*, AIR 1987 SC 962.

2 *Chandan* v. *Aftabuadin*, AIR 1996 SC 591.

3 *Karnataka State Council for Child Welfare* v. *Society of Sister of Charity St. Geroso Convent,* AIR 1994 SC 658 (Adoption by foreigner couple).

bringing up. They do not make the child, a son or daughter of the adopter so as to entitle the child to succeed to the estate of the adopter or make the child responsible for the maintenance of the adopter in his old age. In the eye of law, however, their status remains that of guardian and ward respectively but there is no bar to their calling themselves father/mother and son/daughter which they surely are for all practical purposes. Adoptions of such children by Indians or foreigners have now to be monitored by the Central Adoption Resource Authority established by the Ministry of Women and Child Development and have to be processed in accordance with the guidelines framed by the said Authority.

Stamp Duty

Duty on an instrument recording an adoption or conferring or purporting to confer an authority to adopt is governed by Article 3, Stamp Act. No duty is payable if the fact of adoption is mentioned in a will or if authority or permission to adopt is given by a will.

Registration

The Act does not require the execution of a deed of adoption. If however, a deed is executed, it need not be registered except in U.P. Authority to adopt requires to be registered under Sec. 17(3) of the Registration Act. Where adoption deed is executed and registered, there is rebuttable presumption arising as to the adoption having been made in compliance with the provisions of the Act (Sec. 16).

In *Dina Ji* v. *Daddi*,[1] Apex Court observed that section 17(1)(b) of the Registration Act clearly provides that a document where any right in movable property is either assigned or extinguished will require registration. It could not be disputed that the part of the deed which referred to creation of an immediate right in the adopted son and the divesting of the right of the adoptive mother in the property squarely fell within the ambit of Section 17(1)(b) and therefore under Section 49 of the Registration Act, this could not be admitted if it was not a registered document.

---

1 (1990) 1 SCC 1.

PRECEDENTS

1—Short Form of Adoption, without Recitals

THIS DEED of adoption made on the —— day of ——— BETWEEN AB, etc., (hereinafter called "the adoptive father") of the one part AND EF, etc., (hereinafter called "the natural father") of the other part WITNESSES as under:

1. That the said AB has no son or son's son or son's son's son (*or*, no daughter or son's daughter, *in case a girl is adopted*) living.

2. That the said AB has on the day aforesaid (*or*, on the ———— day of ————) taken in adoption XY the unmarried son of the said EF, aged about ——— years, as his son.

3. That the said EF has on the date aforesaid given the said XY, in adoption to the said AB.

4. That the ceremony of giving and taking in adoption has been duly performed alongwith other religious ceremonies customary with the parties.

5. That the said XY has and shall have from the date of adoption all the legal rights of an adopted son of the said AB.

IN WITNESS WHEREOF, we the said AB and EF have signed this deed on the day and the year first above written.

2—Short form of Adoption, with Recitals

THIS DEED of adoption is made on the ——— day of ——— by AB, etc., of the first part and EF, etc., of the second part.

WHEREAS

1. AB, the party of the first part has no male issue and being now sixty years of age has no expectation of having such issue.

2. Both AB and his wife had long been anxious to adopt a suitable boy as their son.

3. PQ, the wife of AB has consented to the taking in adoption of XY by AB.

4. AB has on the ——— day of ——— taken in adoption XY son of EF, etc., the party of the second part, a boy of 4 years of age, as his son.

5. The said boy, XY, has been given in adoption to the said AB by his natural father, the said EF with the consent of his mother.

6. All the ceremonies, including the giving and taking in adoption of the said XY and *Datta Homam*[1] have been duly performed at the time of adoption, on the ——— day of ——.

NOW THIS DEED WITNESSES and the parties do hereby declare that the said AB has duly adopted the said XY as his son and the said XY has and will have from the date of adoption all the legal rights of an adopted son. IN WITNESS, etc.

3—A Joint Deed by the Natural Mother and Adoptive Father

KNOW ALL MEN BY THESE PRESENTS that we AB, etc., and CD, etc., hereby declare that I the said AB have this day in a meeting of relatives, caste fellows and friends held at ———, duly adopted EF, etc., as my son and I, the said CD being the natural mother of the said EF, his natural father XY having already died, have given the said EF in adoption to the said AB AND WE ALSO record that the ceremony of giving and taking in adoption and other customary ceremonies necessary under the Hindu Law, to which we are subject, have been duly performed AND we declare that henceforth the said EF has ceased to be a member of his family of birth and has all the rights of an adopted son of the said AB.

IN WITNESS WHEREOF, etc.

4—Wife's Consent given before Adoption, without Recitals

KNOW ALL MEN BY THESE PRESENTS that I, AB, etc., wife of CD, etc., hereby consent to the taking of X son of YZ, etc., aged 4 years in adoption by my husband, the said CD, etc., as our son.

IN WITNESS WHEREOF, etc.

5—Wife's consent to Adoption, with Recitals

KNOW ALL MEN BY THESE PRESENTS that I, AB, etc., wife of CD, etc., hereby declare that

WHEREAS—

1. We have no issue of our own and having now become quite aged, have no expectation of having any issue.

---

1 Though *Datta Homam* is no longer insisted on as a matter of law, yet normally such *Yajna* does take place. So if it has taken place there is no harm in mentioning it.

2. Both myself and my husband have long been anxious to adopt a suitable boy as our son.

3. EF son of GH, etc., has a son, XY, etc., 4 years old, who is suitable in every respect and whom the said EF is authorized and willing to give in adoption.

4. My husband is willing to take the said XY in adoption as his son with my consent.

NOW THIS DEED WITNESSES that I hereby freely and willingly give my consent to the taking of the said XY in adoption by my husband as our son.

IN WITNESS WHEREOF, etc.

6—Adoption by a Hindu Widow

THIS DEED of adoption made on the ——— day of ——— by AB, widow of ——— a Hindu by religion ——— aged ——— and resident of ——— hereby declare as follows:

1. That I have no son or son's son or son's son's son (*or*, daughter or son's daughter in case a girl is adopted) living.

(*Or, as the case may be, it may be mentioned that no issue was ever born or that son or sons or daughter or daughters were born but they died during the life time of the husband or after his death*).

2. That I have this day ——— adopted EF, son of GH, a Hindu aged ——— by caste ——— and resident of ——— as my son, the said EF having been given to me in adoption by his father/mother/guardian.

Note: *If it is the father, mention, with the consent of his wife. If it is the guardian, mention his authority.*

3. That the ceremony of giving and taking in adoption and other religious ceremonies were duly performed.

4. That the said EF is aged ——— years and is unmarried and he shall have from this day all legal rights of an adopted son.

IN WITNESS WHEREOF, etc.

7—Adoption by an Unmarried Hindu Woman

Formal part as in Precedent No.6 (except, insert daughter for widow).

1. That I, AB, am the only living daughter of WX, son of YZ, and remained unmarried though attained the age of ——— years.

2. That I have with my free will and consent on this day ——— adopted/taken in adoption EF, ——— (*same as in para 2 of Precedent of No.6*).

3 & 4. Same as in paras 3 & 4 of Precedent No.6.

IN WITNESS WHEREOF, etc.

8—Adoption of an Orphan from a Family or Orphanage[1]

Formal part same as in Precedent No.6 (except, insert son for widow).

1. *Same as in para 1 of Precedent No.6.*

2. That I have this day ——— adopted EF, son of GH, aged —— by caste ——— and resident of ——— as my son. The said EF having been given to me in adoption by testamentary guardian/certificated guardian (*or, if the adoption is of an orphan from any orphanage*), by the President/ Secretary/Manager/Superintendant of ——— orphanage, of ——— city/ town, with the previous permission of ——— court dated ———.

3 & 4. *Same as in paras 3 & 4 of Precedent No.6.*

IN WITNESS WHEREOF, etc.

9—Declaration deed where the child is in the care and custody of a guardian appointed by the court

1. I, AB _______ was appointed Guardian and custody of XY _______ aged _______ was given to me by the District Judge, Agra, vide order dated _______.

2. CD _______ obtained the permission of the District Judge, Agra on _______ to adopt XY as his son.

3. In compliance with the said order dated _______ I, AB gave XY in adoption to CD and performed all the required ceremonies.

IN WITNESS WHEREOF, etc.

1 If the adoption is from some orphanage there should be a certificate of the head of the institution as named earlier certifying that he had satisfied himself that the adoption will be for the welfare of the child and if the child has reached the understanding that he had also obtained the willingness and ascertained the wishes of the child and that permission of the competent court had been obtained. He should further state about the actual adoption and the ceremony of giving and taking. In fact, it will be better that the certificate is of the same authority of the orphanage, who was party to the obtaining of the court's permission and actually gave the child in adoption.

AGREEMENTS

Preliminary Note

An agreement between the parties is an instrument whereby the parties freely agree to perform certain acts or refrain from doing something, unilaterally or bilaterally. The purpose of the instrument is to bind them to the terms and conditions agreed upon. Agreements should, therefore, be drafted as deeds between the parties thereto and not as Deeds Poll.

An agreement is defined in Section 2(e) of the Indian Contract Act, 1872 as "every promise and every set of promises, forming the consideration for each other is an agreement."

In preparing an agreement it is necessary and important that the intention of the parties should be set forth explicitly so as to leave no room for doubt or future controversy. Only a concluded contract can be enforced. An agreement is a legally enforceable contract only if it is made by the free consent of the parties competent to contract, for a lawful consideration and with a lawful object and is not expressly declared by the provisions of the Contract Act or any other law to be void (Sec. 10, Contract Act). The language should be simple and the words used should be definite and precise; the use of loose expression such as "proper", "reasonable", should, as far as possible, be avoided. The essence of a valid agreement is that the parties consciously agree about the subject matter at the same time and in the same sense (*consensus ad idem*).

The provisions of the Contract Act about the essential incidents and legality of agreements (sections 2 to 30) should be studied and nothing should be introduced or left out which would make the agreement void. Where, under an agreement, if any part of single consideration for one or more objects, or any one or any part of any one of several consideration for a single object, is unlawful, the agreement is void (section 24). An agreement made without consideration is void unless it is a deed of gift, duly executed and registered, and made an account of natural love and affection between parties who are near relation to each other; or unless it is a promise in writing to pay a debt barred by law of limitation (section 25). Every agreement in restraint of the marriage of any person, other than minor, is void (section 26). An agreement by which one is restrained from exercising a lawful profession, trade or business of any kind is void unless it is an agreement not to carry on business of which goodwill is sold (section 27). An agreement in restraint of legal proceedings is void unless it is an agreement to refer a dispute to arbitration; or an agreement by which any bank or financial institution stipulates extinguishment of the rights or discharge of any liability under such agreement (section 28). Where, under an agreement, a party agreed to pay the other a sum of money "after deduction as would be agreed upon", it was held that the clause offended against Sec. 29 (Agreement void for uncertainty) and no suit could be brought on such agreement.[1] But, if the material terms of an agreement are clear and specific, omission of certain details which can be worked out by consent of parties or in its absence be settled by court will not invalidate the agreement.[2] However, normally, it is not for the court to make a contract for the parties if the parties have left the terms vague or ambiguous.[3]

Normally, a third party cannot gain any right under a contract,[4] unless he is beneficiary under a trust created by a contract to which he is not a party.[5]

Section 74 Contract Act has sought to cut across the web of rules and presumptions under the Common Law by enacting a uniform principle applicable to all stipulations naming amounts to be paid in case of breach, and stipulations by way of penalty, and according to this principle, even if there is a stipulation by way of liquidated damages, a party complaining of breach of contract can recover only reasonable compensation for the injury sustained by him, the stipulated amount being merely the outside limit. Thus, like a claim for unliquidated damages, a claim for liquidated damages also does not give rise to a debt until the liability is adjudicated and damages assessed by a decree or order of a Court or other adjudicatory authority.[6]

In *Kailash Nath Associates* v. *DDA*,[7] Apex Court has laid the law on compensation of breach of contract under Section 74. Where a sum is named in a contract as a liquidated amount payable by way of damages, the party complaining of a breach can receive as reasonable compensation such liquidated amount only if it is a genuine pre-estimate of damages fixed by both parties and found to be such by the court. In other cases, where a sum is named in a contract as a liquidated amount payable by way of damages, only reasonable compensation can be awarded not exceeding the amount so stated. Similarly, in cases where the amount fixed is in the nature of penalty, only reasonable compensation can be awarded not exceeding the penalty so stated. In both cases, the liquidated amount or penalty is the upper limit beyond which the court cannot grant reasonable compensation.

---

1 *Kovuru* v. *Kumar Krishna*, AIR 1945 Mad 10; *Vimlesh Kumari Kulshreshta* v. *Sambhajirao*, (2008) 5 SCC 58; (Proper description of immovable property not given in the agreement to sell).

2 *Ramchandra* v. *Chinubhai*, AIR 1944 Bom 76, at 82 (Chagla J); [*Compare, Gujarat Ginning Co.* v. *M.H.S. & W. Co.*, 31 BLR 1310; *East India Co.* v. *Nuthum*, 7 Moo PC 482 at 497; *Beer* v. *Bowden*, (1981) 1 All ER 1070 (CA) (increase of rent)].

3 *Dwarkadas & Co.* v. *Dalu Ram*, AIR 1951 Cal 10.

4 *Dunlop Pneumatic Tyre Co.* v. *Selfridge & Co.*, 1915 AC 847; *M.C. Chacko* v. *State Bank*, (1969) 2 SCC 343; *Jamna Das* v. *Ram Autar*, (1911) 39 IA 7, PC.

5 *Khwaja Mohd. Khan* v. *Husaini Begum*, (1910) 37 IA 152 PC, approved in M.C. Chacko, supra.

6 *Union of India* v. *Raman Iron Foundry*, (1974) 2 SCC 231 (para 11); (see also *Rajratha Naranbhai Mills Co. Ltd.* v. *S.T.O.*, (1991) 3 SCC 283.

7 (2015) 4 SCC 136.

Reasonable compensation will be fixed on well-known principles that are applicable to the law of contract, which are to be found inter alia in Section 73 of the Contract Act.

Since Section 74 awards reasonable compensation for damage or loss caused by a breach of contract, damage or loss caused is a sine qua non for the applicability of the section.

The section applies whether a person is a plaintiff or a defendant in a suit. The sum spoken of may already be paid or be payable in future.

While dealing with the expression "whether or not actual damage or loss is proved to have been caused thereby", Apex Court explained that it means that where it is possible to prove actual damage or loss, such proof is not dispensed with. It is only in cases where damage or loss is difficult or impossible to prove that the liquidated amount named in the contract, if a genuine pre-estimate of damage or loss, can be awarded.

Section 20 of the Specific Relief Act, 1963 (as amended by Specific Relief Amendment Act, 2018) makes specific performance of contract a general rule than exception, subject to certain limited grounds. The discretionary jurisdiction of courts to decree specific performance has been done away by the amendment. Section 20 provides for substituted performance of contract, where a contract is broken, the parties who suffer would be entitled to get the contract performed by a third party or by his own agency and to recover expenses and costs including compensation from the party who failed to perform his part of contract.

Sections 23 to 30 of the Contract Act pertain to the legality of agreements. The provisions contained therein have to be borne in mind to ascertain what considerations and objects are lawful and what are not. Agreement between the parties with the object that one of them should wield influence with government to have the *Nawab* recognised as the heir to the estate in return for being given a share in the amount to be recovered by the *Nawab* was nullified being opposed to public policy.

Contract having tendency to injure public welfare is regarded opposite to public policy. The public policy is not static. With the changing time and the needs of the society it varies. The march of law must match with the 'felt needs' of the society: the fact situation.[1]

Agreement between two bidders at an auction sale to bid jointly but not intended to peg down the price or to defraud government to knock out the sale at a lower price was held not to be against public policy and as such not unlawful and void. The agreement, was only to bid jointly, it may be noted, and not to bid against each other.[2]

1 *Rattan Chand Hira Chand* v. *Askar Nawaz Jung*, (1991) 3 SCC 67.

2 *Gurumukh Singh* v. *Amar Singh*, (1991) 3 SCC 79; Halsbury's Laws of England (4th ed. Vol. 9 para 392 at p.266)

Commencement

Agreements generally begin with "An Agreement" or "This Agreement" or "Articles of Agreement" or "Memorandum of Agreement". The latter two expressions are generally used in cases where the covenants are lengthy. After the title follows the date, then the names of the parties with their addresses, as in the case of transfer deed. Then follow recitals, if necessary. (For detailed instructions about parties and recitals see Part II of the Introduction).

The covenants are introduced by some such phrase as:

"WHEREBY the parties mutually agree with each other as follows" (*if there are no recitals, then by* ———)

"NOW THIS AGREEMENT WITNESSES (*or*, THESE PRESENTS WITNESS) and the parties mutually agree as follows:

Agreement to agree

An agreement to enter into an agreement is not enforceable nor does it confer any right upon the parties. Such an agreement does not amount to a concluded contract, hence not enforceable.[1]

Memorandum of Understanding (M.O.U.)

This is a recent development following gradual globalisation of the economy. A MOU is in the nature of a preliminary agreement recording a resolve to explore a desired goal and agreeing to work together to find out the possibilities whether the desired goal can be achieved and whether they can enter into a final agreement to fructify the intended goal. A MOU is also a contract and binds the parties to the stipulations made therein. A MOU usually debars the parties from negotiating the same subject with another party and stresses on confidentiality.

Letter of Intent

Similarly, a Letter of Intent (LOI) may or may not be a concluded contract, depending on the facts and circumstances of the case.[2]Letters of Intent (LOI) are usually issued when bids are invited for a certain work and after evaluation of the bids and/or negotiations, a contractor is selected. A LOI is issued to such contractor informing him that it is intended to award the contract to him and requiring him to comply with certain requirements like depositing security amount, furnishing bank guarantee, etc., before the final contract deed is signed and executed.

Apex Court had held that a letter of intent merely indicates a party's intention

---

1 *Rickmers Verwaltung GMB H.* v. *Indian Oil Corpn.*, AIR 1999 SC 504, (1999) 1 SCC 1 ("draft charter party agreement"); *Speech and Software Technologies (India) Pvt. Ltd.*, v. *Neos Interactive Ltd.*, (2009) 1 SCC 475.

2 *Multichannel (India) Ltd.* v. *Kavitalaya Productions Ltd.*, AIR 1999 Mad 59 (DB) (paras 7, 8, 10); *K. Sriramalu* v. *Ashwatha Narayana*, AIR 1968 SC 1028; *Currimbhay & Co.* v. *Creet*, AIR 1933 PC 29; 69 IA 297.

to enter into a contract with other party in future. Such letter of intent is not intended to bind either party ultimately to enter into any contract......"[1]

Agreement to Sell Immovable Property

See precedents under SALE, *post*.

Mention of Representatives

An agreement can, on the death of promisor, be enforced against his representative (Sec. 37, Contract Act), and on the death of a promisee can be enforced by his legal representative, unless the agreement is of a personal nature. It is, therefore, not strictly necessary though it is usual to mention the representatives or successors-in-title of either party as persons on whose behalf or for whose benefit the contract is made. The assignee of rights under an agreement can enforce them against the other party, but obligations cannot be assigned without the consent of the party in whose favour they arise.[2]

Duplicates

If it is desired that each party should have a copy of the agreement, it should be executed in duplicate, either party signing one of the duplicates and such duplicates being exchanged. Thus the duplicate signed by A is given to B and that signed by B is given to A, but it is better if both the duplicates are signed by both the parties. The duplicates must be the exact reproduction of the original and require signature and attestation in the same manner as the original.

Attestation

An Agreement does not require attestation.

Stamp Duty

For stamp duty see Articles 5 and 6, Stamp Act.

Registration

If an agreement does not by itself create an interest in immovable property, its registration is not compulsory under Sec. 17(2)(v), Registration Act, 1908; but if it creates an interest in immovable property worth Rs.100 or more its registration is compulsory. Other agreements not relating to immovable property are not compulsorily registrable. In U.P., however, an agreement to sell immovable property is also compulsorily registerable if the agreement is accompained by delivery of possession.

---

1 *Dresser Rand S.A.* v. *Bindal Agro Chem Ltd.*, (2006) 1 SCC 751, AIR 2006 SC 871; Also see decision in *Rajasthan Coop. Dairy Federation Ltd.* v. *Maha Laxmi Mingrate Mktg. Service (P) Ltd.*, (1996) 10 SCC 405, AIR 1997 SC 66.

2 *Cheru Komen* v. *Govinden*, 5 MHCR 145 (at 151).

PRECEDENTS

1— Case Stated under Section 90 read with Order XXXVI, Rules 1 and 2, C.P.C.[1]

THIS AGREEMENT made on the ——— day of ——— BETWEEN AB, etc., of the one part AND CD, etc., of the other part.

WHEREAS there is a dispute between the parties, full particulars of which and of the documents bearing on which are stated in the schedule to this deed;

AND WHEREAS the parties are interested in the decision of the following questions arising out of the dispute, namely,

(1)

(2)

(3)

etc., etc.,

AND WHEREAS the estimated value of the property in dispute (*or*, the estimated value of the act about the doing or refraining from doing the parties are in disagreement) is Rs. ———.

AND WHEREAS the parties have agreed that a case be stated for the opinion of the court under Sec. 90 read with Order XXXVI of the Code of Civil Procedure, 1908;

NOW THESE PRESENTS WITNESS and the parties agree as follows:

(*i*) The case as stated in the schedule be referred to the court having jurisdiction for opinion on the questions mentioned above;

(*ii*) If the finding of the court on either of the above questions is in favour of AB in respect of any one or more of the buildings mentioned in para —— of the schedule, then CD shall pay to AB such sum on account of rent in respect of such building or buildings as is mentioned in para ——— of the schedule [or, as the case may be, vide clauses (a), (b) and (c) of Order 30, rule (1)].

1 A case stated is registered and tried as a suit and decided by a judgment followed by a decree.

Schedule

(Parawise statement of facts, documents and dispute)

IN WITNESS WHEREOF the parties hereto have signed this agreement on the dates respectively mentioned against their signatures.

2—Agreement between Government and an Agent for Sale of Government Publications

AN AGREEMENT made on the ——— day of ——— BETWEEN AB, etc., (hereinafter called "the Agent") of the one part AND the Governor of ——— (*name of State*) (hereinafter called "the Government") of the other part.

WHEREAS the Government has at the request of the Agent agreed to appoint him to be agent for the sale of publications of the Government of ——— (*name of State*) (hereinafter called "the State Government") and to supply such publications to the Agent at twenty-five per cent below the published price;

AND WHEREAS such publications are sold by the Government at the published price and it is necessary in the interest of the Government that such publications should not be sold below the published price.

NOW THESE PRESENTS WITNESS as follows:

1. The Government hereby appoints AB as its Agent to sell publications of the State Government on the terms and conditions hereinafter appearing.

2. The Government will supply to the Agent for sale such of the State Government publications as he may require at twenty-five per cent below the published price.

3. The Agent hereby agrees with the Government as follows:

(a) Agent's Covenant not to Sell at Less Price

He will not sell any such State Government publication at less than the published price nor grant any rebate, discount or commission nor otherwise offer any special terms or inducement to purchasers of the said book in order to induce such purchasers to purchase from the Agent instead of the Government Press (*or*, Manager of Publications, etc., *as the case may be*).

(b) Power of Revocation

The Government may at any time revoke the appointment of AB as agent for sale of the State Government publications upon giving to the

Agent ——— months notice in writing of its intention to do so; it shall also be entitled, if it so chooses, to take back from the Agent all State Government publications supplied to him for sale and then unsold at the date of the expiration of the period of such notice after refunding to the Agent the price which he has paid for such publications.

(c) Compensation for Breach

The Agent will if he sells any publication of the State Government at less than its full published price pay to the Government as compensation for breach of this agreement a sum equivalent to the difference between the published price of such publication and the price at which the Agent has actually sold such publication.

IN WITNESS WHEREOF, etc.

3—Agreement for Securing Advertisements

MEMORANDUM of an AGREEMENT dated the —— day of ——, BETWEEN AB, etc., of the one part AND the ——— Co. Ltd., a company registered under the Companies Act, 1956/2013, and having its registered office at ————, (hereinafter called "the Company") of the other part.

WHEREAS the said AB publishes monthly, an agricultural journal called the ——— in Hindi for general circulation particularly among the agricultural classes;

AND WHEREAS the said AB appointed the Company his sole advertising agent for the aforesaid journal on the terms and conditions hereinafter contained.

NOW IT IS HEREBY AGREED between the said AB and the Company as follows:

1. Appointment

The Company will act as the agent of the said AB for the purpose of securing advertisements for the aforesaid journal and will secure contracts for advertising at such rates as it may consider proper and will secure copy and blocks and will give the printer or other person appointed for the purpose necessary instructions with reference to the printing of the said advertisements and will keep records, distribute voucher copies and collect amounts.

PROVIDED that it shall not without the previous consent of the said AB sell space at rates lower than the following rates:

* * * * *

2. Enquiries to be Referred to Company

The said AB will refer to the Company all enquiries about advertisement in the aforesaid journal and except as hereinafter provided shall not accept any advertisements for putting in the said journal except through the Company.

3. English Translation

If the text of any advertisement is set by the Company in English, arrangement will be made by the said AB for rendering the same into Hindi without any extra charge.

4. Space for Advertisement

The space at present sanctioned for letting to advertisers are 16 ordinary pages, two inside covers and one outside cover in each issue of the aforesaid journal but the said AB will favourably consider any representation by the Company for increase of such space.

5. Term

This agreement shall continue in force for a minimum period of —— years and will continue thereafter subject to three months' notice of termination on either side, but in the event of the said AB deciding to cease publication of the aforesaid journal for any reason whatsoever the agreement shall stand determined immediately on the journal ceasing publication.

6. Commission

The Company shall be entitled to a commission of ——— percent on the amount of all bills for advertisements inserted in the aforesaid journal.

7. Bills and Bad Debts

(a) The Company shall within 30 days from the date of delivery to the Company of the voucher copies of any issue of the said journal submit to the manager of the said journal a statement of bills in respect of the advertisements appearing in such issue showing the gross amount of such bills and the net amount payable to the said AB. The said manager will check such statement and return the same after verification. The Company shall pay such amount to the said AB within 15 days of the return of such statement without any deduction for unrealized bill or for bad debts.

(b) If any debt is represented by the Company to be a bad debt, the said AB may on being satisfied in that behalf declare it to be so and after such declaration the share of the amount of such bill paid to the said AB shall be adjusted by deduction from subsequent payments due to the said AB or in any other suitable manner. The decision of the said AB on the question whether a debt is or is not a bad debt shall be final.

8. Refusal of Publication by Editor

The editor of the journal will have the power to refuse publication of any advertisement which in his opinion may be considered obscene or objectionable or of a generally unsuitable character. If the company is dissatisfied with the decision of the editor, the question shall be referred to the said AB whose decision shall be final.

9. Inspection of Company's Books

The said AB and/or any other person deputed by the said AB for the purpose shall be entitled to inspect the books of the Company relating to this contract at any time during the business hours of the Company, and if this agreement continues in force after twelve months the Company shall also before the ——— day of ——— in each year during which this agreement remains in force submit to the said AB, a certificate from a firm of chartered accountants approved by the said AB to the effect that the said firm has audited the accounts of the Company relating to this contract and found them in order.

10. Each Contract to be forwarded by Company

For the purpose of keeping the said AB acquainted with the business booked by the Company and the terms of such booking, a copy of each contract made by the Company with the advertisers shall be forwarded by the Company to the manager of the said journal, and the contract with the advertisers shall be in a form approved by the said AB.

11. Consequence of Termination

In the event of this agreement being terminated at any time except on the ground of the said journal ceasing publication, such termination shall not affect the contracts already made by the Company, and in respect of all contracts as are on the books on the date of termination of the agreement the parties shall perform the duties and observe the covenants to be performed and observed by them respectively under the terms of this agreement.

12. Breach

In case of the Company committing breach of any covenant herein contained, the said AB shall be at liberty immediately to terminate this agreement.

13. Arbitration

All disputes between the parties hereto arising out of this agreement or in relation thereto or regarding the interpretation of any clause hereof for the decision of which no express provision has hereinbefore been made shall be referred to an arbitrator appointed by the ——— Chamber of Commerce and the provisions of the Indian Arbitration and Conciliation Act for the time being in force shall be applicable to such reference.

IN WITNESS WHEREOF the parties hereto have signed this agreement in manner hereinafter appearing and the Company has affixed its common seal on the day and year first above written.

4—Works Contracts[1]

[*This form is in respect of a building work but can be adapted with suitable modifications for any other work*].

AN AGREEMENT made on the ——— day of ——— BETWEEN AB, etc., (hereinafter called "the Employer") of the one part AND CD, etc., (hereinafter called "the Contractor") of the other part. WHEREBY the parties hereto mutually agree as follows:

1. Complete the Works in Workman-like Manner

The Contractor will clear and prepare the site for and will erect and complete in a thorough and workman like manner and with the best material (*or*, with material supplied by the Employer) the works specified in the schedule hereto in accordance with the plans and specifications hereto annexed (hereinafter referred to as "the works").

2. Payment

Subject to the conditions hereinafter appearing, the Employer will pay to the Contractor a sum of Rs. ——— within six months after the Contractor has completed the works in accordance with the terms of this agreement and handed over the same to the Employer.

---

1 For distinction between a works contract and contract of sale, see *Union of India* v. *Central India Machinery Mfg. Co.*, (1977) 2 SCC 847 (Re: contract for the manufacture and supply of wagons to railways).

(*or*, a payment schedule may instead be inserted herewith reference to different stages of the completion of the work or preparations therefor).

3. Incidental Works

The Contractor will do and perform all work incidental to the proper execution and completion of the works including all works rendered necessary in the consequence of the doing of the works and will supply all labour (and material) necessary for the same and no additional payment shall be made for the same.

4. Access to Works

The Contractor will permit the Employer to have access to the works while the same are under construction and to inspect the same.

5. No Variation

The Contractor will not vary or deviate from the said plans and specifications without having first obtained the permission in writing of the Employer.

6. Price Adjustment[1]

(1) The contract price shall be adjusted for increase or decrease in rates and prices of labour, materials, fuels and lubricants in accordance with the following principles and procedures.

(a) The cost of materials and electrical energy supplied by the Employer at fixed prices shall be excluded from the scope of price adjustment.

(b) The price adjustment shall apply only for work carried out within the stipulated time or extended time granted by the Employer under clause 10 hereof and shall not apply to work carried out beyond the stipulated time for reasons attributable to the Contractor.

(c) The price adjustment shall be calculated for work done in accordance herewith.

Or

The price adjustment shall be determined during each quarter in accordance with the following formula:

(*To be omitted if no formula is specified*)

---

1 This is also called "Escalation Clause". The subject is dealt with at length in *Delhi Cloth Mills* v. *Rajasthan SEB*, (1986)2 SCC 431; In some cases escalation has been allowed on grounds of reasonableness even in the absence of such clause: *P.M. Paul* v. *Union of India*, AIR 1989 SC 1034; *C.T. Xavier* v. *P.V. Joseph*, AIR 1995 Ker 140; *Tarapore & Sons* v. *Cochin Shipyard Ltd.*, AIR 1984 SC 1072, (1984) 2 SCC 68.

(2) To the extent that full compensation for any rise or fall in the cost to the Contractor is not covered by the provisions of this or other clauses in the contract, the unit rates and prices included in the contract shall be deemed to include amounts to cover the contingency of such rise or fall in the cost.

(3) (i) The price adjustment for increase or decrease in cost due to labour shall be paid in accordance with the following formula:

* * * * *

(ii) Price adjustment for increase or decrease in cost of materials procured by the contractor other than fuel and lubricants shall be paid in accordance with the following formula:

* * * * *

(iii) Price adjustment for increase or decrease in cost of fuel and lubricants shall be in accordance with the following formula:

* * * * *

(4) If within a period of thirty days from the date of execution of this contract, there occur in India changes to any Central or State Act, Ordinance, rule or other law or any regulation or bye-law of any local or other duly constituted authority, and the introduction of any such Act, Ordinance, rule, regulation or bye-law which causes additional or reduced cost to the Contractor, other than under sub-clauses (1), (2) and (3) of this clause in the execution of the work, such additional or reduced cost shall be certified by the Employer after examining the records, if any, provided by the Contractor and shall be paid by or credited to the Employer and the contract price be adjusted accordingly. Provided that such additional or reduced cost shall not be separately paid or credited if the same shall already have been taken into account in the indexing of any input to the price adjustment formula in accordance with sub-clauses (1), (2) and (3) of this clause.

7. Alteration[1] *of Design*

The contractor will, if so required by order in writing signed by the

---

1 'Alteration' or 'modification', according to various dictionaries such as Webster's Dictionary and Black's Law Dictionary, may involve an increase or decrease in the details but not a change in the general purpose and effect. It would only mean "a small adjustment, a minor or slight change, a qualification or limitation, alteration of a subordinate character", not a change of a vital nature affecting the basic structure: See *S.K. Gupta* v. *K.P. Jain*, (1979) 3 SCC 54 (para 23) (wherein this dictionary meaning adopted by the Delhi High Court in the decision under appeal was held inapplicable to a statutory definition which permitted even an alteration of a basic nature).

Employer, alter the design or size of the works and the materials to be used in constructing the same, provided that he shall not be bound to do so unless the sum to be paid for any extras or to be allowed for any omission has been first fixed by agreement between him and the Employer and, in absence of agreement, the sum to be so paid or allowed shall be settled by ———.

8. Defect

The Contractor shall make good any defects, shrinkage or other faults that may appear in the works within six months after their completion.

9. Materials at Contractor's Risk

While the works are in course of construction and until the Employer takes over the same, they and all materials or plants used or to be used in constructing the same shall remain at the Contractor's risk and he shall not be entitled to any compensation for injury to, or loss or destruction of such works or materials arising from any cause whatever.

10. Extension of Time

If the Contractor requires any extension of time for completing the works he must apply to the Employer within seven days from the date of the occurrence of the event on account of which he desires such extension; and the Employer may, if he thinks such request reasonable, grant such extension of time as he may think necessary.

11. Unsatisfactory Progress

If the Employer is at any time dissatisfied with the progress of the work or with the quality of materials used or of the workmanship he may apply to ———— to depute an Engineer to inspect the works, and if such officer certifies in writing that the rate of progress or the materials used or the workmanship or any or all of them is or are unsatisfactory or not in accordance with this contract, the Employer may then enter upon the site of the works and may employ another builder to complete the same and may pay such builder the cost of such completion out of the sum payable to the Contractor under this agreement or the balance of such sum if advances have been made to the contractor, and, if such cost is more than such sum or balance, then the Contractor will pay the excess to the Employer.

12. Time for Completion

Unless the time is extended under clause 10 hereof, the Contractor will complete a portion of the works of the value of not less than Rs. ——— on or before the ———, and will complete the whole work and will remove from the site of the works all plant, scaffolding, unused materials and rubbish and will leave the works and site clean on or before ———.

13. Default

If the Contractor fails to comply with the provision of clause 12 on or before the dates mentioned therein or within such extended time as may be permitted in accordance with clause 10 hereof, he will pay to the Employer as liquidated damages a sum of Rs. ——— for every day's delay, and the Employer may deduct such sum or sums from any money due to the Contractor under these presents or may recover it otherwise.[1]

14. Running Payments

At the end of each calendar month commencing from the date when the Contractor commences work the Employer will pay to the Contractor a sum equal to 80 per cent of the value as estimated by the parties or in case of disagreement between the parties by ——— of the work executed by the Contractor during the month and the Employer will make final payment to the Contractor within two months from the date when the works are completed.

15. Force majeure

The contractor shall be not responsible for and shall incur no liability of any kind whatsoever for inability to supply for causes beyond its control, and in particular but without prejudice to the generality of the foregoing, by war, strikes, lock-outs, slowdowns, riots or civil commotions, shortage of labour or material, defects in machinery or the working thereof or for delays in supply of bought-out components, transportation difficulties, power failures or Government Regulations encountered by the contractor and its suppliers.

16. Arbitration[2]

If at any time during the progress of the works or after completion

---

1 Liquidated damages is a pre-estimate by the parties as the measure of reasonable compensation. If the compensation contemplated is not by way of penalty or unreasonable the court/arbitrator can grant it even though no loss is proved. *ONGC* v. *SAW Pipes Ltd.*, AIR 2003 SC 2629.

2 See Sec. 56, Contract Act; In *Southern Gas Ltd.* v. *Viswesaraya Iron & Steel Ltd.*, (1998) 9 SCC 555, it was held that the arbitrator should first determine the applicability or otherwise of the '*force majeure*' clause and proceed to determine other questions only in case he finds the *force majeure* clause to be inapplicable.

or the alleged completion thereof and at any time during the continuance of this agreement any disputes or differences arise between the parties hereto in relation to or in connection with this agreement, the same shall be referred to the arbitration of Sri ——— as the sole arbitrator (*or*, three arbitrators, one to be appointed by each party and the third to be appointed by the first two) and the provisions of Arbitration and Conciliation Act 1996, shall apply. The decision so given shall be final and binding upon the parties.

17. Indemnity

The contractor will indemnify the Employer from all claims for injury caused to any person, whether a workman or not, while in or upon the works or the site of the same, and the Employer shall not be bound to defend any claim brought under the Workman's Compensation Act unless the Contractor first deposits with the Employer AB a sum sufficient to cover any liability which the Employer might incur by reason of defending any such claim.

18. Interpretation clause.

The Schedule herein referred to

IN WITNESS WHEREOF, etc.

5—Construction Agreement After Inviting Tenders[1]

[*After describing the parties and giving the necessary recitals an agreement may be drafted on the following lines*]

NOW, therefore it is agreed—

Scope of the Work

The contractor shall perform everything required to be performed and shall provide and furnish all the labour and materials and arrange for tools and equipment required to perform and complete the works (*or*, all works) covered by the contract document in a workmanlike manner and in strict accordance with the drawings and specifications and the general and special conditions of contract, which are made a part of this contract and shall do everything required by this contract in strict compliance of these contract

1 An invitation to tender is a mere attempt to ascertain whether an offer can be obtained within such margin as the building owner or employer is willing to adopt, or, in other words, is an offer to negotiate, an offer to receive offers, an offer to chaffer. It differs from an auction which is a manner of selling or letting property by bids, and usually to the highest bidder by public competition (*P.R. Quenim* v. *M. Kalyan Tandel*, (1974) 2 SCC 169, quoting from Halsbury's Laws of England).

documents and other documents made a part hereof.

Payments

All payments shall be made to the contractor in Indian currency (*or as may be agreed upon*) in accordance with the provisions embodied in the documents made a part of this contract, the sum of Rs. ———— (Rupees ————) or such other sum as may become payable to the contractor under this contract.

This contract consists of the following component parts all of which are as fully a part of this contract as if herein set out verbatim, or if not attached, as if hereto attached.

1. General conditions *of contract. They should be general in nature, such as relating to earnest money, security money, compensation for delay in execution of contract, action which has been agreed upon to be taken for delay, presentation of bills, interim payments, power of inspection, extension of time, sub-contracts, etc.*

2. Special conditions *of contract. They should generally contain an interpretation clause, the extent and scope of the contract, the mutually explanatory nature of the documents forming part of the contract, prices of different works or parcels of work, time for completion of the contract as a whole as well as completion of the particular parcel by a particular time, the contractor's obligations in respect of labour, sanitation, local bye-laws, safety measures, tools, plants, equipment, materials and appliances and perhaps also the programme of the different phases of the work, use of sub-standard material, sub-contracts, supervision of the work, suspension of work, default and variations, etc.*

Special conditions will differ from contract to contract and it is for the parties to settle them. In Government contracts, there may be special conditions for providing certain facilities to the contractor, viz. assisting the contractor in getting the controlled materials required for the work, supplying machinery and other tools and equipment, the means of transport for movement of materials, or assisting him in getting essentiality certificates or the like.

Such conditions should also cover the jurisdiction of the courts[1] *as well as settling the disputes through arbitration.*

3. Contractor's tender *or tenders and all material correspondence relating to the contracts should be made a part of the contract.*

Discrepancies

In case of any discrepancy between the general and special conditions and special conditions and other documents forming part of this contract, the special conditions will prevail.

4. Interpretation clause

IN WITNESS WHEREOF, etc.

6—Agreement for Publication of a Book on Royalty System

AN AGREEMENT made, etc.

WHEREBY IT IS AGREED as follows:

1. Time for Completion

The Author will write and complete a book titled the ———— and will unless prevented by illness or other unavoidable cause deliver the manuscript to the Publisher for printing, so that the completed manuscript may be in the Publisher's hands on the ———. The Author will promptly revise and correct all proof sheets submitted to him by the Publisher.

2. Time for Publication

Subject to the performance, by the Author, of the contract under the preceding clause, the Publisher will on or before the ——— print and publish the said book at his own expense and risk in all things.

3. Paper, Type, etc.

The paper, type, binding and embellishments shall be in accordance with specimens already approved by the Author and the said book will be published at the price of Rs. ——— per copy net.

---

1 Under section 20, C.P.C. a suit arising out of a contract may lie, at the choice of the plaintiff, at one of several places. If, however, the parties have agreed that out of those alternative places the courts only at the specified place shall have jurisdiction such agreement is valid: *Hakam Singh* v. *Gammon (India) Ltd.*, AIR 1971 SC 740 (see Mogha's *Law of Pleadings*, 18th edn., p. 271 under heading Jurisdiction for further implications of such clause).

4. Number of Copies

The first edition will consist of ——— copies, out of which the Publisher shall supply to the Author ——— *gratis* copies for his own use and presentation but not for sale.

5. Royalty[1]

The Publisher shall pay to the Author a royalty of 25 per cent, of the published price in respect of every copy of the first edition sold by the Publisher. Such royalties shall be paid within one month after the dates hereby fixed for rendering accounts by the Publisher.

6. Accounts

The Publisher shall keep proper Account of the sale of the said book and render the same to the Author at the end of each calendar month after the publication and shall at all reasonable times produce all books of accounts for the inspection of the Author who shall be entitled to make copies of or extracts from the same for his own use.

7. Author not to Publish

During the continuance of this agreement the Author shall not publish or authorise the publication of any copy or abridgement or translation of the said book.

8. Copyright

The copyright in the said book shall remain vested in the Author who will indemnify the Publisher against all claims for infringement of copyright or libel in respect of anything contained in the said book.

9. Assignment

This agreement shall not be assignable by the Publisher without permission in writing of the Author.

10. Default in Payment of Royalty

In case the Publisher shall make default in the payment of royalties for one calendar month after due date as appointed under this agreement or becomes insolvent, the Author will have the right to determine this agreement, and on such determination the Author will have the option

---

1 Royalty is "a compensation or portion of the proceeds paid to the owner of a right, as a patent or oil or mineral right, for the use of it and also an agreed portion of the income from a work paid to its author, composer etc., usually a percentage of the retail price of each copy sold" (Random House Dictionary), adopted in *Pradeep C. Mody* v. *Sashikant C. Mody*, AIR 1998 Bom 351 (relying also on Supreme Court decisions to the same effect).

to take all copies of the said book in stock at a fair valuation and if he fails to exercise this option within one month after notice requiring him to do so, such copies shall be sold and the Publisher shall receive half the amount of such valuation or proceeds of sale.

IN WITNESS WHEREOF, etc.

7—Agreement between Author and Publisher for Sale of Copyright and Publication of a Book[1]

AN AGREEMENT made on the ——— day of ———— BETWEEN AB, etc., (hereinafter called the "Author") of the first part and EF, etc., carrying on business as publishers under the firm name of —— at ——— (hereinafter called the "Publisher") of the other part.

WHEREAS it is mutually agreed that the Publishers shall purchase the copyright of the book titled ——— written by the Author, on the following terms:

1. Printing and Publication

The Publishers shall bear the whole expense and risk of the paper and printing of the said book and the publication thereof.

2. Payment to Author

The Publishers shall pay to the Author the sum of Rs. ——— for the first edition of the said book when ——— copies shall have been sold and for the second and every future edition the sum of Rs. ——— to be paid within three months after the day of publication, no edition shall exceed ————— copies and ——— copies of each edition shall be supplied *gratis* to the Author for his own use and for presentation but not for sale.

3. Author to Revise

The author shall revise any new edition of the said work and correct the proofs.

4. Alternative Arrangement for Revision

In case of the death of the Author or his inability to revise the said work or correct the proofs the Publishers shall be at liberty to employ such

1 On assignment of copyright see *Raj Video Vision* v. *K. Mohankrishnan*, AIR 1998 Mad 294 in which it was held that even after a film producer has assigned all rights in the negatives of his film he retains his copyright in the film and can assign T.V. and video rights to a third party.

editors and proof readers as they may think fit and after deducting the payments made to such editors and proof readers, from said sum of Rs.—— the balance shall be paid to the Author or his representatives.

5. Rights of Publisher if Books are not Sold

In case ——— copies of the first edition of the said book shall not be sold within ——— years from the date of publication, the Publishers shall be at liberty to waste the same and shall not be liable to pay the aforesaid sum of Rs. ——— to the Author.

IN WITNESS WHEREOF, etc.

8—Agreement between Firm of Manufacturers and an Agent

THIS AGREEMENT made on this ——— day of ——— BETWEEN AB, etc., CD, etc., and EF, etc., carrying on in partnership the business of manufacture of steel boxes and padlocks under firm name of Bhargava Industrial Works at Aligarh (hereinafter called the "Employer") of the one part AND XY, etc., (hereinafter called the "Agent") of the other part WHEREBY it is agreed as follows:

1. Term of Engagement

The Employer will employ the Agent for a term of ——— years from the date hereof (*or,* from the ——— day of ———) as a travelling agent in the Employer's business of steel boxes and padlocks.

2. Agent to Serve Faithfully

The Agent will serve the Employer during the said term of employment diligently and according to his best abilities in all respects and shall at all times obey the directions of the Employer in regard to such service.

3. To Devote Whole Time

The Agent shall devote the whole of his time, attention and energies to the performance of the duties as such agent and shall not either directly or indirectly be in any way connected with or concerned in any other business or pursuit whatsoever.

4. To Keep Account

The Agent will, subject to the control of the Employer, keep proper books of account and shall make correct entries of the price of goods sold and of all transactions and dealings of and in relation to the said business.

5. To Submit Report

The Agent will forward to the employer every week a statement of all business done by him during the previous week.

6. Salary

The Employer will pay to the Agent a salary of Rs. ——— per mensem payable on the first day of the month following that for which it is due.

7. Commission

The Employer will also pay to the Agent a Commission of ——— per cent on the moneys actually received by the Employer in respect of all original orders obtained by the Agent and a commission of ——— percent on moneys received in respect of repeat orders.

8. Travelling Expenses

The Employer will also pay to the Agent actual reasonable travelling expenses incurred by him in or about the business of the Employer (*or,* the Employer will pay to the Agent in respect of all journeys undertaken by him in or about the business of the Employer one and one-half railway fare of the ordinary second class for journeys performed by rail and at the rate of two rupees per kilometre for journeys exceeding five kilometres performed by road and halting allowance of Rs.50 per day for halts of more than 9 hours in one day) (*or*, the Employer will provide a motor car to the Agent for travelling and will pay him a monthly allowance of Rs. ——— per mensem to cover the pay of the driver and cost of petrol and oil and in the event of any damage to the said car the loss shall be borne by the parties hereto equally and for all journeys undertaken by rail will pay him one and one-half second class airconditioned fare).

9. Jurisdiction of Agent

The Agent will travel in and receive orders from ——— (*name of territory*) and during the continuance of his employment under this agreement the Employer will not allow any other agent to travel in or receive orders from the said territory.

10. Duty to Secure Orders

The Agent will use his best endeavours to obtain orders for the Employer's goods and shall at regular intervals visit the present customers of the Employer in the said territory and also endeavour to secure fresh customers and shall accurately and promptly transmit all orders obtained by him to the Employer. Provided that he shall not be entitled to solicit orders from any place outside the said territory without the direction in writing of the Employer.

11. To Collect Debts

The Agent shall collect debts and receive moneys on behalf of the Employer and give receipts for the same and shall transmit to the Employer all moneys received by him immediately on receipt thereof.

12. Correspondence

The Agent shall deliver over to the Employer all letters and correspondence in any manner relating to the business of the Employer immediately on receipt thereof and shall induce customers and others to address directly to the Employer all correspondence relating to the said business.

13. Not to Undersell

The Agent shall not without the consent in writing of the Employer accept any orders for sale or offer to sell goods at prices less than those appearing in the price lists of the Employer.

14. Absence from Duty

In the event of the Agent being unable to perform his duties for a period of ———— days owing to illness or other unavoidable cause, the Employer may either appoint a substitute to perform the said duties and remunerate him out of the salary of the Agent for such period, or may determine this agreement on payment of a sum equal to one month's salary in addition to salary and commission actually due to him at the date of such determination.

15. Determination of Agreement

Either party hereto may at any time determine this agreement by giving to the other three calender months' notice in writing and the Employer may determine the agreement immediately without any such notice on giving to the Agent three months' salary in lieu of notice with estimated commission for such three months to be calculated on the average commission earned by the Agent during the year preceeding such determination provided that in a case of wilful neglect or refusal of the Agent to perform his duties under this agreement without any justifiable cause or of any other act of misconduct on the part of the Agent, the Employer may terminate the Agent's services without giving such notice or salary or commission as aforesaid.

16. (Arbitration clause if necessary).

IN WITNESS, etc.

9—Agreement for Agency to Sell Goods[1]

THIS AGREEMENT is made on the ——— day of ——— BETWEEN AB, etc., and CD, etc., carrying on business in partnership as ——— under the firm name of Garg and Company of the one part AND EF, etc., (hereinafter called "the Agent") of the other part.

WHEREAS the expression "Successors in business" hereinafter used in relation to the said firm Garg and Company means any one or both of the said AB and CD who after any change or changes in the constitution of the said firm by the death or retirement of a partner or the admission of a new partner or partners shall either alone or in partnership carry on the said business under the firm name of Garg and Company and his or their partners (if any) for the time being in the said business AND the expression "Principals" means Garg and Company or their successors in business;

AND WHEREAS the Agent has agreed with Garg and Company to become the agent of the Principals in the State of Punjab for the sale of ———, manufactured or supplied by them upon the terms and in manner hereinafter mentioned.

NOW THIS DEED WITNESSES and the parties hereto hereby mutually agree as follows:

1. Firm to Supply Goods

The Principals shall from time to time during the term of ——— years from the ———, consign and supply, at their own cost and charge, to the Agent as early as possible after receipt of his order in writing for the same unless they shall be prevented by some just and sufficient cause, such quantities and description of ——— as the Agent shall require.

1 On this type of agreements see discussion in *Bhopal Sugar Industries* v. *S.T.O.*, (1977) 3 SCC 147 (Petroleum agency agreement with Caltex Ltd., held not to create a relationship of principal and agent but one of seller and buyer of goods); See also *Rohtas Industries Ltd.* v. *State of Bihar*, AIR 1963 SC 347; compare form No. 22 *post* for marketing agreement not amounting to agency.

2. Agent to Sell

The Agent shall use his best endeavours to sell and dispose of the goods supplied to him as hereinbefore stated to the best advantage and for the best price obtainable not being less than such prices (if any) as may from time to time be fixed by the Principals and shall in the meantime keep such goods stored in a proper place or places at his own risk.

3. Expenses and Commission

The Principals shall allow or pay to the Agent all reasonable expenses for carriage or delivery of the said goods and for books, stationery and postage and all other reasonable and customary expenses attending the sale thereof or otherwise incurred by him in respect of such sale and shall also allow or pay to him a commission at the rate of ——— per cent upon the net proceeds of sale of such goods after deducting expenses, such commission being chargeable upon moneys actually received and not on outstanding debts.

4. Lien

The Agent shall have a lien or charge for all moneys becoming due to him hereunder upon the goods of the Principals which shall for the time being be in the possession or custody of the Agent.

5. Servants

The Agent shall himself and at his own cost employ such clerks, salesmen and assistants as may be necessary.

6. Accounts and Inspection

The Agent shall keep proper accounts of all goods received by him and of the particulars of the sale thereof and of all sums of money received by him and of all credits given on account of any such goods and of all other matters and transactions concerning the sale of such goods and such accounts shall at all reasonable times be open to the inspection of the Principals or any members of their firm or their representative who shall have full liberty to take copies or extracts of or from the same or any of them.

7. Submission of Accounts

The Agent will in the first week of every quarter render to the Principals a true and proper account of all goods received by him and of all orders received by him and the particulars of all sales and other transactions made and of all moneys received and spent by him for and on account of the said goods during the preceding quarter.

8. Settlement of Accounts

The parties shall on the ——— day of ——— next and thereafter during the continuance of the Agency on the ——— day of ———— and the ——— day of ——— in every year unless prevented by unavoidable cause and then as soon as may be after the removal of such cause, settle accounts respecting the sale of the said goods and other matters aforesaid (*or*, The Agent shall on the —— day of —— and the —— day of ——— in every year submit to the Principal a half yearly statement of account showing all receipts and payments and other dealings and transactions concerning the premises) and the Principals shall have the right to check it with the account books and when such statement of account is approved and signed by the parties it shall be binding on them and shall not afterwards be re-opened unless some manifest error or omission is discovered within one year.

9. Agent not to Work for Another and Principals not to Sell Goods to Another

The Agent, his clerks, sub-agents or servants or any of them shall not during the continuance of the said agency, without the consent in writing of the Principal, buy, sell or deal in ——— directly or indirectly for or on account of any person other than the Principals AND the Principals, their clerks, servants or agents or any of them will not, during the period aforesaid without the consent in writing of the Agents, supply such goods as aforesaid, whether for resale or otherwise, to any person or persons whosoever who shall reside or carry on business in the State of ———.

10. Limit to Credit

The Agent shall not give credit for any goods to any firm for a longer period than ——— months nor for any goods exceeding the value of Rs. —— without the consent in writing of the Principals and shall not give credit for any goods to any person to whom the Principals shall have prohibited him to give credit.

11. Not to Pledge

The Agent shall not without the consent in writing of the Principals pledge any goods consigned or supplied to him as aforesaid.

12. Agent to Obey Principal's Direction

The Agent shall at all times during the continuance of the said agency obey and observe all reasonable directions and instructions which may be given to him by the Principals concerning the sale or disposal of the said goods or otherwise relating to the business of the said agency.

13. Not to Compound Debts

The Agent shall not without the consent in writing of the Principals, compound any debt, obligation or security relating to the business nor shall withdraw or compromise any legal proceeding taken for enforcement of any such debt, etc., as aforesaid nor do any act by which any such debt, etc., as aforesaid may be discharged or diminished in value or prejudiced until the same shall have been fully paid or satisfied.

14. Liability for Loss or Damage

The Agent shall not be liable for any loss or damage which may happen to any goods as aforesaid or which may otherwise be incurred in or about the matters aforesaid unless the same shall be occasioned by his wilful neglect or default.

15. Power to Terminate

Either party hereto shall be at liberty to terminate the aforesaid agency by giving ——— months' notice in writing to the other provided that if either party shall wilfully neglect or refuse to observe or perform any of the agreements and stipulations aforesaid then the other may terminate the said agency upon giving ——— weeks' notice to him. And any notice hereinbefore required to be given to the Principals may be addressed to the firm by its/their name or style or to any partner thereof.

16. To Deliver Goods, Accounts, etc., on Termination of Agency

On the termination of the agency either by expiry of time or by notice as aforesaid, the Agent shall deliver to the Principals all or such of the goods aforesaid as shall remain unsold and all books, accounts and documents relating to the said agency which shall be in his possession or control.

17. Not to Assign Agency

The Agent shall not without the consent in writing of the Principals assign or in any other manner make over the said agency or this contract to any other person.

18. Power of Attorney to Agent

For further effectuating this agreement, the Principals hereby appoint the Agent to be their attorney in the name of the Principals to demand, sue for recovery and receive and give effectual receipts and discharges for all sums which may be due from any person or persons for or on account of goods sold by the Agent as aforesaid and generally to do all such acts and things as may be necessary or proper in relation to the matters aforesaid with power to appoint a substitute or substitutes under him for any of the purposes last aforesaid and the Principals shall ratify and confirm whatever the Agent or his substitute may do or cause to be done in or about the premises.

19. Arbitration

If any question or dispute shall at any time arise between the Agent and the Principals with respect to the meaning or effect of any clause in this agreement or the rights or liabilities of the parties hereto respectively hereunder then such question or dispute shall be referred to the arbitration of ——— whose award shall be conclusive and binding on the parties.

IN WITNESS WHEREOF, etc.

10—Agreement between the Government[1] and a Company for Loan Borrowed for Setting up a Factory

THIS AGREEMENT made this ——— day of ——— BETWEEN the ——— a company within the meaning of the Companies Act, 1956/2013 and having its registered office at ——— (hereinafter called "the Company") of the one part AND THE GOVERNOR OF ——— (hereinafter called "the State Government") of the other part ;

WHEREAS the State Government has on the request of the Company agreed to grant to the Company an advance of Rs. ——— (Rupees ———) for the purpose of setting up a ——— factory in the State of ———.

AND WHEREAS it is agreed that the said advance of Rs. ——— shall be secured by a mortgage of the tangible assets including lands, buildings, plant and machinery of the Company/Director ——— but the completion of mortgage documents cannot be immediately effected and the parties have agreed that till such time as the said security is furnished the Company shall furnish a Bank Guarantee from the ——— Bank, through whom the advance shall be made, for the repayment of the said advance.

---

1 It can also be adapted with suitable modifications for a loan by a financial institution.

AND WHEREAS the Memorandum of Association of the Company did not expressly include in the objects of the Company the power to carry on the business of manufacture of ——— but the Company has at an Extraordinary General Meeting of the shareholders held on the ——— day of ——— 1996 unanimously passed a special resolution to alter the said memorandum by incorporating the said power in the objects of the Company;[1]

AND WHEREAS a copy of the said special resolution has been filed in the office of the Registrar of Companies ———;

AND WHEREAS the Company has agreed that the said loan of Rs. ——— to be advanced by the State Government shall not be withdrawn by the Company from the Bank except after the Government of India have granted a licence to the Company to set up a —— factory in —— State.

NOW THIS DEED WITNESSES as follows:

1. Covenants by Company

In consideration of the State Government agreeing to advance to the Company the amount of Rs. ——— the Company hereby covenants with the Government as follows:

(i) Purpose

That the Company shall utilise the said advance for setting up a —— factory in the State of ——— and for no other purpose.

(ii) Repayment

That the Company shall repay the said principal amount of Rs. —— with interest, which will start accruing from the date the money is paid by the State Government to the ——— Bank (hereinafter called "the Bank") in accordance with sub-para (*vi*) herein at —— per cent per annum by ——— in ——— monthly equated instalments of principal and interest, the first of such repayment instalment shall be due on the first day of ——— PROVIDED THAT in the event of the interest not being paid on the due date, the interest so accrued will be added to the amount of the loan, and the equated instalments will be calculated on that basis.

(iii) Liability in case of Default in Payment

That if any instalments of principal or interest or both as aforesaid are not paid on the due dates, interest on the sum or sums that are in

1 See Sec. 13, Companies Act, 2013.

arrears shall be paid at the rate of ——— per annum for so long as the arrears are not paid, PROVIDED THAT this provision for the payment of enhanced interest shall in no way prejudice or affect the exercise by the State Government of any of the rights or remedies vested in it by law or by this deed.

(iv) Repayment of Whole Amount

That notwithstanding the stipulation regarding payment of ——— monthly instalments as aforesaid, the Company may repay the whole amount of the loan or any portion thereof and the interest that has accrued thereon at any time before the date on which the loan or any portion thereof and the interest that has accrued thereon is due.

(v) Procurement of Licence

That the Company shall obtain a licence from the Government of India for establishing the proposed ——— factory in the State ——— and if the Company shall not be able to obtain such a licence, the loan together with such interest as may be due shall become repayable forthwith.

(vi) Mortgage of Assets & Furnishing of Bank Guarantee

That the Company shall, as soon as possible, and in any case within ——— calendar months from the date of these presents, and upon terms and conditions as are herein provided or may hereafter be required by the State Government, create a mortgage on the tangible assets including lands, buildings, machinery and plant of the Company and on such other assets as may, to the satisfaction of the State Government, be of the value of Rs. —— and till such time as such security is furnished the Company shall furnish a Bank Guarantee from the Bank for the repayment of the aforesaid loan with interest thereon and for keeping the State Government harmless against any and all losses which may result from the failure of the Company to furnish adequate security.

(vii) Hypothecation of Factory's Assets

That the tangible assets including, lands, buildings, plant and machinery of the proposed ——— factory, as and when created, shall also be duly hypothecated with the State Government.

PROVIDED ALWAYS that upon the creation of a mortgage on the assets of the said factory, the security mentioned in sub-para (*vii*) shall be reduced *pro tanto*.

(viii) Insurance of Building and Machinery

That the Company shall at its own cost insure the buildings and machinery offered as security in sub-paras (*vi*) and (*vii*) above with a nationalised general insurance company for the full amount for which such buildings and machinery are hypothecated and the Company shall keep the insurance alive until the whole amount of principal and interest is fully repaid.

(ix) Bar to Re-hypothecation

That the assets hypothecated with the State Government will be kept free from all encumbrances and shall not be re-hypothecated in favour of any other person or as security for any other loan or amount till the dues of the State Government have been paid off in full.

(x) Liability in Case of Abandonment of Purpose

That in case for any reason the scheme is abandoned or the proposed factory is closed after its establishment or in case of default on the part of the Company in the payment of any equated instalment on due date or in case of breach of any of the other conditions and covenants of this agreement, the entire amount of the loan outstanding on that date together with accrued interest shall become recoverable forthwith and it shall be open to the State Government to effect the recovery, in any manner it thinks fit, from the Company or by disposal of the mortgaged or hypothecated assets of the Company either by sale or by public auction PROVIDED THAT if prior to the creating of the mortgage as aforesaid, the scheme for the setting up of the ——— factory, for which purpose the loan is agreed to be advanced, is given up or abandoned, the entire amount of the loan outstanding on that date together with accrued interest shall become recoverable forthwith and it shall be open to the State Government to effect the recovery in any manner it thinks fit, from the Guarantors as well.

2. Condition for Release of Advance by Bank

IT IS HEREBY FURTHER AGREED between the parties hereto:

(*i*) That the sum herein advanced shall remain in deposit and be held by the Bank and the Bank will release the same to the Company only on receipt of specific written instructions from the State Government which will be issued by the State Government when the company has been granted by the Government of India the requisite licence for establishing ——— factory in ——— State, and for establishing ——— factory in ——— State.

(ii) Company to raise Amount Equal to Advance

That the Company shall, over and above the amount to be advanced as aforesaid by the State Government, provide or arrange an amount at least equal to the amount of the advance for the purpose of the erection, establishment and working of the proposed factory.

(iii) Location of Factory

That the proposed ——— factory with all its processes shall be located in the State of ——— at a place to be approved by the State Government.

(iv) Government's Nominees on Board of Directors

That the Company shall, as early as may be, alter its Articles of Association[1] with a view to securing the appointment of two Directors to be nominated by the State Government on the Board of Directors who shall be Directors till such time as the loan including interest has been paid off in full.

(v) Apprenticeship Training

That the Company shall make suitable arrangements for apprenticeship training at the proposed factory in accordance with an agreed plan.

(vi) Settlement of Disputes

That if at any time any dispute, doubt or question shall arise between the Company and the State Government or any person claiming under them, touching or arising out or in respect of this deed or the subject matter thereof, the same shall be referred to an arbitral tribunal consisting of three members, one to be appointed by each party to the agreement, and the third, namely the presiding arbitrator being the Secretary to Government, ——— Judicial Department, and the decision of the arbitrators shall be final and binding on the parties.

PROVIDED ALWAYS and it is hereby agreed that expression "the Company" and "the State Government " herein used shall, whenever such an interpretation would be requisite to give the fullest possible scope and effect to any covenant herein contained, include their respective successors and assigns.

3. Covenants by the Company

The Company hereby assure unto the State Government as follows:

(*i*) That they have been duly authorised by their Board of Directors,

1 See Sec. 14, Companies Act, 2013.

through a resolution dated ——— to raise loan for the purpose of setting up a ——— factory and to mortgage the assets of the Company as security therefor.[1]

(*ii*) That apart from the temporary loan obtained from the Company's Bankers in the ordinary course of business there are no loans contracted or due from the Company.

(*iii*) That the Issued and Paid Up Share Capital of the Company is rupees ———.

(*iv*) That the Free Reserves of the Company are not less than rupees ——.

(*v*) That, subject to the Memorandum of Association and Articles of Association of the Company, the Company has power to establish a ——— factory.

(*vi*) That the Company shall execute all such assurances and documents as may be required by the State Government or be necessary under the Articles of Association of the Company for creating the mortgage as aforesaid.

SIGNED, sealed and delivered by, etc.

11—Agreement for Mutual Promotion of Business

THIS AGREEMENT made on the ______ day of _____ between AB, etc., (hereinafter called the First Party) and CD, etc., (hereinafter called the Second Party).

WHEREAS the First Party is engaged inter-alia in the business of printing and publication of newspaper and periodicals and also organizing various events and activities, including the business of broadcasting on _____ Radio through its different channels namely, _______ in _____ and ______ and also operating other frequencies across India;

WHEREAS the Second Party manages performance of programmes by artists and singers;

WHEREAS, the Second Party has full authority to enter into this agreement on behalf of _______ artists and singers;

WHEREAS, after discussions between these two parties, both of them have agreed to enter into this Agreement for promotion of interest of each other, for performance of live performance by _______ singer, to record

---

1 If the loan together with the moneys already borrowed by the company will exceed the paid up capital and free reserves, then a resolution of the company in a general meeting, will be necessary vide sec 180(1)(c) of Companies Act 2013.

the rights and obligations of each of the parties, First Party, and Second Party on its behalf and on behalf of the singer, have agreed to enter into this Agreement on.following terms and conditions;

NOW THIS AGREEMENT WITNESSES and the parties hereby agree:

1. This Agreement shall be deemed to come into effect from the date of signing of the Agreement and shall remain valid for a period of —————— .

2. The First Party shall promote ———— songs of ———— the singer, over a period of ———— days on its radio station and singer shall give one live performance, over a period of ————.

3. The First Party shall be at liberty to commercially use said live performance of the said singer.

4. The First Party agrees to bear expenses towards Air Travel, Lodging & Boarding, Local Travel of the singer, during the period of live performance.

5. The First Party further agrees to bear expenses for booking of the Venue and entire technical requirement as per advice of the singer.

6. The First Party shall bear professional fee charges of the singer in connection with live performance, but not exceeding a sum of Rs. ———.

7. The singer shall perform with his team, in a live performance to be organised by the First Party on the date, time and place, as per mutual written agreement between the Parties, but on or before the expiry of the Agreement.

8. The Parties agree that except for performance by each party, as noticed above, no other consideration either in the shape of money or in kind shall be payable by any of them.

9. The Parties agree that Standard Terms and Conditions for performance of reciprocal promises, as attached to this agreement, shall form part of this agreement.

10. The Parties agree that all rights, title and interest including intellectual property rights, name, logos, trademarks, copyrights, or other proprietary rights in the content and format shall remain the sole property of First Party and/or its parent company, shareholders, subsidiaries and/or affiliates and the Second Party shall not, itself use and/or permit, authorize and/or allow any third party to use, in any manner, whatsoever except as specified hereunder, and that too without the Party's express and prior written approval.

11. The Parties agree that the copyright and all other associated intellectual property rights including audio visual rights arising out of and/or in connections with this Agreement shall vest in the First Party.

12. The Intellectual property rights in the work developed under this Agreement including sound bites, audio-visual recording etc. shall constitute the absolute property of First Party at all times and First Party shall have absolute and exclusive right to use and commercially exploit such ideas, programming shows, photographs/videos of event organized by the First Party, researches, scripts, voice recordings of the singer

13. The Parties agree that the ownership of all rights, title and interest in the intellectual property in the performance of the singer and the content including transmission, broadcasting rights therein with respect to services performed by the singer shall vest exclusively with the First Party.

14. The Parties further agree that the singer has confirmed that he shall have no objection to his name, voice and photograph being used for planned publicity, in all forms of press or media during the existence of this Agreement.

15. The Parties also agree that the singer has confirmed that he shall make himself available to the First Party on such days, time and place as is mutually agreed between parties, for the purpose of photo-shoot.

16. It is agreed that the First Party shall have a right to raise sponsorship for the event to be performed by the singer.

17. The Parties agree that all information and data learned by either Party under or in relation to this Agreement, or any information, data, and/or matters contained in documents and/or materials to which such party has access to, during the Term, or any aspect whatsoever of either Party's operations (whether existing or future operations) shall be kept and shall be maintained as strictly confidential; and further that same shall not be used, disclosed or made available to any other person or party. Neither Party shall disclose the terms of this Agreement or any confidential or proprietary materials, which it receives from the other party or to which either Party gains access under this Agreement.

18. It is agreed that either Party may terminate this Agreement by a prior written notice of 30 days in the event the other Party has breached any of the terms and conditions of this Agreement and the Party has not cured the breach despite receipt of a prior written notice to cure the breach within 15 days. However, both parties shall continue discharge respective obligation during the said notice period.

19. Any notice or other communication to be given under this Agreement shall be in writing and shall be served by personal delivery

or by facsimile or by prepaid registered post or by courier to the addresses of the Parties specified in Principal Terms or as notified by either Party from time to time. Any notice or communication given under this Agreement shall be deemed to be served/received by the other Party within 48 hours of posting, or immediately upon being faxed if the transmission report indicates that the fax transmission was successful on address in the name clause.

20. The Stamp Duty and registration charges payable on or with respect to this Agreement shall be jointly borne by both the Parties.

21. This Agreement shall be governed by and construed in accordance with the laws of India. The Parties submit to the exclusion jurisdiction of the courts of Delhi.

22. Without prejudice to any other right available to it under the law or under equity, each Party, whosoever commits breach of obligations under this agreement shall, compensate and indemnify, defend and hold harmless the other Party ("Non-Defaulting Party"), its Affiliates, directors, officers and employees, from and against all losses, liabilities, damages, deficiencies, interest, penalties and other costs of expenses arising out of breach of any of the defaulting Party's obligations under this Agreement.

23. It is agreed that the First Party may assign or transfer its rights or obligations under this Agreement to any other party. However, the singer cannot assign or transfer his rights or obligations under this Agreement in any manner.

24. A waiver of any term or provision of, or consent granted under this agreement shall be effective only if it is in writing and signed by the waiving or consenting Party and that too only for the purpose for which it is given.

IN WITNESS WHEREOF, etc.

12—Catering Agreement with an Establishment

THIS AGREEMENT made on the ——— day of ——— BETWEEN AB, etc., of the one part AND CD, etc., (hereinafter called "the Caterer") of the other part.

WHEREAS AB have permitted the Caterer to run a restaurant within the premises owned by AB at ——— (hereinafter called "the restaurant") more fully described at the foot of this agreement, upon the terms and conditions hereinafter appearing:

NOW it is hereby agreed between the parties hereto as follows:

1. Term

This contract shall commence from the ——— day of ——— and shall, except as hereinafter otherwise provided, remain in force for a period of two years ending on the ——— day of ———.

2. Consideration

(a) The Caterer shall for the permission hereunder granted pay AB for such permission a sum of Rs. ——— per month payable in advance on or before the ——— day of each month.

(b) *Rebate*

If the Caterer shall pay to AB the sum under sub-clause (a) above, within the period specified therein then the Caterer shall have to pay only Rs. ——— in that month, the remaining sum being treated as rebate allowed by AB.

(c) *Interest*

If the Caterer shall fail to make the said monthly payment within the period specified in sub-clause (a) above he shall be liable to pay AB interest at 12% p.a. on the outstanding amount.

3. Not to Assign

The Caterer shall not except with the consent of AB obtained beforehand in writing, make sub-contract of any description for the catering hereby contracted for or any part thereof, nor except with such consent as aforesaid assign, sublet or otherwise part with this contract or any interest therein.

4. Menu and Rates

The Caterer shall supply to the public, good and wholesome food according to the standard menu as per Schedule A annexed hereto, and shall charge them at the rates mentioned therein. The parties hereto may vary the said Schedule by mutual agreement and if the parties fail to agree upon such variation, either party will be at liberty to determine this agreement without notice.

5. Inspection

Refreshments and drinks to be supplied by the Caterer shall be wholesome and of good quality to the satisfaction of AB or any person nominated by him for the purpose (hereinafter for brevity's sake called "the Inspecting Officer") and the Inspecting Officer or any other person deputed by him may inspect any provision or foodstuff brought by the Caterer as also cooked food, and take away samples thereof for inspection or analysis. If on examination it is proved that any article of the menu, provision or foodstuff was or is defective or that higher rates than those prescribed in Schedule A annexed read with the provision for variation hereinbefore contained, were or are charged by the Caterer, the Caterer shall pay to AB a sum of Rs. ——— as damages each time such default is proved to the satisfaction of the Inspecting Officer, whose decision shall be binding on the Caterer and AB may in its discretion also terminate this agreement without notice.

6. Manager

The Caterer shall either stay in the premises to look after the arrangements himself or be represented by an experienced Manager.

7. Caterer's Covenant

(1) *Voucher*

All sales made by the Caterer shall be under Vouchers.

(2) *Sales Tax*

Sales Tax, if applicable, on sale of foodstuffs and drinks in the restaurant shall be borne and paid by the Caterer.

(3) *Working Hours*

The restaurant shall remain open during such hours and on such days as the Inspecting Officer may fix.

(4) *Servants*

The Caterer will take all reasonable precautions that the servants and all other persons employed by him to do any work in the restaurant shall be courteous, civil, sober and honest and observe personal cleanliness. Before any person is employed or otherwise engaged by the Caterer in the Restaurant, the Caterer shall require such person to obtain and furnish a certificate (from such medical attendant as the Inspecting Officer may fix) that the person is free from contagious diseases. Such persons or servants as are found in the opinion of the Inspecting Officer guilty of any misconduct or personal uncleanliness or suffering from any contagious disease shall be removed by the Caterer forthwith.

(5) *No Residential Use*

The Caterer shall not use any portion of the Restaurant for residential purposes.

(6) *Uniforms*

The bearers and other servants engaged in the Restaurant by the Caterer shall wear such uniforms as may be prescribed by the Inspecting Officer.

(7) *List of Employees*

The Caterer shall by the ———— day of ——— furnish to the Inspecting Officer a list of persons employed or proposed to be employed by him in the Restaurant together with their temporary and permanent addresses and shall promptly intimate to the Inspecting Officer any change in the said list.

(8) *Cleanliness*

The Caterer shall see that the restaurant pantries and kitchens are clean and shall provide clean table cloth, napkins, etc., which will be changed on every alternate day or earlier if required.

(9) *Electric and Water Charges*

The electric and water installation in the premises shall be maintained by AB but the Caterer will bear and pay the electric and water charges.

(10) *Compliance of Laws*

The Caterer will be responsible to the local authorities including health authorities for complying with laws relating to sanitation and sale of unadulterated or otherwise harmful foodstuffs and drinks and AB will in no case be liable for the same.

(11) *Orders of Inspecting Officer*

The Caterer will comply with all orders that may be given to him by the Inspecting Officer regarding the upkeep and running of the restaurant.

(12) *Cooking*

Cooking will be done only at such place as may be specified by the Inspecting Officer.

(13) *Name*

The name of the restaurant shall be such as may be approved by the Inspecting Officer.

(14) *Erection of Structures*

The Caterer will not erect any temporary or *pucca* structure in the premises without the previous consent in writing of AB. Any such structure shall on expiration or sooner determination of this agreement become the property of AB without payment of any compensation.

8. Articles and Appliances

The sum specified in clause 2 above includes the hire of furniture, coffee machine, refrigerator, gas plant, pressure cooker and utensils described in Schedule B annexed which shall be maintained by the Caterer and returned to AB upon expiration or sooner determination of this Agreement in as good a condition as it is on the date of hire subject to reasonable wear and tear. The Caterer shall not remove the same without the permission of the Inspecting Officer and shall be responsible for any damage to or loss of the said articles and shall be liable to pay to AB such sum of Rs. ——— per day as damages.

9. Breach

Upon breach of any conditions of this agreement by the Caterer, AB will be entitled to determine this agreement forthwith without notice and thereafter the Caterer will be deemed to be a trespasser and in addition will be liable to pay to AB a sum of Rs. ——— per day as damages.

10. Termination Option

This agreement shall be terminable by either party giving to the other, thirty days notice in writing without assigning any reason therefor and without payment of any compensation.

11. Restaurant dues

AB do not undertake any responsibility in the matter of realisation of restaurant charges from the customers.

12. Complaint Book

The Caterer shall keep a complaint book at a conspicuous place in the restaurant in which complaints may be recorded by customers and which shall be open to inspection by the Inspecting Officer.

13. Security

The Caterer has deposited with AB a cash security of Rs. ——— and shall within ——— days of the date of this agreement furnish to AB a personal bond in the sum of Rs. ——— for the faithful performance of this contract. If there shall be any breach of the terms and conditions herein contained and to be observed and performed by the Caterer, AB may, without prejudice to any other rights or remedies in law, forfeit the security deposit and recover the sum under the personal bond and determine this agreement forthwith.

14. Arbitration clause.

15. Interpretation clause.

IN WITNESS WHEREOF, etc.

13—License Agreement for Catering Services

THIS AGREEMENT made on the ——— day of ——— BETWEEN AB, etc., (hereinafter called "the Licensor") of the one part AND CD, etc., (hereinafter called "the Licensee") of the other part.

WHEREAS AB have permitted the licensee to grant him licence for catering services at the premises owned by AB at ———, upon the terms and conditions hereinafter appearing:

NOW, it is hereby agreed between the parties hereto as follows:—

Period of Licence

Term of Licence will be five years, from the date of this agreement.

Licensee will provide the catering services only in the premises and will have the right of user only as a licensee.

Consideration

(a) The licensee shall, for the permission hereunder granted, pay the licensor a sum of Rs. ——— per month payable in advance on or before the ——— day of each month. The licensee shall also pay a sum of Rs. ———, as security deposit within 15 days of this agreement.

The licensee shall deposit Licence Fee/Security Deposit within the stipulated time failing which License would be liable to be terminated.

(b) Rebate

If the licensee shall pay to AB the sum under sub-clause (a) above, within the period specified therein then the licensee shall have to pay only Rs. ——— in that month, the remaining sum being treated as rebate allowed by the licensor.

Mode of Payment

Licensee fee and Security Deposit shall be payable through RTGS/NEFT or Demand Draft or Cheque drawn at ———.

Items to be Sold

The Licensee shall sell the items which are approved by the Licensor and no other item.

The Licensee shall supply to the public, good and wholesome food according to the standard menu as per Schedule A annexed hereto, and shall charge them at the rates mentioned therein.

The parties hereto may vary the said Schedule by mutual agreement and if the parties fail to agree upon such variation, either party will be at liberty to determine this agreement without notice.

In case the licensee is found selling any item other than the approved items, the Licensor or his authorised representative may seize such items. The unauthorised items so seized shall be disposed off as per policy of the Licensor. In addition thereto, penalty may be imposed for such contravention.

Inspection by Licensor or Inspectors

Licensee will also be under obligation to get the premises inspected by Food / Health inspectors, at regular intervals, in addition to having a food Licence from concerned state authorities. Licensee will make available the premises for the inspection by the Licensor or any person so authorised by the Licensor at any time.

Relationship with employees, contractors, sub-contractors of Licensee

The employees, contractors, sub-contractors of the Licensee will not be in any contractual relation with the Licensor.

The Licensor will not be liable for any liability arising under the labour laws or any other law of the land, incurred by the Licensee.

No claim of Compensation by Licensee

In case, Licensee suffers any loss on account of being lawfully restrained by the Licensor, or any competent authority, from indulging in illegal activities or contravention of any law, the licensee shall not be entitled to any compensation for any such loss.

Licensee to Indemnify the Licensor

The Licensee will indemnify the Licensor for any loss or damage caused by Licensee because of his fault or default.

Mode as to any subsequent variation in the terms and conditions

Any verbal or written arrangement abandoning, varying or

supplementing this agreement or any of its terms, shall not be binding on the parties, unless and until the same is endorsed on the agreement or incorporated in a formal instrument and signed by the parties.

General Liability Insurance

The Licensee will bear the costs, throughout the term of the Licence, for a comprehensive general liability insurance, which shall cover injury to or of any persons(s) occuring in the said premises.

Termination due to corrupt and fraudulent practices

If the Licensee has engaged in corrupt or fraudulent practices, in competing for or in executing the License, the Licensor may, after giving 14 days notice to the Licensee, terminate the License.

Refund of Security Deposit

It shall be refunded by the Licensor, without interest, at the time of peaceful vacation of the premises by the Licensee and after settlement of all dues or arrears arising out of the use of the premises by the Licensee.

Requisite Permissions/Certificates from Authorities

Licensee will obtain necessary certificates/permissions, from the concerned authorities, as required by law, such as food Licence, test reports for various food items etc., or required as per local rules and regulations.

In case of any offence on the licensed premises, Licensee will be solely responsible for its penalty and consequences.

Maintenance of record as to gross sales turnover

Licensee will be required to maintain proper record of sales to ascertain the Gross Sales Turnover (Including Tax) and make it available for inspection by the Licensor.

Interest on late payment

Payments of Licence fee, if delayed, will attract interest @24% per annum calculated for the number of days of default, without prejudice to any other right of the Licensor.

Payment of other charges by the Licensee

The Licensee shall pay his other charges such as municipal taxes etc. as and when they are due to the appropriate authorities. In case of default, in payment of any dues, Licensor reserves the right to recover the outstanding amount by deducting it from the Security Deposit / any other amount payable to the Licensee, with interest @ 18% per annum, for the number of days in default until the outstanding payments are cleared.

Recovery of outstanding amount

Licensor reserves the right to recover any other outstanding dues from the Licensee by adjusting the same against any amount / security of the Licensee or any amount payable to the Licensee either under this contract or any other contract.

Compliance with Statutory Obligations

Licensee shall not carry on any unlawful, immoral or illegal activity at the premises.

Licensee shall be responsible for compliance with provisions of Prevention of Food Adulteration Act or any other Act applicable thereto.

Licensee shall also be responsible for compliance with Goods and Services Tax Law, Provident Fund Law, Labour Law or any other law applicable to the Licensee.

Maintenance of Complaint/Suggestion Book

The Licensee shall keep a suggestion/complaint book at a conspicuous place of the premises, where the customers may register their suggestions / complaints, without any difficulty. This suggestion book shall be serially numbered and pre-authenticated by the Licensor.

Arbitration clause

In the event of any dispute or difference arising under these conditions of Licence or in the connection with this Licence the same will be resolved by arbitration, as per the provisions of 'The Arbitration and Conciliation Act, 1996.'

Supervision of Business of Licensee

The Licensee or a duly authorised and competent Manager appointed and paid by the Licensee shall remain present in person to manage or supervise the business to be carried on under the provision of this agreement and to ensure that the obligations of Licensee under the agreement are duly performed and observed.

The licensee shall, from time to time, apprise the Licensor about name(s) of the Manager.

Forfeiture of Security Deposit/Licence fee

In the event of any breach of the said terms and conditions of the Licence, the Licensor shall be entitled to forfeit the whole or the part of the Security Deposit / Licence fee besides terminating or revoking the Licence and debarring the Licensee from participating in the future projects of the Licensor.

Termination of Licence

The Licensor shall also be entitled at any time forthwith to terminate the Licence without notice in any of the following events, that is to say:

(a) in the event of the Licensee being convicted by a court of law under the provisions of criminal procedure code or any other law;

(b) in the event of the Licensee being adjudged insolvent;

(c) Failure to adhere to any of the due dates of payment, specified in the terms and conditions.

Immediately on the determination of this agreement, the Licensee shall peacefully vacate the premises and hand over to the Licensor or its administration all articles in the custody or possession of the Licensee and shall remove all his stores and effects from the said premises.

In default, the Licensor shall be entitled to enter and take possession of the said premises and to lock up the same or remove the furniture or other articles of the Licensee that may be lying there and to dispose of the same by sale or otherwise without being liable, for any damage, and all expenses incurred in connection therewith, shall be deducted by the Licensor from the sale proceeds or from the Security Deposit or pending bills of the Licensee.

Consequences as failure in providing catering service

In the event of failure to provide catering services within a maximum period of ——— days, from the date of this agreement, the licensor reserves the right to annul the Licence and forfeit the Security Deposit, Licence fee. The decision of the licensor will be final and binding in this regard.

14—Agreement to Recane Chairs

THIS AGREEMENT made on the ——— day of ——— BETWEEN AB, etc., (hereinafter called "the Contractor") of the one part AND CD, etc., (hereinafter called "the Second Party") of the other part;

WHEREAS the Contractor has agreed with Second Party to do the recaning of chairs of the office of ———— by Assam cane at the rates and in the manner and at the place hereinafter mentioned on the terms and conditions hereinafter contained;

NOW THESE PRESENTS WITNESS AND the parties hereto hereby agree as follows:

1. Period

This contract is to last for twelve months counted from the —— day of ——— but in the event of any breach of the agreement at any time on the part of the Contractor, the contract shall be determinable summarily by XY on behalf of the Second Party (hereinafter called "the Inspecting Officer") without compensation to the Contractor.

2. Raw material

The Contractor shall use Assam cane for the recaning of chairs, and the cane so used shall be of the quality or sort in every respect equal and answerable to the samples sent with the tender and such as the Inspecting Officer shall approve.

3. Place of Work

The recaning of chairs under this agreement shall be done by the Contractor in the office of ——— situate at ———.

4. Working days

The Contractor shall depute his workmen to do the said recaning work on all working days in the premises of the said office or at such other place or places as may be appointed by the Inspecting Officer.

5. Timely Completion

Conditions as to time for performance whether laid down herein or in any indent issued by the Inspecting Officer hereunder shall always be regarded as of the essence of the contract.

6. Rate

For all the said work done by the Contractor, the Inspecting Officer shall pay to the Contractor at the rate of Rs. ——— (Rupees ———) per seat and at the rate of Rs. ——— (Rupees———) per back recaned. PROVIDED THAT if the Contractor fails to do the recaning work to the entire satisfaction of the Inspecting Officer, the Inspecting Officer shall have the power to reject the said work if it is of defective workmanship or if any material of inferior quality has been used therein. Work rejected on the ground of inferior quality or of defective workmanship shall not be paid for.

7. Delegation of Power

The Inspecting Officer may delegate any or all of his powers under this agreement to any officer or official subordinate to him.

8. Not to Sublet

The Contractor shall not sublet or assign the contract without the permission in writing of the Inspecting Officer.

9. Default

In the event of the work not being in strict accordance with the conditions herein agreed upon or not being done within the time allowed, the Inspecting Officer may deduct or recover from the contractor as liquidated damages and not by way of penalty the sum of Rs. ——— for each and every day upto 25 days during which the said work is not done or bad material is not replaced. Further it shall be lawful for the Inspecting Officer to entrust to any other person the said work at the risk and cost of the contractor, who in addition to the liquidated damages aforesaid shall be liable for any loss or damages caused by the same. If the delay have arisen from any cause which the Inspecting Officer may accept in writing to be reasonable, such additional time may be allowed as may be considered necessary in the circumstances of the case. In such a case he may also forego the whole or any part of the aforesaid liquidated damages but not the other loss or losses.

10. Security

The Contractor shall simultaneously with the execution of this agreement deposit with the Second Party a sum of Rs. ———— as security for the due performance of this contract. In case of non-performance in any form or shape of the covenants and conditions of this contract, the Inspecting Officer shall have power to terminate this contract, and there upon the said sum of Rs. ——— deposited as security for the due performance of this contract may be forfeited by him and upon his doing so shall become the property of the Second Party.

11. Return of Security

The Inspecting Officer is empowered to deduct from such security money any sum that may be fixed by him as being the amount of loss or losses or damages due to the non-performance of one or any of the conditions hereinbefore contained. If not confiscated under the provisions of this contract, the security money or such balance thereof as may be left after making the deduction or deductions aforementioned shall be returned to the contractor after the Inspecting Officer shall have satisfied himself that all the terms of this contract have been duly and faithfully carried out by the contractor.

12. Arbitration clause.

13. Interpretation clause.

IN WITNESS WHEREOF, etc.

15—Agreement to Promote a Company

THIS AGREEMENT made on this ——— day of ——— BETWEEN AB, etc., of the one part AND CD, etc., of the other part;

WHEREAS AB had received a letter of intent from the Government of India for the manufacture of ——— and other allied products at an annual capacity of ———.

AND WHEREAS AB desired that a plant be installed and set up for manufacturing ——— and other allied products so as to give the required annual production of ———.

AND WHEREAS CD being possessed of the requisite technical know-how and management expertise and being fully capable of setting up the desired Plant, offered to install and set up the required Plant which was accepted by AB in accordance with and subject to the terms and conditions as herein contained;

AND WHEREAS both the parties hereto for the aforesaid purpose further agreed to promote a Public Limited Company for the manufacture of the said ——— and other allied products and for marketing the same upon the terms and conditions as herein contained and the said Company was accordingly incorporated under the name and style of EF having its registered office at ——— and duly registered under the Companies Act, 1956/2013;

NOW THEREFORE the parties hereto accordingly agree to abide with and remain bound by the terms and conditions hereinafter contained;

1. CD undertake to instal and set up the ——— and other allied

products manufacturing plant of ——— annual capacity (hereinafter called as "Plant") at ——— latest by ——— (*date*).

2. CD shall set up the plant as aforesaid for and on behalf of EF fully complete so as to go into production latest by ——— in accordance with the terms and conditions of this agreement.

3. The Plant is to be installed and set up as aforesaid by CD for and on behalf of EF, and CD shall give a detailed project report including the descriptions, drawings and detailed cost estimates fully complete in every respect to EF and after the consideration of the said report, EF and CD shall execute a contract in this behalf upon such terms and conditions as may be agreed upon between the said parties in this behalf.

4. (a) The authorised capital of EF is Rs. ——— consisting of ——— equity shares of Rs. ——— each and ——— preference shares of Rs. ——— each. The first issue of the capital of EF shall be of Rs. ——— out of which Rs. ——— will be Equity and Rs. ——— Preference Shares. It is hereby agreed between the parties hereto that whenever share capital is issued for subscription including the first issue, 26% of the Equity thereof shall be subscribed by AB and 25% of the Equity by CD and the balance 49% will be offered to the public or subscribed in such manner as may be desired by EF.

(b) Except with the mutual consent of the parties hereto in writing in this behalf, EF will not alter its share capital or the number of its shares nor shall it in any manner alter or modify the rights, privileges, restrictions or qualifications of any class of shares or issue any further shares to any party.

5. (a) If in addition to the initial capital of EF, further rupee funds are required for implementation of this project, the same may be borrowed and the parties hereto agree that they will use their good offices with various financial institutions in the country in getting the loans sanctioned. If, however, for any reasons the financial resources of EF together with aforesaid assistance are not sufficient to meet the total actual cost of the project then in that event the extra amount needed to meet the cost of project will be provided by AB and CD in equal proportions.

(b) It is further agreed between the parties hereto that in case the Plant is to be expanded further at any stage during the subsistence of this contract, the burden of the required additional cost of expansion shall also be borne by the parties in equal proportions.

6. The Board of Directors of EF shall consist of minimum five directors and maximum eleven directors. For the present EF shall have only

seven directors four of whom shall be nominated by AB and three by CD. When the Board of Directors of EF is to consist of all the eleven directors then out of them four will be nominated by AB and three by CD and the remaining four will be elected by mutual consent of the parties from amongst the other shareholders of EF. The Chairman of the Board of Directors of EF will be nominated by AB and the Managing Director will be nominated by CD from amongst its nominees on the Board.

7. AB and CD shall have the right to remove any of their respective nominees on the Board of Directors of EF and similarly they shall have the right to provide a substitute thereof.

8. EF will be managed through its Managing Director subject to overall control and directions of the Board of Directors of EF.

9. CD will provide the complete technical know-how for implementing and running the Project and Plant and for developing and maintaining a research and development wing for EF and for that purpose CD and EF will enter into a separate contract and CD will receive as remunerations an amount of Rs. ——— for this work from EF on such terms and conditions as may be provided in the aforesaid contract to be entered into between CD and EF.

10. If during the subsistance of this agreement either party hereto desires to part with or transfer its share holding or any part thereof in the equity share capital, such party shall give first option to the other party for the purchase of such shares at the average market value of shares during the last six months preceding the date of offer or at cost plus cumulative interest at the rate of 10% per annum from the date of investment minus the dividends received from EF upto the period of acceptance of the offer to purchase by the party concerned, whichever is higher. The party desiring to part with or transfer its shares or any part thereof shall give to the other party a written notice of such intention specifying the number of shares it is willing to sell and if the other party within thirty days of the receipt of such notice, accepts the offer to purchase such shares the party giving notice shall be bound to sell and transfer such shares to the other party. If the party receiving such notice as aforesaid fails to give such acceptance within thirty days of the receipt of such notice the party giving the notice will be free to sell the shares in question to any other party at any rate within three months after the expiry of the thirty days notice period. However, in the event where any of the parties hereto disposes of, transfers or sells its share holding or any part thereof whereby the requisite percentage of shares (26% for AB and 25% for CD) as required to be taken by the party concerned

under this agreement, falls below by whatever percentage, the benefits and rights conferred on that party by clause 6 of this agreement shall not be available to that party except to such extent and subject to such limitations and restrictions as the Board of Directors of EF may decide in this behalf.

It is also agreed between the parties hereto that if any of the parties sells as aforesaid only a part of its share holding to the other party, the selling party so long as it remains a party to this contract, will have the first option to repurchase the sold shares if the other party intends to sell, at a price to be determined in accordance with the provisions of this clause.

The provisions of this clause shall be subject to clause 12 of this agreement.

11. Duration of this contract shall be for ———— years beginning from ———— and ending on ——— subject to the condition that this contract may be extended further by mutual consent of the parties hereto upon such terms and conditions or with such modifications as may be agreed upon between them.

12. During the first five years of the subsistence of this contract none of the parties hereto shall be empowered to exercise the right to part with or transfer its shareholding or any part thereof in the equity share capital, unless mutually agreed in writing.

13. The parties hereto undertake to exercise or procure the exercise of all voting powers either direct or indirect of themselves respectively, at general meetings, class meetings or any other official meeting of EF (through their respective nominees on the Board of Directors) and in the exercise of the powers of the Directors to pass resolutions by circulation or otherwise so as to give effect to the terms and conditions of this agreement.

14. *Arbitration clause.*

15. *Interpretation clause.*

IN WITNESS WHEREOF, etc.

16—Agreement with Architect

THIS AGREEMENT made on this ——— day of ——— BETWEEN AB, etc. of the one part AND CD, etc. (hereinafter called the Architects) of the other part.

WHEREAS AB intends to construct a multistoreyed building on a plot of land measuring about ———— sq. meters situate at ———.

AND WHEREAS the aforesaid Architects are a reputed firm of architects with long experience in providing professional services;

AND WHEREAS the Architects have, after acquainting themselves with the site, scope and the extent of the work, have agreed to provide to AB all professional services for the completion of the civil works of the construction of the said building (hereinafter referred to as "the said works") and to supervise the construction thereof in the manner and subject to the terms and conditions hereinafter mentioned;

AND WHEREAS AB will at its (*or,* his or her) discretion entrust the execution of the said work either to a construction company or to a firm or any other person (hereinafter called "the Contractor ") as AB may think fit.

Now this deed witnesses and the parties hereto hereby agree as follows:

1. Fee

AB agrees to pay to the Architects as remuneration for the professional services to be rendered by the Architects in relation to the said works and in particular for the services hereinafter mentioned, fees as stipulated in paragraph 3 hereof (the said fees are hereinafter called "the Fees"). The cost of lifts and the air conditioning equipment, if any, will be excluded from the total cost of construction for the purposes of calculating the fees of the Architects.

2. Scope of Work

(a) The Architects agree to supervise the construction of the said works, to attend conferences, prepare working drawings, specifications, large scale detailed drawings, and do all other acts and render professional services in all such matters as may be requisite and appertain to the works of an architect. The supervision of the construction as above stated shall mean supervision and inspection as may be necessary to ensure that the works are being executed in accordance with approved designs, working drawings and specifications.

(b) The services to be rendered by the Architects shall include architectural planning, designing and structural details of:

- *(i)* Civil works.
- *(ii)* Water Supply systems.
- *(iii)* Sanitary installations.
- *(iv)* Electric supply installations.
- *(v)* Fire fighting.

(vi) Ventilation/air conditioning, if required (structural provisions only).

(vii) Laying of telephone conduit.

(viii) Drainage, etc.

(c) In consideration of the fees hereby agreed to be paid to the Architects as aforesaid, the Architects shall faithfully, expeditiously and honestly perform the following professional services pertaining to the said works ;

A. Sketch Stage

(i) Take AB's instructions regarding the requirements of the project as a whole.

(ii) Visit the site.

(iii) Prepare in consultation with AB a plan of accommodation and requirements.

(iv) Examine and take into account legislation, code and standards as they affect the works.

(v) Prepare preliminary draft sketches and notes sufficient to explain the Architects' general understanding of AB's requirements, including an estimate of the cost involved. Estimates of cost prepared from the preliminary draft sketches will simply indicate, from the Architects' experience, the probable cost of the whole works.

(vi) Discuss the draft sketches with AB and make such modifications as may be necessary to satisfy AB regarding his requirements.

B. Preliminary Stage

(i) Obtain from AB, or after approval of AB, prepare at AB's expense, a detailed topographical survey of the site to a scale of 1: 500 and contour interval as may be decided by AB in consultation with the Architects. The survey shall include all necessary data related to the public utility services, lines of streets and pavements, building lines, adjoining properties, obstacles, restrictions, easement rights with respect to access, ventilation and light and boundaries etc.

(ii) Assist in obtaining approval of drawings, designs, estimates, etc., required for proper execution of works from statutory bodies, local and other concerned authorities.

(iii) Obtain from AB or after approval of AB prepare at AB's expense, test site borings, soil tests and such other tests required to provide essential

design data of sub-soil conditions. The Architects shall interpret the said soil test reports and prepare detailed designs of the economic type of foundations for the building. The building structure shall be designed to withstand wind and seismic loads and all designs shall be in accordance with the Indian Standard Code of Practice and where these are not available then in accordance with the international specifications. The Architects will be responsible to ensure the safety of the building.

(iv) Prepare a sketch scheme, Report and Estimate of cost in sufficient details to enable the Architects to proceed with the working drawings stage of the works. (Estimates of cost prepared with sketch schemes are intended for AB's budget forecasting).

(v) Obtain AB's approval of the Sketch Scheme Report and Estimate of cost.

C. Working Drawing Stage

(i) Prepare the necessary drawing and documents in accordance with the requirements of the Contractor.

(ii) Prepare the necessary schedule of quantities and documents in relation to all materials and goods in accordance with the requirements of the Contractor.

(iii) Direct and coordinate the surveying, architectural and engineering work and prepare complete working drawings, schedules (as per ——— Department Specifications and Bill of Quantities) to describe the whole works adequately for the purpose of execution of works.

(iv) Obtain AB's approval for any material deviation in design or cost or working drawings, schedules and specifications.

D. Construction Stage

(i) Supply in advance to the Contractor sufficient copies of the working drawing schedules, specifications, bill of quantities, etc., required to start the work.

(ii) Assist the Contractor in the preparation of the work progress schedule.

(iii) Prepare and supply to the Contractor such further drawings, specifications or details as may be required for the proper execution of work.

(iv) Supervise the construction work to ensure that the works carried out conform in detail to the design and so as to achieve speedy and economical completion of the work.

3. Fees

(a) AB shall pay to the Architects their fees for the above described services as detailed below:

(i)	Design of the buildings and all other work mentioned in clause 2 of this Agreement.	3 per cent of the total cost.
(ii)	Travelling expenses for Sri —— only.	Actual travelling expenses based on Air/ACC fare and taxi fare from —— —— to ——— and back plus Rs.—— per day as incidental charges.

(b) Payment of Fees

Payment to the Architects on account of fee shall be made as follows:

(i)	Upon completion of Sketch stage under Clause 2(c)(A).	One-quarter per cent.
(ii)	Upon completion of the preliminary stage under Clause 2(c)(B).	Three quarters percent inclusive of item (i) above.
(iii)	On completion of working drawings under Clause 2(c)(C)	One percent inclusive of item (ii) above.
(iv)	Detailed estimates and completion of all detailed drawings under clause 2(c)(D).	One and half percent inclusive of item (iii) above.
(v)	Completion of works upto plinth level.	Two percent inclusive of item (iv) above.
(vi)	Completion of works upto the slab level.	Two and a half percent inclusive of item (v) above.
(vii)	Completion of works including finishing.	Three percent inclusive of item (vi) above.

4. Schedule of Time

The Architects undertake to complete their professional services hereunder by the dates mentioned below:

(i) Sketch Stage under Clause 2(c)(A). By ————

(ii) Preliminary drawings and designs under clause 2(c)(B) By ————

(iii) Working drawings under 2(c)(C). By ————

(iv) Detailed estimates and completion of all detailed drawings under clause 2(c)(D). By ————

(v) Supervision of the construction work By ————

5. Construction Cost

The construction cost shall not exceed Rs. ———— per square metre on an average and should conform to the norms of the C.P.W.D. (*or*, as the case may be) for such work.

The construction cost as above stated shall not include:

(a) Cost of land.

(b) The Architects fees.

(c) Any services relating to or cost of fittings or fixtures not designed, planned and supervised by the Architects.

(d) Soil testing fees.

6. Supply of Drawings & Documents

The Architects shall supply free of charge to AB adequate number of copies of all approved drawings alongwith subsequent modifications. Two sets of completion drawings showing all the installations in the building and subsequent corrections, if any, shall also be supplied by the Architects free of charge.

7. Other Architects and Consultants and Assignment

(1) The Architects shall be entitled to collaborate in the performance of this agreement with any other architect, structural consultants, civil or mechanical engineers, quantity surveyors and other consultants with whom they may in good faith enter into partnership relations or other engagements. But AB shall be entitled to withhold permission to any particular architect or engineer, surveyor or other consultant as aforesaid if for reasons stated by AB, AB should bona fide consider it advisable to do so. Any such arrangement shall however not create any contractual obligation between AB and the persons so collaborating and AB shall also not be required to pay any extra sum to the Architects on that account.

(2) The Architects shall not assign or sublet or transfer their interest in this agreement without the permission of AB.

8. Extra Service

AB shall pay to the Architects a reasonable amount mutually agreed upon for any extra services rendered by them if the Architects are required to incur any drafting and other expenses due to any major changes ordered by AB after approval of designs and drawings, provided that the Architects shall obtain written permission from AB to do such work.

9. Structural Soundness

The Architects shall be fully responsible for the structural soundness of the work.

10. Deviations, Alterations, Additions, Omissions and Revisions

The Architects shall not make any deviations, alterations, omissions or additions from or to the approved drawings without the knowledge and prior written consent of AB.

11. Discharge of Functions to be Performed by the Architects

The Architects hereby agree that the fees to be paid as provided herein will be in full discharge of the functions to be performed by them and no claim whatsoever shall lie against AB in respect of any other party collaborating with the Architects relating to the services herein agreed. The Architects shall indemnify and keep indemnified AB against any such claims.

12. Compensation to AB

(i) If the Architects fail to observe the time schedule as per clause 4, they shall be liable to pay to AB compensation of Rs. ——— per day till the work remains incomplete.

(ii) If the Architects abandon the work or become incapacitated from acting as such architects as aforesaid, AB may make full use of all or any drawings and designs prepared by the Architects and AB shall not be liable to pay anything more. If the Architects abandon the contract for any reason whatsoever, the Architects shall be liable to pay such damages to AB as may be assessed by AB upto a maximum of ——— per cent of the total estimated cost of the work.

13. Defects and Deficiencies

The Architects will endeavour to guard AB against any defects and deficiencies in the work of the Contractor, but they are not deemed to guarantee the performance of its contracts.

14. Arbitration

In the event of any question, dispute or difference arising out of the contract between the parties with regard to the interpretation of this contract or the rights, liabilities or duties arising out of it or otherwise, in connection with this contract, the matter shall be referred to two Arbitrators, one to be appointed by each of the parties hereto. The Arbitrators shall appoint a presiding Arbitrator before entering upon the reference. The majority decision of the Arbitrators shall be final and binding on the parties. The provisions of the Arbitration and Conciliation Act 1996 as amended from time to time shall apply to such arbitration. If work under the contract has not been completed when a dispute is referred to arbitration, the work shall continue during the arbitration proceedings and no payment due to the Architects within the provisions of the contract shall be withheld on account of the pendancy of the arbitration proceedings unless authorised or required by the Arbitrators.

15. Interpretation clause. [*However, it is to be moulded in the light of footnote under clause 1 for Fees of this model.*]

IN WITNESS WHEREOF, etc.

17—Agreement for Installation of Hoardings

THIS AGREEMENT made on this ——— day of ——— BETWEEN AB, etc. of the one part AND CD, etc. (hereinafter called the Firm) of the other part.

WHEREAS AB is desirous of having his/its advertisement hoardings installed at selected sites in Uttar Pradesh;

AND WHEREAS the Firm has offered to fabricate, supply, paint and instal the said hoardings and to maintain the same subject to the terms and conditions hereinafter appearing;

NOW THESE PRESENTS WITNESS as follows:—

1. During the period commencing from the ——— day of ——— and ending on ——— the Firm shall whenever so required by AB fabricate, supply, paint and instal the hoardings in accordance with the annexed specifications at such places in Uttar Pradesh as may be specified in the indents sent to the Firm.

2. The Firm shall complete the work of fabrication, supply, painting and installation of each hoarding within such period, not being less than 30 days, as may be specified in the said indents.

3. The painting of the hoardings shall contain such description, design and display as AB may indicate in each indent.

4. The hoardings when installed shall become the property of AB.

5. *(a)* After all the work in respect of a hoarding has been completed the Firm shall request AB to get the installation inspected. If upon

inspection the material and workmanship are found to be in order, AB shall intimate to the Firm that the specified installation has been taken over. PROVIDED THAT if AB shall fail to get the installation inspected within fifteen days from the receipt of notice of completion of the work from the Firm the installation shall be deemed to have been approved and taken over by AB.

(b) If any defect is noticed on inspection then before the taking over, the Firm shall remove the defect immediately and, in any case, before the period as specified in the indent.

6. The Firm hereby undertakes that if during a period of one year from the date of taking over any hoarding the painting on the hoarding shall fade, peel off or wash off or if the hoarding installed shall be damaged by storm or civil commotion or otherwise then and in any such case the defect shall be removed by the Firm within 15 days of receiving intimation, failing which AB may get the same done by other persons on contract or otherwise at the risk and responsibility of the Firm.

7. If during the defect liability period of one year as provided in clause 6 above, the painting fades, peels off or washes off or the hoarding is damaged as above stated and is re-done by the Firm the defect liability period in respect of such hoarding shall be for one year from the date the work is re-done by the Firm.

8. The price of every hoarding fabricated, supplied, painted and installed at selected site including maintenance thereof for one year as aforesaid shall be Rs. ———— which shall be paid to the Firm after the hoarding duly installed is taken over under clause 5(a). PROVIDED THAT a deduction of 10% of the amount shall be made from every such bill towards security deposit which, after making deductions, if any, will be returned to the Firm after the defect liability period of one year as aforesaid is over.

9. AB will be at liberty to get the work inspected at any stage during execution.

10. The Firm shall attend to any defect in the work pointed out to it and shall not use or apply any material rejected or disapproved by AB or his authorised representative.

11. *Arbitration clause.*

12. *Interpretation clause.*

IN WITNESS WHEREOF, etc.

18—Agreement for Purchase of Wooden Cases

This AGREEMENT made on ——— day of ——— BETWEEN AB, etc. (hereinafter called the Purchaser) of the one part AND CD, etc. (hereinafter called the Contractor) of the other part.

WHEREAS the tender of the Contractor for the supply of about —— wooden cases at the rate of Rs. ——— each inclusive of sales tax, stacking and other charges per case has been accepted by the Purchaser.

NOW THIS DEED WITNESSES and the parties hereto hereby agree as follows:

1. That the Contractor shall supply to the Purchaser upto a maximum quantity of ——— wooden cases during the period from —— to —— as per specifications given below and as per sample submitted by the Contractor along with his tender:

Specification	*Internal dimensions*
Type of wood	———
Length	—— cm.
Breadth	—— cm.
Height	—— cm.
Thickness of plank to be used	—— mm.

The wood used in fabrication shall not be less than 15 mm in thickness. The top lid shall be of one piece only while the other sides of the cases should not consist of more than two pieces. The top lid should be temporarily fixed. Iron Patti 1.25 mm thick and 15 mm wide should be fixed with three nails (5 cm long and 12 guage) on three sides of both the long ends and sufficient extension of the same Iron Patti will be left unfixed for fixing the top lid after packing. In joining the pieces to form side panel or in joining side to side panel or side to bottom panel, 4 nails of 12 gauge and 5 cm long shall be used. At each long end side there shall be a small stout rope handle attached by knots through two holes. Ends of nails should not protrude out of wood.

2. Delivery of the cases will be taken at ————.

3. The Contractor shall start the supply immediately after the execution of this agreement in accordance with the Purchaser's requirement and stop the supply as soon as the maximum supply aforesaid has been made within the aforesaid period.

4. The wooden cases supplied by the Contractor shall be inspected by the Purchaser or his authorised representative and if wooden cases are not

found according to the sample and specifications the same will be rejected and the Purchaser will be at liberty to arrange the supply from other parties at the risk and expense of the Contractor or the Purchaser may at his discretion accept the same at such reduced rate as may be mutually agreed upon. PROVIDED THAT the Purchaser shall have the option of stopping the supply at any stage in case he finds that the Contractor is not supplying the wooden cases according to the sample furnished by him.

5. In respect of wooden cases accepted by the Purchaser the payment will be made within 15 days of the receipt of bill from the Contractor.

6. The Contractor shall within three days of the execution of this agreement deposit security money of Rs. ———— with the Purchaser in the form of fixed deposit receipt of any nationalised bank for the due performance of this agreement. But in case the amount of security falls short of the total loss caused to the Purchaser, the Contractor will be liable to indemnify to the extent of total loss caused to the Purchaser. If the Contractor fails at any time to carry out his obligations or defaults in the performance of any terms or conditions hereof the whole or a part of the aforesaid security deposit shall in the discretion of the Purchaser be liable to be forfeited. The security shall, after making deductions, if any, be refunded to the contractor within six months after the expiration or sooner determination of this contract.

7. Any sum of money due and payable to the Contractor including the security returnable to him under this contract may be appropriated by the Purchaser and set off against any claim of the Purchaser for the payment of sum of money arising out of or under any other contract made by the Contractor with the Purchaser.

8. *Arbitration clause.*

9. *Interpretation clause.*

IN WITNESS WHEREOF, etc.

19—Agreement (Lump sum contract) for Fabrication of Bodies on Chassis

THIS AGREEMENT made on the —— day of ——— BETWEEN AB, etc., (hereinafter called "the Contractor") of the one part AND CD, etc., of the other part;

WHEREAS CD requires the fabrication of bodies and cabs on —— chassis complete;

AND WHEREAS the Contractor has agreed to execute upon and

subject to the conditions of contract set out below (hereinafter called "the said conditions") the work shown in the schedules and blue prints annexed hereto and a copy of which has been delivered to the Contractor for the sum of Rs. —— per Chassis plus Goods and Services Tax, if applicable, on the completed works (hereinafter called "the contract sum");

NOW IT IS HEREBY AGREED AS FOLLOWS:

1. In consideration of the contract sum to be paid by CD at the time and in the manner set forth in the said conditions, the Contractor will upon and subject to the said conditions execute and complete the said works.

2. CD will pay to the Contractor, the contract sum or such other sums as shall become payable at the time and in the manner set forth in the said conditions.

3. The said conditions shall be read and construed as forming part of this contract and the parties hereto respectively shall abide by and observe and perform and comply with the terms, stipulations and agreements therein contained and on their part to be observed, performed and complied with respectively.

4. *Conditions of Contract*

i) The Contractor will with his own men and materials execute the work in strict conformity with the annexed specifications and shall deliver the vehicles duly completed on or before ——— as per delivery schedule hereinafter provided.

ii) If any deviation, change or alteration from the specifications is necessary, the Contractor shall obtain prior sanction from CD or his authorised representative (hereinafter called "the Indenting Officer").

iii) The Indenting Officer shall have free access to the place where the work is being executed and he may at any time inspect thereat the materials used, the workmanship and progress of work.

iv)(a) The Contractor shall before using any materials in the fabrication work, get such materials approved by the Indenting Officer and only the materials so approved shall be used in the works. Any delay on the part of the Contractor in furnishing the materials for inspection and approval shall not be a ground for extension of time of delivery but if the approval by the Indenting Officer shall be delayed by more than three days, the Contractor shall be entitled to corresponding extension of time of delivery.

(b) The price is firm and final.

v) The work will be inspected by the Indenting Officer specially at all the stages as will be indicated in O.K. Card. It will be necessary for the Contractor to maintain these O.K. Cards so that the final O.K. of the body built will be given on the basis of these inspections done at various stages.

vi) The Contractor shall attend to any defects in the work pointed out to him and shall not use or apply any material rejected or disapproved by the Indenting Officer.

vii) The Contractor shall give notice to the Indenting Officer when bodies are ready whereupon the same shall be inspected by the Indenting Officer and the defects, if any, pointed out by the Indenting Officer to the Contractor shall be rectified by the Contractor accordingly.

viii) The Contractor shall not paint any body until the same has been inspected by the Indenting Officer, approved and passed as fit for painting.

ix) The Contractor shall get the paint material approved by the Indenting Officer before applying the same to the bodies.

x) The new chassis will be supplied to the Contractor in perfect running condition and free from any mechanical defects. After body building work, the vehicles must be handed over in the same condition. If later on any defect will be found in the bodies while running the vehicle or otherwise it will be set right by the Contractor without any extra charge upto a period of six months from the date of delivery of the vehicle complete by the Contractor to the Indenting Officer.

xi) The Contractor shall be responsible for the safe custody of the chassis given to him for the said work and he will be responsible for any deterioration, loss or shortage of materials and parts of to the said chassis from whatsoever cause arising while the same are in his custody and charge.

xii) Before taking over the chassis for the said work, the contractor shall take at his own cost Comprehensive Insurance Policy from any nationalised insurance company to cover the chassis to be supplied to him against the risks of fire, theft, pilferage, accident and floods, for the sum of Rs. ——— per vehicle. The Comprehensive Insurance Policy shall be assigned in favour of CD. The assignment shall be endorsed on the Policy. The endorsement shall be got registered with the Insurance Company who will make necessary entries on the Policy.

xiii) The Contractor shall within thirty days of the signing of this agreement and in any case before taking over the chassis for the said work, deposit security in a manner acceptable to the Indenting Officer, amounting to Rs.————. This security money shall remain in deposit with the Indenting Officer for a period of six months from the date of delivery of the last completed vehicle to the Indenting Officer.

xiv) The Contractor shall make good at his cost any defects in the fabrication of bodies or the quality or quantity of material used in the execution of the work that is pointed out to the Contractor and on his failure to do so the Indenting Officer may get the defects rectified by some other person on contract or otherwise and the cost thereof will be recoverable from the Contractor.

xv) Pilot sample of body shall be delivered by the Contractor for inspection and final approval within ——— weeks from the receipt of chassis. The balance quantity *i.e.*, ——— Nos. shall be delivered at the rate of ——— Nos. per month commencing after one month of the approval of the pilot sample. The said time of delivery shall be the essence of the contract. The Contractor will deliver the vehicles at the premises of ———.

xvi) The Contractor shall pay by way of liquidated damages to CD a sum of Rs. ——— only per day per vehicle for delay of each day in respect of each vehicle not delivered complete with body on the contracted date of delivery. This sum represents the parties' agreed pre-assessment of the damages that will be suffered by CD from the delay.

xvii) The Indenting Officer may waive off the damages for late delivery of vehicle if, in his opinion, the delay is for reasons beyond the control of the Contractor.

xviii) If called upon to do so the Contractor shall make such alterations in the pilot samples and/or in subsequent bodies as the Indenting Officer may in writing direct, and such alterations shall not vary the rate per body herein agreed but the cost of material only thereby reduced or added shall be deducted from or added to the rate per body as aforesaid at the market rate of such material as are certified by the Indenting Officer.

xix) If the Contractor commits a breach of any of the conditions of this contract the Indenting Officer may forfeit the said security deposit.

5. *Arbitration clause.*

6. *Interpretation clause.*

IN WITNESS WHEREOF, etc.

20—Agreement to Construct a Railway Siding for a Sugar Mill

THIS AGREEMENT made on the ———— day of———— BETWEEN ——— Sugar Mills Co. Ltd., ——— (hereinafter called "the Company", which expression shall include its successors and assigns) of the one part AND the President of India through the General Manager, ——— Railway (hereinafter called "the Railway") of the other part.

WHEREAS the Company has requested the Railway to construct for and at the expense of the Company a railway siding for transport sugarcane for the Company and to maintain the same, and to operate the railway siding at the expense of the Railway and with the rolling stock belonging to the Railway at the haulage rates agreed to by the Company as hereinafter mentioned;

AND WHEREAS the Railway has agreed to accede to the said request of the Company on the terms and conditions hereinafter mentioned, which terms and conditions have been accepted by the Company;

NOW IT IS HEREBY AGREED as follows:

1. Covenants of the Railway

The Railway shall—

(a) supply the rails, crossings, and sleepers which are and will remain its property but the cost of their removal from the ——— branch and their re-laying for the ———— branch, together with the cost of land and all earthwork and masonry works and the usual departmental overhead charges will be met by the Company;

(b) acquire land required for the purpose aforesaid which will vest in the Railway as hereinafter agreed to by the Company;

(c) maintain, at its expense, the branch line and run it;

(d) will not carry any sugarcane on the said line for anyone else besides the Company, but it may transport miscellaneous goods thereon so long as the carriage of sugarcane for the Company is not interfered with thereby;

(e) will reserve two locomotives of ———— make and thirty five 5 MT wagons for the exclusive purpose of carrying sugarcane of the Company on the said branch line.

2. Covenants of the Company

The Company shall—

(a) deposit a sum of Rs. ———— with the ———— prior to the commencement of the construction of the line, to cover the estimated approximate cost of the line, provided that the Company shall be entitled to recover any surplus left after the construction of the line is complete:

(b) pay in advance to the Railway at the beginning of every season in the month of ——— the sum of Rs. ———— to cover the interest charges at ——— percent per annum on the depreciated value at the time of

construction of the branch line of the rails, crossings and sleepers and the rolling stock and on account of the annual depreciation thereon;

(c) guarantee to take a minimum of ———— lakh metric tonnes of sugarcane from the branch line in a year. Should circumstances beyond the control of the Company prevent this minimum carriage being attained, such as a greatly decreased area of cane sown in the reserved area feeding the factory, or a serious failure of the crop therein or break-downs in the Company's factory extending to more than a week at any one time, the Company may ask the Railway in writing to reduce the aforesaid amount for that crushing season and the Railway shall reduce it to such amount as it may in its discretion deem fit to fix;

(d) supply, in case it considers necessary, additional wagons for the line at its own expense to be used by the Railway exclusively for the transport of sugarcane for the Company, PROVIDED THAT it shall do and undertake such repairs thereof as may from time to time be required and the Railway shall not be liable for any damages that may occur to wagons so supplied;

(e) pay the Railway for haulage of sugarcane at the following rates:

(i) For sugarcane transported to the factory of the Company:

For the first six lakh tonnes of cane carried from all way-side stations on this Branch to the Company's weigh-bridge at the rate of Rs. ——— per 5 MT wagon and Rs. —— per 3 MT wagon. Thereafter, at Rs. —— per 5 MT wagon and Rs. ——— per 3 MT wagon for all cane carried over and above the first six lakh metric tonnes.

(ii) For miscellaneous goods carried to and from the factory of the Company:

For such goods carried to the factory of the Company, full rates as in (i) above, and for carriage of such goods from the factory of the Company, half the rates given in (*i*) above when the goods are carried by an empty train returning from the factory of the Company to load up more cane, PROVIDED THAT when a special train will be required to be run for carrying such goods as aforesaid, the Company shall pay full rates as spedcified in (*i*) above.

(f) shall pay to the Railway or such person or persons as the Railway may appoint in this behalf all such sums of money as shall be awarded under the provisions of the Right to fair compensation and transparency in Land Acquisition Rehabilitation and Resettlement Act, 2013 as compensation to any person or persons who may be found on enquiry held under the provisions thereof has interest in the said land, together with all

payments and costs incidental to the acquisition of such land by the Railway, and the land so acquired shall vest in and be the property of the Railway.

3. It being the intention of the parties hereto and being hereby expressly agreed that this agreement shall last and hold good and be binding between them for a period of five years from the crushing season ——— to the crushing season ———.

4. The Railway shall not commence the construction of the railway siding unless the Company shall have performed such of its obligations under this Agreement as ought to be performed prior to the commencement of such construction and the Railway shall be at liberty to refuse to work and maintain the siding and to recover compensation and damages from the Company for breach of any condition, the fulfilment whereof has been hereunto undertaken by the Company.

5. *Arbitration clause.*

IN WITNESS WHEREOF, etc.

21—Agreement with Government for Permission to Pump Canal Water for Industrial Purposes

THIS AGREEMENT made on the ——— day of ——— BETWEEN the Governor of the State of ——— (hereinafter called "the State Government", which expression shall where the context so admits include his successors and assigns) of the one part AND ——— a Company within the meaning of the Companies Act, 1956/2013 (hereinafter called "the Company", which expression shall where the context so admits include its successors and assigns) of the other part;

WHEREAS the Company has installed tubewells in its premises at —— but the quality of water from such tubewells is not suitable for use in the Company's industries at the aforesaid premises;

AND WHEREAS the Company has made an application to the State Government for permission to pump water from the ——— canal and to construct pump house, intake and exit well on the water edge of the said canal and to lay pipes under the service road for the purpose of pumping water from the said canal as aforesaid for use of the Company's industries at the said premises;

AND WHEREAS the State Government has acceded to the aforesaid request of the Company on the terms and conditions hereinafter appearing ;

AND WHEREAS the State Government has also agreed to grant

to the Company on lease the plot of land shown in the annexed plan in —— colour on the terms and conditions contained in the Deed of Lease dated the ——— day of ——— between the same parties as are hereto ;

NOW IT IS HEREBY AGREED AND DECLARED as follows:

1. The State Government hereby grants permission to the Company to pump water from the said canal (hereinafter called "canal water") for use in their industries at the premises hereinbefore mentioned at the rate not exceeding ——— litres of water per hour throughout 24 hours on the following conditions:

(a) The Company will deliver back daily at its own cost in the said canal an equal quantity of water drawn from the Company's tubewells (hereinafter called "tubewell water") but this provision for delivering back tubewell water shall not apply during the period July 10 to October 31 of each year when water is spare to the needs of irrigation.

(b) The Company shall pay to the State Government Rs. ————— per thousand litres of canal water pumped and replaced by tubewell water as stated in sub-clause (a) above.

(c) Should the Company fail to deliver on any calender day an equivalent quantity of tubewell water into the said canal, the Company shall pay to the State Government for such deficiency at the rate of Rs. —— per thousand litres on or before the —— day of every month following, to the Executive Engineer —— or his authorised representative and if the same shall remain in arrear after the due date the Company shall pay interest thereon at ———— per cent per annum, PROVIDED THAT this provision for interest shall not prejudice or affect the exercise by the State Government of any of the rights or remedies vested in it by law or by this deed.

(d) The canal water pumped and the tubewell water delivered back as aforesaid shall be measured by meters as hereinafter provided, all of which shall be read daily by a representative of the said Executive Engineer and a representative of the Company at any fixed time of the day which the said Executive Engineer may decide, at which both the representatives shall be present. The measurement as aforesaid shall be recorded on two separate registers to be provided by each party and both the representatives shall sign both the registers. The measurement so recorded shall not be questioned by the Company. If the Company's representative shall fail to present himself at the appointed time, the measurement recorded by the representative of the said Executive Engineer shall be binding on the Company.

(e) The Company shall at its own cost arrange for pumping canal

water by means of a pumping set and carry the same by means of pipes to the Company's premises.

2. For the purpose of installing equipment for pumping canal water as aforesaid, the State Government hereby grants permission to the Company to construct suitable intake and an exit well on the water edge of the said canal and to lay pipes under the service road connecting the pump house with the intake and the exit well, and the Company hereby covenants to restore the service road to its proper condition at its own cost to the entire satisfaction of the said Executive Engineer within thirty days of its being dismantled or opened for laying pipes as aforesaid. If the Company shall fail to restore the service road as aforesaid it shall be lawful for, but not obligatory upon, the said Executive Engineer to get the same repaired and the cost of such repairs together with usual supervision charges will be recovered from the Company, and a certificate of the said Executive Engineer as to the cost of repairs as aforesaid shall be binding on the Company.

3. For the purpose of constructing a pump house for pumping canal water as aforesaid the State Government has agreed to grant to the Company on lease the plot of land shown in ——— colour in the annexed plan on the terms and conditions contained in the Deed of Lease made on the ——— day of ——— between the parties hereto. If the said Lease Deed is determined by the State Government under the provisions therein contained, this agreement shall also determine.

4. The Company shall at its own cost instal two water meters, one on the intake pipes and the other on the exit pipes at such places as may be directed by the said Executive Engineer.

5. This agreement shall remain in force for a period of ten years from the date hereof, and may be renewed for another term of ten years or more at the request of the Company but at the discretion of the State Government on such terms and conditions as may then be agreed upon.

6. If the Company shall commit a breach of any of the covenants and conditions herein contained and on its part to be observed and performed, the State Government may, notwithstanding the waiver of any previous right, terminate this agreement by giving to the Company three calendar months' notice in writing.

7. Upon the expiration or sooner determination of this agreement, the Company shall with all reasonable despatch and in any case within three calendar months remove all equipment and material and restore the land to its original condition, PROVIDED THAT any equipment or material not

removed within the period aforesaid shall become the property of the State Government without any compensation being payable for it.

8. The Company shall not assign the benefit of this agreement to any one nor shall it use the canal water for any purpose other than for the bonafide use of the Company.

9. *Arbitration clause.*

IN WITNESS WHEREOF, etc.

22—Agreement between a Manufacturer and a Marketer[1]

THIS AGREEMENT entered into on ——— day of ——— two thousand twenty one BETWEEN ————, a company within the meaning of the Companies Act, 1956/2013, having its Registered Office at ——— (hereinafter referred to as the "MANUFACTURER") AND ——— a company within the meaning of the Companies Act, 1956/2013, having its registered office at ———— (hereinafter referred to as the "Marketer"). The expressions "Manufacturer" and "Marketer" shall, wherever the context so permits, mean and include their respective assigns and successors in interest.

WHEREAS the Manufacturer is manufacturing ——— and its attachments in the brand name of ——— (hereinafter called "the Product");

AND WHEREAS the Marketer is doing business in agricultural inputs;

AND WHEREAS both the parties consider it mutually advantageous that the Marketer should undertake the marketing of the Product in a certain territory.

NOW THIS DEED WITNESSES:

1. Territory and Original Purchaser

Subject to the terms hereof, the Manufacturer agrees to sell to the Marketer and the Marketer agrees to buy from the Manufacturer the Product for sale within the territory described hereunder (hereinafter called "the Territory") and in no other place or places:

(a) The Territory covered under this Agreement shall be the States of ———.

(b) "Original Purchaser" shall mean the first buyer of each unit of the Product from the Marketer or directly from the Manufacturer as per advice of the Marketer.

---

1 Compare form No. 9 *ante* for agency to sell goods.

2. Dealership

(a) The Marketer shall work diligently and faithfully to foster and promote sales of the Product purchased by them from the Manufacturer within the Territory and safeguard the Manufacturer's interests to the best of its ability.

(b) The Marketer shall convey to the Manufacturer any information regarding demand or enquiries for the said Product from outside the Territory that may come to its knowledge.

(c) The Marketer shall watch competitors' activities in the Territory and report to the Manufacturer relevant information so as to enable the Manufacturer to take appropriate action for promoting the sale of the Product.

(d) The Marketer hereby guarantees that it shall buy a minimum number of ——— units of the Product every year commencing on ——.

3. Term

Subject to clause 17 below, the term of this Agreement shall be ——— years from ——— to ———. The Agreement shall stand renewed for a further period if, on receipt of advice in this behalf from the Marketer, a letter is issued by the Manufacturer confirming its willingness to renew the Agreement for a further period. Such extension, however, must be asked for by the Marketer 90 days before the expiry date of this Agreement, and at the time of such extension, the Marketer and the Manufacturer may agree to vary the minimum number of units of the Product which the Marketer shall be liable to purchase from the Manufacturer.

4. Limitations

The Marketer shall not, either directly or indirectly and either alone or in conjunction with others, knowingly promote the sale or sell the Product to any person or party outside the Territory nor shall it sell the same to any person or party within the Territory if the Product is to be removed for resale outside the Territory. In the event of such sale, the Manufacturer shall have the option after giving the Marketer an opportunity to explain either to recover in full or in part the discount paid to the Marketer for the Product so sold outside the Territory provided that this right to recover the discount shall be without prejudice to all other rights available to the Manufacturer.

5. Product-Warranty

The Marketer agrees that the only Warranty binding on the

Manufacturer shall be the published warranty of the Manufacturer. The Manufacturer agrees to supply, free of cost, any parts found defective during the Warranty Period under normal operation and service when owned by the Original Purchaser, but no claim for expenditure upon them or consequent damages will be entertained. Defective parts will be sent to the Manufacturer's works at ——— at Marketer's cost. The eventual replacement parts will be sent at Manufacturer's cost. The repairs and/or replacements under Warranty conditions will be carried out by the Marketer free of cost to the Original Purchaser.

6. Price, Commission, etc.

(a) The Marketer shall not charge for the Product and its accessories, prices in excess of the prices stipulated in the Price-list issued by the Manufacturer from time to time plus actual freight charges, insurance, etc., from the Manufacturer's works, Goods and Services Tax, Octroi, other local levies, and such other charges as may be found to be essential and mutually agreed to.

(b) The Manufacturer shall supply spare parts of the Product to the Marketer at Dealers' Prices fixed by the Manufacturer from time to time which are on the basis of F.O.R. destination (by rail or road transport service) and inclusive of Goods and Services Tax. The Marketer shall sell these parts only at the Retail Selling Prices fixed by the Manufacturer plus local Goods and Services Tax and any other local statutory levies.

(c) The Manufacturer shall allow to the Marketer a commission of Rs. ——— (Rupees ———) for each unit of the Product sold to the Marketer or sold to any other party within the Territory as advised by the Marketer. Similar commission allowable on accessories is at the rate of ———per cent of the List Price of the Accessories. The Manufacturer shall pay to the Marketer a further service commission of Rs. ——— per unit product sold after the Marketer has satisfactorily rendered to the Original Purchaser installation, training and other services as prescribed by the Manufacturer.

7. Organisation

(a) The Marketer shall, at its own expense maintain in the Territory such organisation for the sale of the Product, as in the opinion of the Manufacturer, after consulting the Marketer, be deemed to be necessary to thoroughly cover sales and service in the Territory. Such organisation shall include:

(i) the maintenance of upto-date show rooms and stock rooms

commensurate with the size of the Territory and the Product.

(ii) an adequate and properly trained staff and workshop facilities for satisfactory sale and after-sale services of the Product as required by the Manufacturer and to the Manufacturer's sole and entire satisfaction advised from time to time. The Manufacturer reserves the right to appoint its own service dealers for the service of the Product (hereinafter called the "Service Dealer") in the Territory as and when it deems necessary in the interest of the sale promotion of the Product. The Marketer shall pay to the Service Dealer such commission as the Manufacturer may fix for the service of the Product effected by the Service Dealer.

(b) The Marketer shall put in its best effort at all times to obtain maximum sales in the Territory.

(c) The Manufacturer shall have the right any time to depute its representative(s) to visit the Marketer's premises, its branches or its sub-dealers and stockists for purposes of inspecting the show-rooms, relevant records and to make physical checks of branches or the sub-dealers and stockists. The Marketer shall provide all relevant information, assistance and facilities that may be required by the representative(s) of the Manufacturer.

(d) The Marketer shall submit regular stock and service figures as required by the Manufacturer on forms provided by it.

8. Payment

The Marketer shall pay the sale price of the Product, its accessories and spare parts on terms that may be mutually agreed upon.

9. Supply Schedule

The Marketer shall, at least 30 days before the start of each quarter, give a supply schedule to the Manufacturer on a month-wise basis so as to enable the Manufacutrer to plan its production schedule. It shall be open to the Marketer and the Manufacturer to make marginal adjustments in the monthly supply schedule.

10. Despatch by Manufacturer

The Manufacturer shall despatch the quantity to be supplied in each month by the 15th of the month, or in accordance with the mutually agreed delivery schedule. If, however, the Manufacturer fails to deliver the quantity contracted to be supplied before the end of the month to which the supply relates, subject to Clause 9 above and Clause 11 below, the Marketer shall not be bound to its commitment indicated in Clause 2(d) above to the extent of the short-supplied quantity. The Marketer shall, however, have the option to require the Manufacturer to supply and despatch such material, if any, in the subsequent two months. If the Marketer exercises such option, the commitment on the Marketer as per Clause 2 (d) shall continue to operate.

11. Force Majeure

The Manufacturer shall not be responsible for and shall incur no liability of any kind whatsoever for inability to supply for causes beyond its control, and in particular but without prejudice to the generality of the foregoing, by war, strikes, lock-outs, slowdowns, riots or civil commotions, shortage of labour or material, defects in machinery or the working thereof or for delays in supply of bought-out components, transportation difficulties, power failures or Government Regulations encountered by the Manufacturer and its suppliers, and no such delay shall render void any sale hereunder.

12. Purchase from other Sources

The Marketer shall not sell accessories and spare parts not purchased from the Manufacturer or not purchased from sources authorised by the Manufacturer.

13. Trade Marks

The Marketer admits the validity of the copyrights, trade marks and trade names belonging to the Manufacturer in the Product even if not herein listed. The Marketer shall not make use of the said copyrights, trade marks and trade names except with the permission in writing of the Manufacturer and such permission will terminate with the termination of this Agreement.

14. Publicity

(a) Media publicity shall be undertaken by the Manufacturer. Whereas the Marketer shall give necessary advice to the Manufacturer for carrying out publicity, the decision regarding the type, extent and manner of publicity to be undertaken will be solely that of the Manufacturer.

(b) The Marketer will be free to carry out publicity at its own cost. However, the layouts and designs of the advertisement and publicity materials shall be subject to the Manufacturer's approval and supervision. The Marketer shall display conspicuously at, in or on its premises, only such type of signs as may be authorised by the Manufacturer and upon termination of this Agreement shall discontinue representing itself to be an

Authorised Marketer in the Product and shall forthwith remove all the said signs and return to the Manufacturer, without compensation, all such signs whether or not loaned to the Marketer by the Manufacturer. The Marketer will not display or advertise nor permit to be displayed or advertised nor trade in the Product in such a way as in the opinion of the Manufacturer may cause annoyance or injury to the Manufacturer or any of its duly Authorised Marketers.

(c) It is realised by both parties that extensive demonstrations of the working of the Product should be held at various points in the Territory covered by the Agreement. The parties shall mutually agree on the programme for demonstrations and the Manufacturer undertakes to make available a Demonstration Van and a unit of the Product for demonstration purposes and also the personnel required therefor in accordance with an agreed programme. Such programme shall be drawn up from time to time keeping in view the Manufacturer's commitments outside the Territory. The running expenses of the Demonstration Van and the salary, travelling allowances, etc., of the Manufacturer's staff will be met by the Manufacturer. All other local expenses for organising and conducting the demonstration will be met by the Marketer.

15. No Agency Created

Nothing contained in this Agreement shall in any way operate by implication or otherwise to constitute the Marketer as an Agent of the Manufacturer in any respect and for any purpose whatsoever, and the Marketer shall have no right or authority to assume or create obligation of any kind expressed or implied on behalf of the Manufacturer, in any respect whatsoever, except to the extent detailed herein.

16. Assignment

The Marketer agrees that it will not assign this Agreement nor any interest in it, nor any of the rights or liabilities hereunder without the written consent of the Manufacturer.

17. Termination

This Agreement shall remain in force and govern transactions between the parties hereto until cancelled or terminated in the manner hereinafter expressed:

(i) Either party to this Agreement may terminate the Agreement without assigning any reason therefor at any time by giving ninety days' notice in writing to the other.

(ii) The Manufacturer may forthwith without any previous notice terminate this Agreement without prejuduce to its other rights hereunder in any of the following events, viz.

(a) If the Marketer fails to observe and perform any of the conditions and obligations herein stipulated to be observed and performed by it; *or*

(b) If the management or control of the Marketer's business shall be changed so that in the Manufacturer's opinion its interests are likely to be adversely affected; *or*

(c) If the Marketer shall not pay its debts in due course of business; *or*

(d) If the Marketer shall be wound up or commit any act of insolvency or have any insolvency proceedings instituted against it; *or*

(e) If any receiver or trustee be appointed for the Marketer's property or business ; *or*

(f) If the Marketer's property or any part thereof shall be seized or attached in distress or execution of or under process of law.

18. Supplies after Termination

If the Manufacturer after the termination of this Agreement makes any supplies to the Marketer, such supplies shall not imply a continuance or renewal of this Agreement or the extension of appointment of the Marketer.

19. Liability after Termination

In case of termination of this Agreement, the Marketer shall not be discharged of any liability arising out of the Product already delivered to customers by it.

20. Orders on hand at Termination

The Manufacturer may, upon termination of this Agreement, require the Marketer to immediately turn over to the Manufacturer all its unexecuted orders as also those of its sub-dealers and stockists.

21. Previous Contracts

This Agreement supersedes all previous contracts, verbal or written (if any), which may have been made between the parties hereto.

22. Waiver

Any failure on the part of the Manufacturer to enforce at any time the performance by the Marketer of any of the provisions hereof shall in no way be considered to be a waiver of such provisions nor in any way affect the validity of this Agreement or any part thereof or the right of the Manufacturer to enforce thereafter each and every such provision.

23. Security

The Marketer shall give to the Manufacturer a Bank guarantee from a Scheduled Bank, in the form prescribed by the Manufacturer, for a value of Rs. ——— (Rupees ——— only) as security for satisfactory compliance of the terms and conditions of this Agreement.

24. Amendments

Any amendments or alteration to this Agreement shall be valid only if set down in writing and signed by the parties hereto.

25. Arbitration clause

IN WITNESS WHEREOF, etc.

23—Agreement between a Government and a Transport Contractor for the Carriage of Foodgrains[1]

AN AGREEMENT made on the ——— day of ——— BETWEEN the Governor of the State of ——— (hereinafter called "the Government") of the one part and ——— (hereinafter called the "Transport Contractor") of the other part:

WITNESSES as follows:

1. That the Transport Contractor shall carry foodgrains by motor vehicles from one place to another in the same district or in different districts in accordance with the instructions issued, from time to time, by the Regional Food Controller (hereinafter called "the Controller")

2. That the Transport Contractor shall arrange for stacking bags, and for loading the foodgrains into motor vehicles at the place of despatch if so required by the Controller.

3. That the Transport Contractor shall arrange to unload the foodgrains from motor vehicles and to load them into railway wagons or stack them in godowns at destination, if so required by the Controller.

4. That the Transport Contractor shall be liable to compensate the Government for any loss, damage or shortage of the foodgrains during the

---

1 If it is to be executed by a Statutory Corporation such as the Food Corporation of India, substitute "——— a corporation established and incorporated under the ——— Act (hereinafter called the 'the Corporation')," in place of "(Governor of the State of ——— (hereinafter called 'the Government')," and the name of the appropriate officer in place of "Regional Food Controller."

course of handling or transport, and shall also be liable to compensate for any demurrage or wharfage incurred through his negligence.

5. That the Transport Contractor shall arrange for the necessary number of motor vehicles for transporting foodgrains, and shall complete such transport within such time as may be specified by the Controller.

6. That the Transport Contractor shall be paid at the following rates:

A. For transporting foodgrains—

(i) On metalled roads, other than those mentioned in sub-clause (iii) below, at the rate of Rs. —— per quintal per loaded kilometere;

(ii) On *Kachcha* roads, at the rate of Rs. ——— per quintal per loaded kilometre.

(iii) On metalled roads which are in a very bad condition and in respect of which the Controller has certified that the depreciation and running expenses of a motor vehicle plying on it will be equivalent to those of a motor vehicle plying on a *kachcha* road, at the rate of Rs. ——— per quintal per loaded kilometre;

B. For loading and unloading etc.,

(i) For Stacking bags, at ——— per bag;

(ii) For loading into motor vehicles, at ——— per bag; -

(iii) For unloading from motor vehicles, at ——— per bag;

(iv) For loading into railway wagons, at ——— per bag.

7. That the Transport Contractor shall not load more than ——— quintals of foodgrains in a 3-tonne motor vehicle when plying on a *kachcha* road or a road certified under clause 6 *(iii)* by the Controller, and more than —— quintals in such vehicle, when plying on a metalled road.

8. That in case the Transport Contractor transports foodgrains in excess of the limits prescribed in clause 7 above, he shall not be entitled to any transport charges for the excess quantity so transported.

9. That in case the Transport Contractor fails to carry out on any day any of the work mentioned in clauses 1 to 3, the Controller or any other officer authorised by him in this behalf may, without prejudice to any other legal remedy, have the same done in any manner he likes and in every such case the Transport Contractor shall be liable to pay to the Government all such costs, charges or other incidental expenses connected therewith as may be incurred by the Controller or the said officer, together with a sum of Rs. ——— per bag per day as damages.

10. That the Transport Contractor agrees to indemnify the Government against all claims for compensation by or on behalf of any workman employed by him in connection with this contract for injury or death by accident under the Workmen's Compensation Act.

11. That the Transport Contractor shall not sublet, assign or part with this contract.

12. That the Transport Contractor shall within ——— days of the signing of this Agreement deposit in a bank to be approved by the Controller a sum of Rs. ——— in cash or give Government securities of the same value as security for the fulfilment of this Agreement.

13. That the Government shall be entitled to deduct from the pending bills of the Transport Contractor all such sums of money as may be claimed by the Government under the terms of this Agreement. Any sum of money not covered by the amount of the said bills shall be liable to be deducted from his deposit made under clause 12 above.

14. That this Agreement shall remain in force for a period of ——— years from ——— day of ——— 19 ——— and shall be liable to be terminated on 20 days notice in writing on the side of the Transport Contractor and 10 days notice in writing on the side of the Government. But in the event of any breach of any condition herein contained by the Transport Contractor or in the event of any misconduct on his part or on the part of any of his employees, it shall be lawful for the Government to terminate this Agreement forthwith without giving any notice, and in such a case the Transport Contractor shall not be entitled to any compensation whatsoever.

15. That in the case of any dispute or difference which may at any time arise between the parties hereto or any person claiming under them, touching or arising out of or in respect of this Agreement or the subject-matter thereof, such dispute or difference shall be referred to the arbitration of any person nominated by the Secretary to Government of ——— in the Food and Civil Supplies Department and the decision of such arbitrator shall be final and binding on the parties hereto.

16. That for the purposes of this Agreement "Controller" means the Regional Food Controller or Deputy Regional Food Controller having jurisdiction in the area from which the foodgrains are transported.

17. That all expenses for the preparation and execution of this deed, including the stamp duty and conveyancing fee, shall be payable by the Transport Contractor.

IN WITNESS WHEREOF, etc.

24—Memorandum of understanding for bidding for SPA and Health Club

THIS MEMORANDUM OF UNDERSTANDING (MOU) is entered between AB, etc., of one part and CD, etc., (hereinafter called the Technical Collaborator) of the other part.

WHEREAS XY Hotel has invited tenders for setting up a standard SPA and Health Club;

AND WHEREAS AB has expressed his desire to form a Consortium with CD as technical collaborator to bid for the same;

AND WHEREAS CD has reciprocated a similar desire;

This Memorandum of Understanding, therefore, WITNESSETH;

That the following terms and conditions have been agreed upon between the parties named above and are put in writing for future use and reference:

1. AB has agreed to be the Lead Member of the Consortium and will be responsible for all financial obligations connected with this tender/project.

2. CD has agreed to be a part of the Consortium led by AB as a technical collaborator with no financial obligations.

3. All decisions pertaining to the tender/project implementation will be taken by AB and his decision will be final and binding.

4. All costs and expenses relating to the project will be borne by AB.

5. In case this Consortium of AB and CD is selected and is awarded the contract for the SPA and Health Club by the XY Hotel, then CD will grant the requisite franchise to AB. The terms and conditions of the franchise agreement will be decided by mutual consultation/negotiation between the parties hereto and will be finalized within 30 days of being awarded the contract by XY Hotel or prior to submitting the security deposit whichever is earlier. In the event of a deadlock and inability of the parties to conclude the terms of the franchise agreement, both parties will have the right to terminate this MOU.

6. If this Consortium is awarded the contract by XY Hotel and if the terms of Licence Deed to be executed with the said Hotel is not to the satisfaction of AB, then this MOU can be terminated by AB without any obligation to CD.

7. CD has agreed to furnish details about their past experience in setting up and managing an SPA and Health Club of international standards

in Five Star Deluxe Hotels. The note will include details of available expertise and technical know-how of running a SPA and Health Club.

8. CD has agreed to prepare a 'Concept Note' which will provide details about the plans for the SPA and Health Club at the said XY Hotel for which tenders have been invited.

9. AB has agreed to keep the contents of the 'Concept Note' and of the information covered by clause 8 above strictly confidential and not to disclose the same to any one except to the XY Hotel inviting the tender.

10. If any dispute arising under or in relation to this MOU is not resolved through mutual consultation within thirty (30) days of the arising of the dispute, then the same will be adjudicated through arbitration. The venue of the Arbitration shall be New Delhi and laws of India will govern the relationship between the parties in respect of this MOU.

The Arbitral Tribunal shall consist of three arbitrators, each party appointing one arbitrator and the third arbitrator, who shall act as the Presiding Arbitrator, to be appointed by the arbitrators appointed by the parties. The language of the arbitration proceeding shall be English and the award of the majority of arbitrators shall be final and binding on the parties.

IN WITNESS WHEREOF....

25—Live-in Agreement

THIS AGREEMENT made between AB s/o _______ aged about _______ years, r/o _______ hereinafter called the party of the first part and CD widow of Late Shri _______ aged about _______ years r/o _______ hereinafter called the party of the second part

WITNESSETH as under:

1. AB is a widower/divorcee and has two daughters namely _______who are already married and settled in USA;

2. That CD, is a widow whose husband died _______ years ago. She has a son namely_______ who is married and settled in U.K.;

3. That the parties hereto had been living alone in their respective houses with no responsible person to give them company and take care of them;

4. That some months ago the said AB and CD met at a social gathering (or say their families are known to each other for several years etc.) and found compatibility amongst themselves and since then they have met each other several times.

5. That the parties hereto have, with the approval of their respective

children agreed and decided to live together with the following promises to each other:

6. That CD shall move into and reside with AB, in AB's home where he is presently living or in such other house, including the house owned by CD as the parties may mutually agree;

7. That CD will retain full control of the House No._______ situate at _________ and may use the same to her exclusive benefit;

8. That while CD lives with AB, who shall be fully responsible for her maintenance and well being in all respect.

9. That the parties hereto shall be at liberty to visit their respective children, either singly or together, for reasonable number of time;

10. That the respective children of the parties hereto will also be entitled to visit them and stay with them and will be given due love, care, respect and affection;

11. That in case AB predeceases CD, then CD will be entitled to continue to reside in the house of AB during her life time.

12. That the respective movable and immovable properties of either party will on their demise devolve on their natural legal heirs in accordance with law.

13. That, if for any reason whatsoever, any of the parties hereto wishes to withdraw from this relation of companionship, he or she can do so at will. However it is mutually agreed that:

(i) He or she will be allowed a period of one month to move out of the house;

(ii) In case this agreement is terminated after the expiry of ________ years from the commencement hereof, AB will pay to CD a sum of Rs. _______ as alimony and no more.

IN WITNESS WHEREOF the parties have signed and executed this deed of agreement this ___________ day of _________ at ________.

26—Tripartite Agreement
(between Borrower, Bank and Builder of a building)

This agreement made at _______ this _______ day of _______ 2020 amongst (i) Shri _________ S/o Shri _________ residing at _________ (hereinafter referred to as the 'borrower' which expression shall unless repugnant to the context, include his heirs, executors, administrators and assigns) of the first part; and

ii) ____________ (hereinafter referred to as 'the Builder' which term shall include its successors and assigns) of the second part, who is selling the property to the borrower; and

iii) __________, a body corporate constituted under the Banking Companies (Acquisition and Transfer of Undertakings) Act, 1970 having its Head office at __________ and amongst others, has one of its Branch offices at __________ (hereinafter called 'the Bank' which expression shall unless repugnant to the context include its successors and assigns) of the third part.

WHEREAS, the borrower desires to purchase a ready - built flat from the Builder under its __________ scheme.

WHEREAS, The Bank has sanctioned a housing loan of Rs. ________ (Rupees __________) to the borrower for the purchase of said flat, as per terms and conditions agreed under Loan Agreement dated __________ arrived at between the Bank and the borrower (hereinafter referred to as 'the said agreement'), and one of the conditions thereunder is that the borrower shall mortgage, in favour of the bank, the said flat, to be purchased from the Builder.

WHEREAS, The title of the said flat shall be conveyed by the Builder onto the borrower after __________ years from allotment, on payment of total cost of the said flat, as per the demands for payment by Builder as per agreement between the borrower and Builder.

NOW, THIS AGREEMENT WITNESSETH AS UNDER:

In consideration of a sum of Rs. __________ (Rupees __________) already deposited by the borrower with the Builder on __________ as initial payment for the purchase of the said property under the said scheme and a further sum of Rs. ________ (Rupees ________) which is required to be paid by the Bank directly to the Builder, on behalf of borrower as per the demands for payment by the Builder as per agreement between the borrower and Builder, it is hereby agreed to by and amongst the parties as follows:

The Bank will make disbursement of the sanctioned loan by making payment to the Builder directly on behalf of the borrower and any payment made to the Builder shall be deemed to be payments made to the borrower and the borrower shall, in each case, be liable for the amount of loan disbursed on his behalf to the Builder as if the same had been disbursed directly to borrower.

2. It is further agreed by the borrower that the Bank shall not be responsible or liable to ensure or ascertain the progress of construction and mere demand for payment would be sufficient for Bank to effect disbursement as aforesaid.

Without prejudice to the above and notwithstanding anything to the contrary contained herein the Bank may in its sole discretion refuse to disburse the loan until the Borrower has paid his own contribution in full to Builder i.e. the cost of the dwelling unit (including escalation, if any) less the loan.

3. The Builder will maintain a separate account for the borrower and adjust payment of housing loan received by it from the Bank against the cost of the particular flat purchased by the borrower.

4. On completion of the flat, its possession will be handed over to the borrower forthwith alongwith the conveyance of the title thereto on leasehold/freehold basis. Thereafter, the borrower will mortgage the said flat forthwith with the Bank, as security for the said loan, as per the terms and conditions of the said agreement.

5. The cost of the flat, in case exceeds the amount of the sanctioned Housing Loan, shall be borne and paid by the borrower.

6. If the borrower withdraws from the scheme or fails to pay the balance amount representing the difference between the housing loan allowed by the Bank and the actual cost of the flat (including escalation) or dies or allotment of the flat is otherwise cancelled, the entire amount standing to the credit of the borrower (including margin money and borrower's contribution) will be refunded by the Builder to the Bank. The Bank shall refund to the borrower balance amount, if any, after adjusting the entire outstanding dues, including interest, costs and other amount recoverable by the Bank from the borrower.

7. The covenants hereunder shall not be construed to mean and fasten any responsibility upon the Bank to observe the payment schedule, if any, between the Builder and the borrower or make payments to the Builder, as requested. The Bank shall not be responsible for any delay or omission in disbursement on account of breach/default attributable to borrower/society. The borrower shall be responsible to follow-up with the Bank to make disbursement on his behalf, as per arrangement, he may have with the Builder.

8. The Builder will give necessary consent/no objection for mortgage of the flat by the borrower in favour of the Bank.

9. If, for any reason, there is an increase/escalation in the cost of the flat, increase shall be paid and borne by the borrower, without any reference to the Bank and until such increase is paid, the Bank shall have the right to suspend further disbursement of sanctioned loan.

10. The borrower will not further mortgage/charge the said flat to any person/financial institution for raising any loan, without the prior written consent of the Bank.

11. The Builder shall not entertain the request of transfer of the flat of the borrower, without the prior written consent of the Bank.

12. In any event in which any refund becomes due and payable by the Builder to the borrower, under any agreement/arrangement between the borrower and the Builder or otherwise, the Builder agrees not to pay any amount on any account to the borrower/s by way of refund or otherwise, without the written consent of the Bank. In case it is so required by the Bank, any such amount shall be paid by the Builder to the Bank.

IN WITNESS WHEREOF the parties hereto have signed this agreement on the day, month and year first above written.

For other forms of agreement see under the heading of the subject to which the agreement relates. For example, an agreement to sell, will be found under "Sale", an agreement of hire under "Hire", a supplemental agreement for rectification of a document under "Rectification", an agreement of employment under "Service Contracts", and so on.

APPRENTICESHIP

Preliminary Note

Apprentice means a person, who is undergoing apprenticeship training in pursuance of a contract of apprenticeship, Section 2(aa) of Apprentices Act, 1961.

Graduate or technician apprentice means an apprentice who holds, or is undergoing training in order that he may hold a degree or diploma in engineering or technology or equivalent qualification granted by any institution recognised by the Government and undergoes apprenticeship training in any designated trade, Section 2(j).

Every Apprentice undergoing apprenticeship training in a designated trade in an establishment shall be a trainee and is not a worker.

The Apprentices Act, 1961 applies to a "designated trade" which means a trade or occupation or any subject field in engineering or technology specified in that behalf from time to time by Central Government in the official gazette.

A deed is not necessary to bind a person as apprentice for training in any craft, trade, or profession, for a contract can ordinarily be made by parole. But where the period is long, or terms are complicated, it is usual to have a deed embodying the articles of apprenticeship.

A deed is necessary if the Apprentices Act, 1961, is applicable. Such a deed has to be registered with the Apprenticeship Advisor, as per Sec. 4 (4) of the Act. The terms and conditions of such a deed should not be inconsistent with any provisions of the Act of 1961 or the Rules made thereunder, as provided under Sec. 4(3) of the Act.

For cases not covered by the Act, any form may be used.

Apprentice is not a workman

The provisions of section 18 of the Apprentice Act, states that every apprentice undergoing apprenticeship training shall be a trainee and not a worker and that the provision of any law with respect to labour shall not apply to or in relation to such apprentice.

In *Tannery and Footwear Corporation of India Ltd.* v. *Labour Court, Kanpur,*[1] Allahabad High Court has stated that an apprentice appointed under the Act of 1961 would not become apprentice for the purpose of section 2(5) of the Industrial Disputes Act. In fact there is no conflict between section 18 of Apprentice Act and section 2(5) of the Industrial Disputes Act. Under the two

---

1 1994 (2) L.L.J. 1186 para 11.

statutes the expression 'apprentice' is used with a different connotation and meaning.

Qualifications for an apprentice

The person in respect of whom an agreement under the Act can be entered into should not be less than 14 years of age, vide Sec. 3 (a) of the Act, and if he is a minor, the contract must be entered into by his guardian. He must satisfy such standards of education and physical fitness as may be prescribed.

All disputes between the employer and the apprentice are to be referred to the Apprenticeship Advisor, whose decision is appealable to the Apprenticeship Council, as provided under Sec. 20.

Is there is any obligation of employer to offer employment to apprentice?

It is not obligatory on the part of the employer to offer any employment to any apprentice, who has completed the period of his apprenticeship training in his establishment, nor shall it be obligatory on the part of the apprentice to accept an employment under the employer. However, where there is a condition in a contract of apprenticeship that the apprentice shall, after the successful completion of the apprenticeship training, serve the employer, the employer shall, on such completion, be bound to offer suitable employment to the apprentice, and the apprentice shall be bound to serve the employer in that capacity for such period and on such remuneration as may be specified in the contract. Where the Apprenticeship Adviser is of the opinion that such period or remuneration is not reasonable, he may revise the same so as to make it reasonable, and such revised terms and conditions in this regard shall be the agreement between the parties.

An apprentice deed containing stipulation that the apprentice "shall be absorbed in the department if there are vacancies" creates reciprocal obligation on both parties. One must take a broad and common sense view of the terms of employment. It is not proper in such case to indulge in a hair spliting approach and find an escape for defeating the rights of employees.[1] However, the apprentice has to go through examination/interview as provided in the Recruitment Rules.[2]

---

1 *Narinder Kumar* v. *State of Punjab*, AIR 1985 SC 275 (Para 3 & 4)

2 *U.P. Rajya Vidyut Parishad Apprentice Welfare Association* v. *State of U.P.*, AIR 2000 SC 2621.

PRECEDENTS

1—Apprenticeship Deed

THIS APPRENTICESHIP DEED made the —— day of —— BETWEEN AB, etc., (hereinafter called "the apprentice") or, *when the apprentice is a minor*, acting through his guardian CD, (hereinafter called "the guardian") of the one part AND the Governor of ——— (hereinafter called "the Government") of the other part;

WHEREAS the apprentice having completed ———— years' training in Electrical and Mechanical Engineering at the ———— College applied to the Superintending Engineer, Circle I, ——— (hereinafter called "the Superintending Engineer") for practical training at one of the power houses of the ——— Hydro-Electric Scheme;

AND WHEREAS the Superintending Engineer accepted the said application and agreed to give practical training to the apprentice at the power house of the ———— Hydro-Electric Scheme at ———— on the conditions hereinafter appearing;

NOW THIS DEED WITNESSES as follows:

1. Period

The apprentice of his own free will binds himself (*or*, the guardian with the consent of the apprentice binds him) to the Government to receive practical training in Electrical and Mechanical Engineering for a term of at least ———— months from the date of his admission to the power house at ————.

2. Apprentice's Covenants

The apprentice (guardian) covenants with the Government as follows:

(*a*) That he (the apprentice) will during the said term receive no remuneration and shall at the conclusion of his apprenticeship have no claim to any appointment under the Government;

(*b*) That he (the apprentice) will work an eight hour shift in the power house and will sign an attendance register when he comes to work at the power house and when he leaves;

(*c*) That he (the apprentice) will obey and carry out all orders given to him by the officer-in-charge of the power house at ———;

(*d*) That he (the apprentice) will under no circumstances start up or shut down any machine or operate any switch unless ordered to do so by the officer-in-charge of the power house;

(*e*) That he (the apprentice) will keep diaries of work done and experience gained by him and will submit them to such officer and at such intervals as the Superintending Engineer may direct;

(*f*) That in respect of what is not expressly provided herein, the right and liabilities of the apprentice and the Governor, shall be governed by the provisions of the Apprentices Act, 1961 and the rules framed thereunder.

3. Covenants by Government

The Government covenants with the apprentice (guardian) that the apprentice duly and faithfully observing all the conditions of his apprenticeship hereinbefore mentioned, the Government will allow the apprentice to work and obtain practical training in Electrical and Mechanical Engineering at the power house at ——— during the period of the apprenticeship.

IN WITNESS WHEREOF, etc.

2—Ditto, Another form

THIS APPRENTICESHIP DEED made on ——— between A, (the father of B), etc., (called the "Father") and B, etc., (called the "Apprentice") and E, etc., (called the "Employer").

WHEREAS the Father and the Apprentice requested the Employer to take the Apprentice in his trade of manufacture of electrical goods, and the Employer has agreed to it.

NOW THIS DEED WITNESSES as under:

1. Covenants Regarding Training

i) The age of the Apprentice is 15 years. He is willing to learn the trade of manufacture of electrical goods and to work with the Employer for a period of five years. The Father has agreed to the Apprentice so working with the Employer, and the Employer has agreed to train the Apprentice in his trade to the best of his ability during the agreed period of training.

ii) The Father has agreed with the Employer that the Apprentice shall faithfully discharge the duties assigned to him and to the best of his ability shall endeavour to learn the trade.

iii) The Employer shall provide for the boarding and lodging of the Apprentice during the term of the agreement, and shall arrange for his medical expenses in case of illness.

2. Covenants by Employer

In consideration of Rs. ———— paid by the Father to the Employer (who acknowledges its receipt), the Employer covenants that:

(*i*) He will duly instruct the Apprentice in the trade of the manufacture of electrical goods so as to enable the apprentice to work as an independent craftsman in the trade.

(*ii*) He will not inflict any corporal or other punishment on the Apprentice and shall not do anything, which may adversely affect the health of the Apprentice.

(*iii*) He will pay to the Apprentice Rs. ——— per mensem as pocket money during the period the Apprentice is working with him.

SIGNED BY:

ARBITRATION

Preliminary Note

Arbitration is one of the Alternative Dispute Redressal mechanism. Conciliation, Judicial settlement including settlement through Lok Adalat and mediation are the other three.

Parties are free to arrive at an agreement to submit their disputes to arbitration.

The jurisdiction of an arbitral tribunal is basically consensual in character. If the subject matter of the suit is situated within the arbitral jurisdiction of two or more courts, the parties can agree to confine the jurisdiction in one of the competent courts.

Arbitration enables cases to be dealt with speedily, economically and in some instances without lawyers, and with the parties presenting their cases free from legal technicalities with decisions made by experts who know practices, usages and customs of relevant trade or business. It is alternative to time consuming, complex and expensive court procedure.

Previously, Arbitration Act, 1940, was in force. In order to overcome the difficulties in the working of the Arbitration Act, 1940, and to bring it on par with International norms, the Arbitration and Conciliation Act, 1996 has been enacted and the Arbitration Act, 1940 repealed.

The provisions of 1996 Act have to be interpreted uninfluenced by the principles underlying the 1940 Act.[1]

Arbitration Agreement

Arbitration agreement has been defined in Sec. 7 of the Arbitration & Conciliation Act, 1996, as an agreement by the parties to submit to arbitration, all or certain disputes which have arisen or which may arise between them in respect of defined legal relationship, whether contractual or not.

Form of an Arbitration Agreement

The arbitration agreement need not be in any particular form. What is required to be ascertained is the intention of the parties to settle their disputes through arbitration.

An arbitration agreement may be in the form of an arbitration clause in a contract or in the form of a separate agreement (Sec. 7(2)). An arbitration

---

1 *Sunderam Finance Ltd.* v. *NEPC India Ltd.*, AIR 1999 SC 565.

agreement is to be in writing (Sec. 7(3)).

The arbitration agreement may be contained:

(a) in a document signed by the parties;

(b) an exchange of letters, telex, telegrams or other means of telecommunications including communication through electronic means, which provide a record of the agreement; or

(c) an exchange of statements of claim and defence in which the existence of the agreement is alleged by one party and not denied by the other (Sec. 7(4)).

The reference in a contract to a document containing an arbitration clause constitutes an arbitration agreement if the contract is in writing and the reference is such as to make that arbitration clause part of the contract (Sec. 7(5)).

An arbitration agreement, whether contained in the main agreement as an arbitration clause or in a separate document, is an independent agreement. The arbitration clause is distinct from the other clauses in the contract.

So, even if the contract may be void or may get frustrated, the arbitration clause survives as a separate agreement and dispute arising out of such void or frustrated agreement will have to be adjudicated through arbitration. This has been made clear by specific provisions in Sec. 16(1)(a) and (b) of the 1996 Act.

Group of Companies Doctrine

As per the principles of contract law, an agreement entered into by one of the companies in a group, cannot be binding on the other members of the same group, as each company is a separate legal entity which has separate legal rights and liabilities. Similarly, an arbitration agreement is also governed by the same principles, and normally, the company entering into the agreement, would alone be bound by it. However, a non-signatory can be bound by an arbitration agreement on the basis of the "Group of Companies" doctrine, where the conduct of the parties evidences a clear intention of the parties to bind both the signatory as well as the non-signatory parties. The doctrine of 'Group of Companies' had its origins in the 1970's from French arbitration practice. The 'Group of Companies' doctrine indicates the implied consent to an agreement to arbitrate. The circumstances in which the 'Group of Companies' Doctrine could be invoked to bind the non-signatory affiliate of a parent company, or inclusion of a third party to an arbitration, if there is a direct relationship between the party which is a signatory to the arbitration agreement; direct commonality of the subject matter: the composite nature of the transaction between the parties. A 'composite transaction' refers to a transaction which is inter-linked in nature; or, where the performance of the agreement may not be feasible without the aid, execution, and performance of the supplementary or the ancillary agreement, for achieving the common object, and collectively having a bearing on the dispute.[1]

General reference to an earlier contract is not sufficient for incorporation of an arbitration Clause in the later contract. However, a general reference to a standard form would be enough for incorporation of the arbitration clause. (para 19)[2]

The test for determining whether a dispute is one "arising out of the contract" or "in connection with the contract" is as to whether recourse to the contract, by which both the parties are bound, is necessary for the purpose of determining the claim of the party, is justified or otherwise. If it is necessary to take recourse to the terms of the contract for the purposes of deciding the matter in dispute, it must be held that the matter is within scope of the arbitration clause and the arbitrators have jurisdiction to decide that dispute.[3]

Non-arbitrable Disputes

It is significant to note that every dispute cannot be submitted to arbitration. Therefore, while entering into an agreement, relevant law on this point is to be kept in mind, so that a non-arbitrable dispute is not agreed to be submitted to arbitration.

Some examples of non-arbitrable disputes are: (i) disputes relating to rights and liabilities which give rise to or arise out of criminal offences; (ii) matrimonial disputes relating to divorce, judicial separation, restitution of conjugal rights, child custody; (iii) guardianship matters; (iv) insolvency and winding-up matters; (v) testamentary matters (grant of probate, letters of administration and succession certificate); and (vi) eviction or tenancy matters governed by special statutes where the tenant enjoys statutory protection against eviction and only the specified courts are conferred jurisdiction to grant eviction or decide the disputes.[4]

The disputes within the trust, trustees and beneficiaries are not capable of being decided by the arbitrator despite existence of arbitration agreement to that effect between the parties as the remedy provided under the Arbitration Act for deciding such disputes is barred by implication.[5]

While dealing with Section 8 of the Act, if there are serious allegations of fraud which make a virtual case of criminal offence or where allegations of fraud are so complicated that it becomes absolutely essential that such complex issues

---

1. *Mahanagar Telephone Nigam Ltd.* vs. *Canara Bank and Ors.*, AIR 2019 SC 4449; (2020) 12 SCC 767.
2 *Wind Ltd.* v. *Thermocables Ltd.*, (2018) 2 SCC 519; AIR 2018 SC 349.
3 *Union of India* v. *Salween Timber and Construction Co.*, AIR 1969 SC 488; *Ram Baboo Lal* v. *Harish Chandra Burman*, AIR 1974 All 433; *Renusagar Power Co. Ltd.* v. *General Electric Co.*, (1984) 4 SCC 679.
4 *Booz Allen and Hamilton Inc.* v. *SBI Home Finance Limited*, (2011) 5 SCC 532 (para 22)
5 *Vidya Drolia* v. *Durga Trading Corporation*, AIR 2019 SC 3498; *Emaar MGF Land Limited* v. *Aftab Singh* (2019) 12 SCC 751, 2019 (1) SCJ 33, 2019 (133) ALR 228; *Vimal Kishor Shah* v. *Jayesh Dinesh Shah*, (2016) 8 SCC 788.

can be decided only by the civil court on the appreciation of the voluminous evidence that needs to be produced, the court can sidetrack the agreement by dismissing the application Under Section 8 and proceed with the suit on merits. It can be also be done in those cases where there are serious allegations of forgery/fabrication of documents in support of the plea of fraud or where fraud is alleged against the arbitration provision itself or is of such a nature that permeates the entire contract, including the agreement to arbitrate, meaning thereby in those cases where fraud goes to the validity of the contract itself of the entire contract which contains the arbitration Clause or the validity of the arbitration Clause itself.[1]

How reference is made

Arbitration agreement is only a contract to refer while reference is delegation of authority to a named arbitrator.[2] In absence of any usage or custom or trade to the contrary, the implied authority of a partner under section 19(2)(a) Partnership Act does not extend to submit a dispute relating to business of the firm to arbitration. But where one of the partners of a firm entered into a contract on behalf of the firm in the usual course of business and the contract contained an arbitration clause, and the firm filed an application under Sec. 20 of Arbitration Act, 1940, the reference made by the Court to arbitrator was held to be valid.[3]

The new Act, 1996 does not make any provision corresponding to old Sec. 20 for arbitration with the intervention of a court where no suit is pending. However, arbitration in a pending suit can be resorted to, on the initiative of the Court by virtue of Sec. 89(1)(a) CPC as well as on the initiative of the parties. This can also be done through a compromise under O 23 R 3 CPC.

For reference to arbitration by Court, the Arbitration and Conciliation (Amendment) Act, 2015 has brought in substantial changes in the provisions of the Arbitration and Conciliation Act, 1996. As per the amended provision of Sub-section (6A) of Section 11, the power of the court is confined only to examine the existence of the arbitration agreement. It further clarifies that the decision of appointment of an arbitrator will be made by the Supreme Court or the High Court (instead of Chief Justice) and Under Section 11(7), no appeal shall lie against such an appointment.[4]

Disputes – Differences

Only disputes or differences that have arisen between the parties can be got adjudicated through arbitration. A dispute arises when there is claim and a denial and repudiation of claim. The existence of a dispute is essential for appointment of

1 *Zenith Drugs and Allied Agencies Pvt. Ltd.* v. *Nicholas Piramal India Ltd.*, AIR 2019 SC 3498.

2 *Milkfood Ltd.* v. *GMC Ice Cream (P) Ltd*, (2004) 7 SCC 288.

3 *Sanganer Dal & Flour Mill* v. *F.C. Land & others*, (1992), SCC 145.

4 *Duro Felguera S.A.* v. *Gangavaram Port Limited*, (2017) 9 SCC 729, MANU/SC/1352/2017.

an arbitrator. Dispute entails a positive element and assertion in denying, not merely inaction to accede to a claim.[1] However, clarifying this in a later case Hon'ble Supreme Court stated "There is no dispute about the afore mentioned principle but the same would not mean that in every case the claim must be followed by a denial. If a matter is referred to arbitrator within a reasonable time, the party invoking the arbitration clause may proceed on the basis that the other party to the contract has denied or disputed his claim or is otherwise not interested in referring the dispute to the arbitrator.[2]

No new claim can be added after the arbitration has been invoked. It would, therefore, be advisable, for the sake of precaution, to apprise the other side of all the claims, including claim for interest etc., before invoking arbitration.

Term "subject matter of the arbitration" cannot be confused with subject matter of the suit". The purpose of term "subject matter " in Section 2(1)(e) of the Act is to identify the courts having supervisory control over the arbitration proceedings. It refers to a court, which would essentially, be a court of the seat of the arbitration process.

Place for Arbitration

According to the Arbitration and Conciliation Act 1996, the parties are free to agree on any place or seat in India as the place of arbitration, in case of domestic arbitrations [Sec. 20(1)]. In the absence of the parties' agreement thereto, Section 20(2) authorizes the tribunal to determine the place/seat of such arbitration. Section 20(3) enables the tribunal to meet at any place for conducting hearings at a place of convenience in matters such as consultations among its members for hearing witnesses, experts or the parties.[3]

The moment the seat is designated, it is akin to an exclusive jurisdiction clause. Under the Law of Arbitration, unlike the Code of Civil Procedure which applies to suits filed in courts, a reference to "seat" is a concept by which a neutral venue can be chosen by the parties to an arbitration clause. The neutral venue may not in the classical sense have jurisdiction - that is, no part of the cause of action may have arisen at the neutral venue and neither would any of the provisions of Section 16 to 21 of the Code of Civil Procedure be attracted. In arbitration law however, the moment "seat" is determined, the fact that the seat is at Mumbai would vest Mumbai courts with exclusive jurisdiction for purposes of regulating arbitral proceedings arising out of the agreement between the parties. It is well settled that where more than one court has jurisdiction, it is open for parties to

---

1 *Major (Retd) Inder Singh Rekhi* v. *DDA*, 1998 Arbitration Law Reporter 270 SC.

2 *Mcdermott International Inc.* v. *Burn Standard Co. Ltd*, 2006 (2) Arbitration Law Reporter 498 SC

3 *Bharat Aluminium Company* v. *Kaiser Aluminium Technical Service, Inc.*, (2012) 9 SCC 552.

exclude all other courts.[1] Non-use of words like "exclusive jurisdiction", "only", "exclusive", "alone" is not decisive and does not make any material difference.[2]

Option for foreign award may be exercised by the parties to the arbitration agreement only if at least one of them is a foreign national or a company or other body incorporated in a foreign country or a foreign government [See Sec. 2(f), for definition of "international commercial arbitration"].

Domestic Award and International Award

The Supreme Court in *Bharat Aluminium Company* v. *Kaiser Aluminium Technical Service, Inc.*,[3] said that the Arbitration and Conciliation Act, 1996 is designed to give different treatments to "domestic awards" and "foreign awards". It has accepted the territoriality principle which has been adopted in the Model Law of United Nations Commission on International Trade Law (UNCITRAL). Section 2(2) makes a declaration that Part I of the Arbitration Act, 1996 shall apply to all arbitrations which take place within India i.e. it shall apply to both "international arbitrations" which take place in India as well as "domestic arbitrations" which would normally take place in India. This is clear from a number of provisions contained in the Arbitration Act 1996, namely the Preamble of the said Act; proviso and the Explanation to Section 1(2); Sections 2(1)(f); 11(9), 11(12); 28(1)(a) and 28(1)(b). Accordingly, Part I of the Arbitration Act, 1996 would have no application to International Commercial Arbitration held outside India. Therefore, such awards would only be subject to the jurisdiction of the Indian courts when the same are sought to be enforced in India in accordance with the provisions contained in Part II of the Arbitration Act, 1996.

The term "domestic award" can be used in two senses: one to distinguish it from "international award", and the other to distinguish it from a "foreign award". It must also be remembered that "foreign award" may well be a domestic award in the country in which it is rendered. Therefore, Part I of the Arbitration Act, 1996 applies not only to purely domestic arbitrations, i.e., where none of the parties are in any way "foreign" but also to "international commercial arbitrations" covered within Section 2(1)(f) held in India.

The term "international award" does not occur in Part I at all. Therefore, it would appear that the term "domestic award" means an award made in India whether in a purely domestic context, i.e., domestically rendered award in a domestic arbitration or in the international context, i.e., domestically rendered award in an international arbitration. Both the types of awards are liable to be challenged under Section 34 and are enforceable under Section 36 of the

---

1 *Indus Mobile Distribution Private Limited* v. *Datawind Innovations Private Limited* (2017) 7 SCC 678; *Balaji Coke Industry Pvt Ltd* v. *Maa Bhagwati Coke Gujarat Pvt. Ltd.*, (2009) 9 SCC 403.

2 *Brahmani River Pellets Limited* v. *Kamachi Industries Limited*, AIR 2019 SC 3658; *Swastic Gases Pvt. Ltd.* v. *Indian Oil Corporation Ltd.*, (2013) 9 SCC 32.

3 (2012) 9 SCC 552.

Arbitration Act, 1996. Therefore, it seems clear that the object of Section 2(7) is to distinguish the domestic award covered under Part I of the Arbitration Act, 1996 from the "foreign award" covered under Part II of the aforesaid Act; and not to distinguish the "domestic award" from an "international award" rendered in India. In other words, the provision highlights, a clear distinction between Part I and Part II as being applicable in completely different fields and with no overlapping provisions.

In a foreign seated international commercial arbitration, no application for interim relief would be maintainable under Section 9 or any other provision, as applicability of Part I of the Arbitration Act, 1996 is limited to all arbitrations which take place in India, Similarly, no suit for interim injunction simplicitor would be maintainable in India, on the basis of an international commercial arbitration with a seat outside India.

Number of Arbitrators

Under the Arbitration Act, 1940, if a reference was made to two arbitrators then they first appointed an Umpire. The Umpire was to decide the dispute all alone in case of difference arising between the two arbitrators. Until then he had no role. Under the new Act of 1996 either an odd number of arbitrators an appointed by the parties themselves, or they nominate only one each, and the two have to agree on a third arbitrator, all the three acting together throughout. Thus an even number of arbitrators is ruled out (Sec. 10) and the decision of the majority operates as the award (Sec. 29).

Challenge to an award

Section 34 of the Act of 1996 provides remedy to the party aggrieved by the award to challenge the same by way of objections before the court of competent jurisdiction. An arbitral award would be final and binding on the parties unless it is set aside by a competent court on an application made by a party to the arbitral award. Where a party feels aggrieved by an interim award, it can also be challenged by way of objections under section 34 of the Act.

Valuation

The amount of value is required to be and as such should be stated in the award [Sec. 31 (7)].

Stamp Duty

Stamp duty on an agreement of reference is governed by Article 5. Stamp duty on an award is governed by Article 12 of the Schedule to the Stamp Act.

Registration

An agreement of reference does not require registration.

An award would require registration only if it embodies a transaction covered by section 17 (1) (b) or (c) of the Registration Act *i.e.*, if it purports or operates to create or declare, assign, limit or extinguish, whether in present or future, any right, title or interest, whether vested or contingent, of the value of Rs.100 and upwards, to or in immovable property.[1]

Effect of an arbitration clause in a contract requires to be stamped, but not stamped

In *N.N. Global Mercantile Pvt. Ltd.* v. *Indo Unique Flame Ltd.*,[2] the Supreme Court held that since the arbitration agreement was an independent agreement between the parties, and was not chargeable to payment of stamp duty, the non-payment of stamp duty on the commercial contract, would not invalidate the arbitration clause or render it un-enforceable, since it had an independent existence of its own. The view taken by the court on the issue of separability of the arbitration clause on the registration of the substantive contract, ought to have been followed even with respect to the Stamp Act. The non-payment of stamp duty on the substantive contract would not invalidate even the main contrcat. It was a deficiency which was curable on the payment of the requisite Stamp Duty.

1 *Satish Kumar* v. *Surinder Kumar*, (1969) 2 SCR 244, AIR 1970 SC 833.

2 2021 (1) CTC 868, 2021 (1) KLT 324, 2021 1 MLJ 708.

PRECEDENTS

1—General Clauses of Arbitration in an Agreement[1]

(*a*) Every dispute, difference, or question which may at any time arise between the parties hereto or any persons claiming under them, touching or arising out or in respect of this agreement (deed) or the subject-matter thereof[2] shall be referred to the arbitration of XY, etc., or, if he shall be unable or unwilling to act, to another arbitrator, to be agreed upon between the parties or failing agreement, to be nominated by ——— [*or*, failing agreement to three arbitrators, one to be appointed by each party to the difference and the two appointed arbitrators shall appoint the third arbitrator who shall act as the presiding arbitrator and the decision of the arbitrator (*or*, arbitrators) shall be final and binding on the parties].

(*b*) In the event of any dispute, difference or question arising out of or in respect of this agreement or the commission of any breach of any terms thereof or of compensation payable therefor or in any manner whatsoever in connection with it, the same shall be referred to the Chamber of Commerce ——————— (*or*, the Association of ———) for arbitration as provided in Rules framed by the said Chamber (*or* Association) for the purpose. The decision or award so given shall be binding on the parties hereto.

(*c*) All disputes arising between the partners as to the interpretation, operation, or effect of any clause in this deed and/or any other dispute or difference arising between the partners, which cannot be mutually resolved, shall be referred to the arbitration of ———, failing him to any other arbitrator chosen by the partners in writing. The decision of such an arbitrator shall be binding on the partners.

(*d*) In the event of any dispute or difference arising out of or in any way relating to or concerning these presents or the construction or effect of

1 In these forms future disputes are also agreed to be referred, hence it is not necessary for parties to consent again after disputes have arisen: *Banwarilal* v. *P.C. Aggarwal*, (1985) 3 SCC 255; however, for reference of a specific question of law fresh consent is required: *Thawardas* v. *Union of India*, AIR 1955 SC 468; see also, *Shah Construction Co.* v. *Municipal Corpn.*, AIR 1985 Del. 358.

2 The expressions 'arising out of', 'in respect of', 'in connection with', 'in relation to', 'in consequence of', 'concerning' or 'relating to' the contract are of widest amplitude and content and include even questions as to the existence, validity and effect or scope of the arbitration agreement: *Renusagar Power Co.* v. *General Electric Co.*, AIR 1985 SC 1156; *Bindra Builders* v. *D.D.A.*, AIR 1985 Del 370.

these presents (the settlement whereof has not been hereinbefore expressly provided for), the same shall be referred to the sole arbitration of a person appointed by AB.[1] CD will not be entitled to raise objection on any such appointment on the ground that the sole arbitrator is a servant of AB or that he had dealt with the matters to which these presents relate or that in the course of his duties as such servant he had expressed views on all or any of the matters in dispute or difference. In the event of such arbitrator being transferred or vacating his office or refusing or being unable to act for any reason whatsoever, it will be open to AB to appoint another person in his place. The Arbitrator so appointed will be entitled to proceed with the reference from the stage at which it was pending. From time to time, the Arbitrator may, with the consent of both the parties to these presents, extend the time for making the award.

The award of the Arbitrator shall be final and binding on the parties. Subject as aforesaid the Arbitration and Conciliation Act, 1996 and the rules made thereunder shall apply to the arbitration proceedings under this clause.

(*e*) (*i*) [*May be inserted in clause (d) above*]. It is also a term of this contract that no person other than a person appointed by AB as aforesaid should act as arbitrator and if for any reason, that is not possible, the matter is not to be referred to arbitration at all.[2]

(*ii*) It is a term of the contract that the party invoking arbitration shall specify the dispute or disputes to be referred to arbitration under this clause together with the amount or amounts claimed in respect of each dispute.

(*iii*) The work under the contract shall, if reasonably possible, continue during the arbitration proceedings and no payment due or payable to CD shall be withheld on account of such proceeding.

---

1 Such a stipulation is usually made in favour of Government or a public corporation. Its validity has been upheld in *S. Rajan* v. *State of Kerala*, AIR 1992 SC 1918 and *I.D.P.L.* v. *Indo Swiss Manufacturing Co.*, AIR 1996 SC 543. Officers of Government or such corporation even when deciding disputes between their employer and a private party are expected to act fairly and impartially. If however an arbitrator so appointed fails to act fairly he will be committing a breach of Sec. 18, and the award may be set aside under Sec. 34(2). Any challenge earlier is also possible under Sec. 12.

2 Even with a clause (d) or (e) the court can in case, the bias of the arbitrator is established, set aside his appointment and appoint an arbitrator itself, as held in some cases under the old Act. See discussion in *U.P. Co-operative Federation* v. *Sunder Brothers*, AIR 1967 SC 249; *Fertiliser Corpn. of India* v. *Domestic Engineering*, AIR 1970 All 311. Under the 1996 Act, the power vests in the Supreme Court or High Court (instead of Chief Justice) (Sec. 11(6A)).

(*iv*)[1] The Arbitrator shall be deemed to have entered on the reference on the date he issues notice to both the parties fixing the date of the first hearing.

(*v*) The Arbitrator shall give a separate award in respect of each dispute or difference referred to him.

(*vi*)[2] The venue of arbitration shall be such place as may be fixed by the Arbitrator in his sole discretion.

(*f*)[3] Every dispute, difference or question touching or arising out of this deed shall be referred to the sole arbitration of a person nominated by the Legal Remembrancer-cum-Judicial Secretary to Government of —— who shall be a serving officer not lower in rank to that of Joint Legal Remembrancer-cum-Joint Secretary in the Judicial Department.

The arbitrator may from time to time with the consent of the parties enlarge the time for making and publishing the award.

(*g*)[4] If any difference arises as to the amount of any loss or damage such difference shall independently of all other questions be referred to the decision of an arbitrator, to be appointed in writing by the parties, or if they cannot agree upon a single arbitrator to the decision of three persons as arbitrators, one to be appointed by each party and they shall appoint the third arbitrator who shall act as the presiding arbitrator.

(*h*) Except where it has been provided otherwise, any dispute or difference arising out of or in connection with the agreement between the parties including any dispute or difference relating to the interpretation of the agreement or any clause thereof shall be referred to the sole arbitration of a person appointed by the LESSOR, and the provisions of the Arbitration and Conciliation Act, 1996, and the rules framed thereunder and any amendment thereto, from time to time, shall apply. No objection shall be taken on the ground that the arbitrator so appointed is an employee of the LESSOR or is in any way associated with the LESSOR. The award of

---

1 See Sec. 21, Arbitration and Conciliation Act, 1996: "Unless otherwise agreed by the parties, the arbitral proceedings in respect of a particular dispute commence on the date on which a request for that dispute to be referred to arbitration is received by the respondent."

2 See Sec. 20, Arbitration and Conciliation Act, 1996.

3 This form of arbitration clause will be appropriate only in deeds executed between two or more Government companies or other undertakings controlled by the same Government.

4 Such a clause is inapplicable where the insurance company repudiates its liability altogether instead of merely disputing the amount of loss or damage allegedly caused by the fire (*Vulcan Insurance Co. Ltd.* v. *Maharaj Singh*, (1976) 1 SCC 943).

the arbitrator shall be final, conclusive and binding on all the parties. The arbitrator shall be competent to decide whether any matter of dispute or difference referred to him falls within purview of arbitration as provided for above.[1]

(*i*)[2] All claims, disputes, controversies, disagreements or differences between the parties arising out of or in relation to or in connection with this Agreement or a breach thereof shall be determined by arbitration in accordance with the then prevailing rules of Conciliation and Arbitration of the International Chamber of Commerce. The venue of such arbitration shall be London, U.K.

(*j*)[3] "Except where otherwise specified in the contract and subject to powers delegated to him by Agricultural Produce Market Committee, under the Code Rules, then in force the decision of the Chairman shall be final, conclusive, and binding on all parties to the contract upon all questions relating to the meaning of the specifications, designs, and instructions hereinbefore mentioned and as to the quality of workmanship; or materials used on the work or as to any other question, claim, right, matter, thing whatsoever in any way arising out of or relating to the contract, designs, drawings, specifications estimates, instructions, orders or those conditions, failure to execute the same whether arising during the progress of work, or after the completion or abandonment thereof."

(k)[4] In case of any dispute or difference between the parties to the contract, either during the progress or after the completion of the works, or after determination, abandonment, or breach of the contract, as to the interpretation of the contract, or as to any matter or thing arising thereunder, then either party shall forthwith give to the other notice of such dispute or difference and such dispute or difference shall be, and is hereby referred to the arbitration of ——— and the award of such arbitrator shall be final and binding on the parties unless contested by either party in a court of law. Either party may, within a period which shall be fixed by the arbitrator, file before the arbitrator a statement of the case and also all the documents

---

1 The last sentence of this clause will not normally exclude the jurisdiction of the Court to finally decide on the ambit of the arbitrator's powers: Sec. 16 (6) read with Sec. 34.

2 The clause in the Maruti Udyog - case: See *Suzuki Motor Corporation* v. *Union of India*, (1997) 2 Arbi LR 477 (Delhi). Sec. 20 provides for parties to agree on the place where arbitration proceedings shall take place.

3 *Lachmanna B. Horomni* v. *State of Karnataka*, AIR 1998 Kant 405.

4 See *P.V. Subba Naidu* v. *Govt. of A.P.*, (1998) 9 SCC 407 in which a clause in these terms was interpreted. It was held that the arbitration clause was valid though it was very wide and did not confine merely to any question of interpretation of the contract. It also covered any matter or thing arising thereunder.

relating to, or having a bearing on the case. The arbitrator shall have power to view the subject matter of dispute with or without the parties or their agents. The arbitrator shall have also power to open up, review and revise any certificate, opinion, decision, requisition or notice, save in regard to matters expressly excepted and to determine all matters in dispute which shall be submitted to him and of which notice shall have been given as aforesaid.

Clauses not held to be Arbitration Clause[1]

(a)[2] "Except where otherwise specified in the contract the decision of the Superintending Engineer for the time being shall be final, conclusive and binding on all parties to the contract upon all questions relating to the meaning of the specifications, designs, drawings and instructions herein mentioned. The decision of such Engineer as to the quality of workmanship, or materials used on the work, or as to any other question, claim, right, matter or things whatsoever in any way arising out of or relating to the contract, designs, drawings specifications, estimates, instructions, orders or these conditions, or otherwise concerning the works, or the execution or failure to execute the same, whether arising during the progress of the work, or after the completion or abandonment of the contract by the contractor, shall also be final, conclusive and binding on the contractor."

(b)[3] "Implementation will be done in consultation with the financial institutions. For all disputes, clarifications etc., in respect of implementation of this agreement, the same shall be referred to the Chairman, IFCI or his nominees whose decisions will be final and binding on both the groups."

(c) "Except where otherwise specified in the contract, the decision of the Executive Engineer shall be final, conclusive and binding on both the parties to the contract on all questions relating to the meaning, the specification, design, drawings and instructions hereinbefore mentioned,

---

1 It may be noted here that sometimes an officer of the employer, - for instance the Government, is entrusted with powers of supervision in a works contract, and in that capacity he is given certain powers to decide certain questions. Such an empowering clause does not necessarily amount to an arbitration clause. *State of U.P.* v. *Tipper Chand*, (1980) 2 SCC 341, AIR 1980 SC 1522. It should, therefore, be ensured that the clause, if intended to be an arbitration clause, should expressly use either the word "arbitration" or the words "dispute" and "decision" see *Rukmini Bai* v. *Collector*, AIR 1981 SC 479.

2 *State of U.P.* v. *Tipper Chand,* (1980) 2 SCC 341, AIR 1980 SC 1522; *State of Orissa* v. *Damodar Das,* (1996) 2 SCC 216, AIR 1996 SC 942.

3 *K.K. Modi* v. *K.N. Modi*, (1998) 3 SCC 573; It was held, after discussion of authorities, that such a clause did not amount to arbitration agreement but to reference of issues to an expert for decision.

and as to the quality of workmanship or materials used on the work or as to any other questions whatsoever in any way arising out of or relating to the design, drawings, specifications, estimates, instructions, orders or otherwise concerning the works or the execution of failure to execute the same whether arising during the progress of the work, or after the completion thereof or abandonment of the contract by the contractor shall be final and conclusive and binding on the contractor. Decision of the MD of the UPSIC on all other matters shall be final.

(d)[1] "Except as provided in the clause above, the decision of the Managing Director of the UPSIC shall be final, conclusive and binding on both the parties to the contract upon all questions relating to any claim, right, matter or thing in any way arising out of or relating to the contract or these conditions or concerning abandonment of the contract by the contractor and in respect of all other matters arising out of this contract and not specifically mentioned herein."

(For arbitration clause in an Agency Agreement, Works Contract, Electricity Supply Agreement and Partition Deed see respective precedents).

2—Agreement of Reference to Arbitration for Partition of Joint Family Property

THIS AGREEMENT is made on the ——— day of ——— BETWEEN AB, etc., acting for himself and as guardian of EF, etc., a minor, of the first part AND CD, etc., of the second part AND GH, etc., of the third part.

WHEREAS—

Recitals[2]

(1) The said AB, CD, and EF are members of a joint Hindu family and are joint owners of all the property, movable and immovable owned and possessed by them, whether acquired by their ancestors or by themselves in their joint names or by any of them in his separate name, and of all cash and jewellery possessed by them and of all debts outstanding in their favour, described in schedules ——— annexed hereto.

(2) The said AB has by an order of the District Judge of ——— dated the ——— been appointed guardian of the person and property of the

1 *Bharat Bhushan Bansal* v. *U.P. Small Industries Corpn.*, (1999) 2 SCC 166, AIR 1999 SC 899.

2 These italicised headings in this and in the other forms following are not to be reproduced while adapting the draft.

said EF minor who is the son of JK, a deceased brother of the said AB and CD.

(3) The shares of the parties in the property are AB ——— CD ——— EF ———.

(4) Differences have arisen between AB and CD with regard to their state of jointness and they are desirous of having the said family property partitioned.

(5) Under the Hindu Law, the said GH being the mother of the said AB, and CD, and grandmother of EF, is on partition entitled to a one-fourth share in the family property.

(6) The said GH has agreed to take for her life in lieu of the said one-fourth share, property yielding an annual profit of Rs. ——— and a residential house fit for her residence for her life.

(7) The proposed partition will also be for the advantage of the minor EF.

(8) The said AB, acting for himself and as guardian of the said EF minor and considering it to be for the advantage of the said minor and for the benefit of his property, and the said CD and the said GH, have agreed to refer the question of the manner of partition of the aforesaid family property to the arbitration of Shri ———.

NOW IT IS HEREBY AGREED as follows:

(1) Reference & Powers of Arbitrator

The parties hereto hereby refer the question of partition by metes and bounds of aforesaid property to the arbitration and decision of the said Shri ———.

(2) To Reserve House for Mother

The said arbitrator shall select out of the aforesaid joint property, property yielding an annual profit of Rs. ——— and a residential house fit for residence of the said GH and allot the same to the said GH to be held by her for her life, and after her death to be divided equally between the said AB, CD and EF or per stirpes between their heirs.

(3) To Divide Rest

The said arbitrator shall divide the rest of the aforesaid property consisting of immovable and movable property, cash, jewellery, and outstanding debts into three equal shares according to the best of his judgment and allot one such shares each to the said AB, CD, and EF.

(4) To Award Compensation

If necessary for equalizing the shares, the said arbitrator may award such money compensation from one party to another as he may consider necessary.

(5) To Convert Movables into Money

If for any reason the arbitrator finds it inconvenient or inexpedient to divide any movable property, he may convert the same into money and divide such money equally between the said AB, CD, and EF.

(6) To Take Evidence

For the purpose of determining the extent and value of the joint family property and of giving his award the arbitrator may take such evidence and make such investigation and adopt such procedure as he may think proper. (*See note under clause 2 of the next form No.3*).

(7) Place of Arbitration

The place of arbitration shall be ——— or such other place as the arbitrator may decide with the consent of the parties hereto.

(8) Language of the proceedings

The arbitration proceedings will be conducted in —— language.

(9) Arbitrator's Remuneration

The arbitrator shall be paid Rs. ———— per sitting plus reimbursement of expenses on travelling, secretarial assistance etc., incurred by him. All payments to the arbitrator shall be shared by the parties in equal shares.

(10) Award Final

The award made by the arbitrator shall be final binding on the parties.

IN WITNESS, etc.

3—Agreement to Refer Existing Disputes to Arbitration

THIS AGREEMENT is made on the ———— day of ———— 1996 BETWEEN AB, etc., and CD, etc.

WHEREAS—

Recitals

(1) CD has made the following claims against AB:

1. ____________________

2. ____________________

3. ____________________

(2) AB does not admit the said claims of CD;

(3) Disputes have arisen between the parties respecting these claims; and

(4) The parties agree to refer the said disputes to arbitration.

NOW IT IS AGREED between the parties as follows:

1. Reference

All matters in dispute between the parties touching the claims of CD are referred to the award and final determination of XY as arbitrator.

2. Powers of Arbitrator

The arbitrator may take such evidence and make such inquiries[1] as he deems proper. He may proceed *ex parte* in case a party fails, after reasonable notice, to attend before him.

3. Award Final

The award of the arbitrator shall be binding on the parties[2] and this submission shall not be revoked by the death of a party before the making of the award.

IN WITNESS, etc.

4—Agreement of Reference to Three Arbitrators (giving elaborate directions)

THIS AGREEMENT, etc.

WHEREAS—

1. ____________________

2. ____________________ etc.

Describe facts leading to the dispute and showing briefly the nature of the dispute.

3. The parties hereto have agreed to refer the aforesaid matters and dispute to arbitration.

---

1 The expression "such inquiries as he may deem proper" does not include the power of making secret inquiries behind the back of any party. If it is intended to give such power of secret inquiries, it should be stated clearly in the agreement.

2 This is subject to Sec. 34.

NOW IT IS HEREBY AGREED between the parties hereto as follows:

1. Matters of Reference

The following questions and matters are hereby referred to the award and final determination of X, Y and Z, as arbitrators.

(*a*) ——————————

(*b*) ——————————

(*c*) ——————————, etc.

2. Award Final[1]

The decision and award of the arbitrators shall be final and conclusive and binding on the parties hereto.

3. Fee

The arbitrators shall be paid a fee of Rs. ——— and such fees as well as the costs of this reference and other expenses incidental to the arbitration shall be borne and paid by such of the parties or by both parties in such proportion as the arbitrators shall by their award direct.

4. Commencement of Arbitration

The arbitrators shall enter upon the reference on or about the ———.

5. Presiding Arbitrator

The said X shall be the Presiding arbitrator of the tribunal of arbitration.

6. Duties of Presiding Arbitrator

The Presiding Arbitrator shall preside at every meeting of the arbitrators and will be in charge of all the papers and proceedings and will fix dates and times for the sittings of the arbitrators and will issue all notices and summons as required to be issued by the arbitrators under his own signatures.

7. Absence of an Arbitrator[2]

The arbitrators shall hold proceedings and deliberate jointly, but at any sitting of the arbitrators at which only oral evidence is to be recorded or

---

1 Such a clause will not however preclude recourse under Sec. 34 against the award. Sec. 34 is not subject to any agreement to the contrary.

2 The Act does not make any provision regarding quorum. Hence this will be covered by Sec. 19(2).

local inspection is to be made, if any of the arbitrators is unable to be present for any unavoidable reason, then the Presiding Arbitrator may with another arbitrator proceed with the business and report the proceedings at the next joint meeting of the arbitrators.

8. Difference of Opinion

In case of difference of opinion on any point, the opinion of the majority of the arbitrators shall prevail and in case of difference of opinion about the award, the award of the majority shall be deemed the award of the arbitrators and shall be binding.

9. Proceedings before Arbitrators

The parties shall not be entitled to be present at each and every sitting of the arbitrators, and for such sittings, at which their presence may be necessary, due notice shall be given to them by the Presiding arbitrator, but the parties will be entitled to submit written arguments presenting their respective cases to the arbitrators on all the points in dispute and the arbitrators may, if they think it necessary, hear the parties personally or by counsel on any of the points in dispute in arbitration but will not be bound to do so.

10. Documentary Evidence

The arbitrators may, from time to time, call upon any party to submit such documents as they may require for perusal and consideration in connection with the arbitration. The parties will also be entitled to adduce such documentary evidence as they may think fit by such date as the arbitrators may appoint or whenever permitted by the arbitrators to do so thereafter.

11. Award of Money Compensation

The arbitrators will be entitled to award money compensation if absolutely necessary in order to equalize the value of the lots to be allotted to the parties.

12. Land

If the arbitrators are of opinion that it will be more to the advantage of the parties and to the better enjoyment of the property that any land should not be partitioned they will be at liberty to allot the same to one of the parties and to equalize the lot of the other party either by allotment of other house property or by money compensation.

13. Oral Evidence

No oral evidence shall be adduced or taken on the first question of reference (viz. ——————), but the said question shall be determined by the arbitrators on their own interpretation of ——— after seeing and considering such documents as the parties may produce or the arbitrators may like to refer to. On other questions the parties will have a right to produce oral evidence.

14. The submission hereby made shall not be revoked either by the death or incapacity or any act of either party hereto but the said arbitrators shall proceed as if no such act or event had occurred.

IN WITNESS, etc.

5—Appointment of Presiding Arbitrator by Arbitrators (by Endorsement on the Agreement of Reference)

We, the within named arbitrators, in pursuance of the powers given to us by the within contained agreement appoint AB, etc., as Presiding Arbitrator.

6—Appointment of Arbitrator in Other Cases

Whereas some disputes have arisen between the parties and AB has through letter dated ——— appointed X as arbitrator and CD has through letter dated ——— appointed Y as arbitrator for adjudication of such disputes;

And whereas in terms of Sec. 11(3) of the Arbitration & Conciliation Act, 1996, we have to appoint the third arbitrator to act as the Presiding Arbitrator;

Now, We, X and Y, after mutual consultation and agreement, appoint Z, who has consented to act as the Presiding Arbitrator.

7—Award by Sole Arbitrator or Arbitral Tribunal of three or more Arbitrators[1]

Before JK (LM and PQ) ———————— ARBITRATOR(s)

IN THE MATTER OF ARBITRATION

BETWEEN

AB, etc. ———————————————————— *Claimant*

AND

CD, etc. ———————————————————— *Respondent*

By an arbitration agreement dated ———————— certain disputes arising between the parties were referred to me (*or*, to an arbitral tribunal, the parties nominating two of us, namely LM and PQ who jointly appointed JK as the presiding arbitrator).[2]

AB, etc. submitted his claim to us on ——— and CD etc., submitted his defence in a Written Statement to us on ———.[3]

(The respondent has also made a counter claim to the effect that ——

To this, the defence of AB, etc., claimant is that ———).[4]

The parties filed their respective documents and adduced oral evidence. After conclusion of evidence they (*or*, their counsel) advanced arguments before me (us). At the close of arguments on ——— I (we) had (have) reserved my (our) award.

Now after [discussion among ourselves (*these words to be omitted in case of a sole arbitrator*)] perusal of the record and consideration of

---

1 Under the Arbitration Act 1940, non-speaking award was permissible unless otherwise required by the arbitration agreement. On the other hand, Sec. 31 (3), Arbitration and Conciliation Act 1996 requires reasons to be given unless (a) the parties have agreed that reasons are not to be given, or (b) the award is on agreed terms, *i.e.*, based on a compromise.

2 Section 10 of 1996 Act requires that the number of arbitrators shall not be an even number, and unless otherwise stated the arbitral tribunal shall consist of a sole member. Section 11(3) provides for the appointment of the third arbitrator who is to act as the presiding arbitrator. This does away with the system of Umpire who, under the old Act, conducted the arbitration only after the original two arbitrators had differed. It is not necessary that the third arbitrator must always be appointed by the two nominees of the parties. It is open to the parties to agree on all the three/five arbitrators in advance among themselves, as in precedent No.4, ante: Secs. 10 (1) and 11(2).

3 If any 'replication' by claimant was permitted the same should also be mentioned. Further, if there is a counterclaim the same and the defence thereto should also be referred to here.

4 Omit if there is no counter claim.

arguments I (We) am (are) making this award unanimously (*or*, two of us LM and JK are making this agreed award while the remaining member of the arbitral tribunal PQ finding himself unable to agree with us on some points has not signed the award and is appending his dissenting opinion hereto)[1]. (*The words "unanimously" or the alternative phraseology to be omitted in case of sole arbitrator*).

The claimant's case is as follows ———.

The respondent's case is that ———.

The following points (*or*, issues) arise for determination, namely:

1.

2.

3. etc.

Findings

Point (or issue) No. 1:

(Discussion of case, evidence and law, followed by conclusion).[2]

Point (or issue) No. 2, 3 etc.:

(*Similar*)

Conclusion

In the result, I (We) hold that ———.

Award[3]

Accordingly, I (we) award:—

1.

2.

---

1 Section 31(2) requires signatures of the majority with reasons for the omitted signature. There is nothing in the Act about a dissenting opinion, but it seems there can be no objection to a dissenting member appending reasons for his dissent if he so desires.

2 Stating only the conclusion without reasons is not enough. Some inefficient judges and arbitrators think it to be sufficient to state the materials on the record and then to state their conclusion. This is illegal. Reasons, which are the foundation for the conclusion, are absolutely necessary.

3 Sec. 31(7) provides for direction as to interest. Arbitrator can award interest for all four stages: (1) from the stage of accrual of cause of action till filing of the arbitration proceedings (2) during pendency of the proceedings before the arbitrator (3) future interest arising between date of award and date of decree and (4) interest arising from date of decree till realisation of award: *T.P. George* v. *State of Kerala*, AIR 2001 SC 816. Sec. 31(8) provides for direction as to costs. These should be studied. Directions as to these should also be added to the operative portion of the award.

3.

Dated: the ——— day of ———

Place[1] ———

Let a signed copy of this award
be delivered to each party.[2]

Signed[3] ————
Signed ————
Signed ————

1 The place of signing the award shall be the same as was determined under Sec. 20 for arbitration proceedings to take place: Sec. 31(4).

2 Sec. 31(5).

3 Once the award is made and signed it becomes complete and final and the arbitral tribunal cannot then change it: *Satwant Singh* v. *State of Punjab*, (1999) 3 SCC 487 (paras 8 to 11), AIR 1999 SC 2040 (Sec. 14, Arbitration Act, 1940)). This legal position is now subject to the power of the tribunal under Sec. 33 to make any correction to or give an interpretation of a specific point or part of the award.

ASSIGNMENT OF ACTIONABLE CLAIMS, AND OF DECREES, ETC.

Preliminary Note

Definition of "Actionable Claim"

"Actionable claim" has been defined in the Transfer of Property Act, meaning a claim to any debt other than a debt secured by mortgage of immovable property or by hypothecation or pledge of movable property, or to any beneficial interest in movable property not in the possession, either actual or constructive, of the claimant, which the civil courts recognize as affording grounds for relief, whether such debt or beneficial interest be existent, accruing, conditional or contingent (Sec. 3). It includes copyright, patents and trade marks, which are movables being "choses in action".

Distinguished from a mere Right to Sue

It is necessary to note this definition carefully, as under the law, all claims which come under this definition can be transferred while a *mere* right to sue which does not amount to an actionable claim cannot be transferred [Sec. 6 Transfer of Property Act]. For example, a right to recover damages for tort or breach of contract, or to recover mesne profits cannot be assigned, as such damages do not amount to a "debt".

A "debt" is only an obligation to pay a liquidated or certain sum of money, e.g. loan, dower debt, rent.[1]

A contract for sale of goods is ordinarily assignable but not where personal obligations are involved.[2] The rights and obligations under the contract should not be of a personal nature. Rights under a lottery ticket have been held to be assignable as they involve beneficial interests in movable property.[3]

A fixed deposit in bank is an actionable claim.[4] So is the case with arrears of rent,[5] unpaid sale price,[6] amount left with vendee for payment to another, but not

1 *Sahju Sahib* v. *Noordin,* 22 Mad 139.

2 *Khardah Co. Ltd.* v. *Raymon & Co.*, AIR 1962 SC 1810; See also *Delhi Cloth Mills* v. *Harnam Singh*, AIR 1955 SC 590.

3 *H. Anraj* v. *Tamil Nadu Government*, (1986) 1 SCC 414.

4 *Maiyan Dalip* v. *Mohan Bikram*, AIR 1945 All 409.

5 *Madhabilata Devi* v. *Butto Kristo Roy*, AIR 1944 Pat 129, 134; *N.M. Engineer* v. *Narendra Singh Virdi*, AIR 1995 SC 448.

6 *Baij Nath* v. *Permeshwari Dayal*, AIR 1934 Oudh 240.

paid,[1] Provident Fund amount due,[2] arrears of annuity,[3] recovery of earnest money, when vendor fails to execute sale deed,[4] REP Licence/Exim Scrip.[5]

A transfer of a decree is not transfer of an actionable claim.[6] Precedents relating to transfer of decree, etc., are set out hereinafter apart from those relating to actionable claim.

A marine or fire policy cannot be transferred without transfer of the property insured (Sec. 130, exception, and Sec. 135 of the Transfer of Property Act.)

How to assign an actionable claim

Under the Transfer of Property Act, an assignment of an actionable claim must[7] be made by an instrument in writing signed by the transferor or his duly authorized agent [Sec. 130(1)]. However, in the territories to which, vide Sec. 1, that Act does not apply, it may be made orally.

The instrument of transfer need not be attested or registered. No particular form of writing is prescribed. It may be a formal deed of transfer or an endorsement[8] on the deed creating the actionable claim.

The word "transfer" appearing in Sec. 130 connotes a transfer in present. A promise by the debtor to pay money to his creditor, which he, the debtor, might receive a debt due to him by a third person, does not constitute an assignment of the debt so as to charge the debt in the hands of the third person. For example, an undertaking by the debtor to the effect, "I will deposit at your shop all cheques that I may get from the Public Works Department" or "I will be giving you cheques in satisfaction of the money due to you" does not amount to a present transfer or assignment of the debt but merely an agreement to assign in future. In such case the creditor does not get lien on the cheques.

The transfer takes effect from the execution of the instrument irrespective of the notice to the debtor so far as the transferor and the transferee are concerned. The section does not require the transfer to be in any particular form or to be couched in technical language; the transferor's intention should be clearly indicated by the instrument in writing.

---

1 *Agrenath Misir* v. *Ram Ratan Pandey*, AIR 1938 All 544.

2 *Bhupati Mohan Das* v. *Phanindra Chandra Chakravarty*, AIR 1935 Cal 756.

3 *Satindra Nath Choudhury v. Jatindra Nath Chaudhury*, AIR 1935 PC 165.

4 *Chiman Mal* v. *Ganesh*, AIR 1952 Raj 187.

5 *Vikas Sales Corp.* v. *CCT*, (1996) 4 SCC 433.

6 *Jugal Kishore Saraf* v. *Raw Cotton Co. Ltd.*, AIR 1955 SC 376, (per *N.H. Bhagwati J.*, the other two Judges expressing no opinion on this. The judgments also contain good discussion on equitable transfer and transfer by operation of law).

7 The word "only" in the phrase "*only* by the execution of an instrument in writing" occurring in Sec. 130(1) is significant: see *Doraisami* v. *Doraiswami*, AIR 1925 Mad 753.

8 *Hunsraj* v. *Nathoo*, (1907) 9 Bom. L.R. 838, relied on in Mulla's *Transfer of Property Act*, 7th edn., at p. 813.

The words "whether with or without consideration" in Sec. 130 denote that the assignment of an actionable claim may be by gift, as mentioned above, or by sale or mortgage. The transaction is complete and effective upon the execution of the instrument in writing duly signed by the transferor or the authorised agent on his behalf, but it remains open to challenge on ground of fraud, misrepresentation or the like on which any other contract can be impeached.

Warranty of solvency of debtor

Where the transferor of a debt warrants the solvency of a debtor, the warranty, in the absence of a contract to the contrary, applies only to his solvency at the time of the transfer, and is limited, whether the transfer is made for consideration to the amount or value of such consideration, Section 133 of the Transfer of Property Act.

Contents of an Instrument

An instrument of assignment should be drafted as a deed of transfer between the assignor and assignee and should consist of the same parts as a deed of transfer (*see* Introduction, Part II). Particulars as to how the actionable claim has arisen and of the agreement of assignment, if any, may be mentioned in the recitals, though in a simple case recitals may be omitted. The assignor, who may be called either "the assignor" or "transferor", describes himself in the operative part of the deed as claimant in case of debts and as "beneficial owner" in respect of any other interest in movable property as he is entitled to the benefit arising out of the actionable claim. The operative word is "transfers" or "assigns". If the assignment is absolute, the word "absolutely" may be added. If it is as a security the word "absolutely" should be omitted and the conditions of the security should be clearly and expressly stated. The only covenant which is usual in such deeds is one by the assignor to the effect that the debt is still owing and due to the assignor.

If the instrument is not to be a separate one but is to be endorsed on the bond or other deed creating the actionable claim, full particulars of the claim or its basis need not be mentioned but a reference may be made to the "within written bond" or deed.

The instrument of assignment can also be drafted in the form of a deed poll in the first person.

There can only be an assignment of rights arising under a contract but not the "burden of a contract".

In *Jaffer Meher Ali* v. *Budge-Budge Jute Mills Co. Ltd.*,[1] it was observed that the rule as regards the assignability of contracts in this country is that the benefit of a contract, as distinguished from the liability thereunder may be assigned....This rule is however subject to two qualifications: first, that the benefit sought to be assigned is not coupled with any liability or obligation that the assignor is bound to

1 ILR (1906) 33 Cal 702.

fulfil ... that the contract is not one which has been induced by the personal qualifications or considerations as regards the parties to it."

Negotiable Instruments

Negotiable instruments, stocks, shares,[1] debentures or mercantile documents can be transferred according to the law governing them, and the Transfer of Property Act does not apply to their assignment (Sec. 137). For instance, a promissory note may be transferred by endorsement or delivery or if payable to bearer, by delivery only. But this does not mean that a separate deed of transfer will not be effective.[2]

A transferee takes the actionable claim subject to the equities mentioned in Sec. 132, Transfer of Property Act. However a holder in due course under an assignment by endorsement, will not[3] be subject to such equities as Sec. 36, Negotiable Instruments Act provides that every prior party to a negotiable instrument is liable thereon to a holder in due course until the instrument is duly satisfied.

Stamp Duty

Subject to States' variations, stamp duty is payable on the transfer of—

(i) unsecured debt under Article 23; and

(ii) interest secured by a bond, policy of insurance etc., under Article 62, of the Schedule to the Stamp Act.

---

1 But assignment of dividend due on shares is assignment of an actionable claim: *Sheth Dahyabhai* v. *Sheth Ambalal*, AIR 1981 SC 1556, (1981) 3 SCC 644.

2 *Jia Lal* v. *Jag Mohan*, AIR 1937 Oudh 405, 168 IC 922.

3 *Muthar Sahib* v. *Kadir Sahib*, (1905) ILR 28 Mad 544; (1905) 15 MLJ 384; *Akhoy* v. *Haridas*, 18 CWN 494, 22 IC 500.

PRECEDENTS[1]

1—Assignment of a Bond Debt

(In the Form of Deed)

THIS ASSIGNMENT made on the ———— day of ——— BETWEEN AB, etc., (hereinafter called "the assignor") of the one part AND CD, etc., (hereinafter called "the assignee") of the other part.

WITNESSES as follows:

1. In consideration of the sum of Rs. ———— paid by the assignee to the assignor (the receipt of which is hereby acknowledged) the assignor [as claimant] hereby transfers to the assignee ALL that debt due and owing to the assignor by XY, etc., on a bond dated the ——— and all interest due and to become due for the same to the assignee absolutely.

2. The assignor hereby covenants with the assignee that the said debt is still due and owing to the assignor from the said XY.

IN WITNESS WHEREOF, etc.

2—Assignment of a Bond Debt

(In the Form of Deed Poll)

I, AB, etc., in consideration of the sum of Rs. ———— received by me from CD, etc., transfer absolutely to CD, the debt due to me by XY, etc., under a bond dated ———— and all interest due and to become due for the same and the full benefit and advantage thereof and covenants with the transferee that the debt is still due to me from the said XY.

Signed this the ——— day of ————.

3—Assignment of Book Debts in Consideration of a Debt due to the Assignee[2]

THIS ASSIGNMENT is made, etc., (*as in Form 1*).

WHEREAS the assignor has for sometime past carried on the business of ——— at ———— under the name and style ———— and in

1 See also precedents under NOTICE, *post* (Notices of Assignment).

2 Sec. 130 read with the definition of 'actionable claim' in Sec.3, Transfer of Property Act covers transfer of only unsecured debts. If rights as mortgagee are to be transferred, a registered deed will be required: See precedent No. 33 under SALE, post. However the benefit of any pledge of movable with the assignor can be transferred.

connection with such business the several persons whose names are set out in the first column of the schedule hereto have been and now are indebted to him in the several sums set opposite to their respective names in the second column of the said schedule;

AND WHEREAS the assignor had agreed with the assignee to assign to him the said debts in satisfaction of the debt due from the assignor to the assignee under a bond dated ———.

NOW THIS DEED WITNESSES as follows:

1. In consideration of the sum of Rs. ————, due and owing from the assignor to the assignee, from which sum the assignee hereby releases the assignor, the assignor as claimant hereby assigns to the assignee ALL the several debts specified in the schedule hereto and the benefits of all securities for the same and all interest, if any, due and to become due for the same TO HOLD the same to the assignee absolutely.

2. The assignor covenants with the assignee that the said debts hereby assigned are still due and owing to the assignor from the several persons named in the said schedule.

IN WITNESS WHEREOF, etc.

The Schedule herein referred to

Serial No.	Name of Debtor Amount due on the date of this Deed
1	2

4—Assignment of Debts upon Trust to Collect and to Pay sum Due to Assignee and Balance to Assignor

THIS ASSIGNMENT is made on the, etc. (*as in Form* 1).

WHEREAS the assignor is indebted to the assignee in the sum of Rs. ——— due under a mortgage deed dated ———— executed by XY, the deceased father of the assignor.

AND WHEREAS the assignor is entitled to the several debts particulars of which are specified in the schedule hereto and has agreed to assign them to the assignee upon the trust hereinafter declared.

NOW THIS DEED WITNESSES as follows:

1. The assignor, as claimant, hereby transfers to the assignee ALL the several debts or sums of money specified in the third column of the schedule hereto which are owing to the assignor from the several persons whose names are respectively set opposite to the said debts or sums in the

second column of the said schedule and all other sums, if any, due and owing to the assignor from the said several persons and the benefit of all securities for the same and all interest, if any, due and to become due for the debts respectively TO HOLD the same to the assignee absolutely but upon trust to collect the said debts and sums of money and out of the moneys so realized to pay the costs, charges, and expenses of collection and out of the balance to retain and pay himself the said sum of Rs. —— with such further interest as may become due and to pay the surplus (*if any*) to the assignor.

2. The assignor covenants with the assignee that the said debts hereby assigned are still due and owing to the assignor from the several persons named in the said schedule.

IN WITNESS WHEREOF, etc.

The schedule herein referred to

Serial No.	Names of Debtors	Amount due on Date of this Deed	Nature of Debt
1	2	3	4

5—Assignment of Decree obtained by Assignor Benami for Assignee[1]

THIS AGREEMENT is made, etc. (*as in Form* 1).

WHEREAS the assignor instituted in the court of ——— a suit against XY, etc., being original suit No. ——— of ——— and obtained a decree for Rs. ——— and costs;

AND WHEREAS the assignee was the real beneficial owner of the amount claimed in the said suit and the assignor was only a *benamidar* for her;

AND WHEREAS the assignee cannot execute the decree without a deed of assignment from the decree holder, the assignor has agreed to assign the said decree to the assignee.

NOW THIS DEED WITNESSES as follows:

1. In consideration of the premises the assignor hereby assigns to the

1 Entering into any benami transactions is now made a punishable offence and no property held benami is now recoverable by suit: Secs. 3 and 4 Benami Transactions (Prohibition) Act 1988. The only exceptions are purchases of property in the name of the wife or the unmarried daughters, in which case it shall be presumed, unless the contrary is proved, that the property had been purchased for the benefit of the latter: Rebti Devi v. Ram Dutt, (1997) 11 SCC 714. The prohibition is not retrospective: *R. Rajgopal* v. *Padmani,* AIR 1996 SC 238. Also see *C. Gangacharan* v. *C. Narayanan*, AIR 2000 SC 589 (Defendant held to be trustee and not Benamidar).

assignee ALL the benefits and advantages of the said decree full particulars of which are given in the schedule hereto together with the decretal debts due under the said decree and future interest that may be due thereunder and all the rights and interest of the assignor as decree-holder under the said decree TO HOLD the same to the assignee absolutely.

2. The assignor hereby covenants with the assignee that the said decree is in full force and effect, and that the whole of the sum due under the said decree remains owing thereunder.

IN WITNESSES WHEREOF, etc.

The schedule herein referred to

Particulars of the decree hereby assigned

(a) Name of court passing the decree

(b) Name of decree-holder

(c) Name of judgment-debtors

(d) No. of case

(e) Date of decree

Amount due:

Amount mentioned in the decree (including principal money, interest and costs)

Execution costs

Future interest upto—(*date of Assignment Deed*)

6—Assignment of a Final Decree for Sale under Order 34, Rule 5, C.P.C.

THIS AGREEMENT is made, etc. (*as in Form* 1).

WHEREAS the assignor obtained a preliminary decree in suit No. ——— of ——— under Order 34, Rule 4, C.P.C. for sale of certain property specified in the said decree against ——— from the court of ———.

AND WHEREAS on the basis of the said decree the assignor has obtained a final decree under Order 34, Rule 5, C.P.C. for sale of the said property and has put the said final decree in execution;

AND WHEREAS the assignor has agreed to assign and the assignee has agreed to purchase the aforesaid final decree with all the rights and interest of the assignor thereunder for a consideration of Rs. ———.

NOW THIS DEED WITNESSES as follows:

1. In pursuance of the aforesaid agreement and in consideration of the sum of Rs. ———— paid by the assignee to the assignor before or at the time of execution of these presents (the receipt of which the assignor hereby acknowledges) the assignor hereby assigns to the assignee ALL the benefits and advantages of the final decree full particulars of which are given in the schedule hereto together with the decretal debt due under the said decree and future interest that may be due under the same and all the rights and interests of the assignor as decree-holder under the said decree TO HOLD the same to the assignee absolutely.

2. The assignor hereby covenants with the assignee that the said decree is in full force and effect, and that the whole of the sum due under the said decree remains owing thereunder.

IN WITNESS WHEREOF, etc.

The schedule herein referred to

Particulars of the decree hereby assigned;

(*a*) Name of court passing the decree;

(*b*) Name of the decree-holder;

(*c*) Name of judgment-debtor;

(*d*) No. of case;

(*e*) Date of decree;

Amount due

Amount mentioned in the decree (including principal money, interest and costs)

Execution costs

Future interest upto—(*date of Assignment Deed*)

7—Assignment of a Life Policy[1]

THIS ASSIGNMENT is made, etc. (*as in Form* 1).

WHEREAS by a policy of assurance issued by the Life Insurance Corporation of India dated the —— day of ——— and numbered —— the sum of Rs. ———— is assured to be paid on the death of the assignor subject to the payment of the annual premium of Rs. ———.

1 This is permitted by Sec. 38 (1) Insurance Act: either by a separate instrument as in this or in the next precedent, or by endorsement as in the precedent No. 9 *post*. In either case attestation by at least one witness is necessary. Re.: assignment of marine insurance policy, see *New India Assurance Co*.v. *G.N. Sainani*, (1997) 6 SCC 383) (Secs. 52 and 53, Marine Insurance Act 1963), (The policy can be assigned before or after the loss but the assignee must have an insurable interest in the subject matter). Also see precedents under MORTGAGE, *post*.

AND WHEREAS the assignor has agreed with the assignee for the sale to him of the said policy for the price of Rs. ———

NOW THIS DEED WITNESSES as follows:

1. In consideration of Rs. ——— now paid by the assignee to the assignor (the receipt of which is hereby acknowledged) the assignor (as beneficial owner) hereby assigns to the assignee the aforesaid policy of assurance and all moneys assured by or to become payable under or by virtue thereof TO HOLD the same to the assignee absolutely subject to the payment of all future premiums thereon.

2. The assignor covenants with the assignee that the said policy is now valid and in force, and that he will not do/omit or knowingly suffer anything whereby the said policy may become void or voidable or the assignee be prevented from receiving the moneys thereby assured or any bonus or addition thereto.[1]

8—Assignment[2] of Life Policy for Love and Affection

THIS AGREEMENT, etc. (*as in Form* 1).

WHEREAS by a policy of assurance (*as in Form* 7).

AND WHEREAS the assignor had agreed to assign the said policy to the assignee who is the assignor's wife in consideration of his love and affection for her and the assignee has accepted the said assignment.

NOW THIS DEED WITNESSES as follows:

1. In consideration of the love and affection which the assignor has for the assignee, the assignor (as beneficial owner) hereby assigns to the assignee the aforesaid policy of assurance and all moneys assured by or to become payable under or by virtue thereof TO HOLD the same to the assignee absolutely.

2. *Same as in para* 2 *of Form* 7.

IN WITNESS WHEREOF, etc.

---

1 This covenant should be in the negative form. A positive covenant to do and perform all acts necessary for continuing the policy caused trouble when the assignor committed suicide and it was held that as he had not agreed not to do any act so as to make the policy void but had agreed only to do all necessary acts, there was no breach and the assignor's estate was not liable for damages (*Dormay* v. *Borrodail*, (1847) 10 Beav. 335).

2 Mere nomination does not confer title on the nominee. He or she gets only a right to collect the amount due, but the heirs of the deceased can thereafter recover it from the nominee (*Smt. Shobha Sharma* v. *Narain Keshav*, 1978 ALR 586). A bequest or assigment, on the other hand, confers title.

9—Assignment of Policy by Endorsement[1]

I, AB, etc., in consideration of natural love and affection for CD, etc., hereby assign absolutely to the said CD, the within written policy of assurance dated the ———.

Signed ——————

10—Assignment of Patents[2]

THIS ASSIGNMENT of, etc. (*as in Form* 1).

WHEREAS the assignor has invented a process for the manufacture of ——— which was duly registered and entered in the Register of Patents at No ——— on ——— and duly sealed in the Patent Office at ——— and whereas by an agreement dated ——— between the parties to this deed, it has been agreed that the assignor should assign all his rights and interest in the patent above mentioned in favour of the assignee for a consideration of Rs. ———.

NOW THIS DEED WITNESSES as follows:

1. That in consideration of the sum of Rs. ——— paid by the assignee to the assignor (the receipt of which the assignor hereby acknowledges) the assignor, as beneficial and sole owner, hereby assigns to the assignee his title to the said patent and all benefits, rights, privileges and advantages accruing from and pertaining to the said patent TO HOLD the same absolutely.

2. That the assignor covenants that he has not assigned or otherwise dealt with the said patent, and that his title to the said patent subsists, and that nothing has been done to prejudice the rights of the assignee as transferee of the patent to use it exclusively

3. The assignor further covenants that if at any time or times while the said patent is in force, he shall discover, invent or make any improvement or improvements upon the said invention, he shall disclose the same to the assignee and enable the assignee to make such practical use of such method and discovery and do all other acts and execute all such deeds as may be

---

1 As also permitted by section 38(1), Insurance Act, 1938.

2 Under section 68 Patents Act, 1970 a bilateral agreement in writing is necessary. Its registration with the Controller of Patents, Designs and Trade Marks, is also compulsory. On assignment of trade marks, see sections 37 to 45 Trade Marks Act, 1999. Under section 19 of the Copyright Act, 1957 a copyright may be assigned only by in writing which may or may not be bilateral, i.e., it may be executed by the assignor alone. The above form can be adapted mutatis mutandis for assignment of trade mark or copyright as well. (See also precedents under Intellectual Property Rights, post.)

necessary for vesting in the assignee all rights, title and interest in the new invention or improvement and the full and exclusive benefit thereof.

IN WITNESS WHEREOF, etc.

11—Assignment of Registered Trademarks

THIS ASSIGNMENT made on the ———day of ——— between ——— (Registered Proprietor or First Party) and ——— (Registered User or Second party) for the formal recordal of Second Party in the records of the Trademark Registry, as the Registered User of the Trademarks specified below, under the terms of this Agreement.

Whereas, the First Party and Second Party are jointly referred to as Parties.

Whereas, the First Party coined, adopted and is the owner of the trademarks ——— with Trademark Registration No. —— in class —— (hereinafter referred to as the "Trademark").

A printout from the status page of the Trademark Registry is enclosed with this agreement as Annexure A.

Whereas the purpose of this Agreement is to formally appoint the Second Party as a Registered User of the Trademarks;

NOW, THIS DEED WITNESSES, AND THE PARTIES HERETO AGREE AND DECLARE AS FOLLOWS:

1. That the Second Party acknowledges the First Party as the proprietor/owner of the Trademarks;

2. That the First Party seeks to appoint the Second Party as the Registered User of the Trademarks in accordance with section 49 of the Trade Marks Act 1999 and rule 86 of the Rules framed thereunder;

3. That the First Party permits the Second Party to file requisite documents, permissions and applications before the Registrar Trademark, to bring itself on the record of the Trademark Registry as a Registered User of the said Trademarks;

4. The Second Party affirms that it will not alter, obscure, cancel or otherwise interfere with the Trademarks in any manner so as to negatively affect or diminish the rights of the First Party in the Trademarks;

5. That as consideration for the registration as a Registered User, the Second Party shall pay the First Party Rs. —— per annum, with an increase of 10 % every year from the date of signing this instrument;

6. The said Agreement will be deemed effective from the date on which representatives of both Parties sign on the present Agreement;

7. That this agreement shall be valid for 10 years from the date of its signing;

8. That the First Party may terminate this agreement after the expiry of 5 years, by giving a notice in writing to the Second Party, who, upon termination of this Agreement, shall stop representing itself as the Registered User of the Trademarks of the Second Party;

9. The Parties agree that any dispute arising out of this Agreement shall be governed by and interpreted in accordance with the laws of India and the Courts of Delhi shall have exclusive jurisdiction.

IN WITNESS WHEREOF, etc.

12—Assignment of Business and Its Goodwill

THIS ASSIGNMENT, etc. (*as in Form* 1).

WHEREAS the assignor has been carrying on the business of manufacturing electrical equipment for some years past and has earned a goodwill and established a reputation and business connections with various other firms and persons and the assets and liabilities of the said business are as mentioned in the schedule annexed hereto.

AND WHEREAS the assignee has agreed to take the business of the assignor as a running concern along with its goodwill, obligations and outstandings for a consideration of Rs. ———.

NOW THIS DEED WITNESSES as follows:

1. That in pursuance of the said agreement and in consideration of the sum of Rs. ——— paid to the assignor (the receipt of which the assignor hereby acknowledges) the assignor hereby assigns to the assignee:

(*i*) the goodwill of the business;

(*ii*) all the rights, privileges, advantages, and benefits arising out of all pending contracts and engagements;

(*iii*) all debts and outstandings mentioned in the schedule annexed and all other sums which are or may be found due to the assignor in connection with the business;

(*iv*) stock-in-trade, furniture, fixtures of the business;

(*v*) trade-mark in respect of ———.

TO HOLD the same absolutely. The assignor has no right or interest of any kind left in the same.

2. The assignee hereby covenants that he shall pay and discharge all debts, liabilities and outgoings of the said business up to this day and will at

all times keep harmless and indemnified the assignor and his estate and effects from and against all proceedings, costs, claims, expenses and liabilities whatsoever in respect thereof.

3. The assignor hereby covenants and assures the assignee that he shall assist the assignee in claiming and realizing the debts and outstandings of the business and in explaining any items in the account books so as to support any lawful claim in respect of the said debts and outstandings.

IN WITNESS WHEREOF, etc.

13—Assignment of Arrears of House Rent

THIS ASSIGNMENT, etc. (*as in Form* 1).

WHEREAS AB is the owner/landlord of house ——— (*give full description of the house, its boundaries and Number, if any, along with its situation in street mohalla, etc.*). And GH is the tenant from month to month under a lease or rent note dated ——— and is in occupation of the said house at a monthly rent of Rs. ——— payable on ——— day of every month.

WHEREAS the said GH has not paid the rent of the said house for a period commencing from ——— and ending on ——— inspite of repeated demands and a written notice dated ———. The amount of the past rent due comes to Rs. ———.

NOW THIS DEED WITNESSES as follows:

In consideration of Rs. ——— paid by the said assignee CD (the receipt of which is hereby acknowledged) the assignor AB hereby assigns to the said assignee CD the right to recover Rs. ——— due as arrears of rent from the said tenant GH. The said assignee has and shall have all the rights to recover the said arrears of rent with interest and appropriate the same to his use.

IN WITNESS WHEREOF, etc.

ATTORNEY, POWER OF

Preliminary Note

Power of Attorney

A power of attorney is an instrument empowering a specified person or persons to act for and in the name of the person executing it. If the appointment is made for a specified act or acts, the deed is called "special power of attorney". If it is made generally for certain acts, it is called "general power of attorney". When appointment is made by a deed, the deed is termed as a "power of attorney".

By reason of a deed of power of attorney, an agent is formally appointed to act for the principal in one transaction or a series of transactions or to manage the affairs of the principal generally conferring necessary authority upon another person. A deed of power of attorney is executed by the principal in favour of the agent. The agent derives a right to use his name and all acts, deeds and things done by him and subject to the limitations contained in the said deed, the same shall be read as if done by the executor/principal.[1] Except in cases where power of attorney is coupled with interest, it is revocable. An attorney holder may however execute a deed of conveyance in exercise of the power granted under the power of attorney and convey title on behalf of the grantor. He cannot use the power of attorney for his own benefit. He acts in a fiduciary capacity.

Agent and Principal

An "agent" is a person employed to do any act for another, or to represent another in dealings with third persons.

The person for whom such act is done, or who is so represented, is called the "principal".

But, every person who acts for another is not an agent. For example, a domestic servant rendering service to his master, a personal service, is not an agent. Only when a person acts as a representative of the other in creation, modification or termination of contractual obligations, between the other and the third persons, that such a person is an agent.

For rights and liabilities of Agents, See Chap X, Contract Act.

Who can Execute Power of Attorney or employ an Agent

A power of attorney can be executed by any person who is competent to contract. Sec.183 of Contract Act provides that any person, who is of the age of

---

1 *State of Rajasthan* v. *Basant Nahata*, AIR 2005 SC 3401, MANU/SC/0547/ 2005

majority, according to the law to which he is subject, and who is of sound mind, may employ an agent.

Significantly, no consideration is necessary for creation of an agency.

Agency may be implied from the conduct or the relationship between the parties. [1]

Law also provides for creation of sub-agency. A person appointed by and acting under the control of the original agent in the business of the agency is a sub-agent. (Sec.191 of Contract Act).

Delegation would be improper when not authorised and as a result the principal would not be bound by the appointment. Such a person would also not be responsible to the principal. However, agent would be responsible to the principal for any act of such a person to whom delegation was improperly made, the reason being that agent would be the principal towards such a person-a sub agent.

A person who is a sub-agent, is not liable to account to the principal except in very limited circumstances.[2] The sub-agent is responsible for his acts to the agent, but not to the principal, except in case of fraud or wilful wrong.

Partners

If a firm intends to confer any of the following powers to a partner, a power of attorney from all the partners of the firm, will be needed, conferring on him such authority, because the implied authority of partner does not extend to the following, in absence of any usage or custom of trade to the contrary, section 19(1) of the Partnership Act.

(*a*) submit a dispute relating to business of the firm to arbitration;

(*b*) open a banking account on behalf of the firm in his own name;

(*c*) compromise or relinquish any claim or portion of a claim by the firm;

(*d*) withdraw a suit or proceeding filed on behalf of the firm;

(*e*) admit any liability in a suit or proceeding against the firm;

(*f*) acquire immovable property on behalf of the firm;

(*g*) transfer immovable property belonging to the firm; or

(h) enter into partnership on behalf of the firm.

Form of Deed

A power of attorney is executed in the form of a deed poll, usually in the first person and begins either as—"KNOW all men by these presents that I, etc.", or "BY this power of attorney I, etc." The operative words making the appointment are generally introduced directly without any recitals. If recitals become necessary, they should be added after the words "KNOW all men by these presents" thus "That Whereas, etc.," and after recitals the operative part is introduced thus "Now I, the said AB, etc., hereby appoint, etc.," or the deed may be drafted with the heading

---

1 *S.V.R. Mudaliar* v. *Rajabu F. Buhari*, AIR 1995 SC 1607.

2 *Banwari Mukunda Das* v. *Pramatha Nath Bhattacharya*, 1937 SCC OnLine Cal 157.

"THIS POWER OF ATTORNEY is made on the, etc.," then adding the recitals; the operative part is introduced thus "Now this deed witnesses that I appoint, etc."

The powers conferred on the attorney are specifically stated after the appointment, usually in separate paragraphs. Then follows a clause agreeing to adopt the acts and deeds of the attorney and to ratify them. The scope of authority conferred on such an agent is limited to the express terms of the document and in case some ambiguity arises, it may be resolved, from what the terms imply. The purpose of such authority may be looked into to interpret any general terms or words. If there are recitals showing the scope and object of the power, such recitals may be taken to control the general terms in the operative part of the deed.

In drafting the clauses about special powers, great care should therefore be exercised, as a power of attorney is always strictly construed.[1]

An authority given to settle, liquidate or adjust all accounts has been held not to include a power to refer disputes to arbitration. Where, however, a power of wide amplitude has been expressly given in one part of the instrument it cannot be cut down merely because there are ambiguous and uncertain expressions elsewhere.[2] Other rules of interpretation of powers of attorney have already been noticed in the *Introduction,* Part IV *ante*.

Several Attorneys

If several persons are appointed, it is desirable to provide whether they are to act jointly or severally, for in the absence of an express provision authorizing them to act severally, they will be entitled only to act *jointly*.

Duration of Power

Unless expressly or impliedly limited for a particular period, a general power of attorney continues in force until expressly revoked or determined by death of either party. A power of attorney is also automatically revoked if either party becomes insolvent or of unsound mind.

A special power to do an act is determined when the act is done. If it is desired that the power should continue for a particular period or until a certain event happens, an express provision to that effect should be made.

Any person making any payment or doing any act in good faith in pursuance of a power of attorney, shall not be liable in respect of the payment or act, by reason that before the payment or act, the donor of the power had died or become of unsound mind or insolvent or had revoked the power, if the fact of death, unsoundness of mind, insolvency or revocation was not, at the time of payment or act, known to the person making or doing the same.[3]

An irrevocable-power of attorney can also be executed, but the same would

---

1 *Ramanathan* v. *Kumarappa*, AIR 1940 Mad 650; *Syndicate Bank* v. *I.K. Amitha*, AIR 1985 Kant 213.

2 *Syed Abdul Khader* v. *Rami Reddy*, AIR 1979 SC 553 (para 17), (1979) 2 SCC 601.

3 Sec. 3 Powers of Attorney Act, 1882.

be confined to cases where the agent is personally interested in the subject matter of the agency. Such an authority is coupled with interest and cannot, in the absence of an express contract, be terminated to the prejudice of such interest (Sec. 202 Contract Act).

The reason why any power of attorney given for consideration does not lapse after the death of the principal who has executed the same is because once consideration has been received by a person which is a subject matter of the power of attorney, and such interest is created in favour of the agent, agent should not be prejudiced because of the death of the principal inasmuch as the principal has received whatever benefits/consideration which had to be received under the power of attorney.[1]

Irrevocable powers of attorney are also made in respect of so called "Power of Attorney Sales" or "GPA Sales". However, the Apex Court has observed that it is time that an end is put to the pernicious practice of SA/GPA/WILL (Special Power of Attorney/General Power of Attorney/WILL) transactions known as GPA sales. It noted that the observations by the Delhi High Court, in *Asha M. Jain* v. *Canara Bank*[2] that the "concept of power of attorney sales have been recognized as a mode of transaction" when dealing with transactions by way of SA/GPA/WILL are unwarranted and not justified, unintended misleading the general public into thinking that SA/GPA/WILL transactions are some kind of a recognized or accepted mode of transfer and that it can be a valid substitute for a sale deed. Such decisions to the extent they recognize or accept SA/GPA/WILL transactions as concluded transfers, as contrasted from an agreement to transfer, are not good law. It further noted that Transactions of the nature of 'GPA sales' or 'SA/GPA/WILL transfers' do not convey title and do not amount to transfer, nor can they be recognized or valid mode of transfer of immovable property. The immovable property can be legally and lawfully transferred/conveyed only by a registered deed of conveyance.[3]

The Apex Court clarified that their observations are not intended to in any way affect the validity of sale agreements and powers of attorney executed in genuine transactions. For example, a person may give a power of attorney to his spouse, son, daughter, brother, sister or a relative to manage his affairs or to execute a deed of conveyance. A person may enter into a development agreement with a land developer or builder for developing the land either by forming plots or by constructing apartment buildings and in that behalf execute an agreement of sale and grant a Power of Attorney empowering the developer to execute agreements of sale or conveyances in regard to individual plots of land or undivided shares in the land relating to apartments in favor of prospective purchasers. In several States, the

---

1 *Smt. Sudershana Kumari Blagan* v. *Smt. Tulsan Devi Decd Thru LRs*, 2014 SCC OnLine Del 6702

2 94 (2001) DLT 841, MANU/DE/1304/2001.

3 *Suraj Lamp and Industries Pvt. Ltd.* v. *State of Haryana*, AIR 2012 SC 206, 2011 (107) AIC 1, MANU/SC/1222/2011.

execution of such development agreements and powers of attorney are already regulated by law and subjected to specific stamp duty. Their observations regarding 'SA/GPA/WILL transactions' are not intended to apply to such bonafide/genuine transactions. See, e.g., Form No. 13 and 14, *post*, and also see footnote under Form No. 9, *post*.[1]

Authentication and Registration

Power of attorney need not be attested or registered, but if it gives authority to present a document for registration under section 32 of the Registration Act, it must be executed before, and authenticated by, the Registrar or Sub-Registrar, or where the Registration Act is not in force, before any Magistrate, or if it is executed outside India, before a Notary Public or any Court, Judge, Magistrate, Indian Consul or Vice-Consul or representative of Central Government (section 33, Registration Act).

In *Suraj Lamps and Industries (P) Ltd.* v. *State of Haryana*,[2] Supreme Court held that a transaction by way of set of documents consisting of Special Power of Attorney or General Power of Attorney or Will does not convey any title nor creates any interest in an immovable property. It further reiterated that immovable property can be legally and lawfully transferred/conveyed only by a registered deed of conveyance. They cannot be recognised as deeds of title, except to the limited extent of Section 53-A of the Transfer of Property Act. Such transactions cannot be relied upon or made the basis for mutations in municipal or revenue records.

Stamp Duty

Subject to States variations, stamp duty on Power of Attorney is governed by Article 48 of the Schedule 1 to the Stamp Act.

---

1 Section 3, Power of Attorney Act, 1882.

2 AIR 2012 SC 206, 2011 (107) AIC 1.

PRECEDENTS

1—General Clauses of Power of Attorney giving Different Kinds of Authority

[*Any one or more of these clauses may, where necessary, and with necessary modifications, be embodied in any power of attorney*].

1. To Collect Debts

To demand, sue for, enforce payment of, and receive and give effectual receipt and discharge of, all moneys, securities for money, debts and legacies which I now possess or to which I am now entitled or which I may possess or to which I may become entitled or which are or may become due owing, payable or transferable to me from any person or persons.

2. To Receive a Sum of Money

To receive from XY the sum of Rs. ——— which is due to me from him on account of ——— and to give receipt for the same.

3. To Acquire Lands, etc.

From time to time to purchase, take on lease or mortgage or otherwise acquire and hold all such houses, buildings and lands, as shall be thought necessary or expedient for, or in relation to, any of the purposes or objects aforesaid.

4. To Borrow Money

To borrow from time to time such sums of money and on such terms as the said attorney (*or* attorneys) may think expedient for or in relation to any of the purposes or objects aforesaid upon my personal security or the security of any of my property or otherwise or for such purposes, to give, execute and make such mortgages, charges, pledges or other securities with such covenants, powers, and permission as he (they) may think fit and proper subject to the condition that at no time the total amount of the debts borrowed by the said attorney (*or* attorneys) as aforesaid shall be allowed to exceed the limit of Rs. ———.

5. To Manage Trust, Estate

To sell, convert, collect, enter upon or manage or collect or otherwise administer any property movable or immovable which may be vested in me alone or jointly with any other person as a trustee, executor or administrator and to execute and sign any deeds and generally to do any acts which I could lawfully have executed, signed and done in any such capacity.

6. To Let Out Houses and Collect Rents

To collect rents from tenants of houses, shops, plots and compounds belonging to me and to give receipts for the same and to eject tenants from and settle new tenants in the said houses, shops, plots and compounds whenever he considers to be in my interest and to take all necessary legal steps which may be in my interest and which may be required for the purpose.

7. To Appoint Agents and Servants

To appoint and employ any agents, *karindas*, peons or other servants necessary for any of the purposes aforesaid at such remuneration, commission or salary as the said attorney may think proper and from time to time to dismiss or discharge such agents, etc., and to appoint or employ others in their places.

8. To Sell Property

To sell with my permission and consent for proper and adequate consideration any part of my property, to receive the price thereof and to grant receipt or effectual discharge for the same, and to execute and sign and get registered the sale deeds and other deeds necessary to complete the sale.

9. To Sell Goods

To sell and convert into money any goods or things which now belong or at any time or times hereafter shall belong to me.

10. To Draw Bills, etc.

To draw, accept, endorse, negotiate, pay or satisfy any bills of exchange, promissory notes, cheques, drafts, *hundis*, orders for payment or delivery of money, securities, goods, bills of lading or other negotiable or mercantile instruments or securities which may be deemed necessary or proper in the course of or in relation to the aforesaid business or affairs.

11. To Execute a Deed

To execute and sign a deed of sale of —— or of mortgage of —— (*describe briefly the nature of the deed*) to secure —— already prepared and written (*or*, intended shortly to be prepared and written) made (*or*, intended to be made) between ——— and ———.

12. To Execute Deeds Generally

To execute and sign all such deeds as shall be required or may be deemed proper for or in relation to all or any of the matters or purposes aforesaid.

13. To Take and Defend Legal Proceedings[1]

To take, prosecute or defend all legal proceedings touching any of the matters aforesaid or any other matters in which I am or may hereafter be interested or concerned and also, if thought fit to compromise, refer to arbitration, withdraw or confess judgment in, any such proceedings as aforesaid.

14. To Settle and Compromise

To state, settle, adjust, compound, submit to arbitration and compromise, all suits or other legal proceedings, accounts, claims and demands whatsoever which now are, or hereafter shall be, pending between me and any person or persons in such manner as the said attorney shall think fit.

15. To Invest or Deposit Money

To invest any of the said moneys in or upon any of the Government securities, bonds, promissory notes, stocks or mutual funds in my own name and from time to time to vary the said investments or any of them into any other of the same or like nature and in the meantime, pending any such investment, to deposit the said moneys or any part thereof in any scheduled bank which the said attorney may think proper.

16. To Vote at Meetings

To vote at the meetings of any company or companies and otherwise to act as my proxy or representative in respect of any shares, stock or debentures now held or which may hereafter be acquired by me and for that purpose to sign and execute any proxies or other instruments in my name and on my behalf.

---

1 An attorney cannot be empowered by an accused person to appear in a criminal case on his behalf if the court requires his personal presence: *T.C. Mathai* v. *Distt. & Sessions Judge*, (1999) 3 SCC 614, AIR 1999 SC 1385.

17. To Appoint Substitutes

From time to time to appoint and remove at pleasure any substitute or substitutes as attorney or agents under him in respect of all or any of the matters aforesaid, upon such terms and on such salaries or remuneration as he shall think fit.

18. Alternative Appointment in case of Inability etc.

AND in case of the death of the said attorney or of his inability or unwillingness through absence, illness or otherwise to act as my attorney in relation to all or any of the matters aforesaid, then I hereby appoint XY, etc., to act as my attorney in place of the said attorney after his death or during such inability or unwillingness and in the latter case either permanently or from time to time during the subsistence of any such inability or unwillingness (*as the case may be*) unless and until this deed shall be revoked or otherwise determined in like manner as if the name of the said XY had been inserted in this deed instead of the name of the said attorney.

19. To Act Generally

Generally to act as my attorney or agent in relation to the matters aforesaid and all other matters in which I may be interested or concerned and on my behalf to execute and do all deeds, acts or things as fully and effectually in all respects as I myself do if personally present.

20. To Ratify Acts

I hereby for myself, my heirs, executors, administrators and legal representatives ratify and confirm and agree to ratify and confirm whatsoever my said attorney shall do or purport to do by virtue of this deed.

21. Keeping alive Previous Power of Attorney

Provided always that this power of attorney shall not revoke or in any manner affect any previous power of attorney given by me to any other person or persons for any purpose but such other power or powers shall remain and be of the same force and effect as if this deed had not been executed.

22. Limiting Duration

Provided always (*or*, Provided also, *if any other proviso is added before*) that this power of attorney shall remain in force for a period of one year only (*or,* until I return from my trip to Europe where I am proceeding shortly).

23. Restriction on Revocability[1]

And I hereby agree that this power of attorney shall be irrevocable for a period of ———.

2—Special Power (for a Court Case)

KNOW ALL MEN BY THESE PRESENTS that (*or*, BY THIS POWER OF ATTORNEY) I, AB, son of CD, resident of ———being defendant in a civil suit No. ——— of ——— pending in the court of the —— do hereby appoint EF son of GH, resident of ——— my attorney in my name and on my behalf to do or execute all or any of the following acts or things in connection with the said suit:

(*i*) To engage or appoint any legal practitioner to conduct the said case;

(*ii*) To sign, verify and file a written statement or an application for amendment thereof;

(*iii*) To make and present to the court an application in connection with any proceedings in the suit ;

(*iv*) To produce or summon or receive back documentary evidence;

(*v*) To make and file compromise or a confession of judgment or to refer the case to arbitration ;

(*vi*) To deposit or withdraw any money for the purpose of any proceeding;

(*vii*) To file an application for execution of a decree or order passed in the said suit and to sign and verify such application;

(*viii*) To receive any money due to me under such decree or order and to certify payment to the court:

(*ix*) To apply for inspection and inspect documents and records ;

(*x*) To obtain copies of documents and papers ; and

(*xi*) Generally to do all other lawful acts necessary for the conduct of the said case.

AND I hereby agree that all acts, deeds and things lawfully done by my said attorney shall be construed as acts, deeds and things done by me and I undertake to ratify and confirm all and whatsoever that my said attorney shall lawfully do or cause to be done for me by virtue of the power hereby given.

IN WITNESS hereof I have signed this deed on this —— day of ——.

---

1 See Preliminary Note, *ante*, under the topic "Duration of Power" for revocability or otherwise of power of attorney.

3—Special Power to Present a Document for Registration

KNOW ALL MEN BY THESE PRESENTS that (*or*, BY THIS POWER OF ATTORNEY), I, AB, etc., do hereby appoint EF, etc., my attorney on my behalf to appear before the Sub-Registrar of ——— district —— and to present for registration the ——— deed dated —— and executed by me in favour of ——— to admit the execution thereof to do any act that may be necessary for the registration of the said document and to receive it back when it has been duly registered and to sign and deliver a proper receipt for the same.

IN WITNESS, etc.

[*This power is necessary only when a deed is executed by the Principal. Where the Principal appoints an attorney to execute a deed either in the name of the Principal or in his own name, on the Principal's behalf and the Attorney executes the deed himself under a power of attorney in Form No. 4, then a power of attorney in this form is not necessary*].

4—Special Power of Attorney to Execute a Sale Deed

KNOW ALL MEN BY THESE PRESENTS that (*or*, BY THIS POWER OF ATTORNEY) I, AB, etc., hereby appoint CD, etc., as my attorney in my name and on my behalf to do or execute all or any of the acts or things which I have to do in pursuance of an agreement dated —— between me and XY and which are hereinafter mentioned, that is to say:

1. To receive from the purchaser or his heirs or assigns the sum of Rs. ——— being the price agreed to be paid to me by XY for the purchase of (*description of property*) under an agreement dated the ———and to give an effectual receipt and discharge for the same;

2. To execute a proper sale deed of the said property or any other deed or assurance necessary for the completion of the sale of such property and to get the same duly registered;

AND I hereby agree, etc. (*as in Form* 2).

IN WITNESS, etc.

5—General Power of Attorney[1]

KNOW ALL MEN BY THESE PRESENTS that I, AB, etc., appoint EF, etc., my attorney in my name and on my behalf to execute or do all or any of the acts or things hereinafter mentioned, that is to say—

(1) To appear and act in all the courts, civil, revenue or criminal, whether original or appellate, in the registration offices and in any other office of Government or District Board, Municipal Board or any other local authority;

(2) To sign and verify plaints, written statements, petitions of claims and objections, memoranda of appeals and petitions and applications of all kinds and file them in any such court or office;

(3) To appoint any advocate or any other legal practitioner;

(4) To compromise, compound or withdraw cases, to confess judgments and to refer cases to arbitration;

(5) To file and receive back documents, to deposit and withdraw money, and to grant receipts therefor;

(6) To obtain refund of stamp duty or repayment of court fees;

(7) To purchase property at court auction-sales in execution of my decrees up to the amount of the decree;

(8) To take delivery or possession of property in execution of my decrees or of property purchased for me at an auction-sale;

(9) To realize debts due to me, to collect rents from my tenants of houses and land and to receive any money due to me from any other person and to grant receipts and discharges for the same;

(10) To distrain the crops of my tenants for arrears of rent;

(11) To grant leases of my house property, lands agricultural and non-agricultural;

(12) To file suits for rent and ejectment of tenants, and, when expressly instructed by me, other kinds of suits;

(13) To apply to courts and officers for copies of documents and papers;

---

1 The common law principle that "every person who is *sui juris* has a right to appoint an agent for any purpose whatsoever, and he can do so when he is exercising statutory right no less than when he is exercising any other right" does not apply "where the act to be performed is personal in character, or when it is annexed to a public office or to an office involving any fiduciary obligation": *T.C. Mathai* v. *Distt. Judge*, (1999) 3 SCC 614 (para 14), AIR 1999 SC 1385.

(14) To apply for the inspection of and to inspect judicial records;

(15) To accept service of any summons, notice or writ issued by any court or officer against me; and

(16) Generally to do all lawful acts necessary for the above mentioned purposes.

(For forms of other clauses to be inserted, see General Clauses, ante.)

Provided that the powers hereby conferred shall not extend to:

(*a*) granting of an agricultural lease for a term over ——— years or reserving a yearly rent exceeding Rs. ———;

(*b*) granting of a lease of house property for a term over ——— years or reserving a monthly rent exceeding Rs. ———;

(*c*) compromising or withdrawing a claim valued at more than Rs. ——— or involving property of a value exceeding Rs. ———.

(*d*) borrowing any money or hypothecating any property or creating any charge thereon.

AND I hereby agree, etc. (*as in Form* 2).

IN WITNESS, etc.

6—General Power of Attorney for Trademarks

KNOW ALL MEN BY THESE PRESENTS that I, AB, etc., do hereby appoint CD, etc., my attorney in my name and on my behalf, in connection with my trademarks, to execute or do all or any of the acts or things hereinafter mentioned, that is to say:

(1) filing of applications for registration, opposition, rectification, registered users, renewals, restorations, assignments;

(2) applying for legal proceedings certificates;

(3) in connection with any proceedings under the Trade Marks Act and rules framed thereunder, before the Registrar of Trademarks or the Government of India;

(4) all the acts deeds and things, including the appointment of substitutes, as the said Attorney may deem necessary or expedient in connection therewith or incidental thereto;

(5) to take all necessary action for registration and protection of my rights as elucidated above, directly as attorney or through any agent;

(6) to accept service of any summons, notice issued to me by Trade Marks Registry or the Government of India, in connection with my trademarks.

AND I hereby agree, etc., (as in form 2)

7—Appointment of One Attorney in Place of Another[1]

KNOW ALL MEN, etc.

WHEREAS by a power of attorney dated ——— I, AB, etc., appointed CD, etc., as my attorney and gave him certain powers and authorities specified therein with the restrictions and limitations therein mentioned.

AND WHEREAS I am now desirous of appointing EF, etc., as my attorney in place of the said CD, etc.

NOW I hereby revoke all and singular the powers and authorities given by me to said CD, etc., by virtue of the power of attorney dated ——.

AND further I hereby appoint the said EF as my attorney in my name and on my behalf to do all acts and exercise all the powers and authorities mentioned in the aforesaid power of attorney dated ——— with such restrictions and limitations as are mentioned therein, in as effectual a manner as if the name of the said EF had been inserted in the said power of attorney in place of the said CD.

AND I hereby agree that all acts, deeds and things lawfully done by the said EF for me under powers hereby given to him shall be construed as acts, deeds and things done by me and I undertake to ratify and confirm all and whatsoever the said EF shall lawfully do or cause to be done for me by virtue of the powers given by this deed.

IN WITNESS, etc.

8—Deed Giving Further Powers to Attorney

KNOW ALL MEN, etc.

WHEREAS I, AB, etc., have by power of attorney dated the —— appointed CD as my attorney with the powers therein contained AND whereas I am desirous of giving the said CD further powers and authorities hereinafter contained.

---

1 When the authority of an attorney is revoked, it is appropriate to issue to him a notice of revocation and ask him to refrain from doing anything in pursuance of the revoked power of attorney. A public notice may also be published to safeguard the principal's interest.

NOW I, the said AB hereby give to, and vest in, the said CD the following further powers and authorities, that is to say, in my name or on my behalf to do the following acts:

1. ———————

2. ———————

3. ———————

Provided always that nothing herein contained shall in any way prejudice or affect the powers or authorities given or conferred by the aforesaid power of attorney and this power of attorney shall take effect and be in force concurrently with and solely by way of extension and enlargement of the aforesaid power of attorney.

IN WITNESS, etc.

9—Irrevocable Power Coupled with Interest[1] (executed by debtor in favour of Creditor Bank)

KNOW ALL MEN, etc.

WHEREAS I, AB, etc., am very heavily indebted to CD Bank and my liability is partly secured by the pledge of my goods and partly by the equitable mortgage of my immovable properties with the said Bank ;

AND WHEREAS a major part of my said liability is unsecured;

AND WHEREAS I have agreed to appoint CD Bank to be my true and lawful attorney to execute decree in suit No. ——— of ——— and to do the following acts, deeds, matters and things for me, on my behalf and in my name and to credit to my account the sum or sums which may be realised in execution of or under the said decree;

NOW KNOW ALL MEN BY THESE PRESENTS that I do hereby irrevocably constitute, nominate and appoint the said CD Bank and/or any principal officers and/or any other person or persons that may be appointed by the said CD Bank or its assigns from time to time in this behalf to be my true and lawful attorney for me and on my behalf and in my name to represent me therein and do all acts, deeds, matters and things in connection with the execution of the said decree, that is to say:

1. To proceed in execution of the said decree and to proceed to realise and recover the decretal amount.

---

1 Mere description of power of attorney as irrevocable is not conclusive. It will be irrevocable only if it is coupled with interest. Mere right to earn commission is not an interest rendering a grant of authority irrevocable. *(M. John Kotaiah* v. *A. Divakar*, AIR 1985 AP 30). See Sec. 202 Contract Act and Preliminary Note, *ante*, (Duration of Power).

2. To withdraw any amount that may be deposited in any court in the said decree and /or other proceedings in connection with the execution of the said decree or any other order passed or made therein and /or in any Insolvency Court or from the Official Receiver concerning Insolvency of any of the defendants.

10—General Powers of Attorney in connection with Company's Contract Business[1]

KNOW ALL MEN BY THESE PRESENTS THAT we ——— a Company within the meaning of the Companies Act, 1956/2013 having its registered office at ———— send greetings.

WHEREAS we are engaged in the business of manufacturing and supplying of ——— and other equipments to various parties,

AND WHEREAS in course of our said business it is necessary to submit quotations, accept contracts and receive monies from various parties;

AND WHEREAS it has been deemed expedient to appoint some authorised agent for the above purpose;

NOW THEREFORE KNOW ALL MEN that we ——— do hereby nominate, authorise, empower and appoint jointly and severally (one) AB son of CD by occupation one of our Directors residing at —— and (two) EF son of GH by occupation one of our Directors and residing at ——— to be our lawful attorneys and agents jointly and severally for the following purposes namely:

1. In our name and on our behalf to sign all tenders and correspondence relating to any such tender.

2. In our name and on our behalf to accept and execute contracts with any of our customers or prospective customers.

3. In our name and on our behalf to submit bills and receive payments of money due to us and grant valid discharges therefor.

4. In our name and on our behalf to enter into negotiations with any prospective customers and to execute any contract with any customers and if deemed necessary to affix our Common Seal to such or other documents.

---

1 This can be adapted also for powers of attorney executed by a firm, society, co-operative society or other association of persons. So far as a company is concerned, the provisions of Secs. 179, 180 of the Companies Act, 2013 and of the Memorandum and Articles of Association of the Company should also be seen. Further a power of attorney executed on behalf of a company authorising the attorney to execute deeds on its behalf has to bear the common seal of the company (Sec. 22 Companies Act, 2013).

5. In our name and on our behalf to file or make or contest suits or petitions, enter into compromise, refer to arbitration and accept or contest all awards of arbitrators in any matters in which we may or shall be interested.

6. In our name and on our behalf to sign and execute all plaints, written statements, petitions and applications and to sign and subscribe our name thereto.

7. In our name and on our behalf to appoint legal practitioners and other agents for due pursuing of any matters in which we may or shall be interested.

8. In our name and on our behalf to enter into any lawful agreement or contract.

9. In our name and on our behalf to appear before all registering authorities and thereto present for registration and admit execution and otherwise procure valid registration of all documents whether signed by either of them on our behalf.

10. In our name and on our behalf generally to make, do and execute all such acts, deeds and things which either of our said attorneys may or shall deem expedient and lawful for looking after our interest in any matters.

AND we the above named ——— do hereby agree to ratify all such acts, deeds and things to be done by either of our said attorneys AB and EF as if the same were done by us in person.

IN WITNESS WHEREOF, etc.

11—Special Power[1] (for a contract)

KNOW ALL MEN BY THIS POWER OF ATTORNEY THAT we ——— a firm registered under the Partnership Act, 1932 consisting of the partners (1) AB son of CD resident of ———; and (2) EF son of GH resident of ———, hereby appoint and constitute WX son of YZ permanent resident of ——— and at present residing at ——— our lawful attorney.

WHEREAS we ——— have entered into a contract with the Government of ——— detailed below:

1 For appointment of trustees (under a composition with Creditors) as attorney for disposal of the debtor's property, see precedent under TRUSTS, *post*.

(*i*) Details of Contract	Agreement registered in the office of the Superintending Engineer — as Agreement No. ——— of 2004 for the construction of ———
(*ii*) Date of signing of original Contract.	———

AND WHEREAS we ——— have decided to appoint the aforesaid attorney as our lawful attorney for the execution of the said contract.

NOW THEREFORE BY THESE PRESENTS we ——— hereby authorise and empower the said WX as our lawful attorney for us and on our behalf to do the following acts, deeds and things, that is to say:

1. In our name and as our act and deed, to carry out the said contract and to deal with the Government of the State of ———, their officers and other public authorities in matters touching or affecting the said contract or likely to affect or touch the said contract in anyway whatsoever.
2. In our name and as our act and deed, to sign all bills, vouchers, measurement books, accounts and all other papers and documents and instruments in any way concerning or affecting the said contract.
3. To appoint and remove in his absolute discretion any agent in respect of all or any of the matters herein contained upon such terms as he may think fit.
4. To apply for, demand, sue for, recover and receive of and from all and every or any person or persons whomsoever concerned or chargeable therewith all and every sum or sums of money, debts, goods, effects and securities which shall or may belong to or be or become due and payable to us in connection with the said contract.
5. To commence, carry on or defend all acts and other proceedings concerning or touching the said contract. AND to forgo any claims, compound, compromise or submit to arbitration all acts, suits, accounts, claims and disputes between us and any other person or persons in relation to the said contract. And to engage any legal practitioner to appear, plead or act in any case, suit or other proceedings, concerning anything about the said contract.
6. For any of the purposes aforesaid and generally in our name and as our act to draw, endorse and sign any cheque or other negotiable instrument or any investment payable to us and to deposit in and

operate upon the account concerning the said contract at any Bank or elsewhere.

7. AND generally to do, execute and perform all and every other act, matter and thing whatsoever in any way necessary or expedient to be done of every nature or kind arising during the execution of the said contract including completion thereof in all respects as fully and effectually as if We ——— could do it ourselves.

AND WE ——— hereby agree to confirm and ratify all and whatsoever our said attorney or any agents appointed by him under the power in that behalf hereinbefore contained shall lawfully do or cause to be done.

AND WE ——— hereby declare that this power of attorney is executed by us for ——— years from the date hereof and shall not be revocable during the said period except under prior notice thereof to the Government of the State of ———.

IN WITNESS WHEREOF, etc.

12—Power of Attorney required at the time of Incorporation of a Company

We the following Promoters/Subscribers of the ——— (*the proposed Company*) do hereby authorise Sri—— s/o —— r/o ——— to file all papers for registration of the aforesaid Company and to carry out necessary corrections, alterations, amendments in all the documents submitted or to be submitted to the Registrar of Companies, ——— in connection with the registration of the Company. We also hereby declare that all deeds, acts and other things done by him in connection with the registration of the Company shall be binding on us.

Sd/-

Promoters/Subscribers

WITNESS:

13—Irrevocable Power of Attorney in favour of Bank as Security for Financial Accommodation Granted by Bank[1]

KNOW ALL MEN BY THESE PRESENTS (*or*, BY THE POWER OF ATTORNEY) that we ——— a firm registered under the Partnership Act, 1932 consisting of the partners

(1) AB son of CD resident of ———; and

(2) EF son of GH resident of ———, (hereinafter called the Principals) carrying on the business of contractors, send greetings.

WHEREAS we are working as contractors to the Government in its various departments and have entered into certain contracts and will in future enter into other contracts:

AND WHEREAS an arrangement has been made between us and the —— Bank, (hereinafter called the Attorneys) in pursuance of which the attorneys have agreed to finance our contracts and to advance us sums of money against supply bills for payments to be received by us under the contracts issued by the Government in various departments on the conditions inter alia that the attorneys shall have first charge over the cheques in payment of bills and shall also be entitled to realise the amount of the bills direct from the Government and the remittances of such bills will be made direct by the Government to and in name of the attorneys and the attorneys shall repay themselves from such receipts all monies due from us and in consideration of such advances by the attorneys all monies payable to us under the contracts and bills shall be considered under the arrangement as assigned unto the attorneys and we have undertaken not to create any interest, charge, encumbrance or assignment in favour of anyone else over any monies payable or that may become payable to us under the contracts;

AND WHEREAS we, for the purposes of carrying out the terms of the said agreement more effectively and to secure the interest of the attorneys, are desirous of appointing the ——— Bank, as our lawful attorneys;

NOW THEREFORE we do hereby appoint the —— Bank, a corporation established by the—— Act as our lawful attorneys for us, in our name and on our behalf, to do the following acts, deeds and things, that is to say:

---

1 An irrevocable power of attorney in this form and another in the next following form were both the subject of detailed consideration in a three-judge special bench decision in *Miran Bakhsh* v. *Emporer*, AIR 1945 Lah 69 (Stamp Reference). The document was held to be a power of attorney coupled with a mortgage and an agreement, and as such was chargeable under Sec. 5 Stamp Act, with the aggregate amount of duties with which separate instruments, each comprising or relating to one of such distinct matters, would be chargeable.

1. To present and submit supply bills regarding the contracts of the principals to the proper officers, to obtain cheques for sums payable to them under the contracts directly in their own name or in the names of the principals, to cash and receive the amount thereof and to appropriate such receipts towards and in repayment of the advances made or to be made hereafter and all other monies due from the principals to the attorneys in any account whatsoever. No other creditor or representative of ours shall have any concern with such amounts and the payments thereof by the Government, we having undertaken neither to create any encumbrance, interest, charge or assignment over such amounts payable or that may become payable under the contracts taken or to be taken hereafter nor to appoint or authorise any one else to receive payments on our behalf;

2. To ask, demand, sue for, recover and receive, of and from, all and every person all sums of money, which shall or may become due or owing or payable, or that may become payable to the principals under or in connection with the said contracts and to compound and settle all accounts relating to them;

3. To appoint any counsel, lawyer, solicitor or agent to conduct, prosecute or defend in Court or outside Court any claims or actions arising out of the said contracts and to sign all petitions or documents in connection therewith;

4. To execute or sign receipts, acknowledgements and acquittances and sign other documents required for any of the aforesaid purposes on behalf of the principals.

We hereby bind ourselves to allow, ratify and confirm all and whatsoever the attorneys shall lawfully do or cause to be done in execution of the powers given to them. And we further declare that these presents and all powers hereby granted are and shall be irrevocable as long as any claims of the attorneys against us, whether for principal, interest, costs, charges and otherwise, remain outstanding and unpaid.

And we hereby declare and affirm that we have not herebefore created nor shall we in future create any power of attorney in respect of the said contracts in favour of any person or bank and that the monies, bills, dues payable to us or recoverable by us now or in future in respect of the said contracts are free from any prior charge, encumbrance or assignment, of any kind and that we or any person other than the said attorneys shall not have any right to receive, recover, realise the moneys, etc. in respect of the said contracts.

IN WITNESS WHEREOF, etc.

14—Irrevocable Power of Attorney: Another Form

KNOW ALL MEN BY THESE PRESENTS (*or*, BY THIS POWER OF ATTORNEY) that we ——— a firm registered under the Partnership Act, 1932 consisting of the partners

(1) AB son of CD resident of ———, and

(2) EF son of GH resident of ———, (hereinafter called the Principals) carrying on the business of ——— send greetings.

WHEREAS we the said Principals have applied to the ——— Bank for and obtained from it financial accommodations from time to time for the purposes of our aforesaid business.

AND WHEREAS we have requested the said bank to continue the said facilities to us according to their convenience and discretion against the security of ——— and such other things as may be approved by the bank and also against bills submitted by us to the Government Departments and others for goods supplied to them provided we furnish and maintain such margin as may from time to time be fixed by the bank for any or all transactions;

AND WHEREAS the said bank has granted and agreed to continue to grant the said accommodations provided, amongst other things, we vest the said bank with the irrevocable power and discretions as are herein contained;

NOW THEREFORE we do hereby appoint the ——— Bank, a corporation established by the ——— Act (hereinafter called the Attorneys) as our lawful attorneys for us, in our name and on our behalf, to do the following acts, deeds and things, that is to say:

1. To demand and by all legal and effectual means to recover and receive from all and every and any person or persons, firm or firms, corporation or corporations and all other departments of the Government of India and the State Governments all moneys, goods, chattels, which are now and which shall hereafter appear to be due, owing, payable or belonging to us or any moneys or securities for moneys now or hereafter due owing or belonging to us upon any bond or contract, or upon any other account and also to examine, state and settle, all accounts between ourselves and such persons, firms, corporations and Governments, and upon recovery and receipt of any moneys and as our act and deed, from time to time, to sign, execute and deliver such goods and sufficient receipts or other discharges and to do and perform all such other matters and things which may be requisite and on our behalf to sign, execute and deliver any and every deed

or document necessary to constitute the Bank's title to moneys or other property held by the Bank as security;

2. To appoint or substitute in their place from time to time any other attorney and to do all acts, deeds or things which might or could be done by the principals themselves;

And we the principals hereby declare that the principals shall allow, ratify and confirm all and whatsoever the attorneys shall lawfully do or cause to be done, and further that everything which the attorneys shall do or cause to be done in pursuance of the powers given to them shall be valid and effectual in favour of any person claiming the benefit thereof;

And we further declare that the presents and all powers hereby granted are and shall be irrevocable as long as there be any sums whatever due and unpaid by us to the said Bank in respect of advances made by them to us.

IN WITNESS WHEREOF, etc.

BOND

Preliminary Note

A bond is an instrument by which a person obliges himself to pay money or deliver grain or other agricultural produce to another. In section 2(5) Stamp Act, bond is defined as including:

"(*a*) any instrument whereby a person obliges himself to pay money to another, on condition that the obligation shall be void if specified act is performed, or is not performed, as the case may be;[1]

(*b*) any instrument attested by a witness and not payable to order or bearer, whereby a person obliges himself to pay money to another; and

(*c*) any instrument so attested, whereby a person obliges himself to deliver grain or other agricultural produce to another."

Following essentials of a bond came to be noted by Full Bench of Madhya Pradesh High Court in the matter of *Santsingh* v. *Madandas Gyandas Panika*,[2]

The essential of bond are:—

(1) There must be an undertaking to pay;

(2) The sum should be a sum of money but not necessarily certain;

(3) The payment will be to another person named in the instrument;

(4) The maker should sign it;

(5) The instrument must be attested by a witness; and

(6) It must not be payable to order or bearer.

Full Bench of Delhi High Court in the matter of *Hamdard Dawakhana (Wakf) Delhi reference*, [3] while considering the same issue, held:

> "It is trite to say that every bond is an agreement. So is the case with a mortgage or sale or exchange. But what we have to see is whether that agreement has acquired the character of a "bond".
>
> "The test laid down by the learned Chief Justice for distinguishing a "bond" from an "agreement", is: In the former case, in the event of breach the party to the instrument, who had obliged to pay money to the other, is liable to pay the sum stipulated in the instrument. In the latter case, the quantum of damages has to be fixed by the Court.

---

1 This is also the definition of "bond" in Sec. 2 (d), Limitation Act 1963.

2 1976 MPLJ (FB) 238.

3 AIR 1968 Delhi 1 (FB).

In *Udey* v. *Ram Kishan*,[1] Punjab and Haryana High Court observed that:

"No instrument can be a bond within the meaning of Section 2(5)(b) of the Act unless it is one which itself creates an obligation to pay money. The document admitting receipt of money in absence of express promise to pay, may be held to be a receipt but not a bond. The writing in question does not show that the defendant had undertaken any obligation to pay. More so, no such obligation can be inferred from mere acknowledgement of the receipt of the amount."

There are two kinds of bonds, simple and conditional.

Form

A bond is usually drawn up in the form of deed poll. A conditional bond consists of two essential parts, viz. (1) the obligation, and (2) the condition. Sometimes recitals are introduced between the two parts for the purpose of explanation of the conditions which follow them.

Usually the executant is a debtor who executes the bond in favour of the creditor. However, the sum named in the bond is sometimes intended to be a penalty and sometimes liquidated damages. The question, whether a sum stipulated for in a contract is a penalty or liquidated damages, is a question of law. The intention of the parties is material.[2] When it amounts to a penalty, the obligee is not entitled to recover for the breach of conditions the whole amount but only a reasonable compensation not exceeding such sum (vide Section 74, Contract Act). Therefore, it is advisable to fix the sum for which a bond is taken at the maximum figure to which damages apprehended from the breach can possibly go, as the sum entered in the bond is the maximum which the obligee can claim, even if damages actually incurred are larger.

The bond is usually commenced by saying "By this bond I bind myself, etc." or "THIS bond executed by, etc." If a departure from the usual practice prevailing is intended, then any of the different forms given in the Precedents can be adopted for drafting a bond.

A simple bond is to be distinguished from a promissory note (See NEGOTIABLE INSTRUMENTS, *post*) inasmuch as money payable under the bond is not payable to the order of the obligee or to the bearer of the instrument.

Use of Bonds

The object in view in the execution of a bond can as well be served by an agreement. The difference between the two is purely formal. A bond is executed in the form of a deed poll and its conditions are mentioned in an indirect form. In other words, in case of a bond it is not stipulated that the obligor will do this or that and will pay so much as damages or compensation if he does not do so, but that he will pay so much unless he does this or that.

---

1 2000 (2) PLR 179.

2 *K.P. Subbarama Sastri* v. *K.S. Raghvan*, (1987) 2 SCC 424, AIR 1987 SC 1257.

An agreement is executed as a deed between two parties and directly expresses the real obligation intended to be created, e.g., A covenants with B that he will do so and so or will not do so and so, and that if he commits a breach he will pay the sum stipulated. Both forms are equally good, but in some cases the latter is preferable. For security bonds, when the liability is necessarily limited to the amount of security offered, the bond form is more suitable.

Joint Hindu Family

See Preliminary Notes on MORTGAGE page 556, *post*.

Heirs and Representatives

Under Sec. 37, Contract Act, promises bind the representatives of the promisors and the right to enforce a promise descends, under the general law, to the heirs and representatives, unless a contrary intention appears from the contract, either expressly or impliedly. The common instance of a contrary intention being implied from the nature of the contract is that of contracts of a purely personal nature, such as a contract to marry, a contract to paint, etc. It is, therefore, unnecessary to mention the personal representatives or successors in title of the obligor or obligee in the "obligatory" part of the bond. In the "condition" part, however, the "heirs and representatives" of the obligor and the heirs, executors, representatives and assigns of the obligee have to be mentioned, because the condition refers not to the persons upon whom the obligation is binding or for whose benefit it ensures but the persons by whom and to whom the act or acts is or are to be done, by the doing of which the obligation is avoided, and they are not necessarily the same as the persons bound by, or entitled to enforce, the obligation. For instance, if an obligor promises that he will pay a sum of money on a certain date, the promise can be enforced after his death against his representatives (Sec. 37, Contract Act).

Section 40 provides that if it appears from the nature of the case that it was the intention of the parties to any contract that any promise contained in it should be performed by the promisor himself, such promise must be performed by the promisor. Generally, personal performance is expected from the promisor where use of personal skill of the promisor is involved. For example, a contract to sing or marry. In case of death of such a promisor, promise cannot be enforced against legal representatives. In other cases, the promisor or his representative may employ a competent person to perform it. See decision in *CITI Bank NA* v. *Standard Chartered Bank*.[1]

Accord is also a form of an agreement made after breach whereby some consideration other than his legal remedy is to be accepted by the party not at fault, followed by performance of some consideration by way of substitution.[2]

1 (2004) 1 SCC 12.

2 *Union of India* v. *Kishorilal Gupta and Bros*., AIR 1953 Cal 642.

Two Rates of Interest

Sometimes the parties agree that in case of default of payment on a certain date, a higher rate of interest would be payable. Such an agreement is penal under Sec. 74 of the Contract Act. In *Nagewaraswami* v. *Viswasundara*[1] a stipulation to pay compound interest on default was held penal. In order to avoid this possibility of the covenant being regarded as penal it is desirable to mention the higher rate of interest originally and provide that if the debtor shall pay on or before a certain date the principal and interest at a specified lower rate, the creditor would accept such lower rate and would not insist on the higher rate originally fixed. Such a contract is, however, possible only when the deed is between parties and is signed by the creditor also and is not in the form of a deed poll, as the covenant about acceptance of reduced interest is one by the creditor and not by the debtor.

Attestation

The question whether a document is a bond or not is relevant only for payment of stamp duty. A document of the nature mentioned in clauses (b) and (c) of Sec. 2(5) of the Indian Stamp Act becomes a bond only if it is attested by a witness. 'Attested' has been defined in Sec. 3 of The Transfer of Property Act. An ordinary promissory note will, for purposes of stamp duty, be treated as a bond if it is attested by a witness.[2]

Stamp Duty

Article 15 of the Schedule—I to the Stamp Act governs the Stamp Duty on bonds of different valuation. There are separate Articles 34 and 57 for Indemnity Bond and Security Bond respectively.

Security Bond, even if it creates a charge on immovable property, has been held not to amount to mortgage. This would be so only if such bond is signed by the surety alone as provided by Article 57.

For distinction between bond and simple agreement for purposes of the payment of stamp duty under the Stamp Act, reference may be usefully made to the decision of a special bench of seven Judges in *Mahabir Prasad* v. *Peer Bux*.[3]

Registration

Registration is not necessary unless, as in security and hypothecation bonds, any immovable property is charged or hypothecated.

---

1 AIR 1953 SC 370.

2 *Kartey Singh* v. *Iftikhar Ahmad*, AIR 1981 All 386.

3 AIR 1972 All 466.

PRECEDENTS

1—Simple Money Bond for Money Borrowed (Short Form)

I, AB son of CD ——— and resident of ——— (*or*, We, AB, etc., and XY, etc.,) having borrowed Rs. ——— from EF, etc., son of GH —— and resident of ——— (*or*, being indebted to EF, etc., to the extent of Rs.—— due to him on account of the price of ————purchased by me, or under a previous bond dated —————) hereby promise (*or*, ourselves jointly and severally promise) to pay to the said EF the said sum of money on demand (*or*, on the ———, or, within ——— years of this date) with interest thereon from the date of this bond at the rate of ——— per cent per annum with half yearly rests).

Dated the ——— day of ———.

(Signed) —————

Witness —————

Witness —————

2—Simple Money Bond, for Money Due with Recitals

THIS BOND is made on the ——— by me, AB, etc.

Whereas I owe Rs. ——— to EF, etc., on the following accounts:—

(*i*) On account of the principal and interest due under a bond executed by me in his favour on the ———, Rs. ———;

(*ii*) On account of the price of a bullock purchased by me from him on the ———, Rs. ———;

(*iii*) On account of various loans taken by me from him on *bahi khata* from ——— to ———, Rs. ———;

(*iv*) On account of rent for the ——— years, Rs. ———;

(*v*) On account of a decree of the Court of ——— dated —— in his favour and against my deceased father CD, Rs. ——;

NOW in consideration of the aforesaid liabilities, I hereby promise to pay to the said EF the said sum of Rs. ——— within ——— years and interest thereon or on so much thereof as shall for the time being remain unpaid at the rate of ——— percent per annum payable half yearly on the ———— day of ——— and the ——— day of ——— in each year.

AND I hereby agree that in case any interest is not paid on due date the same shall be added to the principal and shall bear interest at the rate and payable on the dates hereinbefore mentioned.

IN WITNESS WHEREOF I, the said AB, have put my signature hereunder.

3—Instalment Bond

I, AB, etc., having borrowed Rs. ——— from CD, etc., hereby promise to pay to the said CD the said sum of Rs. ——— in twelve equal half yearly instalments payable on the ——— and on the ——— in each year (*or*, in twelve instalments of the amounts and payable on the dates hereinafter mentioned) and also on the same dates interest at the rate of ——— percent per annum from the date of this bond on the said sum or on so much thereof as shall remain due on the said dates.

AND I hereby agree that in case I fail to pay up any two consecutive instalments of principal with interest due hereunder on the due dates, the whole amount then due under this bond shall become payable at once.

Details of instalments:

Amount	*Due date*

* * * *

4—Equated Instalments Bond

I, AB, etc., having borrowed Rs. ——— from EF, etc., hereby promise to pay to the said EF the said sum of Rs. ——— and interest at the rate of —— percent per annum in twelve equated instalments of the principal and interest combined of Rs. ——— each payable on the —— day of ———and the ——— day of ——— in each year, the first instalment being payable on the ——— day of ———;

AND I hereby agree that in case any such instalment shall remain in arrears for one month the whole money then due on account of the principal and interest shall thereupon become payable at once.

5—Bond by a Debtor and His Surety for a Loan

THIS BOND is executed on the ——— day of ——— by us AB, etc., (*debtor*) and CD, etc., (*his surety*);

WHEREAS EF, etc., has this day advanced a loan of Rs. ——— to me, the said AB, at the request of my surety the said CD, on the terms and conditions hereinafter appearing;

NOW we the said AB and CD hereby jointly and severally bind ourselves to pay to the said EF the said sum of money on demand with interest thereon from the date of this bond at the rate of ——— per cent per annum with half yearly rests.

6—Bond by a Debtor and His Surety for an Existing Liability

THIS BOND, etc. (*as in Form* 5).

WHEREAS I the said AB owe Rs. ——— to EF, etc., on the following accounts (*as in Form* 2).

AND WHEREAS in consideration of the said EF refraining from instituting a suit for the said sum, I, the said AB, have agreed to give this bond with the said CD as his surety.

NOW we, the said AB and CD, hereby, etc., (*as in Form* 5).

7—Instalment Bond, with Surety, for an Existing Liability (in the Form of a Deed)

THIS BOND is made on the ——— day of ——— BETWEEN AB, etc., (hereinafter called "the debtor") of the first part AND CD, etc., (hereinafter called "the surety") of the second part AND EF, etc., (hereinafter called "the creditor") of the third part.

WHEREAS Rs. ——— is still due to the creditor from the debtor under the decree dated ———, passed in suit No. ——— (*name of parties*) by the court of ——— on account of the arrears of rent for house ———.

AND WHEREAS the lease of the said house has again been settled with the debtor on the debtor agreeing to undertake payment of the said sum due under the said decree.

AND WHEREAS on the application of the debtor, the creditor has agreed to accept an instalment bond with surety for the said sum due under the said decree without interest.

AND WHEREAS in consideration of the creditor having agreed to accept payment of the said sum by instalments, the surety has agreed to guarantee payment of the said sum in accordance with the terms of this bond.

NOW THIS BOND WITNESSES and it is hereby agreed and declared as follows:

1. For consideration aforesaid the debtor and the surety hereby jointly and severally covenant with the creditor to repay to him the said sum of Rs. ——— in six equal half yearly instalments on the —— day of ———

and the ——— day of ——— in each year commencing from the ——— day of ——— next.

2. If any of the said instalments or any part thereof shall be in arrear for thirty days after the said instalments shall have become payable as aforesaid, then the whole of the said sum of Rs. ——— or such part thereof as shall for the time being remain unpaid shall immediately become due and payable with interest thereon at ——— percent per annum up to the date of actual payment thereof and the debtor and the surety hereby jointly and severally covenant to pay the same to the creditor.

IN WITNESS WHEREOF, etc.

8—Bond with Sureties for a Loan Repayable in Equated Instalment with Hypothecation of Property (in the Form of a Deed)

THIS DEED is made on the ——— day of ——— BETWEEN AB, etc., (hereinafter called "the borrower") of the first part AND CD, etc., (first surety) and EF, etc., (second surety) (hereinafter collectively referred to as the "sureties") of the second part AND GH, etc., (hereinafter called "the creditor") of the third part;

WHEREAS the borrower has requested the creditor for the advance of a loan of Rs. ——— repayable with interest at ——— per cent per annum by instalments hereinafter specified ;

AND WHEREAS the sureties have agreed to give security for the repayment of such loan in the manner hereinafter appearing, and the creditor has agreed to advance such loan on such security.

NOW THIS DEED WITNESSES as follows:

1. Covenants

In pursuance of the said agreement and in considerations of the sum of Rs. ——— advanced by the creditor to the borrower (the receipt of which is hereby acknowledged) the borrower and the sureties hereby jointly and severally covenant with the creditor as follows:

(i) To pay in instalments

The borrower and the sureties will pay to the creditor the said sum of Rs. ——— with interest thereon at the rate of ——— per cent per annum computed from the date hereof by four, half yearly instalments of principal and interest combined of Rs. ——— each payable on the following dates:

Instalment			*Due Date*
1st instalment	...	...	... ____________
2nd instalment	...	...	... ____________
3rd instalment	...	...	... ____________
4th instalment	...	...	... ____________

(ii) Penalty for Default

If any of the instalments aforesaid shall be in arrears in whole or part, the whole sum then remaining due to the creditor under this deed on account of principal and interest shall thereupon become payable at once and the borrower and the sureties will be liable jointly and severally to pay the same.

2. Hypothecation

For the consideration aforesaid and in further pursuance of the aforesaid agreement the borrower/first surety/second surety[1] hereby grant(s) and transfer(s) by way of simple mortgage to the creditor ALL that property described in the schedule hereto, to the intent that the said property hereby mortgaged shall remain and be charged by way of simple mortgage as security for the payment to the creditor of the said principal money and interest in accordance with the covenants herein contained.

3. Covenant of No Charge

The borrower/first surety/second surety hereby covenant(s) with the creditor that the said property is free from encumbrances.

4. Enforcement of Mortgagee's Remedies

It is hereby agreed and declared that in case of default in the payment of such sums on account of principal and interest as may become due under the covenant hereinbefore contained the creditor may forthwith enforce against the said property hereby mortgaged or any part thereof, all or any of the remedies of the holder of a simple mortgage.

IN WITNESS, etc.

---

1 If the mortgage is made by one, strike off the other two. If it is made by two, strike off the third and add "and" between the two. If it is made by all the three, substitute "and the sureties" for "first surety/second surety".

9—Bond with Sureties for Loan (in the Form of a Deed) with Provision for Lower Rate of Interest in Case of Punctual Payments

THIS DEED etc. (*as in Form* 8).

WHEREAS the creditor has agreed to advance to the borrower a loan of Rs. ——— repayable in ——— years with interest at the rate hereinafter specified on the security of the sureties.

NOW THIS DEED WITNESSES as follows:

1. In pursuance of the said agreement and in consideration of the said sum of Rs. ——— advanced by the creditor to the borrower (the receipt of which is hereby acknowledged) the borrower hereby covenants with the creditor that he will repay the said sum of Rs. ——— to the creditor within ——— years from this date and will in the meantime and for so long as any part of the said principal sum or any money to be treated as principal hereunder remains unpaid pay interest on the said sum or on so much thereof as shall for the time being remain unpaid at the rate of fifteen per cent per annum half yearly on the ——— and ——— in each year.

PROVIDED ALWAYS that the creditor shall accept interest at the reduced rate of twelve per cent per annum in lieu of the rate of fifteen per cent per annum for any half year in respect of which the borrower shall pay interest at such reduced rate not later than —— days after the due date.

2. In consideration of the creditor advancing the said loan to the borrower the sureties hereby jointly and severally guarantee the repayment of the said loan with interest to the creditor in accordance with the covenant hereinbefore contained.

IN WITNESS WHEREOF, etc.

10—Administration Bond by a Person Obtaining Letters of Administration (section 291, Succession Act)

KNOW ALL MEN that we, AB, etc., and CD, etc., (*surety for the said AB*) hereby bind ourselves jointly and severally to Shri ——— District Judge[1] of ——— for the payment to him or his successor in office of the sum of Rs. ———.

WHEREAS by an order of the court of the said District Judge of——— made on the ——— day of ——— the above named AB has been appointed administrator of the estate of XY deceased subject to the said AB

1 As stated in INTRODUCTION, page 9, *ante*, a court is not a juridical person, hence the bond has to be executed in favour of its presiding judge and his successors in office.

entering into a bond of Rs. ——— with one surety in the same sum for the due collection, entering upon and administrating the estate of the deceased.

AND WHEREAS the said AB had agreed to enter into the above mentioned bond and the said CD has agreed to enter into the said bond as surety for the said AB.

NOW the condition of the above written bond is this that if the said AB do and shall within six months from the grant to him of letters of administration of the estate of XY deceased, or such further time as the said court may appoint, exhibit in the said court an inventory containing a full and true estimate of all the property, in possession, and all the credits, and also all debts owing by any person to which the said AB is entitled as administrator, and do and shall, within one year from the said grant, or such further time as the said court may appoint, exhibit an account of the estate of the said deceased, showing the assets which have come to his hands and the manner in which they have been applied or disposed off and do and shall, justly and truly administer, the said property, credits and estate according to law, and shall deliver and pay to such person or persons, as shall be lawfully entitled thereto, all the rest and residue of the said property, credits and estate which shall be found remaining upon the said administration account, then the above-written bond shall be void but otherwise it shall remain in full force.

Signed, etc.

11—Security Bond Given for the Grant of a Succession Certificate (section 375, Succession Act)

KNOW ALL MEN, etc. (*as in Form* 10)

WHEREAS the court of the said District Judge has on the ——— passed an order for the grant to the said AB of a succession certificate to the estate of XY deceased on condition of the said AB executing a bond with one surety for the amount of Rs. ——— for the purpose hereinafter appearing; AND WHEREAS the said AB has agreed to enter into the above bond and the said CD has agreed to enter into the above bond as surety for the said AB.

NOW the condition of the above bond is this that if the said AB shall justly and truly account for the debts and other securities of the said XY deceased received by him and shall indemnify the persons who may be entitled to the whole or any part of such debts and securities then, the above-written bond shall be void but otherwise it shall remain in full force.

12—Administration Bond by Guardian Appointed Under the Guardians and Wards Act

KNOW ALL MEN, etc., (*as in Form* 10)

WHEREAS by an order of the court of the said District Judge —— made on the —— day of ——— under section 15 of the Guardians and Wards Act, 1890, the above-named AB has, subject to his entering into a bond for Rs.———, with a surety in the same sum, been appointed guardian of the property, movable and immovable of EF, minor son of GH; AND WHEREAS the said AB has agreed to enter into the above written bond, and the said CD has agreed to enter into the same bond as surety for the said AB.

NOW the condition of the above bond is this that if the said AB do and shall justly and truly account whenever called upon to do so for what he may receive in respect of the property of the said EF and do and shall carefully observe, perform and keep all orders and directions of the said court touching or concerning the estate and effects of the said minor and his property, and touching and concerning all such moneys as he, the said AB, shall receive as such guardian as aforesaid, and in all things conduct himself properly, then the above-written bond shall be void but otherwise it shall remain in full force.

13—Security Bond by a Debtor under section 21, Provincial Insolvency Act

KNOW ALL MEN, etc.(*as in Form* 10)

WHEREAS AB has been ordered under Sec. 21(1) of the Provincial Insolvency Act to give reasonable security for his appearance until final orders are made upon the insolvency petition filed by him (*or*, his creditor), AND WHEREAS CD has consented to be the surety for the said AB.

NOW the condition of the above obligation is this that if the said AB shall appear before the court whenever called upon by it to do so, then the above written bond shall be void but otherwise it shall remain in full force.

14—Security Bond by a Receiver Appointed in a Suit: Order 40, Rule 3 (a) C.P.C.[1]

KNOW ALL MEN, etc., (*as in Form* 10)

---

1 It is not necessary for the court to file a suit for recovery of the amount of the bond as under Sec. 145 C.P.C. the court's order is directly executable in the manner provided in the Code for the execution of decrees.

WHEREAS a suit has been filed in the court of the District Judge —— by EF, etc., against GH, etc., for the possession of the immovable and movable property entered in the schedule to the plaint in the said suit;

AND WHEREAS by an order of the said court, AB has been appointed receiver of all the property in suit on the terms and conditions mentioned in the said order and subject to his entering into a bond for Rs. ——— with one surety for the purpose hereinafter appearing;

AND WHEREAS the said AB has agreed to enter into the above bond and the said CD has agreed to enter into the above bond as surety for the said AB.

NOW the condition of the above bond is this that if the said AB shall duly account for all and every sum and sums of money which he shall as such receiver receive on account of the rents and profits of the immovable property and in respect of the movable property mentioned in the plaint in the said suit and shall submit his accounts at such periods and in such form as the said court shall direct and shall duly pay the balances which shall from time to time remain in his hands and such damages for any loss occasioned to the said property by his wilful default or gross negligence as the said court shall direct and shall during the period of his appointment as such receiver fully obey and follow all the orders and directions passed and issued or which may hereafter be passed or issued by the said court to or for the guidance of the said AB as such receiver, then the above written bond shall be void but otherwise it shall remain in full force.

[*Forms of bonds of security for stay of execution by original court, and by appellate court and for courts of appeal (Order 41, Rules 5,6 and10) are given as Forms No.2, 3 and 4 in Appendix G to the Code of Civil Procedure and as they are statutory forms they may be used for these purposes. The Court may execute its order holding the obligor to be in breach of the bond as if such order were a decree (Sec. 145 C.P.C.). Similarly, security bonds under the Code of Criminal Procedure are in prescribed forms No. 3, 12, 13, 28 and 29 in Sch. II to that Code. They all provide for forfeiture of the specified amount to Government. The amount forfeited is recoverable as fine under that Code:* See *Sec. 546 Cr. P.C.*].

15—Cash Security Bond by an Employee of Government (in the Form of Agreement)

THIS AGREEMENT made on this ——— day of ——— BETWEEN AB (hereinafter called "the depositor") of the one part AND the Governor of the Punjab (hereinafter called "the Government") of the other part.

WHEREAS the depositor has been appointed to the post of —— in the ——— Department.

AND WHEREAS it was a condition of his said appointment that the depositor should deposit security to the amount of Rs. ———— for the discharge of his duties in the said appointment.

AND WHEREAS the depositor has made the said deposit in cash (*or,* has paid Rs. ——— in cash and has agreed to pay the balance by monthly instalments of Rs. ———).

NOW THESE PRESENTS WITNESS and parties hereto hereby agree as follows:

(1) Deposit to be Applied to Indemnify

The said deposit or any part thereof may be taken by the Government for the purpose of indemnifying it, the Government, from any loss caused by an act, negligence, or default of the depositor in losing, misappropriateing, injuring, or failing to prevent injury to, any money or property while in his custody or under his supervision as a servant or officer of the said Department, or in permitting or failing to prevent the loss or misappropriation of, or any injury to, any such money or property as aforesaid by any person whosoever.

(2) To Realise Penalty

The said deposit or any part thereof may be applied for the purpose of realising any penalty for which the depositor may become liable under the conditions of his service in force for the time being.

(3) To be Retained for six Months

The said deposit may be retained by the Government for six months after the depositor has either died in the said service or has ceased to be in that service.

(4) To be Repaid

On the expiration of the said period of six months the said deposit will be repaid to the depositor or to the person then entitled to his property after his accounts have been passed by the officer authorised under the rules of the said Department to examine and pass the same and after all sums to which the Government may be entitled under the first two clauses hereof has been deducted therefrom.

(5) Additional Deposit

Any additional sum deposited by the depositor and stated in the schedule hereto and verified by the signature of the depositor and of the officer accepting the same may be applied in the same manner and shall be refunded subject to the same conditions as the said deposit.

(6) Depositor to make up Deficiency

If the said deposit is insufficient for the purpose set forth in the first and second clauses hereof, the depositor will pay to the Government such sum as may be necessary to make up such deficiency.

(7) Repayment not to Exonerate

The repayment either in whole or in part of the said deposit or any additional deposit made under the fifth clause hereof shall not exonerate the depositor or his estate or effects from liability to make good to the Government any loss or damage for which the depositor was liable under the terms of these presents or the rules of the said Department or the conditions of his service and which was not made good before such repayment as aforesaid was made.

IN WITNESS whereof, etc.

16—Personal Security Bond by an Employee, with Sureties, Pending the Execution of a Hypothecation Bond

KNOW ALL MEN that we AB, etc., (Principal), CD, etc., (First Surety) and EF, etc., (Second Surety), bind ourselves jointly and severally to XY, etc., for the payment to the said XY of the sum of Rs. ———.

WHEREAS the above bounden AB was on the ——— day of —— appointed to and now holds and exercises the office of treasurer of the estate of the said XY.

AND WHEREAS the said AB has been called upon to furnish security to the extent of Rs. ——— indemnifying the said XY against all loss and damage which he might suffer by reason of any property entrusted to the care of the said AB in the course of his duties as such treasurer being wasted, embezzled, stolen, misspent or lost dishonestly, negligently or otherwise by the said AB.

AND WHEREAS the said AB has offered such security in landed property and as the verification of the value and adequacy of the security offered by the said AB is likely to take sometime and the execution of the security bond will consequently be delayed.

AND WHEREAS the said XY has called upon the said AB to execute a personal bond with two sureties temporarily for such time as the security bond aforesaid is not executed and registered.

AND WHEREAS the said AB and the said CD and EF as the said AB's sureties have entered into the above written bond in the penal sum of Rs. —— conditioned for the due performance of his duties by the said AB and for the indemnity of the said XY against loss from the acts or defaults of the said AB until such times as the said AB offers adequate security and executes a registered security bond.

NOW the condition of the above-written bond is that if the said AB has whilst in the service of the said XY duly performed and fulfilled the duties assigned to him, or if the said AB and the said CD and EF shall indemnify the said XY from all and every loss and damage caused to the said XY from any act, omission, neglect or default of the said AB in the course of discharge of his duties while in the service of the said XY, or if the said AB shall offer adequate security and execute a regular security bond as promised, then the above-written bond or obligation shall be void and of no effect, otherwise the same shall be and remain in full force.

PROVIDED ALWAYS that immediately on the said AB executing, registering and delivering in the security bond hereinbefore referred to, this bond shall cease to have any effect.

PROVIDED ALSO that neither of them, the said CD and EF, shall be at liberty to terminate their suretyship except upon giving to the said XY six calendar months' notice in writing of his or their intention to do so and their joint and several liability under this bond shall continue in respect of all omissions and defaults on the part of the said AB until the expiration of the said period of six months.

Forbearance of Obligee not to Effect Liability

PROVIDED FURTHER that any forgiveness or forbearance on the part of the said XY or his administrators or executors or any of them towards the said AB in respect of his failure or neglect to perform such services and duties shall not in any way release or exonerate the said CD and EF or either of them or either of their executors or administrators in respect of their or his liability under the above-written bond.

IN WITNESS to the above-written bond and to all the terms and conditions hereinbefore contained we have signed hereunder this ——— day of ———.

17—Security Bond by Sureties on Behalf of a Claimant to Money due from Government to his Deceased Ancestor

KNOW ALL MEN BY THESE PRESENTS that we, AB, etc., CD, etc., and EF, etc., hereby bind ourselves jointly and severally to the

Governor of Assam (hereafter called 'the Government') for the payment to the said Government of the sum of Rs. ———.

WHEREAS XY was at the time of his death in the employment of the Government (*or*, was receiving a pension of Rs. ——— from the Government).

AND WHEREAS the said XY died on the ——— and there was then due to him the sum of Rs. ——— for pay and allowances in respect of his said office (*or*, in respect of his said pension).

AND WHEREAS the above bounden AB (hereinafter called "the Claimant") claims to be entitled to the said sum as heir of the said XY but has not obtained letters of administration of or a succession certificate to the property and effects of the said XY or a succession certificate in respect of his said dues.

AND WHEREAS the Government after making due inquiry is satisfied that the claimant is entitled to the said sum and that it would cause undue delay and hardship if the said Government insisted upon the production by the claimant of letters of administration of or a succession certificate to the property and effects of the XY or a succession certificate in respect of his said dues.

AND WHEREAS the said Government desires to pay the said sum to the claimant but under Government rules and orders it is necessary that the claimant should first execute a bond with two sureties to indemnify the said Government against all claims to the amounts so due as aforesaid to the said XY before the said sum can be paid to the claimant.

NOW THE CONDITION of this bond is that if, after payment has been made to him, the claimant shall refund to the said Government the sum of Rs. ———, if the said Government so requires, and shall in any event indemnify and save the said Government harmless from all liability in respect of the said sum and all costs incurred in consequence of any claim thereto THEN the above written bond or obligation shall be void, otherwise the same shall remain in full force.

IN WITNESS to the above-written bond and the condition thereof we, AB, CD, EF have signed hereunder this ——— day of ——.

18—Security Bond by Surety of the Manager of an Estate (Hypothecating Property)

KNOW ALL MEN BY THESE PRESENTS that I, AB, etc., hereby bind myself to CD, etc., for the payment to the said CD of the sum of Rs. ——— to be paid to the said CD.

WHEREAS EF, etc., has been appointed by the said CD to the post of manager of his estate on the condition that he shall furnish security to the amount of Rs. ——— for the faithful and honest performance of all such duties as may be required of him as such manager as aforesaid.

AND WHEREAS the said AB has in consideration of such appointment being made by the said CD agreed to give security for the said EF, in the manner hereinafter appearing.

NOW THE CONDITION of the above-written bond is that if the said EF shall faithfully and honestly perform all his duties as such manager as aforesaid and shall at all times account for, render and deliver in such manner and to such persons as the said CD may appoint in that behalf all moneys, securities for money and property of any kind whatsoever which he, the said EF, may recover or be entrusted with by virtue of his office as such manager as aforesaid and shall not lose, injure, destroy or in any way take or apply either for his own use or for any purpose other than those for which the same have been received by or entrusted to him any such moneys, securities for money or property as aforesaid then the above written bond or obligation shall be void but otherwise it shall remain in full force and effect.

AND THESE PRESENTS ALSO WITNESS that for the consideration aforesaid and as a security for the payment to the said CD of the said sum of Rs. ——— or any part thereof according to the terms and conditions hereof the said AB (hereinafter called the "mortgagor") hereby transfers to the said CD (hereinafter called the mortgagee) ALL THAT the property described in the schedule hereto, to the intent that the same shall remain and be charged by way of simple mortgage in the manner following, namely that for the purpose of recovering the said sum of Rs. ——— or any such lesser sum as may become due by the mortgagor to the mortgagee by virtue of these presents, the mortgagee may enforce against the said property or any part thereof all or any of the remedies of the holder of a simple mortgage AND the mortgagor hereby covenants with the mortgagee, that the said premises are free from encumbrances PROVIDED ALWAYS that the mortgagor may terminate his aforesaid suretyship on the expiration of six calendar months' notice in writing given by him to the said CD PROVIDED ALSO that notwithstanding the termination of his said suretyship the mortgagor shall remain liable under these presents for any such act or default as aforesaid committed by the said EF before the termination of the mortgagor's suretyship and that for the enforcement of such liability the mortgage hereby created shall continue until released by the mortgagee.

IN WITNESS whereof the said AB has signed hereunder on the ——— day of ———.

19—Security given by a Legatee under a Lost Will to a Purchaser of Bequeathed Property (with Hypothecation)

KNOW ALL MEN, etc. (*as in Form* 10)

WHEREAS by his last will dated the ——— EF devised the lands known as ——— described in the first schedule hereto, to the above bounden AB absolutely;

AND WHEREAS the said EF died on the ——— but probate of the said will was never obtained;

AND WHEREAS the said will has been diligently sought for by the said AB but cannot be found;

AND WHEREAS by a deed dated the ——— all the children of the said EF have released the said lands from any claim which they or any of them might have thereto whether under the said or any other will or by inheritance if the said EF had died intestate;

AND WHEREAS the parties to the said deed of ——— are the only descendants of the said EF;

AND WHEREAS the said AB has in this manner come to be the sole owner of the said lands.

AND WHEREAS by a deed of even date hereto the said AB has sold and transferred the said lands to the said CD absolutely;

AND WHEREAS it has been agreed between AB and CD that for the better protection of the said CD and in addition to the ordinary covenants for title contained in the said sale deed the said AB should execute the above-written bond subject to the condition hereinafter contained.

NOW THE CONDITION of the above-written bond is that if the said AB, his heirs, executors, administrators or assigns do and shall from time to time and at all times hereafter save harmless and keep indemnified the said CD from all suits, losses, costs, charges whatsoever in respect of the said land in case it shall appear that the said will does not devise the said lands to the said AB absolutely or that the said will is for any reason invalid or that the said EF died intestate, then and in such case the above written bond shall be void but otherwise the same shall remain in full force. PROVIDED ALWAYS THAT in the event of any suit being brought or claim being made against the said CD in respect of the said lands for any of the reasons aforesaid the said CD will forthwith give notice of such suit or claim to the said AB or his heirs, executors, administrators or assigns and will at his or their expense diligently contest such suit or claim if required by him or them to do so.

AND WHEREAS CD has required security for the payment of the sum named in the above-written bond, the said AB in consideration of the purchase from him of the said lands by the said CD hereby grants and transfers by way of simple mortgage to the said CD the property mentioned in the schedule hereto to the intent that if the said AB, his heirs, executors, administrators or assigns make default in paying any sum which may become due to the said CD under the conditions of the above-written bond the said CD shall have a right to cause the said property to be sold and the proceeds of the sale applied as far as may be necessary in payment of the said sum AND the said AB and CD hereby agree that all the conditions, covenants and stipulations set forth in the aforesaid bond shall form part of this mortgage.

20—Security Bond with two Sureties, the Principals Agreeing to Deposit Cash Security by Monthly Deduction from Pay

KNOW ALL MEN BY THESE PRESENTS that I AB, etc., (Principal) and CD, etc., (First Surety) and EF, etc., (Second Surety) hereby bind ourselves jointly and severally to the Governor of West Bengal (hereinafter referred to as 'the Government') for the payment to him of the sum of Rs. ———.

WHEREAS the above bounden AB was on the ——— appointed to, and now holds and exercises the office of ———;

AND WHEREAS by virtue of his appointment as such the said AB has, amongst other duties, the care of, and responsibility for the safe and proper handling and keeping in the places appointed for custody of Government property and money;

AND WHEREAS the said AB is bound, whenever called upon to do so, to show to his superior officer that the said property and money is at all times intact in the places aforesaid and is bound to keep true and faithful account of the said property and money;

AND WHEREAS the said AB in consideration of the said appointment has promised to pay the amount of security of Rs. ——— in monthly instalments of not less than 10 per cent of his pay for the purpose of securing and indemnifying the Government against all loss and damage which it might suffer by reason of the said property and money or any part being wasted, embezzled, stolen, misspent, lost dishonestly, negligently, or otherwise by himself, the said AB;

AND WHEREAS the said AB, and the said CD and EF as his sureties, have entered into the above bond, in the penal sum of Rs. ——— conditioned for the due performance by him of the duties of the said office and of the other duties appertaining thereto or lawfully required of him and for the indemnity of the Government against loss from the acts or defaults of the said AB.

NOW THE CONDITION of the above-written bond is that if the said AB has, whilst he has held the post of ———, always duly performed and fulfilled the said duties of the said office and the other duties aforesaid or if the said AB or the said CD and EF shall indemnify the Government from all and every loss or damage which during the time the said AB has held, executed and enjoyed the said office has happened, then the above written bond or obligation shall be void otherwise the same shall be and remain in full force.

PROVIDED ALWAYS and it is hereby agreed and declared that neither of them the said CD and EF shall be at liberty to terminate their suretyship except upon giving to the Government six calendar months' notice in writing of his or their intention to do so, and their joint and several liability under this bond shall continue in respect of all omissions and defaults on the part of the said AB until the expiration of the said period of six months.

AND it is hereby lastly agreed and declared by and between the said AB and the said CD and EF as his sureties and the Government that on the realization of the required security of Rs.—in cash by monthly deductions from the pay of the said AB as aforesaid the above bond will cease to be in operation.

IN WITNESS, etc.

21—Bond by Sureties of a Student Admitted to a College to Secure the Performance of an Agreement

BY THIS BOND we, JK, etc., and LM, etc., (hereinafter called "the sureties") are bound jointly and severally to the trustees of the —— College (hereinafter called "the trustees") for the payment to the trustees of the sum of Rs. ———.

WHEREAS by a deed of agreement dated the ——— executed by the trustees and AB, etc., (*or* XY, etc., acting as guardian of AB, etc.) the trustees have agreed to educate the said AB at the ——— College and to make him certain payments therein stipulated on the terms and conditions therein specified.

AND WHEREAS for the purpose of securing and indemnifying the trustees, their assigns and successors against all loss and damage which they might suffer by reason of the said AB (*or,* the said XY) making default in the observance and performance of any covenant on his part to be performed and contained in the aforesaid agreement and in consideration of the said education and payment to be given and made by the trustees to the said AB it has also been agreed that the sureties should execute the above written bond subject to the condition hereinafter contained.

NOW THE CONDITION of the above written bond is that if the said AB (and the said XY) shall duly and faithfully observe and perform all the stipulations and conditions on his (their) part to be observed and performed and contained in the aforesaid agreement dated the ——— then the above written bond or stipulation shall be void otherwise the same shall remain in full force.

Signed, etc.

22—Bond by Surety for Due Observance by Another of Terms of Partnership Deed

KNOW ALL MEN that I, AB, etc., hereby bind myself to CD, etc., and EF, etc., for the payment to them of Rs. ———.

WHEREAS the said CD and EF have by a deed of partnership dated ——— taken GH, etc., into partnership within the firm styled ——— AND WHEREAS it was part of the arrangement for taking the said GH into the said partnership that the said AB shall enter into and execute a bond for the due observance by the said GH of the terms of the said partnership deed.

NOW THE CONDITION of the above written bond is that if the said GH shall faithfully perform and observe each and every term and all provisions and agreements contained in the said partnership deed and on his part to be performed and observed and if the said AB, his heirs and executors or administrators shall at all times hereafter keep indemnified the said CD and EF and their respective heirs, executors and administrators for all losses, costs, charges and expenses which they or any of them shall or may incur or sustain by reason of the breach or non- performance on the part of the said GH of any of the terms, provisions and agreements aforesaid or by reason of the said GH not doing, performing, observing and complying with any award made by any arbitrator or arbitrators appointed under the terms of the said partnership deed, so and in such manner that he, the said AB, his heirs, executors and administrators shall be answerable to the said CD and EF and their respective heirs, executors and administrators for such losses, etc., in the same manner as if the said AB had been a party to the said partnership deed in the place of the said GH and not further or otherwise AND so that any alteration which may be made in the terms of the said partnership deed or the neglect or forbearance of the said CD and EF in enforcing payment of any sums which may become due to them from the said GH on account of breach or non-performance aforesaid or the giving of time to him for the payment thereof should not release the said AB, his heirs, executors and administrators in respect of his or their liability under the above written bond THEN the above written bond shall be void but otherwise shall remain in full force.

Signed, etc.

23—Bond by a Trainee (if Minor, by His Guardian) with Sureties

KNOW ALL MEN that we AB, etc., (*or*, XY guardian of AB), CD, etc., (surety No.1) and EF, etc., (surety No.2) bind ourselves jointly and severally to the Governor of ——— (hereinafter called "the Government") for payment to the Government of the sum of Rs.———.

WHEREAS the above named bounden AB has under the order ——— notification dated ——— been selected to get training for ——— at ——— in ———.

WHEREAS by a deed of agreement dated ——— executed between the Government and the said bounden AB (*or,* his guardian XY) the Government has agreed to bear all the expenses in relation to the said training including the passage of the said AB at ——— for ——— and to make certain payment to the said AB on the terms and conditions therein specified.

AND WHEREAS for the purpose of securing and indemnifying the Government against all losses and damages which the Government may suffer by reason of the said AB making default in the observance and performance of any covenant on his part to be performed and contained in the said agreement and in consideration of the expenses to be incurred on the said training and payments thereof to be made to the said AB, it has been agreed that the said sureties (CD and EF) should execute the above given bond subject to the condition hereinafter contained.

NOW THE CONDITION of the above-written bond is that if the said AB (*or*, the said XY his guardian) shall duly and faithfully observe all these stipulations and conditions on his part to be observed and performed and contained in the aforesaid agreement dated ——— then the above written bond or stipulation shall be void otherwise the same shall remain in full force.

Signed, etc.

24—Bond not to Carry on Certain Trade or Business within Certain Limits[1]

KNOW ALL MEN, etc. (*as in Form 18*).

WHEREAS by an agreement dated the ———, the said CD has taken the said AB into his employment as Sales Manager of his business as manufacturer and dealer of electrical goods on certain conditions one of which is that the said AB will not set up or carry on the business of sale of electrical goods in the town of ——— (*or*, within ——— km. from the Collectorate of that district) or solicit the customers of the said CD as hereinafter mentioned (*or*, otherwise to pay to the said CD Rs. ——— as liquidated damages), but so that nothing herein contained shall prejudice or affect the right of the said CD, his heirs, executors or administrators or assigns to restrain by injunction any breach by AB of the said agreement and to recover damages from him for any antecedent breach in lieu of taking proceedings under the above written bond.

NOW THE CONDITION of the above written bond is that if the said AB shall not at any time hereafter (*or*, during ——— years from the date of the said bond) directly or indirectly, and either alone or in partnership with, or as agent, clerk or servant of any other person whomsoever or otherwise set up or carry on the trade or business of electrical goods or business thereof or in any way deal in any of the articles of the said trade or business within the town of ——— or within ——— km. from the Collectorate of that district without the consent in writing of the said CD or of the person or persons for the time being carrying on the trade or business now carried on by the said CD at ——— aforesaid being first obtained for that purpose AND if the said AB shall not, either himself or by any other person on his behalf, at any time hereafter (*or*, during the said term of ——— years) solicit or endeavour to obtain the custom of any persons who are now or may hereafter from time to time while the said AB shall be in the service of the said CD be the customers of the said CD (*or*, in the event of the said AB failing to observe any of the conditions hereinbefore expressed) then and in such case if the said AB, his heirs, executors or administrators shall forthwith pay to the said CD, his heirs, executors or administrators Rs. ——

---

1 Sec. 27 Contract Act.

as liquidated damages and not as a penalty THEN the above-written bond shall be void but otherwise it shall remain in full force.

IN WITNESS WHEREOF, etc.

25—Bond with Surety when the Principal proceeds on Leave

KNOW ALL MEN BY THESE PRESENTS that I, AB, etc., (Principal), at present employed as ——— in the office of ——— AND CD, etc., (Surety) do hereby bind ourselves and our respective heirs, executors and administrators, to pay to the Governor of the State of ———, his successors and assigns (hereinafter called "the Government") on demand the sum of Rs. ——— and other expenses, if any, which the Government may incur on the Principal together with interest thereon computed from the day following the expiry of the sanctioned leave at the rate of one per cent over and above the Bank rate in force on the first day of April of the financial year in which the leave has been sanctioned, or, if payment is made in a country other than in India, the equivalent of the said amount in the currency of that country converted at the rate of exchange between that country and India.

WHEREAS the Government has at the request of the above Principal granted him regular leave, followed by extraordinary leave without pay and allowances, for a period of ——— months ——— days with effect from ——— in order to enable him to study at ———.

AND WHEREAS the Government has appointed/will appoint a substitute to perform the duties of ——— (*designation*) during the period of absence of the Principal on extraordinary leave.

AND WHEREAS failure on the part of the Principal to resume duty on the expiry of the period of the extraordinary leave shall be deemed as resignation of the Principal from the service of the Government, but such deemed resignation shall in no way release the Principal or the Surety from their liability hereunder.

AND WHEREAS it has been agreed between the above Principal and Surety of the one part and the Government of the other part that for the better protection of the interest of the Government, the said Principal and the Surety should execute such bond as above written and with such condition as is hereunder written.

NOW THE CONDITION of the above written obligation is that in the event of the Principal failing to rejoin, on the expiry of the period of extraordinary leave, the post originally held by him and serve the Government after rejoining for such period not exceeding a period of ———

years as the Government may require or refusing to serve the Government in any other capacity as may be required by the Government on a salary to which he would be entitled under the rules, the said Principal and/or the Surety or their respective heirs, executors and administrators shall forthwith pay to the Government on demand the said sum of Rs. ——— and other expenses, if any, which the Government may incur on the Principal together with interest thereon as aforesaid.

AND UPON the Principal and/or the Surety making such payment, the above written obligation shall be void and of no effect, otherwise it shall be and remain in full force.

PROVIDED THAT the liability of the Principal and/ or the Surety hereunder shall not be impaired or discharged by reason of the deemed resignation of the Principal upon his failure to resume duty on the expiry of the period of the extraordinary leave.

PROVIDED ALSO that the liability of the Surety hereunder shall not be impaired or discharged by reason of time being granted or for any forbearance, act or omission of the Government or any person authorised by them (whether with or without the consent or knowledge of the Surety) nor shall it be necessary for the Government to proceed against the Principal before proceeding against the Surety for any amounts due hereunder.

This bond shall in all respects be governed by the laws of India for the time being in force and the rights and liabilities hereunder shall, where necessary, be accordingly determined by the appropriate courts in India.

AND it is hereby agreed and declared by the Principal and the Surety that the Government may, on the certificate of the Secretary to the Government in the Administrative Department which shall be final, conclusive and binding, recover all dues hereunder from the Principal and the Surety jointly or severally as arrears of land revenue.[1]

The stamp duty shall be borne by the Government.[2]

IN WITNESS WHEREOF, etc.

---

1 This clause shall be legally enforceable only if there exists, as in U.P., a statutory provision to the effect that any government dues agreed to be recoverable as arrears of revenue, shall be recoverable under Sec. 3(1) (d) of the U.P. Public Moneys (Recovery of Dues) Act, 1972. In the absence of such statutory backing, mere agreement cannot confer jurisdiction on revenue authorities to resort to coercive processes for recovery e.g., arrest, attachment etc., *State of Meghalaya* v. *Orneshwar Das*, 1987 (Supp) SCC 134; *Mohd. Umar* v. *Nagar Palika*, 1998 AIHC 2127 (All-DB).

2 This clause may be inserted if it is desired that no stamp duty may be payable at all: Sec. 3 Stamp Act.

COMPROMISE, COMPOSITION AND FAMILY SETTLEMENT

Preliminary Note

Compromises

A compromise is the settlement of a claim or a dispute between the parties. When it is a settlement of a pending suit, it is evidenced by an application to the court jointly made by all parties in which the terms of the settlement are mentioned. When the claim or dispute is not the subject matter of a suit, or when the settlement goes beyond the scope of a suit, the compromise is made by a deed which is usually drafted in the form of an agreement. Matters which relate to the suit have to be widely construed. These include all matters which form consideration for the adjustment of the suit whether they form its subject matter or not.[1]

When an agreement or compromise is arrived at between the parties, Court is required to pass decree in terms of the compromise. The compromise may be in respect of whole of the suit or part of claim. For example, in a suit for recovery of Rs. 1 lac, defendant pays to the plaintiff Rs. 50,000 by way of settlement or compromise with the plaintiff. Before any such decree is passed, Court is to be satisfied that the agreement or compromise is lawful. Such an agreement has to be in writing and signed by the parties.

Where one party files application before the Court that lawful agreement or compromise has been arrived at or claim of the plaintiff has been satisfied, but the other party denies this submission or opposes the application that adjustment or satisfaction has been arrived at, it is for the Court to decide this question, without delay or unnecessary adjournment. (Order XXIII, rule 3). It is noteworthy that no suit lies for setting aside of decree on the ground that the compromise which led to decree was not lawful.

Section 89 CPC provides that where it appears to the Court that there is possibility of settlement of dispute between the parties and that settlement would be acceptable to the parties, Court is to formulate terms of settlement. Those terms are to be then given to the parties for their observations. After receiving observations of the parties, Court may reformulate terms of possible settlement and refer the same for any of the following modes of Alternative Dispute Resolution:—

1. Arbitration,
2. Conciliation,

---

1 *Bishambhar Nath Agarwal* v. *Kishori Chand*, 1990 (1) ARC 33 (DB) (All); *Pratap Narain Agarwal* v. *Ram Narain*, 1981 ALJ 591 (DB); *Kalyandas* v. *Gangadevi*, AIR 1961 MP 67; *Zakarali* v. *Israr Hussain*, AIR 1947 Nag 53.

3. Settlement (Judicial) including through Lok Adalat;
4. Mediation.

In case of reference for arbitration or conciliation, provisions of Arbitration and Conciliation Act, 1996 do apply. A court has no power, authority or jurisdiction to refer unwilling parties to arbitration, if there is no arbitration agreement. This Court has consistently held that though section 89 of the Code mandates reference to ADR processes, reference to arbitration under section 89 of the Code could only be with the consent of both sides and not otherwise. (paragraph 24)[1]

In case of reference to Lok Adalat, Court is to refer the matter as per provisions of section 20(1) of Legal Services Authority Act, 1987.

In case of judicial settlement, Court is to refer the same to a suitable institution or person. Such institution or person is to be deemed a Lok Adalat and all provisions of Legal Services Authority Act, shall apply.

In case of mediation, Court is to effect a compromise between the parties, while following the prescribed procedure.

All suits and cases of civil nature, whether pending in civil courts or other special Tribunals/Forums, are normally suitable for Alternate Dispute Resolution (ADR) process except the following having regard to their nature, as observed in *Afcons Infrastructure Ltd.* v. *Cherian Varkey Construction Co. (P) Ltd.*[2]

(i) Representative suits under Order 1 Rule 8 CPC which involve public interest or interest of numerous persons who are not parties before the court.

(ii) Disputes relating to election to public offices.

(iii) Cases involving grant of authority by the court after enquiry, as for example, suits for grant of probate or letters of administration.

(iv) Cases involving serious and specific allegations of fraud, fabrication of documents, forgery, impersonation, coercion etc.

(v) Cases requiring protection of courts, as for example, claims against minors, deities and mentally challenged and suits for declaration of title against government.

(vi) Cases involving prosecution for criminal offences.

In case of a representative suit, without leave of the Court, no agreement or compromise can be entered into. Any such agreement or compromise without leave of the Court shall be void. Before granting permission, Court is to issue notice to the interested parties and also to see that the agreement is lawful. Notably, notice is also to be issued to a person, who even if not arrayed as a party in the suit, but who is going to be bound by the decree under any provision of law.

1 *Afcons Infrastructure Ltd.* v. *Cherian Varkey Construction Co. (P) Ltd.*, (2010) 8 SCC 24.

2 (2010) 8 SCC 24

In terms of Order 23 rule 3 C.P.C. a compromise decree may comprehend even matters falling outside the subject matter of the suit but relating to the parties. The "words in writing and signed by the parties" imply that the compromise as above mentioned is valid also where it is signed by the parties' counsel in their cause or by their duly authorised agents.[1]

Compromise decree, if not vitiated by fraud, misrepresentation, misunderstanding or mistake, is binding and operates as resjudicata as also estoppel between the parties. An agreement settling disputes arising out of an earlier contract amounts to accord and satisfaction by a substituted agreement.[2]

If the parties agree to be bound by the terms of the compromise, naturally, they would be also bound by the orders passed by the competent authority or Court, unless, of course, it can be held that the compromise itself was vitiated by fraud, coercion or undue influence.[3]

Composition Deed

A composition deed is an instrument whereby a debtor conveys his property for the benefit of his creditors or secures to the creditors the payment of a composition or dividend on their debts. This is drafted in the usual deed form with recitals and covenants. Where composition or dividend is paid, the debtor and *all* the creditors are made parties, as also the trustee entrusted with the duty of distribution of assets. In case of assignment also, it is better to make *all* the creditors party to the deed, otherwise there is a danger of any one not joining in the deed, filing an application for insolvency as the assignment is itself an act of insolvency under the Act.

Family Settlement or Family Arrangement

Family settlement is a species of compromise. When members of a family compromise their disputes about family property or the property of a relation about the inheritance of which there is a *bona fide* dispute between them, the transaction is known as a family settlement or family arrangement. In *Kale* v. *Deputy Director of Consolidation*,[4] the following propositions were mentioned as some of the requisites of a family settlement:

(1) The family settlement must be a bona fide one so as to resolve family disputes and rival claims by a fair and equitable division or allotment of properties between the various members of the family. The term "family" has to be understood in a wider sense so as to include within its fold not only close relations or legal heirs but even those persons who may have some sort of antecedent title, a semblance of a claim or even if they have a spes succession is so that future disputes are sealed forever.

---

1 *Byram Pestonji Gariwala* v. *Union Bank of India*, (1992) 1 SCC 31, AIR 1991 SC 2234.

2 *Union of India* v. *Kishorilal*, AIR 1959 SC 1362.

3 *Madalappura Kunhikoya v. Kunnamgalam Beebi*, (2015) 15 SCC 684

4 (1976) 3 SCC 119.

(2) The said settlement must be voluntary and should not be induced by fraud, coercion or undue influence;

(3) The family arrangements may be even oral in which case no registration is necessary;

(4) It is well settled that registration would be necessary only if the terms of the family arrangement are reduced into writing. Here also, a distinction should be made between a document containing the terms and recitals of a family arrangement made under the document and a mere memorandum prepared after the family arrangement had already been made either for the purpose of the record or for information of the Court for making necessary mutation. In such a case the memorandum itself does not create or extinguish any rights in immovable properties and therefore does not fall within the mischief of Section 17(2) (Section 17(1)(b) of the Registration Act and is, therefore, not compulsorily registrable;

(5) The members who may be parties to the family arrangement must have some antecedent title, claim or interest even a possible claim in the property which is acknowledged by the parties to the settlement. Even if one of the parties to the settlement has no title but under the arrangement the other party relinquishes all its claims or titles in favour of such a person and acknowledges him to be the sole owner, then the antecedent title must be assumed and the family arrangement will be upheld, and the Courts will find no difficulty in giving assent to the same;

(6) Even if bona fide disputes, present or possible, which may not involve legal claims are settled by a bona fide family arrangement which is fair and equitable, the family arrangement is final and binding on the parties to the settlement.

The courts have, therefore, leaned in favour of upholding a family arrangement instead of disturbing the same on technical or trivial grounds.

It is now well settled that a family arrangement is for saving the honour of the family by the maintenance of peace and harmony and the avoidance of future discord or the preservation of property, hence it will be binding in the absence of fraud, coercion or undue influence. It is wholly unnecessary that a dispute must be existing actually. It would suffice if it is established that there was an actual or possible claim and a counter claim by the parties in settlement, whereof the arrangement as a whole was arrived at, thereby admitting the title in one on whom a particular property has fallen on the assumption of an actual existence in law that he had an anterior title thereof. The parties may either have an actual antecedent title, claim or interest, or even a possible claim in the property which is acknowledged by other parties.

Courts lean strongly in favour of family arrangement.[1] But the family settlement which is accepted by the courts in lieu of partition, is a settlement which

1 *Pullaiah* v. *Narasimham*, AIR 1966 SC 1836; *Shambhu Prasad* v. *Phool Kumari*, AIR 1971 SC 1337; *Krishna Behari Lal* v. *Gulab Chand,* AIR 1971 SC 1041; *Kale* v. *D.D.C.*, supra.

gives share to the parties as per their legal entitlement but not a settlement which is made or purported to have been made to circumvent the law. A partition of the property can only be among the parties who have a pre-existing right to the property.

Where the settlement is with a Hindu widow, it has also to be prudent and reasonable besides being a *bona fide* settlement before it can bind the estate and the reversioner.[1] A compromise effected between brothers, modifying a previous partition of their joint family property, is valid and binding as a family settlement, if there was a genuine dispute, and the compromise was for the benefit of the family as a whole.[2] The Supreme Court dealing with the question, when can a will operate as a family arrangement, observed that it will not do so where there be no dissensions, no contrary claims and no reasonably anticipated disharmony.[3] This was however a case where the will itself disclosed that all the sons of the testator were on amicable terms and there were no dissensions. Their Lordships however accepted that, as held in *Mathuri Pullaiah* v. *Mathuri Narasimham*,[4] "though conflict of legal claims *in praesenti* or *in futuro* is generally a condition for the validity of a family arrangement, it is not necessarily so. Even bonafide disputes, present or possible, which may not involve legal claims will suffice. Members of a joint Hindu family may, to maintain peace or to bring about harmony in the family, enter into such a family arrangement. If such an arrangement is entered into are bonafide and the terms thereof are fair in the circumstances of a particular case, courts will more readily give assent to such an arrangement than to avoid it." An expectation, that such arrangement will result in establishing or ensuring amity and goodwill amongst the relations, can constitute good consideration.

When one of the sons of the family is shown to have not accepted or participated, the family arrangement as a binding agreement among several coparceners must fail. It has been held that a family arrangement between a widow and her daughters is binding on daughters who were parties to it, but not on their minor sons who were not parties to it, not having been represented by their guardians.[5] But if even a minor son takes benefit and gives assent, he cannot later go back on the assent given, on attaining majority. Even where a family arrangement suffers from a legal lacuna or formal defect the rule of estoppel or approbate and reprobate is pressed into service to shut out technical or trivial grounds of objection against it being taken by a person who being a party to it seeks to unsettle a settled dispute and claims to revoke the family arrangement under which he has himself received some material benefits.[6]

No conveyance is necessary for a family arrangement, as a title is presumed

1 *Phool Kuer* v. *Prem Kuer*, AIR 1952 SC 207.
2 *Ramakrishna Raju* v. *Narayana Raju*, AIR 1949 PC 165.
3 *M.N. Aryamurthi* v. *M.L. Subbaraya Setty*, AIR 1972 SC 1279.
4 AIR 1966 SC 1836.
5 *Sahu Madho* v. *Mukund Ram,* AIR 1955 SC 481.
6 *Kale,* v. *D.D.C.* , supra; *Bakshi Ram* v. *Brijlal*, 1994 Supp (3) SCC 198.

already to exist.[1] If an oral compromise has already been arrived at between the parties the document ultimately executed in pursuance of the same may even be unilateral, such as a gift deed or a gift in the garb of a sale deed.[2]

Members of a family

Where the settlement was made between senior members of a family and a compromise was made regarding their rights as well as rights of the other members of their respective branches, it was held binding on all the members and a member who was not a party to it but was beneficially entitled thereunder.[3] The aid of Sec. 23 (c) Specific Relief Act, 1867 was invoked in this case.[4] Persons unborn and illegitimate members of a family are included in the term family. The expression "family" is to be construed widely and is not treated as confined to persons having legal title to the property.[5]

The settlement is binding on the sons and representatives of the parties and on reversioners.[6] It may contain any condition or any division of property. Any term may be agreed upon and provided. Even conditions which would not be valid in the case of deeds of transfer under the ordinary law may be inserted. For instance, a defeasance clause which would be void in a deed of gift or will may be inserted in a family settlement.[7]

A compromise in the nature of a family settlement is not an alienation by one party to another but a family settlement in which each party takes a share of the family property by virtue of an independent title, which is to that extent admitted by the other parties.[8] A family settlement is not a transfer of family property.[9] A memorandum reciting that the parties had appointed 'X' as a *panch* and that they had decided to accept the decision by him, setting out the terms of that decision, and reaffirming their being bound by it, is valid. No formal proceedings under the Arbitration Act are necessary in such a case, and as a memorandum of a past event it could be received in evidence though it was not registered.[10]

---

1 *Sahu Madho* v. *Mukund Ram*, supra.

2 *Mania* v. *Dy. Director Consolidation, U.P.*, AIR 1971 All 151.

3 *Tej Bahadur Khan* v. *Nakko Khan*, AIR 192 Oudh 9, 99 IC 472; *Taraknath* v. *Sushil Chandra*, (1996) 4 SCC 697 (para 4), (one of the brothers living in London can authorize his other brothers to settle the dispute and he was a consenting party to it).

4 *Janki Bala Debya* v. *Maheshwar Das*, AIR 1942 Pat 460, 21 Pat 377; [Note: Old Sec. 23 (c) corresponds to Sec. 15 (c) Specific Relief Act 1963].

5 *Kale* v. *D.D.C.*, supra.

6 *Budh Sagar* v. *Bishun Sahai*, 23 ALJ 141, AIR 1925 All 36, 86 IC 554.

7 *Surender Vikram* v. *Munia*, AIR 1944 Oudh 657.

8 *Hiran Bibi* v. *Sohan Bibi*, AIR 1914 PC 44.

9 *Mahesh Chand* v. *Raj Kumari*, (1996) 8 SCC 128, AIR 1996 SC 869 (para 26); *S.K. Sattar* v. *Gurdappa,* (1996) 6 SCC 373.

10 *Munna Lal* v. *Suraj Bhan*, AIR 1975 SC 1119: (1975) 1 SCC 576; *Kale* v. *D.D.C.*, supra.

Vested and Contingent Rights

It is however expedient to bear in mind the distinction between creation of vested rights and of contingent rights. According to Black's Law Dictionary, 6th Edn. (1990), a contingent estate, interest or right is one "which depends for its effect upon an event which may or may not happen" (p.321), while a vested right is an "immediate or fixed right to present or future enjoyment and one that does not depend on an event that is uncertain". Thus where under a partition deed a father and his three sons got one-fourth share each with rights of alienation, etc., but a later clause added that on the father's death his share will be equally divided among the sons, it was held that the latter provision could not restrain the father from making a gift of his share in his lifetime in favour of one branch only. His right of alienation was a vested right while the sons' right to succeed to his estate was contingent on his leaving any property undisposed of. Creation of an absolute estate in favour of a person is in English Law called a grant in "fee simple".[1] This case also illustrates the principle that unnecessary provisions should not be made in any deed. The later clause was clearly redundant because even without it the sons would have had a right to intestate succession to their father's estate (subject of course to any gift or will by him).

Registration

A composition deed is exempt from compulsory registration [section 17(2)(i)]. But if it amounts to a trust deed, it requires registration under section 5, Indian Trusts Act, 1882.[2] A compromise in a pending suit with respect to subject- matter of the suit is exempt as it is embodied in the decree. If, however, the compromise embodies a transaction of gift or lease of extraneous property the compromise embodying it would require registration.

Family arrangement as such can be arrived at orally. Its terms may be recorded in writing as a memorandum[3] of what had been agreed upon. The memorandum need not be prepared for the purpose of being used as a document on which future title of the parties is to be founded. It is generally drawn as a record of what had been agreed upon in order that there are no hazy notions about it in future. It is only when the family arrangement is brought about by the document itself, that the document requires registration.[4] In that case, it would amount to a document of title; as distinct from this, a mere memorandum of what had been agreed to earlier between the parties does not require compulsory registration under section 17

---

1 *Jaggavarapu Krishna Reddy* v. *Jaggavarapu Chittemma*, 1998 AIHC 3834 (AP).

2 *Govind Ram* v. *Madan Gopal*, AIR 1945 PC 74.

3 In *K.K. Modi* v. *K.N. Modi*, (1998) 3 SCC 573 (para 52); (document described as a "Memorandum of Understanding" was treated as having the effect of a family settlement).

4 *Jamunabai* v. *Sharadabai*, 1998 AIHC 4652 (AP), following, *Kale* v. *D.D.C.*, AIR 1976 SC 807.

Registration Act.[1]

There is no provision of law requiring family settlements to be reduced to writing and registered, though when reduced to writing the question of registration may arise. Binding family arrangements dealing with immovable property worth more than rupees one hundred can be made orally and when so made, no question of registration arises. If, however, it is reduced to the form of writing with the purpose that the terms should be evidenced by it, it required registration and without registration it is inadmissible; but the said family arrangement can be used as corroborative piece of evidence for showing or explaining the conduct of the parties.[2]

Stamp Duty

Stamp Duty is charged on Composition Deed and Family Settlement according to the provisions of Articles 22 and 58 respectively of the Schedule to the Stamp Act, 1899.

---

1 *Tek Bahadur Bhujil* v. *Debi Singh Bhuji*, AIR 1966 SC 292; *Bakhtawar Singh* v. *Gurdev Singh*, (1996) 9 SCC 370.

2 *Subraya M.N.* v. *Vittala M.N.*, (2016) 8 SCC 705; *Thulasidhara* v. *Narayanappa* (2019) 6 SCC 409.

PRECEDENTS

1—Deed of Composition with Creditors

THIS DEED is made on the ——— day of ——— BETWEEN AB, etc., (hereinafter called "the Debtor") of the first part AND CD, etc., (hereinafter called "the Trustee") of the second part, AND all the several persons, firms and companies, being the Creditors of the Debtor, whose names are set out in column 1 and whose signatures are given in column 3 of the schedule hereto (hereinafter called "the Creditors") of the third part:

Recital of Debts

WHEREAS the Debtor is indebted to the Creditors in the sums set opposite their respective names in the second column of the schedule hereto and being unable to pay the Creditors their debts in full has proposed to pay or procure to be paid to the trustee the sum of Rs. ——— to be distributed among the Creditors *pro rata* in proportion to the debts due to them respectively and that such sum may be received by the Creditors in full discharge of their respective debts and claims against the Debtor;

Recital of Composition

AND WHEREAS the Creditors have agreed to accept the offer of the Debtor and to take the said composition in full discharge of their respective debts and in consideration thereof and of the premises to grant to the Debtor the release hereinafter contained.

NOW THIS DEED WITNESSES AS FOLLOWS:

(1) Covenant to Pay to Trustees

The Debtor hereby covenants with the Trustee and the Creditors that he, the Debtor, will on or before the expiration of three months after the execution of this deed pay or cause to be paid to the Trustee the sum of Rs. ——— to be held by the Trustee upon and in trust for the purpose hereinafter declared concerning the same.

(2) Trust

The Trustee shall stand possessed of the said sum of Rs. ——— upon trust to distribute the same among the Creditors whose names are set out in the schedule hereto *pro rata* in proportion to the amounts due to them respectively.

(3) Creditors' Release of Debtor

In further pursuance of the said agreement and in consideration of the premises the Creditors do and each of them does hereby release and discharge the Debtor from all the said debts and from all actions, claims or demands or any of them against the Debtor in respect thereof.

(4) Default of Debtor

If the Debtor shall fail within the specified time to pay or cause to be paid to the Trustee the said sum of Rs. ——— or the debtor is adjudicated insolvent before payment of the whole of the said sum then the release of the said debts hereinbefore contained shall be void and of no effect and the Creditors and each of them shall be free to exercise in respect thereof all such rights and remedies and they and each of them would have been entitled if this deed had never been executed.

(5) Release not to Affect Others

The release hereinbefore contained shall in no respect prejudice the rights of the Creditors or any of them against parties other than the Debtor, and the Creditors hereby expressly reserve all the rights and remedies against any such party or parties.

(6) Arbitration

If any dispute shall arise with regard to any matter or things done under the foregoing provisions or otherwise in relation to this deed the same shall, if the parties fail to agree, be referred to the arbitration of XY.

The Schedule herein referred to

Names and Addresses of Creditors	Amounts of Debt	Signatures

Note: *For a precedent of composition by a debtor assigning his property to the trustees for the benefit of his creditors, see precedent No. 5 under* TRUSTS, etc., *post.*

2—Deed of a Family Settlement between the Widow and a Son of a Deceased Muslim

THIS DEED OF FAMILY SETTLEMENT is made on the —— day of ——— BETWEEN AB, etc., of the one part AND CD, etc., of the other part.

WHEREAS

Recitals

(1) The said CD claims the residential house of her late husband XY and the movable property stocked therein on the basis of an alleged oral gift by the said XY confirmed by a deed dated the ——— and has filed a suit being suit No. ——— of——— in the Court of the ——— against the said AB and two other persons for (*a*) an order directing the defendants to remove the guard posted by them at the said house and certain locks and seals put up by them on the said house, (*b*) a perpetual injunction restraining the defendants from interfering with the plaintiff's use and enjoyment of the said house and the said movable property, and (*c*) the recovery of Rs.— on account of damages for the alleged tortious acts of the defendants;

(2) The said CD threatens to file a suit for recovery of Rs. ——— on account of her dower debt;

(3) As the prosecution of the aforesaid suit now pending in court and the institution of the contemplated suit for dower by the said CD require considerable drain on her purse, and the defence of the two suits is likely to cause unnecessary loss to the said AB, the parties hereto on the advice of mutual relations and friends and after taking competent legal advice have agreed to settle the matters amicably by a family settlement on the terms and conditions hereinafter stated; and

(4) All the conditions of the proposed family settlement have been fully explained to the said CD and the said CD has in consultation with her legal advisers, EF and GH carefully examined and considered the same and has given her free consent to them.[1]

Terms of Settlement

NOW THIS DEED WITNESSES that in pursuance of the aforesaid agreement and in consideration of the settlement arrived at between the parties as hereinbefore recited, the parties hereto hereby agree with each other that they will observe and perform the covenants and conditions hereinafter follows:

(1) The said CD will withdraw her claim for damages preferred in the aforesaid suit No. ——— and the said AB will admit her title to the said house and all the movable property claimed by her in para 6 of the plaint in that suit. The claim with respect of reliefs (*a*) and (*b*) claimed in the said suit shall be decreed and that in respect of relief (*c*) dismissed and each party shall bear its own costs. The parties hereto shall file a petition of compromise in the court to this effect and a decree in terms of reliefs (*a*)

1 Such a clause is expedient in all cases of contracts by *pardanashin* ladies.

and (*b*) claimed in the said suit shall be obtained in favour of the plaintiff and against the said AB by consent;

(2) The said CD will be entitled to Rs. ——— only in full settlement of her claim for dower debt and hereby foregoes the balance of her said claim. The said sum of Rs. ——— shall not be payable in cash but the said CD will be entitled to purchase property of that value with money paid by the said AB in the manner hereinafter provided, and her rights in such property and the devolution of such property after her death will be regulated by the conditions hereinafter provided;

(Here state all the terms and conditions.)

(3) If the said AB shall commit a breach of any of the covenants in clauses ———, the said CD will be entitled to claim her entire dower debt, *i.e.* Rs. —— with interest at —— per cent per annum less any sums already received by her on account of dower debt under the terms of this deed.

IN WITNESS WHEREOF, etc.

3—Deed of a Family Settlement Between Rival Claimants of an Estate

THIS DEED OF FAMILY SETTLEMENT is made on the —— day of ———BETWEEN AB, CD, EF AND GH.

WHEREAS ———

Recitals

(1) XY, owner of the property mentioned in Schedules J, K, L, M, and N died on the ———;

(2) AB claims the whole of the said property as the adopted son of XY and the other parties deny the alleged adoption;

(3) CD claims the whole property as the widow of XY and the other parties deny that she is his widow and assert that she was XY's mistress;

(4) EF claims the whole property as the son of Z, a sister of XY but the other parties deny his claim, alleging that EF is not the son of Z but is the son of Z's husband by another wife;

(5) GH claims the whole property as a collateral of XY;

(6) Each of the four parties has obtained possession of a small portion of the estate of XY and has put in an application for mutation of his name on the whole of the estate;

(7) As the prosecution of the mutation cases and of the civil suits which will necessarily follow, the final decision in the mutation cases will

entail heavy expenditure and is likely to ruin the parties, besides further accentuating the existing disharmony among them, the parties on the advice of mutual friends and relations and after taking competent legal advice to ensure amity and goodwill have agreed to settle the dispute amicably by a family settlement in the following manner.

(8) All the conditions of the proposed family settlement have been fully explained to CD by her counsel Shri ———— and CD has in consultation with Shri ———— fully examined and considered the same and has given her free consent to them.

Terms of Settlement

NOW THIS DEED WITNESSES and the parties agree as follows:

(1) AB, EF and GH shall be absolute owners of the properties mentioned in Schedules J, K and L respectively;

(2) CD shall be owner of the property mentioned in Schedule M for life and shall have no right to alienate except with the consent of AB, EF and GH or in the case of death of either of them, with the consent of the survivor or survivors and of the heirs of the deceased, and on the death of CD, the property shall devolve upon AB, EF and GH or their respective heirs in equal shares;

(3) The property mentioned in Schedule N shall be set apart for the upkeep and other expenses of the temple of ———— at ——— which was built by XY deceased and shall remain in possession of GH in trust for this purpose. GH will apply the whole of the income of the property after deducting Government revenue, cesses, taxes and expenses of collection, on the upkeep of the temple and other necessary expenses in connection with the temple. After the death of GH, his eldest male heir and after him his eldest male heir and so on shall be the trustee provided he is able and willing to act as such trustee.

IN WITNESS WHEREOF, etc.

4—Compromise in a Suit

THIS AGREEMENT made on ——— day of ——— between AB, etc., and CD, etc.,

WHEREAS ———

(1) AB has filed a suit against CD in the court of the Civil Judge Junior Division, Allahabad (suit No. ——— of 1999) for recovery of Rs. —— claiming the amount due to him from CD on account of purchases and sales of wheat made by CD in the *arhat* of AB;

(2) CD has filed a suit No. ——— of 1999 in the Court of the Civil Judge Senior Division, Aligarh, against AB for accounts in respect of the purchase and sale of wheat made by CD in the *arhat* of AB and for recovery of the amount that may be found due to him on settlement of account; and

(3) The parties are desirous of settling their disputes to avoid trouble, inconvenience and expense.

NOW THIS COMPROMISE WITNESSES:

1. The parties agree that suit No. ——— of 1999 filed in the Court of Civil Judge Senior Division Aligarh be dismissed leaving the parties to bear their own costs.

2. That suit No. ——— of 1999 in the Court of the Civil Judge Junior Division, Allahabad, be decreed for Rs. ——— without costs, with future and *pendente lite* interest at 6 per cent per annum and the defendant of the suit should bear his own costs.

3. The parties will file compromise in the Allahabad suit so that a decree may be passed in that suit on its basis.

4 The parties will file copy of this agreement in the Aligarh suit, so that the suit may be dismissed as agreed.

IN WITNESS, etc.

DECLARATION[1]

Preliminary Note

Normally an instrument executed is the outcome of an agreement between two or more parties. Sometimes, however, an instrument in which there is no party to it other than the executant himself may have to be executed. In such an instrument there is no privity between two or more parties. Such an instrument, if declaratory in nature, may be called a "Declaration". Declarations executed when persons change their names or throw their self-acquired property into the hotch-potch of joint family property are some of the illustrations. A declaration may be in the form of deed poll or in the form of an affidavit which will require to be sworn or solemnly affirmed before a Notary Public.

Although strictly speaking, a declaration is not an agreement, yet as a measure of abundant caution it may be assumed to be liable to stamp duty under item 5 of Schedule I to Stamp Act ("Agreement or memorandum of agreement not otherwise provided for") or under the corresponding entry of the Schedule applicable in the particular State.

---

1 *See also*, Release, Relinquishment, Disclaimer *post*.

PRECEDENTS

1—Deed Changing Surname[1]

BY THIS DEED I the undersigned AY (*new name*) etc., lately called AB (*old name*) employed as ——— do hereby for and on behalf of myself and my wife and children and remoter issues wholly renounce, relinquish and abandon the use of my former surname of B (only) and in place thereof do assume from the date hereof the surname of Y and so that I, and my wife and children and remoter issues may hereafter be called, known and distinguished not by my former surname of B (only) but by my assumed surname of Y.

For the purpose of evidencing such my determination I declare that I shall at all times hereafter in all records, deeds and writings and in all proceedings, dealings and transactions private as well as public and upon all occasions whatsoever use and sign the name of Y as my surname in place of and in substitution for my former surname of B (only).

I expressly authorise and request all persons at all times hereafter to designate and address me and my wife and children and remoter issues by such assumed surname of Y accordingly.

IN WITNESS WHEREOF I have hereunto subscribed and adopted name of AY, and have affixed my signatures this ——— day of ———.

2—Declaration Throwing Self-Acquired Property into the Hotch Potch of Hindu Undivided Family[2]

This deed executed by AB, etc., (hereinafter called "the executant") WITNESSES that:

WHEREAS the executant has inherited one-sixth share in certain land-cum-house ancestral property situate at ——— which he is competent to dispose of;

AND WHEREAS the executant has constructed a bungalow at ——— at a total cost of Rs. ——— which is his self-acquired property;

---

1 Such a declaration is sometimes published in newspapers as an advertisement with a view to giving wide publicity.

2 A "Hindu undivided Family", under income tax law is wider than a Hindu coparcenery under Hindu law; it includes wife and unmarried daughters as well. Such declarations were often resorted to earlier as a tax saving device, but later ceased to be advantageous as they amounted to "gift" within the meaning of the Gift Tax Act 1958, *Sec. 4(2)*. However, after the abolition of gift tax in 1998 such deeds may again become useful. The theory of blending is explained in *Pushpa Devi* v. *C.I.T.*, (1977) 4 SCC 184 and *K.V. Narayanan* v. *K.V. Ranganandhan*, (1977) 1 SCC 244.

AND WHEREAS the executant, his wife CD and his sons EF and GH and daughter IJ form a Hindu undivided family and are the members of that family;

AND WHEREAS the executant had always desired to throw his self-acquired properties into the hotch potch of the Hindu undivided family and to treat the same as the property of the said family.

NOW THEREFORE the executant by this deed solemnly declares that the said properties, fully described in the Schedule hereto, have been thrown by the executant into the hotch potch of the Hindu undivided family consisting of himself, his wife, CD and his sons EF and GH and daughter IJ and that the same is the property of the said family, of which the executant is *karta*.

IN WITNESS WHEREOF etc.

Description of Property

Inherited property:

Self-acquired property:

3—Disclaimer of Exclusive Title

WHEREAS by a Deed of Lease dated ——— made between me as the Lessee and the Uttar Pradesh Avas Evam Vikas Parishad as the Lessor registered as No. ——— in book ——— volume ——— on pages ——— to ——— at the ——— office of the Sub-Registrar, Lucknow on the ——— day of——— the Lessor had demised unto the Lessee all that leasehold plot described in the schedule below;

AND WHEREAS the premium and rent of the said plot were paid partly by me and partly by my wife CD and accordingly the aforesaid lease should have been executed in the joint names of myself and my wife aforesaid;

AND WHEREAS at my request the Uttar Pradesh Avas Evam Vikas Parishad have intimated to me vide their letter No. ——— dated ——— that in their records the joint names of myself and my wife aforesaid have been entered as the joint lessees of the plot described in the schedule below.

NOW THEREFORE I, AB, etc., hereby declare that the property described in the schedule below was purchased by me partly *benami* for the said CD, wife of AB, and partly by me, at her instance and partly with her money and therefore it does not belong exclusively to me but belongs jointly to myself and my wife aforesaid AND I hereby disclaim exclusive rights in and title to the same.

Dated this ——— day of ——— 19 ———

Signed by ——— (AB) ———

EASEMENTS

Preliminary Note

Definition

An Easement is a right which the owner or occupier of certain land possesses, as such, for the beneficial enjoyment of that land, to do and continue to do something, or to prevent and continue to prevent something being done, in or upon or in respect of certain other land not his own.

The essence of easement is that it should be a right over property belonging not to the person claiming the easement but to someone else.

For example, A, the owner of a house, has a right of way either over his neighbour B's land or to go on his neighbour B's land, and to take water out of a spring therein, for the purposes connected with the beneficial enjoyment of his house. This is an easement.

Section 6(c) of the Transfer of Property Act, 1882, prescribes that "An easement cannot be transferred apart from the dominant heritage." In other words only an easement cannot be transferred exclusively without transferring the dominant heritage. In other words, a transfer of dominant heritage would automatically pass the easement right also to the person in whose favour such transfer takes place.

How Grant is made

One of the modes of acquiring an easement is by grant. The grant may be made orally or by a deed. The deed may be separate or the grant may be included in a deed relating to the dominant heritage, for example when A sells his land to B he may grant by the same deed a right of way to B for such land over another land of his.

When the transferee of land grants an easement to the transferor, the easement is often mentioned as a "Reservation" or "Exception" from the parcels transferred. This is not strictly correct, as an easement is neither a thing issuing out of the land transferred which can probably be a subject of reservation, nor a parcel of land which can properly be excepted from the transfer. But such reservations and exceptions may be construed as implied re-grant of the easement by the transferee. For burdens annexed to anything taken under a deed bind those who take the benefit. It is however, expedient that the transferee is also made to join in the execution of the deed in such cases so that possibility of dispute be avoided.

Difference between easement by grant and easement of necessity

In *Hero Vinoth* v. *Seshammal*,[1] Apex court observed that the question whether an easement is one acquired by grant (as contrasted from an easement of necessity) does not depend upon absolute necessity of it. It is the nature of the acquisition that is relevant.

Many easements acquired by grant may be absolutely necessary for the enjoyment of the dominant tenement in the sense that it cannot be enjoyed at all without it. That may be the reason for the grant also. But *easement of grant* is a *matter of contract between the parties.*

In the matter of grant the parties are governed by the terms of the grant and not by anything else. The grant may be express or even by necessary implication. Court has held that in either case it will not amount to an easement of necessity under Section 13 of the Act even though it may also be an absolute necessity for the person in whose favour the grant is made.

An easement of necessity is one which is not merely necessary for the reasonable enjoyment of the dominant tenement, but one where dominant tenement cannot be used at all without the easement. The burden of the servient owner in such a case is not on the basis of any concession or grant made by him for consideration or otherwise, but it is by way of a legal obligation enabling the dominant owner to use his land. It is limited to the barest necessity however inconvenient it is irrespective of the question whether a better access could be given by the servient owner or not. When an alternate access becomes available, the legal necessity of burdening the servient owner ceases and the easement of necessity by implication of law is legally withdrawn or extinguished as statutorily recognised in Section 41. Such an easement will last only as long as the absolute necessity exists. Such a legal extinction cannot apply to an acquisition by grant and Section 41 is not applicable in such case.

Mention of Successors

As the burden of an easement runs with the servient tenement into the hands of every person to whom it comes, it is not necessary to mention the representatives or assigns of the grantor. Similarly, as under section 19 of the Easements Act, an easement passes to heirs and transferees of the dominant heritage, it is not necessary to mention the grantee's representatives and assigns, but it would be necessary in States in which the Easements Act is not in force.

Mention of Nature and Purpose

In a deed of grant the nature of the easement and purpose for which it is to be enjoyed should be expressed unless an unlimited enjoyment is intended. In a grant of easement of way the *termini* and the position of the way should be clearly defined. See decision in *Hero Vinoth* v. *Seshammal* (*supra*).

---

1 (2006) 5 SCC 545.

Restrictions to be Expressly Mentioned

As the dominant owner has an implied right to put the subject-matter of easement into such a condition as is necessary to enable him to enjoy the easement for the purpose for which it is granted and such implied right, if not restricted by the grant, may cast an unforeseen burden on the servient tenement, it is advisable to lay down in the grant such restrictions as may be necessary in this respect.

Registration

According to the definition given in Section 2(6) of Registration Act, rights of way and light are expressly included in the definition of immovable property while other easements are not. The definition is however not exhaustive but only illustrative,[1] as it uses the word "includes" and it appears that a deed granting any right of easement will require registration if the value of the right is Rs.100 or above or if the grant amounts to a gift (Sec. 17(1) (*a*) and (*b*) Registration Act). Also see decision in *Sital Chandra* v. *Allen J. Delanney*;[2] *S.K.R.M. Subramanyam Chettiar* v. *Meyyammai Achi*.[3]

Stamp Duty

Chargeability of stamp duty depends upon the nature of the grant of easement. Thus, if the grant amounts to gift, it will be charged with stamp duty according to Article 33 (Gift) of the Schedule to the Stamp Act.

---

1 *State of Orissa* v. *Titaghur Paper Mills*, AIR 1985 SC 1293: 1985 (Supp) SCC 280 (para 100).

2 AIR 1917 Cal. 681.

3 AIR 1943 Mad. 522.

PRECEDENTS

1—Grant of a Right of Way

THIS DEED is made on the ——— day of ——— BETWEEN AB, etc., (called "the grantor") AND CD, etc., (called "the grantee").

Recitals

WHEREAS ———

(1) The grantor is owner and is in possession of a plot of land situate at ——— and entered in the Municipal Registers as No. —— delineated on the annexed plan and coloured red (called "the red land") and on the south of the plot of land runs a public road called the ———.

(2) The grantee is owner and is in possession of a plot of land adjoining the red land on the north and delineated on the plan and coloured blue (called "the blue land"); and

(3) The grantor has agreed with the grantee in consideration of the sum of Rs. ——— to grant to the grantee the right of way mentioned below.

Grant of way

NOW THIS DEED WITNESSES that in pursuance of the said agreement and in consideration of the sum of Rs. ——— paid by the grantee to the grantor (the receipt of which the grantor acknowledges) the grantor grants to the grantee FULL AND FREE right and liberty for him and his successors in title, owners or occupiers for the time being of the blue land, and his and their tenants, servants, visitors and all other persons authorized by him or them in common with the grantor and others having the like right at all times hereafter to pass and re-pass with or without horses, cattle or other animals, carts, carriages or other vehicles laden or unladen of any description over the red land along a path ——— feet wide between the points marked A and B on the plan, which path has been shown on the plan by dotted lines, for the purpose of going from the blue land to the public road called the ——— road and *vice versa* TO HOLD the same to the grantee and his successors in title as appurtenant to the blue land;

PROVIDED ALWAYS that it shall be lawful for the grantor and his successors in title to place and keep gates at the points A and B marked on the said plans, he and they maintaining such gates in proper repair and condition and keeping them open when required for the exercise of the right of way hereby granted.

IN WITNESS WHEREOF, etc.

2—Grant of Easement of Light

THIS DEED (*as in Form* 1).

WITNESSES that in consideration of the sum of Rs. ——— paid by the grantee to the grantor (the receipt of which the grantor hereby acknowledges) the grantor hereby grants to the grantee FULL AND FREE right to the uninterrupted access, transmission and enjoyment of light over and across all that piece of land belonging to the grantor situate at ——— containing —— acres and delineated on the plan annexed hereto and thereon shown as coloured red to the existing windows of the house of the grantee erected on the land adjoining the said land on the north thereof TO HOLD the said easement hereby granted to the aforesaid house.

IN WITNESS WHEREOF etc.

3—Agreement for Preventing Acquisition of Easement

THIS AGREEMENT is made on the ——day of——— BETWEEN AB, etc., of the one part AND CD, etc., of the other part.

Recitals

WHEREAS ———

(1) The said AB is owner of the land situate at ——— and delineated on the plan annexed hereto and thereon coloured blue; and

(2) The said CD is owner of a house adjoining the said land of AB and has recently opened two new windows in his said house which overlook the said land of the said AB but in respect of which (as the said CD hereby admits) no right or easement of light or air over the said land of the said AB has been acquired or exists.

NOW it is hereby mutually agreed between the parties as follows:

1. Covenants not to Erect

The said AB shall not erect on any part of the said land within —— feet of the nearest part of the said house of CD any building or erection any part of which shall be higher than ——— feet above the present ground level of the said land.

2. Not to Enlarge Windows

The said CD shall not without the previous consent in writing of the said AB enlarge the said windows or any of them or open any other windows or apertures in the said house which shall overlook the said land of the said AB.

3. Duration of Agreement

This agreement shall continue to be in force until determined by either party on six months' notice given to the other party and upon determination of this agreement the said CD shall if so requested by the said AB forthwith block up and keep permanently blocked to the satisfaction of the said AB the said windows or such of them as shall be included in such request of the said AB.

4. Running with Land

The benefit and burden of the stipulations in this agreement shall so far as may be possible pass with and bind the said premises of the said AB and CD so as to ensure and bind all persons deriving title thereto from or under the said AB and the said CD respectively.

IN WITNESS WHEREOF, etc.

4—Forms of PARCELS of Different Kinds of Easements

1. Right of Way

FULL AND FREE liberty, right and authority by himself, his servants and agents with receptacles of any kind either on wheels or otherwise to enter into and upon the said piece of land delineated on the said plan and thereon coloured blue and to pass and re-pass to and from the said well along the footpath shown in the said plan and marked thereon with letters XY and to take water from the said well for all domestic purposes.

2. Right to Lay the Footings of a Wall on the Neighbour's Land

FULL AND FREE liberty, right and authority to enter into and upon the said land of the grantor and to excavate the same to the width of —— feet and to a depth of ——— feet along the said boundary between the respective lands of the grantor and the grantee and to lay and forever hereafter to keep laid and maintained in such excavation at a depth of not less than ——— feet from the surface, all such footings and foundations of concrete, bricks, stone or other substance as the grantee shall think fit and proper as the foundation or any part of the foundation of the said intended wall of the said house AND also to erect scaffolding on the said land of the grantor for the purpose of erecting the said wall and to use such scaffolding during the erection of such wall for all usual building purpose AND also to erect such scaffolding and use the same from time to time for repairing and painting the said work after giving two weeks' previous notice to the grantor.

3. Right of Sewage

ALL that free right to using the said sewer or drain for the passage or conveyance of sewage water and soil from the said piece of land of the grantor or any of the lands adjoining such piece of land AND for this purpose to make and forever hereafter to repair and maintain all such connections with the said sewer or drain at the point marked A on the said map as may be reasonable and proper in that behalf making good at his own expense all damage or disturbance which may be caused to the surface of the said piece of land of the grantor in relation to such connection, repairs and maintenance.

4. Rights of Support of a Building

FULL RIGHT AND PRIVILEGE forever hereafter to have whatever building the grantee may at any time hereafter erect on the dominant tenement supported laterally by the subsoil of and minerals in and under the servient tenement.

Note: Any of these forms with necessary changes may be utilised for drafting a deed of grant of easement.

EXCHANGE

Preliminary Note

Exchange is mutual transfer of ownership of one property for the ownership of another. Exchange takes place where two persons owning two separate properties transfer or convey their respective ownership one to the other. In addition to transfer of property, there may be payment of money by one party to equalize the exchange and such payment will not make the exchange lose its character as such.

It is completed in the same manner as sale. A deed of exchange is in fact a deed of double transfers in which one transfer is stated to be the consideration of the other.[1] It should be executed in duplicate, one of the parties taking the original and the other duplicate.

Exchange differs from a sale as in the latter, the price paid is in money while in the former it is paid in kind by way of barter.

A partition is not an exchange within the meaning of Sec. 118 Transfer of Property Act. In partition some of the co-owners possessing an undivided share in several property take by arrangement a specific property in lieu of their shares in all.

On the abolition of estate duty, material changes have been made by various state laws permitting or prohibiting exchanges of certain types of land tenures. Before drafting a deed of exchange in respect of such land the provisions of the applicable state law must be looked into.[2]

Stamp Duty

According to Article 31 (Exchange) of the Schedule to Stamp Act, stamp duty is the same as on a Conveyance (Article 23) for a consideration equal to the value of the property of the greater value. The value of both the properties should be clearly set forth in the deed (Sec. 27). In the absence of an agreement to the contrary, it is borne by both parties in equal shares [Sec. 29(e)].

Registration

Registration is compulsory in case of exchange of immovable property if the property exchanged is valued at Rs. 100 or more (In U.P., it is compulsory in all cases irrespective of value).

---

1 *Income Tax Commissioner* v. *Motor & General Stores Ltd.*, AIR 1968 SC 200 (para 3).

2 *See* Preliminary Note on SALE, *post*.

PRECEDENTS

1—Deed of Exchange

THIS DEED OF EXCHANGE is made on the —— day of —— 19—— BETWEEN AB, etc., of the one part AND CD, etc., of the other part.

WHEREAS the said AB and CD are the absolute owners of the properties described in the first and second schedules hereto respectively;

AND WHEREAS the parties hereto have agreed to exchange the said properties described in the first and second schedules hereto in the manner hereinafter appearing;

NOW THIS DEED WITNESSES as follows:

1. In pursuance of the said agreement and in consideration of the transfer by the said CD hereinafter contained the said AB hereby grants and transfers to the said CD ALL THAT property described in the first schedule hereto TO HOLD the same to the said CD absolutely forever;

2. In further pursuance of the said agreement and in consideration of the transfer by the said AB hereinbefore contained the said CD hereby grants and transfers to the said AB ALL THAT property described in the second schedule hereto TO HOLD the same to the said AB absolutely forever.

3. Each of the parties hereto hereby covenants with the other, FIRST, that the property hereby transferred by him is free from encumbrances; AND (SECONDLY) that the property so transferred by each of them shall be quietly entered upon and held and enjoyed by the other of them and the rents and profits received by the other of them without any interruption or disturbance by the party transferring the same; AND (THIRDLY) that each of the parties hereto will at the request and cost of the other execute every such assurance and do every such act or thing as shall reasonably be required by such other for further or more perfectly assuring to such other the property hereby transferred to him.

4. It is hereby declared that the value of the property mentioned in each first schedule hereto is Rs. ——— and in the second schedule hereto is Rs. ———.

5. The grants hereby made and each of the covenants herein contained shall in the case of each party hereto be binding upon and enure for the

benefit of his heirs, legal representatives, successors and assigns.

IN WITNESS WHEREOF, etc.

The First Schedule herein referred to

* * * *

The Second Schedule herein referred to

* * * *

2—Exchange when Cash Compensation is Paid for Equality[1]

THIS DEED OF EXCHANGE is made, etc. (*as in Form* 1).

WHEREAS ———

The said AB owns the property mentioned in the first schedule hereto valued at Rs.50,000;

The said CD owns the property mentioned in the second schedule hereto valued at Rs.65,000; AND

The parties hereto have agreed to exchange their aforesaid properties with each other with effect from ——— and the said AB has further agreed to pay to the said CD for equality of exchange the sum of Rs.15,000.

NOW THIS DEED WITNESSES as follows:

1. *Same as in para* 1 *of Form* 1.

2. In further pursuance of the said agreement and in consideration of the transfer by the said AB hereinbefore contained and of the sum of Rs.15,000 paid by the said AB to the said CD (the receipt of which the said CD hereby acknowledges) the said CD, etc., (*as in Form 1*);

Same as paras 3, 4 and 5 of Form No. 1.

IN WITNESS WHEREOF, etc.

3—Deed of Exchange when Previous One was Ineffective

THIS DEED OF EXCHANGE is made on the —— day of ——— BETWEEN AB, etc., of the one part AND the Governor of Uttar Pradesh (hereinafter called "the said Government") of the other part;

WHEREAS —

---

1 Such payment of money in part does not detract from the character of the transaction as exchange: *Ismail Shah* v. *Saleh Mohd.*, AIR 1925 Lah 326; *Ram Badan Lal* v. *Kunwar Singh*, AIR 1938 All 229. Where however, the value of the other property is negligible and the main consideration is money, than the transaction will amount to sale: *Nihalu* v. *Bhagwan*, AIR 1936 Lah 234.

(1) Previous Exchange

By an agreement dated the ——— between EF, the then Superintendent of the Central Jail ——— purporting to act on behalf of the said Government and XY the deceased father of the said AB an exchange of the land specified in the first schedule hereto belonging to the said Government and of the land specified in the second schedule hereto belonging to the said XY was effected between the parties to the said agreement and since then the said Government through the Jail Department has been in possession of land specified in the second schedule hereto and the said XY and after him the said AB has been in possession of the land mentioned in the first schedule hereto;

(2) *Doubts*

The said Government has now claimed the land mentioned in the first schedule hereto from the said AB on the ground that the said EF had no authority on behalf of the said Government to transfer the said land by the aforesaid agreement and doubts have thus arisen as to the validity of the aforesaid agreement;

(3) *Agreement to Confirm*

In consideration of the said Government withdrawing all claims to the said land specified in the first schedule and confirming the title of the said AB to the same by a proper deed of conveyance, the said AB has agreed to confirm the title of the said Government to the said land specified in the second schedule;

(4) The said Government of Uttar Pradesh have by G.O. No.—— dated the ——— approved the aforesaid proposal; and

(5) The parties have agreed that the aforesaid agreement should be carried out by a proper deed of exchange;

NOW THIS DEED WITNESSES as follows:

On the lines of Form No.

IN WITNESS WHEREOF, etc.

FOREIGN COLLABORATION

Preliminary Note

Foreign collaboration basically represents a collaboration between the people, organisations or corporations of two countries to join together to do something for common interest. Foreign collaboration could be in the form of technical collaboration or financial collaboration or both.

Technical collaboration could be of the nature of transfer of comprehensive technology wherein the collaborator provides all services right from the supply of equipment till the commissioning of plant including the transfer of technical know-how for the production of goods, training of personnel, grant of trade mark, patent rights, provision of drawings and designs etc.

Financial collaboration is in the form of provision of capital, which can be by way of purchase of shares or by way of setting up of joint venture. Generally, the financial collaboration takes place alongwith technical collaboration from the foreign party.

Foreign collaboration agreement in its tenor and the context is of crucial importance and even decisive to determine whether payment made is of the nature of capital or revenue expenditure, for purposes of the Income Tax Act. The courts accordingly look to this with care.[1]

In broad terms, we can classify the Foreign collaboration agreements into:

1. Share Purchase Agreement

Share Purchase Agreement reflects the agreement for purchase of shares by the foreign party in an existing company so as to join and promote the existing company. Share purchase is generally supplemented by transfer of management support.

2. Joint Venture Agreement

Joint Venture Agreement is entered into between the foreign party and the Indian party to set up projects with equity participation from the foreign party. The foreign party generally also provides technical know-how and management support.

3. Technical Know-How Agreements

Technical know-how transfer agreement which generally include provision of

---

1 *CIT* v. *British India Corporation Ltd.*, (1987) 165 ITR 51 (SC).

drawings and designs, provision of process know-how, training personnel, provision of technicians for supervision of erection and commissioning of plant etc.

Accordingly, for reference the following model agreements are given:

1. Share Purchase Agreement
2. Joint Venture Agreement
3. Technical Collaboration Agreement
4. Supplement to Technical Collaboration Agreement.
5. Consultancy Services.

These agreements as detailed, are just model agreements and need to be developed and elaborated considering the specific need and understanding among the parties.

PRECEDENTS

1—Share Purchase Agreement

THIS SHARE PURCHASE AGREEMENT (hereinafter referred to as the "Agreement") entered into on this ——— day of ——— between ———, a company registered under the Companies Act, 1956 having its registered office at ——— India, (hereinafter referred to as "Seller") of the One Part and a corporation established and registered under the law of ——— having its principal office at ———, (hereinafter referred to as "Purchaser") of the Other Part.

WHEREAS the Seller owns——— equity shares constituting outstanding equity shares of——— a company limited by shares and registered under the Companies Act, 1956 with its registered office at ——— India, (hereinafter referred to as the "Company")

WHEREAS the Seller desires to sell, and the Purchaser desires to purchase ——— per cent (part of the shares) of the said equity shares of the company held by the Seller, (hereinafter referred to as the "Shares") subject to the terms and conditions set forth in this Agreement;

NOW, THEREFORE, in consideration of the premises, the mutual agreements and covenants hereinafter contained, the receipt and sufficiency of which is hereby acknowledged, the Seller and the Purchaser do hereby agree as follows:

1. Sale and Purchase of the Shares

Subject to the terms and conditions set forth in this Agreement, the Seller does hereby agree to sell, assign, transfer and convey to the Purchaser all of its rights, obligations, title and interests in and to the Shares, and the Purchaser do hereby purchase, acquire and accept all of the Seller's rights, obligations, title and interests in and to such Shares. The sale shall be on spot delivery basis.

2. Consideration

(*i*) As consideration for the sale and transfer of the Shares by the Seller, the Purchaser shall pay to the Seller at the rate of Rs. ——— (Rupees ——) per share an aggregate sum of Rs. —— (Rupees ——), which amount shall hereinafter be referred to as the Purchase Price.

(*ii*) Unless otherwise mutually agreed in writing the Purchase Price shall be paid in full, without any adjustment, deduction, set-off or counter-claim.

3. Payments

The Purchase Price shall be paid by the Purchaser to the Seller, as detailed in clause 2 above, on the Closing Date (as defined herein) when all the conditions precedent set forth in clause 5 below are fulfilled.

4. Time and Date of Closing

(*i*) The closing of the transaction provided for in this Agreement shall take place on a date when all the conditions precedent mentioned in Clause 5 hereof have been fulfilled (hereinafter referred to as the "Closing Date") in the office of the company at ———— India by or at such other time, date and/or place as may be mutually agreed upon by the parties hereto in writing.

(*ii*) Simultaneously, on payment of the Purchase Price by the Purchaser to the Seller as set forth in Clause 3, above, the Seller shall deliver to the Purchaser original share certificates of the Shares together with duly executed share transfer deeds and the Seller's receipt acknowledging payment of the Purchase Price by the Purchaser to the Seller.

5. Conditions Precedent to Closing Date

(*i*) On or before the Closing Date following conditions shall have been fulfilled:

(a) All approvals or permissions have been obtained from competent authorities and/or department and/ or ministries of the Government of India relating to the transfer of the shares from the Seller to the Purchaser under this agreement.

(b) The Purchaser has entered into the agreement with the Company for the transfer of technical know-how as per draft enclosed as annexure-A.

(*c*) The technical know-how agreement as per clause 5(i) (b) above is approved by the Government of India.

(ii) The Shares are agreed in principle to be transferred by way of sale by the Seller to the Purchaser under and in accordance with this Agreement by the Board of Directors of the company.

6. Termination

In case the conditions precedent set forth in clause 5 above are not fulfilled or satisfied on or before ———— or such other later date as may be mutually agreed between the parties in writing from time to time, the Seller and the Purchaser shall each have the right to terminate this Agreement.

7. Representation and Warranties of Seller

The Seller hereby represents and warrants to the Purchaser as follows:

(i) The Seller is a corporation, duly organised and validly existing under the Companies Act.

(ii) The Seller has full legal right, power and authority to enter into, execute and deliver this Agreement and to perform the obligations, undertakings and transactions set forth herein, and this Agreement has been duly and validly executed and delivered by the Seller and constitutes its legal, valid and binding obligation, enforceable against it in accordance with its terms.

(iii) The Seller has all requisite power to own and dispose of the Shares to be sold by it.

(iv) The Shares are owned by the Seller free and clear of all pledges, security interest, liens, charges, encumbrances, equities, claims, options or limitations affecting its ability to vote on such shares or to transfer such shares to the Purchaser and all such shares have been validly authorised and issued and are fully paid.

(v) Except for the transaction contemplated by this Agreement there is no subscription, option, warrant, call right, agreement or commitment outstanding in relation to the sale or transfer of the Shares.

(vi) The Balance Sheet of the company as at ————— which have been disclosed to the Purchaser, and which is annexed as Annexure B hereto (hereinafter called the "said balance sheet") gives the true and fair view of the financial position of the company as at ————— (hereinafter called the "said date") and there are no other material liabilities contingent or otherwise as on the said date which have not been disclosed in the said balance sheet and since the said date there has been no material reduction in the aggregate net asset position of the company as set out in the said balance sheet by way of sale, transfer or write off of capital assets except as stated in Annexure C hereto.

(vii) The fixed and other assets of the Company, save and except to the extent disclosed in the said balance sheet, are not subject to any charge or lien or encumbrance whatsoever.

(viii) The Company has not since the said date issued or agreed to issue any shares or given or agreed to give any option or right in respect of

any shares nor issued or agreed to issue or given any option in respect of any debentures or other securities of the Company.

(ix) The Company has not entered into any long term or abnormal contract for undertaking any obligation on or after the said date except as are usual and necessary in the ordinary course of business and in particular and without limiting the generality of the foregoing there are no contracts for purchase of the stocks and stores at prices substantially higher than the market price ruling on dates such contracts were made.

(x) The Company do not have any material debt liabilities, contracts or engagements other than those disclosed in the said balance sheet.

(xi) No material part of the amounts included in the said balance sheet as due from the debtors has been released after the said date on the terms without any debtor paying less than the book value as on the said date or has been written off or treated as irrecoverable or bad debt.

(xii) All returns, particulars of resolutions and other documents required to be delivered by the Company to the Registrar of Companies and other statutory authorities have been duly delivered to such Registrar and authorities.

(xiii) After signing of the agreement till the Closing Date the business and affairs of the Company shall be conducted in the ordinary course of business and there shall be no sale, transfer, assignment and nor shall there be created any lien, charge or encumbrances on the assets and stocks of the Company other than in the normal course of business and unless it is necessary in the interest of the Company.

(xiv) There are no material demands contingent or otherwise on account of outstanding income tax and other taxes or penalties on the Company save and except to the extent disclosed in the said balance sheet.

(xv) All trade marks and registered designs used by the Company in connection with their respective businesses are registered in their respective names and no licence or other rights have been granted or agreed to have been granted to any third party in respect of such trade mark or registered designs.

(xvi) The Company is not engaged in any substantial litigation or arbitration proceedings or prosecutions pending or threatened which will adversely affect its aggregate assets materially.

(xvii) The Company has effectively maintained all insurances necessary and properly required to be effected and maintained by reason of nature of their business and such insurances are in force and effect and there

are no facts or matters which could vitiate and/or lead to repudiation of such insurances.

(xviii) The Company has good and marketable title to all its assets save and except the charges, liens, and encumbrances in favour of lenders as disclosed in the said balance sheet.

(xix) The Company will not prior to the completion of the sale of the Shares pursuant hereto, save and except with the previous consent of the Purchaser or in the normal course of business and subject to the interest of the Company:

(a) create, expend, grant, or issue or agree to create, expend, grant or issue any mortgage, charges, debentures or other securities;

(b) create or issue or agree to issue any shares or give loan or agree to give any option in respect of any shares or loan;

(c) enter into any long term, material or abnormal capital commitments exceeding Rs. ———— other than in the ordinary course of business;

(d) do or suffer anything whereby their financial position shall be rendered less favourable than at the said date save and except in the ordinary course of business;

(e) cause to pass any resolution in General Meeting creating any special rights or privileges in favour of any class of shareholders or particular shareholder;

(f) pay, or agree to pay to its Directors, officers or workmen or any of them, any additional or further remuneration, grant, bonus or allowance other than those in the ordinary course of business;

(g) dispose of any material part of its fixed assets or other assets other than in the ordinary course of business.

(xx) The Seller undertakes that it shall cause the company to make amendments within— days from the date of transfer of shares in the existing Memorandum and Articles of Association of the Company to incorporate the clause mentioned in the annexure-D.

(xxi) The Seller warrants that after the transfer of shares to the Purchaser pursuant to this agreement, the Company shall be managed jointly by the Seller and the Purchaser as per management agreement annexure - E.

8. Disclaimer of Representations and Warranties By the Seller

Save and except the representations and warranties stated in this

Agreement, the Seller makes no other representations or warranties of any kind or nature including without limitation any representations or warranties with regard to the business, financial viability, assets or liabilities of the Company and no statutory or other warranties as to or the business, financial viability, assets or liabilities of the Company shall be implied.

9. Representations and Warranties of the Purchaser

The Purchaser hereby represents and warrants to the Seller as follows:

(i) The Purchaser has full legal right, power and authority to enter into, execute and deliver this Agreement and to perform the obligations, undertakings and transactions set forth herein, and this Agreement has been duly and validly executed and delivered by the Purchaser and constitutes his legal, valid and binding obligation, enforceable against it in accordance with its terms;

(ii) The Purchaser shall cause sufficient funds to be available to acquire and pay for all of the Shares and otherwise to consummate the transactions contemplated by this Agreement on the terms and conditions contemplated hereby;

(iii) Neither the execution and delivery of this Agreement nor the consummation of the transactions contemplated hereby will violate or conflict in India with any Central, State, local or municipal statute, law, ordinance, rule or regulation, or any judgment, order, writ, injunction, award or decree of any court, governmental, quasi-governmental or public agency, arbitrator, tribunal, commission, board, bureau, or other authority applicable to the Purchaser;

(iv) The Purchaser is familiar with the business of the Company and future prospects and has conducted its own due diligence and analysis of the Shares and the businesses in their present conditions as disclosed in the said Balance Sheet;

(v) Save and except what is stated herein, neither the Seller nor any of its agents, affiliates, attorneys, representatives, directors, officers or employees has made any representations or warranties regarding the Company or any of its assets.

10. Expenses

Each party shall pay its or their own expenses (including without limitations, attorneys' fees), in connection with the negotiation, preparation and execution of this Agreement and any amendments or other documents or instruments relating hereto and the transactions contemplated hereby.

11. Obtaining Approvals

Each Party hereto shall at all times exert their best efforts and assist the other to obtain all necessary/requisite approvals permissions, consent of or registration or declaration with, any authority, department or Ministry of Government of India or any third party in connection with the execution, delivery, performance, validity and enforceability of this Agreement and the sale of the Shares pursuant hereto.

12. Miscellaneous Matters

(i) Amendment: This Agreement may not be amended or otherwise altered except pursuant to an instrument in writing signed by each of the parties hereto. This Agreement shall be binding on the respective successors, legal representatives and permitted assigns of the parties, provided that no party shall assign any of its rights, or delegate any obligations hereunder without the prior written consent of the other, and any attempted assignment or delegation without consent shall be null and void. However, such consent shall not be unreasonably withheld.

(ii) Notices: Any notice, request or instruction permitted or required to be given hereunder by any party to the other shall be in writing and shall be deemed sufficiently given if delivered personally, sent by registered or certified mail, postage prepaid, or sent by fax or e-mail to the parties at their respective places of business.

(iii) Delivery: Notice and other communications sent by mail shall be deemed to have been given ———— days after the date on which the same shall be proved to have been posted. Notices and communications sent by fax or e-mail shall be deemed to have been given ——— hours after the same shall be proved to have been sent.

(iv) Headings: The headings contained in this Agreement are inserted for reference purposes only and are not to be considered in interpreting this Agreement.

(v) Counterparts: This Agreement may be executed in one or more counterparts, each of which shall be deemed an original and all of which together shall constitute one and the same instrument. In pleading or proving any provision of this Agreement, it shall not be necessary to produce more than one such counterpart.

(vi) Governing Law: This Agreement shall be governed by and construed and enforced in accordance with the laws of India as to all matters including but not limited to matters of validity, construction, effect, performance and remedies.

(vii) Publicity: Neither party shall issue any press release or announcement or make any other public statement, in each case relating to, connected with or arising out of this Agreement or the matters contained herein, without obtaining the prior written approval of the other party hereto to the contents and the manner of presentation and publication thereof (which approval shall not be unreasonably withheld or delayed), except such release, announcement or statement as may be required by law or the rules or regulations of a national or foreign stock exchange or self-regulatory organisation; provided, further, that nothing herein shall apply to any required communications by any party hereto with any relevant governmental or statutory authority, municipal corporation or any other local authority or any bank or financial or other institution or body.

(viii) Waiver: No delay on the part of the Seller or the Purchaser in exercising any right, power or privilege hereunder shall operate as a waiver thereof, nor shall any waiver on the part of the Seller or the Purchaser of any right, power or privilege hereunder, operate as a waiver of any other right, power or privilege hereunder, nor shall any single or partial exercise of any right, power or privilege hereunder preclude any other or further exercise thereof or the exercise of any other right, power or privilege hereunder. The rights and remedies herein provided are cumulative and are not exclusive of any rights or remedies which the parties hereto may otherwise have at law or in equity.

(ix) Severability: Any provision of this Agreement which is held to be invalid or unenforceable for any reason shall be ineffective to the extent of such invalidity or unenforceability only, without affecting in any way the remaining provisions hereof.

(x) Further Assurances: Subject to the terms and conditions of this Agreement, each of the parties hereto will use all reasonable efforts to take, or cause to be taken, all action, and to do, or cause to be done, all things necessary, proper or advisable under applicable laws and regulations to fulfill its obligations under this Agreement. At any time or from time to time after the Closing Date, without further consideration, each party hereto shall at the request of the other party hereto execute and deliver any further instruments or documents and take all such further action as the Seller may reasonably request in order to more effectively consummate and make effective the transactions contemplated by this Agreement.

(xi) Entire Agreement: This Agreement, all Schedules hereto or thereto, and all other documents and certificates referred to herein or therein constitute the entire understanding and agreement between the parties hereto with respect to the transactions contemplated herein and cancel and

supersede all previous written or oral negotiations, commitments, and writings with respect to the transactions contemplated herein.

13. Arbitration

If any dispute or difference of any kind whatsoever shall arise between the Seller and the Purchaser hereto in connection with or arising out of this Agreement (and whether before or after the termination or breach of this Agreement), including any question regarding the existence of such dispute or difference, such dispute or difference shall be referred to and settled by arbitration as hereafter provided in accordance with the Arbitration and Conciliation Act, 1996 but the existence of any dispute or difference or the initiation or continuance of the arbitration proceeding shall not postpone or delay the performance by thc Parties of their respective obligations pursuant to this Agreement.

The matter would be referred to arbitration of a tribunal of three Arbitrators. The disputing Parties shall appoint one Arbitrator each and the two Arbitrators so appointed shall name the third Arbitrator.

The decision of the majority of Arbitrators so appointed, shall be final and binding upon the disputing Parties. If any of the Arbitrator is unable or incapacitated to act as such by reason of resignation, death or otherwise, a new Arbitrator shall be nominated by the party which had nominated the Arbitrator who is no longer able to serve or by the two Arbitrators nominated by the parties as the case may be. The tribunal with the new Arbitrator so nominated shall continue with the Arbitration proceedings from the stage left by the tribunal with the outgoing Arbitrator and such proceedings shall not be recommenced *de novo*. The arbitration shall be held at ————. The costs and expenses of such arbitration shall be allocated as determined by the Arbitrators.

14. List of Annexures

The following annexures to the agreement form an integral part of the Agreement.

Annexure 'A'	Draft Agreement for transfer of Technical know-how.
Annexure 'B'	Balance Sheet of the company as at ____________.
Annexure 'C'	Details of material reduction in the net asset position of the company after the said date.

Annexure 'D' Amendments to be made in the Memorandum and Articles of Association of the company.

Annexure 'E' Proposed Management Agreement.

IN WITNESS WHEREOF, the parties have caused this Agreement to be duly executed and delivered as of the day of year first above written.

2—Joint Venture Agreement

THIS AGREEMENT made and entered into this —— day of ——— by and between ———— (hereinafter referred to as "PARTY OF THE FIRST PART") a corporation organised and existing under the Companies Act, 1956/2013 having its registered office at ————— and ——— (hereinafter referred to as "PARTY OF THE SECOND PART" a corporation organised and existing under the ———— having its registered office at _____________.

WHEREAS, the party of the FIRST PART and the party of the SECOND PART are desirous to set up a project to manufacture ——— in India.

AND WHEREAS, each party understands that the creation under the laws of India of a limited liability company jointly owned by the parties or their approved associates or nominees and with public participation will be instrumental to the accomplishment of the objective.

AND WHEREAS, the parties have mutually agreed to incorporate a new joint stock company with limited liability under which the project to manufacture ——— shall be taken up.

AND WHEREAS, each party upon agreed ratios, terms and conditions is willing to provide the required capital, technology, equipments and services for the manufacture of ———— in the joint stock company so incorporated.

NOW, THEREFORE, in consideration of the premises and mutual covenants herein contained, the party of the FIRST PART and the party of SECOND PART agree as follows.

1. Definitions

As used in this Agreement, the following terms shall have the following meaning, such meanings to be equally applicable to both the singular and plural forms of the terms defined:

1.1 Joint Company shall mean the Joint Stock Company to be incorporated in India with limited liability by the parties for the manufacture of ——— in accordance with provision of clause 2 of this agreement.

1.2 Associated Company shall mean any company or enterprise owned or controlled by a Party through direct or indirect ownership of at least —— of the stock normally entitled to vote.

1.3 Party shall mean either party of the First Part or party of the Second Part.

1.4 Parties shall mean party of the First Part and party of the Second Part.

1.5 Board shall mean the Board of Directors of the Joint Company.

2. Formation of Joint Stock Company

2.1 The parties (or party of the First Part) shall cause the Joint Company to be incorporated under the provisions of the Companies Act, 1956/2013 in accordance with the terms of this agreement under the name and style of ———— or such other name as may be mutually agreed by both the parties, with Memorandum and Articles of Association, which shall be as per schedule 'A' attached.

2.2 If any of the provisions contained in the Memorandum and Articles of Association as given in the schedule 'A' is not approved by the Registrar of Companies, suitable and desired amendments shall be made therein with mutual consent of both the parties.

2.3 The costs of incorporation of Joint Company shall be borne equally (*or*, by the Party of the First Part).

2.4 The registered office of the Joint Company shall be situated at ———.

3. Objects of the Joint Company

The activities of the Joint Company shall be the manufacture and sale of ———. The joint company shall take up any other object as specified in the object clause of its Memorandum and Articles subject to applicable laws, only after having the consent of both the parties in writing.

4. Cost of the Project and means of Financing

The estimates of the cost of project to be set up by the Joint Company and its means of finance are given in Schedule 'B' attached. The pattern of financing for any cost overrun shall be decided by the parties with mutual consent.

5. Capital Investment

5.1 Capital investment by the Parties in the Joint Company and all obligations pursuant to this agreement are conditional upon the fulfilment of the following conditions on or before ———— or such other date as may be agreed to mutually by the parties.

(a) The requisite approvals from the Government of India for setting up of the project for the manufacture of ———— by the Joint Company are received.

(b) The approval of the Government of India of the Application for Foreign Collaboration is received.

(c) The approval of the Government of India of the Application for Capital Goods Clearance for the import of equipment required is obtained.

(d) The following further approvals from the Government of India and Government of ———— are obtained.

(*Give the list of necessary approvals required for setting up of the project*)

(e) All of the aforesaid approvals must be in a form and content acceptable to both the Parties.

5.2 Immediately after all conditions precedent as set out in clause 5.1 are fulfilled, the parties shall provide capital, in cash, as per the agreed time schedule given in Schedule 'C'. The Time Schedule 'C' may be modified or revised from time to time by the parties with mutual consent in writing.

5.3 The authorised share capital of the Joint Company shall be Rs. ———, which shall be divided, into ——— equity shares of Rs. —— each.

5.4 The parties and their respective associate companies shall respectively subscribe to the issued equity capital of the Joint Company in the following proportions:

Party of the First Part and its associate companies	————
Party of the Second Part and its associate companies	————
Public holdings	————

It is further agreed that nominee of each party participating in any issuance of equity share shall, before acquiring such share of the Joint Company shall agree in writing to be bound by the terms of this agreement.

Subject to the terms hereof, the parties agree to maintain the aforesaid proportions at all times unless otherwise expressedly agreed in writing.

6. Directors

6.1 The number of directors of the Joint Company shall neither be less than ——— nor more than ——— excluding alternate directors. Initially the Board of Directors, ("Board") shall consist of ——— directors, subject to a possible increase in the number of such initial directors to accommodate the nominee directors of the financial institutions or banks, as mutually agreed by the parties.

The initial and successive Boards shall be comprised of ——— directors nominated by the party of the FIRST PART, ——— directors nominated by the party of the SECOND PART and Independent directors elected to the position from a list of candidates mutually acceptable to each party as well as such other directors that may be appointed under rights granted by Joint Company with the mutual agreement of the Parties to financial institutions or banks. Each party shall have the right to appoint alternate directors for each of the directors nominated by such party.

6.2 The Chairman of the Board shall be appointed by the party of the ———, and his term shall not be liable to retirement by rotation.

6.3 The managing Directors shall be appointed by the party of the ———, and his term shall not be liable to retirement by rotation.

6.4 The parties shall jointly nominate for election and appointment of ——— directors, whose office shall be liable to retirement by rotation. Any vacancy caused by such directors being unable or ceasing to hold the office for any reason whatsoever shall be filled by the parties jointly nominating another person for election and appointment to such office.

6.5 Subject to the maximum numbers provided in clause 6.1 above, any additional director or directors may be nominated and appointed by the "Board" only with the mutual agreement of the parties.

6.6 Unless both the parties agree in writing to a shorter notice, ——— clear days notice of every meeting of the Board of Directors or a committee thereof shall be given in writing to every director (including an alternate director) or member of a committee at his usual address, whether in India or abroad. A director abroad shall furnish to the Joint Company an email address at which such notice may be given and communication of notice by the Joint Company at such email address shall be deemed service thereof on such director. Where notice of a meeting is required to be given to a director abroad, the notice shall be given simultaneously by registered Air Mail letter and by email, at the email address provided by such director.

6.7 Every notice convening a meeting of the Board or a committee thereof shall set out the agenda of the business to be transacted at such meeting in full details. Unless otherwise agreed to by the chairman, no item of business shall be transacted at such meeting which has not been stated in full detail in the notice convening the meeting provided that with the prior written consent of the parties, any item of business not included in the agenda may be transacted at that meeting.

6.8 The quorum for the meeting of the Board shall be ——— of its total strength including directors, if any, whose place may be vacant at the time; provided that where at any time the number of directors who have declared an interest in any matter on the agenda exceeds or is equal to one-half of the total strength of directors, then the number of directors who are not so interested, present at the meeting and being not less than two, shall form a quorum for the purpose of that meeting; and further PROVIDED ALWAYS that no such meeting shall proceed to transact any business unless at least ——— each of the directors nominated by each party pursuant to clause 6.1 above or their alternates are present at such meeting, except where for any particular meeting, the said requirement for a quorum is waived in writing by either party in respect of the particular rights under this clause. Provided however, that if a meeting cannot be held due to the absence of the quorum, then upon notice being provided to each director such meeting shall stand postponed to the same day after—weeks at the same time and place or if that day is a public holiday, till the next succeeding day that is not a public holiday at the same time and place.

6.9 Subject to the approval of the Reserve Bank of India, the Joint Company shall bear all the expenses of each visit of all the Directors living abroad to attend the Board Meetings.

6.10 Except in those cases where a resolution is required by law to be passed at a meeting of Board, a resolution shall be taken as duly passed at a meeting of the Board or a Committee of the Board, as the case may be, duly called and constituted in accordance with the provisions of the Companies Act, 1956/2013 and the Article of Association of the Joint Company, if a draft thereof is circulated, together with the relevant papers, if any, to all the directors or to ali members of the committee of the Board as the case may be, and such resolution has been approved by a majority of the directors entitled to vote thereon, including in such majority at least —— each of the directors nominated by either Party pursuant to clause 6.1 above.

6.11 The following business cannot be approved by the Board without the unanimous affirmative vote of the Directors nominated by the Party of the ———— part:

(*a*) Changes in the capital structure of the Joint Company, including issue of shares, reduction of capital, etc.

(*b*) Winding-up, sale or amalgamation of the Joint Company.

(*c*) Change of the Joint Company's registered office.

(*d*) Embarking on a new venture, diversification or expansion.

(*e*) Alteration in the Joint Company's objects clause, as set forth in its Memorandum of Association.

(*f*) Change in the name of the Joint Company.

(*g*) Alteration of the Articles of Association of the Joint Company.

(*h*) Obtaining long-term loans exceeding Rs. ——— other than overdrafts for working capital.

(*i*) Making any loan/advance of Joint Company's funds in excess of Rs. ———.

(*j*) Sale, exchange, surrender or disposal of any asset of the Joint Company, involving a value exceeding Rs. ———.

(*k*) Approval of the annual business plan.

(*l*) Appointment or removal of auditor of the Joint Company.

6.12 The business and operations of the Joint Company shall be conducted in accordance with an annual business plan approved by the Parties.

6.13 The Joint Company shall submit to each party monthly financial report in a form mutually agreed upon between the parties and such other statement and reports containing financial, production or other business information as may from time to time reasonably be requested by either party.

6.14 The Joint Company shall at all times be operated as an independent enterprise for the profit of all its shareholders and all dealings or transactions with or on behalf of any shareholders of the Joint Company shall be on such term no more favourable than would be accorded to any person in the ordinary course of business taking into consideration bulk sales, offers and contracts.

7. Dividend Policy

Subject to the approval of the Board, a minimum of ——— per cent of the surplus available for distribution of dividend shall be distributed by the Joint Company each year as dividend.

8. Records

8.1 The Joint Company shall keep true and accurate accounting records of all operations and such records shall be open for inspection to the parties or to their duly authorised representative at all reasonable times.

8.2 The auditor of Joint Company shall furnish copies of its final reports to the Parties within ———— days after the end of the financial year of the Joint Company.

8.3 Until otherwise agreed to by the parties in writing, the financial year of the Company shall be ending on 31st March every year.

9. Effective Date

As soon as this Agreement is signed, each of the parties shall be obliged to take every reasonable step to co-operate in obtaining the necessary Governmental approvals and licenses provided for in this agreement and to take other steps reasonably necessary to further the objects of this agreement. The parties shall not be obligated, however, to proceed with any other actions required by this Agreement unless otherwise contemplated herein, until the "Effective Date". The "Effective Date" of this Agreement shall be the date mutually determined by the Parties in writing after all the conditions set forth in clause 5.1 of this Agreement have been fulfilled or waived by the Parties.

10. Applications for Approvals

10.1 Party of the FIRST PART shall file all necessary applications for licences and approvals required from the Government of India for the setting up of the project.

10.2 Party of the SECOND PART shall file all necessary applications for any license or approval required under the law of—.

10.3 Each party shall take all reasonable steps to ensure that the requisite approvals are obtained from their respective Government speedily.

10.4 Each party shall co-operate and assist the other party in their efforts of obtaining the requisite approvals. The various informations required by the Governments for the approvals shall be provided by the party concerned speedily and within reasonable time.

11. Transfer of Shares

11.1 It is agreed that neither party shall sell, transfer, assign, mortgage, pledge or otherwise encumber or deal with any or all shares of the Joint Company without consent of the other Party, except as is hereinafter provided:

(*a*) Transfer of the shares by the party to its associate companies or the sale of shares held by the associate company to their concerned party.

(*b*) Transfer of director's qualification share so long as the beneficial ownership of such share is retained by the respective party.

11.2 (*a*) Subject to clause 11.1 above, should a Party or its Associate Company desires to sell any of the shares held by it in the Joint Company, such party shall first offer or have offered the said shares to the other party by notice of the same.

(*b*) Such offer shall contain the price at which the shares for sale are offered by the Party or its Associate Company. The offeree shall within —— days of receipt of the notice of offer accept the offer and pay the price (subject to the provisions of sub-clause (d) below) of the said shares within ———— days of acceptance. In case the offeree desires to accept the offer, without accepting the price contained in the offer, offeree shall within the said period of ——— days, be entitled to exercise its option to purchase the shares subject to the condition that the price of the shares shall be as valued by the auditors of the Joint Company whose valuation shall be final. However, the Party or its Associate Company making the offer shall have the right to withdraw the offer in case the price asked by them is not accepted. The price for the shares shall (subject to the provisions of sub clause (d) below) be paid immediately after —— days of such valuation, unless the party or its Associate Company elects to withdraw its offer within the said ———— days of such valuation.

(*c)* It is expressly agreed that the offeree may nominate any other person to purchase the shares offered to it or any part thereof.

(*d)* In case any approval of an authority in India is required for such sale of shares, the offeree shall make an application for the same within— days after acceptance or the valuation contemplated in sub clause (b) above, as the case may be. The price for the shares shall then be paid within ——— days after receipt by the offeree of the necessary approval(s). If for any reason whatsoever the said approval(s) is (are) not received within ——— days of the making of ————— application (or such further period as agreed to by the parties) the offeror shall be at liberty to withdraw the offer.

(*e)* In the event that the offeree fails for any reason whatsoever to observe any of the time limits set forth hereinabove, the offer shall lapse and the offeror shall be at liberty, for a period of ——— days from the lapse of the offer, to transfer the offered shares to a third party or parties at a price not lower than and/or on conditions not more favourable than those offered in the offer.

12. Competition with the Joint Company

12.1 The party of the FIRST PART or its Associate Companies will not set up any project to manufacture such products as are being or will be produced by the Joint Company in India or abroad except with the written permission of the party of the SECOND PART.

12.2 The party of the SECOND PART or its Associate Company shall not export to India the products manufactured or similar to those manufactured by the Joint Company.

12.3 The party of the SECOND PART or its Associate Company will not set up any other manufacturing facilities either by themselves or with any other person whether resident of India or not for the manufacture of the products being manufactured or to be manufactured by the Joint Company.

12.4 The party of the SECOND PART shall not provide any technical know-how, equipment or any other services to any third party for the purposes of the setting up of projects for the manufacture of the products being manufactured by or to be manufactured by the Joint Company.

12.5 All business confidential or proprietary information received by either Party or their Associate Companies as a result of this agreement or discussions preceding such Agreement, whether direct or indirect, shall be treated by the recipient as confidential and shall not be disclosed in any manner nor used for any purpose except as herein contemplated.

13. Provision of Technical know-how and other services

13.1 It is agreed that the party of the SECOND PART shall provide technical know-how and other services to the Joint Company as per the agreed terms and conditions.

13.2 The party of the SECOND PART shall execute the agreement of provision of technical know-how and other services within 30 days of the incorporation of the Joint Company as per the draft agreement annexed as Schedule 'D' of this agreement.

14. Termination

14.1 This agreement may be terminated as follows:

(i) The Party of the FIRST PART may terminate this Agreement by giving a Notice of Termination in writing to the other Party if:

(a) the Technical know-how and other Services Agreement which is contemplated by the parties to be executed and performed between the Joint Company and the party of the SECOND PART is terminated due to the default of the party of the SECOND PART under such agreement.

(b) if the party of the SECOND PART defaults in the performance of any material undertaking under this Agreement and fails to correct such default to the reasonable satisfaction of the party of the FIRST PART within ——— days after written notice of such default is provided to the party of the SECOND PART.

(ii) The Party of the SECOND PART may terminate this Agreement by giving a Notice of Termination in writing to the other party if:

(a) the Technical know-how and other Services Agreement which is contemplated by the Parties to be executed and performed between the Joint Company and Party of the SECOND PART is terminated due to the default of the Joint Company under such agreement.

(b) if the party of the FIRST PART defaults in the performance of any material undertaking under this Agreement and fails to correct such default to the reasonable satisfaction of the party of the SECOND PART within ——— days after written notice of such default is provided to the party of the FIRST PART.

(iii) Either Party may terminate this Agreement upon ——— days prior written notice to the other Party if any basic premise or term of this Agreement is breached by the other Party and such other Party shall have failed to remedy such breach within ——— days of written notice having been served on the Party in breach, by the party so wishing to terminate the Agreement.

Notwithstanding the foregoing, in any such event, the parties shall endeavour to resolve the differences caused by such breach/defaults and shall negotiate in good faith to determine if there is a method to resolve such differences and correct any breach/defaults so that this Agreement might continue without termination.

14.2 This agreement may be terminated by either Party in the event, due to strike, riot, earthquake, storm, fire, explosion, act of God, war, acts of the Government of India or Government of the ——— or any other cause similar hereto because of which the continued operation of this Agreement or business activities of the joint Company are interrupted, prevented or delayed for a period exceeding ——— months.

14.3 This Agreement may be terminated by either Party in the event that the other Party becomes insolvent or has a Receiver appointed over its assets or execution or distress is levied upon all or substantially all its assets or is ordered to be wound up (except that where any such event is only for the purpose of amalgamation with another or reconstruction and the resultant company is acceptable to the Party desiring termination as a shareholder of Joint Company which acceptance will not be unreasonably withheld).

14.4 This Agreement may be terminated by either Party in the event that there is a deadlock between the Parties with respect to the Management or operations of the Joint Company which deadlock remains unresolved for a period of ——— months following written notice thereof from one Party to the other. In such case this Agreement will automatically terminate at the end of such ——— month period.

14.5 This Agreement may be terminated by either Party in the event that Joint Company becomes insolvent or goes into liquidation or is ordered to be wound up or has a Receiver appointed over or execution or distress is levied upon all or substantially all of its assets.

15. Effect of Termination

15.1 If this Agreement is terminated pursuant to clause 14.1 then unless otherwise agreed, the Party terminating this Agreement shall be entitled to require the Party in breach to sell its own and its Associate Companies' shareholding in the Joint Company to the public at large by a public offer thereof.

15.2 If this Agreement is terminated pursuant to clause 14.2 or 14.4 then unless otherwise agreed, the Party terminating this Agreement shall be entitled to sell its own and its Associate Companies' shareholding in the Joint Company to the public at large by a public offer thereof.

15.3 If this Agreement is terminated pursuant to clause 14.3 then the Party terminating this Agreement shall be entitled to require the Party in default to sell its own and its Associate Companies' shareholding in the Joint Company at the option of the terminating Party.

(*a*) to the terminating party or its Associate Companies on the terms and conditions as set forth in clause 11 hereof; or

(*b*) to the public at large by a Public offer.

16. Arbitration and Applicable Law

16.1 This agreement shall be governed by and construed in accordance with the Laws of India.

16.2 Any dispute arising out or in connection with this agreement, including any question regarding its existence, shall be referred to and finally resolved by arbitration under the Rules of the London Court of International Arbitration, which Rules are deemed to be incorporated by reference into this clause. The tribunal shall consist of three arbitrators, one of whom shall be nominated by each party and the third to be appointed by the London Court of International Arbitration. The arbitration shall take place at ——— and the language of the arbitration shall be English. The parties shall abide by and perform any award rendered by the arbitrators and a judgment may be entered upon the award in any court having jurisdiction.

17. Force Majeure

17.1 If the performance of this Agreement or of any obligation of either party is prevented, restricted or interfered with by reasons of fire, explosion, strike, casualty or accident, epidemic, cyclone, earthquake, flood, or war, revolution, or requirement of any government or any sub-division, authority or representative of any such government; or any other act whatsoever, whether similar or dissimilar to those enumerated, beyond the reasonable control of any or both of the parties hereto; the party so affected, upon giving prompt notice to the other party shall be excused from such performance to the extent of such prevention, restriction or interference for the period it persists provided that the party so affected shall use its best efforts to avoid or remove such causes of non-performance, if possible, and shall continue performance hereunder with the utmost dispatch whenever such causes are removed.

17.2 If the force majeure persists for a continuous period of —months or more, the parties shall meet and decide about the future course of action.

18. Notice

18.1 Unless another form of notice is specified for a specific purpose under this Agreement, notices required or permitted by this Agreement shall be sufficiently given if mailed by registered or certified air mail or postage prepaid and directed by one party to the other party at the respective addresses of business. Either Party may change the address at which notice is to be received by duly notifying the other Party.

19. Miscellaneous Matters

19.1 Non-Agency: Nothing in this Agreement shall be construed to constitute the Joint Company as an agent of any party for any purpose.

19.2 Entire Agreement: This agreement constitutes the entire Agreement between the Parties and supersedes any and all prior agreements and understandings, whether written or oral, between the Parties with respect to the subject matter hereof and no agreement or understanding varying or extending this Agreement shall be binding on any party unless made in writing and signed by a duly authorized officer or representative of each Party, which writing must contain an express reference to this Agreement.

19.3 Assignment: This Agreement and the obligations expressed herein shall not be assigned by either Party except with the prior written consent of the other Party. Notwithstanding the foregoing, any successor in interest to either Party shall be liable to the other Party for the full and proper performance of this Agreement. In the event of any permitted assignment, the Party making the assignment shall continue to be bound jointly and severally with the assignee for the proper performance of the obligations of this Agreement.

19.4 English language: All correspondence and technical documentation between the parties shall be in the English language.

19.5 Continuation of Performance: The parties shall continue performance of their respective obligations herein contained, notwithstanding any arbitration proceeding unless such obligations itself is the subject matter of such arbitration.

19.6 No Waiver: Failure of either party hereto to exercise any right hereunder or to claim for fulfillment of any term hereof will not relieve, exempt or affect in any manner, the rights of the other party including the right to demand at any time strict and complete fulfillment of any or all provisions of this Agreement.

19.7 List of Schedule: The following schedules to the Agreement form an integral part of the agreement:

Schedule 'A' — Cost of Project and Means of Financing

Schedule 'B' — Time schedule for Payment of Capital

Schedule 'C' — Draft Agreement for provision of Technical Know-how and other services.

IN WITNESS WHEREOF, THE PARTIES have caused this Agreement to be executed by their duly authorised representatives in the presence of:

PARTY OF THE FIRST PART	PARTY OF THE SECOND PART

3—Technical Collaboration Agreement

This Agreement is made on this ——— day of ——— by and between —— a corporation organised and existing under the law of —— and having its principal place of business at ——— (hereinafter referred to as 'SELLER' which expression shall unless excluded by or repugnant to the context or meaning thereof include its successors and permitted assigns) of the ONE PART and ——— a company incorporated and existing under the Companies Act, 1956/2013 and having its registered office at ——— (hereinafter referred to as "BUYER" which expression, unless excluded by or repugnant to the context or meaning thereof shall include its successors and permitted assigns) of the OTHER PART.

WHEREAS the SELLER has represented that it is the owner of and possesses technical know-how data, formulae, information, knowledge, experience and skill, necessary and required for manufacture of ——— and also possesses technical know-how, information, data, skills and expertise in respect of erection and commissioning of plants for the aforesaid product.

AND WHEREAS the BUYER desires to obtain and the SELLER has agreed to provide to the BUYER various services in India for erection and commissioning of equipment and plant for the manufacture of ———.

NOW THEREFORE the parties hereto, in consideration of the premises set forth hereinabove and of the mutual covenants and undertaking set forth hereinafter, hereby agree as follows:

1. Definitions

In this Agreement the following expressions shall, unless repugnant to the context thereof, have the meaning as respectively assigned to each of them hereunder:

1.1 Agreement shall mean this Technical Collaboration Agreement including all Annexures hereto and all subsequent amendments hereto made specifically in writing by the authorised representatives of the parties in accordance with the provisions contained herein.

1.2 Process shall mean the process developed and owned by the SELLER for producing the PRODUCT and as briefly described in Annexure 1 to the AGREEMENT.

1.3 Product shall mean the product of the quality and type as specified in Annexure 2 to the AGREEMENT produced according to the PROCESS.

1.4 Plant shall mean the plant to be set up at ——— in India in accordance with the KNOW-HOW for the production of the PRODUCT adopting the PROCESS and having the rated capacity as stipulated in Annexure 3 to the AGREEMENT.

1.5 Site shall mean the site in the State of ——— India at which the PLANT is to be located.

1.6 Technical Documentation shall mean the basic technical documentation designs and drawings in respect of the PROCESS and KNOW-HOW including data, information and process engineering.

1.7 Know-How shall mean all formulae, processes, process description, process parameters and all technical know-how, data, information, basic design and basic engineering, product and raw material specifications, equipment specification for the PLANT, quality control and inspection procedures of the PRODUCT and raw materials, preliminary layout study contained in the "TECHNICAL DOCUMENTATION" and all accumulated knowledge, experience and skill owned or possessed by the SELLER and whether patented/patentable or not.

1.8 Indian Engineering Consultant shall mean the Indian consultant and/or contractor to be appointed by the BUYER, acceptable to the SELLER, or the BUYER itself for inter alia, carrying out the detail design and engineering of the PLANT, assistance in procurement of the INDIGENOUS EQUIPMENT and construction and erection/ supervision of the PLANT.

1.9 Date of Commissioning shall mean the date on which the raw materials have been fed into the PLANT and the first production of the PRODUCT has been commenced.

1.10 Date of Start-up shall mean the date on which, after the DATE OF COMMISSIONING, at least ———— tonnes of the PRODUCT have been produced in the PLANT.

1.11 Date of Acceptance shall mean the date on which the SELLER has successfully proved or is deemed to have proved the performance guarantees as set out in Annexures 2, 3 and 7 to the AGREEMENT in accordance with the provisions of the AGREEMENT and whereupon the PLANT has been accepted by the BUYER and a certificate of PLANT acceptance to this effect has been signed by the BUYER to the SELLER.

1.12 Net sale price means the price realised from the sale of the product net of Goods and Services Tax.

1.13 Effective Date shall mean the date on which this agreement shall come into force and effect in accordance with the provisions of clause 11 hereof.

1.14 Month, Quarter, Year shall have reference to the Roman calendar.

2. Scope of the Agreement

THE AGREEMENT covers, inter alia, the supply of the TECHNICAL DOCUMENTATION, provision of KNOW-HOW and services including provision of SELLER's technicians, training of BUYER's personnel and the grant of licence by the SELLER for the use thereof by the BUYER as provided herein.

3. Seller's Obligations

3.1 The SELLER shall provide to the BUYER the TECHNICAL DOCUMENTATION containing basic designs, drawings and informations in respect of PROCESS and KNOW-HOW and the same shall be delivered at ——— or at such other place outside India as may be mutually agreed by and between both the Parties hereto. The SELLER shall also provide to the BUYER complete know-how and other services including training of BUYER's personnel. The TECHNICAL DOCUMENTATION and KNOW-HOW shall be correct and complete in all respect and shall be such as shall enable the INDIAN ENGINEERING CONSULTANT for performing design, engineering, erection, commissioning, operation, maintenance of the plant and shall enable the BUYER to erect, commission, start-up, operate and maintain the PLANT and to produce thereat the PRODUCT of the quality and quantity, with the consumption of raw materials and utilities as specified herein.

3.2 The SELLER shall deliver the TECHNICAL DOCUMENTATION to the BUYER within ———— from the effective date. On receipt of the TECHNICAL DOCUMENTATION, the BUYER shall issue to the SELLER a receipt thereof. The issue of such receipt by the BUYER to the SELLER shall not however relieve in any manner the SELLER of its obligations of correctness and completeness, and its obligations hereunder, and the SELLER shall, up to the DATE OF ACCEPTANCE, at its cost remove and/or rectify all deficiencies and/or defects therein promptly notwithstanding anything to the contrary contained herein.

3.3 The SELLER shall provide to the BUYER the following technical assistance and services by deputing SELLER'S TECHNICIANS to India for:

(i) Review and checking of all detail design and engineering including all drawings for compliance with the KNOW-HOW to be performed by the INDIAN ENGINEERING CONSULTANT.

(ii) Review and checking of specifications for compliance with the KNOW-HOW of all bought out equipment other than the FOREIGN

EQUIPMENT as approved by the SELLER.

(iii) Provide erection supervision services for the equipment.

(iv) Supervision of commissioning and start-up of the PLANT.

(v) All other services elsewhere provided herein.

3.4 The performance guarantees hereunder of the SELLER shall be provided by the Seller through performance guarantee test run(s) in accordance with the provisions herein contained.

3.5 The TECHNICAL DOCUMENTATION to be provided hereunder by the SELLER shall be supplied to the BUYER outside India in 2 (two only) reproducible copies and 6 (six only) blue prints and in English language.

3.6 The TECHNICAL DOCUMENTATION shall be in metric system.

3.7 The SELLER shall provide and make available to the BUYER after receipt of due notice, whenever required by the BUYER, competent and qualified technicians/specialists (herein referred to as "SELLER's TECHNICIANS") in sufficient number for the purpose of supply of technical supervision services to the BUYER and/or the INDIAN ENGINEERING CONSULTANT and/or its sub-contractor(s) in the performance of the detail engineering, erection, commissioning, start-up and operation of the PLANT and also supervision of performance guarantee test run(s), subject to the provisions of clause 7.3 hereof.

3.8 The SELLER shall, in addition to the aforesaid, as and when required by the BUYER, depute such number of SELLER'S TECHNICIANS as may be required by the BUYER from time to time during the term of AGREEMENT, subject to the provisions of clause 7.3 hereof.

3.9 The SELLER shall not at any time withdraw any of SELLER's TECHNICIANS deputed to the BUYER without the prior written consent of the BUYER which shall not be withheld unreasonably. If however the BUYER is in arrears with any payment by more than ———— days, the SELLER shall be entitled to withdraw any and/or all of SELLER's TECHNICIANS without any further notice.

3.10 SELLER agrees that neither SELLER nor their Technicians shall make any claim against BUYER for any loss and/or damage to SELLER'S property or person caused due to their own negligence. However, SELLER shall be liable for any loss or damage that may be suffered by the person or property of BUYER or third parties due to the negligence of SELLER's TECHNICIANS in the execution of their duties.

3.11 In fulfilling its obligations hereunder, the SELLER shall abide by all applicable code, rules, regulations, directions, notifications, etc., in force in the State of ———— India as made known to the SELLER by the BUYER in writing. In the event of any change(s) in such codes, laws and/or regulations, etc., after the EFFECTIVE DATE which necessarily require changes and/or modification in the TECHNICAL DOCUMENTATION the SELLER shall make all necessary changes and/or modifications therein, subject to the provisions set out in clause 3.12 herein below.

3.12 In the event the SELLER has to make any change and/or modifications relating to the TECHNICAL DOCUMENTATION or KNOW-HOW or any of its obligations under this agreement by reason of any change in applicable codes, laws and regulations or if the BUYER requires any modifications which do not affect the performance guarantee given herein and also do not require any additional cost to be incurred by the SELLER thereunder and also is practically possible for the SELLER, SELLER shall carry out the same within a reasonable time.

However, if such changes or modifications require adjustment in the consideration payable hereto, the SELLER shall submit in writing to the BUYER an estimate of the adjustments in consideration and in time schedule. If such estimates are agreed to, the parties shall enter into a supplementary agreement and only after such agreement has been entered into and approved by the concerned Indian authorities including Reserve Bank of India, if required, the SELLER shall carry out such modifications.

3.13 SELLER undertakes to perpetually supply or arrange to supply at international prices all proprietary raw materials, consumables and components to successfully manufacture the PRODUCT.

4. Training of Buyer's Personnel and Technical Services

4.1 Prior to the Date of Commissioning, SELLER shall upon written request received from the BUYER, arrange to impart training to BUYER's personnel in the manufacture of product and in the inspection, operation and maintenance of the plant and the manufacture, inspection and quality control of the products at SELLER's plants or at the plant of one of its associate companies. The timing of such training visits of BUYER's personnel and the number of BUYER's personnel involved in each such training visit shall be mutually agreed to by the parties hereto and will be limited to ———— man months. All salaries and living and travelling expenses incurred by such BUYER's personnel shall be borne by BUYER. Such training will be imparted in English.

4.2 The personnel sent by BUYER shall be permitted to take notes or make sketches in connection with the information given to them and BUYER shall ensure that their personnel treat such information and notes as strictly confidential and shall not disclose such information to third parties except as provided hereunder.

4.3 SELLER shall, as part of the training of BUYER's personnel, explain the technical documentation, drawings, writings and specification relating to Technical Documentation and Know-how including operation and maintenance manuals to BUYER's personnel and shall impart to them know-how and experience associated with the production of products which is not covered by such technical documentation, drawings, writings and specifications and shall give them an opportunity to acquaint themselves with the techniques relating to the production of PRODUCT. This training will be imparted by qualified and English speaking personnel of SELLER.

4.4 At any/all times during the term of this agreement, SELLER shall, upon written request from BUYER, arrange to provide to the technical personnel of BUYER at its Plant or at the Plant of its associate companies, as per agreed schedule for periods not exceeding in the aggregate ——— man months per year to study the maintenance and operation of machinery and equipment comprised in the plant as also of process and techniques in the TECHNICAL DOCUMENTATION for the production of the PRODUCT, any change or improvement therein used by or known to the SELLER within the scope of this agreement and to confer with SELLER any problems arising out of BUYER's Technical operation and/or practice of Technical Documentation within the scope of this Agreement and to provide advice, clarification and/or additional information sought by such personnel from SELLER. All salaries of such BUYER's personnel and their boarding, lodging, travelling and other expenses shall be borne by BUYER.

4.5 BUYER's personnel shall be subject to SELLER's company regulations at Seller's factory and shall be subject to their laws and customs and shall follow the same at all times during their stay at SELLER's plant.

4.6 SELLER shall familarise BUYER's technicians at SELLER's plant at ——— with the design and engineering as used in the plant as contained in TECHNICAL DOCUMENTATION to enable them to undertake eventual independent performance of the plant.

4.7 The tentative details of training to be provided to BUYER'S personnel in different areas is as per Annexure 4.

5. Grant of Licence

5.1 The SELLER hereby grants to the BUYER a non-exclusive (*or* exclusive) right and licence to manufacture the PRODUCT in the

PLANT with the KNOW-HOW including the PROCESS in India and to sell and market the PRODUCT worldwide except to the countries as mentioned in Annexure-5.

5.2 The SELLER has option to convert the exclusive licence as stipulated in clause 5.1 hereinabove to a non-exclusive right if the BUYER ceases commercial production any time for a continuous period of ——— months after ——— year from the date of START UP.

5.3 The BUYER shall notwithstanding anything to the contrary contained herein be entitled to and shall have the right to use and practice the KNOW-HOW and to manufacture therewith the PRODUCT in the PLANT after the expiry of the term of the AGREEMENT or its earlier termination due to the default of the SELLER without any further payments whatsoever to the SELLER.

5.4 The SELLER hereby grants to the BUYER a non-exclusive right and licence under all its applicable patents, if any, for the respective lives of such patents to the extent applicable to the KNOW-HOW including the PROCESS and the TECHNICAL DOCUMENTATION for the production of the PRODUCT in India and grants to the BUYER the right to market the PRODUCT worldwide (with the exception of the countries as mentioned in Annexure-5) notwithstanding the expiry of the term of the AGREEMENT or its earlier termination due to the default of the SELLER and all the payments due and payable hereunder shall constitute full compensation therefor.

5.5 The BUYER shall be entitled to sub-licence the KNOW-HOW to any other party in India on terms mutually agreed upon in writing by all the parties concerned, including the SELLER, subject to any approval of the Government of India as may be required.

5.6 The SELLER hereby grants to the BUYER the right to the use of a label stating, "manufactured in technical collaboration with ———" for promoting the PRODUCT during the term of the AGREEMENT.

6. Obligations of the Buyer

6.1 The BUYER shall follow in the implementation and practice of the TECHNICAL DOCUMENTATION and KNOW-HOW, the instructions given by the SELLER in respect thereof.

6.2 The BUYER shall at its cost provide the necessary raw materials and utilities as specified in the TECHNICAL DOCUMENTATION, the qualified local personnel necessary for the erection, commissioning and START-UP of the PLANT for the conducting of the performance guarantee test run(s) under the supervision and directives of the SELLER. The SELLER, however, shall supply to the BUYER a written list of all relevant requirements for test run(s) at least ———— months prior to the DATE OF START-UP.

6.3 The BUYER shall procure, obtain and maintain any and all requisite licences, approvals, permits and/or authorisations at its cost as are necessarily required for the fulfilment of SELLER's obligations in India. The SELLER shall provide all such information and assistance which may be required by the BUYER in this regard. Where any application, licence or authorisation is required to be made or obtained by the SELLER, he shall apply for and obtain the same and the BUYER in such a situation shall render all reasonable assistance to the SELLER in this behalf.

6.4 The BUYER shall give to SELLER's and/or its sub-contractors' personnel free access to the PLANT.

6.5 The BUYER shall pay to the SELLER the consideration agreed to be paid as per clause 7 hereof.

6.6 The BUYER agrees that he or his technicians shall not make any claim on the SELLER for any loss and/or damage to BUYER's property or person caused due to their own negligence. However, BUYER shall be liable for any loss or damage that may be suffered by the person or property of SELLER or any of its personnel or third parties due to the negligence of the BUYER's technicians in the execution of their duties.

7. Consideration and Payments

7.1 The BUYER shall pay to the SELLER subject to applicable Indian taxes the following amounts:

(i) a lump sum payment of ——— towards the supply of TECHNICAL DOCUMENTATION;

(ii) a further lump sum payment of ——— towards the provision of KNOW- HOW and services including training of BUYER's personnel and grant of licence.

The aforesaid lump sum payments shall be paid in three equal instalments as detailed below:

(a) 1/3 within ——— days from the date of requisite approval of the collaboration agreement by the Government of India including Reserve Bank of India;

(b) 1/3 within ——— days from the date of transfer of TECHNICAL DOCUMENTATION;

(c) 1/3 within ———— days from the DATE OF START UP.

7.2 During the term of this Agreement the BUYER also agrees to pay to the SELLER within ———— days of the close of each quarter, beginning ——— year after the Effective Date of this Agreement, regardless of the particular manner of manufacture used by BUYER (whether with SELLER's technology or not), an amount ("Periodic payment") equal to ——— percent of the total domestic Net Sale Price of all products sold or otherwise transferred by BUYER to any third party within India during the preceding quarter and ——— percent of the total export Net Sale Price of all products exported or otherwise transferred by Buyer to any third party outside India during the preceding quarter.

Buyer agrees to pay a liquidated late payment charge of ——— percent per annum on all Periodic payments that become overdue.

7.3 In addition to above, the BUYER shall pay Rs. ——— per man-month to the SELLER for the deputation of SELLER's Technicians for supervision services as set out in clause 3.7 and 3.8 hereof. The payment in this regard shall be made by the BUYER to the SELLER within ——— days from the date of presentation of SELLER's bill. The SELLER shall raise the bills on quarterly basis covering the actual man-months served by its technicians during the preceding quarter.

7.4 The basic periodic payments and payments for technicians as provided for in this Agreement shall be made free of any deductions except taxes imposed on SELLER under the law of India which taxes must be deducted from the said payments. In the event of the return of goods to the BUYER by its customers of PRODUCT for which a periodic payment has been made, the BUYER shall be allowed a credit in the amount of such periodic payment from the Periodic payment that next becomes owing from BUYER to SELLER.

The BUYER shall also send to the SELLER an official tax receipt or prescribed tax deduction certificate for all taxes required to be withheld by BUYER on SELLER's behalf.

7.5 The BUYER agrees to keep at its principal office in India, full, true and accurate books of account and records, relating to the manufacture, sale or other disposition of its PRODUCT in such detail as will enable the SELLER to ascertain what periodic payments are due. The SELLER through independent chartered accountants or equivalent agent, of its own selection (or employees thereof) as its duly accredited representatives, shall have access to such records and books during reasonable business hours once in each quarter/calendar year to inspect the same and make excerpts therefrom for the purpose of verifying the accuracy of the reports and payments as required under this Agreement. These accountants may report to SELLER only the amount of Periodic Payments due and payable and SELLER will neither request nor accept any other information.

7.6 The BUYER agrees to make quarterly reports to Seller in respect of all Products for which a Periodic payment is due under this Agreement by virtue of its having been sold or otherwise transferred by BUYER during the preceding quarter. The said reports shall be in such form as SELLER may reasonably request and shall set forth at a minimum:

(a) the total of all Net Sales Prices by BUYER during that quarter; and

(b) the total number of units sold (sales volume) of Product by Buyer during said quarter.

The said reports shall be forwarded to Seller not later than the —— days following the close of each quarter.

8. Patent Indemnity

8.1 The SELLER hereby warrants that the licence granted hereunder by the SELLER to the BUYER and the use and practice by the BUYER of the KNOW-HOW including the PROCESS and/or the TECHNICAL DOCUMENTATION supplied by the SELLER to the BUYER pursuant hereto, does not infringe any patent, copyright, registered design or other industrial property rights of any person in India. In the event that an action, suit or proceeding is brought by any person in India against the BUYER based on any such infringement, the BUYER shall promptly give written notice thereof to the SELLER and the SELLER shall defend the said action for the BUYER at SELLER's cost.

8.2 The BUYER shall fully cooperate with the SELLER in the defence of any such infringement action and shall render all reasonable assistance to the SELLER in all such proceedings and shall have the right to be represented in any such proceedings at its cost and expense.

8.3 Without prejudice to the aforesaid, if at any time any third party raise any objection, claim or demand on any account whatsoever, in respect of the implementation/further implementation of the AGREEMENT, both the Parties hereto shall, without any delay, on receipt of notice of any such objection, claim or demand by any third party, cooperate with each other and determine the manner in which the same should be dealt with.

9. Warranty and Performance Guarantees

9.1 The SELLER warrants that the TECHNICAL DOCUMENTATION, KNOW HOW and other services shall be complete and be such as to enable the INDIAN ENGINEERING CONSULTANT to undertake the detail design and engineering so as to enable the BUYER to erect, commission, startup, operate and maintain the PLANT and to produce thereat the PRODUCT of the quality and in the quantity and with the consumption of raw materials and utilities as guaranteed hereunder.

9.2 The SELLER warrants that the PLANT designed, engineered, erected, commissioned operated and maintained in accordance with the KNOW-HOW and TECHNICAL DOCUMENTATION shall produce the PRODUCT of the quality as provided herein and with the consumption of raw materials and utilities as guaranteed hereunder.

9.3 The PLANT erected, commissioned, operated and maintained in accordance with the KNOW-HOW and TECHNICAL DOCUMENTATION shall produce the PRODUCT of the quality as set out in Annexure 2 hereto and shall have a capacity as set out in Annexure-3 hereto with the consumption of raw materials and utilities as specified in Annexure-7 hereto.

9.4 The performance guarantees and warranties given by SELLER under this Agreement are subject to the following conditions:

(i) The INDIAN ENGINEERING CONSULTANT has performed the engineering in compliance with the KNOW- HOW and TECHNICAL DOCUMENTATION.

(ii) The PLANT is erected, operated and maintained in accordance with the KNOW - HOW and TECHNICAL DOCUMENTATION.

(iii) The raw materials, auxiliary materials and utilities used for the production of the PRODUCT at the PLANT are as per the specifications as set out in Annexure - 6 hereto and such raw materials, auxiliary materials are available continuously in sufficient quantities and in due time.

(iv) The recommended number of qualified and trained personnel of the BUYER are operating the PLANT.

(v) The PLANT has been erected and commissioned under the supervision of SELLER's TECHNICIANS in accordance with the provisions herein contained and minimum ——— man months technical supervision services thereof have been rendered by the SELLER.

9.5 After the erection of the PLANT, it shall be commissioned by the BUYER under the direction and supervision of SELLER's TECHNICIANS. The BUYER shall operate the PLANT and at all times hold the full management responsibility for its operation and the execution of SELLER's written directives given pursuant hereto.

9.6 After the DATE OF COMMISSIONING the PLANT shall be started up by the BUYER under SELLER's supervision.

9.7 Once the PLANT reaches stable operating conditions as indicated by a continuous run of not less than ——— days in achieving a minimum of ——— percent of the designed capacity producing the PRODUCT, both the Parties hereto shall agree upon the date of commencement of the performance test run for proving the performance guarantees given hereunder by the SELLER, and if no agreement is reached as aforesaid, the performance test run shall be held within ten days after the PLANT has run ———— percent of design capacity producing the PRODUCT for a minimum period of seven days as set out hereinabove.

9.8 The detailed procedure for the performance test run shall be agreed in writing by both the Parties hereto well in advance of the commencement thereof. Both the Parties hereto agree that the average figures arrived at for various guarantee figures over the period of the performance test run shall be taken as the basis for determining whether the performance guarantees are met or not.

9.9 The performance test run for proving the performance guarantees hereunder shall be of consecutive days duration. During the performance test run the plant shall be operated by BUYER's personnel under the supervision of SELLER's TECHNICIANS in accordance with SELLER's written operating instructions. Any and all results and/or data during the performance test run shall be jointly compiled by both the Parties hereto and initialled by their authorised representatives.

9.10 If the results of the said performance test run show that the performance specifications as set out in Annexures 2, 3 and 7 hereto are met, the BUYER shall sign a certificate of plant acceptance within ——— days from the date on which the performance test run was completed and the SELLER shall thereupon be deemed to have fulfilled its performance guarantee obligations hereunder. The date on which this certificate has been signed by the BUYER shall be deemed as the DATE OF ACCEPTANCE.

9.11 In case of performance guarantee test being unsuccessful, the parties shall examine the cause of the failure jointly and the party being responsible for the cause shall take necessary action quickly.

9.12 If within a period of ——— months from the date of commissioning of the plant the performance test could not be held under this agreement for reasons attributable to BUYER and guarantees and warranties could not be proved for reasons not attributable to SELLER despite SELLER's best efforts, SELLER will be deemed to have fulfilled its obligation in regard to the performance guarantee provided.

9.13 If the performance guarantees and warranties could not be proved under the performance test held pursuant to this Agreement within ——— months of the date of commissioning of the Plant due to reasons attributable to SELLER or if performance test could not be held or completed within —— months of the commissioning of the Plant for reasons substantially attributable to SELLER, SELLER shall be liable for losses and/or damages that may be suffered or incurred by BUYER and SELLER hereby agrees to indemnify and to keep indemnified BUYER in respect of the said losses and/or damages.

The liquidated damages shall be ————.

9.14 Neither party shall be liable to the other for any indirect or consequential loss or damage.

10. Improvements, Other Technical Assistance and Training

10.1 The SELLER shall provide and disclose to the BUYER free of charge during the term of the AGREEMENT any and all improvements and/or innovations and/or developments and/or modifications to the TECHNICAL DOCUMENTATION and KNOW-HOW including the PROCESS and PRODUCTS and the BUYER shall be entitled to use and practise the same at the PLANT without being required to pay any sum whatsoever to the SELLER for the same.

10.2 During the term of the AGREEMENT the SELLER shall accept BUYER's technical personnel for the exchange of views free of charge regarding operation and maintenance of the PLANT at its existing plants at ——. The timing, the number of persons to be delegated by the BUYER and the duration of such visit(s) shall be mutually agreed by and between both the parties hereto. Any and all cost of such visit(s) including any and all expenses related to travelling, insurance, sustenance, etc., of said personnel shall be borne by the BUYER.

10.3 The SELLER agrees to provide to the BUYER all possible assistance, if so required by the BUYER, for the development of the market for the PRODUCT. The assistance could be in any form including the training of an agreed number of BUYER's sales personnel at its existing plant at ———, supply of any information, such as quality specifications, testing methods relevant to the applications of the PRODUCT, etc. THE SELLER shall also provide to the BUYER any information available in respect of the end use of the PRODUCT. The terms and conditions for visit(s) in connection with such assistance shall be agreed upon between both the parties hereto from case to case in due time.

10.4 In the event of the BUYER being desirous of setting up a research and development laboratory for the PROCESS and the PRODUCT as set out in the AGREEMENT, the SELLER shall provide to the BUYER all necessary assistance for setting up and operation of a research laboratory. The assistance as set out hereinabove shall be such as to provide information on the selection of equipment for such laboratory, to permit BUYER's representatives to visit the SELLER's existing research and development laboratory for a mutually agreed number of man-days on such terms as may be decided mutually between both the parties.

11. Commencement of Agreement

11.1 This Agreement shall come into force and effect on the last day of happening of all of the following events:

a) The Agreement is signed and executed by the parties hereto.

b) The Government of India has taken this Agreement on record.

c) The Agreement is approved by the Government of ———.

12. Term and Termination

12.1 The AGREEMENT shall come into force and effect from the EFFECTIVE DATE and shall remain in full force and effect for a period of ——— years from the Effective Date.

12.2 A party hereto may terminate this Agreement in the event of:

a) The other party committing a substantial breach of this Agreement and failing to rectify the same within ——— days of the receipt of a written notice in this regard from it; or

b) If a creditor takes possession of or a Receiver is appointed on the whole or a substantial part of the undertaking or assets of the other party; or

c) If the other party becomes insolvent or is taken into liquidation or an effective resolution for its winding up is passed by its shareholders; or

d) The sale of the whole or substantial part of the undertaking of the other party for any reason whatsoever.

12.3 Expiration or termination of this Agreement shall be without prejudice to any right which has accrued to the parties hereto with respect of any antecedent breach of any provision of this Agreement by any party hereto.

13. Force Majeure

13.1 Any failure or omission by either party to perform its obligations shall not be deemed to be a breach of the AGREEMENT, if the same is caused by reasons or circumstances constituting *Force Majeure* which shall include but not be limited to acts of God, acts of any Government or any agency thereof, law, order, decree or regulation both present and future of any Government or any agency thereof, fire, war, riots, civil commotion, strikes, lockouts, embargoes, disasters or any other cause beyond the control of the party affected.

13.2 The party claiming *Force Majeure* shall be as soon as possible notify the other party by cable and/or telex/fax of the conditions constituting *Force Majeure* which affect the execution of the AGREEMENT together with expected duration thereof and send at the earliest by registered airmail a detailed report of the *Force Majeure* circumstances.

13.3 When the cause of *Force Majeure* has ceased to exist, the party affected thereby shall immediately inform the other party by cable and/or telex/fax about the same and confirm it by registered airmail. Further, the performance of obligations of the party invoking *Force Majeure* shall, to the extent affected by it, remain suspended during the subsistence of such *Force Majeure* and the period for the performance thereof shall stand extended by the period(s) of delay on account of it.

14. Law and Arbitration

14.1 This AGREEMENT shall be governed by and be interpreted in accordance with the law of India.

14.2 All disputes or differences arising out of or relating to or in connection with this Agreement unless settled amicably by the parties, shall be referred to and settled by arbitration in accordance with the Rules of Arbitration of the International Chamber of Commerce, Paris, by a Board of Arbitrators comprising one nominee each of the parties hereto and third arbitrator to be appointed by the President of the International Court of Arbitration in accordance with the said Rules. The venue of Arbitration shall be ———. All arbitration proceedings shall be in the English language. Judgment upon the award rendered in such arbitration may be entered in any court having jurisdiction in India or ———.

14.3 Any arbitration award made in such arbitration proceeding shall be final and binding on both the parties hereto and shall be enforceable in any court having jurisdiction over the matter.

14.4 During the course of arbitration proceedings both the parties hereto shall continue to execute their respective obligations hereunder, except the obligations in respect of such matter(s) as is/are referred to arbitration.

14.5 The cost of arbitration shall be borne by the party(ies) as determined in the award.

15. Miscellaneous

15.1 The TECHNICAL DOCUMENTATION shall be in metric system and English language and any and all documents and/or correspondence under the AGREEMENT shall be in English.

15.2 The BUYER shall secure and/or assist the SELLER in securing any and all permissions as may be required in India for the performance of SELLER's TECHNICIANS.

15.3 Neither party shall be entitled to transfer or assign its obligations hereunder without the prior consent in writing of the other party.

15.4 Any and all amendments and/or supplements and/or alterations to the AGREEMENT shall be in written form and shall be effectual, if signed by the authorised representatives of both the parties hereto.

15.5 Any and all notices or communications with reference to the AGREEMENT shall be made by registered mail and shall be directed by one party to the other party at the respective address of business.

Either Party may, by a written notice to the other party, change the address for the purpose of notices hereunder.

15.6 The headings and numbers of the clauses hereof and Annexures hereto are for the sake of convenience only and shall not be construed or interpreted as affecting the contents or context or meaning of the provisions hereof.

15.7 Failure of any party at any time to require performance by the other party of any obligations hereunder shall not affect the right of such Party to require performance of that obligation and any failure by any party to notify or to take any action in respect of any breach of any provision of the AGREEMENT shall not be construed as a waiver thereof or of any continuing or succeeding breach of such provision or a waiver of any right under the AGREEMENT.

15.8.1 The BUYER shall keep secret and confidential the KNOW-HOW and the TECHNICAL DOCUMENTATION and shall not disclose the same to any third party without the prior consent in writing of the SELLER.

This secrecy clause shall continue in force until any and all of the KNOW-HOW and the TECHNICAL DOCUMENTATION have become part of the public domain.

15.8.2 The secrecy undertaking as per clause 15.8.1 hereof, however, shall not be applicable and the BUYER shall be under no obligation of secrecy hereunder in respect of any information or knowledge, if such information or knowledge:

— was in lawful possession of the BUYER or its contractors or vendors of equipment prior to the disclosure thereof by the SELLER and has not been obtained by it/them either directly or indirectly from the SELLER; or

— is, after disclosure by the SELLER, lawfully disclosed to the BUYER or its contractors or vendors of equipment by any third party having no obligations of secrecy to the SELLER; or

— has entered before or after the conclusion of the AGREEMENT into the public domain not through any act or omission of the BUYER or its contractors or vendors of equipment.

15.8.3 Disclosure of any part of the KNOW-HOW and/or the TECHNICAL DOCUMENTATION to the authority concerned of India or under appropriate agreements of secrecy to BUYER's engineering consultants or contractors or vendors of equipment or to persons engaged in the erection or commissioning or start up or operation or maintenance of the PLANT shall not be construed as a breach of the secrecy undertaking contained in clause 15.8.1 hereof.

15.8.4 In the event of the BUYER being obliged to provide access to the personnel of the indigenous research and development institution or organisation identified by any statutory authority for the purpose of examining the technology absorption or adaptation or improvement plans, the SELLER shall not have any objection to providing such access to the personnel of such institution or organisation to the PLANT or laboratory of the BUYER. Any disclosure of data to such personnel shall not constitute breach of secrecy.

15.9 If any of the terms or provisions of the AGREEMENT is or becomes void or ineffective, the effectiveness of all other terms and provisions of the AGREEMENT shall not be affected and both the Parties hereto shall use their best efforts to replace any such ineffective or void terms or provisions by effective terms or provisions producing the same or equivalent effects as the effect of the void or ineffective terms or provisions.

15.10 The AGREEMENT provides for any and all liabilities and/or obligations of both the Parties hereto and no obligation and/or liability other than those expressly stipulated in the AGREEMENT shall be assumed by either party.

15.11 The AGREEMENT shall be made in duplicate and both the copies shall be deemed to be originals, one each of which shall be retained by each Party to the AGREEMENT.

16. List of Annexures

16.1 The following Annexures to the AGREEMENT are an integral part of the AGREEMENT.

Annexure 1	Brief description of the PROCESS
Annexure 2	Quality and type of the PRODUCT
Annexure 3	Capacity of the Plant
Annexure 4	Details of training to be provided by the SELLER to BUYER's personnel.
Annexure 5	List of countries where Export is not permitted to the BUYER.
Annexure 6	Specification of the Raw Materials and the Utilities.
Annexure 7	Material Consumption Data

IN WITNESS WHEREOF, both the Parties hereto have duly executed the AGREEMENT on the day and in year first above written.

4—Supplement to Technical Collaboration Agreement

THIS SUPPLEMENTAL AGREEMENT is made this ——— day of ——— by and between ——— a corporation organised and existing under the laws of—— and having its principal place of business at ——, (hereinafter referred to as "SELLER" (which expression shall unless excluded by or repugnant to the context or meaning thereof include its successors and permitted assigns) of the ONE PART and ——— a company incorporated and existing under the laws of India and having its Registered office at ———, India (hereinafter referred to as "BUYER" which expression unless excluded by or repugnant to the context or meaning thereof shall include its successors) of the OTHER PART.

WHEREAS BUYER and SELLER have entered into an agreement dated ——— to provide to BUYER various services abroad for imparting TECHNICAL DOCUMENTATION and various services in India for erection and commissioning of equipments and plant for manufacture of ———;

AND WHEREAS in consideration of SELLER providing TECHNICAL DOCUMENTATION and KNOW-HOW, the BUYER has agreed to pay a lump sum of Rs. ——— inclusive of applicable Indian taxes payable in three instalments as provided in Clause ——— of the

Technical Collaboration Agreement dated——;

AND WHEREAS the BUYER has proposed and SELLER has accepted that clause —— of the said Technical Collaboration Agreement should be amended to provide for revised amount of instalment payments.

NOW therefore it is mutually agreed between the parties that clause ——— of the said Technical Collaboration Agreement dated ——— is substituted by the following new clauses to read as under:

1.
2.
3.
4.
5.

The provisions of this Agreement are supplemental to and not derogative of Technical Collaboration Agreement and to the extent of any inconsistency between the provisions of this agreement and the said agreement, this agreement shall prevail. Save and except as aforesaid the provisions of the Technical Collaboration Agreement shall remain in full force and effect and continue to be binding on the parties.

IN WITNESS WHEREOF the parties hereto have put their hands hereunto on the ———— day of ———— and year first above written.

5—Agreement for Consultancy Services

THIS AGREEMENT for consulting services, as detailed in Appendix A to —— annexed hereto and forming part of this agreement, executed at ———— (name of town) on this ——— day of ———— between AB, ————— represented by ————— hereinafter called the employer and CD, ————— represented by ——— hereinafter called the Consultant:

WITNESSETH THAT

Whereas AB wants to execute a project for ——, as detailed in Appendix A to this agreement and requires a Consultant to advise and assist AB by providing consultancy services needed for the successful implementation/execution of the Project in accordance with the Terms of Reference as detailed in Appendix ——; and

Whereas the Consultant has offered to provide such consultancy services to AB and AB has agreed to appoint CD as Consultant;

Now, therefore, the parties hereto named above, which expression shall include their successors in interest, hereby agree as under:

Article I—Definitions

1. Agreement

Agreement means this deed alongwith the appendices and annexures attached therewith.

2. Project

The project as described and detailed in Appendix 'A' to this agreement.

3. Consultant

Consultant means M/s CD ——————.

4. Principals

Principals means the following officers of the Consultant:

1.

2.

3. etc.

5. Force Majeure

For the purposes of this agreement '*Force Majeure*' shall include strikes, lockouts, industrial disturbances, acts of enemy, wars (whether declared or not), blockades, riots, epidemics, landslides, earthquakes, storms, lightning, floods, wash outs, civil disturbances, explosions and any other event, not within the control of either party, which makes proceeding with the Project or Services impossible or extremely risky.

6. Staff

The members of the Consultant's Project Team other than the principals as detailed in Appendix ——— to this agreement.

7. Local currency means ——————

8. Foreign currency means ——————

9. Billing Rates: } mention details as agreed

10. Reimbursable expenses:

(define any other term as may be necessary)

Article II—Services

2.01 Scope of services: The Consultant shall render to the employer services in performance of this agreement as specified and detailed in the Terms of Reference in Appendix ———; including amendments, adjustments and modifications as may be mutually agreed upon between the parties hereto;

2.02 Standard of Services: The Consultant shall render the services under this agreement of the best internationally accepted professional standards and shall exercise all reasonable professional skill, care, and diligence in the discharge of its obligations.

2.03 Estimated Man-Months: Notwithstanding any other provision herein, the Consultant shall render the Services in accordance with the Work Schedule annexed as Appendix ——— to this agreement, or as otherwise mutually agreed, and depute and make available such number of different classes of staff as specified in Appendix ——— hereto.

Article III—Staff

3.01—Staff: The services shall be performed by the Staff detailed in Appendix— and for the respective period of time indicated therein. The Consultant may, with the prior approval of the employer, make such adjustments as may be appropriate to ensure the efficient performance of the Services, provided that such adjustment will not result in any increase in the cost estimates as referred to in Clause 4.01.

In case any staff resigns, is discharged or withdrawn prior to completing his contract period of service, the Consultant shall promptly nominate and depute a candidate with equivalent or better qualifications and experience acceptable to the employer. The employer shall not be liable for any extra or additional remuneration payable to such substituted staff. The Consultant shall also withdraw and replace any of its Staff who is found by the employer to be unqualified, incompetent or otherwise undesirable.

3.02 However, if any expatriate staff while stationed in India for rendering services under this agreement becomes incapacitated by accident in connection with the performance of duties under this agreement and the same is not due to his wilful misconduct, the employer upon certification of his incapacity by a qualified medical practitioner, may require the consultant that such staff be returned to his point of origin. In such case and in case of a deceased staff, the cost of the staff's return transportation shall be borne by the employer. The resultant replacement, however, shall be at the cost of the consultant.

3.03 Indian Laws, Customs and Traditions: The Consultant's expatriate staff shall not indulge in political activities of India and shall not act against the local laws, customs and traditions.

3.04 Team Leader and Deputy Team Leader: The Consultant shall ensure that at all times during the continuance of this contract, a Team Leader, acceptable to the Employer, remains in charge of the Staff in the

Project Team who shall be responsible for laison between the Consultant and the Employer. There shall also be a Deputy Team Leader-cum-Chief Resident Engineer to be responsible for the daily supervision of the construction, review and monitoring of the progress of the works and the project sites.

Article IV—Payment to Consultant

4.01 An Estimate of the charges for the services rendered under this agreement payable in foreign currency is set forth in Appendix —— while the estimate of such charges payable in local currency is set forth in Appendix ———.

4.02 Ceiling on service charges: Except as may be otherwise agreed upon, payments to the Consultant under this agreement shall not exceed ——— (state the amount in foreign currency) and Rs. ——— in Indian currency. In addition five (5) per cent of the budgetary sums in foreign and Indian currency amounting to —— (state the amounts of foreign currency and Indian currency) respectively is set aside for contingencies.

4.03 Use of Contingency Amount: Payments in respect of costs that exceed the estimates given in Appendix ——— hereto may be chargeable to the contingency account in the respective estimates only if such costs are approved by the Employer.

4.04.1 Remuneration shall be determined on the basis of the time actually spent by the Staff in the performance of the Services after the commencement date thereof (including necessary travel time via the most direct route) at the rates and billing schedules specified in Appendix —— and subject to the following:

(a) Remuneration for the Services for a period of less than one month shall be calculated on a calendar day basis with each calendar day amounting to 1/30th of the month.

4.04.2 Reimbursable expenses shall include:

(i) The cost of full executive class air fare for the Team Leader and Deputy Team Leader and economy class air fare for the other staff by the most direct and expeditious route from the point of origin to ——— or the place of duty in India and return to their point of origin.

(ii) For the air travel of each member of the staff, the cost of excess baggage upto —— kilograms per round trip.

(iii) For any member of the staff spending 12 (twelve) consecutive months or more in the Project, the cost of one round trip for every six months of assignment in the project.

(iv) Miscellaneous travel related expenses, such as cost of transportation to and from airports, airport taxes, passports, visas, travel permits, vaccinations, etc.,

(v) Expenditure incurred on provision of vehicles and accommodation as specified in Appendix.

4.05 Within ———— days of giving notice to proceed, the Employer shall pay to the Consultant a sum of (specify the amount in foreign/local currency) being equal to —— per cent of the contract amount as an advance to cover the mobilisation expenses subject to the Consultant furnishing a Bank Guarantee acceptable to the employer for the amount of such advance. The said amount of advance will be adjusted in ——— equal monthly instalments from the Consultant's monthly invoices which shall be promptly cleared by the Employer within ——— days of the presentation thereof. The value of the Bank Guarantee shall be progressively reduced every ———— month.

4.06.1 The Consultant will submit monthly invoices for the services rendered and reimbursable costs to the Employer with such supporting documents as may be necessary. The invoices shall be duly certified to be correct by the Consultant.

4.06.2 If any invoice includes any items which appear questionable, the Employer shall issue an objection in writing to the Consultant and approve the undisputed balance amount of the invoice. The consultant may resubmit the disputed item in the subsequent invoices with additional supporting documents/submissions.

4.07 Final Payment: Upon completion of the services, the Consultant shall promptly render a final bill/accounting of foreign and local currency costs. Final payment shall be made only after a Certificate of Completion is issued by the Employer which shall not be unduly withheld/delayed.

Article V—Obligations of the Employer

5.01 Taxes and Duties: The Employer agrees and warrants that all payments under this agreement to the Consultant and their staff shall be free from all taxes, duties, fees and other impositions under the laws of India and that the employer will pay taxes and levies payable in respect of such payments directly to the authorities concerned.

5.02 The Employer shall also pay the taxes, duties, etc., leviable in India on the equipment, materials, etc., brought into India by the Consultant or its staff for rendering services under this agreement.

Provided that:

a) The Consultant and its staff shall comply with the relevant laws and regulations of the Government of India in importing such goods into India;

b) The materials brought into India by the Consultant and its staff shall be re-exported out of India and any refund or remission of taxes/duties paid by the Employer in respect thereof shall be receivable by the Employer.

c) If the Consultant or its staff do not re-export such materials, the taxes paid/payable in respect thereof, including penalties, if any, shall be borne by the Consultant and the Employer may set off such amounts against the amounts payable to the Consultant under this agreement.

d) The Employer as well as the Consultant and its Staff shall cooperate and coordinate with each other in compliance of the relevant laws, rules and regulations and supply to each other such documents/information as may be necessary or appropriate.

5.03 The Employer shall assist the Consultant and its Staff for prompt clearance through customs of the equipment, materials, etc., required for the discharge of its obligations under this agreement by the Consultant and also of the personal effects of the Staff except those the import of which is prohibited.

5.04 The Employer shall assist the Consultant's staff in obtaining entry and exit visas, residence and work permits, exchange permits and such other documents as may be necessary for their stay in India for rendering services under this agreement.

5.05 The Employer shall provide to the Consultant and its staff adequate office space at ———— and at the project site/s and such other facilities and services as are stated in Appendix ————.

These will be exclusively at the cost of the Employer.

5.06 The Employer shall supply to the Consultant, the data and information listed in the terms of reference, in time and free of cost and also provide access to any other data required by the Consultant for rendering the services.

5.07 The Employer shall ensure that the Consultant and its staff shall have, at all convenient and appropriate times, free and unimpeded access to all lands and properties as may be necessary for performance of Consultant's duties.

Article VI—Obligations of the Consultant

6.01 Without prejudice to the other provisions of this contract, the Consultant shall:

a) Perform the services under this contract with due care, skill, diligence and speed to ensure that the final works will fully satisfy the requirements of the Project.

b) Will be fully responsible for the consulting and/or engineering services rendered in performance of this contract.

c) Observe and comply with the Indian labour laws applicable regarding workmen's health, and safety, welfare, compensation for death or injury, minimum wages, working hours, etc.

6.02 Recommendations of the Consultant: If any of the recommendations of the Consultant require change or modification in the opinion of the Employer, the same shall be mutually discussed and reappraised, however, that the decision of the Employer shall be final.

6.03 Records: The Consultant shall:

a) Maintain accurate and systematic accounts and records of the costs and expenses incurred by it in connection with the services under this contract.

b) Allow any duly authorised representative of the Employer to inspect/audit such records and accounts at all reasonable times and, if required, furnish copies thereof.

6.04 Progress reports: The Consultant shall furnish to the Employer monthly/quarterly reports about the progress of the project and the services rendered and, whenever required, attend meetings with the Employer to monitor the progress of the project and services.

6.05 Assignment: The Consultant shall not assign or sub-contract any part of the services to be rendered under this contract except with the prior written permission of the Employer. Such permission, if granted shall, however, not relieve the Consultant of its responsibilities and obligations in that regard.

6.06 Prohibition of Activities: The consultant agrees that during the currency of this agreement and during a period of three years from the completion/termination thereof, the Consultant shall not provide services similar to those of this agreement to any other person in India.

6.07 Confidentiality: The parties hereto agree that during the currency of this agreement or during a period of three years after the completion thereof, neither of them shall disclose to any other person the technical data, information, reports, recommendations, etc., exchanged between them without the prior permission of the other party except where the same is to be furnished to law enforcement agencies or their respective superior authorities.

6.08 Status of the Consultant: Nothing in this agreement shall be construed to create the relationship of agent and principal between the Consultant and the Employer. The Consultant and its staff shall be rendering services under this agreement to the Employer as an independent contractor.

6.09 Indemnities:

a) The Consultant shall hold the Employer free from any liabilities, suits, actions, demands, damages, etc., arising from death or injuries to persons or properties or any loss resulting from or caused by the said staff by negligence, and not otherwise, incidental to or in connection with the services under this agreement.

b) The Employer agrees to hold the Consultant free from any liabilities, suits, actions, demands, damages etc., arising from death or injuries to the Consultant or its Staff and their equipment implements or to any other person by the acts of commission or omission of the Employer or its employees incidental to or in connection with the performance of this agreement.

c) The Consultant agrees to indemnify, protect and defend at its costs and expenses the Employer and its employees and agents from all claims and liabilities arising from the acts done by the Consultant under this agreement relating to the use or violation of any copyright and/or patented material.

Article VII—General Conditions

7.01 Laws Applicable: This agreement shall be governed by the laws of India.

7.02 Property Rights:

a) Records like relevant data, maps, diagrams, plans, designs, statistics, specifications and other supporting records or materials prepared during the course of or for the purposes of services shall be the absolute property of the Employer and shall not be used by the Consultant for any other purpose except with the prior written approval of the Employer. On completion of the Project the Consultant shall hand over all such records and materials to the Employer but may retain two copies of the same if so desired.

b) Tools, materials, equipment supplied by the Employer to the Consultant and those purchased by the Consultant and charged to the Employer shall remain the property of Employer and the Consultant shall return the same to the Employer on completion of the project.

7.03 Employer's Control: The employer shall appoint and designate in writing an official who will keep in touch with the progress and implementation of the project and shall act as the medium of communication/coordination with the Consultant and authorised to approve/ disapprove all matters regarding the services under this agreement.

7.04 Insurance: The Employer will not be responsible in respect of any life, health, accident, travel and other insurance for the Consultant and its staff.

7.05 The Employer may at any time by written notice to the Consultant require additional services, make changes or alterations in the scope of services or direct the omission of works of the services covered by this agreement. The consultant on the other hand shall not make any such changes except with the prior written sanction of the Employer.

The Team Leader will closely monitor the staff strength to ensure that no unnecessary or surplus staff is employed.

7.06 Term of the Agreement: It has been estimated that the time required for the completion of the project is ————. This agreement will stand terminated on the expiry of ———— from the date of receipt of the Notice to Proceed by the Consultant unless the Employer grants extension as provided in the following clause.

7.07 Extension of the Term of the Agreement: If there is delay in the rendering of services by the Consultant, it shall promptly notify the Employer of such delay/expected delay and may request for appropriate extension in the term of the agreement. Except in the case of *Force Majeure*, the Employer may grant or refuse extension in its absolute discretion and on such terms as it may think appropriate.

7.08 Completion Certificate: On completion of the services under this agreement to the satisfaction of the Employer, the Employer shall issue, without undue delay, a Certificate of Completion to the Consultant.

7.09 Documentation Expenses: The expenses incurred on the preparation and execution of this agreement shall be borne by the Employer and Consultant in equal shares.

Article VIII—Disputes Settlement and Termination

8.01 Disputes: The parties hereto shall try to settle any disputes arising from or in relation to this agreement amicably by mutual negotiations. In case no such settlement is reached, the disputes and differences shall be settled by arbitration under the provision of Arbitration and Conciliation Act, 1996.

8.02 The place of arbitration will be ——— and ——— shall be the language used in arbitration proceedings.

8.03 Inspite of any dispute/difference between the Employer and the Consultant, the Consultant will continue to perform the services under this agreement.

8.04 Suspension:

8.04.1 The Employer may by ——— days written notice to the Consultant suspend, partly or wholly, payments to the Consultant if there is:

a) a default, failure, or refusal on the part of the Consultant to perform services under this agreement to the satisfaction of the Employer;

b) any other situation like winding up, appointment of receiver, major change in the management of the Consultant as is in the opinion of the Employer likely to threaten or interfere with the proper execution of the project and the rendering of services under this agreement.

8.04.2 In case the Employer fails to clear the invoices submitted by the Consultant within the stipulated time, the Consultant may after —— days written notice to the Employer suspend the services under this agreement.

8.05 Termination of Agreement

8.05.1 By the Employer: a) The Employer may terminate this agreement if any of the conditions mentioned above in the Agreement are violated and continue for a period of ——— days after the Employer issues notice of suspension of payments,

b) The Employer may terminate this agreement by ——— days written notice to the Consultant if because of any event beyond the control of the Employer, the further implementation of the Project is frustrated.

8.05.2 By the Consultant: The Consultant shall promptly notify the Employer in writing any situation/reason beyond its control that makes it impossible for the Consultant to discharge its obligations under this agreement. On confirmation in writing by the Employer of the existence of such circumstances or upon its failure to respond to such notice within —— days from the receipt thereof, the Consultant shall be relieved from all liabilities for failure to carry out its obligations and it may thereafter terminate the Agreement by a written notice of not less than —— days.

8.07.1 Upon receipt of the notice of termination of this Agreement from the Employer, the Consultant shall take immediate steps to wind up its operations in a quick and orderly manner so as to reduce the costs to the minimum.

8.07.2 Upon termination of this Agreement by the Employer, the Consultant shall be entitled to receive from the Employer payment in full for the services rendered prior to the termination and reimbursement of reasonable costs incidental to the winding up of its operations.

8.08 Force Majeure

8.08.1 If any party is temporarily unable by reasons of *force majeure* to meet any of its obligations under this Agreement, and if such party gives to the other party a written notice of the event within —— days of the occurrence thereof, the obligations of the party shall remain suspended for as long as the inability continues.

8.08.2 Neither party shall be liable to the other party for loss or damages sustained by reason of *force majeure* and/or delays resulting therefrom.

Article IX—Execution

9.01 Commencement and Completion: The Consultant will commence the Services within —— days from the receipt of a notice to proceed from the Employer.

The validity of this agreement will come to an end on the expiry of —— months from the date of commencement of the services unless extended in the manner hereinbefore provided.

9.02 Notices and Addresses: All notices under this agreement shall become effective only on receipt by the other party and directed and addressed as under:

Notices to Consultant: Address

Notices to Employer: Address

All notices must be sent by registered post, telegrams, cables, in English language. Notices sent by telegrams, cables will be confirmed through registered post.

The address for the notices, as stated above, may be changed by either party by giving written notice.

9.03 Amendments: No amendment, modification, or alteration in the terms of this agreement shall be valid unless expressed in writing and executed in the same manner as this agreement.

9.04 Counter part: This agreement is executed in ——— copies each of which shall be deemed to be an original,

IN WITNESS WHEREOF the parties have set their hands hereunto on the date and place stated above.

For the Employer

____

For the Consultant

____

In the presence of

____

____

FRANCHISE

Preliminary Note

Franchising, to put it rather broadly, is the permission given by the proprietor of a brand name to another to manufacture and/or sell the product, or provide the service, in his particular area, utilising the brand name and the proprietors' designs, know-how and expertise, while strictly complying with the proprietors' standards as to the quality of the product or service and incidental matters that ensures that the reputation of the product or service is not diminished.

Franchising helps big corporations to expand their business and popularise their brand names without risking large sums of money by way of direct investment. The local dealer, who acts as a franchisee, is able to operate at a lesser cost and utilise his local market knowledge while getting the advantage of financial and technical know-how lent by the franchisor and the good-will attached to the brand name of the latter.

The European Community Commission in its study (1978) has identified five different types of franchise, namely

(1) manufacturer and wholesaler;

(2) manufacturer and retailer;

(3) wholesaler and retailer;

(4) service industry and retailer;

(5) undertaking in the same distributive group (the voluntary chain group).

The Commission has also classified franchises as industrial distribution and service franchises.

Among the well-known foreign brands which have developed franchises in India are McDonald's, K.F.C., Pepsi and Coke. We also have well-known Indian franchises such as Shahnaz Beauty parlours, Titan Watches, Tanishq Jewellery, Tata/Maruti Service Stations, and Raymond/ Bombay Dyeing Showrooms (textiles).

The Competition Commission of India has held that franchisee agreements stand on a different footing as the branding plays a vital role in such arrangements. The franchisee is often seen as an extension of the franchisor and is perceived as a single brand seller e.g. McDonald's sell burgers only of McDonalds and not of KFC. The importance of contractual provisions for protecting the franchisor's know-how, which is likely to have real efficiency benefits, needs to be carefully considered. Thus, the provisions designed to protect know-how and a particular brand value are likely to involve exclusivity in order to prevent the franchisee from unduly appropriating the benefits of this know-how by using it to distribute competing goods or by engaging, directly or indirectly, in activities similar to those of the franchisor.

The question whether it is necessary for a Franchisor to have a uniform Franchise agreement with all its franchisee's or can the terms or clauses be different for different Franchisee's was dealt the Competition Commission of India in *Om Datt Sharma* v. *Adidas AG.*[1] It was held that although there may be certain differences between two franchisee agreements, the differences cannot be termed as abusive unless they are discriminatory within the meaning of section 4(2)(a)(i) and 4(2)(a)(ii) of the Competition Act, 2002.

It may also be pertinent to note that a manufacturer is not be obligated to follow a single template agreement throughout its existence.

In *Classic Motors Ltd.* v. *Maruti Udyog Ltd.*,[2] in relation to the franchise agreement, Hon'ble Court held that the franchise agreements are terminable in character. "

Franchise agreements & Regulation of goods and services

In *EV Motors India Private Limited* v. *Anurag Agarwal*,[3] it was of served that in case of franchise agreements, certain clauses are stipulated to regulate distribution of goods and services. One of such condition may be that the franchisee shall not deal with competing goods. Such a condition is for facilitating the distribution of the goods of the franchiser. It is settled law that such a condition cannot be regarded as the one in restraint of trade.

The Hon'ble Court observed that except in cases where the contract is wholly one sided, normally the doctrine of restraint of trade is not attracted in cases where the restriction is to operate during the period the contract is subsisting and it applies in respect of a restriction which operates after the termination of the contract.

Negative covenants, operative during the period of the contract of employment when the employee is bound to serve his employer exclusively, are generally not regarded as restraint of trade and therefore do not fall under Section 27 of the Contract Act.

A negative covenant that the employee would not engage himself in a trade or business or would not get himself employed by any other master for whom he would perform similar or substantially similar duties is not therefore a restraint of trade unless the contract as aforesaid is unconscionable or excessively harsh or unreasonable or one sided.

1 2014 Comp LR 180 (CCI).
2 65 (1997) DLT 166.
3 2017 SCC OnLine Del 12373.

PRECEDENTS

1—Franchise Agreement to Operate an Outlet

THIS AGREEMENT is made on ——— between AB etc., ———— (hereinafter called "the Franchisor") of the one part and CD etc., ——— (hereinafter called "the Franchisee") of the other part.

WHEREAS the Franchisor is the owner of and possesses the data, formulae, information, knowledge, expertise and technical know-how (hereinafter called "the know-how") in ———— (hereinafter called "the Service");

AND WHEREAS the Franchisor desires to spread the business of the above Services and is willing to grant to the Franchisee the rights set out herein for this purpose;

AND WHEREAS the Franchisee is willing to have those rights with a view to providing the Services from the premises described in the Schedule I hereto (hereinafter called the "Premises") under the name and style of ———— (hereinafter called "the Marks") which is detailed in the Schedule II hereto, as directed in the Franchisor's operation manual.

NOW THEREFORE, in consideration of the covenants hereinafter contained, the parties hereto mutually agree as follows:

1. Interpretation clause

In this Agreement the following expressions shall, unless the context otherwise requires, have the meanings respectively assigned to them hereunder:

1.1 References to the parties hereto shall include, subject to the terms, of this Agreement, their respective successors and assigns.

1.2 'Business' means the business of providing and marketing the Services.

1.3 'Equipment' means the equipment from time to time required by the Franchisee for use in the Business.

1.4 "Manual" means the manual provided by the Franchisor to the Franchisee together with all additions and amendments thereto from time to time.

1.5 "Secret or confidential information" includes confidential information provided by the Franchisor to the Franchisee through letter, correspondence, memorandum or otherwise for the purpose of or relating to the Service connected with the Business.

2. Rights Franchised

Subject to the covenants hereinafter contained the Franchisor grants to the Franchisee the rights to carry on Business, to utilise the know-how and to use the Marks in accordance with the provisions of this Agreement.

3. Period

This Agreement shall subsist for a period of ——— years commencing on ——— day of ——— 2000.

4. Renewal

If after a period of ——— years from the commencement and at least three months before the expiration of this Agreement, the Franchisee requests the Franchisor in writing for renewal of this Agreement, and if the Franchisee has not committed a breach of any terms and conditions of this Agreement, the Franchisor shall renew this Agreement for a further period of ——— years from the date of expiration of this Agreement on such terms and conditions as currently being offered to new Franchisees at that time.

5. Franchisee's Obligations

5.1 Obligation relating to Marks

The Franchisee undertakes that—

(a) he shall use the marks only for the purposes of promoting the Business and Services.

(b) he shall abide by all the reasonable directions of the Franchisor in connection with the use and presentation of Marks.

(c) the equipment regularly used by the Franchisee in the Business and Services shall carry such words, devices or designs and in such colour and manner, as may be directed by the Franchisor.

(d) he shall do nothing which will prejudice or damage the goodwill in the Marks or adversely affect the reputation of the Franchisor.

(e) if he comes to know about the infringement of the Marks by some other person carrying on business in a name and style similar or identical to the Marks he will immediately send information thereof in writing to the Franchisor.

5.2 Obligation relating to Equipment

The Franchisee shall comply with quality specifications for the Equipment as may be prescribed by the Franchisor.

5.3 General Obligations

(a) *Business under the Marks*

The Franchisee shall carry on the Business under the Marks and in no other name and style.

(b) *Business Premises*

The Franchisee shall carry on Business or render Services only in the Premises described in the Schedule or any other premises approved by the Franchiser, and in no other.

(c) *Standards*

The Franchisee shall maintain the highest standards in all matters connected with the Business and render Services relating to Business diligently to the reasonable satisfaction of Franchisor and conform to the requirements of the Franchisor according to the image and reputation of the Franchisor.

(d) *Staff dress*

The Franchisee shall ensure that his personnel comply with all requirements of the Franchisor regarding clothing, cleanliness, appearance, demeanour etc.

(e) *Training*

The Franchisee shall ensure that all his employees are suitably trained by the Franchisor before actually rendering the Services relating to Business.

(f) *Access to customers and personnel*

The Franchisee shall permit the Franchisor and/or his duly authorised agent to interact with the customers and the Franchisee's personnel to know about the Services being provided by the Franchisee.

(g) *Insurance*

The Franchisee shall ensure with a reputed insurance company in an adequate sum against all reasonably foreseeable risks relating to the rendering of Services connected with the Business including product liability arising out of any act, omission or negligence of the Franchisee or any other person for whom Franchisee is responsible. Insurance should cover all liability in respect of death or injury to customers, Franchisee's personnel or third persons and damage to property. Franchisee shall provide copies of such insurance policies and proof of premium payments to the Franchisor upon its request and abide by the directions of the Franchisor in this behalf.

(h) *Indemnity*

The Franchisee shall indemnify and keep indemnified the Franchisor from and against all loss, damage or liability suffered by the Franchisor due to any act, omission or negligence of Franchisee.

(i) *Notice about Franchisee status*

The Franchisee shall clearly indicate on his letter-head and correspondence with the public and customers that he is a Franchisee of the Franchisor. The Franchisee shall prominently display this fact on the notice board at his premises from where Services relating to Business are being rendered by it.

(j) The Franchisee shall not be entitled to demise, assign, or let out the know-how of the Services connected with the Business to any other person.

(k) The Franchisee shall comply with all the reasonable requirements of the Franchisor which are consistent with the terms and conditions of this Agreement and which are necessary for the efficient discharge of the Services connected with the Business.

(l) The Franchisee shall obtain prior written consent of the Franchisor before making any structural change in the trading style of the Franchisor.

6. *Franchisor's obligations*

The Franchisor shall:

(a) assist the Franchisee in establishing and efficiently discharging the Services connected with the Business.

(b) provide to the Franchisee a Manual regarding the Services connected with the Business;

(c) keep the manual upto date with necessary alterations, amendments and improvements;

(d) impart training and refresher courses to the Franchisee and his personnel who are engaged in rendering Services connected with

the business at the cost detailed in Schedule III to this Agreement;

(e) render such reasonable continuing assistance and advice as may be required for the efficient discharge of Services connected with Business;

(f) notify its requirements to the Franchisee from time to time as per provisions of Clause 5.3 (k);

7. Consideration and Payment

The following amounts shall be paid by the Franchisee to the Franchisor:

(i) franchise fee of Rs. ——— on the date of execution of this Agreement;

(ii) monthly fee for Service management equivalent to ——— percent of the previous month's turnover;

(iii) training cost as per provisions of Schedule III to this Agreement;

(iv) monthly contribution of a sum equivalent to ——— percent of the previous month's turnover or Rs. ——— per month/annum whichever is higher, towards Franchisor's Promotion and Advertising Fund.

8. Transfer/demise of business

8.1 The Franchisee shall not be entitled to assign, delegate or transfer the Franchise or any rights or obligations under this Agreement.

8.2 With the prior written permission of the Franchisor the Franchisee may sell or otherwise transfer the Business to any person subject to following conditions:

(a) The proposed transferee should be willing and able to meet the Franchisor's standards in all respects;

(b) The Franchisee has not committed any breach of the terms and conditions or covenants of this Agreement;

(c) The Franchisee shall pay to the Franchisor:

(i) a sum of ——— percent of the sale price, if the Franchisor has introduced the purchaser;

(ii) a sum of ——— percent of the sale price, if the Franchisor has not introduced the purchaser.

8.3.1 Following shall be submitted by the Franchisee to the Franchisor:

(*a*) a copy of the written proposal by the proposed transferee regarding purchase of franchised Business;

(*b*) the proposed transferee's financial status and business experience; and

(*c*) any other information which the Franchisor wants in this regard.

8.3.2 The Franchisor shall have the first option to purchase the franchised Business on the same amount and on the same terms and conditions as the proposed transferee has offered within a period of 30 (thirty) days from the date of receipt of a copy of the written proposal along with other papers as mentioned in Clause 8.3.1 above.

8.3.3 If the Franchisor declines to exercise or fails to exercise such option within a period of 30 (thirty) days as required in Clause 8.3.2, it shall be deemed that the Franchisor has consented to the proposed transfer.

9. Termination

9.1 A party hereto may terminate this Agreement in the event of:

(*a*) The other party committing a substantial breach of this Agreement and failing to rectify the same within ——— days of the receipt of a written notice in this regard from it;

(*b*) If a creditor takes possession of or a Receiver is appointed on the whole or substantial part of the undertaking or assets of the other party;

(*c*) If the other party becomes insolvent or is taken into liquidation or an effective resolution for its winding up is passed by its shareholders.

9.2 Notwithstanding anything contained in Clause 9.1 the Franchisor may terminate this Agreement if:

(*a*) the Franchisee fails to pay any sum to the Franchisor as per provisions of this Agreement within ——— days following its due date;

(*b*) the Franchisee fails to submit any document to the Franchsor as per provisions of this Agreement or as per requirement of Franchisor according to the provisions of this Agreement within ——— days following its due date;

(*c*) The Franchisee winds up or takes any step to wind up the Business;

(*d*) the Franchisor's intellectual property rights relating to the Services are challenged by the Franchisee.

9.3 If a part of this Agreement is held to be void or found to be unenforceable and the Franchisor is of the opinion that the exclusion of unenforceable part of the Agreement will adversely affect the Franchisor's right to receive payment or remuneration for the Franchisor's Mark or its know-how, then the Franchisor shall have right to terminate this Agreement on ——— days notice in writing to the Franchisee.

9.4 ——— days notice shall be required for termination of this Agreement as per provisions of Clauses 9.1 and 9.2 hereinabove.

9.5 Expiration or termination: This Agreement shall be without prejudice to any right or obligation which has accrued to the parties hereto with respect to any antecedent breach of any provision of this Agreement by any party hereto.

9.6 After the termination of this Agreement —

(a) All the documents, papers, stationery or other article bearing the Marks shall be returned by the Franchisee to the Franchisor whether any such document, paper, stationery or other article was supplied by the Franchisor or not;

(b) The Franchisee shall not make use of the Marks;

(c) The Franchisee shall neither pretend nor act like a Franchisee of the Franchisor;

(d) The Franchisee shall neither pretend not act as an associate of the Franchisor;

(e) Any commendations or references provided by the Franchisor to the Franchisee during the subsistence of this Agreement shall not be disclosed to third person.

(f) The Franchisee shall keep secret and confidential the know-how and any technical or confidential information which it has obtained during or as a result of this Agreement and it shall not be disclosed to third persons.

9.7 The secrecy undertaking as per Clause 9.6 (f) hereof, however, shall not be applicable and the Franchisee shall be under no obligation of secrecy hereunder in respect of any information or knowledge, if such information or knowledge:

was in lawful possession of the Franchisee or its agent prior to the disclosure thereof by the Franchisor and had not been obtained by him either directly or indirectly from Franchisor; *or*

is after its disclosure by the Franchisor, lawfully disclosed to the Franchisee or its agent by any third party having no obligations of secrecy to the Franchisor; *or* has entered before or after the expiration or termination of this Agreement into the public domain not through any act of omission of the Franchisee or its agent.

9.8 The Franchisee shall not for a period of ——— years from the date of expiration or termination of this Agreement carry on, directly or indirectly, any business which competes with the Services or is similar to the Business within a radius of ——— kilometres from the premises from where the franchised Business was being carried by the Franchisee.

10. Patent

10.1 The Franchisor hereby warrants that the franchise granted hereunder by the Franchisor to the Franchisee and the use and practice by the Franchisee of the know-how including the process and/or the Manual supplied by the Franchisor to the Franchisee pursuant hereto, does not infringe any patent, copyright, registered design or other intellectual property rights of any person in India. In the event that an action, suit or proceeding is brought by any person in India against the Franchisee based on any such infringement, the Franchisee shall promptly give written notice thereof to the Franchisor and the Franchisor shall defend the said action, suit or proceeding for the Franchisee at the Franchisor's cost.

10.2 The Franchisee shall fully cooperate with the Franchisor in the defence of any such infringement action and shall render all reasonable assistance to the Franchisor in all such proceedings and shall have the right to be represented in any such proceedings at his cost and expense.

10.3 The Manual, photographs, documents, papers and other articles supplied by the Franchisor to the Franchisee during the subsistence of this Agreement is the property of Franchisor. The Franchisee undertakes that it will neither copy it nor permit it to be copied out for any purpose other than the rendering of the Services connected with the Business. The Franchisee further undertakes that he will not disclose the content or concepts of the Manual, know-how and secret and confidential information to any third person and he will not himself make use of it whether directly or indirectly for purposes otherwise than in providing the Services connected with the Business.

11. Entire Agreement

11.1 The manual supplied by the Franchisor to the Franchisee is part of this Agreement.

11.2 This Agreement along with the Manual constitutes the entire Agreement between the parties and supersedes any and all prior agreements and understandings, whether written or oral, between the parties with respect to the subject-matter hereof and no agreement or understanding varying or extending this Agreement shall be binding on any party unless made in writing and signed by a duly authorised officer or representative of that party, which writing must contain an express reference to this Agreement.

12. Severability

Any provision of this Agreement which is held to be invalid or unenforceable for any reason shall be ineffective to the extent of such invalidity or unenforceability only, without affecting in any way the remaining provisions hereof.

13. Warranties

The Franchisee shall give warranty to its customers only to the extent the Franchisee is authorised by the Franchisor in this behalf or as is given in the Manual in force at the relevant time. The Franchisee shall alone be responsible for the warranty given in excess of its authority.

14. Indemnity

The Franchisee shall indemnify and keep the Franchisor fully indemnified against all claims, demands, damages, losses, expenses and costs which the Franchisor may suffer or incur as a result of breach of any provision of this Agreement.

15. Force Majeure

15.1 If the performance of this Agreement or of any obligation of either party is prevented, restricted or interfered with by reasons of fire, explosion, strike, casualty or accident, epidemic, cyclone, earthquake, flood, war or requirement of any Government or authority or representative of any such Government or any other cause whatsoever, beyond the reasonable control of parties hereto, the party so affected, upon giving prompt notice to the other party shall be excused from such performance to the extent of such prevention, restriction or interference for the period it persists, provided that the party so affected shall use its best efforts to avoid or remove such causes of non-performance, if possible, and shall continue performance hereunder with the utmost despatch whenever such causes are removed.

15.2 If the *force majeure* persists for a continuous period of —— days, the Franchisor may require the Franchisee—

(*a*) to pay all the money payable to Franchisor within ——— days from the date of written notice given by the Franchisor to the Franchisee in this behalf; and

(*b*) to stop the Business until further notice by the Franchisor to the Franchisee in this behalf.

16. Arbitration Clause

The Schedules referred to hereinabove:

Schedule I

(Premises)

Schedule II

(Relating to Services Marks)

Schedule III

(Relating to Payment)

IN WITNESS WHEREOF, etc.

2—Franchise Agreement to Operate a Shoppe

THIS AGREEMENT is made on ——— between AB etc., ———— (hereinafter called "the Franchisor") of the one part and CD etc., ———— (hereinafter called "the Franchisee") of the other part.

WHEREAS the Franchisor is the owner of and possesses the data, formulae, information, knowledge, expertise and technical know-how in ————:

AND WHEREAS the Franchisor desires to spread the said business and is willing to grant to the Franchisee the rights set out herein for this purpose;

AND WHEREAS the Franchisee is willing to have those rights with a view to providing the Services from the premises described in the Schedule I hereto.

NOW THEREFORE, in consideration of the covenants hereinafter contained, the parties hereto mutually agree as follows:

1.1 The Franchisor hereby appoints the Franchisee as its non-exclusive Franchisee to handle, store sell the products of the Franchisor and the Franchisee accepts the appointment under this agreement.

1.2 Unless otherwise terminated in accordance with clause 5, the terms of appointment of the Franchisee shall commence from date of execution of this agreement and shall remain in force for a period of 5 years subject to the performance by the Franchisee of the obligation as stimulated in this agreement.

At the discretion of the Franchisor, the terms of this agreement may be extended to such further period on such terms and condition as may be decided then by the Franchisor, which shall be communicated in writing to Franchisee.

1.3 The Franchisee recognizes and acknowledges that the Franchisor has a right to appoint any distributor, stockist, consignment agents, selling agents, and dealer at any time in territory for its products.

1.4 The Franchisee shall not Sub-Franchise and shall not appoint any Sub-Franchisee without written approval from the Franchisor.

1.5 The Franchisee shall not be deemed to be the Sole Selling Dealer. The Franchisee acknowledges that it will not have the status of an agent as provided under section 182 of the Indian Contract Act, 1872. The Agreement between the Franchisor and the Franchisee will be on principal-to-principal basis only.

2. Franchisee Obligations

2.1 The Franchisee shall keep the provisions of this Agreement and all information disclosed to it, concerning the Franchisor, confidential and the Franchisor's assets and businesses and not otherwise publicly available information shall be kept confidential and shall not be disclosed by the Franchisee without prior written consent of the Franchisor, unless otherwise required by law.

2.2 Installation and Maintenance

2.2.1 The Franchise showroom shall be as per designs, specifications and model provided by the Franchisor.

2.2.2 The Franchisee shall be responsible for identifying the premises for opening the SHOPPE. The SHOPPE premises shall be finalized by the Franchisee in consultation with the Regional and Head Office marketing team of the Franchisor.

2.2.3 The Franchisee shall bear all the maintenance charges for the SHOPPE.

2.2.4 The Franchisee shall maintain the SHOPPE and all aspects (interior as well as exterior) in good condition and should not temper with the standardized layout during the terms of this agreement.

2.2.5 The Franchisee shall have some or all of the following elements as advised by the Franchisor - Products Presentation Table, Cash Counter,

Brochure display, Graphic Signage's (value panels), Front Facade, LCD, DVD, Products display table computer with internet facility and landline telephone connectivity.

2.2.6 The Franchisor reserves the right to alter/change any design or display parameters pertaining to the SHOPPE interior or exterior in time with market requirements.

3. Pricing, Invoice and Payment Term

3.1 The Franchisee shall sell all the Franchisor's product range provided in the SHOPPE at the maximum retail price as fixed and communicated by the Franchisor to the Franchisee.

3.2 At the time of dispatch, the Franchisor shall raise its invoice for supply of products on the Franchisee, which shall be dispatched along with other related documents at the time of delivery of the Products to the Franchisee. In case of any discrepancy in the invoice or quality or quantity, then the Franchisee shall within seven working days intimate in writing to the Franchisor, failing which, the amount due under the invoices shall be deemed to have been accepted for payment.

3.3 All payments under such invoices shall be made within the period determined by the Policy of the Franchisor to be announced from time to time from the date of the invoices, by way of cheques payable at par or by demand draft drawn in favor of the Franchisor or through internet banking in the bank account of the Franchisor. In the event of delay in payments beyond stipulated period, then the Franchisee shall pay simple interest at the rate of ——— percent per annum from the due date of payment until the actual payment and/or realization on the outstanding payments to the Franchisor.

3.4 All payments to the Franchisor under this Agreement shall be exclusive of sales, value added, service, consumption tax or taxes or similar nature, which shall be paid for or reimbursed by the Franchisee at the applicable rates.

4. Right of Lien

4.1 Although the risk in the Products passes to the Franchisee from the date of dispatch of the product to the carrier and delivery being taken by the Franchisee, the title to the Products shall pass to the Franchisee only upon receipt of invoice amount by the Franchisor.

4.2 The Franchisor shall have lien on the Products so delivered to the extent of unpaid purchase price of Products and the Franchisor shall be entitled to exercise the lien to recover the unpaid purchase price by taking back the Products and shall be entitled to sell the same to some other dealer and adjust the sum so realized against the unpaid purchase price. This right is without prejudice to the Franchisor's other rights and remedies to recover the outstanding dues and/or other dues and/or the differential price of the Product.

Annexure: Schedule I.

IN WITNESS WHEREOF, etc.

GIFT

Preliminary Note

Gift is defined in Sec. 122 of the Transfer of Property Act, as a voluntary transfer of certain existing movable or immovable property without valuable consideration.[1] It is made by one party and accepted by or on behalf of the other. Without acceptance the transfer is not complete[2] and if the donee dies before acceptance, the gift is void (Sec. 122). The acceptance may be made either orally or implied by conduct (e.g., by taking possession of the property) or in writing. It may be express or implied. The best and the safest course is to join the donee as a party to the deed and state about acceptance in the deed of gift, or if the deed is in the form of a deed poll to have a separate endorsement of acceptance made on the deed and signed by the donee.

A minor may be a donee, and gift in his favour can be accepted by his natural guardian. However, if the gift is onerous, the obligation cannot be enforced against him during his minority; when he becomes major he must either accept the burden or return the gift.[3] A Pujari may accept it on behalf of the Idol.[4]

It has been held that no interest can be created in favour of an unborn person, but when the gift is made to a class or series of persons, some of whom are in existence and some are not, it does not fail in its entirety; it is valid with regard to the persons who are in existence at the time of the testator's death and is invalid as to the rest.[5]

Under the Hindu law, the Karta of a coparcenary can make a gift, by way of reasonable provision for the sake of maintenance of the Karta's daughter regard being had to the financial and other relevant circumstances of the family. This right is not confined to the occasion of marriage. It is regarded a moral obligation which continues to subsist till discharged. The quantity that may be gifted depends on facts of each case.[6] The Explanation to Sec. 30 Hindu Succession Act, which permits the interest of a male Hindu in a Mitakshara coparcenary property to be disposed of by will, does not however extend to gifts.[7] As alienation of joint family

---

1 *Sonia Bhatia* v. *State of U.P.* , AIR 1981 SC 1274, (1981) 2 SCC 585.

2 *Gomatibai* v. *Mattulal*, (1996) 11 SCC 681; AIR 1997 SC 127.

3 Mulla's Transfer of Property Act, 7th Edition p. 786.

4 *Jagadindra Nath Roy* v. *Hemanta Kumari Debi*, 32 Cal 129 PC; See also, *Dhaneshwarbuwa* v. *Charity Commr.*, (1976) 2 SCC 417 (para 27: Trustee accepting the gift on behalf of Sansthan) . See Preliminary notes under TURSTS, etc., *post.*

5 *Bajrang Bahadur Singh* v. *Thakurani Bakhtraj Kuer*, AIR 1953 SC 7 (para 14).

6 *Guramma B.C. Deshmukh* v. *Mallappe*, AIR 1964 SC 510.

7 *M.S.B.Y. Board* v. *Subramania*, AIR 1973 Mad 277.

property can only be for legal necessity or for the benefit of the family, a gift of a substantial i.e., more than reasonable portion of joint family property to charity is invalid.[1] Where, however, a father as Karta made a gift of property in favour of his married daughter, who had become a destitute, the gift whereby he acknowledged his moral liability (even in the absence of legal liability) to maintain her, was upheld.[2]

Gift or Release

Where a Trust deed required the trustees to give the net income from the trust property to 'S' during her lifetime and after her death to transfer the property absolutely to children of 'S', then a release deed, executed by 'S' surrendering her life interest in favour of her children, was held to amount to release and not to a gift. The transaction being unilateral it could not be a gift.[3]

How Drafted

The deed should be drafted as a deed of transfer, with recitals, if necessary. As there is no consideration, it need not be expressed, although consideration of "natural love and affection" is expressed, in all cases of gift to relations, and "consideration of esteem and regard" is expressed, when the gift is in favour of some person, for whom the donor has regard, e.g. when the donee is his religious preceptor.

Property

A gift should be about existing property only and if any future property is included it will be void to the extent of future property. (Section 124 Transfer of Property Act, 1882).

A gift of land with "water", trees, etc., is not, unless expressly specified, to be construed as including running water of a river but only stationary or static water in ponds and wells.[4]

When Gift Revoked or Suspended

A gift is ordinary absolute and irrevocable. However, section 126, Transfer of Property Act, 1882, provides that the donor and donee may agree that on the happening of any specified event which does not depend on the Will of the donor, a gift shall be suspended or revoked; but a gift, which the parties agree shall be revocable wholly or in part, at the mere Will of the donor, is void, wholly or in part, as the case may be. The section further provides that a gift may also be revoked in any of the cases (save want or failure of consideration) in which, if it were

---

1 *Niramathi* v. *Kambalam*, A 1998 Mad 185; cf. *Raghavamma* v. *Chench*, AIR 1964 SC 136 (on bequest); *Kesaram* v. *Jajala*, 1998 AIHC 1780 (AP) (on bequest).

2 *Laxmappa* v. *Balawa*, (1996) 5 SCC 458.

3 *Commr. of Gift Tax* v. *Ansuya Sarabhai*, (1998) 9 SCC 194.

4 *S.N. Ranade* v. *Union of India*, AIR 1964 SC 24.

a contract, it might be rescinded. It is also not revocable if the donee does not honour the donor's pious wish (not expressed as a condition) that the donee shall maintain the donor.[1]

Conditional Gift

A gift may be burdened with obligations. A gift with the condition that the donee shall not alienate the property, the condition itself shall normally be void (Secs. 10 and 12) and the gift cannot be revoked on the ground of its breach.[2]

A grant of land burdened with service may not be resumable, while a grant of land, made by way of remuneration attached to an office, may be resumed with the abolition of that office.[3]

How a Gift is Made

A gift of immovable property of whatever value must be made by a registered deed signed by the donor and attested by at least two witnesses (Sec. 123).[4]

The Transfer of Property Act does not apply to gifts governed by Muslim law which may be made orally, accompanied by delivery of possession.[5] In Muslim law, where the donor (husband) and donee (wife) both live in the house (the subject of gift), mere declaration of fact of delivery of possession is sufficient, and reservation by the donor of his right to reside and manage the property and to collect rents and to change tenants does not detract from his intention to make a valid gift.[6]

When the document is in the nature of a dedication of immovable property to God, the same does not require registration as it constitutes a religious trust and is exempt from registration.

If the gift is not intended to a living person within the meaning of Section 5 of the Transfer of Property Act, the document would not require registration. This view tilted the scale of justice in favour of the appellant Trust as the plot was essentially dedicated to Saibaba for a charitable purpose, although the same was in the form of an unregistered deed of gift.[7]

Under the Mohammedan Law the three essential requisites to make a valid gift are: (1) declaration of the gift by the donor: (2) acceptance of the gift by the donee expressly or impliedly and (3) delivery of possession to and taking possession thereof by the donee actually or constructively. *Hafeeza Bibi* v. *Farid*,

1 *M. Vekatasubbaiah* v. *M. Subbamma*, AIR 1956 AP 195; see also *Tila Bewa* v. *Mana Bewa*, AIR 1962 Orissa 130.

2 *Mt. Brij Devi* v. *Shiva Nanda Prasad*, AIR 1939 All 221.

3 *State of Orissa* v. *Ramchandra*, AIR 1964 SC 685.

4 On 'signature' and 'attestation' see INTRODUCTION Part I-Preliminary, *ante*.

5 *State of U.P.* v. *Syed Abdul Jalil*, (1973) 2 SCC 26; *C.T.D. A. Pathumma* v. *Pokku*, AIR 1998 Ker 134 *Noorbibi* v. *Ayeshabibi*, A 1999 Guj. 27.

6 *Halimbibi* v. *Abdul Rehman*, 1998 AIHC 1553, Guj.

7 *Sainath Mandir Trust* v. *Vijaya*, (2011) 1 SCC 623.

(2011) 5 SCC 654. Under Muslim Law, writing is not essential to the validity of a gift and thus need not be registered under Registration Act. Thus gift may be made orally, whatever may be nature of the property gifted, movable or immovable.

In territories, where Transfer of Property Act does not apply, a gift may be made orally or by an unattested deed. A gift of movable property may be made by a registered deed or by delivery of the property.

A fixed deposit in bank is not a movable property and its gift cannot be made by delivery of the receipt. It is an actionable claim for which a deed is required.[1]

Every assignment without consideration is not a gift.[2] Intention of parties is the determining factor for construction of a gift deed.[3]

Stamp Duty

As per Art. 33, Schedule I, Indian Stamp Act, 1899, stamp duty is same as on a Conveyance (Art. 23) as per amount or value of the consideration of such conveyance as set forth therein or the market value of the property, which is the subject of such conveyance, whichever is greater.

Registration

A gift of any immovable property must be made by a registered deed and attested by two witnesses. (Section 123 of Transfer of Property Act, 1882 and section 17(1)(a). However, section 129 of T.P. Act preserves the rule of Mohammedan Law and excludes the applicability of Section 123 of T.P. Act to a gift by a Mohammedan.

A gift of movable property, maybe effected either by a registered instrument signed as aforesaid or by delivery (section 123 of Transfer of Property Act, 1882).

(*For charitable and religious endowments, also see TRUSTS, etc., post*)

---

1 *Maiyan Dalip Rajeshwari Debi* v. *Mohan Vikram Sah*, AIR 1945 All 409.
2 *Himalaya House Co.* v. *C.C.R. Authority*, (1972) 1 SCC 726.
3 *Ram Gopal* v. *Nandlal*, AIR 1951 SC 139.

PRECEDENTS

1—Deed of Gift for Love and Affection

THIS GIFT is made on the ——— day of ——— BETWEEN AB, etc., (called "the donor") AND CD, etc. (called "the donee").

WHEREAS the donor is owner of the property described in the schedule and out of his paternal affection for his daughter, the donee, he is desirous of making a gift of the said property to the donee at the time of her marriage.

NOW THIS DEED WITNESSES as follows:

1. In consideration of the natural love and affection of the donor for the donee, the donor transfers to the donee free from encumbrances ALL the property described in the schedule TO HOLD the same to the donee absolutely forever.

2. The donee accepts the transfer.

3. The approximate value of the property transferred is Rs. ——[1] (rupees ——— only).

Signed by Donor ——————   Signed by Donee ——————

2—Deed of Gift for a Particular Purpose

THIS GIFT is made on the ——— day of ——— BETWEEN AB, etc., (hereinafter called "the donor") of the one part AND ——, a Society registered under the Societies Registration Act, 1860 (hereinafter called "the donee") of the other part;

WHEREAS the donee has requested the donor to grant to it a building for the accommodation of a school or other educational institution for girls at ———;

AND WHEREAS the donor has agreed to transfer to the donee the land and building described in the schedule hereto for the purpose above-mentioned and only for as long as the premises are used for educational purposes of girls under the control of the donee.

NOW THIS DEED WITNESSES as follows:

1. In pursuance of said agreement the donor hereby transfers to the donee ALL that, etc., TO HOLD the same to the donee and its successors

---

1 It is necessary to state this. See Sec. 27 Stamp Act.

so long as the donee shall use the said land and building for the purpose of education of girls at ———.

2. The donee hereby accepts the said gift and agrees with the donor that if and whenever the donee ceases to use the said land and building premises for the purposes of a school for girls or for any other educational institution for the education of girls under the control of the done, the same shall revert to the donor.

3. *As clause 3* in *Form 1.*

IN WITNESS WHEREOF, etc.

3—Grant of Land for Building a Mosque

THIS GRANT is made on the ——— day of ——— BETWEEN AB, etc., (hereinafter called "the grantor") of the one part AND CD, etc., (hereinafter called "the grantee") of the other part.

WHEREAS the grantee on the ——— day of ——— applied to the grantor for the grant of land for the purpose of building a mosque thereon;

AND WHEREAS the grantor has agreed with the grantee to grant to him for the said purpose the land hereby transferred belonging to the grantor on the terms and conditions hereinafter contained;

AND WHEREAS the grantee has accepted the said grant for the said purpose and on the terms and conditions hereinafter contained.

NOW THIS DEED WITNESSES as follows:

1. Grant of Land

In pursuance of the aforesaid agreement and in consideration of the grantee's covenants hereinafter contained and for the purpose of promoting religious, worship the grantor hereby grants and transfers to the grantee ALL THAT plot of land, etc., TO HOLD the same to the grantee and his successors according to the custom of succession in the management of religious endowments recognized by the religion professed by the grantee for the purpose of a mosque and for no other purpose in accordance with the covenants and the provisions hereinafter contained;

2. Covenants

The grantee hereby covenants with the grantor as follows:

(1) *To Erect Mosque*

He will within ——— years from date hereof erect a mosque of the value of Rs. ——— on the said premises and will not use the said premises for any other purpose whatsoever.

(2) *Open to All*

Such mosque when erected shall be open to all persons professing the religion of the grantee for worship and prayer and for no other purpose.

(3) *To Keep in Repairs*

The grantee and his successors will at all time hereafter keep such mosque in good and substantial repair and will at his or their own cost perform all ceremonies of worship therein according to the religion professed by the grantee.

(4) *Conditions of Reversion of Grant*

a) If the grantee fails to erect a mosque within the said period of —— years, the said premises shall revert to the grantor.

b) If the said premises shall cease to be used for the purpose of a mosque then the said premises and all buildings thereon shall revert to the grantor.

(5) *As clause 3 in Form 1.*

IN WITNESS WHEREOF, etc.

4—Gift to Government with Conditions Attached

THIS DEED OF GIFT, etc.

WHEREAS the donee requires the land described in the schedule hereto for the purpose of constructing an escape of Salempur Minor, Upper Division, Eastern Jamna Canal;

AND WHEREAS the donor has offered to give to the donee the land described in the schedule hereto belonging to him for the aforesaid purpose on the conditions hereinafter appearing and the donee has accepted the said offer.

NOW THIS DEED WITNESSES as follows:

1. In pursuance of the said agreement the donor hereby transfers to the donee ALL THAT land described in the schedule hereto TO HOLD the same absolutely forever subject to the conditions hereinafter contained.

2. The donee hereby covenants with the donor that if at any time the donee no longer requires the said land for use for the purpose aforesaid the donee will return the same to the donor after having removed therefrom the materials of any construction made by the donee thereon.

3. *As clause 3 in Form 1.*

IN WITNESS WHEREOF, etc.

5—Gift in the Form of Deed Poll (Short Form)

I, AB, etc., in consideration of natural love and affection for my sister CD, etc., (hereinafter called "the donee") hereby transfers to the donee ALL that property specified in the schedule hereto TO HOLD the same to the donee absolutely forever (*or*, for her life).

2. *As clause 3 in Form 1.*

The Schedule herein referred to

* * * *

Dated ——————   Signed ——————

I, CD, the donee aforesaid, do hereby accept the above gift.

Dated ——————   Signed ——————

6—Gift to Government for Hospital

THIS DEED OF GIFT made on the ——— day of ——— BETWEEN the Trustees of ——— Charitable Trust, (called "the Donors") AND the Governor of Uttar Pradesh (called "the Donee").

WHEREAS ———

1. The Donors with the permission of the Government of Uttar Pradesh (called "the Government") constructed a *Dharamshala* in the compound of the ——— Medical College and its associated hospitals (collectively called "the College") with a view to donating it to the Government after construction.

2. The Donors offered to transfer to the Donee the *Dharamshala*, which is free from all encumbrance, and the Donee has accepted the offer.

3. By a resolution passed by the Donors at a meeting held on—they have authorized ——— to take necessary action for the transfer of the *Dharamshala* building to the Donee and to sign papers in this connection.

NOW THIS DEED WITNESSES as follows:

1. The Donors transfer to the Donee all the rights and interest in the *Dharamshala* building alongwith the movable and immovable property described in the schedule TO HOLD the same absolutely forever subject to the following terms and conditions:

(a) The Donee shall name the *Dharamshala* as ——— and this name shall not be changed under any circumstances whatsoever.

(b) (*i*) The *Dharamshala* except the shops shall be used only for the stay of the relatives and attendants of the patients visiting the college or being treated there at.

(*ii*) The shops constructed in the *Dharamshala* may either be used for the purpose mentioned in sub-clause (i) or be let out on rent for meeting expenditure on the maintenance and running of the *Dharamshala*.

(c) (*i*) The Donee shall constitute a committee including of at least two nominees of the donors to supervise the running and maintenance of thè *Dharamshala*.

(*ii*) The committee shall function in accordance with the rules to be framed by the Donee.

(d) The Donors shall bear all expenditure on the maintenance and running of the *Dharamshala* up to the date of its transfer to the Donee and the Donee shall bear all expenditure after that date.

(e) The Donors may, with the written permission of the Donee, carry out any repairs to or provide any amenities for the occupants of the *Dharamshala* or make any additional constructions in *Dharamshala* at the cost of the Trust.

(f) If the Government intends to make any additional constructions or alterations in the *Dharamshala* building, it shall first give an offer in writing to the Donors to make the requisite additions or alterations, as the case may be, at the cost of the Trust, in accordance with the plan approved by the Government. If the Donors show their inability or fail to carry out the requisite additions or alterations within a reasonable time, the Government may carry out additions and alterations itself at the Government's cost.

2. *As clause 3 in Form 1.*

3. The Donee shall bear stamp duty[1] and registration charges on this Deed.

4. Unless there is anything repugnant to the subject or context, the expression "Donors" include their respective successors and assigns and the "Donee" include their successors in-office and assigns.

The Schedule

* * *

IN WITNESS WHEREOF, etc.

---

1 As the donee is the Government, this term means that no stamp duty shall be payable on the deed: Sec. 3, Stamp Act.

GUARANTEE

Preliminary Note

A 'contract of guarantee' is a contract to perform a promise or discharge the liability, of a third person in case of his default (Sec. 126, Indian Contract Act, 1872). The person who gives the guarantee is called the 'surety', the person in respect of whose default the guarantee is given is called the 'principal debtor', and the person to whom the guarantee is given is called the 'creditor'. A guarantee may be either oral or written. Guarantee does not include a liability which is incurred independently of a default.

For example, when two persons visit another for shopping. One of them buys some goods and his companion tells the vendor that in case the buyer does not pay, he shall pay for the goods. This is a case of guarantee.

But, where the companion tells the vendor that let the buyer have the goods and he (the buyer) shall pay then this would not amount to guarantee.

In case of guarantee, there must be a recoverable debt. In absence of a principal debt, there cannot be a legal and valid guarantee.

If the guarantee extends to a series of transactions it is called a "Continuing Guarantee" (Sec. 129). In a continuing guarantee, the consideration is supplied from time to time and is therefore divisible, while in case of other guarantees, the consideration is entire and indivisible moving from the person to whom guarantee is given once and for all. (See INDEMNITY *post.*)

A continuing guarantee can be revoked at any time by the surety, as to future transactions by notice to the creditor (Sec. 130). In absence of any contract to the contrary, it is determined on the death of the surety so far as regards future transactions (Sec. 131).

Where management of a company is taken over under a statute, taking over by another would not discharge the guarantors of the company's loans.[1]

In case of a novation of the main contract, even though initially father stood as guarantor for debts of his son's business, on account of subsequent conversion of the business into a company and when the bank consented that the loan be treated as loan of the company and accepted liability of the son and that of his companions, father could be held no more liable as a guarantor.[2]

---

1 *State Bank of India v. Saksaria Sugar Mills Ltd., AIR 1986 SC 868.*

2 *Satish Chandra Jain* v. *National Small Industries Corporation Ltd.*, AIR 2003 SC 623.

A change in the constitution of a debtor firm also determines a continuing guarantee (Sec. 38, Partnership Act). But the revocation is permissible and determination takes place only in the absence of a contract to the contrary. Therefore, if it is intended to keep the continuing guarantee alive in spite of the death of the surety or change in the constitution of the debtor firm, or to guard against a revocation by the surety, an express contract to the contrary should be embodied in the deed of guarantee.

But, a guarantee, for which the consideration is entire and indivisible, is not, except under express stipulation, determinable by notice of revocation or death of the surety or change in the constitution of any firm. Therefore, in the case of such a guarantee any stipulation for revocation or determination will have to be expressly made in the deed.

Liability of a surety is co-extensive with that of the principal debtor, unless it is otherwise provided by the contract. (Sec. 128, Contract Act). Surety would be liable for the whole, which the principal debtor is liable to pay. Similarly, where the principal debtor acknowledges liability, and the acknowledgement extends the prescribed period of limitation to recover the debt, the surety would be liable on the principle that liability of surety is co-extensive with that of the principal debtor.[1]

In case of any variance without the surety's consent in the terms of the contract between the principal debtor and the creditor, the surety is discharged (Sec. 133). Likewise, the surety is discharged by release or discharge of the principal debtor, (Sec. 134), or when the creditor compounds with, or gives time to, or agrees not to sue the principal debtor (Sec. 135), or by the creditor's act or omission impairing the surety's eventual remedy (Sec. 139).

The surety is entitled to the benefit of every security which the creditor has against the principal debtor at the time when the guarantee was given, and if the creditor parts with such security, the guarantor or surety is discharged to the extent of its value (Sec. 141). However, the loss contemplated is by voluntary act of the creditor and not be involuntary act. These rights of the surety can, however, be waived by the surety if the creditor obtains from him a contract to that effect.[2] It is therefore not unusual for banks and financial institutions to obtain such waiver from the guarantors (1997 AIR Jour. 199; article on "Contracting Out" by *V. Adhivorahai*).

In Halsbury's Law of England Fourth Edition (para 335) it has been categorically stated that "A transaction which causes no loss of securities or a loss not attributed to the fault of the creditor, will not discharge the guarantor". Thus

---

1 *Kailash Nath Agarwal* v. *Pradeshiya Industrial & Investment Corporation of U.P.* Ltd., AIR 2003 SC 1886; *Bank of India* v. *Surendra Kumar Mishra*, III 2003 BC 166 (Jhar.).

2 *Citi Bank N.A. New Delhi* v. *Juggilal Kamlapat Jute Mills Company Ltd.*, AIR 1982 Del 487; *T. Raju Setty* v. *Bank of Baroda*, AIR 1992 Kant 108; *Canara Bank* v. *Gokuldas Shenoy*, (1991) 72 CompCas 298.

the loss contemplated under Sec. 141 is by voluntary act of the creditor and not otherwise[1].

Bank guarantee

The Bank guarantee has a dual aspect. It is a contract between the Bank and the beneficiary of the guarantee and it is also a security given to the beneficiary by a third party. It is in the nature of a special contract depending upon the happening of a specific event. The obligations thereunder are independent of the obligations arising out of a specific contract between the parties. This has become the legal base of the banking system and in the world of commerce, it is a well-known business transaction commonly employed.[2]

Stamp Duty

The stamp duty is payable under Article 57 ("Security Bond").

---

1 *Industrial Finance Corporation of India Ltd.* v. *Cannanore Spinning and Weaving Mills Ltd.*, AIR 2002 SC 1841.

2 Syndicate Bank *v.* Vijay Kumar, *(1992) 2 SCC 330; Hindustan Steel Works Construction Ltd.* v. *Tarapore Co.,* AIR 1996 SC 2268, (1996) 5 SCC 34; (The obligation of the Bank is absolute under unconditional guarantee); U.P. State Sugar Corpn. Ltd. *v.* Simac International Ltd., (1997) 1 SCC 568, AIR 1997 SC 1644.

PRECEDENTS

1—Deed of Continuing Guarantee for Securing the Balance due on Account with a Bank[1]

THIS DEED of guarantee made on the ——— day of —— BETWEEN AB, etc., (hereinafter called "the Surety") of the one part AND the ——— Bank having its head-office at ——— (hereinafter called "the Bank") of the other part.

WITNESSES as follows:

Guarantee

In consideration of the Bank opening and keeping a cash credit account of the firm CD, etc., and making advances to and for the accommodation of the said firm CD, the Surety, hereby guarantees to the Bank the payment of all sums of money that may be due from the said firm CD from time to time on the general balance of the said account subject to the covenants hereinafter contained.

The surety and the Bank hereby mutually agree as follows:

(a) *Limiting the Guarantee*

That the liability of the Surety shall not at any time exceed the sum of Rs. ——— with interest thereon at ——— percent per annum.

(b) *Continuing Guarantee*

That the guarantee hereby given shall be a continuing guarantee and shall not be considered as wholly or partially satisfied by the payment or liquidation at any time or times hereafter of any sum or sums of money for the time being due upon such general balance as agreed but shall, subject to the aforesaid limit, extend to cover and be a security for all future sums at any time due hereafter.

(c) *Forbearance of Obligee not to Terminate Surety's Liability*

That the neglect or forbearance of the Bank in enforcing payment of any moneys, the payment whereof is intended to be hereby

1 See also NOTICE, *post* precedents Nos. 54 and 55 for notices determining continuing guarantee.

secured or the giving of time by the Bank for the payment thereof shall not in any way release the Surety of his liability under the guarantee herein contained.

(d) *Guarantee not to be Affected by Change in Constitutions nor by Death of Surety*

(*i*) That the guarantee hereinbefore contained shall not be affected by any change in the constitution of the Bank or in the constitution of the said firm CD.

(*ii*) That the guarantee hereinbefore contained shall not be affected by the death of the Surety but shall continue in force till two calendar months after notice in writing has been given to the Bank by the Surety or his legal representatives as the case may be.

(e) *Settled Account to be Conclusive Evidence*

That any account settled between the Bank and the said firm CD shall be conclusive evidence against the Surety of the amount due on the said account and shall not be questioned by the Surety.

(f) *Interpretation Clause*

That the expressions "Surety" and "Bank" hereinbefore used shall, unless such an interpretation is repugnant to the context, include in the case of the "Surety" his heirs, successors, representative and assigns and in the case of the "Bank" its successors and assigns.

IN WITNESS WHEREOF, etc.

2—Guarantee to a Trading Firm for Supplying Goods to a Shopkeeper (in the Form of a Letter)

To

CD and Co.

New Delhi

Dear Sir,

In consideration of your supplying goods or otherwise giving credit to EF, etc., I hereby guarantee the payment of all sums of moneys that may be due to you on that account on demand with interest at ———— percent per annum till payment but my liability shall not at any time exceed the sum of Rs. ——— with interest at the aforesaid rate.

I also agree that this guarantee, which is to be considered as a continuing guarantee, is not determinable on any payment or payments and shall continue in force in spite of any change in the constitution of your firm and inspite of your granting to EF, etc., time or any other such indulgence, and shall not determine even by my death but shall continue in force until one calendar months' notice to determine it shall be given to you by me or by my legal representative.

Dated ———— Yours faithfully,

(See also Forms of Security Bonds under "Bonds")

3—Guarantee by Directors of a Company to Bankers for Limited Amounts (in the Form of a Letter)

To

The Manager Loans

Punjab National Bank

New Delhi

Dear Sir,

In consideration of your agreeing to grant to the Indian Cold Storage Co. Ltd., Meerut, at our request, a credit overdraft to the extent of Rs. —— we, the undersigned being the Directors of the said company, hereby guarantee to you the payment of all moneys which shall any time be due from the said company to you on the balance of their account with you not exceeding Rs. ——— (such balance to include all interest, commission and other charges and expenses which you may in the course of your business charge in respect of any advance or discount made to the said company or on their account or for keeping the said account with you) and we hereby agree as follows:

(*a*) that this guarantee shall be a continuing guarantee to the extent at any time or times hereafter of any sum or sums of money for the time being due upon such general balance within the limit aforesaid;

(*b*) that this guarantee shall be in force and subsisting whether the whole of the said sum of Rs. ——— shall be actually advanced by you or not; and

(*c*) that you may grant time or other indulgence to or compound with the said company without affecting this guarantee PROVIDED always and we hereby covenant that (1) we shall respectively be liable on this guarantee only to the extent of the sums set opposite to our respective names in the schedule hereto, and (2) that if during the continuance of this guarantee any of us shall die or shall cease to be a director of the said company and if the said company shall be unable to substitute a guarantor or guarantors in his or their place who shall be satisfactory to you, then the said company may pay to you the amount which in the said schedule shall be set opposite to the name or names of the person or persons who shall so die or cease to be a Director or Directors as aforesaid and such payment shall be accepted by you in full satisfaction of all claims against such person or persons in respect of this guarantee.

Signed, etc.

The Schedule herein referred to

Names of Directors	Rs.
AB	——
CD	——
EF	——

Thanking you.

Yours faithfully,

4—Deed of Guarantee by a Bank on Behalf of a Company for the Performance of a Contract[1]

THIS DEED OF GUARANTEE made this ——— day of —— between the Bank of ———— (hereinafter called "the Bank") of the one part, and the Governor of ——— (hereinafter called "the Purchaser") of the other part;

WHEREAS ——— a Company within the meaning of the Companies Act, 1956/2013 having its registered office at ——— (hereinafter called "the Contractor") has by a Deed of Agreement made on the —— agreed with the Purchaser to supply certain Plant, Machinery and Equipment in accordance with the terms, specifications and conditions therein contained;

AND WHEREAS in accordance with the terms and conditions of the aforesaid Agreement the Purchaser has to make to the Contractor an advance payment of UK pounds (*or*, US Dollars) —— equivalent to

1 In *State of Bihar* v. *Hindustan Construction Co.*, AIR 1998 Bom 331 (DB) (para 14), interim injunction was issued, for preventing irretrievable harm and injustice, against invocation (by the employer against the contractor) of a **performance guarantee** where it was clear from the employer's own circular that the construction work had been stopped due to non-availability of funds with the employer. The other guarantee relating to advance received by the contractor was however held to be validly invoked.

Rs. ——— (Rupees ——— only) being equivalent to ——— per cent of the total F.O.B. value of the contract price, and such payment is to be secured by a Bank Guarantee;

AND WHEREAS the Bank has at the request of the Contractor agreed to guarantee the refund of the said advance in case the Plant, Machinery and Equipment of the value aforesaid is not delivered to the Purchaser in accordance with the terms and conditions of the said agreement, and the Purchaser has agreed to make the said advance on such security;

NOW THIS DEED WITNESSES as follows:

1. In consideration of the Purchaser having agreed to advance a sum of ——— to the Contractor, through the Bank, the Bank do hereby guarantee that if the Contractor shall fail to supply to the Purchaser the Plant, Machinery and Equipment of the value of Rs. ——— in accordance with the specifications and conditions contained in the Deed of Agreement dated the ——— and/or any amendments or modifications in the aforesaid Agreement made between the Purchaser and the Contractor on ———, the Bank shall repay to the Purchaser such amount or amounts, as the Bank may be called upon to pay to the maximum aggregate of Rs. ——.

PROVIDED FIRSTLY that the liability of the Bank under this deed shall not at any time exceed the said advance of Rs. ———.

AND PROVIDED SECONDLY that the guarantee hereunder furnished shall be released as soon as the Contractor has supplied to the Purchaser the Plant, Machinery and Equipment of the value of Rs. —— in accordance with the aforesaid Deed of Agreement.

2. This Guarantee of the Bank will come into force immediately upon payment of the sum of Rs. ——— being received by the Bank for and on behalf of the Contractor from the Purchaser and shall continue in force till the supply of Plant, Machinery and Equipment of the value of Rs. ——— aforesaid is effected as testified by documents and invoices (*or*, as certified by the Purchaser).

3. The Guarantee hereinbefore contained shall not be affected by any change in the constitution of the Bank or of the Contractor.

4. Any account settled between the Purchaser and the Contractor shall be the conclusive evidence against the Bank of the amount due and shall not be questioned by the Bank.

5. The neglect or forbearance of the Purchaser in enforcement of payment of any moneys the payment whereof is intended to be hereby secured or the giving of time by the Purchaser for the repayment hereof

shall in no way relieve the Bank of their liability under this Deed.

6. The expressions "the Bank", "the Purchaser" and "Contractor" hereinbefore used shall include their respective successors and assigns.

IN WITNESS WHEREOF ——— for and on behalf of the bank AND SECRETARY TO GOVERNMENT OF ——————— IN ——— DEPARTMENT for and on behalf of the Governor have signed this deed on the day and year first above written.

for AND ON BEHALF OF THE GOVERNOR	*for* AND ON BEHALF OF THE BANK

WITNESS: 1. ——————

WITNESS: 2. ——————

5—Bank Guarantee in Lieu of Earnest Money Deposit for Tender

To,

——————

——————

Sir,

WHEREAS ——— a company within the meaning of the Companies Act, 2013 having its registered office at ——— (hereinafter called "the Tenderer") have in response to your Tender Notice against specification number ——— for ——— offered to supply and/or execute the work as contained in Tenderer's letter No. ——— dated ———;

AND WHEREAS the Tenderer is required to furnish to you, a Bank Guarantee for the sum of Rs. ——— as Earnest Money against the Tenderer's offer as aforesaid;

AND WHEREAS We ——— (*name of Bank*) have, at the request of the Tenderer, agreed to give you this guarantee as hereinafter contained;

NOW THEREFORE in consideration of the premises, We, the undersigned, hereby covenant that the aforesaid tender of the Tenderer shall remain open for acceptance by you during the period of validity as mentioned in the tender or any extension thereof as you and the Tenderer may subsequently agree and if the Tenderer shall for any reason back out, whether expressly or impliedly, from his said tender during the period of its validity or any extension thereof as aforesaid, WE hereby guarantee to you the payment of the sum of Rs. ——— on demand, notwithstanding the existence of any dispute between you or your authorised representative and the Tenderer in this regard[1] AND WE hereby further agree as follows:

(*a*) That you may without affecting this guarantee grant time or other indulgence to or negotiate further with Tenderer in regard to the conditions contained in the said tender and thereby modify these conditions or add thereto any further conditions as may be mutually agreed upon between you and the Tenderer.

(*b*) That the guarantee hereinbefore contained shall not be affected by any change in the constitution of our Bank or in the constitution of the Tenderer.

(*c*) That any account settled between you and the Tenderer shall be conclusive evidence against us (Bank) of the amount due hereunder and shall not be questioned by us.

(*d*) That this guarantee commences from the date hereof and shall remain in force till the Tenderer, if his tender is accepted by you, furnishes the security as required under the said specifications and executes a formal agreement as therein provided or till four months after the period of validity or the extended period of validity, as the case may be, of the tender, whichever of these is earlier.

(*e*) That the expressions "the Tenderer" and "the Bank" herein used shall, unless such an interpretation is repugnant to the subject or context, include their respective successors and assigns.

Yours faithfully,

6—Bank Guarantee in lieu of Security Deposit

THIS DEED OF GUARANTEE made on the ——— day of ——— by ——— (hereinafter called "the Bank") of the one part IN FAVOUR OF AB, etc., of the other part;

WHEREAS by an Agreement No. ——— dated ——— made between (1) CD, etc., (2) EF, etc., all carrying on business in partnership

---

1 This is an unconditional bank guarantee which the bank is bound to honour. This is however subject to two exceptions in which case courts may grant injunction in favour of the bank against encashment. First, a fraud which would vitiate the very foundation of the guarantee. Second, where encashment of the bank guarantee would result in irretrievable harm or injustice to the party on whose behalf the guarantee is given. *U.P. State Corporation Ltd.* v. *Sumac International*, (1997) 1 SCC 568, AIR 1997 SC 1644 (case law); *Dwarikesh Sugar Industries Ltd.* v. *Prem Heavy Enginering Works*, AIR 1997 SC 2477: (1997) 6 SCC 450; *Hindustan Steel Works Construction Ltd.* v. *Tarapore & Co.*, AIR 1996 SC 2268.

under the firm name of ——— at ——— (hereinafter called "the Contractor") and the said AB, the Contractor has undertaken the construction of ———— on the conditions contained in the agreement hereinbefore referred (hereinafter called "the said contract");

AND WHEREAS in accordance with clause ————— of the said contract the Contractor is desirous of furnishing a Bank Guarantee in the sum of Rs. ——— towards security deposit valid upto six months beyond the date of completion of the works under the said contract;

AND WHEREAS AB has agreed to accept a guarantee from the said Bank on condition expressly that the Bank on demand from AB and without demur pay to AB the aforesaid sum of Rs. ———.

AND WHEREAS at the request of the Contractor, the Bank has agreed to give its guarantee as hereinafter contained;

NOW THIS DEED WITNESSES as follows:

1. In consideration of the premises the Bank hereby undertakes to pay to AB on demand the sum of Rs. ———.

2. The Bank shall pay to AB on demand the sum under clause 1 above without demur and without requiring AB to invoke any legal remedy that may be available to it, it being understood and agreed FIRSTLY that AB shall be the sole judge of and as to whether the Contractor has committed breach or breaches, if any, of the terms and conditions of the said contract and the extent of loss, damage, costs, charges and expenses caused to or suffered by or that may be caused to or suffered by AB from time to time and his demand in that regard shall be final and binding on the Bank AND SECONDLY that the right of AB to recover from the Bank any amount under this guarantee shall not be affected or suspended by reason of the fact that any dispute or disputes have been raised by the Contractor with regard to their liability or that proceedings are pending before any tribunal, arbitrator(s) or court with regard thereto or in connection therewith AND THIRDLY that the Bank shall immediately pay the sum under clause 1 above to AB on demand and it shall not be open to the Bank to know the reasons of or to investigate or to go into the merits of the demand or to question or to challenge the demand or to know any facts affecting the demand AND LASTLY that it shall not be open to the Bank to require proof of the liability of the Contractor to pay the amount, before paying the sum demanded under clause 1 above.

3. This guarantee shall come into force immediately and continue in force and remain valid till six months after the completion of all works under the said contract, which according to the terms of the said contract,

should be six months from the probable date of completion viz., the —— day of ——. If, however, the period of the completion of the works under the said contract is for any reason extended and upon such extension if the Contractor fails, before the term of this guarantee expires, to furnish a fresh or renewed guarantee for the extended period, the Bank shall pay to AB the said sum of Rs. ——— or such lesser sum as AB may demand.

4. This guarantee shall not be affected by any change in the constitution of the Bank or of the Contractor.

5. AB and the Contractor will be at liberty to carry out any modifications to the said contract during the term of the said contract and any extension thereof, and notice of such modifications and extensions to the Bank is hereby waived by the Bank.

6. Notwithstanding anything hereinbefore contained, the liability of the Bank under this guarantee is restricted to Rs. ——— (Rupees ——) only and the guarantee shall remain in force till the ————day of —— 19 ———, unless claim or demand under this guarantee is presented to the Bank within six months from that date all the rights of AB under this guarantee shall be forfeited and the Bank shall be released and discharged from all obligations hereunder.

IN WITNESS WHEREOF, etc.

7—Form of Guarantee as Security[1]

Sum of bond (in words and figures)	Contract No. and particulars	Date of contract

KNOW ALL MEN BY THESE PRESENTS, that we ——— having our registered head office at ————— are held and firmly bound unto the Governor of the State of———— (hereinafter called "the Government") in the amount stated above, for the payment of which sum well and truly to be made, we bind ourselves, our administrators and successors, firmly by these presents.

THE CONDITION of this obligation is that whereas ——— having their registered office at ——— (hereinafter called "the Principals") have entered into a certain contract with the Government, numbered and dated as shown above.

1 Only the express terms of the guarantee will be looked into. Sections 91 and 92 Evidence Act disallow any evidence to add to or detract from the express terms: *New India Ass. Co. Ltd.* v. *Kusumanchi Kameshwara Rao*, (1997) 9 SCC 179.

NOW THEREFORE if the Principals shall well and truly perform and fulfil all the undertakings, covenants, terms, conditions and agreement of the said contract during the original term of the said contract and any extension thereof that may be granted by the Government with or without notice to us and during the life of any guarantee required by the contract, and shall also well and truly perform and fulfil all the undertakings, covenants, terms, conditions and agreements of any and all duly authorised modifications of the said contract that may hereafter be made, notice of which (modifications) to us is hereby being waived, then this obligation to be void, otherwise to remain in full force and virtue.

This guarantee shall come into force on ——— and shall remain in force till ———. Any neglect or forbearance of the Government in enforcing payment of any moneys, the payment whereof is intended to be hereby secured or the giving of time by the Government for the payment thereof shall not in any way release the Surety of its liability under the guarantee herein contained.

Any account settled between the Government and the Principals shall be conclusive evidence against us (the Surety) of the amount due hereunder and shall not be questioned by us.

The guarantee herein contained shall not be affected by any change in the constitution of the Principals or the Surety.

This guarantee shall be governed by the laws of India for the time being in force and be subject to the jurisdiction of Indian Courts.

IN WITNESS WHEREOF, etc.

8—Form of Guarantee in favour of State Financial Corporation

THIS DEED OF GUARANTEE made this ——— day of between AB etc. (hereinafter called "the Guarantor") of the one part, and ——— State Financial Corporation etc. (hereinafter called "the Corporation") of the other part.

WHEREAS the Corporation has agreed to grant to ———, a company incorporated under the Companies Act, 1956/2013 having its registered office at —— (hereinafter called the Borrower-Company, which expression shall include its successors and assigns) a term loan of Rs. ——— (Rupees —— only) upon security of a simple mortgage/equitable mortgage and/or deed of hypothecation (hereinafter collectively called "the mortgage");

AND WHEREAS the Guarantor has agreed for the repayment of the above said loan in case of default by the Borrower-Company.

NOW THIS DEED WITNESSES as follows:

1. In consideration of the Corporation having agreed to advance a sum of Rs. ——— to the Borrower-Company, the Guarantor hereby guarantees to the Corporation that if the Borrower-Company fails to repay the above said loan amount, the Guarantor shall repay to the Corporation all such amount that may be due from the Borrower-Company to the Corporation subject to the covenants hereinafter contained.

2. The guarantee herein contained shall be enforceable against the Guarantor notwithstanding that the securities specified in the mortgage or any of them shall at the time when proceedings are taken against the Guarantor hereunder be outstanding or unrealised.

3. The guarantee herein contained shall be enforceable against the Guarantor notwithstanding that no action of any kind has been taken by the Corporation against the Borrower-Company and an intimation in writing sent to the Guarantor by the Corporation that a default or breach has been committed by the Borrower-Company shall be treated as final and conclusive proof of the facts stated therein.

4. The Guarantor hereby agrees that any amount appearing due from the Borrower-Company in the books of accounts of the Corporation kept in the ordinary course of business shall be conclusive evidence against the Guarantor of the amount due on the said account and shall not be questioned by the Guarantor.

5. In order to give effect to the guarantee herein contained the Corporation shall be entitled to act as if the Guarantor was the principal debtor to the Corporation for all payment guaranteed by him as aforesaid to the Corporation.

6. The Guarantor hereby waives all rights which the Guarantor may become entitled to as surety to compete with the Corporation in obtaining payment of the moneys due or to become due to the Corporation in respect of the said loan in favour of the Corporation as against the Borrower-Company.

7. The Guarantor hereby agrees that it shall not be necessary for the Corporation to sue the Borrower-Company before suing the Guarantor for the amount due hereunder.

8. The Guarantor also hereby agrees that the liability to repay the amount due to the Corporation shall arise on demand being made by the Corporation by a registered notice addressed to the Guarantor on its address herein below contained.

9. The Guarantor hereby agrees that any amount due from the Borrower-Company to the Corporation shall be recoverable under the —— (Note: *Mention the name of the Act, if any, under which moneys due to a public sector Corporation under an agreement can be recovered as arrears of land revenue. In the absence of such statutory provision this clause is to be omitted*) Act (as amended from time to time) as arrears of land revenue and further that it shall not be necessary for the Corporation to take recovery proceedings against the Borrower-Company before taking recovery proceedings under the said Act against the Guarantor.[1]

10. The Guarantor further agrees that the relevant provisions of the State Financial Corporation Act, 1951, may be invoked, if needed, against it.

11. Period of guarantee

12. Arbitration clause etc.

IN WITNESS WHEREOF, etc.

9—Form of Counter-Guarantee[2]

IN CONSIDERATION of your having, at our request executed a Guarantee Deed dated ——— in favour of ——— Bank (hereinafter called "the Bank") to secure a loan of Rs. ——— and interest, we hereby covenant and agree with you as under:

(1) That we shall within thirty days of demand pay to you all moneys which you may become liable to pay under the guarantee aforesaid together with interest at one per cent per annum over and above the rate charged by the Bank from us.

(2) That we shall not declare dividend in any year unless the repayment of instalment with interest for that year under the said loan has been paid to the Bank.

(3) That we shall pay to you guarantee commission at the rate of one percent per annum quarterly in advance.

(4) [*Insert other conditions as may be required*].

[*For other forms of Guarantee, see under* BONDS, *ante; under* LICENCE *and* MORTGAGE, *post*].

---

1 A deed in these terms was interpreted in *Pawan Kumar Jain* v. *Pradeshiya Industrial and Investment Corporation of U.P. Ltd.*, AIR 1998 All 57 and it was held that in case of default by the borrower, revenue recovery proceedings can be taken against the guarantor as well.

2 See also, Form No. 8 under INDEMNITY, *post*.

HIRE AND HIRE PURCHASE

Preliminary Note

Hire – Purchase contract is a form of hire contract where the hirer pays by installment to the owner of goods and he has the option to purchase the goods or become the owner of the goods on making certain payments. So it is different from a sale in which the price is to be paid later by installments or in case of credit sale, after the credit period. In case of such a sale, the property passes as soon as the sale is made. However, in case of hire purchase agreement, the property in the goods does not pass when the agreement is made but only when the option is finally exercised.

A contract of hire in respect of movables is a contract of bailment and is governed by the provisions of Chapter IX of the Contract Act.[1] A 'bailment' is the delivery of goods by one person to another for some purpose, upon a contract that they shall, when the purpose is accomplished, be returned or otherwise disposed of according to the directions of the person delivering them. The person delivering the goods is called the 'bailor'. The person to whom they are delivered is called the 'bailee' (section 148, Indian Contract Act, 1872). The provisions of the Contract Act are, however, not exhaustive on bailments. A bailment may arise even without any contract.[2] Houses and shops are also often the subject of hire purchase agreements.[3]

A hire purchase agreement has two elements:

(i) the element of bailment, and

(ii) element of sale,

in the sense that it contemplates eventual sale. The element of sale fructifies when the intending purchaser exercises the option after fulfilling the terms of the agreement. Upon all the terms of the agreement being satisfied, a sale takes place of the goods which till then had only been hired. The property does not pass, it may be noted, when the agreement is made but only passes when the option is finally exercised after compliance with all the terms of the agreement.[4] The intending purchaser is known as the hirer so long as the option to purchase is not exercised. The hirer is not bound to buy, but the other side has the obligation to sell. Under

---

1 The Hire Purchase Act though enacted in 1972 has not yet been brought into force. It may be noted here that this Chapter deals only with movables.

2 *State of Gujarat* v. *Memon Md. Haji Hasan*, AIR 1967 SC 1885: (1967) 3 SCR 938.

3 See SALE *post*.

4 *K.L. Johar* v. *Dy. C.T.O.*, AIR 1965 SC 1082; *Vasantha* v. *V.K. Eleyalwar*, AIR 2001 S 3367

the agreement, possession of the goods is delivered by the owner thereof to the hirer on condition that the agreed amount in periodical instalments being continued to be paid. Before the property passes, the hirer, in the absence of agreement to the contrary, has a right to terminate the agreement.[1]

In this system, the article is let out to the hirer on a monthly hire after making the payment of an initial amount in the form of premium. This amount varies according to the value of the article, as well as the practice prevailing in a particular Company or firm, but the general pattern is to charge 20 to 25 per cent of the value. The remaining balance of the price of the article has to be paid in periodic instalments by way of hire, on the condition that when all the instalments are so paid the property in the article will automatically pass to the hirer. At the same time, there is no obligation on the part of the hirer to pay all the instalments and purchase the article. He has merely an option and may, if he so likes, return the article during the period of hire. In law such an agreement does not amount to sale or an agreement to sell but is treated as a mere contract of bailment with certain variations relating to contemplated sale.[2]

Deed of Hire

The hire deed is drafted in the form of an agreement. The statutory rights and obligations provided in the Contract Act need not be provided in the agreement. For instance, the hirer's responsibility for care of goods (Sec.151), or the option of the owner to terminate the agreement on the hirer's breach of conditions of hire (Sec. 153). All other conditions agreed upon should be clearly mentioned.

Duty of Hirer as Regards Care

Under Sec. 151, the hirer is bound to take as much care of the goods hired as a man of ordinary prudence would, under similar circumstances, take of his own goods of the same bulk, quality and value. Under Sec. 152, the hirer is not responsible for the loss, destruction or deterioration of the goods hired if he has taken such care. A provision to these effects is unnecessary. But if the parties intend to vary the statutory obligations in any way, the exact contract should be entered in the agreement. For instance, they may agree that the hirer shall be liable for loss or damage to the goods, *from whatever cause resulting*, even inspite of the fact he has taken the necessary care. Such a condition is often necessary as it may be difficult for the owner to prove the negligence of the hirer.

Condition of Breach

Under Sec. 153, the contract would be voidable if the hirer does any act *with regard to the goods hired* inconsistent with the conditions of hire. But if it

1 *Dalpat Rai* v. *Manohar Lal*, AIR 1974 Raj. 61; also see *K. Narayan* v. *Laxmi Narasinham*, AIR 1955 Hyd 104 (FB).

2 *Instalment Supply Co. (P) Ltd.* v. *Union of India*, AIR 1962 SC 53 (case covered by Bengal Finance (Sales Tax) Act, 1941).

is intended to provide for the option of termination in any other case, e.g. in case of non-payment of rent or non-insurance of goods, etc., an express condition will be necessary.

Hire Purchase

This is a form of hire contract under which the hire is payable in instalments and an option is given to the hirer to purchase the goods hired or a condition is added that the goods shall become the property of the hirer on the hirer making a certain number of payments. Such agreement should be drafted like hire contracts with the usual conditions, but with a clause or clauses providing for the said option to purchase. The additional clause should be carefully drafted so as to provide for that option or for the property in the goods passing to the hirer on the payment of all the instalments *and* on the hirer duly observing the conditions of hire contract. Two points should be carefully borne in mind in drafting this clause, viz.

(1) *It should not amount to an agreement to buy* but should only give the hirer an option to purchase, for, under the agreement to buy the hirer having got possession of the goods would be able to give good title to anyone who takes the goods on sale or pledge from him without notice of the hire-purchase contract (vide Sec. 30(2) Sale of Goods Act, 1930) and the intention of the owner will thereby be defeated. But if the agreement does not amount to an *agreement to buy* and gives the hirer only an *option to buy*, the hirer cannot give a valid title to anyone, even if the latter takes the goods without notice.[1]

(2) There should be an express stipulation that the property in the goods shall not pass to the hirer until all the instalments have been paid. In the absence of this clause, the power to seize the goods in default of payment of instalments might be held to make the agreement a contract of sale. The owner has vested in himself not only his contractual right under the agreement but also a reversionary interest in the goods which form the subject of agreement.[2]

Similarly, the agreement confers two distinct sets of rights on the hirer, viz.

(1) the benefit of the hiring, which constitutes the bailment part of the contract, and

(2) the option to purchase which it is now established constitutes a separate and proprietary right.

Each of the two interests of both, the owner and the hirer, is capable of separate assignment.

---

1 See *Greenwood* v. *Halguette*, (1874) 12 BLR 42, relied on in *Roopchand Jankidas* v. *The National Bank*, AIR 1919 Cal 540 (at 541, col. 1): 46 Cal 342.

2 *Mc Entire* v. *Crossby*, (1895) AC 457; *D.E. Kasisab* v. *N.T. Engineer*, AIR 1965 Mad 257; See also *K.A. Mathai* v. *Kora Bibbikutty*, (1996) 7 SCC 212 (Financier has right to resume possession of the property, - in this case, a bus, in the event of the purchaser's failure to pay instalments).

Minimum Payment Clause

In order to provide for depreciation of the article taken under the hire purchase agreement, it is usual to insert a "minimum payment" clause which provides that in the event of the determination of the agreement by the hirer or the owner, the hirer shall be liable to pay 50 per cent of the total price after deduction of the instalments already paid by the hirer.

Types of Agreement

The system prevails in two forms. One is where the hirer enters into a direct contract with the owner, while in the other a financier intervenes. The financier advances the money for payment of the price and gets a hire purchase agreement executed in his favour after the hirer has settled the bargain with the owner. The article is delivered to the hirer who takes the responsibility against loss and destruction of the article. Generally, there is a guarantor who also signs the agreement as a surety.

Stamp Duty

The stamp duty is the same as on agreement.

Registration

Registration is not compulsory. However, in U.P. an agreement to sell *immovable* property is compulsorily registrable. Accordingly hire purchase agreement relating to *immovable* property will also require registration in U.P.

PRECEDENTS

1—Agreement to Hire a Spinning Plant

THIS AGREEMENT made, etc.

WHEREAS AB owns a Wool Spinning plant (hereinafter called "the plant") installed on AB's freehold land situate at —— in the town of ——;

AND WHEREAS the said Plant is lying closed for the last several years and CD's offer to take it on hire has been accepted by AB on the conditions hereinafter appearing;

NOW THESE PRESENTS WITNESS as follows:

1. The plant will remain in the use and possession of CD for a period of seven years ending with ——— unless this agreement is sooner terminated under the power reserved in this deed. During the period of the plant remaining in the use and possession of CD, who shall also be entitled to use the land and the building in which the plant is installed. Such use and possession of the land and the building shall be that by way of licence only, the licence being automatically terminable on the expiration or sooner determination of the hire of the plant.

2. CD shall pay to AB as rent for the hire of the said plant the sum of Rs. ——— per year in advance and shall also pay to AB a fee of Rs. ——— per year for the use and possession of the land and the said building.

3. CD will not lend or transfer the plant to any other person.

4. CD will not remove the said plant or any part thereof from the premises where it is presently installed.

5. CD will keep the plant in good order and condition and will, on the expiration of the said term or earlier termination of this agreement, return the same to AB in the same condition in which it has been lent, reasonable wear and tear excepted, and all loss or damage due to breakage or any other cause shall be made good by CD at his own cost.

6. CD will keep the plant insured against damage or loss by fire or theft in the joint names of AB and CD, at least in the sum of Rs. ——— with an Insurance company and shall punctually pay all premia and produce to AB, when required by him, the receipt for the last premium payable in respect of such insurance.

7. If the plant or any part of it is injured or destroyed by fire or lost by

theft all moneys received in respect of such insurance shall be paid forthwith to AB who shall, as the case may require, apply such moneys either in making good the damage done or in replacing the plant or such part by other articles of similar description and value and such substituted articles shall become subject to the provisions of this agreement in the same manner as the articles for which they are substituted.

8. AB or his nominees may at all reasonable times inspect the plant, its working and efficiency and CD will furnish to him or them such information as he or they may require concerning the plant and its working.

9. In case of non-observance or non-performance by CD of any of the provisions of this deed AB may terminate this agreement, seize, and retake possession of the plant and accessories.

10. Any earlier relaxation or indulgence granted by AB to CD shall not in any way prejuduce the rights of AB under this agreement.

11. It is hereby declared that no workman or other labour, whether permanent or temporary, of AB is presently employed in the said plant.

12. A list of the plant and the tools and spares is enclosed as Annexure I.

13. *Arbitration clause.*

14. *Stamp duty clause.*

IN WITNESS WHEREOF, etc.

2—Hire of a Crushing Machine

AN AGREEMENT made on the ——— day of ——— BETWEEN AB, etc., of the one part AND CD, etc., (hereinafter called "the hirer") of the other part;

WHEREBY IT IS AGREED as follows:

1. The said AB shall let to the hirer and the hirer shall take on hire from the said AB for a period of one year from the ——— one crusher (*full description*) (hereinafter called "the crusher").

2. The hirer shall pay to the said AB as rent for the hire of the said crusher the sum of Rs. ——— in advance before the delivery of the said crusher to the hirer.

3. The said crusher shall be delivered to the hirer at the cost of the said AB.

4. The hirer shall keep the said crusher during the period of hire in good order and condition and shall not part with or suffer the same to go out

of his possession and shall keep the same free and exempt from all attachments or other legal process and shall on the expiry of the period of hire, return the same to the said AB in as good a condition as it is at the time of hiring, reasonable wear and tear excepted.

5. In case of non-observance or non-performance by the hirer of any of the provisions hereinbefore contained the said AB shall be at liberty forthwith to terminate this agreement and to retake possession of the said crusher without prejudice to his right to recover damages for breach of agreement.

IN WITNESS WHEREOF, etc.

3—Hire of Electric Fan

AN AGREEMENT made, etc. (*as in Form 2*).

WHEREBY IT IS AGREED as follows:

1. The said AB shall let to the hirer and the hirer shall take on hire from the said AB for a period of —— months from the ——— an electric table fan No. ——— of ——— make ——— model on a monthly rent of Rs. ———.

2. The hirer shall pay the aforesaid rent at the office of the said AB at ——— or at such other place or places as the said AB may from time to time appoint, monthly in advance before the ——— day of every month.

3. For hiring during a portion of a month half rent will be charged if the hiring is for not more than fifteen days and full rent will be charged for hiring for more than fifteen days.

4. The hirer will not let out the fan on hire to any other person nor will he remove it for use outside the limits of the city.

5. If the fan does not suit the requirements of the hirer, he may return it within the first week of hiring and in that case will pay a nominal hire of Rs. ——— for the period of trial.

6. The hirer shall be responsible for any damage caused to the fan, other than ordinary wear and tear due to a reasonable use of the same, and shall in the event of such damage being caused be liable to pay compensation to the said AB.

7. The hirer shall report to the said AB any trouble in the working of the fan and the said AB will get the fan repaired. The hirer will not repair or get it repaired himself.

8. If the hirer does not pay the rent as hereinbefore agreed or is guilty of a breach of any of the covenants by the hirer herein contained, the said

AB may immediately terminate this agreement and the hirer shall thereupon return the fan forthwith to the said AB.

9. Any earlier relaxation or indulgence granted by the said AB to the hirer shall not in any way prejudice his said rights under this agreement.

IN WITNESS WHEREOF, etc.

4—Agreement for Hire (with option to Purchase)

AN AGREEMENT made, etc. (*as in Form 2*).

WHEREBY IT IS AGREED as follows:

1. The owner will let and the hirer will take on hire the goods mentioned in the schedule hereto for the term of ———— years on the terms hereinafter contained.

2. The hirer shall pay to the owner on the execution of this agreement, the sum of Rs. ——— and on the ——— day of every calendar month (or year) during the hiring period the sum of Rs. ——— by way of hire for the said goods.

3. The hirer shall at any time during the hiring have the option of purchasing the said goods for Rs. ——— and in that event the hirer shall receive credit for all sums previously paid by him under the preceding clause. Until a purchase shall have been effected and the price fully paid, the said goods shall remain the property of the owner.

4. During the hiring period, the hirer will—

(*a*) not sell, pledge, charge or in any manner part with the possession of the said goods or any of them;

(*b*) not, without the consent in writing of the owner, remove the said goods or any part thereof from the premises of the hirer at ———;

(*c*) permit the owner or his authorised agents at all reasonable times to inspect and examine the condition of the said goods;

(*d*) keep the goods insured against all losses or damage by fire, tempest or theft up to the value of Rs. ———— with an Insurance Company to be approved by the owner and shall keep the insurance alive during the continuance of the agreement. He shall pay all sums of money received in respect of such insurances to the owner who shall apply such money in making good the loss by replacement of such damaged part or parts or the entire goods of similar description and value, whereupon such substituted part or parts or goods shall become subject to this agreement in the same manner as the original goods.

(*Other conditions settled and necessary according to the nature of the goods*).

5. If the hirer shall make default in the punctual payment in full, of the said monthly hire, or in the observance or performance of any of the provisions of this agreement, on his part to be observed and performed, the hiring shall immediately determine.

6. On the determination of the hiring the owner may without notice or demand retake possession of the said goods and for that purpose may by himself or by his agent or servants, enter into or upon any premises occupied by the hirer and search the same, if necessary, for the hired goods.

7. The hirer may terminate this agreement at any time by returning the said goods at the owner's place of business.

8. If the hiring is terminated by the hirer under Clause 7, such termination shall not prejudice the owner's right to recover the hire upto the date of such termination nor his right to recover damages for any prior breach of this agreement by the hirer, [and the hirer shall not be allowed credit or set off for or on account of any payments previously made by him].

9. (*Minimum Payment Clause as in Form No. 5 below*).

10. Any time or other indulgence granted by the owner shall not prejudice or affect his strict rights under this agreement.

IN WITNESS WHEREOF, etc.

5—Minimum Payment Clause

At the termination of this agreement either at the instance of the hirer or the owner, the hirer shall pay to the owner by way of compensation for depreciation of the said article such sum as with the amount previously paid for hire shall make up a sum equal to not less than one half of total amount payable under the agreement.

6—Agreement for Hire (with option to Purchase) with a Financier and a Guarantor

THIS AGREEMENT made this day ——— BETWEEN AB, etc., (hereinafter called "the owner") of the first part and CD, etc., (hereinafter called "the hirer") of the second part and EF, etc., (hereinafter called "the guarantor") of the third part.

WHEREAS the owner on the request of the hirer has purchased the motor vehicle described in the schedule hereto from the dealer in order to let the same to the hirer on the terms and conditions hereinafter appearing and the guarantor has agreed to guarantee the payment of the hire and performance of other conditions by the hirer in accordance with the terms of this agreement.

WHEREBY in consideration of the above it is agreed between the parties as follows:

Paras 1, 2, 3 *and* 4 *(a), (c) and (d), same as in Form No.* 4. *For para 4 (b) substitute the following:*

(*b*) will keep the vehicle registered in the name of the owner, and pay all taxes, rates, duties and licence fee or any other charges levied by any authority under any law or rules for the time being in force in respect of the said vehicle, during the continuance of the agreement.

Paras 5, 6, 7, 8 *and* 9 *same as in Form No.* 4.

10. The guarantor further agrees that in consideration of the premises, and in case of breach of the terms of this contract by the hirer, he shall restore possession of the vehicle to the owner and shall pay such sums of hire of the vehicle as may have fallen due to the owner along with any other sum that may become payable to the owner.

Para 11 *same as para* 10 *in Form No.* 4.

IN WITNESS WHEREOF, etc.

7—Hire of a Vehicle

AN AGREEMENT made on the ——— day of ——— BETWEEN AB, etc., (hereinafter called "the owner") of the one part and CD, etc., (hereinafter called "the Hirer") of the other part;

WHEREBY IT IS AGREED AS FOLLOWS:—

1. The owner shall let and the hirer shall take on hire the vehicle —— (*full description*) bearing registration No. ——— along with its driver and cleaner from the ——— day of ——— for the term of ——— months hence next ensuing.

2. The hirer shall during the continuance of this agreement pay to the owner by way of rent for the hire of the said vehicle, compensation for the use and depreciation of the same and the pay and all allowances for the driver and cleaner as aforesaid, the sum of Rs. ——— per day.

3. The payment under clause 2 hereinbefore shall be made to the owner within fifteen days after the expiry of the term of this agreement (*or*, by the seventh day of every month).

4. The owner shall at his own expense keep the said vehicle in good and running condition and will keep the hirer indemnified against all loss of or damage to the said vehicle from whatsoever cause the same may arise.

5. The hirer may determine the hiring at any time by returning the said vehicle to the owner, and shall thereupon forthwith pay to the owner all moneys then payable to him under this agreement.

6. The petrol and oil for plying the vehicle will be provided by the hirer.

(*Other conditions as in forms 2 and 3*).

IN WITNESS WHEREOF, etc.

INDEMNITY

Preliminary Note

Indemnity and Guarantee

A contract of indemnity is a contract by which one party promises to save the other from loss caused by the conduct of the promisor himself or by the conduct of any other person (Sec. 124, Contract Act). It differs from a contract of guarantee which is a contract to perform a promise or discharge the liability of a third person in case of the latter's default (Sec. 126).

For example, A contracts to indemnify B against the consequences of any proceedings which C may take against B in respect of a certain sum, this is a contract of indemnity. The person, who gives the indemnity is represented as indemnifier (A) and the person for whose protection the same is given is represented as "indemnity-holder" (B).

Form of Indemnity

Sometimes a separate indemnity bond is executed and sometimes an indemnity clause is inserted in any other deed relating to a transaction from which the contract of indemnity arises, e.g. in a sale deed a covenant to indemnify the purchaser against any loss or damage suffered by any defect in title or by the discovery of any charge.

When separately executed, it may take the form of a deed or may be in the form of a note addressed to the person intended to be indemnified.

The latter form is a simpler one and is generally adopted in banking and commercial transactions. In this form the name of the person addressed is given at the top and under it the covenant is written in the first person, the consideration being stated in the beginning of the covenant. The promisor signs at the end.

Generally, an indemnity is a personal undertaking but sometimes the undertaking is secured by hypothecation of property in which case it is drafted as a mortgage.

Heirs and Successors

If the indemnity relates to any property, e.g. when given to a purchaser of land, it is expressed to be in favour of the other party and his successor-in-title to the property.

In cases of other indemnities, the heirs, successors and assigns of the person to be indemnified are mentioned. The heirs and successors of the person giving the indemnity need not be mentioned as the contract can, after his death, be enforced against his legal representatives (Sec. 37, Contract Act).

In England, indemnity deeds are executed in favour of sureties but this is not necessary in India as, under Sec. 145 of the Contract Act, a contract of indemnity by the principal in favour of the surety is implied in every contract of guarantee by the surety.

Where an indemnity bond executed by a third party in favour of a purchaser of property of a Hindu minor from the minor's guardian provided that if the minor on attaining majority refuses to ratify the sale and loss is caused thereby to the purchaser, the executant would indemnify the purchaser in respect of the sale consideration, and the minor after attaining majority challenged the sale, but the sale was held void for want of valid registration and not on ground of the former minor's refusal to ratify, it was held that no liability accrued on the indemnity bond.[1]

Registration

Registration is not required unless immovable property is hypothecated.

1 *Sri Raja Velugoti S.K. Krishna Yachendra* v. *Apparao*, AIR 1949 PC 234.

PRECEDENTS

1—Indemnity Bond (in the Form of Agreement)

THIS AGREEMENT, etc.

WHEREAS by a deed of lease dated the ——— the said CD demised certain land to the said AB and one XY, since deceased, for a term of nine years from ———;

AND WHEREAS one of the conditions entered in the said lease was that during the first year the said CD will not require the said lessees to pay rent for uncultivated land;

AND WHEREAS though the whole of the demised land was not cultivated during the first year, full rent for that year was realized by the said CD on the alleged ground that the aforesaid condition was not intended to apply to this lease, and that it was by an accidental omission that the same was not scored out of the printed form of lease before execution;

AND WHEREAS the said AB and XY served a notice on the said CD threatening to file a suit against the said CD for refund of the amount of rent so realized from them in violation of the aforesaid condition;

AND WHEREAS as the said XY died leaving behind him, as his heirs, two minor sons KL and MN who are under the natural guardianship of their mother PQ;

AND WHEREAS the said AB and the said PQ on behalf of the said minor sons KL and MN have withdrawn the aforesaid notice and have agreed to forego their claim for the said refund on the said CD agreeing to revise the term of the said lease and to extend the same from nine to twelve years.

AND WHEREAS in consideration of the aforesaid agreement of the said CD the said AB has agreed to indemnify the said CD from any claim which the said minor sons of the said XY may institute for refund of the said amount of rent inspite of the said PQ relinquishing the same on their behalf.

NOW THESE PRESENTS WITNESS that in pursuance of the said agreement and for the consideration aforesaid the said AB hereby agrees always to indemnify and keep harmless the said CD from any claim which the aforesaid KL and MN or either of them or their respective successors or assigns or any of them may at any time institute for the refund of any part of the rent paid by the said AB and XY for the year ——— under the aforesaid deed of lease dated the ———.

IN WITNESS WHEREOF, etc.

2—Indemnity given to a Bank

THIS DEED OF INDEMNITY is made, etc.

WHEREAS a sum of Rs. ——— on account of Insurance Policies on the life of the late EF was collected after the death of the said EF by the said Bank and has since been held by the said Bank as a deposit carrying interest at ——— per cent per annum from the date of realization;

AND WHEREAS EF left at his death a widow GH and two minor sons JK and LM as his heirs.

AND WHEREAS the said AB has by order of the District Judge of ——— dated ——— been appointed a guardian of the person and property of the said JK and LM.

AND WHEREAS the said AB requested the said Bank to pay him the aforesaid deposit with interest due thereon and the said Bank has consented to do so upon the said AB giving such indemnity as is hereinafter contained in case there shall hereafter be a claim against the said Bank by the said JK or LM on their attaining majority or by the said GH for the said deposit or any portion thereof;

NOW THIS DEED WITNESSES that in pursuance of the aforesaid agreement and in consideration of the said Bank paying out the said deposit to the said AB as guardian of the aforementioned JK and LM, the said AB hereby agrees with the said Bank that he will at all times indemnify and keep harmless the said Bank from all claims and demands made and all actions and proceedings taken against the said Bank by the said JK or LM on his attaining majority or by the said GH in respect of the said deposit or any part thereof.

IN WITNESS WHEREOF, etc.

3—Indemnity to Tenant Paying Rent to a Person Whose Title is in Dispute

THIS DEED OF INDEMNITY is made on the ——— day of ——— BETWEEN AB, etc., (hereinafter called "the landlord") of the one part AND CD, etc., (hereinafter called "the tenant") of the other part;

WHEREAS a dispute (*or*, a suit) is now pending between the landlord and certain other persons as to the title to the ——— (*describe the property*) which is now occupied (*or* held) by the tenant (*or*, to the estate of one XY, in which the tenant holds certain land) under a lease thereof dated ——— executed by ———;

AND WHEREAS the tenant has nevertheless agreed to pay to the landlord the rent of the said ——— which is now in arrears and which shall hereafter become due upon the landlord agreeing to indemnify him in respect thereof.

NOW THIS DEED WITNESSES that in consideration of the tenant agreeing to pay the said rent to him, the landlord hereby covenants with the tenant that the landlord will repay on demand to the tenant all such rent, sums of money, costs and damages as the tenant or his assigns shall by due process of law or otherwise be compelled to pay and all costs and damages which he or they shall otherwise sustain by reason of his or their paying the said rent or any part thereof to the landlord in the manner aforesaid.

IN WITNESS WHEREOF, etc.

4—Indemnity given to Drawer of Lost Cheque on Drawing a Second Cheque

(*In First Person*)

To

———

In consideration of your having this day given me a second cheque for Rs. ——— being the amount of a previous cheque No. ——— dated ——— drawn by you in my favour which I have lost, I hereby undertake to refund to you the said sum of Rs. ——— in the event of the earlier cheque being presented to and paid by your banker within ——— months and to indemnify you against all expenses which may be incurred by you in relation thereto.

Dated ——— Signed———

5—Indemnity given to the Railway by a Consignee who has Lost the Railway Receipt

To

The———Railway

In consideration of your having delivered to me the parcel No.——— containing———valued at Rs.———dispatched from———station to my address on or about the———day of———, the Railway receipt for which has been lost, I hereby undertake to hold you (the said ———

Railway) its servants and agents harmless and indemnified against all claims in respect of the said parcel and its contents.

6—Indemnity Bond given by a Shareholder or Debenture holder for Issue of a Duplicate Share or Debenture Certificate or Dividend or Interest Warrant in place of One Lost

To

The Secretary

———— Company

————

We/I, AB, etc. hereby certify that I have lost/misplaced/not received share/debenture certificate/dividend warrant/interest warrant of your company as per details given below:

Application No.	*Folio Allotted*	*Share/debenture Certificate/Dividend/ interest warrant No.*	*Dividend/ interest/ amount*

We/I hereby request you to please issue us/me a duplicate —— against the above ———.

We/I hereby agree to indemnify the Company in the manner hereinafter stated:

We/I have not pledged or deposited by way of security any of the share/debenture certificate relating to the aforesaid shares/debentures nor have sold or transferred any of the said shares/debentures and undertake that We/I shall deliver to you the original share/debenture certificate if and whenever found. (*Or, as the case may be*, We/I have not encashed, negotiated or otherwise dealt in so as to create any adverse claim upon the amount of the dividend/interest warrant).

Now it is hereby agreed that in consideration of the company issuing a duplicate share/debenture certificate/dividend/interest warrant for the said amount, We/I hereby covenant at all times hereafter and from time to time to save, defend and keep indemnified the company and their estates and effects from and against all actions, costs, suits, legal proceedings, claims, demands, charges, damages expenses and liabilities of whatsoever nature which the company may sustain or incur by reason of such issue of duplicate share/debenture certificate/dividend/interest warrant from and against any action which may be brought against the company by any person.

IN WITNESS WHEREOF We/I hereto have hereunto set and subscribed Our/My respective hands at ——— this the —— day of ——— 2000.

WITNESS APPLICANT

7—Indemnity given by a Vendor against Possible Claim of a Co-Sharer Believed to be Dead

THIS DEED OF INDEMNITY is made, etc.

WHEREAS ———

(1) The property described in the schedule hereto was owned by the vendor and his brother D;

(2) The said D left home in 1986 and has not been heard of ever since and is believed to have been dead;

(3) The said D has left no other heir except the vendor;

(4) The vendor agreed to sell the said property to the purchaser and by a separate deed of indemnity to indemnify him against any possible claim of D or any of his heirs; and

(5) In pursuance of the said agreement the vendor executed a deed of sale on the ———.

NOW THIS DEED WITNESSES that in further pursuance of the said agreement and in consideration of the purchaser purchasing the said property, the vendor hereby agrees to keep indemnified and harmless the purchaser, his heirs, successors and assigns against all claims made and action or proceeding commenced by the said D or any person claiming through or under him in respect of the said property and against all costs and expenses incurred by the purchaser, his heirs, successors, or assigns in defending any such claim, action or proceeding.

IN WITNESS, etc.

8—Indemnity by a Company to Indemnify its Managing Director of Guarantees given by him to the Company's Bank[1]

THIS DEED OF INDEMNITY is made, etc.

WHEREAS the said CD at the request of the Board of Directors of the Company of which he is the Managing Director and in consideration of the Company agreeing to give such indemnity as hereinafter appearing has

---

1 See also Form No. 9 (Counter Guarantee) under GUARANTEE, *ante*.

signed or given and may hereinafter from time to time sign or give his promissory note or some other instrument in favour of the ——— Bank (*the bankers of the Company*) by way of guarantee or collateral security for advances made or to be made from time to time by the said bank to or on account of the Company or in respect of other pecuniary accommodation to be from time to time afforded by the said bank to the Company.

NOW THIS DEED WITNESSES as follows:

1. The Company hereby agrees with the said CD that the Company will on demand repay to the said CD all sums which the said CD may have to pay to the said bank or any person or persons by reason of his having signed or given any such promissory note or instrument as aforesaid and will at all times hereafter keep the said CD fully indemnified against all claims or legal proceedings, costs and expenses in respect of any such promissory note or other instrument as aforesaid.

2. The obligations of the Company under the preceding covenant shall not be discharged by reason of the cessation at any time of the guarantees given by the said CD as aforesaid but shall continue in force or revive in the event of subsequent renewal thereof.

3. This deed shall not preclude the said CD from enforcing any other remedy to which he may be or become entitled as a surety under the guarantees given as aforesaid.

IN WITNESS WHEREOF, etc.

9—Indemnity Bond by Employee with Sureties when a Suspended Employee is Reinstated

THIS DEED OF INDEMNITY is made on the ——— day of——— BETWEEN AB, etc., (Bounden) AND CD, etc., and EF, etc., (Sureties) of the one part AND the Governor of the State of—(hereinafter called "the Government") of the other part;

WHEREAS the Bounden above named was in the service of the Government as ———.

AND WHEREAS the Bounden was placed under suspension from service from ——— on certain charges against him;

AND WHEREAS a departmental inquiry was conducted against the Bounden and, as a result of the said inquiry, the Bounden has been reinstated to the post of ——— with effect from ——— vide G.O. No. ——— dated ——— and an adverse entry was made in his character roll;

AND WHEREAS the Government has by G.O. No. —— dated—— sanctioned that the Bounden be paid his full pay for the period of suspension *i.e.*, from ——— to ——— amounting to Rs. ——— but under Government rules and orders it is necessary that the moneys earned through employment by the Bounden during the aforesaid period should be deducted from the payments to be made as aforesaid;

AND WHEREAS the Bounden has denied having earned any money through employment during the above period;

AND WHEREAS the Government is willing to pay to the Bounden the aforesaid sum of Rs. ——— only on condition that the Bounden shall execute a bond with two sureties, being these presents, to indemnify and save harmless the Government from any loss which the Government may incur by reason of any moneys earned through employment as aforesaid not having been paid to the Government;

NOW THIS DEED WITNESSES that in consideration of the Government agreeing to pay to the Bounden the emoluments as aforementioned, the Bounden and the Sureties hereby jointly and severally covenant with the Government that the Bounden shall pay on demand to the Government all moneys which may be discovered to have been earned through employment by the Bounden during the aforementioned period together with all costs and expenses, and the Bounden and the Sureties hereby agree[1] that the Government may, on the certificate of the Secretary to the Government in the Administrative Department, which shall be final, conclusive and binding on the Bounden and the Sureties, recover the same from them jointly or severally as arrears of land revenue.

IN WITNESS WHEREOF, etc.

---

1 This clause will be legally effective only if it is backed by a statutory provision such as that contained in section 3 U.P. Public Moneys (Recovery of Dues) Act 1972, for parties cannot by mere agreement confer jurisdiction of revenue authorities to resort to coercive processes (e.g., arrest, attachment).

THE INSOLVENCY AND BANKRUPTCY CODE

Preliminary Note

To address the issue of stressed entities in India, we have had not only multiple laws like Sick Industrial Companies (Special Provisions) Act, 1985, the Companies Act, 1956 and the Companies Act, 2013 but also RBI formulated mechanisms like corporate debt restructuring (CDR), the joint lenders' forum mechanism, strategic debt restructuring (SDR) to address the issue of stressed entities. However, we have always struggled in debt restructuring and most importantly in providing a smooth exit route to failed companies despite the availability of various such options over the period of time. The prime reason being that these laws were fragmented everywhere without any timelines in place. This created confusion of multiplicity of proceedings amongst the various stakeholders which caused undue delay in the disposal of the matters and further leading to depreciation of assets of the stressed entities besides other economic implications on the economy. The World Bank in 2016 reported that the average time to resolve an insolvency matter in India was four years.

We also have laws like SARFAESI, 2002[1] and Recovery of Debts and Bankruptcy, 1993[2] which were enacted for the benefit of banks and financial institutions with the sole objective of recovering the debt from the borrowers (be it corporates or individuals) but they do not aim to revive the failed companies in the process of recovery.

Individual insolvency and bankruptcy are also dealt under the separate set of laws i.e. vide the Presidency Towns Insolvency Act, 1909, and the Provincial Insolvency Act, 1920.[3]

Therefore, to permanently remove the bottlenecks of the existing laws, *The Insolvency and Bankruptcy Code, 2016* (the **Code**) was enacted on 28th May, 2016. The Code paves the way for much needed reforms while focusing on creditor driven insolvency resolution. The primary aim of the Code is to (i) consolidate all the laws related to Insolvency and Bankruptcy of corporate persons and individuals (including partnership firms) under one roof; (ii) have a solid framework for resolution of a distressed entity in a time bound manner; and (iii) provide a well-defined exit route for companies, whenever required. The Supreme Court, in *Swiss Ribbons Private Limited* v. *Union of India,*[4] observed that the foremost and primary objective of the Code is the reorganization and insolvency resolution of the

---

1 Securitization and Reconstruction of Financial Assets and Enforcement of Security Interest, 2002.

2 Recovery of Debts Due to Banks and Financial Institutions, 1993 was renamed in 2019.

3 They will stand repealed as soon as provisions w.r.t. individuals are notified under the Code.

4 (2019) 4 SCC 17.

corporate debtor in a time bound manner. Liquidation is to be carried out only as a last resort mechanism.

The Code provides a separate framework for corporates and individuals (including partnership firms). However, at present the provisions pertaining to corporate are only effective. The provisions for individuals are still to be notified by the government.[1]

Pillars of IBC

To help the Code achieve its objectives, it is backed by a strong infrastructure ecosystem. It has four strong pillars. They are (1) The Insolvency and Bankruptcy Board of India (IBBI); (2) Adjudicating Authorities which includes National Company Law Tribunal (NCLT) and Debt Recovery Tribunal (DRT); (3) Information Utility (IU); and (4) Insolvency Professionals (IP).

Insolvency Proceedings

Insolvency proceedings of the corporate debtor[2] may be carried out in two stages. At the first stage, an attempt is made to carry out resolution of a corporate since the foremost objective of the Code is "reorganisation". However, on failure to reach a resolution, Liquidation is initiated against the corporate debtor at the second stage.

Corporate Insolvency Resolution Process (CIRP)

On occurrence of a default by the corporate debtor, any creditor (financial or operational) or the debtor itself may initiate CIRP against it by filing an application to the adjudicating authority i.e. National Company Law Tribunal (NCLT).[3] As soon as this process is commenced,[4] there is automatic suspension of powers of the board of directors or partners of the corporate debtor.[5] These powers are exercised through an Interim Resolution Professional (IRP) and later by a Resolution Professional (RP). IRP/RP are also put at helm of affairs of the corporate debtor throughout the CIRP period. Further, during this period, the committee of creditors (CoC) examines the viability of the debtor in question along with the resolution plans submitted by the resolution applicants and takes a final call on the restructuring of the corporate debtor. Any resolution plan, if found to be in tangent with the business in question, is accorded sanction by the CoC and thereafter, put forward to the NCLT for its approval.

---

1 The provisions relating to personal guarantors to corporate debtors (CDs) came into effect on December 1, 2019.

2 Section 3(7) – (i) a company defined under Companies Act, 2013; (ii) LLP defined under Limited Liability Partnership Act, 2008; (iii) any other person incorporated with limited liability under any law.

3 Section 7 (Financial Creditor), section 9 (Operational Creditor), section 10 (Corporate Applicant).

4 Section 5(12) – on the admission of application u/s 7, 9, 10.

5 Section 17(1)(b), Insolvency and Bankruptcy Code, 2016.

Flowchart of CIRP

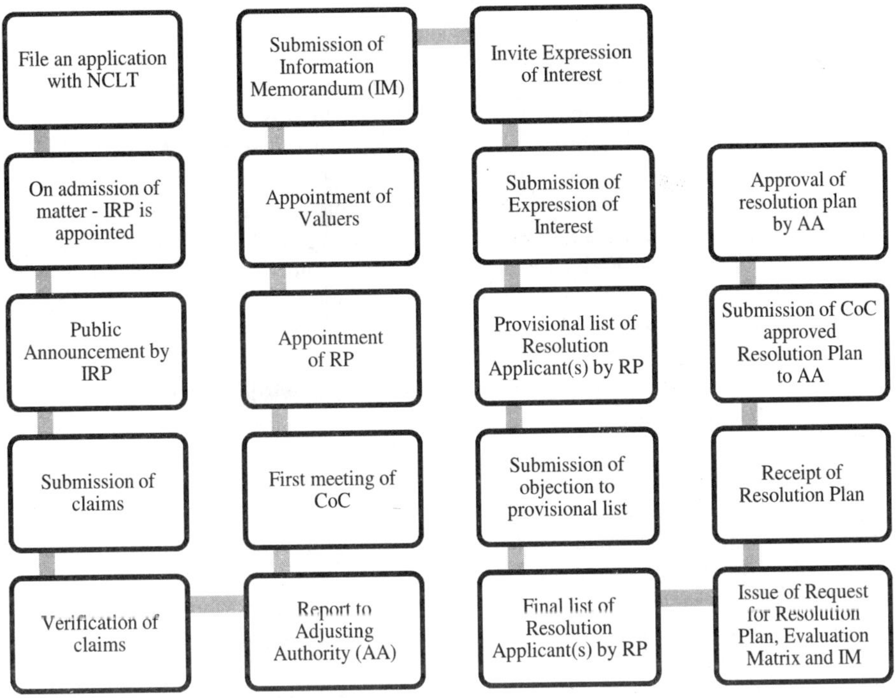

Some of the key elements of the CIRP

- **Minimum threshold** of default for triggering CIRP is 1 crore and above.[1]
- CIRP is a **time bound process** which must be completed within 180 days. An extension of 90 days may be sought further. However, it must mandatorily be completed within 330 days including any extension and any time taken in legal proceedings.[2]
- Once an application of resolution gets admitted by the NCLT, there is a declaration of **Moratorium period** by the NCLT.[3] This continues till either resolution plan is approved by the NCLT or liquidation order is passed against the corporate debtor. During this period, certain actions are barred against the corporate debtor. This ensures that CIRP doesn't get derailed because of other proceedings. Also, moratorium is not applicable against the guarantor of the corporate debtor i.e. simultaneous proceedings

---

1 Section 4. [In the wake of COVID 19 pandemic, the Central Government passed a notification on March 24, 2020 whereby it increased the default amount to 1 crore. However, default amount is one lakh for defaults which took place before 25th March 2020. Also, CIRP was suspended vide section 10A for an year between March 25, 2020 and March 24, 2021 i.e. no CIRP can ever be initiated for defaults taking place during this period].

2 Section 12.

3 Section 13 read with 14, Insolvency and Bankruptcy Code, 2016.

can be initiated against the guarantor, be it corporate or personal.

- The **committee of creditors (CoC)** is constituted by an IRP[1] and it comprises of financial creditors (who are not related party to the corporate debtor) against whom the corporate debtor has made a default. Majority of the approvals (including on the resolution plan), require a vote of not less than sixty six percent of the voting share which is based on the proportion of the financial debt owed to such financial creditor. In *K. Sashidhar* v. *Indian Overseas Bank,*[2] the Supreme Court observed that CoC exercises commercial wisdom while approving or rejecting a resolution plan. Their wisdom is supreme and it cannot be challenged even by the Adjudicating Authority. The legislature, consciously, has not provided any grounds to challenge the commercial wisdom of the individual financial creditors or their collective decision before the Adjudicating Authority. That is made non-justiciable. In *CoC of Essar Steel India Limited* v. *Satish Kumar Gupta,*[3] the Supreme Court reiterated that the wisdom of CoC is supreme in Commercial matters relating to a CIRP.

Resolution plans may be submitted by anyone who is not barred under section 29A of the Code. After a resolution plan is approved and a new management takes over, immunity is provided to the corporate debtor and its assets from prosecution, attachment, confiscation, seizure for the offences committed prior to the commencement of the CIRP.[4]

In *CoC of Essar Steel India Limited* v. *Satish Kumar Gupta,*[5] the Supreme Court also observed that right of subrogation stands extinguished w.r.t. guarantors as resolution is binding on them as well under section 31 of the Code.

In *Ghanshyam Mishra & Sons Pvt. Ltd.* v. *Edelweiss Asset Reconstruction Company,*[6] the Supreme Court observed that any debt owed to the Central Government, State Government or any local authority (including other creditors) which do not form part of the approved resolution plan stand extinguished i.e. no such person shall be entitled to initiate or continue any proceedings against the corporate debtor thereafter.

In *Lalit Kumar Jain* v. *Union of India,*[7] the Supreme Court observed that post the approval of resolution plan, the personal guarantor would not get discharged if the creditors have been unable to recover the whole amount vide the resolution plan. Therefore, insolvency proceedings can be initiated against the personal guarantor.

Withdrawal of application[8] may be allowed at three stages. (1) Before the admission of application by the NCLT; (2) After the admission of application by the NCLT but before the constitution of the CoC; (3) After the constitution of the

---

1 Section 18.
2 (2019) 2 SCC 150, 2019 SCC Online 257.
3 Civil Appeal No. 8766-67/2019 Diary No. 24417/2019 with other Civil Appeals and WP(C)s.
4 Section 32A.
5 *ibid.*
6 Civil Appeal No. 8129 of 2019 and other Appeals.
7 (2021) 167 SCL 1 (SC).
8 Section 12A.

CoC, with the approval creditors holding 90% of voting share. In *Ebix Singapore Private Limited* v. *CoC of Educomp Solutions Private Limited,*[1] the Supreme Court observed that the Adjudicating Authority cannot allow resolution applicant to withdraw or modify the resolution plan once it is approved by the CoC.

Fast Track Resolution Process[2]

Some companies[3] as notified by the Central Government are eligible for resolution under the fast track. The maximum time period for the completion of this process is 90 days and an extension of maximum 45 days can be availed from the NCLT.

Pre-Packaged Insolvency Resolution Process[4]

Since during COVID-19, MSME industries were severely impacted, Pre-Packaged insolvency resolution process was introduced specifically for the benefit of MSMEs.[5] This process is a combination of both formal and informal insolvency resolution process whereby statutory protection is given to a resolution plan i.e. a resolution plan is negotiated between the debtor and its creditors before initiating the formal insolvency resolution process before the NCLT.

The **minimum threshold** of default for triggering this process is also one crore at present. The resolution professional who is appointed for this purpose is required to complete the process within one-hundred twenty days from the pre-packaged insolvency commencement date.

This amendment aims to provide a quick, cost effective and least invasive insolvency regime for the MSMEs.

Liquidation Process

Under the Code, the corporate debtor cannot be liquidated directly unlike the Companies Act, 1956[6] whereby the company was permitted to be wound up on its inability to pay its debts. Every insolvent company is given a fair chance of revival before the liquidation process is commenced against it.

Some of the key elements of Liquidation process

- Section 33 of the Code provides the following grounds on which liquidation may be initiated:

---

1 MANU/SC/0628/2021.

2 Sections 55-58.

3 Start-up company, Small company (paid up share capital up to 50 Lakhs), Unlisted company (up to 1 crore).

4 Chapter III-A has been inserted in the Part II of the Code vide 2021 Amendment to the Code.

5 Micro, Small and Medium Enterprises as defined under section 7(1) of the MSME Development Act, 2006.

6 The corporates were wound up as per section 433 of the Companies Act, 1956 for numerous grounds including on its inability to pay its debt [433(e)] before the enactment of the code. However, post this enactment and notification of section 271 of the Companies Act, 2013 which was made effective from 15th December 2016, winding up of companies is to be done as per the said section of the Companies Act, 2013 on all the grounds except inability to pay its debts which will be dealt under the code.

(i) NCLT doesn't receive a resolution plan for confirmation before expiry of period of CIRP provided under section 12 of the Code; or
(ii) NCLT rejects the resolution plan under section 31 of the Code; or
(iii) CoC takes a decision to liquidate the corporate debtor before confirmation of the resolution plan; or
(iv) When resolution plan approved by the NCLT is contravened by the corporate debtor, any person affected by this contravention can file an application in this regard to the NCLT.

- Entire liquidation process is administered by an insolvency professional who is appointed as a **Liquidator.**[1]
- As soon as Liquidation order is passed by the NCLT, all the powers of the board of directors or partners vest in the liquidator. **Moratorium** is imposed on the proceedings against the corporate debtor and the said order acts as a deemed notice of discharge to all officers, employees, workers (except if business is continued under Liquidation). Further, all the assets of the corporate debtor vest in the Liquidation Estate.[2]
- The Code also provides a **timeline** of one year from the passing of liquidation order within which liquidation process should be completed.[3]
- Since rescuing a business is always advantageous over liquidation, the corporate debtor is provided yet another **opportunity to revive** at the stage of liquidation. There are two possibilities, either as per Schemes and Arrangement under section 230 of the Companies Act or the company is sold as a going concern.[4]
- Sale proceeds from the Liquidation needs to be distributed according to the waterfall mechanism provided under section 53 of the Code.
- Post the liquidation, the corporate is dissolved i.e. its separate legal entity is brought to an end.[5]

Voluntary Liquidation[6]

Unlike the above, corporates may voluntarily initiate liquidation against itself if it not insolvent i.e. no default has been made either because:

(i) The corporate has no debt; or
(ii) The corporate is capable of paying of its debts from the proceeds of assets to be sold in the voluntary liquidation.

Also, directors of the corporate are compulsorily required to give a declaration that the voluntary liquidation is not being carried out to defraud the creditors.

This process is also administered by an insolvency professional who is appointed as a **Liquidator.** He must aim to complete the process within one year of the liquidation commencement date.[7]

---

1 Section 34.
2 Section 36.
3 Regulation 44 of the IBBI (Liquidation process) Regulations, 2016.
4 Regulation 32 of the IBBI (Liquidation process) Regulations, 2016.
5 Section 54.
6 Section 59.
7 Regulation 37 of the IBBI (Voluntary Liquidation Process) Regulations, 2017.

PRECEDENTS

1—Application by Financial Creditor(s) to Initiate Corporate Insolvency Resolution Process[1]

[*Date*]

To,

The National Company Law Tribunal

[*Address*]

From,

[*Names and addresses of the registered offices of the financial creditors]*

In the matter of [name of the corporate debtor]

Subject: Application to initiate corporate insolvency resolution process in the matter of [*name of the corporate debtor*] under the Insolvency and Bankruptcy Code, 2016.

Madam/Sir,

[*Names of the financial creditor(s)*], hereby submit this application to initiate a corporate insolvency resolution process in the matter of [*name of corporate debtor*]. The details for the purpose of this application are set out below:

Part-I
Particulars of Applicant

(To be provided for each Financial Creditor making the Application)

1.	Name of Financial Creditor	
2.	Date of Incorporation of Financial Creditor	
3.	Identification Number of Financial Creditor	
4.	Address of the Registered Office of the Financial Creditor	
5.	Name and Address of the person authorised to submit application on its behalf (enclose authorisation)	
6.	Name and Address of person resident in India authorised to accept the service of process on its behalf (enclose authorisation)	

1 Under section 7 of the Insolvency and Bankruptcy Code, 2016 read with Rule 4 of the Insolvency and Bankruptcy (Application to Adjudicating Authority) Rules, 2016.

Part II
Particulars of the Corporate Debtor

1.	Name of the Corporate Debtor	
2.	Identification Number of Corporate Debtor	
3.	Date of Incorporation of Corporate Debtor	
4.	Nominal share capital and the paid-up share capital of the corporate debtor and/or details of guarantee clause as per memorandum of association (as applicable)	
5.	Address of the Registered Office of the Corporate Debtor	
6.	Details of the Corporate Debtor as per the notification under section 55(2) of the code	
	(i) Assets and income	
	(ii) Class of creditors or amount of debt	
	(iii) Category of corporate person (*where application is under chapter IV of part II of the code*)	

Part-III
Particulars of the Proposed Interim Resolution Professional

1.	Name, Address, Email Address and the Registration Number of the Proposed Interim Resolution Professional	

Part-IV
Particulars of Financial Debt

1.	Total Amount of Debt Granted, Date(s) of Disbursement	
2.	Amount claimed to be in default and the date on which the default occurred (attach the workings for computation of amount and days of default in tabular form)	

Part-V
Particulars of Financial Debt
[Documents, Records and Evidence of Default]

1.	Particulars of security held, if any, the date of its creation, its estimated value as per the creditor. Attach a copy of a certificate of registration of charge issued by the Registrar of Companies (*if the corporate debtor is a company*)
2.	Particulars of an order of a court, tribunal or arbitral panel adjudicating on the default, if any (*attach a copy of the order*)
3.	Record of default with the information utility, if any(*attach a copy of such record*)
4.	Details of succession certificate, or probate of a Will, or letter of administration, or court decree (as may be applicable), under the Indian Succession Act, 1925 (10 of 1925) (*attach a copy*)
5.	The latest and complete copy of the financial contract reflecting all amendments and waivers to date (*attach a copy*)
6.	A rccord of dcfault as availablc with any crcdit information company (*attach a copy*)
7.	Copies of entries in a bankers book in accordance with the bankers books Evidence Act, 1891 (18 of 1891) (*attach a copy*)
8.	List of other documents attached to this application in order to prove the existence of financial debt, the amount and date of default

I, hereby certify that, to the best of my knowledge, [*name of proposed insolvency professional*], is fully qualified and permitted to act as an insolvency professional in accordance with the Insolvency and Bankruptcy Code, 2016 and the associated rules and regulations.

[*Name of the financial creditor]* has paid the requisite fee for this application through *[state means of payment*] on [*date*].

Yours Sincerely,

Signature of person authorised to act on behalf of the financial creditor
Name in block letters
Position with or in relation to the financial creditor
Address of person signing

Instructions

Please attach the following to this application:

Annex I: Copies of all documents referred to in this application.

Annex II: Written communication by the proposed interim resolution professional as set out in Form 2.

Annex III: Proof that the specified application fee has been paid.

Annex IV: Where the application is made jointly, the particulars specified in this form shall be furnished in respect of all the joint applicants along with a copy of authorisation to the financial creditor to file and act on this application on behalf of all the applicants.

2—Written Communication by Proposed Interim Resolution Professional[1]

[*Date*]

To,

The National Company Law Tribunal

[*Address*]

From,

[*Name and address of the registered office of the proposed interim resolution professional*]

In the matter of [*name of the corporate debtor*]

Subject: Written communication in connection with an application to initiate corporate insolvency resolution process in respect of [*name of the corporate debtor*]

Madam/Sir,

I, [*name of proposed interim resolution professional*], an insolvency professional registered with [*name of insolvency professional agency*] having registration number ———, have been proposed as the interim resolution professional by [*name of applicant financial creditor*] in connection with the proposed corporate insolvency resolution process of [*name of the corporate debtor*].

In accordance with rule 9 of the Insolvency and Bankruptcy (Application to Adjudicating Authority) Rules, 2016, I hereby:

(i) agree to accept appointment as the interim resolution professional

1 Under sub rule (1) of rule 9 of the Insolvency and Bankruptcy (Application to Adjudicating Authority) Rules, 2016.

if an order admitting the present application is passed;

(ii) state that the registration number allotted to me by the Board is ——— and that I am currently qualified to practice as an insolvency professional;

(iii) disclose that I am currently serving as an interim resolution professional/resolution professional/liquidator in [*insert number of proceedings*] proceedings;

(iv) certify that there are no disciplinary proceedings pending against me with the Board or [*name of the insolvency professional agency he is a member of*];

(v) affirm that I am eligible to be appointed as a resolution professional in respect of the corporate debtor in accordance with the provisions of the Insolvency and Bankruptcy Board of India (Insolvency Resolution Process for Corporate Persons) Regulations, 2016;

(vi) make the following disclosures in accordance with the code of conduct for insolvency professionals as set out in the Insolvency and Bankruptcy Board of India (Insolvency Professionals) Regulations, 2016;

(Signature of the insolvency professional)

(Name in block letters)

(Name of insolvency professional entity, if applicable)

[Optional certification, if required by the applicant making an application under these Rules]

I, hereby, certify that the facts averred by the applicant in the present application are true, accurate and complete and a default has occurred in respect of the relevant corporate debtor. I have reached this conclusion based on the following facts and/or opinion:

[Please give details].

(Signature of the insolvency professional)

(Name in block letters)

(Name of insolvency professional entity, if applicable)

3—Form of Demand Notice/Invoice Demanding Payment under the Insolvency and Bankruptcy Code, 2016[1]

[*Date*]

To,

[*Name and address of the registered office of the corporate debtor*]

From,

[*Name and address of the registered office of the operational creditor*]

Subject: Demand notice/invoice demanding payment in respect of unpaid operational debt due from [*corporate debtor*] under the Code.

Madam/Sir,

1. This letter is a demand notice/invoice demanding payment of an unpaid operational debt due from [name of corporate debtor].
2. Please find particulars of the unpaid operational debt below:

Particulars of Operational Debt

1.	Total amount of debt, details of transactions on account of which debt fell due, and the date from which such debt fell due	
2.	Amount claimed to be in default and the date on which the default occurred (*attach the workings for computation of default in tabular form*)	
3.	Particulars of security held, if any, the date of its creation, its estimated value as per the creditor. (*Attach a copy of a certificate of registration of charge issued by the registrar of companies if the corporate debtor is a company*)	
4.	Details of retention of title arrangements (*if any*) in respect of goods to which the operational debt refers	
5.	Record of default with the information utility (*if any*)	
6.	Provision of law, contract or other document under which debt has become due	
7.	List of documents attached to this application in order to prove the existence of operational debt and the amount in default	

3. If you dispute the existence or amount of unpaid operational debt (in

1 Under clause (a) of sub-rule (1) of rule 5 of the Insolvency and Bankruptcy (Application to Adjudicating Authority) Rules, 2016.

default) please provide the undersigned, within ten days of the receipt of this letter, of the pendency of the suit or arbitration proceedings in relation to such dispute filed before the receipt of this letter/notice.

4. If you believe that the debt has been repaid before the receipt of this letter, please demonstrate such repayment by sending to us, within ten days of receipt of this letter, the following:

   (iii) an attested copy of the record of electronic transfer of the unpaid amount from the bank account of the corporate debtor; or

   (iv) an attested copy of any record that [*name of the operational creditor*] has received the payment.

5. The undersigned, hereby, attaches a certificate from an information utility confirming that no record of a dispute raised in relation to the relevant operational debt has been filed by any person at any information utility. (if applicable)

6. The undersigned request you to unconditionally repay the unpaid operational debt (in default) in full within ten days from the receipt of this letter failing which we shall initiate a corporate insolvency resolution process in respect of [*name of corporate debtor*].

Yours Sincerely,

Signature of person authorised to act on behalf of the operational creditor
Name in block letters
Position with or in relation to the operational creditor
Address of person signing

Instructions

1. Please serve a copy of this form on the corporate debtor, ten days in advance of filing an application under section 9 of the Code.
2. Please append a copy of such served notice to the application made by the operational creditor to the Adjudicating Authority.

4—Form of Notice with which Invoice Demanding Payment is to attached[1]

[*Date*]

To,

[*Name and address of registered office of the corporate debtor*]

From,

[*Name and address of the operational creditor*]

Subject: Notice attached to invoice demanding payment

Madam/Sir,

[*Name of operational creditor*], hereby provides notice for repayment of the unpaid amount of INR [*insert amount*] that is in default as reflected in the invoice attached to this notice.

In the event you do not repay the debt due to us within ten days of receipt of this notice, we may file an application before the Adjudicating Authority for initiating a corporate insolvency resolution process under section 9 of the Code.

Yours Sincerely,

Signature of person authorised to act on behalf of the operational creditor
Name in block letters
Position with or in relation to the operational creditor
Address of person signing

5—Application by Operational Creditor(s) to initiate Corporate Insolvency Resolution Process[2]

[*Date*]

To,

The National Company Law Tribunal

[*Address*]

From,

[*Name and address for correspondence of the operational creditor*]

In the matter of [*name of the corporate debtor*]

1 Under clause (b) of sub-rule (1) rule 5 of the Insolvency and Bankruptcy (Application to Adjudicating Authority) Rules,2016.

2 Under sub-rule (1) rule 6 of the Insolvency and Bankruptcy (Application to Adjudicating Authority) Rules, 2016.

Subject: Application to initiate corporate insolvency resolution process in respect of [*name of the corporate debtor*] under the Insolvency and Bankruptcy Code, 2016.

Madam/Sir,

[*Name of the operational creditor*], hereby submits this application to initiate a corporate insolvency resolution process in the case of [*name of corporate debtor*]. The details for the purpose of this application are set out below:

Part-I
Particulars of Applicant

1.	Name of operational creditor	
2.	Identification number of operational creditor (if any)	
3.	Address for correspondence of the operational creditor	

Part-II
Particulars of Corporate Debtor

1.	Name of the corporate debtor	
2.	Identification number of corporate debtor	
3.	Date of incorporation of corporate debtor	
4.	Nominal share capital and the paid up share capital of the corporate debtor and/or details of guarantee clause as per memorandum of association (as applicable)	
5.	Address of the registered office of the corporate debtor	
6.	Name, address and authority of person submitting application on behalf of operational creditor (enclose authorisation)	
7.	Name and address of person resident in India authorised to accept the service of process on its behalf (enclose authorisation)	
8.	Details of the corporate debtor as per the notification under section 55(2) of the code: (i) assets and income (ii) class of creditors or amount of debt (iii) category of corporate person *(where application is under chapter IV of part II of the code)*	

Part-III
Particulars of the Proposed Interim Resolution Professional [if Proposed]

1.	Name, Address, Email Address and the Registration Number of the proposed insolvency professional	

Part-IV
Particulars of Operational Debt

1.	Total amount of debt, details of transactions on account of which debt fell due, and the date from which such debt fell due	
2.	Amount claimed to be in default and the date on which the default occurred (*attach the workings for computation of amount and dates of default in tabular form*)	

Part-V
Particulars of Operational Debt
[Documents, Records and Evidence of Default]

1.	Particulars of security held, if any, the date of its creation, its estimated value as per the creditor. (*Attach a copy of a certificate of registration of charge issued by the registrar of companies if the corporate debtor is a company*)	
2.	Details of reservation/retention of title arrangements (if any) in respect of goods to which the operational debt refers	
3.	Particulars of an order of a court, tribunal or arbitral panel adjudicating on the default, if any (*attach a copy of the order*)	
4.	Record of default with the information utility, if any (*attach a copy of such record*)	
5.	Details of succession certificate, or probate of a Will, or letter of administration, or court decree (as may be applicable), under the Indian Succession Act, 1925 (10 of 1925) (*attach a copy*)	
6.	Provision of law, contract or other document under which operational debt has become due	

7.	A statement of bank account where deposits are made or credits received normally by the operational creditor in respect of the debt of the corporate debtor (*attach a copy*)	
8.	List of other documents attached to this application in order to prove the existence of operational debt and the amount in default	

I, [*Name of the operational creditor/person authorised to act on behalf of the operational creditor*] hereby certify that, to the best of my knowledge, [*name of proposed insolvency professional*], is fully qualified and permitted to act as an insolvency professional in accordance with the Code and the rules and regulations made thereunder. [*where applicable*]

[*Name of the operational creditor] has paid the requisite fee for this application through [state means of payment*] on [*date*].

Yours Sincerely,

Signature of person authorised to act on behalf of the operational creditor
Name in block letters
Position with or in relation to the operational creditor
Address of person signing

Instructions

Please attach the following to this application:

Annex I: Copy of the invoice/demand notice as in Form 3 of the Insolvency and Bankruptcy(Application to Adjudicating Authority) Rules, 2016 served on the corporate debtor.

Annex II: Copies of all documents referred to in this application.

Annex III: Copy of the relevant accounts from the banks/financial institutions maintaining accounts of the operational creditor confirming that there is no payment of the relevant unpaid operational debt by the operational debtor, if available.

Annex IV: Affidavit in support of the application in accordance with the Insolvency and Bankruptcy (Application to Adjudicating Authority) Rules, 2016.

Annex V: Written communication by the proposed interim resolution professional as set out in Form 2 of the Insolvency and Bankruptcy (Application to Adjudicating Authority) Rules, 2016. [*where applicable*]

Annex VI: Proof that the specified application fee has been paid.

Note: Where workmen/employees are operational creditors, the application may be made either in an individual capacity or in a joint capacity by one of them who is duly authorised for the purpose.

6—Application by Corporate Applicant to Initiate Corporate Insolvency Resolution Process[1]

[*Date*]

To,

The National Company Law Tribunal

[*Address*]

From,

[*Name and address for correspondence of the corporate applicant*]

In the matter of [name of the corporate debtor]

Subject: Application to initiate corporate insolvency resolution process in respect of [*name of the corporate debtor*] under the Code.

Madam/Sir,

We, hereby submit this application to initiate a corporate insolvency resolution process in respect of [*name of corporate debtor*]. The details for the purpose of this application are set out below:

Part-I
Particulars of the Corporate Applicant

1.	Name address, email address, identification number and address for communication of the corporate applicant	
2.	Name address, email address, identification number and address of the registered office of corporate debtor	
3.	Names and addresses of all directors, promoters, designated partners of the corporate debtor (*as applicable*)	
4.	Date of incorporation of corporate debtor	
5.	Nominal share capital and the paid-up share capital of the corporate debtor and/or details of guarantee clause as per memorandum of association (*as applicable*)	
6.	Name, address and authority of person submitting application on behalf of corporate applicant (*enclose authorisation*)	

1 See sub-rule (1) of rule 7 of the Insolvency and Bankruptcy (Application to Adjudicating Authority) Rules, 2016. Substituted by Notification No. G.S.R 222/(E), dated 14th March, 2019 (w.e.f. 19-03-2019).

7.	Name and address of person resident in India authorised to accept the service of process on its behalf (enclose authorisation)	
8.	Documentation to show that the corporate applicant is authorised to initiate the corporate insolvency resolution process	
9.	Details of the corporate debtor as per the notification under section 55(2) of the code:[1] (i) assets and income (ii) class of creditors or amount of debt (iii) category of corporate person *(where application is under Chapter IV of Part II of the code)*	

Part-II
Particulars of Proposed Interim Resolution Professional

1.	Name, address, email address and the registration number of the proposed interim resolution professional	

Part-III
Particulars of Financial/Operational Debt [Creditor-wise, as Applicable]

1.	Name(s) of Financial/Operational Creditor(s)	
2.	Address of correspondence of the financial/ operational creditor(s)	
3.	Total debt raised and amount in default	
4.	Date when the financial/operational debt was incurred	
5.	Particulars of security held, if any, the date of its creation, its estimated value as per the creditor. (*Attach a copy of a certificate of registration of charge issued by the registrar of companies if the corporate debtor is a company*)	
6.	Details of retention of title arrangements (*if any*) in respect of goods to which the operational debt refers	
7.	Record of default with the information utility, if any	
8.	List of documents attached to this application in order to prove the existence of financial/operational debt and the amount in default	

I, certify that, to the best of my knowledge, [*name of proposed insolvency professional*], is fully qualified and permitted to act as an

1 Inserted by Notification No. G.S.R 222/(E), dated 14th March, 2019 (w.e.f. 19-03-2019).

insolvency professional in accordance with the Code and the associated rules and regulations.

[Name of the corporate applicant] has paid the requisite fee for this application through *[state means of payment]* on [*date*].

Yours Sincerely,

Signature of person authorised to act on behalf of the corporate applicant
Name in block letters
Position with or in relation to the corporate applicant
Address of person signing

Instructions

Attach the following to this application:

Annex I: In case of financial debt, record of default obtained through the information utility or all documents listed in serial number 8 of part III of this application.

Annex II: In case of operational debt, (i) copy of invoice/demand notice served by an operational creditor on the corporate debtor and (ii) record of default obtained through the information utility or all documents listed in serial number 8 of part III of this application.

Annex III: Written communication by the proposed interim resolution professional as set out in Form 2 of the Insolvency and Bankruptcy (Application to Adjudicating Authority) Rules, 2016.

Annex IV: Copy of the relevant books of accounts of the corporate debtor evidencing the default to creditors.

Annex V: Copies of audited financial statements of the corporate debtor for the last two financial years and the provisional financial statements for the current financial year made upto a date not earlier than fourteen days from the date of the application.

Annex VI: A statement of affairs made up to a date not earlier than fourteen days from the date of application including the following document, namely:

- (a) a list of the corporate debtor's assets and liabilities, divided into such categories as are appropriate for easy identification, with estimated values assigned to each category;
- (b) in the case of any property on which a claim against the corporate debtor is wholly or partly secured, particulars of the claim and its amount, and of how and when the security was created;
- (c) the names and addresses of the financial creditors and operational creditors of the corporate debtor, with the amounts due to each of them;

(d) particulars of any debts owed by or to the corporate debtor to or by persons connected with it;

(e) whether any, and if so what, guarantees have been given in relation to the debts of the corporate debtor by other persons, specifying which, if any, of the guarantors is a related party to the corporate debtor and the corporate applicant; and

(f) the names and addresses of the members and partners of the corporate debtor, as the case may be, with details of their respective shareholdings.

Annex VII: A copy of:

(a) relevant extract of any constitutional document or shareholders' agreement that records the authority of the corporate applicant to make this application, where the corporate applicant is a member or partner of the corporate debtor; or

(b) relevant extract of an employment agreement, constitutional document or fillings made to the Registrar of Companies confirming the authority of the corporate applicant to make this application, where the corporate applicant is an individual in charge of managing the operations and resources of the corporate debtor or has control and supervision over the financial affairs of the corporate debtor.

Annex VIII: Affidavit in support of the application in accordance with the Insolvency and Bankruptcy (Application to Adjudicating Authority) Rules, 2016.

Annex IX: Proof that the specified application fee has been paid.

SCHEDULE

[See sub-rule (3) of rule 10]

S. No.	*Applicant*	*Fee payable (in Rs.)*
1.	Application by financial creditor (whether solely or jointly)	25000
2.	Application by operational creditor	2000
3.	Application by corporate debtor	25000

INTELLECTUAL PROPERTY RIGHTS

Preliminary Note

Intellectual property rights are rights given to persons over the creations of their mind. They usually give the creator an exclusive right over the use of his/her creation for a certain period of time. Various forms of intellectual property rights are–

1. Patents
2. Trade Marks
3. Copyright
4. Designs
5. Geographical Indication
6. Plant Variety
7. Trade Secrets

Difference between Assignment and License

The term assignment and license are not interchangeable. An assignment is different from license. An assignment transfers title, however a license merely permits use or permits certain things to be done by licensee.

The primary difference between the two is that a license allow the licensor to maintain their rights and interests in their intellectual property, whereas an assignment transfers all of the assignor's rights and assigns it to the Assignee.

PATENTS

What is a Patent

Patent is an exclusive or monopoly right granted by the Patent Office to an inventor to make, use and distribute his invention for a limited period of time. During this period, the inventor is entitled to exclude anyone from commercially exploiting his invention. A Patent owner has right to prevent others from making, using, selling, offering for sale or importing a process or product(s) in respect of which the patent has been granted.[1]

The person to whom a patent is granted is known as a Patentee.

Nature of Patent Rights

The patent right is territorial in nature i.e. a patent granted in India can only

1 Sec. 48, Patents Act, 1970.

be enforced in India. If the patentee wishes to obtain patents in other countries, he will have to file separate patent applications in countries of his interest, along with necessary fees. A patent in the law is a property right and hence, it can be gifted, inherited, assigned, sold or licensed.

In order to keep the patent in force, prescribed renewal fee is to be paid to the Patent Office every year.

Term of a Patent

A patent in India is granted for a period of twenty years (sec. 53). In India, patent filing and prosecution is governed by the Patents Act, 1970.

Essentials of a Patent

A patent is an exclusive statutory right granted by the Government for an invention[1] that is

(1) New[2],

(2) Involves an inventive step[3] and

(3) Is capable of industrial application[4]

It should not fall within the provisions of sections 3 and 4 of the Patents Act, 1970.

Rationale of the Patent System

Patentee has to describe in the patent application, the invention with such clarity and completeness of all the technical details, that anyone having ordinary skill in the art should by merely reading the description, be able to create the invention.

Before a patent is granted, the invention has to be disclosed at the Patent Office. The price of the grant of the monopoly is the disclosure of the invention at the Patent Office, which after the expiry of the fixed period of the monopoly, passes into the public domain. This enables competitors in the field to manufacture new products or improved products or effect improvements in the manufacturing

---

1 Sec. 2(1)(j) Patents Act, 1970.

2 Sec. 2(1)(l) Patents Act – "New invention" means any invention or technology in respect of a product or process which has not been anticipated by publication in any document or used in the country or elsewhere in the world before the date of filing of the patent application with complete specification, i.e. the subject matter has not fallen in public domain or that it does not form part of the state of the art.

3 Sec. 2(1)(ja) Patents Act, 1970 - "Inventive step" means a feature of an invention that involves technical advance as compared to the existing knowledge or having economic significance or both and that makes the invention not-obvious to a person skilled in the art.

4 Sec 2(1)(ac) Patents Act, 1970 – "capable of industrial application", in relation to an invention, means that the invention is capable of being made or used in an industry.

process thus, avoiding duplication of work, time, costs that is involved in the research.

Assignment of Patent

Property in a patent is purely a creation of the statute. There is no such thing as common law property in a patent. Patent can be transferred from the original patentee to any other person by assignment or by operation of law. The rules of transfer are determined by statute. A patentee can also give licence to others to exploit the patent. Upon a grant of patent to two or more persons each of these persons, in the absence of an agreement to the contrary, is entitled to equal share in the patent: Sec. 50 (1).

In any contract relating to the sale or lease of a patented article, or in a licence to work the patent, it is not lawful to insert certain restrictive conditions regarding the purchase or use of non-patented articles. Such conditions will be void (Sec. 140).

Conveyance or licence referred to above may be terminated, at any time, after the patent is no longer in force, by the purchaser, lessee or licensee of the patent by giving three months' notice to the other side (Sec. 141).

For valid assignment, the following conditions are to be satisfied—

(1) The assignment, mortgage or licence is reduced to writing in a document embodying all the terms and conditions governing the rights and obligations between the parties;

(2) The application for registration of such document is filed in the prescribed manner within six months (unless extended by the Controller) (Sec. 68). When registered, the document takes effect from the date of execution.

A licence granted by a patentee is not valid unless it is in writing and an application for registration of the document embodying the terms of licence is filed with the Controller (Sec. 68).

It may be exclusive, non-exclusive or limited. Exclusive licence has the effect of excluding the other persons including the patentee from the right to use the invention. In a limited licence the limitation may arise as to person, time, price, manufacture, use or sale. A mortgage or other interest may also be created in patent (Sec. 69).

An assignee may sue for infringements.

Co-owners

Where a patent is vested in two or more persons each may, unless an agreement to the contrary is in force, work under the patent without the consent of the other or others, and without accounting to the other or others for the profits he makes [Sec. 50(2)]. A co-sharer cannot assign it to others without the consent of co-owners [Sec. 50(3)]. Hence, the right of each owner as to working and accounting and limitations under which it is to be exercised should be expressly provided in the covenants contained in the deed of assignment creating the co-ownership.

One co-owner may assign his individual share but cannot assign the whole patent to release the rights of the others.

Licence

A patentee has power to grant licence to others to work the patent. The licence should be drafted like any other licence, either as a deed poll, when no covenants by the licensee are required, or as a deed by the parties. All the conditions of the licence, its duration, and the payments agreed upon, whether in a lump sum or a royalty, should be clearly stated.

Compulsory Licence

Section 84 provides that at any time after the expiration of three years from the date of the grant of a patent, any person interested may make an application to the Controller for grant of compulsory licence on patent on any of the following grounds, namely:

(a) that the reasonable requirements of the public with respect to the patented invention have not been satisfied, or

(b) that the patented invention is not available to the public at a reasonably affordable price, or

(c) that the patented invention is not worked in the territory of India.

Revocation of Patents

A patent may be revoked by the High Court, on a petition of any person interested or the Central Government by the Appellate Board or on a counter-claim in a suit for infringement of the patent, on any of the conditions specified in section 64 being satisfied. The controller is also given power to revoke patents, on application by the Central Government or any person interested, on grounds of its not working even after the expiration of two years from the grant of a first compulsory licence (Sec. 85).

TRADE MARK

A trade mark is a distinctive sign, which is used by traders, companies, firms etc. to distinguish their goods and services from those of their competitors. The Trade Marks Act, 1999, defines trade mark as a mark capable of being represented graphically and which is capable of distinguishing the goods and services of one person from those of others and may include shape of goods, their packaging and combination of colours [Sec 2(1)(zb)].

A trade mark is typically a name, word, phrase, logo, symbol, design, image, or a combination of these elements. Apart from the said traditional trade marks, the Indian trade mark law also recognizes unconventional trade marks such as three-dimensional marks, shape marks, colour marks, sound marks and holograms.

The Registrar may accept or refuse the trade mark application subject to the provisions of the Act. An application can be refused/objected by the Registrar on absolute (Sec. 9) or relative grounds of refusal (Sec. 11).

Once the trade mark is registered, it is valid for a period of 10 years from the date of application. The registration can then be renewed for a further period of ten years from the date of expiration of registration or from the last renewal of the registration.

Infringement and Passing off

Registration of trade marks is not mandatory though advisable as it is a prima facie evidence of validity and a constructive notice to the public at large.

Section 29 of the Trade Marks Act, 1999, states various aspects concerning the infringement. "A registered trade mark is infringed by a person who, not being a registered proprietor or a person using by way of permitted use, uses in the course of trade, a mark which is identical with or deceptively similar to the trade mark in relation to goods or services in respect of which the trade mark is registered and in such manner as to render the use of the mark likely to be taken as being used as a trade mark Sec. 29(1). Registration of trade mark is a pre-requisite for seeking the statutory remedy under infringement.

Passing off, on the other hand is a common law remedy wherein registration of trade mark is not required. The fundamental principle behind the tort of passing off is that *'a man is not to sell his goods under the pretense that they are the goods of another man'*. Under passing off remedy apart from proving deceptive similarity, the plaintiff is also required to prove confusion in public and the likelihood of injury to the plaintiff's goodwill.

Trade Mark Licensing in India

Trade mark licensing is the process wherein a registered proprietor of a trade mark, authorizes a third party to use the mark in the course of trade without transferring/assigning the ownership of the mark. The licensing of the trade mark allows the registered proprietor to let others use the mark without assigning the ownership of the mark. The proprietor can also put other limitations on the use of the mark through the terms that he puts into the licensing agreement. For e.g the proprietor may license a trade mark to be used for only particular goods and services.

The term 'license' or 'licensing' is nowhere to be found in the Trade Marks Act, 1999. The concept and the laws governing licensing of trade marks are found in Section 48-55 of the Act. It can be said that the term 'registered user' in the Act is synonymous with the term 'licensee'. Under the 1999 Act, 'permitted use' as defined in section 2(1)(r) means the use of a registered trade mark by a third person as a registered user; as well as, use by a third person by the mere consent of the registered proprietor. The use of the word 'may' in section 48(1) of the Act makes it apparent that registration of a licensing agreement is not mandatory for it to be licensed. The agreement, however, must be in writing as oral licensing is no licensing.

The application for recordal should be made within six months from the date of the license agreement. It shall be made jointly by the licensee and the registered proprietor of the trade mark in Form TM-28 and shall be accompanied by the following documents:

1. The agreement in writing or a duly authenticated copy thereof, entered into between the registered proprietor and the proposed registered user with respect to the permitted use of the trade mark
2. An affidavit by the registered proprietor
3. A Power of Attorney

Well Known Trade Marks[1]

The Trade Mark Registry recognizes well-known trade marks in India on the basis of their international, national and cross border reputation. The Indian Trade Mark Law accords extraordinary protection to trade marks that are "well known" and safeguards them from the vices of infringement or passing off.

The Trade Marks Act, 1999 provides protection to well-known trade marks at two levels"

(1) Against the registration of any similar marks.

(2) Action against the misuse of well-known trade mark

COPYRIGHT

Copyright in any work exists as soon as the work is created in a tangible medium of expression. Copyright does not exist in ideas, concepts, principles, but only in the expression of the ideas etc.

Copyright subsists in the following categories of original work: [2]

(a) Literary work – books, poetry, websites, computer programmes etc.
(b) Artistic work – painting, sculpture, photograph, logo etc.
(c) Dramatic work
(d) Musical work
(e) Cinematograph Films
(f) Sound Recording

Copyright law confers upon the owner of the work, bundle of exclusive rights

---

1 Section 2(1)(zg) - A "well-known trade mark", in relation to any goods or services, means a mark which has become so to the substantial segment of the public which uses such goods or receives such services that the use of such mark in relation to other goods or services would be likely to be taken as indicating a connection in the course of trade or rendering of services between those goods or services and a person using the mark in relation to the first-mentioned goods or services.

2 Section 13 of the Copyright Act, 1957.

in respect of the reproduction of the work and other acts which enables the owner to get financial and other benefits. Section 14 of the Copyright Act lists out certain acts which are the exclusive rights of the copyright owner, i.e. they cannot be done lawfully without his permission. Generally, the acts include reproducing the work (including digital reproduction), issuing copies of the work, performing the work in public or communicating it to the public or making an unauthorised translation etc.

First owner of Copyright

According to Sec. 17, as a general rule, author is the first owner of the Copyright in the work subject to exceptions, for instance in case the work is made in course of the author's employment under a contract of service or apprenticeship, the employer shall, in the absence of any agreement to the contrary, be the first owner of the copyright therein.

Author in relation to various categories of works are as follows:

(i) Literary or dramatic work: the author

(ii) Musical work: the composer

(iii) Artistic work other than a photograph: the artist

(iv) Photograph: person taking the photograph or photographer

(v) Cinematograph film: the producer

(vi) Sound recordings: the producer

(vii) In relation to any literary, dramatic, musical or artistic work which is computer generated, the person who causes the work to be created.

Infringement of Copyright

Under Section 51 of the Copyright Act, the following acts constitute infringement:

(a) *Violation of the exclusive rights:* When any person without a licence or the permission from the copyright owner, exercises economic rights (read with Section 14 of the Copyright Act) of the owner or permits for profit, any place to be used for communication of the work to the public where such communication constitutes an infringement, then it is an infringement of copyright.

(b) *Selling, Distributing or Importing Infringing copies:* If any person, sells, distributes or imports infringing copies of any work, it is an infringement.

Fair Dealing

The Copyright law strives to balance the scale by providing incentives to authors on one hand and providing exceptions to permit reproduction of the copyrighted work or use it in a manner, which but for the exception carved out would have amounted to infringement of copyright. These exceptions are commonly known as 'fair use' or 'fair dealing'.

Section 52 of the Act gives a list of acts which do not constitute infringement of copyright which includes amongst others the following:

(a) Any work used for the purpose of research, personal use, criticism, review, or reporting will be covered under the exception of fair use.

(b) Making copies, back-up copies, or observations of a computer programme, or doing other acts in order to see functionality of the computer programme by a professor.

(c) Reproduction of any work:

- For the purposes of judicial proceedings or reporting a judicial proceedings
- Prepared by any secretariat of a legislature for the use of the members of that legislature
- In a certified copy made or supplied in accordance with any law

(d) Any reading or recitation of extracts of any published literary or dramatic work.

(e) Publishing not more than two short passages from extracts of a work, for a bona fide instructional use by a publisher.

(f) Reproduction of any work as part of an educational instruction where audience primarily comprises of the students, staff, parents or guardians of the student.

(g) Storing of any work in an electronic medium for preserving the work or making not more than three copies of a book by a non-commercial public library, if such book is not available in India.

(h) Reproduction by any library, museum or other place of public access, of any unpublished work for the purposes of research or private study.

Assignment and License of Copyright

The Copyright Act recognizes the transmission of copyright by way of assignment and license.

Under the Copyright Act, no assignment of the copyright in any work shall be valid unless it is in writing signed by the assignor or by his duly authorized agent. The assignment of copyright in any work shall identify such work, and shall specify the rights assigned and the duration and territorial extent of such assignment. If the period and/or territorial extent of assignment of the rights are not specified, it shall be presumed to be 5 years from the date of assignment and presumed to extend within India.[1]

DESIGNS

The Industrial designs refer to that part of a commercial product, which is concerned with the ornamental or aesthetic features of the product and not with its

1 Section 19 of the Copyright Act, 1957.

utility. The Designs Act, 2000 and the Designs Rules, 2001 were enacted to protect new or original design applied on products manufactured by industrial process and to ensure that the artisan, creator, originator of a new or novel design are not deprived of their *bona fide* reward.

An industrial design is registered for a period of fifteen years (a design is initially registered for a period of ten years which can further be extended for five years)[1] and after the registration of an industrial design it shall not be lawful for any person to apply or cause to be applied the design or obvious or fraudulent imitation thereof, to any article in any class of articles in which the design is registered. It is important to note that import of such products is also unlawful and would amount to Piracy of Registered Designs.[2]

"Design" means only the features of shape, configuration, pattern, ornament or composition of lines or colors applied to any article whether in 2-D or 3-D or in both forms, by any industrial process or means, whether manual, mechanical or chemical, separate or combined, which in the finished article appeal to and are judged solely by the eye. It does not include any mode or principle of construction or anything which is in substance a mere mechanical device [Sec. 2(d)].

India follows the system of "first-to-file" and statutory territorial right accrues only on registration.

Assignment of Designs

Under Sec. 30 of the Indian Designs Act, 2000, a person entitled by way of assignments, transmission or other operation of law of copyright can make an application in the prescribed format to the Controller of Designs for transmission of design rights. Section 30(4) states that 'the person registered as the proprietor of a design shall, subject to the provisions of this Act and to any rights appearing from the register to be vested in any other person, have power absolutely to assign, grant licenses as to, or otherwise deal with, the design and to give effectual receipts for any consideration for any such assignment, licence or dealing'.

It is important that the licence or the creation of any other interest in a design is in writing and the application for registration of title under such instrument is filed in the prescribed manner with the Controller within six months from the execution of the instrument. The person who becomes entitled by such license, may file an application in the prescribed form to the Controller to register his title along with original or copies of the instrument, certified by the Notary Public. Such application shall be submitted in Form-12. An instrument, which has not been registered, shall not ordinarily be admissible in any Court as proof of title to copyright in a design or to any interest therein.

1 Section 11 of the Designs Act, 2002.
2 Section 22 of the Designs Act, 2002.

PRECEDENTS

1—Agreement to Sell a Patent Applied for, But not yet Granted

AN AGREEMENT made on the ——— day of ——— BETWEEN AB (hereinafter called "the inventor") of the one part AND CD, etc., (hereinafter called "the assignee") of the other part.

WHEREAS AB is the true and first *inventor* of the invention of ——.

AND WHEREAS the inventor on the ——— made an application bearing number ——— for a patent for the said invention accompanied by a compete specification but the same has not yet been accepted (*or*, and the same has been accepted but a patent has not yet been granted).

Now it is hereby agreed as follows:

1. Agreement to Assign

The inventor shall sell and the assignee shall purchase the said invention and the patent and all the rights and interest of the inventor therein for the sum of Rs. ———and for the payment of the royalty hereinafter mentioned subject to the conditions hereinafter mentioned.

2. Royalty[1]

The assignee shall pay to the inventor during the term of such patent the sum of Rs. ——— for every ——— of whatever size and description manufactured according to the said patent which shall be sold by the assignee.

3. Accounts

The accounts between the parties shall be settled half-yearly on the ———— day of ———— and the ———— day of ————.

4. Covenant to Obtain Patent

The inventor will take all necessary steps for obtaining the patent for the said invention for himself and will then assign the said patent to the assignee and do all other acts and things necessary for the vesting of the same in him.

---

1 Sec. 20(3)(a) makes the mention of the number of the application obligatory.

5. Covenant against Revocation

The assignment shall contain a covenant by the assignee to avoid revocation of the said patent or the granting of compulsory licence and to pay to the inventor as liquidated damages in the event of such revocation and on the grant of any such compulsory licence, the sum of Rs. ——— and Rs. ——— respectively.

6. Covenant to Communicate Improvements

The assignment shall also contain a covenant by the inventor to communicate all improvement in the said invention to the assignee and to assist the assignee to procure patent for the same which shall be vested in the assignee upon the said term as if such improvements had formed part of the original invention.

IN WITNESS WHEREOF, etc.

2—Agreement to Sell a Patent

AN AGREEMENT made on the ——— day of ——— BETWEEN AB, etc., (hereinafter called "the patentee") of the one part AND CD, etc., carrying on business as ——— at ——— (hereinafter called "the assignee") of the other part.

WHEREBY it is agreed as follows:

1. The patentee shall sell and the assignee shall purchase the patentee's patent for ——— No. ——— dated ——— (*or*, the patent, full particulars of which are given in the schedule hereto) for the sum of Rs. ———;

2. The purchase shall be completed on the ——— at ——— when the assignee shall pay the said sum of Rs. ——— to the patentee and the patentee shall execute a deed of assignment and do all such things as may be necessary to vest the said patent in the assignee (*or*, the assignee has paid Rs. ——— to the patentee the receipt of which the patentee hereby acknowledges and will pay the balance of Rs. ——— on the ——— at ——— when the patentee shall execute, etc.).

Rest as in Form 1, *substituting* "patentee" for "inventor".

3—Absolute Assignment of Patent

(*With variation for payment of royalty, and for the case of assignor being himself assignee of the patentee*).

THIS ASSIGNMENT is made on the ——— day of ———

BETWEEN AB, etc., (hereinafter called "the patentee") of the one part AND CD, etc., (hereinafter called "the assignee") of the other part.

WHEREAS the patentee is the inventor of an invention for ——— under the Patent No. ——— dated ——— (*or*, WHEREAS the patentee is entitled by assignment dated ——— duly registered to the patent dated ——— originally granted to XY for ———).

AND WHEREAS the patentee has agreed with the assignee for the sale to him of the said patent and all improvements thereon or further inventions connected therewith for the sum of Rs .———.

NOW THIS DEED WITNESSES as follows:

1. In pursuance of the aforesaid agreement and in consideration of Rs.——— paid by the assignee (the receipt of which the patentee hereby acknowledges) the patentee hereby assigns and transfers to the assignee ALL that the said invention and the said patents for the same with the full and exclusive benefit and advantage thereof and of all and every improvement, extension, renewal thereof TO HOLD the same to the assignee absolutely (subject to the payment of the royalties and moneys hereinafter reserved);

2. The assignee hereby covenants with the patentee as follows:

(a) Covenant to pay royalty—(as in clause 2 of Form 1).

(b) Covenant to keep accounts—(as in clause 3 of Form 1).

(c) Covenant to avoid revocation and grant of compulsory licence—(as in clause 5 of Form 1).

3. The patentee hereby covenants with the assignee as follows:

(*a*) That the said patent is subsisting and is not void or voidable;

(*b*) The patentee shall, whenever required, give to the assignee such assistance and information respecting the said invention and mode of working and using the same and all processes connected therewith as may be necessary for enabling him to use and exercise the said invention to the best advantage;

(*c*) That he will forthwith, from time to time, after marking or discovering any improvements upon the said invention or any further invention relating to ——— disclose the same to the assignee who shall be entitled to the sole and exclusive benefit thereof and if and whenever required by the assignee but at the cost of the assignee will give to the assignee full particulars as to the nature of and mode of performing the same and will, at the option of the assignee, either apply for and endeavour to obtain, or join with the assignee in applying for and obtaining, patent in respect of such improvement or further invention and when and if the same shall be obtained will at the like expense execute and do all instruments, acts and things necessary for vesting the same and the full and exclusive benefit thereof in the assignee;

(*d*) That he will at the expense of the assignee do all such acts and things as may be reasonably required by the assignee for enabling him to obtain and enjoy the exclusive benefit of any extension or further grant of any patents for the time being vested in the assignee by virtue of these presents;

4. The parties hereto hereby agree that wherever the context so admits the expressions "the patentee" and "the assignee" hereinbefore used shall include their respective successors and assigns.

IN WITNESS WHEREOF, etc.

4—Assignment of Share of Patent[1]

THIS ASSIGNMENT, etc. (*as in Form* 3).

WHEREAS the patentee is entitled, etc. (*as in Form* 3).

AND WHEREAS the patentee has agreed to sell to the assignee one half share of and in the said invention and patent for the sum of Rs. ———.

NOW THIS DEED WITNESSES as follow:

1. In consideration of the said sum of Rs. ——— now paid by the assignee to the patentee (the receipt of which is hereby acknowledged) the patentee hereby assigns and transfers to the assignee one-half share or part of and in the said invention and patent TO HOLD the same to the assignee absolutely;

2. The patentee hereby covenants with the assignee that the said patent is valid and subsisting and in full force.

IN WITNESS WHEREOF, etc.

5—Ditto, with Provision for Working Independently

In Form 4, make the following additions:

(1) At the end of the second recital add "upon the terms and conditions hereinafter contained".

(2) At the commencement of the first witnessing clause add "In pursuance of the said agreement".

(3) At the end, add the following covenants as third and subsequent witnessing clauses:

---

1 See also *precedent No. 10 under ASSIGNMENT, ante.*

3. Either of the parties may manufacture and sell ———— under the said patent without accounting to the other for any profits derived therefrom;

4. Neither party shall grant any exclusive licence to manufacture or sell ——— under the said patent without previous consent in writing of the other but any royalties or profits derived by either party under any licence granted as aforesaid shall belong to the party granting such licence who shall not be liable to account to the other party for any part of such royalties or profits;

5. All fees connected with receiving or keeping in force the said patent shall be paid by the parties hereto in proportion to their respective shares in the said patent. If either party shall neglect or refuse to pay his share the other shall, on paying the same, have a first charge upon the share in the patent of the defaulting party for the amount so paid together with interest at ———— per cent per annum.

6. Either party may sell his share to a third person provided that the other party has first been offered and has not agreed to purchase it within ——— days from the date of the offer of the said share or interest at a price not exceeding that which is proposed to be actually received in respect of such sale.

7. *Interpretation clause*—(*as clause* 4 *in Form* 3).

IN WITNESS WHEREOF, etc.

6—Licence to Manufacture under a Patent (by Deed Poll)

KNOW ALL MEN BY THESE PRESENTS that I, AB, etc., in consideration of the sum of Rs. ———— paid by CD, etc., (the receipt of which is hereby acknowledged) hereby grant to the said CD full licence and authority to make use, exercise and vend the invention, the subject of patent No. ——— dated ——— granted to me, for the term of —— years computed from the date of grant.

Dated ————— (*Signature*) —————

7—Licence to Manufacture under a Payment on Royalty[1] System

THIS LICENCE made on the ———— day of———— BETWEEN AB, etc., (hereinafter called "the patentee") of the one part AND CD, etc., (hereinafter called "the licensee") of the other part.

---

1 On meaning of 'royalty', see footnote at p. 92, *ante*.

WHEREAS-

1. In consideration of the royalties hereinafter reserved, the patentee hereby grants to the licensee full (*or,* full and exclusive) licence and authority to make use, exercise and vend ——— under and in accordance with the specification of the patent No. ——— of ——— within the State of West Bengal for a term of ——— years from the date hereof;

2. The parties hereto hereby agree as follows:

(1) The licensee shall on the first day of each quarter of the year, pay to the patentee a royalty of Rs. ——— for every ——— manufactured hereunder and sold during the preceding quarter;

(2) The licensee shall on the first day of each quarter of the year render to the patentee a true and full account of the number of ——— manufactured and sold hereunder during the preceding quarter.

(3) The patentee shall not during the subsistence of this licence make use, exercise or vend or permit or authorise any person or persons other than the licensee to make use, exercise or vend ——— under the said patent within the limits aforesaid;

(4) If the licensee shall commit a breach of his covenant in clause 1 or shall become insolvent or commit an act of insolvency the patentee may by notice in writing determine this licence and thereupon this licence shall forthwith cease and determine;

(5) If the patentee shall not within ——— weeks of receipt of notice to that effect take all such legal proceedings as may be necessary to prevent infringement of the said patent in West Bengal the licensee may at his own cost and expense take such proceedings in the name of the patentee (*or*, the licensee shall be relieved from all further obligation to pay royalties hereunder);

(6) All royalties shall cease if the patentee fails to maintain the said patent or if the said patent is declared, by a competent court, to be void;

(7) This licence is exclusive and non-assignable.

IN WITNESS WHEREOF, etc.

8—Exclusive Patent License Agreement

THIS AGREEMENT made this ——— day of ——— between AB ——— hereinafter called the 'Licensor' AND CD ——— hereinafter called the 'Licencee'.

WHEREAS the Licensor is the owner of the following PATENTED INVENTIONS:

(*details of Licensed Inventions*)

AND WHEREAS the Licencee desires to obtain an exclusive license for the above mentioned Patented Inventions;

NOW THEREFORE, in consideration of the following premises and of the mutual covenants and obligations hereinafter contained, and other good and valuable considerations, the Parties hereto agree as follows:

1. The Licensor hereby grants to the Licencee and the Licencee hereby accepts, subject to the terms and conditions herein recited, an exclusive licence to use, utilise and practice the licensed patented inventions as specified hereinabove for the period of this license.

2. The Licensor shall on the execution of this agreement and not later than —— days thereafter deliver to the Licencee all designs, drawings, technology processes, etc., necessary for the proper use and utilisation of the Licenced Patented Inventions.

3. The Licensor agrees to train and educate —— personnel of the Licensee in the use, utilisation and exploitation of the Licensed Patented Inventions specified hereinabove.

The Licensor further agrees to render appropriate help and guidance to the Licencee in case any problem arises in the use of the technology provided to the Licencee under this agreement.

4. The Licensor agrees that during the term of this Licence, the Licensor shall not make available to any other person the designs, drawings, technology processes, etc., to which this agreement relates.

5. The Licencee shall not assign, transfer the Licence to any one without the prior written permission of the Licensor granted on such terms as the Licensor may deem fit.

6. The Licencee shall not disclose or communicate to any one the designs, drawings, technology, processes, etc., relating to the patented inventions specified hereinabove to any one without the prior written permission of the Licensor granted on such terms as the Licensor may deem fit.

7. The Licencee shall ensure that its personnel maintain secrecy of the designs, drawings, technology, processes, etc., relating to the patented inventions specified hereinabove during the term of this licence and thereafter and use the same only and exclusively for the purposes of this Licence.

8. The Licencee has paid ——— to the Licensor, the receipt of which the Licensor hereby acknowledges, as part payment of Royalty for the grant

of this License and further agreed to pay —— (recite the terms of payment as agreed).

9. This License may be terminated by the Licensor if :

(i) the Licencee defaults in payment of the Royalty in accordance with the terms of this licence and the default continues for more than —— days after the service of a notice of demand by the Licensor on the Licencee.

(ii) the Licencee transfers, assigns or sub-licences, the Licence in violation of the terms hereof.

10. This Licence may be terminated by the Licencee if the Licensor assigns or licences the Patented Inventions mentioned hereinabove to any person or does any other act that reduces the utility of the Patented Inventions to the Licencee.

11. The termination of Licence under clauses 9 and 10 hereof shall take effect from the expiry of —— days from the service of the notice of termination by either party.

12. On the termination of the agreement, the Licencee shall return forthwith to the Licensor all the material like designs, drawings, technology processes, etc., supplied to it by the Licensor and the Licencee shall not thereafter use the same.

13. The Licence may also be terminated by either party by giving written —— months' notice to the other party.

The licence may also be terminated by the Licencee if the patents under this agreement are invalidated by the Competent Authority and termination of the Licence for this reason shall take immediate effect on the service of a notice of termination on the Licensor.

14. (Clauses relating to settlement of disputes, jurisdiction of Courts etc., may be added)

15. The following are the mailing addresses of the parties hereto and notice sent on the same by registered post shall be deemed to be duly served.

Address of Licensor

Address of Licencee

In case there is any change in the mailing address of either party, it shall be forthwith communicated to the other by registered post.

IN WITNESS WHEREOF

9—Trademark License Agreement

This AGREEMENT made on the ——— day of ——— between AB, etc. ———, a ——— corporation having its principal office at ———

(hereinafter referred to as "LICENSOR") and ———, a company incorporated and registered under the laws of India having its registered office at ——— (hereinafter referred to as "USER") and each of which are hereinafter referred to as a "Party" and both of which are herein referred to as the "Parties".

WHEREAS, LICENSOR owns rights in the Trademarks ——, ———, and ——— (hereinafter referred to as the "said trademarks") registered in the ——— and pending under the Trade Marks Act, 1999 details whereof are set out in Annexure "A", in respect of goods set out in the said Annexure "A" and possesses valuable goodwill of the businesses associated therewith due to extensive use of the said Trademark.

WHEREAS, USER desires to obtain a written license from LICENSOR to use the said Trademarks in respect of the Products and Services in connection with the Business in the Republic of India (the terms "Products and Services" and "Business" being defined herein below); and

WHEREAS, LICENSOR is willing to permit USER to make use of the said Trademarks, upon and in relation solely to such Products and Services in connection solely with the Business in India;

WHEREAS, LICENSOR desires that LICENSOR'S ownership of the said Trademarks and the goodwill and reputation associated therewith are maintained and the said Trademarks are fully protected;

NOW, THEREFORE, in consideration of the premises and the mutual covenants expressed herein, and intending to be legally bound, the parties agree as follows:

Article 1. DEFINITIONS

The following definitions shall be applicable throughout this Agreement:

1.01 The term "Trademark" or "Trademarks" shall mean the marks ———, ———, and ——— set out in Annexure A hereto, used to designate the Products and Services specified herein, whether used alone or in combination with other words, names, devices or marks.

1.02 The term "Authorized Trademark" or "Authorized Trademarks" shall mean the marks appearing in the manner illustrated in Annexure "B" hereto.

1.03 The term "Products and Services" shall mean the licensed products and services listed in Annexure "C".

1.04 The term "Business" shall mean the ———.

1.05 The term "Associated Companies" shall mean any company, other than one of the Parties hereto, which are directly or indirectly majority owned, controlled, managed or directed by the named Party, or which are otherwise directly or indirectly under common ownership, control, management or direction with the named Party.

Article 2. PERMISSION TO USE THE AUTHORIZED TRADEMARKS

2.01 *Grant of License*

(i) LICENSOR, to the extent it can lawfully do so, hereby grants to USER during the term of this Agreement, and USER hereby accepts, a non-exclusive, non-transferable, right and license to use the Authorized Trademarks, solely in connection with the purchase, sale and exchange of the Products and Services listed in Annexure C (hereinafter also referred to as the "Licensed Products and Services") for the purpose exclusively of conducting the Business, solely within India.

(ii) No license is granted to USER hereunder to use the Trademarks otherwise than in connection with the Licensed Products and Services, or in a manner other than the Authorized Trademarks. All rights, opportunities and approvals not expressly granted to USER under this Agreement are reserved by LICENSOR.

(iii) USER shall not grant any sub-licenses to use the said Trademarks.

(iv) Nothing in this Agreement shall be deemed or construed to require LICENSOR to grant to USER any right to use the said Trademarks or any other right, which is of a more extensive nature than is possessed by LICENSOR, or which is of any greater extent than which LICENSOR has the lawful right to grant to USER without incurring liability or obligations to others, and the rights herein granted are subject to any rights which may have been acquired by others.

2.02 *Ownership of Authorized Trademarks*

The said Trademarks are the property of LICENSOR, and LICENSOR warrants that it has the legal right to grant the licenses granted herein. USER is only permitted to use the Authorized Trademarks designated in this Agreement without variation. Any rights which arise or are created as a result of the licensed use will accrue to and be owned solely by LICENSOR. USER shall not claim any adverse right, title or interest in the Authorized Trademarks.

Article 3. USE OF TRADEMARKS

3.01 USER shall use the said Trademarks solely upon or in relation to the Licensed Products and Services and USER shall not use the said Trademarks other than in connection with the Licensed Products and Services.

3.02 USER shall use the said Trademarks only as part of the Authorized Trademarks expressly defined herein, without variation in design, wording, colouring or otherwise except with the written consent of LICENSOR and except as may be required by the laws of India.

3.03 USER shall ensure that its use of the Authorized Trademarks are in accordance with the highest standards of ethical business conduct and in a manner to promote and maintain an excellent reputation for the said Trademarks with persons dealing in any way with USER'S products, services, or business.

3.04 USER shall at all times ensure that the Licensed Products and Services sold and the Business are conducted in strict accordance, and in full compliance, with all of the applicable provisions of the laws and regulations of India, and in accordance with this Agreement and such other rules as may be communicated in writing by LICENSOR from time to time.

3.05 USER shall not use the said Trademarks in any manner which would tend to disparage or degrade the reputation associated therewith, or which would impair LICENSOR'S rights therein or its title thereto.

3.06 USER shall use the said Trademarks only in a manner satisfactory to LICENSOR and shall comply with any reasonable written instructions of LICENSOR regarding the manner of its use.

3.07 USER shall not use the said Trademarks linked with, or in close association with any other trademark or trade name, except as may be expressly authorized by LICENSOR. Even in the event of obtaining the express consent of LICENSOR to such use, nothing of such use shall be deemed or construed so as to give USER any rights in the Trademark, and LICENSOR shall at any time be entitled to revoke its consent, giving thirty days notice to USER prior to such revocation.

3.08 Except as authorized herein, USER shall not, either during the term of this Agreement or after the expiration or termination thereof, use or authorize the use of, any trademark or trade name on or in association with any goods, services or business whatsoever, in any country or region of the world, which is either in whole or in part confusingly similar with the said Trademarks or with any other trademarks or trade names of LICENSOR or its Associated Companies, or which is a translation or transliteration into any language of the said Trademarks or of any such confusingly similar trademark or trade name.

3.09 Except as authorized herein, USER shall not, either during the term of this Agreement or after the expiration or termination thereof, use or authorize the use of any mark which is in whole or in part the same as or confusingly similar to the said Trademarks, or which is a translation or transliteration into any language of the said Trademarks or of any confusingly similar mark, as a part of USER'S postal, cable or telex, email, domain name address, or its building name or location.

3.10 USER shall promptly correct, to the satisfaction of LICENSOR, any improper usage of the said Trademarks or other lack of full compliance with this Agreement, upon written notice thereof by LICENSOR.

3.11 USER shall promptly notify LICENSOR of the adoption of any trademark other than the Authorized Trademarks or any change in its trademark during the existence of this Agreement, in which event USER'S rights under this Agreement shall automatically and immediately terminate.

Article 4. RIGHTS IN THE SAID TRADEMARKS

4.01 USER acknowledges and agrees that USER's right to use the said Trademarks in relation to its Products and Services is dependent at all times upon LICENSOR'S authorization and continued consent thereto.

4.02 USER shall provide in all of the instruments creating and governing the existence and operation of its business organization, that in the event that this Agreement with LICENSOR shall expire or be terminated, without being replaced by a new Trademark License Agreement with LICENSOR, then USER shall, without expense to LICENSOR, promptly do all things which are necessary to change its trademark to a mark which does not use the said Trademarks or any mark which is confusingly similar therewith, or which is a translation or transliteration into any language of the said Trademarks or of any mark which is confusingly similar therewith.

4.03 USER acknowledges and agrees that all rights, in and to the said Trademarks, including all of the goodwill of the business associated therewith, are and shall hereafter continue to be the exclusive property of LICENSOR, and that all use of the said Trademarks by USER shall ensure only to the benefit of LICENSOR. USER acknowledges and agrees that it does not have and shall not hereafter claim, acquire or assert any ownership rights in, or permanent right to the use of, the said Trademarks either during the term of this Agreement or after the expiration or termination thereof.

4.04 USER shall execute, acknowledge and deliver all documents and do all things which may be requested by LICENSOR to assist LICENSOR to establish, maintain and safeguard all rights of ownership in and to the said Trademarks, both during the term of this Agreement and after the expiration or termination thereof.

4.05 USER shall not, either during the term of this Agreement or after the expiration or termination thereof for any reason, object to, or interfere in any way with the ownership, registration or use of the said Trademarks by LICENSOR or its licensees, as a trademark, trade name or service mark or for any other purpose whatsoever, either in India or in any other country or region of the world.

4.06 USER shall not, either during the term of this Agreement or after the expiration or termination thereof, register or attempt to register any trademark, trade name or service mark in any country or region of the world, which is either in whole or in part the same as or confusingly similar with the said Trademarks or any mark which is in whole or in part a translation or transliteration into any language, of the said Trademarks or any confusingly similar mark.

Article 5: INSPECTION AND QUALITY

5.01 All Business conducted and all Products and Services provided or sold by USER under the said Trademarks shall conform with uniformly high standards of integrity and quality, which are fully satisfactory to LICENSOR and USER shall strictly adhere to any specifications, directions, and instructions vis-a-vis the products or the services as may be furnished by LICENSOR from time to time.

5.02 USER shall permit LICENSOR and its authorised representatives to enter USER'S premises and branches, during normal business hours to examine all records and operations of USER which relate in any way to USER'S business practices or to the quality and integrity of the products and services sold or provided by USER.

5.03 If LICENSOR notifies USER that USER'S business practices or any products or services sold or provided by USER deviate from LICENSOR'S standards of satisfaction, USER shall exert its best efforts to promptly correct such deviations to the satisfaction of LICENSOR.

5.04 If USER fails to correct, or to submit a satisfactory plan to correct, all deviations in its business, service and product practices and standards, from LICENSOR'S standards of satisfaction, within thirty (30) days after being given written notice thereof, LICENSOR may, at its option, terminate this Agreement.

Article 6: INFRINGEMENTS

6.01 USER shall not give any notification of infringement, or take any other action relating to the infringement by others of the said Trademarks or any other trademarks, trade names, service marks or other intellectual property rights of LICENSOR or its Associated Companies, without obtaining the prior written authorization of LICENSOR.

6.02 USER agrees to cooperate with LICENSOR in any action which LICENSOR may decide to take relating to infringements of the said Trademarks. USER shall inform LICENSOR of any action of others within India, known by USER, which may constitute an infringement of any of trademarks or trade names of LICENSOR.

6.03 In the event that any suit, claim or demand is threatened or brought against USER involving any claim that USER'S use of the said Trademark or Trademarks infringes any rights of others in India, USER shall promptly inform LICENSOR thereof, and LICENSOR shall have the right to take exclusive charge of the defense, at its own expense, of any such suit, claim or demand, and of any negotiations for the settlement thereof. USER shall cooperate fully with LICENSOR in the defense of any such actual or threatened suit, claim or demand or any related proceeding which LICENSOR undertakes.

6.04 In the event of a decision or other determination by LICENSOR or any Court or other competent body in India, that the said Trademark or Trademarks infringes any trademark, trade name or other rights belonging to another, LICENSOR shall have the right to obtain for USER's benefit a license under such rights, or to terminate this Agreement, or take any other action it deems reasonable or prudent to avoid or mitigate such infringement. USER agrees immediately to discontinue the use of the said Trademark and to take all other reasonable and prudent steps to avoid and mitigate all losses, damages, costs and expenses after USER has been notified by LICENSOR of any such determination or decision that the said Trademark infringes rights of another.

Article 7. RESPONSIBILITY & INDEMNIFICATION

7.01 LICENSOR shall not be responsible or liable for any claims, losses, damages, injuries or other liabilities of any kind whatsoever, arising on account of, or in connection with, the exercise by USER of any rights granted hereunder, or for any other acts, faults or omissions of or attributable to USER, including but not limited to any liability for use of the Authorized Trademarks by USER, and USER shall defend, indemnify, release and hold LICENSOR and its Associated Companies harmless from and against all such claims, losses, damages, injuries and other liabilities. In no event shall LICENSOR be liable for any special, incidental or consequential damages of any kind whatsoever arising out of or related to the use of the said Trademarks whether based on warranty, contract, tort or any other legal theory, and whether or not LICENSOR was previously advised of the possibility of such damages.

7.02 LICENSOR shall not be responsible or liable, if USER provides products and services which are inferior in quality to its uniformly high standards of quality or products and services which do not adhere to its specifications, directions, and instructions.

Article 8. AGENCY

Nothing contained in this Agreement shall create or be represented to create an agency relationship between USER and LICENSOR, or any of their Associated Companies, and neither Party shall represent that it is a legal representative or agent of the other Party or any of its Associated Companies for any purpose whatsoever, except as may be otherwise specifically authorized in writing by such other Party.

Article 9. ASSIGNMENT AND SUCCESSION

9.01 This Agreement shall be binding on and ensure to the benefit of the Parties and their permitted successors and assigns.

9.02 This Agreement, and the rights hereunder, shall not be assignable or transferable, in whole or in part, either voluntarily or by operation of law or otherwise, without the written consent of LICENSOR in each instance, and USER shall not attempt to assign, transfer, pledge, sub-license or otherwise dispose of this Agreement or of any of the rights granted hereunder, without the prior written consent of LICENSOR in each instance. Any attempt to make any such disposition of this Agreement or of any of the rights hereunder without the prior written consent of LICENSOR shall be void and may be treated by LICENSOR as a ground for termination of this Agreement.

9.03 LICENSOR shall have the right to administer this Agreement through any of its successors and may assign this Agreement to any person or company which may become the successor to the said Trademark and the Business in relation to the Licensed Products and Services.

Article 10. VALIDITY AND APPROVALS

10.1 USER shall, at its own expense, obtain any approvals and fulfil all other requirements, related to this Agreement which are or may become provided for under any law or regulation now or hereafter existing in the India to enable the Parties to exercise, enforce and enjoy all of the rights and obligations contained in this Agreement.

10.2 In the event that this Agreement or any provision thereof shall be held by final judgment, decree or decision to be invalid, illegal or unenforceable, either Party shall have the right to terminate this Agreement, or both Parties may mutually declare by written notice to each other that such invalidity, illegality, or unenforceability shall not affect any other provisions hereof. In the latter event, this Agreement shall be interpreted and construed as if the provision held to be invalid, illegal, or unenforceable, is not contained herein.

Article 11. DURATION

This Agreement shall become effective on the date first above written, as the effective date and shall be valid for a period of twelve (12) months unless sooner terminated, as provided for herein, by either Party without cause, at any time by giving a written notice of termination to the other Party of at least one month in advance of the effective date of such termination. At the end of the twelve months, the parties would be at liberty to extend the agreement on suitable terms of agreement for another period of twelve months by exchange of letters and such other formalities as desired by the first party. In this way, the parties may continue with this Agreement for as long as they desire.

Article 12. TERMINATION FOR CAUSE

12.01 Either Party may terminate this Agreement for cause if the other Party breaches this Agreement or is in default of any of the provisions hereof, or for any other reason specified herein, by a written notice of termination given to the other Party, not less than one month before such termination is to become effective, and such termination shall become effective on the date specified in such notice unless such breach or default shall be corrected within fifteen days (15 days) of the giving of such notice of termination or within such longer period of time for correcting the breach or default as may be specified for that purpose in such notice.

12.02 Either Party shall have the right, without advance notice, to forthwith terminate this Agreement at any time, by giving the other Party written notice thereof in the event that:

(i) the other Party becomes or is adjudicated to be insolvent or bankrupt, or makes a general assignment for the benefit of creditors, or is placed under judicial management or the control of receivers, liquidators or trustees, or is unable to conduct the business contemplated by this Agreement; or

(ii) this Agreement or any material provision thereof is held by final judgment, decree or decision to be invalid, illegal or unenforceable.

12.03 LICENSOR shall have the right, without advance notice, to forthwith terminate this Agreement at any time, by giving USER written notice of such termination, in the event that:

(i) All or a major portion of USER'S assets are transferred voluntarily or by operation of law; or

(ii) There is a material change in the ownership, management, control or nature of USER'S business, from that existing on the date first above written; or

(iii) This Agreement, or any of the rights granted hereunder, is assigned, transferred, sub-licensed, pledged or otherwise disposed of, or any attempt is made to make any assignment, transfer, sub-license, pledge or other disposition thereof, either voluntarily or by operation of law; or

(iv) USER fails to supply written evidence of the granting of any approval or the fulfillment of any requirement which is provided for under any law or regulation of India, to enable the Parties to exercise, enforce and enjoy all the rights and obligations contained in this Agreement, within one (1) month from the date first above written.

Article 13. ROYALTY

13.01 In consideration of the rights granted to USER under this Agreement, USER shall pay to LICENSOR, an annual trademark licensing fee of ——— payable on ———.

13.02 USER will provide LICENSOR with a certificate from its internal auditors evaluating the net sales and proceeds as of the Products and Services sold and provided by it under the said Trademarks.

13.03 LICENSOR, as aforesaid, shall have the right to inspect the relevant books of accounts of USER to verify the said sales and proceeds record.

Article 14. OBLIGATIONS UPON EXPIRATION OR TERMINATION

Upon expiration or termination of this Agreement for any reason, in addition to any other provisions in this Agreement, relating to such event:

14.01 All rights, privileges, and licenses granted to USER to use the said Trademarks shall automatically stand terminated.

14.02 USER shall discontinue all further use of the Authorized Trademarks, and shall thereafter not conduct business of any kind, or engage in the sale of any goods or services, under or using the said Trademarks,

14.03 USER shall promptly and permanently, at its own expense, remove the said Trademarks, from all its products, invoices, packaging and promotional materials, vehicles, billboards, building signs and other public displays. USER shall thereafter not make any further use of the said Trademarks on stationery, advertising, in telephone or trade directory listings, on the Internet or in, any other manner.

14.04 USER shall not thereafter use any trademark, service mark or trade name which is either in whole or in part the same as or confusingly similar with the said Trademarks, or which is a translation or transliteration thereof into any language.

14.05 USER shall not thereafter object to or interfere in any way with, the ownership, registration or use of the said Trademarks by LICENSOR and its licensees for any purpose whatsoever.

14.06 USER shall, promptly execute, acknowledge and deliver all documents which are requested by LICENSOR to record with appropriate governmental agencies and authorities the fact that USER no longer has any rights in or to the use of the said Trademarks.

Article 15. CONFIDENTIALITY

During the term of this agreement and thereafter USER shall keep confidential all information relating to and arising out of this Agreement. The information received from LICENSOR shall be passed on only to such officers or employees of the USER to whom it is necessary to do so in the normal course of trade and business activity and who shall be held bound by this Confidentiality Clause.

IN WITNESS WHEREOF, the Parties hereto have executed this Agreement by their duly authorized officers or representatives as of the date first above written.

LICENSOR USER

WITNESS 1 __________

WITNESS 2 __________

10—Agreement of Licence between Trade Mark Owner and a Manufacturer

This AGREEMENT is made this —— day of —— between ——— A B & Co. Ltd., a Company registered under the Companies Act, 1956, and having its registered office at ——— hereinafter referred to as 'the Licensor' of the One Part and C carrying on business of ———hereinafter referred has 'the Licensee' of the Other Part

WHEREAS—

1. The Licensor is the proprietor of a trade mark more particularly described in the schedule hereunder written and which is duly registered under the Trade Marks Act 1999.

2. The Licensor is manufacturing and selling the goods viz ——— under the said trade mark.

3. The Licensee who is running a small scale industry has requested the Licensor to grant him a license to manufacture the said goods with the trade mark embossed or printed thereon as is being done by the Licensor and which the Licensor has agreed to do on the following terms and conditions agreed to between the parties hereto.

Now it is agreed by and between the Parties as follows:

1. The Licensor hereby grants to the Licensee a license to manufacture the said goods as a job work by applying the said trade mark, particulars of which are described in the Schedule hereunder written.

2. The Licensee agrees and undertakes that all of the said goods manufactured by the Licensee in his factory at ——— or elsewhere shall be sold to the Licensor and not to anybody else at the price of Rs ——— per item or article. The Licensee undertakes to manufacture and supply to the Licensor a quantity of not less than ——— every month.

3. The goods so manufactured with the said trade mark applied to them will be supplied and delivered by the Licensee to the Licensor at the latter's business premises at ——— at his own costs of transport.

4. The price of the said goods so supplied will be paid by the Licensor against delivery after deducting therefrom the royalty payable by the Licensee to the Licensor as hereinafter provided.

5. The Licensor shall have the right to reject any goods supplied if they are not as per specifications or quality which are made known to the Licensee and in the event of such rejection the Licensee shall take back the rejected goods from the Licensor's premises at his own costs and until such removal they will be at the risk of the Licensee. The Licensor agrees that

during the subsistence of this agreement, the Licensor will not get the said goods manufactured from anybody else.

6. The ownership of the said trade mark will always remain with the Licensor and the Licensee will not pass off the said goods as if he is the owner of the said trade mark.

7. The Licensee will be at liberty to put a label or advertise that the said goods are manufactured by him but it will also be mentioned that the trade mark belongs to the Licensor and that the goods are manufactured for the benefit of the Licensor.

8. In consideration of the Licensor allowing the Licensee to manufacture the said goods with the said trade mark the Licensee agrees to pay to the Licensor by way of royalty a sum equal to ——— per cent of the price of the goods at which they will be sold to the Licensor by the Licensee as aforesaid.

9. The Licensee shall keep an account of the goods manufactured and sold to the Licensor and the price received by him and royalty paid in respect thereof and such account shall be open to inspection by the Licensor from time to time as may be required by the Licensor. The Licensor will also have the right to enter upon the premises of the Licensee where the goods are manufactured and to take inspection of the goods manufactured.

10. This agreement will remain in force for a period of ——— years from the date hereof and on the expiration of the said period or earlier termination thereof as herein provided, the Licensee shall stop manufacturing the said goods under the said trade mark and all the goods till then manufactured and lying undelivered to the Licensor will be delivered to the Licensor in terms of this agreement as aforesaid.

11. If the Licensee commits breach of any term of this agreement, the Licensor will be entitled to terminate this agreement by fifteen days' prior notice in writing to the Licensee and on the expiration of the notice period, this agreement shall stand terminated unless in the meanwhile the breach complained of is remedied to the satisfaction of the Licensor.

12. The Licensee may get himself registered as a registered user under the provisions of the Trade Marks Act 1999 subject to the terms of this agreement.

13. If the Registrar of Trade Marks while registering the Licensee as a registered user puts any condition which is not acceptable to the Licensor, the Licensee will withdraw the application for registration or the Licensor will have the option to terminate this agreement.

14. If any person is found by the Licensee to infringe the said trade mark either by passing off or otherwise, the Licensee will bring that fact to the notice of the Licensor to enable him to take necessary legal action against such person and in that event the Licensee will give all cooperation to the Licensor in prosecuting such action and all the costs thereof will be borne and paid by the parties hereto in equal shares.

15. If the Licensee himself infringes the said trade mark by passing off or otherwise, then notwithstanding anything provided in clause 16 hereof, it will be open to the Licensor to take legal action against him and in such case the Licensee will not be entitled to challenge the ownership of the Licensor in respect of the said trade mark.

16. In the event of any dispute arising out of this agreement, the same will be referred to arbitration of a common Arbitrator if agreed upon or in the absence of such agreement, to two Arbitrators one to be appointed by each party hereto and the Arbitration will be governed by the Arbitration Act for the time being in force.

IN WITNESS WHEREOF the parties have put their respective hands the day and year first hereinabove written.

(The schedule herein referred to)

11—Agreement for Assignment of Copyright in Book for Lump Sum Payment and Royalty

This Agreement for assignment is made at—— this —— day of —— between A, residing at ——— hereinafter referred to as 'the Author' of the One Part and B, carrying on business at ——— hereinafter referred to as the 'Publisher' of the Other Part.

WHEREAS —

1. The Author is writing a book on the subject of ——— and expects to complete the same within a short time.

2. The Publisher has seen the manuscript and synopsis of the book and has proposed to the Author to give him the work of publication and offered to pay consideration partly in lump and partly by royalty in instalments.

3. The Author has agreed to entrust the work of printing and publication to the Publisher and assign the copyright to the Publisher on the following terms and conditions agreed upon between the parties.

Now it is agreed by and between the Parties as follows:

1. The Author agrees to complete the said book which is under process of writing and which is proposed to be named as '———' within a period

of one month from now.

2. On completion of the book within the said period the Author shall hand over the manuscript to the Publisher and the Publisher shall get the said book printed and published at his entire costs and expenses.

3. The Author will be entitled to examine the proofs and to make any additions or alterations in the manuscript or proofs as he may think proper. The printing will not be made final unless and until the Author gives his instructions accordingly.

4. The Publisher agrees and undertakes to prepare the subject index of the book on his own.

5. The Author in consideration of the Publisher paying a lump sum of Rs. ——— and also agreeing to pay royalty as hereinafter mentioned agrees to assign and hereby assigns all his copyright in the said book to the Publisher subject to what is herein provided.

6. The Publisher has in consideration of the Author assigning to the Publisher the copyright in the said book, paid to the Author the said sum of Rs. ——— on the execution of these presents (receipt whereof the Author admits) and agrees to pay as and by way of royalty a sum equal to 10% of the price of each copy of the book sold excluding therefrom the proportionate cost of printing and binding.

7. The amount of royalty will be paid by the Publisher at the end of every six months in respect of the copies sold during that period and he shall also send a statement of account in respect of the copies sold and moneys realised at the end of such period every time.

8. The Author shall be entitled to verify the correctness of the accounts by taking inspection of the books of accounts, vouchers and other papers in connection with the costs of printing and the sale of the books.

9. The Author shall be entitled to ——— copies of the book free of costs. The Publisher shall also furnish free copies of the book to such newspapers, and periodicals as he may think fit, for publishing reviews of the book.

10. The Author agrees and undertakes not to write any other book on the same subject and which would be competing with the book or get it published by any other person so long as the said book which is the subject matter of these presents is being published and sold in the market by the Publisher.

11. The Author agrees to re-edit the said book at the time of publishing second edition thereof and to make it up-to-date when required

by the Publisher but if the Author refuses to do so, the Publisher will be entitled to get the book re-edited, enlarged or abridged through some other author.

12. For all the royalty due and payable by the publisher, the Author will have a charge or lien on all the unsold copies of the book and will be entitled to enforce the said lien or charge through Court.

13. The said royalty will be continued to be paid by the Publisher for subsequent editions of the book but if any subsequent edition is not re-edited by the Author as aforesaid, then the Author will not be entitled to any royalty on subsequent editions.

14. In the event of any dispute or difference between the parties hereto arising out of or in connection with this agreement of whatsoever nature, the same shall be referred to arbitration of a common arbitrator if agreed upon, failing which to two Arbitrators one to be appointed by each party to the Arbitration and the Arbitration shall be governed by the Arbitration Act for the time being in force.

15. This Agreement is executed in duplicate and one copy will remain with thc Author and the other with the Publisher.

IN WITNESS WHEREOF the parties have put their respective hands on the day and year first hereinabove written.

12—Agreement to Assign Rights in Music Composition

This Agreement is made at ——— this ——— day of ——— between A, residing at ———, hereinafter referred to as 'Composer' of the One Part and B, carrying on business at ——— hereinafter referred to as 'the Producer' of the Other Part;

WHEREAS—

1. The Producer has approached the Composer with a request to compose ten songs suitable for the said play and has agreed to purchase the copy right in such songs.

2. The Composer has agreed to compose ten songs and to assign the copyright therein to the Producer on the following terms and conditions agreed to by the Producer.

Now it is agreed by and between the Parties as follows:

1. The Composer agrees and undertakes to compose songs suitable for the said play known by the name of ——— and staged by the Producer. The Producer shall select 10 songs from the songs composed by the Composer.

2. The Composer agrees that on the producer selecting ten songs from the several songs composed by him, he will assign his copyright in such songs to the producer in consideration of the royalty to be paid by the Producer as herein mentioned.

3. The Producer shall pay to the Composer by way of royalty a lump sum of Rs. —— on his delivering the songs in writing and on the composer executing a deed of assignment of the copyright in favour of the Producer.

4. The Producer shall have the exclusive right to use the said songs in his said play as well as to have the songs tape recorded.

5. The Composer covenants and warrants that the said songs will be original. There will be no infringement of copyright of anybody else in such composed songs and he will indemnify the Producer for any claim made against him on account of such infringement.

6. The Producer shall not transfer the copyright in the said songs to anybody else and in the event of the Producer ceasing or stopping performance of the said play for good, the copyright will revert back to the Composer.

7. The Producer however will have the right to use the said songs or any of them at any performance of the said Play as he may think fit.

8. The Producer will be entitled to change the mode or fashion of singing the said songs or any of them and to change the ragas as and when thought fit.

9. On payment of the said amount of royalty, the Composer would execute a Deed of Assignment of copyright and simultaneously hand over the composition of the songs to the Producer.

10. The Composer will complete composition of the songs within one month from the date hereof failing which this agreement shall be cancelled.

11. The Producer shall on receiving the intimation from the Composer that the songs are ready, the Producer shall within two weeks of receipt of such intimation pay the said royalty against execution of the deed of assignment by the Composer.

12. If the Producer commits breach of any term of the agreement, the Composer will have the right to cancel this agreement by giving one month notice to that effect to the Producer and in that event this Agreement will also cease to exist.

IN WITNESS WHEREOF the parties have put their respective hands the day and year first hereinabove written.

(The schedule herein referred to)

13—Assignment of a Design

This DEED OF ASSIGNMENT is made at ——— this ——— day of ——— between A, residing at ———, hereinafter referred to as 'the Assignor' of the One Part and CD & Co. Ltd., a company registered under the Companies Act 1956/2013 and having its registered office at ——— hereinafter referred to as 'the Assignee' of the Other Part.

WHEREAS—

1. The Assignor has prepared a design of a television set and the same is registered under the Designs Act, 1999, under No. ——— in the name of the Assignor as proprietor thereof. The particulars of the design including its picture are given in the Schedule hereunder written.

2. The Assignee intends to manufacture television sets and has requested the Assignor to assign his right to the said design to enable the Assignee to manufacture the sets with the said design and which the Assignor has agreed to do.

NOW THIS DEED WITNESSETH that pursuant to the said agreement and in consideration of the sum of Rs ——— paid by the Assignee to the Assignor, the Assignor hereby assign and transfer unto the Assignee all his rights and title to and interest in the said registered design particulars of which are given in the Schedule hereunder written TO HOLD the same unto and to the use of the Assignee absolutely.

And the Assignor covenants with the Assignee that he will, at the request but at the expense of the Assignee sign, or execute all and further documents and shall do all acts and things as may be required to vest the right and title of the Assignor in respect of the said design in the Assignee to register the said design in any country where such rights subsists and that the said design is of the sole proprietorship of the Assignor and he has full right to assign the same in manner aforesaid.

And that he has not encumbered the same in any way or has not given any license to use the same in favour of anybody else and that he will render all assistance to the Assignee as may be required for the said design being transferred in the name of the Assignee in the register maintained by the Controller under the Designs Act, 1911 and in the event of any infringement thereof by anybody in taking and prosecuting all legal actions to prevent the infringement thereof but at the costs of the Assignee.

IN WITNESS WHEREOF, the Assignor has put his hand the day and year first hereinabove written.

(The schedule herein referred to)

LEASE

Preliminary Note

A lease is a contract between the lessor and the lessee for possession and enjoyment of the profits of the land on one side and recompense by rent or other consideration on the other. The Lessor must be a person competent to contract and also having title or authority to create the grant. Similarly, the lessee must also be a person competent to accept the contract on the date of the lease. Under section 29(b) of the Guardian and Wards Act, a statutory guardian cannot without the previous permission of the court, lease any property for a term exceeding five years or for any term extending more than one year beyond the date on which the ward will cease to be a minor. The powers of an executor or administrator to grant lease are regulated by section 307 of the Indian Succession Act, 1925.

The essential element of a lease are (1) the parties; (2) the subject matter or the immovable property; (3) the demise or partial transfer; (4) the terms and conditions; and (5) rent or the consideration. When the agreement vests in the lessee, a right of possession for a certain time, it operates as a transfer and is lease.

Lease and Agreement for Lease

A document in order to operate as a lease has to be a demise *in presenti.* An agreement to lease not creating a present demise is not a lease and does not require writing or registration.[1] The Supreme Court, while pointing out the distinction between a lease and an agreement for lease observed that a deed may be construed as a lease if contains words of present demise, but if inspite of the words certain things have to be done by the lessor such as carrying out improvements and certain things have also to be done by the lessee, such as giving of sureties, the document must be construed as a mere executory contract and not a lease.[2] The above distinction should be borne in mind while drafting an agreement for lease or a lease deed. The fact that the property demised was to be delivered to the possession of the lessee at a subsequent date is irrelevant for the purpose of determining whether the agreement in question represents a lease or not. Delivery of possession of the property demised is not a condition precedent for coming into operation of a lease. If there is a lease in *presenti*, as distinct from agreement to lease, no question of suit for specific performance arises and the relief instead is for delivery of possession.[3]

---

1 *Rani Hemanta Kumari Debi* v. *Midnapur Zamindari Co. Ltd.*, 1920 (31) CLJ 298, 1920 MWN 66, 46 IA 240).

2 *Tula Ram Rehmal* v. *The State of Bombay*, AIR 1954 SC 496.

3 *H.V. Rajan* v. *C.N. Gopal*, AIR 1975 SC 261, (1975) 4 SCC 302.

Agreement

An agreement for lease (as distinguished from a deed of lease) must be drafted as an ordinary agreement. The property to be leased should be clearly described and the period of lease, the rent and other terms and conditions of tenancy agreed upon must be mentioned. An agreement which only creates a right of getting another document executed creating rights and liabilities in respect of immovable property is an agreement and not a lease requiring registration under section 2(7) of the Registration Act and is therefore admissible in evidence.[1]

Lease how made

A lease of immovable property, under the Transfer of Property Act can be made only by a registered instrument, if it is from year to year or for any term exceeding one year or reserves a yearly rent. Other leases can be made either by a registered instrument or by oral agreement accompanied by delivery of possession (Sec. 107). The State Governments have been empowered to permit any leases of the latter class to be made by unregistered leases or by oral agreements without delivery of possession (Sec. 107). The Transfer of Property Act does not apply to agricultural leases (Sec. 117) which are governed by local Acts.

An unregistered document of lease, in cases where the lease is required to be registered, conveys no title and creates no rights in the lessee; nor can a registered *Kabuliat*, by itself be sufficient to bestow a title upon the lessee or be considered a lease as defined in Sec. 105, Transfer of Property Act.[2] However, such a document can be used for collateral purposes such as to show the nature of possession, the date of its commencement and the rate of rent.[3] Collateral denotes that which is independent of, but subordinate to, an assurance or agreement affecting the same subject matter. If *Kabuliat* is followed by acceptance of rent, a tenancy is created.[4]

Further, a lease should be executed both by the lessor and lessee. However, it has been held that the word "executed" occurring in the third paragraph of Sec. 107 Transfer of Property Act is not synonymous with "signed". Even if a deed has been signed by only one of the parties, it may be deemed to have been *executed* by both the parties, if the transaction was in reality a "bilateral endeavour of both".[5] It is also noteworthy that the definition of lease given in the Registration Act expressly includes a rent note,[6] section 2(7) of the Registration Act.

---

1 *Tiruvenibai* v. *Lilabai*, AIR 1959 SC 620; *Food Corporation of India* v. *Babulal Agarwal*, AIR 1969 SC 620.

2 *Safdar Ali* v. *Ambika Prasad Dube*, AIR 1930 All 618.

3 *Ram Kishore* v. *Ambika Prasad*, AIR 1966 All 515; *Jai Ram Agarwal* v. *VIth Addl. D.J.*, 1987(2) ARC 506; *Zarif Ahmad* v. *Satish Kumar*, AIR 1983 All. 164 (D.B.).

4 *Asa Ram* v. *Ram Kali*, AIR 1958 SC 183; See also *John Mithalal Desai* v. *Dineshbhai*, 1998 AIHC 1995 (Guj) (A rent is a lease as defined in the Registration Act, though not under the Transfer of Property Act.)

5 *Rajendra Pratap Singh* v. *Rameshwar Prasad*, (1998) 7 SCC 602

6 *John Mithalal Desai* v. *Dineshbhai*, 1997 GLH (2) 506, 1997 (3) GLR 279.

Deed of lease

A deed should be drafted as a deed between the landlord and the tenant. They may be called "the lessor" and "the lessee", the terms used in the Transfer of Property Act, but it is open to the parties to use any other expressions such as "landlord" and "tenant". The general requirements of a deed of transfer mentioned in Part II of the Introduction apply to leases also and that Part should therefore be carefully read. A lease deed consists of the same parts as other deeds of transfer except that there is an additional part called the '*reddendum*'. The following special points or modifications should, however, be noted.

(1) *Recitals* are not generally necessary in a deed of lease and should not be inserted except when absolutely necessary in order to mention facts which cannot conveniently be mentioned in the operative part of the deed.

(2) *Consideration*: The practice in England is to mention the consideration of rent and lessee's covenants in the beginning of the *testatum* or witnessing clause thus:

"In consideration of the rent hereby reserved and of the lessee's covenants hereinafter contained the lessor hereby demises, etc."

As the rent reserved and the covenants of the lessee clearly appear from the later part of the lease and it clearly appears from these provisions what is the consideration of the lease, this clause about consideration is not necessary in India. But if a premium is also paid as part of the consideration the fact that such premium is also a part of the consideration and also the acknowledgement of the payment have got to be mentioned as they are not mentioned elsewhere in the lease. In such cases, it will be convenient to mention the whole consideration, *i.e.* the premium, the rent reserved and the lessee's covenants. Similarly, if a lease is made in consideration of the surrender of a previous lease, the consideration should be mentioned. If a premium is *agreed to be paid in future* the same can be mentioned in the *reddendum*.

(3) *Operative Part:* Any words which clearly show the nature of the transfer, that is, the fact that the lessor divests himself of the possession and the lessee shall come into exclusive possession, may be used, e.g. the lessor hereby lets or "demises" or "grants a lease of". The technical words used in England is "demise" and in the absence of any commonly approved expression in India the same may be used here also.

(4) *Habendum:* The commencement and duration of the term of the lease are specified in the habendum, as:

"from the ———— day of ———— for a term of ———— years."

Or if the lease is permanent the words "in perpetuity" are used in place of "for a term of ———— years". If the tenancy is a life tenancy it may be expressed to be "for the life of the lessee". The date of commencement of the term should be clearly specified as "commencing on the ————" or "from the ————".

The date may be the date of the lease in which case it may be expressed as:

"from the date hereof" or it may be a date *prior or subsequent* to the execution of the lease.

A term beginning *from* a specified day is reckoned as exclusive of that day (Sec. 110, Transfer of Property Act,) and if the term begins *on* a day, that day is included and is the first day of the term.

If no term is fixed and the lease is intended to be a year to year or month to month lease, it should be so stated, thus:

"from year to year."

(5) *Reddendum:* After the "TO HOLD" clause technically called the "habendum" and before the covenants, a new clause is added in leases which mentions the rent reserved with the mode and time fixed for payment. This is called the "Reddendum". It begins with the word "Yielding" or "Rendering" or "Paying". In the definition of rent in Sec. 105 of the Transfer of Property Act, the word used is "render" but as "Pay" is the most commonly understood expression, the word "Paying" may be used. "Yielding" however is not used in Indian law and its use in a deed of lease is not therefore recommended. If the consideration is rent in kind or service, the proper word would be "rendering".

If only a yearly rent is mentioned, it will mean that it is payable in one lump sum once a year; therefore if it is intended to be payable in instalments it should be clearly mentioned with the dates on which they should fall due. If no dates are mentioned but only "half yearly" or "quarterly" are mentioned, the rent will fall due in equal parts at these periods reckoned from the commencement of the term.

The rent should be expressed as being payable during the term of the lease by the use of some such words as "during the said term".

The place at which the rent is to be paid should also be mentioned, and if it is not mentioned it will be payable at the house or office or place of business of the lessor. Where a place is mentioned, it is usual to add the words "or at such place or places as the lessor may from time to time appoint in this behalf" to provide for the contingency of the place mentioned being no longer suitable.

In order to safeguard the rights of the landlord evicting a tenant in the interval between two dates for payment of rent, it is better to provide for proportionate payment of rent for the days of occupation by adding to the words of the reddendum the following clause:

"And also paying in the event of the said term being determined between two of the said yearly (*or* monthly or quarterly or half-yearly) days by re-entry (*or* notice) under the terms hereof a proportionate part of the said rent for the fraction of the current year (*or* month or quarter or half year) forthwith on such determination."

Or, simply by addition of the following words "and proportionately for any fraction of a year (month, quarter or half year)".

If the lease is executed sometime after the commencement of tenancy and some rent has already become due and has been paid, it is necessary to add some such words as:

"the first of such payments after the date of this lease in respect of the new current year (month or quarter) to be made on the —— day of ——next."

(6) *Covenants*: The terms and conditions, to which the lease is made subject are given in separate paragraphs, one paragraph containing all the conditions which involve covenants by the lessee, another containing the lessor's covenants; and the third containing mutual covenants by both, if any. Sometimes, it is more convenient to put together all the covenants under the heading "The lessor and the lessee hereby covenant with each other as follows."

There are certain covenants which are usually entered in all leases e.g. the lessee's covenant to pay rent, taxes, etc., and the lessor's covenant for quiet enjoyment. Some of them are so common that even if they are not expressly mentioned they are implied in every lease. They are embodied in section 108 of the Transfer of Property Act[1] in which they are referred to in the form of statutory rights and liabilities of the lessor and the lessee. They may be shortly stated in covenant form as follow:

Implied Covenants

Lessee's Covenants

(1) To disclose material facts enhancing the value of the lessor's interest (clause k).

(2) To pay premium or rent (clause 1).

(3) To keep and restore the property leased in good condition, reasonable wear and tear and damage by irresistible force excepted (clause m).

(4) To permit lessor and his agents to inspect the property (clause m).

(5) To make good defects caused by his act or default within three months of notice by the lessor (clause m).

(6) To inform lessor of any attack of a stranger on lessor's title (clause n).

(7) Not to commit waste or use the property for a purpose other than that for which it is let (clause o).

(8) Not to erect permanent structures (clause p).[2]

(9) To deliver possession on expiry of lease (clause q).

---

1 The provisions of the Transfer of Property Act are subject to overriding provisions of rent control laws relating to urban buildings which are in force in various States.

2 For subsequent permission by lessor to make alterations and additions *see* precedent No. 5 LICENCE, *post*.

Lessor's Covenants

(1) To disclose material defects (clause a).

(2) To give possession (clause b).

(3) To secure possession and quiet enjoyment (clause c).

(4) To allow all accessions to the property to be comprised in the lease (clause d).

(5) To give option to the lessee to avoid lease when the property is destroyed (clause e).[1]

(6) To pay for repairs or allow lessee to deduct the charges from rent if lessor neglects to make any repairs which he is bound to do (clause f).

(7) To pay or allow lessee to deduct from rent any charges paid by him which lessor is bound to pay and which are charged on the demised property (clause g).

(8) To allow lessee to remove fixtures attached by him (clause h).

(9) To allow lessee to remove crops sown by him and standing on determination of lease for an uncertain period (clause i).

(10) To permit lessee to transfer his interest (clause j).

These are statutory covenants which are implied even if not expressly stated.

It is therefore not strictly speaking necessary to insert them in leases governed by the Transfer of Property Act. But these covenants can be varied by contract and any variation must be expressly stated; as also any other conditions and covenants.

In England, the practice is to insert in the lease even those conditions which are ordinarily implied. This is done because they give greater definiteness to the obligations and because they bind the lessee and lessor personally during the continuance of the term even though they may have assigned their rights in the lease to others. But the latter is not consideration in India, as under Sec. 108(j) the lessee remains subject to all the liabilities inspite of a transfer of his interest under the lease. But as the covenants under Sec. 108 are implied only "in the absence of a contract or local usage to the contrary," it is open to party to set up a local usage varying the implied conditions and this may lead to unnecessary disputes and litigation. It is, however, not necessary to set out all the covenants and it would be sufficient to say that

"The lessor and lessee will have the rights and will be subject to the liabilities mentioned in Sec. 108 of the Transfer of Property Act, 1882."

Such a covenant will make the conditions in Sec. 108 applicable to the lease inspite of any local usage to the contrary even in territories where the Transfer of Property Act is not in force. All additional covenants should be inserted separately.

---

1 Destruction of the property makes the lease voidable at the option of the tenant only. It does not automatically put an end to the tenancy: *Dhruvdev* v. *Harmohinder Singh*, AIR 1968 SC 1020; *Hari Krishan* v. *Ramesh Gupta*, 1998 AIHC 2457 (P & H).

If any of the clauses of Sec. 108 is desired to be omitted or varied the same be excluded thus:

"Except clauses —— of the said section which are hereby excluded" and the varied covenant may be inserted as a separate covenant.

It must, however, be clearly understood that where an express covenant is made, no covenant can be implied on the same subject,[1] therefore, the express covenant should be complete in itself.

The additional covenants necessary in a particular lease depend on the nature of the lease and of the demised property. Some of these covenants are usual but most of them are matters of contract. Only such covenants as are legally enforceable can be made. Most tenancies in India are now governed by special local laws,[2] and the tenure and the rights and liabilities under the lease are regulated by statutory provisions. Parties cannot legally contract themselves out of them to the prejudice of the tenant, and it is the duty of conveyancer to satisfy himself that covenants which the parties desire to enter into are not against the provisions of law.

Some of the general important covenants are discussed below:

(i) Covenant to Pay Taxes

The lease should define the mode in which taxes, rates, and other public charges are to be borne by the lessor and lessee respectively. Some taxes are payable under the law by a particular party but there is nothing illegal in the other party undertaking to pay the same and the contract will, as *between the parties to it*, be legal and enforceable. It is thus not unusual for the lessee to undertake to "pay all rates and taxes and cesses charged on the demised premises or payable by the lessor or the lessee in respect thereof." Ordinarily, land revenue, cesses, ground rent, house tax and other cognate dues are payable by the lessor, while water tax, scavenging tax, etc., are payable by the lessee, but it is always better to make a definite contract and embody the same in the lease. It is better to specify all the taxes to be paid by one party and to say in the other party's covenant that he is to pay all the others.

In England the words, "duties", "outgoings", "impositions" or "charges"are used but these words are not in vogue in India. The charges which are generally current in India are, cesses, rates and taxes.

(ii) Covenant to Repair

In practice, the parties always enter into an express covenant for repairs, but if they are satisfied with the statutory provision in clause (f) and (m) of Sec. 108 and do not want any variation they need not mention any specific covenant in this

1 *Standdon* v. *Christmas*, (1847) 10 QB 135 at p.141; *Standard* v. *Forbes*, (1837) 6 Ad. and EL. 572.

2 "Rent control" laws in respect of urban buildings and land laws in respect of agricultural tenancies.

regard. Generally, the liability for certain repairs is thrown on the lessor and for others on the lessee.

Sometimes lessee's covenants are made in general words, e.g., to keep in "good and substantial state of repairs" or to keep in "good and tenantable repairs" or "good repairs" or "habitable repairs". The former covenant, though widely expressed, is construed with reference to the age and general condition of the house at the commencement of the lease, as the lessee has to repair that thing which he took and not to make a new and different thing and the lessee is not bound to make good defects caused by the natural operation of time and the elements upon a house of originally faulty circumstances.[1]

If the duty of repairs is undertaken by the lessor, the exact duty must be clearly and fully stated in the lessor's covenant. In such cases, in case of lessor's default the lessee is entitled to make the repairs and deduct the cost from the rent [section 108 (*f*)]. It is not therefore necessary to make an express covenant to that effect.

(iii) Covenant to Insure Against Fire

In India, such covenants are not frequent except in big towns or in cases of tenancy of commercial buildings, godowns, factories, etc. When a covenant is made, the company from which insurance policy is to be taken and the amount of insurance should be expressed, and the covenant should provide not only for *insurance* but also for punctual payment of *premia*. It should also provide how the insurance money is to be utilized in case a damage by fire takes place. If the duty of insurance is undertaken by the lessor, the lessee must covenant not to do anything on the demised premises which may render any increased or extra premium payable for insurance of the premises or which may make void or voidable any policy for such insurance.

(iv) Covenant about Assignment

Ordinarily, a lessee's right is transferable, except when he has an untransferable right of occupancy, or is a farmer of an estate in respect of which default has been made in payment of revenue [section 108(*j*)], and nothing need be said unless there is a contract to the contrary. Conditions forbidding or restricting transfers are frequently inserted; sometimes transfer is permitted only with the lessor's previous consent in writing. Or the lessee may be required to give notice of transfer to the lessor, or to pay to the lessor a part of the price he gets for the assignment. All such conditions are valid but must be expressly stated in the lease. In a case with the last mentioned condition where the lessee had not paid the part of the price to the lessor, it was held that the transfer was invalid.[2]

---

1 *Lister* v. *Lane*, (1893) 2 QB 212 at P. 217.

2 *Mahendra* v. *Karali*, AIR 1946 Cal 496 (a case of agricultural tenancy under the Bengal Tenancy Act 1885). The legality of the condition may be considered in light of local Rent Control Acts.

(v) Covenant about Use of Property

If the purpose of the lease is stated in the *habendum* it is not necessary to add a covenant that the property shall not be used for any other purpose. Such a covenant usually called "a restrictive covenant" is implied by section 108(*o*). Sometimes a different use is allowed after previous permission of the lessor. If so, an express covenant to that effect is necessary. Sometime the purpose of the lease is not stated in the *habendum* but is stated in a restrictive covenant by the lessee, thus:

"The lessee will use the demised house for residential purposes only, and, except with the previous permission in writing of the lessor, for no other purpose."

(vi) Covenant for Quiet Enjoyment

Sec. 108 *(c)* of the Transfer of Property Act provides that if the lessee pays the rent reserved and performs the contracts binding on him he will hold the property during the time limited by the lease without interruption. This is a covenant for quiet enjoyment which is implied in all leases governed by the Transfer of Property Act, in the absence of an express covenant on the subject.

It is, therefore, not necessary to insert an express covenant in leases governed by the Transfer of Property Act unless it is desired to restrict the implied covenant in any way. But it must be remembered that the interruption, against which protection is afforded, is a lawful interruption and not tortious disturbance by a trespasser, as a tenant has himself a remedy against a trespasser while he has none against a person having a right, e.g., one with a paramount title.[1]

(vii) Covenant for Renewal

This covenant should contain the agreement to renew the lease on the expiry of its present term on such conditions as may be agreed upon. These conditions should be clearly expressed, e.g., the term for which the renewal will be granted, whether any increase will be permissible or the renewal would be on the same rent, whether the lessee should give any notice to the lessor of an intention to exercise the option of having the lease renewed, who would bear the cost of renewal, etc. If the conditions are not mentioned renewal agreement can be enforced on reasonable terms.[2]

Provisos

There are certain covenants which are added as provisos because they control the general terms of the lease, e.g., the stipulation about re-entry on non-payment of rent or on the occurrence of a breach of covenant, or that giving liberty to the parties to determine the tenancy by notice within the term of the lease. These stipulations control the main provision in the habendum fixing a term of the lease

---

1 *Katyani* v. *Udao Kumar*, 52 C 417, 50 IA 160, PC; *British India Corporation* v. *Secy. of State*, AIR 1945 All 425.

2 *Kodamban* v. *English and Scotish*, AIR 1945 Mad 199.

and are really in the nature of proviso to it than an independent covenant. There is, however, no objection if such stipulations are drafted as covenants, e.g., that relating to forfeiture as a lessee's covenant, and that about determination by notice as a covenant by the party against whom the other party is given that power, or if power is given to either then as a covenant by both parties, though it would be more regular and accurate to put them as provisos. Such provisos should indicate their nature of being definite covenants. Also by the addition of words showing an agreement, thus:

"PROVIDED *always and it is hereby agreed that, etc.* (or, *as follows).*"

If the witnessing clause is divided into paragraphs (as in the Precedents in this book) the provisos should also be inserted in separate paragraphs.

The usual matters to be entered in the provisos are the forfeiture clause, the option to determine clause, the clause about suspension of rent in case of fire, and that enabling sub-lessee to pay rent to the superior landlord. The clause for renewal of term is also sometimes included in the provisos but it is more correct to include it in the lessor's covenants.

Sometimes provisos containing covenants by the lessee are added after the lessee's covenants, while others are inserted after the lessor's covenants, but sometimes all the provisos are added at the end. The latter procedure is preferable as in some provisos there may be covenants by both parties.

Forfeiture clause (*commonly called the "Proviso for Re-entry*").

The right of re-entry is reserved usually in cases of default in payment of rent or breach of a covenant, or on the lessee becoming insolvent. In case of default, it is sometimes provided that re-entry can be enforced only if any rent is in arrears for a specified period.

The proviso should be so drafted as simply to give a right of re-entry. Words often used to be inserted authorizing forcible entry or expulsion of the tenant[1] but such authority would not be legal, and no such words are, therefore, necessary. The effect of the proviso is not automatically to determine the tenancy but simply to give the lessor the option to determine it. The tenancy continues until the lessor has given notice in writing to the lessee of his intention to determine the lease [Sec.111(*g*)]. If the lessee does not peaceably surrender possession the lessor will have to sue for it and courts have been given wide powers to relieve the lessee of forfeiture (Sec. 114 and 114A). A clause reserving the rights of the lessor to sue the lessee for damages for breach of contract is also usually added at the end of the proviso though this seems hardly necessary.

Forfeiture clause is always strictly construed. Where, in a lease, there was a condition for re-entry on the insolvency of the lessee, and the lessee's interest was purchased in execution of a decree by X, and thereafter the lessee became

---

1 This was done on the English Pattern, but in India re-entry by force is not legally permissible: See *Lallu Yeshwant Singh* v. *Rao Jagdish Singh*, AIR 1968 SC 620.

insolvent, it was held that the "lessee" for purposes of the condition was, under the circumstances really X, and that as he did not become insolvent, no forfeiture took place.[1]

Devolution of Rights under the Lease

A lease is not a personal contract but is an estate in land which, unless for life, passes to the heirs as any other property and they take it with all the rights and responsibilities attaching to it.[2] Similarly, the lessor's heirs cannot repudiate the lease and are bound by the covenants thereof.

As regards the transferees of lessor's interest, Sec. 109 of the Transfer of Property Act provides that the transferees shall have all the rights of the lessor but will be subject to the liabilities only if the lessee so elects, for the lessee may prefer to make the transferor continue to be liable. A lessee can transfer all his rights and liabilities.[3] In any case, transferee is subject only to such liabilities as arise under covenants "running with the land", e.g., the covenant to pay rent, taxes, to repair, a condition for re-entry. Covenants which are merely personal are not binding on the assignee, e.g., to pay tax in respect of another property or not to keep a building within a certain distance of the demised premises.

However, a lessee shall not, merely by transferring his interest, even absolutely, cease to be subject to any of the liabilities attaching to the lease [Sec. 108(*j*)] unless the lessor releases him, for example, by treating the transferee on the footing of the original lessee. In such a case, a privity of contract is established between the lessor and the transferee and the original lessee is therefore released.

Interpretation Clause

Although, for the above reason, it is rarely necessary to have the successors and assigns of the lessor and lessee mentioned in the lease, yet a practice has grown up for the sake of safety and clarity to insert an interpretation clause providing that where the context so admits the expression the "lessor" shall include the owner for the time being of the lessor's interest in the demised property and the expression the "lessee" shall include his heirs, executors, administrators, and assigns.[4] This is either inserted as a separate covenant clause at the end or is provided for in beginning after the names of the parties, thus—"AB, etc., (hereinafter called the lessor, which expression shall etc."). In the author's opinion a clause somewhat on the above lines should be added as a covenant by both parties or in the provisos. The meaning of the document or of a particular part of it is to be sought for in the document itself. Of course, the document means the document read as a whole and

1 *Hazari Mal* v. *Sada Sukh*, AIR 1925 Cal 750.

2 *Maharaja Tej Chand* v. *Sri Kanth Ghose*, 3 MIA 261.

3 Under rent control laws, however, subletting without the permission of the lessor generally entails forfeiture of the statutory protection of those laws.

4 The word "assigns" should be omitted in respect of lessee where subletting is prohibited either by statute or by express contract.

not piecemeal. In construing instruments you must have regard not to the presumed intention of the parties, but to the meaning of the words which they have used.[1]

Surrender

In many cases a surrender is implied, e.g., when a new lease of the same land is granted to the same lessee, or where a lease is granted to a third party with the assent of the lessee and possession is transferred by the latter to the new lessee.[2]

In a case where the leased premises were mortgaged in favour of the tenant and it was recited in the mortgage deed that the mortgagee undertook to surrender possession if the loan amount was paid within the specified period, it was held that on such payment the lease was to be deemed to be surrendered.[3] It is however a matter of intention whether surrender was to be implied merely by execution of a mortgage in favour of the tenant. There is no automatic merger of the lease and the mortgage; hence unless there is implied or express surrender the right of the tenant will survive the redemption of the mortgage.[4]

Surrender may be made orally by delivery of the property which the lessor accepts. When surrender is made in writing it may be made by a separate deed or by an endorsement on the original deed. After reciting the lease and the consideration and agreement for surrender the lessee in the operative part of the deed "surrenders and yields up the demised premises to the lessor to the intent that the term created by the said lease and the estate and interest of the lessee under or by virtue of the said lease be absolutely and forever extinguished and the said premises may revert to the lessor, and the lessor absolves the lessee from the liabilities under the lease". If there is any other agreement by the lessor in consideration of the lease the same is entered as a covenant by the lessor.

Sometimes surrender is mentioned as a consideration of a new lease. In that case a clause about surrender is added in the new lease. If the surrender is made by endorsement on the lease, no recitals of the lease are necessary.

In case of agricultural tenancies special procedure for surrender is prescribed by local Acts and the same should be followed.[5]

Where a deed contains mixed elements disclosing features of both mortgage and lease, the court will have to find out the predominant intention of the parties from the recitals and the terms in the entire document and from the surrounding circumstances. How the parties or even their representatives in interest treated the

---

1 *Delhi Development Authority* v. *D.C. Kaushish*, (1973) 2 SCC 825. *Also see* Odgers Construction of Deeds and Statutes pp. 28-29 (5th Ed.) and INTRODUCTION, Part IV, *ante*.

2 *P.M.C. Kunhiraman Nair* v. *C.R. Naganatha Iyer*, (1992) 4 SCC 254.

3 *Shaw Mathuradas Mangelal & Co.* v. *N.S. Malage*, (1976) 3 SCC 680, folld. in *Kasilinga* v. *Kaliyaperumal*, 1998 AIHC 4326 (Mad).

4 *Gopalan* v. *Kunimana*, AIR 1996 SC 1659; *Cheriyan Sosamma* v. *Sundaressam Pillai*, (1999) 3 SCC 251: AIR 1999 SC 947.

5 *Mangala Kunhamina Umma* v. *Puthiyaveetil Paru Amma*, AIR 1971 SC 1575.

deed may also be relevant, but the nomenclature given to it by the scribe or even by the parties is not always conclusive.[1]

Stamp Duty

For stamp duty on a lease, including an underlease or sub-lease and any agreement to let or sublet *see* Article 35 with local amendments, if any. For a deed of surrender of lease, see Art. 61.

Registration

All leases from year to year, or for a term exceeding a year, or reserving a yearly rent must be registered (Sec. 107, Transfer of Property Act and Sec. 17(1)(d) Registration Act).

---

1 *Puzhakkal Kuttappu* v. *C. Bhargavi,* (1977) 1 SCC 17; *see also, C.S. Chandrashekharan* v. *George,* AIR 1985 Ker 131; *Mangala,* supra.

PRECEDENTS

1—General Forms of Various Formal Parts of a Lease[1]

Consideration

1. Premium Paid and Rent Reserved

In consideration of the sum of Rs. ——— paid by the lessee to the lessor as premium (the receipt of which is hereby acknowledged) and of the rent and the lessee's covenants hereinafter reserved and contained.

2. Surrender of former Lease

In consideration of the surrender by the lessee of a former lease of the property hereby demised dated the ——— and made between AB, etc., and CD, etc., and of the rent and lessee's covenants hereinafter reserved and contained:

Reservation and Exceptions

1. Excepting and Reserving to the lessor ———

Parcels[2]

1. Trees

ALL timber and fruit trees, saplings, shrubs, and underwood now standing or growing or hereafter to be standing or growing on the demised land with power to enter upon the said land for collecting the fruit and fallen timber but with no power to cut down any trees without the permission of the lessor.

2. Grass

ALL grass now growing or hereafter to grow on the demised land.

3. Minerals

ALL mines, minerals and quarries (including the right, if necessary, to work and get the same by surface workings, the tenant receiving due compensation for all damages sustained through the exercise of this exception).

---

1 *See* Introduction, Part II, and GENERAL FORMS, *ante*.

2 *Ibid.*

4. Right of Way

The use at all times and for all purposes in common with the lessee of the passage of ——— metres width leading from ——— to ——— *or* (ALL ways and rights of way hitherto used or enjoyed over the demised premises).

5. Right of Drainage

The free and uninterrupted passage and running of water and soil from and to other buildings and land of the lessor through the sewers, drains and water course which now are or hereafter may be in or under the demised premises.

6. General Rights

Subject to all rights and easements or re-granted easements belonging to or usually enjoyed with any adjacent property.

Habendum

TO HOLD the same to the lessee from the ——— from year to year; *or*

TO HOLD the same to the lessee from the —— for a term of —— years (months); *or*

TO HOLD the same to the lessee in perpetuity; *or*

TO HOLD the same to the lessee for the life of the lessee.

Reddendum

1. Reserving Rent

PAYING therefor during the said term (tenancy)[1] to the lessor yearly (monthly) and proportionately for any fraction of a year (month) the rent of Rs. ——— to be paid[2] on the ——— day of ——— in each year (month), the first of such payments to be made on the ——— next.

2. Annual Rent Payable in Instalments

PAYING therefor (*as in Form* 1) Rs. ——— by equal quarterly instalments on the ——— day of the months of ——— and in ——— each year, the first of such payments to be made on the ——— next.

---

1 This is suitable when the tenancy is not for a fixed term.

2 If rent is payable in advance add the words "in advance" after "paid" and delete the words "in each year, etc."

3. Alternative more Detailed Form

PAYING therefor during the said term (tenancy) to the lessor the yearly rent of Rs. ——— by equal quarterly instalments on the ——— day of ———, and in each year, the first of such payments to be made on the ——— next and also paying in the event of the said term (tenancy) being determined between two of the said quarterly days by re-entry (*or* notice) under the terms hereof a proportionate part of the said rent for the fraction of the current quarter forthwith on such determination.

4. If lease Executed after Commencement of Tenancy

PAYING therefor each year (*as in Form*1) the first of such payments after the date herein in respect of the now current year (month) to be made on the ——— next.

5. Alternative form

PAYING therefor each year (*as in Form* 1).

Provided that the rent already paid by the lessee in respect of his occupation since the commencement of this tenancy shall be in satisfaction as far as the same extends of the rent already accrued due hereunder.

6. Different Rents

PAYING therefor during each year of the said term (tenancy) to the lessor the respective rents following, that is to say:

1st year Rs. ———.

2nd and 3rd years Rs. ——— yearly.

4th, 5th and 6th years Rs. ——— yearly.

Subsequent years Rs. ——— yearly.

Such respective rents to be paid by equal quarterly, etc. (*as in Form* 2).

7. Premium Agreed to be Paid

PAYING therefor to the lessor the sum of Rs. ——— by way of premium in two equal instalments on the ——— and the——— and during the said term, etc.(*as in above Forms*).

8. Rent to be Determined by Calculation

PAYING therefor during the said term(tenancy) to the lessor yearly rent at Rs. ——— per acre of the demised land actually cultivated by the lessee during such year on the ——— subject to a minimum yearly rent of Rs. ———.

9. Fixing Place of Payment

PAYING therefor during the said term (tenancy) to the lessor at ——— or at such other place or places as the lessor may from time to time appoint in this behalf yearly, etc.,(*as in other Forms*).

10. Rent in Kind

RENDERING during the said term (tenancy) to the lessor at the end of every harvest after the crops have been reaped a half share of the agricultural produce actually grown by the lessee on the demised land.

11. Service

RENDERING during the whole of the said term (entire period of tenancy) to the lessor personal service of a gardener in the lessor's mango grove adjoining the demised land in accordance with the covenants herein contained.

Covenants

(a) By Lessee

1. Covenant to Pay Rent[1]

The lessee will during the said term (*or*, during the continuance of the said tenancy)[2] pay the rent hereby reserved on the days and in the manner aforesaid.

2. Covenant to Pay Taxes[3]

The lessee will during the said term (*or*, during the continuance of the said tenancy) pay all rates, taxes and other charges now payable or hereafter to become payable in respect of the demised premises by the lessor or lessee thereof except the house tax (*or*, except those hereinafter agreed to be paid by the lessor).

3. Covenant to Pay Land Revenue by Lessee

The lessee will during the said term pay the land revenue and cesses now assessed or which may hereafter be assessed on the demised property.

---

1 This covenant is, strictly speaking, not necessary as it is implied by section 108(l), Transfer of Property Act (where that Act is in force).

2 These words are appropriate if the tenancy is not for a fixed term.

3 *See* Preliminary Note on this covenant.

4. Covenant to Repair[1]

The lessee will during the said term (*or*, continuance of the said tenancy) keep the demised premises and the fixtures, paintings and decorations thereof in good and tenantable repair, order and condition (*or*, in as good condition as they were (will be) in when the lessee was (will be) put in possession[2] and will permit the lessor and his agents with or without workmen or others at all reasonable times to enter the demised premises and inspect condition thereof, and will repair and make good all defects of which notice in writing will be given by the lessor to the lessee within ———— calendar months after the giving of such notice.

5. Covenant to Insure[3]

The lessee will insure and shall at all times during the said term (*or*, continuance of the tenancy) keep insured the demised premises with all buildings, erections and fixtures now thereon or which may hereafter be constructed or erected thereon against loss or damage by fire in the sum of Rs. ——— in an Insurance Company approved by the lessor and will, whenever required, produce to the lessor the policy of such insurance and the receipts for the last premium in respect of the same and will apply all money received under the policy in reinstating the premises destroyed or damaged.

6. To Insure against Fire

The lessee will during the said term (tenancy) keep the demised premises insured against loss or damage by fire in the sum of Rs. ——— at least in some Insurance Company of repute and will whenever required produce to the lessor the policy of such insurance and the receipt for the last premium for the same and in case of destruction or damage of any part of the said premises by fire will rebuild or reinstate the same.

7. Not to do Anything to Increase Rate of Insurance

The lessee will not carry on or permit upon the demised premises any trade or occupation or do or suffer any other thing which may render any

---

1 *See* Preliminary Note on this covenant. A covenant for repair is implied by Sec. 108(m) of the Transfer of Property Act. It is however expedient that this express covenant may be inserted as it is more extensive than an implied covenant.

2 Under this covenant it is not sufficient that the premises should remain in a reasonably habitable condition but they should be kept in as good condition as they were when the lessee obtained possession.

3 *See* Preliminary Note on this covenant.

increased or extra premium payable for the insurance of the said premises against fire or which may make void or voidable any policy for such insurance.

8. Not to Commit Waste[1]

The lessee will not at any time during the said term without the consent in writing of the lessor pull down or damage any building belonging to the lessor or cut down or destroy any trees now or hereafter standing or growing on the said premises or open, work or dig for any mines, minerals, quarries, clay, graval or sand in, upon or under the same.

9. To Prevent Loss of Easement

The lessee will during the said term use his best endeavours to prevent any easement of right belonging to or used with the demised premises from being obstructed or lost.

10. To Prevent Encroachment and Acquisition of Easements

The lessee will not allow any encroachment to be made or easement to be acquired on or over the demised premises and if any encroachment or easement shall be made or threatened to be made or anything is done or threatened to be done by any person which if not stopped might confer on him a right of easement against the demised premises the lessee will forthwith give notice thereof to the lessor and permit him and his servants and agents to enter the demised premises to inspect the same.

11. Not to Assign[2]

The lessee will not without the previous consent in writing of the lessor sell, mortgage or sublet or in any other manner transfer or part with the possession of the whole or any part of the demised premises or his interest in the same.

12. Not to Sell or Mortgage but may Sublet

The lessee will not sell or mortgage his interest in the demised premises but may sublet the same from time to time for any term not exceeding ——— years at one time and will not on the expiry of any such term sublet again.

---

1 This is necessary only if the Transfer of Property Act does not apply as section 108(o) implies such a covenant.

2 *See* Preliminary Note on this covenant.

13. To Give Notice of Assignment

The lessee will within ——— months after any transfer or assignment of his interest under this lease give notice in writing to the lessor of such terms of transfer or assignment and of the name and the address of the transferee or assignee.

14. To Give Lessor Right of Pre-emption

The lessee will not sell his interest under this lease without first giving the lessor the option to purchase such interest at the price which any other person is willing to give.

15. To Perform Covenants in Head Lease[1]

The lessee will at all times during the said term duly perform and observe all the covenants affecting the demised premises which are contained in the head lease of the said premises dated ———— on the part of the lessee thereunder to be performed and observed (except the covenants about payment of rent, etc.).

16. To Deliver up Possession[2]

The lessee will on the determination of this lease deliver possession of the demised premises to the lessor in as good condition as it was in when the lessee obtained possession, subject only to the changes caused by reasonable wear and tear or irresistible force.

17. Valuation of Dilapidations

——— days before the expiration or other sooner determination of the term hereby granted a proper estimate or valuation shall be made as between the lessor and the lessee of the amount required to put all the demised premises into such good repair, order, or condition as they ought to be left in, according to the covenants hereinbefore contained and the lessee shall forthwith pay the said amount.

18. Power to Lessor to Repair on Lessee's Default

If the lesee shall at any time make default in the performance of any of the covenants herein contained for or relating to the repair of the said

1 Either a general covenant in this form should be inserted or all the lessee's covenants in the head lease which are intended to be binding on the sub-lessee should be specifically entered in the sub-lease.

2 Necessary only if the implied covenant under section 108 (q) of the Transfer of Property Act does not apply.

premises it shall be lawful for the lessor (but without prejudice to the right of re-entry under the clause hereinafter contained) to enter upon the said premises and repair the same at the expense of the lessee in accordance with the covenant for repair herein contained and the expenses of such repairs shall be repaid by the lessee to the lessor on demand.

(b) By Lessor

1. Absolute Covenant for Quiet Enjoyment[1]

The lessee paying the rent hereby reserved and performing and observing all the covenants by the lessee herein contained may hold and enjoy the demised premises during the said term without any (lawful)[2] interruption by the lessor or any other person whomsoever.

2. Ditto, Even Against Tortious Acts

The lessee paying, etc., (*as in* 1 *above*) without any interruption by the lessor or any person claiming or pretending to claim any right.

3. Qualified Covenant

The lessee performing, etc., (*as in* 1 *above*) without any interruption by the lessor or any person rightfully[3] claiming under or in trust for him.

4. To Pay Land Revenue and Taxes

The lessor will during the said term pay the land revenue, cesses, land or house tax ——— (*mention the taxes payable by the lessor under the contract*), now payable or hereafter to become payable in respect of the demised premises or by the lessor or lessee thereof.

5. To Pay all Taxes Except Some

The lessor will during the said term pay all rates, taxes and other charges now payable or hereafter to become payable in respect of the demised premises by the lessor or lessee thereof except those hereinbefore agreed to be paid by the lessee.

6. To Repair

The lessor will at his own cost keep the demised premises (including

1 *See* Preliminary Note on this covenant. This is not necessary if the lease is governed by the Transfer of Property Act. [see 108 (c)].

2 Not strictly necessary, *see* Preliminary Note; but may be retained.

3 This word is necessary in order to exclude acts done by lessor's successor but not authorised by the lessor, *Naorang* v. *Meik*, 50 Cal 68.

electric installations) in thorough good repair and habitable condition and will in particular annually at such time as the lessee shall direct make such repairs as may be necessary and will also annually after the rains (at such time as the lessee directs) paint such parts of the demised premises both from inside and outside and also all doors, windows and other wooden structures which are painted at the date of this lease and will replace all broken glass panes, bolts etc.

7. To Execute Sanitary Works

And also will at any time during the said term, execute any works which may in the opinion of the Municipal (Sanitary) authorities be necessary in order to put the said premises into good sanitary order and condition.

8. To Replace Fixtures Worn out

The lessor will replace any of the fixtures and fittings specified in the schedule attached hereto which may during the said term become unfit for the purpose for which the same are now used by other fixtures and fittings of a like nature or equal or higher value.

9. To Repair Sanitary Fittings

And will keep the internal sanitary and water apparatus thereof in good and tenantable repair and condition.

10. Dispute about Repairs

Provided that in all cases of dispute as to the necessity or sufficiency of any repairs required by the lessee or done by the lessor, the opinion of ——— shall be final and binding on the parties.

11. Provision on Default of Lessor[1]

Provided that if the lessor shall fail to execute such repairs or to do the painting, etc., hereinbefore referred to, the lessee may serve a notice on the lessor calling upon him to execute and do the same within ——— days of service of such notice and, if the lessor shall fail to execute or do the same, deduct the cost thereof from the rent hereby reserved until the same has been paid off, or otherwise recover the same from the lessor.

1 This is strictly not necessary, in cases governed by the Transfer of Property Act [Sec. 108 (*f*)].

12. To Renew Lease (one Renewal)

If the lessee shall have given to the lessor not less than ——— months' notice in writing prior to the expiration of the term reserved herein expressing a desire to renew the lease and shall have duly observed and performed all the terms and conditions hereof the lessor will grant to the lessee a new lease of the demised premises by way of renewal for a further period of ——— years to commence from the date of expiry hereof at the same rent plus ——— percent thereof and upon the same terms and conditions in all other respects as are reserved and contained herein (excluding only this present covenant for renewal).

13. To Renew Lease, (Several Renewals)

The lessor will at the request and cost of the lessee at the end of the said term and so on from time to time thereafter at the end of such further terms of years as shall be granted execute to the lessee a new lease by way of renewal for a term of ——— years on such covenants and provisions herein contained as shall apply to such renewed lease provided that such renewed term of years as shall be granted shall not with the original term hereby granted exceed in the aggregate the period of ——— years.

14. To Renew Lease, Reserving Enhancement of Rent

The lessor will, etc., (*as in para* 13 *above*) herein contained except that relating to the amount of annual rent reserved as shall apply to such renewed lease, etc., (*as in para* 13 *above*). Provided also that the lessor shall not be bound to grant any such renewal except at the rate of rent current in the neighbourhood at the date of such renewal for property with similar advantages, such rate of rent to be determined in case of dispute by—. (*Or*, except at such enhanced rent not exceeding—percent of the rent payable immediately before such renewal as the lessor may deem reasonable).

(c) By Both Parties

1. Heading of Covenants

It is hereby agreed between the parties as follows; *or,* The lessor and the lessee hereby covenant with each other as follows:

2. General Covenants Extending Rights and Liabilities provided in Transfer of Property Act[1]

It is hereby agreed that in respect of the demised premises the parties hereto shall respectively have all the rights and be subject to all the liabilities of a lessor and of a lessee as set forth in Sec. 108 of the Transfer of Property Act, 1882 except Clauses ——— of the said section which are hereby excluded.

3. Arbitration Clause

It is hereby agreed that if at any time any dispute, doubt or question shall arise between the lessor and the lessee touching the construction, meaning or effect of this deed or any clause thereof or their respective rights and liabilities hereunder the same shall be referred to the sole arbitration of ——— whose decision shall be final and binding on the parties.

4. Contract about Cost of Deed

It is hereby agreed that all costs and expenses incidental to the preparation, execution and registration of this deed shall be payable by the lessor/lessee.

5. Contract about Stamp Duty

It is hereby agreed that the stamp duty, if any, payable on this deed shall be paid by the lessor.[2]

6. Interpretation Clause[3]

It is hereby agreed that whenever such an interpretation would be requisite in order to give the fullest scope and effect legally possible to any covenant or contract herein contained, the expression "the lessor" hereinbefore used includes the owner for the time being of the lessor's interest in the demised premises and the expression "the lessee" hereinbefore used includes his heirs, executors, administrators, and assigns (*or*, permitted assigns); *or*

It is hereby agreed that where the context so requires or admits the

---

1 *See* Preliminary Note.

2 If the lessee is to pay it, no express covenant is necessary (Sec. 29, Stamp Act). If the lessor is Government and it is desired that the lessee should be exempted from the duty, the above covenant may be entered into which will have the desired effect [Sec. 3 Proviso (1)].

3 *See* Preliminary Note on this.

expression "the lessor" shall include his successor-in-title and the expression "the lessee" shall include the lessee's heirs, executors, administrators, and assigns.

7. Interpretation Clause when Guardian or Manager is Lessor

It is hereby, etc., (*as in para* 6) herein contained the expression "the lessor" hereinbefore used includes all persons and the successor-in-title of each and every person on whose behalf the lessor is now entitled to contract and to accept the benefit of a contract in relation to the transaction herein contained whether such persons are named herein or not and the expression "the lessee", etc. (*as in para* 6).

8. Interpretation clause when Guardian or Manager is Lessee

It is hereby, etc., (*as in para* 6) herein contained the expression "the lessee" hereinbefore used includes all persons and the heirs, executors, administrators, and assigns of each and every person on whose behalf the lessee is now entitled to contract and to accept the benefit of a contract in relation to the transaction herein contained, whether such persons are named herein or not.

9. Registration Fee

It is hereby agreed that any fee payable for the registration of this deed will be paid by the lessor/lessee.

Provisos[1]

1. Heading of Proviso

Provided always and it is hereby agreed that[2]

2. For Re-entry[3]

Whenever any part of the rent hereby reserved shall be in arrears for ——— after due date or there shall be a breach of any of the covenants by the lessee herein contained (*or*, the lessee shall be adjudicated insolvent) the lessor may re-enter on the demised premises and determine the lease.[4]

1 See also, Provisos in Preliminary Note of Lease on page 454.

2 If there are several provisos say "agreed as follows:" and state the provisos in separate paragraphs.

3 *See* Preliminary Note, *ante*, sub-heading "Forfeiture Clause (Proviso for Re-entry)".

4 It is usual to add "and thereupon the lease shall absolutely determine." These words are, however not necessary if the lease is governed by Transfer of Property Act as this is the legal effect under section 111.

3. Proviso Excluding Liability after Assignment

That the lessee shall not be liable for the payment of rent hereby reserved or for the performance of any of the covenants hereinbefore contained after he has assigned the said lease (and given notice of assignment as hereinbefore provided).

4. Payment of Rent by Sub-lessee to Superior Landlord

That it shall be lawful for the lessee to pay the rent hereby reserved to the superior landlord whose receipts for such payments shall be in satisfaction or discharge of so much of the rent hereby reserved as shall be expressed in such receipts.

5. Suspension of Rent in case of Fire

That if any part of the demised premises is destroyed or damaged by fire so as to become unfit for use for the purpose for which it has been let, the rent hereby reserved or a fair and just proportion thereof according to the nature and extent of the damage sustained shall from the date of such damage (*or*, the expiration of ——— months from the date of damage) and until the premises shall have been rebuilt or reinstated and made fit for such use be suspended and cease to be payable, and such abatement of rent shall be in full satisfaction of all claims for damages by the lessee against the lessor in respect of such destruction or damage.

6. Option to Determine Lease

If the lessee/lessor shall desire to determine the present tenancy and shall give to the lessor/lessee ——— calendar months' previous notice in writing of such desire (*add in case of lessee*, "and shall upto the time of such determination pay the rent and perform and observe the covenants on his part hereinbefore contained") then immediately on the expiration of such notice this lease shall be void without prejudice to the remedies of either party against the other in respect of any antecedent claim or breach of covenant; *or*

That the tenancy hereby created shall be determinable at the option of the lessor/lessee at any time by his giving to the lessee/lessor ——— calendar months' notice in writing; *or*

That either party may at any time determine the tenancy hereby created by giving to the other ——— calendar months' notice in writing.

7. Contract about Notice and Demands

It is hereby agreed that any demand for payment or notice requiring to be made upon or given to the lessee shall be sufficiently made or given if sent by the lessor or his agent through the post, by registered letter addressed to the lessee at the demised premises (*or* at ———) and that any notice requiring to be given to the lessor shall be sufficiently given if sent by the lessee through the post by registered letter addressed to the lessor at his usual or last known place of residence or business (*or*, at ——) AND that any demand or notice sent by post in either case shall be assumed to have been delivered in the usual course of post.

2—Agreement to Let a House[1]

AN AGREEMENT made the ——— day of ——— BETWEEN AB, etc., (hereinafter called "the lessor") of the one part AND CD, etc., (hereinafter called "the lessee") of the other part.

WHEREBY IT IS AGREED as follows:

1. The lessor shall grant and the lessee shall accept a lease of the house known as No. ———, ——— street and situate in the town of ——— (*or,* fully described in the schedule hereto) for ——— years from the ——— day of ——— at the monthly rent of Rs. ——— payable in advance on the 1st day of each calendar month.

(2) The lessee shall enter into the following covenants:

(*a*) To pay all rates and taxes except the house tax;

(*b*) Not to alter the premises without the lessor's consent;

(*c*) To use the house for residential purposes only;

(*d*) Not to assign or sublet without the lessor's consent.

3. The lessor will enter into the following covenants:

(*a*) To keep the house in repairs;

(*b*) To white-wash and colour-wash every year such parts as are now white-washed or colour-washed;

(c) To paint wood work every third year.

4. The lessor and lessee will expressly covenant:

(a) That they will respectively have the rights and liabilities specified in Sec. 108, Transfer of Property Act, 1882 except in Clauses (*i*), (*j*) and (*m*) thereof; and

(*b*) That the lease will be determinable by either party by three months' notice to the other.

---

1 Such an agreement does not itself constitute a lease, hence it does not require registration: *Food Corporation of India* v. *Babulal*, AIR 1998 MP 23 (DB).

5. The lease shall contain a proviso for re-entry in case of non-payment of rent or breach of a covenant by the lessee.

6. The lease shall be prepared by the lessor at the expense of the lessee and shall be executed by the lessor and lessee on or before the ———.

The Schedule herein referred to

* * * *

IN WITNESS WHEREOF the parties have put their signatures hereinunder on the day and the year first above-written (*or*, on the respective dates mentioned against their signatures).

3—Agreement for Sub-lease of a House[1]

AN AGREEMENT (*as in Form No.* 2).

WHEREBY IT IS AGREED as follows:

1. The lessor shall grant and the lessee shall accept a lease of the premises described in the schedule hereto which are held by the lessor under a lease dated ——— and made between ——— (hereinafter called "the Superior Landlord") and the lessor for ——— years from the ——— day of ——— at the monthly rent of Rs. ——— payable on the first day of the month succeeding that for which it is due.

2. Such lease shall contain the following covenants and provisions:

(a) Covenants by the lessee

Covenant to pay the rent as aforesaid and covenants similar to the lessee's covenants contained in the said head lease so far as they are applicable (except the covenant for payment of rent, and, etc.) so that the lessor shall be put in the place of the superior landlord and a covenant to indemnify the lessor against the observance and performance of the covenants and conditions in the head lease (except as aforesaid) so far as they are applicable.

(b) Covenants by the lessor

For the observance and performance of the lessor's covenants contained in the said head lease except such as under this agreement are imposed on the lessee.

---

1 Such an agreement does not itself constitute a lease, hence it does not require registration: *Food Corporation of India* v. *Babulal*, AIR 1998 MP 23 (DB).

(c) Provisos

For re-entry in case of default in payment of rent or breach of covenants by the lessee and for determination of this tenancy at the option of either party by giving three months' notice.

3. The lease shall be prepared by the lessor at the expense of the lessee and shall be executed by the lessor and lessee on or before the ———.

4. The lessor shall use his best endeavour to obtain the written consent of the superior landlord to the grant of the lease and if such consent cannot be obtained this agreement will become void.[1]

4—Lease of Land for Building Purposes for a Premium and Rent Reserved for a Term, with a Renewal Clause

THIS LEASE made on the ——— day of ——— BETWEEN AB, etc., (hereinafter called "the lessor") of the one part AND CD, etc., (hereinafter called "the lessee") of other part.

WITNESSES as follows:

1. In consideration of the sum of Rs. ——— (Rupees ———) paid as premium before the execution of these presents (the receipt of which the lessor hereby acknowledges) and of the rent hereinafter reserved and of the covenants on the part of the lessee hereinafter contained the lessor hereby demises to the lessee for the purpose of building a house or houses for residence only, ALL that land described in the schedule hereto and for greater clearness delineated on the plan annexed hereto and thereon shown with its boundaries coloured red together with all easements and appurtenances whatever belonging or in any way appurtenant thereto, and the free right of passage at all times and for all purposes to and from the demised land over the land adjoining the demised premises on the east and shown on the plan as coloured blue for the purpose of going from the demised premises to the public road ——— on the west of the said land and *vice versa*, TO HOLD the said premises to the lessee from the ——— day of ——— for a term of ——— years PAYING therefor during the said term the yearly rent of Rs. ——— by equal half yearly payments on the ——— day of ——— and the ——— day of ——— in each year at the office of the lessor or at such other place or places as the lessor may from time to time appoint in this behalf, the first of such payments to be made on

1 Necessary only when under the head lease or under a local Act, a sub-lease without the lessor's consent is prohibited or is a ground for withdrawal of protection of the rent control law from ejectment.

the ——— day of ——— next;

2. Lessee's Covenant

The lessee hereby covenants with the lessor as follows:

(i) To Pay Rent[1]

That he will, during the continuance of this lease, pay to the lessor the yearly rent hereby reserved on the days and in manner hereinbefore appointed.

(ii) To Pay Taxes

That he will, during the said term, pay all rates, taxes and charges of every description now payable or hereafter to become payable in respect of the demised premises or the buildings to be erected thereupon or by the landlord or the tenant in respect thereof.

(iii) To Build House

That he will at a cost of not less than Rs. ——— erect upon the demised premises in a substantial and workman-like manner and in accordance with the plan elevations section and specifications annexed hereto (*or*, to be agreed by the lessor) a dwelling house with necessary outhouses, boundary walls, sewers, drains, garages, etc., and shall complete the same in all respects fit for immediate occupation within ——— months from the date hereof (unless prevented by accident or unavoidable cause and in such case as soon after the said period as practicable)

(iv) Not to Make Additions

That he will not erect or build or permit to be erected or built on the demised premises any building other than those specified in the last clause nor to make any addition to any building at any time existing thereon except with the approval of the lessor.

(v) To Repair

That he will during the term of tenancy hereby created keep the demised premises and all other buildings and structures which may at any time during the said term be erected or constructed on the demised land together with all roads, drains sewers, fences, compound wall and all other appurtenances to the demised premises and the said building and structures in good repair and condition.

---

1 Not strictly necessary if the lease is governed by Transfer of Property Act.

(vi) Not to use for a Different Purpose

That he will not without the consent in writing of the lessor use or permit the use of the said land for any purpose other than that for which it is let and will not without such consent use or permit the use of the said dwelling house or any other buildings that may be erected on the demised premises for the purpose of carrying on any trade or business.

(vii) To Yield up Possession

That he will at the expiration of the said term or sooner determination thereof peaceably and quietly surrender to the lessor the said land after removing any constructions made by him thereon unless the lessor shall express his willingness to purchase the same at the market value of the materials in which case the lessee shall sell the same to the lessor at a valuation to be made by mutual consent or in case of disagreement by arbitration.

(viii) Not to Assign

That he will not assign or sub-let or otherwise part with the premises hereby demised or any constructions erected thereon or any part thereof without the permission in writing of the lessor.

3. Lessor's Covenants

The lessor hereby covenants with the lessee as follows:

(i) For Quiet Enjoyment[1]

That the lessee paying the rent hereby reserved and performing all the covenants by the lessee herein contained may hold and enjoy the demised premises during the said term without any unlawful interruption by the lessor or any other person whosoever.

(ii) For Renewal

That he will at the request and cost of the lessee at the end of the term of ——— years hereby granted and so on from time to time thereafter at the end of each such successive further term of ——— years as shall be granted, execute to the lessee a new lease of the demised premises by way of renewal for the term of ——— years on such covenants and provisos herein contained except that relating to the annual rent reserved as shall apply to such renewed lease PROVIDED that such renewed terms of ——— years as shall be granted shall not with the original term of ——— years exceed

---

1 Not strictly necessary if the lease is governed by Transfer of Property Act.

in the aggregate the period of ——— years. AND PROVIDED ALSO that the lessor shall not be bound to grant any such renewal except at such enhanced rent not exceeding ——— per cent of the rent payable immediately before such renewal as the lessor may deem reasonable.

4. Provisos (Re-entry[1]; Termination)

PROVIDED ALWAYS and it is hereby agreed as follows:

(i) That whenever any part of the rent hereby reserved shall be in arrear for ——— months after due date or there shall be a breach of any of the covenants by the lessee herein contained the lessor may re-enter on the demised premises and determine this lease.

(ii) That the tenancy hereby created shall be determinable at the option of the lessor/lessee (or, either party) by giving to the lessee/lessor (or, the other party) ——— calendar months' notice in writing.

5. Covenants by Parties

It is hereby agreed between the parties as follows:

(i) Service of Notice

That any demand for payment or notice requiring to be made upon or given to the lessee shall be sufficiently made or given if sent by the lessor or his agent through the post by registered letter addressed to the lessee at the demised premises (*or,* at ———), and that notice requiring to be given to the lessor shall be sufficiently given if sent by the lessee through the post by registered letter addressed to the lessor at his usual or last known place of residence or business (*or,* at ———) AND that any demand or notice sent by post in either case shall be assumed to have been delivered in the usual course of post.

(ii) Interpretation Clause

That wherever such an interpretation would be necessary in order to give the fullest scope and effect legally possible to any covenant or contract herein contained the expression "the lessor" hereinbefore used shall include the owner for the time being of the lessor's interest in the demised premises and the expression "the lessee" hereinbefore used shall include his heirs, executors, administrators and permitted assigns.

IN WITNESS WHEREOF the parties hereto have hereunder signed

---

1 See also 'Forfeiture Clause (Proviso for re-entry)' in Preliminary Note of Lease on page 455.

this deed on the dates mentioned against their respective signatures.

The Schedule herein referred to

(Particulars of the plots hereby demised)

5—Lease of Land and Building

THIS LEASE, etc., (*as in Form* 4).

WITNESSES as follows:

1. Demise of Land and Building

The lessor hereby demises to the lessee for ——— and for no other purpose ALL THAT plot of land described in the schedule hereto together with all buildings and trees thereon TO HOLD the same to the lessee from the ——— day of ——— for a term of ——— years PAYING therefor during the said term the yearly rent of Rs. ——— by half yearly payments on the ——— day of ——— and the ——— day of ——— in each year, the first of such payments to be made on the ——— day of ——— next.

2. Lessee's Covenants

The lessee hereby covenants with the lessor as follows:

(i) To Pay Taxes, etc.

During the said term the lessee will pay all rates, taxes and other charges now payable or hereafter to become payable in respect of the said premises.

(ii) To Repair

He will keep the said premises in good condition and complete repair and fit in all respects to be used for ———.

(iii) Not to Transfer

He will not transfer, mortgage or sublet the said premises without having first obtained the consent in writing of the lessor.

3. Provisos for re-entry, option to determine (*as in Form 4*).

4. IT IS HEREBY AGREED between the parties as follows:

(*i*) That in respect of the said premises the parties hereto shall respectively have all the rights and be subject to all the liabilities of a lessor and of a lessee as set forth in section 108, Transfer of Property Act, 1882, except clauses (f), (g) and (i) of the said section which clauses are hereby excluded.

(*ii*) Covenant about notice—(*same as in Form 4*).

(*iii*) Interpretation Clause—(*same as in Form 4*).

IN WITNESS, etc.

6—Lease of Land Already in Lessee's Possession, with Retrospective Effect

THIS LEASE, etc.

WITNESSES as follows:

1. The lessor hereby demises to the lessee ALL that land described in the schedule hereto on which the lessee has built a house and which has been in lessee's possession since ——— TO HOLD the same to the lessee from the beginning of the year ——— for a term of ——— years; PAYING therefor during the said term to the lessor yearly and proportionately for any fraction of a year the rent of Rs. ——— to be paid on the ——— day of —— in each year the first such payment after the date hereof in respect of the new current year to be made on the —— next.

2. Lessee's Covenants

The lessee hereby covenants with the lessor as follows:

(i) To Pay Rent (as in Form 4).

(ii) To Pay Taxes (*as in Form* 4).

(iii) Not to Alter.

The lessee shall not without the consent in writing of the lessor construct any new building or buildings on the demised premises or make any alterations in the buildings now standing thereon.

(iv) Not to make Additions (*as in Form* 4).

(v) To Keep in Repair

The lessee shall keep the building standing on the demised premises in good state of repairs and in habitable condition.

(vi) Not to use for other Purpose

The lessee will not use the said land and buildings otherwise than for residential purposes.

(vii) To Yield up

That the lessee will on the expiration of the said term or sooner determination thereof peaceably and quietly surrender to the lessor the said land after removing his building materials therefrom unless the lessor within three months preceding such expiry or within 15 days of such determination notifies his intention of purchasing the same at a cost to be determined in the manner hereinafter prescribed in Clause 4 hereof.

3. Lessor's Covenants

As in para 3 *of Form* 4.

4. Provisos

PROVIDED ALWAYS and it is hereby agreed as follows:

(i) Proviso for Re-entry (*as in para* 4 *of Form* 4).

(ii) Option to Determine

That the lessor may at any time after six months' previous notice in writing to the lessee determine the tenancy hereby created and shall in such case pay to the lessee as compensation such cost of any building or buildings standing on the demised premises on the date of such determination as may be mutually agreed upon or in case of disagreement as may be determined by ——— and on such payment being made such buildings shall vest in the lessor.

5. Covenant about notice and interpretation clause (*same as in para 5 of Form* 4).

IN WITNESS WHEREOF (*as in Form* 4).

7—Lease of Land for Playground

THIS LEASE made on the ——— day of ——— BETWEEN AB, etc., (hereinafter called "the lessor") of the one part AND ———, of the——— High School, a society registered under the Societies Registration Act, 1860 such Secretary being authorised by the governing body of the society by resolution dated ——— in this behalf,[1] (hereinafter called "the lessee") of the other part;

WITNESSES as follows:

1. The lessor hereby demises to the lessee for use as playground for the said ——— High School and for no other purpose ALL that land described in the schedule hereto To HOLD the same to the lessee from the ——— day of ——— for a term of ——— years PAYING therefor the yearly rent of Rs. ——— on the ——— day of ——— in each year at the office of the lessor, or at such other place or places as the lessor may from time to time appoint in this behalf.

1 Under section 5 of the Societies Registration Act, the property of the society, if not vested in trustees, shall be deemed to be vested in its governing body.

2. Right of Re-entry

PROVIDED ALWAYS AND IT IS HEREBY AGREED that if the annual rent hereby reserved shall remain in arrears for a period of 30 days or if the demised land is at any time used otherwise than as a playground for the said ——— High School, the lessor may re-enter on the demised premises and determine this lease.

3. Interpretation Clause

It is hereby agreed that wherever such an interpretation would be necessary in order to give the fullest scope and effect legally possible to any covenant or contract herein contained the expression "the lessor" hereinbefore used shall include the owner for the time being of the lessor's interest in the demised premises and the expression "the lessee" hereinbefore used shall include all persons from time to time acting as Secretary of the said society.

IN WITNESS WHEREOF, etc.

8—Fresh Lease of New Land in Consideration of the Surrender of Another Lease

THIS LEASE made, etc., (*as in Form* 4).

WITNESSES as follows:

1. In consideration of the lease hereinafter granted by the lessor, the lessee hereby relinquishes from his tenancy and surrenders to the lessor possession of the land held by him as lessee under the lease dated the ———.

2. In consideration of the aforesaid surrender by the lessee and of the rent hereby reserved and the covenants herein contained the lessor hereby demises to the lessee ALL that land described in the Schedule hereto TO HOLD the same to the lessee from the ——— day of ——— for the term of ——— years PAYING therefor during the said term the annual rent of Rs. ——— in two equal instalments on the ——— day of ——— and the ——— day of ——— in each year at the ——— or at such other place or places as the lessor may from time to time appoint in this behalf.

Covenants and Provisos

* * * *

9—New Lease on Modified Terms in Consideration of the Surrender of an Old Lease by the Lessee and a Third Person (with Recitals)

THIS LEASE is made on the ——— day of ——— BETWEEN AB, etc., (hereinafter called "the lessor") of the first part AND CD, etc., (hereinafter called "the lessee") of the second part AND EF, etc., of the third part.

WHEREAS—

(1) By a lease dated the ——— the lessor demised the land described in the schedule hereto to one X, etc., for building purposes for a period of ——— years and the said X erected some buildings thereon;

(2) By a deed of sale the said X transferred his rights and interest in the said land under the said lease and also the buildings standing on the said land to the lessee and the said EF.

(3) The lessor has now agreed with the lessee and the said EF that on the lessee and the said EF surrendering the aforesaid lease the lessor will grant to the lessee a fresh lease of the said land on the modified terms and conditions hereinafter contained.

NOW THIS DEED WITNESSES as follows:

(1) In pursuance of the aforesaid agreement and in consideration of the lease hereafter granted to the lessee, the lessee and the said EF hereby surrender and yield up to the lessor all the land comprised in the aforesaid lease dated ——— TO the intent that the said term created by the said lease and all the estate and interest of the lessee and the said EF in the said land under or by virtue of the aforesaid lease may be absolutely and forever extinguished from the date hereof and to the further intent that the lessor may forthwith grant to the lessee a new lease of the said land.

(2) In further pursuance of the aforesaid agreement and in consideration of the surrender hereinbefore contained, etc., (*as in para* 2 *of Form* 8).

IN WITNESS WHEREOF, etc.

10—Lease of Land in Favour of a Club

THIS LEASE made on the ——— day of ——— BETWEEN AB, (hereinafter called "the lessor") of the one part AND the ——— Club[1]

---

1 If the Club is a registered company or society, it should join in its own name. If not, either all the members should join or the Secretary or President may enter into the lease in his own name and not merely as Secretary or President.

at ———, a society registered under the Societies Registration Act (*or,* company within the meaning of the Companies Act, 1956) (hereinafter called "the lessee") through ——— Secretary of the said club of the other part.

WITNESSES as follows:

1. Demise of Land

The lessor hereby demises to the lessee ALL that land described in the schedule hereto TO HOLD the premises hereby demised to the lessee for the purpose of the said ——— Club from the day of ——— for the term of ——— years; PAYING therefor during the said term the yearly rent of Rs. ——— by monthly payments of Rs. ——— on the ——— day of every month.

2. Lessee's Covenants

The lessee hereby covenants with the lessor as follows:

(i) To Pay Rent

That he will during the said term pay to the lessor the yearly rent hereby reserved on the days and in the manner hereinbefore appointed;

(ii) To Pay Interest

That if any monthly instalment of the rent hereby reserved or any part thereof shall at any time be in arrears and unpaid for the period of one calendar month next after the day whereon the same shall have become due the lessee shall pay interest at the rate of ——— per cent per annum;

(iii) To Pay Taxes

That he will pay all rates, taxes and other charges (except land tax) now chargeable or hereafter to be chargeable in respect of the demised premises;

(iv) Not to Build

That the lessee will not, without the previous consent in writing of the lessor, erect or suffer to be erected on any part of the said demised premises any building other than and except the building or structure already erected for the Club and shown in the plan annexed hereto;

(v) Not to use for Other Purposes

That the demised premises shall be used only for the purpose of a club as aforesaid and for no other purpose;

(vi) Not to Transfer

That he will not transfer or sublet his rights under this lease without the written consent of the lessor;

(vii) To Yield up

That he will on the expiration or sooner determination of the said term peaceably surrender and yield up the demised premises to the lessor, and in such an event the lessor may, at his option, either purchase the buildings, water pipes and other structures or fixtures belonging to the lessee and standing on the demised land upon the valuation of the lessee or may permit the lessee to remove the same.

3. Lessor's Covenants

The lessor hereby covenants with the lessee as follows:

(i) For Quiet Enjoyment

That the lessee paying the rent hereby reserved and performing and observing the covenants and conditions herein contained and on his part to be performed and observed shall and may peaceably and quietly hold, possess and enjoy the said demised premises during the said term in the manner aforesaid without any unlawful interruption or disturbance by the lessor or any person or persons whomsoever;

(ii) To Pay Land Tax

That the lessor shall pay the land tax now imposed or hereafter to be imposed on the demised premises.

4. Provisos

PROVIDED ALWAYS, etc., (*Clause for re-entry and option to determine as in para* 4 *of Form* 4).

5. Interpretation clause — As in para 5 (ii) of Form 4.

IN WITNESS WHEREOF, etc.

11—Lease of Land for Building a House for a Government Servant with Condition to Sublet the same to Government[1]

THIS LEASE made on the ——— day of ———BETWEEN the Governor of Uttar Pradesh (hereinafter called "the lessor") of the one part AND AB, etc., (hereinafter called "the lessee") of the other part.

WITNESSES as follows:

1. Demise of Land

The lessor hereby demises to the lessee ALL THAT plot of land described in the schedule hereto and with the boundaries thereof for greater clearness delineated on the plan annexed hereto and thereon coloured red TO HOLD the said premises to the lessee from the ——— day of ——— for the term of ——— years subject to the conditions hereinafter mentioned PAYING therefor during the said term the yearly rent of Rs. ——— by equal half-yearly payments on the ——— day of ——— and the ——— day of ——— in each year at the office of the Collector of ——— or at such other place or places as such Collector may from time to time appoint in this behalf, the first of such payments to be made on the ——— day of ———.

2. Lessee's Covenants

The lessee hereby covenants with the lessor as follows:

(1) To Pay Rent

That during the said term he will pay the yearly rent hereby reserved on the days and in the manner hereinbefore appointed;

(2) To Pay Taxes

That he will pay and discharge all rates, taxes and other charges which now are or hereafter may be payable in respect of the said premises or the buildings to be erected thereon by the lessor or lessee in respect thereof, except for the period during which the said buildings have been sublet by the lessee to the lessor under the covenant hereinafter following;

(3) To Construct House

That he will within ——— calendar months next after the date of this deed at his expense and at an outlay of not less than Rs. ——— in a good

---

1 *Cf. State Bank of India* v. *Aditya Finance and Leasing Co.,* AIR 1999 Del 18 (case of Bank getting building constructed for being leased to it).

substantial and workmanlike manner and to the satisfaction of the Collector for the time being of the district of ——— (hereinafter called "the Collector") erect and complete on the said premises a dwelling house with suitable outbuildings according to a plan and elevation approved by the Collector;

(4) To Lay Water and Electricity

That he will within the aforesaid period of ——— calendar months at his own expense lay out water pipes at such places on the demised premises as the Collector shall direct and will have complete electric installations on the premises with points, switches and plugs at such places as the Collector shall direct (*or*, that whenever facilities for laying out water or electric installations or both on the premises are offered and the Collector so requires, the lessee will at his expense lay out water pipes at such places as the Collector shall direct and/or will have complete electric installations in the house with points, switches and plugs at such places as the Collector shall direct within such time as may be fixed by the Collector);

(5) Not to make Alterations

That no part of the elevation or plan of such dwelling house or out buildings shall at any time be altered or varied from the original elevation or plan thereof without the consent in writing of the Collector and no other buildings shall be erected on the said premises without the like consent;

(6) To Repair

That he will at all times repair, and keep in good and substantial condition and repair, such dwelling house and out-buildings and also the boundary and other walls, sewers, drains, rails, gates, fences and fixtures of or connected with the same, and shall in particular execute all necessary repairs and do all necessary painting of walls, exteriors, doors, windows, etc. annually before the ——— day of ——— at a cost of not less than Rs. ———;

(7) To Permit Lessor to Inspect

That he will permit the lessor and his agent in the day-time after ——— hours' previous notice of his or their intention so to do, to enter into or upon the premises and view the condition of such buildings and also the boundary and other walls, sewers, drains or want of repair there found, which defects or want of repair the lessee will within three calendar months after such notice repair and rectify accordingly;

(8) Not to use House except for Dwelling

That he will not at any time carry on or permit to be carried on upon the said premises any trade or business whatsoever or use the same for any other purpose than as a private dwelling without the consent in writing of the Collector first had and obtained;

(9) Not to Assign House

That he will not, except with the permission in writing of the lessor, assign or otherwise part with the premises or the said building or any part of them otherwise than by a sub-lease from month to month terminable by 15 days' notice expiring with the end of a calendar month and will not permit any other person to occupy the same except on an express condition to vacate it on 15 days' notice;

(10) To Sublet House to Government

That he will sublet the said building and premises to the lessor for the residence of a Government servant whenever required to do so by the Collector at a monthly rent of Rs. ——— and will deliver possession of the same to the lessor or his agent on one calendar months' notice in writing served upon him by the Collector.

(11) Lessor's Right to Repair on Lessee's Default

That if at any time during the aforesaid sub-tenancy of the lessor the lessee shall in breach of the covenant hereinbefore contained refuse or neglect to execute such repairs as the Collector shall require, it shall be lawful for the Collector to serve upon him a notice in writing requiring him to execute such repairs within a specified time, and in case of the lessee's default, to execute such repairs and to deduct the cost of the same from the monthly rent payable by the lessor to the lessee until the same has been paid off.

(12) To Yield up

That, subject to the covenant regarding renewal of the lease hereinafter contained, the lessee shall on the expiry of the term hereby reserved or sooner determination of this lease peaceably surrender possession of the demised premises with such buildings thereon as may be standing at the time to the lessor;

3. Lessor's Covenants

The lessor hereby covenants with the lessee as follows:

(1) To Pay Taxes

That he will during the period of his sub-tenancy pay all rates, taxes and other charges which now are or which may hereafter become payable in respect of the said premises or the buildings to be erected thereon;

(2) To Renew Lease

That he will at the request and cost of the lessee at the end of the said term of —— years and so on from time to time hereafter at the end of each successive term of —— years that may be granted execute to the lessee a new lease of the said premises by way of renewal for the term of —— years PROVIDED that such renewed term of years as may be granted shall not with the original term of ——— years hereby granted exceed in the aggregate the period of ——— years AND that the lessor shall not be bound to grant any renewal except at such enhanced rent not exceeding 50 per cent of the rent payable during the period immediately preceding the renewal as may be assessed by the Collector regard being had to the circumstances of the demised land and to the market value of similar plots in the neighbourhood, which assessment shall be final, save that where the estimated value of the plot, calculated at ——— times the proposed annual rent, shall exceed Rs. ——— the lessee shall have a right of appeal to the Commissioner of the ——— division AND save as to the amount of rent thereby reserved and as to the term thereby granted every renewed lease of the said premises shall contain such of the covenants, provisions and conditions in these presents contained as shall be applicable;

4. Provisos

PROVIDED ALWAYS, etc., Proviso for re-entry [*as in Form* 4 Proviso (i)].

5. Interpretation clause [*as in Form* 4, clause 5 (ii)].

The Schedule herein referred to

(Description of the land leased)

IN WITNESS WHEREOF, etc.

12—Perpetual Lease of Land

THIS LEASE made on the ——— day of ———— BETWEEN AB, etc., (hereinafter called "the lessor") of the one part AND CD, etc., (hereinafter called "the lessee") of the other part,

WITNESSES as follows:

1. Demise of Land

The lessor hereby demises to the lessee ALL THAT plot of land described in the schedule hereto and delineated on the plan annexed hereto and thereon shown with its boundaries coloured red TO HOLD the said premises from the date of this deed in perpetuity PAYING therefor the yearly rent of Rs. ——— on the ——— day of ——— in each year.

2. Lessee's Covenants

The lessee hereby covenants with the lessor as follows:

(i) To Pay Rent

That he will pay the rent hereby reserved on the date hereinbefore mentioned.

(ii) To Pay Rates, Taxes, etc.

That he will pay all rates hereby reserved on the date hereinbefore mentioned.

3. Proviso for Re-entry

PROVIDED ALWAYS that whenever any part of the rent hereby reserved shall be in arrears for one month the lessor may re-enter on the demised land and determine this lease.

4. Interpretation clause (as in Form 4).

IN WITNESS WHEREOF, etc.

13—Grant of Land Free of Rent in Lieu of Maintenance

THIS DEED OF GRANT is made on the ——— day of ——— BETWEEN AB, etc., (hereinafter called "the grantor") of the one part AND CD, etc., (hereinafter called "the grantee") of the other part.

WHEREAS—

Recitals

(1) By deed dated ——— day of ——— purporting to be made between the grantor (then a minor) and the grantee and executed on behalf of the grantor by his mother ——— purporting to act as his guardian, certain lands described therein were granted to the grantee for maintenance;

(2) The grantor brought a suit No. ——— of ——— against the grantee in the Court of the ——— to have the said deed set aside and cancelled;

(3) The parties agreed to compromise the same upon the terms that the said deed should be set aside and that the grantor should pay to the grantee a *guzara* or maintenance of Rs. ——— during her life and should also grant to her for her life a lease in respect of an area of ——— situate in ——— to be held by her free of rent for maintenance but with non-transferable rights and subject to the condition that no sub-lease of her rights in such area should be valid or have any effect after her death;

(4) A deed setting forth the terms of the said compromise was filed in the said Court on the ——— and a decree in terms of the said deed was thereupon passed.

NOW THIS DEED WITNESSES as follows:

1. Grant

That in pursuance of the said compromise decree the grantor hereby grants and transfers to the grantee ALL THAT land described in the schedule hereto TO HOLD the same to the grantee for her life subject to the terms and conditions hereinafter set forth.

2. Parties' Covenants

IT IS HEREBY AGREED AND DECLARED between the parties hereto as follows:

(i) Not to Pay any Rent

The said land shall be held and enjoyed by the grantee without the payment of rent or of any sum in the nature of rent to the grantor;

(ii) To Pay Revenue, etc.

The grantee shall pay all revenue, cesses, rates, taxes and other charges now payable or hereafter to be payable in respect of the said land during the period of this grant;

(iii) Not to Sublet, etc.

That the grantee shall not sublet, assign or mortgage any of her rights hereunder without having first obtained the permission in writing of the grantor.

(iv) Not to Grant Lease

That the grantee shall not grant or attempt to grant any lease of any part of the said land to any person except an ordinary cultivating lease and then only for a period of not more than ——— years;

(v) Not to Build

That the grantee shall not erect or construct any buildings or plant any trees upon the said land or permit or suffer any other person to do so unless she has first obtained the written permission of the grantor;

(vi) Not to Commit Waste

That the grantee shall not do, or permit or suffer any other person to do, any act or thing which might injure the said lands or decrease the value thereof;

(vii) To Realize Rent, etc.

That except as hereinbefore provided the grantee shall have powers necessary to enable her to realize for her own benefit the rents and profits of the said land;

(viii) That on the death of the grantee the said land and any building erected and trees planted thereon by the grantee or with her consent shall immediately revert to and vest in the grantor without the payment of any compensation whatever to any person claiming through or under the grantee.

3. Provisos

PROVIDED ALWAYS, etc., (*Proviso for re-entry as in para* 4(i) *of Form* 4).

4. Interpretation clause (as in para 5(ii) of Form 4)

IN WITNESS WHEREOF, etc.

14—Lease of a Brickfield

THIS LEASE, etc. (*as in Form* 4).

WITNESSES as follows:

1. Demise of Land

The lessor hereby demises to the lessee the plot of land described in the schedule hereto together with the liberties and with the reservation and exceptions hereinafter mentioned TO HOLD the said premises to the lessee from the ——— day of ———— for the term of ———— years PAYING therefor the rents and royalties hereinafter mentioned.

2. Rights of Lessee

The following liberties are included in the said demise:

(i) Lessee's Rights to get Earth and make Bricks

To get from the said land earth, clay and other materials to be used in the manufacture of bricks and to manufacture the same into bricks or tiles on any part of the said land and to sell and dispose of the bricks and tiles so manufactured but not, without the permission of the lessor, to dig any part of the said land to a depth exceeding ——— meter from the surface;

(ii) To Erect Machinery

To erect, construct and maintain such engines, machinery, kiln, clamps, ovens, workshops, buildings or cottages and other things necessary for the purpose of manufacturing, storing or selling bricks and to form such roads, communications and other conveniences on the said land as may be necessary or convenient;

(iii) To use Water and make Water Courses

For the purpose aforesaid and for the purposes of any building now or hereafter to be erected on the said land to use any water in or under the demised land and to divert the same and to make, construct or maintain any water-courses, ponds or reservoirs but not so as to interfere with the rights of adjoining owners or occupiers in respect of such water; and

(iv) General

Generally to do all things which shall be convenient or necessary for the purposes aforesaid.

3. Reservation by Lessor

The following are excepted and reserved to the landlord out of this demise—

(i) Reservation of Mines, etc.

All mines and minerals and other substances not hereinbefore expressly authorised to be got from the demised land by the lessee; and

(ii) Lessor to Work Excepted Substance

Liberty for the lessor, his tenants and agents to search for, work, carry away and dispose of the excepted substance and for such purposes to do all necessary acts on the demised land PROVIDED that in so doing the lessor shall cause as little obstruction as possible to the lessee in the use and enjoyment of his rights hereunder and will pay reasonable compensation for any damages caused by any such obstruction the amount thereof which in case of difference shall be settled by arbitration as hereinafter provided.

4. Lessee's Covenants

The lessee hereby covenants with the lessor as follows:

(i) To Pay Rent and Royalty

(a) The fixed yearly rent of Rs. ——— payable in equal half-yearly instalments on the ——— day of ——— and the ——— day of ——— in each year.

(b) A royalty to be paid on the aforesaid half yearly dates of Rs. ——— for every thousand bricks in excess of ——— and of Rs. ——— for every thousand tiles in excess of ——— which shall be manufactured on the demised land during the half year preceding such payment PROVIDED that no royalty shall be paid in respect of bricks and tiles used in any building or other erection or constructions on the demised land.

(ii) To Pay Rates, Taxes, etc.

That he will pay all existing and future rates, taxes and duties imposed or charged on the demised premises or the produce thereof or the rents and royalties hereby reserved or upon the owner or occupier in respect thereof;

(iii) Fencing

That he will fence off the demised premises from the adjoining lands and will keep the fences in good repair and condition.

(iv) To Remove Surface and Restore it

That he will before digging or opening any part of the land carefully remove the surface soil to a depth of at least ——— centimetres and lay aside and preserve the same and will after working out such part of the land forthwith level the same and replace the surface soil thereof so as to make the same fit for agricultural purposes.

(v) Not to Remove Earth, etc.

That he will not remove any earth, clay or other materials from the demised premises but will manufacture the same into bricks and tiles only on the demised premises.

(vi) To Indemnify

That he will keep the lessor indemnified against all claims, suits, damages and expenses arising out of the use of the demised land for the aforesaid purposes or in respect of any nuisance apprehended therefrom or alleged to be occasioned thereby.

(vii) To keep Accounts

That he will always keep accurate accounts showing the number of bricks and tiles manufactured on the demised premises and the number of those in respect of which exemption from royalties is claimed, the date of manufacture and other matters necessary for calculating the royalties payable hereunder and will at all reasonable times and on the lessor's request grant inspection of the same to the lessor or his agents and will permit them to take copies or extracts therefrom.

(viii) To Permit Inspection

That he will permit the lessor or his agents at all reasonable times to enter upon the demised premises to inspect the same and the works carried on and bricks and tiles manufactured therefrom.

(ix) Not to assign —as in Form 4, clause 2 (viii).

(x) To Yield up

That he will at the determination of this lease deliver up the demised premises with all kilns, clamps and other buildings and erections in such conditions as shall be in accordance with the provision of this deed save that the lessee shall if so required by the lessor remove any kilns, clamps and other erections and restore in the manner hereinbefore provided the surface of any land which has been worked and not restored.

5. Lessor's Covenants

The lessor hereby covenants with the lessee as follows:

(i) Covenant for quiet enjoyment—as in Form, 4 clause 3 (i).

(ii) Lessee to be Indemnified

That he will keep the lessee indemnified against all claims, suits and demands made by other tenants of the lessor (*or,* by any person) in respect of injury or loss alleged to be caused by the proper exercise by the lessee of his rights and liberties hereunder.

(iii) Lessee to take away Bricks, etc.

The lessee will on determination of this lease be entitled to take away all bricks, tiles, engines, machinery and other fixtures and all plants and things whatsoever except buildings, etc.

6. Provisos

PROVIDED ALWAYS and it is hereby agreed as follows:

(i) Power of re-entry—as in Form 4, Proviso (i).

(ii) Option to Surrender

That the lessee may at any time and from time to time during the said term surrender to the lessor any part of the demised land after restoring the surface thereof as hereinbefore provided and the rent will thereupon be reduced by Rs. ——— per square metre of the land so surrendered.

(iii) Option to Determine

If at any time any suit filed against the lessee for any damage or injury apprehended or alleged to be caused by reason of the proper exercise of any of the rights and liberties hereby granted is decreed, then the lessee may forthwith determine the tenancy without notice.

7. Parties' Covenants

It is hereby agreed between the parties as follows:

(i) *Arbitration Clause —as in para* 3 *of General Forms of Covenants by both parties,*

(ii) *Service of Notice —as in Form* 4, *clause* 5 (i).

(iii) *Interpretation Clause —as in Form* 4, *clause* 5 (ii).

IN WITNESS WHEREOF, etc.

15—Lease of Dwelling House

THIS LEASE, etc., (*as in Form* 4).

WITNESSES as follows—

1. Demise of dwelling house

The lessor hereby demises to the lessee ALL that dwelling house with the land fully described in the schedule hereto together with all outhouses, pucca well, motor garage, pathways, passage, garden and other appurtenances thereof, situate at ——— TO HOLD the same to the lessee from the ——— day of ——— for the term of ——— years (*or*, year to year) PAYING therefor during the said term the monthly rent of Rs. ——— (Rupees ———) payable on the first day of the month succeeding that for which the rent is due;

2. To Pay Taxes, etc.

The lessee hereby agrees that he will, during the said term (tenancy[1]), pay all rates, taxes and other charges excluding the house tax which now are or may hereafter become payable in respect of the demised property;

3. Lessor's Covenants

The lessor hereby agrees as follows:

(i) To Keep in Repairs

That the lessor shall keep the premises in good and substantial repairs during the said term and shall annually whitewash and do all necessary repairs to the outhouses and demised premises and on the lessee giving the lessor notice in writing of any special decays, defects and want of repair the lessor will within one calendar month from the receipt of such notice repair and amend the same;

(ii) When to Repair

That the lessor shall repair, when necessary, the well, the passages, pathways and the road connecting the public road with the house hereby demised and shall get the well cleaned at least once a year;

(iii) Grass

That the grass of the compound of the demised premises will be at the disposal of the lessee who will have every right to appropriate or to sell the same to any person he likes;

4. Provisos

Provisos for re-entry and option to determine—as in para 4 *of Form* 4.

5. Application of Sec. 108,Transfer of Property Act.

It is hereby agreed between the parties that in respect of the demised premises the parties hereto shall respectively have all the rights and be subject to all the liabilities of a lessor and of a lessee as set forth in section 108, Transfer of Property Act, 1882, except Clause (*m*) thereof which is hereby excluded.

6. Interpretation clause —as in clause 5 (ii) of Form 4.

IN WITNESS WHEREOF, etc.

---

1 If no term is fixed.

16—Lease of a Bungalow for Residence

THIS LEASE, etc., (*as in Form* 4).

1. Demise of Dwelling House

The lessor hereby demises to the lessee for residential purposes and for no other purpose ALL that the dwelling house situate at and known as No. ———, ——— Road, at which premises contain by measurement ——— sq. mts. or thereabout and for greater clearness are delineated on the map or plan annexed hereto and thereon shown with their boundaries coloured red together with the grounds, garden, trees, fences, hedges, ditches, wells, easements and other appurtenances whatsoever belonging to the said dwelling house and premises or usually held or enjoyed therewith TO HOLD the same to the lessee from the ——— day of ——— for the term of ——— years (*or*, from year to year, *or*, from month to month) from the ——— day of ———) PAYING therefor the monthly rent of Rs.——— on the last date of each month beginning from the ——— day of ———.

2. Lessee's Covenants

The lessee hereby agrees with the lessor as follows:

(i) To Maintain

That he will maintain the grounds and gardens appertaining to the said premises in the condition in which they are at the date of these presents subject to deterioration by natural causes beyond the control of the lessee;

(ii) To Pay Taxes, etc.

That he will pay all rates, taxes and other charges now payable or hereafter to become payable in respect of the demised premises except the house tax.

(iii) Not to Assign

That he will not without the previous consent in writing of the lessor, transfer or sublet or otherwise part with possession of the demised premises.

(iv) To use for Residential Purpose only

That he will use the demised premises for residential purposes[1] and for no other purpose except with the consent in writing of the lessor.

3. Lessor's Covenants

The lessor hereby agrees with the lessee as follows:

(i) To Maintain

That he will during the said term (tenancy[2]) maintain the demised premises in good and habitable condition and shall execute all necessary repairs including annual white-washing and colour-washing, plastering, painting, etc., and shall renew all broken panes, fittings, bolts, etc.;

(ii) To Maintain Electric Installations

That he will during the said term (tenancy) maintain the electric installations in the said premises and supply at his own expense such electric fans as may be required by the lessee;

(iii) To Repair

That he will carry out all immediate necessary repairs to the said premises to the entire satisfaction of the lessee;

4. Parties' Covenants

It is hereby agreed between the parties as follows:

(i) Application of Sec. 108, Transfer of Property Act

That in respect of the demised premises the parties hereto shall respectively have all the rights and be subject to all the liabilities of a lessor and of a lessee as set forth in section 108 of the Transfer of Property Act, 1882, except Clauses (*j*) and (*m*) thereof which are hereby excluded.

(ii) Interpretation clause—as in para 5 (ii) of Form 4.

5. Provisos for re-entry—as in para 4 (i) of Form 4.

IN WITNESS WHEREOF, etc.

---

1 A clause that "the lessee shall use the premises for the purpose of residential personal office only and not for commercial purposes" was held in *V.S. Talwar v. Prem Chandra Sharma,* (1984) 2 SCC 420 not to amount to grant of the lease for composite (residential and business office) purposes. The use of the word 'personal' before 'office' was intended to covey the idea that the tenancy was not for the purpose of accommodating a place of business.

2 If there is no fixed term.

17—Lease of a Furnished House

THIS LEASE, etc., *(as in Form 4).*

WITNESSES as follows:

1. Demise of Furnished House

As in para 1 of Form 16, adding before the words "To HOLD" the words "furnished as stated in the inventory contained in the schedule hereto".

2. Lessee's Covenants

The lessee hereby agrees with the lessor as follows:

Clauses (i) to (iv) of clause 2 of Form 16, adding

(v) Breakages and Damage

That he will replace and make good all breakages, deficiencies and damage to the furniture, fittings and effects in the dwelling house and premises which may happen during the period of his tenancy except by reasonable use and wear (and damage by accidental fire).

(vi) To yield up

That at the expiration of the said tenancy he will deliver up to the lessor possession of the demised premises with the whole of the said furniture and effects according to the said inventory in as sound, perfect and good condition as they now are in (*or,* as they were at the commencement of the tenancy, *if the tenancy commenced before the execution of the lease*) except as aforesaid.

(vii) Infectious or Contagious Disease

That in the event of any infectious or contagious disease which may require notification by virtue of any law, bye-law or rule thereunder, happening in the said house during the said tenancy, he will give written notice thereof or any other information which may be required relative thereto to the lessor before or immediately upon expiration of the tenancy and pay to the lessor the expenses of disinfecting the premises and replacing any article and things belonging to the lessor the destruction of which may be rendered necessary by such illness or may be incurred by such disinfecting and in case of default in giving such notice as aforesaid, pay to the lessor in addition the sum of Rs. ———— as liquidated damages.

(viii) Not to Let out

That the lessee shall not let out, lend or otherwise part with the possession of or remove from the demised premises any article of the said furniture, fittings or effects to any person or persons whatsoever without the previous consent in writing of the lessor nor shall allow the same to be attached by legal authority or under colour of a legal authority.

3. Lessor's Covenants

The lessor hereby agrees with the lessee as follows:

As in Form 16, adding.

(iv) That he will replace such of the articles stated in the said inventory as may become useless by reasonable use and wear (*or,* as may be damaged by accidental fire) during the term of the tenancy.

4-5. As in Form 16.

IN WITNESS WHEREOF, etc.

18—Lease-cum-Management Agreement for Hotel

THIS AGREEMENT MADE BETWEEN AB ——— hereinafter called the "Lessor" and CD ——— hereinafter called the "Transferor" and XY ——— hereinafter called "Lesee".

WITNESSETH as under:

WHEREAS the Lessor owns the land measuring ——— bearing Municipal No. and situate on ——— in the town of ———, bounded as at the foot of this deed and more fully delienated in the map annexed hereto as Annexure A and the buildings and other structures situate thereon and more fully detailed in the building plans annexed hereto as Annexure B together with all rights, easements and appurtenances whatsoever to the said property and collectively called as the 'lease premises'; AND

WHEREAS the Transferor has been running a Five Star Delux Hotel in the aforesaid premises known as Hotel ——— and the Transferor owns the requisite licences, permits, etc., and movable properties, plant machinery, furniture and fittings, electrical and other goods, telephones, television sets, vehicles, crockery, cutlery, linen and other furnishings, paintings, decorations etc., as detailed in Annexure C to this deed; AND

WHEREAS the Lessor is desirous of giving the lease premises on lease and the Transferor is desirous of transfering its hotel business and all Properties detailed in Annexure C to the Lessee; AND

WHEREAS the Lessee is desirous of acquiring the lease premises on lease and of purchasing the hotel business along with the goods mentioned in Annexure C;

NOW THIS DEED made on this ——— day of ——— witnesseth and it is agreed as under:

1. The Lessor grants and the Lessee takes on lease land measuring —- acres or thereabouts situate at ——— in the town of ——— bounded as at the foot of this deed and more fully delienated in the map annexed hereto as Annexure A and the buildings and other structures situate on the said land and more fully detailed in the building plans annexed hereto as Annexure B together with all rights, easements and appurtenances whatsoever TO HOLD the same for a period ——— years commencing from ——— for a consideration:

(*a*) A sum of Rs. —— as lease rent per annum for the first —— years of the lease and thereafter the lease rent as enhanced from time to time as herein provided under clause 7.

(*b*) Payment of ——— per cent of the gross turnover of the hotel business or a guaranteed sum of Rs.—— per annum whichever is higher.

'Gross turnover' for the purposes of this clause would mean receipts from restaurants, bars, room tarrif, convention and meeting rooms, health and sports facilities, excluding taxes.

(*c*) Interest free refundable deposit of Rs. ————.

2. The Transferor —— conveys and transfers to the Lessee all movable properties, plant and machinery, furniture, fittings and furnishings, electrical and other goods and telephones, television sets, vehicles, crockery, cutlery, linen and other furnishings, paintings, decorations, etc., as detailed in the list Annexure C to this deed and all debts and liabilities, stock in trade, cash in hand and in bank, securities, investments, etc., as shown in the Balance Sheet of ——— Hotel as on ——— signed by the parties and all licences, permits etc. concerned with the said Hotel business, and goodwill for a lump sum consideration of Rs. ———.

3. The Transferor agrees and promises not to carry on any Hotel/Restaurant business in the town of ——— or within ———— kms of the municipal limits of the town of ———— after the commencement of this lease.

4. The Lessee has deposited the sum of Rs. ——— as interest free deposit vide cheque No. ——— drawn on the ——— with the Lessor

which the Lessor hereby acknowledges.

5. The Lessee has also paid the sum of Rs. ——— to the Transferor by cheque No. —— dated —— drawn on —— as consideration for the transfer of its assets and rights as stated above, the receipt of which the Transferor hereby acknowledges.

6. The yearly lease rent of Rs. —— will be paid by the Lessee in four equal instalments on or before the —, —, — and —— (mention the four due dates of instalments). All payments will be made by crossed account payee cheques or pay orders or bank demand drafts payable at ———.

In the case of non-payment of any sum due towards lease rent, the Lessor will be entitled to appropriate and realise such sum out of the amount of security deposit and notify the same to the Lessee whereupon the Lessee shall be bound to make up the amount of security within a period of —— days after the receipt of notice. If the Lessee fails to make up the security deposit within the said period of ——— days, then, notwithstanding any other provision in this deed, the Lessee shall be liable to pay interest @ —— per cent per annum from the date on which the amount of lease rent had become payable. The payments of Lease rent to the lessor shall be clear of all deductions except those statutorily required.

7. The lease rent shall be liable to upward revision on the expiry of every ——— years by ———— per cent. The first period of years —— will for this purpose commence on the 1st day of ———— following the commencement of this lease.

8. The amount of security deposit with the Lessor will also be increased correspondingly with the increase in the lease rent by ———— per cent and the Lessee will be liable to pay to the Lessor the additional amount by way of security deposit within ——— days of the receipt of notice of increase. In case of default the Lessee shall be liable to pay interest on the said sum @ ———— per cent per annum from the date of receipt of notice of increase to the date of payment.

9. The amount of security deposit shall be returned to the Lessee on expiry of the lease and on the Lessee delivering peaceful possession of the lease premises in good condition.

10. The part of the lease rent @ ——— per cent of the gross turnover shall be payable along with the instalments of lease rent on the dates specified in clause 6 above.

11. The term of the Lease cum Management Agreement shall be renewable for one term of ——— years at the option of the Lessee provided the lessee exercises its option by notice in writing delivered to the

Lessor ——— months prior to the expiry of the first term of the lease and provided the Lessee is not in default entitling the Lessor to terminate the lease or unless the Lessor has already determined the lease.

12. The Lessee shall be entitled to peaceful possession and use of the lease premises. It is understood and agreed that the lease premises shall be used only for running a Five Star Deluxe Hotel and for such allied or ancillary purposes as are common in such hotel and tourist business.

13. The Lessee shall not change the name of the hotel i.e. ———, but it may with the written permission of the Lessor prefix or suffix its own brand name to ———.

14. The Lessee shall keep and maintain the lease premises properly and according to the standards prescribed/prevalent for Five Star Deluxe Hotels and shall run and manage the hotel business in the lease premises in conformity with such standards.

15. The Lessee shall be entitled to use the available Floor Area Ratio (FAR) as permissible at all relevant times according to the laws/regulations in force and make additions alterations to the leased buildings after obtaining necessary clearances/permission, etc., from the concerned authorities. In case the Lessee intends to carry out major alterations or additions to the existing structure or buildings and/or wants to make any change in the architectural or structural features of the leased buildings, prior approval of the Lessor shall be necessary. Such permission/approval shall not be unreasonably withheld. Such additions will become part of the leased premises and vest in the Lessor and no compensation therefor shall be payable by the Lessor to the Lessee on the termination or determination of the lease in any manner whatsoever.

16. The Lessee shall at all times keep the lease premises duly and sufficiently insured against damage by fire, riots, and natural calamaties like flood, earthquake, etc. The insurer shall be a company of repute registered and incorporated in India. The insurance premium shall be payable by the Lessee and the policies of insurance shall be in favour of the Lessor.

17. In case the lease premises or any part thereof is partially destroyed or damaged by flood, earthquake, riot or by any other cause whatsoever, the Lessee shall repair, restore and redo the same at its own cost and expense as expeditiously as possible. A notice of such damage shall, however, be given to the Lessor soon after the occurrence. The Lessor shall reimburse the Lessee for any such works to the extent of compensation received from the insurer.

18. The Lessee shall be responsible for complying with all laws

applicable to the lease premises and business including municipal laws, laws relating to environment, public nuisance, public morale.

19. The Lessor and the Transferor shall be liable to pay all taxes and other liabilities for the period upto the day preceeding the commencement of this lease. All liabilities relating to the lease premises and hotel business arising thereafter shall be borne by the Lessee.

20. The Lessee shall immediately on the commencement of the lease get all requisite permits, licenses, electric and telephone, internet connections, etc. transferred/issued in its name and the Lessor and Transferor shall render all necessary help and cooperation in that regard as may be required.

21. All amounts of security deposits in connection with electric, telephone and other connections, licenses, permits, etc., deposited by the Lessor/Transferor shall enure for the benefit of the Lessee.

22. The Lessee shall not mortgage, transfer, sublet or otherwise alienate the lease premises. The Lessee may, however, let out commercial shops/advertising spaces for such uses only as are permissible to the Lessee under this deed. All such leases/licences shall be limited in their term granted to the Lessee and they shall stand determined/terminated on the expiry/ determination/ termination of this lease.

23. The Lessee shall not create any easement on the lease premises and shall not allow any person to acquire such right. The Lessee shall also keep the lease premises free from any trespass and keep the Lessor informed of any such acts and take proper legal action to protect the property from such acts.

24. It is envisioned that on the commencement of the lease all the employees of ——— Hotel employed by the Transferor will continue in their employment and will become the employees of the Lessee with the same rights and liabilities as they have including the existing voluntary retirement scheme applicable to employees of ——— Hotel. This will, however, not apply to the managerial staff who may be dealt with according to their terms of contract with ——— Hotel.

25. The Lessor or any person authorised by him shall upon reasonable notice to the Lessee have the right of entry into the leased premises for purposes of inspection thereof.

26. The Lessor excepts and reserves unto himself all mines minerals, coals, gold-washing earth, oils, queries in or under the lease premises.

27. If by fire, tempest or flood, or violence of an army or of a mob,

any material part of the property be wholly destroyed or rendered substantially and permanently unfit for the purpose for which it has been let, the lease shall, at the option of the Lessee, be void.

28. The Lessor shall be entitled to terminate the lease only in the following circumstances:

(i) If the lease rent hereby reserved or any part thereof shall remain unpaid for ——— days after becoming payable and the shortfall in the security deposit is not made up till the expiry of ——— days after receipt of notice in terms of clause 6 of this deed.

(ii) If the Lessee has after notice of not less than ——— days in writing from the Lessor has failed to remedy any other breach of covenant of this deed.

(iii) If the Lessee has carried out any major alterations to the existing structures without the Lessor's permission in writing or has materially altered or damaged any architectural or structural features of the lease premises.

(iv) If the Lessee's business or management undergoes such material change as would adversely affect the business of leased hotel.

(v) If the Lessee has gone into liquidation.

29. On the expiry/ termination of the term of the lease, the Lessee shall deliver peaceful possession of the lease premises and the hotel assets like plant and machinery equipment, furniture, fittings and furnishings, electrical and electronic goods, telephones, television sets, vehicles, crockery, cutlery paintings, decoration materials, etc. The Lessee will be entitled to receive from the Lessor the value of such goods as determined by an approved valuer appointed by the Lessor.

30. All disputes or differences arising out of this agreement or relating thereto, if not settled mutually, shall be referred for adjudication by an arbitral tribunal consisting of three arbitrators, one to be appointed by the Lessor, one to be appointed by the Lessee and third by the two arbitrators jointly. The such third arbitrator shall be the Presiding Arbitrator. The arbitration proceedings shall be governed by the Arbitration & Conciliation Act, 1996.

31. The place of arbitration shall be ————. The language of the arbitration proceedings shall be ———.

32. All notices, demands and other communications shall be in writing addressed to the other party and delivered personally or sent by registered/speed post or telegrams.

All communications despatched through telegrams, cables, fax shall be confirmed through letters by registered/speed post.

Any party may change its address by giving written notice to the other party.

33. The expressions Lessor and Lessee in this deed will include their respective assignees, legal representatives and successors in interest as the case may be.

34. The costs of the execution of this deed, including the stamp duty and the registration fees, if any, payable thereon shall be borne by the Lessee.

Boundaries of the Lease Premises:

Bounded on: The North by
The South by
The East by
The West by

Annexure A
Annexure B
Annexure C

IN WITNESS WHEREOF

19—Form of Rent Note[1]

THIS RENT NOTE executed by me, AB, etc., (hereinafter called "the lessee") contains the terms and conditions agreed to between the lessor and the lessee as follows:-

1. Term

That the lessor has agreed to let and the lessee has agreed to occupy the house described in the schedule below for a period of eleven months commencing from the —— day of —— and the possession of the said house has been delivered to the lessee by the lessor.

2. Rent

That the lessee shall pay punctually on or before the 10th day of each month, the rent of Rs.———— in advance to the lessor at such place as the lessor may from time to time intimate to the lessee and failing such intimation the rent shall be paid to the lessor's authorised representative.

1 *See* Preliminary Note as regards legal implications of unilateral rent note.

3. Repairs

That the lessee shall keep the said house in proper state of repairs.

4. Not to Sublet

That the lessee shall not sublet or deliver possession of the house to any other person except with the previous written consent of the lessor.

5. To Vacate on Expiration of Term

That the lessee shall vacate the house at the expiry of the aforesaid period of eleven months provided that the lessee shall vacate the same earlier on receipt of one month's notice from the lessor to vacate the house and the lessee shall deliver vacant possession of the house to the lessor on the expiry of the notice period as aforesaid.

6. Notice if Lessee Vacates before Term Expires

That in case the lessee should desire to vacate the house prior to the expiry of the period of eleven months, the lessee shall give notice thereof to the lessor at least one month prior to vacating the house and delivering vacant possession of the same to the lessor.

7. Damages for use and occupation

That in case the lessee omits or fails to deliver vacant possession of the house to the lessor on the expiration or sooner determination of the lease, the lessee shall be liable to pay to the lessor as damages for use and occupation a sum equivalent to double the amount of rent for the period of continued occupation by the lessee or any other person on his behalf till the date of the recovery of the possession of the house by the lessor.

IN WITNESS WHEREOF, etc.

20—Tenancy in the form of Letter by Prospective Tenant

AB, etc. (*address*)

Dear Sir,

I gather that you would be willing to let your bungalow situate at—— on the following conditions:

1. That the rent will be Rs. ——— per month.

2. That the tenant will punctually pay on or before the 10th of each month the aforesaid rent to you or to your authorised agent.

3. That the tenant shall pay all taxes, rates and impositions whatsoever in respect of the said premises payable by the owner or occupier thereof.

4. That the tenant shall not sublet or deliver possession of the said premises or any part thereof to any other person except with your previous written consent.

5. That the tenant shall keep the said premises in proper state of repairs.

6. That the tenant will keep the electric fans, installations and sanitary fittings in proper working order and should any damage happen to the same or to the wash basins, sinks, glass panes, etc., the tenant shall at his own cost replace the same with equipment and material of the same specifications.

7. That the said premises shall be let out for eleven months only and no further on the conditions herein contained.

8. That the tenant will vacate the said premises earlier on receipt of one month's notice from you and shall deliver vacant possession of the premises on the expiry of the period fixed in the notice.

9. That in case the tenant should desire to vacate the premises prior to the expiry of the period of 11 months mentioned above, the tenant shall give notice thereof to you at least one month prior to vacating the premises and delivering the possession of the same to you.

I hereby agree to the above terms and conditions and request you kindly to give me possession of the said premises as early as possible.

Yours faithfully,

(————)

Dated: ———— Address: ————

21—Lease of Land by Government for Building a House and Lease of the House by Lessee to Government

THIS LEASE made on the ——— day of ——— BETWEEN the Governor of Uttar Pradesh (hereinafter called "the lessor") of the one part AND CD, etc., (hereinafter called "the lessee") of the other part.

WITNESSES as follows:

1. Demise of Land

The lessor hereby demises to the lessee ALL THAT plot of land containing about ——— Sq. Mts. in the town of ——— and described in the schedule hereto and delinated on the plan annexed hereto and thereon coloured red on which the lessee has built a house for the residence of the Superintendent of Police of the ——— district TO HOLD the same to the lessee from the ——— day of ——— for the term of ——— years PAYING therefor during the said term a yearly rent of Rs. ——— on the first day of ——— in each year, the first of such payments to be made on the ——— day of ——— next.

2. Sub-lease to Lessor

The lessee hereby sublets to the lessor ALL that the aforesaid plot of land with all the buildings and constructions erected and standing thereon TO HOLD the same to the lessor for the term of the lease hereinbefore recited PAYING therefor the monthly rent of Rs. ——— on the 1st day of the month succeeding that for which the rent is due, the first of such payments to be made on the ——— next.

3. Lessee's Covenants

The lessee hereby covenants with the lessor as follows:

(i) To Pay Taxes, etc.

That he will pay all rates, taxes and other charges now payable or hereafter to become payable in respect of the said premises or of any buildings now or hereafter to be erected thereon by the landlord or tenant in respect thereof;

(ii) To Keep in Repair

That he will at all times keep in good and substantial repair both externally and internally the houses and outbuildings and also the electric installations on the said premises and in particular will keep the roofs of all buildings water-tight and will white-wash such buildings both inside and outside every year after the rains and will maintain the electric installations in such repairs as will prevent leakage or waste of electric current PROVIDED that if at any time the lessee shall fail to execute such repairs and white-washing as are specified in the covenant hereinbefore contained the lessor after giving 14 days' notice to the lessee may execute the same and deduct the cost thereof from the rent payable by the lessor until such cost has been thereby paid off.

4. Lessor's Covenants

(i) To Pay Water Tax

The lessor hereby covenants with the lessee that when the said premises are occupied, he will pay the water rate and conservancy (scavenging) taxes payable in respect of the said premises and also the electric charges payable in respect of the same.

5. Provisos

PROVIDED ALWAYS and it is hereby agreed as follows:

(i) Option to Purchase Buildings

That the lessor may at any time upon giving not less than one month's notice in writing to the lessee purchase from the lessee all buildings erected by the lessee upon the said premises at a value which shall take into account the rate of rent payable by him to lessee for the said buildings and the market value of the lessee's interest then subsisting under this demise, which value shall be fixed in case the parties cannot agree by the arbitration of a board of three arbitrators, one to be nominated by each of the parties hereto, and the third appointed by such arbitrators or if either the lessor or the lessee shall neglect to appoint an arbitrator within two months after being served with a notice by the other requiring him to do so (such notice to be served on the lessee either personally or by leaving it at or posting by registered post to his last known address) then by the sole arbitration of the arbitrator appointed by such other of them, which arbitration shall be final, and immediately upon the payment by the lessor to the lessee of such value as aforesaid the demise shall absolutely determine.

(ii) Re-entry

That whenever any part of the rent hereby reserved and payable by the lessee shall be in arrears for a period of thirty days or there shall be a breach by the lessee of any of the covenants by the lessee herein contained the lessor may re-enter upon the said premises and determine this lease and on such determination all erections, buildings and fixtures on the said premises shall be forfeited to the lessor without the payment of any compensation whatever by him for or in respect of the same.

6. Interpretation Clause

It is hereby agreed between the parties that wherever the context so admits the expression "the lessor" shall include his successors and assigns and the expression "the lessee" shall include his heirs, executors, administrators and assigns.

IN WITNESS WHEREOF, etc.

22—Clauses about Buying Lessee's Structures on Determination of Tenancy and Settling Price by Arbitration

The following modification shall be made in the ordinary lease:

1. To lessee's covenants add—

(i) "The lessee will at the expiration or sooner determination of the said term peaceably and quietly surrender the said premises to the lessor together with all such erections or buildings and all such fixtures thereon or therein as may then be upon the said premises as the lessor shall desire to take over at a valuation according to the option hereinbefore reserved to the lessor, but subject to the proviso for re-entry, hereinafter contained."

"That if the lessor shall not desire to take over such erections, buildings or fixtures, it shall be lawful for the lessee to remove the same within —— months (but not later) after the expiration or determination of the said term."

2. To the lessor's covenants add—

(i) That the lessor may take over all or any of the erections, buildings and fixtures standing on the said premises at the expiration or sooner determination of the said term as he shall select on paying for them the market price to be fixed by mutual agreement and if the parties disagree by the arbitration of a board of three arbitrators, one to be named by the lessor and the other by the lessee and the third appointed by such arbitrators or if either of them, the lessor or the lessee, shall neglect to appoint an arbitrator within a fortnight after being served with a notice from the other of them requiring him to do so, then by the sole arbitration of the arbitrator appointed by the party serving such notice.

23—Lease of a Mill with Fixed and Movable Machinery, with the Concurrence of Mortgagee of Part of the Property[1]

THIS DEED OF LEASE is made on the ——— day of ——— BETWEEN AB, etc., (hereinafter called the "lessor") of the first part AND CD, etc., (hereinafter called the "mortgagee") of the second part AND EF, etc., (hereinafter called "the lessee") of the third part.

---

1 Such a composite lease of building along with the equipment, or lease of a factory including lease of a building alongwith the machinary, is valid: *Bhagyashree Combines* v. *Distt. Magistrate*, AIR 1998 Kant 328 (DB); followed *Uttamchand* v. *S.M. Lalwani*, AIR 1965 SC 716; *Dwaraka Prasad* v. *Dwaraka Das*, AIR 1975 SC 1758. Held that such a lease does not amount to a lease of a building within the meaning of rent control law.

WHEREAS—

(1) The lessor is the owner of the mill and fixed machinery and other property described in the first and second schedules hereto and of all the machinery and movable property described in the third schedule hereto;

(2) The mortgagee is in possession of the mill and fixed machinery and properties described in the first and second schedules hereto under a mortgage deed dated ——— executed by the lessor for a term of ten years;

(3) The lessor has now agreed to grant a lease of all the properties mentioned in the first, second and third schedules hereto to the lessee; AND

(4) The mortgagee has, at the request of the lessor, agreed to join in the manner hereinafter appearing in the lease of the said premises described in the first and second schedules hereto.

NOW THIS DEED WITNESSES as follows:

(1) Demise of Mill and Machinery

In consideration of the rent hereinafter reserved and of the covenants on the part of the lessee hereinafter contained the lessor with the consent (hereby testified) of the mortgagee so far as regards the premises described in the first and second schedules hereto hereby demises to the lessee all that mill and machinery fixed and movable and all and every other property described in the first, second and third schedules hereto TO HOLD the same to the lessee from the ——— day of ———for a term of 20 years PAYING yearly during the said term and so in proportion for any less time than a year the rent of Rs. ——— for the properties mentioned in the first and second schedules hereto and the rent of Rs. ———— for the property mentioned in the third schedule hereto by equal quarterly instalments on the first days of January, April, July and October in each year the first of such payments to be made on the first day of January next.

(2) Lessee's Covenant

The lessee hereby covenants with the lessor as follows:

(i) To Pay Rent

To pay during the term hereby granted on the days hereinbefore appointed the quarterly rent of Rs. ——— in respect of the property mentioned in the third schedule to the lessor and the yearly rent of Rs. —— in respect of the properties mentioned in the first and second schedules hereto to the mortgagee during the continuance of the said mortgage and to the lessor thereafter.

(ii) To Pay Taxes, etc.—as in clause 2 (ii) of Form 4.

(iii) Not to make additions—as in clause 2 (iv) of Form 4.

(iv) To Keep in Repairs

As in clause 2 (*v*) *of Form* 4 adding "and also all machinery whether fixed or not and other movable properties hereby demised save and except in case of fire, storm, tempest and earthquake affecting the premises mentioned in the first and second schedules hereto," before the words "in good repair and condition".

(v) To Permit Lessor and Mortgagee to Inspect, etc.

To permit the mortgagee as regards the premises described in the first and second schedules hereto and the lessor as regards all the premises hereby demised with his agents to enter demised premises and examine the state of repairs and conditions thereof and of all machineries and other movable property hereby demised and to repair and make good all defects of which notice in writing shall have been given by the mortgagee or lessor as the case may be to the lessee within ——— months after the giving of such notice.

(vi) To Permit Lessor to Repair on Lessee's Default

To permit the lessor as regards all the property hereby demised, in case of lessee's default to make repair in accordance with the covenant herein before contained, to enter upon the said premises and repair the same and the machineries whether fixed or not and all other moveable property hereby demised in accordance with the aforesaid covenant for repair and to pay to the lessor on demand all expenses incurred by the lessor on such repairs.

(vii) To Insure

The insure, etc., (*as in clause* 5 *in Lessee's General Covenants on page* 463 *ante*) adding after the words "erected thereon" the words "and all machinery fixed or not and all other movable property hereby demised."

(viii) To Deliver Possession on Determination

On the determination of this lease to deliver up possession, etc., (*as in Clause* 16 *in Lessee's General Covenants on page* 465 *ante*).

(ix) To Comply with Requirements of Law Regarding Factories

To comply with requirements of the law for the time being in force regarding factories and their working imposed upon the owner of the demised premises and at all times during the said term to indemnify and keep indemnified the lessor and the mortgagee against any breach or non-observance thereof.

(x) To estimate dilapidation— As in clause 17 in General Covenants of the Lessee on page 465 ante.

3. Lessor's Covenants

The lessor hereby covenants with the lessee as follows:

(*i*) *For Quiet Enjoyment*

As in clause 3(*i*) *of Form* 4.

(*ii*) *For Renewal*

As in clause 3(*ii*) *of Form* 4.

(*iii*) *For Purchasing Working Stock*

The lessor will on the expiration or sooner determination of the term of this tenancy take and purchase from the lessee all the working stock upon the said demised premises at a valuation as working stock.

4. Proviso

PROVIDED ALWAYS and it is hereby agreed that—

(i) For Re-entry

As in Clause 2 *of the Proviso at page 470 ante.*

(ii) Option to Determine Lease

If the lessor shall at the end of the first ———— year desire to determine the tenancy hereby created, etc., (*as in clause* 6 *of the Provisos at page 471 ante*).

(*iii*) The lessor shall be entitled, on giving written notice of his intention in that behalf to the lessee at least one calendar month before the determination of the present tenancy or within one week of the determination thereof by re-entry, to purchase from the lessee any additional machinery or effects of the nature of the machinery or effects hereby demised which may during the term of this tenancy be put or erected in or upon the premises by the lessee at a valuation to be made by three persons one to be appointed by each and the third to be appointed by those two persons and in case the lessor shall not purchase the same it shall be lawful for the lessee to remove the same within reasonable time.

(iv) Suspension of Rent in Case of Fire

As in clause 5 *of the Provisos at page 471 ante.*

5. Parties Covenant

It is hereby agreed between the parties as follows:

(*i*) *Arbitration Clause*

As in clause 3 *of covenants by both parties at page 469 ante.*

(*ii*) *Cost of Deed*

As in clause 4 *of covenants by both parties at page 469 ante.*

(*iii*) *Cost of Stamp Duty*

As in clause 5 *of covenants by both parties at page 469 ante.*

(iv) *Interpretation Clause*

As in clause 6 *of covenants by both parties at page 469 ante.*

IN WITNESS WHEREOF, etc.

24—Lease of an Equipment[1]

THIS DEED OF LEASE, etc., (*as in Form* 4).

1. Definitions

In this lease, unless the context otherwise requires, the following expressions shall have the following meanings, namely:

(i) Commencement Date

The commencement date shall be the earliest of (*a*) the date of last payment by the lessor to the manufacturer, or (*b*) the date of delivery or installation of the equipment, or (*c*) that date which is seven days after the date on which written intimation is sent by the manufacturer to the lessor and/or the lessee that the equipment is ready for delivery with the manufacturer.

(ii) Equipment

The equipment described in the schedule to this lease, purchased by

---

1 It does not amount to lease of immovable property. In *Board of Revenue* v. *K. Venkataswami Naidu*, AIR 1955 Mad 620 (FB) a lease of properties relating to a touring cinema was held not to be a lease of immovable property. In *C.R.K. Parsad* v. *Sub-Collector*, AIR 1985 AP 390, an agreement for distribution, exploitation, screening and exhibition of a film for a certain period was held not to be a lease or mortgage of immovable property.

the lessor at the request of the lessee, from the manufacturers named in the schedule, leased to the lessee for industrial use and (where the context so admits) any individual items comprised in the equipment including all alterations, replacements and/or additions during the period of this lease.

2. Terms of Lease

(i) Commencement of Lease

The lessor hereby gives on lease, and the lessee hereby takes on lease, the equipment, for a fixed period of ——— from the commencement date, subject to the terms, conditions, covenants and stipulations contained herein and in the schedule.

(ii) To Pay Rent and Interest

The lessee shall pay to the lessor from the commencement date, lease rentals specified in the schedule, regularly and punctually, without any deduction or abatement, irrespective of whether the equipment is in use by the lessee or not.

Arrears of lease rentals shall carry interest at the rate of ——— per cent per annum, compounded with monthly rests, from the due date specified in the schedule till the date of actual payment.

(iii) To Yield up Possession

Upon termination of this lease by efflux of time, or otherwise, the lessee shall, at its own cost and expense, forthwith, deliver or cause to be delivered to the lessor the equipment, at such time and place as may be directed by the lessor, in good repair, order and condition (subject to normal wear and tear).

3. Lessee's Warranties

The lessee warrants that:

(*i*) The execution of this lease and the use and operation of the equipment by the lessee will not:

(a) contravene any provision of any statutes, rules and regulations which the lessee is subject to and the lessee's Memorandum and the Articles of Association;

(b) result in any breach of any agreement or arrangement to which the lessee is a party.

(*ii*) The lessee has obtained all consents, licences, approvals, etc., as are necessary for or in connection with the execution, validity and enforceability of this lease and for the storage, installation, use and operation of the equipment and undertakes to keep them effective and in force during the period of this lease and till the equipment is delivered back to the lessor in good order and condition.

4. Lessee's Covenants

The lessee shall:

(i) Not to Remove

Keep the equipment, at all times, in its control at its plant specified in the schedule and not remove the same therefrom without the prior written permission of the lessor;

(ii) Affix Lessor's Name plate

Affix a name plate or other mark on the equipment identifying the sole and exclusive ownership thereof of the lessor and not allow or permit the same to be removed or defaced;

(iii) Not to Claim Ownership

Hold the equipment as the bailee of the lessor and not claim any right, title or interest in the equipment other than that of a lessee or contest the lessor's sole and exclusive ownership thereof;

(iv) To Repair and Keep in Good Condition

Use and operate the equipment carefully and maintain the same in good working condition and repair at its own cost and expense, and comply with all statutory and other requirements of law, rules, regulations and directions applicable to the storage or installation or governing use and operation of the equipment, and not to do or omit to be done any act or thing by which the warranties would be invalidated or become unenforceable wholly or partly.

(v) To Pay Taxes, etc.

Punctually and duly pay or cause to be paid all rates, taxes, licence fees, surcharges, registration charges and other outgoings payable in respect of the equipment or the storage, installation, use or operation thereof or of the premises where the same is kept and on demand produce to the lessor all receipts and other evidence of such payment;

(vi) To Insure

Insure the equipment in the name of the lessor for its full replacement value, against all risks including transit, erection, fire, riot, theft, civil commotion and such other risks (including third party risks) as the lessor may require and pay all insurance premia and renew the insurance policies from time to time, under advice to lessor and not do or omit to do or be done or permit or suffer any act, deed or thing which might or could prejudicially vitiate or affect any such insurance.

(vii) Authorise Lessor to Act in Case of Claim

In the event of any claim arising under any such insurance, give to the lessor immediate written intimation thereof and comply with the instructions of the lessor in connection therewith and permit and hereby authorise the lessor to take all steps, actions and proceedings and adjust or compromise any such claim as the lessor may think fit and to receive any moneys payable in respect thereof and to give effectual receipts and discharge therefor and generally to act for and on behalf of the lessee in respect of all such claims as the lessor may think fit. The lessor shall be entitled to receive and retain to the exclusion of the lessee and without thereby divesting itself of the property in the equipment or in the salvage thereof all moneys payable with respect to such claims.

(viii) Reimburse on Failure to Insure

In the event of failure on the part of the lessee to insure the equipment or to pay the insurance premia, then the lessor may insure the equipment and/or pay the insurance premia as above and shall forthwith on receipt of a notice of demand from the lessor reimburse all sums so paid by it together with interest thereon at the rate of ———— per cent per annum from the date of such payment by the lessor.

(ix) To Allow Inspection

Permit the lessor or all persons authorised by the lessor at all reasonable times (immediately in case of an emergency) to inspect, view and examine the state and condition of the equipment and for the purpose, permit entry in the premises where the equipment is used, stored or lying.

(x) Not to Transfer or Encumber

Not transfer, assign or otherwise dispose of or purport to transfer, assign or dispose of the lessee's rights or obligations or interest hereunder by way of mortgage, charge or sub-lease, sale or other assignment, hypothecation, pledge, hire, encumbrance, conducting arrangement, licence, or otherwise in any manner part with the possession of the equipment or any part thereof or allow or purport to allow or create any lien, charge, attachment or other claim of whatsoever nature on the equipment or any part thereof.

(xi) Indemnify Lessor

Indemnify and keep indemnified the lessor, at all times, against any loss or claim or demand arising out of the storage, installations, use or operation of the equipment, and hold the lessor harmless, against all losses, damages, claims, penalties, expenses, suits or proceedings of whatsoever nature made, suffered or incurred consequent thereupon and for this purpose take out such workmen's compensation or third party insurance cover as may be necessary, customary or the practice in the business carried on by the lessee or as may be directed by the lessor, in that behalf.

(xii) To Pay Costs, etc.

On demand pay to the lessor all costs, charges and expenses incurred by the lessor in connection with the equipment or for the preservation, protection or enforcement of the lessor's rights or for re-taking or repossessing of the equipment, with interest thereon at the rate of ——— per cent per annum from the date of the incurring such costs, charges and expenses by the lessor till payment.

(xiii) Not to Claim Lessor's Statutory Allowance, deduction, etc.

Not claim any relief by way of any deduction, allowance or grant available to the lessor as owner of the equipment, under the Income-tax Act, 1961 or under any other statute, rules, regulations or guidelines issued by the Government of India or any statutory authority and not to do or omit to be done any act, deed or thing whereby the lessor is deprived wholly or partly and that the lessee shall, at the end of each financial year of the lease, provide to the lessor such information as it may require to claim relief by way of any deduction, allowance or grant, as the owner of the equipment, and the lessee undertakes to comply with and observe, at all times, the terms and conditions to be complied with or observed in respect of the use and operation of the equipment to entitle the lessor to obtain such relief.

(xiv) To Furnish Audited Accounts, etc.

Furnish to the lessor its audited Balance Sheet and Profit and Loss Account simultaneously with the issuance thereof to the shareholders of the lessee and also such other information as may be required by the lessor from time to time.

5. Acceptance of the Equipment

(i) The lessor hereby appoints the lessee as its agent to inspect, receive delivery and installation of the equipment from the manufacturer. By accepting the equipment the lessee shall be deemed to have examined the equipment and to have found it complete, in proper order and condition and entirely fit for its purpose and the lessee does not and will not, at any time, have any claim against the lessor in respect of or arising out of the equipment.

(ii) Consequence of Failure to take Delivery

In the event that the lessee shall refuse or be unable for any reason to accept delivery and installation of the equipment, other than for reason of the manufacturer failing to supply the same in satisfactory order and condition, the lessor shall be entitled to terminate this lease at any time, within one month thereafter, by a notice in writing to the lessee and the lessee shall, on demand, pay to the lessor all costs of the equipment together with interest thereon at the rate of ——— per cent per annum, and expenses incurred by the lessor for insuring, transporting, storing and maintaining the equipment and for its disposal and/or lease to third party or in any other manner whatsoever, without prejudice to the lessor's remedies for damages for breach of contract.

(iii) Lessor not Responsible for Delay in Delivery

The lessor shall not be responsible for any direct, indirect or consequential loss to the lessee or any third party arising from any delay in delivery and/or installation of the equipment either by the action of the manufacturer or otherwise howsoever or by reason of any delay in the commencement.

6. Lessee's Confirmations

The lessee acknowledges, represents, declares, agrees and confirms that:

(i) Suitability of Equipment

The equipment is of the required size, design, capacity and manufacture, suitable for its purpose and is selected by the lessee relying entirely on its own judgement and not on the statements or representations, if any, made by the lessor or its agents or servants.

(ii) Selection of Equipment

The lessor is not the manufacturer or dealer of the equipment and that the essential function of the lessor in this lease is to purchase the equipment selected by the lessee from the manufacturer designated by the lessee.

(iii) Lessor's Liability Excluded

The lessor shall in no way be liable, or responsible to the lessee for any liability, claim, loss, damage, or expense of any kind or nature whatsoever arising from the transportation and delivery of the equipment, lease of the equipment, its storage, installation, use or operation or its failure to operate or perform or otherwise howsoever.

(iv) Lessor's Ownership Acknowledged

As between the lessor and the lessee and their respective successors in title, the equipment shall remain the personal property of and shall continue to be in the ownership of the lessor.

7. Imposts, Taxes and Other Clauses

(*i*) The lessee shall during the period of this lease and till the equipment is delivered back to the lessor in good working order and condition, bear all imposts, charges and other duties, taxes and penalties as may be levied from time to time by the Government or any other authority pertaining to or in respect of this lease.

(ii) Lessee to Pay Sales Tax, etc.

The lessee agrees that the transaction covered by this lease is not understood to be a sale eligible to tax under the existing GST laws. If, however, by reason of any amendment of any law, Central or State, this transaction is held to be exigible to tax, as a sale or otherwise, either in whole or in part, or any input or material or equipment used or supplied in execution of or in connection with the lease are exigible to tax, the lessee shall pay such tax immediately upon the same becoming payable,.

(iii) To Reimburse Lessor

If the lessee fails to pay monies referred to in (*i*) and (*ii*) above, the lessor may pay the same and the lessee shall reimburse all sums so paid together with interest thereon at the rate of ——— per cent per annum from the date of payment till such reimbursement.

8. Termination by Default

The lessor shall be entitled without prejudice to any other rights or remedies which the lessor may have under this lease or otherwise in law, to terminate this lease if the lessee fails or neglects to observe or perform or commits or allows to be committed a breach of any of the terms, conditions, provisions, or stipulations of this lease on its part to be observed and performed (other than failure to pay any sum hereunder when due and payable) and if such breach is remediable, fails to remedy the same within fourteen days of notice by the lessor specifying such default and requiring such default to be remedied.

9. Consequence of Termination by Default

Upon termination of the lease (other than by efflux of time) consequent upon default hereunder by the lessee, the lessee shall forthwith pay to the lessor:

(*i*) a sum equal to the total amount of rent payable during the term of this lease which on termination had not been paid plus a default premium equal to 10 per cent of the rentals payable under this agreement which on termination were unpaid and past due.

(*ii*) the cost of all repairs and maintenance of the equipment to render and maintain it in good working order and condition and all costs, charges and expenses incurred by the lessor in re-possessing the equipment and in enforcing its remedies howsoever occasioned. The parties hereto agree and record that the amounts to be paid by the lessee to the lessor as aforesaid have been *bona fide* and satisfactorily estimated to be the proper and reasonable amount that may be suffered by the lessor as and by way of liquidated damages.

Notwithstanding anything to the contrary herein contained, in the event of such termination the lessor shall also be entitled to sell, re-lease or otherwise dispose of the equipment in such manner as the lessor may think fit and the lessor shall not be bound to account to the lessee in any manner whatsoever.

10. Time to be of Essence

Time shall be of essence of this lease in so far as it relates to the observance or performance by the lessee of all or any of its obligations hereunder.

11. Registration Charges, etc.

The lessee shall pay to the lessor upon demand the stamp duty and registration charges, if any, payable on this lease and its duplicate and all lease deeds, agreement deeds, writings and documents executed by and between the parties hereto in respect of the equipment.

12. Jurisdiction

It is agreed by and between the parties that the civil courts at ——— shall have the exclusive jurisdiction in respect of any matter, claim or dispute arising out of or in any way relating to this lease.

IN WITNESS WHEREOF, etc.

25—Lease of Tube Well to Irrigation Department for the Purpose of Working it (Lessee Paying Royalty)

THIS LEASE made, etc.

WITNESSES as follows:

1. Demise of Tube Well

The lessor hereby demises to the lessee ALL that tube-well standing on plot No.——— in village ———, District ——— with the pumping plant erected thereon and all machineries, accessories and fixtures appertaining thereto together with the land on which the said tube well, machineries, accessories and fixtures stand all existing watercourses used in carrying water of the said tube-well to different fields TO HOLD the same to the lessee from the ——— for the term of ——— years PAYING therefor during the said term by way of rent the royalty hereinafter mentioned on the dates hereinafter specified.

2. Lessee's Covenants

The lessee hereby covenants with the lessor as follows:

(i) To Keep in Repairs

To maintain the demised premises including the said machinery and accessories in proper repairs and working order and condition;

(ii) To Pay all Charges

To keep his own staff for running the pumps and to pay all charges for the energy consumed by the motor;

(iii) Royalty

To pay to the lessor a royalty of 80 paisa for every unit of energy consumed by the lessee in pumping water from the said tube well, whether the water is used on the lessee's field or otherwise, such royalty to be determined by the meter reading on the ——— and the ——— and to be paid on the ——— and the ——— following in each year.

3. Proviso

PROVIDED ALWAYS *and it is hereby agreed between the parties hereto as follows:*

(i) Termination if Well becomes Useless

If the said tube-well at any time fails to give any supply of the water or gives so little water that it becomes necessary to replace it and the lessor does not on being called upon to do so pay the cost of replacing it, the lessee may determine this lease.

(ii) Proviso for re-entry—as in Clasue 4 (i) of Form 4.

4. Arbitration

It is hereby agreed between the parties hereto as follows:

(i) Any dispute between the parties hereto regarding the terms of this lease or the necessity of replacing the tube-well or any other matter arising out of this contract shall be referred to the Chief Engineer, Irrigation Department, Western Circle, whose decision thereon shall be final and binding on the parties.

(ii) Interpretation clause—as in Clause 5 *(ii) of Form* 4.

IN WITNESS WHEREOF, etc.

26— Lease by or to Limited Company

Necessary modifications

1. In Parties, the Company will be described as "the ——— Company Limited, a Company within the meaning of the Companies Act, 1956, and having its registered office at ——— (hereinafter referred to as "the Company") and should be described throughout as the Company instead of lessor or lessee.

2. The proviso for re-entry if the lessee is a Company will instead of insolvency provide for the contingency "if the Company shall enter into liquidation whether compulsory or voluntary or if their assigns not being a Company shall be adjudged insolvents, etc."

3. In the interpretation clause "the Company" shall include "its assigns."

4. The "service of notice" clause will provide for a notice on the Company being left at its registered office.

5. The lease will otherwise be as if it was by one or two joint tenants.

27—Lease on behalf of a Minor[1]

THIS LEASE is made on the ——— day of ——— BETWEEN XY, etc., acting as guardian of the property of AB, etc., a minor (who is hereinafter called "the lessor") of the one part AND CD, etc., (hereinafter called "the lessee") of the other part.

WHEREAS—

1. The lessor is a minor and the said XY is his father and natural guardian under the Hindu Law (*or*, has been appointed as the guardian of his property by an order of the District Judge of ——— dated the ——) (*or*, by the Will of MN, the deceased father of the lessor dated the ———).

2. The said XY acting on behalf of the lessor has agreed with the lessee to grant a lease of the property mentioned in the schedule hereto.

3. The District Judge of ———— has by his order dated ———— granted previous permission to the said XY to grant the proposed lease.[2]

NOW THIS DEED WITNESSES as follows:

1. The said XY on behalf of the lessor and in exercise of his power as natural guardian (*or*, the power conferred on him by the aforesaid Will dated the ———) (*or*, conferred on him, by the Guardians and Wards Act, 1890) (*or*, with the previous permission of the said District Judge granted by him by his order dated the ———)[3] hereby demises, etc., (*as in appropriate Form of lease*).

2. *Lessor's covenants as in the appropriate Form of lease.*

---

1 A minor cannot grant or accept a lease, as acceptance also involves covenants on the part of the lessee. The guardian of his property may grant a lease. The guardian may, in case of a Hindu, be his natural guardian who has under section 8 (2) (b) of the Hindu Minority and Guardianship Act, 1956, no power to grant leases for any term exceeding five years or extending more than one year beyond the date on which the minor will attain majority, except with the previous permission of the court. He may also be guardian appointed by will or other instrument or by court. If he is also declared guardian under the Guardians and Wards Act, the court may, notwithstanding any restriction in the instrument of his appointment, grant him permission to grant a lease (Sec. 28). A lease for a longer term requires the court's previous permission (Sec. 29). The lease may be made either in the name of the minor or guardian but in the latter case it should be made expressly on minor's behalf, [vide Introduction, Part II: (c) Parties to the deed: (vii) Minors, *ante*].

2 Necessary in case of natural guardian of Hindu minor or if the guardian has been appointed or declared by Court and the lease is for more than five years or extends more than one year beyond the ward's minority, or the lease is prohibited by the instrument of appointment and the court grants permission notwithstanding this prohibition.

3 Necessary if the certificated guardian is not authorised to grant the lease without court's permission.

3. The said XY on behalf of and so as to bind the lessor but so as not to impose any liability on himself except as to his own acts or default hereby covenants with the lessee as follows:

(*As in appropriate Form of lease*),

4. *Provisos, etc.*

As in appropriate form of lease, except that power of re-entry should be given to the lessor and not to the guardian.

IN WITNESS WHEREOF, etc.

28—Lease on behalf of Mentally ill Person[1]

THIS LEASE made on the ——— day of ——— BETWEEN XY, etc., Manager of the property of AB, etc., a mentally ill person (who is hereinafter called "the lessor") appointed by an order of the District Judge of ——— dated ——— acting on behalf of the lessor of the one part AND CD, etc., (hereinafter called "the lessee") of the other part.

WITNESSES as follows:

1. The said XY, acting on behalf of the lessor under permission granted to him in this behalf by the District Judge of ——— by his order dated ——— hereby demises, etc.,

Other clauses as in Form 26.

29—Lease by Trustees[2]

THIS LEASE made on the ——— day of ——— by AB, etc., CD, etc., and EF, etc., trustees of the estate of XY appointed as such by a deed of trust dated the ——— executed by the said XY, acting under the power conferred on them by the said deed of trust (hereinafter called "the lessor"), etc., AND, etc.

Other clauses as in appropriate Form of lease

1 The manager of the property of a mentally ill person appointed by court can alone grant a lease of such person's and that too with the court's permission (Sec. 59, Mental Health Act).

2 Sec. 36 of the Trusts Act 1882 (General authority of trustee) provides that except with the permission of the principal civil court of original jurisdiction, no trustee shall lease trust property for a term exceeding 21 years, nor without reserving the best yearly rent that can be reasonably obtained.

30—Lease by Managing Trustees of a Charitable Institution[1]

THIS LEASE is made on the ——— day of ——— BETWEEN AB and CD managing trustees acting on behalf of the trustees of the Mayaram Female Hospital Trust (hereinafter called "the lessors"), etc.

WHEREAS—

1. One XY, owner of a large estate including the land hereby demised by a deed of endowment dated the ——— created a trust called the Mayaram Female Hospital Trust and endowed the said estate for the upkeep of the said Mayaram Female Hospital at ——— and appointed the lessors and certain other persons as trustees for carrying out the objects of the said trust.

2. By a scheme of management settled by an order of the District Judge of ——— dated ——— the lessors have been appointed managing trustees for the management of the said estate and have been empowered to grant lease of the land comprised in the said estate.

NOW THIS DEED WITNESSES as follows:

1. The lessors as such managing trustees as aforesaid and acting under the powers granted to them under the aforesaid scheme of management on behalf of all the trustees of the said Mayaram Female Hospital Trust hereby demise, etc., *as in appropriate Form of lease.*

31—Lease by Way of Renewal—When the Original Lease has not yet Expired

(*With variation if there has been a derivation of the interests of the lessor and the lessee*).

THIS LEASE is made on the ——— day of ——— BETWEEN *(as in Form* 4*).*

WHEREAS—

1. By a lease dated ——— the property described in the schedule thereto was demised by AB, etc., to CD, etc., for a term of ——— years subject to the rent thereby reserved and the lessee's covenants therein contained.

2. The interest of the said CD in the said property is now vested in the

---

1 The Trusts Act 1882 does not apply to public or private religious or charitable endowments. They are governed by personal law and by the Charitable and Religious Trusts Act 1920, Charitable Endowments Act 1890 and the Religious Endowments Act 1863 apart from various State enactments and Sec. 92, C.P.C.

lessee, and that of the said AB in the lessor.[1]

3. The lessee has now requested the lessor to grant a lease to him (in accordance with the lessor's covenant in this behalf contained in the aforesaid lease)[2] for a further period of ——— years from the date of expiry of the term of the aforesaid lease on the terms hereinafter expressed (which the lessor has agreed to do).[3]

NOW THIS DEED WITNESSES as follows:

1. The lessor hereby demises to the lessee ALL those premises demised by the aforesaid lease (with the same exceptions and reservations as are therein expressed) TO HOLD the same to the lessee from the ——— for a term of ——— years subject to the payment in the same manner and on the same days of a yearly rent of the same amount as that reserved by the aforesaid lease (*or,* a yearly rent of Rs. ———) and subject to and with the benefit of such covenants (other than the covenant for renewal), provisos and conditions as are contained in the aforesaid lease.

2. It is hereby mutually agreed by and between the lessor and the lessee that they will respectively perform and observe the several covenants, provisos and conditions in the aforesaid lease (except the ——) as fully as if the same were repeated at length in this lease with such modifications only as are necessary to make them applicable to this demise and the parties hereto.

3. PROVIDED ALWAYS that if the aforesaid lease is determined under the proviso for re-entry therein contained this deed shall become absolutely void.

IN WITNESS WHEREOF, etc.

32—Lease by Reference to Expired Lease

THIS LEASE etc., (*as in Form* 4).

WITNESSES as follows:

1. The lessor hereby demises, etc., (*as in Form* 4).

2. Except as to the term of years hereby granted and the rent hereby reserved this demise is made upon the same terms and subject to the same covenants, provisos and conditions as were contained in the lease dated the —— day of ——— and made between the parties hereto (*or,* between

---

1 Omit if the parties are original lessor and lessee.

2 These words may be omitted if there is no renewal clause in existing lease.

3 If the renewal is in accordance with a renewal clause in the existing lease, these words may be omitted.

AB, etc., and CD, etc.,) as if the same were herein set forth at length with such modifications only as are necessary to make same applicable to the present demise and the parties hereto.

3. The lessee hereby covenants with the lessor to pay the rent hereby reserved on the dates and in manner aforesaid.

4. The lessor and the lessee hereby agree with each other that they will respectively perform and observe the several covenants, provisos and conditions subject to which the demise is made as aforesaid as ought on his part to be observed and performed.

IN WITNESS WHEREOF, etc.

33—Surrender of Lease by Endorsement on the Lease

(With variation for the case of death of original parties)

In consideration of the sum of Rs. ——— paid by the within-named lessor to within-named lessee (*or,* by AB, etc., the successor-in-title of the within-named lessor to CD, etc., the successor-in-title of the within-named lessee), the receipt of which the said lessee (*or,* CD) hereby acknowledges, the said lessee (*or,* CD) hereby surrenders and yields up to the said lessor (*or,* AB) ALL the premises comprised in the within-written lease to the intent that the said lease and the estate and interests of the said lessee (*or,* CD) in the said premises thereunder be forever extinguished AND the said lessee (*or,* CD) hereby releases the said lessor (*or,* AB) from all obligations arising under the within-written lease AND the said lessor (*or,* AB) hereby releases the said lessee (*or,* CD) from the claims, demands and liabilities in respect of the within-written lease.

IN WITNESS WHEREOF, etc.

34—Surrender of Lease, by a Separate Deed

THIS DEED OF SURRENDER is made on the —— day of ——— BETWEEN AB, etc. (hereinafter called "the lessee") of the one part AND CD, etc. (hereinafter called "the lessor") of the other part.

WHEREAS the lessor granted to the lessee a ——— years/perpetual lease of the land mentioned in the schedule hereto on an annual rent of Rs. ———;

AND WHEREAS the lessee has agreed with the lessor to surrender to him the said land by relinquishing all the right and interest which the lessee holds in respect of the same under the lease hereinbefore recited in consideration of a sum of Rs. ———.

NOW THIS DEED WITNESSES as follows:

1. In pursuance of the aforesaid agreement and in consideration of the sum of Rs. ——— paid by the lessor to the lessee (the receipt of which the lessee hereby acknowledges) the lessee hereby surrenders and yields up to the lessor the property mentioned in the schedule hereto and demised by the lease hereinbefore recited with all the appurtenances thereto belonging TO the intent that the said term/perpetuity created by the said lease and all the estate and interest of the lessee in the said property under or by virtue of the said lease may be absolutely and forever extinguished from the date hereof and the said property may revert to the lessor.

2. The lessee hereby releases the lessor from all obligations arising under the said lease.

IN WITNESS WHEREOF, etc.

35—Surrender of a Portion of Demised Land and Proportionate Reduction of Rent

THIS DEED OF SURRENDER made, etc., (*as in Form* 34).

Recital of Lease

WHEREAS by a deed of lease dated ——— the lessor granted a heritable and non-transferable permanent lease of the land described in the schedule hereto to the lessee on an annual rent of Rs. ———;

AND WHEREAS the aforesaid permanent lease comprised among other lands the plot No. ——— containing an area of ——— but as the same has been in actual possession of XY and his ancestors as statutory tenants the lessee could not obtain possession thereof;

Agreement to Surrender a Part

AND WHEREAS the lessee has agreed with the lessor for the surrender to him of the said plot No. ——— in consideration of the reduction of rent hereinafter agreed to be made.

NOW THIS DEED WITNESSES as follows:

1. Surrender

In pursuance of the said agreement and in consideration of the reduction of rent hereinafter agreed to be made, the lessee hereby surrenders and yields up to the lessor the said plot No. ——— etc., and all the estate, right, title, interest, claim or demand whatsoever of the lessee into, out of or upon the said plot TO the intent that the perpetuity created by the said permanent lease as to the said plot and all estate and interest of the lessee in the said plot under or by virtue of the said permanent lease be absolutely and forever extinguished from the date hereof and the said plot may revert to the lessor.

2. Parties' Covenants

It is hereby agreed and declared as follows:

(i) *Reduction of Rent*
In consideration of the surrender hereinbefore contained the yearly rent of Rs. ——— reserved by the said permanent lease shall be from the year ——— *Fasli,* be reduced to the sum of Rs. ——— payable at the time and in the manner mentioned in the said permanent lease.

(ii) *Other Covenants to Remain in Force*
All the covenants and conditions contained in the said permanent lease shall continue in force in respect of and so far as they apply to the land remaining subject to the said permanent lease with such modifications as may be necessary in consequence of these presents.

IN WITNESS WHEREOF, etc.

36—Surrender of Lease Accepted in Consideration of Lessee Delivering His Building, etc.

THIS DEED OF SURRENDER, etc., (*as in Form* 34).

Recital

WHEREAS by a lease dated the ——— the lessor demised to the lessee the land described in the schedule hereto for a term of ——— years.

AND WHEREAS the lessee spent over Rs. ——— to turn the said land into a successful farm by reclaiming it, making *Kachcha* road and a small building on it and fixing a small sugar centrifugal, rice huller, persian wheels, etc., but on account of floods in the river, hard and clay nature of the soil and *gaudar* grass the enterprise has been a total failure and further investment of money on it is now beyond the means of the lessee and owing to personal circumstances he was unable to cultivate the land for the past two years or to do anything on it;

AND WHEREAS in view of the aforesaid unfortunate circumstances the lessor has made a grant of Rs. ——— to the lessee as an act of grace and at the request of the lessee agreed to accept a surrender of the said lease for the remainder of the term thereof and to relinquish and forego all his rights under the said lease on the lessee abandoning all claims for compensation for buildings, structures and other improvements made upon the demised land.

NOW THIS DEED WITNESSES as follows:

1. Surrender

In consideration of the lessor relinquishing and foregoing all demands, rights or claims accruing to him under the said lease the lessee hereby surrenders and yields up to the lessor ALL that land comprised in and demised by the aforesaid lease and described in the schedule hereto with all building, well and other constructions erected, sunk and made on the said land and such other things as may be fixed on the land and other improvements made by the lessee thereon TO the intent that the term created by the said lease and all the estate and interest of the lessee in the said land under or by virtue of the said lease be absolutely and for ever extinguished and the said land may revert to the lessor with the aforesaid buildings, well, constructions, fixtures and improvements;

2. Release by Lessor

The lessor hereby releases the lessee, his heirs, executors, administrators and assigns from all claims, demands and liability arising under or in respect of the aforesaid lease;

3. Lessee's Relinquishment of Buildings, etc.

The lessee hereby relinquishes all claims to compensation for any buildings, wells, constructions, fixtures and improvements erected, sunk and made by him on the said land.

IN WITNESS WHEREOF, etc.,

37—Deed Altering Covenants in Lease

AN AGREEMENT made on the ——— day of ——— BETWEEN AB, etc., (hereinafter called "the lessor") of the one part AND CD, etc., (hereinafter called "the lessee") of the other part.

WHEREAS this deed is supplemental to the deed of lease dated —— made between the parties hereto;

AND WHEREAS the parties hereto have agreed that the said deed of lease be varied and modified in manner hereinafter appearing.

NOW THIS DEED WITNESSES as follows:

1. Sub-clause ——— of clause ——— of the aforesaid lease shall cease to have effect.

2. There shall be substituted for sub-clause ——— of clause ——— of the aforesaid lease the following sub-clause, namely ——

(*Set out the new sub-clause.*)

3. The annual rent reserved by the aforesaid lease shall with effect from ——— be reduced (*or*, increased) from Rs. ——— to Rs. ———.

4. Save as hereinbefore modified the aforesaid lease shall continue in full force and effect.

IN WITNESS WHEREOF, etc.

LICENCE

Preliminary Note

Licence

Where one person grants to another, or to a definite number of other persons, a right to do or continue to do, in or upon the immovable property of the grantor, something which would in the absence of such right, be unlawful, and such right does not amount to an easement or an interest in the property, the right is called a licence (Sec. 52, Indian Easement Act, 1882).

Licence differs from a lease, as under a lease an interest in the property is transferred while no interest is transferred under a licence, the effect of which is only to make an action lawful which would otherwise be unlawful. The distinction between a lease and licence has been brought out by the Supreme Court in various cases, and it has been held[1] that if a document gives only a right to use the property in a particular way or under particular terms while it remains in possession and control of the owner thereof it will be a licence. The licensee's occupation does not create in his favour any estate or interest in the property. Even in cases of exclusive possession, though *prima facie* the grantee is to be considered a tenant, yet he will not be held to be so if the circumstances and the conduct of the parties negative any intention to create a tenancy. For ascertaining the intention the substance of the document must be preferred to the form.[2]

Revocation

In absence of a contract to the contrary, a licence is, unlike a lease, generally revocable without notice, but when a licence is coupled with a transfer of interest in property and such transfer of property is still in force, or the licensee has, acting upon the licence, has executed a work of a permanent character and incurred

---

1 *Associated Hotels* v. *R.N. Kapoor*, AIR 1959 SC 1262; M.N. *Clubawala* v. *Fida Hussain*, AIR 1965 SC 610; *Sohan Lal Naraindas* v. *Laxmidas Raghunath*, 1971 (1) SCC 276; *Qudartullah* v. *M.B. Bareilly*, 1974 (1) SCC 202; *Sridhar* v. *Shri Jagannath Temple*, (1976) 3 SCC 485; *Board of Revenue* v. *A.M. Ansari*, (1976) 3 SCC 512; *The Corporation of Calicut* v. *K. Sreenivasan*, AIR 2002 SC 2051.

2 *Qudrat Ullah* v. *Municipal Board*, AIR 1974 SC 396; *Khalil Ahmed* v. *Tufeilhussein*, AIR 1988 SC 184; *Vayallakath* v. *Illikkal*, AIR 1996 SC 3288; *Basappa* v. *Gangadhar*, 1998 AIHC 2989 (Kant); (*Held* shop given on licence, not lease); *Shyam Sunder* v. *Delta International Ltd.*, AIR 1998 Cal 233 (DB), reversed in AIR 1999 SC 2607 (document of Licence not treated lease); *Board of Revenue* v. *A.M. Ansari*, AIR 1976 SC 1813; *Puran Singh* v. *S.B. Kriplani*, (1991) 2 SCC 180; *B.V.D'Souza* v. *Antonio Fernandes*, (1989) 3 SCC 574, AIR 1989 SC 1816.

expenses in the execution, then such licences are not revocable (Section 60, Indian Easement Act, 1882). The revocation of a licence may be express or implied (section 61). Any restrictions on the power of revocation, such as that of previous notice or payment of compensation should therefore be expressly provided in the licence.

A licence is simply a permission to use land. It allows someone access to the land of another for an agreed purpose. It is an authority given to a person that justifies what would otherwise be a trespass. A licence does not confer any interest in land.

A licence is not really a contract, but a lower species of property interest recognised by a grant to use and occupy premises for an agreed purpose. It is a permission to use something, to do a particular thing, or to carry on a trade or business to their common advantage. It is not a tenancy or a contract stricto sensu of the status of lease. It may appear to look like one but is not in effect.[1]

A licence is deemed to have been revoked in the following situation (Section 62, Indian Easement Act, 1882):

(a) when, from a cause preceding the grant of it, the grantor ceases to have any interest in the property affected by the licence;

(b) when the licensee releases it, expressly or impliedly, to the grantor or his representative;

(c) where it has been granted for a limited period, or acquired on condition that it shall become void on the performance or non-performance of a specified act, and the period expires, or the condition is fulfilled;

(d) where the property affected by the licence is destroyed or by superior force so permanently altered that the licensee can no longer exercise his right;

(e) where the licensee becomes entitled to the absolute ownership of the property affected by the licence;

(f) where the licence is granted for a specified purpose and the purpose is attained or abandoned, or becomes impracticable;

(g) where the licence is granted to the licensee as holding a particular office, employment or character, and such office, employment or character ceases to exist;

(h) where the licence totally ceases to be used as such for an unbroken period of twenty years, and such cessation is not in pursuance of a contract between the grantor and the licensee;

(i) in the case of an accessory licence, when the interest or right to which it is accessory ceases to exist.

---

1 *Ravi Bansal* v. *Maa Bhagwati Associates*, 2014 SCC OnLine P&H 7643, MANU/PH/0239/2014.

Statutory Provision

The statutory provisions governing licences are contained in the Indian Easement Act, 1882, Chapter VI. In States, where this Act does not apply, courts rely upon English common law and the general principles as embodied in the Act are also applied even though the Act as such does not apply in term.[1]

Form of Licence

No special form of grant is prescribed. It may be granted orally or by an agreement in writing or by a covenant contained in any other deed, such as lease, sale, etc. If it is granted in writing, the writing should be in the form of a deed or agreement or in the simple form of a deed poll. If no fee is to be paid and the licensee has not to enter into any covenants, the form of deed poll would be suitable, but if the licensee is to pay any fee and the licence is for a fixed term or revocable only by notice, a deed or agreement is preferable.

The deed may be described as "THIS LICENCE" or "THE DEED of LICENCE" or simply as "THIS DEED" and the parties as "Licensor" and "Licensee" or "Owner" and "Licensee" or "Grantor" and "Grantee".

Recitals

In a simple deed, recitals will be rarely necessary.

Consideration

A licence may be for consideration (though this is not necessary). If so, it should be mentioned.

Operative Words

The operative words may be "licenses and authorizes to do" or "grants liberty and licence to do, etc.", or "grants leave and licence to do, etc." The exact liberty given, the property on which it is to be exercised, and the conditions imposed on the exercise should be clearly expressed in the deed. If there is a long list of the powers and authority given by the licence the same may be incorporated in a schedule to be referred to in the deed. The deed should make it clear that it is a licence and not a lease or a grant.

Devolution of Right

A licence is generally not heritable and transferable. However, a licence to attend a place of public entertainment is transferable (Sec. 56). A contract to the contrary should, therefore, be expressly stated. As a licence granted to A cannot be exercised by his servants or agents (Sec. 56), the servants and agents should also be expressly mentioned along with the licensee.

---

1 *Sital Chandra Chaudhry* v. *Allen J. Delanney*, 34 IC 450; *Maung Chan Nayem* v. *Maung Pure*, 114 IC 519.

A licence is purely a personal right between the licensor and the licensee; so a transferee from the licensor is not as such bound by the licence (Sec. 59).

Stamp Duty

If a licence is contained in any deed, such as in a deed of sale or lease. it does not constitute a matter distinct from the subject matter of such deed but is ancillary to it, hence no separate stamp duty is required under Sec. 5 Stamp Act in respect of the covenants relating to the licence, but if a separate deed is executed it will be chargeable with the same duty as an agreement not otherwise provided for (vide Article 5).

Registration

A mere deed of licence need not be registered unless any right, title or interest in immovable property of the value of Rs.100 or more is created, declared, assigned, limited or extinguished (Sec. 17, Registration Act).

PRECEDENTS

1—Licence to Play Cricket, in the form of a Deed Poll

I, AB, etc., owner in possession of the land described in the schedule hereto hereby license and authorize all members for the time being of the ——— Club by themselves, their servants, agents and friends with all proper equipment necessary for the game of cricket, such as bats, wickets, balls, roller, etc., to enter and to go upon the said land at all times between the ——— day of ——— and the ——— day of ——— in every year so long as this licence shall be unrevoked and to practise and play the game of cricket and as far as may be proper for that purpose to cut and mow the grass growing there and to roll the said field and do all things incidental to practising and playing the said game doing no unnecessary damage to the said land or anything lying or growing thereon.

The Schedule herein referred to.

*****

Signed by owner ——— on the ———.

2—Ditto, in Deed Form

THIS DEED OF LICENCE made on the ——— day of ——— BETWEEN AB, etc., (hereinafter called "the licensor", which term shall include his heirs, representatives, successors and assigns) of the one part AND CD, EF, GH, etc., members of the ——— Club, ——— (hereinafter called "the licensees" which term shall include all persons who may for the time being be the members of the said Club) of the other part.

WITNESSES as follows:

1. Permit to Play Cricket

The Licensor hereby licenses and authorises the licensees at all times during the continuance of this licence and so long as the ——— Club ——— (hereinafter called "the Club") continues to exist by themselves and by the servants and agents of the Club to enter upon that plot of land in ——— known as the cricket lawn and measuring approximately ——— by ——— metres and bounded on the north by ——— on the south by ——— on the east by ——— and on the west by ——— and there to practise and play the game of cricket and to roll the said plot and do all things incidental to practising and playing the game of cricket and no other.

2. Licensee's Covenants

The licensees hereby agree with the licensor as follows:

(a) Not to Waste

The licensees shall not commit any waste on or cause any damage to the said land.

(b) Licensor may Revoke

The licensor shall be at liberty at any time to put an end to this licence by giving to the licensees such notice as he may consider reasonable, and any notice delivered to the Honorary Secretary of the Club or to any other office-bearer of the Club or left at the office of the Club will be deemed to be sufficient notice to the licensees.

(c) Licensee to Quit if Land Required

If the said land is required by the licensor temporarily for any purpose, the licensees shall quit the same and suspend its use as aforesaid for such time as the licensor may direct but during the period of such suspension the licensor shall not be responsible for the maintenance of the grounds and shall not be bound to incur any expense on its maintenance other than to meet his own requirements.

(d) To Submit Programme

The licensees shall at the beginning of every year submit to the licensor a programme of their yearly functions, and fixtures.

(e) The licensees and every one using the said land on their behalf under this licence shall refrain from the use of the grounds when they are unfit for play and the decision of the licensor on the question of such unfitness shall be final.

IN WITNESS WHEREOF, etc.

3—Licence to Build and Maintain a Seed Store

THIS LICENCE is made on the ——— day of ——— BETWEEN AB, etc., (hereinafter called "the licensor") of the one part AND CD, etc., (hereinafter called "the licensee") of the other part.

WHEREAS the licensor desired the licensee to open a seed store in ——— and the licensee has agreed with the licensor to do so upon being given a suitable site for such store and the necessary permission to build thereon.

NOW THIS DEED WITNESSES as follows:

1. Grant of Easement

In pursuance of the said agreement the licensor hereby grants to the licensee LEAVE AND LICENCE to build and maintain a seed store in the compound known as ——— and situate in ——— now in the possession of the licensor and upon that part of the said compound which is shown within red lines on the plan annexed hereto and to carry on the business of buying, selling and storing seeds in such store as aforesaid and also to construct a road from such store to the point marked A on the said plan and to erect and maintain a gate at the said point together with full rights of passage along such road and from such store for the licensee, his servants and agents and all other persons coming to such store for the purpose of buying, selling, delivering or removing seed with trucks, tractor, trollies, carts, or other means of transport.

2. Licensee not to use for Different Purpose

The licensee hereby covenants with the licensor that he will not use the said site for any purpose other than the purpose aforesaid and that if he ceases to do so he will surrender the same to the licensor after removing all buildings therefrom and clearing the said site of all foundations or materials of buildings erected by him thereon.

3. Quiet Enjoyment

The licensor hereby covenants with the licensee that as long as the licensee performs and observes the terms and conditions hereinbefore contained the licensor will not in any way hinder him in the use and enjoyment of the said site and of the licence hereinbefore contained AND will if he desires to surrender the said site, permit him to remove the materials of all buildings erected by him thereon

IN WITNESS WHEREOF, etc.

4—Licence to Construct Road on the Licensor's Land

AN AGREEMENT made on the ——— day of ——— BETWEEN AB, etc., (hereinafter called "the grantor") of the one part AND CD, etc., (hereinafter called "the grantee") of the other part;

Recitals

WHEREAS the grantee has applied to the grantor for liberty to construct, maintain and use a road across the land described in the schedule hereto between the points marked A and B on the plan annexed hereto and along the route between the said points which route is delineated on the said plan and thereon coloured red, which road is required for the better and more convenient working of the Sugar Factory of the grantee called the ——— factory;

AND WHEREAS such road if constructed would also be useful for the purposes of the grantor's estate;

AND WHEREAS the grantor has therefore agreed to grant such liberty as aforesaid to the extent and subject to the conditions hereinafter set forth and the grantee has likewise agreed to accept the grant on such conditions:

NOW THESE PRESENTS WITNESS as follows:

1. Grant of Easement

The grantor hereby grants to the grantee full licence to construct and maintain a road across the said land between the said points and along the said route and also a right of way along the same for pedestrian or vehicular traffic or by whatever means at all times for the grantee, his servants, agents and customers and TO HAVE and exercise such licence and right of way for as long as such road shall be required for any of the purposes of the grantee in working and managing the said Sugar Factory but no longer.

2. Grantee's Covenants

It is hereby agreed and declared that the aforesaid grant is subject to the following conditions all of which the grantee hereby covenants with the grantor to observe and perform:

(i) *To put up Notices*
As soon as such road shall be ready for use, the grantee will put up and will at all times thereafter maintain in good and legible condition notices in Hindi and English and in a form to be approved by the grantor at each terminus of such road stating that the same is a private road maintained for the use of the grantee and that any use of the same by members of the public is merely permissive;

(ii) *To Stop Traffic*
That the grantee will at least once in every year and for a continuous period of not less than twenty-four hours stop all traffic along such road from either terminus thereof except traffic by the grantee, his servants, agents and customers or by the grantor and his servants and agents and will on every such

occasion post a person at each such terminus and will both by notice and by the agency of such person explain that traffic is stopped in order to prevent the acquisition by the public of any right to use such road for any purpose whatever;

(iii) Right to Revoke

Upon any breach of either of the conditions hereinbefore contained the grantor may, notwithstanding the waiver of any previous right of revocation, revoke the aforesaid grant and thereupon the same shall become void.

3. Grantor's Covenants

The grantor hereby covenants with the grantee as follows:

(i) That so long as the conditions hereinbefore contained are observed the aforesaid grant will not be revoked;

(ii) Payment

The grantor will every year pay either half the cost of the repair and maintenance of such road during the year or will contribute towards the same the sum of Rs. ———, whichever sum shall be less;

(iii) Grantee to Prevent use

Except as hereinbefore provided the grantee shall not be bound to prevent or control the use of such road by any person nor shall be in any way responsible for any damage done by any person using such road other than persons in the employment or subject to the control of the grantee;

(iv) Option to Surrender

The grantee or his successors may at any time surrender his or their rights under these presents and that nothing herein contained shall impose upon him or them any obligations to construct or to maintain such a road as aforesaid after such rights have been surrendered.

4. Parties' Covenants

The parties hereby agree that subject to the conditions hereinbefore mentioned the grantee shall repair and maintain the road in a good condition by carrying out necessary repairs and the sole responsibility in this behalf shall be that of the grantee. Non-payment of repair and maintenance contribution by the grantor under clause 3(*ii*) shall be no ground for not maintaining and keeping the road in good repairs.

It is further agreed between the parties that if the grantor shall fail to pay half of the repair and the maintenance cost of the road under clause 3 (*ii*) the grantee may recover the same from grantor through a court of law with interest at the rate of 18 percent per annum, compounded yearly.

5. Interpretation Clause

It is hereby agreed that where the context so requires or admits the expression "the grantor" hereinbefore used includes the owners for the time being of the said land on which this licence is granted; and the expression "the grantee" hereinbefore used includes his heirs, executors, administrators and assigns.

IN WITNESS WHEREOF, etc.

5—Licence to make Alterations and Additions in Demised Premises[1]

THIS LICENCE is made on the ——— day of ——— BETWEEN AB, etc., (hereinafter called "the lessor") of the one part AND CD, etc., (hereinafter called "the lessee") of the other part.

WHEREAS—

(1) By a deed of lease dated ——— the lessor (*or*, one MN predecessor-in-title of the lessor) demised the house described in the schedule hereto to the lessee (*or*, one GH the predecessor-in-title of the lessee).

(2) The said lease contained a covenant by the lessee not to make any structural additions or alterations to the said house without the previous permission of the lessor in writing.

(3) On the request of the lessee the lessor has agreed to grant the lessee permission to make the additions and alterations specified in the schedule hereto on the conditions hereinafter contained.

NOW THIS DEED WITNESSES as follows:

In pursuance of the said agreement the lessor grants to the lessee licence to execute in and upon the said premises the several alterations and works specified in the schedule hereto on condition that the same shall be completed within ——— months from the date hereof in conformity with the plan and specifications already submitted to and accepted by the lessor, which plan and specifications are annexed hereto and signed by the parties.

1 See Preliminary Note on LEASE: Implied covenants.

1. Lessee's Covenants

The lessee hereby covenants with the lessor as follows:

(*i*) That he will complete the said alterations and additions within the period and in the manner hereinbefore specified;

(*ii*) That in carrying out such alterations and additions he will do as little injury as possible to the existing structure of the said building and will make good any damage done or caused to the said building by the execution of such alterations and additions;

(*iii*) That in addition to rent reserved in the aforesaid deed of lease he will pay an additional rent of Rs.——— per mensem along with the rent so reserved and in the manner provided in the said lease.

(*iv*) That on the determination of the said lease unless released from compliance with this stipulation by the lessor, he will at his own cost reinstate and make good the demised premises and restore the same to the same state and condition as they are now in and as if the several additions and alterations hereby authorized had not been made [*or*, that on the termination of the lessee's tenancy of the said building, by the act of either of the parties hereto except in the case provided by Sec. 111 (c) of the Transfer of Property Act[1], the lessee will hand over to the lessor all such additions as aforesaid, (if carried out) in good condition and repair (reasonable wear and tear excepted) and shall not be entitled to any compensation or payment for value or cost of such alterations or additions].

2. Parties' Covenants

It is hereby agreed that the lessor's covenants and conditions contained in the said lease which are now applicable to the premises comprised therein shall continue to be applicable to the same when and as altered and shall be applicable to all additions which may be made thereto.

The Schedule hereinabove referred to.

* * * * *

IN WITNESS WHEREOF, etc.

1 Sec. 111 (c) provides for automatic determination of the lease on the termination of the interest of the lessor in the property.

6—Licence for Grazing and Appropriation of Fruits (with a Surety for the Licensee)

AN AGREEMENT made the ——— day of ——— BETWEEN AB, etc., (hereinafter called "the licensor") of the first part AND CD, etc., (hereinafter called "the licensee") of the second part and EF, etc. (hereinafter called "the surety") of the third part.

WHEREBY the parties hereto agree as follows:

(1) During a period of —— months/years commencing from the —— day of ———— next the licensor will permit the licensee to do the acts and things specified in the first schedule hereto over all the land described in the second schedule hereto.

(2) The licensee will pay the licensor for such permission the sum of Rs. ——— by ——— instalments, payable as follows:

Rs. ——— on the ——— day of ——— 20 ———

Rs. ——— on the ——— day of ——— 20 ———

Rs. ——— on the ——— day of ——— 20 ———

(3) The licensee will be liable to pay for any damage done by him or his servants or agents or cattle, during the period of this licence, to any trees, shrubs, plants, culverts, drains or other property of the licensor on the said land and will accept as final the decision of XY[1] as to his such liability and as to the amount of such liability and will pay the said amount within ——— days after being required by the licensor to do so.

(4) If the licensee makes default in payment of any instalment mentioned in clause (2), or of any sum which he is liable to pay under clause (3) hereof, he will be liable to pay interest on such sum at one percent per mensem from the date of default to that of actual payment, and the licensor shall also be at liberty to revoke this license and the licensee shall thereupon forfeit all his rights hereunder and shall not be entitled to any compensation by reason of such forfeiture.

(5) Water will be supplied to the licensee from the tube well at —— and the licensor will take all reasonable care to maintain an adequate supply but he shall not be liable for any damage or loss which may be caused by any deficiency in the water supply and the licensee will not be entitled to any remission or compensation for such damage.

(6) The licensee will not be entitled to any remission or compensation

---

1 Such a clause makes him a referee and not an arbitrator. Clauses (6) and (8) are also similar in this respect.

on account of damage by storm, insect attack or other natural calamity unless such damage is of exceptional severity, in which case he will get a reasonable remission or compensation, and in case of disagreement about the liability of the licensor or as to the amount of remission or compensation allowable to the licensee, the matter shall be referred to XY whose decision shall be final.

(7) The licensee shall not sublet this contract either in part or in whole, unless the permission in writing of the lessor is previously obtained.

(8) The licensor may at his option determine this agreement at any time after one week's notice and shall in such case compensate the licensee (if the licensee is not in default) either by payment in money or by giving him over other land the same rights as are hereby given to him, and the licensee will accept as final the decision of the said XY concerning the amount to be paid or the land to be given, as the case may be.

(9)[1] The surety in consideration of the licensor having given the licensee the permission hereinbefore mentioned agrees with and guarantees to the licensor that the licensee will duly pay all sums payable by him under the covenants hereinbefore contained and that in case the licensee makes default in the payment of any such sum the surety will pay the same to the licensor.

The first schedule herein referred to

(*Description of the rights given*)

(*a*) To cut and sell grass for profit.

(*b*) To gather and sell fruit for profit (except fruit of—trees).

(*c*) To graze cattle and sheep (but no other animals).

(*d*) To graze animals of any kind (except goats and elephants).

The second schedule herein referred to

(Description of the land to which this agreement relates).

IN WITNESS WHEREOF, etc.

7—Licence for Hotel Shop[2]

THIS DEED OF LICENCE is made at ———— on this the —— day

1 If there is no surety then this clause is to be omitted and also the words "and EF, etc. ..... third part" in the enumeration of parties in the beginning.

2 *It does not amount to a lease: Om Prakash v. Ravinder Kumar*, 1995 Supp. (4) SCC 115; *Swarn Singh* v. *Madan Singh,* 1995 Supp (1) SCC 306; *Delta International Ltd.* v. *Shyam Sunder*, AIR 1999 SC 2607.

of ——— between AB HOTELS LIMITED, a public limited company incorporated under the Companies Act, 1956 and having its registered office at ———, hereinafter called "the Licensor" (which expression shall include its successors and assigns) of the ONE PART and CD, etc., (*the constitution and status of the licensee to be defined*), hereinafter called "the Licensee" (which expression shall include its successors and assigns) of the OTHER PART.

WHEREAS the Licensor is operating a 5-star deluxe hotel known as ——— at ——— on the plot of land admeasuring 20,000 sq. metres leased out to the Licensor by the ——— Development Authority under the perpetual lease deed dated the ——— day of ——— and in which the licensor is also required to have a shopping plaza as essential facility to the hotel customers;

AND WHEREAS the Board of Directors of the Licensor have decided to give on licence basis shops in the shopping plaza to intending parties to use the shops for the specified business purposes;

AND WHEREAS the Licensee is desirous to use as Licensee Shop No. ——— (measuring———sq. metres) in the said shopping plaza (hereinafter referred to as "the stipulated space");

NOW THIS AGREEMENT WITNESSES AND IT IS HEREBY AGREED, DECLARED AND RECORDED AS FOLLOWS:

1. In consideration of the periodical payments hereinafter agreed to be paid by the Licensee and other Licensee's undertakings hereinafter set out, the Licensor hereby licenses and authorises the Licensee to enter upon and use the stipulated space for the purposes of carrying on ——— (hereinafter called "the authorised purpose") on the days and during the hours to be determined by the Licensor from time to time. Any change in the authorised purpose shall be made only with the permission in writing of the Licensor.

2. The Licence under this agreement shall be operative for a period of 5 (five) years from the date the stipulated space is made available to the licensee (hereinafter referred to as "commencement date") for carrying out the authorised purpose. At the option of the Licensee the licence under this Agreement shall be renewed for an additional period of not exceeding 5 (five) years at a time.

3. During the currency of this licence, the licensee hereby agrees with the Licensor and undertakes as follows:—

(*a*) To pay to the Licensor a sum of Rs. ——— (Rupees ——— only) by the 10th day of every month, the first of such payments to be made on commencement date;

(*b*) If default is made in paying the said amount in time, interest at 24% p.a. shall be chargeable from the due date(s) to the actual date of payment.

(*c*) Not to use the stipulated space for any purpose other than for the authorised purpose;

(*d*) To obtain and to keep in force all permissions and licences which may be required by law for use of the stipulated space and to comply with any condition which may be attached to any such permission or licence;

(*e*) To manage and conduct the stipulated space so as to preserve the reputation of the Licensor and its hotel and to abide by the rules and regulations framed by the Licensor from time to time and that nothing shall be done, permitted or committed contrary to any provision made by or under any statute or law for the time being in force or rules and regulations framed by the Licensor and in particular not to use or permit the stipulated space to be used for any form of unlawful activities;

(*f*) Not to make any alterations or additions to the stipulated space or to remove therefrom any of the Licensor's fixtures or fittings therein;

(*g*) Not to alter the original colour of the outside of the stipulated space or the facade and front elevation nor erect sun-screens, curtains or blinds on the exterior nor paste any bills, advertisements, posters, notices, cuttings, etc., on the glasses, nor permit the same to be made, affixed or altered or erected in any circumstances;

(*h*) To have the scheme, specification and the layout for decor, for interior decoration and furnishing of the stipulated space approved by the Licensor and to keep the same-as approved by the Licensor keeping in view the high standard of a 5-star luxury hotel, and to carry out, at its own expense, such repair or renovation work as the Licensor may direct as a result of inspection by its representative(s) and that in default the Licensor shall be entitled to carry out such repairs or renovations and to recover the costs, charges and expenses thereof from the Licensee;

(*i*) To forthwith remove or cause to be removed any goods, articles or exhibits exhibited or exposed for sale or being sold in the stipulated space, which in the opinion of the Licensor are obnoxious, obscene or undesirable;

(*j*) Not to store or cause to be stored any hazardous, combustible or dangerous goods in stipulated space nor use any gas, kerosene or electric stove or appliances for preparing any food or beverage item or for any other purpose;

(*k*) Not to hold any auction, bids or such other activities without prior written consent of the Licensor.

(*l*) Not to display, affix paint or exhibit any name or writing or anything upon the exterior of the stipulated space without obtaining prior written consent of the Licensor:

(*m*) Not to employ for work or otherwise allow any person at the stipulated space who is not of good character and behaviour and/or suffering from any contagious, infectious disease or is not suitably attired or otherwise unsuitable to be seen in a modern 5-star luxury hotel;

(*n*) To forthwith submit, at the requisition of the Licensor any member of its staff for medical examination by a doctor of the Licensor's choice at the cost of the Licensee:

(*o*) Shall use such route or passage only to go to or come out of the hotel premises (for reaching the stipulated space) or any toilet or wash-room as is stipulated by the Licensor for use by persons working at the stipulated space;

(*p*) To pay or cause to be paid charges for electricity (including meter hire charges), telephone calls, and other facilities/ utilities provided by the Licensor at the stipulated space immediately on receipt of bills/demand by the Licensor. In case of default, the Licensor may at its discretion withdraw the facilities/utilities;

(*q*) Not to do or permit to be done any act which may invalidate or in any way affect the insurance of the building or property wherein the stipulated space is located;

(*r*) Not to throw dirt, rubbish, garbage, refuse or permit the same to be thrown in the stipulated space or in the verandah or the passage or in any other portion of the shopping plaza or hotel;

(*s*) In the event of any damage or injury being caused to the stipulated space or any property of the Licensor by the Licensee or his servants or agents or any one upon the stipulated space with the acceptance or implied consent of the Licensee or as a result of the use of the premises for unauthorised purposes, the Licensee shall at its own expense make good all such damage or injury and in the event of his failure to do so within 15 (fifteen) days after the occurrence of such damage, the Licensor may make good such injury/damage and the Licensee shall indemnify the Licensor against all such costs and charges and expenses in respect thereof.

(*t*) To charge the customers reasonable price for the goods sold or services rendered and in the event of any complaint, to satisfy the Licensor about the reasonableness of the price and to refund to the customer any amount in excess of the price which is considered reasonable by the Licensor.

(*u*) To forthwith on the expiry of the licence or its earlier termination by the licensor vacate the stipulated space and remove all its wares, equipments furnishings, etc., and in default the Licensor's representatives shall be fully entitled to get the stipulated space vacated without being liable to damages or otherwise; and

(*v*) To take out a policy of insurance in the joint names of the Licensor and the Licensee against all liability in respect of any damage or loss which may be suffered by any person other than the Company or the Licensee by reason or arising directly or indirectly out of the use of the stipulated space for the authorised purpose and to keep the Licensor indemnified against all such liability.

4. The Licensor hereby agrees with the Licensee as follows:

(*a*) To permit or cause to permit the Licensee, his servants and agents to enter and use the stipulated space;

(*b*) To keep or cause to be kept the premises, in which the stipulated space licenced to the Licensee is situated, in good condition;

(*c*) To provide the following facilities/services:—

(*i*) Central air-conditioning facilities during business hours;

(*ii*) Cleaning and keeping in neat and tidy condition common passages, lobbies and entrances around the stipulated space;

(*iii*) Looking after and attending to the electricity, water and sanitary fittings and pumping requirements in the common passages, lobbies and entrance around the stipulated space; and

(*iv*) Providing watch and ward and the maintenance services for the shopping area, provided that the Licensor shall not in any way be responsible in case of any theft, pilferage or loss.

PROVIDED that the air-conditioning and telephone services may be shut off and cut off, after giving 24 (twenty four) hours' notice in writing, for the purpose of altering, repairing services or overhauling any apparatus, machine, plant or installations;

PROVIDED FURTHER that in the event of failure of the central air-conditioning or the telephone installations due to any reason beyond the control of the Licensor, the Licensee shall have no recourse against the Licensor for non-provision of the above facilities/services; and

(*d*) To permit the Licensee to use the common portions such as entrances, passages, stairways in the shopping plaza as are specifically designated by the Licensor from time to time.

5. (*a*) As security for proper maintenance of the stipulated space and proper conduct and complete compliance of terms and conditions of the Licence herein contained the Licensee shall pay to the Licensor an interest free security deposit of Rs. ——— (Rupees ————— only) in four equal instalments as per the details given below:—

1st Instalment of Rs. ———	Payable at the Commencement of this Licence deed.
2nd Instalment of Rs. ———	Payable on or before ——.
3rd Instalment of Rs. ———	Payable on or before ——.
4th Instalment or Rs. ———	Payable on or before ——.

(*b*) The Licensee shall maintain the said deposits at all times during the continuance of the licence.

(*c*) The Licensor reserves the right to allow extension for such period as it may deem fit for paying the aforesaid instalments by the licensee at its sole discretion. However, interest @ 24% p.a. shall be charged from the due date (s) to the actual date of payments.

(*d*) If the Licensee fails to pay the aforesaid instalments in time the Licensor shall have the right to terminate the License and the full amount of security deposit made under this Licence with the Licensor shall stand forfeited on such termination and the Licensee shall not be entitled to raise any dispute in this regard.

(*e*) On the expity of the period of the licence and the vacation of the stipulated space by the licensee in good and proper condition the

Licensor shall refund the security deposit to the Licensee. If the security deposit is not refunded within 30 days from the date of expiry of this Licence and vacation of the stipulated space the Licensor shall be liable to pay an interest which would be 2% per annum higher than the prevailing bank lending rate from the date of the vacation of the stipulated space to the date of the payment.

6. The Licensee shall have the right to assign/transfer his/its right under this Licence with the written consent of the Licensor on such terms and conditions as the licensor may agree to.

7. The Licensee may bring upon the stipulated space such equipment as is necessary for the use of the stipulated space for the authorised purpose, provided that while upon the stipulated space all such equipment shall be at the risk of the Licensee and the Licensor shall not be liable for any damage/injury to such equipment.

8. The Licensor shall have the right to increase the amount of consideration set out in clause 3 (a) hereof on the ——— day of —— and thereafter every 5 (five) years [in case term of the Licence is renewed beyond the initial period of 5 (five) years], provided, however, that such increase shall not exceed 25% (twenty-five percent) of the amount so being charged.

9. The licensee shall observe and adhere to the special and general conditions as per Annexures I and II respectively during the licence period of the shop.

10. The Licensor shall have the right to terminate the licence in case any of the terms of the Licence is contravened by the Licensee by giving 30 (thirty) days' notice in writing to the Licensee to remove the breaches of the terms contravened, and on failure of the licensee to remove the said breaches within 30 (thirty) days, the Licence will stand terminated. In case the Licensee is interested in terminating the licence, the Licensee may do so by giving 60 (sixty) days' notice in writing to the Licensor and the Licence shall stand terminated on such expiry of the notice.

11. That the Licensee is a sole-proprietary/partnership/company. Name(s) of the sole-proprietor/partners/directors/controling shareholders as on date of the signing of this agreement have been furnished to the Licensor.

The Licensee hereby nominates Shri ——— partner (*director*) of the Licensee (hereinafter known as "the nominee") who shall be the person who will deal with the Licensor on behalf of the Licensee for the purposes of this Agreement. The Licensee shall notify, in writing, to the Licensor in case he/it desires any change in the nominee as proposed by him/it. The change will become effective only after the licensor has confirmed in writing its acceptance of the name of the new nominee.

12. That in case of any dispute, difference, between the parties, with regard to any matter including interpretation of this agreement and the clarifications thereof, the same shall be referred to the arbitration of the Chairman of the Licensor or any person appointed by the Chairman[1] whose decision shall be final and binding between the parties and shall not be questioned in any court of law.

13. Notwithstanding anything contained hereinbefore the Licensor shall have the right to create charges/mortgages as and by way of first charge on its land, premises and the buildings (including the shops) constructed and to be constructed, in favour of the Financial Institutions and Banks as Security for their term loans advanced/to be advanced to the Licensor for the completion of its hotel project hereinbefore mentioned.

IN WITNESS WHEREOF, etc.

---

1 It will not be expedient to have nominees of both parties as arbitrators because in that case the two nominees will have to appoint a third arbitrator who will act as the presiding arbitrator while the Chairman of the Licensor will become an ordinary member of the arbitral tribunal: Sec. 11 (3), Arbitration and Conciliation Act 1996.

MORTGAGE, CHARGE, HYPOTHECATION AND PLEDGE

Preliminary Note

Mortgage

Definition of Mortgage

A mortgage is a transfer of an interest in specific immovable property as security for the repayment of money advanced or to be advanced by way of loan, or an existing or future debt, or the performance of an engagement which may give rise to a pecuniary liability (Sec. 58, Transfer of Property Act).

This mode of transfer, so far as immovable property is concerned is governed by the provisions of Chapter IV of the Transfer of Property Act, 1882 which applies to the whole of India except the States of Punjab and Haryana.

The Act is, however, not exhaustive and the principles of common law on which it is based are applied in areas and situations to which the Act does not apply.

The right created by the transfer is accessory to the right to recover the debt. The nature of the right transferred depends upon the form of a mortgage. In case of a deed of a composite character containing mixed features of a mortgage as well as lease the dominant intention of the parties has to be gathered from the recitals and the terms in the entire document and also possibly from how the parties or their representatives treated the deed. The nomenclature given by them is not always conclusive. Where the essential feature, namely, that the property transferred is a security for repayment of debt is absent, the deed cannot be held to be a mortgage.[1]

The following are the different forms of mortgage in vogue in India.

Forms of Mortgages

(1) *Simple Mortgage:* In this form, possession is not transferred but the mortgagor covenants personally to pay the debt and interest, and power is given to the mortgagee to have the property sold for the realisation of his dues in case the mortgagor makes default.

(2) *Usufructuary mortgage:* In this form, possession is delivered to the mortgagee who retains possession until satisfaction of the debt—the mortgagee taking the usufruct in lieu of interest, or, part payment of the principal, or partly in payment of interest and partly in part payment of the principal. The mortgagor is not personally liable to pay the debt and the mortgagee is not entitled, during the term of the mortgage, to demand his mortgage money.

---

1 *Puzhakkal Kuttappu* v. *C. Bhargavi*, (1977) 1 SCC 17.

(3) *Mortgage by conditional sale:*[1] In this form, the property is ostensibly sold subject to the condition that on default in payment of the mortgage money on a certain date, the sale shall become absolute, or that on such payment the sale shall become void, or that on such payment the buyer shall transfer the property to the seller. It is essential that the said condition be embodied in the document, which purports to effect the sale. Generally if the contract for re-purchase is recorded in a separate document the transaction is not treated as a mortgage by conditional sale, but a sale with condition of re-purchase. The mortgagee remains in possession, and in case of default of mortgagor's covenant, can sue for foreclosure. If the mortgagor pays the money within the time fixed by court, the property is re-transferred to him, otherwise the mortgagee becomes its absolute owner.

(4) *English mortgage*: In this form there is a covenant to repay the mortgage money on a certain date, and property is transferred absolutely to the mortgagee, subject to the proviso that the mortgagee will re-transfer it to the mortgagor upon payment of the mortgage money as agreed.

(5) *Equitable mortgage:* In this form, the mortgagor delivers to creditor or his agent documents of his title deeds of immovable property, with intent to create a security thereon, the transaction is called a mortgage by deposit of title deeds. This is permissible in certain towns mentioned in section 58 (f), Transfer of Property Act, 1882, namely Calcutta, Madras and Bombay and in any other towns, like Ahmedabad, Kanpur, Allahabad, Lucknow, Coimbatore, Madurai, Cochin, which the State Governments concerned have by notification in the Official Gazette, specify in this behalf. This restriction as to specified towns relates not to the sites of the property but to the place where the title deeds may be delivered; the property may be situated elsewhere.

Mere memorandum recording it is not required to be registered. If a contract is executed then registration is necessary.[2]

(6) *Anomalous mortgage:* A mortgage which is not a simple mortgage, a mortgage by conditional sale, an usufructuary mortgage, an English mortgage or a mortgage by deposit of title-deeds within the meaning of this section is called an anomalous mortgage, section 58(g), Transfer of Property Act, 1882.

Who may Mortgage

Any person who is not under any disability, or any company or association or body of individuals, who has an interest in immovable property can mortgage that interest. Idols, in whom any property is vested, are also recognized as juristic

---

1 On whether a deed is mortgage by conditional sale or sale with condition of repurchase see *Tamboli Ramanlal Motilal* v. *Ghanchi Chimanlal*, 1993 Supp. (1) SCC 295; *Chunchun Jha* v. *Ebadat Ali*, AIR 1954 SC 345; See also *Vidhyadhar* v. *Manikrao*, (1999) 3 SCC 573; AIR 1999 SC 1441 (mortgage by conditional sale)

2 *V.G. Rao* v. *Andhra Bank*, AIR 1971 SC 1613.

persons capable of transferring and accepting transfers of property.[1] But no one can mortgage more interest than he himself has, e.g. a lessee can mortgage his leasehold right only and a life estate owner cannot make a mortgage so as to be effective after his death. A person not capable of making a contract, e.g. a minor or a lunatic, cannot make a mortgage but the guardian or manager of such person's property can mortgage the property, subject to such restrictions as may be imposed by law or by the deed or order of his appointment. The manager of a joint Hindu family can mortgage the family property under certain circumstances recognised in the Hindu Law. A partner in a commercial firm can mortgage the firm property to secure a partnership debt. A Corporation can only mortgage so far as it is expressly or impliedly authorized to do so.

Joint Hindu Family

According to the Dayabhaga School of Hindu Law, each coparcener has a right to alienate by sale or mortgage his separate share in the joint property, and as a son does not acquire an interest in family property by birth, the father has absolute power of alienation.

According to the Mitakshara law, a coparcener cannot alienate (though he can make a will of it) his undivided share in joint family property except in Western, Central and Southern India; and joint family property can be alienated only by all the coparceners or by the father or manager (*Karta*) under certain circumstances. A father can make an alienation only for payment of his antecedent debts[2] (not tainted with illegality or immorality), or for a legal necessity, or for the benefit of the family.

A manager (*Karta*) has the same powers under both the schools, that is, he can alienate the family property only for a legal necessity, or for the benefit of the family, or for a family necessity.

A father can alienate property to pay off old debts provided they are not tainted with illegality or immorality, but any other manager cannot do so unless the debts were contracted for a legal necessity. Of course, a father or a manager can make any alienation with the consent of all the coparceners. A person taking a mortgage from the manager of a joint Hindu family or, in the case of a family governed by Mitakshara law, from a father, should therefore satisfy himself as to the existence of the circumstances under which the manager or father makes the mortgage, and it is preferable to have such circumstances carefully recited in the deed of mortgage to avoid future trouble. The fact that the property to be mortgaged belongs to a joint Hindu family, the school by which the family is governed, the status and position of the mortgagor in the family and the

1 *Bhoagat Rao* v *Shri Ram Chandra*, 96 IC 1004; *Pramatha Nath* v *Pradhyamma*, 67 IC 309, 52 C 809; *Narsinha* v. *Venkatalingum*, 50 M 687, 103 IC 302, (see also Preliminary Note under, GIFT, *ante*).

2 See discussion in *Gangadharan* v. *Janardhana*, (1996) 9 SCC 53: AIR 1996 SC 2127.

circumstances under which the mortgagor is justified in making the mortgage should be narrated in the recitals, as also the making of a bona fide inquiry by the mortgagee to satisfy himself about the existence of legal necessity.

As held in *Sm. Kamala Kumari* v. *Harekrishna*,[1] even the mother of a sole coparcener (who is a minor) being a guardian has no rights of a *karta* to alienate the joint family property. She can do so as a guardian only with the permission of the court. An alienation without such permission is voidable: Sec. 8 (2) Hindu Minority and Guardianship Act 1956.[2]

Who may be a Mortgagee

Any person capable of holding property may take a mortgage, unless he is disqualified by any special law from doing so. A minor may be a mortgagee, but as he cannot enter into any contract, the mortgage should not involve any covenant by him.[3]

Property to be Mortgaged

Any interest in any property, which is capable of being transferred may be the subject of mortgage. The Transfer of Property Act, however, deals only with immovable property. According to the definition in General Clauses Act as modified by Transfer of Property Act "immovable property" includes "land, benefits to arise out of land and things attached to the earth" but does not include "standing timber, growing crops or grass." All other property is included in movable property according to General Clauses Act. Annual allowance charged on land, right to collect dues at a fair held on land, a *haat* or market, right to collect rent of land, life interest in the income of land, right of way, ferry, fishery, lessee's interest in land have all been held to be "immovable property". If the mortgage of any property or interest in it is forbidden by law it cannot be mortgaged, e.g., lessee's right, the mortgage of which is forbidden by terms of the lease.

Only 'interest in specific immovable property' can be mortgaged (Sec. 58). 'Specific' and 'Specified', which amount to the same thing, include property which is 'clearly defined and capable of identification'. As per Latin maxim *certiem est quod certiem reddi potest*, property must be regarded as certain if it can be ascertained.[4]

---

1 AIR 1998 Ori 196.

2 See also Preliminary Note on NEGOTIABLE INSTRUMENTS, *post*.

3 *Raghav Chariar* v. *Srinivas*, 40 Mad 308, 26 IC 921; *Zafar Ahsan* v. *Zubaida*, 27 ALJ 1114, 121 IC 398, AIR 1929 All 604.

4 *Miran Bakhsh* v. *Emperor*, AIR 1945 Lah 69 (SB), at 74 (holding that a works contractor who had completed some work and was to complete the rest could mortgage the amount that had already accrued due to him by then, though not ascertained. He could not however mortgage amounts that might fall due in future. So far as the latter are concerned, they were not amounts in existence, hence were not property, and only an agreement could be executed in respect of the same. Pledge was ruled out as there

Where a mortgage deed purported to encumber properties X and Y and assured that the mortgagor shall not transfer or assign X and Y in future and further recited that property Z had not been transferred or encumbered till then and that should any cause of action arise the mortgagee would be competent to realise the full amount by selling X, Y and Z, it was held that not only X and Y but Z also stood mortgaged by the deed.[1]

Movable Property

Mortgage of movables is permitted. (*See* note "Mortgage of movables" below).

How Mortgage is made

A mortgage of immovable property (other than a mortgage by deposit of title-deeds), where the principal money secured is Rs.100 or more, can be effected only by a registered instrument, signed by the mortgagor and attested by at least two witnesses. If the principal money is less than Rs.100, the mortgage may be made either by a registered instrument, signed and attested as aforesaid, or by delivery of the property. (Sec. 59 Transfer of Property Act, 1882). However, a simple mortgage of immovable property must always be made by a registered instrument as there is no delivery of property in simple mortgage. Where the Transfer of Property Act does not apply, the mortgage can be made in any way, unless a particular mode is prescribed by any special or local law governing the mortgage.

Equitable mortgage is made by deposit of title deeds with the creditor with an agreement (oral or written) that the property covered by the deed would be security for the debt. If this is a written agreement it would amount to a mortgage deed, but if it is only a memo written after the oral agreement of mortgage, it will not be a mortgage deed. In England a memo always accompanies deposits of title deeds and in this country too, it is better to adopt this practice. Care should be taken to draft it so as to show that it does not constitute the bargain between the parties but is merely the record of an already completed transaction. In that case it would not require registration otherwise it will require registration if for Rs.100 or more.[2]

Mortgage Deed

A deed of mortgage may be drafted either as a deed poll on behalf of the mortgagor in favour of the mortgagee or as a deed between mortgagor and mortgagee as parties, though even in the latter case it need not be signed by the mortgagee unless it contains any covenants by him (in which case a deed poll will always be unsuitable).

---

was no transfer of possession, actual or constructive, which is necessary in case of a pledge within the meaning of Sec. 172 Contract Act).

1 *Monimala Devi* v *Indu Bala*, AIR 1964 SC 1295.

2 *Veeramachineni Gangadhara Rao* v. *The Andhra Bank Ltd.*, AIR1971 SC 1613; *Pentala Githavardhana Rao* v. *The Andhra Bank Ltd.*, AIR 1973 AP 245.

In the case of equitable mortgage, a memorandum is usually executed by the mortgagor recording the deposit of title deeds to secure the specified mortgage money. The general requirements of a deed of transfer mentioned in Part II of the Introduction apply to mortgage also and they should therefore be carefully read. A deed of mortgage ordinarily consists of the same parts as any other deed of transfer. (*See* Introduction Part II).

Requirements of a Mortgage Deed

In the form of a deed poll, the loan or the existing liability intended to be secured is mentioned in the beginning as consideration, and then follows the covenant to repay the loan or discharge the liability and to pay interest. In a purely usufructuary mortgage, there is no personal covenant to pay but the debt alone may be recited. This is followed by the operative words creating the mortgage, and then any special covenants entered into by the mortgagor. In the form of a bilateral deed, after the description of the deed (which should be described as a "Mortgage") date, and parties (usually called "mortgagor" and "mortgagee" or "borrower" and "lender") follow recitals, if any, though in a simple deed of mortgage recitals are hardly necessary.

The recitals would be necessary in the case of a joint Hindu family or an owner acting through manager or guardian, or a trustee or *mutawalli*.

It is further necessary to mention the circumstances under which the mortgagor is competent to make the mortgage. If the property consists of leasehold or mortgagee rights or any other right short of absolute ownership, the lease or earlier mortgage or the particulars and extent of the right, as the case may be should be mentioned.

Then follow the witnessing clauses. The first witnessing clause contains the covenant to repay the loan or discharge the liability, which would be unnecessary in a purely usufructuary mortgage, and the contract about payment of interest. The fact of the loan having been taken or of the existence of liability is stated in the beginning of the covenant as a consideration of the covenant, unless it is mentioned in the recitals. In the second witnessing clause, the operative words of transfer, the parcels or description of the mortgaged property, and the nature and extent of the interest transferred should be mentioned. In the subsequent clauses, covenants describing the rights and liabilities of the parties may be entered, and at the end an interpretation clause.

Covenant to Pay

The date fixed for payment, or, if the payment is to be in instalments, the amount and date of each instalment, the place (if any) fixed for payment and any other manner agreed upon for making the payments, the rate of interest stipulated, the dates fixed for payment of interest, and the condition about compound interest should be clearly specified in the same way as is done in the case of a bond.

Consideration

If the consideration is a loan or existing liability, it should be sufficiently indicated by the first witnessing clause, but if the consideration is a future advance or the performance of a future obligation, it should be stated clearly in the recitals. In such cases the maximum amount to be secured should be stated, as the mortgagee cannot get priority for a larger amount than that stated in the mortgage deed against a subsequent mortgagee (Sec. 79).

Operative Words

As a mortgage is a transfer of interest in property, words importing transfer should be used, and it is better to say "transfer by way of simple mortgage (*or* usufructuary mortgage)", etc. The exact interest transferred is indicated after the parcels by expressing the "intent", or by adding a "habendum". In the case of *simple* mortgage it is sufficient to say "to the intent that the said property shall remain and be charged as security for the payment to the mortgagee of, etc.". In the case of a *usufructuary* mortgage, the transfer should be "to the intent that the said property shall remain in possession of the mortgagee until the principal sum of Rs. ——— and interest has been paid off in the manner hereinafter mentioned." In the case of an *English mortgage*, a habendum is added providing that the mortgagee is "to hold the said property absolutely" with a proviso "that if the mortgagor pays, etc. ——— the mortgagee shall reconvey the said property to the mortgagor". In a *mortgage by conditional sale,* the conveyance is either as in an English mortgage or, "subject to the conditions that the aforesaid transfer will be void if the mortgagor pays, etc." or, "to the intent that if the mortgagor fails to pay the said sum, etc., as hereinafter provided the transfer hereby made shall be regarded as an absolute transfer by way of sale".

Mortgagor's Title

The interest of the mortgagor in the property which he mortgages should be disclosed either by a recital of his title or, if there are no recitals, in the operative part by the addition of suitable words to the word "mortgagor" in the beginning, such "as owner" or an "absolute owner", after the parcels. The only statutory contract implied by a mortgage is that the interest which the mortgagor professes to transfer subsists and that the mortgagor has power to transfer it [Sec. 65(*a*)], and all that is necessary to be indicated is the interest which is professed to be mortgaged.

Covenants

The rights and obligations intended to be created in the parties should be provided for in the covenants. There are certain rights and liabilities which are expressly provided in Sec. 65 (implied contracts by the mortgagor), Sec. 65-A (mortgagor's power of lease), Sec. 66 (waste by mortgagor in possession), Sec. 67 (mortgagee's right to foreclosure or sale), Sec. 67-A (mortgagee when bound to bring one suit on several mortgages), Sec. 68 (right to sue for mortgage money),

Sec. 69 (power of sale without the intervention of court), Sec. 69-A (right to appoint Receiver), Sec. 70 (right to accession to mortgaged property), Sec. 71 (right to renewal of lease), Sec. 72 (right of mortgagee in possession to spend money), Sec. 73 (right to proceeds of revenue sale or compensation on acquisition), and Sec. 76 (liabilities of mortgagee in possession) of the Transfer of Property Act. These matters need not be expressly provided in the mortgage deed, (except perhaps in places in which the Transfer of Property Act is not in force, though even in these territories, as the principles underlying the Act will apply) as the rights and liabilities prescribed in the Transfer of Property Act will be implied in the absence of a contract to the contrary. It is, however, safe in the territories, where the Act is not in force, to insert a general clause providing that the mortgagor and the mortgagee will have the rights and be subject to the liabilities respectively provided in the Transfer of Property Act, 1882 and that this deed shall be deemed to be a deed of ————mortgage as defined therein. Even in the territories where the Transfer of Property Act applies, it would be better to indicate precisely the nature of the transaction by making some such provision as "that the deed shall be read and construed as a simple (*or*, usufructuary) Mortgage as defined in the Transfer of Property Act". If any special covenants are entered into as in an anomalous mortgage, they should be expressly mentioned. No covenant which has the effect of operating as a clog on redemption will be valid.[1]

Covenant for title

This is generally always entered in all deeds, but in view of Sec. 65(*a*) which, in the absence of a contract to the contrary, implies such a contract in all mortgages, it is unnecessary to insert it in territories where the Transfer of Property Act is in force. This implied covenant is of the same kind as the implied covenant of title by the vendor. It is to the effect that the interest which the mortgagor professes to transfer subsists, and that the mortgagor has power to transfer it.

Interpretation Clause

As in the case of leases, it is proper to insert an interpretation clause either in the heading along with the names of parties, or at the end as a covenant, although for the purpose of enforcement of rights under the Transfer of Property Act this is not, strictly speaking, essential, as the rights and liabilities of a mortgagor and mortgagee as specified in Chapter IV of the Transfer of Property Act can be enforced by or against persons deriving title through them (Sec. 59A, Sec. 65, para 2), unless it is otherwise expressly mentioned, e.g., the transferee of a mortgagor is not bound personally by the mortgagor's covenant to pay [proviso to Sec. 68(1)].

For the purpose of enforcing special covenants not covered by the Transfer of Property Act, and in territories where the Transfer of Property Act is not in force, it is safer to insert an interpretation clause. The simple form of such clause is as follows:

1 *Shivdev Singh* v. *Sucha Singh*, AIR 2000 SC 1935.

"The expressions "the mortgagor" and "the mortgagee" shall, where the context so admits, include the persons deriving title under the mortgagor and mortgagee respectively," *or*

"Unless there is anything repugnant in the context, the expressions "the mortgagor" and "the mortgagee" hereinbefore used include their respective heirs, representatives, successors and assigns."

In the case of corporations the words, "heirs" and "representatives" should be omitted. Where the person making the contract is doing so in a representative character, e.g., as guardian, manager, etc., the expression denoting such persons should include "all persons, and the heirs, representatives, successors and assigns of every person upon whose behalf he is entitled to contract or to accept the benefit of a contract in relation to the subject-matter of the transaction." The words "Wherever such an interpretation would be requisite in order to give the fullest scope and effect legally possible to any covenant or contract herein contained", recommended for interpretation clause in the case of leases, are recommended in mortgage deeds also.

Reconveyance

Reconveyance of the mortgaged property to the mortgagor is not absolutely necessary to complete the redemption of a mortgage. If the mortgage money is repaid, the debt is wiped off, its security automatically vanishes, but the mortgage deed must be returned preferably along with an endorsement of repayment.

A reconveyance may be endorsed on the mortgage deed itself or may be made by a separate deed. If it is made by endorsement there need be no recitals but if it is made by a separate deed, the mortgage deed must be recited. If the person redeeming is not the original mortgagor, his title should be traced to show how he has a right to redeem, and similarly, derivation of the mortgagee's title should be recited, if he is not the original mortgagee. In the operative part the mortgagee "conveys" or "transfers" or, if the property is leasehold "assigns" the same to the mortgagor to hold it freed and discharged from his claims under the mortgage. Sometimes the word "releases" and "surrenders" are also used.

Mortgagor has a right to redeem the mortgage provided the right conferred in favour of mortgagor has not been extinguished by act of the parties or by decree of the Court, as per Proviso to Section 60 of the TP Act.

Mortgage of Movables[1]

The Transfer of Property Act is not exhaustive on the subject of mortgage or charge. While it deals with the mortgage of immovable property it does not deal with mortgage of movables at all. It cannot, therefore, be regarded as forbidding a mortgage of movable property. A mortgage of movables (such as machinery and plant, stock in trade, floating stock policy) is a perfectly valid transaction even

1 See also "Pledge and Hypothecation", *post*.

though possession is not delivered and the mortgage is only a hypothecation.[1] Such a mortgagee can obtain decree for sale[2] and a mortgagee in possession can sell the movables without the intervention of a court if the mortgagor fails to pay inspite of notice.[3] But a mortgagee without possession is liable to be defeated by a bona fide purchaser without notice.[4] Machinery and plant attached to earth have been held to be immovable property and governed as such by the law of transfer relating to immovable property.[5]

Even movables not in existence (e.g., future crops, machinery to be fixed, etc.) can be mortgaged, for such mortgage will be a contract to assign property when it will come into existence and when the property will come into existence the contract will become a complete assignment.[6]

Shares of companies are included in England in the description of "Choses in action" and can be transferred as "goods".[7] They can therefore be mortgaged by a proper deed of mortgage creating a charge on them. As a mortgagee of goods without possession is defeated by a *bona fide* purchaser without notice it is always safer to obtain delivery of the share certificates also with blank transfer deeds signed by the mortgagor, which can be completed when necessary by the signature of the transferee. This right of completing the transfer which is a chose in action is also included in the definition of "goods"[8] and can be transferred by the mortgagee by sale in case mortgagor makes default in payment of the debt. It is safer to give this power of sale expressly by the mortgage deed and such a contract would be valid as section 69 of Transfer of Property Act cannot apply to a mortgage of movables, although even if no such express power is given, it is implied in the mortgage.[9] The mortgagor may even agree that if the shares are not redeemed by a particular date the title of the mortgagee to them will become absolute. In such cases the deed is drafted very much in the form of an English mortgage, *i.e.*, the shares are transferred to the mortgagee absolutely subject to the right of redemption.

A mortgage of movables is distinct from a pledge, inasmuch as in the former,

---

1 *Tahilram* v. *D'Mello*, 18 BLR 587, 37 IC 231; *In the matter of Ambrose Summers*, 23 C 592; *Co-operative Hindustan Bank* v. *Surendra Nath*, AIR 1932 Cal 524; *Chinni Venkatchalam Chetty* v. *Athivarapu Venkatrami Redd*, AIR 1940 Mad 929.

2 *Basavireddy* v. *Kamaraju*, 64 MLJ 86, AIR 1933 Mad 241.

3 *In re Ali Mohamed*, AIR 1932 Bom 613.

4 *Sreeram* v. *Bamireddi*, (1918) 35 MLJ 450; *K.M.S. Mallayan Chettiar* v. *Sivarama Pillai Krishna Pillai*, AIR 1955 Trav. Coch. 162; *Naraiah* v. *Venkataramiah*, (1919) 42 Mad 59.

5 18 *Official Liquidator* v. *Krishna Deo*, AIR 1959 All 247.

6 *Babu Ram* v. *Ram Sarup*, AIR 1926 All 164; *Co-operative Hindustan Bank* v. *Surendra Nath*, 1932 (1) Cal 526.

7 *Manekji* v. *Wadilal*, 50 B 360 PC.

8 *Manekji* v. *Wadilal*, 50 B 360 PC.

9 *In re Ali Mohamad*, AIR 1932 Bom 613.

the mortgagee acquires general property in the goods mortgaged subject to the right of redemption, while in the latter case the pledgee has only the special property, *i.e.*, right to retain goods as a security.[1]

Ordinarily, when possession is relinquished the right of the pledgee is extinguished or waived, while a mortgagee's rights subsist even without possession. Delivery of possession of goods is necessary in pledge but not in hypothecation.[2] A subsequent pledge has priority over a previous hypothecation.[3] The facts and circumstances determine whether the transaction is a mortgage or a pledge.[4]

CHARGE

Where immovable property of one person is by act of parties or operation of law made security for the payment of money to another, and the transaction does not amount to a mortgage, the latter person is said to have a charge on the property; and all the provisions hereinbefore contained which apply to a simple mortgage shall, so far as may be, apply to such charge (section 100, Transfer of Property Act 1882). Thus, in a charge, property of one person is made security for the payment of money to another.

Here we are concerned only with a charge created by act of parties and not with charge created by operation of law or by a decree.

Distinguished from Mortgage

A mortgage is a transfer of an interest in specific immovable property, while in a charge there is no such transfer but only the creation of a right of payment out of certain property.[5] A mortgage is good against subsequent transferees while a charge is good only against a transferee with notice of the charge, or a volunteer with or without notice.[6] A subsequent mortgagee with notice of a prior charge takes the mortgage subject to the charge.[7]

No particular words are necessary to create a charge but the property and also the payment to be secured should be specified though, there is no transfer of an interest in the property. In order that a charge may be created there must be evidence of intention disclosed by the deed that a specified property or fund belonging to a person was made liable to satisfy the debt due by him.[8] A mere

---

1 *T. Radhakrisnan Chettiar* v. *The Official Liquidator Madras, Peoples Bank Ltd.*, AIR 1943 Mad 73; *Raja Kakarlapudi Venkata Sudarsana Sundra Narasayyamma Guru* v. *Andhra Bank Ltd., Vijayawada*, AIR 1960 AP 273.

2 *Jammu & Kashmir Bank Ltd.* v. *Tek Chand,* AIR 1959 J & K 67 (69).

3 *Co-operative Hindustan Bank v. Surendra Nath*, AIR 1932 Cal 524, ILR 59 Cal 667.

4 *Jageshwar Thakur* v. *Maha Bharat Thakur*, AIR 1950 Pat 32 (37).

5 *U.P Govt.*v. *Manmohan Das*, AIR 1941 All 345, 196 IC 425.

6 *Kishan Lal* v. *Ganga Ram*, (1891) ILR 13 All 28.

7 *D. Shanker Mote* v. *A.C. Datar*, 1975 (2) SCR 224.

8 *M.C. Chacko* v. *State Bank of Travancore*, (1969) 2 SCC 343; See also *Dattatreya Mote* v. *Anand Datar*, (1974) 2 SCC 799.

agreement to mortgage certain property in future for satisfaction of certain dues does not however create a charge,[1] though a suit for specific performance may lie on the contract. If "all the property" of a person "movable or immovable" is mentioned the description is not vague but is sufficiently specific and it is not necessary that every item of the property should be specified.[2] If the deed creating charge recites an earlier equitable mortgage by deposit of title deeds in respect of some of the immovable property charged and further provides for reconveyance of the properties then it will be construed as a deed of mortgage even if it is described as one of hypothecation.[3]

Further Charge

Sometimes the same mortgagee advances further sums of money to the mortgagor on the same security and on the same conditions. The deed to secure this is called "a deed of further charge." Usually a separate deed is executed, reciting the first mortgage, the new loan, terms of its repayment and making the principal and interest a further charge on the same security to be enforced in the same way. When a usufructuary mortgagee advances a further loan on interest and the parties agree that the amount due for principal and interest on the latter bond should be added to the mortgage money payable on redemption of the usufructuary mortgage, in such a case, the usufructuary mortgage cannot be redeemed without payment of the money due on account of the later loans, but such loans should be definitely secured by hypothecation of the mortgaged property.

Floating Charges

While a specific charge is one that fastens on ascertained and definite property, or property capable of being ascertained and defined, (with the consequence, as in case of a mortgage, that the debtor cannot dispose of the specified assets covered by the charge except subject to the charge) a floating charge is ambulatory and shifting in its nature, hovering over and, so to speak, floating with the property which it is intended to affect (which may be both present and future) until some event occurs or some act is done which causes it to settle and fasten on the subject of the charge within its reach and grasp.[4] Thus, a floating charge is generally executed in respect of work in progress, stock-in-trade or book debts, while a specific (or fixed) charge covers land, building and installed machinery, etc. The debtor executant of a floating charge can continue to dispose of

---

1 *J.K Ltd.* v. *New Kaiser-e-Hind Spinning and Weaving Co.*, (1969) 2 SCR 866.

2 *Narasimhamurthi* v. *Satyanandan*, AIR 1941 Mad 794.

3 *Chittavalsa Jute Mills* v. *Commissioner*, AIR 1985 AP 391 (SB).

4 *Illingworth* v. *Houldsworth*, 1904 AC 355; *In re, Yorkshire Wool-combers Association*, (1903) 2 Ch 284; *Imperial Bank* v. *B.N. Bank*, AIR 1931 Cal 223; *G. Bhor & Co.* v. *U.B.I.*, AIR 1961 Cal 308; *George Barker* v. *Eynon*, (1974) 1 All ER 900 (CA); See *Re. ELS Ltd.*, (1994) 2 All ER 833 (for difference between charge before crystallisation and its operation after crystallisation).

its stock-in-trade as if the charges did not exist, but as soon as the charge crystallises, it will fix upon whichever specific assets comprise the executant's stock-in-trade at the moment of crystallisation.[1]

The floating charge crystallises or becomes fixed on any of following events happening, namely,

(a) default on the part of the debtor,

(b) debtor ceasing business, becoming bankrupt or commencing of liquidation proceedings against debtor company,

(c) debenture-holder appointing a receiver or applying to the court to appoint a receiver over the property or business of debtor.

A floating charge may be created over the entire undertaking of the debtor, *i.e.*, all assets, whether fixed or current, or over "all the property now belonging to or hereafter acquired by" the executant.[2]

It is possible in law for a mortgagor, by way of continuing security for further advances, to grant to a mortgagee a charge on future book debts in a form which creates in equity a specific charge on the proceeds of debts or other like assets as soon as received. In that case the mortgagor will be prevented from transferring such assets except subject to the encumbrance. A clause providing that "during the continuance of this security the company shall pay into its account with the bank all moneys which it may receive in respect of book debts and other debts hereby charged and shall not without the prior consent of the bank (creditor) in writing purport to charge or assign the same", has thus been upheld.

Unless the floating charge contains a prohibition against the creation of subsequent charge ranking in priority or *pari passu*, and the fixed chargee has notice of such prohibition, a subsequent fixed charge will have priority over an earlier floating charge.[3] Notice of such prohibition can be ensured by getting a special resolution of the debtor company passed in respect of the creation of the floating charge including such prohibition[4] and/or by the floating charge taking possession of the title deeds and other documents of title to the assets charged[5] where it be possible to do so.

PLEDGE (PAWN) AND HYPOTHECATION[6]

The bailment of goods as security for payment of a debt or performance of a promise is called "pledge" (Sec. 172, Indian Contract Act). No writing is required

---

1 Sheldon and Fidler's Practice and Law of Banking, 11th Edn. (ELBS), p. 435; Chorely's Law of Banking, 6th Edn., p. 312; Reeday's Banking, 4th Edn., pp. 142-147.

2 *In re, Panama, New Zealand, etc. Co.*, 1870 LR 5 Ch 318.

3 Sheldon and Fidler's Practice and Law of Banking 11th edn. (ELBS), pp. 441-442.

4 Milnes Holden's Law of Banking, 5th edn., Vol. 2, p. 359.

5 Sheldon and Fidler, *op. cit.*, p. 442.

6 *See also* "Mortgage of Movables", *ante*.

for a pledge but the bailment may be accompanied by a memorandum or a collateral agreement containing the terms of the pledge. In such a memorandum *or* agreement the articles pawned, the payment to be secured by the pledge, the conditions of such payment, and any special terms of the pledge should be given. The power of sale is statutory and need not be provided in the agreement.

In the case of share certificates, in order to constitute a valid pledge, there should be such delivery of possession to the pledgee, by virtue of which he can effectively exercise the power of sale for realizing the debt. Assignment would therefore be necessary.[1]

Under Sec. 176, a pawnee may in case of pawner's default, either, bring a suit for recovery of the debt retaining the goods as a collateral security, or may sell the goods after notice and realise any balance by suit.

Hypothecation as such is not referred to in the Transfer of Property Act or in the Indian Contract Act.

The position of a pawn broker or pawnee has been explained by the Supreme Court in a case on sales tax.[2]

Unlike a mortgage, a pledge or hypothecation does not have the effect of transferring the property in favour of the pledgee or hypothecatee.[3] The pledge or hypothecation, however, creates a special property in the goods in his favour. In the case of pledge, the special feature is the right to keep possession of the pledged goods and to dispose them of, for the realisation of the debt for which it is held as security. In the case of hypothecation, possession remains with the hypothecator but the hypothecatee has the right to take possession of the hypothecated property and to sell it for the realisation of the debt secured by hypothecation either on its own or through court.[4]

While in case of pledge, transfer of actual or constructive possession over goods to the lender is essential, in the case of hypothecation, the possession remains with the borrower. Thus pledge may not be possible where the goods are in the temporary custody of a third party[5] or where they are so stored in the borrower's own warehouse that they cannot be sealed off in such a way as to enable

---

1 *Krishna* v. *Kunhunni*, AIR 1941 Mad 394.

2 *Karnataka Pawnbroker Association* v. *State of Karnataka*, AIR 1999 SC 201.

3 *Balkrishna Gupta* v. *Swedeshi Polytex Ltd.*, (1985) 2 SCC 167 (para 33) (relying on the Court's earlier decisions).

4 *Syndicate Bank* v. *Official Liquidator*, AIR 1985 Del 256; *Miran Baksh* v. *Emp.*, AIR 1945 Lah 69 (SB), *Board of Revenue* v. *Hindustan Construction Co.*, AIR 1985 Ker 2 86 (SB) relg. on *Harish Chandra* v. *Punjab National Bank*, AIR 1958 All 864 (DB).

5 *In re, Hemilton Young & Co.*, (1905) 2 KB 772 (Borrower's cloth was with bleachers. Borrower gave to the bank "letters of lien" accompanied by the bleacher's receipts for the goods. Bank gave notice of the lien to the bleachers. Held, effective as hypothecation, though subsequently borrower adjudicated bankrupt).

the bank to become a pledgee,[1] or where the goods are such as must be used constantly by the borrower in order to enable him to make his living and repay the loan (as in the case of a taxi or a truck purchased out of the loan). Security over the goods may be created by the execution either of a letter of hypothecation, also called a letter of lien[2] or of a formal deed.

It may be noted here that although the expression "hypothecation bond" is now used in respect of movables only, there is nothing in the legal meaning of the word 'hypothecate' to confine or inhibit its use in respect of either movable or immovable property.[3] It is thus that the word 'hypothecates' has been used in some of the precedents in deeds relating to immovable property also (See for Instance precedents No. 4, 5, 6, 16).

Stamp Duty

The duty on a mortgage deed is payable by the mortgagor (Sec. 29). Pledge and Hypothecation are chargeable under Article 6 and not under the Article relating to Mortgage.[4] In the Central Schedule, Art. 40 of Schedule 1 of The Stamps Act, is the relevant provision (but see local Amendments).

Registration

Under the Transfer of Property Act, a simple mortgage deed and all other mortgage deeds (except mortgage by deposit of title deeds) securing Rupees one hundred or more should always be registered (Sec. 59). Even in territories where that Act is not in force, registration is necessary where the money secured is Rs.100 or more (Sec. 17 Registration Act). If an equitable mortgage (*i.e.* mortgage by deposit of title deeds) which can be made orally is made by a deed, the deed needs registration if the money secured is Rs.100, or more (Sec. 17), but a memorandum of deposit of title deeds if drafted in such a way as to be merely the record of an already completed transaction, same would not require registration. In other words, if the writing is merely a statement that the mortgage has been effected or a statement of facts from which the contract of mortgage can be inferred, it would not require registration. But if the memo embodies such terms and is signed and delivered at such time and place and in such circumstances as to lead legitimately to the conclusion that it constitutes the agreement between the parties, it would

---

1 Chorley's Law of Banking, 6th edn., p. 329.

2 Sheldon and Fidler's Practice and Law of Banking, 11th edn., p. 481.

3 According to Black's Law Dictionary (6th , 1990 edn.), p. 742, "hypotheca" was a term of Roman law denoting a mortgage, whether of lands or of goods, in which the subject of mortgage remained in the possession of the mortgagor. The expression "hypothecation bond" is however "a bond in the contract of *bottomry or respondentia*", which contracts relate to hypothecation of a ship or its cargo as security for the repayment of a loan.

4 *Board of Revenue* v. *Hindustan Construction Co.*, AIR 1985 Ker 286 (SB), relg, on *Harish Chandra* v. *Punjab National Bank*, AIR 1958 All 864 (DB).

require registration.10[1]

A reconveyance requires registration if the consideration is Rs.100 or more (Sec. 17).

A receipt for mortgage money whether separate or endorsed on the mortgage deed does not require registration unless it by itself purports to extinguish the mortgage of the value of Rs.100 or more [Sec. 17(2)(XI)],

A deed creating a charge over immovable property requires registration if the amount of the charge is Rs.100 or more.

It may be noted here that the condition of "Rs.100 or more" has, due to inflation, now become meaningless, and has therefore been omitted in U.P. by U.P. Act No. 57 of 1976.

A mortgage of movables does not require registration.

A charge or a mortgage by a company requires also to be registered with the Registrar of Companies under section 77 Companies Act, 2013, failing which it shall not be taken into account by the liquidator and any creditor of the company. However, this shall not prejudice any contract or obligation for the repayment of the money secured by a charge.

---

1 *Obla* v. *Narayanna*, AIR 1931 PC 36.

GENERAL FORMS OF DIFFERENT PARTS OF A MORTGAGE DEED

Formal Parts[1]

Recitals

1. Title to Mortgaged Property as Owner[2]

WHEREAS the mortgagor is absolute owner of the property described in the schedule hereto.

2. Derivation of Title

WHEREAS the property described in the schedule hereto originally belonged to one AB, etc., on whose death in (year) ——— it devolved on his sons CD and EF as his heirs.

AND WHEREAS in a partition made between the said CD and EF by a deed of partition dated ——— the said property was allotted exclusively to the said EF;

AND WHEREAS the said EF sold the same to GH by a deed of sale dated the ————;

AND WHEREAS one JK brought a civil suit for pre-emption of the said sale and obtained a decree against the said GH and in execution of the said decree obtained possession;

AND WHEREAS the said JK has by a deed dated ——— made a gift of the said property to the mortgagor and the mortgagor has been in possession as absolute owner since the date of the said deed of gift.

3. Title as Lessee

WHEREAS by a lease dated the ————— made between AB, etc., as lessor and the mortgagor as lessee the property described in the schedule hereto was demised to the mortgagor from the ———— day of ———— for the term of —— years subject to the payment of the rent thereby reserved and the covenants by the lessee and conditions therein contained.

---

1 *See* also, GENERAL FORMS (immediately after Introduction, pp. 52-64, *ante*).

2 Recitals of title are not always necessary (covenant as to title being implied), but should always be given when the mortgagor is not the absolute owner.

4. Partly as Owner, Partly as Lessee

WHEREAS by a lease dated ——— one AB, etc., demised to the mortgagor the land described in the schedule hereto from the ——— day of ——— for the term of ——— years subject to payment of rent thereby reserved and the covenants by the lessee and the conditions therein contained;

AND WHEREAS the lessee has built on the said land a dwelling house with out-houses, garage and guest house.

5. Derivation of Title to Leasehold Property

WHEREAS by a lease, etc., (*as in No. 3, substituting the words "CD etc.", for the word "mortgagor"*);

AND WHEREAS on the death of the said CD his rights and interest in the said land under the said lease devolved on his son EF who sold the same by a deed of sale dated the —— to one GH and on the death of the said GH the same were inherited by his nephew JK who by a Will dated the —— bequeathed the same to the mortgagor;

AND WHEREAS the said JK has died on the ——— and since then the mortgagor has been in possession of the said property under the said will.

Or,

WHEREAS by a lease, etc., (*as in No.3, substituting the words "CD, etc.," for the word "mortgagor"*);

AND WHEREAS by diverse transfers, operation of law and events and ultimately by a Will dated the ——— and made by one JK, etc., the rights and interests of the lessee in the said land under the said lease have become vested in the mortgagor.

6. Title as Mortgagee

WHEREAS by a mortgage deed dated ——— one AB, etc., transferred to one CD, etc., by way of usufructuary mortgage the property described in the schedule hereto to secure a debt of Rs. ——— on certain conditions therein mentioned;

AND WHEREAS on the death of the said CD his rights under the aforesaid mortgage devolved on his son EF who has transferred the same to the mortgagor by a deed of sale dated ——— and the mortgagor is thus now in possession of the said property as mortgagee under the aforesaid mortgage.

7. Title to Life Policy

WHEREAS the mortgagor is entitled to the policy or several policies of assurance on his life hereby mortgaged (*or*, mentioned in the schedule hereto) and has handed the same to the mortgagee.

8. Mortgagor's Right as Executor

WHEREAS by his Will dated the ——— day of ——— XY, etc., deceased appointed the mortgagors to be executors thereof and *inter alia* devised the property described in the schedule hereto to them upon the trust therein declared;

AND WHEREAS the said XY died on the ——— without having altered or revoked the said Will which was duly proved by the mortgagor in the Court of District Judge of ——— and a probate of the same was duly obtained[1] on the ———.

9. Mortgagor's Right as Administrator

WHEREAS XY, the owner of the property described in the schedule hereto by his Will dated the ———, devised and bequeathed the said property in the manner herein set forth but did not thereby appoint any executor of his said Will;

AND WHEREAS the said XY died on the ——— without having revoked or altered his said Will and on the ———, letters of administration with the said Will annexed were granted to the mortgagor by the Court of the District Judge of ———.

10. Mortgagor's Right as Guardian

WHEREAS the said AB minor is owner of the property described in the schedule hereto;

AND WHEREAS by an order of the District Judge of ——— dated the ——— the mortgagor has been appointed guardian of the property of the said AB;

AND WHEREAS by an order dated ——— the said District Judge has granted to the mortgagor permission to make the mortgage hereby intended to be made;

11. Mortgagor's Right as Manager of Joint Hindu Family

WHEREAS the mortgagor and AB, CD and EF form a joint Hindu family governed by the Mitakshara School of Hindu Law of which the

1 *See* Preliminary Note on WILLS, *post*, on when probate is required and when it is not.

mortgagor is the manager;

AND WHEREAS the property described in the schedule hereto belongs to the said Joint Hindu family.[1]

12. Agreement for Loan

WHEREAS the mortgagee has agreed with the mortgagor to lend to him the sum of Rs. ——— upon having the repayment thereof with interest thereon at the rate hereinafter mentioned secured in the manner hereinafter appearing.

13. Agreement to Secure Old Debts

WHEREAS the mortgagor owes to the mortgagee the sum to Rs. —— on account of a loan taken by him under a promissory note (*or*, bond) dated ———, and it has been agreed that the repayment thereof with interest at the rate hereinafter mentioned shall be secured in the manner hereinafter appearing.

14. Agreement to Secure Old and Present Debts

WHEREAS the mortgagor owes the mortgagee the sum of Rs. ——— as per details given in the First Schedule hereto and the mortgagee has agreed to advance a further sum of Rs. ———— on having the repayment of the total sum of Rs. ———— with interest thereon at the rate hereinafter mentioned, secured in the manner hereinafter appearing.

15. Agreement to Secure Present and Future Advances

WHEREAS the mortgagee has agreed with the mortgagor to lend to him the sum of Rs. ———— upon having the repayment thereof and of every other sum which may be advanced in pursuance of the covenant by the mortgagee hereinafter contained with interest thereon at the rate hereinafter mentioned, secured in the manner hereinafter appearing;

Or

WHEREAS the mortgagee has agreed to lend to the mortgagor the further sum of Rs. ———— (*or*, such further sums of money as may be required by the mortgagor not exceeding the total sum of Rs. ————) upon having the repayment thereof with interest thereon at the rate hereinafter mentioned, secured in the manner hereinafter appearing;

Or

---

1 In such a case details of legal necessity or benefit to the estate are also to be recited in justification of the mortgage (See recitals No. 17, 18 *post*).

WHEREAS the principal sum secured by the aforesaid deed of mortgage still remains due to the mortgagee;

AND WHEREAS the mortgagee on the application of the mortgagor, has agreed to lend to the mortgagor a further sum of Rs. ——— upon having the same and the interest thereon at the rate hereinafter mentioned secured by a further charge on the property comprised in the aforesaid deed of mortgage.

16. Joining of Surety

WHEREAS the surety has agreed to join this deed as surety for the mortgagor in the manner hereinafter appearing.

17. Recitals of Legal Necessity

WHEREAS the mortgagor requires a loan of Rs. ——— to meet the expenses of his daughter's marriage (*or*, to pay land revenue of the villages ———, *or*, to meet the expenses of higher technical education of his son).

WHEREAS the mortgagee, after making bona fide inquiries has satisfied himself as to the existence of the said legal necessity.

18. Recitals of Antecedent Debts of Father[1]

WHEREAS the mortgagor's deceased father had borrowed Rs.——— from AB, etc., on a bond dated ——— and Rs. ——— from CD, etc., on a promissory note dated ——— and a sum of Rs. ——— is now due to the said AB and Rs.——— to the said CD on account of the aforesaid loans;

AND WHEREAS in order to pay off the aforesaid debts the mortgagor desired to raise a loan of Rs. ——— and the mortgagee agreed to advance the said loan on having the repayment thereof with interest thereon at the rate hereinafter mentioned secured in the manner hereinafter appearing.

19. Transfer of Shares Mortgaged

WHEREAS in pursuance of the said agreement the mortgagor has transferred to the mortgagee the shares specified in the schedule hereto and has deposited with him the share scrips of the said shares together with duly executed transfers thereof enabling the mortgagee to have his name registered as a shareholder in respect thereof and to deal with the said shares.

1 See note under recital No. 11 *ante*.

20. Agreement for Reconveyance

WHEREAS the principal sum of Rs. ——— secured by the aforesaid deed of mortgage (*or*, a sum of Rs. ——— is now due under the aforesaid deed of mortgage) and the mortgagor is desirous of paying the same and obtaining a reconveyance of the mortgaged property.

21. Agreement for Release of Part of Property

WHEREAS the mortgagor having paid Rs. ——— to the mortgagee, the mortgagee has agreed to release from the mortgage, the property specified in the schedule hereto from the charge created by the hereinbefore recited deed of mortgage.

Consideration, Receipt

1. Present Debt (when no Recitals)

In consideration of the sum of Rs. ——— now advanced by the mortgagee to the mortgagor (the receipt of which the mortgagor hereby acknowledges).

2. Consideration to be Paid at Registration

In consideration of the sum of Rs. ——— to be paid by the mortgagee at the time of the registration of the deed.

3. Partly Paid before and Partly to be Paid at Registration

In consideration of the sum of Rs. ——— out of which Rs. ——— has been paid to the mortgagor before the execution hereof (the receipt of which is hereby acknowledged), Rs. ——— has been left in the mortgagee's hands for payment to the various creditors named in the first schedule hereto and Rs. ——— agreed to be paid by the mortgagee at the time of registration hereof.

Or

In consideration of the sum of Rs. ——— out of which a sum of Rs. —— has already been paid to the mortgagor on ——— (the receipt of which the mortgagor hereby acknowledges) and the balance is to be paid as follows:

Rs. —— on the —— day ———.

Rs. —— on the —— day ———.

4. Payments Detailed in Schedule

In consideration of the sum of Rs. ——— particulars of the payments of which are given in the schedule hereto.

5. Present and Past Debts

In consideration of the sum of Rs. ——— due to the mortgagee on account of, etc., (from which the mortgagee hereby releases the mortgagor) and of the further sum of Rs. ——— advanced by the, etc.,(*as in No.*1)

6. To Pay off Old Creditors

In consideration of the sum of Rs. ————— left in the hands of the mortgagee to pay off the various creditors of the mortgagor named in the first schedule hereto, which sum the mortgagee hereby agrees to pay to the said creditors.

7. Present and Past Debts with Recitals

In pursuance of the aforesaid agreement and in consideration of the sum of Rs. ——— due as aforesaid and of Rs. ——— now advanced by the mortgagee, etc.,(*as in No.*1)

8. Present and Future Advance

In consideration of the sum of Rs. ———— advanced etc., (*as in No.* 1) and of the mortgagee's covenant hereinafter contained for the advance of a further sum of Rs. ———— on the conditions hereinafter mentioned.

Parcels[1]

A. Covenant to Pay

1. Repayment of Principal

(*i*) The Mortgagor shall pay to the Mortgagee the principal sum on —— (*date*).

(*ii*) The Mortgagor shall repay to the Mortgagee the principal sum in instalments of Rs. ——— each on the 1st January every year, commencing from 1st January, 2001.

2. Repayment of Interest

(*i*) The Mortgagor shall pay to the Mortgagee interest at 12% per annum on the principal sum or so much as remains owing in half yearly instalments on 1st January and 1st July every year.

1 *See* INTRODUCTION, Part II, page 21 *ante*.

(ii) Where the Mortgagor pays on the dates specified in sub-clause (i) interest at the rate of 9% per annum, the Mortgagee shall accept the interest so paid in satisfaction of the Mortgagor's liability to pay interest.[1]

3. Principal with Interest

The mortgagor will pay to the mortgagee the said sum of Rs. —— with interest at ——— percent per annum on the ——— day of ——— (*or*, within ——— years from the date hereof) (*or*, on demand).

4. Repayment of Principal on Fixed Date and Interest Meantime[2]

The mortgagor will pay the mortgagee the said sum of Rs. ——— on the ———— and will in the meantime pay interest thereon or on such sum as may for the time remain unpaid at the rate of ——— percent per annum from the date hereof (*or*, from the ————) by yearly payment (*or*, by half yearly payments) on the ———— day of ——— and on the ——— day of ——— in each year and also so long as any part of the said principal money or sum to be treated as such remains unpaid.

5. Compound Interest

Any sums due on account of interest not paid on due date (*or*, within ——— days after due date) shall be treated as principal and added to the principal sum hereby secured and bear interest at the rate and payable on the yearly (half yearly) dates aforesaid.

6. To Pay Principal and Interest in Instalments

The mortgagor will pay to the mortgagee the said principal sum of Rs. ——— in annual instalment of Rs. ———— each on the ———— day of ——— in each year beginning from the ——— day of ——— next (*or*, by the instalments and on the dates mentioned below *or*, in the first schedule hereto) and will pay interest on the said sum or on so much thereof as shall from time to time remain unpaid at the rate of ——— percent per annum from the date hereof on the ——— day of ——— in each year along with the instalment of the principal (*or*, on the dates hereinafter fixed for payment of the instalments of the principal) so that upon each such day the interest up to that day shall be paid together with the instalments of the principal then payable as aforesaid.

---

1 An alternative form is given in Covenants and Provisos, No. 5, page 579.

2 Such mortgages are popularly called "Interest Only or Standing Mortgages" in England.

7. To Pay by Equated Instalments of Principal and Interest[1]

The mortgagor will pay the said principal sum of Rs. ——— with interest at ——— percent per annum in annual (half yearly) equated instalments of (Rs. ——— of the principal and interest combined on the ——— day of —— and the ——— day of ———) in each year.

8. Whole to become due on Default

If any interest or any instalment of the principal is not paid within—— days of due date, the sum then due to the mortgagee hereunder on account of principal and interest shall immediately become payable.

9. Covenant by Surety

The surety hereby covenants with the mortgagee that if default shall at any time be made in payment of any sum becoming payable by the mortgagor in accordance with the mortgagor's covenants hereinbefore contained then the surety will on demand pay the said sum to the mortgagee.

B. Covenants and Provisos

1. Against Redemption within a Term[2]

The mortgagor shall not be entitled to pay off the said sum of Rs.—or any part thereof (*or*, to redeem this mortgage) within ——— years, (*or*, before the ——— day of ———) unless the mortgagee takes any steps to enforce this security.

---

1 Such mortgages are popularly called "Fixed Instalment Mortgages" in England. An innovation adopted by Building Societies in England is Retail Prices Index Linked Mortgages, under which the capital outstanding on a mortgage is increased to reflect any movement in the retail prices index: see *Nationwide Bldg. Society* v. *Registrar of Friendly Society,* (1983) 3 All ER 296; *Multiservice Bookbinding Ltd.* v. *Marden,* (1979) Ch 84.

2 Section 60 of the Transfer of Property Act confers on the mortgagor, right of redemption which is a statutory right. It is a settled law in England and in India that a mortgage cannot be made altogether irredeemable or redemption made illusory. The period should not be unreasonable long. A mortgage deed stipulating redemption after a period of 99 years was held to be a clog on the equity of redemption, *Shivdev Singh* v. *Sucha Singh*, AIR 2000 SC 1935; *Seth Ganga Dhar* v. *Shanker Lal*, AIR 1958 SC 770; See also *Jayasingh Dnyanu Mhuprekar* v. *Krishna Babji Patil*, AIR 1985 SC 1646 (Right to redemption can come to an end only in a manner known to law: either by a contract between the parties or by merger or by a statutory provision debarring redemption); folld. in *Ch. Sambaiah* v. *Marapaka*, 1998 AIHC 3635 (AP) (Right to redemption lost by acquiescence: allowing mortgagee to make constructions over a period of 26 years).

2. Mortgagee for a Term

Neither the mortgagor shall be entitled to redeem nor the mortgagee shall be entitled to call for any part of his mortgage money within ——— years of the date hereof.

3. Option to Pay within Time

Provided always that the mortgagor may at any time pay to the mortgagee any sum of not less than Rs. ——— on account of the moneys hereby secured and that all sums so paid shall be applied first in reduction or payment of the interest and costs then due under these presents and then in reduction or payment of the principal money hereby secured.

4. Covenant to make Further Advances

The mortgagee will from time to time advance to the mortgagor such further sum or sums as he may require not exceeding in all the sum of Rs. ——— by monthly instalments of Rs. ——— each payable on the ——— day of each calendar month (*or*, by the instalments at the time and in the manner provided in the schedule) (*or*, at such time and in such instalments as the mortgagor shall require provided that in no one calendar month shall the mortgagee be bound to advance more than Rs. ———).

5. Reduction of Interest in case of Punctual Payment[1]

Provided that the mortgagee shall accept interest at the rate of ——— per cent per annum in lieu of the higher rate hereby appointed for any year (half year) in respect of which the mortgagor shall pay interest at such reduced rate not later than the due date (*or*, ——— days after due date) as to which time is to be of the essence of the contract.

6. Surety to be Liable to Mortgagee as Principal Debtor

Although as between the surety and the mortgagor, the surety is only a surety, yet as between the surety and the mortgagee, the surety shall be considered to be the principal debtor for the moneys hereby secured so that the surety shall not be released by time being given to the mortgagor or by any other variation in the provisions of this deed or any other act, omission, matter or thing whatsoever whereby the surety as surety only would have been discharged.

7. Limiting Surety's Liability

The surety shall not be liable hereunder to pay a larger sum than

1 An alternative form is given in Parcels No. 2 (ii), page 577.

Rs. ——— in all, with further interest on the same at the rate herein provided from the date of demand for payment being made upon him until payment.

8. Power of Sale (where Transfer of Property Act does not Apply)

If the mortgagor fails to pay the principal sum hereby secured with interest when the same shall become payable under the terms of this deed or if and whenever interest for ——— months remains unpaid, the mortgagee shall have power without the intervention of court to take possession of the mortgaged property and to sell or concur with any other person in selling the mortgaged property or any part thereof either together or in lots and either by public auction or by private contract subject to such conditions concerning title or evidence of title or any other matter as the mortgagee thinks fit, with power to vary any contract for sale and to buy in or at any auction or to rescind contract for sale and to resell without being liable for any loss occasioned thereby, and to realize the amount due to the mortgagee from such sale proceeds after defraying the necessary expenses properly incurred by him as incidental to the sale or any attempted sale and after discharging any prior encumbrance to which the sale is not made subject. Provided that such power of sale shall not be exercised unless and until notice in writing requiring payment of the money in arrears has been served on the mortgagor and default has been made in payment for three months after such service.

9. Power of Sale (where Transfer of Property Act Applies)[1]

If the mortgagor fails to pay the principal sum with interest after it has become payable under the provision of this deed, the mortgagee shall, in addition to any other remedy available to him under the law, have power to sell without the intervention of court, the mortgaged property or any part thereof for realization of the money due to him hereunder.

10. Appointment of Receiver (where Transfer of Property Act does not Apply)

In lieu of exercising the power of sale hereinbefore conferred, the mortgagee may appoint ——— or any other person he considers proper as

1 Sec. 69: This power is available to a mortgagee in the following cases:

(a) English mortgage: Where neither party is a Hindu, Muslim or Buddhist, etc. (*Note:* A company or corporation has no religion or caste).

(b) Where power expressly conferred and the mortgagee is Government;

(c) Where power expressly conferred and the property or any part thereof is situate in a Presidency town or Delhi, New Delhi or Ahmedabad or any other notified town.

receiver of the income of the mortgaged property or any part thereof with power to realize the said income and out of it to discharge all rents, taxes, and land revenue, rates and outgoings whatever payable in respect of such property or part, to pay interest on all prior mortgages of the property of which he is the receiver, to pay his own commission at the rate of ——— percent on gross realization, to pay all premia on insurance policies on such property or part and the cost of necessary repairs, and to expend the balance first in liquidation or payment of the interest due under this deed and then in liquidation or payment of the principal money due hereunder, and to pay the residue, if any, to the mortgagor;

11. Appointment of Receiver (where Transfer of Property Act Applies)[1]

In case the mortgagee shall have power under the law to appoint a receiver of the mortgaged property or any part thereof, he shall appoint Shri ——— as such receiver provided he is then alive and is able and willing to act as such.

12. Mortgagor's Covenant to Insure

During the continuance of the mortgage the mortgagor will keep the mortgaged buildings insured against damage by fire in the name(s) of the mortgagor (and mortgagee) in the sum of Rs. ——— with the ——— Insurance Company or such other company as the mortgagee may approve and will punctually pay all premia on such insurance and will produce to the mortgagee on demand the policy of such insurance and the receipt for the last premium so paid. Provided always that if the mortgagor shall make default in any of the above matters, the mortgagee may in his discretion insure and keep insured all or any of the said buildings to the amount aforesaid and that the expenses of so doing shall be repaid to him by the mortgagor on demand and until so paid shall be added to the principal money hereby secured and bear interest accordingly and be secured in the like manner as the said principal.

Provided also that any money received under any such insurance as aforesaid shall at the option of the mortgagee be applied either in and towards payment of the moneys hereby secured or the replacing or reinstating the property in respect of which the moneys have been paid.

Or

(1) The Mortgagor shall—

(*a*) insure and keep insured the mortgaged buildings against damage

1 Sec. 69 A, Transfer of Property Act.

by fire in the name of the mortgagee with ——— Insurance Company or with an insurance office nominated by the mortgagee in a sum of Rs. ———; and

(*b*) deliver to the mortgagee the policy of insurance and deliver to him three days before the policy expires a receipt for the payment of the premium to renew that policy.

(2) Where a sum of money is receivable under a policy effected under the last preceding sub-clause the mortgagee may apply the money—

(*a*) in repairing or rebuilding the building damaged; *or*

(*b*) towards payment of the principal and interest; or

(*c*) partly for purpose specified in para (*a*) and partly for purpose specified in para (*b*).

(3) The Mortgagor appoints the mortgagee his attorney—

(*a*) to demand, sue for, and receive money payable under the policy; and

(*b*) to settle and compromise all claims in relation to the policy.

(4) The Mortgagor shall not do anything that makes or may make the policy of insurance void or voidable.

13. Mortgagor's Covenant to Repair

During the continuance of the mortgage, the mortgagor will keep the mortgaged buildings in good and substantial repair and if he shall neglect to do so the mortgagee may at his discretion (either recall the moneys due hereunder and realise the same by enforcement of this mortgage or otherwise, or), enter upon the said premises from time to time in order to repair and keep in repair the said buildings without thereby becoming liable as a usufructuary mortgagee and the expenses of his so doing shall be paid by the mortgagor on demand and until so repaid shall be added to the principal moneys hereby secured and bear interest accordingly and be secured in the like manner as the said principal.

14. Covenant to give Possession to Usufructuary Mortgagee after Redeeming Prior Mortgage

The mortgagor will pay off the said prior mortgage of ——— and redeem the mortgaged property and deliver the same into the possession of the mortgagee and get the mutation of names effected in the revenue/municipal records in favour of the mortgagee.

15. Covenant to Pay Mortgagor's Creditors and Indemnity

The mortgagee will pay to all the creditors hereinbefore mentioned (*or*, mentioned in the schedule hereto) the moneys hereinbefore mentioned (*or*, mentioned it the said schedule) as being payable to them respectively and will indemnify and save harmless the mortgagor from all claims and demands of the said creditors and each of them in respect of the said moneys.

16. Mortgagee not to Cut Trees

The mortgagee may cut from the mortgaged properties such trees as may be needed for agricultural purposes or the cutting of which may be necessary for the management of the property but will not be entitled to cut any other trees.

17. Purchase of Arrears of Rent by Mortgagor at the Time of Redemption

Any rent of the mortgaged property for the period of the mortgage remaining unrealized but being legally recoverable at the date of redemption shall be purchased by the mortgagor from the mortgagee at a price equal to ——— percent of the total amount of such unrealized rents.

18. Covenant against Encumbrances

The mortgaged property is free from encumbrances (except those specified in the schedule hereto, subject to which this mortgage is made).

19. Taxes

The Mortgagor shall pay all rates, taxes, assessments and outgoings (whether apportionable or not), imposed or to be imposed on the mortgaged property.

20. Restrictions on Lease

The Mortgagor shall not lease the property except with the written consent of the mortgagee.

21. Covenant to Reconvey

Where the Mortgagor—

(*a*) repays to the mortgagee the principal sum;

(*b*) until the date of payment of the principal sum, pays to the mortgagee interest at the rate specified in clause ———; and

(*c*) complies with the covenants specified in this deed, the mortgagee, shall, at the request and cost of the Mortgagor, execute a statutory discharge as a reconveyance of the property.

PRECEDENTS

1—Simple Mortgage Deed for a Cash/Loan, with variation for Old Debt or Partly Old Debt and Partly Cash Loan (in the Form of Deed Poll)

I, AB son of CD, resident of ——— having borrowed Rs. ——— from EF, son of GH, resident of ——— (*or,* being indebted to the said EF in the sum of Rs. ——— due to him on account of ———), (*or*, being indebted to the said EF in the sum of Rs. ——— due on a bond dated——— and having borrowed to pay Rs. ——— from him) hereby promise to pay to the said EF the said sum of money (*or*, the sum of Rs. ———) on demand (*or*, on the ——— or within ——— years from this date) with interest thereon from this date at the rate of ——— percent per annum (compoundable half yearly).

AND for the consideration aforesaid and as security for the aforesaid loan, I hereby transfer by way of simple mortgage to the said EF, ALL that property described in the schedule hereto to the intent that in case default is made in the payment of any sum due hereunder, the said EF may enforce against the said premises all or any of the remedies of a simple mortgagee.

The schedule herein referred to

(Description of the mortgaged property)

Dated this the ——— day of ———.

Sd.———.

(Mortgagor)

Witnesses 1. ________

2. ________

2— Ditto (Consideration mentioned in the Schedule, Payment by Instalments)

I, AB, etc., being indebted to CD, etc., in the sum of Rs. ——— as per details in the first schedule hereto hereby agree to repay the said sum of Rs. ——— without interest in monthly instalments of Rs. ——— each payable on the ——— day of each month commencing from the day of ——— next, and also agree that in case of default in the payment of any two of the aforesaid instalments, the whole money then remaining due hereunder shall become payable at once and interest at ——— percent per annum will be charged on such money from the date of its so becoming payable at once.

AND for the consideration aforesaid, etc., (*as in Form* 1).

The first schedule herein referred to

(Details of liability)

(1)	Due to the mortgagee on account of price of cloth purchased by mortgagor on the ———	Rs. ———
(2)	Due to the mortgagee from the mortgagor on account of *bahi khata* account	Rs. ———
(3)	Due to the mortgagee on account of bond dated ———	Rs. ———
(4)	Borrowed from the mortgagee at the time of execution of this deed	Rs. ———
	Total	Rs. ———

The second schedule herein referred to

(Details of mortgaged property)

Dated this the ——— day of ———.

sd/-
(Mortgagor)

Witnesses 1. ___________

2. ___________

3—Simple Mortgage Deed (Ordinary Form without Recitals) with Several Variations of the Consideration

THIS DEED OF MORTGAGE made on the ——— day of ——— BETWEEN AB, etc., (hereinafter called "the mortgagor") of the one part AND CD, etc., (hereinafter called "the mortgagee") of the other part.

WITNESSES as follows:

I. Consideration

In consideration of the sum of Rs. ——— borrowed by the mortgagor from the mortgagee (the receipt of which the mortgagor hereby acknowledges) (*or,* in consideration of the sum of Rs. ——— due from the mortgagor to the mortgagee under a bond dated ——— and of the sum of Rs. ——— due to the mortgagee on account of a decree obtained by him in suit No. ——— of ——— from the Court of the ——— on the ———, and of Rs. ———— borrowed in cash by the mortgagor from the mortgagee) (*or,* in consideration of a cash loan of Rs. ———— to be advanced by the mortgagee to the mortgagor at the time of the registration of this deed and of Rs. ——— agreed to be paid by the mortgagee to the several creditors of the mortgagor named in the schedule hereto on account of the debts specified in the said schedule) (*or,* in consideration of the sum of Rs. ———— due to the mortgagee as per details given in the schedule hereto) the mortgagor hereby covenants with the mortgagee as follows:

(1) *Covenant to Pay Principal and Interest*

That the mortgagor will pay to the mortgagee the said sum of Rs. ——— on the ——— day of ———, and in the meantime interest thereon or on so much thereof as shall, for the time being, remain unpaid at the rate of —— percent per annum by half yearly payments on the —— day of —— and the —— day of ——— in each year, and also so long as any part of the said principal money or sum to be treated as such remains due under this deed;

(2) *Compound Interest*

That any interest not paid on (*or,* within ——— days after) due date shall be treated as principal and added to the principal sum hereby secured and bear interest at the rate and payable on the half-yearly dates aforesaid provided that this provision for the payment of compound interest shall in no way prejudice or affect the exercise by the mortgagee of any of rights or remedies vested in him by law or by this deed;

(3) *Costs*

That the mortgagor will on demand pay all reasonable costs incidental to this mortgage;

(4) *Whole to become due in Case of Default*

That in case any interest or any sum payable on account of costs shall be in arrear for thirty days, the whole sum secured by these presents shall thereupon become payable at once.

II. Mortgage Clause

For the consideration aforesaid the mortgagor hereby transfers by way of simple mortgage to the mortgagee all that property described in the first schedule hereto belonging to the mortgagor TO THE INTENT that the said premises shall remain and be charged as security for the payment to the mortgage of the said principal money, interest and costs, in accordance with the covenants hereinbefore contained.

III. Mortgagor's Covenants

The mortgagor hereby covenants with the mortgagee as follows:

(i) *Free from Encumbrances*

That the said premises are free from encumbrances (except those specified in the second schedule hereto, subject to which this mortgage in made).

(ii) *Mortgagee's Remedy*

That in case of default either in payment of the sum becoming payable under Clause 1 (4) or in payment thereof on the date hereinbefore provided (whether such default may have been made before or not) the mortgagee may forthwith enforce against the said premises or any part thereof all or any of the remedies of the holder of a simple mortgage, as provided in the Transfer of Property Act, 1882 and this deed shall be read and construed as a simple mortgage as defined by the said Act.

IV. Mortgagor's Right to Pay before Time

PROVIDED ALWAYS that the mortgagor may, at any time, pay to the mortgagee any sum of not less than Rs. ——— on account of the moneys hereby secured, and that all sum so paid shall be applied first in reduction or payment of the interest and costs then due under these presents and then in reduction or payment of the principal money hereby secured.

Reduced Interest

[Provided also that the mortgagee shall accept interest at the reduced rate of ——— percent per annum in lieu of the normal rate hereby appointed for any half year in respect of which the mortgagor shall pay interest at such reduced rate not later than the due date (*or,* ——— days after due date) as to which time is to be of the essence of the contract.][1]

[The mortgagee hereby covenants with the mortgagor that he will duly pay to the several creditors of the mortgagor hereinbefore named (*or,* named in the schedule hereto) the several sums of money left with him for payment out of the mortgage money and will always indemnify and save harmless the mortgagor and his property from all claims and demands of the

1 Where parties agree that in case of non-payment of interest on due date a higher rate shall be payable it is preferable in order to take the case out of Sec. 74, Contract Act (*i.e.,* in order that the higher rate may not be deemed to be penal) to adopt this device of providing the higher rate in the beginning and adding a proviso for acceptance of the lower rate.

said creditors or any of them in respect of such moneys or part thereof].[1]

V. Interpretation Clause

It is hereby agreed that wherever such an interpretation would be requisite in order to give the fullest scope and effect legally possible to any covenant or contract herein contained, the expressions "the mortgagor" and "the mortgagee" hereinbefore used include their respective heirs, executors, administrators and assigns.

The first schedule herein referred to

(Description of property or properties mortgaged by this deed).

The second schedule herein referred to

(Particulars of encumbrances)

The third schedule herein referred to

(Particulars of consideration) *as in the first schedule to Form* 2

IN WITNESS WHEREOF the parties hereto have hereunder put their signatures (*or*, the mortgagor has signed this deed) the day and year first above written (*or*, on the dates respectively mentioned against their signatures).

4—Simple Mortgage Deed in Lieu of Rent Decree with Agreement to pay the Sum due with Interest in Instalments, with Debtor and Surety Jointly Mortgaging their Property

THIS DEED OF MORTGAGE is made on the ——— day of —— BETWEEN AB, etc., (hereinafter called "the mortgagor") of the first part AND CD, etc., (hereinafter called "the mortgagee") of the second part AND EF, etc., (hereinafter called "the surety") of the third part.

WHEREAS—

(1) Debt

The aforesaid AB is indebted to the mortgagee to the extent of Rs. ——— due under a rent decree dated ——— passed by the court of ——;

(2) Agreement to pay in Instalments

The aforesaid AB not being in a position to pay the aforesaid decretal debt requested the mortgagee for permission to pay the same in ten equal annual instalments with interest at ——— percent per annum;

1 To be added if any part of the mortgaged money has been left for payment to creditors.

(3) Agreement for surety

The aforesaid EF in consideration of the mortgagee agreeing to accept payment in such instalments agreed to stand surety for payment of the aforesaid amount by the said AB to the mortgagee; and

(4) Hypothecation of the Property

The mortgagee agreed to accept the payment of the aforesaid decretal amount in ten equal annual instalments on the payment thereof being guaranteed by the aforesaid EF and secured by the hypothecation of the property described in the schedule hereto in the manner hereinafter appearing.

NOW THIS DEED WITNESSES as follows:

I. In pursuance of the said agreement and in consideration of the sum of Rs.——— due to the mortgagee from the aforesaid AB, the aforesaid AB hereby covenants with the mortgagee as follows:

(1) *Payment of Principal*
He will pay to the mortgagee the said sum of Rs. ——— in ten equal annual instalments payable on the ——— in each year;

(2) *Payment of Interest*
He will pay interest on the aforesaid sum or on such sum thereof as for the time being remains unpaid at the rate of ——percent per annum;

(3) *Time for Payment*
The whole amount due on account of interest on the dates of the annual instalments of the principal shall be paid along with such instalments;

(4) *Whole to become due on Default*
If any instalment is not paid on due date with the interest then due, the whole of the money thus remaining due shall become payable at once; and

(5) *Costs*
He will on demand pay reasonable costs incidental to this mortgage.

II. Surety Clause

In consideration of the mortgagee having agreed to accept the payment of the said decretal debt from the said AB in ten instalments as aforesaid, the said EF hereby guarantees the repayment of the same to the mortgagee in accordance with terms of the covenants hereinbefore mentioned.

III. Mortgage Clause

For the consideration aforesaid and in pursuance of the said agreement the aforesaid AB and EF (hereinafter jointly called "the mortgagors") hereby grant and transfer by way of simple mortgage to the mortgagee ALL that property described in the schedule hereto and jointly belonging to them TO the intent that the said premises shall remain and be charged by way of simple mortgage as security for the payment to the mortgagee of the said decretal debt and costs in accordance with the covenants hereinafter contained.

IV. Mortgagee's Remedy

The mortgagor hereby covenants with the mortgagee as follows:

(i) The said premises are free from encumbrances.

(ii) If the mortgagors shall make default in payment of any sum when becoming due as hereinbefore provided then the mortgagee may forthwith enforce against the said premises or against any portion of them all or any of the remedies of a holder of a simple mortgage and these presents shall be read and construed as a simple mortgage as defined by the Transfer of Property Act, 1882.

V. Interpretation clause—(as in Form 3).

IN WITNESS WHEREOF, etc.

5—Simple Mortgage of Property Purchased with a Loan Advanced on a Simple Money Bond on Condition of such Mortgage (the Simple Bond remaining Operative)

THIS DEED OF MORTGAGE is made, etc., (*an in Form* 3).

WHEREAS the mortgagee advanced to the mortgagor the sum of Rs. ——— for the purchase of ——— on the terms and conditions mentioned in the bond dated the ——— of ——— executed by the mortgagor (hereinafter referred to as the said "bond");

AND WHEREAS one of the conditions on which the said loan was advanced was that the mortgagor would within one month of the advance, purchase the said property for which the said loan was advanced and would hypothecate the same in favour of the mortgagee as security for repayment of the said loan with interest in accordance with the covenants contained in the said "bond";

AND WHEREAS the mortgagor has purchased the said property fully described in the schedule hereto.

NOW THIS DEED WITNESSES as follows:

1. In pursuance of the aforesaid agreement and in consideration of the said loan the mortgagor hereby grants and transfers to the mortgagee ALL that property described in the schedule hereto with all rights, easements and appurtenances thereto to the intent that the said premises shall remain and be charged by way of simple mortgage as security for the payment to the mortgagee of the said loan with interest thereon in accordance with the covenants contained in the said bond.

2. The mortgagor hereby covenants with the mortgagee as follows:

(1) that the said property described in the schedule hereto is free from encumbrances; AND

(2) for the purpose of recovering any sum that may become due to the mortgagee under the terms of the said bond the mortgagee may forthwith enforce against the said property described in the schedule hereto all or any of the remedies of the holder of a simple mortgage.

3. Interpretation clause—(as in Form 3).

IN WITNESS WHEREOF, etc.

6—Simple Mortgage Deed by Surety for Securing the Performance of Conditions of State Scholarship

THIS DEED OF MORTGAGE is made on the ——— day of —— BETWEEN XY, etc., (hereinafter called "the mortgagor") of the one part AND the Governor of West Bengal (hereinafter called "the mortgagee") of the other part

WHEREAS—

Recitals

(1) The Government of West Bengal has agreed to grant a State technical scholarship to AB, son of CD ——— etc.;

(2) Under the rule governing the grant of such scholarship each scholar or his parent or guardian is required to deposit Rs. 15,000 so that in the event of the scholar failing to secure employment on his return to India, funds at the rate of Rs. 1,500 per mensem may be available for ten months for his maintenance;

(3) The said AB or his father having been unable to deposit the said amount, the said Government by G.O. No. —— dated —— have waived the said condition of deposit provided that CD the

father of the said AB secured the payment of the said sum of Rs. 15,000 for the maintenance of the said AB on return to India by hypothecation of immovable property; and

(4) The mortgagor has in consideration of the said Government granting a State technical scholarship to the said AB agreed to furnish the required security in the manner hereinafter appearing;

NOW THIS DEED WITNESSES as follows:

1. Covenant to Pay a Maximum Sum

The mortgagor hereby agrees that in the event of the said AB not securing any employment on his return to India after completion of the training for which the State technical scholarship shall be awarded to him the mortgagor will pay to the mortgagee such sum not exceeding Rs. 15,000 as may be requisite for the maintenace of the said AB at the rate of Rs. 1,500 per mensem for such period as the said AB may remain out of employment during the ten months following his arrival in India;

2. Mortgage to Secure Sum Due

For the consideration aforesaid and as a security for the payment to the mortgagee of the said sum of Rs. ———— according to the terms and conditions hereof the mortgagor hereby transfers to the mortgagee ALL that property described in the schedule hereto to the intent that the same shall remain and be charged by way of mortgage in the manner following, namely that for the purpose of recovering the said sum of Rs. ——— or any lesser sum as may become due by the mortgagor to the mortgagee by virtue of these presents the mortgagee may at his option either sell the said property or any part thereof without the intervention of any court or take the rents and profits thereof for his own use until he shall have thereby or otherwise recovered any sum which may be due to him by the mortgagor by virtue of these presents.

3. The mortgagor hereby covenants that the said premises are free from encumbrances.

4. PROVIDED ALWAYS and it is hereby agreed that unless there is anything repugnant in the context the expression "the mortgagor" hereinbefore used shall include his heirs, representatives, successors and assigns, and the expression "the mortgagee" hereinbefore used shall include his successors and assigns.

IN WITNESS WHEREOF, etc.

7—Consolidation of Several Simple Mortgages into One

THIS DEED OF MORTGAGE is made, etc., (*as in Form* 3).

WHEREAS—

Recitals of Old Mortgages

(1) By deed dated the ——— the mortgagor mortgaged to the mortgagee the property described in Part A of the schedule hereto to secure the payment of a sum of Rs. ——— lent to the mortgagor by the mortgagee with compound interest thereon at the rate of ——— with half yearly rests;

(2) By a second deed dated the ——— the mortgagor mortgaged to the mortgagee the property described in Part B of the schedule hereto to secure the payment of another sum of Rs. ——— lent by the mortgagee to the mortgagor with compound interest thereon at the rate of ——— with half yearly rests;

(3) By a third deed dated the ——— the mortgagor mortgaged to the mortgagee the property described in Part C of the schedule hereto to secure the payment of a third sum of Rs. ——— with compound interest thereon at the rate of ——— with half yearly rests;

Sum Due

No part of the principal sums secured by the aforesaid three mortgages has been repaid;

The mortgagor on ——— paid to the mortgagee a sum of Rs. —— (as the mortgagee hereby admits) on account of interest leaving a sum of Rs. ——— now due for interest, making in all the sum of Rs. ——— now due for principal and interest;

Agreement to Mortgage

The mortgagee has agreed with the mortgagor to abstain from taking legal proceedings to realize the said sum of Rs. ——— upon having the repayment of the same with interest thereon at the rate of ——— secured in the manner hereinafter appearing;

NOW THIS DEED WITNESSES as follows:

(*Rest as in Form* 4).

The Schedule herein referred to.

IN WITNESS WHEREOF, etc.

8—Simple Mortgage Deed by a Pardanashin Lady in Pursuance of the Terms of a Compromise

THIS DEED OF MORTGAGE is made,. etc., (*as in Form* 3).

WHEREAS—

(1) In suit No. 27 of 1995 pending in the Court of the Civil Judge at ——— a joint decree was passed on the ——— in favour of the mortgagee and EF, etc., GH, etc., and JK, etc., against the mortgagor and her deceased husband XY for Rs. ——— with costs and interest from the date of suit upto the date of realisation;

(2) By virtue of the consent decree passed in suit No. 26 of 1996 in *re:* EF and four others *versus* CD, the mortgagee became solely and wholly entitled to realize the money due under the decree pased in suit No. 27 of 1995 as aforesaid;

(3) XY the husband of the mortgagor died and the mortgagor became the heir and owner of the the property left by the aforesaid XY;

(4) On the ——— mortgagee applied for execution of the decree in suit No. 27 of 1995 aforesaid against the mortgagor for Rs. ———;

(5) The mortgagor after consultation with her near relations and legal advisers and after fully understanding the transaction and realizing its effect on her interest and considering it to be for her benefit entered into a compromise with the mortgagee whereby the aforesaid decree was agreed to be satisfied by the mortgagor executing in favour of the mortgagee (1) a sale deed in respect of certain lands in village ——— for a price calculated at 25 times the annual net profits, and (2) this mortgage deed on the terms and conditions hereinafter contained for the balance of the money due to the mortgagee under the aforesaid decree;

AND WHEREAS in pursuance of the agreement in the aforesaid compromise and in part satisfaction of the aforesaid decree the mortgagor executed a sale deed of the said lands in village ——— for a consideration of Rs. ———.

NOW THIS DEED WITNESSES a follows:

1. In further pursuance of the aforesaid agreement and in consideration of the said sum of Rs. ——— remaining due to the mortgagee from the mortgagor on account of the aforesaid decree, the mortgagor hereby covenants with the mortgagee (*a*) that the mortgagor will pay to the mortgagee the said sum of Rs. ——— by six monthly instalments of Rs. —— each payable on the ——— and the ——— in each year commencing from the ——— and the last instalment of the remaining

Rs. ——— payable on the ———; and (*b*) that in case any two consecutive instalments hereinbefore mentioned be in arrears in whole or in part, then the whole sum secured by this deed then remaining unpaid shall become payable at once.

[*Rest as in Form* 3 *with necessary modifications in* III(*ii*)].

9—Simple Mortgage of Joint Family Property by Father for Legal Necessity and Antecedent Debt[1]

THIS MORTGAGE is made, etc., (*as in Form* 3).

WHEREAS—

Recitals of Status of Family

(1) The mortgagor and his sons, EF, GH and JK (minor) form a joint Hindu family governed by the Mitakshara School of Hindu law;

(2) The property mentioned in the schedule hereto is the joint ancestral property of the said family;

(3) The mortgagor's family carries on the ancestral business of ——;

(4) For the purpose of the said business the mortgagor borrowed Rs. ——— from the mortgagee on a pronote dated the ——— and the amount of the said loan with interest now due to the mortgagee comes to Rs. ——.

Necessity for the Loan

(5) The mortgagor is now in need of Rs. ———— for the following purposes, viz., Rs. ———— for the marriage of his daughter XY to be celebrated in the month of ————— next, Rs. ————— for payment of Government revenue in respect of the said family's land in villages ——; and Rs. ——— for the expenses of sending his son GH to the Indian Institute of Technology for education in electrical engineering;

(6) The mortgagee has made *bona fide* enquiries both as regards the ancestral nature of the business as well as the existence of the legal necessity. He has satisfied himself that the business of the family is ancestral and that the money is needed for the purposes aforesaid.

Agreement for Loan

(7) The mortgagor applied to the mortgagee for a loan of Rs. ——— for the aforesaid purposes and the mortgagee has agreed to advance the said

---

1 *See* Preliminary Note. Though a father may have power under the law to make the mortgage, it is always safer to join all the members of the family as mortgagors.

loan on an interest of ——— percent per annum on the mortgagor securing the repayment of the same as well as of the aforesaid debt of Rs. ——— with interest, by mortgage of the property described in the schedule hereto in the manner hereinafter appearing.

NOW THIS DEED WITNESSES as follows:

Covenants to Pay, etc.

In pursuance of the said agreement and in consideration of the sum of Rs. —— due to the mortgagee under the promissory note dated —— and of a further loan of Rs. ——— advanced to the mortgagor (the receipt of which the mortgagor hereby acknowledges) the mortgagor hereby covenants with the mortgagee as follows:

Rest as in Form 3 *except clause* V *which should run as follows:*

Interpretation Clause

PROVIDED ALWAYS that unless such an interpretation be inconsistent with the context the expression "the mortgagor" hereinbefore used includes all persons and the heirs, successors, representatives and assigns of each and every person on whose behalf the mortgagor is now entitled to contract or to accept the benefit of a contract in relation to the transaction herein contained whether such persons are named herein or not and the expression "the mortgagee" hereinbefore used includes his heirs, successors, representatives and assigns.

The schedule herein referred to.

IN WITNESS WHEREOF, etc.

10—Simple Mortgage of Joint Family Property, All Members of the Family Joining

THIS MORTGAGE is made on the ——— day of ——— BETWEEN AB, etc., EF, etc., GH, etc., and JK, etc., a minor acting through his father and natural guardian the said AB (hereinafter called "the mortgagors") of the one part AND CD, etc., (hereinafter called "the mortgagee") of the other part.

WHEREAS—

(1) The mortgagors form a joint Hindu family governed by the Mitakshara School of Hindu Law;

(2) *(As in Form 9);*

(3) The said family also own and carry on through the said AB an ancestral cloth business;

(4) *(As in Form 9, Substituting "the said AB" for "the mortgagor");*

(5) *(As in form 9, substituting "mortgagors" for "mortgagor" and "the said AB's daughter" for "his daughter", and "the said GH" for "his son GH").*

Rest as in Form 9, substituting "mortgagors" for "mortgagor".

11—Simple Mortgage by Manager of a Joint Hindu Family, Other Members also Joining

THIS MORTGAGE, etc. (*as in Form* 10), substituting for "acting through the said AB, the manager of his joint family" for the words "acting through his father, etc.")

WHEREAS—

(1) The said AB, EF, GH and JK form a joint Hindu family governed by the Mitakshara School of Hindu Law and the said AB is the manager of the said family.

(2) LM was the common ancestor. He had two sons, X and Y both now dead. The said AB and EF are the sons of the said X and the said GH and JK are the sons of the said Y.

[*Rest as in Nos.*(2), (3), (4) *etc. of Form* 9]

12—Mortgage to Secure an Annuity (Giving Option of Sale or of Taking Possession and Providing for Appointment of Trustees)

THIS DEED OF MORTGAGE is (*as in Form* 3).

WHEREAS—

Liability of Mortgagor

(1) The mortgagor and XY deceased brother of the mortgagor and husband of the mortgagee formed a joint Hindu family governed by the Mitakshara School of Hindu law;

(2) The whole joint ancestral property of the said family is now in possession of the mortgagor as the sole surviving male member and the mortgagor is therefore under a legal obligation to maintain the mortgagee;

Agreement to give Annuity

(3) The mortgagee has been living separately from the mortgagor and at the suggestion and on the advice of relations and friends of the family, the mortgagor has agreed to pay the mortgagee a maintenance allowance of

Rs. ——— per annum and to secure the same in the manner hereinafter appearing.

NOW THIS DEED WITNESSES as follows:

I. Covenant to Pay

In pursuance of the said agreement and in fulfilment of his legal obligation to provide for the maintenace of the mortgagee, the mortgagor hereby covenants with the mortgagee to pay to the mortgagee a monthly allowance of Rs. ——— on or before the ——— day of each month during the life of the mortgagee;

II. Mortgage Clause

The mortgagor hereby transfers by way of simple mortgage to the mortgagee the property described in the Schedule hereto together with all rights, easements and appurtenances thereto belonging, to the intent that the same shall remain and be charged in the manner hereinafter appearing as security for the payment of the said monthly allowance to the mortgagee in the manner herein mentioned;

III. Enforcement of Mortgage

It is hereby agreed that if and whenever the said monthly allowance or any part thereof shall be in arrear or unpaid for the space of three months after the same shall have become due the mortgagee may for the purpose of recovering the same either, (*i*) enter into possession of and hold all or any part of the said property and take the rents and profits thereof for her own use until she shall have thereby or otherwise realized all arrears of the said monthly allowance after having first taken for her own use out of such rents and profits the said allowance of Rs. ——— for every month during which she is so in possession or (*ii*) may at her option enforce against the said property the remedy available to a mortgagee;

IV. Sale Proceeds to be Paid to Trustees

It is hereby agreed that if the mortgagee elects to sell the said property then after all arrears of the said monthly allowance have been first paid to the mortgagee the proceeds of such sale or so much thereof as the court ordering such sale may deem to be necessary for the purpose hereinafter appearing shall be paid to such trustees as such court may appoint to be applied by them under the directions of such court in paying out of the capital or income thereof (if invested by order of such court) the said monthly allowance to the mortgagee during her life and the balance, if any, of the proceeds of such sale shall be paid to the mortgagor and on the death of the mortgagee any money or investments in the hands of such trustees for the purpose aforesaid shall be held by them in trust for the mortgagor.

V. Interpretation Clause

PROVIDED ALWAYS and it is hereby agreed that wherever such an interpretation would be requisite in order to give the fullest scope and effect legally possible to any covenant or contract herein contained the expression "the mortgagor" hereinbefore used includes the owner or owners for the time being of the property mortgaged and the expression "the mortgagee" hereinbefore used includes her heirs, executors, administrators and assigns.[1]

The schedule herein referred to.

IN WITNESS WHEREOF, ETC.

13—Simple Mortgage Deed for Loan Partly Advanced and Partly to be Advanced, with Promise to give Usufructuary Mortgage when Full Loan Advanced

THIS DEED OF MORTGAGE is made, etc. (*as in Form* 3).

WHEREAS—

Agreement for Loan

(1) The mortgagor desired to raise a loan of Rs. ——— bearing interest at the rate of ——— percent per annum on the usufructuary mortgage of the property mentioned in the first schedule hereto in order to pay off the debts shown in the second schedule hereto with which the said property is encumbered;

(2) The mortgagee has agreed to lend the said sum of Rs. ——— on the terms aforesaid;

(3) The mortgagee not finding it convenient to advance the aforesaid loan of Rs. ——— in a lump sum it was agreed between the mortgagor and the mortgagee that the mortgagee should advance the aforesaid loan of Rs. ——— piecemeal on the execution by the mortgagor of pronotes pending the execution and registration of the deed of usufructuary mortgage for the aforesaid loan of Rs. ——— after the said loan has been advanced in full and as soon as the loans referred to in the second schedule have been

1 As the maintenance is personal and is for the life of the mortgagee it cannot be assigned [Sec. 6 (*dd*), Transfer of Property Act], but as arrears of maintenance can be assigned and can also be claimed on the death of the widow by her personal heirs, the interpretation clause is necessary to provide for the case of arrears.

paid off and the property in the first schedule hereto redeemed from their charge;

(4) The mortgagee has up to date advanced to the mortgagor Rs. —— only as part of the said loan of Rs. ———.

NOW THIS DEED WITNESSES as follows:

1. In pursuance of the aforesaid agreement and for the consideration aforesaid the parties hereto hereby agree as follows:

(1) Agreement of Future Advances

The mortgagee will advance to the mortgagor the balance of Rs. —— of the aforesaid loan of Rs. ——— piece-meal on the execution of pronotes by the mortgagor.

(2) Agreement for Usufructuary Mortgage

The mortgagor immediately on the receipt of the aforesaid loan of Rs. ———— in full shall have the property shown in the first schedule hereto released from the loans described in the second schedule hereto and shall mortgage the same with possession by the execution of a usufructuary mortgage deed in favour of the mortgagee; AND

(3) Payment in case of Default

If the mortgagor shall fail immediately on the advance of the aforesaid loan of Rs. ————— in full to have the property in the first schedule hereto released from the loans detailed in the second schedule hereto and to mortgage the same with possession in favour of the mortgagee, the mortgagor shall repay to the mortgagee the said sum of Rs. ———— with interest at ——— percent per annum thereon and shall also pay by way of consolidated damages and not by way of penalty a sum of Rs. ———.

II. Mortgage

In consideration of the sum of Rs. ——— already advanced and of Rs. ——— hereby agreed to be advanced by the mortgagee, the mortgagor hereby grants and transfers by way of simple mortgage to the mortgagee ALL that property described in the first schedule hereto to the intent that the said premises shall remain charged with the payment of all sums which may become due and payable to the mortgagee on account of principal and interest or consolidated damages under the terms hereinbefore contained.

III. Default Clause

IT IS HEREBY AGREED that if the said mortgagor fails to mortgage with possession the property mentioned in the first schedule hereto under the terms hereinbefore contained and fails to pay the principal, interest and consolidated damages becoming due and payable under the terms hereinbefore contained the mortgagee may enforce against the said property all or any of the remedies of the holder of a simple mortgage but that if the mortgagor executes a deed of usufructuary mortgage and deliver possession of the said property of the mortgagor free from the encumbrances mentioned in the second schedule hereto the simple mortgage hereby contained shall be deemed to be extinguished.

The first schedule herein referred to.

* * * * *

The second schedule herein referred to.

* * * * *

IV. Interpretation clause—(as in Form 3).

IN WITNESS WHEREOF, etc.

(*For security bonds hypothecating property—see under BOND*)

14—Simple Mortgage with an Option to turn it into Usufructuary Mortgage in case of Default in Payment on Due Date

THIS MORTGAGE made, etc., (*as in Form* 3).

WITNESSES as follows:

I and II. (*as in Form* 3).

III. (*i*) (*as in Form* 3).

(*ii*) (*as in Form 3*) with the following addition:

"Or may at his option take possession of the said premises and remain in possession as a usufructuary mortgagee until the said sum and interest due hereunder are fully paid off by the usufruct of the said property in the manner hereinafter mentioned or otherwise and in that case the mortgagee shall have all the rights of a usufructuary mortgagee and this mortgage shall thenceforth be deemed to be a usufructuary mortgage."

IV. The mortgagee hereby covenants with the mortgagor that he will on entering into possession of the mortgaged property collect the rents and other moneys accruing due and payable upon the said property with all care and diligence and out of the rents and moneys thus collected will pay the Government revenue, cesses and taxes assessed, imposed and charged on the mortgaged property and defray the cost of collection and management (which shall in no case exceed ———— percent of the total rents to be collected) and the cost, if any, incurred in any suit relating to the said premises in a civil or revenue court and will apply the balance first in the reduction or payment of the interest due hereunder and then in the reduction or payment of the principal money hereby secured.

V. *Interpretation clause*—(*as in Form* 3).

IN WITNESS WHEREOF, etc.

15—Simple Mortgage of Leasehold Land with House Built by the Mortgagor

THIS MORTGAGE is made, etc., (*as in Form* 3).

WHEREAS—

(1) By a deed of lease dated the ——— day of ——— XY, etc., demised the land described in the schedule hereto to the mortgagor for the term of ——— years on the terms and conditions mentioned in the said lease.

(2) After obtaining the aforesaid lease the mortgagor built a *pucca* house with garage, outhouse and tubewell on the demised land and has since been in possession of the same.

(3) The mortgagee has agreed with the mortgagor to lend to him the sum of Rs. ——— upon having the repayment thereof with interest thereon at the rate hereinafter mentioned secured in the manner hereinafter appearing.

NOW THIS DEED WITNESSES as follows:

I. In pursuance of the said agreement and in consideration of the sum of Rs. ——— etc. (*as in Form* 4).

II. For the consideration aforesaid the mortgagor as lessee under the aforesaid lease in respect of the said land and as owner in respect of the said house hereby assigns and transfers by way of simple mortgage ALL that land and house described, etc. (*Rest as in Form* 3).

16—Hypothecation Bond Giving Additional Security

THIS DEED is made, etc., (*as in Form* 3).

Recitals of Mortgage

WHEREAS the mortgagor borrowed Rs. ——— from the mortgagee and executed a simple mortgage deed in favour of the mortgagee on the ——— under which all the property described in the ——— Schedule to the aforesaid mortgage deed was transferred by way of simple mortgage to the mortgagee to the intent that the said premises should remain and be charged by way of simple mortgage as security for the payment to the mortgagee of the said principal sum and interest and costs in accordance with the covenants contained in the aforesaid mortgage deed;

Insufficiency of Security

AND WHEREAS owing to a general fall in the market value of property (*or*, owing to non-payment of interest by the mortgagor and consequent swelling up of the amount due to the mortgagee) the said property described in the ———— schedule to the aforesaid mortgage deed is no longer sufficient as security for the said debt;

(*or*, owing to a wrong calculation of the market value due to the non-exclusion of remissions from the rents the properties described in the —— schedule to the aforesaid mortgage deed were then considered to be sufficient as security for the amount of the aforesaid mortgage deed but on a correct calculation having now been made on the basis of rents after excluding the remissions it has now transpired that the said properties are not sufficient as such security as aforesaid);

Agreement for Additional Security

AND WHEREAS it is now agreed between the mortgagor and the mortgagee that the mortgagor shall hypothecate the property specified in the schedule hereto by way of additional security for the amount due to the mortgagee under the aforesaid mortgage deed.

NOW THIS DEED WITNESSES as follows:

1. Mortgage of Additional Property

In pursuance of the said agreement and in further consideration of the said loan of Rs. ———— the mortgagor hereby transfers by way of simple mortgage to the mortgagee ALL that property described in the schedule hereto with all rights, easements and appurtenances thereto to the intent that the said premises shall remain and be charged by way of simple mortgage as further security in addition to the property described in the ———— schedule to the aforesaid mortgage deed for the payment to the mortgagee of the moneys payable under aforesaid deed of mortgage in accordance with the covenants therein contained;

2. Covenant against Encumbrance

The mortgagor hereby covenants with the mortgagee that the property described in the schedule hereto is free from encumbrances;

3. Remedy of Mortgagee

IT IS HEREBY AGREED and declared that in all cases in which the mortgagee becomes entitled under the terms of the aforesaid mortgage deed of the ——— to enforce the remedies of the holder of a simple mortgage against the property described in the ——— schedule to the aforesaid mortgage deed, he will also be entitled to enforce all or any of such remedies against the property described in the schedule hereto in the same way as if the said property had been entered in the ——— schedule to the aforesaid mortgage deed;

The schedule herein referred to.

4. Interpretation clause—(as in Form 3).

IN WITNESS WHEREOF, etc.

17—Simple Mortgage or Hypothecation of Machinery with Provision for Insurance

THIS DEED OF MORTGAGE is made, etc.

WITNESSES as follows—

I. Consideration (as in Form 3).

II. Hypothecation

For the consideration aforesaid the mortgagor hereby hypothecates and charges ALL that machinery, plant, engines, etc., described in the schedule hereto of which he is the absolute owner to the intent that all such property shall remain and form additional security in the manner hereinafter appearing for the payment to the mortgagee of the said principal money, interest and costs in the manner aforesaid.

III. Mortgagor's Covenants

The mortgagor hereby covenants with the mortgagee as follows:

(1) Covenant against Encumbrance

The said property described in the schedule hereto is free from encumbrances;

(2) To Keep in Repairs and Working Order

The mortgagor will at all times during the continuance of this security maintain and keep in good and working order and repair, and if necessary, replace the machinery described in the schedule hereto and all plants, engines and machinery which shall at any time during the continuance of the security be brought upon or used in the premises described in the schedule hereto, whether in addition to or in place of any existing plants, engines and machinery shall, if the property of the mortgagor, become included in the schedule hereto, remain part of the security hereby created, and be subject to the powers, provisions and covenants herein contained and relating to the said security;

(3) To Insure

The mortgagor will at all times during the continuance of this security at his own expense insure and keep insured in the name of the mortgagee with an insurance company all the property described in the schedule hereto against fire to the amount of Rs. ————.

(4) To Pay Premia

During the continuance of this security the mortgagor will pay all premia and sums of money necessary for keeping such insurance in force and will deliver to the mortgagee the receipt of every such payment within seven days after the same shall have become due;

(5) In case of Default Mortgagee may Insure

If the mortgagor shall neglect or refuse to effect such insurance as aforesaid or to keep the same in force by making such payments as aforesaid or to deliver such receipt as aforesaid, to the mortgagee, it shall be lawful for the mortgagee to insure all such property as aforesaid to the amount aforesaid or to the amount of any deficiency and to pay all premia on such insurance;

(6) To Reimburse Expenses

The mortgagor will, on demand, repay to the mortgagee all moneys expended by the mortgagee in or about such insurance as aforesaid and all other costs and expenses properly incurred by him hereunder and will pay interest at ——— percent per annum upon any such sum until the same shall have been repaid by the mortgagor to the mortgagee;

(7) Security for the Expenses Incurred by Mortgagee

Until the amount of any such premia, costs, charges and expenses have been paid by the mortgagor to the mortgagee, the same shall be secured upon all the property enumerated in the schedule hereto in like manner as the principal sum of Rs. ——— is hereby secured;

(8) Application of Money Received from Insurance

All money received under any insurance of any part of the property enumerated in the schedule hereto shall at the option of the mortgagee be applied either in or towards the payment of the moneys hereby secured or in or towards replacing or reinstating the property in respect of which such insurance money is paid by the company; AND

(9) Default Clause

In case of default either in payment of the sum becoming payable under Clause III (4) or in payment of the principal money hereby secured with interest on the date hereinbefore mentioned (whether such default may have been made before or not) the mortgagee shall have power without the intervention of any court to take possession of the hypothecated property and to sell or concur with any other person in selling the same or any part thereof either together or in lots and either by public auction or by private contract subject to such conditions concerning title or evidence of title or other matter as the mortgagee thinks fit with power to vary any contract for sale and to buy it at any auction or to rescind any contract for sale and to re-sell without being liable for any loss occasioned thereby, and to realize the amount due to the mortgagee from such sale proceeds after defraying the necessary expenses.

IV. Provisos—(as in Form 3).

V. Interpretation clause—(as in Form 3).

The schedule herein referred to.

IN WITNESS WHEREOF, etc.

18—Simple Mortgage or Hypothecation of all Stock in Trade (Present and Future), Goodwill and Takings of Business

THIS DEED OF MORTGAGE is made on the ——— day of ——— between AB, etc., CD, etc., and EF, etc., carrying on business as photo-engravers, block-makers, printers and stationers under the name and style of AB and Sons at the premises No. ————, Aminabad Park, Lucknow (hereinafter called "the mortgagors") of the one part AND XY, etc. (hereinafter called "the mortgagee") of the other part.

"WITNESSES as follows:

I. *Consideration* (*as in Form* 3).

II. For the consideration aforesaid, the mortgagors hereby hypothecate and charge ALL the goodwill of the business carried on by the mortgagors at the said premises No. ——— Aminabad Park or at any other premises to which the said business may hereafter be shifted AND the whole stock in trade of the said business including all plants, machinery, fittings, furniture, etc., which at present is or which may hereafter be brought on the premises at which the said business is carried on for the purpose of the said business AND ALSO all moneys to be received by or to become owing to the mortgagors in respect of the said business to the intent that all such property shall remain and form additional security in the manner hereinafter appearing for the payment to the mortgagee of the said principal money, interest and costs in the manner aforesaid.

III. Mortgagors' Covenant

The mortgagors hereby covenant with the mortgagee as follows:

(1) The said property described in the schedule hereto is free from encumbrances.

(2) *as in* III (2) *of Form No.* 17 *with the following modifications*:

For "machinery described in the schedule hereto" substitute "machinery hereby mortgaged," for "premises described in the schedule hereto" substitute "premises at which the mortgagors' said business is for the time being carried on," omit the words "included in the schedule hereto."

(3) to (6) *as in* III (3) to (6) *of Form No.*17.

(7) and (8) *as in* III (7) and (8) *of Form No.*17 substituting "hereby mortgaged" for "enumerated in the schedule hereto."

(9) During the continuance of this security the mortgagors will carry on the said business and will keep proper books of account of the said business and make full entries therein of all the dealings and transactions of the said business and will keep such books and all letters, papers and documents belonging or relating to the said business upon the premises at which the said business is for the time being carried on and will at any time if required produce the same for the inspection of the mortgagee and allow him or any person appointed in writing by him to have free access thereto and to take copies and extracts of and from the same.

(10) *as in* III (9) *of Form* 17.

IV. Mortgagor's Right to Pay before Time—(as in Form 3).

V. Interpretation Clause—(as in Form 3)

IN WITNESS WHEREOF, etc.

19—Ditto, When Loan is Agreed to be Repaid in Monthly Instalments and Receiver is Appointed

THIS DEED OF MORTGAGE is made on the day of ——— BETWEEN AB, etc., (hereinafter called "the mortgagor") of the first part, XY, etc., (hereinafter called "the mortgagee") of the second part, AND GH, etc., (hereinafter called "the Receiver") of the third part.

WITNESSES as follows:

I. In consideration of the sum of Rs. ——— borrowed by the mortgagor from the mortgagee (the receipt of which the mortgagor hereby acknowledges), the mortgagor hereby covenants with the mortgagee as follows:

(1) That the mortgagor will pay to the mortgagee within a term of —— months the said principal sum of Rs. ——— by equal monthly instalments of Rs. ——— each, the first of such instalments to be paid on the first day of ——— until the whole principal sum has been fully paid off and shall along with each said instalments of the principal pay interest at the rate of ——— percent per annum on the said principal sum or on so much thereof as shall from time to time remain unpaid.

(2) If at any time any of the aforesaid instalments or interest or any part thereof respectively shall be in arrears and unpaid for the period of thirty days after due date, then the whole of the said principal and interest remaining unpaid shall forthwith become payable and shall be paid with interest at the aforesaid rate by the mortgagor to the mortgagee on demand.

II. (*as in Form* 18),

III. (1—8) (*as in Form* 18).

(9) In case of default in payment of the sum becoming payable under clause I (2) the mortgagee shall have power, etc., (*as in cl*ause III (9) *of Form* 17).

(10) In consideration of the premises the mortgagee with the concurrence of the mortgagor hereby appoints the Official Receiver to be receiver of the profits and income of the said business of the mortgagor and of all moneys becoming due to the mortgagor in respect of the said business from the persons liable to pay the same. PROVIDED ALWAYS that the

receiver shall out of the moneys received by him in each month, after deducting his own remuneration at the rate of 5 percent of total income received and other reasonable costs and expenses, pay the instalment of the moneys hereby secured which is payable on the first day of the next month and all other moneys for the time being owing under this security.

IV and V (*as in Form* 3).

IN WITNESS WHEREOF, etc.

20—Mortgage of Shares for Securing Past and Future Trade Debts
(When only blank transfer is given)

THIS MORTGAGE, etc., (*as in Form* 3).

WHEREAS the mortgagor is indebted to the mortgagee in several sums of money amounting to Rs. ——— for goods sold, moneys advanced and otherwise, and in order to induce the mortgagee to continue his dealing with the mortgagor and for the purpose of securing the payment of all such moneys as are or shall at any time hereafter be due or owing from the mortgagor to the mortgagee with interest thereon as hereinafter mentioned the mortgagor has agreed to mortgage the shares specified in the schedule hereto to the mortgagee and has deposited with the mortgagee the said share certificates together with transfer deeds in blank to the said shares and has agreed to execute this deed.

NOW THIS DEED made in consideration of the mortgagor being indebted as aforesaid and of the recited agreement WITNESSES as follows:

1. The mortgagor hereby agrees with the mortgagee to pay to him or any person authorised by him in this behalf on demand all and every sum or sums of money which are now or shall at any time hereafter be owing from the mortgagor to the mortgagee in respect of goods sold, advances made or deemed to have been made or on any other account whatsoever together with interest on the same respectively at the rate of ——— percent per annum from the time or respective times of the same having becoming due.

2. The mortgagor hereby charges all the shares specified in the schedule hereto with the repayment to the mortgagee of the moneys hereinbefore covenanted to be paid by the mortgagor to the mortgagee PROVIDED that on payment of all moneys due to the mortgagee from the mortgagor with interest thereon as aforesaid on demand or without any demand before the mortgagee sells such shares or completes the blank transfer deed under the power hereinafter reserved, the mortgagee shall deliver back to the mortgagor the said certificates of the shares mentioned in the schedule hereto with the blank transfer deeds relating to them.

3. The parties hereto hereby mutually agree with each other as follows:

(*i*) That the mortgagor will, during the continuance of this security, duly and punctually pay all calls and instalments that may be made or become due in respect of any of the shares hereby mortgaged or that in default of his so doing the mortgagee may make such payments and all sums paid by him for this purpose shall for the purposes of the covenants of this deed be deemed to have been advanced by him to the mortgagor.

(*ii*) In case of the mortgagor's default in payment under covenant No.1 hereinbefore contained, the mortgagee will be at liberty to sell the said shares in the open market or may himself purchase them at the current market rate of the stock exchange and the mortgagee may in that case complete the blank transfer deeds by inserting the name of the purchaser or inserting his own name as the case may be and may cause such transfer to be registered and the sale proceeds shall after deducting all costs and charges incurred in making the sale and registration of the shares shall be credited to the amount then due to the mortgagee from the mortgagor.

(*iii*) That the mortgagor shall, if required by the mortgagee, permit all or any of the shares specified in the schedule hereto which have not yet been fully paid up to be revested in the mortgagor in such manner as the mortgagee shall think fit.

(*iv*) That the mortgagor will indemnify the mortgagee, his executors, administrators and assigns against all costs and liabilities which may be incurred or sustained in respect of the mortgaged shares.

The schedule herein referred to.

IN WITNESS WHEREOF, etc.

21—Mortgage of Shares in a Company for Money Borrowed to Purchase the Shares (when Shares Transferred)

THIS MORTGAGE, etc., (*as in Form* 3).

WHEREAS the mortgagor in order to purchase ———— shares in the ——— Company Limited required the sum of Rs. ——— and the mortgagee advanced to him a loan of Rs. ———— on the terms and conditions hereinafter appearing and on having the repayment thereof with interest secured by the mortgage of the shares when purchased by the mortgagor.

2. The mortgagor has purchased——ordinary shares numbered —— to ——— inclusive in ——— Company Limited and has transfered them to the mortgagee and delivered the same with transfer deed duly executed.

NOW THIS DEED WITNESSES and the parties hereto hereby agree as follows:

(1) Covenant for Payment of Principal

That the mortgagor will repay the aforesaid sum of Rs. ———— in —— monthly instalments of Rs. ——— each payable on the ——— day of each month beginning from the ——— day of ——— next.

(2) Covenant for Payment of Interest

(*a*) That the mortgagor will pay interest on the sum of Rs. ——— or on so much thereof as shall remain unpaid at the rate of ——— percent per annum;

(*b*) That the whole amount of interest due hereunder on the date of each monthly instalment of the principal hereinbefore fixed shall be paid along with such instalment.

(3) Costs

That the mortgagor will on demand pay all reasonable costs incidental to this mortgage.

(4) Transfer of Shares

That the aforesaid transfer of the said shares has been made by the mortgagor to the mortgagee as a security for repayment of the said sum of Rs. —— with interest and costs in the manner hereinbefore stated and on the express condition that upon payment of all sums due to the mortgagee hereunder the mortgagee will at the request and cost of the mortgagor re-transfer the said shares to the mortgagor or as the mortgagor shall direct.

(5) Right of Sale to Mortgagee

That whenever any money becomes payable hereunder and the same is not paid, it shall be lawful for the mortgagee to sell and transfer all or any of the shares hereby mortgaged without the consent of the mortgagor at the market price then current and to pay himself the amount due to him with proper costs and expenses of realisation and other proper and usual charges.

(6) Covenant to Pay Call Money

That the mortgagor will duly pay all sums which may during the continuance of this security become payable by reason of any call in respect of the said shares and any money which the mortgagee shall notwithstanding this agreement be called upon to pay and shall pay in respect of any such call shall be repaid by the mortgagor with interest at the rate aforesaid on demand and until so repaid shall be a charge on the shares hereby mortgaged.

22—Mortgage by Conditional Sale[1]

THIS MORTGAGE made, etc. (*as in Form* 3).

WITNESSES as follows:

1. In consideration of the sum of Rs. ——— borrowed by the mortgagor from the mortgagee (the receipt of which the mortgagor hereby acknowledges) the mortgagor hereby transfers to the mortgagee ALL that property described in the schedule hereto TO HOLD the same to the mortgagee absolutely forever subject to the conditions hereby expressly declared by the parties hereto that if and when the mortgagor repays the said sum of Rs. ——— to the mortgagee with interest thereon at the rate of ——— percent per annum compoundable annually (half yearly) on the —— day of —— (and the —— day of ——) the transfer hereby made shall become null and void (*or*, the mortgagee will at the request and cost of the mortgagor re-transfer the said property to the mortgagor) [*or*, transfers by way of mortgage by conditional sale the property described in the schedule hereto on the condition that if the mortgagor shall fail to repay the said sum of Rs. ——— with interest thereon at the rate of —— percent per annum compoundable annually (half yearly) on the —— day of —— (and the —— day of ——) within —— years from this date (*or*, on or before the ——— day of ———) then the transfer hereby made shall become an absolute sale in favour of the mortgagee].

2. The mortgagor hereby covenants with the mortgagee that the said property is free from encumbrances.

---

1 This is a form suitable for a simple case. In case of mortgage by the guardian, manager of joint Hindu family, etc., the necessary recitals as given in Forms 9, 10 and 11 should be inserted with necessary verbal changes. [Compare this with Form No. 33 (English Mortgage), *post*, and see footnote thereto explaining the difference between the two]. In a mortgage by conditional sale, the condition precedent is that there must be an ostensible sale. It must contain a condition that in default of payment of mortgage money on a certain date, the sale shall become absolute and on condition that on such payment being made, the sale shall become void, or on condition that on such payment being made the buyer shall transfer the property to seller. In such a transaction the debt subsists and a right to redeem remains with the debtor. In case of a sale with condition of repurchase there is a sale outright with an agreement to repurchase (*Tulsi* v. *Chandrika Prasad*, (2006) 8 SCC 322).

3. *Interpretation clause*—(*as in Form* 3).

IN WITNESS WHEREOF, etc.

23—Mortgage by Conditional Sale by Father of Joint Hindu Family, with a Personal Covenant to Pay[1]

THIS MORTGAGE is made (*as in Form* 3).

Recitals (*as in Form* 9).

NOW THIS DEED WITNESSES as follows:

I. (*as in Form* 3).

II. In further pursuance of the said agreement and for the consideration aforesaid the mortgagor hereby transfers to the mortgagee ALL that property described in the schedule (or, first schedule) hereto TO THE INTENT that the said premises shall remain and be charged as security in the manner hereinafter mentioned for the payment to the mortgagee of the principal money, interest and costs in accordance with the covenant hereinafter contained.

III. (*as in Form* 3) substituting for the words "may forthwith enforce and this deed shall be read, etc.," at the end of (ii) the following words:

"may foreclose the mortgage hereby made and convert the same into an absolute sale in the mortgagee's favour." and add:

"(*iii*) If the mortgagor pays the principal and interest due hereunder on the date hereinbefore fixed, the transfer hereby made shall become null and void (*or*, the mortgagee shall re-transfer the said property to the mortgagor)."

IV and V (*as in Form* 3).

IN WITNESS WHEREOF, etc.

24—Usufructuary Mortgage[2]— Profits Liquidating Interest only

THIS MORTGAGE made, etc., (*as in Form* 3).

WITNESSES as follows:

1 This is a form suitable for a simple case. In cases of mortgages by father or manager of joint Hindu family, the recitals should be taken *mutatis mutandis* from Forms 9, 10, 11. In this form the mortgagee has no right to sue for the mortgage money.

2 This is an 'anomalous mortgage' and takes effect both as a simple mortgage as well as a conditional sale, the remedy of the mortgagee being both sale as well as foreclosure.

I. Mortgage Clause

In consideration of the sum of Rs. ——— borrowed by the mortgagor from the mortgagee (the receipt of which the mortgagor hereby acknowledges), the mortgagor hereby transfers by way of usufructuary mortgage to the mortgagee ALL that property described in the schedule hereto TO the intent that the said premises shall remain in possession of the mortgagee as security for the repayment to the mortgagee of the said sum of Rs. ——— in accordance with the provisions hereinafter contained.

II. Mortgagor's Covenants

The mortgagor hereby covenants with the mortgagee as follows:

(*i*) *Covenant against Encumbrances*
The said property hereby mortgaged is free from encumbrances (except the encumbrances mentioned in the second schedule hereto);

(*ii*) *Appropriation of Income*
All the rents and profits of the mortgaged property collected by the mortgagee will after paying the Government revenue and cesses and other taxes assessed, imposed or charged on the said property and defraying the cost of collection and management and the costs, if any, incurred in any suit relating to the said property in the civil or revenue court, be appropriated by the mortgagee in lieu of interest on the said sum of Rs. ———.

III. Redemption

The mortgagee hereby covenants with the mortgagor that the mortgagor may redeem the aforesaid mortgage at any time after ——— years (*or*, in the month of *Jeth* in any year after ——— years) on repayment of the said sum of Rs. ———.

IV. Parties' Covenants

It is hereby agreed between the parties as follows:

(1) That the parties shall have all such rights and be subject to all such liabilities of a mortgagor and mortgagee provided in the Transfer of Property Act, 1882 as may be applicable to them.

(2) That any rents of the mortgaged property for the period of the mortgage remaining unrealized but being legally recoverable at the date of redemption shall be purchased by the mortgagor from

the mortgagee at a price equal to 75 percent of the total amount of such unrealised rents.

V. Interpretation clause—(as in Form 3).

The schedule herein referred to.

IN WITNESS WHEREOF, etc.

25—Usufructuary Mortgage (Interest Fixed, Profits Liquidating both Principal and Interest)

THIS MORTGAGE made, etc., (*as in Form* 3).

WITNESSES as follows:

I. Mortgage Clause

In consideration of the sum Rs. ——— borrowed by the mortgagor from the mortgagee (the receipt of which the mortgagor hereby acknowledges) the mortgagor hereby transfers by way of usufructuary mortgage to the mortgagee ALL that property described in the schedule hereto TO THE INTENT that the said premises shall remain in possession of the mortgagee as security for the payment of the said sum of Rs. ——— and interest hereinafter mentioned.

II. Mortgagor's Covenants

The mortgagor hereby covenants with the mortgagee as follows:

(1) *Covenant against Encumbrances.* (*as in Form* 24).

(2) *Covenant to Pay Interest*

Interest at the rate of ——— percent per annum shall be payable from the date hereof on the said sum of Rs. ——— or on so much thereof as shall for the time being remain unpaid on the ——— day of ——— and the ——— day of ——— in each year, and any interest not paid by the mortgagor on due date and not realized from the profits of the mortgaged property in the manner herein provided will be added to the principal and shall bear interest at the said rate and be payable on the half yearly dates aforesaid.

III. Mortgagee's Covenants

The mortgagee hereby covenants with the mortgagor as follows:

(1) Appropriation of Income

He will on entering into possession of the mortgaged property collect the rents and other moneys accruing due and payable upon the said property with all care and diligence and out of the rents and moneys thus collected will pay the Government revenue, cesses and taxes assessed, imposed and charged on the mortgaged property and defray the costs of collection and management (which shall in no case exceed ——— percent of the total rents to be collected) and the costs if any incurred in any suit relating to the said premises in a civil or revenue court and will apply the balance first in the reduction or payment of the interest due hereunder and then in the reduction or payment of the principal money hereby secured.

(2) Payments by Mortgagor

The mortgagor may at any time after five years from the date hereof pay to the mortgagee any sum of money not less than Rs. ——— on account of the moneys hereby secured and all sums so paid shall be applied first in reduction of the interest then due hereunder and then in reduction or payment of the principal.

(3) Redemption

On the principal moneys and interest hereby secured being paid off in the manner hereinbefore mentioned or otherwise, the mortgagee will re-transfer the mortgaged property to the mortgagor and will put him in possession (provided that nothing herein contained shall entitle the mortgagor to be put in possession before the end of the *Fasli* year in which the said moneys and interest have been paid off).[1]

IV. *Parties' Covenants—(as in clause* IV (1) *of Form* 24).

V. *Interpretation clause—(as in Form* 3).

The schedule herein referred to.

IN WITNESS WHEREOF, etc.

1 Necessary if property is agricultural.

26—Usufructuary Mortgage by a Hindu Widow,[1] Reversioner Consenting (Mortgage Money Left with Mortgagee to pay off Old Debts)

THIS MORTGAGE is made on the ——— day of ——— BETWEEN AB, etc., (hereinafter called "the mortgagor") of the first part, AND EF, etc., (hereinafter called "the reversioner") of the second part AND CD, etc.,(hereinafter called "the mortgagee") of the third part.

WHEREAS—

Recital about Mortgagor's Estate

(1) XY, the deceased husband of the mortgagor was the owner of the property described in the schedule hereto;

(2) The said XY who was a HINDU governed by the Mitakshara school of Hindu Law died leaving the mortgagor as his widow and legatee under a Will dated ——— which laid down that the mortgagor shall have in the property only a Hindu widow's estate as understood in Hindu Law prior to the enactment of the Hindu Succession Act and not full ownership;

(3) The said EF is the brother's son and is the present next reversioner of the said XY;

Necessity for the Mortgage

(4) The said XY was at the time of his death indebted to the several persons whose names with particulars of their debts are mentioned below:

(*a*) GH, etc., for a loan taken on a bond dated ——— at an interest of 15 percent per annum, total sum due till date being Rs. ———;

(*b*) JK, etc., for a loan taken on a simple mortgage deed dated—at an interest of 12 percent per annum, total sum due till date being

1 A Hindu widow who has not become absolute owner under section 14 of the Hindu Succession Act, 1956, can mortgage the property inherited by her only in case of legal necessity or for the benefit of her estate. This is so only if any property is acquired by way of gift or under a will or any other instrument or under a decree or order of a civil court or under an award which prescribes only a restricted estate for her, vide section 14(2). When after her death a mortgage made by her is impeached by the reversioners, the mortgagee can succeed only on proof of actual legal necessity or benefit to the estate or of the fact that he had made proper and *bona fide* inquiry as to the existence of such necessity. Consent of the next reversioner is not by itself sufficient to bind other reversioners but would be good evidence of the existence of a necessity justifying the mortgage. In a mortgage by her all circumstances showing the necessity for the mortgage should be recited, as in a mortgage by the manager of a joint family. If the next reversioner agrees he should be made party to the mortgage.

Rs. ———;

(*c*) LM, etc., for a loan taken on a promissory note dated ——— at an interest of 18 percent per annum, total sum due till date being Rs. ———;

(*d*) NP & Co. for Rs. ——— being the balance of the price of a motor car purchased by the said XY carrying interest at 12 percent per annum, total sum now due being Rs. ———.

(5) The total annual income of the property left by the said XY is Rs. ——— which is barely sufficient for the maintenance of the mortgagor and the burden of interest on the aforesaid debts is increasing day by day;

(6) A part of the residential house of the mortgagor has fallen during the recent rains and a sum of Rs. ——— is needed for its repair and prevention of further damage;

Agreement for Loan

(7) The mortgagee has agreed to advance to the mortgagor a sum of Rs. ——— to liquidate the aforesaid debts and to meet the expenses of the said repairs on the repayment thereof with interest at 9 percent per annum being secured by a usufructuary mortgage of the property described in the schedule hereto in the manner hereinafter appearing and on the said EF also consenting to the said mortgage;

Consent of Reversioner

(8) Having regard to the necessity for raising the said loan and to the immense benefit to the estate resulting therefrom, the said EF has agreed to give his consent to the said mortgage and to join in this mortgage deed as a token of such consent;

NOW THIS DEED WITNESSES as follows:

I. *Covenant for Payment*

In pursuance of the said agreement and in consideration of the sum of Rs.——— out of which a sum of Rs. ——— has been retained by the mortgagee for payment to the various creditors hereinbefore mentioned and Rs. ——— has been paid by the mortgagee to the mortgagor (the receipt of which the mortgagor hereby acknowledges) the mortgagor with the consent and concurrence of the said EF hereby testified hereby transfers by way of usufructuary mortgage (*Rest as in clause* I *of Form* 25).

II, III and IV (*as in Form* 25).

V. *Covenant to Pay Creditors*

The mortgagee hereby covenants that he will pay and discharge the various debts specified in para 4 of the recitals hereof and will always indemnify and save harmless the mortgagor and her property from all claims, demands and costs in respect of the said debts or under the bonds, promissory notes or mortgage deeds by which they are secured.

VI. *Interpretation clause—(as in Form* 3).

The schedule herein referred to.

IN WITNESS WHEREOF, etc.

27—Usufructuary Mortgage, with a Personal Covenant to Pay by the Manager of a Joint Hindu Family, all Members Joining[1]

THIS DEED OF MORTGAGE is made etc., (*as in Form* 10).

Recitals (*as in Form* 10).

NOW THIS DEED WITNESSES as follows;

I. Mortgagor's Covenant

In pursuance of the said agreement and in consideration of the sum of Rs. ——— consisting of Rs. ——— due to the mortgagee on the pronote dated ——— and Rs. ——— now advanced by the mortgagee to the mortgagors (the receipt of which the mortgagors hereby acknowledges) the mortgagors hereby covenant with the mortgagee—

— that the mortgagors will pay to the mortgagee the said sum of Rs. ——— within ——— years of the date hereof and interest thereon or on so much thereof as shall for the time being remain unpaid at the rate of ——— percent per annum in the manner hereinafter appearing; and

— that the mortgagors will, on demand, pay all reasonable costs incidental to this mortgage;

II. Mortgage Clause

For the consideration aforesaid and in further pursuance of the said agreement the mortgagors hereby grant and transfer by way of simple as well as usufructuary mortgage to the mortgagee ALL that property described in the schedule hereto TO THE INTENT that the said premises

1 This is 'an anomalous mortgage' being a combination of simple and usufructuary mortgage.

shall remain in possession of the mortgagee and be charged by way of simple as well as usufructuary mortgage as security for the payment to the mortgagee of the said principal money and interest in accordance with the covenants herein contained.

III. Covenant against Encumbrances

The mortgagors hereby covenant with the mortgagee that the said premises are free from encumbrances (except the encumbrances mentioned in the second schedule hereto to which this mortgage is subject).

IV. Liquidation of Mortgage Money

It is hereby agreed and declared FIRST that the said premises shall remain in possession of the mortgagee until the said principal money and interest have been fully paid off either by the usufruct of the property in the manner hereinafter mentioned or otherwise and that if and when the said sum of Rs. ——— with interest thereon shall be liquidated in the manner herein provided out of the income of the said property or be paid to the mortgagee or partly so liquidated and partly so paid the said property shall at the request and cost of the mortgagors be transferred to them, AND (SECONDLY) that if the said sum of Rs. ——— with interest thereon shall not be liquidated in the manner herein provided or paid to the mortgagee within the aforesaid period of ten years, the mortgagee may forthwith enforce against the said premises all or any of the remedies of the holder of a simple mortgage and these presents shall in that case be read and construed also as a simple mortgage as defined by the Transfer of Property Act, 1882.

V. Mortgagee's Covenant—

The mortgagee hereby covenants with the mortgagor as follows (*As II in Form 24*)

VI. Parties' Covenants

It is hereby agreed between the parties as follows (*As IV in Form 24*)

VII. Interpretation Clause—(As in Form 9).

The Schedule herein referred to.

IN WITNESS WHEREOF, etc.

28—Usufructuary Mortgage for a Fixed Term, on Condition that the Principal and Interest would be satisfied by the Usufruct

THIS MORTGAGE is made, etc. (*as in Form* 3).

WITNESSES as follows:

I. Mortgage Clause

(*As in Form* 24) with the addition of the words "for the term of —— years" before the parcels.

II. Mortgagor's Covenants

The mortgagor hereby covenants with the mortgagee that the said property is free from encumbrances (except those mentioned in the second schedule hereto, to which this mortgage is subject).

III. Mortgagee's Covenants

It is hereby agreed as follows:

(1) The mortgagee will collect the rents and profits of the mortgaged property and after paying the land revenue, cesses and other taxes assessed, imposed or charged on the said property and defraying the cost of collection and management and all other costs and expenses incurred by the mortgagee in suits in connection therewith, appropriate the balance in liquidation of his aforesaid debt.

(2) On the expiry of ——— years from the date hereof, the whole of the aforesaid debt shall be deemed to have been fully paid off by the usufruct of the mortgaged property and the mortgagee will at the cost of the mortgagor re-transfer the said property to the mortgagor discharged from the aforesaid debt and all claims and demands in respect thereof.

IV. Parties' Covenants—(*as in* IV (1) *in Form* 24).

V. Interpretation clause—(*as in Form* 3).

The schedule herein referred to.

IN WITNESS WHEREOF, etc.

29—Usufructuary Mortgage of Leasehold Land and House[1]

THIS MORTGAGE is made, etc., (*as in Form* 3).

Recitals— (*as in Form* 15).

NOW THIS DEED WITNESSES as follows:

1. In pursuance of the aforesaid agreement and in consideration of the sum of Rs. ——— borrowed by the mortgagor from the mortgagee (the receipt of which is hereby acknowledged) the mortgagor hereby (*i*) assigns to the mortgagee ALL the said leasehold land described in the schedule hereto TO HOLD the same to the mortgagee for the unexpired residue of the term of the said lease, and (*ii*) transfers to the mortgagee ALL that house, garage, outhouses, stables and well standing on the said land and described in the schedule hereto TO HOLD the same to the mortgagee, in both cases as a usufructuary mortgagee in possession on the terms and conditions hereinafter mentioned.

(*Rest as in Form* 25).

30—Memo to Accompany Deposit of Title Deeds (to Secure a Loan or Further Advances or Current Account or Money to be due in Business Transaction) (Requiring Registration)[2]

THIS MEMORANDUM made by me AB, etc., WITNESSES as follows:

The title deeds mentioned in the schedule hereto relating to the property fully described in the second schedule hereto have been delivered and deposited by me today to and with CD, etc., for securing the payment to him on the ——— day of ——— of the sum of Rs. ——— borrowed by me today with interest thereon at ——— percent per annum and (also, for the payment to him of any further sum that I may borrow from him from time to time with interest thereon at the aforesaid rate) (*or,* the payment to

---

1 Sometimes the landlord may execute a usufructuary mortgage in favour of the tenant, stipulating that the rent payable by the tenant was to be adjusted against the interest payable by the mortgagor. It has been held that in such cases, the rights of the lessee and those of the mortgagee are not automatically merged, unless the deed specifically provides for relinquishment of his rights under lease. In the absence of such specific provision the redemption of the mortgage does not entitle the mortgagor to get possession, as the ex-mortgagee will continue to have rights as tenant: *Chambangi Applaswamy Naidu* v. *Behara*, (1984) 4 SCC 382; *Nand Lal* v. *Sukhdev*, 1987 (Supp) SCC 87.

2 This is also popularly called Equitable Mortgage, though the Transfer of Property Act does not use that expression. *See* next two precedents in which the need for registration is obviated. (*See* also Preliminary Note, *ante*.)

him of all such sums of money as are now due or shall from time to time or at any time be due to the said CD from me either on current account or for money advanced or paid or in respect of bills, drafts, or notes accepted paid or discounted, interest, commission or any other usual or lawful charges together with all cost and expenses which may be incurred in respect of the premises).

The schedule referred to herein.

Dated the ——— Signed ———

31—Memo of Deposit of Title Deeds in Pursuance of an Equitable Mortgage already Effected (not Requiring Registration)

Modify the preceding precedent in the following manner:

1. Between the words "CD, etc.", and "for securing" add the words "in pursuance of oral agreement previously made with him."

2. Omit the words "at ——— percent per annum" and "at the aforesaid rate."

3. After the words "payment to him" wherever they occur, add "in accordance with the aforesaid oral agreement."

32—Memorandum to Accompany Deposit of Title Deeds to Secure a Loan (Short Form which will not require Registration)[1]

I, AB, etc., hereby declare that, as agreed upon in person, I have this day deposited the title deeds specified in the sub-joined list with you to secure the repayment to you on demand (*or*, on the ————) of the sum of Rs. ——— already lent by you to me together with interest thereon (*or*, to secure the repayment with interest of the sum of Rs. ——— borrowed by me from you this day on the execution of a promissory note).

The list referred to hereinabove.

1 *V.G. Rao* v. *Andhra Bank*, AIR 1971 SC 1613 , (1971) 1 SCC 874 (para 17), relying on *Rachpal* v. *Bhagwan Das*, AIR 1950 SC 272 and other cases; *United Bank of India* v. *Lakharam & Co.*, AIR 1965 SC 1591; *Deb Dutt Seal* v. *Ramanlal*, (1969) 3 SCC 821, AIR 1970 SC 659, relying on *United Bank of India*, supra.

33—English Mortgage[1]

THIS MORTGAGE made, etc., (*as in Form* 3).

WTINESSES as follows:

I. Consideration

(*as in Form* 3).

II. Mortgage Clause

For the consideration aforesaid the mortgagor hereby transfers to the mortgagee ALL that property described in the schedule (first schedule) hereto belonging to the mortgagor TO HOLD the same to the mortgagee absolutely subject to the condition that if the said sum of Rs. ——— with interest shall be paid on the day hereinbefore mentioned in accordance with the covenant hereinbefore contained the said premises shall at the request and cost of the mortgagor be reconveyed to him.

III. Mortgagor's Covenant

(1) The mortgagor hereby covenants with the mortgagee that the said premises are free from encumbrances (except those specified in the second schedule hereto subject to which this mortgage in made).

(2) Add, if necessary, a clause giving *power of sale* (*as in clause* 8 *or* 9 *of the General Forms of Covenants and Provisos on page 580 ante*).

(3) Add, if necessary a clause for *appointment of receiver* (*as in clause* 10 *or* 11 *of the General Forms of Covenants and Provisos on page 580 and 581 ante*).

IV. Interpretation Clause—(as in Form 3)

---

1 This form of mortgage is in vogue mainly in the three Presidency towns. It is apt to be confused with a mortgage by conditional sale. But there is a basic difference between the two. In an English mortgage there is an immediate transfer *of ownership* and on repayment the property has to be reconveyed to the mortgagor. In a mortgage by conditional sale, on the other hand, there is a present transfer *of interest in the property* and the ownership is transferred only subsequently on default in repayment of debt; thus on repayment no deed of reconveyance is necessary, only a release or receipt should suffice.

34—English Mortgage of an Insurance Policy[1]

THIS MORTGAGE, etc., (*as in Form* 3).

WHEREAS the mortgagor is entitled to the policy of life insurance hereinafter described;

AND WHEREAS at the request of the mortgagor, the mortgagee has agreed to lend him the sum of Rs. ———— upon having the repayment thereof with interest secured by a mortgage of the said policy in the manner hereinafter appearing.

NOW THIS DEED WITNESSES as follows:

I. Covenant to Pay

In pursuance of the said agreement and (*as clause I of Form* 3).

II. Mortgage Clause

In further pursuance of the said agreement and for the consideration aforesaid the mortgagor hereby assigns to the mortgagee ALL that policy of assurance (hereinafter called the "said policy") effected with the Life Insurance Corporation dated the ——— day of ——— and numbered ——— whereby the life of the mortgagor is insured in the sum of Rs. ———— and all moneys including bonuses accrued and to accrue hereafter which shall become payable under the said policy TO HOLD the same to the mortgagee absolutely subject to the condition that if the said sum of Rs. ———— with interest shall be paid on the day hereinbefore mentioned in accordance with the covenant hereinbefore contained, the said policy shall at the request and cost of the mortgagor be re-assigned to him.

III. Mortgagor's Covenants

The mortgagor hereby covenants with the mortgagee as follows:

(i) Covenant to Pay Premia

That he will duly pay the premia and other moneys payable for keeping up the said policy or any substituted policy in force and produce the receipts for the same to the mortgagee on demand and will not do or suffer anything whereby the said policy may become voidable or void;

(ii) Covenant to Renew Void Policy

That if any such policy is or shall become voidable or void, the

---

1 Also see precedent No.7 and 8 under ASSIGNMENT OF ACTIONABLE CLAIMS *ante*, and also footnotes thereunder, and precedent No.49 *post*.

mortgagor will immediately at his own cost do all things necessary for restoring or renewing the same and will deliver any substituted policy to the mortgagee and such substituted policy and the moneys to become payable under the same shall be subject to the covenant hereinbefore contained in the same manner and to the same extent as the policy hereby mortgaged and the moneys to become payable thereunder;

(iii) Mortgagee's Right in Case of Default

That in case of default on the part of the mortgagor in the performance of any of the above covenants the mortgagee may at the cost of the mortgagor do what is necessary to make good such default, and all costs and expenses incurred in so doing with interest at ——— percent per annum from the date they are incurred to that of payment by the mortgagor shall be charged on the said policy or renewed policy.

IV. Interpretation clause—(as in Form 3).

IN WITNESS WHEREOF, etc.

35—Mortgage of Share in a Partnership Business

THIS MORTGAGE is made, etc., (*as in Form* 3).

WHEREAS—

(1) The mortgagor and certain other persons are carrying on in partnership the business of manufacture of ice and running of Cold Storage at Hapur District under the firm name of Indian Cold Storage and the said partnership has been formed under a deed of partnership dated the ——— on the terms and conditions mentioned therein.

(2) The mortgagor is indebted to the mortgagee in the sum of Rs. 5,000 under a bond dated ———;

(3) The mortgagor has requested the mortgagee to lend to him the further sum of Rs.10,000 to enable him to bring an additional capital of Rs.10,000 into the said partnership business which the mortgagee has agreed to do on having the repayment of the said sum of Rs.5,000 so owing to him as aforesaid as well as the said sum of Rs.10,000 to be advanced by him with interest secured in the manner hereinafter appearing.

NOW THIS DEED made in pursuance of the said agreement and in consideration of the sum of Rs.5,000 so owing to the mortgagee as aforesaid and of the sum of Rs.10,000 now paid by the mortgagee to the mortgagor (the receipt of which the mortgagor hereby acknowledges) WITNESSES as follows:

The mortgagor covenants with the mortgagee as follows:

1. *Covenant about payment of Rs.* 15,000 *with interest* [*as in* I (1) *and* (2) *of Form* 3].

2. The mortgagor hereby assigns to the mortgagee ALL his interest in the capital of the said partnership business of Indian Cold Storage including the sum of Rs.7,000 now standing to the credit of the mortgagor in the books of the said partnership business, the said sum of Rs.10,000 so to be brought in by him as an additional capital as aforesaid and all such further moneys as from time to time hereafter be brought into the said partnership business by the mortgagor whether by accumulation of profits or otherwise AND all the interest due or to accrue due in respect of such capital AND all the share and interest of the mortgagor in all and every one of the debts, property and effects of every description, present as well as future, payable or belonging to the said partnership TO HOLD to the mortgagee absolutely subject to redemption on payment of the said sum of Rs.15,000 with interest on the day hereinbefore mentioned in accordance with the covenants hereinbefore contained.

3. The mortgagee hereby covenants with the mortgagor that upon payment by the mortgagor of all sums due to the mortgagee hereunder in the manner hereinbefore stipulated the mortgagee shall, at the request and cost of the mortgagor, re-assign the mortgaged share to the mortgagor.

4. The mortgagor hereby covenants with the mortgagee that he will at all times during the continuance of this security, give to the mortgagee all such information as to business and assets of the said partnership firm of Indian Cold Storage as he shall reasonably require and as it shall be lawful for the mortgagor to give and also if all the partners in the said firm shall consent will allow the mortgagee to inspect the partnership books and to make copies and extracts from them.16[1]

IN WITNESS WHEREOF, etc.

1 Consent of other partners is necessary because a mortgagee of a partner's interest is not entitled to interfere in the conduct of the business or to require accounts, or to inspect the books of the firm: Section 29 of the Partnership Act.

36—Sub-Mortgage (Simple Mortgage of Usufructuary Mortgage)[1]

THIS MORTGAGE, etc. (*as in Form* 3).

WHEREAS—

By a deed of usufructuary mortgage dated the ——— XY, etc., owner of the property described in the schedule hereto mortgaged the same to the mortgagor for Rs. ——— and agreed *inter alia* that the usufruct of the said property should be taken by the mortgagor in lieu of interest on the said sum of Rs. ——— and that the mortgage should be redeemable at any time after ——— years on payment of the said sum of Rs. ———;

The mortgagor has since been in possession of the said property and the said principal sum of Rs. ——— is still due to him on the said mortgage;

The mortgagee has agreed to lend to the mortgagor a sum of Rs. ——— upon having the repayment thereof with interest secured in the manner hereinafter appearing.

NOW THIS DEED WITNESSES as follows:

I. Covenant to Pay

In pursuance of the aforesaid agreement and in consideration of the sum of Rs. ——— advanced by the mortgagee (the receipt of which the mortgagor hereby acknowledges) the mortgagor hereby covenants, etc., [*as in Form* 3 clause I (1) & (2)].

II. Sub-Mortgage

In further pursuance of the aforesaid agreement and for the consideration aforesaid the mortgagor hereby assigns to the mortgagee ALL that debt secured by the aforesaid deed of usufructuary mortgage and all the rights, remedies and securities expressly or impliedly contained in or conferred upon the mortgagor by the aforesaid deed of usufructuary mortgage TO THE INTENT, etc.,

(*Rest as in Form* 3).

---

1 Sub-mortgage means a mortgage of the mortgagee rights. The sub-mortgagee acquires all the rights and remedies of the original mortgagee who cannot exercise those rights so long as the sub-mortgage subsists. The sub-mortgagee can enforce the original mortgage against the original mortgagor, the original mortgagee remaining only in the position of a surety.

37—Sub-Mortgage (Usufructuary Mortgage of Usufructuary Mortgage)

Commencement and recitals—(as in Form 36).

NOW THIS DEED WITNESSES as follows:

I. In pursuance of the aforesaid agreement and in consideration of the sum of Rs. ——— advanced by the mortgagee (the receipt of which the mortgagor hereby acknowledges) the mortgagor hereby (*i*) assigns to the mortgagee ALL that debt secured by the aforesaid deed of usufructuary mortgage and all the rights, remedies and securities expressly or impliedly contained in or conferred upon the mortgagor by the aforesaid deed of usufructuary mortgage TO HOLD the same to the mortgagee subject to the right of redemption hereinafter provided, and (*ii*) transfers to the mortgagee ALL that property comprised in the aforesaid deed of usufructuary mortgage TO HOLD the same to the mortgagee as usufructuary mortgagee on the terms and conditions hereinafter contained and subject to such right of redemption as subsists by virtue of the aforesaid deed of usufructuary mortgage and to the right of redemption by the mortgagor hereinafter provided.

II. *Covenants as in Form* 25 *or any other covenants agreed upon.*

38—Agreement of Pledge of Movables

MEMORANDUM OF AGREEMENT made the ——— day of ——— BETWEEN AB, etc., (hereinafter called "the borrower") of the one part AND CD, etc., (hereinafter called "the lender") of the other part.

WHEREBY IT IS AGREED as follows:

1. Pledge Clause

The lender has lent the sum of Rs. ——— (the receipt of which the borrower hereby acknowledges) and the borrower has delivered to the lender the articles belonging to the borrower and specified in the schedule hereto (*or,* the goods specified in the schedule hereto stored in the godown at ——— the key of which has been handed over by the borrower in token of such delivery) by way of pledge for securing the payment on or before the ——— day of ———.

(*a*) *Loan*
The said loan of Rs. ———;

(*b*) *Interest*
Interest thereon from this date at the rate of ——— percent per annum, compoundable half yearly on the ——— and the ———

in each year;

(*c*) *Expenses of Warehousing*

The expenses of warehousing the said goods;

(*d*) *Expenses of Repairs*

The expenses of keeping the said articles in a good state of repair and in proper working order.[1]

(*e*) *Other Costs*

All other costs, charges and expenses (if any) which the lender may be entitled by law to add to his security.

2. Covenant to Pay

In consideration of the said loan the borrower hereby personally promises to repay the said several items specified in the last preceding clause;

3. Lender's Liability for Losses

The lender shall not be liable to the borrower for any involuntary losses which may occur during his custody of the said articles (goods) or by reason of the sale thereof.

4. Power of Sale

(*a*) The power of sale conferred by law on the lender shall be exercisable by public auction or private contract in respect of the entire articles (goods) in one lot or in several lots at the discretion of the lender;

(*b*) Before exercising such power of sale as aforesaid the lender shall give at least one month's notice to the borrower.[2]

IN WITNESS WHEREOF, etc.

39—Agreement of Pledge of Movables, of a Printing Press (Another Form)

THIS DEED made, etc., (*as in Form* 38).

WITNESSES as follows:

1. Covenant to Pay

In consideration of the loan of Rs. ——— advanced by the lender to

1 As may be applicable.

2 In the absence of such a contract, the borrower is entitled to a reasonable notice under section 176, Contract Act. It is better to make a definite contract to avoid disputes as to what is a "reasonable" notice.

the borrower, the borrower hereby covenants with the lender that he will repay the said loan on or before ———, with interest at ——— percent per annum from the date hereof in half yearly payments on the ——— and the ——— in each year and interest at the rate and payable on the dates aforesaid.

2. Pledge Clause

For the consideration aforesaid the borrower hereby delivers to the lender by way of pledge as defined in section 172 of the Indian Contract Act, 1872, ALL that Printing Press and other connected movable property set forth in the schedule hereto to be held by him as security for the repayment of the aforesaid loan with interest in the manner herein provided.

3. Borrower Permitted to use the Pledged Article

The lender hereby permits the borrower to use the said property and the borrower hereby covenants that during the continuance of this security so long as he will use the said property he will at his own expense maintain and keep the same in substantial order and repair, and will from time to time during the continuance of this security replace all such of the plant, engines, machinery, type, utensils and implements of trade set forth in the schedule hereto as may from decay, destruction or other cause become useless or unsuitable for the purpose for which they were intended with new substitutes or proper plant, engines, machinery, type, utensils and implements respectively so that the work of the printing press hereby pledged continues to be carried on as efficiently as it is carried on now.

4. Insurance

Provision for insurance—[*as clause* III (3 to 5) *of Form* 17]

5. Addition to be Included in Security

The borrower hereby covenants that all plants, engines, machinery, type, utensils and implements of trade which shall at any time during the continuance of this security be brought upon and used in the said printing press shall become included in this security and be subject to the powers and covenants herein contained.

6. Rights of Pawnee

The borrower further covenants with the lender that in case any interest payable hereunder is not paid within 30 days after the due date, the whole sum hereby secured shall become payable at once, and in case of default in the payment of the whole sum becoming so payable or in the payment of the principal money hereby secured with interest thereon on the date aforesaid or in the performance of any of the covenants by the borrower hereinbefore contained the lender may enforce all or any of the remedies of a pawnee provided by law provided that in case of sale of any part of the pledged property, a previous notice of two months shall be given to the borrower.

7. Interpretation clause—(as in Form 3).

The schedule herein referred to.

IN WITNESS WHEREOF etc.

40—Reconveyance (Mortgagee Foregoing his Claim to Arrears of Rent)[1]

THIS RECONVEYANCE is made on the ——— day of ——— BETWEEN AB, etc., (hereinafter called "the mortgagee") of the one part AND CD, etc., (hereinafter called "the mortgagor") of the other part.

WHEREAS the mortgagor usufructuarily mortgaged in favour of XY, deceased husband of the mortgagee the property described in the schedule hereto by a mortgage deed dated the ——— for a sum of Rs. ———.

AND WHEREAS the said XY has died and the mortgagee being his widow and the sole heir has agreed to accept the sum of Rs. ——— only in full discharge of all her claims under the aforesaid mortgage deed and also to forego her claim to the amount of the arrears of rent which the mortgagor is under the terms of the aforesaid mortgage deed bound to pay to the mortgagee at the time of redemption.

NOW THIS DEED WITNESSES as follows:

1. In consideration of the sum of Rs. ——— paid by the mortgagor (the receipt of which the mortgagee hereby acknowledges) the mortgagee hereby reconveys to the mortgagor ALL the said mortgaged property described in the schedule hereto TO HOLD the same to the mortgagor forever freed and absolutely discharged from all principal moneys and interest secured by the said deed of mortgage dated the ——— and all claims and demands on account thereof.

2. The mortgagee hereby covenants with the mortgagor that she or her

1 Such reconveyance can be effected also by an endorsement on the mortgage deed itself. (see form 30 and 31, *ante*). Right of reconveyance can be transferred to a third person (*Habiba Khatoon* v. *Ubaidul Haq*, JT 1997 (7) SC 298).

deceased husband XY has not done or knowingly suffered or been party or privy to any act, deed or thing whereby the said property or any part thereof is, can, or may be encumbered.

3. For the consideration aforesaid the mortgagee hereby assigns to the mortgagor all the arrears of rent of the mortgaged property particulars of which are detailed in the second schedule hereto.

4. *Interpretation clause*—(*as in Form* 3).

The schedule herein referred to.

IN WITNESS, etc.

41—Release of Part of the Mortgaged Property by the Mortgagee in Favour of a Purchaser (Mortgagor joining)[1]

THIS RELEASE is made on the ——— day of ——— BETWEEN AB, etc., (hereinafter called "the mortgagee") of the first part AND EF, etc., (hereinafter called "the mortgagor") of the second part AND CD, etc., of the third part;

WHEREAS by a deed of mortgage dated the ——— the mortgagor mortgaged to the mortgagee ALL that property described in the schedule hereto together with other property belonging to him to secure a loan of Rs. ——— with interest;

AND WHEREAS the mortgagor has by a deed of sale dated the——sold the property described in the schedule hereto to the said CD;

AND WHEREAS at the request of the mortgagor the mortgagee has agreed to release the said property from his security on the said CD paying to the mortgagee the sum of Rs. ——— in part payment of the debt due to him on the aforesaid deed of mortgage.

NOW THIS DEED WITNESSES as follows:

1. In pursuance of the said agreement and in consideration of the sum of Rs. ——— paid by the said CD to the mortgagee (the receipt of which the mortgagee hereby acknowledges and which the mortgagee will credit to the debt payable to him under the aforesaid deed of mortgage) the mortgagee hereby assigns and releases to the said CD ALL that property described in the schedule hereto TO HOLD the same to the said CD absolutely freed and discharged from the aforesaid deed of mortgage and from all moneys secured thereby and all claims and demands in respect thereof.

---

1 In such cases it is safer to join the mortgagor to avoid future dispute about apportionment of the mortgage debt on the remaining property.

2. It is hereby declared that nothing herein contained shall prejudicially affect the security of the mortgagee under the aforesaid deed of mortgage upon the remaining property for the balance of the debt now payable and interest hereinafter to accrue due.

The schedule herein referred to.

IN WITNESS WHEREOF, etc.

42—Agreement Reducing Rate of Interest and Extending Time of Payment

AN AGREEMENT made on the ——— day of ——— BETWEEN AB, etc., (hereinafter called "the mortgagor ") of the one part AND CD, etc., (hereinafter called "the mortgagee") of the other part.

WHEREAS by a deed of mortgage dated the ——— to which this deed is supplemental (and which is hereinafter called "the Principal Deed") the mortgagor mortgaged the property therein specified to secure a loan of Rs. ——— and agreed to repay the same with interest at 12 percent per annum within ten years.

AND WHEREAS owing to a general fall in the rate of interest, the parties have agreed to reduce the rate of interest stipulated in the Principal Deed to 9 percent per annum compoundable annually instead of half yearly as therein provided and also to extend the time of payment by another two years.

NOW THESE PRESENTS WITNESS and the parties hereto hereby agree as follows:

(1) With effect from the ——— the interest payable under the Principal Deed shall run at the rate of 9 percent per annum instead of 12 percent per annum as therein provided, and shall be compoundable yearly instead of half yearly as therein provided.

(2) The principal and interest secured by the Principal Deed shall be payable within twelve years of the date of the Principal Deed instead of within ten years as therein provided.

(3) Save as varied as aforesaid, all the conditions and covenants of the Principal Deed shall remain in full force and effect.

IN WITNESS WHEREOF, etc.

43—Agreement Extending Time of Payment, Mortgagor Agreeing to Pay Higher Rate of Interest

AN AGREEMENT made on the ———, etc.

WHEREAS by a deed of mortgage dated ——— the mortgagor mortgaged certain property specified therein in favour of the mortgagee for a sum of Rs.——— payable within fifteen years of the date of the said deed of mortgage, and bearing interest at five percent per annum;

AND WHEREAS the mortgagor finding it difficult to liquidate the said debt of Rs. ——— within the aforesaid period of fifteen years requested the mortgagee to extend the time of payment by two years. *i.e.* up to the ——— in consideration of the mortgagor paying interest at the rate of six percent per annum instead of five percent per annum as provided in the aforesaid deed of mortgage dated the ——— and the mortgagee has agreed to do the same.

NOW THESE PRESENTS WITNESS as follows:

1. In consideration of the mortgagor paying interest at the rate of six percent per annum from and after the date of these presents the mortgagee hereby extends the time for payment of the said loan secured by the aforesaid deed of mortgage dated ——— from the ——— to the ———.

2. In consideration of the extension of time granted as aforesaid the mortgagor hereby agrees to pay interest on the said loan secured by the aforesaid mortgage deed at the rate of six percent per annum from the date of these presents instead of five percent per annum as mentioned in the aforesaid mortgage deed.

3. It is hereby agreed and declared that save and except so far as the same is expressly varied by these presents the aforesaid mortgage deed dated the ——— and everything contained therein shall remain in full force and effect.

IN WITNESS WHEREOF, etc.

44—Charge Clause

After providing for an agreement to pay money in the appropriate deed relating to any transaction, add the following clause—

"The ——— hereby declares that the property described in the schedule hereto shall henceforth be a security for and be charged with the payment of the said sum (annuity) of Rs. ——— hereinbefore agreed to be paid."

Or

"To secure the payment of the money (annuity) hereinbefore agreed to be paid, the ——— hereby charges the land described in the schedule hereto."

45—Deed of Further Charge (With Variation for Security for Future Advances)

THIS DEED OF FURTHER CHARGE is made, etc., (*as in Form* 3).

(1) By a deed of mortgage dated the ——— day of ———the mortgagor, mortgaged by way of simple mortgage to the mortgagee the property described in the schedule hereto to secure a loan of Rs. ——— with interest at the rate and on the conditions mentioned in the said deed of mortgage.

(2) The said sum of Rs. ——— still remains due to the mortgagee on the aforesaid deed of mortgage but all interest thereon has been paid up to date (*or,* the sum of Rs. ——— is now due on account of principal and interest on the aforesaid deed of mortgage).

(3) The mortgagee has agreed to lend to the mortgagor a further sum of Rs. ——— upon the same security and on the terms hereinafter expressed.

(4) It has also been agreed between the parties hereto that security should at the same time be given for any future advances the mortgagee may make to the mortgagor up to the limit of Rs. ———.

NOW THIS DEED WITNESSES as follows:

1. In pursuance of the said agreement and in consideration of the sum of Rs. ——— advanced by the mortgagee (the receipt of which the mortgagor hereby acknowledges) the mortgagor hereby covenants, etc. (*Covenant to Pay - as in clause* I *of Form* 3).

2. The mortgagor hereby declares that all the property comprised in the aforesaid deed of mortgage shall henceforth be a security for and be charged with the payment of the said sum of Rs. ——— now lent with interest due hereunder (and all such further sums of money not exceeding in the aggregate the sum of Rs. ——— as may be hereafter lent by the mortgagee to the mortgagor with interest thereon) as well as the payment of the sums secured by the aforesaid deed of mortgage (and that no part of the said property shall be redeemable until both the said sums have been fully paid to the lender).[1]

3. All the powers, provisions and covenants contained or implied in the aforesaid deed of mortgage in relation to the moneys secured thereby shall be applicable to the said sum of Rs. ——— hereby secured and the interest thereon (and also to all such further sums as may be advanced under the covenant hereinbefore contained with interest thereon) and to this

---

1 Necessary in case of English mortgage or mortgage by conditional sale.

security as fully as if the same had been herein set out and specifically made applicable thereto.

IN WITNESS, etc.

46—Memorandum of Further Charge Endorsed on the Mortgage Deed

I, the within named AB hereby charge the within mortgaged property with the payment of the further sum of Rs. ——— this day advanced to me by the within named CD with interest thereon at the rate of ——— percent per annum AND I declare that all the covenants, powers, and provisions contained in the within-written deed shall operate and take effect in like manner for securing payment of the moneys hereby secured as if the same moneys had formed part of the moneys secured by the within-written mortgage.

IN WITNESS WHEREOF I the said AB have signed this endorsement on the ——— day of ———.

47—Further Charge on a Usufructuary Mortgage (when Interest Stipulated)

THIS DEED, etc. (*as in Form* 3).

WHEREAS—

(1) By a deed of mortgage dated ——— the mortgagor has mortgaged by way of usufructuary mortgage the property described in the schedule thereto for Rs. ——— on condition that he will appropriate the usufruct of the said property in lieu of interest on the said sums.

(2) The mortgagee has agreed to lend to the mortgagor a further sum of Rs. ——— upon the same security and on the terms hereinafter expressed.

NOW THIS DEED WITNESSES as follows:

1. In consideration of the sum of Rs. ——— now borrowed by the mortgagor from the mortgagee (the receipt of which is hereby acknowledged) the mortgagor hereby covenants with the mortgagee that he will pay the said sum with interest thereon at ——— percent per annum at the time of redemption of the usufructuary mortgage hereinbefore mentioned.

2. The mortgagor hereby declares that all the property comprised in the aforesaid usufructuary mortgage shall henceforth be a security for and be charged with the payment of the said sum of Rs. ——— and interest due hereunder as well.

3. It is hereby agreed that the said usufructuary mortgage shall not be redeemed without payment of the moneys due hereunder along with the mortgage money due under the said usufructuary mortgage.

IN WITNESS, etc.

48—Further Charge on a Usufructuary Mortgage (when no Interest is Agreed to be Paid on the Further Advance)

THIS DEED, etc., (*as in Form* 3).

WHEREAS—

(1) (*as in Form* 47)

(2) The mortgagee has agreed to lend to the mortgagor a further sum of Rs. ——— on the security of the aforesaid mortgage and on condition that the usufruct of mortgaged property shall be deemed to liquidate the interest on the said sum of Rs. ——— also.

NOW THIS DEED WITNESSES as follows:

1. In consideration of the sum of Rs. ——— now advanced by the mortgagee to the mortgagor, the mortgagor declares that the said sum of Rs. ——— shall be a further charge on the property comprised in the aforesaid usufructuary mortgage, and shall be added to the principal sum secured by the aforesaid mortgage so that the said mortgage shall not be redeemed without payment of the total sum of Rs. ———.

2. It is hereby agreed that the mortgagee shall appropriate the usufruct of the said mortgaged property as well in lieu of interest on the sum now lent by him as on the sum secured by the aforesaid deed of usufructuary mortgage and that no further interest shall be payable on the sum now lent by him.

IN WITNESS, etc.

49—Memo Creating a Charge on Life Policy to Secure a Loan taken from an Insurance Co.[1]

To,

The ________________ Co.

I, AB, etc., hereby declare and agree that you have this day advanced to me the sum of Rs. ——— on account of the sum insured by the Policy No. ——— dated ——— and that the said sum has been advanced on compound interest at ——— percent per annum payable every year

1 Also see precedent No. 34 *ante*.

on the ———— with annual rests on the condition that any sum on account of principal and interest remaining unpaid on the date on which the sum insured by the said policy become payable may be deducted from the said sum insured AND I hereby charge all moneys to become payable under the said policy with the payment of the principal and interest due on account of the said loan under the terms aforesaid AND I further agree that any sum which may hereafter be added as bonus or profits to the said policy shall remain as an addition to the sum insured until all sums due to you on this security shall have been fully paid and satisfied.

50—Memorandum Creating a Charge on Property to Secure a Current or Cash Credit Account with a Bank

To

The ———————— Bank.

I, AB, etc., hereby charge my interest in the property described in the schedule hereto (*or,* in the deeds mentioned below which I have deposited with you) with the payment to you, on demand, of the balance which on my current cash credit account with you shall for the time being be in respect of bills, notes or drafts, accepted, paid or discounted or advances made to me or for my use or accommodation and for interest, commission or other usual banker's charges or otherwise, together with interest on the said balance from the date of such demand being made or left till the date of payment at the rate of ———— percent per annum.

Dated ——— (Sd.) AB

The schedule referred to above

* * * * *

51—Deed of Appointment of Receiver by Mortgagee (Section 69A, Transfer of Property Act) (if Receiver named in the Mortgage Deed)

THIS DEED OF APPOINTMENT is made by me AB, etc., on the day of ———.

WHEREAS by a deed of mortgage dated the —— day of ——— and made between CD, etc., of the one part AND me, of the other part, the said CD mortgaged to me the property described in the schedule hereto.

AND WHEREAS XY, etc., was named in the aforesaid mortgage deed as the person to be appointed a receiver of the income of the mortgaged property and the said XY has signified his willingness and is able to act as such receiver.

AND WHEREAS the mortgage money due under the aforesaid mortgage deed has not yet been fully paid and a large sum is still owing to me thereunder.

NOW THIS DEED WITNESSES that in exercise of the power conferred on me in that behalf by law (*or*, by the terms of the said mortgage deed) and of every other power vested in me in that behalf I hereby appoint the said XY to be the receiver of the property described in the schedule hereto with all the powers of a receiver appointed under and by virtue of Sec. 69A of the Transfer of Property Act, 1882 and with all the rights, duties and obligations and remuneration as are therein mentioned (*or, if Transfer of Property Act does not apply*, "under the terms of the aforesaid mortgage deed").

IN WITNESS WHEREOF, etc.

52—Deed of Appointment of Receiver by Mortgagee (if Receiver is not Named in the Mortgage Deed)

THIS DEED is made on the ——— day of ——— BETWEEN AB, etc., (mortgagor) of the first part, CD, etc., (mortgagee) of the second part AND XY, etc., (receiver) of the third part.

WHEREAS (*recite the mortgage and the power of sale that is given therein*).

AND WHEREAS the mortgagee considers it expedient to appoint a receiver of the mortgaged property and the mortgagor has consented to the appointment of the said XY as such receiver.

NOW THIS DEED WITNESSES that the mortgagee with the consent and concurrence of the mortgagor hereby appoints the said XY as receiver of the property mentioned in the said mortgage deed with the following powers and duties:

etc., etc., etc.,

53—Deed of Hypothecation of Construction Plant

THIS DEED made on this —— day of —— 20 —— BETWEEN AB, etc., (hereinafter called "the Contractor" which expression shall unless the context otherwise requires include its successors and assigns) of the one part AND the Governor of the State of ——— (hereinafter called "the Government" which expression shall unless the context otherwise requires include his successors and assigns) of the other part.

Recitals

WHEREAS the parties hereto entered into an agreement dated ——— (hereinafter called the Principal Agreement) for the construction of ———.

AND WHEREAS under clause ——— of the Principal Agreement, the Contractor has applied to the Government for an interest free loan of Rs. ——— as advance for the construction of the plant and for the equipment described in the Schedule hereto specifically acquired by the Contractor for the works and brought to site.

AND WHEREAS one of the conditions on which the said loan of Rs. ——— is to be granted by the Government to the contractor is that the Contractor shall hypothecate the plant and equipment described in the Schedule hereto in favour of the Government until such time as the work under the Principal Agreement is completed and accepted by the Government.

AND WHEREAS the Contractor has represented that he is the owner of the plant and equipment described in the schedule hereto.

NOW THIS INDENTURE WITNESSES as follows:—

1. Hypothecation

In pursuance of the said Principal Agreement and in consideration of the premises, the Contractor hereby hypothecates, assigns and transfers to the Government the plant and equipment described in the schedule hereto to the intent that the same shall remain and form security for repayment to the Government of the said loan of Rs. ———.

2. Contractor's Covenants

The Contractor hereby agrees, declares and covenants with the Government as follows:

(a) Repayment

The Contractor shall repay to the Government the said loan of Rs. ——— and agrees that the said loan be recovered by the Government by making deductions in the manner provided in clause ——— of the Principal Agreement and other conditions of the Principal Agreement from the claims made by the Contractor against the Government for "on account" payment.

(b) Absolute Owner

The Contractor has paid in full the purchase price of the plant and equipment described in the Schedule hereto and each and every one of them and that the same are the absolute property of the Contractor and that the same have not been sold, pledged, mortgaged or transferred or in any way dealt with by the Contractor.

(*c*) *Not to Transfer*

So long as the plant and equipment described in the Schedule hereto remain assigned and hypothecated to the Government, the Contractor shall not sell, pledge, hypothecate, transfer, part with or in any way deal with the plant and equipment described in the Schedule hereto.

(*d*) *Default*

If the said loan of Rs. ——— shall not be repaid by the Contractor or recovered in the manner described in clause —— of the Principal Agreement due to any reason whatsoever or the said Principal Agreement has been determined earlier or cancelled or if the Contractor shall sell, pledge, mortgage, transfer, part with or in any way deal with the said plant and equipment or any part thereof or shall remove the same or any part thereof without the written permission of the Engineer-in-charge, or the Contractor or any of its partners is adjudged insolvent [or liquidation or winding up proceedings (*applicable in case the contractor is a Compnay*) are apprehended or commenced against the Contractor Company] or makes any composition or arrangement with its creditors or the Contractor shall commit breach of any of the terms and conditions or covenants as herein contained or in any of the said plant and equipment or if any other property whatsoever belonging to the Contractor has been sold or attached for a period of not less than 21 days in execution of the decree of any Court for payment of money, or if the Contractor abandons the said work, the whole of the said loan of Rs. ——— or such part thereof as may have remained unpaid or unrecovered shall forthwith become due and payable.

(*e*) *Sale of Plant and Equipment*

The Government may on the happening of any of the events mentioned in the preceding sub-clause(d) or if the said loan or any part thereof becomes due and payable and the same has not been repaid or recovered or cannot be recovered as provided in the said conditions, seize and take possession of the said plant and equipment (and either remain in possession thereof without removing the same or else may remove the same) and sell the said plant and equipment or any of them either by public auction or private contract and may, out of the sale proceeds, retain the balance of the said loan then remaining unpaid and unrecovered and all costs, charges and expenses and payments incurred or made in maintaining, defending or protecting the rights of the Government hereunder and shall pay over the surplus, if any, to the Contractor.

(*f*) *Insurance*

The Contractor shall at all times during the continuance of the security and at his expense insure and keep insured the plant and equipment described in the Schedule hereto for the full value thereof in the joint names of the Contractor and the Government with an insurance company against the risk of loss or damage from whatever cause as provided in the Principal Agreement. During the continuance of the security the Contractor shall pay all premia and sums of money necessary for keeping such insurance in force and the insurance policy and receipts in original for premia paid shall be deposited with the Engineer-in-charge. The Contractor shall assign all his rights, title and interest in the policy to the Government.

(*g*) *Prevent Damage*

The Contractor shall not permit or suffer the said plant and equipment or any part thereof to be destroyed or damaged or used or to be used or to deteriorate in a greater degree than it would deteriorate by reasonable wear and tear thereof in the performance of the Principal Agreement.

(*h*) *Replacement*

In the event of any damage or loss happening to the said plant and equipment or any part thereof the Contractor shall forthwith have the same repaired or replaced as the case may be or arrange for the payment of the entire amount recovered or to be recovered from the insurance company to the Government towards the payment of the said loan of Rs. ———.

(*i*) *Recovery of Loan*

If the sale proceeds realised under sub-clause (e) above or the insurance money recovered shall not be sufficient to repay the entire outstanding amount of the loan or if the said hypothecated property or any part thereof shall be removed or the Government shall be precluded from seizing the same whether by destruction, theft or otherwise, the Government shall be at liberty to recover the amounts due as arrears of land revenue.[1]

3. Upon repayment or recovery in full of the amount secured on account of this hypothecation deed and on completion of the work under the contract mentioned above and its acceptance by the Government, the said plant and equipment, (unless the Government has exercised its right to take over the plant and equipment for the construction of the said works at thirty percent of its original cost as per provisions of the Principal Agreement), shall stand released from the hypothecation but this is without prejudice to the right of the Government under any other conditions of the Principal Agreement.

The schedule referred to above:

Sl. No.	Particulars of plant & equipment	No.	Purchase price/ price considered reasonable by Engineer-in-charge	Total	Advance price
1	2	3	4	5	6

IN WITNESS WHEREOF, the parties hereto have executed these presents on the day and year first above written.

54—Deed Creating Floating Charge

THIS DEED made on the ——— day of ——— BETWEEN AB, etc., of the one part AND CD, etc., of the other part;

WITNESSES as follows:—

1. In consideration of the sum of Rs. ——— advanced by CD to AB (receipt of which AB hereby acknowledges), AB hereby covenants with CD as follows:

(*a*) *Repayment*

That AB will pay to CD the said sum of Rs. ——— together with interest at ——— percent per annum in seven instalments of Rs. —— each of principal with interest on the outstanding sum up-to-date on the ——— day of ——— in each year, the

1 Such a clause will be legally effective only if there is statutory backing for it, such as that contained in section 3(1) (*d*), U.P. Public Moneys (Recovery of Dues) Act, 1972.

first of such payments to be made on the ——— day of ———.

(*b*) *Utilization*

That AB shall utilise the aforesaid sum of Rs. —— for —— alone and shall not utilise it for any other purpose whatsoever.

(*c*) *Earlier Repayment*

That notwithstanding the stipulation regarding payment of annual instalments and interest contained in sub-clause(a) above, AB may repay the whole amount of the loan or a portion thereof or interest thereon at any time before the date on which the loan or any instalment thereof or its interest falls due for payment.

PROVIDED ALWAYS that if there shall be a breach on the part of AB of any of the terms of this deed or any instalment or interest is in arrears for three months after the due date or if there is a reasonable apprehension that AB is unable to pay his debts or that (applicable in case of a company) liquidation or winding up proceedings may be commenced against AB, CD may, notwithstanding anything to the contrary said in this deed, order AB to repay in full forthwith the outstanding amount of the loan and interest.

2. Floating Charge

For the consideration aforesaid and in pursuance of the said agreement AB hereby assigns to CD by way of floating charge ALL THAT the property of AB, fully described together with approximate value in the Schedule hereto and such other assets as may be created from the said loan TO HOLD the same upto CD absolutely subject only to the proviso for redemption hereinafter contained.

3. Free from Encumbrances

That the property hereby charged is free from encumbrances and AB will at all times during the continuance of this deed maintain and keep in good state of repairs and in proper working order the said property.

4. Discharge

That if AB shall pay to CD the said principal sum with interest thereon in accordance with the covenants hereinbefore contained, CD will at the request and cost of AB duly discharge their security.

5. When Charge becomes Fixed

That the said floating charge will become fixed and immediately enforceable upon the happening of any of the following events:

(a) If AB having received in writing notice under the proviso to clause 1 aforesaid to pay all principal money with interest, makes default in payment of the same.

(b) If AB, being a company, goes into liquidation except for the purpose of reconstruction or amalgamation.

6. *Insurance clause.*

7. *Arbitration clause.*

8. *Interpretation clause.*

The schedule herein referred to.

IN WITNESS WHEREOF etc.

NEGOTIABLE INSTRUMENTS

Preliminary Note

Negotiable Instruments

A "negotiable instrument" means a bill of exchange, promissory note or cheque payable either to order or to bearer (section 13, Negotiable Instruments Act, 1881). It is not necessary that it should be expressly stated to be payable to the order of a person. If a bill or promissory note or cheque is payable to a particular person and there is nothing to indicate the intention that it is not transferable, it is payable to order, and is negotiable. If there is anything to indicate that it is not a negotiable instrument but an ordinary actionable claim, then the rules relating to negotiable instruments do not apply to it.

Cheque is a bill of exchange drawn on a specified banker and payable on demand and the Act, therefore, practically deals with two kinds of instruments, the promissory notes and bills of exchange. The broad distinction between the two is that in the former the executant makes promise himself while in the latter he directs a third person to pay.

The following definitions are given in the Act.

Definition of Pronote

A "promissory note" is an instrument in writing, (not being a bank note or currency note), containing an unconditional undertaking, signed by the maker, to pay a certain sum of money only to, or to the order of, a certain person, or to the bearer of the instrument (Sec. 4).

There must be an express undertaking to pay the amount mentioned in the instrument before it can be held to be a promissory note. A mere implied undertaking, by the use of word "debt" or "pronote" or "acknowledgement" in the instrument is not sufficient.[1] In case the terms are "I acknowledge myself to be indebted to X for Rs. 500, to be paid on demand for value received", the instrument will be a promissory note.

An instrument bearing one-anna revenue stamp (which was the stamp duty then payable) was in these terms "I had borrowed a sum of Rs. 50 bearing interest at the rate of annas four percent per mensem from B on 1st March, 1939 and have therefore executed this pronote so that it may serve as evidence". It was held that this instrument was not a promissory note as it did not contain an unconditional

1 *Akbar Khan* v. *Attar Singh,* AIR 1936 PC 171; *Lakhami Das* v. *Lakha Ram*, AIR 1935 All 410; *B.B. Lohar* v. *Prem Prakash Goyal*, AIR 1999 Sikkim 11.

undertaking to pay.[1]

Definition of Bill of Exchange

A "bill of exchange" is an instrument in writing containing an unconditional order, signed by the maker, directing a certain person to pay a certain sum of money only to, or to the order of, a certain person or to the bearer of the instrument (Sec.5).

Essentials of a Bill or Note

The following are the essential requisites of a bill or promissory note-

(i) It must be for payment of *money* alone;

(ii) The sum to be paid must be certain;

(iii) The promise, or order must be absolute and unconditional;

(iv) The maker or drawer must be a certain person;

(v) The payee and drawee must be certain persons.

Mode of Transfer or Negotiation

A bill of exchange, cheque or promissory note which is negotiable may be transferred by endorsement and delivery if the instrument is payable to order, or, by delivery only if it is payable to bearer (Secs.46 to 48). An endorsement may be in any form and mere signature of the endorser is sufficient. In the latter case, the endorsement is said to be "in blank" or general endorsement, as against an endorsement "in full" or special endorsement in which the name of the person in whose favour the instrument is endorsed is also mentioned. An instrument endorsed in blank may be negotiated further by mere delivery or the blank endorsement may be converted into a full endorsement in favour of another person by writing above the endorser's signature a direction to pay to another person as endorsee. Mere delivery with intention to transfer the property in the instrument will constitute effective endorsement.

Deed of Transfer

Section 137, Transfer of Property Act saves negotiable instruments from the other provisions of the Chapter on *Actionable Claims*. However, the Act does not apply to some territories. It must further be remembered that a transferee by negotiation under the Negotiable Instruments Act takes the instrument free from the liabilities and equities affecting the transferor and thus in certain cases stands in a better position than his transferor, while a transferee other than an endorsee takes it subject to all the liabilities and equities affecting the assignor.

1 *Bachan Singh* v. *Ram Avadh*, AIR 1949 All 431.

Capacity of Parties

(a) Agent

A person can be made liable on a negotiable instrument by a duly authorised agent *acting in his name* (Sec. 27). The last four words are important and the name of the person to be made liable should clearly appear in the instrument. It will not be sufficient that the name is disclosed in such a way that on a fair interpretation of the instrument he appears to be liable. The agent should also clearly indicate that he is not personally liable, otherwise the mere fact of his signing the instrument will make himself personally liable upon it (Sec. 28). Where a *hundi* was signed by "G.V. Athole, Managing Proprietor, Ganga Dhar and B. Friends" it was held that Athole was personally liable.[1]

(b) Corporation/Companies

Though a corporation is a person capable of entering into contract, it cannot bind itself by making, endorsing or accepting a negotiable instrument except in cases in which under the law for the time being in force it is so empowered (Sec. 26). If the corporation is a Company within the meaning of the Companies Act, its capacity is determined with reference to the memorandum and articles of association.

If a corporation exceeds its power and executes an instrument, the act is ultra vires and even a bona fide holder cannot make the corporation liable.

Section 22 of Companies Act, 2013 provides that a bill of exchange, *hundi* or promissory note shall be deemed to have been made, accepted, drawn or endorsed on behalf of a company if made, accepted, drawn, or endorsed in the name of, or on behalf of or on account of, the company by any person acting under its authority, express or implied. A company may, by writing under its common seal, if any, authorize any person, either generally or in respect of any specified matters, as its attorney, to execute other deeds on its behalf in any place either in or outside India.

Provided that in case a company does not have a common seal, the authorization under this sub-section (2) of Section 22 shall be made by two directors or by a director and the Company Secretary, wherever the company has appointed a Company Secretary. A deed signed by such an attorney on behalf of the company and under his seal shall bind the company.

(c) Firm

Firms are governed by the provisions of the Partnership Act. A partner of a trading firm is liable as a party to a negotiable instrument if the name of the firm appears on the instrument, as every partner can bind his co-partners by his acts which are done in the usual way for carrying on the business of the firm (Sec. 19). *The executant should, however, sign expressly as a partner and the name of the firm should appear on the face of the instrument* (Sec. 22). If it was not executed

---

1 *Sita Ram* v. *Chimman Das*, AIR 1928 B 516, 30 BLR 1300, 52 B 640.

in the name of the firm, the latter will not be bound even if the money was borrowed for a purpose binding on the firm.[1] If the executant signs as "Managing Partner" of the firm then the intention to bind the firm is presumed.[2]

(d) Legal Representatives

A legal representative of a deceased person signing a negotiable instrument is liable personally, unless he expressly limits his liability to the extent of the assets received by him (Sec. 29). It will not be sufficient for the executant merely to describe himself as an executor or administrator.[3] The personal liability can be excluded by adding the words "without recourse" or "without recourse to me personally" to the signature, or by expressly stating in the body of the promissory note that the executant will be liable to the extent of the assets of the deceased.

(e) Persons of unsound mind and Minors

Every person who is capable of entering into a contract (Secs. 10, 11, 12 Contract Act) may incur liability under a negotiable instrument (Sec. 26 Negotiable Instruments Act). A bill executed by a person of unsound mind will therefore be void even against a *bona fide* transferee. But a minor may draw, endorse, deliver and negotiate an instrument so as to bind all parties except himself. The holder of a bill drawn by a minor is therefore entitled to receive payment from the drawee and, if necessary, to enforce it against any party but the minor. A minor is, however, not precluded from accepting the benefit of a negotiable instrument and can sue all the parties liable under it.[4] A *de facto* guardian cannot execute a negotiable instrument on behalf of a minor.[5]

Presentment

Promissory Notes, bills of exchange and cheques must be presented to the maker, acceptor or drawee thereof respectively, by or on behalf of the holder. Only after such presentment they become liable under it. In default of such presentment, the other parties there to are not liable thereon to such holder. (sections 61 to 64, Negotiable Instruments Act, 1881.) When a promissory note is payable on demand, and is not payable at a specified place, no presentment is necessary in order to charge the maker (Sec. 64 exception). Other cases in which no presentment is necessary are given in Sec. 76.

Notice of Dishonour

When an instrument is dishonoured, notice of dishonour must be given to

---

1 Cf *Mt Suraj Bahu* v. *Jaitley*, AIR 1946 All 372.

2 *Chandan* v. *Mt. Krishna Kumari*, AIR 1944 Oudh 273; *Vattumalli* v. *Medrarpu*, AIR 2003 AP 46.

3 *Kayya Lal Mudi* v. *Subhara Yadu*, AIR 1926 M 390.

4 *Ulfat Rai* v. *Gauri Shankar*, 33 A 657; *Cf. Raghav* v. *Srinivas*, 40 M 308.

5 *Mynemi* v. *Kondamudi*, AIR 1946 Mad 1 (F.B.).

the parties sought to be made liable, but no such notice is necessary to the maker of a pronote or the drawee or acceptor of a bill (Sec. 93). Other cases in which notice of dishonour is unnecessary are given in Sec. 98.

Contents of Notice of Dishonour and how to be given

There must be something in the notice itself that there has been failure of payment on presentment and therefore dishonour of the promissory note.[1]

Section 94 stipulates the mode in which notice may be given. It may be oral or written. If written, notice may be sent by post. It may be in any form, but it must inform the party to whom it is given either in express terms or by reasonable intendment, that the instrument has been dishonoured,

It provides that notice of dishonour may be given to a duly authorised agent of the person to whom it is required to be given, or,

(i) where he has died, to his legal representative, or

(ii) where he has been declared an insolvent, his assignee; and in what way, and that he will be held liable thereon; and it must be given within a reasonable time after dishonour, at the place of business or (in case such party has no place of business) at the residence of the party for whom it is intended.

Bill or Note how Drafted

While drafting of a promissory note or bill of exchange, the point mentioned below should be kept in mind. Care should also be taken to include all the essential ingredients of the negotiable instrument detailed below.

Date and Place

The date and place of a promissory note or bill is generally entered at the right-hand top corner. Sometimes, in promissory notes they are given at the end. They are not an essential part of the instrument, though it is always preferable to enter them, and their omission does not invalidate the instrument. If no date is given, date of delivery will be considered to be its date and it may be filled in by the payee (section 20).

Amount

The amount of the bill or note is usually entered in words in the body and in figures at the left hand top corner. Sometimes, in promissory notes, it is written only in the body both in words and figures. It may be mentioned either way, but as a safeguard against mistake or fraud it is better to enter it both in words and figures.

In case of discrepancy, the amount in words shall be deemed to be the correct amount (Sec.18). Care should be taken that nothing except money should be

---

1 *Kottan* v. *Kannan*, 1950 MWN 161.

undertaken to be delivered, otherwise the instrument, will be invalid as a negotiable instrument, though in the case of such a promissory note it may, if attested and stamped, be used as a bond. The amount must be *certain*. A promise to pay "Rs. —— or such amount as may be found due" or "Rs. ———— after deducting such amount as may be found due to me on account of ———" will not be in order in a promissory note.

Section 20, Negotiable Instruments Act provides that where one person signs and delivers to another a paper stamped in accordance with the law relating to negotiable instruments, either wholly blank or having written thereon an incomplete negotiable instrument, he thereby gives prima facie authority to the holder thereof to make or complete, as the case may be, for any amount specified therein and not exceeding the amount covered by the stamp.

Payee

The name of the payee is mentioned in the body, either by personal name or by official designation, but it should be certain or ascertainable. A negotiable instrument may be made payable to two or more payees jointly, or it may be made payable in the alternative to one of two, or one or some of several payees. [Sec. 13(2)]. If the payment is to be made to the bearer, the words "or bearer" are added.

If it is intended to be payable to the order of the payee, the words "or order" are added or we might say "to the order of ———" [vide section 13(1), Expl. (3)], but the addition of the words "or order" is not essential so long as a bill or note is negotiable, for, even if it is payable to a particular person, it can be endorsed by the payee to anyone else [Sec. 13(1), Expl. (1)].

However, if there is anything to show that it is not negotiable it cannot be endorsed. For example, when it is expressly stated that it shall be payable to the payee "only". In such cases, the rules relating to Negotiable Instruments do not apply and the pronote is like any other actionable claim.

Besides the name, sufficient description, (e.g. his or her father's name or her husband's name, occupation and residence) necessary for identification, should also be added.

Sometimes a promissory note is drafted in the form of a letter in which case the name of the payee is mentioned as the heading as "Dear Shri ———", "To Shri ———" and he is referred to in the body by the pronoun "you".

Sometimes a promissory note is delivered to another person duly signed and stamped and with the amount payable mentioned therein but without the name of the payee, the intention being that such other person may insert his or any other person's name as payee. This procedure is perfectly regular and the person to whom such paper is delivered is entitled to convert it into a promissory note payable to himself or to a third person (Secs. 4, 20, Negotiable Instruments Act).[1]

Unconditional Promise

In a promissory note there should be an unconditional promise to pay. If the promissory note being in the form of a letter simply contains a request for the loan and an undertaking to repay it with interest, there is no unconditional promise as the promise is dependent on the advance of the loan.[2] A mere acknowledgment of a debt is not a promise to pay. The payment may be promised on demand, or on a particular date, or after a particular period from a certain event, or in instalments payable on certain dates, but if payment is agreed on the happening of an uncertain event (e.g. seven days after my marriage with A), it will not be an "unconditional undertaking". There is no objection if no time is fixed for payment, for in that case the money is payable on demand (Sec. 19). If the money is payable "on demand" the phrase does not import a condition to make the actual demand,[3] but the money is payable at once.

Payable to Bearer on Demand

Notwithstanding anything contained in the Negotiable Instruments Act, 1881, no person other than the Bank or as expressly authorised by this Act (Reserve Bank of India Act), the Central Government shall make or issue any promissory note payable to the bearer of the instrument. Provided that cheques or drafts, including hundis, payable to bearer on demand or otherwise may be drawn on a person's account with a bank or agent. (section 31).

Several Executants

Where there are more than one executants of a promissory note, it should be clearly stated whether the undertaking by them is joint or joint and several. If the note begins with "we promise" and is signed at the end by two persons, they are jointly liable. If it begins with the words "I promise" and is signed by two persons, it would be considered that each is jointly and severally liable.

Order in Case of Bill

The drawer's order to pay to the drawee must also be unconditional. The order may be to pay "on demand" or so many days "after date" or "after sight".

Name of Drawee of Bill

The name and address of the drawee of a bill is mentioned either at the top in the same form in which letters are addressed. e.g.:

"To

AB, etc."

or at the bottom left-hand corner.

---

1 *Hriday* v. *Kailash*, AIR 1940 Pat 377, 186 IC 809.

2 *Sarju* v. *Sukhulal*, AIR 1924 Pat 96, 79 IC 420.

3 *Perumal* v. *Alagirisami*, 20 M 245.

The name must be certain, must be distinctly written with the addition of address, etc., sufficient for identification.

For bills drawn in fictitious name, *see* Sec. 42, Negotiable Instruments Act.

Consideration

A negotiable instrument is, until the contrary is proved, presumed to be made, drawn, accepted, endorsed or negotiated for consideration [Sec. 118(a)], and it is not necessary to recite the consideration in the bill or note.[1] This presumption is not available where the actual consideration is different from that recited, and the real consideration can be proved by other evidence.[2] It is not usual to recite it in bills, but in promissory notes it is sometimes mentioned, and the practice is good as affording evidence against a possible plea of want of consideration and as enabling the payee to sue on the original consideration, in case the pronote is found to be defective or inadmissible in evidence.

Mostly where a pronote is executed for a loan, a separate receipt is also executed acknowledging the loan. This serves a useful purpose inasmuch as, if the pronote is, for any reason, inadmissible in evidence, the creditor can prove the debt by the receipt and sue for money paid and received *i.e.* for the original consideration.[3] Besides the transaction can be made more secure by having the receipt attested. But the pronote itself should not be attested, for, if pronote is attested, it requires the stamp duty of a bond.[4] [Sec. 2(5) (b), (c), Stamp Act].

Section 139 of Negotiable Instruments Act, mandates that unless the contrary is proved, it is to be presumed that the holder of a cheque, received the cheque for the discharge, in whole or in part, of any debt or other liability. The presumption contemplated under Section 139 is a rebuttable presumption. However, the onus of proving that the cheque was not in discharge of any debt or other liability is on the accused drawer of the cheque.[5]

Interest

If interest is agreed to be paid, the rate must be specified. It will be payable from the date on which the money becomes due, which, in the case of agreement to pay on demand, is the date of the instrument. In case rate of interest is not specified in the negotiable instrument, then notwithstanding any agreement relating to interest between the parties, interest will be calculated at the rate of 18% per annum

1 *Lal Girwal Lal* v. *Dau Dayal*, AIR 1935 All 509; *Lala Ram Nath* v. *Lala Ramchander Mal*, AIR 1935 All 154.

2 *K.P.O. Moideankutty* v. *Pappu Manjooram*, (1996) 8 SCC 586.

3 *See*, e.g., *Gulab Gir* v. *Nath Mal*, AIR 1932 Nag 33 (per Bose A.J.C., later Judge Supreme Court), See notes under Negotiable Instruments in Mogha's Pleadings (18th, Edn), pp. 564-574.

4 *Jageshwar* v. *Collector*, AIR 1966 All 392.

5 *Bir Singh* v. *Mukesh Kumar*, (2019) 4 SCC 197; *Hiten P. Dalal* v. *Bratindranath Banerjee*, (2001) 6 SCC 16.

from the date on which the same ought to have been paid by the party charged until tender or realization of the amount due thereon or until such date after the institution of a suit to recover such amount as the court directs. (Sec. 80)

Name of the Maker and Signature

The name of the maker or drawer is sometimes mentioned separately from the signature, but this is not strictly necessary so long as the name clearly appears from the signature. But in promissory notes given for loans, the name of the maker, with additions, is generally mentioned in the beginning as "I, AB, etc." In that case also, signature is necessary at the end. Signature may be full or only initials or mark. In the latter cases, it is better to write down the full name also under the signatures. This is particularly necessary if the name of the maker is not mentioned in the body.

Inchoate Instruments, Alteration

Unlike any other instrument, a negotiable instrument may be signed by the maker or drawer in blank. All that is necessary is that the signatures should be put on a paper stamped with the requisite stamp and the paper should be delivered by the maker or drawer to another person. The paper may be wholly blank or blank with regard to any particulars, e.g., date, amount, etc. The person to whom it is delivered has the right to write a promissory note or bill on it or to fill in the blanks and the only limit to the amount is that covered by the stamp duty (*see* Sec. 20). Any omission in the bill or note can therefore be made good by the payee under this section, but no material alteration in a negotiable instrument is permissible, and, if one is found to have been made, the instrument becomes void against anyone who is a party thereto at the time of such alteration and who has not consented thereto, unless the alteration was made in order to carry out the common intention (Sec. 87).[1]

Attestation

A bill or promissory note need not be attested. If it is attested by a witness and is not payable to order it will fall under the definition of a bond, as given in the Indian Stamp Act, and will therefore be chargeable with duty as a bond.

Bills in Set

Sometimes bills are drawn in parts, each part being numbered and containing a provision that it shall continue to be payable only so long as the others remain unpaid. All the parts together make a set, and the whole set constitutes only one bill and is extinguished when one of the parts would be extinguished (Sec. 132). The object of the set is to avoid delay and inconvenience resulting from loss or miscarriage of the bill and to enable the holder to send the bill by different conveyance to the drawee to expedite presentment for acceptance and payment.

---

1 *See also,* INTRODUCTION, PART IV: 'Material Alteration in Deed', page 49].

Foreign bills are as a rule drawn in sets.

Holder in due course

"Holder in due course" means any person who for consideration became the possessor of a promissory note, bill of exchange or cheque before the amount mentioned in it became payable, and without having sufficient cause to believe that any defect existed in the title of the person from whom he derived his title (section 9 read with 118(g), Negotiable Instruments Act, 1881). The condition entails that he should act in good faith and with reasonable caution. Mere failure to prove good faith or absence of negligence on his part does not negate his claim, unless, of course, the court finds that the negligence was gross and extra-ordinary and that in face thereof there could be no sufficient cause to believe that the title was free from being defective.[1]

Section 131

Collection of Cheques (Sec.131) and drafts (Sec.131A) by a banker on behalf of its customer after the account is opened and the relationship of banker and customer has been established is protected where the banker in good faith and without negligence, receives payment for the customer. In such an event, the banker does not incur any liability to the true owner of the cheque or draft by reason only of having received such payment.[2] However, the banker who receives payment based on electronic image has a duty to verify *prima facie* genuinness of the cheque to be truncated and any fraud, forgery or tampering apparent on the face of the instrument that can be verified with due diligence and ordinary care (Explanation II)[3]

Dishonour of cheque

It is well settled law that if cheques were not issued for discharge of the any debt or liability but only by way of security, then offence under section 138 of the Act is not made out for dishonor of cheques.[4] It is clear from the aforesaid section read with the explanation that the debt or other liability means a legally enforceable debt or other liability and cheques issued as security cannot be said to be issued for clearing any such liability. However, every offence punishable under this Act shall be compoundable (section 147).[5]

---

1 *U. Ponnappa Moothan Sons Palghat* v. *Catholic Syrian Bank Ltd.*, (1991) 1 SCC 113.

2 *Indian Overseas Bank* v. *Industrial Chain Concern*, (1990) 1 SCC 484.

3 *Negotiable Instruments Amendment Act, 2002.*

4 *Jitendra Sing Flora* v. *Ravikant Talwar*, 2001 (1) M.P.L.J. 229 M.P., *M.S. Narayan Menon @ Mani* v. *State of Kerala*, 2006 (4) M.P.L.J. (S.C.) 97 and *Vijay* v. *Laxmanchand*, 2013 (2) M.P.L.J. (S.C.) 615 and *Shobha Chouhan* v. *Gopichand Khatri*, 2016 SCC OnLine MP 11939

5 *Vinay Devanna Nayak* v. *Ryot Seva Sahakari Bank Ltd.*, AIR 2008 SC 716.

PRECEDENTS

1—Bill of Exchange Payable on Demand

Lucknow

January 31, 2021

Rs. ————

Pay to XY, etc., or order (*or*, pay to XY, etc., or bearer) (*or*, pay to my order), (*or*, pay to bearer), on demand (*or*, at sight) (*or*, on presentation) the sum of Rs. ——— (*in words*)

To

CD, etc. (*drawee*). (Signed) ——— AB (*drawer*)

2—Bill of Exchange, Payable after Date (with Interest)

Agra,

January 15, 2021

Rs. ————

——— days (months) after date pay to XY, etc., or order (*or*, pay to XY, etc., or bearer) (*or*, pay to my order) (*or*, pay to bearer) the sum of Rs. ——— (*in words*), with interest at ——— percent per annum.

To

CD, etc. (*drawee*). (Signed) ——— AB (*drawer*)

3—Bill of Exchange, Payable after Sight

——— (*Date*)

——— (*place*),

Rs. ———

——— days (months) after sight pay to, etc., (*as in Form* 2).

4—Bill of Exchange Payable to Any One of Several Payees

Agra

January 15, 2021

Rs.———

——— days (months) after date pay AB, etc., or CD, etc., or EF, or the order of any one of them, the sum of Rs.———(*in words*).

To

XY, etc. (*drawee*). (Signed) ——— M (*drawer*)

5—Bill of Exchange where the Drawer and Payee is the Same Person

Lucknow

January 31, 2021

Pay self (*or*, to my order) the sum of Rs.——(*in words*) only.

To (Signed) ——— AB

———

6—Bill of Exchange Payable to Bearer

Allahabad

May 14, 2021

Rs. ———

——— days after sight (*or*, after date)[1] pay the bearer the sum of Rs. ——— (*in words*) only.

To (Signed) ——— XY, etc.

———

7—Foreign Bill of Exchange

(*Drawn in Set of three Parts*)

First part

No.————— Exchange for £

Mumbai,

January 15, 2021

——— months after sight of this first of exchange (the second and third of the same date remaining unpaid), pay to CD, etc., or to his order ——— pounds sterling (*in words*) (and charge the same to account of XY against your letter of credit No. ——— dated ———).

To AB, etc. (*drawee*) Signed ——— (*drawer*)

1 A purely bearer bill cannot be made payable *on demand* (Sec. 31 Reserve Bank of India Act, 1934).

Second and Third Parts

Same as first part substituting for the words "the first of exchange (the second and third of the same date remaining unpaid" the words "the second of exchange (the first and third of the same date remaining unpaid)" *or* "the third of exchange (the first and second of the same date remaining unpaid)."

8—Promissory Note Payable on Demand

Allahabad,
January 20, 2021

Rs. ———

On demand I promise to pay CD, etc., (*or*, to CD, etc., or order) the sum of Rs. ——— (*in words*) with interest at ——— percent per annum.

Signature & Address

9—Promissory Note, for a Loan

Allahabad,
January 20, 2021

Rs. ———

In consideration of the loan of Rs. ——— advanced by CD, etc., to me, I promise to repay the said loan of Rs. ——— (*in words*) with interest at ——— percent per annum to the said CD or order.

(Signed) ——— *drawer*

10—Promissory Note Payable on a Fixed Date or in Instalments

Allahabad,
January 13, 2021

Rs. ———

I, AB, etc., promise to pay to CD, etc., or order the sum of Rs. —— (*in words*) on the ——— (*or*, ——— month after date) (*or*, in twelve equal instalments of Rs. ——— (*in words*) each payable on the first day of every month commencing from the first day of February, 1996).

(Signed) —— *drawer*

11—Promissory Note, with Details of Consideration

I, AB, etc., hereby promise to pay on demand (*or*, within ——— years from this date) to CD, etc., (or order) the sum of Rs. ——— (*in words*) with interest at ——— percent per annum on account of the consideration received as specified below—

(1) Rs. ——— due from me to the said CD on account of a promissory note dated ———.
(2) Rs. ——— due from me to the said CD on account of the price of cloth purchased on ———.
(3) Rs. ——— due from me to the said CD on *bahi khata* account.
(4) Rs. ——— now borrowed in cash by me from the said CD.

Date: 3rd of June 1996.

Place: Agra Signed —— *drawer*

12—Promissory Note, in the Form of a Letter

Allahabad
January 28, 1996

Dear Shri CD, etc.

Whereas you have advanced to me today a loan of Rs. ——— (*in words*) I hereby promise to repay the same to you on demand with interest at ——— percent per mensem.

Yours sincerely

Signed ————

AB s/o.—————, resident of ———

13—Joint Promissory Note

Agra
May 5, 1996

Rs. ———

On demand (*or*, ———months after date) (*or*,——— days after sight) we hereby promise to pay to CD, etc., or order the sum of Rs.——— (*in words*).

Name and address of drawers	Signatures of drawers
1. ———	1. ———
2. ———	2. ———

Or,

Whereas we, AB, etc., CD, etc., and EF, etc., owe Rs. ——— to XY, etc., as detailed below:

1. ———
2. ———

We hereby promise to pay on demand (*or*, ——— years after date) the said sum of Rs. ——— (*in words*) to the said XY with interest at —— percent per annum.

Date: 3rd June, 2021

Place: Agra

Signed AB ———

CD ———

EF ———

14—Joint and Several Promissory Note

In Form 13 *for the words* "we hereby promise" *substitute the words* "we jointly and severally promise".

15—Receipt of Consideration of a Promissory Note

I, AB, etc., acknowledge to have received this day the sum of Rs. —— (*in words*) from CD, etc., on account of the consideration of the promissory note executed by me today in favour of the said CD.

Dated the ——— day of ———.

Witness ———

Signed ——— (AB)

(1) ———

(2) ———

Or

Received this day sum of Rs. ——— (*in words*) etc., (*as in the Form above*).

Signed ——— AB

(S/o. —————

resident of ——— etc.)

16— General Endorsement

"(Signed) —— AB"

17— Specific Endorsement

"Pay to XY or order

Signed ——— AB"

Or,

"Pay to order of XY—

Signed ——— AB"

Or,

"Pay to XY—

Signed ——— AB"

Or,

"Pay to XY or bearer

Signed ——— AB"

18—Restrictive Endorsement

"Pay to XY only

Signed ——— AB"

19—General and Absolute Acceptance

(1) (Signed) ——— "AB"

(2) Accepted (Signed) ——— "AB"

20—Partial Acceptance

Accepted as to Rs. ————— only.

Signed ——— AB.

(For precedents of Notice of dishonor of Bill or cheque, see under Notice)

NOTICE

Preliminary Note

Notice when given

A notice is given by one person to another sometimes because the law requires such notice to be given, sometimes because such notice is agreed upon by contract between the parties, sometimes as a matter of precaution with a view to have a claim amicably settled, if possible. When a notice is given under any law, e.g., in a suit against Government or Railway or under a contract, it should strictly correspond with the requirements of the law or terms of the contract. It is always preferable to use the very words of the statute or contract in drafting the notice.

How drafted

A notice is drafted generally in the first person as a communication addressed to the person to whom it is intended to be given. Sometime the ordinary form of a letter is used. A notice may be drafted even in the third person. The acts of which notice is intended to be given should be stated concisely and clearly, and the claim or demand of the notice-giver should be clearly and specifically made. In addition to this if any other fact is provided by the contract or statute to be entered in the notice, the same should be mentioned.

By Agent or Pleader

Notice may be given either by the party or by his agent or pleader but it must be on behalf of the principal. An agent must be specifically authorised to give such notice, and, although there is nothing to prevent authority being given orally, it is always safe to have it given in writing. A pleader must be instructed by his client to give the notice, but no *vakalatnama* or written power is necessary. He can act on oral instructions, but in order to safeguard their own interests, pleaders are advised to have a regular instruction book in which they should record in writing the instructions received and showing the action taken thereon. The instructions may be signed by the client. When an agent gives notice he must give it "As agent for and on behalf of ———" and when an advocate or solicitor gives notice he must give it "As Advocate/Solicitor for and behalf of ————" or "Under instructions from ———".

A Notice by a pleader generally starts with the opening sentence "Under instructions from my client Sri/Sm./Km. ——— son/wife/daughter of ———— (occupation) ———— resident of ————, I hereby give you the following notice." The paragraphs following this sentence should first set out, parawise, the relevant and material facts as in a plaint, and later, the occasion for giving the notice (corresponding to the para on "cause of action" in a plaint), and then the demand (corresponding to the prayer, i.e., the relief clause in a plaint), and finally the threat that unless the addressee meets the demand within the stated period "my client will be compelled to file a suit (*or*, take necessary legal proceedings) and you will be responsible for all costs and other consequences".

Restrictions on the landlord's right to evict a tenant from certain accommodations have been placed by local laws. Amendment has also been made in Sec. 106 of Transfer of Property Act by a local amendment in the State of U.P. providing 30 days, period of notice (instead of 15 days).[1] Before drafting a notice to evict, these provisions should be looked into and a proper notice should be given.

Defective legal notice

The notice terminating the tenancy has to be liberally interpreted because the only object of such notice is to give a 15 days period (in case of month to month tenancy) for vacation of the premises by the tenant.

To ensure that no technicalities are raised by the tenant with respect to service of legal notice terminating the tenancy, the legislature amended Section 106 of the Transfer of Property Act, 1882 by Act 3 of 2003 whereby no defence was permitted with respect to defective legal notice as long as a suit for possession was filed after 15 days of service of notice.[2]

Service of Notice

As to service of notice, the best mode is personal service. The next best is service by post, in which case it should be sent in a registered cover, acknowledgement due, addressed to the usual place of residence or business of the addressee. Sometimes special modes of service, e.g., leaving it at certain premises, sending it by post, or service on a relation or servant is provided in the law or contract, in which case the notice should be served in one of such ways. When a contract is made between the parties which provides for service of notice by one party on another, it is always better to provide for mode of service also. In case of service by post, although there will always be a presumption (which is rebuttable) that a letter addressed to the usual address of a person, if not returned in due course of post, was delivered to him, it is always better to provide for this also in the agreement.

Notice to Terminate Tenancy - when not Required

No notice is required to determine a tenancy which is for a fixed term. If the contract provides that the tenant would leave possession whenever required, in which case a mere demand is sufficient and notice is not necessary. Notice to quit is only one of the modes in which a tenancy could be determined. Section 106 only

---

1 The words `expiring with the month of tenancy' have been deleted by Act III of 2003.

2 *Venus Sugar Ltd.* v. *Nishi Chopra* 2011 SCC OnLine Del 1221.

recognizes two kinds of tenancies, one yearly tenancy and the other monthly tenancy. There are cases which do not come within the ambit of section 106 and they are governed by the terms of the contract of tenancy. It is only in cases where there is no contract as to notice that the provisions of section 106 would be applicable; but where there is a contract as to giving notice or waiving notice, the parties are governed by the terms of the contract and the law enacted in section 106, Transfer of Property Act, cannot apply. Where the contract was that the tenant should surrender the property whenever required, the provisions as to notice in section 106 cannot apply to it.[1] No notice is needed to a servant occupying quarters given by the master, as service occupation is not tenancy.[2]

When Notice Required

A notice is required only (1) when there is a condition of notice in the lease; (2) there is local custom or usage; (3) the tenancy is one from year to year or month to month; or (4) a forfeiture has been incurred and the landlord wishes to take advantage of it and to eject the tenant on that ground (see also the local amendments to Transfer of Property Act and rent control laws overriding that Act). Where the tenancy automatically determined on the expiry of the stipulated period but the lessee continued to hold the property on payment of rent, it was held the lease got renewed from month to month and its termination could only be by giving a valid notice.[3]

Length of Notice to Quit

In case there is a condition of notice in the lease or it is required under a local custom or usage, then such notice as stipulated in contract or required by custom or usage should be given.

In the case of periodic leases, *i.e.*, in case of tenancy from year to year or month to month, the provisions of Transfer of Property Act are to be looked into. Sec. 106 applies for agricultural and manufacturing purposes, as well as leases for other purposes. (Agricultural leases are, however, excepted from the operation of Transfer of Property Act and are regulated by local laws relating to agricultural tenures.)

Agricultural purposes include field tillage, gardens, coffee plantations[4] and indigo plantations. Manufacturing purposes include, making or manufacturing by aid of machinery, articles of trade and commerce.[5] Manufacturing purpose within

---

1 *Moosa Kutty* v. *Thekke*, 110 IC 398; AIR 1928 Mad 687; *Kuda Baksh* v. *Abid Hussain*, 120 C 279, 3 IC 837; *S.K. Ramachandra Mudaliar* v. *J. Anjamma*, 2020 (4) LW 448, MANU/TN/0758/2020.

2 *B.M. Lall* v. *Dunlop Co.,* AIR 1968 SC 175, (1968) 1 SCR 23 (servant is bare licensee).

3 Burmah Shell Distributing v. *Khaja Midhat Noor,* (1988) 3 SCC 44.

4 *Murugesa Chetti* v. *Chinnathambi Goundan*, 24 Mad. 421.

5 *Jayanti Hosiery Mills* v. *Upendra Chandra Das*, AIR 1946 Cal 317; *William Jacks and Co.* v. *Joosab Mahomed*, 48 Bom 38.

the meaning of section 106, means the making or fabricating articles or materials by physical labour or skill or by mechanical power vendible and useful as such.[1]

In the absence of contract or local law or usage to the contrary the leases for agricultural or manufacturing purposes are deemed to be from year to year, terminable by giving six months' notice and the leases for other purposes are deemed to be from month to month, terminable by fifteen days' notice to commence from the date of the service of notice.[2] In computing the period of yearly tenancy, the date on which the tenancy commenced, has to be excluded.[3] A house tenancy is presumed to be from month to month terminable by 15 days' notice. The fact that the rent of a house is payable annually is immaterial and is not sufficient to rebut the presumption of a monthly tenancy terminable by 15 days' notice.[4]

In U.P. on account of local amendment to Transfer of Property Act, vide U.P. Act 24 of 1954, 30 days' notice is necessary. In computation of 30 days the date on which notice is served shall be excluded.[5]

Form and Construction of Notice to Quit

The notice should be in writing and should be signed by or on behalf of the person giving it (Sec. 106). The party on whose behalf it is given should be clearly named and described. It may be given by a pleader or solicitor acting on behalf of his client. If the notice is given by a pleader or other agent, the name of the principal and the authority of the pleader or agent should be disclosed.

The property to which it refers should be specified.

The language of the notice should be clear and specific. Ambiguous phrases like "to vacate by ——— (*date*) or upto ——— (*date*)" should not be used as these expressions are likely to render the notice invalid. Notice to quit is not vitiated by use of present tense to terminate; the interpretation is not to be pedantic.[6] It is not necessary to specify any reason for terminating the tenancy and nothing unnecessary need be stated.

Notice by whom and to whom

If there are several landlords the notice should be on behalf of all. The notice to quit must be given by or on behalf of all the co-owners, but where lease was granted by a co-owner claiming or professing to be the sole owner or

---

1 *Allenbury Engineers Pvt. Ltd.*, v. *R.K. Dalmia*, AIR 1973 SC 425 (para 8).

2 The words `expiring with the month of tenancy' has been deleted by Amendment by Act III of 2003.

3 *Dattonpant Gapalvarao Devakate* v. *Vithal Rao Maruthirao Janagaval*, (1975) 2 SCC 246.

4 *Mohendra* v. *Narendra*, 50 IC 918; *Mangal Singh* v. *Atra*, 3 LLJ 222, 60 IC 226; *Chinti* v. *Kripa Shankar*, AIR 1941 Pat 488, 194 IC 300.

5 *Shiv Narain* v. *Chandrika Prasad*, AIR 1973 All 155.

6 *Abdul Jalil* v. *Haji Abdul Jalil*, AIR 1974 All 402; *Lakshmi Shankar* v. *J.C. Sharma*, 1980 ARC 43; *Bipat* v. *A.D. J.*, AIR 1980 All 142.

without disclosing other co-owners, the notice to quit given by him is sufficient to determine the lease,[1] as the grantor of the lease is the sole landlord or lessor though not the sole owner.[2] In case of a deity being the landlord any one *shebait* can act on its behalf if the others are either unable or unwilling to act to protect the interest of the deity.[3]

The notice to quit is to be addressed to the tenant. But when there are more than one tenant, before framing notice to quit it would be necessary to ascertain whether they are joint tenants or they are tenants-in-common.

In case of joint tenants, "tenants have unity of title, unity of commencement of title, unity of interest so as in law to have equal shares in the joint estate, unity of possession, as well of every part as of the whole, and right of survivorship",[4] "Tenants in common have only unity of possession; they may have unequal shares, and there is no right of survivorship. Each tenant in common could make a lease in respect of his own share alone, the interest of each being separate and distinct, and if tenants in common all joined in one lease it operated as a lease by each, of his respective share, and a confirmation by each as the shares of the others". In a case where a joint lease was executed by two tenants a notice to terminate tenancy to one of them was held to be good.[5] The Supreme Court has held that on death of a Mohamadan, his estate devolves on his heirs who succeed to the estate as tenants in common in specific shares.[6] Similarly, on death of original tenant, tenancy rights were inherited by his heirs who became tenants in common; notice to quit given to one of the heirs was held not sufficient and valid notice to all heirs or tenants in common.[7] In case of tenants in common, the notice should be sent to all jointly, but if it cannot be served personally and has to be sent by post, separate copies may be sent to each. But if for a long time only some of the heirs remained in occupation and paid rent and were recognised by the landlord as tenants, the other heirs who made no claim, may be deemed to have surrendered their tenancy.[8]

Notice by assignee of the Landlord—when there is no attornment

Though by virtue of Section 116 of the Evidence Act, the tenant is estopped from challenging the title of his landlord, yet the tenant is entitled to challenge the

1 *Nana Lal Girdhar Lal* v. *Gulamnabi Jamalbhai Motorwala*, AIR 1973 Guj 131 (F.B.)

2 *Sri Ram Pasricha* v. *Jagnnath*, (1976) 4 SCC 184; *Subhendu Pd. Roy Choudhury* v. *Kamla Bala*, (1978) 2 SCC 89.

3 *Mool Chand* v. *A.D.J.*, 1986 AWC 723 (DB).

4 See also *Badri Narain* v. *Rameshwar*, AIR 1951 SC 186 (para 10).

5 *Kanji Manji* v. *The Trustees of the Port of Bombay*, AIR 1963 SC 468; *H.C. Pandey* v. *G.C. Paul*, 1989 (2) ARC 26 (S.C.).

6 *Syed Shah Gulam Ghouse Mohiuddin* v. *Syed Shah Ahmad Mohiuddin Kamisul Qadri*, AIR 1971 SC 2184, (1971) 1 SCC 597.

7 *Ramesh Chand Bose* v. *Gopeshwar Prasad Sharma*, 1976 (2) ALR 711, AIR 1977 All 38.

8 *Bundoo* v. *Akbar Ali*, 1978 ALJ 215 (implied surrender).

derivative title of an assignee of the original landlord of the demised property in an action brought by the assignee against the tenant for his eviction under the rent laws. However, this right of a tenant is subject to one caveat that the tenant has not attorned to the assignee. If the tenant pays rent to the assignee or otherwise accepts the assignee's title over the demised property, then it results in creation of the attornment which, in turn, deprives the tenant to challenge the derivative title of the landlord.

How to be Served

The notice should be sent by post or tendered or delivered personally to the party to whom it is addressed or to one of his family members or servants at his residence, or, if this is not practicable, it be affixed to a conspicuous part of the demised property (Sec. 106, Transfer of Property Act) or may be served in any other manner specially agreed upon. It is always better to provide in the lease some easy and simple mode of service of notices. Notice to company under registered post is considered valid.[1]

Notice of Re-entry

If a lessee renounces his character as such by setting up a title in himself or in a third person or breaks an express condition of the lease, the breach of which entitles the lessor under the terms of the lease to re-enter, or adjucated an insolvent and the lease provides that in such event the lessor may re-enter, the lessor has a right to terminate the tenancy by giving notice in writing of his intention to do so [Sec. 111(*g*), Transfer of Property Act]. Although the giving of such notice may not be provided in the lease, yet the tenancy does not determine automatically by a breach, but the breach simply makes the lease voidable and the forfeiture is not complete, unless the lessor gives notice of his option to determine the lease. In such notice, the ground on which the lessor claims forfeiture should be stated. The lessor should clearly state that he desires to determine the lease. It is better, though not absolutely necessary, to state the date on which the lessor wants the lessee to surrender possession.

Stamp Duty

No Stamp duty is required on any notice.

---

1 *Kulkarni Patterns (Pvt.) Ltd.* v. *Vasant Baburao*, AIR 1992 SC 1097.

PRECEDENTS

A—NOTICE TO TERMINATE TENANCY

1—Notice to Quit by Landlord

To

CD, etc., (*name, description and address of the tenant*).

I, AB, etc., (*or*, AB, etc., EF, etc., and GH, etc.) give you notice to quit and deliver up possession of the house known as No. ——, ——— road, situate at ——— of which you are now my (our) tenant on the —— day of ——— next (or after the end of 15 days from the date of the service of this notice).

Signature of Landlord

Date ———

2—Notice to Quit, by Landlord's Agent[1]

To

CD, etc.

I, XY, etc., as agent for and on behalf of AB, etc., hereby give you notice to quit and deliver up possession of the house in *Mohalla* ——— in the city of ——— which you hold as the said AB's tenant under a lease dated ——— on the day of ——— next (*or*, after the end of 15 days from the date of the service of this notice).

3—Notice to Quit by Tenant

To

AB, etc.

I, CD, etc., hereby give you notice that I shall quit and deliver up possession of the house known as —— and situate at ——— and now held by me as your tenant on the, etc., (*as in Form* 1).

1 *See also* precedent No. 50 *post*: "Notice through Advocate/Solicitor, Generally".

4—Notice by Either Party to Determine Lease in Accordance with a Condition of the Lease

To

———————

I, the undersigned, give you notice that I desire that the term of lease created by the deed of lease dated ——— and made between you and myself shall determine on the ——— in accordance with the proviso (condition) in this behalf contained in the said deed of lease, and I hereby require you to (*or*, and I hereby give you notice that I shall) quit and deliver possession of the said premises on the said date.

5—Ditto, Another Form

In pursuance of a power contained in the lease dated ——— under which the house known as ——— and situate at ——— thereby demised is held, I hereby give notice that it is my intention to determine the said lease and to put an end to the term thereby created on the ——— and I hereby require, etc., (*as in Form* 4).

6—Notice to Demand Possession on the Expiry of a Lease

I, the undersigned, owner of the premises comprised in the lease dated ——— hereby give you notice that the said lease expired by efflux of time on the ——— day of ——— and I hereby demand immediate possession of the said premises and also give notice that you will be held responsible for all damages which may be sustained by me by reason of your wilfully retaining possession thereof as well as for breach by you of the covenants contained in the lease.

7—Notice of Determination of Tenancy for Breach of Covenants

To CD, etc.

I, the undersigned, give you notice as follows:

1. The lease dated the ——— day of ——— and made between myself of the one part and yourself of the other part under which you hold the ——— (*describe the property*), as a lessee. The lease contains a covenant by the lessee to the effect that you will not use the said premises except for the purpose of residence and a further covenant that in case of a breach of the aforesaid covenant, the lessor would have a right of re-entry (*or,* a covenant to the effect that ———).

2. You have started a soap factory on the said premises since the ——

and have so committed a breach of the said covenant [*or*, you have ——— (*specify the act of breach*)] (*or, if there are several such acts say,* you have committed the several acts and omissions specified in the schedule hereto and such acts and omissions constitute a breach of the said covenant).

3. In pursuance of the aforesaid covenant for re-entry, I, from the date given hereunder determine the said lease and I require you to quit and deliver up possession to me of the said premises on the ——— (*or,* within ——— days of the service of this notice).

8—Notice of Determination of Tenancy, for Denial of Title

To CD, etc.

I, the undersigned give you notice as follows:

1. By a lease dated the ———, I demised the land described below to your deceased father EF on a perpetual lease for building a house.

2. The said EF built a house and on his death you succeeded to it as well as to the leasehold rights under the aforesaid lease.

3. By a sale deed dated ——— you have now sold the said house on the said land to one XY and in the sale deed you have described yourself as the owner of the said land also and have professed to sell to the said XY proprietary rights in the said land and have thereby renounced your character as lessee.

4. For the reason aforesaid I, etc., (*as in para* 3 *of Form* 7).

B—MISCELLANEOUS NOTICES BETWEEN LANDLORD AND TENANT

9— Notice to Repair by Lessee[1]

To CD, etc.

As pleader for and on behalf of AB, etc., I hereby give you notice and require you within ——— days (months) from the date of service of this notice to execute or cause to be executed the repairs detailed below and all other repairs which you are bound to execute under the covenant by you in that behalf contained in a lease dated ——— and made between yourself and the said AB (And that if you fail to comply with this notice the said AB will execute the same or cause the same to be executed and deduct the cost

1 This is necessary only where the Transfer of Property Act does not apply, as otherwise a statutory right in that behalf is given by Sec.108 (f) of that Act. The local rent control laws should also be consulted on the subject.

thereof from the rent payable to you or otherwise recover it from you).

Details of repairs ———.

10—Notice to Repair by Lessor

To CD, etc.

I, AB, etc., hereby give you notice and require you in pursuance of the covenant contained in a lease dated ——— and made between yourself and myself within ——— months from the date hereof to put in good and substantial repair and condition the house comprised in the said lease and in particular that you do in a workmanlike manner the several repairs and amendments mentioned in the schedule hereto annexed AND I further give notice that if you make default in remedying such breach of covenant in manner mentioned above, I shall enter upon the said premises in accordance with the said covenant and execute the said work at your expense as therein provided.

(*The schedule herein referred to*)

(Specification of repairs and amendments)

11—Notice by Tenant of Election to take Renewed Lease

To AB, etc., (*name and address of lanllord*)

I, the undersigned, give you notice that pursuant to the proviso (covenant) for renewal contained in a deed of lease dated ——— and made between yourself and myself I elect to accept a renewed lease of the property comprised in the said deed of lease for a further term of ——— years on the terms and conditions specified in the said lease and I hereby require you to grant the said lease to me accordingly.

12—Notice by Landlord of Election to Purchase Fixtures

To CD, etc., (*name and address of tenant*)

I, the undersigned, give you notice that I intend on the determination of the term created by a deed of lease dated ——— and made between myself and yourself to purchase such of the fixtures erected by you on the premises thereby demised as are specified in the schedule hereto in accordance with and on the terms specified in the proviso (covenant) in that behalf contained in the said lease.

The schedule herein referred to.

13—Notice of Assignment[1] by Tenant

To AB, etc., (*name and address of lessor*)

I, the undersigned, give you notice that by a deed of assignment dated the ———— I have assigned to XY, etc., all my rights and interest under the deed of lease dated ———— made between yourself and myself in the property comprised in the said lease.

C—MORTGAGOR AND MORTGAGEE

14—Notice of Demand of Mortgage Money

To AB, etc., (*mortgagor*)

I, CD, etc. (*or*, as pleader and agent for and on behalf of CD, etc.) hereby demand of you immediate payment of the sum of Rs. ———— due to me (*or*, to the said CD) under a mortgage deed dated ———— executed by you with interest payable according to the term of the said mortgage deed.

15—Notice of Demand of Mortgage Money, when Parties are Representatives of the Original Mortgagor and Mortgagee

To AB, etc.

I, CD, etc., (*or*, as pleader and agent for and on behalf of CD, etc.) hereby give you notice as follows:

1. By a deed of mortgage dated ———— one EF owner of the property, described in the schedule thereto, mortgaged the said property to one GH for Rs. ———— repayable with interest at the rate therein specified.

2. On the death of the said GH his son JK succeeded to his rights and interest under the aforesaid mortgage, and subsequently by a deed of sale dated ———— the said JK assigned the said rights and interest with the said mortgage debt to me (*or,* the said CD).

3. At an auction sale held on the ———— in execution of a decree against the said EF the rights and interest of the said EF in the said property were purchased by you subject to the encumbrance created by the said mortgage deed.

4. I hereby demand of you payment of the principal and interest due to

---

1 The expression "assignment" is not confined to actionable claims (See ASSIGNMENT OF ACTIONABLE CLAIMS, ante) but may be used for transfer of any movable or immovable property and includes assignment of lease.

me (*or*, the said CD) under the aforesaid mortgage deed within 15 days, failing which I (*or*, the said CD) shall (*or*, I have instruction to) institute a suit for recovery of the same by sale of the mortgaged property.

16—Notice to Exercise Powers of Sale by Mortgagee

At the end of the notice of demand as in Form 14 *add, the following* or *for the words "failing which, etc.," in para* 4 *of Form* 15, *substitute the following:*

"AND in default of you paying the said amount for a period of three calendar months from the service hereof I intend (*or*, I have instructions on behalf of the said CD) to sell the said mortgaged property or such portion thereof as I may think fit in pursuance of the power of sale conferred upon me (*or*, CD) by the said deed of mortgage (*or*, by law)."

17—Notice by Mortgagee to Tenant to Pay Rent to Him

To XY (*name and address of tenant*)

I, CD, etc., (*or*, as pleader and agent for and on behalf of CD, etc.) hereby give you notice that under a mortgage dated ——— made by AB, etc., I (*or*, the said CD) as mortgagee have (has) become entitled to the receipt of the rent of the (*describe the property*) which you hold as tenant of the said AB and I require you to pay to me (*or*, the said CD) all rent now due and henceforth to become due in respect of the said property until you shall receive further notice from me (*or*, the said CD) and on no account to pay such rent to the said AB or any person on his behalf.

18—Notice to Tenant by Mortgagor

To

AB, etc.

WHEREAS I have mortgaged to XY, etc., the house situate at —— which you hold on lease from me, I hereby authorize and request you to forthwith attorn and become tenant of the said XY during the continuance of the said mortgage, to pay to the said XY, his heirs, executors, administrators or assigns all such rent as now is or hereafter shall be payable from you in respect of the said house and for so doing this shall be to you a sufficient warrant and authority.

19—Notice by Mortgagee Calling upon Mortgagor to Furnish Further Security

To

XY, etc.

I, AB, etc., hereby give you notice that the security furnished by you under the mortgage deed dated the ——— executed by you in my favour has been rendered insufficient in respect of the sum now due under the said mortgage (by Rs. ——— approximately) and you are, therefore, hereby called upon to furnish, within one month of the receipt of this notice, further security enough to render the said security sufficient for the sum due under the mortgage. Please take notice that in default of your compliance with the demand, legal proceedings will be taken against you for recovery of the mortgage money payable under the said mortgage deed.

20—Notice by Mortgagee of Transfer of Mortgage

To AB, etc. (*mortgagor*)

I, CD, etc., hereby give you notice that by a deed of sale dated ——— the debt due to me under the mortgage deed dated ——— executed by you has been transferred by me with all the interest due thereon and the security for the same to GH, etc., absolutely to whom all payments of principal and interest must in future be made.

D—SALE OF LAND AND GOODS

21—Notice to Complete a Purchase by Vendor

To ______________AB, etc.

(*Purchaser*)

I, CD, etc., (*or*, as pleader for and on behalf of CD, etc.) hereby give you notice that I am (the said CD is) willing and ready to execute a sale deed in your favour or as you may direct, of (*briefly describe the property, or simply say*) the property contracted to be purchased by you by an agreement dated the ——— and registered on the ——— in accordance with the terms of the said agreement AND that I (the said CD) hereby require(s) you forthwith to tender such sale deed for execution and to pay the balance of the price in accordance with the terms of the said agreement AND that if you fail to comply with this notice within —— days from the date hereof or its receipt I (he) shall (will) then forfeit the deposit of Rs. ——— paid by you as earnest money and either rescind the contract or resell the property in accordance with the provisions of the said agreement and claim from you the deficiency in price (if any) on such resale and all expenses attending the resale and any attempted resale and all costs, losses, damages and expenses incurred by me (him) by reason of your delay or default in performing the said agreement [*or*, I (he) shall (will) file a suit against you for specific performance of the contract and damages] [*or* will seek such relief as I (he) may be entitled to in law].

22—Notice to Complete Purchase by Purchaser

I, AB, etc., (*or*, as pleader for and on behalf of AB, etc.,) hereby give you notice that I am (he is) willing and ready to complete the purchase of (*briefly describe the property, or simply say*) the property contracted to be purchased by me (him) from you by an agreement dated the ——— in accordance with the terms of the said agreement AND that I (he) require(s) you to complete the same AND that if you fail to complete the same within ——— days from the date hereof, I (the said AB) will bring a suit for specific performance of the contract and damages [*or*, will seek such relief as I (he) may be entitled to in law].

23—Notice by Purchaser to Tenant of Property Purchased for payment of Rent to Purchaser

I hereby give you notice that under a deed of sale dated ——— and registered on the ——— the house known as ——— and situate at ——— held by you under a lease dated ——— made by AB, etc., was sold by the said AB to me AND that all rent now due or to become due from the date of the said sale in respect of the said house must be paid to me or my authorised agent and not to the said AB or anyone on his behalf.

24—Notice by Seller or Donor to Tenant to Attorn to Transferee

To

AB, etc.

WHEREAS I have now sold to XY, etc., (*or*, made a gift to XY, etc.) of the house situate at ——— which you hold on lease from me, I hereby authorise and request you to forthwith attorn and become tenant of the said XY and henceforth to pay to the said XY his heirs, executors, administrators, or assigns all such rent as now is or hereafter shall become due from you in respect of the said premises and for so doing this shall be to you a sufficient warrant and authority.

25—Notice of Sale of Business to Vendor's Creditors

I, AB, etc., (*or*, as pleader for and on behalf of AB, etc.), hereby give you notice that the business of a ——— herebefore carried on by me (the said AB) at ——— under the name and style of ——— was as from the ——— sold by me (the said AB) to CD, etc., who will in future carry on the said business under the name and style of —— AND I further give you notice that I (the said AB) will not be liable for any debts or liabilities incurred or contracts entered by the said CD or any other person whatsoever in connection with the said business after the ——— (*date*).

For notices of Assignment of Actionable Claims, see under Assignment of Actionable Claims, Decrees, etc.

26—Notice of Intended Purchase to a Possible Pre-Emptor[1]

To

XY, etc.

For and on behalf of my client AB, etc., I hereby give you notice that subject to the option of purchase hereby given to you, the said AB has agreed to sell his property mentioned below to CD for the price of Rs. —— AND that in case you wish to purchase the said property at the said price please communicate your assent to me or to the said AB forthwith AND that if you fail so to communicate your assent within —— days of the receipt of this notice the said AB will presume that you waive whatever right of pre-emption you may have and he will be at liberty to sell the said

1 The right of pre-emption arises under some statute or under the Mohammedan Law or under a custom or contract. Such a statutory right has been held to be valid by the Supreme Court except insofar as it is based on vicinage1 or consanguinity1 in other words it is valid only in favour of cosharers and tenants. If a person having such right fails to avail of it when the property is offered to him he loses his right of pre-emption, unless the property is sold at a less price than that demanded from him. Therefore, in order to avoid future claims, it is always better to give notice of intended sale to all pre-emptors, though the giving of such notice is not obligatory and waiver can always be proved by an oral refusal or other conduct. The property, the price agreed upon, and the name of the vendee, should be mentioned in the notice. In Haryana1 and Oudh1 it is not necessary to mention the name of vendee. In Haryana and Oudh such notice is given through court and reply is also given through court within three months. (*See* Sec. 10, and 11, Oudh Laws Act and Sec. 20, Punjab Pre-emption Act). In M.P. the notice may be given direct, and unless reply is given within one month the right of pre-emption is extinguished. Provisions for preferential purchase/pre-emption are also contained in sections 3 and 4 of The Partition Act, 1893, as well as in section 22 of the Hindu Succession Act, 1956.

property to CD or anyone else for the said price.

Description of property

* * * * *

27—Reply of Pre-Emptor Agreeing to Purchase

In reply to your notice dated ——— I hereby give you notice that I am willing to purchase the property mentioned in your said notice for the price mentioned therein.

28—Reply Objecting to the Price

In reply to your notice dated ——— I hereby give you notice that I am willing to purchase the property mentioned in your said notice but I do not consider that the price mentioned in your said notice is correct or genuine. Therefore, I am willing to pay Rs. ——— which according to my information is the price really agreed upon between you and the said CD or such other price as may be proved to have been so agreed upon or a fair and reasonable price.

29—Reply Challenging the Title of the Vendor and also Reserving the Right of Pre-Emption

In reply to your notice dated ——— I hereby give you notice that the property mentioned in your said notice does not belong to you but belongs to me and that, therefore, there is no question of my purchasing it from you. I further give you notice that if you will sell the same to any person I shall take such legal action as I may be advised to take and will also in the alternative claim to prempt it at such price as may have been actually paid or promised by the vendee or as may be proved to be fair and reasonable.

30—Notice of Appropriation of Goods to Contract

We hereby give you notice that we have today set aside for you and appropriated to the contract of the ——— made between you and our firm, the following goods and that the same are ready for delivery to you here at any time between the hours of ——— and ——— (*or*, for despatch to you according to your instructions).

(*Description and quantity of goods*)

31—Notice by Seller to Buyer to take Delivery

The undermentioned goods being ready for delivery, you are hereby requested to take delivery thereof without further delay. If they are not taken within ——— days from the date of receipt of the notice I shall hold you responsible for any loss incurred by me in consequence and also for my charges for the custody of the said goods.

32—Notice of Buyer to Seller of His Intention to Treat the Seller's Non-fulfilment of a Condition as Breach of Warranty[1]

I hereby give you notice that the condition that ——— contained in clause ——— of the contract made between you and me on the ——— has not been fulfilled. I have, however, elected to accept the goods and to treat the breach of condition as a breach of warranty only. By reason of such breach of warranty I have sustained damages to the extent of Rs. ——— which I claim to be entitled to recover from you.

33—Notice of Re-sale of Goods by Seller

WHEREAS on the ——— you purchased ——— (*specify goods*) from me and agreed to pay for and take delivery of the same within two weeks, and whereas you have not yet paid for the same and as per account given below Rs. ——— are now due to me from you, I hereby demand payment of the same and I hereby give you notice that if you fail to make the payment by the ——— day of ——— the goods purchased by you and now lying at your risk in my godown at ——— shall be resold by public auction at ——— (*place*) at ——— (*time*) on ——— (*date*) and you shall be liable for all loss that may take place on such resale.

Account above referred to

* * * *

E—ARBITRATION

34—Notice Calling upon a Person Designated in the Arbitration Clause to Appoint an Arbitrator (Sec. 11 of the 1996 Act)

Calcutta

September 3, 1996

To
The President
Chamber of Commerce
Calcutta

1 See Sec. 13 Sale of Goods Act. For the difference between a condition and warranty, see also Sec.12.

Dear Sir,

By an agreement in writing between us made on ——— we, the undersigned, had agreed to refer all future disputes between us to the arbitration of a person to be nominated by you. As differences have now arisen between us, we request you kindly to nominate a person to act as an arbitrator for the purpose of the aforesaid reference and intimate us of such appointment within ——— days of the receipt to this notice.

35—Appointment of Arbitrator pursuant to Arbitration Clause (Sec. 11)

To XY, etc.

WHEREAS disputes and differences (*or*, certain differences detailed at the foot of this notice) have arisen between us, the undersigned AB, etc., and CD, etc., within the meaning of the arbitration clause contained in a deed dated ——— and made between us and we are desirous of having the said disputes settled by arbitration.

Now, therefore, in pursuance of the provisions of the said deed we hereby jointly nominate and appoint you to be the sole arbitrator to determine all such matters in difference between us as aforesaid and we hereby call upon you to act as such arbitrator.

36—Notice Calling upon the Other Party to Appoint Arbitrator (Sec. 11)

I AB, etc., (*or*, as pleader for and on behalf of AB, etc.) hereby give you notice that I have (*or*, the said AB has) this day appointed XY, etc., to be the arbitrator on my (his) behalf to settle by arbitration in pursuance of the proviso in that behalf contained in the deed of ——— dated the ——— the disputes and differences that are pending between us (you and him) AND I hereby require you within thirty days from the service of this notice to appoint an arbitrator to act on your behalf in the matter of the said disputes and differences failing which I shall apply to the Hon'ble Chief Justice of the ——— High Court (or the person/institution if any designated by him)[1] to make the necessary appointment under section 11 of the Arbitration and Conciliation Act 1996.

1 In the case of an international commercial agreement the request will have to be made to the Chief Justice of India instead, vide Sec. 11 (12) (a).

37—Notice to Appoint Arbitrator in Place of One Refusing to Act or Becoming Incapable of Acting or Who Dies (Sec. 15 read with Sec. 11)

In the matter of arbitration between AB, etc., and CD, etc.

To CD, etc.

Take notice that XY the arbitrator appointed by you in this matter having refused to act (*or* having become incapable of acting by becoming insane) (*or,* having died) (*or*, having left for Africa to accept a long-term appointment there) I, the above named AB, hereby request you to appoint an arbitrator to act in place of the said XY and that if the appointment is not made by you within thirty days from the service of this notice I shall apply to the Hon'ble Chief Justice of the ——— High Court for the appointment of an arbitrator in the place of the said XY.

F—PARTNERSHIP

38—Notice of Intention to Determine Partnership (Sec. 43 Partnership Act 1932)

I hereby give you notice that I intend to dissolve as from the ——— (*or,* the date of service of this notice on you) the partnership subsisting between you and me in the business of ——— carried on at ——— under the name and style of ———.

39—Public Notice of Dissolution of Partnership (Sec. 45)

PUBLIC NOTICE IS HEREBY GIVEN that the partnership heretofore subsisting between the undersigned and CD, etc., and EF, etc., carrying on business as ——— at ——— under the firm name of —— is dissolved by mutual consent (*or*, by the death of the said CD) (*or*, by efflux of time) as from the day of ————.

40—Public Notice of Retirement of Partner, if the Business is to be continued by Remaining Partners (Sec. 32)

PUBLIC NOTICE IS HEREBY GIVEN that from the partnership heretofore subsisting between the undersigned and CD, etc., and EF, etc., carrying on business as ——— at ——— under the firm name of ——, the said CD has retired with the consent of all the other partners; and ceases to have any interest in the said business and all debts due to and owned by the said firm will be received and paid respectively by the undersigned and the said EF who will continue to carry on the said business as partners under the same old firm's name.

41—Notice of Retirement [Sec. 32 (1) (c)]

Take notice that with effect from the ————, I intend to retire from the partnership established between you and me by deed of Partnership dated ————.

Or,

I hereby give you notice under Clause ———— of our Partnership deed dated the ———— of my intention to retire from the partnership as from and immediately after the ———— next being the end of the current year of partnership (*or,* on the ———— next).

42—Public Notice of Election by a Minor on Attaining Majority[1]

PUBLIC NOTICE IS HEREBY GIVEN that I, the undersigned, having been admitted to the benefits of the partnership subsisting between AB, CD, EF and GH carrying on business as ——— at ——— under the firm name of ——— and having now attained majority on the ——— (and having on the ——— came to know of my having been admitted to the benefits of the said partnership) do hereby elect to become (*or,* not to become) a partner in the said partnership.

43—Notice to the Registrar of Firms about Changes in the Constitution of Firm [Sec. 63 (1)]

I, CD, etc., hereby give you notice that with effect from the ——— day of ———— the following change has occurred in the constitution of the registered firm known as ———— and carrying on business as ——— at ———.

AB, a partner in the said firm, has retired and in his place XY has been taken as a partner.

(*Or,* AB, a partner in the said firm, has died and in his place his son XY has been made a partner.)

(*Or,* AB, a partner in the said firm, has under the authority conferred

1 A minor who is admitted to benefits of a partnership may give public notice within six months of attaining majority or of obtaining knowledge that he had been so admitted, whichever date is later, that he has elected to become or not to become a partner in the firm and such notice shall determine his position as regards the firm. If he fails to give such notice he shall become a partner on the expiry of the said six months [Sec. 30(5)].

by clause ——— of the Deed of Partnership dated ——— been expelled from the said firm.)

44—Public Notice of Dissolution[1]

PUBLIC NOTICE IS HEREBY GIVEN that I, the undersigned, have retired from the firm known as ——— and carrying on business as ——— at ———.

Or

PUBLIC NOTICE IS HEREBY GIVEN that the firm known as —— and carrying on business as ——— at ——— has been dissolved in consequence of ———.

G—ASSIGNMENT

45—Notice of Assignment of Debt by the Assignor

To,

AB, etc. (*debtor*)

I, the undersigned hereby give notice that by an instrument in writing dated the——I have assigned absolutely to XY, etc., the bond of —— executed by you in my favour and the debt due to me from you thereunder with interest already accrued and hereafter to accrue thereon (*or,* the sum of Rs. ——— and interest due to me on account of, etc.).

(*or*, the decree for Rs. ——— interest and costs passed on the ——— by the court of —— in my favour against you in suit No. ——— of ———).

And I require you henceforth in due course to pay the same to the said XY.

46—Notice of Assignment of Debt by Assignee

To

AB, etc. (*debtor*)

I, the undersigned, hereby give notice that by an instrument in writing dated the ——— executed in my favour by CD, etc., the said CD has assigned to me absolutely, etc., (*as in previous form*) and I require you in

---

1 See Sec. 32(3), Sec. 45 Partnership Act. Unless public notice is given the ex-partners continue to be liable as such to third parties for any act done by them which would have been an act of the firm if done before the dissolution: *Vinayak Keshav Paranjape* v. *Dena Bank,* AIR 1998 Bom 356 (paras 11-12); *Central United Bank* v. *Venkataram Naidu*, AIR 1963 Mad 302 (DB).

due course to pay such principal sum and all interest due and to become due thereon to me.

47—Notice of Assignment, (General Form applicable to both cases)

To

AB, etc. (*debtor*)

Notice is hereby given to you that CD, etc., has by an instrument in writing dated the ——— absolutely assigned to EF, etc., the bond dated the ——— executed by you in the said CD's favour and the debt due to him thereunder with interest already accrued and hereafter to accrue thereon (*or*, the decree obtained by the said CD against you from the Court of the Civil Judge at Aligarh being decree No. ——— dated ———) (*or*, the benefit of the contract of sale of 200 bars of silver made by you in favour of the said CD on the ——— to be delivered on the ——— at the rate of ———).

48—Notice by Assignor of a Legacy

To

AB, etc., the executor of the Will of XY deceased.

I, the undersigned, hereby give you notice that by an instrument in writing dated the ——— the legacy of the sum of Rs. ——— bequeathed to me by the Will of XY, etc., was assigned by me absolutely to CD, etc., and I hereby request you to pay the sum to the said CD as and when the same shall become payable together with such interest (if any) as may become accrued at the date of payment.

49—Notice to Insurance Company of Assignment of Policy

Dear Sir

I, the undersigned AB, etc., hereby give you notice that by a deed of assignment dated the ——— the policy of life insurance effected by CD, etc., with your corporation for the sum of Rs. ——— dated the ——— and numbered ——— and all moneys assured by or to become payable under the said policy were assigned by the said CD to me absolutely (*or*, by way of mortgage) and I request you to note the assignment in your books and to acknowledge receipt of this notice.

H—MISCELLANEOUS NOTICES[1]

50—Notice Through Advocate/Solicitor, Generally

Dear Sir

Under instructions of my client EF, etc. (*or*, As advised by my client AB, etc.), I hereby give you notice that (continue as in the other forms).

51—Notice of Demand by a Creditor's Pleader

Under instructions from AB, etc., I hereby require you to pay to him the sum of Rs. ——— borrowed by your deceased father CD from the said AB on a promissory note (bond) dated the ——— together with all interest due in respect thereof on the date of payment AND I hereby give you notice that if you make default in doing so for ——— days after the receipt of this notice I have instructions to file a suit for recovery of the amount due to the said AB as aforesaid in a competent court of law.

52—Notice of Demand of Possession of Property and Mesne Profits

I am instructed by AB, etc., to state as follows:

WHEREAS—

1. The land and house property detailed at the foot of this notice originally belonged to one XY deceased.

2. On the death of the said XY on the ——— one CD has taken wrongful possession of the said property and had got his name recorded in the village papers as an adopted son of XY.

3. The said CD wrongfully sold the said property to you.

4. The said CD is not the adopted son of the said XY, and the said AB, being the sister's son of the deceased XY is his legal heir and entitled to possession of the said property.

Now, therefore, as pleader for and on behalf of the said AB, I hereby require you to deliver back the said property to the said AB and pay him mesne profits of the said property from the date of your possession AND I hereby give you notice that in case you fail to do so for one month, after the receipt of this notice, the said AB will institute a civil suit against you for recovery of the property and mesne profits.

1 Several notices in this part are preparatory to filing a suit in Civil Court. For law on the respective topics, see also Mogha's Law of Pleadings, 18th Edition (notes below precedents of plaints).

53—Notice Demanding Possession of Property Held Under a Voidable Sale[1]

I am instructed by AB, etc., to state as follows:

WHEREAS you are in possession of the property detailed at the foot of this notice under a deed of sale dated —— executed by Srimati———;

AND WHEREAS the said Smt. ————, having acquired the said property from her decased husband XY under a Will which granted to her only a limited estate in the same, was not competent to transfer the same beyond her life;

AND WHEREAS the said sale was not made for any legal necessity and is not therefore binding on the reversioners of the said XY;

AND WHEREAS the said Smt. ——— has died on ———;

AND WHEREAS the said AB is the reversionary heir of the said XY and entitled to the said property after the death of the said Smt. ———.

Now, therefore, as pleader for and on behalf of the said AB, I hereby give you this notice that the said AB hereby impeaches the said sale and requires you forthwith to deliver the said property to him AND I further give you notice that if you fail to so deliver the property and to pay mesne profits of the said property up to the date of delivery of possession, the said AB will institute a suit against you for possession of the said property and mesne profits.

54—Notice Determining a Continuing Guarantee given to a Banker[2]

Take notice that I hereby discontinue and revoke the guarantee dated the ——— whereby I guaranteed to you the payment of all moneys then or at any time due to you from AB, etc., on the balance of his account with you and I hereby give you further notice not to make any further advances or payments to or on account of or give further credit to the said AB or incur or allow to be incurred any further liability under the said guarantee.

---

1 In such cases when the person in possession is not a trespasser but holds a valid title until it is challenged by another person, no mesne profits are recoverable until the title is challenged and recovery of property is demanded. Therefore in all such cases notice is necessary, otherwise the court will not allow mesne profits for the period before the date of suit (*Bhirgu* v. *Narsingh*, 14 ALJ 1161, AIR 1917 All 479).

2 A continuing guarantee may at any time be revoked as to future transactions by notice to the creditor (Sec.130, Indian Contract Act) but such revocation does not affect the liability already incurred up to the date of such revocation. See also GUARANTEE, *ante*, Precedent No. 1.

55—Notice Determining a Continuing Guarantee, given to an Employer

Take notice that I hereby determine and revoke the guarantee dated ——— whereby I guaranteed to you the fidelity of AB, etc., as the manager of your estate and the payment of any sum that may become due to you on account of loss or damage sustained by you by reasons of any defalcation, mis-appropriation or any other wrongful act of the said AB, etc., in the course of his employment as such manager and I hereby give you further notice that I shall not be liable for any such loss or damage sustained by you on or after this date.

56—Notice Claiming Damages for Wrongful Dismissal

To

The ——— Co. Ltd.

I am instructed by my client Shri ——— to state as follows:

Whereas my client Shri ——— was employed by you as Manager of the ——— Mill at ——— owned by you under a contract of employment dated the ——— and continued to be in such employment upto the ——— day of ——— AND whereas by an order dated ——— the Managing Director of the said Mill wrongfully dismissed him against the terms of the aforesaid contract and in pursuance of the said order relieved him of his duties on the day of ———.

I am instructed to request you to either reinstate my aforesaid client Shri ——— in service and to pay his salary for the period from the date of his wrongful dismissal to the date of reinstatement or pay him Rs. ——— as damages for wrongful dismissal.

Please take notice that in default of your compliance with the aforesaid request within one month from the receipt of this notice my client will be compelled to seek his legal remedy by filing a suit against you for recovery of Rs. ——— as damages for wrongful dismissal.

57—Notice Claiming Damages for Defamation

To

The Editor & Publisher of ———.

I am instructed by my client Shri ——— to state as follows.

Whereas in your paper "The Observer" of the 3rd January 1999, you have published an article headed "Jobbery in the Education Department" in which you have made the following defamatory remarks about my client

Shri ———— Director of Education of ————.

(*a*) * * *

(*b*) * * *

(*c*) * * *

AND whereas these remarks are highly defamatory of my said client who has on account of them suffered in his reputation and has been lowered in the estimation of his friends and the general public; I have been instructed by the said Shri —— to demand of you, which I hereby do, within —— days from the receipt of this notice, a sum of Rs. ——— as damages and an unqualified apology duly and prominently published in "The Observer".

Please take notice that in default of your compliance with this notice, legal action will be taken either to prosecute you for defamation in a criminal court or to sue you for damages as my aforesaid client may be advised.

58—Notice of Claim under Sec. 106 of the Railways Act, 1989[1]

Notice of Claim for refund of overchange or compensation for loss, destruction or deterioration of goods to the General Manager Northern Railways/Eastern Railway, New Delhi/Calcutta.

AB son of CD carrying on the business of ——— residing in house No. ——— of Mohalla ——— street ——— at ——— hereby gives notice of his claim for compensation for loss as required by Sec.106 of the Indian Railways Act.

1. That AB booked a consignment of ——— packages/tins (*mention the nature of the consignment*) from ——— a station of ——— Railway to ——— a station on ———— Railways on ——— under R.R. No. ——— dated ———.

---

1 The notice has to be given within a period of six months from the date of entrustment of the goods, Sec. 106 (1). The notice should actually reach the administration within time, not merely be posted within time: *Khandelwal Ferro Alloys* v. *Union of India*, AIR 1999 Bom 50, follg. *Union of India* v. *Amin Chand Pyarelal*, AIR 1974 P&H 190 and distg. *Union of India* v. *Sha Vastimull Harakchand*, AIR 1959 Mys 13 (case of non-delivery, for which it was held that no notice was necessary). The notice has to be served (a) on the railway administration to which the goods are entrusted for carriage; or (b) on the railway administration on whose railway the destination lies; or (c) the railway administration on whose railway the loss/damage occurs, or in case of a Zonal Railway, on the General Manager or any of the railway servants authorized by the General Manager, section 192.

2. That he was consignor and the consignee under the said R.R. of the said consignment.

3. That at the time of delivery at ——— station ——— packages/tins were not delivered while ——— packages/tins had been badly damaged which caused loss to the said AB. The said AB hereby makes a claim for compensation for loss due to short delivery/non-delivery of ——— packages/tins and for damages to ——— packages/tins. He claims a sum of Rs. ——— for the same.

59—Notice under Sec.106 of the Railways Act (Another Form)

Notice on behalf of AB, etc., (*give full address*) under Sec.106, Indian Railways Act, for compensation for loss, etc., ——— to the General Manager ——— Railway ———.

Dear Sir,

I despatched a consignment consisting of ——— from ——— station to ——— station both on ——— Railway (*or*, the former being on ——— Railway and the latter being on ——— Railway) in my name as a consignor and consignee on ——— by means of R.R. No. ——— dated ———.

The said consignment should in the ordinary course have reached the destination within ——— days but the consignment remained undelivered (*or*, it was short delivered by ——— even after a lapse of ——— days) and according to the endorsement made on the R.R. by the Railway authorities at the destination the consignment is not traceable.

That the loss of the consignment (*or*, short delivery) is totally due to the misconduct or neglect of the Railway administration and I hereby make a claim for compensation for the loss due to non-delivery (*or*, short delivery) the details of which are being given below. I claim a sum of Rs. ——— as the price and Rs.———for damages.

60—Notice under Sec. 106 of the Railway Act (Another form)

To

The General Manager
Northern Railway/Eastern Railway
New Delhi/Calcutta

I, AB etc., hereby give you notice of my claim for compensation for loss as required by Sec.106 of the Indian Railways Act.

(1) That I booked a consignment consisting of ——— packages from —— a station on Northern Railways to ——— a station on Eastern Railways on —— under R.R. No. ——— dated ———.

(2) That I was the consignor and consignee both under the said R.R. of the said consignment.

(3) That at the time of delivery at ——— station ——— packages were not delivered at all, while ——— packages had been badly damaged which caused loss to me.

(4) That I hereby make a claim for compensation for loss due to short delivery/ non-delivery of——— packages and for damage to —— packages.

I claim a sum of Rs. ——— for the same.

61—Notice of Suit Against Government[1] (Sec. 80 C.P.C.)

To

The Collector of ——— /The Secretary to Government of ———.

As Advocate for and on behalf of AB etc., I hereby give you notice that unless the sum of Rs. ——— is refunded to him, the said AB will on the expiry of two months from the date of service of this notice institute a suit in a Civil Court of competent jurisdiction against the State Government for the refund of Rs. ——— and for the award of interest on that sum at the rate of ——— percent per annum from the ——— by way of damages, on the following cause of action:

(1) The said AB is the owner of the land described in the schedule below.

---

1 At least two months' previous notice of suit against the Government is necessary under sub-section (1) of Sec. 80 C.P.C. A suit to obtain an urgent or immediate relief, may be instituted with the leave of the court, without serving the notice [Sub-Sec.(2) of Sec. 80 C.P.C.] Such notice should state the name, description, and place of residence of the plaintiff, the cause of action (which means a short statement of the facts which constitute the ground on which the claim will be based), and the relief which is intended to be claimed, and may be given by pleader or agent on his behalf. It is not necessary that it should be addressed to a State Government or Union of India so long as it clearly states against whom the threatened suit will be instituted. The notice shall be delivered to or left at the office of the concerned authority (Sec. 80, C.P.C.). If the facts are long, it is sometimes more convenient to attach to the notice a draft plaint and refer to it in the notice which, in such a case, need not be detailed.

(2) The said AB has by a deed dated the ——— mortgaged the said land with possession to one EF, etc., and since the date of mortgage the said EF and not AB has been in possession thereof;

(3) The said EF failed to pay the Government revenue due in respect of the said land for the years ——— *Fasli*;

(4) Instead of taking proceedings for recovery of the said revenue from the said EF who was legally liable for it, the *Tahsildar* of ——— attached the movable property of the said AB.

(5) The said AB had to deposit and he did deposit under protest in writing in the ——— the said sum of Rs. ——— being the revenue for the said years in respect of the said land in order to save his movable property and have it released from attachment.

(6) As the payment was made by the said AB under coercion he is entitled to have it refunded.

The schedule referred to herein.

62—Notice of Suit Against Government, (Another Form)

To ———

I, AB, etc., (*or*, As Advocate for and on behalf of AB, etc.) hereby give you notice that unless proper and satisfactory amends are made, I (the said AB) will after the expiry of two months from the date of service of this notice, institute a civil suit in a court of competent jurisdiction on the cause of action and for the reliefs appearing from the draft plaint appended hereto, which should be read as part of this notice.

(*Draft Plaint*)

63—Notice of Suit Against a Public officer[1]

To

CD, etc., Sub-Inspector in charge of ——, Police Station, District——.

As Advocate for and on behalf of AB, etc., and under his instructions I hereby give you notice as follows:

1. That in ——— while you were Station Officer of the Police Station ——— you maliciously and without any reasonable or probable cause arrested the said AB and searched his house and prosecuted him on a false charge of murder of his wife.

2. That while the said AB was in your custody in the police lock-up at ——— you abused and beat him, gave him no food, did not allow him to sleep and caused him other inconvenience and tortures in order to extort money from him and, when he did not agree to pay you the money demanded by you as bribe, you challaned him on the said charge.

3. That after a protracted trial at which you gave false evidence and produced suborned witnesses the said AB was acquitted, the Sessions Judge finding that the case against him was false.

4. That the said AB had to undergo great physical and mental suffering while he was in the lock-up and as undertrial prisoner and had to spend Rs.50,000 in his defence.

5. The said AB, therefore, demands from you Rs.50,000 as damages for assault and battery, Rs.50,000 as damages for his physical and mental

---

1 It is not every suit against a public officer for which a previous notice is required, but such notice is required only if the suit is in respect of any act purporting to be done by the public officer in his official capacity, and the object is to make him personally liable for such act. Therefore though a receiver is a public officer and notice is necessary for a suit against him in respect of acts done by him as such, *Asia Khatun* v. *Amarendra Nath*, AIR 1940 Cal 578, no notice is necessary for a suit against a receiver for possession of property vested in him by order of the court, *Bhuban* v. *Biraj*, 1940 AC 1, 44 CWN 74. The notice should be in the same form as a notice of suit against the Government. The cause of action should clearly indicate that the claim is in respect of an act done by the defendant in his official capacity. In a suit for damages against a public officer using defamatory language, insulting and assaulting his subordinates, no notice is necessary as it is not an act purporting to be done by such public officer in his official capacity, *Narayan Hari* v. *Yeshawant Raoji Naik*, AIR 1928 Bom 352. On the same principle sanction under Sec. 197, Cr. P.C. is not necessary before a public officer can be prosecuted for an offence of taking bribe under Sec. 161 of the Indian Penal Code, *Lumbardur Zutshi* v. *King*, 1950 ALJ 120; *Gill* v. *King*, 75 IA 61. Notice under Sec. 80 C.P.C. is necessary in suits on contract also, *Revati Mohan* v. *Jatindra Mohan*, AIR 1934 PC 96.

suffering during the period of trial and Rs.50,000 the cost incurred by him in his defence, total Rs.1,50,000, and gives you notice that if you do not pay this amount or make other suitable amends to the satisfaction of the said AB, the said AB will on the expiry of two months from the date of service of this notice file a suit against you for the recovery of Rs.1,50,000 as damages for assault and battery and malicious prosecution in the Court of the Civil Judge (Senior Division) at Agra.

64—Notice Demanding Delivery of Movable Property Deposited for Safe Custody

I, AB, etc., (*or*, as Advocate for and on behalf of AB, etc., and under instructions from him) hereby require you to deliver up to me (the said AB) within ——— days from the service of this notice upon you the several articles set forth in the inventory hereunder written which were entrusted to you by me (him) for safe custody AND FURTHER TAKE notice that if you fail to comply with this demand I (the said AB) shall (will) institute such proceedings against you as I (he) may be advised.

The inventory referred to herein.

65—Notice to Creditors of a Deceased Person Inviting Claims by Executors[1]

Notice is hereby given that all persons having claims against the estate of XY deceased who died on the ——— and whose Will was proved in the Court of District Judge of ——— by the undersigned, the executor therein named are required to send particulars thereof in writing to the undersigned on or before the ——— next, after which date the undersigned will proceed to distribute the assets having regard only to the claims of which he shall then have had notice.

66—Notice to Creditors of a Deceased Person Inviting Claims by Administrator

Notice is hereby given that all persons having claims against the estate of XY etc., deceased who died on the ——— and Letters of Administration of whose estate were granted on the ——— by the Court of the District Judge of ——— to the undersigned are hereby required to send, etc., (*as in Form* 65).

1 See Preliminary Note under WILLS, *post* for when taking out a probate is obligatory and when it is not.

67—Notice Requiring Abatement and Removal of a Nuisance

I, AB, etc., (*or*, as Advocate for and on behalf of AB, etc., and under his instructions) hereby require you to remove the nuisance and obstruction described at the foot of this notice. AND I give you notice that in default of your so doing within ——— days from the service of this notice I (the said AB) shall (will) take such steps as I (he) may be advised to secure the abatement, removal and discontinuance of such nuisance and obstruction and to recover such damages as I have (he has) sustained or may sustain by reason of the said nuisance and obstruction.

(*Description of the nuisance and obstruction. For example*). Obstruction to the light and air of the notice-giver's house situate at —— passing through the windows in the western wall of the said house which you have blocked by building a wall alongside the said house.

Or, obstruction caused by you to the notice-giver's right of way from the house at ——— to the public highway known as ——— by constructing your new house.

Or, nuisance caused by flowing the water of the kitchen and latrine of your house at ——— to my land on the west of the said house by constructing two water spouts in the western wall of your house.

68—Notice Requiring Abatement and Removal of a Nuisance (Another Form)

I, AB, etc., hereby give you notice as follows:

1. That I own a house in *mohalla* ——— in the city of ——— and have been in possession of it for the last 50 years.

2. That I have been residing in the said house with my family and my ladies who observe strict *purdah* and do not appear before the public and they have always been enjoying this seclusion from outsiders while residing in the said house.

3. That you have recently built a room on the roof of your house to the east of my house and in the western wall of the newly built room opened three windows overlooking the residential rooms, kitchen and the courtyard of the *zanana* portion of my house.

4. I, therefore, require you to close the said windows and give you notice that if you fail to do so within ——— days of the receipt of this notice, I shall file a suit in the court for closing the said windows, damages and such other reliefs as I may be entitled to in respect of the aforesaid invasion of my right of privacy.

69—Notice of Dishonour of Bill to Drawer[1]

To

CD, etc.

I hereby give you notice that a bill of exchange No. —— dated —— drawn by you on AB, etc., for Rs. —— payable to me —— months after date has been dishonoured by non-acceptance (*or*, by non-payment).

70—Notice of Dishonour of Bill to Endorser

To,

EF, etc. (*endorser*)

I, hereby give you notice that the bill of exchange No. ——— dated the ——— drawn by AB, etc., on CD, etc., for Rs. ——— payable to XY, etc., or order ——— months after date and bearing your endorsement has been dishonoured by non-acceptance (*or*, non-payment).

71—Notice of Dishonour of a Cheque

To

AB, etc.

I hereby give you notice that a cheque No. —— dated the ——— of ——— drawn by you on the ——— Bank for Rs. ——— payable to CD, etc., or order and endorsed by the said CD to me has been dishonoured by non-payment.

(*For notice of Protest, see Statutory forms, prescribed under Sec.*101, *Negotiable Instruments Act*).

72—Notice of Dishonour of Cheque under 138 of Negotiable Act

To

CD, etc.

1. I, hereby give you notice that your cheque No. ——— dated ——— for Rs. ——— drawn on ——— Bank in my favour towards

---

1 A notice of dishonour is necessary in the case of negotiable instruments. However, it is not necessary in cases mentioned in section 98, Negotiable Instruments Act. Such notice may be given to the party intended to be charged or his authorized agent, or in case of his death, his legal representatives and in case of insolvency, to his assignee or receiver. It may be sent by post to his place of business or, if there is no place of business, to his place of residence (Sec. 94). See also Preliminary Note under NEGOTIABLE INSTRUMENTS, *ante*.

the payment of the goods purchased by you from my shop has been returned unpaid with the remarks 'insufficient funds'.

2. That my Bank informed me about the dishonour of the cheque on ———.

3. That you are requested to make the payment of the amount of the aforesaid cheque to me within fifteen days of the receipt of this notice failing which I may file complaint, under section 138 Negotiable Instrument Act, against you in the appropriate court.

73—Notice of Sale of Pledged Articles

To

AB, etc. (*pledgee*).

Whereas on ——— you borrowed Rs. ———— from me on pledge of the articles mentioned in the inventory below and whereas per account given below Rs. ——— are now due to me from you on account of the balance of the said debt and interest, I hereby demand the said amount from you and give you notice that in case you fail to make the payment by the ——— day of ——— the said articles shall be sold by public auction to the highest bidder at —— (*place*) at ——— (*time*) on ——— (*date*) (*or*, shall be sold by me privately at the best obtainable price) for realization of my dues and if the same are not satisfied from the sale proceeds after deducting the expenses incurred in sale or attempted sale the deficiency shall be recovered from you.

Account above referred to

* * * *

Inventory above referred to

* * * *

74—Public Notice of Termination of Agent's Authority

PUBLIC NOTICE IS HEREBY GIVEN that CD, etc., who was in the service of the undersigned as Sale Agent (*or*, as rent collector, *or*, a *Mukhtar Am*) has ceased to be in my service from the —— day of ——— and he has no authority whatsoever to transact any business or to receive any money or to act in any way for or on my behalf (and the power of attorney executed by me in his favour on the ——— has been revoked).

75—Public Notice of Sale of Business by Heirs

PUBLIC NOTICE IS HEREBY GIVEN that AB, etc., and CD, etc.,

the heirs and legal representatives of the deceased XY, etc., have sold to the undersigned the business of ——— lately carried on by the said XY at ——— and that all amounts now due and all debts now owing to the said business should be paid to the undersigned at its place of business AND further that all debts owing by the said business will be paid and discharged by the undersigned at the said place of business.

76—Public Notice by Father Repudiating the Debts of Son

PUBLIC NOTICE IS HEREBY GIVEN that my son AB, etc., has separated from me and has no claim or title to any of the properties possessed by me all of which are self-acquired properties and therefore neither myself nor any of the properties possessed by me shall be liable for any debts the said AB may hereafter contract or incur and anyone advancing money to him either personally or on the security of the said properties shall do so at his own risk.

PARTITION

Preliminary Note

What is a Partition

Partition is the process by which property, which is held in undivided shares by joint tenants, tenants in common, or coparceners, is divided amongst them so that each co-owner thenceforth holds a divided share in severalty instead of an undivided share in the whole.

It is possible that only one out of several co-owners may desire a partition and the others prefer to remain joint. In such a case, the property is divided only in two lots, one for the co-owner separating and the other jointly for the others.

Earlier Section 23 of Hindu Succession Act provided that right of female heir (specified in Class I of the Schedule) to claim partition of dwelling house shall not arise until the male heirs choose to divide their respective shares therein; but the female heir was entitled to a right of residence therein.

This special provision respecting dwelling houses stands repealed by Hindu Succession (Amendment) Act, 2005 w.e.f. 9.9.2005.

How is Partition made

Partition may be made either by an agreement—oral or written, or through court, or by arbitration. If parties cannot agree, anyone or more of them may file a suit for partition in the court.

Joint tenancy and tenants in common

The term joint tenants denotes unity of title, possession, interest and commencement of title whereas in tenants in common, there may be unity of possession and commencement of title, but the other two features namely the unity of the title and unity of interest would be absent. It was held that "the basic distinction between joint tenants and tenants-in-common is that in the case of joint tenants there is unity of the title and possession while in the case of tenants in common there is unity of possession but no unity of title". It was accordingly held that a notice under Section 106 of the T.P. Act on one of several tenants in common would not effectively terminate the tenancy of the other.[1] On the death of a tenant, his heirs succeed to his right not as joint tenants but as tenant-in-common.

While dealing with ordinary tenancies one frequently comes across cases in which two or more persons hold a demise under one lease. In such a case it is

---

1 *Kamla Devi* v. *Vimal Kumar Jain*, 1997 (29) ALR 154; 1996 (2) ARC 572; MANU/UP/1869/1996.

well settled that in the absence of a clear provision to the contrary, the entire body of tenants constitutes a single tenant, qua the landlord, for certain purposes. As between themselves their rights may be specified, they might hold the tenancy in well defined shares capable of separate enjoyment or transmission to the respective heirs of each, as if it were his separate property. But qua the, landlord they constitute one persona.[1]

This rule is equally applicable to an occupancy tenure where there is a unity of tenancy with a plurality of parties possessing well-defined shares. The rule which has been laid down in the majority of rulings is that in the case of a "joint" occupancy tenancy, the tenants, as between themselves, hold their shares independently of each other, and on the death of any one of them, his share passes to his own "heir" or "heirs" under section 59(1) and (2) Punjab Tenancy Act, 1887; but as against the landlord they or their "heirs" taken together, constitute a single tenant.[2]

Deed of Partition

No particular form of deed is necessary to effect a partition and it is sufficient if the intention to divide and to hold the property in separate lots in severalty is clearly indicated.

The deed takes the form of transfer or release by each co owner of his share in the joint property allotted to the other. In the case of joint tenants or co-parceners, each "releases and conveys" his share in the property allotted to the others in favour of the latter. In the case of tenants in common, a "grant" is made instead of "release". The reason is obvious. In the case of joint tenants there is no defined share which a co-owner can grant or transfer, as it is in the case of tenants in common.[3]

It is advisable to execute a partition deed in duplicate, triplicate, etc., each of which is treated as an original, so that each party may take one of them. If it is not executed in duplicates, one party keeps the deed, and in such cases he should by a clause in the partition deed undertake to permit others to inspect and take copies thereof.

Recitals

A deed of partition generally contains recitals showing the title of the parties to the joint property, their respective share in it, and a desire or agreement to partition it. Reference is also often made to the proceedings prior to the execution

---

1 *Moti Lal* v. *Kartar Singh*, AIR 1930 Lah 515; 127 IC1; MANU/LA/0136/1930.

2 *Moti Lal* v. *Kartar Singh*, AIR 1930 Lah 515; 127 IC1; MANU/LA/0136/1930.

3 For difference between the two, see *Venkatakrishna* v. *Satyayathi*, AIR 1968 SC 751; *Ram Awalamb* v. *Jata Shankar*, AIR 1969 All 526 (FB); See also Sec. 45 Transfer of Property Act, Sec. 106, Indian Succession Act. In "joint tenancy" there is right of survivorship but not so in a "tenancy in common" where the shares are fixed.

of the deed, e.g., the preparation and drawing of lots. These recitals should be carefully drafted.

Operative Words and Transfer Clause

After the recitals follow the witnessing clauses. The first contains the operative part of the deed containing the agreement to hold different lots in severalty and the release or grant by each co-owner in favour of the others with the usual habendum, which should entitle the transferee to hold the lot allotted to him in severalty.

When the property is divided into two lots it is easy to effect the partition by two clauses of reciprocal grant or release but such clauses are likely to become complicated when there are several lots, as in that case as many conveyance clauses will be necessary as there are permutations and combinations of the co-owners.

For instance, if lots 1, 2, 3 and 4 are allotted to A, B, C and D respectively, B,C, and D will convey their shares in lot 1 to A; A, C and D their shares in lot 2 to B; A, B and D their shares in lot 3 to C; A, B and C their shares in lot 4 to D. In such cases it may be found easier to have one clause agreeing to hold the different lots by different co-owner as absolute owner in severalty, and another general clause expressing a grant or release of each co-owner of his share in the lot allotted to others. (*As clause 1 and 2 in Form 2, post*)

Money Compensation

Sometimes money compensation has to be paid by one co-owner to another for equality of partition to bring about equitable adjustment. This is known as "owelty". This may be recited in the recitals, and, if it has already been paid, an acknowledgment will be inserted in the conveyance clause relating to the grant or release by the persons receiving the consideration. If it is agreed to be paid in future the agreement should be definitely mentioned in the witnessing clauses as a covenant by the party agreeing to pay. Such provision of owelty ordinarily creates a lien or a charge on the land taken under the partition.

Covenants

The usual covenant in a deed of partition are covenants about encumbrances on the property, apportionment of the debts or continuance of the charges, covenant for further assurance, covenant for quiet enjoyment, about custody of title deeds and the right of production. In a partition of house property, covenants about easements of necessity may be necessary. If the property is leasehold property, covenant about payment of rent and performance of covenants of the lease are generally necessary. Any special covenant about any other necessary matter may be inserted in the usual way. A covenant that one co-owner transferring his share will give the option of first refusal to the other is valid.[1]

---

1 *Rattanlal* v. *Ramanuj Das*, AIR 1944 Nag 187.

In the case of dwelling houses the legislature has itself provided (Sec. 4, Partition Act 1893) that if a cosharer has transferred his undivided share in the family dwelling house to a stranger and that stranger then files a suit for partition, the Court shall allow any cosharer to buy that share from the plaintiff instead of dividing the house for separating that stranger's share. If the stranger transferee does not apply for separation of his share, the provisions of Sec. 4 would not come in operation.[1] This provision extends to all families and not merely to Hindu families.

The value of each lot must be mentioned, either in the schedules in which the lots are mentioned, or in the recitals, or in a covenant, as may be convenient. The various lots of property allotted to each co-owner should be mentioned in separate schedules, and should be prepared with the same precision as "Parcels" in any conveyance.

Parties to the Deed

All co-owners should be parties to a deed for partition. If some of them are minors they may be represented by their guardians. The act of the guardian in this respect is generally binding on the minor, if the partition is to the advantage of the minor and is fair and equitable. If it is not, the minor has a right to get it re-opened on attaining majority. The necessity for the partition should in such cases be clearly mentioned in the recitals.

Title Deeds

Title deeds relating to the property falling to the lot of any party should be handed over to that party. If there are any title deeds which relate to properties falling to the shares of several co-sharers, one of the parties should by mutual consent, preferably expressed in the deed itself, retain them, undertaking their safe custody and to allow others to make inspection and take copies. However, it is not absolutely necessary to add such a covenant to the deed itself and a partition deed would not be invalid for want of it.

Stamp Duty

Same as on a Bond for the amount of the value of the share or shares of the property. The largest share remaining separated after the property is partitioned or if there are two or more shares of equal value and not smaller than any of the other shares, then one of such equal shares shall be deemed to be that from which the other shares are separated: Provided always that— Where an instrument of partition containing an agreement to divide property in severalty is executed and a partition is effected in pursuance of such agreement, the duty chargeable upon the instrument effecting such partition shall be reduced by the amount of duty paid in

---

1 *Babulal* v. *Habibnoor Khan*, AIR 2000 SC 2684, relied on *Ghanteshwar Ghost* v. *Madan Mohan Ghosh*, AIR 1997 SC 471.

respect of the first instrument, but shall not be less than the amount provided by the local amendments made by the States in Article 45, of the Stamp Act, Schedule I.

Duplicates will be stamped as provided in Article 25 of Stamp Act, Schedule I, but the value of the stamp on the original should be denoted on each duplicate (Sec. 16).

In the absence of a contract to the contrary, stamp duty is payable by the parties to the deed in proportion to their respective shares in the whole property partitioned [Sec. 29(g)].

Registration

A partition of joint property is not an exchange within the meaning of Sec. 118, Transfer of Property Act and therefore, partition can be effected orally and need not be in writing. If, however, it is effected by an instrument in writing, a deed of partition of immovable property of the value of Rs. 100 or upwards requires registration. However, a partition of a joint Hindu family property has been held not to amount to transfer.[1] Still, it will be expedient to have such a partition deed registered. A writing which contains a mere statement of partition previously made does not require registration.[2] A mere list of properties allotted at partition is not a deed of partition and does not require registration.[3]

An unregistered deed of partition by which the parties purported to effect a partition of their properties fell within the purview of section 49(*a*), Registration Act and though the deed was admissible in evidence for proving the factum of partition, it could not be used for proving that a particular property was allotted to a member upon partition as his share.[4]

A partition deed of movable property does not require registration.

If a partition includes both movable and immovable properties and the deed is not registered, it cannot be relied on even in support of a claim to movable property if the partition is one and indivisible, but it is otherwise, if the partition of movables is separate.[5]

It remains ope to parties to effect partition orally and, thereafter, to record the factum of having made the division in the form of a memorandum. That would not require registration. The memorandum requires careful drafting so that it may not give the appearance of being the deed of partition in itself. For distinction between a deed of partition and memorandum of partition see Family Settlement (*Supra*).

---

1 *C.I.T.* v. *Keshavlal*, AIR 1965 SC 866; *Sarin* v. *Ajit Kumar*, AIR 1966 SC 432.

2 *Runganayaki* v. *Rukmani*, 45 MLJ 100, 72 IC 456; *Yendapalli* v. *Yendapalli*, AIR 1958 AP 147; See Preliminary Note under COMPROMISE etc., *ante*.

3 *Kshetra Mohan* v. *Tufani*, 37 CWN 112, 144 IC 863.

4 *Gopinath Sharma* v. *Hangsa Sharma*, AIR 1950 Assam 129.

5 *Pothi* v. *Nagarana*, 30 MLJ 62, 32 IC 486; *Caramchand* v. *Uma Datt*, 1932 ALJ 45, 138 IC 369.

PRECEDENTS

1—Deed of Partition between Two Tenants in Common

THIS PARTITION is made on the ——— day of ——— BETWEEN AB, etc., of the one part and CD, etc., of the other part.

WHEREAS—

Recitals

(1) The properties mentioned in the first and second schedules hereto belonged to one XY, etc.

(2) The said XY died on the ——— leaving behind him the said AB, his son and the said CD, his daughter as his only heirs who inherited the said property under the Mohammedan Law in the shares of two-third and one-thirds respectively;

(3) The parties hereto have agreed to divide the said properties in the manner hereinafter appearing; and

(4) It has been agreed between the parties that the sum of Rs. ——— should be paid by the said AB to the said CD for equality of partition.

NOW THIS DEED WITNESSES as follows:

Conveyance

1. In pursuance of the said agreement and in consideration of the transfer by the said CD hereinafter contained the said AB hereby grants and conveys to the said CD ALL THAT the undivided two-thirds share and interest of the said AB in the property described in schedule A hereto containing ——— square metres and delineated on the plan annexed hereto and thereon shown with its boundaries coloured red together with all buildings TO HOLD the same to the said CD henceforth in severalty.

2. In further pursuance of the said agreement and in consideration of the transfer by the said AB hereinbefore contained and the payment of Rs. ——— by the said AB (the receipt of which is hereby acknowledged) the said CD hereby grants and conveys to the said AB ALL THAT the undivided one-third share and interest of the said CD in the property described in the schedule B hereto containing ——— square metres and delineated on the plan hereto annexed and thereon shown with its boundaries coloured green together with all buildings thereon TO HOLD

the same to the said AB henceforth in severalty.

3. Covenants

It is hereby agreed between the parties as follows:

(1) Encumbrances

There is no encumbrance or charge on the property hereby partitioned and that if any encumbrance or charge is found to attach to any part of such property both the parties shall be liable for the same in proportion to their shares in the joint property (*Or,* the property hereby allotted to each party has been allotted to it subject to any encumbrance or charge attaching thereto and the other party shall not be liable for any part of the same).

(2) Quiet Enjoyment

The property hereby allotted to each party shall be entered upon and henceforth held in severalty by such party without any interruption or disturbance by the other party or any one claiming through or under him.

(3) Further Assurance

Each party will at the cost of the person requiring the same do every such act or thing as may reasonably be required for further or more perfectly assuring the property hereby transferred by it to the other.

(4) Custody of Partition Deed

The said AB shall have the custody of this deed together with the maps annexed thereto and will at the request and cost of the said CD produce the same for inspection and will produce the same in evidence.

(5) Production of Title Deeds

Each of the parties hereto will at the request of the other produce for inspection by the other and produce in evidence in legal proceedings any title deed or document in his possession and in any way affecting the *title* of the party requiring such production to the property hereby transferred to it (*or,* The title deeds of the property partitioned shall be retained by the said AB who undertakes, at the request of any other party, to produce the same for inspection by such other party and to allow the latter to take copies thereof).

(6) Interpretation Clause

Wherever such an interpretation would be necessary in order to give the fullest scope and effect legally possible to any covenant or contract herein contained, the expressions "the said AB" and "the said CD" hereinbefore used include the heirs, successors, representatives and assigns of the said AB and the said CD respectively.

4. Value of Lots

It is hereby declared that the values of the properties mentioned in the first and second schedule hereto are Rs. —— and Rs. —— respectively.

5. Arrears of Rent

It is hereby agreed that each party will be entitled to realize the arrears of rent in respect of the property allotted to it and the other party hereby assigns to it its undivided right and interest in such arrears.[1]

The schedule herein referred to.

IN WITNESS WHEREOF, etc.

2—Partition Between Three Hindu Coparceners (One being Minor), and Mother[2]

THIS DEED OF PARTITION is made on the —— day of —— BETWEEN AB, etc., of the first part, CD, etc., of the second part, EF, etc., a minor, acting through his father and natural guardian the said AB, of the third part AND GH, etc., of the fourth part.

WHEREAS—

(1) The said AB and his sons the said CD and EF form a joint Hindu family, and the said GH is the wife of the said AB and mother of the said CD and EF;

(2) The movable and immovable properties mentioned in the first, second, third and fourth schedules hereto is the joint property of the said family, part of it being ancestral property and part having been acquired by the family with joint funds or earnings of individual members thrown into the common stock;

(3) The family also owns a sugar factory at —— which has been closed for some time but there are outstanding debts of the factory which are entered in the books of the factory;

(4) Owing to diverse disputes between the said AB and CD and quarrels between the said GH and the wife of the said CD, the said CD has

---

1 This is necessary if the property is in possession of tenants and there are arrears of rent.

2 A daughter of a coparcener has been granted the status of a coparcener by birth and can claim a share in the coparcenary property equal to the son. She is also entitled to claim partition of the dwelling house (The Hindu Succession Amendments Act, 2005).

for some time past been living separately from others and it is now expedient that the family property should be partitioned;

(5) The said partition is also advantageous and beneficial to the interest of the said EF minor;

(6) Under the law the said GH being the mother of the said CD and EF is also entitled to a share in the said property on partition and each of the parties hereto is, therefore, entitled to a one-fourth share;

(7) On the advice of the friends of the family, the parties agreed to divide the said property amicably, and with this object the said AB prepared four equal lots of the said joint property and it was agreed that they should be allotted to the parties by drawing of lots; and

(8) Lots were accordingly drawn and the lots mentioned in the first, second, third and fourth schedules were drawn by the said AB, CD, EF and GH respectively.

NOW THIS DEED WITNESSES as follows:

1. In pursuance of the aforesaid agreement the parties hereto hereby agree and declare that the said AB, CD, EF and GH shall henceforth be separate owners of the properties mentioned in the first, second, third and fourth schedules hereto respectively and each of them shall hold and enjoy the property so allotted to him in severalty and free and discharged from all claims and demands of the others thereto or concerning therewith.

2. Each of the said parties AB, CD, EF and GH hereby releases and conveys to the others its undivided share and interest in the property hereby allotted to such other parties.

3. *Covenants, etc.*

(*As in* Form 1 *and any special covenants*).

4. It is hereby declared that the value of the properties entered in each of the first, second, third and fourth schedules is Rs. ————.

5. *Arrears of Rent*

(*As in Form* 1, *if necessary*).

The schedules herein referred to.

3—Separation of the Share of One Co-owner from the Rest of the Estate

THIS DEED OF PARTITION is made on the ——— day of ——— BETWEEN AB, etc., and CD and EF minor sons of the said AB acting through their natural guardian the said AB of the one part AND XY, etc., of the other part.

WHEREAS—

(1) The late MN uncle of the said XY and father of the said AB was the owner of the properties mentioned in the first and second schedules hereto which are valued at Rs. ———;

(2) Disputes having arisen between the said XY and AB about the right to succeed to the said property which were settled by a compromise effected between them on the ———, under which it was agreed that the said XY should get a 1/6th share in the said estate of the said MN and the remaining 5/6th should remain with the said AB;

(3) The said CD and EF being the sons of the AB have rights by birth in the said 5/6th share;

(4) The said AB, being in possession of the said entire estate has been paying 1/6th share of the net profits thereof to the said XY; and

(5) The said XY being desirous of separating her 1/6th share by partition, applied to the said AB and the said AB accordingly prepared certain lots of partition, out of which one lot comprising the property described in the first schedule hereto and representing approximately 1/6th share of the entire estate comprised in the first and second schedules was selected by the said XY, and the said AB on his own behalf and on behalf of the said CD and EF has agreed that the same should be given to her and the parties have further agreed that as the value of the property in the first schedule exceeds 1/6th of the entire estate by Rs. ——— the said XY should pay that sum to the said AB, CD and EF and that the said sum be deducted from the amount of her share of profits payable by the said AB, CD and EF for the year ———.

NOW THIS DEED WITNESSES as follows:

1. In pursuance of the aforesaid agreement and in consideration of the transfer by the said XY hereinafter contained and of the sum of Rs. ——— to be paid by the said XY as hereinafter stipulated, the said AB on his own behalf and on behalf of the said CD and EF hereby grants and conveys to the said XY ALL that undivided 1/6th share of the said AB, CD and EF in the property mentioned in the first schedule hereto TO HOLD the same to the said XY henceforth in severalty.

2. In further pursuance of the aforesaid agreement and in consideration of the transfer hereinbefore contained the said XY hereby grants and conveys to the said AB, CD and EF ALL that the undivided 5/6th share in the property described in the second schedule hereto TO HOLD the same to the said AB, CD and EF henceforth in severalty.

3. The said AB, on his own behalf and on behalf of the said CD and EF and the said XY, hereby agree with each other as follows:

(1) The said AB, CD and EF may deduct from the profits payable by them, to the said XY for the year ——— a sum of Rs. ——— payable by her as hereinbefore mentioned;

(*Other covenants as in Form* 1 *or any special covenant*).

The schedule herein referred to.

IN WITNESS WHEREOF, etc.

4—Confirmation of a Partition Already made (some Co-Sharers being Minor Members of a Joint Hindu Family) when the Parties were Tenants in Common

THIS DEED OF PARTITION is made on the ——— day of ——— BETWEEN AB acting on his own behalf and as manager of a joint Hindu family governed by the Mitakshara School of Hindu Law and consisting of himself and his three minor brothers CD, EF and GH, sons of XY and residents of ——— (hereinafter in this capacity called the first party) of the one part AND JK, etc., of the other part;

WHEREAS—

(1) The said AB, CD, EF and GH and their aforesaid father XY on the one hand and the said JK on the other were owners in equal shares of the property mentioned in the two lists called Lot No. 1 and Lot No. 2 annexed hereto;

(2) The said JK and the said XY now deceased and the then manager of the joint Hindu family consisting of himself and his aforesaid sons AB, CD, EF and GH being desirous of effecting a partition of the said property, the said two Lots Nos. 1 and 2 were prepared and by a drawing of lots on the ——— in the presence of the said XY and said JK, Lot No. 1 fell to the share of the said XY and his aforesaid sons and Lot No. 2 fell to the share of JK;

(3) The said XY and the said JK agreed that partition should be effected in accordance with the aforesaid lots as drawn in the manner aforesaid;

(4) After the death of the said XY mutation was effected in the Revenue papers with the consent of the parties hereto in accordance with partition carried out in manner aforesaid, *i.e.,* the name of JK was entered on the property mentioned in Lot No. 2 and the names of AB, CD, EF and GH on property mentioned in Lot No. 1;

(5) The parties hereto have now agreed that in order to confirm the aforesaid partition carried out in the manner aforesaid a formal deed of partition should be drawn up and executed.

NOW THIS DEED WITNESSES as follows:

1. In pursuance of the said agreement and in consideration of the transfer hereinafter contained by the said JK, the first party hereby confirms the aforesaid partition and grants and conveys to the said JK as from the date of the said partition, *i.e.*, the ——— day of ———, ALL THAT the undivided share and interest of the said AB, CD, EF and GH in the property described in the list called Lot No. 2 annexed hereto TO HOLD the same to the said JK thenceforth in severalty;

2. In further pursuance of the said agreement and in consideration of the transfer by the first party hereinbefore contained, the said JK hereby confirms the aforesaid partition and grants and conveys to the said AB, CD, EF and GH as from the date of the said partition, *i.e.* the ——— day of ———, ALL that undivided share and interest of the said JK in the property described in the list called Lot No. 1 annexed hereto TO HOLD the same to the said AB, CD, EF and GH thenceforth in severalty.

3 and 4.(*as in Form* 1).

IN WITNESS WHEREOF, etc.

5—Partition of Leasehold Property

THIS DEED OF PARTITION, etc. (*as in Form* 1).

WHEREAS—

(1) By a deed of lease dated ——— one XY, etc., demised the land described in the first and second schedules hereto to the said AB and one CD, deceased father of the said EF, to be held by them as tenants in common in equal shares for the term of ——— years on the terms and conditions mentioned in the said deed of lease.

(2) The said AB and CD had obtained the lease of the said land for the construction of a sugar factory thereon in partnership but before this intention could be carried out the said CD died on the ———;

(3) The said EF has inherited the leasehold rights of the said CD in said land but he does not wish to join with the said AB in the construction of a sugar factory;

(4) The parties now want to build two residential houses separately on the demised land and have therefore agreed to make a division of the said land in the manner hereinafter appearing;

(5) It has also been agreed between the said AB and EF that a sum of Rs. ——— should be paid by the said AB to the said EF for equality of partition.

NOW THIS DEED WITNESSES as follows:

1. In pursuance of the aforesaid agreement and in consideration of the assignment by the said EF hereinafter contained, the said AB hereby grants and assigns to the said EF ALL that the undivided share and interest of the said AB of and in the leasehold land described in the first schedule hereto and delineated on the map annexed hereto and thereon shown as coloured red TO HOLD the same to the said EF henceforth in severalty for all the residue now unexpired of the said term of ——— years granted by the aforesaid lease subject nevertheless to the payment of the apportioned yearly rent of Rs. ——— and to the performance and observance of such of the covenants and provisions and conditions contained in the said deed of lease and to be performed by the lessee as affect the land described in the first schedule hereto.

2. In further pursuance of the said agreement and in consideration of the sum of Rs. ——— paid by the said AB (the receipt of which is hereby acknowledged) and of the assignment by the said AB hereinbefore contained the said EF hereby grants and assigns to the said AB ALL, etc., (*as in Clause* 1, *substituting "second schedule" for "first schedule"*).

3. Each of the parties hereto hereby covenants with the other as follows:

(1) That during the continuance of the said term of ——— years and of any renewal thereof they will duly pay such part of the said yearly rent of Rs. ——— reserved by the said lease as is hereby apportioned to be made payable by them at the time and in the manner provided in the said lease.

(2) That during the said term and renewal, they will perform and observe the covenants and conditions contained in the said lease and to be performed and observed by the lessee so far as such covenant and condition in any way relate to the leasehold land assigned to him under this partition.

(3) That if and whenever on account of non-performance or non-observance of any of the covenants and conditions aforesaid by any of the parties hereto the other of them shall be called upon to pay and shall pay such apportioned part of the rent or any part thereof or shall incur any costs, charges, damages or expenses in respect of the covenants and conditions affecting the premises hereby assigned to the party so in default and in every such case such party will forthwith repay such sums of money, costs,

charges, damages and expenses so paid or incurred to the party so paying or so incurring the same.

(4) *Other covenants as necessary.*

5. Interpretation clause (*as in clause 3* (*6*) *of Form 1*)

(*Rest as in Form 1*)

The schedule herein referred to.

IN WITNESS WHEREOF, etc.

6—General Clauses in Partition Deed Relating to Debts

There are no debts owing by the family. If in respect of the transaction ———— (specify details) any amount is found due and payable to 'X' that amount is to be paid by AB and he alone and the properties in Schedule A (allotted to him) alone will be answerable for that amount.[1]

1 Such clause does not create a charge in favour of 'X' on the properties in Schedule A but is intended to confer a right of indemnity upon other members of the family if 'X' sought to enforce the liability against them: *M.C. Chacko* v. *State Bank of Travancore*, (1969) 2 SCC 343; *Akella Suryanarayana Rao* v. *Dwarampudi*, 55 Mad 436.

PARTNERSHIP

Preliminary Note

Definition

A partnership is the relation between persons who have agreed to share the profits of a business carried on by all or any of them acting for all. (Sec. 4 of the Indian Partnership Act, 1932).

In *Chimanram Motilal* v. *Jayantilal Chhaganlal*,[1] Bombay High Court observed that partnership requires three elements: (a) an agreement entered into by the persons concerned; (b) distribution of the profits of the business; (c) management of business by all or any one of them acting for all, i.e. mutual agency. The element of mutual agency is most essential and it distinguishes partnership from other type of contractual relationship between the parties. One partner is not only an agent of the firm but also of the other partners. One partner can always bind another partner in any matter which falls within the scope of the partnership business, subject to any limitation under Section 20 of the Act. The agreement to share profit of a business is also an essential element of partnership. Societies and clubs whose object is not to acquire profit are not partnership. Section 5 of the Partnership Act, expressly provides that the relation of partnership arises from contract and not from status. The sharing of profits by joint owners of a property does not, therefore, make persons partners. The Act does not apply to a trading joint Hindu family[2] as that relationship arises from status and not from agreement.

Persons who have entered into partnership with one another are individually called "partners" and collectively "a firm" and the name under which their business is carried on is called the "firm name". In *Kylasa Sarabhaiah* v. *CIT*, [3] Hon'ble Apex Court observed that a firm is strictly not a person and that it is an association of persons.

It is not merely the name given to a deed which determines its character, and if the essential element of a partnership contract is omitted, the transaction will not be partnership contract though it may be called by that name. For example, in a case in which plaintiff advanced money and was to get interest on it at a fixed rate which was described as his share of profit and was to supervise the accounts and the actual business was done by the defendant, it was held that there was no partnership as there was no share in the profits as such.[4]

---

1 (1939) 41 Bom LR 899 AIR 1939 Bom 410.

2 *Nanchand Gangarm* v. *M.M. Sadalge*, (1976) 2 SCC 429.

3 AIR 1965 SC 1411, (1965) 56 ITR 219.

4 *Karnidan* v. *Sailaja Kant*, AIR 1940 Pat 683.

Deed of Partnership

Partnership can be created by oral agreement, but it is always safe, in order to avoid future disputes, to have a proper deed of partnership drawn up. It is executed by all the partners and is drafted as an agreement by them to carry on a business in partnership on certain terms and conditions. The nature of the business, the capital and the shares of the partners in the profit and loss, should be clearly specified and all the terms and conditions on which the business is to be carried on should be clearly mentioned.

Parties

Section 464 of the Companies Act prohibits partnership of persons exceeding 100 for the purpose of carrying on any business that has for its object the acquisition of gain unless it is registered as a company under this Act or is formed under any other law for the time being in force. Every member carrying on business in contravention of this section shall be punishable with fine which may extend to one lakh rupees and shall also be personally liable for all liabilities incurred in such business.

All the partners should join in the execution of the partnership deed. New partners can be admitted and also can retire during the continuance of the partnership. The term on which new partners are admitted should be stipulated and clearly stated in the deed, if one is drawn up.

A minor cannot be a partner but he may be admitted to the benefits of partnership.[1] His rights on such admission are laid down in section 30 of the Partnership Act. On attaining majority, he should give notice whether he does or does not elect to become a partner. Such notice must be given within six months of attaining majority or obtaining knowledge of his having been admitted to the benefits of the partnership, whichever is later. If no notice is given, he shall become a partner in the firm on the expiry of the said six months [Sec. 30 (5)].

A firm cannot be a partner,[2] but a joint Hindu family may enter into partnership with a stranger but not with an individual member of the same family in his individual capacity.[3]

It is not necessary that the duration of the partnership should be fixed beforehand. When no term is fixed and no provision is made for dissolution, the partnership is called a "partnership at will" and such partnership can be dissolved by notice (Sec. 43). It should be clearly stated whether the business of partnership actually exists at the time or it is intended to start a new business. In the latter case, it is better to state when the business is intended to be started. Until the business actually comes into existence there can be no partnership and relations between the promoters of a business before the business is started are governed by general rules

---

1 *Ram Gopal* v. *Baij Nath*, AIR 1937 Cal 396, 172 IC 532.

2 *Hakmaji* v. *Punnaji*, 40 BLR 995, 178 IC 419, AIR 1938 Bom 453.

3 *In re: Lachman Das*, AIR 1945 Lah 61.

of contract and not by the law of partnership.[1]

Business

The business should be clearly defined. Business includes every trade, occupation and profession. It should not be immoral, or illegal or unlawful, or against public policy, as the contract to carry on such business will be illegal and not enforceable.

Firm Name

The name under which a partnership carries on business is the firm's name. Any name may be chosen, but the name should not contain any words expressing or implying the sanction, approval or patronage of the Government of India or the State Government, (Sec. 58, Partnership Act). State amendments to section 58 should also be looked into. The firm name is only a matter of convenience, as a partnership firm has not, unlike a company, a legal existence distinct from the partners but firms can sue or be sued in the name of the firm under a special enabling procedure given in Order XXX of the C.P.C.

Registration of Firm

Registration of a firm as referred to under Sec. 58, Indian Partnership Act, 1932, is not compulsory, but registration of the firm is a condition precedent to the right to institute a suit to enforce a right arising from a contract or conferred by the Act. Sec. 69 is mandatory. Section 69 does not affect right of third party to proceed against the firm or its partners, even though unregistered.

The expression "other proceedings" in Section 69(3) of the Partnership Act, and the ban imposed under the Section 69 of the Partnership Act can have no application to the arbitral proceedings as well as arbitration award.[2]

Terms of Partnership and Contents of Deed

Terms should be carefully settled and entered in the partnership deed. They will always depend on the nature of the business and it is not possible to lay down definitely what they should be. But as a general rule provision may be made for:

(*a*) Nature of business, duration of partnership, and name of firm.

(*b*) Shares of partners.

(*c*) Provision about capital and interest on capital.

(*d*) Banking account of the firm.

(*e*) Authority to draw upon the account and sign cheques.

(*f*) The method of keeping accounts and making up annual accounts or balance sheets.

---

1 *R.R. Sarna* v. *J.Reuben*, AIR 1946 Oudh 68.

2 *Umesh Goel* v. *Himachal Pradesh Cooperative Group Housing Society Limited*, (2016) 11 SCC 313.

(*g*) Management of business.

(*h*) Duties of Partners to each other (including respective covenants).

(*i*) Outgoings and profits.

(*j*) Arrangement on death of a partner or dissolution of partnership.

(*k*) Retirement and expulsion of partners.[1]

(*l*) Winding up.[2]

(*m*) Mode of service of notice.

(*n*) Arbitration.

Statutory provisions exists in the Indian Partnership Act, 1932, for some of these matters and it is not necessary to make an express provision in respect thereof, unless the partners agree to vary such of them as can legally be so varied. For instance, the following agreements are implied in all partnership contracts:

(1) That the partners will carry on the business to the greatest advantage (Sec. 9).

(2) That they will be just and faithful to each other (Sec. 9).

(3) That they will render true account and full information of all things affecting the firm to any partner or his legal representative (Sec. 9).

(4) That every partner shall indemnify the firm for loss caused by his fraud or wilful neglect in the conduct of the business [Secs. 10 and 13(*f*)].

(5) That every partner has a right to take part in the business [Sec. 12(*a*)].

(6) That every partner is bound to attend diligently to his duties [Sec. 12(*b*)].

(7) That all differences shall be decided by a majority of the partners, but no change in the nature of business may be made without the consent of all [Sec. 12(*c*)].

(8) That every partner will have access to, and will be entitled to inspect and take copies of the accounts [Sec. 12(*d*)].

(9) That partners shall not take any remuneration [Sec. 13(*a*)].

(10) That partners will share the profits and losses equally [Sec. 13(*b*)].

(11) That interest on capital shall be payable out of profits only [Sec. 13(*c*)].

(12) That a partner is entitled to interest at 6 percent per annum on advances above the capital [Sec. 13(*d*)].

(13) That the firm will indemnify a partner in respect of payments made in

---

1 *Vishnu Chandra* v. *Chandrika Prasad*, AIR 1983 SC 523, (1983) 1 SCC 22 [Sec. 32 (1) (b) of Act relied on].

2 If partnership is constituted for a specific job, e.g. execution of a works agreement, it comes to an end with the completion of the job: *Deoki Prasad Rajgarhiah* v. *Anar Dei Poddar*, AIR 1999 Pat 22 (case law). It is different from a partnership at will.

the ordinary course of business or for protecting the firm from loss [Sec. 13(*e*)].

(14) That the profits of the firm will be held exclusively for the purposes of the business (Sec. 15).

(15) That a partner deriving profits from any transaction of the firm or from the use of firm property or by carrying on business of the nature as and competing with that of the firm shall account to the firm for all profits so made (Sec. 16).

(16) That the mutual rights and liabilities of the partners remain the same (*a*) inspite of a change in its constitution, (*b*) after the expiry of the fixed term, and (*c*) in respect of new undertakings or adventures (Sec. 17).

(17) That a partner has authority in an emergency to do all acts necessary for protecting the firm from loss (Sec. 21.)

Items (1) to (4) and (17) cannot be altered by contract, except item (4) in respect of "wilful neglect". All others are subject to contract to the contrary, and a contrary agreement varying the implied agreements may be made and recorded.

Sec. 19(2) provides that "in the absence of any usage or custom of trade to the contrary the implied authority of a partner does not empower him to:

(*a*) submit a dispute relating to the business of the firm to arbitration;

(*b*) open a banking account on behalf of the firm in his own name;

(*c*) compromise or relinquish any claim or portion of a claim by the firm;

(*d*) withdraw a suit or proceeding filed on behalf of the firm;

(*e*) admit any liability in a suit or proceeding against the firm;

(*f*) acquire immovable property on behalf of the firm;

(*g*) transfer immovable property belonging to the firm; or

(*h*) enter into partnership on behalf of the firm;

Accordingly, if authority to do any of these things is sought to be conferred on any partner it is necessary to make specific provision in that behalf in the deed, as it is unsafe and uncertain to rely merely on "usage or custom of trade to the contrary" which may not always be easy to prove.

Although it is not necessary to mention in the deed anything which is implied by law, yet sometimes, in order to make the deed a complete code of direction fully intelligible to the lay man, for whom and not the lawyers, it is drafted, it is thought advisable to incorporate all the terms and conditions in the deed.

To determine whether a group of persons is or is not a firm, or whether a person is or is not a partner in a firm regard shall be had to the real relation between the parties as shown by all the facts taken together, section 6 of the Partnership Act. Vesting of the exclusive power and control, by agreement of the parties, in one partner or the operation of firm account by one of the partners alone does not detract from the factum of existence of partnership. Sec. 11 provides for determination of rights and duties of the partners by contract between them. Sec. 12 (Conduct of business) and Sec. 13 (Mutual rights and liabilities) are also both subject to contract between the partners. Thus law does not require that the power of all the partners be identical.[1] The partners might agree to share the profits in any manner.

Co-ownership is distinct from partnership inasmuch as—

(i) Co-ownership is not necessarily the result of agreement, but partnership is;

(ii) Co-ownership does not necessarily involve community of profit or loss, but partnership does;

(iii) One co-owner can, without consent of the other, transfer his interest to a stranger, a partner cannot do this.

The relationship among the partners is contractual. To constitute partnership, it is not incumbent that each partner contributes capital in the firm. The partnership sails primarily upon mutual confidence. It is illegal if constituted for some purpose opposed to public policy or the law. A partner cannot obtain private benefit at the expense of the firm. In all transactions which affect the partnership, he has to put in his best. With the co-partners he is to share the benefits.

Stamp Duty

The deeds should be written on stamp paper of the requisite value as required by Article 46.

Registration

Registration under the Indian Registration Act is not compulsory. But if the deed of partnership or deed of dissolution of partnership relates to immovable property, then registration is compulsory.[2]

A document recording previous fact of dissolution of partnership and the relinquishment of the interest of the partners affecting immovable properties does not require registration.[3]

Difference between dissolution and reconstitution

The dissolution and reconstitution of a partnership are two different legal concepts.

In *Tyresoles (India),*[4] a Division Bench of the Madras High Court observed that the dissolution puts an end to the partnership, but reconstitution keeps it subsisting, though in another form. A dissolution followed by some of the erstwhile

---

1 *Steel Brothers & Co.* v. *C.I.T.*, AIR 1958 SC 315.

2 See, however, footnote under Form 5, *post*.

3 *Addanki Narayanappa* v. *Bhaskara Krishnappa*, AIR 1966 SC 1300.

4 (1963) 49 ITR 515 (Mad)

partners taking over the assets and liabilities of the dissolved partnership and forming themselves into a partnership is not reconstitution of the original partnership. The partnership formed after the dissolution is a new partnership and not a continuation of the old partnership, for it would be a contradiction in terms to say that what ceased to exist was continued.

A reconstitution of a firm of partnership necessarily implies that the firm never became extinct. What it denotes is a structural alteration of the membership of the firm, by addition or reduction of members, and an incidental redistribution of the shares of the partners."

When the widow of a deceased partner was inducted in the partnership and another partnership deed was drawn up, then it was held that the existing firm was not dissolved or ceased to exist or totally new firm came into existence.[1]

---

1 *Sharad Vasant Kotak* v. *Ramniklal Mohanlal Chawda*, (1998) 2 SCC 171.

GENERAL FORMS OF VARIOUS CLAUSES IN PARTNERSHIP DEED

1. Establishment of Partnership between Two Partners

The said AB, etc., and CD, etc., will become and remain partners in the business of ——— from the ——— day of ——— during the term of ——— years (*or*, during their joint lives) under the firm name of ——— subject to determination as hereinafter provided.

2. Establishment of Partnership between Three or more Partners

The said AB, etc., CD, etc., EF, etc. and GH, etc., and the survivors of them will become and remain partners in the business of (*or, if business is already existing,* in continuation of the business carried on for ——— years by the said AB and CD) from the ——— day of ——— during the term of ——— years if they or any two or more of them shall so long live (*or*, during so long as they or any two or more of them shall live) under the firm name of ——— subject to determination as hereinafter provided.

3. Shares in Profits & Losses[1]

The partners shall be entitled to the net profits of the said business and shall be liable for losses in the following proportions viz. AB, ——— percent, CD, ——— percent, EF, ——— percent, etc. (*or*, in equal share).

4. Capital

The capital of the firm shall be Rs. ——— which shall be contributed by the several partners in the following proportions, viz. AB, Rs. ———, CD, Rs. ———, EF, Rs. ———, etc. (*or,* in equal shares).

5. Interest on Capital

Interest at the rate of ——— percent per annum shall be paid to each partner on the capital for the time being standing to his credit out of the gross profits of the business and such interest shall be cumulative so that any deficiency in one year shall be made up, out of the gross profits of any succeeding year or years.

6. Loans by Partners or Profits Left

If any partner shall at any time advance to the firm any sum or sums

---

1 In the absence of an express agreement the shares of partners in profits and losses are equal [Sec. 13(b)].

beyond the amount of capital which he has agreed to contribute or, with the consent of other partners or majority of them, leave in the firm any part of the net profits carried to his credit at any annual general account, the same shall be considered as a debt due to him from the firm and shall bear interest at ———— percent per annum payable annually but any such sum so advanced or left undrawn shall not be called in or withdrawn by him without giving ——— months' written notice to the other partners and he shall be bound to accept repayment of or to withdraw the same on a like notice being given to him by the other partners, and, at the expiration of such last mentioned notice, interest shall cease to be payable thereon.

7. Stock in Trade if Business existing at Commencement of Partnership

The stock in trade, plants, machinery and other things belonging to the said business at the commencement of the partnership (particulars whereof are entered in the schedule hereto) shall become the property of the firm and shall be taken over and adopted by the firm at Rs. ——— (*or,* at a valuation to be made by ————) as part of the capital to be contributed by the said ———— (*former owner*).

8. Where Capital of the New Partnership Consists Wholly of the Assets and Liabilities of an Old Firm

All the assets belonging to the said business, lately carried on by the said AB, the particulars of which are specified in the first schedule hereto, shall become the property and assets of the firm and all the debts and liabilities of the said business mentioned in the second schedule hereto shall become the debts and liabilities of the firm. The said AB shall be credited in the books of the firm with the sum of Rs. 78,000 (being one half of the net value of the assets after deducting the said debts and liabilities) as so much capital brought in by him and each of the said CD, EF and GH shall pay to the said AB the sum of Rs. 26,000 (being one-third of the other half of the said net value) as a premium for his admitance into the said partnership and shall be credited with that amount as so much capital brought in by him. The said AB, his heirs, executors and legal representatives shall, if and when required so to do, at the cost of the firm duly transfer or otherwise assure the said property in such manner as effectually to vest the same in the firm as part of the partnership assets and until this is done shall hold the same in trust for the firm.

9. Increase in Capital

If at any time or times hereafter it shall be determined by the partners (*or* by a majority of the partners) to increase the capital of the firm the additional capital required shall, unless otherwise agreed, be advanced by the partners in equal shares (*or*, in proportion of the shares held by them in the initial capital).

10. Place of Business

The business of the firm shall be carried on at ———— or at such other place or places as the partners shall from time to time determine.

11. Reserve Fund

Out of the net profits of the said business as determined on settlement of every annual account, a sum calculated at ——— percent of such net profit shall be set apart and carried to a separate account to be called "the reserve fund" which shall from time to time be applied for the purpose of meeting extraordinary losses or expenses or for such other purposes and in such manner as the partners shall direct and subject thereto shall belong to the partners in the proportion in which they are entitled to profits. PROVIDED that whenever the reserve fund shall amount to Rs. ——— the same shall not be further augmented unless all the partners shall so agree.

12. Drawings by Partner

Each partner shall be entitled to draw out of the partnership business any sum or sums of money not exceeding Rs. ——— per month for his own use, such sums to be duly accounted for on each succeeding settlement of account and division of profits of the partnership and any excess of the drawings found on such settlement shall be refunded (with interest at —— percent per annum).

13. Attention to Business by Partner

The said partners AB and CD shall, at all times during the partnership, devote the whole of their time and attention to the said partnership business and diligently and faithfully employ themselves therein and carry on the same for the greatest advantage of the partnership and the said EF shall give such amount of supervision and attention to the said business as may be necessary for the efficient management thereof and except to that extent shall not be bound to personal attendance or participation therein, and the said GH shall not be bound to attend to the said business any further than he shall think proper.

14. Sleeping Partner

The said XY shall not be required to interfere with the carrying on management or conduct of the said business and shall not sign in the name of the firm.

15. Partners not to carry on Rival Business

No partner shall without the consent in writing of the other (*or*, others) carry on or be connected with, directly or indirectly, in any business of ——— except on account and for the benefit of the partnership.

16. Share not Transferable

No partner shall without the consent in writing of the other (*or*, others) assign or mortgage his share or interest in the partnership (except to any person whom he is authorised under the provisions hereinafter contained to introduce into the partnership, *or*, except to another partner).

17. Partners not to Contract beyond a Limit

No partner shall without the consent in writing of the other (*or*, others) buy, order or contract for any property or goods or article for the firm exceeding Rs. ——— in value.

18. Partner not to give Credit or have dealing

No partner shall lend money or give credit to or have any dealings on behalf of the partnership with any person or company to whom the other partner or partners shall previously have forbidden him to trust or deal with.

19. Keeping of Accounts

Proper books of account shall be kept by the partners and entries made therein of all such transactions and things as are usually entered in books of account kept by the persons engaged in concerns of a similar nature. The said books of account and all letters, papers and documents belonging to the firm shall be kept at the place of business of the firm and shall at all times be open to inspection by any partner or his agent who shall be entitled to take extracts and copies of the same.

20. Annual Accounts

On the ——— day of each year during the continuance of the partnership, an account shall be taken of all the capital, assets and liabilities and of the profits and losses of the partnership so that actual receipts and payments alone shall be taken into account (*or,* including therein the profits earned or losses incurred but not actually received and paid) for the preceding year and shall be signed by each partner. Such account when signed shall be binding on the partners (*or,* and a copy of such account shall be furnished to each partner who shall be bound thereby) unless some manifest error shall be discovered within ——— months in which case such error shall be rectified. As soon as the annual general account shall have been signed by the partners the net profits (if any) of the business shall be divided between them in accordance with the provision of this deed. (Provided that if any partner refuses to sign the general account without assigning any valid reason for such refusal, a copy of the general account shall be posted to him by registered post and the account shall be deemed to be signed by him on the date of such posting).

21. Power to Dissolve in case of Losses, etc.

If at any time owing to losses or any cause whatsoever, one-fourth of the entire capital of the partnership has been sunk or reasonable apprehension shall be entertained that a call would require to be made for further capital to the extent of Rs. ——— in order to carry on the work and business of the partnership, a majority in value of the partners may require the partnership to be dissolved and wound up as if the same had expired by efflux of time.

22. Provision for Death or Voluntary Retirement of one Partner

If any partner shall die or voluntarily retire, an account and statement shall be taken and made out of his share of the capital and effects of the partnership and of all unpaid interest and profits belonging to him up to the time of his death or retirement for which purpose a valuation shall be made of any assets or effects requiring valuation and of the goodwill and the amount found to be due or owing to the deceased or retiring partner shall be paid by the remaining partner or partners to him or his representatives as the case may be within ——— calendar months from his death or retirement with interest from such death or retirement until payment at ——— per cent per annum, and on such payment the share of the deceased or retiring partner in the property or effects shall vest in the remaining partner or partners in the proportion (if more than one) in which they shall have contributed to the purchase thereof. The cost for carrying this provision into effect shall be borne by the remaining partner or partners and the out-going partner or the representatives of the deceased partner in shares proportionate to their shares in the capital.

23. Option of Representatives of Deceased Partner to be Sleeping Partner

If any partner shall die during the continuance of the partnership, his representatives shall have the option to be declared by notice in writing given to the surviving partners within ———— calendar months after his death of their succeeding to his share in the said business as from his death as sleeping partners, *i.e.*, as partners without the power to interfere in or having any control over the conduct or management of the said business, and if such option is so exercised the said business shall be carried on during the residue of the term of partnership as nearly as may be according to the provisions of this deed with the said representatives of the deceased as sleeping partners from the date of the death of the deceased, and all proper instruments for carrying the provisions of this present clause into effect shall be executed or made between them and the surviving partner or partners.

24. Outgoing Partner not to carry on Business

An out going partner, the amount or value of whose share in the partnership business shall have been paid or provided for in accordance with the covenants in this deed, shall not during the remainder of the term of the partnership carry on or engage or be interested directly or indirectly in the business of ———— within ———— kilometres of the principal place of business of the said partnership.

25. Option to Purchase Share of Retiring, Deceased or Insolvent Partner

If during the continuance of the partnership any (either, *if there are two partners*) partner shall retire or die or become insolvent then the remaining partner or partners shall have the option (to be exercised by notice in writing to the retiring partner or to the legal representatives of the deceased partner or to the receiver of his estate, as the case may be, within a month after the retirement, death or insolvency) to purchase the share of the other partner at the date of his retirement, death or insolvency in the capital and assets of the partnership on the following terms:

(*a*) The purchase price shall be the amount at which such share shall stand in the last balance sheet which shall have been prepared prior to retirement, death or insolvency or if the retirement, death or insolvency shall occur before the taking of the first annual general account, the amount credited to him as his share in the capital up to the date of his retirement, death or insolvency, *plus* the amount of interest on the aforesaid sums at the rate of ———— percent per annum from the date of the last general account or from the commencement of the partnership as the case may be or, in the case of further capital, from the date when the same was credited upto the date of retirement, death or insolvency (*or*, a sum equal to the amount of the share of profits of the said partner since the taking of the last general account or the commencement of the partnership as the case may be), *minus* any drawings by the said partner during the current year of the partnership such drawings being debited so far as possible against the sum payable in place of current profits.

(*b*) Of the purchase price the sum payable as interest or current profits shall be paid on the exercise of the option and the balance by —— equal instalments at intervals of ——— months from the date of the exercise of the option, with interest at ——— per cent per annum from such date.

(*c*) The purchasing partner shall enter into a covenant to indemnify the said partner or his legal representatives or the receiver of his estate as the case may be, from the debts, engagements and liabilities of the partnership, both existing and future.

(*d*) The surviving partner shall secure the payment of the said purchase price and interest and the performance of the said covenant of indemnity by a floating charge on the assets present and future of the said business.

26. *Provision for vesting Assets in one Partner on Dissolution*

Upon dissolution of the partnership in any event not otherwise herein provided for, the said business and the assets and goodwill thereof, shall vest absolutely in the said CD if he shall be living subject to the discharge by him of the partnership debts and liabilities and to the payment by him to each of the other partners in satisfaction of the latter's share in the partnership business of the amount to which such partner would have become entitled as an outgoing partner under the provisions of this deed.

27. *Provisions for Partners in Succession to Succeed to Whole Business on Determination of Partnership*

Upon dissolution of partnership by efflux of time, the said AB shall have the option, to be signified in writing to the other partner or partners not more than ——— not less than——— calendar months before the expiration thereof, to succeed to the whole of the said business, AND in case AB refuses or neglects to exercise such option, to be signified in like manner not less than ———— calendar months before the expiration of the partnership; CD shall have the like option to be signified in like manner before the expiration of the partnership AND in case he too refuses or neglects to exercise such option then the said EF shall have the like option to be signified in like manner before the expiration of the partnership; AND in case any partner shall elect to succeed to the said business as aforesaid a general account and valuation shall be taken and made at the expiration of the partnership at the expense of the partnership of the assets and liabilities thereof and the partner so succeeding to the said business shall within —— months of the making of such valuation pay to the other partner (*or,* to each of the other partners) the sum which is found to be the value of his share of the capital, goodwill, interest and profits after making provision for all the liabilities of the partnership AND on such payment being made the whole of the assets and goodwill of the partnership shall as from the date of such expiration, become the sole property of the partner so succeeding to the said business AND the partner so succeeding shall indemnify the other partner or partners against all the outstanding liabilities of the partnership on that day and such assurances and instruments (if any) as shall be necessary for vesting in the partner so succeeding all the assets of the partnership and for indemnifying the outgoing partner or partners against all liabilities of the partnership and for releasing each other from all claims on account of the partnership shall be executed by the parties at their joint expense.

28. Provision for Continuance of Partnership by Surviving Partners on Death, Retirement, or Insolvency

If during the continuance of the partnership any partner shall die or become insolvent or retire, the share of the deceased or outgoing partner shall, as from his so dying or ceasing to be a partner, belong to the remaining partners, in shares proportionate to their shares in the profits of the partnership, and the partnership shall be continued between the remaining partners under the provisions of this deed so far as applicable, and the outgoing partner or his estate or the legal representatives of the deceased partner (as the case may be) shall be entitled to a sum equal to the value of the share of such outgoing or deceased partner in the said partnership on the date of his retirement, insolvency, or death as the case may be; such value shall be the amount, etc., (*continue as in Clause (a) of para No.*25).

29. Mode of Valuing Goodwill

The value of the goodwill of the business shall, unless otherwise agreed, be taken to be three times the average net yearly profits of the said business during the ——— years preceding the date on which valuation is made or from the commencement of the partnership if less than that time.

30. Mutual Release in respect of Former Deed of Partnership

In consideration of the premises the said AB and CD do and each of them does hereby mutually release and discharge the other of them, his heirs, executors, administrators and legal representatives from all claims and demands, actions and proceedings whatsoever for or in respect of the covenants contained in the deed of partnership dated the ——— under which the said business has hitherto been carried which is intended to be wholly suspended by this deed.

31. Notice

Any notice hereby required or authorised to be given to any of the said partners shall be sufficiently given by leaving the same addressed to him at the principal place of business of the said firm or by sending the same by registered post to his usual or last known address.

32. Arbitration

All disputes and questions in connection with the partnership of this deed arising between the partners or between any one of them and the legal representatives of the other or others or between their respective legal representatives and whether during or after the partnership shall be referred to the arbitration of three arbitrators, one to be appointed by each party, and the third who shall be the presiding arbitrator, appointed by those two arbitrators.

PRECEDENTS

1—Deed of Partnership Between Two Persons Setting up a New Business[1]

THIS DEED OF PARTNERSHIP made on the ——— day of ——— BETWEEN AB, etc., of the one part AND CD, etc., of the other part.

WITNESSES AND it is hereby mutually agreed that the said parties shall become partners upon the following terms:

1. Business and its Place

The partnership business shall be that of ——— and shall be carried on at ———— or at such other place or places as the partners may from time to time agree upon.

2. Name

The name of the firm shall be ————.

3. Term

The partnership shall commence on the ——— day of ——— and shall continue for a term of ——— years[2] determinable nevertheless as hereinafter provided (*or*, and thereafter until determined as hereinafter provided).

4. Capital

The capital of the partnership shall be a sum of Rs. ——— and shall be provided by and belong to the partners in equal shares (*or*, in the following proportion);

If at any time hereafter any further capital shall be required for the purposes of partnership the same shall, unless otherwise agreed, be contributed by the parties in the said shares (proportion).

---

1 This is a comprehensive form. In a simple case some of the conditions entered herein will not be needed and may be left out or suitably modified.

2 Sec. 42 (a) provides that "Subject to contract between the partners a firm is dissolved— if constituted for a fixed term, by the expiry of that term." Other clauses of this section provide for other contingencies in which the firm is dissolved.

5. Interest on Capital

As clause 5 of the General Forms of various clauses in Partnership Deed.

6. Profits and Losses

The profits and losses of the firm (including loss of capital) shall be divided between and borne by the partners in proportion to the capital for the time being credited to them in the partnership books.

7. Drawings by Partner

As clause 12 of the General Forms of various clauses in Partnership Deed.

8. Books of Account

All necessary and proper books of account shall be kept properly posted up and shall not be removed from the place of business without the consent of the partners.[1]

9. Annual Accounts

As clause 20 of the General Forms of various clauses in Partnership Deed.

10. Manager

The said AB shall be the manager of the said partnership business and shall devote his whole time and attention to the management and shall receive a salary of Rs. ——— per mensem for his services (and he shall manage the business according to the best of his ability and judgment).

11. Duties of Partners[2]

Each partner shall—

(*a*) diligently attend to the business and devote his whole time and attention thereto;

(*b*) Punctually pay his separate debts and indemnify the other partners and the assets of the firm against the same and all expenses therefor;

---

1 The words "and each partner shall have access to and shall be entitled to take copies of and extracts from such account books" are also ordinarily added; but as the right is statutory as provided in section 12(*d*), it is not strictly necessary.

2 For statutory duties (Relations of Partners to One Another), see also Chapter III of the Partnership Act.

(*c*) Upon every reasonable request, inform the other partners of all letters, accounts, writings and other things which shall come to his hands or knowledge concerning the business of the partnership.

12. Acts forbidden

Neither partner shall without the consent of the other:

(*a*) Either directly or indirectly engage or be concerned or interested in any other business or occupation;

(*b*) Take any apprentice or hire or (except in cases of gross misconduct) dismiss any agent or servant of the firm;

(*c*) Lend any of the moneys or deliver upon credit any of the goods of the firm to any person or persons whom the other partner shall have previously forbidden him to trust;

(*d*) Except in the ordinary course of business give any security or promise for the payment of money on account of the firm;

(*e*) Stand surety or furnish guarantee for any person or do or knowingly suffer anything whereby the partnership property may be endangered;

(*f*) Assign or charge his share in the assets or profits of the firm;

(*g*) Draw or accept or endorse any bill of exchange or promissory note on account of the firm;

(*h*) Sign any cheque on behalf of the firm for a sum exceeding Rs. ————;

(*i*) Remit the whole or any part of any debt or sum due to the firm;

(*j*) Except in the ordinary course of trade, dispose by pledge, sale or otherwise any part of the partnership property;

(*k*) Buy, order or contract for any immovable property or any goods or articles for the use of the firm exceeding the value of Rs. ——;

(*l*) Undertake any journey or voyage on account of the firm necessitating an absence of more than ———— days from the head office of the firm.

13. Notice to Determine

After the expiration of the said term of ———— years the partnership may be determined by either party giving to the other not less than ——— months' notice in writing (expiring on any anniversary of the commencement of the partnership) and on the expiration of such notice, the partnership shall determine accordingly.[1]

14. Determination in Certain Events

If either party shall—

(*a*) Commit a breach of any of the provisions of clause 11 and 12 hereto;

(*b*) Commit an act of insolvency; or

(*c*) Become physically or mentally unfit to attend to the business of the partnership; or

(*d*) Do or suffer any act which would under the law be a ground for dissolution of the partnership by the court, then and in any such case the other partner may within ———— calendar months after becoming aware thereof by notice in writing determine the partnership and in that case he shall have the option (to be exercised at the time of giving such notice) of purchasing the share of the other partner in the capital and assets of the business upon the like term as are set forth in the next clause hereof in relation to purchase by a surviving partner of the share of a deceased partner.

15. Option to Purchase Share of Retiring, Deceased or Insolvent Partner

As clause 25 of the General Forms of various clauses in Partnership Deed.

16. Dissolution

If the option to purchase is not exercised as aforesaid or if the partnership shall be determined or expire during the joint lives of the partners, the partnership shall be wound up and the assets distributed as provided in the Indian Partnership Act, 1932.

17. Notice

As clause 31 of the General Forms of various clauses in Partnership Deed.

18. Arbitration

As clause 32 of the General Forms of various clauses in Partnership Deed.

IN WITNESS WHEREOF, etc.

---

1 This is necessary if the partnership is to continue even after the term fixed until determined (as provided in brackets in clause 3). If the partnership is at will, Sec. 43 provides for its determination by notice, and no express provision in the deed is necessary for that purpose.

2—Introduction of a New Partner in an Existing Partnership

THIS DEED OF PARTNERSHIP is made on the —— day of —— BETWEEN AB, etc., of the first part, AND CD, etc., of the second part AND EF, etc., of the third part.

Recitals of Old Partnership

WHEREAS the said AB and CD are now and have of sometime past been carrying on the business of ——— in partnership together at ——— under the firm name of ——— (hereinafter called "the old partnership") under a deed of partnership dated the —————.

Agreement about New Partnership

AND WHEREAS it has been mutually agreed between the parties hereto that the said EF shall enter the said business as a partner therein upon the terms hereinafter contained;

AND WHEREAS the property of the old partnership has been transferred and the goods in possession of the old partnership have been delivered to the said AB, CD and EF as part of the assets of the partnership hereby constituted;

AND THIS DEED WITNESSES that the parties hereto hereby mutually agree as follows:

1. Term

The partnership hereby constituted (hereinafter called "the new partnership") will commence (*or*, shall be deemed to have commenced) on the ——— day of ——— and from such date the deed of partnership dated ——— shall be (*or*, should be deemed to have been) superseded by this deed, and shall continue for the term of ——— years;

2. Name

The firm name of the new partnership shall be ———.

3. Capital

The capital of the new partnership shall be Rs. ———— where of Rs. ——— represents the capital of the old partnership and shall belong as to Rs. ——— to the said AB and as to Rs. ——— to the said CD and the balance of Rs. ——— shall be contributed by and belong to the said EF and the said sums shall be credited to the said partners in the books of the new partnership.

4. Interest

As clause 5 of the General Forms of various clauses in Partnership Deed.

5. Debts of Old Partnership

The said AB and CD shall discharge all the liabilities of the old partnership and shall indemnify and keep indemnified the said EF and the assets and the property of the new partnership against such liabilities and against all proceedings, costs, claims and expenses in respect thereof;

6. Profits of Old Partnership

All profits of the old partnership up to the commencement of the new partnership including profits earned but not actually distributed between the partners shall belong to the said AB and CD in the proportions in which they would be entitled thereto under the deed of partnership dated ———;

7. Profits of New Partnership

The profits and losses of the new partnership shall be divided and borne between the partners in the following proportions, namely the said AB ———, the said CD ——— and the said EF ———.

8, 9, 10, 11, 12 and 13 (Conditions about accounts, management, duties of partners, etc., *as in Form* 1 *mutatis mutandis*).

14. Death or Insolvency of one Partner

(*a*) If during the continuance of the partnership any one of the partners shall die or become insolvent, his share in the goodwill, capital and assets and undivided profits of the partnership shall belong to the surviving or solvent partners in shares proportionate to their own shares of property in the partnership or in such other proportions as they may agree and the partnership so constituted shall continue between them under the provisions of this deed so far as applicable.

(*b*) The legal representatives of the deceased or the receiver of insolvent partner shall be entitled to the fair value of the share of deceased or insolvent partner as at the date of death or insolvency in the goodwill, capital and assets and undivided profits of the partnership, including the profits and losses earned or incurred but not actually received or paid, after taking into account and making allowance for current drawings by such partner and any moneys owing by him to the partnership and the current liabilities to the partnership.

(*c*) The said fair value shall be certified by the auditors for the time being of the partnership and the certificate shall be binding upon and conclusive against the surviving or solvent partners and the representatives of the deceased partner or the insolvent partner or the receiver of his estate.

(*d*) The amount so certified shall be paid rateably by the surviving or solvent partners in proportion to their shares in the partnership.

(*e*) All deeds of release, indemnity and instruments necessary to give effect to the provisions of this clause shall be executed by the parties requisite and all costs of carrying out this clause into effect shall be charged as to one half against the deceased or insolvent partner and as to the remaining half against the surviving or solvent partners.

16, 17 and 18 (*Conditions about dissolution, notice, arbitration—as in Form* 1).

IN WITNESS WHEREOF, etc.

3—A Simple Form of Deed of Partnership of a Small Dairy Business

THIS DEED OF PARTNERSHIP made on the ——— day of ——— BETWEEN AB, etc., of the one part AND CD, etc., of the other part.

WITNESSES that it is hereby mutually agreed that the said AB and CD shall become partners in a dairy business upon the following terms:

1. Business

The partnership business shall be that of Dairy Farm consisting of the maintenance and upkeep of cattle, sale of milk, production and sale of cream and butter and such other work as the parties may agree upon and shall be carried on at ——— or at such other place or places as the partners may from time to time agree upon.

2. Term

The duration of partnership shall in the first instance be three years from the date hereof provided that the parties shall be at liberty to extend the said period by mutual consent from time to time.

3. Name

The name of the firm shall be ———.

4. Capital

The capital of the partnership shall consist of Rs. ——— brought into the business in equal shares by each of the partners which sum shall be credited to him as his share of the capital, and such further sum as either partner shall with the consent of the other partner from time to time contribute for partnership purposes which shall be credited to his capital account.

5. Interest on Capital

As clause 5 of the General Forms of various clauses in Partnership Deed.

6. Profits and Losses

The net profits of the business shall be divided between the partners equally and they shall, in like proportion, bear all losses including loss of capital.

7. Management

The management shall be carried on jointly and both the parties shall be active partners. The said AB shall be in charge of accounts and the said CD shall be in charge of the management of the dairy farm, but the parties may by mutual consent allot to each of them such duties as they may think necessary.

8. Work of Partnership

Any work to be done under the agreement or under any subsequent agreement by any partner may be done by the father or other relative of that partner or by any agent or servant appointed by him but the pay of any such agent or servant shall not be debited to the partnership account. Provided that if any partner shall fail to do the work assigned to him or to make satisfactory arrangement for that work, the other partner may do that work or have the same done by his agents or servants at his own cost and such other partner shall in that case be paid Rs. ——— per month as his pay for doing the additional work or having it done and such pay shall be part of the partnership expenditure.

9. Accounts

The accounts of the partnership business shall be taken half-yearly in the months of ——— and ——— in each year and profits or losses shall be determined. Any profit due to either partner may be taken by him or left as part of the capital of the business in which case interest shall be paid to him thereon as under clause 5 hereof.

10. Partners not to do Separate Business

Neither of the partners shall do any separate dairy business or allied business on his own account.

11. Dissolution

The partnership may be dissolved during the aforesaid term of three years if both partners mutually agree to such dissolution.

12. Winding up

At the time of dissolution of the partnership the business will be wound up in the following manner:

(*i*) Out of the assets of the firm, the debts of the firm shall be paid first and out of the balance the capital contributed by each partner will be paid to him with interest.

(*ii*) The balance after paying off the debts and capital with interest will be divided equally between the partners.

(*iii*) The cattle belonging to the partnership may be either purchased by any partner at a valuation agreed upon between the parties or may be divided equally between the partners or may be sold. The division will be made according to the average yield of milk by each cattle, the average to be calculated on the preceding year's yield.

(*iv*) If one of the partners wishes to continue the business alone he can, at the time of winding up, claim the following privileges:

(*a*) He can retain the milk vans and delivery cycles on payment to the other partner half the value thereof less deduction at ——— percent per year from the date of purchase on account of depreciation of value;

(*b*) In the division of cattle he will have the right to take two cows and two buffaloes of his own choice;

(*c*) He will be entitled to have a lease of the other partner's share of such lands and buildings as shall have been used for dairy purposes at the time of dissolution, for a period of six months at such rent as may be agreed upon and if the partners cannot agree as to the rent, then at such rent as may be determined by —————;

(*d*) He will have a right to purchase the other partner's half share in all machines, furniture and appliances at the original cost price less a deduction of 10 percent per year from the date of original purchase in the case of machines and appliances and 5 per cent per year in the case of furniture.

IN WITNESS WHEREOF, etc.

4—Deed of Partnership between Several Persons for Starting Sugar Factory

THIS DEED OF PARTNERSHIP is made on the —— day of —— BETWEEN AB, etc., of the first part, CD, etc., of the second part, EF, etc., of the third part, GH, etc., of the fourth part and JK, etc., of the fifth part.

WHEREAS—

1. The parties hereto have agreed to carry on in partnership the business of the manufacture of sugar at ——— and for this purpose to construct a sugar factory.

2. In pursuance of the said agreement the said AB and CD have acquired land measuring ———— *bighas* situate in plot No. ———— in village ——— pargana ——— district——— for Rs. ———— by a sale deed dated —————.

NOW THIS DEED WITNESSES and the parties hereto hereby mutually agree with each other as follows:

1. The said partnership shall be carried under the name of ———.

2. The total capital of the partnership shall be Rs. ——— which shall be payable by each partner in proportion to his share in the partnership.

3. The shares of the partners in the partnership shall be as follows:

AB..........one-fourth

CD..........one-fourth

EF..........one-sixth

GH..........one-sixth

JK..........one-sixth

4. The land purchased under the said sale deed dated ———— shall remain the property of the partnership and is hereby transferred by the said AB and CD to the said AB, CD, EF, GH and JK to be held by them as part of the property of the partnership.

5. The sum of Rs. ———— paid by each of the said AB and CD as the price of the said land shall be credited to their respective shares in the capital of partnership.

6. The said AB shall do the work of construction of the building, of purchase and planning of the machinery and other work necessary for equipping the sugar factory and putting it in working order and shall be responsible for maintaining the building and the factory in proper order and good repair and in perfect working condition during the continuance of the partnership.

7. The said CD shall be the manager of the sugar factory and shall run the business of the partnership to the best of his ability and shall devote the whole of his time diligently to it.

8. The said CD will have full discretion to appoint and dismiss servants and agents for carrying on the business of the partnership on such pay and terms as may be approved by the majority of the partners.

9. The said AB shall be entitled to 5 percent and the said CD to 10 per cent of the net profits of the partnership as remuneration for their services and out of the balance, 15 per cent shall be kept in reserve fund and 70 per cent shall be divided amongst the partners in proportion to their shares in the partnership.

10. The reserve fund shall be utilized for renewal of any part of the building or machinery of the sugar factory and any balance thereof remaining at the date of dissolution of the partnership shall be dealt with as part of the assets of the partnership.

11. In case the said AB or CD is found negligent in the performance of his duties or guilty of misconduct, he may be removed by the majority of the partners and in case of such removal or of voluntary resignation or death of the said AB or CD the remaining partners may by majority of votes appoint another partner in his place on the same terms or employ an outsider on such pay or terms as they may determine.

12. The partnership shall continue for ten years and thereafter until determined as hereinafter provided.

13. If any partner shall be desirous of selling his share in the partnership he shall offer it first to all the remaining partners and if any partner shall desire to purchase it, he shall sell it to such partner at a fair valuation. In case more than one partner desire to purchase it, the same shall be transferred to them in equal shares. In case no partner shall desire to purchase it, the same may be transferred to any one and the transferee shall be admitted to the partnership on the same terms as are contained therein.

(Other terms regarding accounts, management, drawings, notice, arbitration, death of partners, dissolution of partnership, etc., *as in Form* 1 *mutatis mutandis*).

5—Deed of Dissolution of Partnership between Two Partners, One Taking over the Share of the Other[1]

THIS DEED made on the ———— day of ———— BETWEEN AB etc., of one part and CD, etc., of the other part.

WITNESSES as follows:

1. The parties hereto hereby declare that the partnership between them carried on under the deed of partnership dated ———— shall dissolve by mutual consent as from the date hereof and the said business shall henceforth be carried on by the said AB alone.

2. In consideration of the sum of Rs. ———— now paid by the said AB to the said CD (the receipt of which the said CD hereby acknowledges) and of the sum of the Rs. ———— hereinafter agreed to be paid by the said AB to the said CD, the said CD hereby assigns to the said AB ALL that the share and interest of the said CD in the said partnership and the business, goodwill,[2] property, assets and book debts thereof and other debts and claims of the partnership outstanding against other persons TO HOLD the same to the said AB absolutely.[3]

3. On the said AB paying to the said CD the said sum of Rs. ———— together with interest as hereinafter agreed the said CD shall by a separate deed transfer absolutely to the said AB all his share and interest in the immovable property belonging to the said partnership.

---

1 Such taking over on dissolution of a partnership results only from distribution of surplus assets of the partnership (Sec. 46 and 48 Partnership Act) and is by way of adjustment of the rights of partners and therefore does not amount to transfer of property: *C.I.T.* v. *Dewas Cine Corporation*, AIR 1968 SC 676; *Malabar Fisheries Co.* v. *C.I.T.*, AIR 1980 SC 170.

2 For an interesting precedent in which continuing partner AB agreed to pay to the retiring partner CD a share in the net profits of the business in consideration for the goodwill, see *Devidas Vithaldas* v. *C.I.T.*, (1972) 3 SCC 457. The payments made to CD were held to be in the nature of royalty for licence to use the goodwill and as such were admissible as revenue expenditure for income tax purposes.

3 In such deeds it is also usual to include a clause appointing the continuing partner attorney for the retiring partner for realizing the assets or giving an authority to the continuing partner to realise all the assets and debts, etc., of the partnership but this is, it is submitted, not strictly necessary in view of the assignment by the retiring partner of all his rights and interest in the partnership in favour of the continuing partner which gives the assignee full right to sue (Sec. 130, Transfer of Property Act). In England it is considered proper to insert this clause in spite of assignment because there an assignee cannot sue until he has given notice of assignment to the debtor and it may be difficult to give such notice to all the debtors of the partnership. In India such notice is not necessary to enable an assignee to sue.

4. The said AB shall pay to the said CD, the said sum of Rs. ——— on the ——— together with interest on the said sum of Rs. ——— or the balance thereof for the time being remaining unpaid at the rate of ——— percent per annum from the date hereof.

5. The said AB hereby covenants with the said CD to pay, discharge and fulfill all debts, liabilities and obligations of the partnership and all times hereafter effectually to indemnify and keep indemnified the said CD and his legal representatives and their estate and property therefrom and from all proceedings, costs, claims and expenses in respect thereof.

6. Each of the parties hereto hereby releases the other from all proceedings, accounts, costs, claims and demands in respect of the partnership but without prejudice to any rights or remedies under the provisions of this deed.

7. The said CD shall not during the period of ———— years from the date hereof carry on or engage or be concerned or in any way interest himself directly or indirectly in the business of a ————.

8. Whenever the context so admits or requires the expression "the said AB" hereinbefore used shall include besides the said AB, his successor or successors for the time being in the said business so intended to be carried on by him as aforesaid.

(*For notices relating to Partnership, see under "Notice"*)

IN WITNESS WHEREOF, etc.

RECEIPTS

Preliminary Notes

Definition of Receipt

A receipt is any note, memorandum or writing acknowledging receipt of any money, bill of exchange, cheque, promissory note or any other movable property in full or partial satisfaction or discharge of any debt or demand.

How Drafted

It is sometimes endorsed on the deed to which the payment relates, e.g. payment of rent may be endorsed on a deed of lease or repayment of loan on the back of the bond. Sometimes a separate deed is executed. When money is paid as consideration of a transaction endorsed by a deed (e.g. sale, mortgage) the acknowledgment is usually incorporated in the deed itself. For example, "In consideration of the sum of Rs. ——— paid by the purchaser to the vendor (the receipt of which the vendor hereby acknowledges, etc.)."

The drafting of a separate receipt is also a simple matter as all that a receipt need contain are the amount of money or specification of other movable property received, the date of receipt, the name of the person paying or delivering it and the account on which the payment is made. The name of the person receiving the payment or delivery need not be separately mentioned if it sufficiently appears from the signatures at the end, or it may be mentioned in the body of the receipt.

The date of receipt is usually mentioned at the end or sometimes in the body of the receipt.

When the person granting the receipt is an agent, this should be clearly stated.

Precautions

Care should always be taken that the receipt does not contain any matter which may convert it in any other kind of deed mentioned in the Stamp Act. Otherwise, it shall be chargeable with enhanced duty as such or may even require registration.

For example, if in a receipt for earnest money on a contract of sale of land, a covenant to sell the land is also added, stamp duty will be levied as on an agreement and in Uttar Pradesh the document will require registration.

But there is no objection to reciting any agreement already made with all its terms so long as the writing does not amount to a definite agreement *in itself*. For example, a vendor might say that he has made a contract for selling his land to the purchaser for Rs. ———, and has received Rs. ———as part price or as earnest money, but he should not say that he will execute a sale deed or will sell the land on receipt of the balance of the price, etc.

If a receipt is required to be given under a special law, e.g. receipts for rent of agricultural holding, and the law prescribes a particular form of receipt or any particulars to be mentioned in it, it should be given in such form and should contain such particulars.

Should be Signed

A receipt should be signed by the person granting it, and, though attestation is not legally necessary, it is always safe to have it attested by one or two witnesses. Even if it is not signed, so long as it can be proved by handwriting or otherwise that it was issued by a particular person, it will amount to a receipt issued by such person.

Obligation to give Receipt

A person who makes a payment or delivers any movable property is entitled to a receipt therefor, and if a receipt is demanded and not given the person refusing or neglecting to give the same is guilty of criminal offence, for which he may be punishable with fine up to Rs. 100 (Sec. 65, Stamp Act).

Stamp Duty

If the amount of money paid or value of the property delivered does not exceed Rs.5000, no stamp duty is payable, but if it exceeds Rs. 5000, stamp duty, of one rupee is payable (Article 53). The duty is payable by the person executing the receipt (Sec. 29).

Cancellation of Stamp

The adhesive stamp should be cancelled by the person affixing it, or by the person executing the receipt, by writing on or across the stamp his name or initials with the date of his so writing, or in any other effectual manner, so that the stamp cannot be used again. If the stamp is not cancelled, the receipt will be deemed to be unstamped (Sec. 12). An unstamped receipt can be admitted in evidence only on payment of a penalty (Sec. 35).

Registration

If a receipt is for money paid on account of the creation, declaration, assignment, limitation, or extinction, of any right, title or interest, whether vested or contingent, of the value of Rs. 100 or upwards, to or in immovable property, registration is compulsory [Sec. 17(1)(*c*)]; otherwise a receipt does not require registration. A receipt for part of the debt does not require registration as it does not extinguish the mortgage. But full payment of a mortgage debt also does not require registration, if the receipt *does not purport to extinguish the mortgage*, section 17(2)(xi) Registration Act (even though it may evidence payment, the effect of which is to extinguish the mortgage).[1] Care should therefore be taken to say nothing in the receipt which might be taken as purporting to extinguish the mortgage, e.g. the statement that "I will return the mortgage deed"[2] *or*, "I have now ceased to have any right to field No. 172 under the mortgage-deed."[3]

---

1 See discussion in *Totaram Jawaharlal Kalwar* v. *Harishchandra Harkisan Raje Khatri*, AIR 1937 Nag 402; MANU/NA/0235/1936.

2 *Jwala Prasad* v. *Mohan Lal*, AIR 1926 All 693.

3 *Totaram Jawaharlal Kalwar* v. *Harichandra Harkisan Raje Khatri*, AIR 1937 Nag 402; MANU/NA/0235/1936.

PRECEDENTS

1—Receipt of a Bond Debt

Received this ———— day ———— from AB, etc., (*name and address*) the sum of Rupees Two thousand (Rs. 2,000) on account of principal and interest due to me under the bond dated the ————.

(*Affix stamp and write signature and date across it).*

Or

I, CD, etc., (*name and address*) hereby acknowledge to have received from AB, etc., this day of ———— the sum of Rs. ———— (*words and figures*) on account of, etc., (*as in Form* 1)

2—Receipt for Balance of Account

Received this day from AB, etc., the sum of Rs. ———— (*words and figures*) being the balance of account due from him to me at this date.

3—General Receipt in Full

Received this day from AB, etc., the sum of Rs. ———— (*words and figures*) in full discharge of all claims which I have against him up to date.

4—Receipt of Mortgage Money

(*See under mortgage: General forms: "Consideration, Receipt"*).

5—Receipt for Part Payment of a Loan

Received, etc., (*as in above Forms*) on account of payment in part of the debt due to me under the bond dated ————.

6—Receipt for Payment of an Instalment

Received, etc., (*as in other Forms*) on account of the instalment due under the bond dated ———— on the ———— day of ————.

7—Receipt for Rent

Received, etc., (*as in other Forms*) on account of rent of the house situate in ———— for the month of ———— besides the sum of Rs. ———— on account of water tax.

8—Receipt by Agent

Received this day from AB, etc., the sum of Rs. ——— on account of rent of a house situate in ——— for the month of ——— due to CD, etc.

Dated ——— (Signed) ———

Agent for the said CD

9—Receipt for Price or Part of Price of Goods to be Made and Delivered

Received this day from AB, etc., the sum of Rs. ——— the price (*or*, on account of price) of three tables and one chest of drawers to be built by me as per specification dated the ——— and to be delivered to him on or before the ——— (*or*, on receipt of Rs. ——— on account of the balance of the price).

10—Receipt for Earnest Money for Sale of a House (with Recitals about Agreement to Sell)

WHEREAS I, AB, etc., have agreed to sell to CD, etc., my house situate at ——— for Rs. ——— and have agreed to receive Rs. ——— as earnest money and it has been agreed that the balance of the price shall be paid and the sale deed executed on or before the———. Now, I hereby acknowledge receipt of the said sum of Rs. ——— as earnest money.

11—Receipt Endorsed on a Bond

Received this day from the within named CD, Rs. ——— on account of (*or*, towards part payment of) the debt due under the within written bond (*or*, on account of interest due to me under the within written bond on the ———).

12—Receipt Signed by the Payer and Payee[1]

The within named CD has paid and the within named AB has received this day Rs. ——— towards, etc.

(Signed) CD (Signed) AB

1 Signature of payer is sometimes obtained with a view to extending the period of limitation under Sec. 19 of the Limitation Act, 1963.

13—Receipt of a Debt

Borrowed and received from CD, etc., today the sum of Rs. ——— repayable within ——— years with interest at ——— percent per annum.

14—Receipt for Money Paid on Account of Work to be Done

Received this day from CD, etc., Rs. ——— on account of cost of repairs to be carried by me to the house of the said CD as per my estimate dated the ———.

15—Receipt for Price of a Watch with a Warranty

Received this day from AB, etc., Rs. ——— the price of a gold watch warranted by us to keep correct time within two minutes per week for twelve calendar months from this date.

for GD & Co.

Dated ———

(Sd.) CDF

16—Receipt of Title Deeds by Mortgagor from Mortgagee

I, AB, etc., hereby acknowledge that I have this day received from CD, etc., all the documents of title relating to the ——— (*describe the property*) mortgaged by me to the said CD by a deed of mortgage dated ——— which mortgage I have this day paid off.

17—Receipt by a Legatee with full Discharge to the Executor

Received this day from AB, etc., executor of the Will of my late father XY the sum of Rs. ——— being my share of proceeds of the property of the said XY AND having carefully examined the accounts of the said executor with the vouchers, I hereby approve the same and accept the above-mentioned sum in full satisfaction of all my claims against the said AB on account of property of the said XY.

RECTIFICATION AND MODIFICATION OF DEEDS

Preliminary Note

Sometimes accidental mistakes crop up in a deed which require to be corrected, or the parties may agree to modify or vary the terms of any previous deed, e.g. to reduce the rate of interest or to extend the period of payment or to extend the period of performance of contract. In all such cases, the object is achieved by entering into a supplemental agreement. This is drafted like other agreements. The former deed, which it is intended to correct or modify, should be recited, as also the mistake or agreement to modify or vary its terms. Then, in the operative part, the corrections intended to be made, or the changes intended to be introduced, should be detailed with an agreement that the original deed should be so read and construed as if such corrections or changes had been made. It is usual to add, at the end, a clause agreeing that the former deed shall remain in full force and effect subject to the variations made by the agreement, but, strictly speaking, this clause is not absolutely necessary.

The original deed is called the principal deed and the agreement is supplemental to it. Usually it is expressly stated in the agreement that it is supplemental to the principal deed but this, too, is not necessary.

If the parties to the agreement are not the original parties to the principal deed but their successors, recitals should be made to show the derivation of title.

Stamp Duty

The supplemental deed is chargeable with the same stamp duty as an agreement. However if a supplemental deed corrects a purely clerical error then concessional rate of duty is provided for, in U.P. vide Article 34-A, Schedule I-B, Schedule Uttar Pradesh; See similar provisions in other State amendments.

Registration

If the principal deed was registered, the supplemental deed should also be registered.[1] If unregistered, it will remain inoperative.

---

1 *Durga Prasad* v. *Rajendra Narain*, 49 IA 223, 41 C 493, 21 IC 750; *Dat* v. *Gopal,* 14 ALJ 57; *Tika Ram* v. *Deputy Commissioner of Barabanki*, 26 C 707, 26 IA 97; *Sadaruddin* v. *Chajju,* 31 A 13; *Yegnanaryana* v. *Suppan Chetty*, 52 MLJ 244, 100 IC 54, AIR 1927 Mad 111; *Afsar* v. *Bechalal,* 7 Luck 16, 132 IC 66, AIR 1931 Oudh 286.

PRECEDENTS

1—Agreement Correcting Mistakes in a Sale Deed

AN AGREEMENT made on the ——— day of ——— BETWEEN AB, etc., (hereinafter called the "vendor") of the one part AND CD, etc., (hereinafter called "the purchaser") of the other part;

WHEREAS by a deed of sale dated the ——— and made between the same persons as are parties hereto and in the same order (hereinafter called "the principal deed") the vendor transferred to the purchaser the entire property ——— in *pargana* ——— district ——— and the principal deed has been registered at No. ——— in Book No. ———Volume No. 1 pages ——— to ——— in the Sub-Registrar's office at ———;

AND WHEREAS certain mistakes have accidentally crept in the principal deed which the parties have now agreed to rectify, in the manner hereinafter appearing.

NOW THESE PRESENTS WITNESS and the parties hereto hereby agree as follows:

1. That the principal deed shall be so read and construed as if—

(*a*) For the word "Radha Mohan Das" wherever the same occurs in the principal deed the word "Radha Raman Das" were substituted.

(*b*) Between the words "the vendor hereby transfers to the purchaser all that" and the words "TO HOLD the same" there were inserted the words "the property described in the schedule hereto."

(*c*) In the schedule to the principal deed for the figure and word "386 *bighas*" shown in the column of the area of the property sold, the figure and word "424 *bighas*" were substituted.

2. That as rectified and modified as aforesaid the principal deed shall remain in full force and effect.

IN WITNESS WHEREOF the parties hereto have signed the agreement on the date first hereinbefore mentioned.

2—Agreement Correcting Two Previous Deeds

AN AGREEMENT made the ——— day of ——— BETWEEN AB, etc., (hereinafter called "the mortgagor") of the one part AND CD, etc., (hereinafter called "the mortgagee") of the other part;

WHEREAS this agreement is supplemental to the deed of mortgage made on the ——— between the same parties and in the same order and registered at No. ——— Book No. —— and Volume No. ——— pages —— in the Sub-Registrar's office at ——— (hereinafter referred to as "the first principal deed") and also to the deed of additional mortgage dated —— made between the same parties and in the same order and registered at, etc., (hereinafter referred to as "the second principal deed");

AND WHEREAS in the schedule to the first principal deed the property entered as item No. 5 has by an accidental slip been wrongly described both as regards its name and also as regards the particulars of rent, revenue and profits thereof;

AND WHEREAS in the Schedule A to the second principal deed in which the same property has been included and entered as item No. 4, though the name of the village has been correctly shown, the other particulars about rent, revenue and profits have been taken from the schedule to the first principal deed and wrongly shown;

AND WHEREAS the parties have now agreed that the aforesaid mistake in the first principal deed and the second principal deed should be corrected in the manner hereinafter mentioned.

NOW THIS DEED WITNESSES and the parties hereto hereby agree as follows:

1. That the first principal deed shall be so read and construed as if in the schedule thereto for the entry at No. 5 the following entry were substituted;

* * * *

2. That the second principal deed shall be so read and construed as if in Schedule A thereto for the figures in columns 6, 7 and 8 (viz. those of rent, revenue and profits) relating to village Mirzapur, the figures "——" "———" and "———" respectively were substituted.

3. That as varied aforesaid the first principal deed and the second principal deed shall be fully binding between the parties and shall have full force and effect.

IN WITNESS WHEREOF, etc.

3—Modifying a Previous Deed by Extending Time for Performance of a Contract (One Party being Different from the Original)

THIS AGREEMENT made the ——— day of ——— BETWEEN the Governor of Uttar Pradesh (hereinafter called "the Governor") of the one part AND AB, etc., (hereinafter called "the buyer") of the other part;

WHEREAS this deed is supplemental to the deed of sale made on the ——— day of ——— between the Secretary of State for India in Council of the one part AND the buyer of the other part (hereinafter called "the principal deed") relating to the produce of the ——— forest;

AND WHEREAS since the passing of the Constitution of India all contracts relating to the property vested in the State for the administration of a State are to be made in the name of the Governor;

AND WHEREAS by clause 4 of the principal deed the buyer is required to convert the forest produce purchased by him and to remove the same beyond the limits of the specially fire protected area by the ——— day of ———, and to remove the same beyond the limits of the forest division and beyond such *chaukis* as may be decided on and recorded in writing by the Forest Officer before sunset on the ——— day of ———;

AND WHEREAS it has now been agreed between the parties to extend the said dates, the former of them to ——— day of ——— and the latter of them to ——— day of ———.

NOW THESE PRESENTS WITNESS and the parties hereto hereby mutually agree as follows:

(1) That the principal deed shall be so read and construed as if in clause 4 thereof "the ——— day of ———" were substituted for "the ———day of ———" and "the ——— day of ———" were substituted for "the day of ———".

(2) That save as varied as hereinbefore provided the principal deed and all terms and conditions thereof shall continue to be binding and in full force and effect.

IN WITNESS WHEREOF, etc.

4—Agreement Modifying Previous Agreement by Extending the Period of Supply of Goods

AN AGREEMENT made on the ——— day of———, etc., which is supplemental to an agreement made on the ——— between the parties hereto and in the same order (hereinafter called "the principal agreement").

WHEREAS under the terms of the principal agreement the said CD advanced a sum of Rs. ——— to the said AB on the terms and conditions therein specified, one of them being that during a term of five years from the ——— the said AB would if so required sell to the said CD in each year certain quantity of wheat of a certain kind and that in case of default would pay to the said CD as compensation a sum of Rs. ——— for every quintal of wheat by which the quantity delivered by him would fall short of the quantity agreed upon;

AND WHEREAS default has been made by the said AB in the delivery of the said quantity of ——— in the year ———;

AND WHEREAS the said AB has represented that the said default was due to circumstances beyond his control and requested the said CD that the term of the principal agreement be extended by two years;

AND WHEREAS the said CD has agreed to grant extension of the term of the principal agreement as prayed by the said AB and the parties have agreed that the said extension should be secured by a supplemental agreement modifying the principal agreement;

NOW THESE PRESENTS WITNESS and the parties hereto hereby agree as follows:

1. That clause ——— of the principal agreement shall be so read and construed as if for the words "five years" the word "seven years" were substituted.

2. That as varied and modified as aforesaid the principal agreement shall remain fully binding on the parties and of full force and effect.

IN WITNESS WHEREOF, etc.

5—Supplementary Agreement Varying Rate of Interest on a Mortgage Debt and the Time of Payment

(See Precedents Nos. 42 and 43 under MORTGAGE).

RELEASE, RELINQUISHMENT, DISCLAIMER[1]

Preliminary Note

A deed of Release is an instrument whereby a person renounces a claim upon another person or against a specified property. A release deed can only feed title but cannot transfer title.[2] Release must be in favour of a person, who had already title to the estate, the effect of which is only to enlarge the right. Release does not vest in a person a title where it did not exist. [3] However, a deed called a deed of release can, by using words of sufficient amplitude, transfer title to one having no title before the transfer. In *Kuppuswamy Chettiar* v. *A.S.P.A. Arumugam Chettiar*, [4] the Apex Court observed that release was without any consideration. But property may be transferred without consideration. Such a transfer is a gift.

When considered from the point of view of the releasor, it may be said to be a "relinquishment", as the releasor relinquishes a certain right which he has or may be, entitled to enforce.

When considered from the point of view of the person in whose favour the transaction operates, it is a "release" as it releases him or his property from an obligation or a liability.

The deeds in the nature of Release, Relinquishment or even disclaimer are ordinarily executed by an ostensible owner like a *benamidar* in favour of the real owner or by two or more contesting claimants to the same property,[5] or by a Hindu widow surrendering her widow's estate in favour of next reversioner,[6] or even by a Hindu son disclaiming any right in his father's self-acquired property[7] or his right to succeed to the property.[8] A minor is not competent to release his share in property.[9] A Hindu father by executing a deed of release in favour of his sons

---

1 See also DECLARATION, *ante*.

2 *Hutchi Gowder* v. *Bheema Gowder*, MANU/TN/0466/1959; (1959) 2 MLJ 324.

3 *S.P. Chinnathambiar* v. *V.R.P. Chinnathambiar*, AIR 1954 Mad 5, MANU/TN/0085/1954.

4 AIR 1967 SC 1395, MANU/SC/0211/1966.

5 *Jiban Kunwar* v. *Gobind Das*, 38 All 56 F.B.

6 *Jwala Bank Ltd.* v. *Sheobodh Chandra Banerji*, AIR 1947 All 104.

7 *Rajagopala Pillai* v. *Pakkiam Ammal*, (1976) 1 SCC 299, AIR 1975 SC 895.

8 *Chinnathayi* v. *Kulasekhara*, AIR 1952 SC 29.

9 *Wali Singh* v. *Sohan Singh*, AIR 1954 SC 263; See also, *S. Shanmugam Pillai* v. *K. Shanmugam*, AIR 1972 SC 2069, (1973)2 SCC 312 on rectification by minor on attaining majority.

may abandon his rights in his self-acquired property and impress it with the character of joint family property.[1]

It is a well settled rule of interpretation of deeds of release that however wide and general the covenant of release may be, its operation must be restricted to the rights which are in contemplation or in controversy between the parties and would not cover or comprehend rights which were not in the minds of the parties at that time. The general words of a release are limited to that thing or those things which were specially in the contemplation of the parties at the time when the release was given, though they were not mentioned in the recitals.[2] The deed has to be construed strictly consistent with its contents and the purpose thereof.

Thus if what was released was right in a Hindu father's self-acquired property it would not operate in respect of that property which the father subsequently threw into joint family hotchpotch. Likewise if what was surrendered was right to succeed to a certain estate as heir it could not amount to renunciation of the executant's contingent right of succeeding to it by survivorship as and when occasion arose.[3]

A deed of release should be drafted either simply as a deed poll, or as a deed to which both the releasor as well as the person in whose favour the release is made are made parties. A deed of release should be drafted generally in the same form as deeds of transfer. However if a deed is bilateral it may be construed to be a gift, while a unilateral release cannot amount to a gift.[4]

Parties

All persons interested, whether as beneficiaries, or as trustees, or otherwise, in the subject of the release should, as a general rule, be made parties to the deed and should execute the deed. When there are several co-promisees (as co-mortgagees, co-partners, co-sharers), all must join in giving a release.

Recitals

The recitals in a release should show fully and precisely the circumstances upon which the release is based. This is necessary as the general words of release will be controlled by the recitals.

Consideration

Unless there is a definite monetary consideration (in which case the same should be stated, and its receipt should be acknowledged), it is usual to express a release as made in consideration "of the premises", *i.e.* of the facts stated in the recitals.

---

1 *Rajagopala*, supra.

2 Norton on Deeds (II Edn.) p. 206 rel. on in *Chinnathayi,* supra (also relying on Halsbury's Laws of England, III Edn., Vol 7, para 345); *Rajagopala,* supra.

3 Chinnathayi, supra.

4 *Commr. of Gift Tax* v. *Ansuya Sarabhai*, (1998) 9 SCC 194.

Operative Words

No special words are necessary so long as the intention is clearly expressed. The words in general use are "release", "discharge" "relinquish". Release of a person or his property from "all suits, proceedings claims and demands", generally extinguishes all rights of action, titles, conditions, etc., then existing.

Release and Receipt

There is a distinction between release and receipt. A release extinguishes a claim whereas a receipt is simply an evidence of payment.

Release and Gift

Renouncement by one of the co-sharers of joint agricultural land in favour of the other cosharer was held in the undernoted case[1] to be a release and not a gift.

Execution

The deed should be executed by all releasors (co-promisees). If some do not sign, it would ordinarily not be binding on them unless there is anything to indicate that it was intended to bind them. In all cases, in which there is an apprehension that some persons will not execute the deed, it should be provided that non-execution by any party should not affect its operation as against those who execute it.

Several Co-promisors

When there are several co-promisors, a release of one does not discharge the others; therefore, if it is intended to discharge all, the release should be of all the co-promisors, whether they are all made parties to the deed or not.

Stamp Duty

The relevant provision is Article 55 of Schedule 1[That has to be read with Sec.23-A]. State amendments to the Schedule should be consulted.

By whom Payable

The duty is, in the absence of a contract, payable by the person making or executing the deed, *i.e.* the releasor (Sec. 29).

Registration

A release must be registered when the amount of the claim to, or interest in, immovable property which is extinguished is of the value of Rs.100 or upwards [Sec. 17(1)(*b*) Registration Act].

If the release is of a right in movable property, or from a personal obligation or, is relinquishment of a personal right, it need not be registered.

---

1 *State* v. *Alokik Jain*, AIR 1998 Raj 348.

PRECEDENTS

1—Mutual Release by Two Persons

THIS RELEASE made on the ——— day of ——— BETWEEN AB, etc., of the one part AND CD, etc., of the other part WITNESSES that each of them the said AB and CD hereby releases the other of them, from all sums of money, accounts, proceedings, claims and demands whatsoever which either of them, at any time had or has by reason or in respect of (*here state business or matter e.g.*) the partnership of ——— at ——— *or*, the agency of sale of books heretofore held by the said AB from the said CD, *or*, (any act, cause, matter or thing[1].)

It is hereby declared that amount or value of the claim hereby renounced is Rs. ———.[2]

IN WITNESS WHEREOF, etc.

2—Mutual Rclcasc by Three Persons

THIS RELEASE, etc., (*as in Form* 1).

WITNESSES that everyone of the said AB, CD, and EF, does and do hereby release each of the others from all sums of money, accounts, proceeding, claims and demands whatsoever which any one or two of them at any time had or has upto the date hereof against the others or either of the others of them for or by reason etc., (*as in Form* 1).

It is hereby declared (*as in Form* 1)

3—Release by Creditors to a Debtor, Conditional on Composition of Debts

THIS RELEASE is made on the ——— day of ——— BETWEEN AB., etc., CD, etc., EF, etc., GH, etc., (hereinafter called "the creditors") of the one part AND XY, etc., (hereinafter called "the debtor") of the other part;

WHEREAS the debtor is indebted to the creditors in several sums specified against their respective names in the schedule hereto;

---

1 If a general release from all claims is intended then these words within brackets may be used instead.

2 This is necessary only if the amount or value does not exceed Rs.1,000 because beyond that value a fixed stamp duty is levied (see however local amendments to Article 55).

AND WHEREAS the creditors have agreed to accept a composition of ——— paise in the rupee in full discharge of their said debts.

NOW THIS DEED WITNESSES as follows:

1. The debtor agrees on or before the ——— day of ——— to pay to each of creditors who shall execute this deed before that date the composition of ——— paise in the rupee on his debt specified in the schedule hereto.

2. Each of the creditors hereby agrees to accept such composition in full satisfaction of his said debt.

3. If such composition be duly paid each of the creditors hereby releases the debtor from his debt.

4. This release shall be binding and effectual though not executed by all creditors and though all or any of the non-executing creditors may be paid in full.

5. If the said composition shall not be duly paid at the time and in manner aforesaid or if before the ——— day of ——— the debtor shall have been adjudged insolvent then this deed shall be void.

The schedule herein referred to

Creditor's name —— Amount of debt —— Amount of Composition

IN WITNESS WHEREOF, etc.

4—Release of a Bond Obligation when the Bond is Lost[1]

TO ALL WHOM IT MAY CONCERN, I, AB, etc., send greetings.

WHEREAS by their bond or obligation dated the ——— CD, etc., and EF, etc., bound themselves to the said AB for payment to him to the sum of Rs. ———;

AND WHEREAS the said sum has been paid with interest in full discharge of the said bond;

AND WHEREAS the said bond having been lost or mislaid cannot be delivered up to the said CD and EF.

1 If the bond is forthcoming the simplest thing is to return it, but when it is lost or mislaid, the obligor may require a release. If the bond was a simple money bond, a mere receipt of the money due thereon may be sufficient, but if the bond is in English form consisting of a bond and an obligation, a release in this form may be required. When there are several joint obligors, the release in favour of one does not discharge the others (Sec.44 Contract Act). It is doubtful if one of the joint promisees can give a valid discharge of the claims of others [Sec. 45]. A release should therefore be made by all the joint promisees so that there may be no possibility of doubt about it.

NOW THESE PRESENTS WITNESS that I, the said AB, for the consideration aforesaid, hereby release and forever discharge the said CD and EF and each of them from the obligation of the said recited bond for all sums thereunder payable to me or my executors, administrators and assigns.

IN WITNESS WHEREOF, etc.

5—Release of a Guardian by a Minor on Becoming Major

THIS RELEASE is made on the ——— day of ——— BETWEEN AB, etc., of the one part AND CD, etc., of the other part;

WHEREAS by an order of the District Judge of ——— dated——— in the matter of ———— minor, it was ordered that the said CD be appointed guardian of the property of the said AB during his minority;

AND WHEREAS the property of the said AB consisted of agricultural land, house property, movables, outstanding debts and cash;

AND WHEREAS since his appointment as such guardian the said CD has administered the said property diligently and kept correct accounts of the income and expenditure and has with a portion of the income so received purchased Government securities and the rest has been deposited in the Bank in his own name;

AND WHEREAS the said AB has on the ——— day of ——— attained majority;

AND WHEREAS the said AB has now gone through the accounts kept by the said CD and has satisfied himself as to their correctness and the said CD has delivered to the said AB all the title deeds to immovable property and the movable property and cash due to him and has transferred into his name all the securities and bank accounts and has put the said AB in possession of all the agricultural land, house property and has delivered to him all the papers, registers, accounts, receipts and vouchers relating to the management of the said property of the said AB during the said AB's minority;

AND WHEREAS the said AB has agreed to execute the release hereinafter contained.

NOW THIS DEED WITNESSES that in pursuance of the said agreement, the said AB hereby releases and forever discharges the said CD from all suits, proceedings, claims, demands or accounts whatsoever for or on account of the movable and immovable property and cash of the said AB or the management thereof or for conversion, sale, application, accumulation and investment thereof or for or in respect of the rents, profits, income or accumulation of income thereof respectively or for or in respect of any act or thing at any time done or omitted or neglected by the said CD in relation to the premises.

IN WITNESS WHEREOF, etc.

6—Release from Certain Obligations Contained in a Contract[1]

THIS RELEASE, etc. (*as in Form* 5).

WHEREAS by an agreement made between the parties hereto on the ——— the said CD agreed to supply 1,80,000 cubic metres of *semal* logs to the said AB.

AND WHEREAS the said AB has now agreed to release the said CD from the obligation to supply 30,000 cubic metres of *semal* logs out of the contracted supply hereinbefore mentioned.

NOW THIS DEED WITNESSES as follows:

(1) The said AB hereby releases the said CD from so much of his obligation under the aforesaid deed of agreement dated the ——— as relates to the supply of 30,000 cubic metres of *semal* logs.

(2) The parties hereto hereby agree that the remaining obligations under the aforesaid deed of agreement dated the ——— shall continue to be binding and of full effect.

IN WITNESS WHEREOF, etc.

7—Release in Consideration of a Transfer

THIS RELEASE, etc., (*as in Form* 5).

WHEREAS by an agreement entered into between the parties hereto on the ——— and registered on the ——— the said CD agreed on the expiration of five years from the date of registration of the said agreement to transfer to the releasor certain property therein specified on certain terms therein mentioned and the releasor agreed on the execution of a deed of such transfer by the said CD to execute a deed of release releasing the estate described in the schedule hereto from every claim and demand whether by inheritance or agreement or otherwise which he might have for or about any share in the said estate other than the properties agreed to be so transferred.

AND WHEREAS in performance of the agreement hereinbefore recited, the said CD has this day transferred by a formal deed of transfer

1 See also RESCISSION OF CONTRACT, *post*.

the said property specified in the said agreement to the releasor on the terms therein mentioned.

NOW THIS DEED WITNESSES that in pursuance of the agreement hereinbefore mentioned and in consideration of the said transfer, the releasor hereby releases, transfers and confirms the estate described in the schedule hereto TO HOLD the same to the said CD freed from every claim and demand whether by inheritance or under any agreement or otherwise which the releasor may have had at the date of the agreement hereinbefore recited or now has against the said estate or any part of it.

The schedule herein referred to.

IN WITNESS WHEREOF, etc.

8—Deed Declaring that Executant has no Right in Certain Land Transferred to him by his Father Relinquishing all Rights under the Deed of Transfer

AN AGREEMENT made on the ——— day of ——— BETWEEN AB, etc., of the first part AND CD, etc., of the second part AND ——— Bank having its registered office at ——— of the third part;

WHEREAS the said CD in anticipation of the threatened attachment of his property in proceedings for recovery of revenue executed on the —— a fictitious deed of transfer styled a *tamlik namah* in favour of his son, the said AB in respect of lands in villages X,Y and Z fully described in the schedule hereto;

AND WHEREAS the said *tamlik namah* was never intended to pass any title to the said AB and consequently the latter did not take possession or obtain mutation in respect of the land of the said villages and the same are still in possession of the said CD;

AND WHEREAS the said CD executed on the ——— a deed of mortgage in favour of the Bank of the sum of Rs. ——— hypothecating among other property the said lands in the villages X, Y and Z;

AND WHEREAS the Bank having come to know of the said *tamlik namah* has threatened to repudiate the said transaction of mortgage unless the said AB disclaims all rights under the said *tamlik namah*;

AND WHEREAS the said CD has requested the said AB to execute such a deed of disclaimer and the said AB has agreed to do so;

NOW THESE PRESENTS WITNESS that in pursuance of the said agreement and in consideration of the Bank's forbearance to repudiate the said mortgage, the said AB hereby declares and assures the Bank that the said *tamlik namah* executed by the said CD on the ——— and registered on the ——— is a fictitious transaction and does not confer any title on the said AB;

AND the said AB hereby disclaims and relinquishes in favour of the said CD all rights in the said lands in the villages X,Y and Z which the said *tamlik namah* may be deemed to have conferred on him.

The schedule herein referred to.

IN WITNESS WHEREOF, etc.

9—Release of a Covenant in a Deed by Endorsement on the Deed

I, the within-named AB, do hereby release and forever discharge the within named CD and his heirs, executors, administrators and assigns, from the within written covenant entered into by the said CD to, etc., (*specify the act*) (*Or*, not to, etc.,) and from all suits, proceedings, accounts, claims or demands for or on account of or in respect of the said covenant. The value of the claim renounced is Rs. ———.[1]

Dated ———

(Signed) —— AB

10—Release from a Contract for Re-purchase Contained in a Sale Deed, in Consideration of Release from a Debt

THIS RELEASE is made on the —— day of —— BETWEEN AB, etc., (hereinafter called "the vendor") of the one part AND CD, etc., (hereinafter called "the purchaser") of the other part;

WHEREAS the vendor executed a sale deed in favour of the purchaser purporting to sell to him his property in village ——— for Rs. ——— and the said sale deed had been registered at No. ——— in book No. ——— volume No. ——— on pages ——— in the Sub-Registrar's office at———;

AND WHEREAS in the aforesaid sale deed a condition was inserted that if the vendor repaid the consideration money with the expenses of execution and registration of the sale deed within twenty years from the date of the sale deed, the purchaser or his heirs would re-transfer the property sold to the vendor;

AND WHEREAS as the said condition was added to the sale

1 Necessary only if it does not exceed Rs.1,000, because beyond that value a fixed stamp duty is levied (See, however, local amendments of Article 55).

deed after it had been written but before registration, there is a dispute between the parties about its validity;

AND WHEREAS in view of the said dispute the vendor has agreed with the purchaser to release the purchaser of the said condition in the aforesaid sale deed in consideration of the purchaser releasing the vendor and his property from the principal and interest due under the promissory note executed by him for Rs. ——— in favour of the purchaser on the ——;

NOW THIS DEED WITNESSES that in pursuance of the aforesaid agreement, the purchaser hereby releases the vendor and his property from the principal and interest due to the purchaser under the promissory note dated ——— AND the vendor hereby releases and forever discharges the purchaser and his heirs from the covenant that the purchaser or his heirs shall re-transfer the property sold to the vendor on the latter repaying the purchase money with expenses of execution and registration of the sale deed contained in the aforesaid sale deed dated the ——— and from all suits, proceedings, claims or demands for or on account of or in respect of the said covenant;

PROVIDED ALWAYS, etc. (*Interpretation clause*).

IN WITNESS WHEREOF, etc.

11—Release by Lessor of Breach of Lease Covenants[1]

THIS DEED OF RELEASE is made, etc.

(*After names of parties and recital of the lease and also of the covenants of the lease which have been broken*).

AND WHEREAS recently the lessee has committed a breach of the hereinbefore recited covenant of the said lease whereby a right of action of and of re-entry and forfeiture has or may have arisen to the lessor AND WHEREAS the lessor has agreed to execute the release hereinafter contained NOW THIS DEED WITNESSES that in pursuance of the said agreement the lessor hereby releases and waives all right and title of action, re-entry and forfeiture, and other claims and demands whatsoever which the lessor now has or might have against the lessee or any person or persons claiming under or by virtue of the said lease for or by reason of any breach of any covenant contained in the said lease by the lessee AND also does ratify or confirm the said lease PROVIDED ALWAYS that nothing herein contained shall prejudice or affect any of the rights or remedies of the lessor under the covenants, conditions and provisos of the said lease in respect of

---

1 See precedents of LEASE, *ante*.

any future breach of any covenant or agreement on the part of the lessee therein contained.

IN WITNESS, etc.

12—Surrender by a Hindu Widow of her Life Estate to Accelerate Reversioner's Succession[1]

THIS DEED OF SURRENDER is made on the ——— day of ——— BETWEEN AB, etc., of the one part AND CD, etc., EF, etc., and GH, etc., (hereinafter called "the reversioners") of the other part;

WHEREAS the property specified in the schedule hereto of the value of Rs. ——— is the whole estate of XY the deceased husband of the said AB;

AND WHEREAS ever since the death of the said XY, AB has been in possession of the said property under his will conferring on her, only a life estate therein as a Hindu widow;

AND WHEREAS the said reversioners are the only nearest reversioners of the XY and the said AB is desirous of releasing and determining her life interest in the said property in order to accelerate the succession thereto of the reversioners.

NOW THIS DEED WITNESSES that in pursuance of such desire and in consideration of the natural love and affection of the said AB for the reversioners, the said AB as life owner of the said property hereby releases and surrenders to the reversioners ALL that property described in the schedule hereto and all the rights, interest, claim and demand of her husband, the said XY thereto or therein to the intent that the said property may become immediately vested in the reversioners as absolute owners thereof.

The schedule herein referred to.

IN WITNESS WHEREOF, etc.

---

1 Strictly speaking this is a form of conveyance. The surrender should be *bonafide*, of the *whole* estate, and in favour of the *whole* body of nearest reversioners. With the statutory acquisition of absolute estate by Hindu widow under Sec. 14(1) of the Hindu Succession Act, 1956, this precedent would be relevant only in cases referred to in Sec. 14(2).

13—Compromise of a Threatened Claim by Government Relinquishing Land and the other Party giving up his Mesne Profits, with Indemnity Clause against Claim of Government's Lessee

THIS RELEASE made this ——— day of ——— BETWEEN the Governor of Uttar Pradesh (hereinafter called "the State Government") of the one part AND AB, etc., of the other part;

WHEREAS the State Government has been in possession of the market land described in the schedule hereto and valued approximately at Rs. ——— since the year 1988 and has let out the said land to one CD for a term ending with the year ———;

AND WHEREAS AB claims the said land as his property and has served the Collector of ——— with a notice under Sec. 80 of the Code of Civil Procedure, 1908, threatening to institute a suit against the State Government for possession of the said land and for recovery of Rs.——— on account of mesne profits;

AND WHEREAS the State Government are advised that AB has a good claim to the said land;

AND WHEREAS the State Government has agreed to relinquish all claims to the said land and to give up possession thereof in consideration of AB not taking any legal steps in the matter and withdrawing his claim to mesne profits.

NOW THIS DEED WITNESSES as follows:

1. In pursuance of the said agreement and in consideration of the premises the State Government hereby relinquishes, surrenders and transfers to AB all the rights, title and interest that the State Government may have in the market land described in the schedule hereto TO HOLD the said land to AB, his heirs, successors and assigns forever.

2. The Governor hereby covenants with AB that the said lands shall be quietly entered upon and held and enjoyed and the rents and profits thereof received without any interruption or disturbance by the State Government or any person claiming through or in trust for it AND that it has given notice of the cancellation of the lease and of the relinquishment of all proprietary rights in the said land by the Governor in favour of AB.

3. In pursuance of the said agreement and in consideration of the relinquishment and transfer hereinbefore contained, AB hereby relinquishes all claims to mesne profits in respect of the said land for the period from the date of possession of the State Government upto the date of this deed.

4. AB hereby agrees that he will indemnify and save harmless the State Government against any claims by the said CD in respect of any loss or damage suffered by the said CD in consequence of being dispossessed of the said land before the expiry of the term of his lease and also in respect of all costs, charges and expenses which the State Government may incur or for which it may become liable in respect of any such claim.

5. PROVIDED ALWAYS and it is hereby agreed that in each of the covenants hereinbefore contained the expression "the State Government" includes its successors and assigns and AB includes his heirs, successors, representatives and assigns.

The schedule herein referred to.

IN WITNESS WHEREOF, etc.

14—Release of Property from Charge for Maintenance under Wills

THIS RELEASE made on the ——— day of ——— BETWEEN AB, etc., CD, etc., EF, etc., GH, etc., and JK, etc., (hereinafter called "the releasors") of the one part AND XY, etc., of the other part;

WHEREAS PQ the grandfather of the said XY executed three Wills on the ——— day of———, the ———day of ———, and the ——— day of ——— respectively and under the said Wills provided for the payment of Rs.1,500 per month as maintenance to each of his three daughters named RS, TU, and VW respectively and after their deaths to their respective children, and by the said Wills charged the payment of the said amounts of maintenance on the property described in lists I and II in the schedule hereto;

AND WHEREAS the said RS having died the maintenance allowance of Rs.1,500 per mensem allowed to her has devolved on her daughter the aforesaid AB;

AND WHEREAS the said TU having died, her maintenance allowance of Rs.1,500 per mensem has devolved on her sons and daughter the aforesaid CD, EF and GH;

AND WHEREAS the said VW having died her maintenance allowance of Rs.1,500 per mensem has devolved on her daughter JK;

AND WHEREAS the said XY has agreed to sell the property described in list I of the schedule hereto free from all encumbrances and charges:

AND WHEREAS at the request of the said XY the releasors

have agreed to release the said property from their claim for maintenance aforesaid;

NOW THIS DEED WITNESSES that in pursuance of the aforesaid agreement the releasors hereby release the said property described in list I of the schedule hereto from the charge of the hereinbefore recited maintenance allowances created by or under the hereinbefore recited Wills of the said PQ and from every claim which the releasors or any of them have for the same.

PROVIDED THAT AND IT IS HEREBY AGREED that the expression "the releasors" hereinbefore used includes their heirs, representatives, successors and assigns.

The schedule herein referred to.

IN WITNESS WHEREOF, etc.

15—Release of Part of Mortgaged Property from Mortgage

(*See Form* 41 *under* MORTGAGE)

16—Disclaimer by Members of a Joint Family of any Right in the Separate Property of a Member

We, AB, etc., CD, etc., and EF, etc., being members of a joint Hindu family with GH, etc., hereby declare that the property purchased by the said GH under a sale deed dated ——— from XY for Rs.—— has been purchased by him with his own separate money and is his separate property and not the property of the said joint Hindu family and each of us hereby disclaim all rights in and title to the same.

17—Disclaimer of Title by a *Benamidar*[1]

I, AB, etc., hereby declare that the property described in the schedule hereto and purchased by me at an auction sale in execution of decree No. ——— dated ——— of the court of ——— for Rs. ——— was purchased by me *benami* for CD, etc., at his instance and with his money and therefore belongs exclusively to him and I hereby disclaim all rights in and title to the same.

1 Though under the Prohibition of Benami Property Transactions Act, 1988 benami transactions have been banned, a disclaimer of title by a benamidar in favour of true owner will be in order: Cf *Sankara Hali Institute* v. *Kishori Lal*, (1996) 7 SCC 55 (para 5). See also precedent No.7 under SALE, *post*.

18—Disclaimer of Right, Coupled with Relinquishment

AN AGREEMENT dated the ——— day of ——— BETWEEN AB, etc., CD, etc., and EF, etc., of the one part AND the Governor of Uttar Pradesh (hereinafter called "the State Government") of the other part;

WHEREAS the house mentioned and described in the schedule hereto was built by the said AB and was his separate and exclusive property;

AND WHEREAS by a deed of sale dated the ——— the said AB absolutely transferred the said house to XY, the widow of the late GH, one of the sons of the said AB;

AND WHEREAS on his appointment as ——— at ——— the State Government demanded security from the said CD and the said XY stood surety for the said CD and hypothecated the said house in favour of the State Government as security;

AND WHEREAS the said AB, being a member of a joint Hindu family, the State Government were advised that the other members of the said joint family might claim a right in the said house and might dispute the power of the said AB to sell the same to the said XY or they or the said AB might impeach the said sale on any other ground and the State Government refused to accept the security offered by the said XY as sufficient until all the members of the said joint family executed a deed of disclaimer of any right to the said house and assured the State Government that the said XY had a good and indivisible title to the said house;

AND WHEREAS the parties hereto of the first part being all the present members of the said joint Hindu family of the said AB have, in consideration of the State Government accepting the said security, agreed to execute the required deed of disclaimer and to give the required assurance;

NOW THESE PRESENTS WITNESS as follows:

(1) The parties hereto of the first part hereby state and declare that the house mentioned and described in the schedule hereto was on the ——— (*date*) the absolute and exclusive property of the said AB and assure the State Government that the transfer made by the said AB by the said sale deed of the ——— in favour of the said XY was a valid transaction and conferred a good and absolute title on the said XY to the said house;

(2) If the said house be regarded as being part of the property of the said joint Hindu family and the said CD and EF as having a right to impeach the said transfer, the said CD and EF hereby relinquish such right and confirm the said transfer.

The schedule herein referred to.

IN WITNESS WHEREOF, etc.

RESCISSION OF CONTRACT

Preliminary Note

The word 'rescinds' implies an express and unequivocal cancellation of contract. A contract can, by consent of parties, be rescinded and each party is thereupon released from its obligation to perform its part of such contract, section 62 of the Indian Contract Act, 1872. The simplest way of making the rescission is to endorse the mutual agreement of the parties on the deed of contract, or if there is no deed of contract, or it is not at hand, a separate deed of rescission may be written and executed by both the parties. The deed should recite the contract, and the agreement to rescind it. In the operative part, the parties agree and declare that the contract be rescinded. The parties also release each other from their obligations. The deed must be stamped as a deed of release.

Sometimes a contract is rescinded by one party only, e.g. when a contract is voidable at the option of a party, he may rescind it and restore such benefit as he may have received under the contract (Sec. 64, Contract Act). This rule is applied as a rule of equity and good conscience. But the contract must be rescinded as a whole. A party to a contract cannot both avoid the contract and retain the benefit received under it. The rescission of a voidable may be made by communication of the repudiation to the other party (see Sec.66). In such cases the communication may be made by notice, but the rescission must be clear and unequivocal. Upon a voidable contract being rescinded, the avoidance is effective not from the date of rescission but from the date of the original transaction.

A contract may be rescinded by bringing suit for rescission. For rescission through court, see Sections 27, 28, 29 and 30, Specific Relief Act, 1963.

PRECEDENTS

1—Rescission of Contract, by Endorsement

The parties within named hereby mutually agree and declare that the within written agreement be and is hereby rescinded and each of the said parties hereby releases the other from the obligation to perform that other's part of the contract under the within written agreement.

2—Rescission of an Agreement, by Separate Deed

AN AGREEMENT made the ———— day of ———— BETWEEN AB, etc., of the one part AND CD, etc., of the other part;

WHEREAS by an agreement made on the ————— between the said AB and the said CD (hereinafter referred to as the principal agreement) the said AB agreed to sell and the said CD agreed to buy certain quantity of timber of the kind and quantity and upon the conditions therein mentioned;

AND WHEREAS the said CD proposed to the said AB that the aforesaid agreement be rescinded and the parties be released from the performance of their respective parts of the contract under the said agreement and the said AB accepted the said proposal and agreed to rescind the aforesaid principal agreement;

NOW THESE PRESENTS WITNESS that in pursuance of the aforesaid agreement the parties hereto hereby agree and declare that the aforesaid principal agreement dated the ————— be and is hereby rescinded AND that each party hereby releases the other from the obligation to perform its part of the contract under the aforesaid agreement.

IN WITNESS WHEREOF, etc.

3—Rescission of a Contract by One of the Parties by Notice

To

AB, etc.

WHEREAS you induced the undersigned to purchase your proprietary rights in the house situate in village ——— *pargana* —— District ——— for Rs.50,000 on the representation that the same was free from encumbrances;

AND WHEREAS it has since been discovered that the said property is subject to an encumbrance of Rs.15,000 and interest created by a simple mortgage deed executed by your deceased father XY on the ———;

AND WHEREAS the said encumbrance, though now twenty years old, has been kept alive by your acknowledging in writing under your signature the liability under the said mortgage deed in a letter written by you on the ——— to Z;

AND WHEREAS as the undersigned was induced to purchase the property by your false representation the falsity of which he could not detect at that time as he had no occasion or reason to make a search in the Registration office for more than twelve years past, the contract of purchase is voidable at the option of the undersigned;

Now the undersigned hereby repudiates and rescinds the said contract of sale and calls upon you to refund to him the sum of Rs.20,000 paid to you on account of the price of the property. The undersigned is prepared to return possession of the said property on your making a refund of the said price.

SALE

Preliminary Note

Sale is defined in the Transfer of Property Act as a transfer of ownership in "exchange for a price paid or promised, or part paid and part promised" (Sec. 54). Almost all the High Courts in India have held that the word 'price' used in this section has the same import as in old Sec. 77 of the Contract Act [now, Sec. 2(10), Sale of Goods Act], that is, money consideration. It need not necessarily be paid in cash, but must be such as may be ascertainable in terms of money.[1] It may be in lieu of existing debt,[2] or a set-off in a decree,[3] or in discharge of an existing mortgage on the property sold,[4] or in lieu of dower.[5] Even if no part of consideration is paid and the whole is to be paid in future, it will still be a sale.[6] The price is an essential ingredient of sale. If no price is paid or promised the transaction will not be covered by the definition of sale. It is permissible, however, that the parties may agree to get the price determined in a particular manner, or they stipulate to pay the market price.[7] In a case, the property was transferred on the condition that all expenses of the litigation will be borne by the transferee and after successful termination of the case 50 per cent of the value will be paid to the vendor. This was upheld as a sale.[8] In case of part payment of price and non-payment of the balance, Patna High Court upheld the transaction as that of sale.[9]

"Sale" of any kind of movable property, except actionable claims and money, is a transfer by the seller of the property in goods[10] to the buyer for a price, and "price" means money consideration.[11]

"Sale" of actionable claims is treated in a separate chapter in the Transfer of Property Act, as assignment of actionable claims, and this has been dealt with

---

1 *Madam Pillai* v. *Badrakali Ammal*, AIR 1922 Mad 311; *Rajjo* v. *Lajja*, AIR 1928 All 204.

2 *Matta Sura Reddi* v. *Mana Rama Narasu*, AIR 1937 Mad 714.

3 *Thakar Dass* v. *Ram Rakha Mal*, AIR 1937 Pun 287 (Lah).

4 *Alama Chand* v. *Chhajju*, AIR 1923 All 530.

5 *Saiful Bibi* v. *Abdul Aziz Khan*, 1931 ALJ 951; *Ghulam Abbas* v. *Mt. Razia Begum*, AIR 1951 All 86.

6 *Chandrashankar Manishankar* v. *Abhla Mathur*, AIR 1952 Bom 56.

7 *Ram Sundar Saha* v. *Kali Narain Sen Choudhury*, AIR 1927 Cal 889.

8 *Beni Madho* v. *A.U. John*, AIR 1947 All 110; *Unnao Commercial Bank Ltd., Unnao* v. *Kailash Nath*, AIR 1955 All 393.

9 *Raj Kumar Singh* v. *Uchit Tatwa*, AIR 1951 Pat 454.

10 As defined in the Sale of Goods Act: Sec. 2 (7) read with Sec. 4.

11 Sec. 2(10) *ibid.*

in this book also separately under "ASSIGNMENT OF ACTIONABLE CLAIMS, etc.", *ante*. In this part it is proposed to deal only with sale of immovable property and sale of goods.

SALE OF IMMOVABLE PROPERTY

Law Applicable

"Immovable property" is defined in Sec. 3(26) of the General Clauses Act 1897, as including "land, benefits to arise out of land, and things attached to the earth or permanently fastened to anything attached to earth." The only difference in the Transfer of Property Act definition is that it excludes standing timber, growing crops or grass (Sec. 3, Transfer of Property Act).

While trees and shrubs are expressly included in the definition of "attached to the earth" in the Transfer of Property Act, "standing timber" is expressly excluded. This is so because timber is intended to be cut away for commercial purposes, hence it is not treated as immovable property. As for machinery, furnishings and fixtures the question "depends on the circumstances of the case and mainly on two circumstances, as indicating the intention, namely, the degree of annexation and the object of the annexation.[1] If a thing is imbedded in the earth or attached to what is so imbedded for the permanent beneficial enjoyment of that to which it is attached then it is part of the immovable property. If the attachment is merely for the beneficial enjoyment of the chattel itself, then it remains a chattel, even though fixed for the time being so that it may be enjoyed".[2]

"Mortgage debt" is excluded from the definition of "actionable claims" given in the Transfer of Property Act. Its sale will therefore be governed, not by the Chapter dealing with assignment of actionable claims, but by this Chapter and so is the case with the sale of all intangible rights not amounting to actionable claims, and also with grants of *profits a prendre*.[3]

In territories in which the Transfer of Property Act is not in force the general principles of the Act, though not its technical requirements, have been freely applied as rules of justice, equity and good conscience.[4]

---

1 *Hollond* v. *Hodgson*, (1872) 7 C.P. 328 at 334 (per Blackburn J.). Similar view in *Leigh* v. *Taylor*, (1902) AC 157 at 161, H.L.; *Narayana Sa* v. *Balaguruswami*, AIR 1924 Mad 187; *Meghraj* v. *Krishna Chandra*, AIR 1924 All 365.

2 *Subrohmaniam Firm* v. *Chindambaram*, AIR 1940 Mad 527 At 529 (Wadsworth J.), Similar view in *Md. Ibrahim* v. *N.C. Fibre Trading Co.*, AIR 1944 Mad 492; *Board of Revenue* v. *Venkataswami Naidu*, AIR 1955 Mad 620 (FB); *Bamadv* v. *Manorama*, AIR 1974 AP 226 (DB).

3 See *State of Orissa* v. *Titaghur Paper Mills*, 1985 Supp SCC 280, AIR 1985 SC 1293, (Distinction between sale of standing timber, which are goods, and grant of rights in forest land containing timber, explained).

4 *Kadir Moiddin* v. *Nepear*, 26 C1; *Mohammad Abdulla* v. *Mohammad Yasin*, 141 IC 377; *Ratanchand* v. *Smail*, 149 IC 853.

How made

Under the Transfer of Property Act, a sale of tangible immovable property of a value less than Rs. 100 can be made either by a registered instrument, or by delivery of the property. All other sales of immovable property can be made only by a registered instrument (Sec. 54). In the territories where the Transfer of Property Act is not in force a sale may be made in any way, i.e., orally or by unregistered deed but if it is made in writing and relates to property of a value exceeding Rs.100 then it must be registered under Sec. 17 of the Registration Act.

Delivery of property can be made in any way possible according to the nature of property. If it is in possession of tenants, symbolical possession is sufficient. If it is in possession of the purchaser himself (e.g. as mortgagee or lessee), it is sufficient if the vendor, by appropriate acts and directions, converts that possession into that of a vendee.[1]

When a sale is made by an unregistered deed and also possession is delivered, the vendee cannot rely on delivery of possession as a proof of sale, as the terms of the sale cannot be proved, the deed being inadmissible even for that purpose.[2]

Sale is different from exchange as in the former, the price paid is in money; in the latter, it is paid in kind by way of barter.

Contract for Sale

Every sale of immovable property is usually preceded by a contract or an agreement for sale, *i.e.* agreement to sell, which means a contract that a sale of such property shall take place on the terms settled between the parties. It rarely happens that the terms are settled when the sale deed is being written. They are invariably settled before-hand and very often recorded in writing either in the form of a memorandum or a regular agreement, but this is not legally necessary in India (except in Uttar Pradesh, vide U.P. Amending Act. No. 57 of 1976) and a suit for specific performance of a contract to sell or buy land, or for damages for its breach, can be instituted even if the contract is oral. It is however, always safe to have a formal agreement drawn up in writing. This is all the more desirable because the relief of specific performance is discretionary and is not granted unless the evidence and proof of the contract is absolutely clear and certain.[3] Such an agreement to sell or a contract *for* sale (as distinguished from a contract *of* sale) does not by itself create any interest or a charge on the property agreed to be sold[4], (Sec. 54, Transfer of Property Act). It merely creates a right in the purchaser to compel the vendor to complete the sale by a proper sale deed and this right is heritable and assignable. But, if the purchaser under a written and signed agreement

---

1 *Kulachandra Ghosh* v. *Jogendera Chandra Ghosh*, 60 C 384, 144 IC 155, ILR 1933 Cal 411; *Sheik Dawood* v. *Moideen*, 48 MLJ 264, 87 IC 331.

2 *Tribhovan* v. *Shankar*, AIR 1943 Bom 43.

3 *K. Basavarajappa* v. *Tax Recovery Commr.*, (1996) 11 SCC 632.

4 *Ganesh Shet* v. *Dr. C.S.G.K. Sethy*, (1998) 5 SCC 381 (paras 13 and 14).

to sell takes possession of the property agreed to be sold, the doctrine of part performance will prevent the vendor from ejecting him even though no sale deed has been executed (Sec. 53 A, Transfer of Property Act).

Hire Purchase Agreement relating to Immovable Property

Public bodies like housing boards and development authorities often give the less affluent sections of the public the facility of buying houses and shops on hire purchase basis. Such hire purchase agreements are in the nature of agreements to sell, the consideration being payable in instalments, with transfer of possession. When the entire amount is so paid up the agreement to sell is implemented and a sale deed is executed. If the transferee is unable to keep up the payments or to adhere to other terms of the contract he becomes liable to ejectment and the vendor gets the right to resell, the purchaser being liable for any loss on such resale. A precedent of such a transaction has also been given, *post.* (Hire purchase agreements relating to movables have already been dealt with under the title HIRE AND HIRE PURCHASE, *ante*).

How Drafted and its Contents

An agreement for sale is drafted like any other agreement. It should clearly show:

(1) who are the parties to the contract,
(2) the subject-matter,
(3) the intention to sell and buy,
(4) the price agreed and how it is to be paid;
(5) and other terms of the contract.

Parties

The seller must be a person competent to transfer, *i.e.*

(1) he must be competent to contract, *i.e.*, must be major, of sound mind, and not disqualified from contracting by any law to which he is subject, (Sec. 11, Contract Act), and

(2) he must have title to the property, or authority to transfer it, if not his own (Sec. 7, Transfer of Property Act).

The buyer must be a person capable of holding property and not legally disqualified to be a transferee. Examples of persons legally disqualified are officers having duty to perform in connection with a sale (Order 21, Rule 73, C.P.C.).

A minor is not disqualified to be a transferee though he cannot enter into a contract.[1] If the sale has been negotiated and the contract has been made by his guardian or any other person on his behalf, the actual sale deed may be executed

1 *Ulfat Rai* v. *Gauri Shankar*, 33 AIR 657, 11 IC 20; *Munia* v. *Perumal*, 37 M 390, 26 IC 195; Raghav v. *Srinivas*, 40 M 308, 36 IC 931; *Collector of Merrut* v. *Lala Hardian Singh*, AIR 1945 All 156.

in his favour, provided the sale deed does not contain any covenant by the purchaser. Under Hindu Law and also otherwise, a minor's guardian can enter into a contract for sale on behalf of the minor if the contract is for the benefit of the minor.[1]

The names of both the parties to the contract namely, the person agreeing to sell and person agreeing to purchase, should be given. Though, strictly speaking, the terms "vendor" and "purchaser" are applicable after a sale has actually been made, yet they are used both in coveyances as well as in statute, e.g. in Sec. 55, Transfer of Property Act and Sec. 13, Specific Relief Act, there is no objection to the use of the expression "vendor" and "seller", and "purchaser" and "buyer".

Subject Matter

"Subject matter" means the property agreed to be sold. The purchaser should satisfy himself that the property he agrees to purchase is by its nature transferable and its transfer is not forbidden by law. Properties which cannot be transferred are detailed in Sec. 6 of the Transfer of Property Act. The right of a Muslim widow to retain possession in lieu of dower is not saleable.[2]

It is not necessary that the parcels should be described with the same precision as in a sale deed, yet a description sufficient for the proper identification of the property should be given, and in this respect it is always better to err on the side of prolixity than to err on the side of brevity.

Intention to Sell and Buy

The agreement to sell and buy should be clearly expressed. In India, where unilateral deeds are common, the agreement is generally made by the vendor to sell the property and no agreement is made by the purchaser to purchase it. The conduct of the purchaser in taking such an agreement and paying earnest money thereupon amounts to an agreement by him to buy the property, but it is always preferable to have agreement to purchase also embodied in the deed and to have the agreement signed by the purchaser also[3].

Price

The price may either be fixed in a lump sum or a rate may be specified and the total price may be left for calculation at the time of the execution of the sale deed, or it may be provided that the price will be that at which the property may be valued by a particular person or in a particular manner. If a particular person is named, provision should be made for the contingency of such person's death

---

1 *Sri Kakulam Subrahmanyam* v. *Kurra Subba Rao*, AIR 1948 PC 95; *Manik Chandra* v. *Ramchandra*, AIR 1981 SC 519, (1980) 4 SCC 22.

2 *Abdul Samad* v. *Alimuddin*, AIR 1944 Pat 174.

3 *M.S. Gopal Chetty* v. *Raman,* AIR 1989 Mad. 169.

or inability or refusal to make the valuation, otherwise the contract will fall through.[1] A contract, however, for sale "at a fair valuation" is valid and enforceable[2] and in such cases in case of disagreement between the parties or difficulty of a satisfactory valuation, the Court will make the valuation when enforcing the contract.

As required by Sec. 29 Contract Act, the meaning of the agreement should be either certain or be capable of being made certain, failing which it will be void for uncertainty. Hence, preferably, the price should be mentioned in the sale deed itself.

Any contract about the manner in which the price is to be paid should be stated. In the absence of any such stipulation, the seller can insist on the payment to be made at the time of completion of the sale [Sec. 55 (5) (b), Transfer of Property Act, 1882].

If price is mentioned in the sale deed as having been paid but this recital is found incorrect, the sale deed is not rendered invalid thereby; the sale stands and the price is recoverable and is a charge upon the property in the hands of the buyer.[3]

Earnest Money

If part of the price is paid as earnest money the same may be mentioned in the agreement and a separate receipt is not necessary.

Any Other Terms

The insertion of all material terms, both of the agreement to sell and buy, as well as of the proposed sale deed, is very important.

The terms of the agreement usually provided are:

(a) the time fixed for completing the sale, the time and mode of payment of the price,

(b) the penalty for not completing the sale,

(c) the liability of the parties for expenses of the sale deed (conveyancing fee, stamp, registration, etc.),

(d) conditions about investigation of title, if the same has not been investigated before the agreement.

If any covenants are to be entered in the sale deed the same may also be provided in the agreement, otherwise the vendor or purchaser may very well refuse to have them inserted, e.g. an indemnity clause against encumbrances or defect in title.

---

1 *Faith* v. *Midland Rail Co.*, (1875) 20 Eq. 100.

2 *Wilks* v. *Davis*, (1817) 3 Mer 507.

3 *Narain Prasad* v. D.D.C., 1998 AIHC 921 (All), relg. on *Baij Nath* v. *Paltu*, (1908) 30 All 125 (DB); *Sukalu* v. *Punam*, AIR 1961 MP 176; *Motilal* v. *Ugrah Narain*, AIR 1950 Pat 288.

Encumbrances

If the sale is to be subject to encumbrances, the encumbrances should be specified. If it is to be free from encumbrances, that fact should be stated, as the remedy under Sec. 13 of the Specific Relief Act may not be available unless the sale is expressly made free from encumbrances.

Investigation of Title

The title of the vendor should be carefully examined before a contract is made. It is the duty of the vendor to inform the purchaser of any *material* defect in the property or his title thereto of which he is aware but the purchaser is not cognizant, and which the purchaser could not have himself discovered *i.e. latent* defects as opposed to *patent* defects [Sec. 55(1)(a), Transfer of Property Act, 1882].

If the defect is such as the purchaser could easily discover himself, if he had taken reasonable care, there is no duty on the vendor. In view of this law, independently of what the vendor is bound to do, the purchaser should, in his own interest carefully inspect the property and investigate the vendor's title thereto by inspecting village or municipal records, title deeds, etc., and should also find out encumbrances by making a search of the registers in the Registration Office.

Sometimes, it is not considered advisable to delay the execution of the agreement by investigation. In such cases, the agreement to purchase may be made expressly subject to the title of the vendor being found on investigation to be good and the vendor's assertion or representations about the title and encumbrances being verified. In such cases, the manner in which title is to be investigated may be agreed upon and mentioned in the agreement to avoid future trouble and disputes. If this is done, it will be better to fix the period for this purpose.

Sometimes, in order to avoid settling such details, parties agree that the seller should show a title to the satisfaction of the buyer's solicitor or pleader. This does not make the arbitrary opinion of the solicitor or pleader final, but the reasonable meaning of the condition is to claim the purchaser's right of investigating title with professional assistance and of refusing to complete the sale, if the seller's title is proved to be bad.[1] If the seller shows that there was such a title tendered as made it unreasonable for the solicitor not to approve of it, it is sufficient even if the solicitor withholds his approval.[2]

Sometime the buyer agrees to accept the title, as it is, and this is a valid contract.[3] But this condition does not relieve the seller of the obligation under Sec. 55(1) (*a*) of disclosure,[4] or of giving as good a title as he can *e.g.*, by paying off

1 *Hussey* v. *Horne Payne*, (1879) 3 App. Cas. 311, 322.

2 *Apro* v. *Promotho*, 18 CWN 568, 24 IC 452; *Treacher & Co.* v. *Mahomedally,* 35 B 110, 7 IC 669.

3 *Motivahoo* v. *Vinayak*, 12 B 1; *Indra Narain* v. *Badan,* 47 IC 340.

4 *Hume* v. *Pocock*, (1888) 1 Ch. App. 379.

a mortgage unless the property is sold subject to it.[1] Nor will the condition be enforceable if he has no title at all,[2] and a *fortiori*, if he knows he has none [Sec. 17(1)(*a*), Specific Relief Act).

How Investigation into Title is made in the Absence of a Contract

If the manner of investigation of title has not been agreed upon between the parties, ordinarily the vendor should be required to produce his title deeds. If he has purchased the property himself from another, he must be in possession of the sale deed. If it is not forthcoming, a copy can be obtained from registration officer. The title of his vendor should then be traced, a clue to which may be found in the sale deed itself, and, if there is no reference to it in the sale deed, it should be independently investigated.

In this way, the claim should be pursued as far back as possible, and if title of the vendor and his predecessors-in-title for over a considerable period is established, the title is made out. Ordinarily the period of prescription for acquisition of title is 12 years, but as the period can always be extended by the minority or insanity of the person entitled, it is advisable not to be satisfied by title and possession of only 12 years, unless there is a very clear case of a definite and undisputed possession traceable to some title for over 12 years.

In case of property entered in any public register, such as a house in a municipal or cantonment register, or agricultural land in village registers, such registers should be scrutinized, and the names of the vendor and his successive predecessors-in-title should be seen. If any name is omitted, or added the same should be satisfactorily accounted for. When a sale deed is found to have been made by the heir of a person entered as proprietor in the register, it should be ascertained whether such heir was the only heir of that person, or if there were other heirs, what about them and of their shares in the property. This is all the more necessary in the case of Muslims amongst whom property devolves on several heirs in different small shares.

In case it is found that at some stage the property had vested in the Government, it should either be shown as to how Government came to part with the title, or definite adverse possession for over 60 years (under the Limitation Act, 1908, now reduced to 30 years under the Act of 1963) should be established. If the Government's lease in favour of vendor has expired and is yet to be renewed the purchase may be expressed to be conditional on the vendor obtaining the renewal of the lease. It will be a condition precedent and until it is fulfilled there would be no concluded contract.[3] When the land is vacant one and of no present use to the owner, proof of adverse possession is difficult and a purchaser should not be satisfied without proof of actual title.

1 *Goold* v. *Birmigham Bating Co.*, (1888) 4 TLR 413.
2 *Motivahoo* v. *Vinayak*, 12 B 1.
3 *Aberfozle Plantations Ltd.* v. *Cherg*, (1960) AC 115 PC.

In tracing title through successive title deeds or entries in successive registers of property, extreme care should be taken to be satisfied as to the identity of the property as described in the several title deeds or registers. The purchaser should thus satisfy himself that the vendor has power to sell the property. Many cases are coming to light where imposters have duped people by selling property by impersonating themselves as the true owner. Before paying any sum as earnest money the prospective buyer must, therefore, satisfy himself that he is dealing with a genuine person. A physical and close inspection of the property to be purchased is also necessary to see who is in possession thereof and under what right and how the property is being used and can be used.

After satisfying himself about the title of the vendor and his power to sell, the next point on which a purchaser should satisfy himself is, whether there are any charges or encumbrances on the property. On this point the vendor should be questioned and his representation should be embodied in the agreement and the sale deed. As there can be no charge or encumbrances without registration, it is not difficult to find this out by a search of the registers in the registration office. Registers of at least 12 years must be searched, but it would be profitable to search the registers further back if possible, as sometimes there is a period fixed for payment in a mortgage deed, and the 12 years would run from the expiry of that period, or limitation is extended by part payment or acknowledgment. It is always advisable to have a declaration by the vendor about the encumbrances. In places where the Transfer of Property Act applies, Sec. 55 (1) (*g*) provides that it is the vendor's duty to discharge all encumbrances, unless the property is sold subject to them.

Transferability of Right or Contract

A right to buy or sell under a contract for sale is assignable, but, though the assignee would be entitled to enforce the right, yet the assignor cannot relieve himself of the obligation, as an obligation is not assignable except with the consent of the other party. In transactions of sale of immovable property, time is not the essence of the contract. Where, however, reciprocal promise is made by way of a 'concession' the compliance with the reciprocal obligation could be secured strictly within the stipulated time frame.[1]

Stamp

An agreement for sale of immovable property should be stamped as an agreement with the duty prescribed under Article 5 of Schedule I of the Indian Stamp Act. The rate is different in different States due to local amendments and it may be looked into.

In the Union Territories, a conveyance in the nature of part performance as defined in Sec. 53A of the Transfer of Property Act, 1882, has to bear

1 *Indira Kaur* v. *Sheo Lal Kapoor*, (1988) 2 SCC 488.

ninety percent of the duty payable on a conveyance (See Art. 23A inserted by Act 48 of 2001).

Registration

An Agreement for sale of immovable property need not be registered (Sec. 17(2)(v) Registration Act) except in States where there is some local amendment as in U.P. by the U.P. Act 1957 of 1976, and in Gujarat vide Gujarat Act 7 of 1982.

An agreement to sell where possession is transferred to the prospective buyer in part performance of the agreement as contemplated in Sec.53A of the Transfer of Property Act, 1882, is compulsorily registrable, section 17(1A) of the Registration Act as added by Amendment in 2001.

SALE THROUGH POWER OF ATTORNEY[1]

In metropolitan and other bigger cities Development Boards or Authorities have been created by the State Governments for planned development of the cities. These Authorities acquire land to develop and then give on long lease to actual users. Therefore in the lease of land, houses or flats for housing and other purposes, a clause in inserted by which the lessor is prohibited to transfer the property. In such cases many transactions take place without execution of a sale deed between the parties.

The transferor receives the sale consideration, transfers possession to the purchaser and executes a power of attorney and some other documents in his favour. An agreement to sell or a mere receipt for the sale consideration, the receipt itself mentioning the broad details of the proposed transfer, is issued by the transferor. Thereafter because of the provisions of section 53-A of the Transfer of Property Act, the transferee obtains valuable rights by virtue of "part performance" of the contract. Section 53-A is as follows:

"Where any person contracts to transfer for consideration any immovable property by writing signed by him or on his behalf from which the terms necessary to constitute the transfer can be ascertained with reasonable certainty, and the transferee has, in part performance of the contract, taken possession of the property or any part thereof, or the transferee being already in possession, continues in possession in part performance of the contract and has done some act in furtherance of the contract, and the transferee has performed or is willing to perform his part of the contract, then, notwithstanding that where there is an instrument of transfer, that the transfer has not been completed in the manner prescribed therefor by the law for the time being in force, the transferor or any person claiming under him shall be debarred from enforcing against the transferee and persons claiming under him any right in respect of the property of which the transferee has taken or continued in possession, other than a right expressly provided by the terms of the contract:

---

1 See also preliminary note on Attorney, Power of, page 201.

Provided that nothing in this section shall affect the rights of a transferee for consideration who has no notice of the contract or of the part performance thereof."

By the power of attorney the transferee gets right to enter into subsequent transactions of transfer etc. He has got an indefeasible right to defend his possession from the transferor though not against a transferee without notice, (vide the proviso quoted above). The power of attorney being coupled with an interest and for consideration is in law irrevocable.

However, the Apex Court has observed that it is time that an end is put to the pernicious practice of SA/GPA/WILL (Special Power of Attorney/General Power of Attorney/WILL) transactions known as GPA sales. It noted that the observations by the Delhi High Court, in *Asha M. Jain* v. *Canara Bank*[1] that the "concept of power of attorney sales have been recognised as a mode of transaction" when dealing with transactions by way of SA/GPA/WILL are unwarranted and not justified, unintended misleading the general public into thinking that SA/GPA/WILL transactions are some kind of a recognized or accepted mode of transfer and that it can be a valid substitute for a sale deed. Such decisions to the extent they recognize or accept SA/GPA/WILL transactions as concluded transfers, as contrasted from an agreement to transfer, are not good law. It further noted that Transactions of the nature of GPA sales' or 'SA/GPA/WILL transfers' do not convey title and do not amount to transfer, nor can they be recognized or valid mode of transfer of immovable property. The immovable property can be legally and lawfully transferred/conveyed only by a registered deed of conveyance.[2]

The Apex Court clarified that their observations are not intended to in any way affect the validity of sale agreements and powers of attorney executed in genuine transactions. For example, a person may give a power of attorney to his spouse, son, daughter, brother, sister or a relative to manage his affairs or to execute a deed of conveyance. A person may enter into a development agreement with a land developer or builder for developing the land either by forming plots or by constructing apartment buildings and in that behalf execute an agreement of sale and grant a Power of Attorney empowering the developer to execute agreements of sale or conveyances in regard to individual plots of land or undivided shares in the land relating to apartments in favour of prospective purchasers. In several States, the execution of such development agreements and powers of attorney are already regulated by law and subjected to specific stamp duty. Their observations regarding 'SA/GPA/WILL transactions' are not intended to apply to such bonafide/genuine transactions.

Sometimes the transferee also obtains from the transferor a Will. Under that Will the transferor bequeaths the property in favour of the transferee. Such a Will is, however, *not advisable* from the point of view of the transferee as it is always

---

1 94 (2001) DLT 841, MANU/DE/1304/2001.

2 *Suraj Lamp and Industries Pvt. Ltd.* v. *State of Haryana*, AIR 2012 SC 206, 2011 (107) AIC 1, MANU/SC/1222/2011.

revocable and comes into effect only upon the death of the testator.

Although this informal mode of transfer is *not recommended*, specimen forms are given here by way of recognising the reality.

For giving effect to such transactions the following documents are normally needed:

1. Agreement for sale.
2. Power of Attorney.
3. Special Power of Attorney.
4. Possession Letter.
5. Will.

SALE DEED

Duty to Prepare Conveyance

In the absence of a contract to the contrary, it is the duty of the purchaser and not of the vendor, to prepare the conveyance or sale deed and to tender it to the vendor for execution at a proper time and place, and the vendor is bound to execute the same on payment to him of the amount due in respect of the price [Sec. 5(1)(*d*), Transfer of Property Act]. The cost of preparing the sale deed is generally borne by the purchaser but the parties may agree otherwise. In any case, even if the vendor is to bear the cost, the duty of preparing the conveyance always falls upon the purchasers, unless there is an express contract to the contrary.

Points to be Considered before Drafting a Sale Deed

A conveyancer should carefully consider the following points before drafting a sale deed:

(1) Whether the vendor is competent to contract and is not suffering from any disability;

(2) Whether he is competent to sell the particular property. If he is not a full owner and has only a limited interest, he should either sell the limited interest only, if it is saleable, or should procure the consent and concurrence of the owner of the remaining interest;

(3) If the vendor cannot sell, except under certain circumstances or without some sanction, e.g. a guardian, or a trustee, or a corporation, what these circumstances are which empower him to sell, and what are the formalities which the vendor is bound to comply with, and whether such circumstances exist and such formalities have been complied with;

(4) Whether the property, from its nature, is transferable;

(5) Whether the purchaser is a person capable of holding the property;

(6) What is the full and correct description of the property;

(7) What is the consideration and how is it to be paid;

(8) Whether there are any encumbrances, and what has been settled about them;

(9) Whether any particular terms are settled and whether they are legally valid. For example, they may not operate as a restraint against alienation (Sec. 10), or direction to enjoy in a particular manner (Sec. 11), Transfer of Property Act; and

(10) What has been settled about the cost of drawing up the conveyance, stamp duty and registration fee.

Form of Sale Deed

In India, the traditional vernacular form of a sale deed is like that of a deed poll, in which the vendor directly says in the first person that he has sold such and such property to such and such person for such and such price. This is not executed by the purchaser, even though it may contain any covenants binding on the purchaser; and it has been held that the very fact of a purchaser having accepted the deed and entered into possession of the property under it makes all its conditions binding on him; but there is always the risk of the purchase being repudiated by the purchaser before taking possession. The form in use in England, which is the usual form of a deed between two parties is, however, much better and should be adopted. Though it is proper that it be signed by the purchaser also, yet that is not necessary, unless it contains any covenants by the purchaser, or any reservations from the grant (e.g. an easement over the property sold), in which case the purchaser should sign it.[1] As the signature of the purchaser is not, however, necessary under the law, the sale deed will be valid even without its execution by the purchaser. Even if the purchaser signs the sale deed, but does not appear at the registration and the acknowledgment is made before the Sub-Registrar by the vendor alone, the deed is not invalid.

Contents of a Sale Deed

A sale deed consists of the following parts: Description of the deed, Date, Parties, Recitals, (if any), Testatum, Consideration, Receipt, Operative Words, Parcels, Exceptions and reservations (if any), Habendum, Covenants (if any), and Testimonium.

For a detailed consideration of each of these parts, the reader is referred to Part II of the Introduction, which should be carefully read. It is unnecessary to repeat here all that has been said there, and all that has been stated there fully applies to a deed of sale. He should also refer to what has been stated above under "Contract for Sale". It is necessary only to make a few additional observations.

Recital of Vendor's Title

It has been stated in the INTRODUCTION, *ante*, that in a simple case, when the vendor is the absolute owner, no recital of title need be made. In such cases

---

1 See also Preliminary Note under EASEMENTS, *ante*.

it would be advisable to indicate the title of the vendor in the operative part of the deed by describing the vendor as absolute owner thus: "The vendor as absolute owner hereby transfers by way of sale, etc." Its advantages would be, not only to clearly show the title of the vendor, but also to indicate, without the use of words of limitation used in English conveyances, what amount of interest has been transferred to the purchaser, as when it is stated that the vendor is the absolute owner, and the deed does not show that any smaller interest is transferred, the transfer will pass the absolute ownership to the purchaser (Sec. 8). This would no doubt be the consequence even if these words were omitted, but then, if a dispute arises, it would have to be inquired what were the exact rights of the vendor at the time of sale.

Operative Words

The word "conveys" is used in England and is no doubt quite sufficient but, as that word is not used in our Transfer of Property Act, it would be advisable to use the word "transfer", which is simple and equally clear and has been used in Indian statutes. To make the operative words more expressive of the transaction, we might say "transfers by way of sale".

Several Vendors

Where there are several co-owners[1] in a property which is sold, it will be sufficient to say that "the vendors hereby transfer to the purchaser, etc." but it will be more correct, precise, and careful to say that "each of the vendors so far as relates to his own share and interest in the property hereby sold, hereby transfers to the purchaser, etc." This will be all right if the whole share of each of the vendors in the property is sold, but greater care is required where the vendors sell a lesser share then they hold. For example, if A holds one half share and B and C one-fourth each in an estate and they sell one eighth to D, the question will be, out of which shares will this one-eighth share be made.

If nothing is said in the sale deed, and the sale deed is executed in the ordinary terms, the transfer takes effect on all the shares proportionately to the extent of shares, and to give effect to the sale of one-eighth, one-sixteenth share will be taken from the share of A, and 1/32 from each of the shares of B and C (Sec. 47).

If it is desired, that this proportion should be varied, this should be expressly provided in the operative part thus:

"The several vendors hereinbefore mentioned as to their shares hereinafter specified in the property hereby sold, namely, the said A as to a 10 percent undivided share thereof, the said B as to 8 percent undivided share thereof, and the

1 Joint owners are also owners and each of them is, in the eye of law, deemed to be in possession of the every part of the composite property: *Kochkunju Nair* v. *Koshy Alexender*, (1999) 3 SCC 482 (para 10), AIR 1999 SC 2272.

said C as to 7 percent undivided share thereof hereby transfer by way of sale to the purchaser ALL that 25 percent share in the estate, etc."

In such cases the several vendors would be entitled to the consideration also in proportion to the shares sold by them (Sec. 46).

Habendum, when several Purchasers

If there are several purchasers it may be necessary to define the interest which each is to take under the sale. Sec. 45 of the Transfer of Property Act provides, that if the consideration comes out of a fund belonging jointly to all the purchasers, they are entitled to the same shares as they held in the fund, and, where such consideration is paid out of separate funds belonging to them, they are entitled to the property in proportion to the shares of the consideration advanced by them respectively. In the absence of any evidence of interest in the common fund or shares in which the consideration was advanced, the purchasers are presumed to be equally interested in the property. It is expressly provided by this section that these rules are to operate only "in the absence of a contract to the contrary". Therefore, any express provision in the sale deed will override them, and it is necessary that if the purchasers have separate shares in the money paid as consideration, the same should be specified thus:

"In consideration of Rs. 10,000 paid to the vendor by the purchasers in equal shares (*or*, in the proportions hereinafter mentioned *viz.*, Rs. 5,000 by AB, Rs. 2,500 by CD and Rs. 2,500 by EF) (the receipt of which amount is hereby acknowledged by the vendor), etc." If this is done, it is immaterial whether the shares which the purchaser is to hold are not defined in the *habendum*, though it may be better to define them also thus:

"To hold the same to the purchasers as tenants in common[1] in equal shares (*or*, in the following undivided shares, *i.e.* to the said AB, one-half and to the said CD and EF one-quarter each)."

If the fund, out of which the price is paid, is a joint undivided fund and the purchasers are to hold the property not as tenants in common, but as joint tenants as in the case of a purchase by a joint Hindu family, it is unnecessary to say anything about the consideration, and in the *habendum* it is sufficient to name the purchasers with or without the addition of the word 'jointly', thus "To hold the same to the purchasers (*or*, purchasers jointly)."

Words of Limitation

It is sufficient to say "To hold the same to the purchaser absolutely for ever" or "as absolute owner". Even the words "by way of sale" after the word "transfer"

---

1 The distinction between "tenants in common" and "joint tenants" mainly is that the rule of survivorship applies to joint tenants, while it does not apply to tenants in common. Tenants in common have fixed defined shares (See Preliminary Note under PARTITION, *ante*).

in the operative part are not necessary, as "sale" implies absolute transfer of ownership.

Conditions

If there is any condition (e.g., payment of rent, revenue or mortgage amount by the purchaser) subject to which the sale is made, the same should be expressed immediately after and as part of the *habendum,* thus, "subject to the payment of, etc.", or, if there are several conditions, "subject to the conditions hereinafter mentioned" (mentioning the conditions as covenants).

Sale of Joint Hindu Family property

See Preliminary Notes on MORTGAGE page 556, *ante*.

Sale by Government

In all sales of land by Government it is usual to add in the *habendum* that the purchaser is to hold the land "subject to the payment of such land revenue, cesses and taxes as are or may be assessed or imposed on the said land", unless it is intended that the land should always be revenue free and tax free, which is rarely the case. If the condition is not added the right of Government to assess the land to revenue or to impose a land tax on it in future may be disputed by the parties.

Sale of Leasehold Property

In the *habendum* of the sale deeds relating to leasehold property, the purchaser is to hold the land, not absolutely forever, but, "for the residue term of the said lease, subject to the rent reserved by the lease and to the covenants and conditions contained in the said lease to be performed and observed by the lessee".

COVENANTS IN A SALE DEED

Implied Covenants

The usual covenants in a sale deed are covenant for title, covenant for quiet enjoyment, covenant against encumbrances and covenant for further assurance.

In India, in every sale, it is implied that the seller covenants that the interest which he professes to transfer to the buyer subsists and that he has power to transfer the same [Sec. 55 (2)]. It has been held that even if the buyer knew of any defect in the seller's title at the time of contract, still he may, under this implied covenant, hold the seller responsible if he is dispossessed by reason of such defect in title, and may claim either damages or return of the price.[1] This implied covenant

---

1 *Kalka* v. *Namdar*, 1933 ALJ 938, AIR 1933 All 389; *Basaradi* v. *Enajaddi*, 25 C 298; *Mohamad Ali* v. *Venkatapatri*, 30 MLJ 449, 60 IC 235; *Muhammad Ibrahim* v. *Nakched*, 7 ALJ 752, 6 IC 890; *Subharya* v. *Rajagopala*, 38 M 887, 23 IC 570; *Shahu Avdesh* v. *S. Zakaul Husnain*, AIR 1944 All 243; *Deep Chandra* v. *Rukndaula*

amounts to an absolute warranty of title proposed to be transferred. For example, if a seller transfers land as his absolute property and it turns out to be his occupancy holding, or if he sells a mortgagee's interest and it is found out that mortgage was invalid, if dispossessed or disturbed by a person entitled, the buyer is entitled to return of his purchase money or to damages.

Exception

But in a sale made by a person in a fiduciary character (e.g. a trustee or a guardian), no such covenant for title is implied. The only covenant in such cases is, that the seller has done no act whereby the property is encumbered or whereby he is hindered from transferring it [Proviso to Sec. 55 (2)].

Other Implied Covenants

In addition to the covenant mentioned above, there are certain other rights and liabilities of the vendor and purchaser which are, in the absence of a contract to the contrary, implied by the statute (Transfer of Property Act). They are as follows:

(1) Apportionment of Rent between Vendor and Purchaser

In the absence of a contract or local usage to the contrary, any rent, annuities or other periodical income which the vendor is authorised to receive from the property sold, shall be deemed to accrue from day to day, and vendor will be entitled to the rent or other income upto the date transfer takes effect, and the purchaser will be entitled to the rent or other income after that date. However, the rent or income will remain payable on the days appointed for payment (Sec. 36, Transfer of Property Act).

(2) Apportionment of Right in Properties sold to Different Persons

If, by reason of a sale or several sales, a property is severed and several portions pass to several persons, the benefit of an obligation relating to the property as a whole shall also pass proportionately to the several owners, e.g. the rent will be apportioned, but if the obligation is indivisible, it shall be performed for the benefit of such one of the several owners as they shall jointly designate for the purpose (Sec. 37).

(3) Duty to Deliver Possession

The vendor is bound to give, on being so required, the purchaser or his nominee, such possession of the property as its nature admits [Sec. 55(1)(*f*)].

In case of a share in joint property, no actual delivery of possession is possible, but the purchaser acquires the right of joint possession or joint enjoyment as his vendor enjoyed and a right to demand partition.

Shamsher Jang Nawab Mohammad Sajjad Ali Khan, AIR 1951 All 93 (FB); *Shanker Lal* v. *Jethmal*, AIR 1961 Raj 196; *Dr. Gwasha Lal* v. *Karter Singh*, AIR 1961 JK 66.

If the share is a share in a dwelling house belonging to an undivided family, the purchaser will not be entitled to joint possession (Sec. 44, second paragraph).

In *Hardeo Rai* v. *Sakuntala Devi*,[1] Hon'ble Apex Court observed that even a coparcenary interest can be transferred subject to the condition that the purchaser without the consent of his other coparceners cannot get possession. He acquires a right to sue for partition.

(4) To Pay Rent

All public charges and rents are to be paid by the vendor upto the date the property passes to the purchaser and by the purchaser thereafter [Secs. 55(1)(*g*) and 55(5)(*d*)].

(5) To Discharge Encumbrances

If the property is sold free from encumbrances, the vendor is to discharge the encumbrances, and pay interest; if it is sold subject to encumbrances, the purchaser is to discharge the encumbrances, and pay interest after the date of passing of ownership in the property to him [Secs. 55(1)(*g*) and 55(5)(*d*)].

(6) Title Deeds

The vendor is bound, on payment of price by the purchaser, to deliver to the purchaser all title deeds, unless the vendor retains any part of the property comprised in the title deeds, in which case he is entitled to retain the title deeds, or, where the property is sold to different purchasers, in which case the title deeds are retained by the purchaser of the lot of greatest value [Sec. 53(3)].

(7) To Produce Title Deeds

The seller, or the purchaser of the lot of the greatest value retaining the title deeds is bound to produce them and to furnish copies to the purchaser at the latter's cost [Sec. 55(3)].

(8) Charge for Unpaid Price

The vendor is entitled to a charge on the property in the hands of the purchaser for any unpaid purchase money, and for interest on the same, from the date on which possession has been delivered to the purchaser [Sec. 55(4)(*b*)].

(9) Right of Rents and Profits

Rents and profits of the property belong to the vendor till the ownership of the property passes to the purchaser, and thereafter to the purchaser [Secs. 55(4)(*a*), 55(6)(*a*)].

1 (2008) 7 SCC 46.

(10) Right to Increase in Value

Any increase in value of the property, after ownership has passed to the purchaser, belongs to the Purchaser [Sec. 55(6)(*a*)].

(11) Charge for Price Paid and Earnest Money

Unless the purchaser has improperly declined to accept delivery, he is entitled to a charge on the property for the amount of any purchase money paid by him and for interest on such amount, and, when he properly declines to accept delivery, also for earnest money and for cost of a suit for specific performance, if awarded [Sec.55(6)(*b*)].

(12) Further Assurances: Rights of Purchaser or Lessee against person with no title or imperfect title

Where a person contracts to sell or let certain immovable property haying no title or only an imperfect title, and the vendor or lessor subsequently acquires any interest in the property, the purchaser or lessee may compel him to make good the contract out of such interest acquired subsequently, section 13(a) Specific Relief Act. Where the vendor professes to sell unencumbered property, but the property is mortgaged for an amount not exceeding the purchase money and the vendor only has y a right to redeem it, the purchaser may compel him to redeem the mortgage and to obtain a valid discharge, and, where necessary, also a conveyance from the mortgagee, section 13(a) Specific Relief Act.

No express provision regarding the above matters need be made in the sale deed, unless—

(1) It is intended to vary or modify such rights and liabilities as are implied under the above provisions;

(2) The property is situate in a territory in which the Transfer of Property Act is not in force. Although, as the general principles of the Act have been held to apply in such territories also, the above provisions, which only lay down common sense principles, will apply, yet in order to be on the safe side an express provision about any matter on which the parties intend to stipulate may be inserted.

It would thus appear that in a simple deed of sale no covenants are necessary where the Transfer of Property Act applies.

Express Covenants

In places, where the Transfer of Property Act is in force, it is, therefore, unnecessary to insert an express covenant for title unless it is intended to enlarge or restrict the covenant or to make special provisions for the case of breach. Such enlargement or restriction of the implied covenant by express contract is permissible, as the implied covenant arises only "in the absence of a contract to the contrary". But all such express covenants should be clear, unequivocal and definite. Though ordinarily an express covenant overrides an implied covenant on the same subject,[1] yet it has been held that the implied covenant cannot be got rid of, except by clear and unambiguous expression, and, in the absence of such clear expression, an express covenant will not be held to be over and above the implied covenant.[2] The express covenant, in order to override the implied covenant, must be on the same subject; therefore a covenant for quiet enjoyment only will not exclude the implied covenant for title. For instance, an express covenant that in case of any dispute arising about the possession of the land, the seller will have it settled,[3] and an express covenant in a sale of mortgagee's interest that the seller will make good any sums found to have been paid to him by the mortgagor,[4] were held to be only express covenants for quiet enjoyment which did not override the implied covenant for title. Similarly, the covenant that in case any person came forward as a co-partner or co-sharer and brought a claim and the property passed out of the vendee's hands or if an encumbrance was found, the vendor should refund the price with costs was held by the Privy Council not to override the implied covenant for title so as to negative the claim of the vendee for a sum larger than price paid by him to discharge a prior encumbrance.[5] Likewise the implied covenant was held not to be excluded in a case where the express covenant referred to ouster by a partner or cosharer while the vendee was actually ousted by a reversioner of a Hindu widow.[6] The High Court held that "in order to exclude the operation of the statutory liability of the vendor, a contract, covenant or agreement must so clearly be inconsistent with the statutory rules as to lead to the inference that it had been made to qualify the generality of the law".

Express provision may be necessary if the seller is to pay any interest on the price, in case the title is found to be defective, or if provision for the refund of the proportionate price is to be made, in case of the purchaser losing a fraction of the property sold.

Although, as in those territories also where the Transfer of Property Act is not in force, its principles apply and therefore, the implied covenant for title will be available, yet it is safer to have an express covenant for title and quiet possession.

Quiet Enjoyment

A general covenant for quiet enjoyment is not implied by the Transfer of Property Act and can, therefore, attach only by express covenant.

Though in case of disturbance by a stranger having a better title than the

1 *Subramania Aiyar* v. *Saminatha Aiyar*, (1898) ILR 21 Mad 69, (1897) 7 MLJ 319, MANU/TN/0090/1897.

2 *Mahomed Ali Sheriff* v. *Budharaju Venkatapathi Raju*, (1920) 39 MLJ 449, MANU/TN/0097/1920.

3 *Raghava Aiyangar* v. *Samachariar*, 1914 MWN 57, 22 IC 42.

4 *Bala Gurumurthy* v. *Ramakrishna*, 41 MLJ 267, 69 IC 473, AIR 1921 Mad 277.

5 *Bhagwati* v. *Banarsidas*, 50 A 371, 55 IC 135, 108 IC 687, AIR 1928 PC 98, (1928) 54 MLJ 689.

6 *Nand Ram* v. *Parshottam Das*, 145 IC 615, 1933 ALJ 201, AIR 1933 All 203.

vendor, a purchaser can sue his vendor on the implied warranty of title even if there is no express covenant for quiet enjoyment, yet there is a distinct advantage in having an express covenant for quiet enjoyment, and that is in the matter of limitation. An implied covenant for title by a vendor who has no title is broken on the day the sale is made and a suit upon it should be filed within three years of the sale (Article 55, Limitation Act, 1963), and when disturbance actually takes place after six years, the purchaser may find that he has no remedy against the vendor. If, however, there is an express covenant for quiet enjoyment, it is not broken until the purchaser is actually disturbed.

But in order to be fully effective the covenant should be against disturbance, not by the vendor and persons claiming under him, but also against all persons showing paramount title, i.e. against lawful disturbance by any person whomsoever. As regards strangers, a vendor can, of course, covenant against *lawful* disturbance and not against tortious disturbance for which the purchaser has his own remedy against the tort-feasor; but against himself and persons claiming under him he should be liable for *all* kinds of disturbance.

Encumbrances

Section 55(1)(g) makes the seller bound to discharge all encumbrances on the property existing on the date of sale, unless the property is sold subject to such encumbrances. It follows that, if nothing is mentioned in the deed about encumbrances, the provisions of the Transfer of Property Act in Sec. 55(1)(g) and 55(2) will imply a contract that there are no encumbrances, and if there are found to be any, the seller must discharge them. For this reason, it is not necessary for the seller to say that he transfers the property free from encumbrances. But if there are encumbrances, it would be better to provide whether the sale is subject to them and the purchaser is liable to discharge them, or the sale is free from encumbrances and the vendor will himself discharge them. In the former case, there should further be a covenant by the purchaser to indemnify the vendor from any claim under the encumbrances.

An express covenant for title or free from encumbrances cannot be contradicted by oral evidence. Therefore, if there is an express covenant against encumbrances, the seller will not be able to show that the buyer knew of the encumbrances at the time of sale and cannot sue on that covenant, because he would be barred by Sec. 92, Evidence Act from proving the same.[1] It is therefore always advantageous to have an express covenant.

Covenant for Further Assurances

Under a covenant for further assurance, a vendor who has sold a defective title can be called upon to convey such title as he afterwards acquires, even though he acquires it by purchase for consideration, and, can be required to complete

---

1 *Thammineni* v. *Dhavala*, AIR 1945 Mad 205.

the title or to discharge the encumbrances. He can also be compelled to produce title deeds, or to defend his title if any third party assails it.

Section 43, Transfer of Property Act provides that when a person fraudulently or erroneously represents that he is authorised to transfer certain immovable property and professes to transfer it for consideration, such transfer shall, at the option of the transferee, operate on any interest which the transferor may acquire in such property at any time during which the contract of transfer subsists. The subsequently acquired interest does not automatically become included in the sale, but this can only be claimed by the purchaser *at his option*. Therefore, the purchaser may require the vendor to execute a deed of transfer of such subsequently acquired right. Sec. 13(1)(a) of the Specific Relief Act, 1963 makes a statutory provision for this right and no express contract of further assurance is therefore necessary for this purpose, nor for the right to compel the seller to discharge encumbrances [Sec. 13(1)(c), Specific Relief Act, 1963]. Still, a careful conveyancer would consider it safe to include an express covenant for further assurance in all sale deeds.

SPECIAL COVENANTS

In addition to the usual covenants, which are either implied in every sale or are expressly entered, special covenants about any matter connected with the sale or the property sold may be entered into by the parties in particular cases. They are purely matters of contract. The parties are at liberty to enter into any contract, provided the same is legally enforceable at law, i.e. it is not one of the agreements which is void under the Contract Act, or a contract which will not be enforceable under the Transfer of Property Act [Secs. 10 and 11].

Condition Restraining Alienation

A condition restraining the purchaser or his successor from parting with, or disposing of, his interest in the property is void, if the restraint is absolute, but if the restraint is partial, e.g., a prohibition of alienation to a particular class, or a condition not to sell out of the family, the condition is valid.1 But a restraint of alienation for a particular period or time is void, as it is not a partial restraint but an absolute one though limited in point of time (Sec. 10, Transfer of Property Act).

A plot in an industrial estate was sold to an intending entrepreneur by an Industrial Development Corporation subject to the following conditions:

"That the allottee shall start on the said site construction of the building for setting up the aforesaid industry within a period of six months and complete the construction thereof within two years from the date of issue of the allotment letter,

---

1 *Mohammad Raza* v. *Mst. Abbas Bandi*, 7 Luck 257, 36 CWN 734, 59 IA 236, 1932 ALJ 709, 137 IC 321, AIR 1932 PC 158; *Ratanlal Kanhaiyalal Bania* v. *Ramanujdas Ramchandra*, AIR 1944 Nag 187; *Mahamud Ali Majumdar* v. *Brikodar Nath*, AIR 1960 Assam 178.

the plans of which shall be in accordance with the rules made and with the directions given from time to time by the Town and Country Planning and Urban Estates Department in this respect and approved by the Director, Town & Country Planning Department or any other officer duly authorised by him in this behalf. Further, the allottee shall complete the erection and installation of machinery and commence production within a period of three years from the date of allotment of the plot, failing which the plot shall be liable to be resumed by the Corporation:

Provided that the time under this clause may be extended by the MD, HSIDC Ltd., in case the failure to complete the building and commencement of production by the stipulated date was due to reasons beyond the control of the allottee.

The Corporation shall also have the right to call for periodical reports every six months from the allottee starting from one year after the date of delivery about the progress in implementation of the project and if, after hearing the allottee, in the opinion of the MD, the progress is found to be unsatisfactory, he may order the plot resumed".

It was held[1] that the clause was not hit by Sec. 11, Transfer of Property Act as that section is attracted only when an absolute interest is created in favour of the vendee. Moreover such a clause is saved by Sec. 31 read with Illustration (b) thereof. It was further held that the contract of sale in such a case was not assignable without the consent of the vendor.

Restriction on Enjoyment

Though a restriction that the property sold shall be enjoyed in a particular manner is void, yet an exception has been made in Sec. 11 in favour of any direction made in respect of one piece of immovable property for the purpose of securing the beneficial enjoyment of another piece of such property. Such a condition would be enforceable even against a transferee of the purchaser with notice, provided it is a negative covenant, e.g. a covenant not to build or not to do any act (Sec. 40) but, not an affirmative covenant, e.g. a covenant to pull down, when required by the vendor, rooms over a passage between the house of the vendor and the house sold.

Sale of Flats and Apartments: Development Agreements

Various such restrictions on enjoyment of the property transferred are now usually imposed in the case of flats or apartments sold to different persons. These restrictions are for the mutual benefit of the various transferees. Some States have enacted special statutes for apartments (Maharashtra, Karnataka, Delhi, Gujarat, W. Bengal, U.P., etc.) Some aspects of such transactions relating to ownership of flats

1 *Indu Kakkar* v. *Haryana S.I.D.C.*, (1999) 2 SCC 37, AIR 1999 SC 296; Following *Khordah Co.* v. *Rayman & Co.*, AIR 1962 SC 1810.

have been dealt with by the Courts in the undernoted cases.[1] Several systems are in vogue in this regard. One, the requisite number under the applicable cooperative societies law (which differs from State to State) forms a cooperative society which acquires a large plot of land on either ownership or long lease basis. They then divide it into several plots which are distributed among members of the society by mutual consent, and the members then build houses on them. The roads dividing the plots, common spaces, lift, staircase and other amenities including provision for society's servants like guard, liftmen, etc. are agreed upon between them.

Another system is for the owner or developer of the big plot to float a scheme. He undertakes to construct the flats or shops but enters into agreements with intending purchasers in advance and obtains the sale consideration from them in agreed instalments. Here, arrangements in regard to common spaces and other amenities, including formation of a co-operative society as above, are settled in advance by the builder, while the purchasers accept them as part of the bargain. Whatever the system adopted, suitable deeds can be drafted by modification and adaptation from the given specimens of agreement to sell, sale deed, lease deed, power of attorney etc. Relevant State laws on flats and on co-operative housing societies, town planning, building regulations, etc. should be consulted. See also Forms No. 42, 43 and 45(a) & (b), *post*; on development agreement, see footnote to Form No. 24 and 45(a), *post*.

Contract of Pre-emption

A contract of pre-emption is sometimes entered in a sale deed. Such a contract, amounting only to a partial restraint on alienation, is not void, nor does it offend against the rule of perpetuity, if the pre-emptor is to purchase the property at the market price, but it will be void if the pre-emptor is given the right to purchase it at a specified price which is below market price.[2] Such a contract, besides being binding on the parties and their legal representatives, creates an obligation arising out of the contract and is enforceable under Sec. 40 against a purchaser for value with notice or against a gratuitous transferee. However, the benefit of a covenant for pre-emption cannot be transferred [Sec.6(*d*)], because the transfer of such a right to an outsider defeats the very object of the right of pre-emption, namely to prevent the introduction of strangers as co-sharers or neighbours.

---

1 *Ramesh Himmatlal Shah* v. *Harsukh Jadhavji Joshi*, (1975) 2 SCC 105, AIR 1975 SC 1470; *Vrajlal* v. *Jaswantlal*, AIR 1977 Guj 131; *Contessa Knitwear* v. *Udyog Mandir Co-operative Housing Society*, AIR 1980 Bom 374; *Mulshandar* v. *Juvansingh*, AIR 1980 Guj 62 (FB); *CSR Estates Flat Owners' Association* v. *Hyderabad Urban Development Authority*, AIR 1999 AP 61.

2 See 70th Report (on Transfer of Property Act) of the Law Commission of India (1977) headed by Chief Justice Gajendragadkar, relying (in paras 9A, 10, 11, 12, 29 and 30 of Chap. 17) on English and Indian cases.

Examples of Special Covenants in Special Cases

Property subject to Liabilities

If the property sold is subject to restrictive covenants, the purchaser must covenant with the vendor to observe the restrictions, so that the vendor will still remain liable after the sale. In other words, the purchaser must give the vendor sufficient indemnity in respect of the restrictive covenants.

Sale of Equity of Redemption

In a sale of equity of redemption or of a property subject to a mortgage, the purchaser must give an indemnity to the vendor against the claim of the mortgagee.

Sale of Leasehold

In case of sale of lessee's rights, the vendor remains liable to pay rent and to perform the covenants and conditions of the original lease, unless the sale is made with the consent of the lessor and the lessor releases the vendor. The purchaser should, therefore, give an indemnity to the vendor against breaches of covenants in the lease. The vendor should also covenant that he has done nothing to incur forfeiture or to invalidate the lease and that rents have been paid and all covenants performed by him upto the date of sale.

Restrictive Covenants

When a person sells part of his property, and retains adjoining property, and desires to protect the latter from being depreciated by acts of the purchaser, the purchaser may be required to enter into covenants restricting his right to use the property purchased by him in any manner agreed upon. Such restrictions may be for the benefit of the vendor, or, in case the vendor sells his property in lots, for the benefit of the other similar purchasers. Such restrictive covenants are usually called for where portions of land are sold to different persons for building purposes in pursuance of a general scheme of development. It has already been stated above that such covenants are binding on transferees with notice under Sec. 40, Transfer of Property Act, if they are of a negative character, but covenants of an affirmative character are not binding on transferees. (Also see Sec. 11). In case of sales of different parts of a property to different persons, such restrictive covenants may be enforced by one purchaser against another, if—(1) both derive title under a common vendor, (2) before selling the lands now owned by them the vendor laid out his estate or a defined portion of it for sale in lots, subject to restrictions intended to be imposed on all the lots, and consistent only with a general scheme of development, (3) the restrictions were intended by the common vendor to be, and were, for the benefit of all the lots, and (4) both the purchasers purchased on the footing that the restrictions were to enure for the benefit of the other lots.[1]

In *Anil Sen Gupta* v. *Dhirendra Nath Basak*,[2] there was an identical covenant in the deed of transfer in favour of each transferee in the following form:

"To construct his building at least 10 feet off from the road constructed by the landlord and which is at least 15 feet in width and to keep at least 8 feet of land open on each side of the premises and to keep 10 feet land open on the back and altogether to keep at least one half of the demised premises open at all times from any structures thereon and not to plant any tree from which timber may be made in the space reserved as open on the four sides of demised land."

This restrictive covenant was wider than the restrictions imposed by the municipal building regulations. It was held to be nonetheless binding on the respective transferees and to be enforceable by each against the others.

It is, therefore, necessary that, in all such cases, full facts which necessitate such restrictive covenants should be recited and the object of having such covenants clearly expressed. The covenants should also be clearly worded, so as to avoid future disputes. In addition to such covenants by the purchaser with the vendor, a declaration that the purchaser shall be entitled to the benefit of similar covenants entered into by the other purchasers, and that, as regards any lot sold and conveyed, the vendor shall be subject to like restrictions, should be entered in the sale deed.

Interpretation Clause

So far as sale is concerned it is not necessary to mention the heirs, successors and assigns of the vendor or purchaser. The moment a vendor transfers his property, it vests in the purchaser, and the vendor is completely divested of it. His heirs can never claim it back and the purchaser's heirs take it in the ordinary course without any contract of the vendor to that effect.

The necessity of the mention of heirs, etc., arises only in case of covenants. In the case of some covenants which are personal, the personal heirs are bound without being expressly mentioned, but not necessarily the assigns, nor can the assigns of the covenantee enforce them. There are certain covenants which run with the land, i.e. they can be enforced, in absence of a contract to the contrary, by any one in whom the property sold vests for the time being. Such is the implied covenants of title by the vendor [Sec. 55(2), Transfer of Property Act]. In the case of such covenants, successors and assigns are not necessary to be expressly mentioned. Therefore, it appears that it would be only in rare case that the mention

---

1 See in this connection *Venkiah* v. *Krishnamoorthy*, (1915) 38 M. 141; *Cooveryi* v. *Bhianji*, (1880) 6 B 528; *Torbay Hotel* v. *Jenkins*, (1927) 2 Ch 225 at 240; *Chambers* v. *Randall*, (1923) 1 Ch 149 at 156, (1922) All ER Rep 565; *In Re Wembley Park Estate Co's Transfer*, (1968) 1 All ER 457; See, however *Bhagwat Prasad* v. *Damodar Das*, AIR 1976 All 417.

2 (1998) 8 SCC 547.

of successors and assigns will really be necessary and they will be bound generally, even if not mentioned. However, it is always safe to make an express provision. This is done either shortly by adding to the description of parties in the beginning the words "which expression shall where the context so requires or permits include his heirs, successors, representatives and assigns", or, by inserting a separate Interpretation Clause at the end thus:

"It is hereby agreed that wherever such an interpretation would be requisite in order to give the fullest scope and effect legally possible to any covenant or contract herein contained, the expressions "the vendor" and "the purchaser" hereinbefore used include respectively the heirs, successors, representatives and assigns of the vendor and the purchaser."

Stamp Duty[1]

Stamp duty is levied on a sale deed of immovable property, not being a sale deed of interest under a mortgage deed, as in Art. 23, Schedule I, Indian Stamps Act.

If property is sold subject to a mortgage the amount of the mortgage will be considered to be part of consideration (Sec. 24, Indian Stamps Act, 1899). If the property is sold to the mortgagee the stamp duty payable will be on the total consideration *minus* the duty already paid on the mortgage deed (proviso to Sec. 24).

In the case of sale of interest secured by a mortgage deed, the duty is payable by the person making or executing the instrument. In all other cases of sale, the duty is payable by the purchaser (Sec. 29).

Registration

It is compulsory if the value of the interest sold is Rs.100 or more, otherwise not.

SALE OF GOODS

Law Applicable

The statutory provisions relating to the sale of goods were formerly contained in a Chapter of the Contract Act. In 1930, a special Act, called the Sale of Goods Act, 1930, was enacted by which the law relating to the sale of goods was amended and defined. This Act has replaced the Chapter on Sale in the Contract Act, but the other sections of the Contract Act governing contracts generally are applicable to contracts of sale of goods also (Sec.3, Sale of Goods Act).

Sale and Agreement

Where the property in the goods is transferred from the seller to the buyer,

1 See also local amendments in Indian Stamps Act, 1899.

the contract is called a *sale*, but, where the transfer is to take place at a future time or subject to some condition thereafter to be fulfilled, the contract is an *agreement to sell* [Sec. 4(3)]. When the time elapses or the conditions are fulfilled, the property in the goods is transferred and the agreement becomes a sale, an executory contract becomes an executed contract. Goods existing at the time of sale as well as future goods, i.e. those which are expected to arrive, or to be produced, or to be manufactured or made by the seller, may be sold. In the case of the latter, the contract of sale operates as an agreement to sell. A reference may also be made to Sec. 25 of the Sale of Goods Act. A seller may reserve a right of disposal of the goods by consigning, them in his own name or that of an agent as a consignee, or by taking the bill of lading to his own order. In both the cases the property is not appropriated to the contract and the seller retains the right to deal with the goods.[1]

For difference between a contract of sale of goods and a contract for works and services see the undernoted cases[2] in which the question assumed importance in connection with liability to sales tax. The contracts were for manufacture and supply of wagons, etc., and their incidents were discussed in these cases.

How made

Subject to the provision of any law for the time being in force, sale or an agreement to sell may be made either in writing, or by word of mouth, or partly in writing and partly by word of mouth or may be implied from the conduct of parties [Sec. 5(2)]. Writing is not, therefore, necessary in any case, whatever may be the nature or value of the goods. Sales are made orally every day by the purchaser paying the price and the seller delivering the goods. Even in cases when the sale is made on credit, formal deed is rarely drawn up. For law on auction of unredeemed pawned goods see the undernoted case.[3]

Agreement to Sell

An agreement to sell is generally drawn up in writing when the property is of large value, or is not in existence at the time of the agreement, though this is not legally necessary.

Such an agreement is drafted like an ordinary agreement. The parties are the seller and the buyer, both of whom must be persons capable of making a contract. The property to be sold, the price fixed, the time and manner fixed for payment of the price and for delivery of property, should be clearly specified, and any other conditions agreed upon e.g. the condition about warranty, and about quality or fitness of the goods sold, should be clearly mentioned as covenants. As to time of delivery, it is always safe to express or to indicate clearly whether it is to be of the

1 *Carona Sahu Co. Pvt. Ltd.* v. *State of Maharastra*, AIR 1966 SC 1153.

2 *C.C.T.* v. *Hindustan Aeronautics Ltd.*, (1972) 1 SCC 395; *State of Gujarat* v. *Variety Body Builders*, (1976) 3 SCC 500; *State of Gujarat* v. *Kailash Engineering Co.*, (1967) 1 SCR 543; *Union of India* v. *C.I. Machinery Co.*, (1977) 2 SCC 847.

3 *Karnataka Pawnbrokers Association* v. *State of Karnataka*, AIR 1999 SC 201.

essence of the contract or not, as the working out of the rights of the parties often depend on that question, and sometimes, when the terms of the contract are not explicit, it becomes difficult to determine whether the parties had intended to regard time as of the essence of the contract or not. Time fixed for payment is generally regarded as not being of the essence of the contract, unless the intention appears from the terms of the contract i.e., there is an express contract to that effect (Sec. 11, Sale of Goods Act, 1930). Therefore, if it is intended to make the time of payment as of the essence of the contract, an express covenant to that effect will be necessary.

Condition or Warranty

A stipulation or covenant with reference to the goods may be either in the nature of a condition or of a warranty. The difference between the two is important. A condition is a stipulation essential to the main purpose of the contract, the breach of which empowers the other party to repudiate the contract; a warranty is a stipulation collateral to the main purpose of the contract, the breach of which gives the other party a right to claim damages, but not to repudiate the contract (Sec. 12). The covenants should be so framed as to indicate clearly what they are intended to be. However, if a stipulation is essentially a condition, it will not become a warranty by the parties calling it a warranty [Sec. 12(4)]. A breach of contract as to the goods being of merchantable quality and the failure to deliver part of the goods contracted to be sold, amounts only to breaches of warranty and not of condition.[1]

Title to Goods

In every contract of sale of goods, there is an implied warranty of title of the seller and of freedom from encumbrances, and an implied contract for quiet enjoyment, just as in a contract of sale of land. The implied warranty is provided by Sec. 14, Sale of Goods Act, 1930 and consists of—

(*a*) in case of sale, an implied condition that the seller has a right to sell the goods, and in the case of agreement to sell that he will have a right to sell at the time when the property is to pass;

(*b*) an implied warranty that the buyer shall have and enjoy quiet possession of the goods; and

(*c*) an implied warranty that the goods shall be free from any charge or encumbrance in favour of any third party not declared or known to the buyer before, or at the time when, the contract is made.

An express contract on these points is not necessary, unless it is intended to vary the above implied conditions.

Other Implied Covenants

The other conditions implied in every contract for sale, besides the warranty

---

1 *Harnarain* v. *Firm Radha Kisan*, AIR 1949 Nag 178.

for title referred to above, are:

(*a*) In a contract for sale of goods by description, that the goods shall correspond with the description (Sec. 15);

(*b*) Where the buyer expresses the purpose of his requirement and relies on the seller's skill or judgment, that the goods shall be reasonably fit for such purpose, (except in the case of a patented article) [Sec. 16(1)];

(*c*) Where goods are bought by description, that the goods shall be of merchantable quality, except that when the buyer has examined the goods, there is no implied condition as regards defects which such examination ought to have revealed [Sec. 16(2)];

(*d*) In case of sale by sample, that the bulk shall correspond with the sample in quality, that the buyer shall have reasonable opportunity of comparing the bulk with the sample, and that the goods shall be free from any patent defect rendering them unmerchantable (Sec. 17).

No express contract about these matters is necessary, unless it is desired to vary the implied conditions.

Rights and Liabilities of Seller and Buyer

The rights and liabilities of the seller and buyer under a contract or agreement to sell are provided for in the Sale of Goods Act, but it is open to the parties to negate or vary them or any of them by express contract (Sec. 62); hence any such contract should be expressly and clearly made and mentioned in the deed of contract.

Power of re-sale in case buyer does not take delivery may be given in any form, and although ordinarily the power can be exercised only within a reasonable time, there is nothing illegal in an express agreement that it may be exercised *at any time,* even after an unreasonable lapse of time.[1] Clause for forfeiture of earnest money on breach of contract by vendee is not invalid.[2]

Trade Usage

Where any right, duty or liability would arise under a contract of sale by implication of law, it may be negatived or varied by express agreement or by the course of dealing between the parties, or by usage, if the usage is such as to bind both parties to the contract (Sec. 82, Sale of Goods Act, 1930).

Stamp Duty

An agreement for sale is chargeable like any other agreement.

Sale deeds of movables are in most States chargeable with the same duty as sale deeds of immovable property, as both are included in the definition of

1 *Ralli Bros.* v. *Firm Bhagwandas*, AIR 1945 Lah 35.

2 *Municipal Committee, Khurai* v. *Firm Kalu Ram*, AIR 1944 Nag 73.

conveyance as given in the Stamp Act. (State Amendments should be consulted). But where the conveyance recites that movables have already been transferred by delivery, they do not pass under the conveyance and are not liable to duty.[1]

Registration

Not compulsory.

1 See arguments and discussion in In Re: A Reference from the Board of Revenue under Section 48 of the Stamp Act, 1879 (corresponding to Sec. 57 of the Stamp Act, 1899) 1895 ILR 23 Cal 283, MANUAA/B/0128/1895.

GENERAL FORMS OF DIFFERENT PARTS OF A SALE DEED

Formal Parts[1]

Recitals of Title

See General Forms of Recitals under MORTGAGE, page 570.

Introductory Recitals

1. Contract of Sale of Freehold Property

WHEREAS (by an agreement dated ————) the vendor has agreed to sell to the purchaser the property described in the schedule hereto (*or*, the property hereby intended to be transferred) free from encumbrances (except as hereinafter mentioned) for the sum of Rs. ————.

2. Contract of Leasehold Rights

WHEREAS the vendor has agreed with the purchaser for the sale to him for the sum of Rs. ———— of the premises comprised in the hereinbefore recited lease (*or*, several or respective leases hereinbefore recited) for all the residue now unexpired of the term thereby granted subject to the rent reserved by and the covenants and conditions contained in the said lease (*or*, leases).

3. Alternative Shorter Form

WHEREAS the vendor has agreed to sell to the purchaser for the sum of Rs. ———— all his rights and interests under the aforesaid lease.

4. Recital where Vendor is not the Original Lessee

WHEREAS the vendor in whom the property comprised in the hereinbefore recited lease is now (*or, where there have been several successive assignments,* has become) vested as estate owner in respect of the said term of ——— years has agreed with the purchaser for the sale to him of his estate in the said property for the sum of Rs. ————.

---

1 See also General Forms (immediately after INTRODUCTION, *ante* page 5).

5. Contract for Sale of both Freehold and Leasehold Properties

WHEREAS the vendor as owner of the property described in the first schedule and as lessee of the property described in the second schedule hereto has agreed with the purchaser for the sale to him of the property described in the first schedule hereto and of his rights and interests in the property described in the second schedule hereto under the lease hereinbefore recited for the sum of Rs. ———.

6. Contract by Trustees

WHEREAS the vendors as trustees under the said Will of said AB deceased and in exercise of the power of sale therein contained have agreed, etc. (*as in para* 1).

7. Contract when both Parties are Trustees

WHEREAS the vendors as trustees under the said Will of said AB deceased and in exercise of the power of sale therein contained have agreed to sell and the purchasers as the present trustees of a settlement dated —— and in exercise of the powers therein contained have agreed to purchase, etc.

8. Contract by Mortgagee under Power of Sale

WHEREAS the vendor in exercise of the power conferred on him by the said mortgage in that behalf has agreed with the purchaser for the sale to him of the property mentioned in the schedule hereto free from encumbrances for the sum of Rs. ———.

9. Contract of Sale with Consent of Another

WHEREAS the vendor (with the consent hereby testified of the said AB) has agreed, etc.; *or,*

WHEREAS the vendor has agreed, etc. (*as in para* 1);

AND WHEREAS the said AB (being the next reversioner of the said ————) has given his consent and concurrence to the said sale.

10. Sale by Auction

WHEREAS at an auction held by the Collector of —— on the—— the said property was put up to sale and at such sale the purchaser being the highest bidder was declared purchaser of the same for Rs. —————.

11. Contract of Assignment of Contract of Sale

WHEREAS one XY contracted with the vendor for the sale to him of the property described in the schedule hereto free from encumbrances for the sum of Rs. ——— but no sale deed thereof has yet been executed AND WHEREAS the vendor has agreed with the purchaser to transfer to him the benefit of the said contract upon the term of the purchaser paying to him, the vendor, the sum of Rs. ——— and paying direct to the said XY the said sum of Rs. ——— at the time of the execution of the sale deed.

12. Agreement to have Sale Deed in Favour of Another Person

WHEREAS the vendor has agreed with the said AB to sell to him, etc. (*as in para* 1).

AND WHEREAS the said AB has assigned the benefits of the said contract to the purchaser and has therefore requested the vendor to execute a sale deed in favour of the purchaser.

(*or*, AND WHEREAS the said AB has requested the vendor to execute a sale deed in pursuance of the said agreement in favour of the purchaser).

13. Agreement about payment of Price by Instalments with Interest[1]

WHEREAS it has been agreed that the said sum of Rs. ——— shall be payable as follows:

The sum of Rs. ——— upon the execution of this deed, the sum of Rs. ——— at the time of registration of this deed, and the balance thereof in four annual instalments of Rs. ——— each on the ——— day of ——— in each year beginning from the ——— day of ——— next with interest on the principal sum for the time being remaining unpaid at the rate of —— per cent per annum to commence from the date of this deed and to be payable annually with the instalments of the principal.

14. Payment Partly to Vendor, Partly to his Nominees and Partly Credited by Purchaser to himself

WHEREAS it has been agreed that out of the said sum of Rs. ——— the sum of Rs. ——— should be paid by the purchaser to the vendor at the time of the registration of this deed, the sum of Rs. ——— should be retained for payment to XY, the creditor of the vendor on account of a mortgage deed dated ———, and the sum of Rs. ——— should be

1 Ordinarily this recital is not necessary as the details of the consideration can be fully set out in the witnessing clause. It may, however, be considered proper for the sake of clearness to have the agreement about payment of the price separately recited, and this would be so when the details are lengthy or complicated.

credited by the purchaser to himself on account of the principal and interest due to him from the vendor under a bond dated ———.

15. Legal necessity to Sale by Hindu father

WHEREAS the vendor is in need of Rs. ——— for the expenses of the marriage of his daughter (*or*, for sending his eldest son XY to the Indian Institute of Technology at ——— for higher education) (*or*, for payment of land revenue due for the year ——— in respect of the land ——— which belongs to the said joint family).

16. Antecedent Debt of Father

WHEREAS the vendor's deceased father had borrowed Rs. —— from AB, etc., on a bond dated ——— and Rs. ——— from CD, etc., on a promissory note dated ——— and a sum of Rs. ——— is now due to the said AB and a sum of Rs. ——— to the said CD on account of the said loans; AND WHEREAS the said AB and CD are pressing for payment of the same and threaten to bring suits for their recovery; AND WHEREAS the vendor not being able to obtain a loan to pay off the said debts on satisfactory terms, has agreed with the purchaser to sell to him the said property for the sum of Rs. ——— in order to pay off the said debts.

17. Valuation of Machinery and Trees

WHEREAS by the said agreement it was agreed that all trees standing on the said land (*or*, the plant and machinery of the said Sugar Mills) shall be purchased by the purchaser at a valuation to be made as therein mentioned and the said trees (*or*, plant and machinery) have accordingly been valued at Rs. ———.

18. Apportionment of Rent of the Property sold

WHEREAS it has been agreed between the parties that the apportioned part of the annual rent payable by the tenant for the part of the land agreed to be sold shall be Rs. ——— and the said tenant has also agreed to this apportionment (*or*, but that the consent of the tenant is not required to this apportionment).

19. Apportionment of Rent Payable on Account of Property sold

WHEREAS it has been agreed between the parties, with the consent of the lessor, that the apportioned part of the annual rent payable under the aforesaid lease for which the purchaser should be liable on account of the property hereby sold shall be Rs. ———.

20. Agreement for Joining the Mortgagee

WHEREAS it has been agreed that out of the said price, a sum of Rs. ———— shall be paid to the mortgagee and that the mortgagee shall join in this deed in manner hereinafter appearing;

[*or*, that the said price of Rs. ————— shall be paid to the mortgagee in part discharge of the said mortgage debt (*or*, that out of the said price of Rs. ————— a sum of Rs. ———— shall be paid to the mortgagee in part discharge of the said debt) (*or*, that the whole of the said price shall be paid to the vendor and the mortgagee shall release the said property from his security), and that the mortgagee shall join in this deed in the manner hereinafter appearing].

21. Sale of Freehold Right

The vendor is the absolute owner of the property described in the schedule with unlimited freehold rights subject only to the mortgages hereinafter referred to but otherwise free from encumbrances.

22. Sale when Mortgagee Joins

The vendor has agreed to sell to the purchaser his absolute ownership rights in the property free from encumbrances for Rs. ———— and B, the lender has agreed to join in for the purpose of discharging mortgages.

Consideration, Receipt

See General Forms (after Introduction) pages 20 and 21.

Parcels

See General Forms (immediately after Introduction) page 21.

Exceptions and Reservations

1. Heading

(a) Excepting and reserving to the vendor, etc.; *or*,

(b) Subject nevertheless to the exceptions and reservations hereinafter contained.[1]

---

1 This form (b) will be suitable where either the exceptions and reservations are numerous or lengthy and detailed, or themselves subject to exceptions and savings, which can be more properly put in as provisos to the covenants containing the exceptions and reservations. In a simple case the exceptions and savings may be added after the parcels and the Form (a) above should be used.

2. A right of way

Except and reserving to the vendor absolutely full and free right and liberty at all times and for all purposes connected with the use and occupation of his house to the west of the said land, with or without horses, carts, carriages and motor and other vehicles, whether used for pleasure or for trade or business purposes, and either laden or unladen, and whether belonging to the vendor or to his visitors or to persons residing in that house or to persons coming to transact business with him, to go, pass and repass along over and upon the path marked ABC on the said plan which leads from the said house to the public road called the ————.

3. Minerals with Right of Surface Working[1]

Except and reserving to the vendor the absolute ownership of all mines and minerals in or under the land hereby sold with full liberty and power at all times to enter upon the said land or any part thereof to search for, dig, raise, make merchantable and carry away the said mines and minerals, and with full liberty and power to make, sink, maintain and use all such pits, shafts, levels, drains, watercourses and reservoirs and to construct, erect, maintain and use all such spoil, tanks, rail road, tram roads and other roads, bridges, building works and conveniences over the said land or any part thereof as may be necessary or convenient for all or any of the purposes aforesaid from time to time, subject, nevertheless to payment to the purchaser or his successor in title and his and their lessees and tenants reasonable and adequate compensation for all damages thereby done or occasioned to the said land or any buildings thereon.

4. Minerals with Right of Underground Working[2]

Except and reserving to the vendor the absolute ownership of all mines and minerals in and under the said land hereby sold with full power and authority to work and get the same mines and minerals by underground workings only and without entering upon or in any manner affecting or exercising any rights or provisions whatsoever in or over the surface of the said beds (and making compensation, *as in Para* 3).

5. Reservation to Take Water

Except and reserving to the vendor and all persons, occupying the vendor's house to the west of the said land marked on the plan by red

1 On mines and minerals, consult the Mines and Minerals (Regulation and Development) Act 1957 and the rules made thereunder.

2 *Ibid.*

colour with full and free right and liberty at all times hereafter of taking the water from the well (*or*, tank) distinguished on the said plan by blue colour with liberty from time to time to pass and repass upon the said land for the purpose of taking and bringing water from the said well to the said house.

6. Right of Using Staircase

Except and reserving to the vendor the full and free right of using the staircase marked on the said plan by blue colour for the purpose of going to and coming from the upper storey of the vendor's house adjoining the said house hereby sold on the west and marked on the said plan by red colour.

7. Right of Way

In pursuance of the agreement herein and in consideration of Rs.—— paid by the purchaser to the vendor (who acknowledges the receipt of the same), the vendor conveys to the purchaser by way of sale his rights of absolute ownership in the property described in the schedule, excepting the mines and minerals under that land, but together with the benefit of—

(*a*) the right of way granted by the deed dated ——— between A and B;

(*b*) restrictive covenant contained in deed dated ——— between ——— and ————, but subject to;

(*c*) restrictive covenant contained in the deed dated ———— between ————— and ————;

(*d*) right of way granted by the deed dated —— between —— and —————.

Habendum

1. Ordinary Form

TO HOLD the same to the purchaser absolutely forever (*or*, as absolute owner).

2. Several Joint Purchasers

TO HOLD the same to the purchasers absolutely forever as joint owners.

3. Several Persons in Equal Shares

TO HOLD the same to the purchasers absolutely forever as owners in common in equal shares.

4. Several Persons in Unequal Shares

TO HOLD the same to the purchasers absolutely forever as owners in common in the following undivided shares, i.e. to the said AB one-third share, to the said CD, one-half share and to the said EF one-sixth share.

5. Several Persons in Different Portions

TO HOLD the same to the purchasers as absolute owners in separate portions specified below, that is to say the portion shown as coloured red on the plan hereto to the said AB and the portion shown as coloured green to the said CD.

6. Subject to Payment of Dues

TO HOLD the same to the purchaser absolutely forever (*or*, as absolute owner) subject to the payment of such land revenue, cesses and taxes as may be assessed or imposed thereon.

7. Subject to Obligations[1]

TO HOLD, etc., the same to the purchaser absolutely for ever (*or*, as absolute owner) subject to the obligations and restrictions hereinafter expressed and imposed upon the purchasers as obligations intended to be binding in perpetuity on the property hereby sold.

8. Subject to Mortgage[2]

TO HOLD etc., subject to the hereinbefore recited mortgage and the principal sum of Rs. ———— now owing on the security thereof and the interest due or to become due on such sum.

9. Subject to Easements[3]

TO HOLD, etc., subject to the rights and easements to which the said property is now subject as aforesaid (*or*, to the rights and easements vested in the owners of adjoining property under or by virtue of the deeds specified in the schedule B hereto).

---

1 When any restrictive covenants on the enjoyment of the property are made they should be inserted in particular as covenants but referred to in the habendum also as in this form.

2 When property is sold subject to an encumbrance, the mortgage should be mentioned in the recitals.

3 If there are any easements in favour of third persons to whom the property is subject, the same should be recited in the recitals, or if there are several deeds creating such easements, the same should be mentioned in schedule.

10. Leasehold Property

TO HOLD the same to the purchaser for all the residue now unexpired of the said term of ——— years granted by the said lease subject henceforth (*or*, as from the ————) to the payment of rent reserved by, and the performance and observance of the covenants on the part of the lessee contained in the said lease.

11. Sale of Part of Leased Property and Apportionment of Rent

TO HOLD, etc., subject if and so far as subsisting, to a lease dated —— whereby the said property (together with other property not sold) was demised to XY, etc., at the yearly rent of Rs. ——— of which the yearly rent of Rs. ———— shall be the apportioned part to be henceforth payable in respect of the said property hereby sold and with the benefits of such apportioned rent and all powers and rights for the recovery thereof and of the covenants and conditions by the lessee contained in the said lease so far as the same relate to the property sold.

12. Partly Leasehold and Partly Freehold[1]

TO HOLD the said land for all the residue, etc., (*as in Form* 10) and the said house and other buildings absolutely forever but subject to such covenants in the aforesaid lease as may relate to such house and buildings.[2]

13. Where Mortgagee also joins and gives up his Mortgage

TO HOLD, etc. (*as in para* 1 *above*) discharged from all principal moneys and interest intended to be secured by and from all claims and demands under the hereinbefore recited mortgage.

14. Restricting Implied Grant of Easement, etc.[3]

TO HOLD, etc., subject to the provision and declaration hereinafter

---

1 For instance, where land is taken on lease for building a house and a house is built thereupon, and both are sold.

2 Sometimes a building lease contains a covenant that in case of breach of a condition the lease would be determined and the buildings will also vest in the lessor. In such cases this will be necessary.

3 Under Sec. 8 of the Transfer of Property Act certain rights and things implied by it go with the property "unless a different intention is expressed or necessarily implied". If it is intended that any such right or thing should not be transferred to the purchaser, the same should be expressly excepted from the sale. If the rights and things are several it would be more convenient simply to say "*subject to the provisions and declaration hereinafter contained*" and to mention all such rights in the provisos after the covenants.

contained, that is to say, PROVIDED ALWAYS and it is hereby declared that the purchaser shall not be entitled to, etc. (*state the rights which are not to pass*), and the sale shall not be deemed or construed to imply the grant of any such right or thing.

15. Exceptions and Restrictions Mentioned with Parcels

TO HOLD, etc., subject to the exceptions and reservations herein-before mentioned.

16. Exceptions and Restrictions not Mentioned with Parcels[1]

TO HOLD, etc., subject to the exceptions and reservations hereinafter contained that is to say,

The vendor reserves,

(1)

(2)

(3)

etc., etc.

17. Subject to Terms and Conditions

TO HOLD, etc., subject to the several terms and conditions hereinafter contained.

18. Sale of Mortgagee's Right

TO HOLD, etc., subject to such right or equity of redemption as is now subsisting in the said property under or by virtue of the hereinbefore recited deed of mortgage.

19. Sale on Trust

TO HOLD the same to the purchaser on trust for the said hospital.

(*Or*, TO HOLD the same to the purchaser upon trust that the income of the said property shall be used by the purchaser for, etc.)

(*Or*, TO HOLD the same to the purchaser upon trust that the said land shall be used for building a school under the scheme hereinbefore mentioned and on the constitution of a proper trust for the said school, the said land shall form part of the property of the said trust.)

---

1 Exceptions and reservations are generally mentioned after the Parcels; but if they are long, it may be convenient to mention them separately after the habendum. In the former case para 15 and in the latter para 16 of the habendum should be used.

Production of Title Deeds[1]

1. Covenant by Vendor when Deeds Retained by him

The vendor will upon every reasonable request of the purchaser and at the cost of the person making the request produce all or any of the documents of title relating to the property sold which are specified in the schedule hereto and which have been retained by the vendor and furnish such true copies or extracts therefrom as the purchaser may require, and will, in the meantime, keep the said documents safe, uncancelled and undefaced unless prevented from so doing by one or other inevitable accident.

2. Covenant when Deed Retained by Another Purchaser

It is hereby agreed that as the documents of title specified in the schedule hereto relating to the property hereby sold cover also other properties which have been sold by the vendor to the other persons, all the said documents shall be delivered to XY one of the other such purchasers.

AND the vendor covenants with the purchaser that the said XY will upon any reasonable request, etc., (*as in Form* 1, *substituting the words* which have been/will be delivered to the said XY" *for the words* "which have been retained by the vendor").

3. Covenant of Indemnity by Purchaser retaining Title Deeds

The documents of title specified in the ——— schedule hereto having been delivered to the purchaser, the purchaser hereby covenants with the vendor that he will upon every reasonable request of the purchaser of any other property covered by the said documents, and at the cost of the person making the request, produce all or any of the said documents and furnish

---

1 These covenants are implied by Sec. 55 (3) and need not be entered in territories where the Transfer of Property Act is in force. Under the said sub-section if properties covered by a document of title are sold to different persons, the purchaser of the property of the highest value has the right to have the title deeds and he is bound to produce them. But the parties may agree that the title deeds may be retained by any other purchaser, in which case an express covenant that he shall produce them and grant copies should be entered. In such cases, Form 2 may be employed. As such purchaser will not generally be a party to other sales, the covenant can be on behalf of the vendor alone, and the vendor should obtain a covenant of indemnity from the purchaser relating to the title deeds (*as in Form* 3). This will be necessary only where the Transfer of Property Act is not in force or where any purchaser other than that of the highest value retains the title deeds. As there may be a dispute as to what title deeds a person has in his possession it is always safe to specify the documents in the sale deed.

such copies, etc., (*as in Form* 1). AND further agrees to keep the vendor indemnified against any compensation or damages he may have to pay and all costs he may have to incur by reason of the purchaser's default in fulfilling this obligation.

4. Acknowledgment of Title Deeds[1]

The vendor hereby acknowledges that he has retained possession of the documents of title mentioned in the ——— schedule hereto which relate to the property hereby sold and to other property.

Special Covenants

1. Title[2]

The vendor hereby covenants with the purchaser that he is the owner of the property hereby sold and has power to sell the same;

(*Or,* The vendor hereby covenants with the purchaser that the title which is hereby transferred subsists and that he has power to transfer the same.)

2. Quiet Enjoyment

The vendor hereby covenants with the purchaser that the said premises shall be quietly entered into and upon and held and enjoyed and the rents and profits received therefrom by the purchaser without any interruption or disturbance by the vendor or any person claiming through or under him and without any lawful disturbance or interruption by any other person whomsoever.

3. Against Encumbrances[3]

The vendor hereby covenants that the property hereby sold is free from encumbrances (except those hereinbefore mentioned, *or*, mentioned in ——— schedule hereto, subject to which this sale is made).

---

1 This acknowledgment will be of advantage to avoid future dispute about the number and character of title deeds in possession of the vendor. When the vendor retains any title deeds it is always safe to specify them in the sale deed.

2 A covenant for title is implied by Sec. 55(2) and is not strictly necessary except in territories where the Transfer of Property Act is not in force (*See* Preliminary notes).

3 *See* Preliminary notes.

4. Further Assurance[1]

The vendor will at the cost of the person requiring the same execute and do every assurance or thing necessary for further or more perfectly assuring the said property to the purchaser his heirs or assigns, as by him or them shall be reasonably required.

5. Limiting Liability under Implied Covenant for Title

It is hereby agreed that the liability of the vendor under the implied covenant for title shall be limited to the amount of the sale price, *i.e.,* Rs.————.

Or,

In case the purchaser is deprived of the whole or any part of the property hereby sold by reason of any defect found in the title of the vendor or of any encumbrance or charge on the same to which this sale is not subject, the vendor will pay to the purchaser by way of damages the whole amount of the sale price or such part of it as shall bear the same proportion to the whole as such part of the property shall bear to the whole property, as the case may be, with interest from the date of the purchaser's dispossession at the rate of ———— per cent per annum, and that the liability of the vendor under his implied covenant for title will not extend any further.

6. Contracting out of Implied Covenant

It is hereby agreed that the vendor gives no warranty of his title and the warranty implied by law shall not apply and that the purchaser accepts such title as the vendor has.

7. Several Liability of Several Vendors

It is hereby agreed between the parties hereto that the liability of the vendors for breach of the implied covenant for title shall not be joint and several but each vendor shall be liable only in respect of his share in the said property (*or*, the portion of the said property which belongs to him).

8. Covenant by a Person Selling in Fiduciary Character[2]

The vendor hereby covenants with the purchaser that he has done no act whereby the property hereby sold is encumbered or whereby he is

---

1 This covenant is not strictly necessary but as a precaution a careful conveyancer would insert it (*See* Preliminary notes).

2 This is not strictly necessary where the Transfer of Property Act applies as it is implied by the proviso to Sec. 55 (2). In fact, in case of persons in fiduciary character this is the only covenant of title implied by law.

debarred from transferring it to the purchaser.

9. Covenant by Vendor for Title[1]

The vendor hereby covenants with the purchaser that the interest which is hereby transferred to the purchaser subsists and that he has the power to transfer it.

10. Cost of Repairing Road or Staircase in which Right of Passage is Reserved

It is hereby agreed that in consideration of the right of passage hereinbefore reserved, the vendor will pay to the purchaser every year half the cost incurred by the latter in maintaining in proper repairs the said staircase (*or*, the said road) the amount of such cost in case of disagreement to be determined by arbitration.

11. Covenant not to Build but to Keep Land Open

The purchaser hereby covenants with the vendor that he will not erect any wall or other building upon the land hereby sold to the North of or opposite to the window recently constructed in the Northern wall of the house shown on the plan by red colour nearer to the said wall than the dotted line shown on the said plan between points A and D nor erect any building upon or overhanging the said land coloured blue on the said plan and such land shall always be kept open.

12. Covenant for Assistance in Mutation

The vendor will support any application made by the purchaser for mutation of names on the property hereby sold and will at the cost of the person requiring the same do all that he may be required to do for obtaining mutation in favour of the purchaser.

13. Covenant for Mutation at Vendor's Expense

The vendor will at his own expense get mutation of names made in the village registers in favour of the purchaser in respect of the property hereby sold.

---

1 A person in fiduciary character, e.g. guardian or trustee, does not necessarily enter into a covenant of title nor is such covenant implied, but a purchaser may insist and the vendor may agree to guarantee the title by an express covenant like this.

14. Contract of Pre-emption[1]

The purchaser shall not sell the said property to any person other than the vendor unless he has first offered the same to the vendor and the vendor has declined or neglected to purchase the same at the price offered by such other person.

15. Covenant about Common Walls of House

It is hereby agreed that all walls separating the house hereby sold and the house of the vendor adjoining it on the West shall be deemed to be common walls of the parties and shall be maintained and repaired at the joint cost of the parties.

16. Agreement to Pay Price Reserved for Future

The purchaser will pay the said sum of Rs. ——— being the balance of the said price to the vendor on the ————, (*or*, in the following instalments), and will in the meantime pay interest thereon (*or* on so much thereof as for the time being remains unpaid) at the rate of ——— per cent per annum.

17. Cost of Stamp and Registration[2]

It is hereby agreed that the cost of stamp and registration of this deed shall be borne by the vendor (*or*, by the vendor and the purchaser in equal shares).

18. Payment of Mortgage Money

The purchaser hereby covenants with the vendor that the purchaser will pay to the said mortgagee or his successor in title, on such payment being lawfully demanded, all his dues under the aforesaid deed of mortgage, and will at all times keep the vendor indemnified against the same and against all suits proceedings, costs, charges, claims and demands whatsoever in respect thereof.

---

1 *See* Preliminary notes.

2 Under Sec. 29 (c) of the Stamp Act, it is the purchaser who has to bear this cost. But this is subject to a contract to the contrary. This form is to be used in case of a contract to the contrary.

19. Indemnifying Against Restrictive Covenants[1]

The purchaser hereby covenants with the vendor (with the object of affording to the vendor and his representatives a full and sufficient indemnity, but not further or otherwise),[2] that the purchaser will at all times hereafter duly perform and observe the covenants by the vendor and restrictive provisos of the said deed of, etc., (*nature of deed*) contained in relation to the property hereby sold and will at all times keep the vendor and his representatives indemnified against all suits, proceedings, costs, charges, claims and demands in respect of the said covenants and restrictive provisos or any of them.

20. Reserved to Vendor to Destroy Access of Light

It is hereby agreed and declared that the access and use of light from and over the adjoining property of the vendor, to and for the Land hereby sold and any building for the time being erected and standing thereupon shall henceforth be enjoyed by the purchaser and his successors-in-title under and by virtue only of the consent of the vendor hereby given and that the vendor or his successors-in-title or owners or occupiers of the adjoining property shall be at liberty at any time hereafter to interfere with or destroy such access or use of light by making erections on buildings or altering existing buildings on such adjoining land without any formal revocation of the consent hereby given.

21. Restrictive Covenant by Purchaser

The purchaser and his successors-in-title will at all times hereafter observe and perform the following stipulations and regulations in relation to the land and property hereby sold (*or*, the stipulations and regulations in relation to the lands and property hereby sold contained in the ——— schedule hereto).

22. Form of Restrictive Covenant to be annexed to Land

The purchaser to the intent and so as to bind (so far as practicable) the land hereby sold into whosesoever hands the same may come and to benefit and protect the other land delineated on the plan hereto annexed (but not

1 Sometimes the property sold is subject to restrictive covenants contained in the sale deed by which the vendor had himself purchased the property. Such covenants should now be performed by the purchaser and the vendor should be indemnified against the consequence of the purchaser's non-performance.

2 The words within brackets are necessary to prevent the vendor from enforcing the performance of covenants or claiming damages even if he has not suffered any damage.

so as to render the purchaser personally liable to damages for any breach of covenant committed after he shall have parted with all interest in the property in respect of which such breach shall occur)[1] hereby covenants with the vendor as follows:-

23. Covenant for Sale to be Void on Non-fulfilment of Condition of Building

PROVIDED ALWAYS and it is hereby agreed that if the purchaser shall make default in erecting and completing in accordance with the covenant by the purchaser in that behalf hereinbefore contained and within the time hereinbefore specified the said buildings or any of them so to be erected and completed as aforesaid the sale hereby made shall be void and the said land shall immediately thereupon vest in the vendor, and all materials then standing or lying upon the said land if not removed by the purchaser within two months shall become the property of the vendor.

24. Assignment of Restrictive Covenant

The vendor (so far as he is able) assigns to the purchaser the benefit of the restrictive covenant contained in the deed dated —— between ——and ———— (so far as it is subsisting and capable of being enforced).

Agreement to Sell

1. Investigation of Title

(a) The title shall begin with a sale deed dated ——— and the purchaser shall not inquire into or require the production of the earlier title.

(b) The title shall begin with the Will of XY, etc., dated ——— and the purchaser shall *presume* that the said XY was on the ——— absolute owner of the property.

(c) The vendor has been in undisturbed possession of the property for over 30 years without acknowledging the title of any other person and the purchaser shall assume that the vendor has acquired title by prescription.

(d) The vendor's title is well known and shall be accepted by the purchaser.

(e) The vendor's title shall not be investigated beyond 30 years.

(f) Certified copies of deeds by the purchaser shall be accepted in place of the original.

1 The words in the brackets will be necessary if the personal liability of the covenantor is to be limited.

2. Price Fixed by Valuation

(a) The price of the trees shall be fixed according to a valuation of the said trees to be made by ——— and in case of his refusal, neglect or inability to make a valuation by ———.

(b) The price shall be Rs. ——— for the house and such price for the furniture and fixture according to a valuation by ——— and (*as in* (a) *above*).

3. Reservation of Minerals

The property is subject to a reservation of mines and minerals and power of working the same contained in a sale deed dated ———.

4. Reservation of Way in Favour of Vendor

The sale shall be subject to reservation to the vendor of a right of way for all purposes over the property to be sold between the points marked A and B on the plan annexed hereto.

5. Exception of Light and Air

The purchaser shall not be entitled to any right or easement of light or air otherwise which would restrict or in any way interfere with the due use for building or for any other purpose on or of the adjoining land of the vendor.

6. Restrictive Covenants

(a) The property is agreed to be sold subject to the restrictive covenants contained in a deed of sale dated ——— a copy of which has been supplied to the purchaser and will be attached to the sale deed (*or*, and the covenants shall be entered in a schedule to the sale deed).

New Restrictive Covenants

(b) The property is agreed to be sold subject to the restrictions and explanations set out in the schedule hereto.

7. Power of Attorney

The vendor being in England, the sale deed will be executed by his attorney under a power of attorney duly executed by the vendor.

8. Vendee to obtain permission (Cantonment land)

The vendee undertakes to obtain permission from the Military Estates Officer for the sale.[1]

---

1 *Rameshwar Swaroop* v. *Saroj Tyagi*, AIR 1998 SC 3389.

PRECEDENTS OF AGREEMENTS[1]

1—Agreement to Sell a House[2]

AN AGREEMENT made on the ——— day of ——— BETWEEN AB, etc., (hereinafter called "the vendor") of the one part AND CD, etc., (hereinafter called "the purchaser") of the other part.

WHEREBY the parties hereto mutually agree as follows:

(1) The vendor will sell and the purchaser will buy ALL that, etc., (*describe the house*) with all the rights belonging or appurtenant thereto.

(2) The sale will be free from encumbrances.

(3) The price will be Rs. ——— of which Rs. ——— has been paid by way of earnest money to the vendor (the receipt of which the vendor hereby acknowledges) and the balance shall be paid at the time of execution of the sale deed.

(4) The title of the vendor as absolute owner shall be accepted by the purchaser without any further investigation (*or*, the vendor shall deliver to the purchaser within one month certified copies of all documents of his title to the said property, of the Municipal register in which the said property is entered, and any other documentary evidence proving his title, and this agreement is subject to the purchaser's pleader being satisfied as to the absolute title of the vendor).

(5) The property is believed and shall be taken to be correctly described and is sold subject to all *outgoings*[3], easements, restrictions and rights affecting the same and if any error, misstatement or omission shall be discovered the same shall not annul the sale nor shall any compensation be allowed in respect thereof.

(6) The vendor will reserve to himself a right of way for his adjoining house for all purposes over the property agreed to be sold between the points marked A and B on the plan attached herewith.

---

1 In these precedents only general covenants are given. If there is any special covenant on any subject, the same should be expressed. Some general forms of clauses relating to special covenants have been given before (pp. 812 to 817). See also footnote below Form Nos. 24 and 45(a), *post* explaining 'development agreements' relating to land.

2 The agreement should be bilateral. A unilateral agreement may be treated as a mere gratuitous 'undertaking': *S.M. Gopal Chetty* v. *Ramesh*, AIR 1998 Mad 169.

3 Meaning 'expenditures' (Black's Law Dictionary, 1990 edn. p. 1101).

(7) The purchaser shall in the sale deed enter into the restrictive covenants set out in the second schedule hereto for the benefit of the adjoining property of the vendor.

(8) The purchase shall be completed on the ——— day of ——— by the purchaser paying the balance of the price and the vendor executing the sale deed.[1]

(9) All expenses for preparation of the sale deed and the cost of stamp and registration charges shall be borne by the purchaser.

(10) If from any default of the purchaser the purchase shall not be completed on the date fixed, the purchaser shall pay interest on the unpaid balance of the price at ——— per cent per annum upto the date of completion of sale.

(11) If the purchaser shall fail to comply with the terms and conditions of this agreement his earnest money will be forfeited and the vendor will be at liberty to resell the property and recover the deficiency in price and expenses of resale from the purchaser (*or*, if the deficiency in price and expenses of resale exceed the amount of earnest money, recover the excess) and any excess in price on resale shall belong to the vendor.

IN WITNESS WHEREOF, etc.

2—Agreement for Sale of Leasehold

AN AGREEMENT made, etc., (*as in Form* 1).

WHEREBY the parties hereto mutually agree as follows:

1. The vendor will sell and the purchaser will buy ALL, etc., as the same are held for the residue of a term of ——— years from the ——— day of ——— granted by a lease dated the ——— and made between XY, etc., of the one part and the vendor of the other part at the yearly rent of Rs. ——— and subject to the covenants and conditions therein contained and on the part of the lessee to be observed and performed.

2 and 3. (*as in Form* 1).

4. The purchaser having seen a certified copy of the said lease shall be deemed to have full notice of the contents thereof and of the state of the property as to repairs, insurance and all other matters, and shall accept

---

1 In regard to contracts for sale of immovable property, time is not of the essence of the contract: *Ardeshir H. Mana* v. *Flora Sassoon*, AIR 1928 PC 208, 55 I.A. 360. However in a contract of reconveyance, time is of the essence: *Bismillah Begum* v. *Rahmatullah Khan*, (1998) 2 SCC 226, AIR 1998 SC 970, reiterated in *Babu Ram* v. *Indra Pal Singh*, (1998) 6 SCC 358 (para 37), AIR 1998 SC 3021.

for the last rent accruing due previously to the date fixed for completion of the sale as conclusive evidence of the performance and observance of all the covenants and conditions contained in the said lease and of the effectual waiver of breach of any covenant or condition upto the date of actual completion without proof of title or authority of the person giving the receipt.

5. (*as* 4 *in Form* 1).

(*Rest mutatis mutandis as in Form* 1).

3—Agreement for Hire Purchase of House

THIS AGREEMENT TO SELL entered on this —— day of ——— between the ——— Authority ——— through its ——— (hereinafter referred to as "the Vendor") of the one part and AB, etc., (hereinafter referred to as "the Purchaser") of the other part.

Whereas the Vendor is a body corporate duly constituted under the provisions of law to promote and secure the development of land according to plan, and has acquired in the interest of public at large according to provisions of the Right to Fair Compensation and Transparency in Land Acquisition, Rehabilitation and Resettlement Act, 2013 and has constructed/shall construct a house under the ——— scheme and shall also transfer the land of the said house as freehold land in favour of the Purchaser.

And Whereas the Purchaser has applied to purchase the house with land and has also deposited the requisite amount towards his registration.

And Whereas the house No. ——— bearing an area of ——— sq. mt. in ——— Scheme ——— was allotted by the Vendor on hire purchase basis for a total sale consideration for Rs. ——— payable by the Purchaser to the Vendor and the Purchaser has agreed with the Vendor to purchase it on the terms and conditions hereinafter contained:

NOW THIS DEED WITNESS AS FOLLOWS:

1. That the Vendor will sell the house with land No. ——— bearing an area of ——— sq. mt. situated in ——— scheme ——— more specifically described in the Schedule at the foot of this deed in favour of the Purchaser as freehold property for a consideration for Rs. ——— along with all the rights, fixtures and appurtenants thereto in favour of the Purchaser free from all encumbrances.

2. That the Purchaser has made part payment of sale consideration amount to the Vendor amounting to Rs. ——— so far, and the balance

amount shall be obtained by the Vendor from the purchaser in ——— equal monthly instalments payable in advance within the first week of each calendar month.

3. That possession of the house hereby agreed to be sold in favour of the Purchaser has been delivered to the Purchaser.

4. That the Purchaser shall from time to time and at all times during the said term of ——— years pay and discharge all rates, charges and assessments of whatsoever description which are now or which may at any time in future during the said term be assessed, charged or imposed according to law by any authority duly constituted and authorised to do so regarding the said land with house.

5. That upon payment of all the instalments in respect of the demised property by the Purchaser, the Vendor will execute a sale deed of the said house with land in favour of the Purchaser.

6. That all the expenses for preparation of sale deed and incidental charges for the registration of the document including stamps, fees and any other expenses whichsoever it may be required, shall be borne exclusively by the Purchaser.

7. That the Purchaser shall abide by all the rules and regulations made in this regard by the Vendor including the provisions contained in any Government orders of the State Government of ——— as issued from time to time which shall be fully applicable and binding upon the Purchaser.

8. That during the pendency of this agreement the Purchaser shall not make any addition or alterations in the house or its structures and shall not in any manner reduce the open spaces provided in or around the said house or structures without the written permission of the Vendor.

9. That in case the Purchaser commits default in payment of three successive instalments or otherwise fails to comply with the terms and conditions of this agreement, this agreement shall stand terminated and the instalments paid shall be forfeited and the Vendor shall be at liberty to re-sell the aforesaid demised house with land and also recover any deficiency in the price obtained from such resale and the expenses of resale from the Purchaser.

10. That during the pendency of this agreement the Purchaser shall not in any manner transfer the possession of the house to any other person or let out the whole or any part of the said house without the previous written consent from the Vendor.

11. That the Purchaser shall keep the said house in good and

substantial repair and shall use the house and land for residential purposes only and shall not at any time carry on or permit to be carried on in the said house or any part thereof any trade or profession or establish any office or otherwise contravene the land use as provided in the Master Plan.

12. The Purchaser shall also not use or permit to be used the said land or house for public religious purposes in any manner.

13. That in view of the fact that to promote and secure the development of ——— (*name of area*), the land was acquired according to provisions of the Right to Fair Compensation and Transparency in Land Acquisition, Rehabilitation and Resettlement Act, 2013 and the valuation of the aforesaid plot was fixed according to the then rates at the time of allotment and compensation granted to the former owners of the land, but references, appeals and writ petitions are pending before courts of law and in case of any increase in compensation, solatium or in the rate of interest payable to former owners of the land the liability to pay the aforesaid increased amount of compensation solatium or interest shall automatically shift upon the Purchaser according to the proportion of the land in the lay-out-plan and the Purchaser shall make payment as per demand letter issued by the Vendor in this regard.[1]

14. That in case of any dispute regarding the terms of this agreement the Chairman of the Vendor Authority shall be sole arbitrator whose decision shall be final and binding on both the parties.

15. That the courts established in the local limits of district ——— shall have exclusive jurisdiction to try any suit or entertain other legal proceeding in respect of or arising out of this agreement.

16. That the terms "Vendor" and "Purchaser" hereinbefore used in this deed shall respectively mean and include the Vendor Authority itself and its administrators and the Purchaser and his legal representatives, heirs, successors and assigns.

The schedule herein referred to.

IN WITNESS WHEREOF ——— for and on behalf of the Vendor and the Purchaser have signed this deed on the dates mentioned against their respective signatures.

---

1 On a clause for escalation of cost see also footnote to the precedent on Works Contract under AGREEMENT, *ante*; Also see *Indore Development Authority* v. *Sadhana Agarwal*, (1995) 3 SCC 1; *Shiv Pal Karan* v. *State*, AIR 1988 All 268.

PRECEDENTS OF SALE DEEDS[1]

1—Simple Deed of Sale of a House, without Recitals

THIS DEED OF SALE made on the ——— day of ——— BETWEEN AB, etc., (hereinafter called "the vendor") of the one part AND CD, etc., (hereinafter called "the purchaser") of the other part.

WITNESSES as follows:

1. In consideration of the sum of Rs. ———— paid by the purchaser to the vendor on the ——— day of ——— (the receipt of which the vendor hereby acknowledges) the vendor as owner hereby transfers to the purchaser by way of sale ALL that *pucca* house standing on the land measuring 27 metres by 10 metres fully described in the schedule hereto annexed and thereon shown with its boundaries coloured red TO HOLD the same to the purchaser as absolute owner.

2. The vendor hereby covenants with the purchaser as follows:

(1) The said premises shall be quietly entered into and upon and held and enjoyed and the rents and profits received therefrom by the purchaser without any interruption or disturbance by the vendor or any person claiming through or under him and without any lawful disturbance or interruption by any other person whomsoever;

(2) The vendor will at the cost of the person requiring the same, execute and do every such assurance or thing necessary for further more perfectly assuring the said premises to the purchaser, his heirs or assigns as may reasonably be required;

[(3) The interest hereby transferred subsists and the vendor has power to sell the same;

(4) The property hereby sold is free from encumbrances].[2]

3. PROVIDED ALWAYS and it is hereby agreed that wherever such an interpretation would be requisite to give the fullest possible scope and effect to any contract or covenant herein contained the expressions "the vendor" and "the purchaser" hereinbefore used include their respective heirs, legal representative, successors and assigns.

---

1 These precedents contain ordinary conditions. If any special covenants are agreed, they should be added. Forms of different kinds of such covenants are given on pp. 812-817 *ante*.

2 (3) and (4) are not strictly necessary where the Transfer of Property Act applies vide Sec. 55 (2), Transfer of Property Act.

The schedule herein referred to

(Description of the property)

IN WITNESS WHEREOF the parties hereto have signed this deed on the dates mentioned against their respective signatures.

2—Sale Deed, when Part of Consideration Retained by Vendee for Payment to a Prior Mortgagee and part Agreed to be Paid Afterwards, with Recital of Title

THIS DEED OF SALE is made on the, etc., (*as in Form* 1).

WHEREAS the vendor is owner of the land described in the schedule hereto.

AND WHEREAS by a mortgage bond dated the ——— executed by the vendor in favour of one EF the said land was mortgaged to secure the principal sum of Rs. ——— and interest in accordance with the covenants therein contained.

AND WHEREAS the said principal sum of Rs. ——— with interest thereon from the date of the aforesaid bond upto the date hereof remains owing on the security of the said bond;

AND WHEREAS the vendor has agreed with the purchaser for the sale to him of the said land free from encumbrances for the sum of Rs. ——— of which the sum of Rs. ——— has been agreed to be retained by the purchaser for the redemption of the said mortgage of the said EF.

NOW THIS DEED WITNESSES as follows:

1. In consideration of the price of Rs. ———, out of which the sum of Rs. ——— has been paid by the purchaser to the vendor (the receipt of which the vendor hereby acknowledges) and the sum of Rs. ——— has been retained by the purchaser for payment to the said EF in pursuance of the aforesaid agreement and the remaining Rs. ——— will be paid by the purchaser to the vendor within three months, the vendor hereby transfers by way of sale to the purchaser ALL that property described in the schedule hereto TO HOLD the same to the purchaser as absolute owner.

2. The vendor hereby covenants with the purchaser as follows:

(1)

(2)

(3) The said premises are free from encumbrances except the encumbrance created by the aforesaid mortgage deed;

(4) If the amount due to EF mortgagee on the said mortgage bond

dated ——— on the date of execution of this deed is found to exceed Rs. ——— the vendor will pay the excess to the purchaser with interest at ——— per cent per annum from the date hereof.

3. The purchaser hereby covenants with the vendor as follows:

(1) He will pay the said sum of Rs. ——— to the vendor within three months from the date hereof; and

(2) He will at all times keep indemnified the vendor and his estate from and against the claim of the said EF under the aforesaid mortgage deed dated the ———.

4. PROVIDED ALWAYS, etc., (*Interpretation clause as in Form* 1).

The schedule herein referred to

IN WITNESS WHEREOF, etc.

3—Sale Deed where Consideration Partly Paid, Partly Retained for Creditors and Partly Set Off

THIS DEED OF SALE is made, etc., (*as in Form* 1).

WHEREAS the vendor borrowed Rs. ——— from the purchaser on an interest of ——— per cent per annum and by a deed of mortgage dated ——— mortgaged the property described in schedule B hereto to secure the said loan of Rs. ——— and interest;

AND WHEREAS a sum of Rs. ——— is now due on account of the said loan and interest thereon;

AND WHEREAS the vendor being the owner of the property described in schedule A hereto has agreed to sell and the purchaser has agreed to buy the said property for a consideration of Rs. ———;

NOW THIS DEED WITNESSES as follows:

1. In consideration of the said sum of Rs. ——— out of which the sum of Rs. ——— has been retained by the purchaser in full satisfaction of his claim under the aforesaid deed of mortgage (from which the purchaser hereby releases the vendor and the said property mentioned in schedule B)[1] and the sum of Rs. ——— has been retained by him for payment to the various creditors of the vendor whose names and particulars of whose debts are set forth in schedule C hereto annexed and the balance of Rs. ——— has been paid at the time of the execution of this deed by the purchaser to the vendor (the receipt whereof the vendor hereby acknowledges) the vendor hereby transfers, etc., (*as in Form* 2).

1 If the property mortgaged is the same which is sold, Form 34, *post,* may be adopted.

2. The vendor hereby covenants etc., (*as in Form* 1).

3. The purchaser hereby covenants with vendor as follows:

(1) The purchaser will pay the sum of Rs. ———— to the various creditors of the vendor named in the schedule C hereto and will at all times hereafter keep indemnified the vendor and his estate from and against the claims of such creditors to the extent of the amounts respectively mentioned against the name of each in the said schedule C.

4. In consideration of the transfer by the vendor hereinbefore contained the purchaser hereby releases the vendor and his estate from every obligation concerning the said sum of Rs. ———— lent by the purchaser to the vendor as hereinbefore recited and any interest thereon whether such obligation is imposed by the deed of mortgage hereinbefore recited or not.

5. PROVIDED ALWAYS, etc., (*as* 3 *in Form* 1).

The schedule A, B and C herein referred to

IN WITNESS WHEREOF, etc.

4—Sale Deed when Part of Consideration is Paid before Execution and Part is Agreed to be Paid after Registration

THIS DEED OF SALE, etc., (*as in Form* 1).

WITNESSES as follows:

1. In consideration of the sum of Rs. 10,000 part of the price of Rs. 65,000 paid before the execution of this deed by the purchaser to the vendor (the receipt of which the vendor hereby acknowledges) and of the sum of Rs. 55,000 being the remainder of the said price to be paid by the purchaser to the vendor within two months from the registration of the deed, the vendor as owner hereby transfers, etc., (*as in Form* 2).

2. The vendor hereby covenants with the purchaser as follows:

(1) and (2) (*as in Form* 1).

(3) The said premises are free from encumbrances, charges, claims and liens except the lien in favour of the vendor in respect of the sum of Rs. 55,000 being the unpaid balance of purchase money due hereunder.

3. The purchaser hereby covenants with the vendor that he, the purchaser, will pay to the vendor within two months of the registration of this deed the sum of Rs. 55,000.

4. PROVIDED, etc., (*as in* 3 *of Form* 1).

The schedule herein referred to.

IN WITNESS WHEREOF, etc.

5—Sale Deed where a Portion of the Price is Left for a Creditor (who is also a Party to the Sale Deed)

THIS DEED OF SALE made on the ——— day of ——— BETWEEN AB, etc., (hereinafter called "the vendor") of the first part AND CD, etc., (hereinafter called "the creditor") of the second part AND EF, etc., (hereinafter called "the purchaser") of the third part.

WHEREAS the vendor being the owner of the property described in the schedule hereto has agreed to sell and the purchaser has agreed to buy the said property for the sum of Rs. ———;

AND WHEREAS the purchaser being unable to pay more than Rs. ——— of the said purchase money at the date of these presents, and the vendor being indebted to the creditor to the extent of Rs. ——— and upwards it has been agreed between the vendor and the purchaser that the purchaser shall pay the balance of the said purchase money, namely Rs. ——— to the creditor in part discharge of the vendor's said debt to the creditor together with interest at the rate of ——— per cent per annum till payment.

NOW THIS DEED WITNESSES as follows:

1. In consideration of the sum of Rs. ——— paid by the purchaser to the vendor on or before the date hereof (the receipt of which is hereby acknowledged) and of the sum of Rs. ——— to be paid by the purchaser with interest at the rate aforesaid to the creditor for the credit of the vendor in the manner hereinafter agreed the vendor hereby transfers, etc., (*as in Form* 2).

2. The vendor hereby covenants with the purchaser, etc., (*as in Form* 1).

3. The purchaser hereby covenants with the vendor that the purchaser will pay to the creditor the said sum of Rs. ——— within ——— years from the date of these presents and will in the meantime pay to the creditor interest thereon or on so much thereof as may for the time being remain unpaid at the rate of ———per cent per annum and will indemnify the vendor from any claim or demand in respect of the same or any part thereof.

4. The creditor hereby covenants with the vendor that if the purchaser pays to the creditor interest at the rate aforesaid upon the said sum of Rs. ——— and pays the whole of the said sum to the creditor within a period of ——— years from the date of these presents the creditor will not require payment from the vendor of the said sum of Rs. ——— or any

interest thereon and will give the vendor credit for such payments on account for discharging in part the vendor's debt to the creditor.

5. The vendor hereby covenants with the creditor that if the purchaser makes default in paying the said sum or in paying interest thereon in accordance with the covenants hereinbefore contained the vendor will himself pay such sum to the creditor or so much thereof as may be unpaid together with interest at the rate aforesaid.

6. PROVIDED ALWAYS and it is hereby agreed between the vendor and the purchaser that nothing herein contained shall affect or amount to a release of the charge to which the vendor is entitled under the law for the said sum of Rs. ——— or such part thereof as may remain unpaid and for interest thereon at the rate aforesaid until the said sum with interest has been paid in full by the purchaser as hereinbefore provided.

7. PROVIDED ALSO, etc., (*as in* 3 *of Form* 1).

The schedule herein referred to.

IN WITNESS WHEREOF etc.

6—Sale Deed - Consideration Agreed to be Paid in a Particular Way

THIS DEED OF SALE made, etc., (*as in Form* 1)

WITNESSES as follows:

1. In consideration of the sum of Rs. ———agreed to be paid by the purchaser to the vendor in the manner hereinafter provided the vendor as proprietor hereby transfers, etc., (*as in Form* 2).

2. The vendor hereby covenants, etc., (*as in Form* 1).

3. The purchaser hereby covenants with the vendor as follows:

(1) That he will pay the aforesaid consideration of Rs. ———, etc., (*describe the mode of payment agreed upon*).

4. PROVIDED, etc., (*As in* 3 *of Form* 1).

The schedule herein referred to.

IN WITNESS WHEREOF, etc.

7—Sale Deed by *Benamidar* and *Beneficiary*[1]

THIS DEED OF SALE is made on the ——— day of ——— BETWEEN AB, etc., (hereinafter called "the *benamidar*") of the first part AND CD, etc., (hereinafter called "the vendor") of the second part AND EF, etc., (hereinafter called "the purchaser") of the third part.

WHEREAS the property described in the schedule hereto was purchased by the vendor from one XY under a deed of sale dated —— but as the vendor was then in Government service and under the rules of his service was not competent to make the purchase without permission of the Government, the purchase was made fictitiously in the name of the *benamidar* for and on behalf of the vendor;

(*or*, WHEREAS as the *benamidar* hereby admits the property described in the schedule hereto really belongs to the vendor although the name of the *benamidar* is fictitiously recorded in the revenue records as the owner thereof);

AND WHEREAS the vendor has agreed with the purchaser to sell the said property to him for the sum of Rs. ————;

AND WHEREAS the *benamidar* has, at the request of the vendor agreed to join in the sale of the said property for the purpose of perfecting the title of the purchaser thereto;

NOW THIS DEED WITNESSES as follows:

1. In pursuance of the said agreement and in consideration of the said sum of Rs. ——— paid before the execution hereof by the purchaser to the vendor (the receipt whereof the vendor hereby acknowledges) the vendor hereby transfers to the purchaser and at the request of the vendor the *benamidar* hereby releases to the purchaser ALL that, etc., (*as in Form* 2).

2. The vendor hereby covenants with the purchaser (*as in* 1 *of Form* 1).

3. The *benamidar* likewise covenants with the purchaser that the said premises shall be quietly entered upon and held and enjoyed and the rents and profits received by the purchaser without any interruption by him or any one claiming through or under him.

4. The vendor and the *benamidar* respectively each for himself but not for the other, covenant with the purchaser that he will at the cost of the person requiring the same execute and do every assurance or thing necessary for further or more perfectly assuring the said premises to

---

1 The Prohibition of Benami Property Transactions Act, 1988, does not in any way affect the benamidar's voluntary offer to join in such a transaction: See foot note under precedent No.17 under RELEASE, *ante*.

the purchaser, his heirs or assigns as by him or them shall reasonably be required.

5. PROVIDED ALWAYS (*as in* 3 *of Form* 1)

The schedule herein referred to.

IN WITNESS WHEREOF, etc.

8—Sale Deed by a Pardanashin Lady under the Terms of a Compromise in Lieu of a Decree

THIS DEED OF SALE is made, etc., (*as in Form* 1).

WHEREAS—

(1) In suit No. ——— of ——— pending in the Court of the ——— a joint decree was passed on the ——— in favour of EF, GH, JK and the purchaser against the vendor and her deceased husband for Rs. ——— with costs and interest from the date of suit upto date of realisation;

(2) By virtue of the consent decree passed by the Court of —— in Suit No.——— of ——— *in re*: EF and 4 others versus CD, the purchaser became solely and wholly entitled to realise the money due under the decree passed in Suit No.——— of ——— aforesaid;

(3) The said husband of the vendor having since died the vendor became the heir and owner of the property left by him;

(4) On the ——— the purchaser applied for execution of the decree in Suit No. ——— of ——— aforesaid against the vendor for Rs.———;

(5) The vendor after consultation with her near relations and legal advisers and after fully understanding and realising the effect of the transaction on her interest and considering it to be for her benefit entered into a compromise with the purchaser whereunder the aforesaid decree was agreed to be satisfied by the vendor executing in favour of the purchaser this sale deed in respect of the property mentioned in the schedule hereto in full satisfaction of the amount of the aforesaid decree;

(6) The said compromise has been embodied in a petition dated ——— presented jointly by the vendor and purchaser to the court of the ——— and duly verified and recorded by the presiding officer of the said court on the ———;

NOW THIS DEED WITNESSES as follows:

1. In pursuance of the agreement in the said compromise and in consideration of Rs. ——— credited by the purchaser towards full satisfaction of his aforesaid decree the vendor hereby transfers to the

purchaser, etc., (*as in Form* 1).

2. The vendor hereby covenants, etc., (*as in Form* 1).

3. The purchaser hereby covenants with the vendor that he will immediately after the registration of this deed certify satisfaction of the said decree to the Court in which the said execution application is pending.

4. PROVIDED ALWAYS, etc., (*as in* 3 *of Form* 1).

The schedule herein referred to.

IN WITNESS WHEREOF, etc.

9—Sale Deed by Attorney[1]

THIS DEED OF SALE is made, etc., (*as in Form* 1).

WHEREAS the vendor is the owner of the property described in the schedule hereto under a deed of sale dated the ——— executed by one EF;

AND WHEREAS the vendor by a deed dated the ——— and registered at the office of ——— on the ——— appointed XY his attorney to sell the said property, to receive and give receipt for the purchase money thereof and to execute and present for registration deed of sale thereof;

AND WHEREAS the vendor by the said XY his attorney has agreed with the purchaser for the sale to him of the said property for the sum of Rs. ———.

NOW THIS DEED WITNESSES as follows:

1. That in pursuance of the aforesaid agreement and in consideration of Rs. ——— paid by the purchaser to the said XY as such attorney as aforesaid (the receipt of which the vendor by the said XY hereby acknowledges) the vendor by the said XY as such attorney as aforesaid hereby transfers, etc., (*as in Form* 1).

2. The vendor by the said XY as such attorney as aforesaid hereby covenants with the purchaser as follows:

Rest as in Form 1.

10—Sale by Guardian of a Minor[2]

THIS DEED OF SALE is made on the ——— BETWEEN AB,

1 The sale should be in the name of the vendor and not in that of his attorney.

2 With regard to a minor's undivided interest in joint Hindu family property, see discussion in *Sri Narayan Bal* v. *Sridhar*, (1996) 8 SCC 54 explaining the scheme of Secs. 6, 7 and 8 Hindu Minority & Guardianship Act.

etc., a minor acting through XY, etc., his mother and natural guardian (*or*, his guardian appointed by the District Judge of ———— by an order dated ————) (hereinafter called "the vendor") of the one part AND CD, etc., (hereinafter called "the purchaser") of the other part.

WHEREAS the vendor is the owner of the property described in the second schedule hereto;

AND WHEREAS the vendor is a minor and is indebted to the several persons named in the first schedule hereto and the burden of interest on the said debts is increasing;

AND WHEREAS in order to pay off the said debts, the said XY has agreed on behalf of the vendor to sell to the said CD the property described in the second schedule hereto for the sum of Rs. ———— (AND WHEREAS the District Judge of ———— has by an order dated ———— permitted the said XY to make the said sale).

NOW THIS DEED WITNESSES as follows:

1. (*as in Form* 9, substituting "guardian" for "attorney").

2. The said XY for and on behalf of the vendor hereby covenants with the purchaser as follows:

(1) The vendor is the owner of the property described in the said schedule and is competent to transfer the same.[1]

(2) and (3) (*as in* 1 *and* 2 *of Form* 1).

3. Interpretation clause (*as in Form* 1).

The schedules herein referred to.

IN WITNESS WHEREOF, etc.

11—Sale by a Person on His Own Behalf and as Guardian of a Minor

THIS DEED OF SALE is made on the ———— BETWEEN AB, etc., and CD, etc., a minor acting by his guardian the said AB (hereinafter jointly called "the vendors") of the one part AND XY, etc., (hereinafter called "the purchaser") of the other part;

WHEREAS the vendors are joint owners of the property described in the schedule hereto;

AND WHEREAS the said CD is a minor and the said AB is the

---

1 This may be required from the guardian personally as the sale being made by a guardian there is no implied covenant for title by the vendor under Sec. 55(2), Transfer of Property Act.

certificated guardian of his property appointed by order of the District Judge of ——— dated ———;

AND WHEREAS the said AB acting for himself and as guardian of the said CD has agreed with the purchaser for the sale to him of the property described in the schedule hereto for the price of Rs. ———;

AND WHEREAS the District Judge of ——— has by an order dated the ——— permitted the said AB to make the said sale in respect of the share of the said CD;

NOW THIS DEED WITNESSES as follows:

1. In pursuance of the aforesaid agreement and in consideration of the sum of Rs. ——— paid by the purchaser to the said AB (the receipt of which the vendors hereby acknowledge) the vendors hereby transfer, etc., (*as in Form* 1).

2. *As in Form* 10, substituting "acting for himself and as guardian of the said CD" instead of "for and on behalf of the vendor".

3. (*As in Form* 1).

The schedule herein referred to.

IN WITNESS WHEREOF, etc.

12—Sale on behalf of a Mentally Ill Person

THIS DEED OF SALE is made on the ——— BETWEEN AB, etc., a mentally ill person acting through XY, etc., manager of his estate (hereinafter called "the vendor"), etc., (*as in Form* 1).

WHEREAS by an inquisition taken before the District Judge of Agra, the vendor was found to be a mentally ill person and by order of the said Judge dated ——— the said XY was appointed to be the manager of his estate.

AND WHEREAS it is necessary to raise a sum of Rs. ——— to pay off the debts of the vendor which amount approximately to Rs. ——— and to defray the necessary expenses for the maintenance and support of the vendor and his family.

AND WHEREAS by an order dated the ——— the said District Judge has authorised the said XY to raise the said sum of Rs. ——— by sale of the property of the vendor described in the schedule hereto.

AND WHEREAS the said XY has agreed to sell to the purchaser the said property for the sum of Rs. ———.

NOW THIS DEED WITNESSES as follows:

1. In pursuance of the said agreement and the order aforesaid and in consideration of the sum of Rs. ———— paid by the purchaser to the said XY as such manager as aforesaid (the receipt of which the vendor by the said XY hereby acknowledges) the vendor acting by the said XY as such manager as aforesaid hereby transfers to the purchaser ALL that, etc., (*as in Form* 1).

2. The said XY, etc., (*as in Form* 10).

3. (As in Form 1)

The schedule herein referred to.

IN WITNESS WHEREOF, etc.

13—Sale of Joint Family Property by Father for a Legal Necessity and Antecedent Debt

THIS DEED OF SALE is made on, etc., (*as in Form* 1).

WHEREAS—

(1) The vendor and his minor sons EF, GH and JK form joint Hindu family governed by the Mitakshara School of Hindu Law;

(2) The property mentioned in the schedule hereto is the joint ancestral property of the said family;

(3) The vendor also carries on the business of *Khandsari* (sugar manufacture) which is his ancestral business;

(4) For the purpose of the said business the vendor borrowed Rs. —— from the purchaser on a promisssory note dated the——and the amount of the said loan with interest now due to the purchaser comes to Rs. ———;

(5) The vendor is now in need of Rs. ——— for the following purposes, viz. Rs. ———— for the marriage of his daughter XY to be celebrated in the month of ———— next, Rs. ———— for payment of Government revenue in respect of the said family's land in villages ——— and Rs. ———— for the preliminary expenses of sending his son GH to England for education in Electrical Engineering; and

(6) As there is no other means of raising the said money the vendor has, in order to pay off the said loan and to raise a sum of Rs. ———— for the above mentioned purposes, agreed with the purchaser to sell to him the said property described in the schedule hereto for the sum of Rs. ————;

NOW THIS DEED WITNESSES as follows:

1. In consideration of the sum of Rs. ————— due to the purchaser on account of the said loan (from which the purchaser hereby releases the

vendor) and of the sum of Rs. ———— to be paid by the purchaser to the vendor at the time of registration of this deed, the vendor hereby transfers, etc., (*as in Form* 2).

2. *As in Form* 1.

3. *As in Form* 1.

The schedule herein referred to.

IN WITNESS WHEREOF, etc.

14—Sale by Manager of Joint Family, other Members joining

THIS DEED OF SALE is made on the ——— day of ——— BETWEEN AB, etc., EF, etc., GH, etc., and JK, etc., a minor acting through the said AB, the manager of his joint family (hereinafter called the "Vendors") of the one part AND CD, etc., (hereinafter called "the purchaser") of the other part.

WHEREAS—

(1) LM was the common ancestor. He had two sons X and Z both now dead. The said AB and EF are the sons of the said X and the said GH and JK are the sons of the said Z;

(2) The said AB, EF, GH and JK form a joint Hindu family governed by the Mitakshara school of Hindu law and the said AB is the manager;

(3) *As in para* 2 *of Form* 13;

(4) The said family also owns and carries on through the said AB an ancestral business of *Khandsari*;

(5) *As in* 4 *of Form* 13, *substituting* "the said AB" for "the vendor";

(6) *As in* 5 *of Form* 13 *substituting* "the vendors" for "the vendor", "the said AB's daughter" for "his daughter" and "the said GH" for "his son GH";

(7) The purchaser has made bonafide enquiries both as regards the ancestral nature of the business as well as the existence of the legal necessity. He has satisfied himself that the business of the family is ancestral and that the money is needed for the purpose aforesaid.

Rest as in Form 13, *substituting* "vendors" for "vendor".

15—Sale by Several Joint Owners (Tenants in Common or Joint Tenants)[1]

THIS DEED OF SALE is made, etc., (*as in Form* 1).

---

1 On distinction between joint tenants and tenants in common, see Preliminary Note on Partition page 698, *ante*.

WHEREAS the vendors are owners of the property described in the schedule hereto as tenants in common in equal shares (*or*, as joint tenants) and they have agreed to sell the same to the purchaser at the price of Rs.———;

NOW THIS DEED WITNESSES as follows:

1. In consideration of Rs. ———— paid by the purchaser to the vendors (the receipt of which the vendors hereby acknowledge) each of them the vendors so far as relates to his own share, estate or interest in the property hereby sold (but so as to make each of them liable by way of damages in respect of every breach of implied covenant to the extent of one-third only of such damages) hereby transfers, etc.

(*Rest as in other forms*).

16—Sale of Insolvent's Property by an Official Receiver

THIS DEED OF SALE is made on the ———— BETWEEN AB, etc., Official Receiver for the district of ———— (hereinafter called "the vendor") of the one part AND CD, etc., (hereinafter called "the purchaser") of the other part.

WHEREAS on the date of the order next hereinafter recited XY, etc., was absolute owner of the property described in the schedule hereto;

AND WHEREAS by an order of the District Judge of ——— made on the ——— day of ——— the said XY was adjudicated insolvent and the vendor was appointed receiver of his estate;

AND WHEREAS the vendor has agreed to sell the said property to the purchaser at the price of Rs.————;

NOW THIS DEED WITNESSES that in pursuance of the aforesaid agreement and in consideration of Rs. ——— paid by the purchaser to the vendor (the receipt of which the vendor hereby acknowledges) the vendor as official receiver and by virtue of the powers conferred on him by law in this behalf hereby transfer, etc.

(*Rest as in other Forms*).

17—Sale by Liquidator of Land of a Company in Voluntary Liquidation[1]

THIS DEED OF SALE is made on the ——— day of ——— BETWEEN the ——— Company Limited, in liquidation (hereinafter called "the Company") acting through AB, etc., its Liquidator of the one part AND CD, etc., (hereinafter called "the purchaser") of the other part.

When the Voluntary Liquidation is being done under Section 59 of the Insolvency and Bankruptcy Code, 2016

[WHEREAS at an ordinary/extraordinary[2] general meeting of the Company held on the ——— day of ———, it was resolved by a resolution/special resolution[3] duly passed that the Company should be wound up voluntarily and the said AB was appointed the Liquidator of the Company for the purpose of such winding up;

AND WHEREAS creditors representing atleast two-thirds in value of the debt of the company, have approved the said resolution dated ——— at a duly convened meeting held on ———]; *Or*

---

1 Inspite of winding up, whether voluntary or by order of the Court, the property of the Company remains vested in the Company and does not vest in the Liquidator or Official Liquidator. (Unlike the Official Receiver of the estate of an insolvent as in Form No. 16 above). The sale should, therefore, be in the name of the Company and not the Liquidator, though it is made through the Liquidator. The Liquidator should, therefore, not be made a party to the deed. In case of a liquidation under Section 271 Companies Act, 2013 (whether voluntary or otherwise), the power of an Official Liquidator to sell the Company's property is subject to the directions and over-all control of the Tribunal Section 290(l)(c) and (2) Companies Act, 2013. A similar power is exercised by the Tribunal in case of a liquidation under Chapter III, Part II Insolvency and in case of a voluntary liquidation under Section 59 Insolvency & Bankruptcy Code, 2016, the Liquidator of a Company may sell with the sanction of a special resolution of the Company. Section 59 Insolvency and Bankruptcy Code, 2016 deals with voluntary liquidation of corporate persons, giving the compliances and requirements which must be fulfilled. A covenant to the effect that the Liquidator has done nothing to charge or encumber the estate and one about production of title deeds are added but they are implied by section 55(2) and Sec. 55(3) Proviso Transfer of Property Act, 1882. They should be added where Transfer of Property Act, 1882 does not apply.

2 Section 59(3)(c), Insolvency and Bankruptcy Code 2016, provides that a resolution to liquidate voluntarily must be passed at a "General Meeting". This may be either at an Annual General Meeting or an Extra-Ordinary General Meeting.

3 Section 59(3)(c)(ii), Insolvency and Bankruptcy Code 2016, requires a "resolution", not a "special resolution", in the case where the voluntary liquidation of the Company is as a result of expiry of the period of its duration, if any, fixed by its articles or on the occurrence of any event in respect of which the articles provide that the company shall be dissolved.

When voluntary liquidation is taking place under Section 271(a) of the Companies Act

[WHEREAS at an ordinary/extraordinary[1] general meeting of the Company held on the ——— day of ———, it was resolved by a special resolution that the Company be wound up by the National Company Law Tribunal under Section 271(a) of the Companies Act, 2013;

WHEREAS the Hon'ble National Company Law Tribunal, ——— Bench has, *vide* Order dated ——— in C.P. No. —— of ——, appointed AB, etc., the provisional liquidator/Company Liquidator of the Company for the purposes of such voluntary winding up:

WHEREAS AB, etc. is therefore authorized and has the power to enter into the present deed of sale]

AND WHEREAS the land described in the schedule hereto is the property of the Company and the said AB, on behalf of the Company has agreed to sell the said land to the purchaser for Rs. ———

NOW THIS DEED WITNESSES as follows:

1. In consideration of Rs. ——— paid by the purchaser to the said AB, (the receipt of which the said AB on behalf of the Company hereby acknowledges) the Company acting by the said AB, hereby transfers, etc.

(*Rest as in other Forms*)

18—Sale by Liquidator of Land of a Company in Compulsory Liquidation

THIS DEED, etc. (*as in Form* 17).

When liquidation has been ordered under any provision of Section 271 of the Companies Act, 2013 other than sub-section (a) thereof.

[WHEREAS by an order dated the ——— passed by Hon'ble Mr. Justice ———, a Judge of High Court at ———/the Hon'ble National Company Law Tribunal, ——— Bench[2] in C.P. No. —— of ——, it was ordered that the Company be wound up by the Court/Tribunal under the provisions of the Companies Act, 2013 and the said AB, etc. was duly

1 Section 271(a), Companies Act, 2013 requires that the "special resolution" be passed at a "General Meeting". This be an Annual General Meeting or an Extra-Ordinary General Meeting.

2 Depending on whether the winding up proceeding stood transferred to the NCLT under the Companies (Transfer of Pending Proceedings) Rules, 2016

appointed liquidator of the Company for the purpose of such winding up;] [1]

Or

When liquidation has been ordered following an unsuccessful Corporate Insolvency Resolution Process under Chapter III of Part II of the IBC.

[WHEREAS by an order dated the ——— passed by the Hon'ble National Company Law Tribunal, ——— Bench in C.P. No. —— of ——, it was ordered that the Company be liquidated under Chapter III Part II of the Insolvency and Bankruptcy Code, 2016 and the said AB, etc., was duly appointed liquidator of the Company for the purpose of such liquidation]

AND WHEREAS by an order dated the—the Hon'ble High Court at ——— /National Company Law Tribunal, ——— Bench authorised the said AB to effect a sale of the property described in the schedule hereto belonging to the Company by private contract and for the price of Rs. —— AND WHEREAS the said AB in the name and on behalf of the Company has agreed with the purchaser for the sale to him of the said property described in the schedule hereto for the sum of Rs. ——.

NOW THIS DEED WITNESSES (as in Form 17).

19—Sale Deed by Treasurer, Charitable Endowments

THIS DEED OF SALE is made, etc., (*as in Form* 1).

WHEREAS the property described in the schedule hereto and forming part of the Moradabad High School Endowment Trust Fund was vested in the vendor by the Government of the Uttar Pradesh by G.O. No. ———— dated ———;

AND WHEREAS the said Government by G.O. No. ——— dated —— authorised the vendor under Sec. 10 of the Charitable Endowments Act, 1890, to sell the said property through the Collector of Moradabad;

AND WHEREAS the vendor acting through the Collector of Moradabad has agreed to sell and the purchaser has agreed to purchase the said property for the sum of Rs. ———— which sum has been deposited by the purchaser in the Government Treasury at Moradabad to the credit of the vendor;

NOW THIS DEED WITNESSES that in consideration of Rs. ——— paid by the purchaser as aforesaid (the receipt of which the vendor hereby acknowledges) the vendor transfers, etc.

(*Rest as in other Forms*)

---

1 For winding up under Section 271(a) of the Companies Act, 2013, see the previous precedent.

20—Sale by Trustees

THIS DEED OF SALE is made on the ——— day of ——— BETWEEN AB, etc., CD, etc., EF, etc., trustees of the Arya Charitable Hospital, Agra (hereinafter called "the vendor") of the one part AND GH, etc., (hereinafter called "the purchaser") of the other part.

WHEREAS—

(1) Under a deed of sale dated —————, PQ, RS and TU, the then trustees of the said Arya Charitable Hospital, Agra (hereinafter called "the said hospital") purchased from one XY the land described in the schedule hereto for Rs. ————— from the funds of the said hospital and the said land vested in the said trustees in trust for the general purposes of the said hospital;

(2) By an order of the District Judge, Agra, dated ————the said trustees were removed from the trusteeship of the said hospital and the vendors were appointed trustees thereof and the whole of property of the said trust including the said land vested in the vendors;

(3) The said land was purchased for extending the eye-ward of the said hospital but at a general meeting of the governors of the said hospital who were appointed by the aforesaid order of the District judge dated ———— for the management and administration of the hospital affairs it was unanimously resolved that an eye-ward was no longer required and that the said land was not required for any other purpose of the said hospital and that it was for the benefit of the said hospital that the same should be sold;

(4) The said District Judge of Agra has by an order dated —— authorised the vendors to sell the said land; and

(5) The vendors have therefore agreed to sell the said land to the purchaser for Rs. —————;

NOW THIS DEED WITNESSES as follows:

1. In pursuance of the said agreement and in consideration of Rs. —— paid by the purchaser (the receipt of which the vendors hereby acknowledge) the vendors under the direction of the said governors and under the said authority of the said District Judge of Agra and as trustees hereby transfer to the purchaser, etc., (*as in Form* 2).

(*Rest as in other Forms*).

21—Sale by One Tenant in Common or Joint Tenant to Another

THIS DEED OF SALE is made, etc., (*as in Form* 1).

WHEREAS under a Will dated the ——— of XY who died on the —— and whose said Will was proved[1] in the Court of the District Judge of ——— on the ———— the parties hereto are owners in possession of the property described in the schedule hereto as tenants in common in equal shares (*or*, as joint tenants);[2]

AND WHEREAS the vendor has agreed to sell his share and interest in the said property to the purchaser at the price of Rs. ———.

NOW THIS DEED WITNESSES as follows:

1. In consideration of the sum of Rs. ———— paid by the purchaser to the vendor (the receipt of which the vendor hereby acknowledges) the vendor hereby (*in case of tenant in common*) transfers, (*or, in the case of joint tenant*, releases and transfers) to the purchaser ALL the said estate and interest of the vendor of and in ALL that property described in the schedule hereto TO HOLD the same to the purchaser absolutely to the intent that the purchaser may henceforth become the sole and absolute owner of the said property freed from any estate or right of the vendor therein.

(*Rest as in other Forms*).

22—Sale to Several Persons Purchasing as Tenants in Common (in Equal or Unequal Shares)

THIS DEED OF SALE is made, etc., (*as in Form* 1).

WHEREAS the vendor is owner of the property described in the schedule hereto and has agreed to sell the same to the purchasers for Rs. ———;

[If the sale is to be made in unequal shares, AND WHEREAS the purchasers have provided the said purchase money in the shares and proportions following namely, the said AB Rs. ————— the said CD Rs. ———, and the said EF Rs. ————— and have requested that the said property should be transferred to them in the proportions hereinbefore appearing].

NOW THIS DEED WITNESSES as follows:

1. In consideration of Rs. ———— paid to the vendor by the purchasers in equal shares, (*or*, in the proportions hereinbefore mentioned)

---

1 Taking out a probate is not compulsory in the case of Muslim Wills. It is also not compulsory in the case of Wills of Parsis, Hindus, Sikhs, Jains and Buddhists except in Presidency towns, etc. (See Preliminary Note of WILLS, page 957 *post*.)

2 On distinction between joint tenants and tenants in common, see Preliminary Note on Partition, page 698 *ante*.

(the receipt of which the vendor is hereby acknowledges) the vendor hereby transfers to the purchasers ALL that property described in the schedule hereto TO HOLD the same to the purchasers as absolute owners in equal shares (*or*, in the following undivided shares that is to say the said AB one-half and the said CD one-third and the said EF one-sixth).

(*Rest as in other Forms*).

23—Sale Deed when Different Portions of Properties are Sold to Different Purchasers

THIS DEED OF SALE is made, etc., (*as in Form* 1).

WHEREAS the vendor being owner of the property described in the first schedule hereto has agreed with the purchasers for the sale to them of the said property in different portions as detailed against the names of the several purchasers in column 2 of the second schedule hereto for the prices respectively specified in column 3 thereof, the total of which is Rs. ———;

NOW THIS DEED WITNESSES that in pursuance of the said agreement and in consideration of the total sum of Rs. ———— paid before the execution of these presents by the purchasers in the proportions specified against their names in column 3 of the second schedule hereto (the receipt of which the vendor hereby acknowledges) the vendor hereby transfers to purchasers ALL the property described in the first schedule hereto TO HOLD the same to the purchasers in separate portions as specified against the names of the several purchasers in column 2 of the second schedule hereto, the position of each of such portions being more clearly delineated on the map hereto annexed by the area of such portions shown thereon in separate colours specified against the name of each purchaser in column 4 of the second schedule hereto.

(*Rest as in other Forms*).

The first schedule herein referred to

(Description of the whole property)

The second schedule herein referred to

Names of purchasers	Portions of property sold to each purchaser	Price paid by each purchaser	Colour by which the portion of each is shown on the annexed map

IN WITNESS WHEREOF, etc.

24—Sale to Sub-Purchaser[1]

THIS DEED OF SALE is made on the ——— day of ——— BETWEEN AB, etc., (hereinafter called "the vendor") of the first part AND CD, etc., (hereinafter called "the purchaser") of the second part AND EF, etc., (hereinafter called "the sub-purchaser") of the third part;

WHEREAS the vendor being the absolute owner of the property described in the schedule hereto has agreed to sell the same to the purchaser for Rs. 50,000 and the purchaser has agreed to resell the same to the sub-purchaser for Rs. 60,000;

NOW THIS DEED WITNESSES as follows:

1. In consideration of Rs. 50,000 paid by the sub-purchaser to the vendor under the direction of the purchaser and of Rs. 10,000 paid by the sub-purchaser to the purchaser (the receipt of which sums respectively, the vendor and the purchaser hereby acknowledge) the vendor, by the direction of the purchaser, hereby transfers, and the purchaser hereby confirms, to the sub-purchaser ALL that, etc., TO HOLD the same to sub-purchaser absolutely forever;

(*Covenants as usual between vendor and sub-purchaser). The purchaser need not enter into any covenants except the following:*

"The purchaser covenants with the sub-purchaser that the purchaser has not created any encumbrance or charge on the said property."

(*Rest as in other Forms*).

25—Sale Deed of Government Land Sold at an Auction Sale

THIS DEED OF SALE is made on the ——— day of ——— BETWEEN the Governor of West Bengal (hereinafter called "the vendor") of the one part AND CD, etc., (hereinafter called "the purchaser") of the other part.

---

1 When before the execution of a sale deed the purchaser has agreed to resell the property to a third person, it is unnecessary to have two sale deeds and the seller may be requested to execute a deed in favour of the sub-purchaser in this form. Sometimes now-a-days the owner enters into a contract with a developer or builder for development of land. The land is not sold outright to the developer or builder but possession is given to him with permission to build apartments or shops, etc. The developer is given the right to finalise deals for sale, to the ultimate purchasers, of the apartments or shops so built. The sale deeds are then executed either by the owner alone or by the owner and developer jointly [as in *Ajmera Housing Corporation* v. *Amrit Patel*, (1998) 6 SCC 500, para 3] to those ultimate purchasers directly. See also Forms No. 42, 43 and 45, *post* and Preliminary Note, sub-head "Sale of Flats and Apartments, Development Agreements", page 792 *ante*.

WHEREAS—

(1) The land described in the schedule hereto vests in the State of West Bengal for the purpose of the Government of West Bengal;

(2) The said land was put up to auction sale by the Collector of —— district on behalf of the Government of West Bengal and the purchaser's bid of Rs. ———— being the highest was accepted;

(3) The said sale has been confirmed by the said Government by G.O. No. ———— dated ————;

(4) The purchaser has deposited the said sum of Rs. ———— into the Government Treasury at ———— to the credit of the said Government;

NOW THIS DEED WITNESSES as follows:

1. In pursuance of the said auction sale and in consideration of the sum of Rs. ———— paid by the purchaser as aforesaid (the receipt of which the vendor hereby acknowledges) the vendor hereby transfers to the purchaser the land described in the schedule hereto TO HOLD the same to the purchaser as absolute owner subject to the payment of such Government revenue, cesses and taxes as may be assessed or imposed thereon.

2. *As in Form* 1.

PROVIDED ALWAYS and it is hereby agreed that in each of the covenants herein contained the expression "the vendor" hereinbefore used includes his successors and assigns and the expression "the purchaser" hereinbefore used includes his heir, representatives, successors and assigns

The schedule herein referred to.

IN WITNESS WHEREOF, etc.

26—Sale of Leasehold Land

THIS DEED OF SALE is made, etc., (*as in Form* 1).

WHEREAS the vendor is in possession of all the land described in the schedule hereto under a lease dated ———— granted to the vendor by EF, etc., at the yearly rent of Rs. ———— for the term of ———— years subject to covenants by the lessee and conditions therein contained;

AND WHEREAS the vendor has agreed with the purchaser for the sale to him for the sum of Rs. ———— of the land described in the schedule hereto and comprised in the aforesaid lease;

NOW THIS DEED WITNESSES as follows:

1. In consideration of the sum of Rs. ———— to be paid at the time of the registration of this deed by the purchaser to the vendor, the vendor as

lessee hereby transfers to the purchaser ALL the said land described in the schedule hereto and comprised in the aforementioned lease TO HOLD the same to the purchaser for the residue now unexpired of the said term of ——— years subject henceforth to the payment of the rent reserved by and the performance and observance of covenants and conditions on the part of the lessee contained in the aforesaid lease.

2. The vendor hereby covenants with the purchaser as follows:

(1) That the rents, covenants and conditions by and in the said deed of lease reserved and contained have on the part of the vendor been duly paid and observed and performed up to the date hereof and that he has done nothing to incur forfeiture or to invalidate the lease;

(2) That the land hereby transferred shall be quietly entered into and upon and held and enjoyed either in its present state or by having house or bungalow built upon it without any interruption or disturbance by the vendor or any person claiming through or in trust for him;

(3) That the vendor will at the cost of the person requiring the same, execute and do every such assurance or thing necessary for the further or more perfectly assuring the said property to the purchaser, his successors and assigns as by him or them shall be reasonably required.

3. The purchaser hereby covenants with the vendor (FIRST) that he the purchaser will at all times hereafter during the subsistence of the said lease pay the yearly rent reserved by the said lease and observe and perform all the covenants and conditions contained in the said lease and henceforth on the part of the lessee to be observed and performed, AND (SECONDLY) that he will always hereafter keep indemnified the vendor from and against the payment of the said rent and the observance and performance of the said covenants and conditions and all actions, claims and demands whatsoever for or on account of the same or in any way relating thereto.

4. PROVIDED ALWAYS, etc., Interpretation clause (*as in Form* 1).

The schedule herein referred to

IN WITNESS WHEREOF, etc.

27—Sale of Lessee's Rights in Land and of Proprietary Rights in House Standing thereon

THIS DEED OF SALE is made, etc., (*as in Form* 1).

WHEREAS—

(1) By a lease dated the ——— the land described in the schedule

hereto was demised by the owners in favour of XY for the term of ninety years from the ——— at the annual rent of Rs. ——— and on the terms and conditions specified in the said lease;

(2) The said XY constructed a bungalow on the said land;

(3) By a sale deed dated the ——— the said XY sold the aforesaid bungalow, out-houses and buildings standing on the said land and also assigned all his lessee's rights in the said land under the aforesaid lease to the vendor;

(4) The vendor has agreed with the purchaser to assign the said lessee's rights and to sell the said bungalow, out-houses, buildings, etc., for a total price of Rs. ———.

NOW THIS DEED WITNESSES as follows:

1. In pursuance of the said agreement and in consideration of the sum of Rs. ——— paid by the purchaser to the vendor (the receipt of which the vendor hereby acknowledges) the vendor as lessee hereby assigns to the purchaser ALL the land described in the schedule hereto and delineated on the plan hereto annexed and thereon shown as coloured red TO HOLD the same to the purchaser for the unexpired residue of the term of the lease subject henceforth to the payment of the annual rent thereby reserved and to the covenants and conditions therein contained and on the part of the lessee to be observed and performed.

2. In further pursuance of the said agreement and for the consideration aforesaid the vendor as owner hereby transfers to the purchaser ALL that bungalow, outhouses and buildings standing upon the aforesaid land and described in the schedule hereto TO HOLD the same to the purchaser as absolute owner but subject to such covenants in the aforesaid lease as may relate to such bungalow and buildings.

3, 4 and 5 (*As in* 2, 3 *and* 4 *of Form* 26).

The schedule herein referred to

IN WITNESS WHEREOF, etc.

28—Sale of Leasehold Property (Another Form)

WHEREAS, etc. (*as in Form No.* 26)

AND WHEREAS etc. (*as in Form No.* 26).

NOW THIS DEED made on the ——— day of ——— BETWEEN the aforesaid lessee AND XY, etc., (hereinafter called "the Purchaser").

WITNESSES that in consideration of Rs. ——— paid by the

purchaser to the lessee (the receipt of which is hereby acknowledged) the lessee hereby assigns to the purchaser ALL that property comprised in the aforesaid lease TO HOLD the same to the said purchaser for the residue now unexpired of the term of ——— years therein mentioned, subject to the payment of the rent and performance and observance of the lessee's covenants and conditions reserved and contained in the said lease AND the purchaser hereby agrees to keep the lessee, his heirs, executors and successors indemnified against the said rent, covenants and conditions and all such proceedings, claims and expenses in respect thereof.

IN WITNESS WHEREOF, etc.

29—Sale of Leasehold Property, the Lessor also Joining to Release the Lessee and to take New Covenants from the Purchaser

THIS DEED OF SALE is made on the ——— day of ——— BETWEEN AB, etc., (hereinafter called "the vendor") of the first part AND CD, etc., (hereinafter called "the purchaser") of the second part AND EF, etc., (hereinafter called "the lessor") of the third part.

WHEREAS (*as in Form* 26 *substituting the words* "the lessor" *for the words* "EF, etc.").

AND WHEREAS the lessor agreed to release the vendor from the rent and covenants and conditions on his part entered in the said lease and to accept the said rent and the performance of the said covenants from the purchaser;

NOW THIS DEED WITNESSES as follows:

1. In consideration of, etc., (*as in Form* 26).

2. *As in Form* 1.

3. In consideration of the covenant by the purchaser hereinafter contained, the lessor hereby releases the vendor, his estate and effects from all liability in respect of the rent reserved by and the covenants and conditions contained in the aforesaid lease and all claims and demands in respect of any breach whether present or future of any such covenant or conditions.

PROVIDED that the release hereinbefore contained shall not affect the said covenants and conditions so far as the same are binding on the said demised property and the persons from time to time in possession thereof but have effect only as regards the personal liability of the vendor, his heirs, executors and successors thereunder.

PROVIDED ALSO that neither the said release nor anything herein contained shall prejudice or affect the right of the lessor or his heirs, executors, successors and assigns to re-enter upon the said demised property for non-payment of rent or breach of covenants or conditions reserved and contained in the said lease;[1]

4. The purchaser hereby covenants with the lessor henceforth to pay the rent reserved by the aforesaid lease on the days and in the manner therein provided and to observe all the covenants and conditions therein contained and on the lessee's part to be performed and observed and also agrees that the lessor, his heirs, executors, successors and assigns will have the power of re-entry provided in the said lease under circumstances therein stated.

5. PROVIDED ALWAYS, etc. (*As* 3 *in Form* 1, *adding reference to the lessor*).

IN WITNESS, etc. (*As in other forms*).

30—Sale of Part of Leasehold Property held under One Lease, Rent being Apportioned

THIS DEED OF SALE is made, etc., (*as in Form* 1).

WHEREAS by a deed of lease dated the ——— day of ——— one PQ, etc., demised ALL that, etc., to the vendor for the term of ——— years from the ——— at the yearly rent of Rs. ——— and subject to the covenants and conditions therein contained.

AND WHEREAS the vendor has agreed with the purchaser for the sale to him of the property described in the schedule hereto being part of the property comprised in the said lease for Rs. ——— subject to the yearly rent of Rs. ——— part of the said yearly rent of Rs. ——— and on the terms and conditions hereinafter contained.

NOW THIS DEED WITNESSES as follows:

1. In consideration of the sum of Rs. ——— to be paid at the time of the registration of this deed by the purchaser to the vendor, the vendor as lessee hereby transfers to the purchaser ALL the said land described in the schedule hereto and comprised in the above mentioned lease TO HOLD the same to the purchaser for the residue now un-expired of the said term of ——— years subject to the yearly rent of Rs. ——— reserved by the lease and to the performance and observance of the covenants and conditions on the part of the lessee contained in the aforesaid lease.

---

1 This proviso may be omitted if the lessor also agrees not to enforce any penalty against the property on account of any past breach.

2. The vendor hereby covenants with the purchaser (*as in Form* 26).

3. The vendor and the purchaser hereby covenant with each other as follows:

(1) The vendor will pay Rs. ———— and the purchaser Rs. ——— out of the said yearly rent of Rs. ———— reserved by the said lease.

(2) The purchaser and the vendor will perform and observe all the covenants and conditions contained in the said lease and on the part of the lessee to be performed and observed so far as the same relate the premises hereby sold and those not hereby sold respectively.

(3) The purchaser and the vendor will indemnify each other against all claims and demands for or on account of the non-payment of the said rent and the non-performance of the said covenants and conditions so far as they relate to the portions of the property comprised in the said lease belonging to them respectively.

(4) All moneys which may become payable either to the vendor or the purchaser under the respective covenants or indemnity hereinbefore contained shall be a charge on the portion of the property comprised in the lease belonging to the other of them.

(5) Interpretation clause (*as in Form* 1).

The schedule herein referred to.

IN WITNESS WHEREOF, etc. (as in other Forms)

31—Sale of Leasehold Property, when Rent is Apportioned with the Consent of the Lessor

THIS DEED OF SALE is made on the ———— day of ——— BETWEEN AB, etc., (hereinafter called "the vendor") of the first part AND CD, etc., (hereinafter called "the purchaser") of the second part AND PQ, etc., (hereinafter called "the lessor") of the third part.

WHEREAS (*as in Form* 30, substituting the words "the lessor" for "one PQ, etc.");

AND WHEREAS the vendor has agreed with the purchaser for sale to him of the property described in the schedule hereto being part of the property comprised in the said lease for Rs. ————;

AND WHEREAS it has been agreed between the vendor and purchaser with the consent of the lessor that the said yearly rent of Rs. ———— reserved by the said lease should be apportioned between the part of the demised property sold to the purchaser and that remaining with the vendor in the manner hereinafter appearing;

NOW THIS DEED WITNESSES as follows:

1. (*As in Form* 30)

2. (*As in Form* 26)

3. The parties hereto hereby agree as follows:

(1) The yearly rent reserved by the said lease shall be apportioned in such manner that Rs. ——— shall henceforth be payable in respect of the property hereby sold and Rs. ———— in respect of the remaining property comprised in the said lease and the covenants and conditions on the part of the lessee contained in the said lease shall be so read that no breach of any covenant or conditions on the part of the vendor shall give rise to any right of re-entry on the premises hereby sold to the purchaser.

(2) The rights, powers and remedies conferred on the lessor by the lease or otherwise shall continue in full force, but shall extend and apply to the hereby apportioned part of the said rent and the said several parts of the property for which such apportioned parts of the rent are hereby expressed to be payable as fully as they applied to the whole of such rent and the whole of such property.

(3) Interpretation clause—(*as in Form* 29).

The schedule herein referred to.

IN WITNESS WHEREOF, etc. (*As in other forms*)

32—Sale of Factory with Business on "As Is, Where Is" Basis[1]

THIS SALE DEED is made on ——— between ——— a company within the meaning of the Companies Act 1956/2013 and having its registered office at ——— (hereinafter called "the Vendor") of the one part AND ——— a Company within the meaning of the Companies Act 1956/2013 and having its registered office at ——— (hereinafter called "the Purchaser") of the second part.

WHEREAS the Vendor had obtained ——— acres of land situated at ——— on lease by a deed dated ——— from ——— Development Authority (hereinafter referred to as "the Development Authority") for a period of ——— years on an annual rental of Rs. ——— for the purposes of setting up a ——— factory on the terms and conditions contained therein;

AND WHEREAS the Vendor installed a ——— factory on the above

1 A somewhat similar transaction is the subject of decision of stamp duty in *Duncan Industries Ltd.* v. *State of U.P.*, AIR 1998 All 72.

said land consisting of a manufacturing plant with an aggregate installed capacity of ——— and has been engaged in the business of running of the said factory and selling its products;

AND WHEREAS the Vendor has agreed to sell his above said business as a going concern on "as is, where is" basis and the purchaser has agreed to purchase it which comprises:

(a) the said land together with the plant described in the Schedule hereunder;

(b) the power plant and all other movable capital assets including vehicles, furniture, air conditioners, stand-by systems, pipelines and railway siding relating to the said factory;

(c) all stocks of raw material, finished and semi-finished goods, work in process, stores and spares of all kinds relating thereto;

(d) all other current assets including cash in hand, book debts, outstanding claims, bills, and loans and advances relating thereto;

(e) all industrial licences, import licences, excise licences, storage licences, factory licences, permissions and all other tangible and intangible benefits pertaining thereto, with the research and development registration for Research and Development Centre to the extent transferable and relating exclusively to the said business;

(f) all rights in leaseholds and tenancies pertaining to the said business to the extent transferable;

(g) the technology package comprising technical information, drawings, designs, reports, operating manuals, process know-how, trade marks, formulas, efficiency improvement techniques, pollution control and environmental control manuals and instructions as are owned by the Vendor on this date and/or used by the Vendor in the said business with free rights to use and disclose in India as on the date hereof;

(h) all current liabilities relating exclusively to the said business;

NOW THIS DEED WITNESSES as follows:

1. That in consideration of the sum of Rs. ——— paid by the Purchaser to the Vendor, the receipt whereof the Vendor hereby acknowledges, the Vendor does hereby grants, transfer, convey, assure and assign unto and in favour of the Purchaser ALL THAT premises, buildings, lands, immovable structures more fully and particularly described in the Schedule hereunder together with all property rights, title and interests mentioned hereinabove TO HAVE and TO HOLD unto the Purchaser the said business including the said factory as a going on concern on "as is,

where is" basis on this day, absolutely and forever free from all encumbrances, charges, liens, attachments or trusts of whatsoever nature.

2. That the Vendor has handed over possession of the said business and factory together with all movable assets comprised in the above said business to the Purchaser.

3. That the Vendor and Purchaser have executed a separate agreement with the Development Authority to ensure that the Purchaser shall pay directly to the Development Authority the enhanced rent of Rs. ——— per annum payable in respect of the said land for the remainder of the period of lease.

4. That the Vendor hereby covenants with the Purchaser that notwithstanding any act, deal, matter or thing whatsoever that the Vendor may have made, done, committed and/or knowingly or willingly suffered to the contrary, the Vendor now has good right, full power and absolute authority to convey and transfer all the lands, buildings, premises, immovable structures, movable properties, rights and interests, etc., hereby conveyed or transferred or expressed or intended so to be unto and to the use of the Purchaser in the manner aforesaid and the Purchaser shall from time to time and at all times hereinafter peaceably and quietly possess and enjoy the said properties without any hindrance, interruption, disturbance, claims or demands whatsoever from or by the Vendor or by any person claiming through the Vendor.

5. That the Vendor does hereby covenant with the Purchaser that the Vendor shall and will from time to time and at all times hereafter at the request and expenses of the Purchaser, its successors or assigns make, do, acknowledge and execute or cause to be done, execute all such acts, deeds and things whatsoever for further more and effectively or satisfactorily assuring the aforesaid properties unto the Purchaser as shall be reasonably required.

6. That the Purchaser covenants to the Vendor to be bound by all the covenants and obligations cast upon the Vendor as the Lessee of the said land and to indemnify and hold the Vendor harmless from any breach thereof.

The schedule herein referred to:

IN WITNESS WHEREOF etc.

33—Sale of Mortgagee Rights under a Usufructuary Mortgage

THIS DEED OF SALE is made, etc., (*as in Form* 1)

WHEREAS by a deed of mortgage dated ————, one XY usufructuarily mortgaged the property mentioned in the schedule hereto to the vendor for Rs. ————.

AND WHEREAS the vendor has agreed with the purchaser to assign and transfer to him the said mortgage debt and all his right, title and interest under the hereinbefore recited deed of mortgage for the sum of Rs. ———;

NOW THIS DEED WITNESSES as follows:

1. In pursuance of the said agreement and in consideration of the sum of Rs. ———— paid on or before the execution of these presents by the purchaser to the vendor (the receipt of which the vendor hereby acknowledges) the vendor hereby assigns to the purchaser ALL THAT principal sum of Rs.———— secured by the hereinbefore recited deed of mortgage and the full benefit of all powers, rights, remedies and securities contained in the said deed of mortgage and thereby expressly or impliedly conferred upon the vendor TO HOLD the same to the purchaser absolutely.

2. In further pursuance of the said agreement and for the consideration aforesaid the vendor hereby transfers to the purchaser ALL that property comprised in the said deed of mortgage and set forth in the schedule hereto and all the estate, right, title and interest of the vendor to and upon the same TO HOLD the same to the purchaser subject to such right or equity of redemption as is now subsisting in the said property under or by virtue of the said deed of mortgage.

3. The vendor hereby covenants with the purchaser as follows:

(1) and (2) (*as in Form* 1).

(3) The vendor has not at any time hereinbefore done or executed or knowingly suffered or been party or privy to anything whereby the said principal sum and the property hereby respectively assigned and transferred or any part thereof respectively is, can or may be released, affected or encumbered in any way howsoever.

4. PROVIDED ALWAYS, Interpretation clause, etc. (*as in Form* 1).

The schedule herein referred to.

IN WITNESS WHEREOF, etc.

34—Sale of a Mortgaged Property to the Mortgagee

THIS DEED OF SALE, etc. (*as in Form* 1).

WHEREAS the vendor is the owner of the property described in the schedule hereto;

AND WHEREAS by a deed dated ——— the said property was usfructuarily mortgaged to PQ the ancestor of the purchaser for the sum of Rs. ——— by XY the ancestor of the vendor;

AND WHEREAS the said sum of Rs. ——— is still due and owing under the said usufructuary mortgage deed;

AND WHEREAS the vendor has agreed with the purchaser for sale to him of the said property for the sum of Rs. ——— and it has been agreed that out of the said sum of Rs. ——— the sum of Rs. ——— shall be retained by the purchaser on account of his debt due under the said mortgage deed.

NOW THIS DEED WITNESSES as follows:

1. In pursuance of the said agreement and in consideration of the said sum of Rs. ——— retained by the purchaser in full satisfaction of the mortgage debt remaining due and owing to him upon the said mortgage deed (which mortgage debt the purchaser hereby declares to be fully satisfied accordingly and from which the purchaser hereby releases the vendor) and also in consideration of the sum of Rs. ——— paid to the vendor by the purchaser in cash before the execution of these presents (the receipt of which sum the vendor hereby acknowledges) the vendor hereby transfers by way of sale to the purchaser ALL his rights, title and interest in the property described in the schedule hereto TO HOLD the same to the purchaser (*rest as in Form* 1).

35—Sale of a Mortgaged Property to the Mortgagee—Another Form

THIS DEED OF SALE is made, etc. (*as in Form* 1).

WHEREAS the vendor is the owner of the property described in the schedule hereto.

AND WHEREAS the same property is subject to a mortgage made in a deed dated ——— by PQ the deceased father of the vendor in favour of XY the predecessor-in-title of the purchaser for securing the sum of Rs.——— and interest thereon at the rate specified in the deed of mortgage;

AND WHEREAS a sum of Rs. ——— is now due to the purchaser on account of principal and interest due under the said mortgage;

AND WHEREAS the vendor has agreed with the purchaser for the sale to him of the said property for the sum of Rs. ——— out of which the purchaser is to pay Rs. ——— in cash to the vendor and to credit the remaining sum of Rs. ——— towards his said debt from which the purchaser has agreed to release the vendor;

NOW THIS DEED WITNESSES as follows;

1. In pursuance of the said agreement and in consideration of Rs.—— paid by the purchaser to the vendor (the receipt of which the vendor hereby acknowledges) and of the release by the purchaser hereinafter contained the vendor hereby transfers to the purchaser the said property described in the schedule hereto TO HOLD the same absolutely freed from all rights or equity of redemption and from all claims and demands of the vendor under the said mortgage.

2. The purchaser hereby releases the vendor from liability of the said debt due under the aforesaid mortgage deed and from all suits, costs, claims and demands whatsoever in respect thereof or otherwise under the said mortgage.

3. The purchaser hereby declares that the said mortgage shall forthwith merge in the absolute title hereby transferred to him and shall be deemed to be forever extinguished.

(*Rest as in other Forms*).

36—Sale of Mortgaged Property, Mortgage to be Satisfied out of Consideration, Mortgagee Joining

THIS DEED OF SALE is made on the ——— day of ——— BETWEEN AB, etc., (hereinafter called "the vendor") of the first part AND XY, etc., (hereinafter called "the mortgagee") of the second part AND CD, etc., (hereinafter called "the purchaser") of the third part.

WHEREAS—

(1) The vendor is the absolute owner of the property described in the schedule hereto;

(2) By a deed of mortgage dated ———— the vendor mortgaged the said property to the mortgagee to secure payment of Rs. ———— with interest at the rate therein mentioned;

(3) The amount now due under the said mortgage deed on account of the principal and interest is Rs. ————;

(4) The vendor has agreed to sell the said property to the purchaser free from encumbrances for Rs. ————;

(5) It has been agreed between the parties hereto that out of the aforesaid sum of Rs. ———— the sum of Rs. ———— shall be paid to the mortgagee and that the mortgagee shall also join the deed;

NOW THIS DEED WITNESSES as follows:

1. In consideration of the sum of Rs. ———— paid by the purchaser as follows viz., the sum of Rs. ———— by the direction of the vendor to the mortgagee (the receipt of which sum the mortgagee hereby acknowledges) and the sum of Rs. ———— to the vendor (the receipt of which sum and the payment of the sum of Rs. ———— to the mortgagee the vendor hereby acknowledges) the vendor as owner hereby transfers and the mortgagee as mortgagee and by the direction of the vendor hereby transfers and releases to the purchaser ALL that, etc., TO HOLD the same to the purchaser as absolute owner discharged from all the principal money and interest secured by the aforesaid mortgage and from all claims and demands thereunder.

(*Rest as in other Forms*).

37—Sale of Mortgaged Property, Mortgagee Joining and Releasing Vendor on Purchaser Agreeing to Pay the Mortgage Money

THIS DEED OF SALE, etc., (*as in Form* 36).

(1), (2) and (3) (*Same as in Form* 36).

(4) The vendor has agreed to sell the said property to the purchaser subject to the said mortgage but free from all other encumbrances at the price of Rs. ————;

(5) The mortgagee at the request of the vendor and the purchaser and in consideration of the covenants by the purchaser hereinafter contained has agreed to join in this deed for the purpose of releasing the vendor in manner hereinafter appearing.

NOW THIS DEED WITNESSES as follows:

1. In consideration of Rs. ———— paid by the purchaser to the vendor (the receipt of which the vendor hereby acknowledges), the vendor hereby transfers, etc., TO HOLD the same to the purchaser subject to the aforesaid mortgage and the principal thereby secured and all interest now due and henceforth to become due in respect thereof.

2. The purchaser hereby covenants with the mortgagee to pay to him on the ———— day of ———— next the said sum of Rs. ———— now due under the aforesaid deed of mortgage and to pay in the meantime and until the whole of the said amount has been paid, interest on the said amount or on so much thereof as shall remain for the time being payable at the rate of —— percent per annum by equal half yearly payments on the ———— and the —— in each year.

3. The mortgagee hereby releases the vendor from his covenant to pay principal and interest contained in the aforesaid deed of mortgage and from all claims and demands under or in respect thereof.

4 and 5. Covenants and Interpretation clause - (*as in clauses* 2 *and* 3 *of Form* 1, (however, in clause 2(4), for the word "encumbrances" the words "any other encumbrances" shall be substituted and in clause 3, reference to the mortgagee shall be added).

38—Sale of Mortgaged Property, Mortgagee Relying on the Rest of the Security and Releasing the Property Sold

THIS DEED OF SALE, etc., (*as in Form* 36).

WHEREAS—

(1) (*as in Form* 36);

(2) (*Same as in Form* 36, *adding the words* "together with other properties" after the words "the said property");

(3) The vendor has agreed to sell the said property to the purchaser for Rs. ————;

(4) The mortgagee being satisfied that the other property comprised in his mortgage is sufficient security for the money due to him thereunder has agreed to join herein to release the property hereby intended to be sold.

NOW THIS DEED WITNESSES as follows:

1. In consideration of Rs. ——— paid to the vendor by the purchaser (the receipt of which the vendor hereby acknowledges) the vendor as owner, etc., (*as in Form* 36).

2. The mortgagee who retains possession of the several documents specified in the second schedule hereto will, upon every reasonable request of the purchaser, and at the cost of the person making the request, produce all or any of such documents and furnish such true copies or extracts therefrom as the purchaser may require and will, in the meantime, keep the said documents safe and undefiled unless prevented from so doing by one or other cause beyond his control.

3. Covenants and Interpretation clause—(*as in Form* 1).

39—Sale of Mortgaged Property by Mortgagee under Power of Sale given by the Mortgage Deed

THIS DEED OF SALE is made, etc., (*as in Form* 1).

WHEREAS by a deed of mortgage dated the ——— and made between

AB, etc., of the one part and the vendor of the other part, the property described in the schedule hereto with other property was mortgaged to the vendor for securing the principal sum of Rs. ——— and interest;

AND WHEREAS by the aforesaid deed of mortgage, it was agreed that the mortgagee should in certain events (which have happened) have power to sell without the intervention of the Court the property comprised in the said mortgage or part thereof for the realisation of the money due to him under the said mortgage;

AND WHEREAS on the ——— the vendor has served on the said AB a notice in writing requiring payment of the principal money secured by the aforesaid mortgage and default has been made by the said AB in payment thereof for more than three months after service of the said notice (*or*, AND WHEREAS a sum of Rs. ——— due on account of interest under the said mortgage deed has been in arrears for over three months);[1]

AND WHEREAS the vendor having power of sale under the aforesaid provision of the said mortgage deed and under Sec. 69 of the Transfer of Property Act, 1882, has agreed to sell to the purchaser the property described in the schedule hereto for the sum of Rs. ———;

NOW THIS DEED WITNESSES as follows:

1. In consideration of the sum of Rs. ——— paid by the purchaser to the vendor (the receipt of which the vendor hereby acknowledge) the vendor as mortgagee in exercise of the hereinbefore recited power of sale hereby transfers, etc., TO HOLD the same to the purchaser as absolute owner freed from all right of redemption and from all claims whatsoever under the aforesaid deed of mortgage.

(*Covenants and provisos as necessary*).

40—Sale Deed, Vendor Reserving a Right of Way on the Land Sold for the Benefit of a Third Person

THIS DEED OF SALE, etc., (*as in Form* 1).

WITNESSES as follows:

1. In consideration, etc., the vendor as owner hereby transfers to the purchaser ALL THAT, etc.

---

1 This amount due should be at least Rs. 500 and unpaid for three months after becoming due, Sec. 69, Transfer of Property Act. The mortgagee has also an alternative power of appointing a Receiver of the income of the property, vide Sec. 69A.

RESERVING nevertheless to XY, etc., a perpetual right of way in common with the purchaser at all times and for all purposes from and to the public highway on the ———over and across that portion of the road running from the main gate to the house hereby sold which is marked on the plan annexed hereto by letters ABC throughout the length of their respective plots subject to the payment by the said XY of a fair proportion of the expenses of maintaining and keeping the said way over and across the aforesaid portions of the said road in repair TO HOLD, etc.

(*Covenants and provisions as necessary*)

41—Sale of Property Subject to Restrictive Covenants

THIS DEED OF SALE is made, etc., (*as in Form* 1).

WHEREAS by a deed of sale dated ——— the property hereby intended to be sold was with other property purchased by the vendor from PQ, etc., and under the said deed of sale, the vendor entered into certain covenants and stipulations about the user of the said property and otherwise;

AND WHEREAS the vendor has agreed with the purchaser for the sale to him for the sum of Rs. ——— the property described in the schedule hereto subject to covenants and stipulations as hereinafter expressed.

NOW THIS DEED WITNESSES as follows:

1. In consideration, etc., (*as in Form* 1) *adding,* "subject to the said covenants and stipulations contained in the said deed of sale dated ———.

2. The purchaser hereby covenants with the vendor but by way of indemnity only that he will at all times hereafter duly perform and observe the said covenants and stipulations on the part of the vendor contained in the said deed of sale and will keep the vendor and his representatives indemnified against all suits, proceedings, costs, claims and demands whatsoever in respect of the said covenants and stipulations.

3. Covenants and Interpretation clause, etc. (*as in Form* 1).

42—Sale by Housing Board or Development Authority[1] of a Plot of Land, Part of an Estate laid out in Building Lots, Sold Subject to Restrictive Covenants by the Purchaser

THIS DEED OF SALE is made on the ——— day of ——— BETWEEN the ——— of ——— (hereinafter called "the Board"/ "Authority") of the one part AND CD, etc., (hereinafter called "the purchaser") of the other part.

WHEREAS—

(1) By a resolution dated ——— the Board/Authority resolved that the plot of land measuring about ——— acres situate at ——— and delineated on the plan annexed hereto which vested in the Board/Authority should be laid out in thirty lots as shown on the said plan for building purposes and roads be constructed and main sewers be laid beneath the same to the intent that each of the said lots should be used for building a dwelling house according to a general building scheme and that the owner or occupier for the time being of each such lot should be bound by the stipulations and restrictions contained in the second schedule hereto for the benefit and protection of the owner or occupier of every other of the said lots and of the Board/Authority.

(2) The Board/Authority put the said lots to auction sale on the ——— day of ——— at which sale lot Nos. ——— were sold at the price of Rs. ——— subject to the stipulations and restrictions contained in the second schedule hereto.

NOW THIS DEED WITNESSES as follows:

1. In consideration of the sum of Rs. ——— paid to the Board/Authority by the purchaser (the receipt of which the Board/Authority hereby acknowledges) the Board/Authority hereby transfers to the purchaser ALL that piece of land fully described in the first schedule hereto and delineated on the plan annexed hereto and thereon coloured red marked lot No. 30 TO HOLD the same to the purchaser subject to the performance and observance of the stipulations and restrictions specified in the second schedule hereto so far as the same are binding upon the purchaser.

2. The vendor hereby covenants, etc., (*as in Forms* 1).

---

1 The vendor can also be a municipal corporation or improvement trust. In that case "Corporation" or "Trust" may be mentioned in place of "Board/Authority" wherever occurring. The same form can be adapted with suitable modifications for sale by private builders, whether of plots or of built apartments. See also footnotes under Form No. 24, *ante* and Form No. 45(a), *post* explaining 'development agreements'.

3. The vendor as to the plot of land remaining vested in it to which the stipulations and restrictions mentioned in the second schedule hereto relate and the purchaser as to the land hereby sold hereby mutually covenant with each other and the purchaser also hereby covenants with the owner or owners for the time being of any other land to which the benefit of the said stipulations and restrictions is attached to perform and observe the said stipulations and restrictions mentioned in the second schedule hereto, but so that the said covenants shall not be personally binding upon the Board/Authority and the purchaser respectively except during the time of his or its respective ownership of the pieces of land where to the same respectively relate.

4. It is hereby agreed that unless there is anything repugnant in the subject or context the expression "the Board"/"Authority" used herein shall include its successors and assigns and the expression "the purchaser" shall include his heirs, representatives, successors and assigns.

The first schedule herein referred to

(Description of the land sold)

The second schedule herein referred to

Covenants

1. The purchaser will observe the building line shown upon the said plan except in regard to ordinary structural dressings, bay-windows or porches. No erection or building or portion thereof except as aforesaid shall project upon or overhang the space between the building house and road boundary as marked in the said plan.

2. The purchaser will within ———— months from the date of this sale deed erect and afterwards maintain on the said land one side wall as shown on the said plan and marked ———— within the boundary.

3. Fences adjoining the road and side fences so far as such side fences lie in front of the building line shall be dwarf walls not exceeding ———— metres in height with such irons thereon not exceeding on the whole ———— metres in height as shall be approved by the vendor's officers authorised in that behalf. All other fences shall be brick walls —— centimetres thick and ———— metres high and not more than ———— metres above the level of the footpath.

4. The purchaser will within ———— months build a dwelling house on the said land on an area of not less than ———— square metres and according to the elevations and plan approved by the ————.

5. The purchaser shall not make any alteration in the elevations or plan

of the said building except with the previous consent of ———;

6. The purchaser shall not use the house to be built on the said land or any part thereof otherwise than as a dwelling house and shall not use any part of the said land for carrying out any trade or business.

7. If any part of the said land shall be used for roads or approaches, the purchaser shall pave, make and complete at his own expense such roads or approaches to the satisfaction of the Board/Authority.

IN WITNESS WHEREOF, etc.

43—Deed of Mutual Covenants by Purchasers of various parts of a Building Site Leased out under a Building Scheme of Statutory Body for Observance of Restrictive Stipulations, the Vendor Covenanting in respect of Unsold Lots

THIS DEED is made on the ——— day of ——— BETWEEN the several persons who have or hereafter shall have signed their names in the first schedule hereto (all of them being hereinafter collectively referred to as the purchasers) of the one part AND the Municipal Board of ——— (hereinafter called "the Board")[1] of the other part.

WHEREAS—

(1) (*As in Form* 42); AND

(2) The Board has sold or intends to sell the said lots upon the term that the respective purchasers of the respective lots shall enter into and become bound by the said stipulations and restrictions and that the Board shall enter into and become bound by the same to the extent hereinafter appearing;

NOW THIS DEED WITNESSES as follows:

1. Each of the purchasers for himself, his heirs and assigns, to the intent that this covenant shall bind the lot purchased by him and the owner or owners thereof for the time being and all persons claiming through/under or in trust for him or them and shall enure for the benefit and protection of any and all other lots delineated on the said plan and the owner or owners of

1 If the vendor is a Housing Board, Improvement Trust, Development Authority or Housing Cooperative Society, then suitable words may be substituted as in Form No. 42, *ante*. The same form can be adapted with suitable modifications for sale of apartments by a co-operative society to its members by separate similar sale deeds (without the intervention of any local body or other authority). The provisions of various Apartments/Flats Ownership Acts in force in the States concerned may also be consulted (e.g., in U.P., Maharashtra, Karnataka, Delhi, W. Bengal and Gujarat).

such other lots and all persons claiming through under or in trust for such owner or owners, subject nevertheless as in clause 4 hereof mentioned, hereby covenants with every other of the purchasers, his or her heirs and assigns, and also as a separate covenant with the Board, its successors and assigns, that the covenanting purchaser will at all times hereafter perform and observe the stipulations and restrictions contained in the second schedule hereto so far as regards the lot purchased by or belonging to the covenanting purchaser.

2. In respect of any lot not sold by the Board and not entered in the first schedule hereto the Board and its successors and assigns shall be deemed to have entered into and become bound by the said stipulations and restrictions so far as they are of a negative character as if it was for the time being the purchasers of such lot.

3. The Board hereby covenants that if and when any of the lots remaining unsold shall be sold it shall be sold upon the term that the purchaser thereof shall sign his name in the first schedule hereto.

4. Neither the Board nor the covenanting purchaser nor their representatives or successors shall be liable for any breach of stipulations or restrictions contained in the second schedule hereto which may happen after they have disposed of the lot or lots in respect of which such covenant has been entered.

The first schedule herein referred to

No. of lot on plan	Name of purchaser	Signature of purchaser	Witness	Date of signature

The second schedule herein referred to

(Stipulations and Restrictions)

IN WITNESS WHEREOF ———— for and on behalf of the Board has signed this deed and the Board has affixed its common seal on this deed on the date first hereinbefore mentioned and the respective purchasers have put their signatures on the dates set opposite to their respective signatures in the first schedule hereto.

44—Deed of Cancellation of a Sale, with Reconveyance by Purchaser

THIS DEED, etc., (*as in Form* 1).

WHEREAS by a deed of sale dated the ——— registered in the office of the ——— on the ———, the vendor transferred the property described in the schedule hereto to the purchaser for a consideration of Rs. ——— retained by the purchaser to be applied in manner therein specified;

AND WHEREAS one EF represented to the vendor that under the law of pre-emption he had a preferential right of purchase as against the purchaser and offered to purchase the said property for the said price;

AND WHEREAS the vendor has been advised that the claim of the said EF is valid and to avoid future litigation it would be better to cancel the sale made in favour of the purchaser under the aforesaid deed of sale and to transfer the property in favour of the said EF;

AND WHEREAS the purchaser has agreed with the vendor to have the aforesaid deed of sale cancelled and to reconvey the said property to the vendor in consideration of the vendor releasing the purchaser from the obligations arising under the covenants by the purchaser contained in the aforesaid deed of sale.

NOW THIS DEED WITNESSES that in pursuance of the said agreement and for the consideration aforesaid the parties hereto hereby agree that the aforesaid deed of sale be and is hereby cancelled AND the purchaser hereby reconveys and transfers to the vendor ALL the property described in the schedule hereto TO HOLD the same to the vendor forever;

AND the vendor hereby releases the purchaser from the obligation under the covenants by the purchaser contained in the aforesaid deed of sale;

PROVIDED ALWAYS, etc.

The schedule herein referred to.

IN WITNESS WHEREOF, etc.

45(a)—Development Agreement[1]

This AGREEMENT is made at ——— on this ——— day of —— between AB, etc., hereinafter referred to as "the Owner" of the one part and CD etc., hereinafter referred to as "the Developers" of the other part;

WHEREAS the Owner is the proprietor in possession of land being plot No. ——— etc., situated at ——— fully described in the Schedule hereunder and desires to develop it by constructing a building thereon on Flat Ownership basis;

And Whereas the Developers have offered to develop the said land on the following terms and conditions:

NOW THEREFORE IT IS HEREBY AGREED BETWEEN THE PARTIES AS FOLLOWS:

1. The Owner hereby agrees to entrust and hand over to the Developers the work and right of development of the said land on the terms contained herein.

2. The Developers hereby agree to develop or cause to be developed the said property for and on behalf of the Owner on the terms mentioned herein and as permitted by the concerned authorities, by constructing a building thereon and other premises on Flat Ownership basis and then to sell the said flats to the Developers' own nominees. The Developers agree that they will obtain at their own cost and on their responsibility but in the name of the Owner and on his behalf whatever other permissions are required from any authority to develop the property.

3. The Developers will pay to the Owner a sum of Rs. ——— as consideration and out of it pay Rs. ——— as earnest money in part payment on execution of this Agreement and the balance of Rs. ——— will be paid in the following manner:

---

1 The documentation normally effected for a development of any land are (1) Development Agreement and (2) Allotment Agreement:

(1) Development Agreement is between the owner of the land (site) or old building (to be pulled down) and the developer. Under this agreement the owner gives the developer the right to build a multistoreyed complex (of flats or offices, shops etc.) and to allot them (generally, even before the construction is complete) to the prospective purchasers. The owner promises to execute transfer deeds direct to such allottees chosen by the developer, though the sale money from the allottees is received by the developer. (The allottees are also made members of a co-operative society or other like association with common mutual obligations among themselves as set out in the allotment agreements):

(2) The Allotment Agreement is between the developer and each allottee.

(Payment details)

4. The Developers shall not start any work on the said property unless the requisite permissions and certificates are issued by the concerned authorities.

5. Any external development of the said site and any construction thereon shall be at the cost and risk of the Developers. The Developers shall be at liberty to make necessary applications for the purpose of obtaining requisite permissions for the said work to the authorities concerned at their own cost in the name of the Owner, and the Owner shall join in such applications but the responsibility of obtaining such permissions will be on the Developers and at their cost.

6. The Owner hereby gives licence and permission to the Developers to enter upon the said land and the authority to commence, carry on and complete development thereof (including laying of roads, drainage, sewerage, water pipes and electricity cables) in accordance with duly sanctioned building plans.

7. If the Developers or their agents commit any breach of any of the terms and conditions of this Agreement then the Owner may terminate this agreement and forfeit all moneys paid thereunder and on such termination the license and permission given to the Developers as aforesaid shall stand revoked.

8. The Owner shall at the request of the Developers sign and execute from time to time any amended plans that may be required and other applications for construction of any structures on the said land for being sanctioned and approved by any authorities provided that all costs, charges and expenses incurred in this connection shall be borne and paid by the Developers alone.

9. The Developers shall indemnify and keep indemnified the Owner from and against all civil, criminal or administrative proceedings, fines, penalties, and all costs, charges, expenses, and damages incurred or suffered by the Owner in the course of such development.

10. The Owner shall, if required by the Developers, execute a power of attorney in favour of the Developers or their delegate giving all necessary powers for carrying out the work of development in all respects.

11. The Developers shall be at liberty to sell or allot the flats or any other structures in the building to be constructed on the said land to any parties at such price and on such terms and conditions and provisions as the Developers may think fit subject to any terms that may be imposed by any authority. All such allotments shall be made by the Developers at their own

risk and they alone shall be liable and responsible to such party or parties in connection with all dealings between them and such purchasers or allottees.

12. The Developers shall be entitled to put up or permit to be put up any hoardings or boards upon the said property advertising that the said complex is being developed by them, but shall not mention the name of the Owner in any manner. The Owner will be entitled to remove the board or hoardings forthwith if the Developers mention the Owner's name therein.

13. The Owner shall directly execute and deliver a deed or deeds of conveyance in favour of the Developers or their nominees including a co-operative society of purchasers of flats and other premises erected by the Developers. The Developers hereby agree to join in such Deeds as Confirming Party if required.

14. The Developers shall for any period after the date of this Agreement pay all Municipal and other taxes and all other charges, rates or cesses that may be levied by any authority in respect of the said building on the Owner.

15. The Developers shall indemnify the Owner and keep him indemnified against all losses, damages, costs, charges, expenses that may be incurred or suffered by the Owner on account of any breach of any of these terms and conditions.

IN WITNESS WHEREOF ETC.

45(b)—Agreement of Allotment

This Agreement is made at ——— on this ——— day of ——— between AB etc., ——— (hereinafter referred to as the "Developer" which expression shall, unless the context otherwise requires, be deemed to include its executors, successors and assigns) of the one part acting through its Attorney; AND CD etc., ——— (hereinafter referred to as "The Allottee" which expression shall, unless the context otherwise requires, be deemed to include its successors, assigns, administrators) of the other part acting through ———.

WHEREAS the Developer is developing a plot of land admeasuring —— in ——— approved for commercial use by constructing thereon a multistoried commercial complex called "——" in accordance with the building plans as approved by the —— (site plan enclosed as schedule-1).

AND WHEREAS the Allottee has applied to the Developer for the allotment of office space in ——— admeasuring ——— sq. metres (Super Area), more or less, at site on ——— floor in the (*name of complex*) which is under construction, (hereinafter referred to as the "*Premises*").

AND WHEREAS the Allottee has inspected the plot, tentative building plans, and other documents relating to title and competency of the Developer.

AND WHEREAS the Developer has represented to the Allottee that the Developer is the rightful owner and in possession of the land on which the Developer proposes to build the said complex;

NOW THEREFORE IT IS HEREBY AGREED BY AND BETWEEN THE PARTIES HERETO AS FOLLOWS:

1. That the Developer hereby allots to the Allottee the "Premises" in ——— measuring in the aggregate super built up area of approximately ——— sq. metres on ——— floor(s) being constructed in the (*name of complex*), as more particularly described in schedule II hereto, @ Rs. —— per sq. metre.

2. That the aforesaid price shall remain fixed and shall not be subject to change notwithstanding escalation in the cost of material and labour during the period of construction and also includes the cost of Fire Fighting and Electric Sub-station, but subject to clause 12 thereof.

3. That the above price is also inclusive of the External Development Charges (EDC) as laid down by the ——— which is Rs. ——— per acre, as on date. However in case there is any enhancement in the above EDC charges, the same shall be charged on pro rata basis of the saleable area of the Allottee.

4. That the aforesaid area is tentative and subject to change, as per Clause-14 hereof.

5. That if there are any additional levies, rates, taxes, charges, cesses or fees as assessed and attributable to the Developer as a consequence of Government statutory or other local authority's orders or statutory provision, the same, if applicable, shall also be paid by the Allottee.

6. That the Allottee agrees that for the purpose of calculating the sale price in respect of the said "Premises" in the said Complex, the super area shall include the covered area, inclusive of the columns and walls, the area utilised for common use services and facilities, that is to say, areas under staircases, circulation areas, walls, lifts, shafts, passages, corridors, and lobbies. The ownership of the terrace above the top floor shall remain with the Developer.

7. That the Allottee has agreed to pay a sum of Rs. ——— only, being the booking amount of the said "Premises", the receipt of which the Developer hereby acknowledges, and the Allottee shall pay the remaining

sale price as per the Instalment schedule described in Annexure-III hereto or as and when demanded by the Developer.

8. That the Allottee shall pay to the Developer by NEFT or RTGS or cheque/demand draft payable at ———, the instalments as detailed in Annexure-III and other sums payable under this Agreement and agreed to be paid by the Allottee.

9. That the timely payment of instalments and other charges mentioned herein are of the essence of this Agreement. It shall be incumbent on the Allottee to comply with the terms of payment and other terms and conditions for sale. In case of any breach of the terms of this Agreement, including delay in the payment of instalments and other charges as specified herein, the Allottee shall be liable to pay interest calculated from the due date of outstanding amount at the rate of 15% per annum compounded at the time of every succeeding instalment.

10. However, if the Allottee fails to pay the instalments and other charges with interest within three months from the due date of the outstanding amount, the Developer may forfeit the amount of earnest money (which is 10% of the sale consideration) deposited by the Allottee with the Developer, and the allotment shall thereupon stand cancelled and the Allottee shall be left with no lien, right, title or claim whatsoever in the said "Premises" and the Developer shall be entitled to resell the said "Premises" at its sole discretion. The amounts, if any, paid over and above the earnest money, shall however, be refunded to the Allottee by the Developer without any interest or compensation whatsoever.

11. That the Developer shall adjust the instalment amount received from the Allottee, first towards interest due, if any, and then towards the sale consideration of the "Premises". The sale deed shall however be executed only after all the outstandings under various heads herein have been paid in full.

12. That at present the fire safety measures at the said ——— Complex have been provided as per existing Fire Safety Code/Regulations. If, however, due to any subsequent legislation, Government Regulations, orders, directives or guidelines, or if deemed necessary by the Developer, any further fire safety measures are undertaken, the proportionate charges in respect thereof shall also be payable on demand by the Allottee.

13. That the Developer shall undertake the maintenance of the said ——— Complex either by itself or with the help of a MAINTENANCE AGENCY appointed by the DEVELOPER. For this purpose the Allottee agrees to sign a separate Maintenance Agreement which shall contain

the full scope of Maintenance of the Complex and shall pay the maintenance charges as decided by the Developer or the Maintenance Agency appointed by the Developer calculated on the super area basis purchased by the Allottee.

14. That the Allottee has seen and accepted the Building Plans, Building Designs and specifications shown to him and agrees that the Developer may make such variations, additions, deletions, alterations and modifications therein as may be directed by any competent authority, and the Allottee hereby gives his consent to such variations, additions, deletions, alterations and modifications. Further if as a result of the above mentioned alterations, there is either reduction or increase in the super area of the said "Premises" in the Complex or its location, no claim, monetary or otherwise, will be raised or accepted by either party except that the original agreed rate per sq. metre and other charges will be applicable on any increase or decrease in area. The Developer shall be liable to refund without interest only the extra price and other proportionate charges recovered from the Allottee. Likewise, the Developer shall be entitle to recover from the Allottee the additional price and other proportionate charges, as the case may be, without interest.

15. That the Developer confirms that the said Complex is to be a fully air-conditioned building and to have hundred percent generator based power back-up.

16. That the possession of the "Premises" shall be delivered to the Allottee in ——— years time from the date of signing of this Agreement, provided all amounts due and payable by the Allottee under this Agreement are paid to the Developer. Further, that the Developer shall give notice to the Allottee about the date of handing over possession, and the Allottee shall himself or through its authorised representative take possession of the "Premises". That the parties agree that in the event of the Allottee failing to accept and taking over possession of the "Premises" by such date as intimated to him by the Developer, the possession of the said "Premises" shall be deemed for the purposes of this Agreement to have been handed over by the Developer to the Allottee on the said date.

17. However, if the completion of the "Premises" is delayed for reasons of *force majeure* including go slow, work to rule, strike, lockout, civil commotion or by reasons of war or enemy action, terrorist action or any act of God, or delay in grant of completion or occupation certificate by the Government or any other public or competent authority or for any reason beyond the control of the Developer, the Developer shall be entitled to a reasonable extension of time of delivery of possession of the said

"Premises" in the said Complex.

18. (a) The Allottee agrees that after receiving the written notice from the Developer regarding the possession of the "Premises" in the said Complex the Allottee fails or neglects to take possession of the "Premises" within 90 days of service of the notice, the Allottee shall be liable to pay holding charges equivalent to 75% of the Maintenance Charges, and the "Premises" shall lie at the risk and cost of the Allottee after the expiry of the said period of 90 days. The holding charges shall be in addition to the amount payable by the Allottee as its share of the Government, municipal charges and maintenance charges.

(b) That the Developer shall execute the Sale Deed and have it registered in favour of the Allottee within a reasonable time after completion of the construction of the said "Premises" in the said Complex and after receipt from the Allottee of the full sale consideration and other dues, as also the Maintenance Charges as mentioned herein and the full cost of the registration charges, miscellaneous expenses and any other charges as mentioned in this agreement.

19. That it is mutually agreed that save and except in respect of the said "Premises" hereby agreed to be acquired by the Allottee, the Allottee shall have no claim, right, title or interest of any nature or kind whatsoever except right of ingress and egress over or in respect of land, open spaces and all or any of the common areas and basement in the said Complex, the possession whereof shall remain with the Developer who will maintain and upkeep the same until the same are taken over by any other body or by any legally constituted association of all the Allottee of the said Complex. This is subject to the provision of any Act relating to apartments governing the said Complex or rules framed thereunder, which shall govern the rights, title and obligations covered by this clause.

20. The Maintenance Charges shall *inter alia* include the following:

(a) Open Area Maintenance Charges: These charges relate to the maintenance of open spaces within the boundary wall of the said Complex, such as maintenance of compound wall, landscaping, electrification, water supply, tubewell, sewerage, drainage, roads and paths and other services including security and open car parking within the boundary walls but not outside the building.

(b) Common Area Maintenance Charges: These charges relate to the operation and maintenance of various services in the common areas viz., lifts, fire fighting equipment and other services inside the building including security, common area house-keeping, garbage disposal, etc. However, the maintenance of the area inside the Allottee's office space/Premises is the responsibility of the Allottee.

(c) **Maintenance charges of Basement and Common Services in the Basement:** These charges shall inter alia relate to maintenance and operation of various services in the basement like Diesal Generating Sets, Air Conditioning Plant, Electric Sub Station, Pumps, Fire Rooms and other services including Car Parking and Security in the Basement.

21. That the Developer shall maintain the said Complex for a period of three years and shall recover the maintenance charges, six months in advance, from the Allottee of said "Premises" and the Allottee hereby agrees to pay maintenance charges in advance.

22. That the tentative cost of maintenance charges per sq. metre per month works out to ———. The cost shall be determined six months before the handing over of possession of the premises taking into consideration the cost index increase of fuel rates, electricity rates and Minimum Wages then prevailing.

23. That the Allottee shall also pay before the due date the meter hire charges and the bills of consumption of electricity as recorded in the meters provided separately for recording consumption of power and electricity in the "Premises".

24. That the right of the Allottee to use the common facilities and services shall be subject to the payment of the maintenance charges as mentioned above and as decided by the Developer or the Maintenance Agency appointed by the Developer. Should these maintenance charges be not paid regularly or in the form as decided by the Developer or the Maintenance Agency appointed by the Developer, the Allottee shall have no right to use the common facilities or services. In other words, this right is not an integral part of sale and the same shall be available only on regular payment of the charges as envisaged herein.

25. That in the interest of all Allottees and other lawful Occupants of all premises comprised in the Complex, the Developer or the Maintenance Agency appointed by the Developer shall have the authority to deal with unlawful entrants, loiterers, peddlers, etc. and in order to deal more effectively with the security of the Complex and maintenance of order therein, to regulate and restrict their entry at the outer gate itself. In case of insistence by any person to enter, the security staff of the Complex will be at liberty to call upon the Allottee or other Occupant to come to the gate and personally escort such person from the gate to his office space and assume the responsibility of escorting them out as well.

26. That the internal security of the "Premises" and of its occupants or visitors or of the material kept therein and their safety shall be sole responsibility of the Allottee.

27. That Developer shall be entitled to connect the electric, water, sanitary and drainage fittings on the additional building(s) allowed on the additional land being attached to the said Complex, with the existing electric, water, sanitary and drainage sources but at the Developer's own cost.

28. That from the date of possession of the "Premises" the Allottee shall be responsible for the insurance of his "Premises" against fire, earthquake, riots, civil commotion, militant action etc., and of any persons and things in the Premises.

29. That the Allottee can assign, transfer, lease or part with possession of the "Premises" with the prior consent of the Developer, which consent shall not be unreasonably withheld. In such an event it shall be the responsibility of the Allottee to continue to pay any charges pertaining to the "Premises" of whatsoever nature payable under this Agreement to the Developer. Further the Allottee shall not sub-divide the "Premises" in parts without the prior consent of the Developer except any partition, additions, alterations as stipulated in clause 38 hereunder.

30. That the Allottee shall carry out day to day maintenance of the "Premises" and the fixtures and fittings installed therein and the normal maintenance, including painting and distempering and polishing the interiors, of the "Premises" at its own cost.

31. That the Allottee shall permit the Developer or the Maintenance Agency so appointed by the Developer and their agents at all reasonable hours, to enter the "Premises" for the purpose of inspection or maintenance.

32. That the Allottee shall use the "Premises" for office purposes only and not carry on or permit to be carried on in the "Premises" or in any part thereof any activities which shall be or are likely to be unlawful, obnoxious or to cause nuisance, annoyance or disturbance to other occupants of the Block wherein the "premises" are situated or store any goods of hazardous or combustible nature or which are so heavy as to affect the construction or the structure of the said Block or any part thereof or in any manner interfere in the common use. The usage of the "Premises" for office shall be unrestricted and uninterrupted and shall be made available at all times of day and night to the Allottee, its employees, servants, representatives, customers, visitors and invitees.

33. That the Allottee shall display its name and address of its

registered office only at such places as mutually decided between him and the Developer and not put up any name or sign board, publicity or advertisement material on the external facade of the block or anywhere in the common areas without the prior approval of the Developer in writing.

34. That the Developer shall plan and distribute its electrical loads in conformity with the electrical systems installed by the Developer.

35. That should any modifications, additions, alterations be required in the fire-fighting equipment, electrical and other systems installed, the Developer shall if feasible make such changes and be entitled to recover from the Allottee all additional costs on this account.

36. Except in the event of a mechanical defect or electrical failure or for any reason beyond its control, the Developer or Maintenance Agency shall provide air-conditioning facilities and the lift facilities to the "Premises" during the normal office hours i.e. between ——— on all week days except ———.

37. That subject to the Allottee paying all amounts mentioned herein and observing and performing the terms, conditions and covenants contained herein he shall be entitled to hold, use and enjoy the "Premises" and every part thereof without any interruption by the Developer or any person or persons claiming under it or for or on its behalf.

38. That the Allottee shall be free to carry out at his own cost but without damaging the main structure of the "Premises"/Block as well as the False Ceiling/Sprinkler system provided inside the "Premises", any erection of internal partitions and other internal alterations and additions which are not visible from outside, as may be considered by him to be necessary for his business:

PROVIDED THAT if any such additions or alterations, require the prior approval or permission of any Municipality or any other local body or other Authority, the Allottee shall not carry out such additions or alterations or erections except after obtaining the approval or permission or complying with the rules and regulations, of such Municipal or local body or Government authority.

39. That if any amount payable by the Allottee under this Agreement shall be in arrears and unpaid for a period of 30 days after the same has become due, or if the Allottee shall omit to perform, observe any covenant or condition under this Agreement and shall continue to do so for 30 days after written notice received in respect thereof, or the Allottee is adjudicated an insolvent, the Developer may forthwith re-enter upon the Premises or upon any part thereof and this agreement shall stand determined but without

prejudice to any claim which the Developer may have against the Allottee in respect of any such breach, non-performance or non-observance of such covenants or conditions.

40. That all costs, charges and expenses payable on or in respect of this agreement and on all other instruments and deeds to be executed pursuant to this agreement, including stamp duty and registration charges on this agreement and the sale deed to be executed, shall be borne by the Allottee.

41. That the Allottee shall comply with all legal requirements for purchase of immovable property, wherever applicable, after execution of the agreement herein and sign all applications, forms, affidavits, undertakings etc., for the said purpose. This includes in particular the requirements of Sec. 269 UC of the Income Tax Act if so applicable and the Allottee shall sign any Form as and when required by the Developer.

42. This agreement constitutes the entire agreement between the parties and revokes and supersedes all previous discussions, correspondence and agreements, if any between the parties, concerning the matters covered herein. The terms and conditions embodied in this Agreement shall be incorporated in the sale deed and shall form part thereof.

43. That the Allottee shall abide by the laws of the land including any local enactments in respect of this agreement and the "Premises". The Developer may, after notice in writing to the Allottee, inspect the "Premises" from time to time at frequencies considered necessary by the Developer and should there be any contravention, the Allottee will ensure compliance with the requirements as per the applicable laws. Any penalities levied by the Government, State, Municipal Body etc., as a result of non-compliance by the Allottee in respect of the "Premises" will be borne by the Allottee.

44. That any notice, letter or communication to be made, served or communicated unto the Developer under these presents shall be deemed to be duly made, served or communicated only if the notice or letter or communication is addressed to the Developer at the address shown above or changed addresses as may be intimated by the Developer in this behalf and sent by registered post. Similarly any notice, letter or communication to the Allottee shall be deemed to be made, served or communicated only if the same are addressed to the address of the Allottee as mentioned above, and thereafter when the corporate office of the Allottee is shifted to the "Premises" at the said address and sent by registered post.

IN WITNESS WHEREOF ETC.

46(1)—Agreement for Sale

(For Sale through Power of Attorney)[1]

This Agreement to Sell is made at ——— on ——— BETWEEN AB, etc., ——— (hereinafter called the First Party) of the one part and CD, etc., ——— (hereinafter called the Second Party) of the other part.

The expressions "First Party" and "Second Party", wherever they occur in the body of this agreement shall except where the context otherwise requires, include their respective successors, executors, administrators, and assigns.

Whereas the First Party is the owner and in possession of Flat No. ——— with reserved parking situated at ——— allotted by —— Development Authority, vide ———;

And Whereas the First Party has agreed to sell, transfer and convey his rights, interests, liens and title in the said flat to the Second Party for a consideration of Rs. ———;

And Whereas the Second Party has agreed to purchase, acquire and possess the same from the First Party on the following terms and conditions;

NOW THIS AGREEMENT WITNESSES AS UNDER:

1. That the entire sale consideration amount has been received by the First Party from the Second Party prior to the execution of this agreement The First Party has received payment as under:—

Amount	Draft/Pay order/Cheque No.	Drawn on

2. That the First Party has delivered vacant peaceful physical possession of the said flat unto the Second Party at the spot along with all the original documents related thereto.

3. That the First Party has assured the Second Party that he is the sole and absolute owner of the said flat (with leasehold rights in the land beneath it) and that the same is free from all encumbrances or agreements, or court injunctions, attachments or disputes.

4. That the First Party shall not have any rights, interest or liens on the said property henceforth and the Second Party shall be its sole owner henceforth for all intents and purposes and the Second Party only shall

1 For giving effect to such transactions, the following documents are normally needed: (1) Agreement for sale, (2) Power of Attorney, (3) Special Power of Attorney, (4) Possession Letter, (5) Will. See also, Preliminary Note, page 779.

henceforth be liable and responsible for all the dues and demands in respect thereof from the date of the execution of this Agreement. However, if any dues in respect of the said flat be found outstanding for any period prior to the execution of this agreement the same shall be borne and paid by the First Party.

5. That the First Party shall authorise the Second party to apply for and get the execution of conveyance deed, the permission for the transfer of the said flat and lease-hold rights in the land thereunder in favour of the Second Party or his nominee and execute proper deed(s) for conveying the same in favour of the Second Party or his nominee within one month from the date of grant of sale permission and to get the same registered in the office of the competent registering authority anywhere in India, at the cost of the Second Party.

6. That all the expenses whatsoever for the transfer of the said flat including Municipal/Corporation taxes, stamp duty, court fee, registration fee, any charges levied by the ——— Development Authority for unearned increase or other fees or charges shall be borne by the Second Party.

7. That on instructions from Second Party, the First Party has appointed him (*or*, his nominee, EF, etc.) as attorney for the management, control and supervision of the affairs of the said flat and for the completion of the sale, transfer, registration of the said property in favour of the Second Party or his nominee. The First Party shall not cancel, withdraw or revoke the powers conferred upon said attorney.

8. That the First Party hereby declares that all payments due prior to execution of this agreement, payable to the ——— Development Authority as claimed by it have been paid by the First Party as on the date of the execution of this deed and no amount in respect of the flat is due and payable to the said authority or any other statutory, local or other authority or undertaking for any electrical or water connection, etc., secured by the First Party.

9. That the First Party shall assist the Second Party in obtaining the Income Tax Clearance Certificate, to sell the property in favour of the Second Party or his nomiee(s) as and when required.

10. That the First Party assures the Second Party that the property hereby agreed to be sold is his self-acquired property and as such he is competent to sell the same and that if someone else establishes any right title or interest in the said property as owner or otherwise, then the First Party shall be liable and responsible to make good any loss thereby suffered by the Second Party.

11. That the First Party shall assist the Second Party in obtaining permission to sell the said property in favour of the Second Party or his nominee from the said Development Authority or any other concerned authority.

12. That the Second Party is hereby authorised to nominate any person in whose favour the First Party shall execute and register a valid Sale Deed/Deed of Apartment and/or Lease/Sub-Lease Deed for the Flat without any further permission or consent or payment of any amounts from the Second Party to the First Party. Such nomination shall be absolutely binding on the First Party and all persons claiming through him.

13. That the Second Party is hereby authorised to assign all his rights, title and interest under this Agreement in favour of any person without any further permission or consent from or payment of any amount to the First Party. Such assignment shall be absolutely binding on the First Party and all persons claiming through him.

14. The First Party hereby undertakes, to pay revenue, ground rent, house tax, municipal taxes, water and electricity charges etc., till the date of this Agreement whether assessed, demanded or levied at present or any time in future and not to mortgage, equitably mortgage, lease, or rent out, charge or encumber or otherwise deal with the said Flat to the detriment of the Second Party and his rights thereunder.

15. That all the relevant original documents in respect of the said Flat have been handed over by the First Party to the Second Party.

16. That this Agreement to Sell is irrevocable, and binding on both the parties and their respective heirs, successors and assigns.

17. *Arbitration Clause*

18. That all disputes shall be subject to the jurisdiction of courts at ——— only.

IN WITNESS WHEREOF, etc.

46(2)—Power of Attorney

(For Sale through Power of Attorney)

Be it known to all whom it may concern that I, AB, etc., —— do hereby nominate, appoint and constitute CD, etc., ———— as my lawful and legal attorney and authorise him to lawfully do all or any of the following acts, deeds and things for and on my behalf and in my name in respect of my flat/plot, etc., ——— allotted in my favour by ——— Development Authority/Housing Board.

1. To have the physical possession of the said flat/plot and to represent me before any office/authority or the State or Central Government or local authority or development authority or the water or sewerage authority or the police or any court in connection with the said flat/plot in any matter whatsoever and to make any statement, application, affidavit or undertaking for and on my behalf and in my name in respect of the said flat/plot or any matter connected therewith or incidental thereto.

2. To get connected, stopped, transferred any water, sewer or electric power connection or any other service in the said flat/plot and for that purpose to do all acts, deeds and things which may be considered to him necessary for the same including the tendering of securities and payments and receiving refund of the excess, if any, in his own name or in my name as may be considered necessary or expedient.

3. To pay the lease money, ground rent, house tax or any other dues in respect of my said flat or the land beneath the same (*or*, my said plot) and to get the receipt thereof in his own name or in my name as may be considered necessary or expedient.

4. To get the lease deed or any supplemental deed or conveyance deed of the said flat/plot from the office of the ——— Authority, in this regard and to sign it and get the same registered in the office of the Registrar or Sub-Registrar concerned.

5. To make any additions or alterations in the existing structure after seeking permission from the ——— Authority and for the purpose to apply for and get plan(s) sanctioned if required and engage any Architect or labour or contractor for the purpose.

6. To get the property assessed for house tax, to pay the same and to get the refund thereof if paid in excess under his own signature and in his name or in my name as he may consider necessary or expedient.

7. To deal with all relevant matters with all the local, competent, revenue and other authorities in respect thereof.

8. To let out the said flat/plot in full or in part to any intended tenant(s), to receive rents in his own name and appropriate the same as he deems fit and issue receipts thereof, under his own signature and deal with the tenant(s) in any lawful manner.

9. To negotiate, agree to sell or dispose of or transfer by way of exchange, sale, lease (whether permanent or for a fixed period or from year to year or month to month) in accordance with law, the flat/plot or any part thereof on such terms as he may in his sole discretion deem fit and proper, with any person whosoever and to enter into and sign any agreement with

any intending transferee, to receive earnest money, consideration amount or premium amount in his own name and give receipts therefor.

10. To apply for and get Income Tax Clearance Certificate, if so required, for the sale or otherwise transfer of my said flat/plot from the office of the concerned Income Tax Officer and for that purpose to do all acts, deeds and things which may be considered necessary for the purpose.

11. To apply for and get permission for sale or No Objection Certificate or other requisite permissions from the office of any authority in this regard for the sale or otherwise transfer of my rights, share, interests, liens and titles in the said flat/plot or any part thereof, in favour of any intending purchaser or his nominee(s).

12. To execute, sign and present for registration before proper Registering Authority, a proper Sale or other Conveyance Deed for conveying my rights, interests, liens and titles in the said property or any part thereof, in his own name or in favour of the intending purchaser(s) and for the purpose of conveying the same absolutely and for ever, in favour of the intending purchaser(s) or his nominee(s), to do all other acts, deeds and things which may be considered necessary for the purpose including but not limited to receiving and appropriating the consideration thereof, and to admitting the receipt thereof, and delivering the possession thereof, to said purchaser(s) or his nominee(s), either physical or constructive as may be feasible.

13. To institute or defend any suit or other proceeding in any court of law in any matter concerning my said flat/plot or any matter connected therewith or incidental thereto and for that purpose to appoint any advocate or attorney and to make any statement, application, affidavit or undertaking for and on my behalf and in my name.

14. To apply for insurance of the said premises or any fittings or fixtures or appliances or other articles stored or found therein and to make, pursue and receive the amounts of all claims therein from the insurer under his own signature.

15. To apply and get freehold certificate of the said flat from the concerned authority and for the purpose to make any application, affidavit, undertaking, indemnity bond or declaration and execute conveyance deed before the competent authority and pay the requisite fee or other charges, if any.

16. To execute, sign, affirm, verify, institute and present all kinds of plaints, writs, complaints, petitions, revisions, written statements, appeals, applications, affidavits etc., in any Court of Law *i.e.* Civil Criminal or

Revenue and/or Tribunal or arbitration on or in any matter concerning my said flat/plot or any matter connected therewith or incidental thereto, and further to do the above in his own name as, when and where the same is relevant or pertinent.

17. To execute a ratification deed of any deed(s) executed in respect of the said flat/plot and to get the same registered in the office of any competent Registering Authority.

18. To appoint any other person(s) in my name as my attorney authorising him/her/them to do all or any of the acts, deeds and things, whether specifically mentioned herein or not, which in the opinion of my said attorney ought to be done, executed or performed, in respect of my said flat/plot or any matter connected therewith or incidental thereto, and to cancel, withdraw or revoke the powers conferred upon the attorney(s) so appointed.

19. The attorney appointed by him under the last foregoing clause shall have the authority to execute Power of Attorney in favour of any other person(s) conferring all the powers conferred on my attorney by me. Such attorney so appointed shall also have similar power, and so on.

20. To mortgage the said flat/plot as per law, by way of deposit of title deeds or otherwise, and to sign on all relevant documents, to receive the mortgage amount and to complete all other formalities in this regard.

21. To apply for and get mutation from any one or more of the appropriate authorities such as, ———————— Development Authority, ———————— Municipal Corporation, Sewer and Water Supply Authority, Electricity or any other undertaking/authority for the flat/plot ownership, house tax, water or electric connection in the name of the purchaser.

22. To mortgage, assign, encumber, transfer in any other manner whatsoever the said property in favour of any person(s) or financial institution(s).

23. That my attorney is also authorised to raise loan for any purpose whatsoever and also to stand as guarantor and thus mortgage, assign, encumber the said property to secure the loan amount.

24. To do all such things which may be conducive to the effectual performance of the aforesaid functions.

25. This Power of Attorney shall be irrevocable.

I do hereby unconditionally agree, declare and undertake to ratify all acts, deeds and things lawfully done by my attorney in exercise of power or authority under this Deed, as if the same had been done by me and the same shall be binding on me, my heirs and my successors-in-interest.

And I, the executant, do hereby specifically affirm that the acts, deeds and things lawfully done or got done by my attorney or any other person appointed, authorised or retained by him, by virtue of this power of attorney, in respect of the said flat/plot, be construed as acts, deeds and things done by me.

IN WITNESS WHEREOF etc.

Or,

KNOW ALL MEN BY THESE PRESENTS that, I, AB, etc., do hereby constitute and appoint CD, etc., as my attorney (hereinafter referred to as the said Attorney) in my name and on my behalf to execute or do all or any of the acts or things hereinafter mentioned.

WHEREAS I am owner and was in possession of a house No. —— which is briefly described in the schedule hereto;

AND WHEREAS by an agreement dated ———— executed by and between me and the said Attorney I have contracted with the said Attorney to sell the above said house to him;

AND WHEREAS in consideration of Rs. ——— received by me from the said Attorney I have delivered vacant possession of the said house to the said Attorney;

AND WHEREAS due to certain reasons I am for the present unable to execute a sale deed in favour of the said Attorney;

AND WHEREAS the said Attorney has requested me to execute this irrevocable Power of Attorney in his favour to which I have agreed;

NOW THESE PRESENTS WITNESS as follows:—

In consideration of the said sum of Rs. ——— (the receipt whereof I hereby acknowledge) and in pursuance of agreement dated ——— executed between me and the said Attorney, I hereby nominate, authorise and empower the said Attorney as my lawful attorney for me and on my behalf to do the following acts, deeds and things, that is to say—

1. To manage and administer the said house;

2. To let out the said house and collect rents from tenants if any, of the said house and to give receipts for the same and to eject tenants from and settle new tenants in the said house whenever he considers fit and to take all necessary legal steps which may be considered necessary by him;

3. To appoint and employ any agent or servants as may be considered by him to be necessary for any of the purposes aforesaid or purposes

hereinafter mentioned on such terms as to remuneration, commission or otherwise as the said attorney may think proper and from time to time to dismiss or discharge them, and to appoint or employ others in their places;

4. To sell, mortgage or otherwise transfer or give on licence or to deal otherwise with or in respect of the said house and to receive any consideration therefor and to grant receipt or effectual discharge for the same, and where he considers necessary, to execute and sign and get registered the deeds necessary to complete the transaction;

5. To negotiate in my name and on my behalf with any prospective purchaser, mortgagee, lessee or other transferee or licensee of the said house and to execute any contract with any such person when needed.

6. In my name and on my behalf to institute or contest or enter into suits or petitions, or compromise, or refer to arbitration and accept or contest all awards of arbitration in any matter in respect of the said house;

7. In my name and on my behalf to sign and execute all plaints, written statements, petitions and applications in respect of the said house and to sign and subscribe my name thereto.

8. In my name and on my behalf to appoint legal practitioner and other agent for due pursuing of any matter in respect of the said house;

9. In my name and on my behalf to appear before all registering authorities and thereto present for registration and admit execution and otherwise procure valid registration of all documents in respect of the said house or executed as aforesaid by him on my behalf;

10. To deposit all rates, taxes and charges relating to the said house;

11. To accept service of any summons, notice or writ issued by any court or officer against me in respect of the said house;

12. Generally to act as my attorney or agent in relation to the matters aforesaid and all other matters in respect of the said house in which I may be interested or concerned and on my behalf to execute and do all deeds, acts and things as fully and effectually in all respects as I myself would do if personally present.

AND I hereby for myself, my heirs, executors, administrators and legal representatives ratify and confirm and agree to ratify and confirm whatsoever the said attorney shall do or purport to do by virtue of this deed.

Schedule

(Description of house)

IN WITNESS WHEREOF, etc.

46(3)—Special Power of Attorney

(For Sale through Power of Attorney)

Be it known to all to whom it may concern that I, AB, etc., do hereby nominate, constitute and appoint CD, etc., as my Special Attorney in respect of Flat No. ——— with reserved parking situtated at ——— allotted by ——— Development Authority, vide ———:

To manage, control and supervise the affairs of my said property and for the purpose, to have the physical possession thereof, to represent me before any office/authority of any State or Central Government (including police department), authority or local authority which may be connected or concerned with the said flat in any manner whatsoever and to make any statement, application, affidavit or undertaking for and on my behalf and in my name in respect of the said flat or any matter connected therewith or incidental thereto.

The acts, deeds and things lawfully done or got done by my attorney by virtue of these presents for any purpose aforesaid shall be construed as acts, deeds and things done by me.

That this special power of attorney shall be irrevocable.

IN WITNESS WHEREOF I, the executant, have put my hands on these presents in the presence of the following witnesses—

46(4)—Possession Letter

(For Sale through Power of Attorney)

BE IT KNOWN TO ALL THAT I, AB etc., do hereby hand over the vacant physical possession of Flat No. ——— with reserved parking situated at ———— to CD, etc., as per terms and conditions of the Agreement to sell dated ———.

Place:

Date:

WITNESSES: POSSESSION HANDED OVER

1. (Signed) —— AB, etc.

2. POSSESSION TAKEN OVER

(Signed) —— CD, etc.

46(5)—Will

(For Sale through Power of Attorney)

This WILL is made and executed here at ——— on ——— by AB, etc. (hereinafter called "the Testator") of the one part in favour of CD, etc., (hereinafter called "the Executor") of the other part—

WHEREAS I (the said AB) am owner and in possession of Flat No. —— etc., with lease hold rights in the land there under and reserved parking, allotted by ——— Development Authority, vide ———.

I of my own volition hereby make this WILL that after my death my rights, shares, interests, liens and titles in the said flat shall devolve on the Executor who may then get the same mutated or substituted and transferred in his own name as owner and lessee, in the records of the ——— Development Authority, ——— Municipal Corporation, ——— Electricity undertaking or any other concerned authorities on the basis of this WILL or its certified true copy.

That I further declare that if the said Executor predeceases me, then my rights, interests, liens and titles in the said flat shall devolve on the legal heirs of the EXECUTOR, who may then get the same mutated and transferred in his/her own name as owner and lessee/s in the records of the concerned authorities on the basis of this WILL, without any objection by my legal heirs and successors. I hereby declare that my other legal heirs have no right or title in the subject-matter of this will and that the same is my self-acquired personal property.

That I further declare that this is my FIRST and LAST WILL in respect of the said flat and the land beneath the same and it has been executed by me of my own consent, without any force, fraud, compulsion, coercion or allurement from any quarter whatsoever, while in possession of sound health and disposing mind.

This WILL has been made specifically in respect of the said property only, and this WILL shall not be construed to extend to or relate to any of my other properties in any manner whatsoever.

IN WITNESS WHEREOF, I, the TESTATOR have put my hands on this WILL on the date, month and year hereinabove first mentioned in the presence of the following witnesses who have signed and attested the WILL in my presence.

WITNESSES: (Testator)

1.

2.

SALE OF GOODS

General Forms of Miscellaneous Clauses in a Contract for the Sale of Goods

1. Time[1]

The time hereinbefore mentioned within which the buyer is to pay for the said goods shall be of the essence of this contract.

2. Condition

It is hereby agreed that the stipulation hereinbefore contained as to the quality of the goods is a condition of the contract the breach of which shall give the buyer the right to treat the contract as repudiated.

3. Warranty

It is hereby agreed that the stipulation hereinbefore contained as to the quality of the goods is not to be regarded as a condition but as merely a warranty, the breach of which will not give the buyer the right to repudiate the contract.

4. Goods to be Manufactured According to Specifications

The said ——— shall be manufactured in a good workmanlike manner according to the specifications of the best material and to the entire satisfaction of the buyer. If the buyer shall in good faith be dissatisfied with the said ——— on delivery, he shall be entitled to reject the same.

5. Effect of Non-conformity with Contract

It is hereby agreed that the failure by the seller to perform any material part of this contract shall entitle the buyer at his option either within —— days after delivery thereof to reject the goods and repudiate the contract or to retain the goods subject to a right to compensation or damages for breach of contract.

6. Sample

The said ——— shall correspond with the sample which has been sealed by the buyer and placed with the seller.

---

1 *See*, Preliminary Note.

7. Description

The description hereinbefore given of the said goods has been given only by way of identification thereof and not so as to constitute this contract as a sale by description.

8. Acceptance and Rejection

The buyer may return the goods within ———— days of delivery if they are not according to the contract giving notice to the seller in what respects they are not according to the contract. If the goods are not returned within the said period the buyer shall be bound to accept them.

9. Delivery when Goods with Bailee

Delivery shall be sufficient if made by the seller handing to the buyer a delivery order or transferring to the buyer the warrant of the delivery of the said goods.

10. Risk in Transit

The said goods shall be delivered to the buyer at ———— provided that from the time of despatch thereof from the seller's place and until such delivery the risk of any loss and damage to or deterioration of the said goods from whatever cause shall be borne by the buyer.

11. Lien

The seller shall be entitled to retain possession of the said goods until payment in full.

12. Trial of Machinery

The said machine shall within ———— days after delivery be tried by the buyer by working it in the proper and usual manner during a period of ———— days. If it shall fail to work efficiently the buyer may reject it. If the buyer fails to make such trial, or the trial does not disclose any defects, the buyer shall be bound to accept it.

13. Prevention of Delivery by Strike, etc.

Should the seller be prevented from delivering the goods at the time hereby fixed by reason of lock out, strike, riot, mutiny, fire or any other unexpected cause beyond his control, the time for delivery shall be extended until the operation of such cause has ceased or the seller may at his option cancel the contract by giving notice to the buyer in writing before the expiry of the period fixed for delivery.

PRECEDENTS OF SALE OF GOODS

1—Agreement between a Manufacturer and a Wholesale Dealer for Exclusive Supply of Goods Manufactured[1]

AN AGREEMENT made on the ——— day of ——— BETWEEN AB, etc., (hereinafter called "the seller") of the one part AND CD, etc., (hereinafter called "the buyer") of the other part,

WHEREBY it is agreed as follows:

1. The seller will sell and the buyer will buy the whole of the seller's existing stock of ——— at the price of Rs. ——— per ———;

2. The seller agrees with the buyer that he will not for the period of one year from the date hereof make or sell for or to any person (including any firm or company) other than the buyer at ——— any ——— similar in pattern and description to any of those hereby agreed to be sold.

3. If the buyer at any time or times during the period of one year from the date hereof require a further supply of any ——— manufactured in accordance with any of said pattern the seller will manufacture and sell the same to the buyer at the same price per ——— as the buyer is to pay for the seller's existing stock.

4. All goods to be supplied under this contract shall be paid for in cash upon delivery.

IN WITNESS WHEREOF, etc.

2—Agreement for the Manufacture and Supply of Furniture

AN AGREEMENT, etc., (*as in Form* 1).

WHEREBY it is agreed as follows:

1. The seller will make and sell to the buyer and the buyer will buy from the seller the furniture detailed in the schedule hereto.

2. The said furniture shall be made in accordance with the specifications and drawings attached hereto and signed by the parties and shall be made of the best materials and workmanship throughout.

3. The seller shall make by way of sample of each class of furniture

---

1 For agreement between manufacturer and marketer, see under AGREEMENT, precedent No. 22.

mentioned in the schedule hereto and shall deliver the same to the buyer at ——— within one month from this date. The buyer shall be entitled within one week from the date of such delivery to reject any of them as are not approved by him and the seller will prepare another such piece of furniture as has been rejected and deliver the same within 15 days of the notice of rejection and if this piece is also rejected within three days of delivery, the contract for the manufacture and sale of the class of furniture the samples of which have been so rejected shall stand cancelled. If the samples made and delivered by the seller are approved or not rejected within the appointed time, the remaining furniture agreed to be made shall be made in accordance with such samples.

4. All the furniture shall be made and delivered to the buyer at —— on the ——— and the time in this respect shall be of the essence of the contract.

5. The buyer shall pay the price on delivery of the furniture at the rates specified in the schedule hereto.

6. If the seller shall fail to deliver the samples within one month as hereinbefore provided or fail to deliver all the furniture on or before the date hereinbefore fixed the buyer shall be entitled to cancel this contract.

The schedule herein referred to

IN WITNESS, etc.

3—Agreement to Supply Grain

AN AGREEMENT, etc., (*as in Form* 1).

WHEREBY it is agreed as follows:

1. The seller will supply to the buyer ——— quintals of wheat according to the samples sealed in bottles with the seal of the seller and placed with the buyer and in bottles sealed with the seal of the buyer and placed with the seller, on the terms and conditions hereinafter mentioned.

2. The total quantity of wheat agreed to be supplied shall be delivered to the buyer within ——— months from this date in such instalments and on such dates as the buyer may from time to time order provided that such orders should be served on the seller at least one week before the date fixed for delivery of any instalment.

3. The buyer shall pay for the wheat supplied by the seller at the rate of Rs. ——— per quintal. Payments for each instalment shall be made within one week of the delivery.

4. If any wheat supplied by the seller is not according to the sample,

the buyer will have the option, to be exercised within one week, of delivery of either rejecting the same and purchasing the same quantity of wheat from the market at the risk of the seller or accepting the same on such reduced rate of price as may be mutually agreed upon.

5. The time fixed for delivery of any instalment of wheat shall in each case be regarded as of the essence of the contract, and if the seller shall fail to deliver the wheat on such date, the buyer may annul the whole of this contract and purchase the wheat from any other person including any firm or company and claim the difference in price and any expenses and damages incurred by him from the seller.

IN WITNESS, etc.

4—Agreement to Sell Business with Goodwill

AN AGREEMENT, etc., (*as in Form* 1).

WHEREBY it is agreed as follows:

1. The seller will sell and the purchaser will buy ————.

(1) The goodwill of the business of ———— now carried on by the seller at ———— under the firm name of ———— and the right to use the said firm name and to represent the seller as carrying on the said business in succession to the seller.

(2) The benefit of all contracts and engagements entered into with the seller in respect of the said business and all book debts now owing to the seller in respect of the said business.

(3) All the office furniture and shop equipment, plant, machinery, motors and vehicles and other things specified in the inventory attached hereto except the stock-in-trade which shall be on the business premises or in use in connection with the said business on the date hereinafter fixed for completion of the sale (hereinafter called "the date of completion").

2. The purchase price shall be Rs. ———— of which Rs. ———— shall be paid to the seller upon execution of this deed and the balance by instalments in the manner hereinafter provided, that is, etc.

3. The stock-in-trade of the said business upon the business premises on the date of completion other than the stock sold but not yet removed shall be taken over and purchased by the buyer at a valuation to be made at the joint expense of parties by ———— but the completion of the sale shall not be delayed on account of waiting for such valuation.

4. The sale shall be completed on the ———— day of ———— and, on the payment of the balance of the purchase price with the price of the stock-

in-trade according to valuation, the seller will permit the buyer to enter into possession of the business premises and will deliver to him the property hereby agreed to be sold.

5. Upon completion of the sale, the seller will, if required by the buyer, and at the buyer's expense, execute a proper deed of transfer of the premises and shall send to the customers of the seller in connection with the said business a circular announcing the transfer of the goodwill and business to the buyer.

6. The seller will carry on the said business at his own risk and for his own benefit until the completion of sale.

7. All books of account and of reference to customers and other documents shall on completion of the sale be delivered to the buyer.

8. If completion does not, by reason of the buyer's default take place within one month of the date hereinbefore fixed therefor, the seller will be at liberty to determine this agreement and to forfeit the said deposit.

9. No error, mis-statement nor omission in the description of the premises hereby agreed to be sold shall be a ground for avoiding the sale but such compensation shall be paid therefor as may be fixed by AB who shall be the arbitrator for this purpose.

10. The seller shall not, at any time during a period of ——— years,[1] after the completion of the sale, carry on, either solely or as agent for or partner with any other person or persons, directly or indirectly, the business of —— or be in any way concerned or interested in any similar business within a radius of ———— kms from ———— aforesaid.

IN WITNESS, etc.

5—Sale of Standing Timber

THIS SALE DEED made on the ——— day of ———— BETWEEN AB, etc., (hereinafter called "the seller") of the one part AND CD, etc., (hereinafter called "the buyer") of the other part.

WITNESSES as follows:

1. The seller hereby sells to the purchaser the following timber trees standing on the plots mentioned in the schedule hereto that is to say, fifty *Shisham* trees, twenty *Deodar* trees, forty *Jamun* trees, fifty old Mango trees, and thirty *Tun* trees.

---

1 The restraint is protected by Exception 1 to Sec. 27, Contract Act within reasonable limits.

2. The trees hereby sold have been marked by the seller and shown to the buyer on the spot. The remaining trees on said plots have been counted in the presence of buyer and the number of trees on each plot has been noted against the same in the schedule hereto. The buyer shall not cut any of such remaining trees.

3. The price fixed is Rs. ——— of which Rs. ——— shall be paid on the execution of this deed and the balance on the ——— day of ———.

4. The seller grants to the buyer, his sub-buyer, if any, his or his sub-buyer's agents, servants, workmen and labourers full and free liberty to enter upon the said plots to fell and cut down, grub up and work up the said trees and also to have free ingress and egress with or without horses, carts, tractors, trollies, trucks and other means of transport to enter into and upon the said plots for the purpose of taking and carrying away the said trees and wood, and also to sink saw-pits in such places as shall be appointed by the seller or his agent.

5. The whole of the timber shall be cut down and removed from the said plots within ——— months from this date and anything remaining on the land after that date shall vest in the seller. The buyer shall also fill up any saw-pits sunk by him and shall clear the land within the said period.

6. The trees shall be felled close to the ground with as much care as possible in a proper customary and workman like manner and at the sole cost of the buyer and no trees shall be rooted up without the consent of the seller.

7. The buyer shall pay compensation to the seller for all damage done to the remaining timber or to cattle on the land and for all losses or damage that the seller or his tenants may sustain by the carelessness or negligence of the buyer, his sub-buyers, his or his sub-buyer's agents, workmen, labourers or servants.

The schedule herein referred to.

IN WITNESS, etc.

6—Sale of Business as a Going Concern with Goodwill and Stock-in-Trade and also of Lease-Hold Rights in Business Premises[1]

THIS SALE DEED is made, etc., (*as in Form* 5)

WHEREAS—

1 The rent control law in force in the State should be consulted in respect of transfer of lease-hold rights in the premises.

(1) By a deed of lease made on the ——— day of ——— between EF as lessor and the seller as lessee the house and land situate at ——— and fully described in the said deed of lease and now in the occupation of the seller was leased out to the seller;

(2) The seller now carries on the business of ——— on the said demised premises;

(3) The seller has agreed to sell to the buyer for the price of Rs. 57,000 and on the terms and conditions hereinafter mentioned all the rights in the said premises under the aforesaid deed of lease for the remaining term of the said lease AND also all his interest and goodwill in the said business of ——— AND also the book and other debts and rights in the contracts of the said business which are more particularly described in the books of accounts and other books which have been delivered to the purchaser AND also all office furniture and shop equipment, etc., other than the stock in trade present on the date of completion of sale;

(4) The seller has also agreed for sale to the buyer all his other stock in trade of the said business present on the said business premises on the date of completion of sale at a valuation to be made by one XY as arbitrator and the said XY has now valued the said stock in trade at Rs. 1,22,000.

NOW THIS DEED WITNESSES as follows:

1. In pursuance of the aforesaid agreement and in consideration of the price of Rs. 1,79,000 paid by the buyer to the seller (the receipt of which the seller hereby acknowledges) the seller hereby transfers to the buyer—

(*i*) All the said house and land described in the schedule hereto and comprised in the aforementioned lease TO HOLD the same to the buyer for the residue now unexpired of the term of the said lease subject henceforth to the payment of the rent reserved by the said lease and the performance and observance of covenants and conditions on the part of the lessee contained in the aforesaid lease; and

(*ii*) All the beneficial interest and goodwill of the seller in the said business of ——— AND also all the book and other debts to which the seller is now entitled on account of the said business with all the securities for the said debts and the full benefit of all contracts entered into with, or orders given to, the seller in connection with the said business AND also all the stock in trade, goods, fittings, articles and things, etc., belonging to the seller and relating to the said business TO HOLD the same to the buyer absolutely.

2. The seller hereby agrees as follows:

(*i*) that he will not during the term of ——— years from the date hereof either solely or as agent for or partner with any other person or persons, directly or indirectly, carry on the business of ——— or be in any way concerned or interested in any similar business within a radius of ——— kms. from ——— aforesaid;

(*ii*) that the amount and particulars of the debts due and owing to and from the seller on account of the said business and the particulars of the contracts and engagements to which he is liable in respect of the said business are correctly stated and set forth in the books of account and other books delivered to the buyer and that the seller will indemnify the buyer against all sums he may have to pay on account of such debts, contract or engagement in excess of the amounts shown in the said books.

3. The buyer hereby agrees as follows:

(*i*) that he will pay the rent reserved in, and observe and perform terms and covenants of, the said deed of lease and on his part to be observed and performed and shall keep the seller indemnified against all rents, claims or demands on account of any omission on his part to pay the rent or observe or perform the said covenants.

(*ii*) that he will pay every debt and sum of money appearing in the said books of account for which the seller is liable and shall perform all the contracts and engagement hereinbefore mentioned and shall at all times keep the seller indemnified against all claims and liabilities in respect thereof.

The schedule herein referred to.

IN WITNESS, etc.

SEPARATION DEED

Preliminary Note

A Separation Deed is an arrangement between husband and wife to live apart on certain conditions.

With the advancement in Indian social structure and the constitutional guarantee of 'equality before the law' as well as the passing of the Hindu Marriage Act in 1955, the concept of agreed separation is gradually gaining acceptance. Though marriage amongst Hindus still continues to be a religious sacrament yet the law has introduced such major changes as to permit judicial separation (Sec. 10), nullification of marriage (Sec. 11 & 12) and divorce (Sec. 13), and under a later amendment, even divorce by mutual consent (Sec. 13B). Similar provisions exist in the Special Marriage Act. The provisions of the Hindu Adoptions and Maintenance Act, 1956 (Sec. 18) and Code of Criminal Procedure, 1973 (Sec. 125) also contemplate separate living by mutual consent or in specified circumstances. Thus execution of a deed of separation can be useful so that neither party may be able to accuse the other of "desertion". Welfare of the children, their education and upbringing, their preferences depending on their age and understanding should be a primary consideration. Both husband and wife might agree, as was ordered in the undernoted case[1], to give their individual though divided attention to the children.

How Drafted

The deed should be executed either as a deed poll or as an agreement between husband and wife, and both should consent to live apart on conditions to be expressly stated therein, and the agreement should be revocable on a reconciliation between the parties and on the commencement of cohabitation. Such deed is executed either after the parties have actually commenced to live apart or immediately before actual separation, because a deed which is not followed immediately by actual separation will be void, as an agreement for future separation.

Trustees

As even a married woman may now contract as a *feme sole,* (*i.e.,* in the same manner as an unmarried woman), and hold property, the joining of trustees is not necessary. If, however, trustees are joined, as in many cases that may be considered desirable, the wife should make a covenant with the husband as well as with the trustees. The creation of a trust may be useful particularly where the husband

---

1 *Chandrakala Menon* v. Capt. *Vipin Menon*, JT 1993 (1) SC 229, (1993) 2 SCC 6.

proposes or agrees to pay a lump sum which may be so invested by the trustee(s) that a monthly return therefrom is sufficient to pay maintenance to the wife and any children left into her custody under the arrangement.

Annuity

An annuity is generally granted to the wife for her maintenance but it is made to determine on the wife becoming unchaste. An express condition is, however, necessary to that effect.

Stamp Duty

A separation deed is an agreement and is chargeable with stamp duty as such (*see* Note on "Agreements"). If a clause for payment of annuity is incorporated and the agreement is attested, an additional *ad valorem* duty at the rate of that payable on a bond on the total amount of allowance payable during the period of first twelve years should be paid (Sec. 25 (*c*) Stamp Act).

Registration

Registration of a separation deed is not compulsory.

PRECEDENTS

1—Separation Deed between Husband and Wife

THIS DEED OF SEPARATION made on the ——— day of ——— BETWEEN AB, etc., (hereinafter called "the husband") of the one part AND CD, etc., (hereinafter called "the wife") of the other part.

WHEREAS differences have arisen between the husband and the wife and they have mutually agreed to live apart from each other and to enter into the arrangement hereinafter contained.

AND WHEREAS the husband has by the wife three children namely, EF, GH and JK.

NOW THIS DEED WITNESSES and the parties hereto mutually agree as follows:

1. The wife may at all times hereafter live separate and apart from the husband and in all respects free from the control and authority of the husband.

2. Neither of them shall molest or interfere with the other nor will bring a suit for restitution of conjugal rights against the other.

3. The wife shall at all times hereafter have the sole custody and control of the aforesaid children and of their education and upbringing during their minority but shall allow the husband at all convenient and reasonable times free access and communication with them (or, the wife shall hereafter have the sole custody and control of the aforesaid children, provided that they shall as and when they respectively attain the age of ——— years be placed at the expense of the husband at such school as he shall from time to time determine and such of the said children as shall for the time being be at school shall pass their holidays at such places and in such manner as the husband shall direct).

4. The husband shall pay to the wife during her life and so long as she shall continue to live a chaste life and perform and observe the conditions and terms herein contained the monthly allowance of Rs. ——— for her maintenance on the Ist day of each month in advance.

5. The husband shall pay to the wife along with the monthly payments stipulated in clause 4 hereof a further monthly sum of Rs. ——— for the maintenance and education of each of the said children until he or she attains the age of ——— years and the wife shall out of such sum maintain

and educate the said children and shall also keep the husband indemnified from and against all claims and demands in respect of the maintenance and education of such children. Provided that if any of the said children before attaining the said age of ——— years dies or is settled in life and begins to earn his or her own livelihood or in the case of female child EF marries, the allowance herein stipulated to be paid for his or her maintenance shall cease to be payable.

6. The wife shall be at liberty forthwith to remove from the husband's house all her wearing apparel, jewellery and personal effects and also such of the further and other household goods and effects at the said house as belong to her as her separate property.

7. The wife shall pay and discharge all debts and liabilities incurred by her after the date hereof and keep the husband, his heirs, executors and administrators indemnified therefrom and if the husband has to pay any such debts or liabilities he will be at liberty to deduct the same from the maintenance allowance of the wife.

8. If the parties shall be reconciled and return to cohabitation or if their marriage shall be dissolved or they shall be judicially separated by reason of any misconduct of the wife occurring after the date hereof then and in any such case all the covenants and provisions herein contained shall become void but without prejudice to the right of any party to take proceedings in respect of any antecedent breach of any such covenant or provision.

9. This deed shall be revoked by the death of the wife (*or*, by the death of either of the parties hereto).

IN WITNESS WHEREOF, etc.

2—Separation Deed between Husband and Wife with a Trustee

THIS DEED OF SEPARATION is made on the ——— day of ——— BETWEEN AB, etc., (hereinafter called "the husband") of the first part AND CD, etc., (hereinafter called "the wife") of the second part AND EF, etc., (hereinafter called "the trustee") of the third part.

WHEREAS (*as in Form* 1).

NOW THIS DEED WITNESSES and the husband and wife hereby covenant with each other and separately with the trustee, and the trustee so far as the agreements and provisions hereinafter contained are or ought to be performed or observed by the wife or the trustee or their respective executors or administrators or any of them hereby covenants with the husband as follows:

1-3 (*As in Form* 1).

4. The husband shall during the life of the wife and so long as she remains chaste pay to the trustee the annuity of Rs. ——— in trust for the wife as her separate estate. The said annuity shall be paid in advance by equal monthly instalments on the 1st day of each month and the wife shall have no power during her coverture to anticipate[1] the same.

Or

[4 (*i*) The husband will pay to the trustee on demand the sum of Rs. ——— with interest thereon until payment at the rate of ——— per cent per annum from the date of the deed and until such demand is made and is complied with will pay to the trustee interest at the said rate by monthly payment on the principal moneys for the time being remaining due on this covenant;

(*ii*) The trustee shall invest the principal money paid to him hereunder in or upon ——— and may at his discretion withdraw the money and invest it in or upon any other investment of any nature hereby authorised;

(*iii*) The trustee shall pay the income of the investment and also the interest received by him from the husband to the wife during the joint life of the husband and wife and so long as the wife remains chaste without power of anticipation;

(*iv*) After the death of the husband or wife the trustee shall hold the said investments and the principal money and interest received by him hereunder in trust for the survivor of them PROVIDED THAT the wife shall not have power to dispose of such reversionary interest by way of anticipation;

(*v*) The trustee shall not require payment of the said principal sum or any part thereof if and so long as the husband shall pay the interest thereon or as the unpaid part thereof within 15 days after the same shall become payable.]

5. The wife shall out of the provision made for her by this deed maintain herself and defray all the expenses of all kinds.

6. (*As in Form* 1).

7. The wife shall pay and discharge all her debts and liabilities incurred by her after the date hereof and she and the trustee will at all times hereafter keep the husband indemnified, etc., (*as in Form* 1).

8-9 (*As in Form* 1).

IN WITNESS WHEREOF, etc.

---

1 In conveyancing "anticipation" means "the act of assigning, charging or otherwise dealing with income before it becomes due" Black's Law Dictionary, VIth edn, page 93.

SERVICE CONTRACT

Preliminary Note

Contents of a Service Contract

Service contracts are drafted in the same way as other agreements. The terms of employment should be definitely fixed and clearly expressed and nothing should be left to presumptions. They are required to be both affirmative (describing the acts and duties to be performed) as well as negative (putting restrictions on the acts of the employee during and/or after the term of employment). It is therefore necessary to make provision for:

(1) exact designation of the employee with brief description, so as to distinguish if the employee falls or does not within the definition of 'workman' as provided in labours laws or say, Industrial Disputes Act;

(2) the time or period of employment;

(3) the remuneration and other perquisites, if any, including pay, allowances, commission, rent free house, conveyance, etc.;

(4) duties of employment;

(5) powers of the employee;

(6) leave and the terms on which it will be granted;

(7) modes and grounds of determining the employment during the term; and

(8) restrictive covenants.

The terms of a service contract should be as explicit as possible and should be easily intelligible to a lay man. Unlike other agreements and legal documents which need not contain matters presumed or implied by law, it is better in such an agreement to specify even such matters and all other matters so as to make it a complete code, embodying the rights and duties of each party.

In respect of Government service, normally no formal contract is executed and only an appointment order is issued and the terms of service are thereafter governed by statutory rules and Government order. The same is the position of statutory corporations as employers. Service under government[1] or a statutory corporation[2] is primarily a matter of status, even though its origin be contractual, and the employer generally has the statutory power to alter the conditions of service unilaterally though subject to certain limitations.

However, contractual employment on special terms is also permissible, vide Article 310 (2) of the Constitution. In such a contract, there is no objection to refer

---

1 *Roshan Lal Tandon* v. *Union of India*, (1968) 1 SCR 125, AIR 1967 SC 1889.

2 *Sirsi Municipality* v. *Tellis*, AIR 1973 SC 855; *Sukhdeo Singh* v. *Bhagatram*, AIR 1975 SC 1331.

to any rules of service governing the particular class of service and referring to them as governing relations between the parties on any particular point, instead of repeating them in the form of covenants, because such rules are well known to all Government servants and are well understood by them, e.g., we may say that the employee will in all respects be bound by the Manual of Government Orders and rules relating to the conduct of Government servants; or the employee will be allowed travelling allowance at the rates admissible to a Government servant of the second class under Fundamental and Subsidiary Rules contained in volume II of the Financial Handbook.

An interesting illustration of contractual appointment in Government service is furnished by a case[1] in which the State Government permitted the Ministers to appoint persons of their choice in their respective establishments. The order for appointment provided that it shall be temporary, co-terminous with the tenure of the concerned Minister. Following election new Government took over and their services were terminated. The Supreme Court upheld the contention of the State to the effect that the appointment was purely contractual co-terminous with the tenure of the Ministers establishment at whose choice and instance they were appointed. The employees could not be deemed to be temporary Government servants within the meaning of the Service Rule.

Period of Service—This may be definite or indefinite. If no period is fixed or an indefinite period is stated, e.g., "so long as the parties respectively please", the contract is terminable by a reasonable notice on either side. What is a reasonable notice varies in different cases, according to the character of the employment and the general custom, from 15 days to six months. When no term is fixed it is always proper to provide for determination by notice. In such a case, and also in case option of determination is reserved during the term, the period of notice should be settled and expressed in the agreement. It is not permissible, where the employer is Government or a statutory corporation or other instrumentality of the State, to provide for termination of services of a permanent employee by a mere notice without formal inquiry into the charges against him (see footnote in precedent No. 4).

Tenure means a term during which an office is held. Once a person is appointed to a tenure post, his appointment commences when he joins and it ends on completion of the tenure unless curtailed on justifiable grounds. Such a person does not superannuate.[2]

Remuneration—This may be a fixed monthly salary, or fees or commission, or salary as well as fees or commission. Sometimes in business firms, employees are allowed a share in the profits in addition to a fixed salary. All these should be clearly provided.

Leave—Conditions and grounds on which, and the period for which leave

1 *State of Gujarat* v. *P.J. Kampavat*, (1992) 3 SCC 226, AIR 1992 SC 1685.
2 *Dr. L.P. Agarwal* v. *Union of India*, (1992) 3 SCC 526, AIR 1992 SC 1872.

may be granted as well as allowance payable during leave should be stated. In the case of Government servants engaged on contract, the leave rules applicable to permanent Government Servants in general may be applied but as there are different rules for different classes of Government Servants those applicable should be clearly referred to, or if they are not lengthy, they may be embodied in the agreement in the form of a covenant.

Determination of Employment

The grounds on which the employment may be determined during the term are generally misconduct, negligence, or want of medical fitness. Subject to what has been stated earlier, it may also be determined at pleasure by notice, without giving any ground. In the case of misconduct[1] or neglect, no notice is required, but, provision may be made for framing charges and taking defence as in the case of Government Servants. As an employee is entitled to damages for wrongful dismissal if the termination of the service is not properly made, provision in this respect should be carefully worded.

Transfer from one Employer to Another

A contract for service is incapable of transfer unilaterally. Such a transfer of service from one employer to another can, in the absence of any statutory provision in that behalf, only be effected by a tripartite agreement between the employer, the employee and the third party.[2] Transfer cannot be made unilaterally from one cadre to another which alters, varies or modifies the terms and conditions of service. It would be necessary to accord opportunity to the government servant to exercise his option.[3]

Restrictive Covenants

Under this head are included covenants not to undertake any other work or service, not to divulge the master's secrets or to make improper use of his trade secrets or information about the master's affairs. Such latter covenants may be not only for the term of employment but also for subsequent reasonable periods.

Agreements in Restraint of Trade

In drafting restrictive covenants it is necessary to see that they are not illegal. Agreements in restraint of trade are void under Sec. 27, Contract Act, and should not be inserted in an agreement. However any covenant that the employee, during the course of employment, shall not directly or indirectly promote or help in any similar business will be lawful. It will be deemed to be in the interest of the employer and not a restraint on trade or business.[4] A covenant that the employee

1 *State of Punjab* v. *Ram Singh*, (1992) 4 SCC 54, AIR 1992 SC 2188 (misconduct discussed in detail).

2 *Pyarchand Kesarimal* v. *Omkar Laxman*, (1969) 2 SCR 272, AIR 1970 SC 823.

3 *Shankar Pandurang Jadhav* v. *Vice Admiral*, JT 1991 (1) SC 301.

4 *Charlesworth* v. *Mac Donald*, 23 Bom 103.

shall not join any firm of the employer's competitors or run a similar business of his own directly or indirectly for a period of two years at the place of his last posting after he leaves the company was interpreted to mean that it did not cover a case of termination of service by the employer as it was confined to the employee's voluntarily leaving the company.[1] In view of this construction the majority did not think it necessary to consider the validity of this partial restraint of trade, but the concurring judgment of A.P. Sen, J. discussed the law on the subject and held that as the agreement in question was not a "goodwill of business" type of contract it did not fall within Exception I to Sec. 27 and was therefore void.[2] Some other decisions on the subject are noted below.[3]

Effect of Labour Laws

In the process of complete rationalization of Labour Laws in India, all earlier Labour acts have now been repealed by framing the relevant provisions of existing laws into four labour codes which are:

(1) Code of Wages, 2019

(2) Code on Social Security, 2020

(3) Occupational Safety, Health and Working Conditions Code, 2020

(4) Industrial Relations Code, 2020.

In drawing up a service contract for a person falling within the definition of these Codes, the provisions of the relevant codes must be kept in mind. Any term of contract contrary to the statutory provisions will be null and void, as it is not open to an employee to contract out of the safeguards provided by the Legislature for his protection.

Section 9A of Industrial Disputes Act provides how an employer shall effect change in the condition of service of a workmen.

Stamp Duty

Duty on an agreement for contract of service is the same as that for an ordinary agreement (*see* note on "agreements").

Registration

Not compulsory.

---

1 *Superintendence Company of India* v. *Krishna Murgai*, (1981) 2 SCC 246, AIR 1980 SC 1717.

2 *Superintendence Company of India* v. *Krishna Murgai*, (1981) 2 SCC 246, AIR 1980 SC 1717; See also, *Niranjan Shanker Golikari* v. *Century Spinning and Manufacturing Company*, AIR 1967 SC 1098, and other cases cited in the judgment of A.P. Sen, J. in *Superintendence Co. supra.*

3 *Niranjan Shankar* v. *Century Spinning & Mfg. Co.*, AIR 1967 SC 1098; *A.B.C. Laminart Ltd.* v. *A.P. Agencies*, AIR 1989 SC 1239; *Gujarat Bottling Co.* v. *Coca Cola*, AIR 1995 SC 2372, (1995) 5 SCC 545.

PRECEDENTS

1—Agreement of Service of Municipal Engineer

THIS AGREEMENT is made on the ——— day of ——— BETWEEN the Municipal Board of ——— (hereinafter called "the Board") of the one part AND AB, etc., (hereinafter called "the Engineer") of the other part.

WHEREAS the Board has engaged with effect from the ——— day of ——— the Engineer to serve the Board in the capacity of Municipal Engineer at the pay and upon the terms and conditions hereinafter appearing;

AND WHEREAS the said appointment, salary and conditions have been approved by the State Government.

NOW THIS AGREEMENT WITNESSES and the parties hereto hereby agree as follows:

1. That the Engineer will remain in the service of the Board for a period of five years from the ——— day of ———;

PROVIDED that the first year of such service shall be regarded as a period of probation and if at the end of that year the Board is not satisfied with his service, it may terminate this agreement without any notice.

2. That the Engineer will submit himself to the orders of the Board and of the officers and authorities under whom he may from time to time be placed by the Board and will at all times obey the rules lawfully prescribed for the time being by the Board regarding the duties to be performed by the Engineer.

3. That the Engineer will employ himself efficiently and diligently and to the best of his ability as a Municipal Engineer and will devote his whole time to the duties of the service and will not engage directly or indirectly in any trade, business or occupation on his own account and will not (except in case of accident or sickness certified by competent medical authority) absent himself from his said duties without having first obtained permission from the Board or its authorised officer.

4. That in the event of misconduct on the part of the Engineer or of a breach of any of the terms and conditions herein specified the Board may at any time dispense with his services after due inquiry and observance of the conditions laid down in the ——— Municipalities Act or the rules made

thereunder in this behalf, and the order of the Board dispensing with his services shall be subject to such appeal as may for the time being be provided by the said Act or rules.

5. That the Board will pay the Engineer so long as he shall remain in the service and actually perform his duties, salary at the rate of Rs. —— per mensem which may, at the option of the Board be increased after three years of approved service.

6. That subject to the condition that the Engineer maintains a motor car for the performance of his duties as Municipal Engineer, the Board shall pay him a conveyance allowance of Rs. ———— per mensem.

7. That in the matter of leave and other matters not provided for in this agreement the Engineer shall be governed by the rules, regulations and bye-laws lawfully made from time to time by the State Government or the Board in this behalf.

8. That either party to the agreement may terminate this agreement by giving to the other three months' notice in writing of its intention to do so and on the expiration of such notice this agreement shall be determined. Provided that the Board may pay to the Engineer three months' salary in lieu of such notice, and thereupon this agreement shall stand determined forthwith.

IN WITNESS WHEREOF, etc.

2—Deed of Appointment of an Engineer under Government

AN AGREEMENT made on the ———— day of ———— BETWEEN the Governor of Uttar Pradesh of the one part AND AB, etc., at present residing at ———— in the district of ——— (hereinafter called "the Engineer") of the other part.

WHEREBY it is hereby agreed as follows:

1. That the Engineer will remain in the service of the Government of Uttar Pradesh (hereinafter called "the Government") for a period of —— years from the day of ————;

2. That the Engineer will submit himself to the orders of the Government and of the officers and authorities under whom he may from time to time be placed by the Government and will at all times obey the rules prescribed for the time being for the regulation of the branch of the public service to which he may belong and will from time to time proceed to any part of India to which he may be required to proceed.

3. That he will employ himself efficiently and diligently and to the best of his ability as Executive Electrical Engineer and that he will devote his whole time to the duties of the service and will not engage directly or indirectly in any trade, business or occupation on his own account and that he will not (except in case of accident or sickness certified by competent medical authority) absent himself from his said duties without having first obtained permission from the Government or their authorised officer.

4. That in the event of misconduct on the part of the Engineer or of a breach of term of any of the conditions herein specified the Government may at any time dispense with his services after due enquiry.

5. That it shall be lawful for the Government, if satisfied on the medical evidence before them that he is unfit and is likely for a considerable period to continue unfit by reason of ill-health for the discharge of his duties, to determine the service under this agreement (the satisfaction of the Government in that behalf being conclusive) and thereupon his services shall be terminated and the Engineer shall be entitled to only three months' salary by way of compensation.

6. That the Government will pay the Engineer so long as he shall remain in the service and actually perform his duties, salary at the rate of Rs.——— per mensem during the first year, Rs. —— per mensem during the second year, and Rs. ——— per mensem during the third and subsequent years.

(*or*, that the scale of the pay of the Engineer, so long as he shall remain in service and perform his duties shall be Rs. 24,000-1,000-30,000 and that the Engineer will start in this scale at the stage of Rs. —— per mensem and will get this pay rising to Rs. 24,000 per mensem by annual increments of Rs. 1,000).

7. That the Government will pay the Engineer so long as he actually performs his duties travelling allowance on the following scale, subject to the condition that he maintains and uses a motor car for all journeys performed by him in the discharge of his duties when the journeys are within his jurisdiction and it is practicable to use a motor car—

(*a*) a conveyance allowance of Rs. 2,500 per mensem;

(*b*) a mileage allowance of Rs. 8 per km., for journeys performed by road in the discharge of his duties;

(*c*) a daily allowance at the rate allowed under the Rules for first class officers.

(*d*) mileage and daily allowance at the rate ordinarily admissible under the Rule to officers of the first class on duty by rail or road when the journeys are outside his jurisdiction or it is impracticable to use a car.

(*e*) for journeys partly by road and partly by rail within his jurisdiction a mileage allowance of Rs. 8 per km. for the road journey and railway fare at the rates admissible under the Rule to a first class officer.

8. That if the Engineer shall on the expiration of the term of this agreement leave the said service with approval of the Government and having satisfactorily at all times performed his duties and shall actually quit the said service or if his service is terminated within the term of this agreement otherwise than by himself, he shall be provided with a first class passage to any place in India provided that he claims such passage within three months from the determination of his service.

9. That the Engineer will be entitled during the said term of his engagement to leave on average pay upto 1/11th of period spent on duty (upto a maximum of four months at a time) to which may be added leave on medical certificate on average or half average pay up to the maximum of three months reckoned in terms of leave on average pay.

10. That he shall not be entitled to any pension, gratuity or bonus on retirement but that while this agreement is in force he shall subscribe to a Provident Fund at the rate of one-tenth of his pay each month the Government adding a half yearly contribution at the rate of one hundred per cent of his subscription for the half year. Interest at such rate as the Government may from time to time fix will be calculated monthly and added yearly to the account. The amount at his credit in the Fund will be paid to him on his quitting the service or to his legal representatives in the event of his death whilst in the service.

PROVIDED that the whole or any part of the Government contribution and interest and increment accrued thereon may be withheld to meet a liability incurred to the Government or in case he is dismissed from the service.

IN WITNESS WHEREOF, etc.

3—Contract of Employment of College Staff[1]

(With reference to rules of the College)

AN AGREEMENT made on the ———— day of ———— BETWEEN the Committee of Management of the ———— college

1 See Preliminary Note regarding teachers of Government-aided educational institution.

(hereinafter called "the Committee") of the one part AND AB, etc., of the other part.

WHEREBY IT IS AGREED as follows:

1. That the Committee hereby appoints the said AB to be —— in the said College upon the following scale of salary and increments namely the sum of Rs. ——— per mensem upto the month of ——— inclusive and thereafter by annual increments of rupees ——— per mensem upto Rs. ——— per mensem.

2. That the said AB shall assist the principal of the said College with zeal and efficiency in all matters pertaining to instruction and discipline and shall in addition perform when called upon to do so any other such services as may reasonably be required of him by the said Principal in the furtherance of the interest of the said ——— College.

3. That the said AB shall not at any time during his employment under this agreement directly or indirectly engage in any other employment save of the said College.

4. That the period of employment of the said AB under this agreement shall be regulated by the rules for retirement passed by the Committee on the ——— day of ——— which shall be deemed to be incorporated herein PROVIDED NEVERTHELESS that in the event of the President of Committee being satisfied after a report from the Principal of the said College that the said AB is not performing his duties with zeal or efficiency or that he is a person unfit to be retained in employment in the said College the said President may require the said AB to show cause why his services should not be dispensed with under this agreement and upon the said President deciding against the said AB, this agreement shall terminate and the decision of the President in this respect shall be final.

5. That the said AB accepts the conditions of services, rights, and privileges which now obtain in the said college with reference to leave rules, Provident Fund regulations, retirement allowances and so forth and which are contained in the published Rules of the said College which shall be deemed to be incorporated herein and agrees to abide by all such conditions in so far as they may affect his services.

IN WITNESS WHEREOF, etc.

4—Contract of Employment of Manager of a Business Concern

AN AGREEMENT made on the ——— day of ——— BETWEEN AB, etc., (hereinafter called "the Principal") of the one part

AND CD, etc., (hereinafter called "the Manager") of the other part.

WHEREBY it is hereby agreed as follows:

1. The Manager shall during the term of —— years from the —— day of ——— next (now last past, *if the appointment is to take effect from a back date*) continue to serve the Principal as manager of business of ——— at ———— or any other place and shall give his whole time and attention to the said business and shall use his best endeavour to improve and extend the same and shall in all respects diligently and faithfully obey and observe all lawful orders and instructions of the Principal in relation to the conduct of the said business and shall not without his consent divulge any secrets or dealings relating thereto.

2. The Manager shall keep at the place of business at ———— proper books of accounts showing all goods and moneys received and delivered and disbursed by him with necessary particulars of all such transactions and shall duly account for all moneys belonging to the Principal and coming into the hands or power of the manager and shall forthwith pay the same to the Principal or his bankers for the time being except only such moneys as the Manager shall be authorised by the Principal to retain for the immediate requirements of the said business.

3. The Principal shall pay to the Manager during the continuance of his engagement and provided he shall duly observe and perform the agreements herein on his part contained, the salary of Rs. ——— per mensem on the first day of every calendar month commencing from the first day of ———— without any deduction except such as he will be bound to make under the Income Tax law for the time being in force, AND shall also pay the Manager at the end of each year during the aforesaid period a further sum equal to —— per cent on the gross sales for the said year (*or*, on the net profits of the said business for the said year if any, after making such deductions as are properly made according to the usual custom of the said business in the estimation of net profits) PROVIDED ALWAYS that upon the death or termination of the engagement of the Manager before the expiration of the said period of ——— years, the Principal shall forthwith pay to him or his heirs, executors, administrators or other legal representatives as the case may be, in respect of the services of the Manager for the whole or any part of the current month a due proportion of the salary of Rs. ——— per mensem together with such further sum in lieu of such percentage as aforesaid as shall bear the same proportion to the estimated gross sales (net profits) for the then current year as the part of the said year during which he has served shall bear to the whole year, the gross sales (net profits) being calculated on average of the past three years.

4. The Principal shall during the continuance of the Manager's engagement provide him with a suitable furnished house for residence free of rent, rates and taxes (except the charges for electricity consumed by him or of extra water used by him) and the Manager shall reside in the said house.

5. The Manager shall make such tours as may be necessary in the interest of the said business or as he may be directed by the Principal to make, and the Principal shall pay him all reasonable expenses actually incurred in undertaking such tours (*or*, a travelling allowance at Rs. 8 per km. for all journeys by road and one and one half first class fare for journeys performed by rail and a halting allowance of Rs. 1,500 per diem when a halt of not less than 8 hours is made at one place).

6. The Manager shall be entitled during his engagement to leave on full pay for a period equal to 1/12th of the period of service rendered and to a further leave on half pay in case of illness or incapacity to be proved to the satisfaction of the Principal for a period upto 15 days in one year.

7. Either party hereto may terminate the engagement of the Manager at any time before the expiration of the said term of ——— years on giving or sending by registered post to the other party three calendar months' notice in writing, such notice to be given or sent in the case of the Principal to his house at ————— and in case of the Manager to his place of business or residence provided by the Principal and on the expiration of the said three months from the date of giving or posting such notice the said engagement shall terminate provided that the Principal may terminate the said engagement at any time on payment of three months' pay in advance in lieu of such notice as aforesaid.[1]

8. If the Manager at any time wilfully neglects or refuses or from illness or other cause become or be unable to perform any of the duties under this engagement the Principal may suspend his salary (and sum by way of percentage) during such neglect, negligence or inability as aforesaid and may further immediately terminate the engagement of the Manager without giving any such notice or making such payment of salary in advance as hereinbefore provided.

---

1 The validity of such a clause was not upheld in case of a State undertaking: *Central Inland Water Transport Corporation* v. *Brojo Nath Ganguly*, (1986) 3 SCC 156. Although observations in the judgement are wide enough to cover even private employers the extension of its ratio to purely private employment would be contrary to the common law of master and servant and Sec. 14(i) (*b*) Specific Relief Act, 1963. See also, *S. Dutt* v. *Delhi University*, AIR 1958 SC 1050 and *Steel Industrials Kerala Ltd.* v. *Rebello*, (1985) 2 SCC 363 (para 19).

9. The Manager will at his own expense find and provide two respectable sureties to the amount of Rs. ——— each for his good conduct and for the due performance by him of this engagement and if he fails to do so for a period of three months from this date the Principal may terminate his services forthwith.

IN WITNESS, etc.

5—Renewal of Term of Service of an Employee (either on Old Terms or New Terms)

THIS AGREEMENT is made, etc.

WHEREAS the said CD has served the said AB as ——— under an agreement dated the ——— between the parties hereto;

AND WHEREAS the term of the said CD's engagement under the said agreement having expired on the ———, it has been agreed that the said AB shall re-engage, the said CD upon the terms and conditions hereinafter appearing (*or*, upon the terms and conditions contained in the said agreement dated the ———).

NOW THESE PRESENTS WITNESS and the parties hereto hereby agree as follows:

(1) The said CD shall serve the said AB as ——— for one year from the ———.

(2)

(3)

etc.

(*or*, 2. Terms and conditions of the said agreement shall be the same as are contained in the aforesaid agreement of the parties dated ——— in so far as they may be applicable to the employment under this agreement and all the terms and conditions contained in the said agreement shall be deemed to have been incorporated in this agreement).

IN WITNESS WHEREOF, etc.

6—Agreement Cancelling Employment (Endorsed on Service Agreement)

AN AGREEMENT made on the ——— day of ——— BETWEEN the within-named parties.

WHEREBY it is agreed as follows:

1. The employment of the Engineer by the Board under the within-

named agreement shall cease as from the date hereof and from the same date all the provisions of the within-named agreement shall cease to have effect;

2. In consideration of the sum of Rs. ———— paid by the Board to the Engineer (the receipt of which the Engineer hereby acknowledges) the Engineer releases the Board from all claims and demands under the within written agreement whether in respect of salary, allowance, compensation, damages or otherwise;

3. The Engineer shall on or before the ————day of ———— deliver up possession of the quarters occupied by him under the within written agreement and in default shall pay to the Board as liquidated damages the sum of Rs. ———— for every day after that date during which he shall retain possession thereof.

IN WITNESS WHEREOF, etc.

7—Service Agreement with Confidentiality Clause

AN AGREEMENT made on this ——— day of ——— BETWEEN the ——— a company incorporated under Companies Act, 2013 and having its registered office at ——— (hereinafter called "the Company") of the one part AND AB, etc., (hereinafter called "the Employee") of the other part.

WHEREAS the Company manufactures ALP and ZNP by using white/yellow phosphorous through a process not known to others;

AND WHEREAS the Company wants to employ a Chemical Engineer to supervise the same while ensuring that such Employee should maintain secrecy and confidentiality to which the employee has agreed.

NOW THESE PRESENTS WITNESS AS follows:

1. The Employee shall serve the Company as ——— for a period of —— years from the ———

2. The Employee shall not during the tenure of his employment or for a period of one year thereafter either join any business of the Company's competitors or run any business of his own using any confidential or secret information including any secret process or formula acquired in the course of his employment with the Company.[1]

---

1 Care should be taken in drafting this clause in view of the provisions of sec. 27 of Contract Act. Such restraint during the period of employment is perfectly valid and can be enforced by injunction, vide Sec. 42 of Specific Relief Act, 1963. However as regards negative covenants operative after the cessation of employment, they must be

3. The Employee shall return all papers and documents of the Company and not retain any copies or extracts therefrom upon termination of his services.

IN WITNESS WHEREOF, etc.

reasonable (*Superintendence Company of India* v. *Krishan Murgai*, AIR 1980 SC 1717, (1981) 2 SCC 246; *Sandhya Organic Chemicals P. Ltd.* v. *United Phosphorous Ltd.*, AIR 1997 Guj. 177).

TRUSTS INCLUDING SETTLEMENTS, ENDOWMENTS AND WAQFS

Preliminary Note

A trust is defined in Indian Trusts Act 1882[1] as an obligation annexed to the ownership of property, and arising out of a confidence reposed in and accepted by the owner or declared and accepted by him, for the benefit of another, or of another and the owner (Section 3). Thus, there are three essential ingredients:

(i) a declaration of trust,

(ii) existence of property, which is the subject of trust, and

(iii) the beneficiary (also called "*cestui que trust*").

The purpose of the trust should always be lawful, whether for the benefit of the public or an individual. The person creating the trust must be legally competent to contract and a trust may be created on behalf a minor with the permission of the Principal Civil Court of original jurisdiction (Sec. 7 Indian Trusts Act).

Every person capable of holding property may be a trustee, but if the trust involves the exercise of discretion he cannot execute it unless he is competent to contract (Sec. 10).

The Government cannot be a trustee[2] nor can a Government servant in his official capacity, act as trustee of a mosque, temple or religious institution (Sec. 22, Religious Endowments Act, 1863).

A corporation can both create trust and be a trustee. An insolvent can also be a trustee and the trust property is not affected by his insolvency. It is not advisable to appoint the beneficiary *cestui que trust* as trustees. Every trust of which the purpose is unlawful will be void, and, if the trust is created for both lawful and unlawful purposes and the two purposes cannot be separated, the whole trust would be void (Sec. 4).

Any property which is transferable can be the subject of trust, whether it is movable or immovable, but a mere beneficial interest under a subsisting trust cannot be made subject [illegible] trust.

The beneficiary of the trust may be any person capable of holding property. Such person may be a sentient being or a juristic person or even a deity.

---

1 This Act governs only private trusts as Sec. 1 mentions that nothing herein contained affects public or private religious or charitable endowments or to trusts to distribute prizes taken in war among the captors.

2 *Viziaramarju* v. *The Secretary of State*, 8 Mad 525 PC.

A trust may also be created for a religious or charitable object and the beneficiaries, in such cases, are the public or class of the public, interested in it.

Whether Public or Private

A trust may be either public or private. The criterion for deciding whether a particular trust is or is not of a private nature is whether the said trust is or is not for the benefit of individuals. It is the extensiveness of the object which may indicate the public nature of a trust. If a trust is intended to benefit a large and extensive section of the community it cannot be treated as a family trust.[1]

A private trust is trust for the private convenience and support of individuals or families while a public trust is for the benefit of the public at large or some class of it answering a particular description, the object being to benefit an uncertain and fluctuating body and the trust being of a permanent and definite character.[2]

A clear picture in mind of distinction between private and public trust should help in drawing the trust. The crucial point to be seen is whether it is intended by the founder that specified individuals are to have the right of worship at the shrine, or the general public or any specified portion thereof.[3]

If the endowment is in favour of the idol itself "proof of user by the public without interference would be cogent evidence that the dedication was in favour of the public", though "the mere fact that the public is allowed to visit a Temple Thakurdwara cannot necessarily indicate that the trust is public as opposed to private.[4]

When property is dedicated for the worship of a family idol, it is a private and not a public endowment as the persons entitled to worship the deity can only be the members of the family. A consideration may also be whether the idol is installed not in the precincts of the residential quarter but in a separate building raised for that very purpose on vacant site.[5]

Following are some of the features, taken in consideration in this connection[6]—

(a) location of the temple with reference to the residence of the person claiming rights of private ownership:

---

1 *Prakash Chandra Nag* v. *Subodh Chandra Nag*, AIR 1937 Cal 67; *State of Bihar* v. *Charusila Dasi*, AIR 1959 SC 1002 (case of temple); *Narain Bhagwantrao* v. *Gopal Vinayak*, AIR 1960 SC 100; *Dhaneshwarbua* v. *Charity Commissioner*, (1976) 2 SCC 417; *Shivprasad* v. *Leelabai*, AIR 1998 Bom 131; *Bala Shankar* v. *Charity Commissioner*, 1995 (Supp.) 1 SCC 485.

2 *Farman Ali* v. *Md. Raza Khan*, 1949 ALJ 453 at 457.

3 *Deoki Nandan* v. *Murlidhar*, AIR 1957 SC 133;

4 *Babu Bhagwan Din* v. *Gir Har Saroop*, AIR 1940 PC 7.

5 *Jammi Raja Rao* v. *Sri Anjaneya Swami Temple*, (1992) 3 SCC 14, AIR 1992 SC 1110.

6 *Hari Bhanu Maharaj of Baroda* v. *Charity Commissioner, Ahmedabad*, (1986) 4 SCC 162.

(b) the size of the construction and its proportion to the entire extent of the property;

(c) the nature of the grants made to the endowment:

(d) the identity of the individuals for whom the *Samadhi* in question has been raised;

(e) The ownership of the property in question.

The character is to be ascertained of the time of its origin. The private character of the institution is not affected subsequently in the absence of clear and definite evidence that later the dedication came to be for the use of the public.

Property belonging to public religious or charitable endowment, cannot ordinarily be disposed of by negotiation; this has preferably to be by public auction with reserve price fixed having regard to the market value. That is one of the noteworthy incidents of such endowment.[1] How did the founder treat the property and how did the descendants treat it are relevant, as also, as to whether the income of the endowed lands been continuously applied to the objects of the dedication.

A trust may also be partly private and partly public. Apart from the instance of *Wakf Alal Alad* (discussed below), even a non-Muslim is not barred, for instance, from making a trust private up to his life time, and after his death, public.

How Trust is Created

Under the Indian Trusts Act, 1882, a trust in relation to immovable property may be declared by a non-testamentary instrument in writing, signed by the author of the trust or the trustee and registered, or by a Will of the author of the trust or of the trustee (Sec. 5). No particular form or language is required to create a trust. What is essential is a clear intention of the author. A trust in relation to movable property can be created either in the same way as that of immovable property or by transfer of the ownership of the property to the trustee (Sec. 5).

In places where the Trusts Act does not apply, a trust of immovable property may be created orally if the author of the trust is himself the trustee and consequently no transfer of the property is involved, and all that is required is only a declaration of trust.[2]

If a stranger is appointed as trustee, a transfer of property is necessary and the conveyance must be made according to the law of Transfer of Property, e.g., if it amounts to gift, it must be made as a gift in favour of the trustee.

Instrument of Trust

An instrument of trust is drafted either as a deed poll or as a regular deed between the author of trust and the trustees. Where trustees are strangers and a transfer of property is involved, it is better to draft the deed as a deed between the

1 *Chenchu Rami Reddy* v. *Govt. of A.P.*, (1986) 3 SCC 391.

2 *Madonji* v. *Tribhowan*, 36 B 396.

author of trust and the trustees. Where the author is to be the trustee himself and the deed requires a mere declaration of trust, it is drafted as a deed poll. No specific words are necessary, but, whatever the words used, the deed should contain with reasonable certainty: (a) an intention to create a trust, (b) the purpose of the trust, (c) the beneficiary, (d) the names of the trustees, (e) the trust property, and (f) transfer of the legal ownership of the property to the trustee unless the trust declared by Will or the author is himself the trustee. [Sec. 6 of the Indian Trusts Act]

Declaration of Trust

The most important and vital part of a trust is the expression of an intention to create a trust which should be expressed in the deed in unequivocal language and with reasonable certainty. No particular or technical words are necessary but the words used must be definite and unequivocal. This intention is expressed clearly in the recitals of the deed and in the operative part also. If the trustee is a stranger the property is transferred to him "upon trust". If the author is himself the trustee, he declares in the operative part that he "dedicates" or "sets apart" the property in trust for such and such purpose and constitutes himself as the trustee.

Acceptance of Trust

Acceptance of trust by a trustee may be either express, e.g. by executing the deed of trust or by verbal assent, or be inferred from conduct, e.g., by entering into possession of the property and on the duties as trustee. But it is always safer to have the deed of trust executed by the trustee also.

Directions in Respect of Trust

Different directions are given to the trustees by the author as to the manner in which the trust is to be worked. These are the conditions and provisions of the trust and vary in different kinds of trusts according to the circumstances. Provision is also usually made for appointment of new trustees.

Revocation or Extinguishment of Trust

A trust created by Will may be revoked at the pleasure of the testator. A trust otherwise created can be revoked only (a) where all the beneficiaries are competent to contract then by their consent; or (b) by exercise of a power of revocation expressly reserved in the deed; or (c) where the trust is for the payment of the debts of the author of the trust, but no communication has been made with the creditors then at the pleasure of the author of the trust (Sec 78, Indian Trusts Act).

A trust is extinguished (a) when its purpose is completely fulfilled; or (b) when its purpose becomes unlawful; or (c) when the fulfillment of its purpose becomes impossible by destruction of the trust-property or otherwise; or (d) when the trust, being revocable, is expressly revoked (Sec 77, Indian Trusts Act).

If the trust property is to be applied for author's own benefit, the trust can be revoked. A power of revocation may with advantage always be reserved in the deed.

A public charitable trust cannot however, be revoked, nor be otherwise adversely affected by a subsequent deed.[1] After having settled the property by a settlement deed the settler has no title left in it and is, therefore, not competent to bequeath it, for such bequest will amount to implied revocation of the settlement.[2]

Both testamentary and non-testamentary gifts for public charitable purposes must be saved by wider interpretation of court applying the doctrine of *Cy-pres* (as near as), *i.e.*, giving effect to the general intention *via* another method that closely approximates the one specified. Because, public interest is served that way.[3] Where only a conditional gift was made, if the condition fails, the gift will not take effect.

Hindu Endowments

While a trust can be created for charitable and religious purposes by transferring property to the trustees and defining the objects of the trust as laid down above, yet religious and charitable endowments under the Hindu and Mohammedan law can be created in accordance with the law and usage relating thereto. This is a fundamental difference between the juridical conception on which the English law relating to trust is based and that which forms the foundation of the Hindu and Mohammedan systems, and for this reason the rules applicable to *waqfs* and Hindu religious endowments have been deliberately exempted from the scope of the Indian Trusts Act, (Sec. 1).

Under the Hindu law a gift can be made to a deity installed or to be installed in a temple, and deity or idol is recognized by courts as a juristic person capable of holding property, and property dedicated to an idol belongs to the idol and not to the *shebait* who is in the position of a manager only and not that of a trustee.[4] Similarly a *math* is also a juristic person and gift of property can be made to it instead of a trust. It is not necessary that the idol be in existence at the time of creating the trust.[5] Sometimes, a dedication is made and also trustees are appointed with definite directions for spending the income of the dedicated property for the purposes of the deity in a particular way. Sometimes the donor appoints himself as the first trustee. There is nothing illegal in this. There is also nothing illegal in the donor as *shebait* of a temple continuing to reside in the house, in a portion of which the idol is installed, for the convenient management of the trust[6] and in appointing his heirs as *shebaits* to succeed him one after another and allow them also to reside in the house likewise. In spite of such provisions, the dedication may be held to be absolute. But, if the deed, as a whole, shows that only a charge is created on the

---

1 *Sri Agasthyar Trust* v. *C.I.T.*, (1998) 5 SCC 588 (paras 14 to 16).

2 *Dagani Ramadas* v. *P. Daveed*, (1998) 8 SCC 465.

3 *State of U.P.* v. *Bansidhar*, AIR 1974 SC 1084.

4 *Angurbala* v. *Debabrata*, AIR 1951 SC 293.

5 *Ratan Sen* v. *Suraj Bhan*, AIR 1944 All 1; *Jagdish* v.*Mt. Kausilla*, AIR 1947 All 317.

6 *Nirupama Ghosh* v. *Purnima Ghosh*, (1973) 3 SCC 411, AIR 1972 SC 1412.

property or there is a mere trust to receive and apply a portion of the income for the specified religious or charitable purpose and there is no divesting of property then the dedication may be held to be partial.[1] Though, as regards the property of the temple he is in the position of a trustee.

A *shebait* is different from a trustee in that *(a)* the property does not vest in him but in the idol or the institution, while in case of a trust, the property vests in the trustee for the benefit of *cestui que trust,* (the beneficiaries) *(b)* the *shebait* is a manager and not a trustee, *(c)* the *shebait* has not only duties to discharge in connection with the endowment, but he has a beneficial interest in the debutter property and almost invariably has a share in its usufruct which depends upon the terms of the grant or upon custom or usage. His rights and interest have the character of proprietary rights, and except as otherwise provided by the founder or by usage or custom, *shebaitship*, like any other species of heritable property, follows the line of inheritance from the founder.[2]

In this connection, observations made by Hon'ble Apex Court, in *Nirupama Ghoshe* v. *Purnima Ghoshe*,[3] are interesting and instructive. Their lordships observed that where a pious settlor with a large family but few properties is torn between his desire to make a dedication in the name of his titulary deity, on the one hand, and his natural inclination to make a provision for the members of his family, on the other, and bearing both considerations in mind executes a deed of settlement, a favourite device with such settlor is to constitute his heirs as *shebaits* of the deity and give them a right of residence permanently though in the capacity of *shebaits*. In all such cases courts must decide principally on the wording of the Settlement Deed whether the settlor intended to create an absolute dedication in favour of the deity or only a partial dedication. It was further pointed out that *shebaits* are merely managers of the deity and are not expected to spend out of their pocket for the upkeep of the deity. They might spend out of devotion to the deity, but there is no legal obligation on them in that behalf. In these circumstances, a settlor intending an absolute dedication in favour of a deity or charity would not be more concerned that his heirs live in the house from generation to generation along with their families, but would be more concerned for the welfare of the deity and the permanent maintenance of the building in which the deity is housed.

In *Radhakanta Deb* v. *Commissioner of Hindu Religious Endowments*,[4] the following tests have been laid down to determine whether an endowment is of a private or of a public nature:

---

1 See discussion of case law in *Sappani Mohd. Mohideen* v. *R.V. Sethusubramania Pillai*, (1974) 1 SCC 615, AIR 1974 SC 740; See also *Menakuru Dasaratharami Reddi* v. *D. Subba Rao*, AIR 1957 SC 797, 1957 SCR 1122.

2 *Angurbala* v. *Debabrata*, AIR 1951 SC 293; *Shambhu Charan Shukla* v. *Sri Thakur Ladli Radha Chandar Madan Gopal*, (1985) 1 SCC 524 (Shebait right may as well be bequeathed by will.)

3 AIR 1972 SC 1412: (1973) 3 SCC 411

4 AIR 1981 SC 798 (para 14 at pages 801-2).

1. Where the origin of the endowment cannot be ascertained, the question is whether the user of the temple by members of the public is as of right;

2. The fact that the control and management vests either in a large body of persons or in the members of the public, and the founder does not retain any control over the management. Allied to this may be a circumstance where the evidence shows that there is provision for a scheme to be framed by associating the members of the public at large.

3. Where, however, a document is available to prove the nature and origin of the endowment and the recitals of the document show that the control and management of the temple are retained with the founder or his descendants, and that extensive properties are dedicated for the purpose of the maintenance of the temple belonging to the founder himself. This will be a conclusive proof to show that the endowment was of a private nature.

4. Where the evidence shows that the founder of the endowment did not make any stipulation for offerings or contributions to be made by members of the public to the temple, this would be an important intrinsic circumstance to indicate the private nature of the endowment.[1]

How Made

Property can be dedicated to a temple either by giving it to the trustees and executing a deed of trust in the usual way, or by dedicating it to the idol itself. In the latter case, a deed of dedication, though not absolutely necessary, is expedient to have one executed instead of leaving the dedication to be inferred from the use of the property and conduct of the donor and the *Shebaits*. No particular words are required for dedication, and either it may take the form of a gift to the idol or the property should be expressly set apart for, or dedicated to, the religious and charitable purposes, which should be clearly specified. The undernoted cases,[2] contain an exhaustive discussion on ascertainment of the intention of the author as to whether an absolute *debutter* of the properties was created with directions to *shebaits* regarding application of moneys or a trust was created vesting the properties in the trustees. Debutter means literally 'belonging to a deity'.

It is not necessary that the image of the deity should have been installed in a temple, but the deity should be named,[3] nor is an endowment affected by the destruction or mutilation of the idol, and a new idol may be installed in its place.[4]

Charitable gifts, e.g., those for *sadabarat, dharamshala, pathshala* may be

---

1 *State of Bihar* v. *Biseshwar Das*, AIR 1973 SC 2057; *Deelip Kumar & Co.* v. *Mulla Gulamali Trust*, 1998 AIHC 1073 (Mad.); *Marua Dei* v. *Muralidhar Nanda*, AIR 1999 SC 329, (1999) 1 SCC 377.

2 *C.I.T.* v. *Jagannath Jee*, (1977) 2 SCC 519; *Ramkishorelal* v. *Kamalnarayan*, AIR 1963 SC 890.

3 *Sarab Sukh Das* v. *Ram Prasad*, 46 AIR 130, 78 IC 118.

4 *Puran Chandra* v. *Gopal Lal*, 8 CLJ 369.

joined with religious gifts[1] but if they are separately made they should be made in the form of trusts.

Waqfs

Waqf is the tying up of the property in the ownership of God the almighty and the devotion of the property for the benefit of human beings. The right of ownership passes from the donor to God immediately when a proper *waqf* is made and the manager of the *waqf*, who is called *mutwalli*, is only the manager or governor and not a trustee in the strict sense in which that word is used in English law.[2]

There are two kinds of *waqfs* (1) *public waqf* which is a dedication of property for public purposes, e.g., the maintenance of a mosque, orphanage, *imambara*, etc., and (2) *Private waqf*, which is for the benefit of the settlor's family and descendants. The latter kind of *waqf* is valid if the ultimate benefit, in case of there remaining no descendant, however distant is reserved for the public and for any other religious purposes or charitable purpose of a permanent character. Such a waqf is called *waqf alal aulad* and is recognized by the Mussalman Waqf Validating Act, 1913. A *waqf* exclusively for the benefit of the family or descendants of the settlor is not valid, therefore, the device of reserving an ultimate dedication to charity is adopted so as to bring the *waqf* under the Act and make it valid.[3] The maintenance and support of the family, children or descendants of the *waqif* are not pious purpose.[4] The whole of the property must be given to charity as ultimate bequest.[5] It should also be noted that the reservation may be for the maintenance and support of the *waqif* and descendants and not for the absolute use of the settlor for his life. In the latter case, the gift would be void. If there was no intention to dedicate and the *waqfnama* was never acted upon and the deed was meant to be a shield against possible claims there would be no valid *Waqf*,[6] but once a valid *Waqf* is created it is not open to the *Waqif* to subsequently revoke it and deal with the property as its owner.[7]

No form is prescribed by the Mohammedan law for making a valid *waqf*. It may be made orally or by a deed *inter vivos* or by will. If a deed or *waqfnama* is written, all that is necessary is that the object of the *waqf* should be clearly

---

1 *C.I.T.* v. *Jagannathjee*, (1977) 2 SCC 519.

2 *Vidya Vaauthi T. Swamgal* v. *B. Ayyar*, AIR 1922 PC 123; *Aliah Rakhi* v. *Shah Mohd.*, AIR 1934 PC 77; *Nawab Zan Yar Jung* v. *Director of Endowments*, AIR 1963 SC 985.

3 *Mohammad Ali* v. *Dinesh*, AIR 1940 Cal 417; *Trustees of Sahebzadi Oalia Kulsum Trust* v. *C.E.O.*, (1998) 6 SCC 267, AIR 1998 SC 2986 (Such a trust is not violative of Secs. 13 and 14, Transfer of Property Act which apply only to transfers *inter vivos* and not to such trusts).

4 *Mohiuddin* v. *Sofia*, AIR 1940 Cal 501.

5 *Abdul Karim* v. *Rahimabai*, AIR 1946 Bom 342.

6 *Mohd. Ali Mohd Khan* v. *Mst. Bismillah Begam*, AIR 1930 PC 255.

7 *Beli Ram & Bros* v. *Md. Afzal*, AIR 1948 PC 168.

specified and the property should be clearly defined. No particular words are necessary to indicate the grant but it is advisable to use the word *waqf* which has a well-known and recognised meaning though it is not necessary.[1] The *Waqif* should actually divest himself of the property and a mere declaration of intention by itself will not constitute a *waqf*, though the dedication need not be express and may be inferred from long use[2] and other facts and circumstances.[3]

A *waqf* made while the *waqif* is suffering from death illness (*marzul maut*) is valid only to the extent of 1/3rd of the assets, unless assented to by the heirs.

Any Muslim who has attained puberty, though not majority, can make a *waqf*. A woman can also make a *waqf*.

Requirements of Valid Waqf

A *waqf* should be certain as to the property endowed, unconditional, and not subject to an option. It must have a final object which cannot fail and the object must be expressly stated. The dedication must be absolute and present, and not contingent or conditional. The *waqf* can be of any kind of property but the dedication must be permanent. A decree is property of too precarious a nature to admit of a permanent dedication.[4] *Waqf* must according to Shia law, be accompanied by delivery of possession, though this is not necessary under the Sunni law. The office of a *mutwalli* is not necessarily heritable. The deed of *waqf* should provide for the appointment or nomination of a *mutwalli*. Sometimes it is provided that a *mutwalli* should nominate his successor. If there is no provision in the deed of *waqf*, or if the directions given therein fail, court will appoint a *mutwalli*.

Dedication for a mosque

With regard to a mosque in order to create a valid dedication of a public nature the following conditions are to be satisfied[5]:-

(i) the founder declares his intention to dedicate a property for the purpose of a mosque.

(ii) the founder divests himself completely from the ownership of the property;

(iii) the founder provides for a separate entrance to enable the public to enter the mosque.

Founder's permission or the bare act of allowing the members of Muslim community to offer prayers amounts to a complete delivery of possession. Mosque becomes consecrated for public worship either by delivery of possession or the

1 *Mt. Khurshed Jahan* v. *Qamqam Ali*, AIR 1947 Oudh 17.

2 *Mohammad Shah* v. *Fasihuddin*, AIR 1956 SC 713.

3 *Muhammad Imdad* v. *Mt. Bismillah*, AIR 1946 All 468.

4 *Ghulam* v. *Hafiz Abdul Rashid*, AIR 1947 All 127.

5 *Syed Mohd. Salie Labbai* v. *Mohd. Hanifa*, (1976) 4 SCC 780.

dedication to *waqf*. Subsequent to the complete dedication to the mosque as a place of public worship, any reservation or condition imposed by the owner would be deemed to be void.

As to when a graveyard is to be deemed public, see decision in *Syed Mohd. Salie Labbai* v. *Mohd. Hanifa,* supra.

In the case of *waqf*, the usufruct only can be spent; in case of gift the corpus of the property itself may be consumed. Without delivery of possession, gift is incomplete.

Treasurer of Charitable Endowments

In case of trusts established for charitable, or partly charitable and partly religious purposes (but not exclusively for religious teaching or worship), the trust property may, by an application to the State Government under Sec. 4, Charitable Endowments Act 1890, be vested in the officer called the Treasurer of Charitable Endowments to be held by him in trust for the objects of the trust (Sec. 3). He is a corporation sole (*ibid*). A scheme is prepared by the Government with the concurrence of the founder, for the administration of the said property and application of the income to the objects of the trust, but the Treasurer is not required to administer the property (Sec. 5). In such cases no deed of trust is necessary.

Marriage and Family Settlements

Marriage and family settlement are species of settlements by way of trust. When an annuity is settled on a wife, it is not necessary to have any trustees and the annuity may be settled by agreement to which the husband and wife are parties. Certain antenupital and post-nuptial arrangements are however made in England by way of settlement and in these, as well as in cases of family settlements for the benefit of children trustees are usually introduced. Property is transferred to them in trust for the wife and children. Such settlements are not common in India. In all such settlements, provision is usually made for a resulting trust in favour of the settlor or his legal heirs in case of death of the beneficiaries. In case of children, the children are usually made the beneficiaries on attaining majority or in case of females on marriage, and, until then the trustees spend the income of trust property on their maintenance and education. Whatever provision is intended to be made should be clearly expressed.

Other Settlements

Settlement of property in lieu of right to maintenance does not amount to transfer by way of sale or gift.[1] A settlement deed providing that the property will be held and enjoyed by the settlor's wife and "after her by her son and his descendants from generation to generation, for all time" was held to create only a

---

1 *State of U.P.* v. *Rajkumar R.R. Brahma*, (1969) 2 SCC 818.

life estate and not an absolute estate in her favour; the absolute estate was given to their son subject to the life estate in her favour.[1]

It was provided that after the death of the daughter-in-law "the members of her family" shall be the owners of the property given to her by the settlement deed, it was held that the property would devolve not on her collaterals but on her daughter's son as the nearest member of her family.[2]

Stamp Duty

Settlement is defined in the Stamp Act as meaning "any non-testamentary disposition in respect of movable or immovable property, made: (*a*) in consideration of marriage, (*b*) for the purpose of distributing property of the settlor among his family or those for whom he wishes to provide, or for the purpose of providing for some person dependent on him, or (*c*) for any religious or charitable purpose." For a deed of settlement, or endowment which falls within the definition, the stamp duty payable is that as on a bond for a sum equal to the amount or value of the property settled as set forth in the deed (Article 58).

For declaration of trust not amounting to settlement, see Article 64, Schedule I, Indian Stamp Act.

Registration

Registration of a deed of trust involving immovable property is compulsory under the Indian Trusts Act, (Sec. 5). In cases of trusts not covered by the Act (e.g., *waqfs*, or religious or charitable trusts), registration would be compulsory under the Registration Act if the value of the property involved is Rs. 100 or more.

If a trust is created by a Will, registration is not necessary.

---

1 *A. Sreenivasa Pai* v. *Saraswathi Ammal*, AIR 1985 SC 1359.

2 *L. Babu Ram* v. *Raghunathji*, AIR 1976 SC 1734, (1976) 3 SCC 492.

GENERAL FORMS

Various Forms of Recitals in Deeds of Trust

1. Intended Marriage

WHEREAS a marriage is intended shortly to be solemnized between the said AB and the said CD.

2. Marriage and Agreement for Settlement

WHEREAS the husband and wife were married on the ——— of ——— and previous to such marriage they agreed to make a settlement as is hereinafter contained.

3. Transfer of Securities Passing by Delivery

AND WHEREAS pursuant to an agreement made for the intended marriage, the bonds mentioned in the schedule hereto belonging to the husband have been delivered by him to the trustees to the intent that the same shall be held in trust for the husband until the intended marriage and after the solemnization thereof upon the trusts hereinafter expressed.

Or,

AND WHEREAS the said AB has endorsed and made over to the trustees, the securities particulars of which are set forth in the schedule hereto to be held by the trustees upon trust and in the manner hereinafter expressed.

4. Agreement to Assign Property by Husband and Wife

AND WHEREAS for the intended marriage it was agreed that the properties of the husband and wife hereinafter mentioned shall be assigned to the Trustees upon the trusts hereinafter declared concerning the same (respectively).

5. Agreement to Pay Annual Sum

AND WHEREAS for the intended marriage it was further agreed that the said AB shall enter into such covenant as is hereinafter contained for the payment to the trustees, the annual sum hereinafter mentioned to be held and applied by them upon the trusts and in the manner hereinafter expressed.

6. Statement about Children

AND WHEREAS there has been five children from the said marriage, viz., AB, CD and EF, sons and GH and JK daughters of whom AB and GH are major and married the others are still minor and unmarried.

7. Agreement for Settlement on Wife

AND WHEREAS for the intended marriage it was agreed that all the said premises shall be settled by the husband in the manner hereinafter appearing.

8. Debutter Settlement

AND WHEREAS the said AB has erected a temple at ——— and has established a deity by the name of ——— in the said temple and is desirous of dedicating the properties mentioned in the schedule hereto to the said deity for the expenses of the said temple and to secure the worship of the said deity in the said temple and to make a settlement of the said property in the manner hereinafter appearing;

9. Trust for Erecting a Temple

AND WHEREAS the said AB is desirous of erecting a temple at ——— and of installing the idol of ——— therein and has decided to dedicate the property mentioned in the schedule hereto for the cost of the construction of the temple and of the maintenance thereof and for the expenses of the worship and other necessary expenses in the manner hereinafter appearing.

10. Making a Further Provision

AND WHEREAS the founder is desirous of making such further provision as is hereinafter contained for the maintenance of the said temple and *dharamshala* and for performance of such acts of devotion and charity and celebration of such festivals connected with the said worship to be conducted and on such scale as specified in the ——— schedule hereto;

11. Payment of Money for Founding Scholarships

AND WHEREAS the founder has paid the sum of Rs.——— to the trustees to the intent that the same shall be dedicated in perpetuity for the promotion and encouragement of education at the ——— College at ——— by founding scholarships in the manner hereinafter appearing.

12. Founding Beds in Hospital

AND WHEREAS the donor is desirous of establishing an endowment fund for the endowment of beds in the ———— hospital (hereinafter called "the Hospital") and the maintenance of the same for patients who may be unable to pay fees and rent charged by the hospital;

AND WHEREAS the donor has for this purpose paid Rs. ——— (*or*, endowed and delivered the securities mentioned in the ——— schedule hereto) to the trustees upon the trust and subject to the powers and provisions hereinafter declared and expressed, concerning the same;

13. Waqf Alal Aulad

WHEREAS with the object of attaining *Kurbat* or nearness to God and reward in the next world, I desire to make a *waqf* of the properties mentioned in the schedule hereto for the maintenance and support of my descendants with the ultimate reservation for the public charitable purposes hereinafter mentioned;

14. Waqf of Mosque

AND WHEREAS the *Waqif* of the property hereinafter described to be used as a mosque for the benefit of the Muslim community and for the use of the said community in the manner hereinafter appearing;

15. General Waqf

AND WHEREAS the *Waqif* is desirous of making a *waqf* of the properties described in the schedule hereto for the public religious and charitable purposes hereinafter mentioned;

16. Statement of Value of the Property[1]

AND WHEREAS the value of the said property (*or*, the property described in the schedule) is Rs. ————.

Miscellaneous Clauses and Conditions of Trust

1. Trust of Separate Funds of the Wife and Husband for Life of each

During the joint lives of the husband and wife the trustees shall pay the income of the property described in the first schedule hereto and the property for the time being representing the same (hereinafter called "the

---

1 This is necessary for calculation of stamp duty and is required by Sec. 27, Stamp Act. The statement may be made either as a recital or as a declaration, or the value may be mentioned along with the description of the property.

husband's fortune") to the husband and his assigns and shall pay the income of the property described in the second schedule hereto and the property for the time being representing the same (hereinafter called "the wife's fortune") to the wife and after the death of such one of them the husband or wife as shall first die shall pay the income of his or her fortune to the survivor of them and his or her assigns during his or her life but so that during marriage this interest hereby given to the wife shall be without power of anticipation.[1]

2. Annuity to Wife

During the joint lives of the husband and wife the trustees shall out of the income of the said property for the time being representing the same pay an annuity of Rs. ——— to the wife without power of anticipation from the date of marriage such annuity to be payable in equal monthly instalments on the ——— day of each month and shall during such joint lives pay the residue of such income to the husband and his assigns.

3. Trust in Favour of Children

The trustees shall hold the property hereby settled IN TRUST for all or any of the children or children of the intended marriage who being male attain the age of eighteen years or being female attain that age or marry, and if more than one, in equal shares.

4. Maintenance and Accumulation

The trustees shall after the death of husband and wife apply the whole or such part as they think fit of the income of the share in the trust property to which any child of the intended marriage shall for the time being be entitled in expectancy under the trust hereinbefore declared for and towards his or her maintenance, education or benefit and may either themselves apply the same or may pay the same to the guardian or guardians of such child for the purpose aforesaid without seeing to the application thereof (and shall invest the surplus income (if any) thereof in any investment hereby authorised in augmentation of the capital or share).

5. Investment of Trust Fund

The trustees shall forthwith invest the trust fund in any of the forms of investment allowed by law (*or*, in one of the investments mentioned in —— schedule hereto) and may from time to time vary such investment for others

1 In conveyancing "anticipation" means "the act of assigning, charging or otherwise dealing with income before it becomes due" (Black's Law Dictionary, VI edn., p. 93)

of a like nature as often as they shall deem expedient.

Or

All moneys received by the trustees and not required for immediate expenditure for the purposes of the trust may at the discretion of the trustees be invested in any of the forms, etc., (*as in para* 5).

6. To Sell Securities

The trustees shall be at liberty at their discretion to call in and sell any securities hereby transferred and re-invest the sale proceeds in any other securities or deposit the same in any nationalised bank.

7. Not to Sell

The turstees shall have no power to sell, mortgage or otherwise transfer the immovable property hereby settled or any part thereof but they shall be at liberty to grant leases for terms not exceeding seven years.

8. To Sell

The trustees shall have power if they think fit to sell the immovable and movable property subject to the trust hereby created and all money received by such sale shall form part of the trust fund and shall be applicable accordingly.

9. To Purchase

The trustees may at any time or when they think expedient, apply any part of the trust fund in acquiring by purchase or on lease or otherwise any land and all land so acquired shall be transferred or demised to or otherwise vested in the trustees or such other persons as they shall from time to time direct.

10. Appointment of New Trustees

If and whenever the number of the trustees shall be reduced below ———, the continuing trustees shall appoint such number of new trustees as shall be required to make up the total number for the time being to ———.

Or,

In case of any vacancy in the board of trustees caused by death, resignation or otherwise, the same shall be filled up by nomination by the remaining trustees.

11. Trustees to Act by Majority of Votes[1]

All or any of the trusts and powers vested in or exercisable by the trustees hereunder shall be capable of being performed or exercised by a majority of the trustees hereof for the time being and any action or decision of such majority shall be as valid and effective as it would have been if done by all the trustees.

12. Power to make Rules

Subject as aforesaid the trustees shall from time to time make and alter rules and regulations with regard to the conduct of the business and all matters in respect of which any power or duty is hereby vested in them as they may think proper.

13. Cy-pres

If the object for which this trust has been created shall fail and cannot be fulfilled the trustees shall be at liberty to apply the trust fund and the property which is the subject of this trust to any other object of alike nature which the trustees shall consider proper.

14. Power of Revocation

The settlor may at any time or times hereafter by any deed or deeds revocable or irrevocable or by Will or conduct expressly referring to this power or the property subject thereto appoint such new or other trustees and concerning the trust fund (*or*, the property hereby settled or any part thereof) as he may think fit.

---

1 Sec. 48 Trusts Act provides that all trustees must act jointly except where the instrument of trust otherwise provides. Hence this clause.

PRECEDENTS

[*In these Precedents only trusts created inter vivos are dealt with; Precedents of those created by Will will be found in the next part relating to Wills*]

1—Marriage Settlement under which prospective Husband's Father Agrees to Pay an Annuity to the prospective Wife

THIS SETTLEMENT is made on the ——— day of ——— BETWEEN AB, etc., (hereinafter called "the settlor") of the first part AND CD, etc., of the second part AND EF, etc., of the third part.

WHEREAS a marriage has been fixed up between CD and EF and during the negotiations for the marriage it was agreed (between the settlor and the father of the EF) that the settlor will enter into an agreement to pay an annuity of Rs. ——— to EF during the continuance of her marriage with CD;

NOW THIS DEED WITNESSES that in pursuance of the agreement and in consideration of the intended marriage the settlor covenants with CD and EF and as a separate covenant with each of them as follows:

1. The settlor will during his life (*or*, the settlor his heirs, executors, administrators will) from and after the solemnization of the marriage and during the subsistence of that marriage pay to EF without power of anticipation an annuity of Rs. ———.

2. The annuity shall be deemed to accrue from day to day and shall be payable monthly by equal instalments on the first day of every month, the first payment (if necessary of an apportioned part of the said annuity) to be made on the first day of the month next following the month in which the marriage is solemnized.

3. If EF becomes insolvent or does or attempts to do or suffer anything or any event happens whereby the annuity, or its part becomes vested in or payable to some other person or cease to become payable to EF then the annuity shall forthwith cease to be payable.

4. The settlor as owner of the property mentioned in the schedule hereto, hereby charges the same with the payment of the annuity.

5. If marriage between CD and EF is not solemnized within ——

months this settlement shall become void and of no effect.

The schedule herein referred to.

IN WITNESS WHEREOF, etc.

2—Post-Nuptial Settlement by Husband on himself, his Wife and Children

THIS SETTLEMENT made on the ——— day of ——— BETWEEN AB, etc., (hereinafter called "the Settlor") of the first part AND CD, etc., (hereinafter called "the wife") of the second part AND EF, etc., HI, etc., LM, etc., and OP, etc., (hereinafter called "the trustees," which expression shall include the trustee or trustees for the time being) of the third part.

WITNESSES that in consideration of natural love and affection of the settlor for his wife and children and for other good considerations the settlor as owner hereby transfers to the Trustees ALL that property described in the schedule hereto valued at Rs. ——— TO HOLD the same to the Trustees upon trust and subject to the powers and provisions hereinafter expressed, viz.:

(1) The Trustees shall first discharge out of the income or capital of the property hereby settled after paying land revenue, cesses and taxes and other outgoings and expenses of realisation all the debts of the settlor due on the date hereof.

(2) The trustees may in their absolute and unfettered discretion either allow the said property or any part or parts thereof to remain as actually invested or may sell, call in or convert into money the same and invest the net sale proceeds thereof in the names of the trustees in or upon any investments they think proper.

(3) Subject to the provisions contained in clause (1) the trustees shall hold the income of the property settled and the property for the time being representing the same for the benefit of the settlor and the wife during their lives and after the death of either of them for the benefit of the survivor.

(4) After the death of the settlor and the wife the trustees shall hold the said property and the capital and income of the trust fund in trust for all the children of the settlor who shall attain the age of eighteen years in equal shares, and in the meantime shall apply the income of the said property towards the maintenance and education of the said children during their minority and invest the surplus income, if any, in such investments as they think fit.

(5) If there shall be no child of the settlor then subject to the trusts and

provisions herein contained the trustees shall hold the said property and all trust funds and income for the legal heirs of the settlor surviving the settlor and the wife (*or*, the legal heirs of the settlor or the wife whoever shall die last).

(6) The trustees may, after the death of the settlor and the wife, from time to time by mortgage or sale of the said property hereby settled raise any moneys necessary for the maintenance and education of the settlor's children during their minority.

(7) The power of appointing a new trustee or new trustees hereof shall vest in the settlor and after his death in the wife if she survives him and after the death of both in the person or persons for the time being entitled to the trust funds if of full age, and if there shall be no such person then in the court or any other officer having jurisdiction in this behalf under the law for the time being in force PROVIDED THAT whenever a vacancy shall happen amongst the trustees by death or any other means a new trustee shall forthwith be appointed to fill such vacancy.

(8) The settlor may at any time in his lifetime or by will revoke all or any of the trusts powers or provisions hereinbefore declared and by the same or any other deed or will declare such new or other trust powers or provisions concerning the property hereinbefore settled as he shall think fit.

The schedule herein referred to.

IN WITNESS WHEREOF, etc.

3—Settlement of Property for the Benefit of Minor Children

THIS SETTLEMENT made on the ——— day of ——— BETWEEN AB, etc., (hereinafter called "the settlor") of the one part AND CD, etc., EF, etc., GH, etc., (hereinafter called "the Trustees" which expression shall include the trustee or trustees for the time being) of the other part.

WITNESSES as follows:

1. In consideration of the natural love and affection for his children named X, Y and Z who are all minors and were born on the ———, the ——— and the ——— respectively, the settlor hereby transfers and assigns the property described in the schedule hereto which belongs to the settlor to the trustees upon trust and subject to the powers and provisions hereinafter expressed and declared.

2. The Trustees shall not transfer the immovable property hereby

transferred except in case of absolute and unavoidable necessity and with the permission of the settlor or in case of his death his wife and in case of the death of both with the permission of the District Judge having jurisdiction in the matter.

3. The Trustees may sell the movable properties mentioned in the schedule hereto as necessity may arise and may in their absolute discretion either allow the money and securities to remain deposited and invested as they at present are or may withdraw the said money or any part thereof and deposit it elsewhere or invest it in any safe security and may sell or convert into money and security or part thereof and invest the net sale proceeds thereof in the name of the Trustees in or upon such investments as they think proper.

4. The Trustees shall hold the said property mentioned in the schedule hereto or any property representing the same in trust for such of the settlor's children viz., X, Y and Z, in equal shares, when they shall attain the age of 18 years, in equal shares.

5. The Trustees shall apply the income of the property hereby transferred to them or the property representing the same towards the maintenance and education of the settlor's said children during their minority and invest the surplus income, if any, in such investments as they think fit.

6. The settlement hereby made shall be irrevocable.

7. The power of appointing new trustee or trustees shall be vested in the settlor or after his death in his wife if she survives him.

8. It is hereby declared that the value of the aforesaid property is Rs. ————.

The schedule herein referred to.

IN WITNESS WHEREOF, etc.

4—Private Trust for Management and Preservation of Property

THIS DEED OF TRUST etc. (*as in Form 3*).

WHEREAS the said AB owns and possesses all that property detailed and specified in the schedule hereto which is his self-acquired property and over which he has full disposing power under the Hindu law;

AND WHEREAS the said AB has for some time past been keeping very indifferent health and is unable to look after his affairs and has lost all hopes of a complete recovery;

AND WHEREAS his only son CD has long been subject to epileptic fits is now a man of weak intellect and of almost unsound mind totally incapable of managing the household and estate affairs;

AND WHEREAS for the aforesaid reasons and with the object of making proper and adequate provision for the due management, protection, preservation and disposition of his estate the said AB is desirous of creating a trust in respect of his aforesaid property in manner hereinafter appearing;

AND WHEREAS the total value of the aforesaid property is Rs. —— as detailed in the schedule hereto.

NOW THIS DEED WITNESSES as follows:

1. The said AB hereby transfers ALL that property described in the schedule hereto (hereinafter referred to as "the trust property") to the trustees TO HOLD the same in trust for the said AB and after his death upon the trust hereinafter declared concerning the same with and subject to such powers and limitations as are hereinafter specified.

2. The Trustees shall by themselves or through an agent or agents employed by them manage and deal with the trust property in such manner as might be most beneficial to the interest of the trust and shall realise the rent, dividend, interest and other income accruing from the trust property and the said AB shall make such formal endorsements and execute such documents and do every such thing as may be legally necessary to enable the trustees to realize such income.

PROVIDED that so long as the said AB or his wife shall be alive and in full possession of his senses, the trustees shall not be competent to sell, mortgage or otherwise transfer any portion of the residential house except with his express consent if he is alive and able to give consent or with the consent of his wife in case he is dead or is unable to give his consent.

3. During the said AB's life time the trustees shall spend the income of the trust property in such manner as the said AB may direct and in case he is not able to give any directions the said income shall be spent on the maintenance of the said AB, his wife, his son, his son's wife and such other members of his family as may for the time being be in existence and dependent on him and on all religious, social and customary needs of the family such as *mundan* and marriage of members of the family, *bhat* and *chhuchak* of the children of his daughters, etc.,

4. After the death of the said AB the income of the trust property shall be spent on the maintenance of his wife, his son the said CD, the said CD's wife and such other members of his family as may be in existence and on all such religious, social and customary needs of the family as aforesaid.

5. If at any time the trustees find that the income of the trust property is not sufficient for the objects of the trust as hereinbefore recited, they shall be at liberty to draw upon the cash mentioned in the schedule hereto or to raise money by disposing of such stocks, shares or securities mentioned in the said schedule as they may think proper, provided that except in cases of sudden, urgent and unavoidable necessity they shall not be entitled to raise more than rupees ten thousand in any one year by drawing upon such cash or disposing of such stocks, shares or securities.

6. Whenever on account of death or other cause, the office of trustee becomes vacant, the said AB if he is alive and in proper senses and after his death or if he is not in his proper senses the remaining trustees shall appoint a new trustee and if they cannot agree about the appointment of a new trustee or fail to appoint one within a reasonable time, the court may appoint a new trustee in accordance with the law for the time being in force in this behalf and in making such appointment the trustees or the court shall give due weight to the wishes, if any, of the said AB's wife and wife of the said CD expressed in this behalf.

Pending the appointment of a new trustee the remaining trustees shall continue to administer the trust.

7. On the death of both the said AB and his son the said CD this trust shall cease and the trust property or such portion of it as may be in existence shall immediately vest as follows:

* * * * *

8. The said AB hereby expressly reserves to himself the power to revoke or modify at any time and at his pleasure the trust hereby created but such revocation or modification will not affect any acts already done by the trustees in execution of the trust.

The schedule herein referred to.

IN WITNESS WHEREOF parties have signed this deed on the ——— day of —————.

5—Assignment of Property by a Debtor for the Benefit of his Creditors[1]

THIS DEED is made on the ———— day of ———— BETWEEN AB, etc., (hereinafter called "the Debtor") of the first part AND CD, etc., and GH, etc., (hereinafter called "the Trustees") of the second part

1 See also precedent No. 1 under "COMPROMISE, COMPOSITION AND FAMILY SETTLEMENT", page 258 *ante*.

AND the several persons, firms, and companies mentioned in the First schedule hereto (hereinafter called "the Creditors") of the third part.

WHEREAS the Debtor being unable to pay to the Creditors, their debts in full has proposed to them to make an assignment of his property for their benefit in the manner hereinafter contained and the proposal has been accepted by the Creditors.

NOW THIS DEED WITNESSES as follows:

1. The Debtor hereby transfers all that property described in the second schedule hereto to the Trustees upon the trust hereinafter declared with and subject to such powers and limitations as are hereinafter specified.

2. The Trustees shall collect, call in, sell and convert into money the property hereby transferred and after defraying the necessary expenses shall distribute the net assets proportionately amongst the creditors according to such rules as are applicable to the administration of estates in insolvency proceedings and shall stand possessed of the balance thereof (if any) upon trust for the Debtor.

3. The Trustees may postpone the sale of all or any of the property so long as they think fit and may at their discretion lease, manage or otherwise deal with the trust property in such manner as they think fit. They shall also have the power to raise money by mortgage of all or any of the trust property for the purpose of discharging the liabilities of the Debtor and for repairs and other expenses incidental to the management of the property.

4. The Trustees may carry on and manage the business of the Debtor and may employ the Debtor or any other person in the management and may pay to him such remuneration as they determine.

5. For the purpose of collection of debts owing to the Debtor, the Trustees may bring any suit or other proceedings in court or may refer any dispute with any person in relation to any such debt to arbitration or may enter into any compromise or arrangement in relation to any such debt.

6. The Debtor hereby appoints the Trustees jointly and any two or more and each of them severally his attorneys and attorney in his name and on his behalf to execute any deed or document or instrument which the trustees may deem necessary for the due performance of the trusts hereof.

7. The Creditors hereby do and each of them does hereby release and discharge the Debtor from all the said debts and from all actions, claims, demands or any other proceeding whatever by the Creditors or any of them against the Debtor in respect thereof; Provided that this release shall in no respect prejudice the rights of the Creditors or any of them against parties

other than the Debtor and the Creditors hereby expressly reserve all their rights and remedies against any such party or parties.

8. The Trustees shall, in the administration of the trust hereby created, act according to their unanimous judgment and in case of difference of opinion, according to the opinion of the majority of them.

The schedule herein referred to

The First Schedule

(Names of Creditors)

The Second Schedule

(Details of Property assigned)

IN WITNESS, etc.

6—Deed of Trust about Government Grant-in-Aid to a Roman Catholic Church[1]

THIS DEED OF TRUST is made on the ——— day of ——— BETWEEN AB Roman Catholic Bishop of Allahabad (hereinafter called "the Bishop") of the one part AND the Governor of Uttar Pradesh (hereinafter called "the Government" which expression includes its successors and assigns) of the other part.

WHEREAS the Bishop applied to the Government for the grant of money for building a Roman Catholic Church in Allahabad Cantonment;

AND WHEREAS the said Government by G.O. No. ——— dated ——— sanctioned the grant-in-aid of Rs. ——— towards the construction and electric installation of the said Roman Catholic Church on condition of the execution of this deed of trust.

NOW THESE PRESENTS WITNESS and the parties hereto hereby agree as follows:

1. That the Bishop will apply the whole of the aforesaid grant on the construction and electrification of the building of the said Church.

2. That the Bishop shall hold the said building upon trust to permit the same to be used in perpetuity as a Roman Catholic Church for the benefit and use of Roman Catholics residing or being in the neighbourhood of the

---

1 Normally in a secular State such a grant-in-aid would not now be permissible (*see* Preamble and Article 27 of the Constitution). But if places of worship are destroyed in a communal riot, etc., Government may be justified in spending public funds on restoration of those temples, mosques, churches or gurudwaras (*K. Raghunath* v. *State of Kerala*, AIR 1974 Ker 48, 1972 Ker LT 442). Suitable recitals should be made according to the facts of the case.

said hereditament.

3. That on the death of the Bishop or on his ceasing to hold the office of the Roman Catholic Bishop of Allahabad, the said building shall vest in the person appointed for the time being to the office of Roman Catholic Bishop of Allahabad upon the same trust as aforesaid.

4. That the said Church shall be maintained by the Bishop or any other person for the time holding the office of the Roman Catholic Bishop of Allahabad from collections, donations or any other fund at his disposal for the purpose.

5. That if at any time the said building ceases to be used as a Roman Catholic Church the Government will be at liberty to claim a refund of the aforesaid grant and the said building shall remain charged with the repayment of the aforesaid amount of grant to the Government and the Government shall for the purpose of realising the amount of the aforesaid grant be entitled to enforce against the said building all the remedies of a charge holder.

IN WITNESS WHEREOF, etc.

7—Deed of Endowment of Property for a Hospital to be Built by the Founder and to be Managed by Zila Panchayat

THIS DEED OF TRUST is made on the ——— day of ——— BETWEEN AB, etc., (hereinafter called "the founder") of the one part AND the Zila Panchayat of ——— (hereinafter called "the Panchayat") of the other part.

WHEREAS the founder had always had a keen and earnest desire to serve the people of the locality round about the village of ——— within an approximate radius of twenty kilometres;

AND WHEREAS the best method of service in the opinion of the founder is the rendering of better medical aid which, at present, is practically denied to the aforesaid locality;

AND WHEREAS this can best be done by the opening of a well-equipped hospital on modern lines;

AND WHEREAS on the founder providing a building for the said hospital and making a gift of the properties hereinafter specified and valued at Rs. ——— for the purposes of the hospital the Panchayat has agreed to make a contribution for the recurring expenses of the hospital and the Government of Uttar Pradesh (hereinafter called "the Government") has also promised to make a non-recurring grant for equipment of the hospital and also to make a recurring grant for the upkeep and maintenance of the same.

NOW THIS DEED WITNESSES as follows:

1. The founder hereby transfers to the Panchayat ALL those properties detailed in the schedule hereto TO HOLD the same to the Panchayat upon trust that the proceeds and income of the said properties after deducting bad debts, expenses of realisation and litigation, etc., (if any) shall be used exclusively for the maintenance and upkeep of the hospital hereinafter mentioned.

2. The founder hereby undertakes to construct suitable buildings for the said hospital at village ———— according to plan sanctioned and approved by the ———, on or about the ———— at a cost of not less than Rs. ——— and on its completion to transfer the same to the Panchayat upon trust that the same shall be used for the purposes of the said hospital.

3. The Panchayat hereby agrees that on the said building being completed and transferred to the Panchayat as hereinbefore agreed, the Panchayat shall open a hospital in the said building to be called ———— Hospital, and that the name of the said hospital shall never be changed notwithstanding any change in its management or constitution.

4. The Panchayat hereby agrees that it will manage the said properties properly and with due diligence through its agents and will spend the entire net proceeds accruing therefrom on the upkeep of the said hospital. The Panchayat further agrees to keep the buildings of the said hospital at all times in proper repair and will also meet all recurring or non-recurring charges that may be necessary for this purpose.

5. It is further declared that in case the Government thinks that it would be to the interest and benefit of the said hospital, the Panchayat may, with the previous approval of the Government, dispose of the properties hereby transferred in any manner advised by the Government, and in such contingency the total sale proceeds shall be deposited in a Bank approved by the Government or invested in some secure and profitable manner approved by Government.

6. If at any time the Government is of opinion that the said hospital is not being managed efficiently and properly and in consequence withdraws its grant the Government will have the full authority to take charge of all the properties hereby conveyed or of the money into which the same may have been converted under the preceding clause and either to run the hospital itself or to have it run by any other body constituted by the order of the Government.

7. That for the better and more efficient management of the hospital for all time to come it is also declared that there shall be a Board of Visitors consisting of the District Magistrate, ———, as the President and CD, EF, and GH and the founder as members. After the death of the founder one of the descendants of the founder nominated by the District Magistrate will take the place of the deceased and similarly after the death of any such descendants one of his descendants, and so on, nominated as aforesaid, shall take the place of the deceased as a member of the Board of Visitors, and in case of the non-existence of any such descendant, or on the occurrence of vacancy in the office of any other member, the remaining members shall appoint any suitable man to fill up the vacancy.

8. The main function of the Board of Visitors shall be to inspect the hospital to see that the Panchayat is properly and efficiently managing the hospital and spending on it the amount contributed for the purpose and to give such advice and direction to the Panchayat for the efficient, proper and economical administration of the hospital as it thinks proper and the Panchayat shall accept such advice and obey such directions as far as possible and as far as the funds will permit.

9. That it would be within the competence of the Panchayat to appoint, remove and dismiss, medical and other staff for the said hospital.

The schedule herein referred to

IN WITNESS WHEREOF, etc.

8—Deed of Settlement for Establishing a Girls' School

THIS DEED OF TRUST is made on the ——— day of ——— BETWEEN AB, etc., (hereinafter called "the settlor") of the one part AND CD, etc., and EF, etc., and GH, etc., (hereinafter called "the Trustees" which expression shall include the survivor or survivors of them and the administrators and executors of the last survivor or the trustee or trustees for the time being of the trust hereby created) of the other part.

WHEREAS the settlor is owner of the immovable property described in the first schedule hereto and of the land described in the second schedule hereto and of the securities mentioned in the third schedule hereto;

AND WHEREAS the settlor being desirous of establishing a Girls' High School at ——— has decided to settle irrevocably the said property, land and securities for this purpose in the manner hereinafter following;

AND WHEREAS the settlor has endorsed in favour of and delivered to the trustees the said securities mentioned in the third schedule hereto;

AND WHEREAS the total value of the properties mentioned in the first, second and third schedules hereto is Rs. ——— as detailed in the said schedules.

NOW THIS DEED WITNESSES as follows:

1. In pursuance of the said desire of the settlor, the settlor hereby transfers and assigns to the trustees ALL that property described in the first schedule hereto AND ALL that land described in the second schedule hereto AND ALL the securities described in the third schedule hereto TO HOLD the same to the Trustees upon the trust and with and subject to the powers, provisions and agreements hereinafter declared and expressed concerning the same.

2. The Trustees shall within one year from this date construct on the land described in the second schedule hereto a suitable building for a Girls' School at a cost of not more than Rs. ——— to be raised by sale of such of the securities mentioned in the third schedule hereto as the Trustees may think proper.

3. The Trustees shall establish a Girls' High School in the said building and any initial cost of establishing such school shall be met from the income of the property described in the first schedule and the securities described in the third schedule hereto and if such income is not sufficient, from the sale proceeds of such securities as the trustees may consider it necessary to sell for the purpose.

4. The Trustees shall manage the said property mentioned in the first schedule hereto and after paying Government revenue, cesses, taxes and all expenses of collection and management shall use the balance of the income as well as the income from such of the securities mentioned in the third schedule hereto as may remain unsold or of any other securities into which the same may hereafter be converted by them shall be used for the expenses of the said Girls' School and any balance remaining after making such expense, shall be deposited in such bank and invested in such manner as the Trustees may consider proper.

5. The Trustees shall have power to convert such securities mentioned in the third schedule hereto as they think necessary into other securities or into money but they shall not have power to sell, mortgage or otherwise transfer the property described in the first schedule hereto except with the permission of the District Judge having jurisdiction.

6. In case of any vacancy amongst the trustees occasioned by death, resignation or incapacity of any trustee or otherwise the settlor shall appoint another trustee to fill up the vacancy and after his death the remaining

trustees shall make the appointment.

(*Any other conditions suitable and necessary*).

The schedule herein referred to

IN WITNESS WHEREOF, etc.

9—Trust Deed Establishing a Scholarship

THIS DEED OF TRUST is made etc. (*as in Form 3*)

WITNESSES as follows:

1. The trustees shall hold the sum of Rs. ———— this day paid to them by the founder upon trust to apply the income thereof in perpetuity for the promotion and encouragement of education in the ———— University in the manner hereinafter appearing.

2. The Trustees shall invest the said sum of Rs. ———— in any investment permitted by law and may at any time and from time to time vary any of such investments for others of a like nature.

3. The said sum of Rs. ———— and the investment representing the same as ———— aforesaid shall be called the Trust Fund and are hereinafter referred to as the Trust Fund.

4. The trustees shall out of the income of the trust fund first pay all costs and expenses of or incidental to the management of the trust fund and the income thereof and shall apply the balance in establishing a scholarship (hereinafter called the ——— scholarship) of the monthly value of Rs. ———— to be from time to time awarded in the manner hereinafter mentioned to a student entering the said University as an undergraduate and to be held and enjoyed as hereinafter provided.

5. The scholarship shall be awarded at such intervals and as the result of such examination and in such manner and shall be held and enjoyed for such period and upon and subject to such terms and conditions as shall from time to time be prescribed by regulations to be made by the said University and in default of such regulations as the trustees shall determine.

6. The trustees may at any time and from time to time set apart as sinking fund the whole or any part of the surplus income produced by the trust fund in any year not required to meet the cost of the said scholarship and may invest any sums so set apart and the resulting income thereof in the names of the trustees in the manner aforesaid with power at any time to vary such investments.

7. The trustees may at any time sell any investment representing the capital or income of the sinking fund and apply the proceeds thereof or the

capital or income of the sinking fund as though the same were income produced by the trust fund during the then current year.

8. So much of the income of the trust fund in any year as is not required for the aforesaid scholarship or sinking fund shall from time to time be applied for the grant of any such other scholarship and in such manner as the University may from time to time direct.

9. The trustees may with the concurrence of the Chancellor of the said University at any time wholly or partially vary any of the purposes for which the income of the trust fund is to be applied and such income or part thereof shall then be applied to such other purpose provided that the same shall not be applied to any purpose unless the same is conducive to the promotion or encouragement of education at the said University.

10. In case of the occurrence of any vacancy amongst trustees by reason of death or resignation of any trustee or for any other cause, the founder will have the right to appoint a new trustee and after the death of the founder the remaining trustees shall by a majority of votes appoint a new trustee and in case of equality of votes, the appointment shall be made by the Chancellor of the said University (*or*, by the Court having jurisdiction in this behalf).

IN WITNESS WHEREOF, etc.

10—Endowment to a Deity in a Temple

THIS DEED OF ENDOWMENT is made on the ——— day of ——— by AB, etc.

WHEREAS I have created (*or*, am desirous of creating) a temple at ——— and have established (*or*, and am establishing) a deity by the name of Shri Kishori Ramanji Maharaj in the said temple.

AND WHEREAS I am desirous of dedicating the properties mentioned in the first and second schedules hereto to the said deity (and for the cost of construction of the said temple) and to secure the worship of the said deity in the said temple and of making a religious endowment of the said properties in the manner hereinafter appearing.

AND WHEREAS the value of the said properties is Rs. ———.

NOW THIS DEED WITNESSES and hereby declares as follows:

1. In pursuance of my said desire I hereby grant, set apart, dedicate and appoint ALL that land and house property described in the first schedule and all those securities and movable property described in the second schedule hereto to and for the worship of the said deity absolutely forever in the manner hereinafter contained.

2. I hereby constitute and appoint myself the first *shebait* for the purpose aforesaid and direct that after my death my eldest son and after his death his eldest male descendant in the male line shall succeed successively as *shebait* and that if any *shebait* dies without leaving any male descendant then his widow and after her death the eldest of the male heirs of the last male *shebait* shall succeed and failing such male heirs, any officer of Government appointed by the Government or court will be the *shebait* who will have the power to appoint *sub-shebaits* under him, removable at his pleasure. If any person entitled to succeed is a minor, then the person who is guardian of the property of such minor shall be the *shebait* during the term of such person's minority.

3. The *shebait* shall not have power to sell or mortgage or otherwise transfer the properties hereinbefore dedicated except in case of urgent necessity and with the permission of the District Judge for the time being of ———.

4. If any person entitled to be a *shebait* shall renounce the Hindu religion or transfer any portion of the dedicated property in violation of the condition hereinbefore recited then he shall for the purposes of this deed be considered to be dead and the person next entitled to succeed as *shebait* shall succeed.

5. The *shebait* for the time being shall hold the said properties hereinbefore dedicated in trust to manage the same to the best advantage with full power to let out the same and in the event of an involuntary transfer of any portion of the immovable property, to invest the value or price thereof or any compensation received therefor in landed property or in securities of the Government of India and will have power to vary such investments from time to time.

6. The income of the said properties hereinbefore dedicated shall be applied first in the maintenance and repair of the said property and the payment of land revenue, cesses, taxes and other outgoings in respect of the same and the *shebait* after deducting a remuneration for himself of ——— percent of the gross income and collections shall lay out and spend the remainder of the said income in the daily worship of the said deity and in defraying the expenses of the usual festivals in the manner and according to the customs of the family with full liberty to apply a portion of such income to the improvement of the said property hereinbefore dedicated or to purchase other property to be included in the said dedication.

The schedule herein referred to

IN WITNESS WHEREOF, etc.

11—Declaration of Public Trust in Property Already used as a Charitable Institution

THIS DEED is made on the ——— day of ——— by me, AB, etc.

WHEREAS three years ago my deceased father CD constructed a building for a *dharamshala* at ———— with shops attached thereto;

AND WHEREAS since the said building has been used as a *dharamshala* for the free accommodation of all Hindu travellers and visitors and the income from the rent of the said shops is spent on the upkeep of the said building and the pay of the *chaukidar*;

AND WHEREAS it is considered expedient to make a formal dedication of the said building and shops to the purpose for which they were constructed and to make a more definite provision for the upkeep of the said *dharamshala*;

NOW THIS DEED WITNESSES that I grant, dedicate and set apart the building and shops fully described in the schedule herto to and for the purposes hereinafter mentioned in the manner hereinafter contained and declare as follows:

1. The said building shall forever be used as a *dharamshala* for the free accommodation of Hindu visitors and travellers in accordance with such rules as may from time to time be made by the trustee for the time being.

2. I shall be the Manager or trustee of the said *dharamshala* and shops during my life and after my death my eldest male descendant in the male line and failing him any other person in my family who may be fit to act as such trustee will be the trustee.

3. The trustee for the time being shall keep the said *dharamshala* building in good state of repairs and in clean and sanitary condition and will employ a *chaukidar* and such other servants as may be necessary to look after the said building and the comfort of the lodgers as he may consider necessary.

4. The income of the said shops shall after defraying the necessary expenses of collection be applied to the upkeep and necessary expenses of the said *dharamshala* and any surplus remaining after defraying all such expenses shall be used either in improvement of the said building and shops or in providing additional comforts to the visitors and travellers and no part of the said income shall in any case be appropriated by the trustee to his own use.

The schedule herein referred to

IN WITNESS WHEREOF, etc.

12—Waqf Alal Aulad

THIS DEED OF WAQF is made on the ——— day of ———— by AB, etc., (hereinafter called "the *Waqif*").

WHEREAS the *waqif* is the absolute owner of the immovable property mentioned in the first schedule hereto and of the shares, securities and other movable property mentioned in the second schedule hereto.

AND WHEREAS the *waqif* has no debts and the dower debt of his wife also has been partly paid to her and partly relinquished by her by the deed dated —————.

AND WHEREAS the *waqif* is desirous of making a *Waqf* of the said properties for the maintenance and support of himself and his descendants and in the event of extinction of the line of his descendants for the benefit of the poor Muslims of ————— in manner hereinafter appearing.

AND WHEREAS the total value of the said properties as per details given in the schedules hereto is Rs. —————.

NOW THIS DEED WITNESSES that the *waqif* hereby makes a settlement by way of *waqf* of ALL immovable properties, shares, securities and movables mentioned in the first and the second schedules hereto and extinguishes all his rights of ownership therein and declares as follows:

1. That the aforesaid property shall no longer be the private property of anyone but shall be *waqf* for the maintenance and support of the *waqif*, his family, children and descendants and in case of extinction of his line of descendants for the benefit of the poor of the ———— belonging to Muslim faith.

2. That the *waqif* hereby appoints and constitutes himself the sole *mutwalli* of the said *waqf* during his life with absolute power of management thereof and shall appropriate the income of the said property to his own use.

3. That after the death of the *waqif*, any person nominated by the *waqif* in his lifetime or failing such nomination, his eldest son or failing him the eldest male descendant and failing a male descendant a female descendant of the *waqif* in the male line of descendants or failing her the eldest male descendant in the female line of descendants and failing him the eldest female shall be the *mutwalli*.

4. The second and subsequent *mutwallis* shall have power to nominate their successors and failing such nomination the descendants in the order given in Clause 3 shall be the *mutwalli*.

5. The *mutwalli* for the time being shall manage the *waqf* property to

the best of his ability and in case he is a minor or person of unsound mind his guardian appointed by the Court shall manage the property on his behalf.

6. That after payment of revenue, cesses, rates, taxes and necessary expenses of management, the profits and income of the said property shall be divided by the *mutwalli* amongst the *waqif's* descendants according to their shares under the Muslim Law.

7. That the *mutwalli* shall have no power to sell, mortgage or in any other way transfer or charge the immovable property mentioned in the first schedule hereto or any part thereof except by lease for a period not exceeding seven years at a time but he may call in and convert into cash the property mentioned in the second schedule hereto and deposit the money in any nationalised bank or invest it in such securities as he may deem fit or may purchase immovable property and all such money, securities and immovable property into which the property mentioned in the said schedule may be so converted shall be deemed to be part of the *waqf* hereby made, as if the same were included in the first schedule hereto.

8. That the descendants of the *waqif* will have no right to transfer or charge in any manner their shares of the income and profits of the *waqf* property.

9. That on the extinction of the line of descendants of the *waqif*, the *mutwalli* for the time being shall use the income and profits of the aforesaid property for the sole use and benefit of the Muslims of the city of ——— in such manner as he shall think fit.

The schedule herein referred to

IN WITNESS WHEREOF the *Waqif* has signed this deed on the date first above written.

13—Waqf for Public Purposes

THIS DEED OF WAQF, etc., (*as in Form* 12).

WHEREAS, etc., (*as in Form* 12).

AND WHEREAS the *waqif* having no wife or children is desirous of making *waqf* of his said properties for the sake of God for charitable purposes hereinafter mentioned;

AND WHEREAS the total value, etc., (*as in Form* 12).

NOW THIS DEED WITNESSES that the *waqif* purely for the sake of God and in order to get religious benefit in the next world hereby makes a *waqf* of the properties mentioned in the first and second schedule hereto and extinguishes all his rights of ownership therein and declares as follows:

1. That out of the money specified in the second schedule and the proceeds of sale of such of the securities mentioned in the second schedule as the *mutwalli* may think proper to sell, Rs. ——— shall be spent on the construction of a mosque on the land near ———, mentioned in the first schedule, and the mosque so constructed shall be used as a public mosque for saying prayers by all Muslims without any distinction of sect or school of thought.

2. That the income of the aforesaid property shall be applied in perpetuity to the following purposes:

(*a*) Rs. —— per annum for the upkeep of the *Imambara* at ———;

(*b*) Rs. ——— per annum for the expenses of *majlis* and other celebrations in connection with the Muharram;

(*c*) Rs. ——— per annum to be paid to the Shia Orphanage at ——— so long as it exists and if it ceases to exist to any other Muslim Orphanage in India according to the discretion of the *mutwalli* for the time being;

(*d*) Rs. —— per annum to be paid to the Islamia High School at —— or if the said school ceases to exist to any other Islamia school at the discretion of the *mutwalli* for the time being;

(*e*) Rs. ——— per annum on feeding the poor Muslims;

(*f*) Rs. ——— per annum on the expenses of poor pilgrims proceeding to *Kaaba Sharif*;

(*g*) Rs. ——— per annum on the upkeep and maintenance of the mosque to be constructed as provided in clause 1.

(3) The *waqif* hereby appoints AB, etc., as the *mutwalli* of the said *waqf* and has delivered possession of the aforesaid *waqf* property to him as such *mutwalli.*

4. The said *mutwalli* and each *mutwalli* after him will have power to nominate his successor and the successor so nominated will be the *mutwalli.* Failing a nomination in any case or if the person so nominated becomes unfit or incapable to act as *mutwalli*, the Court may appoint a *mutwalli.*

5. The *mutwalli* for the time being shall manage the *waqf* property to the best of his ability and shall after payment of revenue, cesses, rates, taxes and necessary expenses of management first pay out of the surplus an allowance of Rs. ——— per annum to himself for his services as such *mutwalli* and shall apply the residue to the several expenses mentioned in clause 2 hereof and any surplus remaining over after meeting all the said expenses shall form part of the *waqf* fund.

6. If the profits and income of the *waqf* property in any year proves insufficient for meeting all the aforesaid expenses, the *mutwalli* shall be at liberty to draw upon the *waqf* fund and if that also is not sufficient the expenditure referred to in sub-clause (*f*) of clause 2 shall be reduced, and if a further reduction becomes necessary the expenses referred to in sub-clauses (*b*), (*c*) and (*d*) will also be proportionately reduced;

7 and 8. (*as in Form* 12).

The Schedule herein referred to

IN WITNESS WHEREOF, etc.

14—Appointment of a New Trustee

THIS DEED OF APPOINTMENT is made on the day of ——— BETWEEN AB, etc., CD, etc., and EF, etc., (hereinafter called "the continuing trustees") of the one part AND GH, etc., (hereinafter called "the new trustee") of the other part.

WHEREAS by a deed of trust dated ——— made by XY, the continuing trustees and one LM were appointed trustees;

AND WHEREAS by the said deed it was provided that in case of a vacancy amongst the said trustees, the surviving trustees shall have power to appoint a new trustee to fill up the same.

AND WHEREAS the said LM has died on the ——— (*or*, has on the ——— resigned the office of trustee), (*or*, has become insane) (*or*, has been sentenced to imprisonment for life).

NOW THIS DEED WITNESSES that the continuing trustees in exercise of the powers conferred on them by the aforesaid deed of trust, hereby appoint the new trustee as a trustee of the said trust for all the purposes for which the said LM was trustee thereof jointly with the continuing trustees AND declare that henceforth the continuing trustees and new trustee shall hold the trust property as trustees under the aforesaid deed of trust and exercise all the powers and perform all the duties of trustees specified in the aforesaid deed of trust.

IN WITNESS WHEREOF, etc.

15—Revocation of Trust, by Endorsement[1]

I, the within named AB, etc., acting with the consent hereby testified of the within named beneficiaries X, Y and Z (*or*, acting under the power of revocation reserved in the within-written deed of trust) hereby revoke the trust created by the within-written deed of trust.

16—Revocation of Trust by a Separate Deed

THIS DEED is made on the ——— day of ——— BETWEEN AB, etc., (hereinafter called "the Settlor") of the one part AND CD, etc., (hereinafter called "the Trustee") of the other part.

WHEREAS by a deed of trust dated ———— the Settlor transferred his property specified therein to the Trustee upon trust to sell the same and with the proceeds of the sale to pay the debts due from the Settlor to the several creditors named in the said deed;

AND WHEREAS the trust created as aforesaid has not yet been communicated to any of the aforesaid creditors;

AND WHEREAS the Settlor now desires to revoke the said trust and to make other arrangements for the discharge of his aforesaid debts.

NOW THIS DEED WITNESSES that the Settlor hereby revokes the trust created by the aforesaid deed of trust.

IN WITNESS WHEREOF, etc.

17—Trust Deed for Charitable Objects

THIS DEED made on the ———— day of ———— BETWEEN AB, etc., (hereinafter called "the Settlor") of the one part AND (1) CD etc., (2) EF etc., (3) GH etc. (hereinafter called "the Trustees") of the other part;

WHEREAS the Settlor is absolutely entitled to the Fixed Deposits described in the Schedule hereto and is desirous of declaring the trust of the said sum of Rs. ————— together with other sums which the Settlor may from time to time deliver to the Trustees for such purpose and the income from such sums;

AND WHEREAS the Trustees have agreed to be the trustees and the Settlor has agreed to transfer and deliver the property described in the Schedule hereto to the Trustees to the intent that the same shall be held by

---

1 Sec. 78, Trusts Act permits revocation of a non-testamentary trust, where all the beneficiaries are competent to contract, with their consent, or if a power of revocation has been expressly reserved, or in the case of trust for payment to creditors, until it has been communicated to them.

them upon trust and subject to the powers, provisions and stipulations hereinafter declared and contained of and concerning the same;

NOW THIS DEED WITNESSES as follows:

1. The said Trust shall be known as ————.

2. Only the income by and out of and not the corpus of the Trust Fund shall be spent on the objects of the Trust.

3. The Trustees shall apply the net income of the corpus for the purposes of giving financial assistance to poor and needy people, to ailing persons having no means or little means to get their treatment, to poor students who cannot prosecute their further studies for want of money, to widows who do not earn and who have no male members to support them, to persons in distress affected by floods or earthquakes or other acts of God, and also to religious institutions for erection of rooms or cottages in their premises and to educational institutions for purposes of establishing scholarships and generally to help hospitals and other charitable institutions financially.

4. (1) For so long as the Settlor shall live and shall not himself resign or become incapacitated, he shall be the Trustee Chairman of the said Trust and shall alone exercise the powers of applying or expending the trust fund for the purposes hereinbefore mentioned. During his life time, for so long as he shall be the Trustee Chairman, the other trustees shall not be entitled to question his act or omission in applying or expending the trust fund for the purposes aforesaid or to question whether or not the moneys applied or expended or to be applied on any person, institution or body was or is a deserving case to be benefited by the trust fund.

(2) After the death of the Settlor or of his resignation or incapacitation, the said trustee or trustees for the time being shall elect one from amongst themselves to be the Trustee Chairman but such Trustee Chairman shall be a relative of the Settlor and shall be entitled to exercise only such powers as the majority of the trustees for the time being may in a duly constituted meeting decide.

(3) During his life time the Settlor shall have power at any time and from time to time to remove any trustee without assigning any reason and to appoint a substitute.

5. The trustees may at any time make such arrangements, draw up such schemes and make and frame such rules as they shall in their uncontrolled discretion think fit for the administration of the charity hereby constituted and the management of the Trust Fund and may at any time amend alter or repeal any of the said arrangements, schemes or rules as they shall think fit.

6. All receipts to the Trust Fund, other than the income from the corpus, shall be signed by at least two trustees.

7. Proper accounts showing all receipts received and disbursements made on account of the charity hereby constituted shall be kept by the trustees and shall be duly audited with all necessary vouchers every year by such auditor or auditors as the trustees shall appoint from amongst themselves or other persons or themselves jointly with other persons or if the trustees shall consider it necessary or expedient by a professional accountant whom they may employ and pay for the purpose.

8. Subject to the provisions of clause 4(3), if the trustees or any of them or any trustees or trustee of this deed shall die or desire to be discharged from trusteeship or refuse or neglect or become incapable or unfit to act as trustee under this deed the surviving or continuing trustees or trustee for the time being under this deed (and for this purpose any retiring or refusing trustee shall if willing to act in the execution of this power be considered a continuing trustee) shall appoint new trustees or a new trustee in the place of the trustees or trustee so dying or desiring to be discharged or refusing or neglecting or becoming incapable or unfit to act as aforesaid and upon every such appointment the number of trustees may be increased or diminished but not to less than five in number and upon every such appointment the trust property shall as soon as circumstances shall conveniently admit be transferred to or vested in the trustees or trustee for the time being. This present power shall be additional to and shall not prevent the execution or exercise of any statutory power to appoint new trustees for the time being in force. PROVIDED ALWAYS that for so long as the Settlor shall continue to be the Trustee Chairman, he shall have the absolute discretion of appointing any person to be a trustee in place of any trustee ceasing to act as aforesaid or of increasing the number of trustees and appointing persons thereto.

9. (1) The Trustees may from time to time appoint any one of their member to be their Secretary without remuneration.

(2) The Trustees shall keep a minute book of their proceedings.

(3) Subject to the provisions of clause 4, three trustees excluding the Trustee Chairman shall form the quorum and the opinion of the majority shall prevail.

10. The Trustees may convert the corpus of the Trust Fund by investing in such securities as are mentioned in Sec. 20 of The Indian Trusts Act, 1882.

The schedule herein referred to

IN WITNESS WHEREOF etc.

[*For other forms of trusts see under WILLS*].

WILLS

Preliminary Note

What is Will

Will is a disposition of property made by a person during his life but which is intended and takes effect after his death. Will has been defined in Sec. 2 (h) of the Indian Succession Act 1925 as "the legal declaration of the intention of a testator with respect to his property, which he desires to be carried into effect after his death".

A Will takes effect on the death of the executant and during his life-time, it is alterable or revocable at any moment, having no legal effect whatsoever. Where, however, a document though entitled a Will also nominated the *shebait* of a temple, it was held[1] that such nomination was immediately effective and was not postponed till after the executant's death and that unless the power to cancel the nomination was expressly reserved, it could not be cancelled.

A Will is a secret and confidential document which the executant is never ordered to produce.[2]

The Law Applicable

In order to be a valid disposition of immovable property, a Will must be made in conformity with the law of the country in which the property is situate, and in order to be a valid disposition of movable property, it must be made in conformity with the law of the testator's domicile. Therefore, when the question of the validity of a Will is to be considered with regard to (*i*) testamentary capacity of the testator, (*ii*) the heritable quality of the property, and (*iii*) the formalities and constitution of a deed of will, it is necessary to consider it with reference to the law applicable as laid down above. The country of domicile is the country of domicile at the time of making the Will and subsequent change of domicile does not affect the validity of a Will previously made.

When a man has got immovable property in one country and has a domicile in another, it is more convenient and advisable for him to make two Wills, one relating to immovable property and one to movable property. The law of the country which is to govern a Will should be carefully studied or understood before drafting it.

---

1 *Rambir Das* v. *Kalyan Das*, (1997) 4 SCC 102.

2 *Hubert P. James* v. *Ghulam Hussein Pakseema*, 1949 ALJ 148 (PC), AIR 1949 PC 151.

How Will is made in India

Wills by all persons except Hindus, Buddhists, Sikhs, Jains and Muslims are governed by the Indian Succession Act, 1925. The more important provisions of that Act relating to Wills, including that which relates to the form of a Will, have, however, been applied to Wills made by Hindus, Buddhists, Sikhs and Jains as well (Sec. 57).

Following formalities are prescribed by the Indian Succession Act for a Will:

(1) The will should be made in writing. However, a soldier or airman in active service or a mariner at sea can make privileged Will or oral Will. (Sec. 63, 65).

(2) It should be signed or marked by the testator or by some other person in his presence and by his direction [Sec. 63(a)]. The signature should be so placed that it should appear that it was intended thereby to give effect to the writing as a will [Sec. 63(*b*)]. The best place is at the foot or end of the writing.

(3) It should be attested by two or more persons, each of whom has seen the testator making his signature or mark, or has seen some other person signing the will in the presence and direction of the testator, or has received from the testator a personal acknowledgment of his signature or mark or the signature of such other person. Each of the attesting witnesses should sign the will in the presence of the testator, but it is not necessary that more than one witness should be present at the same time [Sec. 63(*c*)].

In a case where the attesting witnesses' signatures appeared above the thumb mark of the testator it was held that the attestation was invalid as the witnesses appeared to have signed it even before the executant.[1]

How Will is Drafted

No particular form of Will is prescribed by law, but the ordinary form in vogue in England which has been followed for centuries may be usefully adopted. The language employed should be as simple as possible and free from technical words and be easily intelligible to a lay man. Since, in many cases Will is made by persons at death bed, if it is full of technical expressions and not easily intelligible to a lay man, it can be challenged on the ground that the testator did not clearly understand it and its effect.

Parts of a Will

A Will is drafted as a deed poll in the first person and generally consists of the following parts:

1. Commencement

A Will is commenced thus:

"This is the last Will of me, AB, etc., made this the —— day of ——" and

---

1 *Mangal Singh* v. *Nathu Singh*, (1998) 8 SCC 598.

the first clause to follow is that revoking previous disposition thus:

"I hereby revoke all former Wills and Codicils made by me."

There is also an alternative form thus:

"I, AB, etc., hereby revoke all former Wills and codicils made by me and declare that this is my last Will" (*or,* and by this last Will bequeath all my property, etc.).[1]

In this case the date is placed at the end.

The revocation of previous wills and codicils must be expressly and definitely made and it is not sufficient to say that this will is the last will as that statement does not amount to a revocation of a former Will. The intention to revoke a Will should be expressly declared (Sec. 70, Indian Succession Act).

2. Clause about appointment of executor and trustees and guardians

If the will contains a trust, trustees should be appointed, and if executors of the Will are appointed the same persons may be appointed trustees. It is not necessary that an executor should be appointed, but the great advantage of appointing an executor is that the executor is entitled to get a probate of the Will to enable him to administer the estate of the deceased without giving any security, while if no executor is appointed, no probate can be granted (Sec. 222), and letters of administration will be necessary (Secs. 232 and 234), which will not be granted without an administration bond (Sec. 291).

Probate cannot be granted to a minor or a person of unsound mind nor to any association of individuals unless it is a company satisfying notified criteria. (Sec. 223). No such person should, therefore, be appointed executor, but there is no objection to the appointment of a minor "if and when he shall attain the age of majority".

Any number of persons may be appointed executors. The previous consent of an executor should be obtained as no one is bound to accept the duties of an executor or trustee.

There is no objection to the appointment of one of the beneficiaries as an executor. The appointment may be in the alternative to provide for the contingency of the executor dying during the lifetime of the testator or refusing to act.

It may be pointed out here that Sec. 213 provides that no right as executor or legatee can be established in any court unless a probate or letters of administration have been obtained. This section, however, does not apply to Wills made by Muhammadans or Indian Christians or to those Wills of Hindus, Sikhs, Jains, Buddhists and Parsis which are made outside the Presidency towns of Calcutta, Chennai and Mumbai.

If a testator wants to appoint a guardian for his minor children, he can do so

---

1 This form is traditionally used even where the testator never made any will or codicil earlier.

by his Will; such guardian can get a certificate of guardianship.

3. Legacies and Devises

In English law, a bequest of movables is called a "legacy" and a bequest of land and other immovable property is called a "devise". Legacies and devises are either "specific" or "general". The Indian Succession Act 1925 however uses the term "legacy" to cover both movable and immovable property: (See illustrations to Sec. 142). A specific legacy is the bequest of a definite thing or property out of the testator's estate. It consists of a specified part of the testator's property (Sec.142). The other bequests are general legacy.

A clause of bequest is generally commenced thus:

"I give, etc." or "I bequeath, etc."

The bequest may be made either absolutely or for life, or on trust. It is more convenient to set out the *bequests on trust* after all the other bequests and annuities.

4. General Provisions

After bequests, annuities and trust clauses, general clauses should be added as necessary, e.g., those relating to the appointment of trustees, powers of trustees. Investment clauses, power of sale, etc.

5. Testimonium

Testimonium is the last part of a Will. Date is sometimes mentioned in the testimonium, sometimes in the beginning as in deeds.

6. Signature and Attestation

Signature and attestation are placed at the end of a Will, signature immediately after the testimonium and attestation after the signatures. No particular form of attestation is prescribed by law, but the best and safest thing would be to state correctly and fully how the witnesses have attested the Will. *i.e.*, whether the Will was signed by the testator in their presence or the testator acknowledged his signature thus:

"Signed by the above named testator in our presence at the same time and each of us has in the presence of the testator signed his name hereunder as witness." See also INTRODUCTION, Part II "Signatures and Attestation" page 26 and "Testimonium" under General Forms of attestation, page 53.

Recitals

Recitals will rarely be required in a will and are not inserted in an ordinary English Will. If, however, any recitals are considered necessary, they should be added to the relevant clause. For instance, if a power of appointment given to a widow by her husband's Will is exercised, the husband's Will may be recited in the beginning of the clause in which the power is exercised, thus:

"WHEREAS by his Will dated ————, my deceased husband, AB, had given me power to appoint guardian of my minor son XY. Now in exercise of that power, I appoint etc."

or, "WHEREAS my late husband XY had begun to construct a building for a *dharamshala* which he could not complete and had directed me by his Will dated ———— to finish it and dedicate it to a *dharamshala* and to make suitable provision for its upkeep.

AND WHEREAS the building is now complete but I have not been able to make suitable provision for the current expenses of the *dharamshala*. Now I hereby bequeath the following securities to the aforesaid trustees upon trust etc."

If, however, the recitals are general and not applicable to any clause in particular, e.g., recital about title to property they may, if absolutely necessary, be added immediately after commencement, thus "Whereas I am owner, etc., I hereby make the following bequests and trust in respect of the said property."

A recital in a Will about the legatee being her adopted son is certainly a piece of admissible evidence but is not conclusive evidence of the adoption. However, the bequest in his favour may nevertheless be given effect to if the Court finds that the motive for the execution of the Will was not merely the recognition by the testator of his relationship, through adoption, with the devisee but mainly the existence of feelings of love and affection for him.[1]

Corrections

All obliterations, interlineations and other alterations made in the Will must be executed in the same way as Will, *i.e.*, must be signed by the testator and attested by witnesses (Sec. 71). This can be done, if there are one or two alterations, by the testator and witnesses signing on the margin opposite the alteration but if there are several alterations it would be more convenient to make a memorandum at the end, showing by reference to the serial number of the lines and the alterations made, and to have this memorandum signed by the testator and attested by witnesses (Proviso to Sec. 71).

Points to be Considered before Drafting

Before drafting a Will it is necessary to consider-

(1) whether the testator is competent to make a Will,

(2) whether the property which he wishes to bequeath is that which is legally bequeathable and which the testator is competent to bequeath,

(3) whether the devisees are legally competent to take the devises,

(4) whether the interests which the testator wishes to create can legally be created,

(5) Whether the conditions which the testator wishes to impose can legally be imposed,[2] and

---

1 *Banwarilal* v. *Tirlok Chand*, (1980) 1 SCC 349.

2 See Sections 126 to 140, Indian Succession Act.

(6) whether the machinery desired to be employed for carrying out his wishes is sufficient and legally sound.

If the description as a whole or any part of a deed or document fails to ascertain the object of the writer or the parties, no meaning can be extracted and the document or the clause must be rejected for uncertainty. Although a document which is vague or meaningless must be rejected, the courts often strive hard to construe them generously in order to make sense of them and give effect to them.[1]

Who can make a Will

Every person of sound mind not being a minor can make a Will (Sec. 59, Indian Succession Act, 1925, which applies to all except Muslims; for Muslim Law see, sub-heading, 'Muslim Law' *infra*; for Hindu coparcener see 'Bequeathable Property' *infra*). A person may, however, be disqualified by any local law from disposing of his property, or may be entitled to do so only with some permission or under certain restrictions.

By a man of "unsound mind" is meant not necessary a lunatic, idiot or insane person but also a man who, though otherwise quite sane, is not at the moment of executing the deed, by reason of illness, in his proper senses and competent to understand what he is doing. It is necessary that he should be in a sound disposing condition which means that he must also be conscious of the various claims persons have upon his property and must be capable of realising the extent of the property disposed of under the Will.[2] Mere old age is no evidence of incapacity to make a Will.[3] When a Will is made by a sick person, it is advisable to provide satisfactory evidence that the man is in his proper senses and able to understand what he declares. For this purpose, it would be best, if practicable, to have the Will attested by the medical attendant, who may also append a certificate at the foot of the Will that he has satisfied himself that the testator is in his proper senses. A Will or any part of a Will, the making of which is caused by fraud or coercion or by such importunity as to take away the free agency of the testator, Will be void (Sec. 61). A practice has therefore grown in India to say that the testator makes the Will without any persuasion, fraud or coercion, but such a statement is not strictly necessary.

Joint, Mutual, Reciprocal Wills

Joint Wills—A joint Will is a Will made by two or more testators contained in a single document, duly executed by each testator, and disposing either of their separate properties or of their joint property. It is not, however, recognised in English law as a single Will. It is in effect two or more Wills, and it operates on the

1 See also, *Pramod Kumar Bhatia* v. *Om Prakash*, (1980) 1 SCC 412 (missing words supplied in a will where intention clear).

2 *Pt. Parshotam Ram* v. *L. Keshodas*, AIR 1945 Lah 3; *Krishna Kumari Sinha* v. *Kayastha Pathshala*, AIR 1966 All 570.

3 *Ram Nath Das* v. *Ram Nagina Chaubey*, AIR 1962 Pat 481.

death of each testator as his Will disposing of his own separate property; on the death of the first to die it is admitted to probate as his own Will and on the death of the survivor, if no fresh Will has been made, it is admitted to probate as the disposition of the property of the survivor. Joint Wills are now rarely, if ever, made.

Mutual Wills—Wills are mutual when the testators confer on each other reciprocal benefits, which may be absolute benefits in each other's property, or life interests with the same ultimate disposition of each estate on the death of the survivor. Apparently, a mutual Will in the strict sense of the term is a joint Will, but, where by agreement or arrangement similar provisions are made by separate Wills, these are also conveniently known as mutual Wills. Wills which by agreement confer benefit on persons other than the testators, without the testators conferring benefits on each other, can also be mutual Wills. Where there is an agreement not to revoke mutual Wills and one party dies having stood by the agreement, a survivor is bound by it.

The concept of mutual Wills have been explained by the Supreme Court in *Shiva Nath Prasad* v. *State of WB*[1] as under:

> "A Will on its own terms is inherently revocable during the life time of the testator. However, "Mutual Wills" and "secret trusts" are doctrines evolved in equity to overcome the problems of revocability of Wills and to prevent frauds. mutual Wills and secret trusts belong to the same category of cases. The doctrine of mutual Wills is to the effect that where two individuals agree as to the disposal of their assets and execute mutual Wills in pursuance of the agreement, on the death of the first testator (T-1), the property of the survivor testator (T-2), the subject matter of the agreement, is held on an implied trust for the beneficiary named in the Wills. T-2 may alter his/her Will because a Will is inherently revocable, but if he/she does so, his/her representative will take the assets subject to the trust. The rationale for imposing a "constructive trust" in such circumstances is that equity will not allow T-2 to commit a fraud by going back on her agreement with T-1. Since the assets received by T-2 on the death of T-1, were bequeathed to T-2 on the basis of the agreement not to revoke the Will of T-1, it would be a fraud for T-2 to take the benefit, while failing to observe the agreement and equity intervenes to prevent this fraud."

Bequeathable Property[2]

All property, movable and immovable of which a man is owner can be disposed of by him by Will except such as is legally non-transferable, such as an

1 (2006) 2 SCC 757.

2 Sec. 90 Succession Act provides for increase, diminution or other change in the description of the property between the execution of the will and the death of the testator: See *Lachhman Singh* v. *Raja Ram Singh*, AIR 1999 SC 1756, (1999) 3 SCC 517 (para 5).

occupancy tenancy.[1] If a man has only a life interest in a property, he cannot make a Will of it. According to *Mitakshara* Law, a Hindu coparcener, earlier, could not dispose of his undivided coparcenary interest even if the other coparceners consented. The position has now been changed. Sec. 30 (Explanation) of the Hindu Succession Act, 1956, says that any Hindu may dispose of by Will or other testamentary disposition, any property which is capable of being so disposed of by him in accordance with law. The explanation to the section makes it clear that the interest of a male Hindu in a *Mitakshara* co-parcenary property shall be deemed to be property capable of being disposed of by him. A sole surviving coparcener may bequeath the joint family property, and a subsequent adoption will not amount to revocation of the Will. To the extent the testator oversteps his right in devising certain property the Will would be inoperative but would operate in respect of the rest.[2] A property which has already been settled earlier under a settlement deed is no longer bequeathable.[3]

Rules of construction of a Will

In *Rajendra Prasad Bose* v. *Gopal Prasad Sen*,[4] it was laid down that "the duty of the court is to ascertain the intention from the words used in the document". Further it was held that once the construction is settled, the court is bound to carry out the intention as expressed and no other."[5]

Who can be Devisee

Any person can be a devisee, including a minor, or a mentally ill person. A corporation, a Hindu deity and any other juristic person can take a bequest. So far as Hindus are concerned the Hindu Disposition of Property Act, 1916 permits disposition of property by Will even in favour of a person not in existence at the time of such disposition provided it is not in breach of the provisions of Secs. 113, 114, 115 and 116 of the Indian Succession Act, 1925. Section 113 provides that where a bequest is made to a person not in existence at the time of the testator's death, subject to a prior bequest contained in the Will, the later bequest shall be void unless it comprises the whole of the remaining interest of the testator in the thing bequeathed. Section 114 lays down the *rule against perpetuity,* namely, that no bequest is valid whereby the vesting of the thing bequeathed may be delayed beyond the lifetime of one or more persons living at the testator's death and

---

1 *Sangappa* v. *Land Tribunal*, AIR 1998 SC 3229.

2 *Banwari Lal* v. *Trilok Chand*, (1980) 1 SCC 349.

3 *Dagani Ramadas* v. *P. Daveed*, (1998) 8 SCC 465.

4 AIR 1930 PC 242. 1930 SCC OnLine PC 54

5 Also see decision in *Navneet Lal* v. *Gokul*, (1976) 1 SCC 630; *Ram Gopal* v. *Nand Lal*, AIR 1951 SC 139; *Venkata Narasimha Appa Row* v. *Parthasarathy Appa Row*, 1913 SCC OnLine PC 39: (1913-14) 41 IA 51: 21 IC 339; *Gnambal Ammal* v. *T. Raju Ayyar*, AIR 1951 SC 103; *Raj Bajrang Bahadur Singh* v. *Bakhtraj Kuer*, AIR 1953 SC 7; *Pearey Lal* v. *Rameshwar Das*, AIR 1963 SC 1703; *Ramachandra Shenoy* v. *Hilda Brite*, AIR 1964 SC 1323.

the minority of some person who shall be in existence at the expiration of that period and to whom, if he attains full age, the thing bequeathed is to belong. Sections 115 and 116 make consequential provisions.

Joint devisees

Unless expressly mentioned otherwise in the Will, the joint devisees will take the property as tenants in common and not as joint tenants.[1]

Person to Whom Probate or Letters of Administration cannot be granted

Probate or letters of administration cannot be granted to any person who is a minor or of unsound mind, nor to an association of individuals unless it is a company which satisfies the conditions prescribed by rules to be made by the State Government in this behalf (Secs. 223 and 236, Indian Succession Act). A statutory corporation is however, not an association of individuals but is a "person", and probate or letters of administration can be granted to it.[2]

It may be added that taking of a probate or letters of administration is not obligatory except when the Will is made or the property is situated in Bombay or Chennai presidency towns or within the territories which were under the Lt. Governor of Bengal at the time the Succession Act was passed.[3]

Legality of Interest Created

In this connection, it is necessary to bear in mind the provision in Sec. 112-117 (which apply to Hindus, Buddhists, Sikhs and Jains also), and to see that the bequests do not conflict with them. Sec. 118 (which does not apply to Hindus, Buddhists, Sikhs and Jains) provides that a man having a nephew or niece or any nearer relative shall not have power to bequeath any property to religious or charitable uses except by a Will executed not less than twelve months before his death and deposited within six months from its execution in some place provided by law for the safe custody of Wills of living persons. However, the provision has been held to be violative of the constitution and as such void.[4]

Sufficiency of Provisions

The provisions relating to bequests made and trusts created by the Will should be complete. For example, when trustees are appointed, the Will should provide for the appointment of new trustees and for the conduct of business by the trustees by the opinion of a majority. It should give sufficient power to them,

---

1 *Amal Krishna* v. *Ganesh Chandra*, AIR 1998 Cal. at 228, relying on *Boddu Venkatakrishna Rao* v. *Boddu*, AIR 1968 SC 751 and *Syed Shah Ghulam Ghouse* v. *Syed Shah Ahmad*, AIR 1971 SC 2184 (para 12); Sec. 19 Hindu Succession Act also relied on.

2 *Benaras Hindu University* v. *Gouri Datt Joshi*, 1949 ALJ 523, AIR 1950 All 196.

3 *Jagdish Chandra* v. *Punjab National Bank*, AIR 1998 Delhi 266 (para 24).

4 *John Vallamattom* v. *Union of India*, AIR 2003 SC 2902.

according to the nature of the property, to manage it properly and carry out the testator's directions regarding the disposal or uses of the property or its income. Powers of sale, of reinvestment, employing agents, etc., may also be necessary in certain cases.

The interest conveyed should be clearly defined. This is particularly necessary in the case of Wills by Hindus in favour of their wives. If the intention is that the wife should take an absolute interest it should be clearly so expressed. Saying that the wife shall be "full and absolute owner" is sufficient to convey absolute title,[1] but even the words "*malik*" and "*Waris*" may be held to be consistent with conferment of a life estate only if the other terms of the will so indicate.[2] Where a will provides that after the testator's death his widow shall be "exclusive owner" and "full owner" and after her death "whatever property remains shall be owned" by the testator's nephews and also that she and they shall not be entitled to sell it, the widow was held to be full owner and the prohibition against selling was disregarded as repugnant to the absolute gift to her.[3] In construing the true intention of testator, it is permissible to deduce the fair import of the document by reading it as a whole.[4]

Where it is clear on the face of a Will that the testator has not accurately or completely expressed his meaning by the words he has used, and it is also clear what are the words which he has omitted, those words may be supplied (by the court) in order to effectuate the intention, as collected from the context.[5]

It is one of the cardinal principles of construction of Wills[6] that to the extent that it is legally possible, effect should be given to every disposition contained in the Will unless the law prevents effect being given to it. Of course, if there are two repugnant provisions conferring successive interests, if the first interest created is valid the subsequent interest cannot take effect but a Court of construction will proceed to the farthest extent to avoid repugnancy, so that effect could be given as far as possible to every testamentary intention contained in the Will. It is for this reason that where there is a bequest to "A" even though it be in terms apparently absolute followed by a gift of the same to "B" absolutely "on" or "after" or "at" A's

---

1 *Bai Kevli* v. *Dalsukh Ram*, AIR 1945 Bom 178.

2 *Arun Kumar* v. *Shrinivas*, AIR 2003 SC 2528 *(approved the principles for construction of Wills Summarised in Navneet Lal* v. *Gokul*, (1976) 1 SCC 630; *Ramkishorelal* v. *Kamalnarayan*, AIR 1963 SC 891 (case Law on when "*Malik*" may not imply proprietary rights).

3 *Jagat Singh* v. *Sangat Singh*, AIR 1940 PC 70.

4 *Bishun Singh* v. *Mangla Nain*, AIR 1945 PC 30; *Usha Subbarao* v. *B.E. Vishveswariah*, AIR 1996 SC 2260.

5 Jarman on Will, 8th Edn., 592, relying on *Pramod Kumar Bhatia* v. *Om Prakash*, (1980) 1 SCC 412.

6 Sections 74 to 111 Succession Act lay down statutory rules of construction of wills. Excepting sections 91 to 94, 97, 99 and 100 all these sections apply to construction of Hindu wills as well (See schedule III to the Act read with Sec. 57).

death, "A" is prima facie held to take a life interest and "B" an interest in remainder, the apparently absolute interest of "A" being cut down to accommodate the interest created in favour of "B".[1] It is however always safe to express the intention clearly and in unmistakable terms.

On distinction between creation of vested interests and contingent interests, see p. 268, *ante*.

Proof of Will

The law settled with regard to proof of a Will is that the mode to prove a Will does not ordinarily differ from that of proving any other document except as to the special requirement prescribed under Sec. 68 of the Evidence Act. The onus to prove the Will is on the propounder.[2] In the absence of suspicious circumstances surrounding the execution of the Will, proof of testamentary capacity and signature of the testator as required by law are sufficient to discharge the onus. The onus is on the propounder to clear the mist arising due to suspicious circumstances by explaining the same to the courts' satisfaction. The burden of proving existence of undue influence, fraud, collusion, unsoundness of mind or absence of disposing state of mind is on the person challenging the Will.[3]

Attestation can only follow the execution.[4] If attestation has preceded the execution of the Will, it is not valid.

Section 63 of the Succession Act requires a Will to be attested. However, it cannot be used as evidence until one attesting witness, at least, has been called for the purpose of proving its execution, if there be an attesting witness alive, and subject to the process of the court and capable of giving evidence, section 68, Indian Evidence Act, 1872.

Muslim Law

Under the Muslim Law, the power to make bequests is limited to one third of the net assets. Where, however, there are no heirs (or among, Sunnis, if the only heir is the spouse) upon whom two-thirds share is to devolve in the ordinary course, or when there are heirs but all of them agree and give their consent, the limit of one third may be exceeded. The consent in such a case is to be given in the case of Sunnis, after the testator's death, but in the case of Shias, such consent may be given during the lifetime of the testator also. If the heirs are minors at the time of testator's death, consent must be given only after attaining majority. A guardian is not competent to give consent on behalf of a minor. Muslim law does not recognise a conditional Will. For detailed rules regarding rateable abatement in case one or

---

1 *Ramachandra Shenoy* v. *Hilda Brite*, AIR 1964 SC 1323; folld. in *A. Sreenivasa Pai* v. *Saraswathi Ammal*, AIR 1985 SC 1359.

2 *Gurdial Singh* v. *Smt. Rattan Kaur*, AIR 1996 P&H 265.

3 *Meenakshiammal* v. *Chandrashekharan*, (2005) 1 SCC 280.

4 *Virendra Singh* v. *Kashibai*, AIR 1998 MP 324 (DB); *Mangal Singh* v. *Nathu Singh*, (1998) 8 SCC 598.

more Wills exceed the "bequeathable third" works on Muslim Law may be consulted.

Codicil

Codicil is a supplement to a Will. When a testator wishes to make some slight alteration in his Will, e.g., change in the number of trustees or absolute or partial revocation of a gift or a bequest of an additional item of property, he should do so by executing a Codicil to his Will, making the additions or alterations and expressly confirming the original Will. When the alterations are considerable, it is best to write a fresh Will revoking the former one. Codicil requires the same formalities (signature and attestation) as a Will and is usually commenced thus: "I, AB, etc., hereby declare that this is my *first (second or third* as the case may be) Codicil to the Will dated ———".

Stamp Duty

No Stamp duty is required on a Will.

Registration

The registration of a Will is optional (Sec. 18).[1] There are special provisions in Part IX of the Registration Act under which a testator may deposit his Will in a sealed cover with the Registrar. On the death of the testator any person can apply to have the Will opened and copied in the Register. The Court can also require the production of such a Will from the Registrar who will open it and send it to the Court after copying it out in his Register.

---

1 *Rani Purnima Devi* v. *Kumar Khagendra Naryan Deb,* AIR 1962 SC 567; *Shakuntala Devi* v. *Ladly Mohan Mathur, (1986) All CJ 189.*

GENERAL FORMS OF DIFFERENT PARTS AND CLAUSES OF WILL

1. Introductory Clauses

a) *Commencement*

I, AB, etc., declare this to be my last Will which I make this ——— day of ————— hereby revoking all other Wills and Codicils heretofore made by me.

Or,

I, AB, etc., hereby revoke all former Wills and Codicils made by me and declare that this is my last Will.

Or,

This is the last Will of me AB, etc., made this the ——— day of ——.

Or,

I, hereby revoke all former Wills and Codicils made by me.

Or,

I, AB, etc., hereby revoke all former Wills and Codicils made by me and by this last Will bequeath all my property, etc.

Or,

I declare this to be the first (*or,* second) Codicil to my Will dated —— (and which is modified by a Codicil dated —————).

2. Appointment of Executors and Trustees

a) Executor

I appoint CD, etc., sole executor of this my Will (*or,* CD, etc., EF, and GH, etc., executors[1] of this my Will).

b) Executor and Trustee

I appoint CD, etc., EF, etc., GH, etc., to be the executors and trustees of this Will.

---

1 Where more executors than one are appointed, any transfer of property by them can be made only jointly: *K. Leelavathy Bai* v. *P.V. Gangadharen*, (1999) 3 SCC 548, AIR 1999 SC 1267.

c) On Attaining Majority

I appoint CD, etc., and EF, etc., and also my son XY, etc., if and when he shall attain majority to be the executors and trustees of this my Will.

d) Guardian

I appoint my trustees hereinbefore named to be the guardian of my minor children to act jointly with my wife.

3. Specific Legacies

a) Absolute

I give to CD, etc., absolutely ————.

b) For life

I bequeath the use and enjoyment of all my furniture, etc., to my wife ———— during her life (*or* widowhood) and declare that after her death (*or*, remarriage) the same shall fall into my residuary estate.

c) Release of Debt

I release and forgive to ———— or to his representatives if he should die in my lifetime whatever amount may remain owing to me at my death on the bond executed by him for Rs. ——— on the ——— and, I direct my trustees to cancel and deliver up the said bond to him or them.

4. Specific Devises

a) Devise of Property

I bequeath to CD, etc., all that property described in the first schedule hereto.

b) Subject to legacies, etc.

I bequeath to CD, etc., all that property described in the first schedule hereto subject to and charged with the payment to XY of legacy of Rs. —— (*or,* subject to the payment of several annuities and legacies hereby charged and made payable out of the said property).

c) Bequest of Leasehold

I give my leasehold land described in the first schedule hereto for all the residue which shall be unexpired at my death of the term for which the said land is held subject to the rent reserved by and the covenants and conditions contained in the lease under which the same is held.

d) Of Trade and Business

I bequeath to —— the goodwill of my trade and business of —— and the stock in trade, machinery, plant and effects therein or belonging thereto together with the lease of the shop and building situate at ——— in which the said business is carried on or which is used for the purpose thereof and the benefit of all contracts subsisting in respect of the said business and all book debts and moneys due to me in respect thereof or standing to the credit of my business account at my death, the said ——— discharging and indemnifying my general estate from debts and liabilities due or subsisting in respect of the said business at my death.

5. *General Legacies*

a) Pecuniary legacies

I give to CD, etc., the sum of Rs. ————.

b) Several Legacies

I give the following legacies namely;

(*i*) to CD, etc., the sum of Rs. ————;

(*ii*) to EF, etc., the sum of Rs. ————.

c) On Trust

I give to the trustees the sum of Rs. ———— upon the trust hereinafter declared concerning the same.

d) Alternative Bequest

I give to CD, etc., the sum of Rs. ———— but if the said CD shall die before me then I give his legacy to his children or child, if any, living at the time of my death.

e) On Majority

I give the sum of Rs. ———— to CD, etc., if and when he shall attain the age of eighteen.

f) In Trust to Invest

I give to my trustees the sum of Rs. ——— upon trust to invest the same in or upon any of the investments hereby authorised with power to vary any such investment AND I declare that my trustees shall hold the said sum of Rs. ———— and investments and income thereof in trust for CD, etc., if and when he attains the age of eighteen, but if the said CD shall die under the age of eighteen then I declare that the said sum of Rs. ——— and the investment and income thereof shall sink into and form part of my residuary fund.

g) Priority of Legacies

The several pecuniary legacies hereinbefore given to the said ——— shall have priority in the order in which the same are hereinbefore given but so that legacies given to a class shall have no priority as between the members of such class.

h) Direction in case of Deficiency

If the moneys to arise from the sale and conversion hereby directed or otherwise forming part of my estate shall not be sufficient to pay all the legacies hereby given then the said legacies shall be proportionately reduced (*or,* the said legacies given to CD, etc., and EF, etc., and GH, etc., shall abate proportionately in exoneration of the remaining legacies).

6. Legacies to Charity

a) To Orphanage

I give to the ——— orphanage the sum of Rs. ———.

b) Several Legacies

I give the following charitable legacies, namely:

(*i*) To the ——— the sum of Rs. ———;

(*ii*) To the ——— the sum of Rs. ———.

c) Legacy Invested for the Poor

I give to my trustees the sum of Rs. ——— upon trust to invest the same and apply the yearly income thereof for the benefit of the poor and deserving widows.

d) Legacy on Several Trusts

I give to my trustees the sum of Rs. ——— to be expended by them at their absolute discretion for all or any of the following purposes, namely ——— etc.

e) Dedication to Deity

I direct that the property described in the second schedule hereto shall be dedicated to the deity of Shri Radha Krishanji Maharaj in the temple at ——— and shall be set apart and income thereof applied for the upkeep of the said temple and the expenses of worship of the said deity and the expenses of the annual festivals of the said temple.

7. Annuities

a) Bequest of Annuity

I give to CD, etc., during his life an annuity of Rs. ——— to begin from my death (and to be payable in equal monthly instalments thereof).

b) To wife

I give to my wife CD during her life and so long as she does not remarry an annuity of Rs. ——— without power of anticipation[1] to begin from my death.

c) To wife, Reducible on Remarriage

I give to my wife CD an annuity of Rs. ——— during her widowhood beginning from my death and in the event of her marrying again then during the remainder of her life a reduced annuity of Rs. ——— in either case without power of anticipation.

d) To Two Persons or Survivors

I give to CD, etc., and EF, etc., and the survivor of them an annuity of Rs. ——— during their joint lives and the life of the survivor to begin from my death.

e) Charge on Property

I give to CD, etc., during his life an annuity of Rs. ——— to begin from my death to be charged against and payable out of my property described in the third schedule hereto.

8. Bequest of Residue

a) To an Individual

I bequeath and devise all my movable and immovable property whatsoever and wheresoever not otherwise disposed of by this my Will or any Codicil hereto to CD, etc., absolutely (*or*, to CD for his life and after his death to EF, etc., absolutely).

---

1 In conveyancing "anticipation" means "the act of assigning, charging or otherwise dealing with income before it becomes due." (Black's Law Dictionary, VI edition, page 93).

b) On Trust

I bequeath etc., (*as in a above*) to my trustees upon the trust hereinafter declared concerning the same, that is to say ————.

9. General Clauses relating to Trust or Trustees' Powers

a) Introductory Clause

My trustees shall hold the residue of the said money and investments for the time being representing the same and of such part of my estate as shall for the time being remain unsold and uninvested upon the trust hereinafter declared that is to say ————.

b) Life Interest

My trustees shall pay the income of the said sum of Rs. ———— (*or*, the said shares and securities and the property representing the same) to my wife the said CD during her life and so long as she remains my widow without power of anticipation.

Or,

My trustees shall out of the income of the trust fund accruing during the lifetime of CD, etc., pay an annuity of Rs. ———— to XY during his life, such annuity to commence from the death of my said wife and to be payable by monthly payments.

c) Trust for Sale and Conversion of Property

Upon trust my trustees shall sell, call in, collect, and convert into money, the said movable and immovable property at such time or times and in such manner as they shall think fit and I direct that the income of such of the said property as for the time being shall remain unsold shall be applied as if the same were income arising from investments hereinafter directed to be made of the proceeds of sale thereof.

d) Payment of Debts, and to make Investments

The trustees shall out of the moneys to arise from the sale, calling in and conversion of or forming part of my said property pay my funeral and testamentary expenses and debts and the legacies given by this my Will or Codicil hereto and other moneys which under or by virtue of any direction or bequest are payable out of my general estate, and to invest the residue in or upon any of the investments hereby authorised with power to vary such investments of a nature hereby authorised.

e) Trust for Children[1]

After the death of my wife, the trustees shall stand possessed of the capital and future income of the trust fund in TRUST for all or any of my children who being male attain the age of 18 years or being female attain that age or marry if more than one in equal shares (*or,* for all or any of my children or child if more than one in equal shares).

Or,

After the death of my wife the trustees shall stand possessed of the capital and future income of the trust fund in TRUST for my issue in such shares and in such manner as my wife shall by deed or Will appoint AND in default of any such appointment for all or any of my children or child if more than one in equal shares.

f) Giving Predeceased Child's Share to his Representative

If any child of mine shall have died in my lifetime leaving issue living at my death, the share which such child would have taken shall be held in TRUST for his or her legal representatives as part of his or her present estate.

g) Trust for Spendthrift Son

I give the sum of Rs. ——— to my trustees upon TRUST that they shall invest the same at their discretion in any investment hereby authorised with power from time to time to vary such investment AND shall from time to time during the life of my son CD or during such shorter period or periods either continuous or discontinuous as they shall think fit pay all or any part of the income of the said sum of Rs. ——— and the investments thereof upon protective trusts for the said CD with power from time to time to pay or apply any part of the capital thereof for the benefit of the said CD as if they were the beneficial owners of such income and capital.

After the death of the said CD my trustees shall pay the income of the said sum of Rs. ——— and the investments thereof or such part thereof as shall remain undisposed of to his widow during her life without power of anticipation and after her death to the children of A who being male, etc.

---

1 In case of a bequest to a plurality of persons, the presumption is that they take the property as joint tenants, with a right of survivorship (and not as tenants in common), unless there are words showing the contrary: Sec 106 Succession Act; the rule has been recognised in the cases of Christians, (*Arakal* v. *Domingo*, 34 M 80), Parsees (*Navroji* v. *Perozbai*, 23 B 80) and Muslims (*Jusali* v. *Fatima Bai*, AIR 1948 B 53), but not so in case of Hindus (*Amal Krishna* v. *Ganesh Chandra*, AIR 1998 Cal. at 221 DB).

In the event of the failure or determination of the trust hereinbefore declared and contained the said money or investment or such part thereof as shall remain undisposed of shall sink into my residuary estate.

h) Maintenance and Accumulation during Minority

My trustees may apply all or any part of the income of the share to which any minor shall be entitled in expectancy or would if of full age be entitled to possession under the trust hereinbefore contained for his or her maintenance, education or benefit in such manner as they think fit and shall invest the surplus in any investments hereby authorised in anticipation of the capital of such share.

i) Investment Clause

Trust moneys may be invested in or upon the following securities:

j) Power to Purchase Furniture

Trust money may at the request of my wife be laid out to an amount not exceeding Rs. ———— in the purchase of ————.

k) Power to Lend

Trust money may at any time be lent to the said ———— for the purposes of his business of —— to an amount not exceeding Rs. ——— from such fund and at such rate of interest and upon such terms as the trustees may think fit.

l) To Act by Majority[1]

Any of the powers and authorities hereby given to or vested in my trustees may at any time be exercised by a majority of my trustees.

m) Power to Appoint new Trustees

The power of appointing a new trustee of this my Will shall be vested in my wife during her life.

Or,

The power of appointing a new trustee of this my Will shall be exercised by the remaining trustees with the concurrence of my said wife if she is alive.

---

1 Section 48 Trust Act provides that all trustees must act jointly unless the instrument of trust otherwise provides.

10. Testimonium and Attestation

a) Will

IN WITNESS WHEREOF I, the said ———, have put my signatures to this my Will (to each sheet of this my Will on the day, the year first above written (*or*, on the ————).

b) Codicil

IN WITNESS WHEREOF I, the said ——— have signed this Codicil on the ————.

c) Attestation of Signature

Signed by the above named AB in our presence[1] and each of us has in the presence of the testator signed his name hereunder as attesting witnesses.

d) Attestation on Acknowledgment

The said AB has personally acknowledged to us separately having made the above signature to this Will and each of us has on such acknowledgment and in the presence of the said AB signed this Will hereunder as an attesting witness.

e) Where Another Person Signs for the Testator

Signed by CD, etc., with the name of the above named testator as his last Will in the presence of and by the direction of the testator and in our presence and each of us has in the presence of the testator signed his name hereunder as attesting witnesses.

f) When the Testator is Illiterate or Blind

Signed by the above named testator with his mark as his last Will after the same had first been read over and explained to him in our presence and had appeared to be perfectly understood and approved by him in our presence and each of us (*as in para e*).

g) Attestation of Alterations

The interlineations between the ——— and ——— lines of page ——— and the alteration in the ——— line of page and the erasure in the ——— line of page ———— having been previously made has been signed by the above named, etc. (*as in para c*).

---

1 It is possible for the testator to acknowledge his signature to an attesting witness who may not have actually seen the testator sign the Will. In that case however each attesting witness will make a separate attestation, and the one who has not seen the testator signing it but has only received the testator's personal acknowledgement will state so.

PRECEDENTS

1—Simple Will giving All Property to One Person

I, AB, etc., hereby revoke all former Wills and Codicils made by me and by this my last Will bequeath and devise all my movable and immovable property whatsoever and wheresoever to my wife (*or,* to CD, etc.,) absolutely and appoint her (him) sole executrix (executor) of this my Will.

IN WITNESS WHEREOF I have signed this will hereunder on the ———— day of ————.

Sd. ————

Signed by the above named testator in our presence and each of us has in the presence of the testator signed his name hereunder as an attesting witness.

1.

2.

2—Will Bequeathing All Property to Wife for Life and thereafter to Others, with Annuities to Several Persons

This is the last Will of me, AB, etc., made this the ———— day of ————.

1. I hereby revoke all former Wills and Codicils made by me.[1]

2. I bequeath all my money and other movable property whatsoever and wheresoever to my wife XY absolutely.

3. I devise all my lands and other immovable property to my wife XY for her life and after her death to my daughter CD absolutely and if the said CD shall die before my said wife then to my nephew GH.

4. I bequeath the following annuities to commence from the date of my death and to be paid in equal monthly payments:

(*a*) To my daughter CD, etc., an annuity of Rs. ———— to be paid during her life;

(*b*) To my sister EF, etc., an annuity of Rs. ———— during her

---

1 These words are traditionally used even where no former Will or Codicil was made at all.

life and after her death to be continued to her son, if any, or sons, if more than one, in equal shares;

(*c*) To my nephew GH, etc., an annuity of Rs. ——— during his life;

(*d*) To my old servant JK, etc., an annuity of Rs. ——— during his life;

IN WITNESS WHEREOF, I the said AB have signed this Will hereunder the day and year first above written.

(*Attestation as in Form* 1).

3—Will with Pecuniary Legacies, Annuities and Trust for Wife and Children

THIS is the last Will etc. (*as in Form* 2).

1. *As in Form* 2.

2. I appoint AB, etc., CD, etc., and EF, etc., to be my executors and trustees.

3. I bequeath all my household goods and cattle to my wife absolutely.

4. I bequeath my books, clothes, watch and personal jewellery to my eldest son KL.

5. I bequeath—

(*a*) Rs. ——— to my wife absolutely to be paid as soon as possible;

(*b*) Rs. ——— to each of my executors who shall prove my Will.

(*c*) To each of my servants who at my death shall have been in my employment for not less than three years immediately preceding my death, three months' salary in addition to the wages then due or accruing.

6. I bequeath to my said wife a life annuity of Rs. ——— and to my sister MN a life annuity of Rs. ——— both of which shall commence from my death, such annuities to be secured by the appropriation of investments sufficient to ensure the same out of income but in the event of a subsequent deficiency of income the capital of this appropriated fund to be liable. After such appropriation any residuary estate shall be free of the said annuities.

7. All the residue of my property, movable and immovable is to be converted into money by my executors and after payment of my debts, funeral and testamentary expenses is to be invested and settled on the following trusts:

(*a*) To pay the income to my said wife during her life (*or* widowhood).

(*b*) Subject hereto in trust to pay or divide the corpus to or between all my children or who being male shall attain majority or being female shall attain majority or previously marry, the share which would have belonged to any child already dead or who may die before me, leaving issue, to go to such issue by substitution *per stirpes*.[1]

(*c*) The shares of each daughter to be retained upon the usual trust for life for her separate and unalienable use with power by Will to give her husband a life or lesser interest with remainder to her issue as she may by deed or Will appoint and so far as such power shall not be exercised, to her children at majority with remainder, in default of such child becoming absolutely entitled, to such persons as such daughter may by Will appoint, with remainder, in default of appointment, to her legal heirs as if she had died unmarried and intestate and her share had belonged to her absolutely.

8. During her life my said wife is to have the power of appointing a new trustee in case of any vacancy.

IN WITNESS WHEREOF, etc.

Attestation as usual.

4—Will by a Sonless Hindu Leaving Several Legacies and also making Religious and Charitable Bequests

This is the last Will, etc., (*as in Form* 2).

1. *As in Form* 2.

2. I appoint AB, etc., and CD, etc., and EF, etc., to be the executors and trustees of this my Will.

3. I appoint the said trustees as guardian of my children jointly with my wife.

4. I bequeath—

(*a*) to my friend X, all my books;

(*b*) to my son-in law Y, my motorcar, watch with chain, drawing room furniture, silver and china dinner and tea sets and my bungalow situate at ——————;

(*c*) to my daughter P, wife of the said Y, the agricultural land described in the first schedule hereto.

5. I bequeath the following pecuniary legacies:

---

1 "*per stirpes*", as distinguished from 'per capita', means, in a representative capacity. In other words, members of each branch get one share. *Cf.* Sec. 10 Rule 3 and Sec. 19 (a), Hindu Succession Act.

(*a*) to each of my trustees who shall prove my Will and act in the trust thereof, the sum of Rs. ————;

(*b*) to each of my servants HJ and KL, the sum of Rs. ————; and

(*c*) to my sister Q for the marriage of her daughter, if the daughter is in existence and un-married at the date of my death, Rs. ————.

6. I bequeath the following charitable legacies:

(*a*) to the ———— hospital Rs. ————;

(*b*) to the ———— Orphanage Rs. ————;

(*c*) to the ———— Girls' School at ———— Rs. ————;

(*d*) to the ———— Temple at ———— Rs. ————.

7. I bequeath the following annuities (*as clause* 4 *in Form* 2).

8. I bequeath all my money in deposit in the various banks and all shares and securities to the trustees upon trust to utilise the same for the expenses of ceremonies in connection with my funeral and *shradh* and payment of all my debts and the pecuniary legacies hereby bequeathed and the balance in founding a charitable hospital to be called the ———— hospital. For this purpose the trustees will have power to sell the said securities.

9. I release and forgive to GH or to his representatives if he dies before me, the amount that may at the time of my death be due to me from him on his bond for Rs. ———— dated ———— and direct my trustees to cancel and deliver up the bond to him.

10. I bequeath all my agricultural land described in the second schedule hereto to the trustees upon trust to apply the net income thereof after payment of the land revenue, cesses, taxes and necessary charges of collection to the current expenses of the said hospital, and to invest the savings left after meeting such expenses in a sinking fund for the benefit of the said hospital.

11. Whereas my deceased father PQ had built a *dharamshala* which has since been maintained by me but no permanent provision for its maintenance has yet been made either by deceased father or by me, I hereby bequeath the property described in the fourth schedule hereto to the trustees upon trust to apply the net income thereof to the maintenance and upkeep of the said *dharamshala* and the comfort of the public using the same, according to their best judgment and discretion.

12. I bequeath my property movable and immovable whatsoever and wheresoever existing at the time of my death and not otherwise disposed of

by this Will to my wife absolutely (*or,* for her life without any power of alienation and after her death to my grandson MN, being the son of my daughter AB).

13. I hereby give power to my wife the said ST to appoint a new trustee or new trustees on the occurrence of any vacancy in the office of trustees.

14. I direct that if there is any difference of opinion between any trustees in any matter concerning this Will or the management of property hereby bequeathed or the execution of any trust hereby created, the opinion of the majority shall prevail.[1]

IN WITNESS etc.

Attestation as usual.

5—Codicil Substituting a Trustee for one Appointed by the will

I, AB, etc., declare this to be a first Codicil to my Will dated the —— day of ———.

WHEREAS by my Will I have appointed CD as one of the executors and trustees and have given him a legacy of Rs. ——— if he acts.

AND WHEREAS the said CD has died.

1. Now I hereby revoke the appointment of the said CD as one of the executors and trustees of my Will and appoint KL, etc., to be the executor and trustee thereof in place of the CD and I bequeath to the said KL a legacy of Rs. ——— if he acts as such executor and trustee.

2. I hereby revoke the legacy of Rs. ——— given to the said CD by the said Will.

3. I hereby declare that my said Will and all the provisions contained therein shall be construed and take effect as if the name of the said KL were substituted therein as an executor and trustee thereof for the name of CD.

4. In all other respects I confirm my said Will.

IN WITNESS. etc.

Attestation as usual.

6—Codicil Altering certain Bequests

I, AB, etc., declare this to be a second Codicil to my Will dated

---

1 See Preliminary Note, *ante*, sub-heading "To act by majority".

the ———— which was modified by the first Codicil dated the ————.

WHEREAS by the said Will I bequeathed-

(*a*) a specific legacy of Rs. ———— to my daughter CD;

(*b*) a share in my residuary estate to my son KL.

AND WHEREAS the said CD has died and since the execution of my Will I have had cause to be displeased with the conduct of my son KL and do not therefore desire to leave any share of my estate to him.

NOW I direct that—

(1) I hereby revoke the legacy of Rs. ———— to the said CD and bequeath the said legacy to the said CD's daughter EF;

(2) I revoke the devise of a share in my residuary estate in favour of my son KL;

(3) In all other respects I confirm my said Will and the first Codicil aforesaid.

IN WITNESS, etc.

Attestation as usual.

7—Codicil correcting clerical errors

1. I declare this to be a first Codicil to my Will dated ————;

2. I declare that my said Will shall be read and construed and take effect in all respects as if,

(*a*) the word "———" had been inserted after the word "——" in line ———— of page ———— thereof;

(*b*) the words "————" had been substituted for the words "——" in the ———— line of the ———— page thereof.

3. In all other respects I confirm my said Will.

IN WITNESS WHEREOF, etc.

Attestation as usual.

8—Revocation of Will

I, AB, etc., hereby revoke the Will made by me bearing date —— and modified by a Codicil dated ———— and all other testamentary dispostions whatsoever hereinbefore made by me and declare it to be my intention to die intestate.

IN WITNESS, etc.

Attestation as in Will.

9—Will Reviving a Will and Codicil previously Revoked

1. I, AB, etc., declare this to be my last Will.

2. I hereby revive and confirm the Will dated ——— and the Codicils thereto dated ——— and ———, formerly made by me, which said Will and codicils I had revoked by a deed dated ———.

IN WITNESS, etc.

Attestation as usual.

INDEX

Figures written within brackets refer to Notes, and those without brackets to precedents